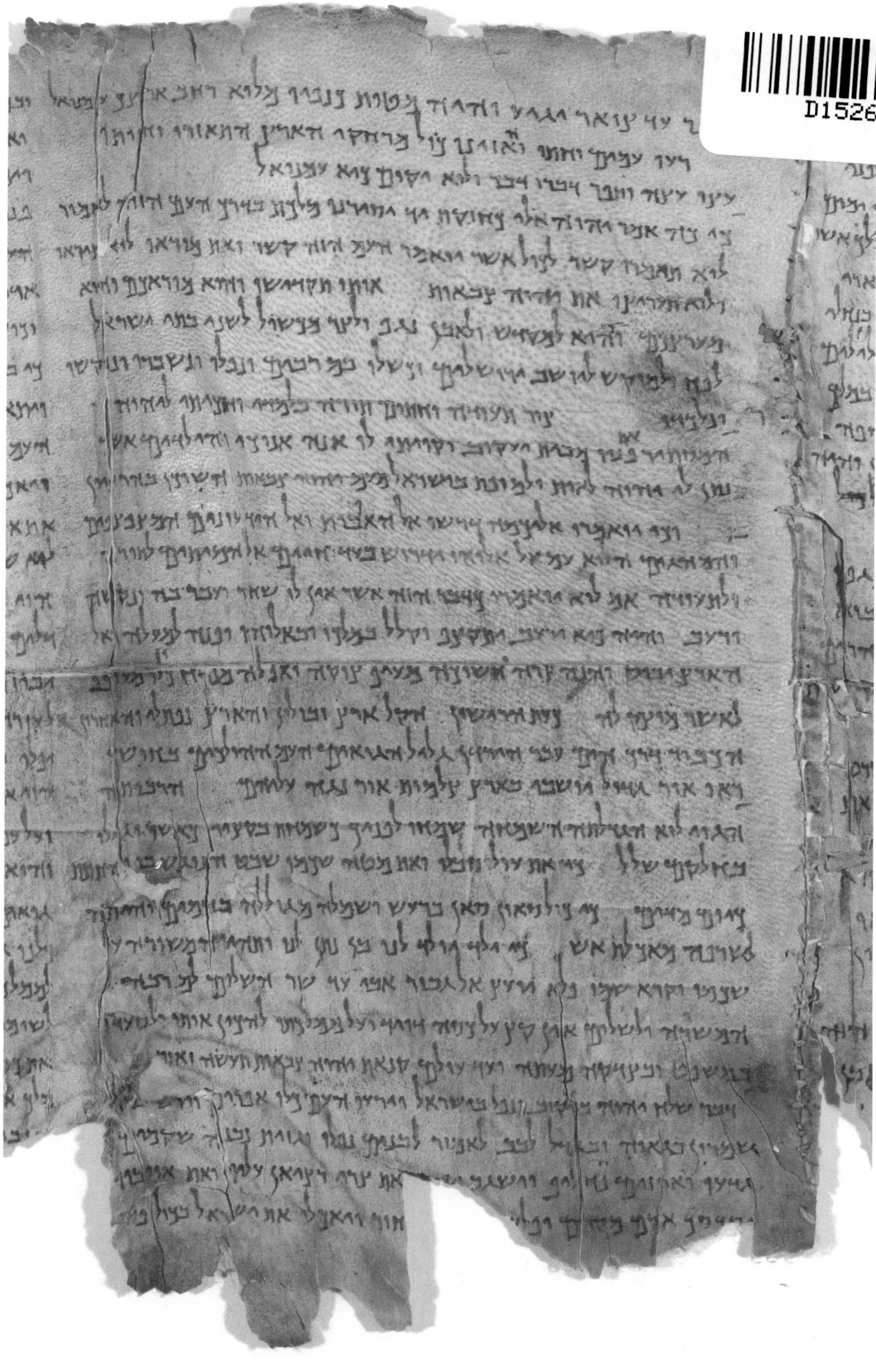

Hermeneia
—A Critical
and Historical
Commentary
on the Bible

First Isaiah

A Commentary

by J. J. M. Roberts

Edited by
Peter Machinist

Fortress Press   Minneapolis

First Isaiah
A Commentary

Cover and interior design by Kenneth Hiebert
Typesetting and page composition by
The HK Scriptorium

Library of Congress cataloging-in-publication data is available

Print ISBN: 978-0-8006-6080-2

eISBN: 978-1-5064-0290-1

The paper used in this publication meets the minimum requirements of American National Standard for Information Sciences—Permanence of paper for Printed Library Materials, ANSI Z329.48–1984.

Manufactured in the U.S.A.

■ *To Kathryn, my beloved wife, who has endured my complete absorption in finishing this lifetime work with far more patience and grace than I deserved.*

Jim Roberts has been a major scholar in biblical studies for more than four and a half decades, internationally recognized for his scholarship and teaching. He trained at Abilene Christian College (BA) and Harvard University (STB, PhD), where in the context of a broad study of religion and theology, he focused on the religions, history, and languages of the ancient Near East, especially the Old Testament/Hebrew Bible, ancient Israel and Canaan, and ancient Mesopotamia (Assyriology). His faculty positions have taken him to Dartmouth College, the Johns Hopkins University, the University of Toronto, and Princeton Theological Seminary—at the last serving for twenty-five years as the William Henry Green Professor of Old Testament Literature until his retirement in 2004. In addition, he has been honored with appointments as visiting professor or lecturer at many colleges, universities, and seminaries in the United States, Europe, and South Africa, including the Yale and Harvard Divinity Schools, the Austin Presbyterian Theological Seminary, the University of Stellenbosch, and the University of Vienna.

The Old Testament/Hebrew Bible is the core of Roberts's scholarship and teaching, and he brings to it a multifaceted approach, centered on comparative study of the Bible in the larger ancient Near Eastern world, on close textual analysis, grounded in an acute literary, philological, and theological sensitivity, and on the implications of historical study of the Bible for present issues and religious communities. All these are on display in his extensive and ongoing bibliography. Here are three examples. The first is the book entitled *The Hand of the Lord*, which Roberts wrote with Patrick D. Miller Jr.

(1977). It sheds striking new light on the much-discussed "Ark Narrative" of 1 Samuel, especially on the function of the ark as a divine symbol, by a penetrating examination of comparable Mesopotamian narratives. The book has become a model for what judicious comparative study can reveal. Then there is Roberts's commentary on the prophetic books of Nahum, Habakkuk, and Zephaniah, in the Old Testament Library series (1990). What is particularly valuable in this book is that it clarifies not simply the standard Masoretic Text but also the ancient versions in Hebrew, Greek, Latin, and Aramaic and how they understood the often-difficult verses in the three prophets. A third example is the book *The Bible and the Ancient Near East: Collected Essays* (2002). Here Roberts has gathered a number of his studies on comparative history, mostly published earlier, which emphasize issues and texts concerned with prophecy and monarchy in biblical Israel and Mesopotamia. Among the studies are a previously unpublished comprehensive edition and translation of the known prophetic texts from the ancient Mesopotamian/Syrian city of Mari, crucial for understanding prophecy in the Hebrew Bible, and several essays on the theology of kingship, Jerusalem, and temple in Judean Israel (the "Zion theology"), which establish its foundational importance for the history and culture of ancient Judah and the Hebrew Bible as a whole. In the Zion group also are several essays about the book of Isaiah, which, along with a number of other essays on Isaiah published elsewhere, offer a window on the scholarly workshop from which Roberts has now given us his magnum opus, the Hermeneia commentary on the First Isaiah.

Endpapers

The photographs at the front and back of *First Isaiah* are from 1QIsa[a], the Great Isaiah Scroll from Qumran Cave 1. The front photograph is of the text of Isaiah 8:8—9:11, and the back photograph is the text of Isaiah 33:1-24. Both photographs have been published in John C. Trever, *Scrolls from Qumran Cave I: The Great Isaiah Scroll, The Order of the Community, The Pesher to Habakkuk* (Jerusalem: Albright Institute of Archaeological Research and Shrine of the Book, 1972), plates VIII and XXVII. Shrine of the Book / photo © The Israel Museum, Jerusalem, by Ardon Bar-Hama.

Contents
First Isaiah

■ **Commentary**

■ **Back Matter**

The name *Hermeneia,* Greek ἑρμενεία, has been chosen as the title of the commentary series to which this volume belongs. The word *Hermeneia* has a rich background in the history of biblical interpretation as a term used in the ancient Greek-speaking world for the detailed, systematic exposition of a scriptural work. It is hoped that the series, like its name, will carry forward this old and venerable tradition. A second, entirely practical reason for selecting the name lies in the desire to avoid a long descriptive title and its inevitable acronym, or worse, an unpronounceable abbreviation.

The series is designed to be a critical and historical commentary to the Bible without arbitrary limits in size or scope. It will utilize the full range of philological and historical tools, including textual criticism (often slighted in modern commentaries), the methods of the history of tradition (including genre and prosodic analysis), and the history of religion.

Hermeneia is designed for the serious student of the Bible. It will make full use of ancient Semitic and classical languages; at the same time, English translations of all comparative materials—Greek, Latin, Canaanite, or Akkadian—will be supplied alongside the citation of the source in its original language. Insofar as possible, the aim is to provide the student or scholar with full critical discussion of each problem of interpretation and with the primary data upon which the discussion is based.

Hermeneia is designed to be international and interconfessional in the selection of authors; its editorial boards were formed with this end in view. Occasionally the series will offer translations of distinguished commentaries which originally appeared in languages other than English. Published volumes of the series will be revised continually, and eventually, new commentaries will replace older works in order to preserve the currency of the series. Commentaries are also being assigned for important literary works in the categories of apocryphal and pseudepigraphical works relating to the Old and New Testaments, including some of Essene or Gnostic authorship.

The editors of *Hermeneia* impose no systematic-theological perspective upon the series (directly, or indirectly by selection of authors). It is expected that authors will struggle to lay bare the ancient meaning of a biblical work or pericope. In this way the text's human relevance should become transparent, as is always the case in competent historical discourse. However, the series eschews for itself homiletical translation of the Bible.

The editors are heavily indebted to Fortress Press for its energy and courage in taking up an expensive, long-term project, the rewards of which will accrue chiefly to the field of biblical scholarship.

The editor responsible for this volume is Peter Machinist of Harvard University.

Peter Machinist
For the Old Testament
Editorial Board

Helmut Koester
For the New Testament
Editorial Board

Reference Codes

1. Abbreviations

AASOR	*Annual of the American Schools of Oriental Research*
AAT	Ägypten und Altes Testament
AB	Anchor Bible
ABD	*The Anchor Bible Dictionary* (ed. David Noel Freedman; 6 vols.; New York: Doubleday, 1992)
ACEBTSup	Amsterdamse cahiers voor exegese en bijbelse theologie, Supplement
AcOr	*Acta Orientalia*
AEM	*Archives épistolaires de Mari*
ÄF	Ägyptologische Forschungen
AfO	*Archiv für Orientforschung*
AfOB	Archiv für Orientforschung Beiheft
ÄgAbh	Ägyptische Abhandlungen
AHw	Wolfram van Soden, *Akkadisches Handwörterbuch* (3 vols.; Wiesbaden: Harrassowitz, 1965–81)
AJSL	*American Journal of Semitic Languages and Literatures*
AJT	*American Journal of Theology*
Akk.	Akkadian
ALBO	Analecta Lovaniensia Biblica et Orientalia
AnBib	Analecta Biblica
ANEP	*The Ancient Near East in Pictures Relating to the Old Testament* (ed. James B. Pritchard; 2nd ed.; Princeton: Princeton University Press, 1994)
ANET	*Ancient Near Eastern Texts Relating to the Old Testament* (ed. James B. Pritchard; 3rd ed.; Princeton: Princeton University Press, 1969)
Ang	*Angelicum*
AnnStEbr	*Annuario di studi ebraici*
AnOr	Analecta Orientalia
Anton	*Antonianum*
AO	Der alte Orient
AOAT	Alter Orient und Altes Testament
AOS	American Oriental Series
AR	*Archiv für Religionswissenschaft*
ArBib	Aramaic Bible
ARE	*Ancient Records of Egypt* (ed. James Henry Breasted; 5 vols.; Chicago: University of Chicago Press, 1906–7; repr., New York: Russell & Russell, 1962)
ArOr	*Archiv Orientální*
ASAE	*Annales du service des antiquités de l'Egypte*
ASOR	American Schools of Oriental Research
AsSeign	*Assemblées du Seigneur*
ASTI	*Annual of the Swedish Theological Institute*
ATA	Alttestamentliche Abhandlungen
ATANT	Abhandlungen zur Theologie des Alten und Neuen Testaments
ATD	Das Alte Testament Deutsch
ATDan	Acta theologica Danica
ATR	*Anglican Theological Review*
ATSAT	Arbeiten zu Text und Sprache im alten Testament
Aug	*Augustinianum*
AuOr	*Aula Orientalis*
AUSS	*Andrews University Seminary Studies*
AV	Authorized Version
AYBRL	Anchor Yale Bible Reference Library
AZ	*Archäologische Zeitung*
AzTh	Arbeiten zur Theologie
BA	*Biblical Archaeologist*
BAR	*Biblical Archaeology Review*
BASOR	*Bulletin of the American Schools of Oriental Research*
BAT	Die Botschaft des Alten Testaments
BBB	Bonner biblische Beiträge
BBR	*Bulletin for Biblical Research*
BCE	Before the Common Era
BDB	Francis Brown, S. R. Driver, and Charles A. Briggs, *A Hebrew and English Lexicon of the Old Testament* (Oxford: Clarendon, 1907)
BEATAJ	Beiträge zur Erforschung des Alten Testaments und des antiken Judentums
BeO	*Bibbia e oriente*
BETL	Bibliotheca ephemeridum theologicarum lovaniensium
BetM	*Bet Mikra*
BEvT	Beiträge zur evangelischen Theologie
BFCT	Beiträge zur Förderung christlicher Theologie
BHH	*Biblisch-historisches Handwörterbuch: Landeskunde, Geschichte, Religion, Kultur* (ed. Bo Reicke and Leonhard Rost; 4 vols.; Göttingen: Vandenhoeck & Ruprecht, 1962–66)
BHK	*Biblia Hebraica* (ed. Rudolph Kittel; Leipzig: Hinrichs, 1905–6)

BHQ	*Biblia Hebraica Quinta* (ed. Adrian Schenker et al.; Stuttgart: Deutsche Bibelgesellschaft, 2004–)	COuT	Comentaar op het Oude Testament
		CQR	*Church Quarterly Review*
BHS	*Biblia Hebraica Stuttgartensia* (ed. Karl Elliger and Wilhelm Rudolph; Stuttgart: Deutsche Bibelgesellschaft, 1983)	*CTA*	*Corpus des tablettes en cunéiformes alphabétiques découvertes à Ras Shamra-Ugarit de 1929 à 1939* (ed. Andrée Herdner; MRS 10; Paris: Geuthner, 1963)
BHT	Beiträge zur historischen Theologie	*CTom*	*La ciencia tomista*
		CTQ	*Concordia Theological Quarterly*
Bib	*Biblica*	*CTR*	*Criswell Theological Review*
BiBh	*Bible Bhashyam*	DBAT	*Dielheimer Blätter zum Alten Testament und seiner Rezeption in der Alten Kirche*
BibInt	*Biblical Interpretation*		
BibLeb	*Bibel und Leben*		
BibOr	Biblica et Orientalia	*DBSup*	*Dictionnaire de la Bible: Supplément* (ed. Louis Pirot and André Robert; Paris: Letouzey & Ané, 1928–)
BibS(N)	Biblische Studien (Neukirchen)		
BIFAO	*Bulletin de l'Institut français d'archéologie orientale*		
BIOSCS	*Bulletin of the International Organization for Septuagint and Cognate Studies*	DD	*Dor le Dor*
		DDD	*Dictionary of Deities and Demons in the Bible* (ed. Karel van der Toorn, Bob Becking, and Pieter W. van der Horst; Leiden: Brill, 1995; 2nd rev. ed., Grand Rapids: Eerdmans, 1999)
BIS	Biblical Interpretation Series		
BJRL	*Bulletin of the John Rylands Library of Manchester*		
BJS	Brown Judaic Studies		
BK	*Bibel und Kirche*	*Did*	*Didaskalia*
BKAT	Biblischer Kommentar, Altes Testament	DJD	Discoveries in the Judaean Desert
		DSD	*Dead Sea Discoveries*
BN	*Biblische Notizen*	*DTT*	*Dansk teologisk tiddskrift*
BRev	*Bible Reviw*	EBib	Etudes bibliques
BSac	*Bibliotheca Sacra*	EdF	Erträge der Forschung
BSOAS	*Bulletin of the School of Oriental and African Studies*	EHAT	Exegetisches Handbuch zum Alten Testament
BT	*Bible Translator*	*EncJud*	*Encyclopaedia Judaica* (New York: Macmillan, 1971–72)
BTB	*Biblical Theology Bulletin*		
BurH	*Buried History*	*ErIsr*	*Eretz Israel*
BV	*Biblical Viewpoint*	*EstBíb*	*Estudios bíblicos*
BWA(N)T	Beiträge zur Wissenschaft vom Alten (und Neuen) Testament	*EstEcl*	*Estudios eclesiásticos*
		EstTeo	*Estudios teológicos*
BZAW	Beihefte zur Zeitschrift für die alttestamentliche Wissenschaft	ETL	*Ephemerides Theologicae Lovanienses*
c.	*circa*	*ETR*	*Etudes théologiques et religieuses*
CAD	*The Assyrian Dictionary of the Oriental Institute of the University of Chicago* (Chicago: Oriental Institute of the University of Chicago, 1956–2006)	Eusebius *Praep. evang.*	*Praeparatio evangelica*
		EVO	*Egitto e vicino oriente*
		EvT	*Evangelische Theologie*
		ExAu	*Ex Auditu*
CB	*Cultura Biblica*	*ExpTim*	*Expository Times*
CBC	Cambridge Bible Commentary	FAT	Forschungen zum Alten Testament
CBET	Contributions to Biblical Exegesis and Theology	FB	Forschung zur Bibel
CBQ	*Catholic Biblical Quarterly*	*FF*	*Forschungen und Fortschritte*
CBQMS	Catholic Biblical Quarterly Monograph Series	*FO*	*Folia Orientalia*
		FoiVie	*Foi et vie*
CHANE	Culture and History of the Ancient Near East	FOTL	Forms of the Old Testament Literature
ChrCent	*The Christian Century*	GKC	*Gesenius' Hebrew Grammar* (ed. Emil Kautzsch; trans. A. E. Cowley; Oxford: Clarendon, 1910)
ConBOT	Coniectanea Biblica: Old Testament Series		

HALAT	Ludwig Koehler, Walter Baumgartner, and Johann J. Stamm, *Hebräisches und aramäisches Lexikon zum Alten Testament* (3rd ed.; Leiden: Brill, 1995, 2004)	*JCS*	*Journal of Cuneiform Studies*
		JEA	*Journal of Egyptian Archaeology*
		JEOL	*Jahrbericht van het Vooraziatisch-Egyptisch Gezelschap*
		Jerome (Hieronymus)	
		Comm. Isa.	*Commentariorum in Isaiam*
HALOT	Ludwig Koehler, Walter Baumgartner, and Johann J. Stamm, *The Hebrew and Aramaic Lexicon of the Old Testament* (trans. and ed. under the supervision of Mervyn E. J. Richardson; 4 vols.; Leiden: Brill, 1994–99)	*JETS*	*Journal of the Evangelical Theological Society*
		JHNES	Johns Hopkins Near Eastern Studies
		JJS	*Journal of Jewish Studies*
		JNES	*Journal of Near Eastern Studies*
		JNSL	*Journal of Northwest Semitic Languages*
HANE	History of the Ancient Near East		
HANE/S	History of the Ancient Near East: Studies	*JPOS*	*Journal of the Palestine Oriental Society*
HAR	*Hebrew Annual Review*	JPS	Jewish Publication Society Version
HBS	Herders biblische Studien		
HBT	*Horizons in Biblical Theology*	*JQR*	*Jewish Quarterly Review*
HDR	Harvard Dissertations in Religion	*JR*	*Journal of Religion*
Herm	*Hermanthena*	JSJSup	Journal for the Study of Judaism Supplement
HeyJ	*Heythrop Journal*		
HKAT	Göttinger Handkommentar zum Alten Testament	*JSOT*	*Journal for the Study of the Old Testament*
HO	Handbuch der Orientalistik	JSOTSup	Journal for the Study of the Old Testament Supplement Series
HR	*History of Religions*		
HS	*Hebrew Studies*	*JSR*	*Journal for the Study of Religion*
HSM	Harvard Semitic Monographs	*JSS*	*Journal of Semitic Studies*
HThKat	Herders theologischer Kommentar zum Alten Testament	*JTS*	*Journal of Theological Studies*
		KAT	Kommentar zum Alten Testament
HUCA	*Hebrew Union College Annual*		
IBC	Interpretation: A Bible Commentary for Teaching and Preaching	*KD*	*Kerygma und Dogma*
		KHC	Kurzer Hand-Commentar zum Alten Testament
ICC	International Critical Commentary		
		KJV	King James Version
IDB	*The Interpreter's Dictionary of the Bible* (ed. George A. Buttrick; 4 vols.; New York: Abingdon, 1962)	KR	B. Kennicott, *Vetus Testamentum Hebraicum, cum variis lectionibus* (2 vols.; Oxford: Clarendon, 1776–80); J. B. de Rossi, *Variae Lectiones Veteris Testamenti librorum* (4 vols.; Parma: Ex Regio Tipographeo, 1784).
IDS	*In die Skriflig*		
IEJ	*Israel Exploration Journal*		
Int	*Interpretation*		
IOS	*Israel Oriental Studies*		
JAC	*Jahrbuch für Antike und Christentum*	*KTU*	*Die keilalphabetischen Texte aus Ugarit* (ed. Manfried Dietrich, Oswald Loretz, and Joaquín Sanmartín; Münster: Ugarit-Verlag, 1995)
JANES	*Journal of the Ancient Near Eastern Society*		
JANESCU	*Journal of the Ancient Near Eastern Society of Columbia University*		
		LD	Lectio divina
JAOS	*Journal of the American Oriental Society*	*Leš*	*Lešonenu*
		LHBOTS	Library of Hebrew Bible/Old Testament Studies
JARCE	*Journal of the American Research Center in Egypt*		
		LQ	*Lutheran Quarterly*
Jastrow	Marcus Jastrow, *A Dictionary of the Targumim, the Talmud Babli and Yerushalmi, and the Midrashic Literature* (2 vols.; New York: Pardes, 1950)	*LRb*	*Lutherischer Rundblick*
		LumVie	*Lumière et vie*
		LXX	Septuagint
		MdB	*Le Monde de la Bible*
		MEAH	*Miscelánea de estudios arabes y hebraicos*
JBL	*Journal of Biblical Literature*		
JBR	*Journal of Bible and Religion*		

MGWJ	*Monatschrift für Geschichte und Wissenschaft des Judentums*
MIO	*Mitteilungen des Instituts für Orientforschung*
MPT	*Monatsschrift für Pastoraltheologie*
MRS	Mission de Ras Shamra
MT	Masoretic Text
MTZ	*Münchener theologische Zeitschrift*
MUSJ	*Mélanges de l'Université Saint-Joseph*
MVAG	Mitteilungen der Vorderasiatisch-ägyptischen Gesellschaft
NAB	New American Bible
NC	*Nouvelle Clio*
NCB	New Century Bible
NEASB	*Near Eastern Archaeological Society Bulletin*
NEB	New English Bible
NEchtB	Neue Echter Bibel
NedTT	*Nederlands theologisch tijdschrift*
NGTT	*Nederduitse gereformeerde teologiese tydskrif*
NICOT	New International Commentary on the Old Testament
NIDB	*The New Interpreter's Dictionary of the Bible* (ed. Katharine Doob Sakenfeld; 5 vols.; Nashville: Abingdon, 2006–9)
NIV	New International Version
NKZ	*Neue kirchliche Zeitschrift*
NorTT	*Norsk Teologisk Tidsskrift*
NRSV	New Revised Standard Version
NRT	*La nouvelle revue théologique*
n.s.	new series
NThSt	*Nieuwe theologische studien*
NTS	*New Testament Studies*
NTT	*Norsk Teologisk Tidsskrift*
OBO	Orbis biblicus et orientalis
OIP	Oriental Institute Publications
OLP	*Orientalia Lovaniensia Periodica*
OLZ	*Orientalische Literaturzeitung*
Or	*Orientalia*
OrAnt	*Oriens Antiquus*
OTE	*Old Testament Essays*
OTL	Old Testament Library
OTM	Old Testament Message
OTS	Oudtestamentische Studiën
OTS	*Oudtestamentische Studiën*
OTWSA	*Ou Testamentiese Werkgemeenskap van Suid-Afrika*
Pauly-W	*Paulys Real-encyclopädie der classischen altertumswissenschaft* (Stuttgart: J. B. Metzler, 1920–)
PEQ	*Palestine Exploration Quarterly*
PIBA	*Proceedings of the Irish Biblical Association*
PJ	*Palästina-Jahrbuch*
Presb	*Presbyterion*
Proof	*Prooftexts*
PRSt	*Perspectives in Religious Studies*
PSB	*Princeton Seminary Bulletin*
PTMS	Pittsburgh Theological Monograph Series
PTSDSSP	Princeton Theological Seminary Dead Sea Scrolls Project
PzB	*Protokolle zur Bibel*
QD	Quaestiones Disputatae
RA	*Revue d'assyriologie et d'archéologie orientale*
RB	*Revue biblique*
RCB	*Revista de cultura bíblica*
REB	*Revista eclesiástica brasileira*
REJ	*Revue des études juives*
ResQ	*Restoration Quarterly*
RevExp	*Review and Expositor*
RevistB	*Revista bíblica*
RevQ	*Revue de Qumran*
RGG³	*Die Religion in Geschichte und Gegenwart* (ed. Kurt Galling; 3rd ed.; Tübingen: Mohr Siebeck, 1957–65)
RHA	*Revue hittite et asianique*
RHPR	*Revue d'histoire et de philosophie religieuses*
RHR	*Revue de l'histoire des religions*
RIMB	Royal Inscriptions of Mesopotamia, Babylonian Periods
RINAP	Royal Inscriptions of the New-Assyrian Period
RivB	*Rivista biblica italiana*
RlA	*Reallexikon der Assyriologie* (ed. Erich Ebeling et al.; Berlin: de Gruyter, 1928–)
RLC	*Revue de littérature comparée*
RocTK	*Roczniki teologiczno-kanoniczne*
RSR	*Recherches de science religieuse*
RSV	Revised Standard Version
RTL	*Revue théologique de Louvain*
RTP	*Revue de théologie et de philosophie*
RTR	*Reformed Theological Review*
SAA	State Archives of Assyria
SAAB	*State Archives of Assyria Bulletin*
SAAS	State Archives of Assyria Studies
Salm	*Salmanticensis*
SANT	Studien zum Alten und Neuen Testament
SB	Sources biblique
SBFLA	*Studii Biblici Franciscani Liber Annuus*
SBL	Society of Biblical Literature
SBLDS	Society of Biblical Literature Dissertation Series
SBLEJL	Society of Biblical Literature Early Judaism and Its Literature
SBLSP	*Society of Biblical Literature Seminar Papers*
SBLSymS	Society of Biblical Literature Symposium Series
SBS	Stuttgarter Bibelstudien

SBT	Studies in Biblical Theology
ScEs	*Science et esprit*
Scr	*Scripture*
ScrB	*Scripture Bulletin*
ScrHier	Scripta Hierosolymitana
SCS	Septuagint and Cognate Studies
SEÅ	*Svensk exegetisk årsbok*
Sef	*Sefarad*
SHCANE	Studies in the History and Culture of the Ancient Near East
SHR	Studies in the History of Religions
SJOT	*Scandinavian Journal of the Old Testament*
SJT	*Scottish Journal of Theology*
SMSR	*Studi e materiali di storia delle religioni*
SOTSMS	Society for Old Testament Studies Monograph Series
SP	*Sacra Pagina*
SPAW	Sitzungsberichte der preussischen Akademie der Wissenschaften
SSN	Studia Semitica Neerlandica
ST	*Studia Theologica*
STDJ	Studies on the Texts of the Desert of Judah
StOr	Studies in Oriental Religions
SubBib	Subsidia Biblica
Syr.	Syriac
TA	*Tel Aviv*
TB	Theologische Bücherei
TBC	Torch Bible Commentaries
TBei	*Theologische Beiträge*
TBl	*Theologische Blätter*
TBT	*The Bible Today*
TCS	Texts from Cuneiform Sources
TD	*Theology Digest*
TDNT	*Theological Dictionary of the New Testament* (ed. Gerhard Kittel and Gerhard Friedrich; trans. Geoffrey W. Bromiley; 10 vols.; Grand Rapids: Eerdmans, 1964–76)
TDOT	*Theological Dictionary of the Old Testament* (ed. G. Johannes Botterweck and Helmer Ringgren; trans. John T. Willis et al.; Grand Rapids: Eerdmans, 1974–2006)
TEV	Today's English Version
Tg.	Targum
TGl	*Theologie und Glaube*
THAT	*Theologisches Handwörterbuch zum Alten Testament* (ed. Ernst Jenni and Claus westermann; Munich: C. Kaiser, 1971–).
Theol	*Theologica*
ThSt	Theologische Studiën
ThWAT	*Theologisches Wörterbuch zum Alten Testament* (ed. G. Johannes Botterweck and Helmer Ringgren; Stuttgart: Kohlhammer, 1970–)
ThWNT	*Theologisches Wörterbuch zum Neuen Testament* (ed. Gerhard Kittel and Gerhard Friedrich; Stuttgart: Kohlhammer, 1923–79)
TLZ	*Theologische Literaturzeitung*
TPQ	*Theologisch-praktische Quartalschift*
TQ	*Theologische Quartalschrift*
TRu	*Theologische Rundschau*
TSK	*Theologische Studien und Kritiken*
TThSt	Trierer theologische Studien
TTZ	*Trierer theologische Zeitschrift*
TynBul	*Tyndale Bulletin*
TZ	*Theologische Zeitschrift*
UBL	Ugaritisch-biblische Literatur
UF	*Ugarit-Forschungen*
VAB	Vorderasiatische Bibliothek
VC	*Vigiliae Christianae*
VD	*Verbum Domini*
VF	*Verkündigung und Forschung*
Vg.	Vulgate
VH	*Vivens Homo*
VT	*Vetus Testamentum*
VTSup	Supplements to Vetus Testamentum
WAW	Writings from the Ancient World
WD	*Wort und Dienst*
WMANT	Wissenschaftliche Monographien zum Alten und Neuen Testament
WO	*Die Welt des Orients*
WTJ	*Westminster Theological Journal*
WUNT	Wissenschaftliche Unversuchungen zum Neuen Testament
WZKM	*Wiener Zeitschrift für die Kunde des Morgenlandes*
ZAH	*Zeitschrift für Althebräistik*
ZÄS	*Zeitschrift für ägyptische Sprache und Altertumskunde*
ZAW	*Zeitschrift für die alttestamentliche Wissenschaft*
ZBK	Zürcher Bibelkommentare
ZDMG	*Zeitschrift der deutschen morgenländischen Gesellschaft*
ZDMGSup	Zeitschrift der deutschen morgenländischen Gesellschaft Supplementbände
ZDPV	*Zeitschrift des deutschen Palästina-Vereins*
ZKT	*Zeitschrift für katholische Theologie*
ZNW	*Zeitschrift für die neutestamentliche Wissenschaft und die Kunde der älteren Kirche*
ZRGG	*Zeitschrift für Religions- und Geistesgeschichte*
ZST	*Zeitschrift für systematische Theologie*
ZTK	*Zeitschrift für Theologie und Kirche*
ZWT	*Zeitschrift für wissenschaftliche Theologie*

2. Short Titles

Commentaries

Auvray
    Paul Auvray, *Isaïe 1–39* (SB; Paris: Gabalda, 1972).

Beuken, *Jesaja 1–12*
    W. A. M. Beuken, *Jesaja 1–12* (HThKAT; Freiburg: Herder, 2003).

Beuken, *Jesaja 13–27*
    W. A. M. Beuken, *Jesaja 13–27* (HThKAT; Freiburg: Herder, 2007).

Beuken, *Jesaja 28–39*
    W. A. M. Beuken, *Jesaja 28–39* (HThKAT; Freiburg: Herder, 2010).

Bewer
    J. A. Bewer, *The Book of Isaiah,* vols. 3–4 of *Harper's Annotated Bible* (New York: Harper & Bros., 1950).

Blenkinsopp
    Joseph Blenkinsopp, *Isaiah 1–39: A New Translation with Introduction and Commentary* (AB 19; New York: Doubleday, 2000).

Bruno
    Arvid Bruno, *Jesaja: Eine rhythmische und textkritische Untersuchung* (Stockholm: Almqvist & Wiksell, 1953).

Buhl
    Frants Buhl, *Jesaja* (2nd ed.; Copenhagen: Gyldendal, 1912).

Cheyne
    T. K. Cheyne, *The Book of the Prophet Isaiah* (5th ed.; New York: Dodd, Mead, 1904).

Childs
    Brevard S. Childs, *Isaiah* (OTL; Louisville: Westminster John Knox, 2001).

Clements
    Ronald E. Clements, *Isaiah 1–39* (NCB; Grand Rapids: Eerdmans, 1980).

Conrad
    Edgar W. Conrad, *Reading Isaiah* (Overtures to Biblical Theology; Minneapolis: Fortress Press, 1991).

Delitzsch, *Jesaia*
    Franz Delitzsch, *Biblischer Commentar über den Propheten Jesaia* (Leipzig: Dörffling & Frank, 1869).

Delitzsch, *Prophecies of Isaiah*
    Franz Delitzsch, *Biblical Commentary on the Prophecies of Isaiah* (trans. James Martin; Grand Rapids: Eerdmans, 1949).

Dillmann, 5th ed.
    August Dillmann, *Der Prophet Jesaia* (5th ed.; Kurzgefasstes exegetisches Handbuch zum Alten Testament 5; Leipzig: S. Hirzel, 1890).

Dillmann, 6th ed.
    August Dillmann, *Der Prophet Jesaia* (6th ed., rev. and ed. Rudolf Kittel; Kurzgefasstes exegetisches Handbuch zum Alten Testament 5; Leipzig: S. Hirzel, 1898).

Döderlein
    J. C. Döderlein, *Esaias, ex recensione textus Hebraei* (Altorfi, 1789).

Duhm
    Bernhard Duhm, *Das Buch Jesaia* (3rd ed.; HKAT 3.1; Göttingen: Vandenhoeck & Ruprecht, 1914).

Ehrlich, *Randglossen*
    Arnold B. Ehrlich, *Randglossen zur hebräischen Bibel, textkritisches, sprachliches und sachliches,* vol. 4, *Jesaia, Jeremia* (Leipzig: Hinrichs, 1912).

Eichrodt, *Jesaja 1–12*
    Walther Eichrodt, *Der Heilige in Israel: Jesaja 1–12* (BAT 17.1; Stuttgart: Calwer, 1960).

Eichrodt, *Jesaja 13–23 und 28–39*
    Walther Eichrodt, *Der Herr der Geschichte: Jesaja 13–23 und 28–39* (BAT 17.2; Stuttgart: Calwer, 1967).

Eusebius
    Eusebius Pamphili of Caesaria, *Der Jesajakommentar,* vol. 9 of *Eusebius Werke* (ed. J. Ziegler; Berlin: Akademie, 1975).

Feldmann
    Franz Feldmann, *Das Buch Isaias* (2 vols.; EHAT 14; Münster: Aschendorff, 1925–26).

Fohrer
    Georg Fohrer, *Das Buch Jesaja* (3 vols.; ZBK;. Zurich: Zwingli, 1960–64; 2nd ed., 1962–1967).

Gesenius
    Wilhelm Gesenius, *Der Prophet Jesaia* (Leipzig: Vogel, 1829).

Gray
    George Buchanan Gray, *A Critical and Exegetical Commentary on the Book of Isaiah I–XXXIX* (ICC; Edinburgh: T&T Clark, 1912).

Guthe
    Hermann Guthe, *Jesaja* (Tübingen: Mohr, 1907).

Hayes and Irvine
    John H. Hayes and Stuart A. Irvine, *Isaiah, the Eighth-Century Prophet: His Times and His Preaching* (Nashville: Abingdon, 1987).

Herbert
    A. S. Herbert, *The Book of the Prophet Isaiah, Chapters 1–39* (CBC; Cambridge: Cambridge University Press, 1973).

Herntrich
    Volkmar Herntrich, *Der Prophet Jesaja: Kapitel 1–12* (ATD 17; Göttingen: Vandenhoeck & Ruprecht, 1950).

Hertzberg
    Hans Wilhelm Hertzberg, *Der Erste Jesaja* (3rd ed.; Leipzig: Schloessmann, 1955).

Hitzig
    Ferdinand Hitzig, *Der Prophet Jesaja* (Heidelberg: Winter, 1833).

Ibn Ezra
    Ibn Ezra (Abraham ben Meir), *Commentary of Ibn Ezra on Isaiah* (in Hebrew; trans. M. Friedlander; 2nd ed.; New York: Feldheim, 1966).

Jensen
    Joseph Jensen, *Isaiah 1–39* (OTM 8; Wilmington, DE: Michael Glazier, 1984).

Jerome

    Jerome, *Commentaires de Jerome sur le prophete Isaie* (ed. R. Gryson and P.-A. Deproost; Aus der Geschichte der lateinischen Bibel 23, 27, 30, 35, 36; Freiburg: Herder, 1993–).

Kaiser, *Jesaja 1–12*

    Otto Kaiser, *Der Prophet Jesaja: Kapitel 1–12* (2nd ed.; ATD 17; Göttingen: Vandenhoeck & Ruprecht, 1963).

Kaiser, *Jesaja 13–39*

    Otto Kaiser, *Der Prophet Jesaja: Kapitel 13–39* (ATD 18; Göttingen: Vandenhoeck & Ruprecht, 1973).

Kaiser, *Isaiah 1–12*

    Otto Kaiser, *Isaiah 1–12* (trans. R. A. Wilson; 2nd ed.; OTL; Philadelphia: Westminster, 1983).

Kaiser, *Isaiah 13–39*

    Otto Kaiser, *Isaiah 13–39* (trans. R. A. Wilson; 2nd ed.; OTL; Philadelphia: Westminster, 1983).

Kelley

    P. H. Kelley, "Isaiah," in *The Broadman Bible Commentary* (ed. Clifton J. Allen et al.; 12 vols.; Nashville: Broadman, 1969–72) 5:149–374.

Kilian, *Jesaja 1–39*

    Rudolf Kilian, *Jesaja 1–39* (EdF 200; Darmstadt: Wissenschaftliche Buchgesellschaft, 1983).

Kilian, *Jesaja 1–12*

    Rudolf Kilian, *Jesaja 1–12* (NEchtB 17; Würzburg: Echter, 1986).

Kilian, *Jesaja II: 13–39*

    Rudolf Kilian, *Jesaja II: 13–39* (NEchtB 32; Würzburg: Echter, 1994).

Kimchi

    David Kimchi, *The Commentary of David Kimchi on Isaiah* (in Hebrew with introduction in English; ed. L. Finkelstein; Columbia University Oriental Studies 19; New York: Columbia University Press, 1926; repr., New York: AMS Press, 1966).

Kissane

    Edward J. Kissane, *The Book of Isaiah* (rev. ed.; 2 vols.; Dublin: Browne & Nolan, 1960).

König

    Eduard König, *Das Buch Jesaja* (Gütersloh: Bertelsmann, 1926).

Leslie

    Elmer Archibald Leslie, *Isaiah, Chronologically Arranged, Translated and Interpreted* (New York: Abingdon, 1963).

Luther

    Martin Luther, *Der Prophet Jesaia,* vols. 25, 31.2 of *D. Martin Luthers Werke* (Kritische Gesamtausgabe 25; Weimar: H. Böhlau, 1883) 87–401.

Luther, *Lectures on Isaiah*

    Martin Luther, *Lectures on Isaiah Chs. 1–39,* vol. 16 of *Luther's Works* (ed. and trans. J. Pelikan and H. C. Oswald; St. Louis: Concordia, 1969).

Luzzatto, *Commentary*

    S. D. Luzzatto, *Commentary on the Book of Isaiah* (in Hebrew; 1855; repr., Tel Aviv: Davir, 1970).

Luzzatto, *Il profeta Isaia*

    S. D. Luzzatto, *Il profeta Isaia volgarizzato e commentato ad uso degli'Israelit.* (Padua: A. Bianchi, 1867).

Macpherson

    Ann Macpherson, *Prophets* (Scripture Discussion Commentary 2, 4; London: Sheed & Ward, 1971–72).

Marti

    D. Karl Marti, *Das Buch Jesaja* (KHC 10; Tübingen: Mohr Siebeck, 1900).

Mauchline

    John Mauchline, *Isaiah 1–39: Introduction and Commentary* (TBC; London: SCM, 1962).

Motyer

    J. Alec Motyer, *The Prophecy of Isaiah: An Introduction and Commentary* (Downers Grove, IL: InterVarsity, 1993).

Nägelsbach

    C. W. E. Nägelsbach, *Der Prophet Jesaja* (Leipzig: Klasing, 1877).

Oswalt

    John N. Oswalt, *The Book of Isaiah, Chapters 1–39* (NICOT; Grand Rapids: Eerdmans, 1986).

Procksch

    Otto Procksch, *Jesaia I übersetzt und erklärt* (KAT 9.1; Leipzig: A. Deichert, 1930).

Schoors

    Antoon Schoors, *Jesaja* (De boeken van het Oude Testament; Roermond: J. J. Romen & Zonen, 1972).

Scott

    R. B. Y. Scott, "The Book of Isaiah," in George A. Buttrick et al., eds., *The Interpreter's Bible* (12 vols.; Nashville: Abingdon, 1956) 5:149–381.

Seitz

    Christopher R. Seitz, *Isaiah 1–39* (IBC; Louisville: John Knox, 1993).

Snijders

    L. A. Snijders, *Jesaja,* vol. 1 (2nd ed.; De Prediking van het Oude Testament; Nijkerk: Callenbach, 1979).

Steinmann

    Jean Steinmann, *Le prophète Isaïe: Sa vie, son oeuvre et son temps* (LD 5; Paris: Cerf, 1955).

Sweeney

    Marvin A. Sweeney, *Isaiah 1–39, with an Introduction to Prophetic Literature* (FOTL 16; Grand Rapids: Eerdmans, 1996).

Watts, *Isaiah 1–33*

    John D. W. Watts, *Isaiah 1–33* (WBC 24; Waco, TX: Word Books, 1985; rev. ed., 2005).

Watts, *Isaiah 34–36*

    John D. W. Watts, *Isaiah 34–66* (WBC 25; Waco, TX: Word Books, 1987).

Wildberger

    Hans Wildberger, *Jesaja* (3 vols.; BKAT 10.1–3; Neukirchen-Vluyn: Neukirchener Verlag, 1972–82).

Wildberger, *Isaiah 1–12; 13–27; 28–39*
Hans Wildberger, *Isaiah 1–12; 13–27; 28–39* (trans. T. H. Trapp; 3 vols.; Continental Commentary; Minneapolis: Fortress Press, 1991–2002).

Williamson
H. G. M. Williamson, *A Critical and Exegetical Commentary on Isaiah 1–27* (3 vols.; ICC 23; London: T&T Clark, 2006).

Wright
George Ernest Wright, *The Book of Isaiah* (Layman's Bible Commentary 11; Richmond: John Knox, 1964).

Young
E. J. Young, *The Book of Isaiah* (3 vols.; NICOT; Grand Rapids: Eerdmans, 1965–72).

Ziegler
Joseph Ziegler, ed., *Isaias* (Septuaginta 14; Göttingen: Vandenhoeck & Ruprecht, 1939).

Ziegler, 3rd ed.
Joseph Ziegler, ed., *Isaias* (3rd ed.; Septuaginta: Vetus Testamentum Graecum Auctoritate Academiae Scientiarium Gottingensis 14; Göttingen: Vandenhoeck & Ruprecht, 1983).

Ziegler, *Isaias*
Joseph Ziegler, *Isaias* (Echter-Bibel; Würzburg: Echter, 1948).

Text Critical

Baer, "It's All About Us!"
D. A. Baer, "It's All About Us! Nationalistic Exegesis in the Greek Isaiah 1–12," in *SBLSP 2001* (Atlanta: Society of Biblical Literature, 2001) 197–219.

Baer, "With Due Respect"
D. A. Baer, "With Due Respect: Speaking about God in LXX Isaiah," *AAR/SBL Abstracts 1998* (Atlanta: Scholars Press, 1998) 326.

Baillet et al., *Les "petites grottes"*
M. Baillet, J. T. Milik, and R. de Vaux, eds., *Les "petites grottes" de Qumrân* (DJD 3; Oxford: Clarendon, 1962).

Barnett, *Sculptures of Aššur-nasir-apli II*
R. D. Barnett, *The Sculptures of Aššur-nasir-apli II, 883–859 B.C., Tiglath-pileser III, 745–727 B.C., [and] Esarhaddon, 681–669 B.C., From the Central and South-West Palaces at Nimrud* (London: Trustees of the British Museum, 1962).

Barthélemy and Milik, *Qumran Cave 1*
D. Barthélemy and J. T. Milik, *Qumran Cave 1* (DJD 1; Oxford: Clarendon, 1955).

Benoit et al., *Murabba'at*
P. Benoit, J. T. Milik, and R. de Vaux, eds., *Les grottes de Murabba'at* (DJD 2; Oxford: Clarendon, 1961).

Brock, *Isaiah*
S. P. Brock, ed., *Isaiah* (Old Testament in Syriac according to the Peshiṭta Version 3.1; Leiden: Brill, 1987).

Brock, "Text History"
S. P. Brock, "Text History and Text Division in Peshiṭta Isaiah," in *The Peshiṭta: Its Early Text and History. Papers Read at the "Peshiṭta Symposium" Held at Leiden 30-31 August, 1985* (ed. P. B. Dirksen and M. J. Mulder; Monographs of the Peshiṭta Institute, Leiden 4; Leiden: Brill, 1988) 49–80.

Brownlee, *Meaning*
W. H. Brownlee, *The Meaning of the Qumran Scrolls for the Bible: With Special Attention to the Book of Isaiah* (New York: Oxford University Press, 1964).

Burrows, *Isaiah Manuscript*
Millar Burrows et al., eds., *The Dead Sea Scrolls of St. Mark's Monastery*, vol. 1, *The Isaiah Manuscript and the Habakkuk Commentary* (New Haven: ASOR, 1950).

Burrows, "Variant Readings"
Millar Burrows, "Variant Readings in the Isaiah Manuscript," *BASOR* 111 (1948–49) 16–24; 113 (1949) 24–32.

Charlesworth, *Bible and the Dead Sea Scrolls*
James H. Charlesworth, ed., *The Bible and the Dead Sea Scrolls*, vol. 1, *Scripture and the Scrolls. The Second Princeton Symposium on Judaism and Christian Origins* (Waco, TX: Baylor University Press, 2006).

Chilton, *Glory of Israel*
Bruce D. Chilton, *The Glory of Israel: The Theology and Provenience of the Isaiah Targum* (JSOTSup 23; Sheffield: JSOT Press, 1982).

Chilton, *Isaiah Targum*
Bruce D. Chilton, *The Isaiah Targum: Introduction, Translation, Apparatus, and Notes* (ArBib 11; Wilmington, DE: Glazier, 1987).

Cohen, "Philological Reevaluation"
C. Cohen, "A Philological Reevaluation of Some Significant DSS Variants of the MT in Isa 1–5," in T. Muraoka and J. F. Elwolde, eds., *Diggers at the Well: Proceedings of a Third International Symposium on the Hebrew of the Dead Sea Scrolls and Ben Sira* (STDJ 36; Leiden: Brill, 2000) 40–55.

Cross, *Scrolls from Qumran Cave I*
F. M. Cross et al., eds., *Scrolls from Qumran Cave I: The Great Isaiah Scroll, The Order of the Community, The Pesher to Habakkuk, from Photographs by John C. Trever* (Jerusalem: Albright Institute of Archaeological Research and the Shrine of the Book, 1972).

Dalman, *Arbeit und Sitte*
Gustaf Dalman, *Arbeit und Sitte in Palästina* (7 vols.; Gütersloh: C. Bertelsmann, 1928–39).

Driver, "Hebrew Notes"
G. R. Driver, "Hebrew Notes," *VT* 1 (1951) 241–50.

Driver, "Isaiah 1–39: Problems"
G. R. Driver, "Isaiah 1–39: Textual and Linguistic Problems," *JSS* 13 (1968) 36–57.

Driver, "Isaianic Problems"
G. R. Driver, "Isaianic Problems," in G. Wiesner, ed., *Festschrift für Wilhelm Eilers* (Wiesbaden: Harrassowitz, 1967) 43–57.

Driver, "Linguistic and Textual Problems"
G. R. Driver, "Linguistic and Textual Problems: Isaiah I–XXXIX," *JTS* 38 (1937) 36–50.

Driver, "Prophets and Proverbs"
G. R. Driver, "Hebrew Notes on Prophets and Proverbs," *JTS* 41 (1940) 162–75.

Field, *Origenis Hexaplorum*
F. Field, *Origenis Hexaplorum quae supersunt,* vol. 2 (1875; repr., Oxford: Oxford University Press, 1964).

Fischer, *Buch Isaias*
Johann Fischer, *In welcher Schrift lag das Buch Isaias den LXX vor?* (BZAW 56; Giessen: A. Töpelmann, 1930).

Flint, "Book of Isaiah"
Peter W. Flint, "The Book of Isaiah in the Dead Sea Scrolls," in Edward D. Herbert and Emanuel Tov, eds., *The Bible as Book: The Hebrew Bible and the Judaean Desert Discoveries* (London: British Library, 2002) 229–51.

Flint, "Isaiah Scrolls"
Peter W. Flint, "The Isaiah Scrolls from the Judean Desert," in C. C. Broyles and C. A. Evans, eds., *Writing and Reading the Scroll of Isaiah: Studies of an Interpretive Tradition* (2 vols.; VTSup 70; Leiden: Brill, 1997) 2:481–89.

Flint et al., *Isaiah Scrolls*
P. W. Flint, E. Ulrich, and M. G. Abegg, *Qumran Cave 1.II: The Isaiah Scrolls* (DJD 32; Oxford: Clarendon, 2010).

García Martínez, "Le livre d'Isaïe"
F. García Martínez, "Le livre d'Isaïe à Qomrân: Les textes, l'influence," *MdB* 49 (1987) 43–45.

Gelston, "Peshitta of Isaiah"
A. Gelston, "Was the Peshitta of Isaiah of Christian Origin?" in C. C. Broyles and C. A. Evans, eds., *Writing and Reading the Scroll of Isaiah: Studies of an Interpretive Tradition* (2 vols.; VTSup 70; Leiden: Brill, 1997) 2:563–82.

Gesenius, *Grammar*
GKC
E. Kautzsch and A. E. Cowley, eds., *Gesenius' Hebrew Grammar* (2nd ed.; Oxford: Clarendon, 1910; repr., 1988).

Gesenius, *Handwörterbuch*
Wilhelm Gesenius, *Hebräisches und aramäisches Handwörterbuch über das Alte Testament* (18th ed.; Berlin: Springer, 1987).

Gonçalves, "Isaiah Scroll"
F. J. Gonçalves, "Isaiah Scroll," *ABD* 3:470–72.

Gordon, *Ancient Versions*
R. P. Gordon, *Hebrew Bible and Ancient Versions: Selected Essays of Robert P. Gordon* (SOTSMS; Aldershot: Ashgate, 2006).

Goshen-Gottstein, *Isaiah*
Moshe H. Goshen-Gottstein, ed., *The Book of Isaiah* (Hebrew University Bible; Jerusalem: Magnes Press, Hebrew University, 1995).

Goshen-Gottstein, "Die Jesaja Rolle"
Moshe H. Goshen-Gottstein, "Die Jesaja Rolle und das Problem der hebräischen Bibelhandschriften," *Bib* 35 (1954) 429–42.

Gryson, "Esaias"
R. Gryson, "Esaias," in *Vetus Latina Beuron 12* (Freiburg im Br.: Herder, 1987).

Irwin, *Isaiah 28–33*
William Henry Irwin, *Isaiah 28–33: Translation with Philological Notes* (BibOr 30; Rome: Biblical Institute Press, 1977).

James, "Critical Examination"
F. D. James, "A Critical Examination of the Text of Isaiah" (PhD diss., Boston University, 1959).

Joüon-Muraoka
P. Joüon and T. Muraoka, *A Grammar of Biblical Hebrew* (2 vols.; SubBib 14; Rome: Pontifical Biblical Institute, 1993).

van der Kooij, *Die alten Textzeugen*
Arie van der Kooij, *Die alten Textzeugen des Jesajabuches* (OBO 35; Freiburg: Universitätsverlag; Göttingen: Vandenhoeck & Ruprecht, 1981).

van der Kooij, "Septuagint of Isaiah"
Arie van der Kooij, "The Septuagint of Isaiah: Translation and Interpretation," in J. Vermeylen et al., eds., *Le livre d'Isaïe: Les oracles et leurs relectures. Unité et complexité de l'ouvrage* (BETL 81; Leuven: Leuven University Press, 1989) 127–33.

van der Kooij, "Interpretation"
Arie van der Kooij, "Interpretation of the Book of Isaiah in the Septuagint and Other Ancient Versions," in *SBLSP 2001* (Atlanta: Society of Biblical Literature, 2001) 220–39.

van der Kooij, "Isaiah in the Septuagint"
Arie van der Kooij, "Isaiah in the Septuagint," in C. C. Broyles and C. A. Evans, eds., *Writing and Reading the Scroll of Isaiah: Studies of an Interpretive Tradition* (2 vols.; VTSup 70; Leiden: Brill, 1997) 2:513–29.

van der Kooij, "Old Greek of Isaiah"
Arie van der Kooij, "The Old Greek of Isaiah in Relation to the Qumran Texts of Isaiah: Some General Comments," in G. J. Brooke and B. Lindars, eds., *Septuagint, Scrolls and Cognate Writings: Papers Presented to the International Symposium on the Septuagint and Its Relations to the Dead Sea Scrolls and Other Writings, Manchester, 1990* (SCS 33; Atlanta: Scholars Press, 1992) 195–213.

van der Kooij and van der Meer, *Old Greek of Isaiah*
Arie van der Kooij and M. van der Meer, eds., *The Old Greek of Isaiah: Issues and Perspectives. Papers Read at the Conference on the Septuagint of Isaiah, Held in Leiden 10-11 April 2008* (CBET 55; Leuven: Peeters, 2010).

Kutscher, *Language and Linguistic Background*
E. Y. Kutscher, *The Language and Linguistic Background of the Isaiah Scroll (1QIsaᵃ).* STDJ 6. Leiden: Brill, 1974.

Laberge, *La Septante d'Isaïe*
Léo Laberge, *La Septante d'Isaïe 28–33: Étude de tradition textuelle* (Ottawa: L. Laberge, 1978).

van der Meer, *Isaiah in Context*
    M. N. van der Meer et al. (eds)., *Isaiah in Context: Studies in Honour of Arie van der Kooij on the Occasion of His Sixty-fifth Birthday* (VTSup 138; Leiden: Brill, 2010).

das Neves, *A teologia da tradução*
    Joaquim Carreira Marcelino das Neves, *A teologia da tradução grega dos setenta no livro de Isaías: (cap. 24 de Isaías)* (Lisbon: Universidade Católica Protuguesa, 1973).

Olley, "Hear the Word"
    J. W. Olley, "Hear the Word of JHWH: The Structure of the Book of Isaiah in 1QIsaᵃ," *VT* 43 (1993) 19–49.

Parry and Qimron, *Great Isaiah Scroll*
    D. W. Parry and E. Qimron, eds., *The Great Isaiah Scroll (1QIsaᵃ): A New Edition* (STDJ 32; Leiden: Brill, 1999).

Porter and Pearson, "Isaiah through Greek Eyes"
    S. L. Porter and B. W. R. Pearson, "Isaiah through Greek Eyes: The Septuagint of Isaiah," in C. C. Broyles and C. A. Evans, eds., *Writing and Reading the Scroll of Isaiah: Studies of an Interpretive Tradition* (2 vols.; VTSup 70; Leiden: Brill, 1997) 2:531–46.

Rahlfs
    A. Rahlfs, ed., *Septuaginta* (9th ed.; Stuttgart: Württembergische Bibelanstalt, 1935).

B. J. Roberts, "Second Isaiah Scroll"
    B. J. Roberts, "The Second Isaiah Scroll from Qumran (1QIsaᵇ)," *BJRL* 42 (1959) 132–44.

Rubinstein, "Theological Aspect"
    A. Rubinstein, "The Theological Aspect of Some Variant Readings in the Isaiah Scroll," *JJS* 6 (1955) 187–200.

Schweitzer, "Mythology"
    S. J. Schweitzer, "Mythology in the Old Greek of Isaiah: The Technique of Translation," *CBQ* 66 (2004) 214–30.

Seeligmann, *Septuagint Version*
    Isac L. Seeligmann, *The Septuagint Version of Isaiah: A Discussion of Its Problems* (Leiden: Brill, 1948).

Seeligmann, *Septuagint Version and Cognate Studies*
    Isac L. Seeligmann, *The Septuagint Version of Isaiah and Cognate Studies* (ed. R. Hanhart and H. Spieckermann; FAT 40; Tübingen: Mohr Siebeck, 2004).

Skehan, "Text of Isaias"
    Patrick W. Skehan, "The Text of Isaias at Qumrân," *CBQ* 17 (1955) 158–63.

Skehan, "Textual Problems"
    Patrick W. Skehan, "Some Textual Problems in Isaia," *CBQ* 22 (1960) 47–55.

Skehan and Ulrich, "Isaiah"
    P. W. Skehan and E. Ulrich, "Isaiah," in E. Ulrich et al., eds., *Qumran Cave 4.X: The Prophets* (DJD 15; Oxford: Clarendon, 1997).

Sperber, *Bible in Aramaic*
    A. Sperber, ed., *The Bible in Aramaic*, vol. 3, *The Latter Prophets according to Targum Jonathan* (Leiden: Brill, 1962).

Stenning, *Targum of Isaiah*
    J. F. Stenning, ed. and trans., *The Targum of Isaiah* (Oxford: Clarendon, 1949).

Sukenik, *Dead Sea Scrolls of the Hebrew University*
    E. L. Sukenik, ed., *The Dead Sea Scrolls of the Hebrew University* (Jerusalem: Magnes Press, Hebrew University, 1955).

Tadmor, *Inscriptions of Tiglath-pileser III*
    Hayim Tadmor, *The Inscriptions of Tiglath-pileser III King of Assyria: Critical Edition, with Introductions, Translations, and Commentary* (Jerusalem: Israel Academy of Sciences and Humanities, 1994).

Tadmor and Yamada, RINAP 1
    Hayim Tadmor and Shigeo Yamada, *The Royal Inscriptions of Tiglath-pileser III (744–727 BC) and Shalmaneser V (726–722 BC), Kings of Assyria* (RINAP 1; Winona Lake, IN: Eisenbrauns, 2011).

Talmon, "Observations"
    S. Talmon, "Observations on Variant Readings in the Isaiah Scroll (1QIsaᵃ)," in Talmon, *The World of Qumrân from Within: Collected Studies* (Jerusalem: Magnes; Leiden: Brill, 1989) 117–30.

Tov, "Text of Isaiah at Qumran"
    Emanuel Tov, "The Text of Isaiah at Qumran," in C. C. Broyles and C. A. Evans, eds., *Writing and Reading the Scroll of Isaiah: Studies of an Interpretive Tradition* (2 vols.; VTSup 70; Leiden: Brill, 1997). 2:491–511.

Troxel, *LXX-Isaiah*
    Ronald L. Troxel, *LXX-Isaiah as Translation and Interpretation: The Strategies of the Translator of the Septuagint of Isaiah* (JSJSup 124; Leiden: Brill, 2008).

Ulrich, "Index"
    Eugene Ulrich, "An Index to the Contents of the Isaiah Manuscripts from the Judean Desert," in C. C. Broyles and C. A. Evans, eds., *Writing and Reading the Scroll of Isaiah: Studies of an Interpretive Tradition* (2 vols.; VTSup 70; Leiden: Brill, 1997) 2:477.

Ulrich, *Qumran Cave 4.X*
    Eugene Ulrich et al., eds., *Qumran Cave 4.X: The Prophets* (DJD 15; Oxford: Clarendon, 1997).

de Waard, *Handbook on Isaiah*
    J. de Waard, *A Handbook on Isaiah* (Textual Criticism and the Translator 1; Winona Lake, IN: Eisenbrauns, 1997).

Weber, *Biblia Sacra*
    O. Weber, ed., *Biblia Sacra iuxta vulgatem versionem*, vol. 2 (Stuttgart: Württembergische Bibelanstalt, 1969).

Ziegler, *Isaias,* 1st ed.
    Joseph Ziegler, ed., *Isaias* (Septuaginta 14; Göttingen: Vandenhoeck & Ruprecht, 1939).

Ziegler, *Isaias,* 3rd ed.
> Joseph Ziegler, ed., *Isaias* (3rd ed.; Septuaginta: Vetus Testamentum Graecum Auctoritate Academiae Scientiarium Gottingensis 14; Göttingen: Vandenhoeck & Ruprecht, 1983).

Ziegler, *Die jüngeren griechischen Übersetzungen*
> J. Ziegler, *Die jüngeren griechischen Übersetzungen als Vorlagen der Vulgata in den prophetischen Schriften,* Beilage zum Personal- und Vorlesungs-Verzeichnis der Staatl. Akademie zu Braunsberg (Ostpr.) W.-S., 1943/44.

Ziegler, *Septuaginta des Buches Isaias*
> J. Ziegler, *Untersuchungen zur Septuaginta des Buches Isaias* (ATA 12.3; Münster: Aschendorff, 1934).

Ziegler, *Sylloge*
> J. Ziegler, *Sylloge: Gesammelte Aufsätze zur Septuaginta* (Mitteilungen des Septuaginta-Unternehmens der Akademie der Wissenschaften in Göttingen 10; Göttingen: Vandenhoeck & Ruprecht, 1971).

Ziegler, *Textkritische Notizen*
> J. Ziegler, *Textkritische Notizen zu den jüngeren griechischen Übersetzungen des Buches Isaias* (Septuaginta-Arbeiten 1; Göttingen: Vandenhoeck & Ruprecht, 1930).

Ziegler, "Die Vorlage der Isaias-Septuaginta"
> J. Ziegler, "Die Vorlage der Isaias-Septuaginta (LXX) und die erste Isaias-Rolle von Qumran (1QIsaᵃ)," *JBL* 78 (1959) 34–59.

Zion Tradition

Batto and K. L. Roberts, *David and Zion*
> Bernard F. Batto and Kathryn L. Roberts, eds., *David and Zion: Biblical Studies in Honor of J. J. M. Roberts* (Winona Lake, IN: Eisenbrauns, 2004).

Ollenburger, *Zion*
> Ben C. Ollenburger, *Zion, the City of the Great King: A Theological Symbol of the Jerusalemite Cult* (JSOT-Sup 41; Sheffield: JSOT Press, 1987).

J. J. M. Roberts, "Davidic Origin"
> J. J. M. Roberts, "The Davidic Origin of the Zion Tradition," *JBL* 92 (1973) 329–44.

J. J. M. Roberts, "Public Opinion"
> J. J. M. Roberts, "Public Opinion, Royal Apologetics, and Imperial Ideology: A Political Analysis of the Portrait of David, A Man after God's Own Heart," *Theology Today* 69 (2012) 1–17.

J. J. M. Roberts, "Solomon's Jerusalem"
> J. J. M. Roberts, "Solomon's Jerusalem and the Zion Tradition," in A. G. Vaughn and A. F. Killebrew, eds., *Jerusalem in Bible and Archaeology: The First Temple Period* (SBLSymS 18; Atlanta: Society of Biblical Literature, 2003) 163–70.

J. J. M. Roberts, "Zion"
> J. J. M. Roberts, "Zion in the Theology of the Davidic Solomonic Empire," in W. H. Ishida, ed., *Studies in the Period of David and Solomon and Other Essays: Papers Read at the International Symposium for Biblical Studies, Tokyo, 5–7 December 1979* (Tokyo: Yamakawa-Shuppansha; Winona Lake, IN: Eisenbrauns, 1982) 93–108.

Rohland, "Die Bedeutung der Erwählungstraditionen Israels"
> Edzard Rohland, "Die Bedeutung der Erwählungstraditionen Israels für die Eschatologie der alttestamentlichen Propheten" (PhD diss., Heidelberg, 1956).

Stager, "Jerusalem and the Garden"
> Lawrence E. Stager, "Jerusalem and the Garden of Eden," *ErIsr* 26 (1999) 183*–94.*

Stager, "Jerusalem as Eden"
> Lawrence E. Stager, "Jerusalem as Eden," *BAR* 26, no. 3 (2000) 36–47.

Wanke, *Die Zionstheologie*
> Günther Wanke, *Die Zionstheologie der Korachiten in ihrem traditionsgeschichtlichen Zusammenhang* (BZAW 97; Berlin: A. Töpelmann, 1966).

Covenant Theology and Covenant Lawsuit

De Roche, "Yahweh's *rîb*,"
> Michael De Roche, "Yahweh's *rîb* against Israel: A Reassessment of the So-Called 'Prophetic Lawsuit' in the Preexilic Prophets," *JBL* 102 (1983) 563–74.

Harvey, *Le plaidoyer prophétique*
> Julien Harvey, *Le plaidoyer prophétique contre Israël après la rupture de l'alliance* (Bruges: Desclee de Brouwer, 1967).

Harvey, "Le 'Rib-Pattern'"
> Julien Harvey, "Le 'Rib-Pattern': Réquisitoire prophétique sur la rupture de l'alliance," *Bib* 43 (1962) 172–96.

Hillers, *Covenant*
> Delbert R. Hillers, *Covenant: The History of a Biblical Idea* (Seminars in the History of Ideas; Baltimore: Johns Hopkins Press, 1969).

Huffmon, "Covenant Lawsuit"
> H. B. Huffmon, "The Covenant Lawsuit in the Prophets," *JBL* 78 (1959) 285–95.

Koch, *Vertrag, Treueid, und Bund*
> Christoph Koch, *Vertrag, Treueid, und Bund: Studien zur Rezeption des altorientalischen Vertragsrechts im Deuteronomium und zur Ausbildung der Bundestheologie im Alten Testament* (BZAW 383; Berlin: de Gruyter, 2008).

Kutsch, *Verheissung und Gesetz*
> Ernst Kutsch, *Verheissung und Gesetz: Untersuchung zum sogenannten "Bund" im Alten Testament* (BZAW 131; Berlin: de Gruyter, 1973).

Limburg, "Root *rîb*"
> James Limburg, "The Root *rîb* and the Prophetic Lawsuit Speeches," *JBL* 88 (1969) 291–304.

McCarthy, *Treaty and Covenant*
> Dennis J. McCarthy, *Treaty and Covenant: A Study in Form in the Ancient Oriental Documents and in the Old Testament* (AnBib 21; Rome: Pontifical Biblical Institute, 1963; rev. ed., 1978).

Mendenhall, "Ancient Oriental and Biblical Law"
> George E. Mendenhall, "Ancient Oriental and Biblical Law," *BA* 17 (1954) 26–46.

Mendenhall, "Covenant Forms"
George E. Mendenhall, "Covenant Forms in Israelite Tradition," *BA* 17 (1954) 50–76.

Nielsen, *Yahweh as Prosecutor*
Kirsten Nielsen, *Yahweh as Prosecutor and Judge: An Investigation of the Prophetic Lawsuit (Rîb-Pattern)* (JSOTSup 9; Sheffield: Department of Biblical Studies, University of Sheffield, 1978).

Otte, *Der Begriff berît*
Marianne Otte, *Der Begriff berît in der jüngeren alttestamentlichen Forschung: Aspekte der Forschungsgeschichte unter besonderer Berücksichtigung der semantischen Fragestellung bei Ernst Kutsch* (Frankfurt am Main: P. Lang, 2005).

Perlitt, *Bundestheologie*
Lothar Perlitt, *Bundestheologie im Alten Testament* (WMANT 36; Neukirchen-Vluyn: Neukirchener Verlag, 1969).

Rignell, "Isaiah Chapter I"
L. G. Rignell, "Isaiah Chapter I: Some Exegetical Remarks with Special Reference to the Relationship between the Text and the Book of Deuteronomy," *ST* 11 (1957) 140–58.

J. J. M. Roberts, "Form, Syntax"
J. J. M. Roberts, "Form, Syntax and Redaction in Isaiah 1:2-20," *PSB* 3 (1982) 293–306.

Wright, "Lawsuit of God"
G. Ernest Wright, "The Lawsuit of God: A Form-Critical Study of Deuteronomy 32," in Bernhard W. Anderson and Walter Harrelson, eds., *Israel's Prophetic Heritage: Essays in Honor of James Muilenburg* (New York: Harper, 1962) 26–67.

General Bibliography

Ackroyd, "Isaiah I–XII"
P. Ackroyd, "Isaiah I–XII: Presentation of a Prophet," in *Congress Volume: Göttingen 1977* (VTSup 29; Leiden: Brill, 1978) 16–48.

Alt, *Kleine Schriften*
Albrecht Alt, *Kleine Schriften zur Geschichte des Volkes Israel* (3 vols.; Munich: C. H. Beck, 1953–59; 3rd ed., 1964).

Anderson and Harrelson, *Israel's Prophetic Heritage*
Bernhard W. Anderson and Walter Harrelson, eds., *Israel's Prophetic Heritage: Essays in Honor of James Muilenburg* (New York: Harper, 1962).

Asurmendi, *La guerra siro-efraimita*
Jesús María Asurmendi, *La guerra siro-efraimita: Historia y profetas* (Institución San Jerónimo 13; Valencia: Institución San Jerónimo para la Investigación Biblica, 1982).

Balentine and Barton, *Language, Theologie, and the Bible*
S. E. Balentine and J. Barton, eds., *Language, Theologie, and the Bible* (Oxford: Clarendon, 1994).

Barrick and Spencer, *In the Shelter of Elyon*
W. Boyd Barrick and John R. Spencer, eds., *In the Shelter of Elyon: Essays on Ancient Palestinian Life and Literature in Honor of G. W. Ahlström* (JSOTSup 31; Sheffield: JSOT Press, 1984).

Bartelt, *Book around Immanuel*
Andrew H. Bartelt, *The Book around Immanuel: Style and Structure in Isaiah 2–12* (Biblical and Judaic Studies from the University of California, San Diego 4; Winona Lake, IN: Eisenbrauns, 1995).

Barth, *Die Jesaja-Worte*
Hermann Barth, *Die Jesaja-Worte in der Josiazeit: Israel und Asshur als Thema einer Produktiven Neuinterpretation des Jesajaüberlieferung* (WMANT 48; Neukirchen-Vluyn: Neukirchener Verlag, 1977).

Barthel, *Prophetenwort*
Jörg Barthel, *Prophetenwort und Geschichte: Die Jesajaüberlieferung in Jes 6–8 und 28–31* (FAT 19; Tübingen: Mohr Siebeck, 1997).

Beck, *Fortunate the Eyes*
Astrid B. Beck et al., eds., *Fortunate the Eyes That See: Essays in Honor of David Noel Freedman in Celebration of His Seventieth Birthday* (Grand Rapids: Eerdmanns, 1995).

J. Becker, *Isaias*
Joachim Becker, *Isaias: Der Prophet und sein Buch* (SBS 30; Stuttgart: Katholisches Bibelwerk, 1968).

U. Becker, *Jesaja*
U. Becker, *Jesaja–Von der Botschaft zum Deuterojesaja* (BWANT 4.25; Stuttgart: Kohlhammer, 1938).

Beckman, *Hittite Diplomatic Texts*
Gary Beckman, *Hittite Diplomatic Texts* (WAW; Atlanta: Scholars Press, 1996).

Berges, *Das Buch Jesaja*
U. Berges, *Das Buch Jesaja: Komposition und Endgestalt* (HBS 16; Freiburg: Herder, 1998).

Beuken, "Isa 30"
W. Beuken, "Isa 30: A Prophetic Oracle Transmitted in Two Successive Paradigms," in C. Broyles and C. Evans, eds., *Writing and Reading the Scroll of Isaiah: Studies of an Interpretive Tradition* (2 vols.; VTSup 70; Leiden: Brill, 1997) 1:369–97.

Blum et al., *Die hebräische Bibel*
E. Blum et al., eds., *Die hebräische Bibel und ihre zweifache Nachgeschichte: Festschrift für Rolf Rendtorff zum 65. Geburtstag* (Neukirchen-Vluyn: Neukirchener Verlag, 1990).

Böhnke and Heinz, *Im Gespräch*
M. Böhnke and H. Heinz, eds., *Im Gespräch mit dem dreineinen Gott: Elemente einer trinitarischen Theologie. Festschrift für 65. Geburtstag von Wilhelm Breuning* (Düsseldorff: Patmos, 1985).

Borger, *Die Inschriften Asarhaddons*
Riekele Borger, *Die Inschriften Asarhaddons, Königs von Assyrien* (AfOB 9; Graz: E. Weidner, 1956).

Broyles and Evans, *Writing and Reading*
C. C. Broyles and C. A. Evans, eds., *Writing and Reading the Scroll of Isaiah: Studies of an Interpretive Tradition* (2 vols.; VTSup 70; Leiden: Brill, 1997).

Brunet, *Essai sur l'Isaïe*
G. Brunet, *Essai sur l'Isaïe de l'histoire: Études de quelques textes, notamment dans Is 7,8 et 22 (I. l'Emmanuel: II. le Siloé)* (Paris: A. and J. Picard, 1975).

Budde, *Jesaja's Erleben*
K. Budde, *Jesaja's Erleben: Eine gemeinverständliche Auslegung der Denkschrift des Propheten (Kap. 6:1–9:6)* (Gotha: Klotz, 1928).

Carr, "Reading Isaiah"
David M. Carr, "Reading Isaiah from Beginning (Isaiah 1) to End (Isaiah 65–66): Multiple Modern Possibilities," in Roy F. Melugin and Marvin A. Sweeney, eds., *New Visions of Isaiah* (JSOTSup 214; Sheffield: Sheffield Academic Press, 1996) 189–96.

Carrez, *De la torah*
M. Carrez et al., eds., *De la torah au messie* (Paris: Desclée, 1981).

Chan, "Rhetorical Reversal"
Michael Chan, "Rhetorical Reversal and Usurpation: Isaiah 10:5-34 and the Use of Neo-Assyrian Royal Idiom in the Construction of an Anti-Assyrian Theology," *JBL* 128 (2009) 717–33.

Charlesworth, *Messiah*
James H. Charlesworth, ed., *The Messiah: Developments in Earliest Judaism and Christianity. The First Princeton Symposium on Judaism and Christian Origins* (Minneapolis: Fortress Press, 1992).

Childs, *Assyrian Crisis*
Brevard S. Childs, *Isaiah and the Assyrian Crisis* (SBT 2/3; Naperville, IL: Allenson, 1967).

Childs, *Struggle to Understand*
Brevard S. Childs, *The Struggle to Understand Isaiah as Christian Scripture* (Grand Rapids: Eerdmans, 2004).

Clements, *Isaiah and the Deliverance*
Ronald E. Clements, *Isaiah and the Deliverance of Jerusalem: A Study of the Interpretation of Prophecy in the Old Testament* (JSOTSup 13; Sheffield: JSOT Press, 1980).

Cogan and Tadmor, *II Kings*
Mordechai Cogan and Hayim Tadmor, *II Kings: A New Translation with Introduction and Commentary* (AB 11; Garden City, NY: Doubleday, 1988).

Coggins, *Israel's Prophetic Tradition*
Richard Coggins et al., eds., *Israel's Prophetic Tradition: Essays in Honour of Peter R. Ackroyd* (Cambridge: Cambridge University Press, 1982).

Cohen and Westbrook, *Isaiah's Vision of Peace*
Raymond Cohen and Raymond Westbrook, eds., *Isaiah's Vision of Peace in Biblical and Modern International Relations: Swords into Plowshares* (Culture and Religion in International Relations; New York: Palgrave Macmillan, 2008).

Conrad, "Prophet, Redactor"
E. W. Conrad, "Prophet, Redactor and Audience: Reforming the Notion of Isaiah's Formation," in Roy F. Melugin and Marvin A. Sweeney, eds., *New Visions of Isaiah* (JSOTSup 214; Sheffield: Sheffield Academic Press, 1996) 305–26.

Conrad and Newing, *Perspective on Language*
Edgar W. Conrad and Edward G. Newing, eds., *Perspectives on Language and Text: Essays and Poems in Honor of Francis I. Andersen's Sixtieth Birthday, July 28, 1985* (Winona Lake, IN: Eisenbrauns, 1987).

Coppens, "Le messianisme royal"
Joseph Coppens, "Le messianisme royal," *NRT* 90 (1968) 30–49, 82–85, 225–51, 479–512, 622–50, 834–63, 936–75 = *Le messianisme royal* (LD 54; Paris: Cerf, 1968).

Cross, *Canaanite Myth*
Frank Moore Cross, *Canaanite Myth and Hebrew Epic: Essays in the History of the Religion of Israel* (Cambridge, MA: Harvard University Press, 1973).

Darr, *Isaiah's Vision*
Katheryn Pfisterer Darr, *Isaiah's Vision and the Family of God* (Literary Currents in Biblical Interpretation; Louisville: Westminster John Knox, 1994).

Dearman, *Property Rights*
J. Andrew Dearman, *Property Rights in the Eighth-Century Prophets: The Conflict and Its Background* (SBLDS 106; Atlanta: Scholars Press, 1981).

Diedrich and Willmes, *Ich bewirke das Heil*
F. Diedrich and B. Willmes, eds., *Ich bewirke das Heil und erschaffe das Unheil (Jesaja 45,7): Studien zur Botschaft der Propheten* (FB 88; Würzburg: Echter, 1998).

Dietrich, *Jesaja und die Politik*
Walter Dietrich, *Jesaja und die Politik* (BEvT 74; Munich: C. Kaiser, 1976).

Dobbs-Allsopp et al., *Hebrew Inscriptions*
F. W. Dobbs-Allsopp, J. J. M. Roberts, C. L. Seow, and R. E. Whitaker, eds., *Hebrew Inscriptions: Texts from the Biblical Period of the Monarchy with Concordance* (New Haven: Yale University Press, 2005).

Donner, *Israel unter den Völkern*
Herbert Donner, *Israel unter den Völkern: Die Stellung der klassischen Propheten des 8. Jahrhunderts v. Chr. zur Aussenpolitik der Könige von Israel und Juda* (VTSup 11; Leiden: Brill, 1964).

Driver, *Isaiah: His Life*
S. R. Driver, *Isaiah: His Life and Times and the Writings Which Bear His Name* (New York: Randolph, 1883).

Durand, *AEM 1/1*
Jean-Marie Durand, *Archives épistolaires de Mari 1/1* (Archives royales de Mari 26; Paris: Editions Recherche sur les civilisations, 1988).

Eaton, "Origin"
J. H. Eaton, "The Origin of the Book of Isaiah," *VT* 9 (1959) 138–57.

Erlandsson, *Burden of Babylon*
S. Erlandsson, *The Burden of Babylon: A Study of Isaiah 13:2–14:23* (ConBOT 4; Lund: Gleerup, 1970).

Exum and Williamson, *Reading from Right to Left*
J. Cheryl Exum and H. G. M. Williamson, eds., *Reading from Right to Left: Essays on the Hebrew Bible in Honour of David J. A. Clines* (JSOTSup 373; London: Sheffield Academic Press, 2003).

Fales and Postgate
F. M. Fales and J. N. Postgate, *Imperial Administrative Records, Part II* (SAA 11; Helsinki: Helsinki University Press, 1995).

Fey, *Amos and Jesaja*
 R. Fey, *Amos und Jesaja: Abhängigkeit und Eigenstän-
 digkeit des Jesaja* (WMANT 12; Neukirchen-Vluyn:
 Neukirchener Verlag, 1963).
Fohrer, "Neue Literatur"
 Georg Fohrer, "Neue Literatur zur alttestamentli-
 chen Prophetie," *TRu* 45 (1980) 1–39, 108–15.
Fohrer, *Studien zur alttestamentlichen Prophetie*
 Georg Fohrer, *Studien zur alttestamentlichen Prophetie
 (1949–1965)* (BZAW 99; Berlin: A. Töpelmann,
 1967).
Fohrer, *Die symbolischen Handlungen*
 Georg Fohrer, *Die symbolischen Handlungen der
 Propheten* (ATANT 25; Zurich: Zwingli, 1953; 2nd
 ed., 1968).
Frame, "Inscription of Sargon II"
 Grant Frame, "The Inscription of Sargon II at Tang-
 i Var," *Or* 68 (1999) 31–37.
Frame, *Rulers of Babylonia*
 Grant Frame, *Rulers of Babylonia: From the Second
 Dynasty of Isin to the End of Assyrian Domination
 (1157–612 BC)* (RIMB 2; Toronto: University of
 Toronto Press, 1995).
Franklin, "Room V Reliefs"
 N. Franklin, "The Room V Reliefs at Dur-Sharruken
 and Sargon II's Western Campaigns," *TA* 21 (1994)
 255–75.
Fuchs, *Die Annalen*
 Andreas Fuchs, *Die Annalen des Jahres 711 v. Chr.
 nach Prismenfragmenten aus Ninive und Assur* (SAAS
 8; Helsinki: Neo-Assyrian Text Corpus Project,
 1998).
Fuchs, *Die Inschriften Sargons II*
 Andreas Fuchs, *Die Inschriften Sargons II. aus Khor-
 sabad* (Göttingen: Cuvillier, 1994).
Gallagher, *Sennacherib's Campaign*
 William R. Gallagher, *Sennacherib's Campaign to
 Judah: New Studies* (SHCANE 18; Leiden: Brill,
 1999).
Gitay, *Isaiah and His Audience*
 Yehoshua Gitay, *Isaiah and His Audience: The Struc-
 ture and Meaning of Isaiah 1–12* (SSN 30; Assen: Van
 Gorcum, 1991).
Goedicke, *Near Eastern Studies*
 H. Goedicke, ed., *Near Eastern Studies in Honor of
 William Foxwell Albright* (Baltimore: Johns Hopkins
 Press, 1971).
Gordon, "Place Is Too Small"
 Robert P. Gordon, *"The Place Is Too Small for Us":
 The Israelite Prophets in Recent Scholarship* (Sources
 for Biblical and Theological Study 5; Winona Lake,
 IN: Eisenbrauns, 1995).
Gottwald, *All the Kingdoms*
 N. K. Gottwald, *All the Kingdoms of the Earth: Israelite
 Prophecy and International Relations in the Ancient
 Near East* (New York: Harper & Row, 1964).
Gray, *Canaanites*
 John Gray, *The Canaanites* (New York: Praeger,
 1964).

Grayson, *Assyrian and Babylonian Chronicles*
 A. Kirk Grayson, *Assyrian and Babylonian Chronicles*
 (TCS 5; Locust Valley, NY: J. J. Augustin, 1975).
Grayson and Novotny, RINAP 3/1
 A. Kirk Grayson and Jamie Novotny, *The Royal
 Inscriptions of Sennacherib, King of Assyria (704–681),
 Part 1* (RINAP 3.1; Winona Lake, IN: Eisenbrauns,
 2012).
Grayson and Novotny, RINAP 3/2
 A. Kirk Grayson and Jamie Novotny, *The Royal
 Inscriptions of Sennacherib, King of Assyria (704–681
 BC), Part 2* (RINAP 3/2; Winona Lake, IN: Eisen-
 brauns, 2014).
Gressmann, *Der Messias*
 Hugo Gressmann, *Der Messias* (FRLANT 43; Göt-
 tingen: Vandenhoeck & Ruprecht, 1929).
Hardmeier, "Verkündigung und Schrift"
 Christof Hardmeier, "Verkündigung und Schrift
 bei Jesaja: Zur Entstehung der Schriftprophetie als
 Oppositionsliteratur im alten Israel," *TGI* 73 (1983)
 119–34.
Hausmann and Zobel, *Alttestamentlicher Glaube*
 Jutta Hausmann and Hans-Jürgen Zogel, eds.,
 *Alttestamentlicher Glaube und biblische Theologie:
 Festschrift für Horst Dietrich Preuss zum 65. Geburtstag*
 (Stuttgart: Kohlhammer, 1992).
H. W. Hoffmann, *Die Intention*
 H. W. Hoffmann, *Die Intention der Verkündigung
 Jesajas* (BZAW 136; Berlin: de Gruyter, 1974).
Høgenhaven, *Gott und Volk*
 Jesper Høgenhaven, *Gott und Volk bei Jesaja: Eine
 Untersuchung zur biblischen Theologie* (ATDan 24;
 Leiden: Brill, 1988).
Holladay, *Scroll of Prophetic Heritage*
 W. L. Holladay, *Isaiah: Scroll of a Prophetic Heritage*
 (Grand Rapids: Eerdmans, 1978).
Huffmon, *Quest for the Kingdom*
 H. B. Huffmon et al., eds., *The Quest for the King-
 dom of God: Studies in Honor of George E. Mendenhall*
 (Winona Lake, IN: Eisenbrauns, 1983).
Irvine, *Isaiah, Ahaz*
 Stuart A. Irvine, *Isaiah, Ahaz, and the Syro-
 Ephraimitic Crisis* (SBLDS 123; Atlanta: Scholars
 Press, 1990).
Jacobson, "Iconography"
 Rolf A. Jacobson, "A Rose by Any Other Name:
 Iconography and the Interpretation of Isaiah 28:1-
 6," in Martti Nissinen and Charles E. Carter, eds.,
 *Images and Prophecy in the Ancient Eastern Mediter-
 ranean* (FRLANT 233; Göttingen: Vandenhoeck &
 Ruprecht, 2009) 125–46.
Janzen, *Mourning Cry*
 Waldemar Janzen, *Mourning Cry and Woe Oracle*
 (BZAW 125; Berlin: de Gruyter, 1972).
Jensen *Use of tôrâ*
 Joseph Jensen, *The Use of tôrâ by Isaiah: His Debate
 with the Wisdom Tradition* (CBQMS 3; Washington,
 DC: Catholic Biblical Association of America,
 1973).

Katzenstein, *History of Tyre*
H. J. Katzenstein, *The History of Tyre, from the Beginning of the Second Millennium B.C.E. until the Fall of the Neo-Babylonian Empire in 539 B.C.E.* (2nd rev. ed.; Beer Sheva: Ben-Gurion University of the Negev Press, 1997).

Keel, *Jahweh-Visionen*
Othmar Keel, *Jahwe-Visionen und Siegelkunst: Eine neue Deutung der Majestätsschilderungen in Jes 6, Ez 1 und Sach 5* (SBS 84/85; Stuttgart: Katholisches Bibelwerk, 1977).

Kelle and Moore, *Israel's Prophets*
Brad E. Kelle and Megan Bishop Moore, eds., *Israel's Prophets and Israel's Past: Essays on the Relationship of Prophetic Texts and Israelite History in Honor of John H. Hayes* (LHBOTS 446; New York: T&T Clark, 2006).

King and Stager, *Life in Biblical Israel*
Philip J. King and Lawrence E. Stager, *Life in Biblical Israel* (Library of Ancient Israel; Louisville: Westminster John Knox, 2001).

Kitchen, *Third Intermediate*
K. A. Kitchen, *The Third Intermediate Period in Egypt, 1100–650 B.C.* (2nd ed. with suppl.; Warminster: Aris & Phillips, 1986; 3rd ed., 1995).

Laato, *Star Is Rising*
Antti Laato, *A Star Is Rising: The Historical Development of the Old Testament Royal Ideology and the Rise of the Jewish Messianic Expectations* (University of South Florida International Studies in Formative Christianity and Judaism 5; Atlanta: Scholars Press, 1997).

Laato, *Who Is Immanuel?*
Antti Laato, *Who Is Immanuel? The Rise and the Foundering of Isaiah's Messianic Expectations* (Åbo: Åbo Academy Press, 1988).

Lack, *La symbolique du livre d'Isaïe*
Rémi Lack, *La symbolique du livre d'Isaïe: Essai sur l'image littéraire comme élément de structuration* (AnBib 59; Rome: Biblical Institute Press, 1973).

Leichty, *RINAP 4*
Erle Leichty, *The Royal Inscriptions of Esarhaddon, King of Assyria (680–669 BC)* (RINAP 4; Winona Lake, IN: Eisenbrauns, 2011).

Lindblom, *Immanuel Section*
Johannes Lindblom, *A Study on the Immanuel Section in Isaiah: Isa. vii, 1–ix, 6* (Scripta Minora Regiae Societatis Humaniorum Litterarum Lundensis 4; Lund: Gleerup, 1957).

Loretz, *Der Prolog*
Oswald Loretz, *Der Prolog des Jesaja Buches (1, 1-2, 5): Ugaritologische und kolometrische Studien zum Jesaja-Buch* (UBL 1; Altenberg: CIS-Verlag, 1984).

Luckenbill, *Annals*
Daniel David Luckenbill, *The Annals of Sennacherib* (OIP 2; Chicago: University of Chicago Press, 1924).

Machinist, "Assyria and Its Image"
Peter Machinist, "Assyria and Its Image in the First Isaiah," *JAOS* 103 (1982) 719–37.

Melugin and Sweeney, *New Visions of Isaiah*
Roy F. Melugin and Marvin A. Sweeney, eds., *New Visions of Isaiah* (JSOTSup 214; Sheffield: Sheffield Academic Press, 1996).

Metzger, *Königsthron*
Martin Metzger, *Königsthron und Gottesthron: Thronformen und Throndarstellungen im Ägypten und im Vorderen Orient im dritten und zweiten Jahrtausend vor Christus und deren Bedeutung für das Verständnis von Aussagen über den Thron im Alten Testament* (2 vols.; AOAT 15.1–2; Kevelaer: Butzon & Bercker; Neukirchen-Vluyn: Neukirchener Verlag, 1985).

Millard, *Eponyms*
Alan Millard, *The Eponyms of the Assyrian Empire 910–612 B.C.* (SAAS 2; Helsinki: Neo-Assyrian Text Corpus Project, 1994).

Mowinckel, *He That Cometh*
Sigmund Mowinckel, *He That Cometh: The Messiah Concept in the Old Testament and Later Judaism* (Nashville: Abingdon, 1956).

Mowinckel, "Die Komposition des Jesajabuches"
Sigmund Mowinckel, "Die Komposition des Jesaja-buches Kap. 1–39," *AcOr* 11 (1933) 267–92.

O'Connell, *Concentricity and Continuity*
Robert H. O'Connell, *Concentricity and Continuity: The Literary Structure of Isaiah* (JSOTSup 188; Sheffield: Sheffield Academic Press, 1994).

Olyan and Culley, "A Wise and Discerning Mind"
Saul M. Olyan and Robert C. Culley, eds., *"A Wise and Discerning Mind": Essays in Honor of Burke O. Long* (BJS 325; Providence, RI: Brown Judaic Studies, 2000).

Postma, *New Things*
F. Postma et al., eds., *The New Things: Eschatology in Old Testament Prophecy. Festschrift for Henk Leene* (ACEBTSup 3; Maastricht: Shaker, 2002).

Rainey and Notley, *Sacred Bridge*
Anson F. Rainey and R. Steven Notley, *The Sacred Bridge: Carta's Atlas of the Biblical World* (Jerusalem: Carta, 2006) 233.

Reid, *Prophets and Paradigms*
Stephen B. Reid, ed., *Prophets and Paradigms: Essays in Honor of Gene M. Tucker* (JSOTSup 229; Sheffield: Sheffield Academic Press, 1996).

J. J. M. Roberts, *Bible and the Ancient Near East*
J. J. M. Roberts, *The Bible and the Ancient Near East: Collected Essays* (Winona Lake, IN: Eisenbrauns, 2002).

J. J. M. Roberts, "Double Entendre"
J. J. M. Roberts, "Double Entendre in First Isaiah," *CBQ* 54 (1992) 39–48.

J. J. M. Roberts, "Egypt, Assyria, Isaiah"
J. J. M. Roberts, "Egypt, Assyria, Isaiah, and the Ashdod Affair: An Alternative Proposal," in Andrew G. Vaughn and Ann E. Killebrew, *Jerusalem in Bible and Archaeology: The First Temple Period* (SBLSymS 18; Atlanta: Society of Biblical Literature, 2003) 265–83.

J. J. M. Roberts "Egyptian and Nubian Oracles"
J. J. M. Roberts, "Egyptian and Nubian Oracles," in Brad E. Kelle and Megan Bishop Moore, eds., *Israel's Prophets and Israel's Past: Essays on the Relationship of Prophetic Texts and Israelite History in Honor of John H. Hayes* (LHBOTS 446; New York: T&T Clark, 2006) 201–9.

J. J. M. Roberts, "Importance of Isaiah"
J. J. M. Roberts, "The Importance of Isaiah at Qumran," in James H. Charlesworth, ed., *The Bible and the Dead Sea Scrolls: The Princeton Symposium on the Dead Sea Scrolls* (Scripture and the Scrolls 1; Waco, TX: Baylor University Press, 2006) 273–86.

J. J. M. Roberts, "Isaiah, National Security"
J. J. M. Roberts, "Isaiah, National Security, and the Politics of Fear," in Robert Jewett, ed., *The Bible and the American Future* (Eugene, OR: Cascade, 2009) 72–91.

J. J. M. Roberts, "Prophets and Kings"
J. J. M. Roberts, "Prophets and Kings: A New Look at the Royal Persecution of Prophets against Its Near Eastern Background," in B. A. Strawn and N. R. Bowen, eds., *A God So Near: Essays on Old Testament Theology in Honor of Patrick D. Miller* (Winona Lake, IN: Eisenbrauns, 2003) 341–54.

J. J. M. Roberts, "Rod That Smote"
J. J. M. Roberts, "The Rod That Smote Philistia: Isaiah 14:28–32," in David S. Vanderhooft and Abraham Winitzer, eds., *Literature as Politics, Politics as Literature: Essays on the Ancient Near East in Honor of Peter Machinist* (Winona Lake, IN: Eisenbrauns, 2013) 381–95.

J. J. M. Roberts, "Security and Justice"
J. J. M. Roberts, "Security and Justice in Isaiah," *Stone-Campbell Journal* 13 (2010) 71–79.

J. J. M. Roberts, "Whose Child?"
J. J. M. Roberts, "Whose Child Is This? Reflections on the Speaking Voice in Isaiah 9:5," *HTR* 90 (1997) 115–29.

J. J. M. Roberts, "Yahweh's Foundation"
J. J. M. Roberts, "Yahweh's Foundation in Zion (Isaiah 28:16)," *JBL* 106 (1987) 27–45; reprinted in *The Bible and the Ancient Near East: Collected Essays* (Winona Lake, IN: Eisenbrauns, 2002) 292–310.

Schunck and Augustin, *Goldene Äpfel*
K.-D. Schunck and M. Augustin, eds., *Goldene Äpfel in silbernen Schalen: Collected Communications to the XIIIth Congress of the International Organization for the Study of the Old Testament, Leuven 1989* (BEATAJ 20; Frankfurt am Main: P. Lang, 1992).

Simons, *Geographical and Topographical Texts*
J. Simons, *The Geographical and Topographical Texts of the Old Testament* (Studia Francisci Scholten memoriae dicata 2; Leiden: Brill, 1959).

Skilton, *Law and the Prophets*
John H. Skilton, ed., *The Law and the Prophets: Old Testament Studies Prepared in Honor of Oswald Thompson Allis* (Nutley, NJ: Presbyterian and Reformed, 1974).

Stager, *Ashkelon 1*
Lawrence E. Stager et al., eds., *Ashkelon 1: Introduction and Overview (1985–2006)* (Leon Levy Expedition to Ashkelon; Winona Lake, IN: Eisenbrauns, 2008).

Stansell, "Isaiah 32"
Gary Stansell, "Isaiah 32: Creative Redaction in the Isaian Traditions," in *SBLSP 1983* (Chico, CA: Scholars Press, 1983) 1–12.

Strong and Tuell, *Constituting the Community*
John T. Strong and Steven S. Tuell, eds., *Constituting the Community: Studies on the Polity of Ancient Israel in Honor of S. Dean McBride, Jr.* (Winona Lake, IN: Eisenbrauns, 2005).

Sweeney, *Isaiah 1–4*
Marvin A. Sweeney, *Isaiah 1–4 and the Post-Exilic Understanding of the Isaianic Tradition* (BZAW 171; Berlin: de Gruyter, 1988).

Tadmor, "Campaigns of Sargon II"
Hayim Tadmor, "The Campaigns of Sargon II of Assur: A Chronological-Historical Study," *JCS* 12 (1958) 22–40, 77–100.

Tadmor et al., "Sin of Sargon"
Hayim Tadmor, Benno Landsberger, and Simo Parpola, "The Sin of Sargon and Sennacherib's Last Will," *SAAB* 3 (1989) 3–51.

Thiele, *Mysterious Numbers*
Edwin R. Thiele, *The Mysterious Numbers of the Hebrew Kings* (Chicago: University of Chicago Press, 1951; 2nd ed., Grand Rapids: Eerdmans, 1965; 3rd ed., Grand Rapids: Zondervan, 1983).

Thiele, *Mysterious Numbers*
E. R. Thiele, *The Mysterious Numbers of the Hebrew Kings: A Reconstruction of the Chronology of the Kings of Israel and Judah* (rev. ed.; Grand Rapids: Eerdmans, 1965).

Török, *Kingdom of Kush*
László Török, *The Kingdom of Kush: Handbook of the Nabatan-Meriotic Civilization* (HO 1: Der Nahe und Mittlere Osten 31; Leiden: Brill, 1977).

Tucker, "Prophecy"
Gene M. Tucker, "Prophecy and the Prophetic Literature," in Douglas A. Knight and Gene M. Tucker, eds., *The Hebrew Bible and Its Modern Interpreters* (Philadelphia: Fortress Press; Chico, CA: Scholars Press, 1985) 325–68.

Tur-Sinai, "Contribution to the Understanding"
N. H. Tur-Sinai, "A Contribution to the Understanding of Isaiah I–XII," in C. Rabin, ed., *Studies in the Bible* (ScrHier 8; Jerusalem: Magnes Press, 1961) 154–88.

Vanel, "Tâbeʾél en Is VII 6"
A. Vanel, "Tâbeʾél en Is VII 6 et le roi Tubail de Tyr," in *Studies on Prophecy* (VTSup 26; Leiden: Brill, 1974) 17–24.

van Ruiten and Vervenne, *Studies in the Book of Isaiah*
J. van Ruiten and M. Vervenne, eds., *Studies in the Book of Isaiah: Festschrift Willem A. M. Beuken* (BETL 132; Leuven: Leuven University Press/Peeters, 1997).

Vermeylen, *Du prophète Isaïe*
J. Vermeylen, *Du prophète Isaïe à l'apocalyptique* (2 vols.; EBib; Paris: Gabalda, 1977–78).

Vermeylen, *Book of Isaiah*
J. Vermeylen, *Book of Isaiah = Le livre d'Isaïe: les oracles et leur relectures. Unité et complexité de l'ouvrage* (BETL 81; Leuven: Leuven University Press/Peeters, 1989).

Vollmer, *Geschichtliche Rückblicke*
J. Vollmer, *Geschichtliche Rückblicke und Motive in der Prophetie des Amos, Hosea und Jesaja* (BZAW 119; Berlin: de Gruyter, 1971).

Watts and House, *Forming Prophetic Literature*
James W. Watts and Paul R. House, eds., *Forming Prophetic Literature: Essays on Isaiah and the Twelve in Honor of John D. W. Watts* (JSOTSup 235; Sheffield: Sheffield Academic Press, 1996).

Westermann, *Basic Forms*
Claus Westermann, *Basic Forms of Prophetic Speech* (trans. H. C. White; Philadelphia: Westminster, 1967; repr., Louisville: Westminster John Knox, 1991).

Whedbee, *Isaiah and Wisdom*
J. W. Whedbee, *Isaiah and Wisdom* (Nashville: Abingdon, 1971).

Wiklander, *Prophecy as Literature*
Bertil Wiklander, *Prophecy as Literature: A Text-Linguistic and Rhetorical Approach to Isaiah 2–4* (ConBOT 22; Malmö: Gleerup, 1984).

Williamson, *Book Called Isaiah*
H. G. M. Williamson, *The Book Called Isaiah: Deutero-Isaiah's Role in Composition and Redaction* (Oxford: Clarendon, 1994).

Williamson, "Isaiah and the Wise"
H. G. M. Williamson, "Isaiah and the Wise," in John Day, Robert P. Gordon, and H. G. M. Williamson, eds., *Wisdom in Ancient Israel: Essays in Honour of J. A. Emerton* (Cambridge: Cambridge University Press, 1995) 133–41.

Willis, "First Pericope"
John T. Willis, "The First Pericope in the Book of Isaiah," *VT* 34 (1984) 63–77.

Willis, *Instruction Shall Go Forth*
John T. Willis, *Instruction Shall Go Forth: Studies in Micah and Isaiah* (ed. M. Hamilton and T. M. Willis; Eugene, OR: Pickwick, 2014.

Wong, *Road to Peace*
Gordon C. I. Wong, *The Road to Peace: Pastoral Reflections on Isaiah 1–12* (Singapore: Gordon C. I. Wong, 2009).

Wood, *From Babel to Babylon*
Joyce R. Wood et al., eds., *From Babel to Babylon: Essays on Biblical History and Literature in Honour of Brian Peckham* (LHBOTS 455; New York: T&T Clark, 2006).

My friends like to kid me that I have been working on this commentary on Isaiah 1–39 for even more years than the eighth-century BCE prophet, Isaiah of Jerusalem, remained active as a prophet. There is some plausibility to the charge. I began my serious work on Isaiah in a joint seminar led by my colleague at Johns Hopkins, Delbert R. Hillers, in the mid-1970s, and I accepted a contract to write a theological commentary on Isaiah 1–39 in 1978–79, while I was teaching at the University of Toronto. During the first half of a year-long sabbatical in Austin, Texas, in the late 1980s, I produced a long manuscript of this Isaiah commentary, but when the editors rejected the manuscript as insufficiently theological, I switched to the minor prophets and completed my OTL commentary on Nahum, Habakkuk, and Zephaniah. On returning to Princeton Theological Seminary following the sabbatical, I was eventually offered the contract to produce the Hermeneia commentary on Isaiah 1–39, and I have been working on the commentary ever since. So I have been seriously working on this commentary for about thirty-five years. The ministry of Isaiah of Jerusalem, however, was actually slightly longer than that, depending on the disputed dates of its beginning and end. If Uzziah died in 738 BCE, as I argue, Isaiah's ministry began in that year at the latest, and it continued through at least 701 BCE, and perhaps to as late as 686 BCE. At the shortest, Isaiah's ministry lasted some thirty-eight years, but it was perhaps as long as fifty-two years. In either case, Isaiah was active as a prophet longer, even if not by much, than I was active in my work on this commentary.

The length of my work on this commentary has some bearing on the finished product. Early on I tried to read everything written on Isaiah. At Johns Hopkins and the University of Toronto I had access to fine libraries, and as a full Professor at Princeton Theological Seminary for twenty-five years, I had access both to an excellent research library and to the help of graduate assistants. At a certain point, however, I had to make a choice, as one of my teachers, G. Ernest Wright, once put it, whether to be a reader or a writer. The choice was less difficult when I retired from Princeton Theological Seminary and eventually found myself in Grand Haven, Michigan, far removed from a decent research library. I have tried to keep up with the literature on Isaiah, but discerning readers will probably detect gaps of important literature that I have missed entirely or to which I have given insufficient attention. Given the long gestation period between the beginning of my research and the final product, it is also likely that I have forgotten the ultimate sources of some of the ideas that have shaped my thought on Isaiah. Any scholar stands on the shoulders of those who preceded him or her, and even where I may inadvertently fail adequately to credit the ultimate sources of my ideas, I am under no illusions that my ideas are genuinely original. Original ideas in a field with a history of interpretation of more than two thousand years are few and far between.

In a related way, the length of Isaiah's ministry has a significant bearing on the way in which one should look at the collection of Isaiah's oracles. If Isaiah continued his ministry for fifty years, or even only for some thirty-eight years, that is a long ministry. His inaugural vision is dated to the year of Uzziah's death, in my view 738 BCE, and a number of his oracles were originally given during the crisis of the Syro-Ephraimitic War in 735–732 BCE. Others clearly date to the Ashdod crisis of 715–711 BCE, and still others are linked to the death of Sargon II in 705 BCE, or to Sennacherib's third campaign in 701 BCE. If Isaiah remained active over that long a period of time, it is likely, as any preacher should acknowledge, that the prophet would have had occasion to reedit and reuse older oracles, or, at the very least, to reuse the same themes, motifs, and vocabulary, in later, somewhat analogous contexts. Isaiah 28:1-6 is the perfect example of such a reuse of an early oracle in a later context, and it is by no means the only example. Jeremiah is reported to have dictated a scroll to his scribe Baruch in the fourth year of Jehoiakim (c. 605 BCE) that included all the oracles he had given from the beginning of his ministry in the time of Josiah until the day of his dictation of the scroll. One cannot help but wonder how much his earliest oracles were reshaped by the prophet to be more relevant to the time of his dictation (Jer 36:1-3). When that scroll was burned, Jeremiah is reported to have dictated another scroll with all the same material plus the addition of many similar words (Jer 36:32). Again one is faced with the question how much the earlier oracles were reshaped by the prophet to make them more relevant for the time of their publication. In the case of Isaiah, we are told that he sealed a scroll, presumably with oracles associated with his children with symbolic names during the Syro-Ephraimitic crisis (Isa 8:16-18), and that he again wrote down his oracle(s) at the time of Hezekiah's rebellion

1

against Sennacherib as a witness for the future (Isa 30:8-9). Given Isaiah's very long ministry, it is not just later editors and redactors who may have altered the prophet's oracles; Isaiah himself may have, and most probably, did reedit and update many of his earlier oracles to make them relevant again to new situations in the life of the people to whom he ministered. Any such reworking, unless it is done in an almost impossibly thorough manner, is likely to leave awkward traces that allow one in some cases to intuit the earlier context that the oracle originally served.

Methodology

The previous paragraph bears on the dominant methodology adopted in this commentary. In my opinion, the methodology one adopts is largely contingent on the nature of the document one is interpreting. Apart from the Isaiah Apocalypse in chaps. 24–27 and similar material in chaps. 34–35, Isaiah 1–39 is marked by a whole series of chronological notices connecting Isaiah's oracles to a specific time or specific events—Isa 1:1; 6:1; 7:1-2; 14:28; 20:1; 36:1. Moreover, even oracles lacking such precise chronological notices are often so clearly linked by their content to these particular crises or to other events well known from the historical record of the period that they obviously refer to them. In most cases, the contents of the oracles suggest that the oracles actually date to the general period of those background events rather than being much later references back to a far earlier setting. Thus, many oracles may be dated with a fair degree of certainty and accuracy. Given this situation, the dominant approach of this commentary is the classic historical-critical method. Historical reconstruction does involve hypotheses, as any reconstruction does, but at least it is based on material in the public record. Historical events were public events, and no matter how differently they may have been interpreted by different participants in these events, there was a public aspect to them that is to some extent still preserved in the Israelite, Assyrian, Egyptian, and other sources that reflect these events.

In contrast, this commentary spends relatively little time on the editorial process by which the material in Isaiah 1–39 reached its present shape. Much contemporary scholarship focuses on the complete book of Isaiah (chaps. 1–66) as a unified literary composition and attempts to unravel the centuries-long editorial and redactional process by which the book grew into its final form. One could point to any number of books (e.g., Ulrich Berges, *Das Buch Jesaja: Komposition und Endgestalt* [HBS 16; Freiburg: Herder, 1998]; Brevard Childs, *The Struggle to Understand Isaiah as Christian Scripture* [Grand Rapids: Eerdmans, 2004]; Roy F. Melugin and Marvin A. Sweeney, eds., *New Visions of Isaiah* [JSOTSup 214; Sheffield: Sheffield Academic Press, 1996]; Jacques Vermeylen, *Du prophète Isaïe à l'apocalyptique* [2 vols.; EBib; Paris: Gabalda, 1977–78]; and H. G. M. Williamson, *The Book Called Isaiah: Deutero-Isaiah's Role in Composition and Redaction* [Oxford: Clarendon, 1994]).To take a different example, Marvin A. Sweeney in his commentary (1996) reconstructs a historical development involving four major editions of Isaiah: (1) the final form of the book produced in relation to the reforms of Ezra and Nehemiah in the mid- to late fifth century BCE; (2) a late-sixth-century edition produced in conjunction with the return of Babylonian exiles to Jerusalem and the building of the Second Temple; (3) a late-seventh-century edition written to support King Josiah's reform; and (4) various texts that stem from the eighth-century prophet, though this earliest written material may never have constituted a single unified written edition. In part, my unwillingness to get deeply embroiled in this discussion about the larger book and the process of its formation is no doubt due to the historical accident that my commentary covers only chaps. 1–39, not the whole book of Isaiah. On the other hand, I have deep reservations about many of the underlying assumptions undergirding this quest. I am not convinced that the ancient Judean and Jewish audiences that heard or, in rarer cases, read the oracles in the Isaianic collection in whatever edition were as enthralled by elaborate book-length literary coherence as modern scholars and contemporary readers are,[1] and I am

---

1   See David M. Carr's astute observations on the differences between ancient and modern readers, "Reading Isaiah from Beginning (Isaiah 1) to End (Isaiah 65–66): Multiple Modern Possibilities," in Roy F. Melugin and Marvin A. Sweeney, eds., *New Visions of Isaiah* (JSOTSup 214; Sheffield: Sheffield Academic Press, 1996) 189–218, esp. 193–96.

amazed at the confidence with which scholars can reconstruct the editorial growth of a biblical book over the centuries with the barest minimum of actual evidence. It is not that I consider this process unimportant or uninteresting; it is more that I consider the details of this process to be largely unrecoverable. In general, in the absence of a trail of early datable and evolving manuscripts, the editorial process behind a particular book is both private and largely unrecoverable. Even with modern books that go through several editions, where each datable edition is available for comparative study, it is often difficult to determine why certain changes to the books took place. The confidence with which many modern scholars, who lack any datable manuscripts earlier than the final form of Isaiah, reconstruct hypothetical redactors living at particular periods, who make particular editorial changes in the service of some equally hypothetically reconstructed theological interest, strikes me as extreme hubris. If it were true, how could one know it? Even when it comes to the rationale and history behind the structure and shaping of discrete smaller units consisting of more than one oracle, whether of Isaiah 2–4 (Sweeney), Isaiah 1–12 (Peter Ackroyd, Yehoshua Gitay), Isaiah 2–12 (A. H. Bartelt), or any other extended unit, such reconstructions are often mutually exclusive and seldom convince more than a small circle of adherents.[2] For this reason I have focused primarily on individual oracles, not on larger literary structures, and only occasionally, when I thought the text justified it, on a small collection of related oracles. There are places in Isaiah where I think one can detect secondary editorial work on an original oracle, and I am quite willing to reflect on the nature of that secondary editing, but I think one's claims about such editing,

particularly as it involves larger and larger blocks of material, should be quite modest.

The Eighth-Century Isaiah of Jerusalem and the Book of Isaiah

Nonetheless, even if the redactional and editorial process behind the present form of the book of Isaiah is unrecoverable in precise detail with the evidence at hand and the degree of genuine coherence in the book qua book remains disputed, that does not deny that the growth of the book was complex and took place in stages. Since the groundbreaking work of Bernhard Duhm,[3] it has come to be generally recognized today that not all of the book of Isaiah stems from the eighth-century BCE prophet from Jerusalem. Chapters 40–55 of Isaiah, because of their two references to Cyrus the Great (44:28; 45:1) and their message of comfort to a discouraged Jewish community portrayed as in bondage in Babylon, which is seen as the dominant enemy in this section of the book (47:1), are normally dated somewhere between 550 and 539 BCE.[4] Cyrus the Persian first came to prominence by his defeat of his Median overlord Astyages (550 BCE), and his imminent threat to Babylon became blindingly obvious only with his surprisingly rapid conquest of the Lydian empire (545 BCE). Moreover, his audience's obvious resistance to the prophet's message makes more sense before 539 BCE, when Cyrus's conquest of Babylon and his following edict allowing the Jewish exiles in Babylon to return home would appear to have confirmed the broad outlines of the Second Isaiah's message.[5] Chapters 56–66 are normally dated even later, after 539 BCE, because they seem to presuppose an audience and a writer (or writers) who are no longer in Babylon but once again resident in the

---

2 Marvin A. Sweeney, *Isaiah 1–4 and the Post-Exilic Understanding of the Isaianic Tradition* (BZAW 171; Berlin: de Gruyter, 1988); P. Ackroyd, "Isaiah I–XII: Presentation of a Prophet," in *Congress Volume: Göttingen 1977* (VTSup 29; Leiden: Brill, 1978) 16–48; Yehoshua Gitay, *Isaiah and His Audience: The Structure and Meaning of Isaiah 1–12* (SSN 30; Assen: Van Gorcum, 1991); Andrew H. Bartelt, *The Book around Immanuel: Style and Structure in Isaiah 2–12* (Biblical and Judaic Studies from the University of California, San Diego 4; Winona Lake, IN: Eisenbrauns, 1995).

3 Bernhard Duhm, *Das Buch Jesaia* (3rd ed.; HKAT 3.1; Göttingen: Vandenhoeck & Ruprecht, 1914; 1st ed., 1892).

4 See Klaus Baltzer, *Deutero-Jesaja* (KAT 10.2; Gütersloh: Gütersloher Verlagshaus, 1999) 57, though Baltzer himself dates the section somewhat later, between 450 and 400 BCE. For the more common dating, see R. N. Whybray, *Isaiah 40–66* (NCB; Greenwood, NC: Attic Press, 1975) 20–23.

5 Hans Barstad argues for a Judean setting for the author and audience of this material, but his views remain a distinctly minority and extreme position (*The Babylonian Captivity of the Book of Isaiah: "Exilic" Judah and the Provenance of Isaiah 40–55* [Oslo: Novus: Instituttet for sammenlignende kulturforskning, 1997]).

Judean homeland.[6] The historical context presupposed by these two blocks of material are totally different from that of Isaiah 1–39, and the literary style of this material is also quite distinct from that characteristic of chaps. 1–39.

It is also true, however, that not everything in Isaiah 1–39 may be attributed to Isaiah of Jerusalem. Chapters 24–27, the so-called little Isaiah Apocalypse, is normally dated later than Isaiah of Jerusalem, though there is little agreement on its precise date.[7] The material is difficult to date because of a lack of unambiguous historical allusions, but my inclination is to date it to the end of the seventh and beginning of the sixth century, approximately seventy-five to a hundred years later than the eighth-century prophet. Isaiah 34–35, which has points of contact with both chaps. 40–55 and 24–27, also appears to be later than Isaiah of Jerusalem. The mainly prose traditions about Isaiah in chaps. 36–39, though they may contain some genuine words of Isaiah, also date from sometime after the death of Isaiah. In their present form, which mentions the death of Sennacherib, which occurred at least five years after the death of Isaiah, they could not be the work of the eighth-century prophet but probably represent traditions about him codified by disciples as much as a generation after his death. Within the remaining material in chaps. 1–23; 28–33, there are other passages, both large and small, that many scholars dismiss as later, non-Isaianic expansions, glosses, and later reinterpretations, but apart from chap. 13 and some minor expansion at the beginning of chap. 14, I am far more reluctant to late date any of this material. Some of it is problematic and questionable, as will be discussed in the commentary, but far more of it can be attributed to Isaiah of Jerusalem than is often admitted.

Theological Influences on Isaiah of Jerusalem
People who grow up in a religious culture are influenced by the dominant theological currents of their day, and Isaiah of Jerusalem was no exception to that rule. Isaiah was a Jerusalemite with close contacts to the royal court, and therefore the major influence on his thought appears to have been the royal theology cultivated in the Davidic court, the theological construct that I refer to as the Zion Tradition.[8] This was a political as well as a theological construct, originally created in the days of the Davidic imperial expansion to legitimate that expansion theologically, then maintained and refined under Solomon, and preserved by Solomon's Judean successors as the ideal despite the breakup of the empire and the collapse of the political reality that had initially given credence to the construct. There were three main points to this construct: (1) Yahweh was the imperial God, king of all the gods and ruler over all the nations; (2) Yahweh had chosen David as his earthly vice-regent and had made an eternal covenant with him that one of his descendants would always sit on David's throne as Yahweh's ruler on earth; and (3) Yahweh had chosen Jerusalem as his imperial capital and earthly dwelling place. Each of these points was developed and elaborated in the theology. The first point was linked to the earlier motif according to which Yahweh had chosen Israel as his special people (Deut 32:8-9), and the gods of the other nations were reduced to mere members of Yahweh's court, the heavenly host or armies (צְבָאוֹת, ṣĕbāʾôt) of Yahweh of Hosts (*YHWH ṣĕbāʾôt*). If they rebelled or failed in carrying out the divine emperor's judgments, even though they were gods, they were still subject to the imperial God's judicial imposition of the death penalty (Psalm 82). In a similar manner, the human rulers of these other nations were expected to submit to the imperial God and his chosen Davidic ruler (Psalm 2). On point 2, there were expectations about the moral nature of the rule that David's descendants would exercise, since they were supposed to render the judgment of Yahweh (Ps 72:1-4) and share in his conquest of the powers of chaos and evil (Ps 89:26). There were also expectations about the exaltation and fertility of Jerusalem as the dwelling place of Yahweh. Most especially, the security of the city was assured, since Yahweh dwelled there and, as the imperial deity, was expected to defend his city against all its enemies (Psalms 46; 48; 76; 132).

---

6 See Joseph Blenkinsopp, *Isaiah 56–66: A New Translation with Introduction and Commentary* (AB 19B; New York: Doubleday, 2003) 43.

7 See the discussion and bibliography in that section of this commentary.

8 See my "Public Opinion, Royal Apologetics, and Imperial Ideology: A Political Portrait of David, 'A Man after God's Own Heart,'" *Theology Today* 69 (2012) 116–32, and the earlier articles cited there on p. 131 n. 37.

In Isaiah's inaugural vision, he sees the divine king, the huge and majestic Yahweh of Hosts, whose glory fills the whole earth, sitting on a high and exalted throne in the temple in Jerusalem (Isa 6:1-5). This Yahweh founded Zion (14:32) and lives in Mount Zion (8:18). His choice of David and Zion means that the plots of Rezin of Damascus and the son of Remaliah of Samaria will come to nought (7:7-9), for Yahweh is with his people in Zion (Immanuel—God is with us—Isa 7:10-17; 8:8b-10; cf. Ps 46:8, 10—Yahweh of Hosts is with us, the God of Jacob is our stronghold). Even the sins that necessitate the purification and refining of Jerusalem will not nullify God's choice of his city (Isa 1:21-28) any more than Isaiah's unclean lips nullified God's choice of him as his prophetic messenger (6:5-7). When Jerusalem, in the process of its purification by fire (1:25-26), is on the very brink of death at the hands of the hated Assyrians, Yahweh will intervene to punish the arrogant Assyrian club, which God used merely to discipline Zion (10:5-12), miraculously delivering his chosen city in the process (14:24-27; 29:1-8; 31:1-9). In days to come, Yahweh's choice of and elevation of Zion will be evident to the whole world (2:2-6), and the nations in order to inquire of Yahweh will come to Zion and to the root of Jesse that remains standing as a signal flag (11:10). This new David and his royal officials will rule with the justice of Yahweh (9:1-6; 11:1-10; 32:1-8) on the throne of David and over his kingdom to establish it forever (9:6). Where Isaiah differed from his contemporaries in the appropriation of this theological construct is in his insistence that the Davidic rule must be marked by the justice of God, that God's city must be kept pure and fit for the divine king to reside in it. Justice and righteousness were the crucial measurements for Yahweh's firm foundation of Zion (28:16-17). These elements of responsibility were also a part of the theological tradition, but there was a tendency in the popular tradition, perhaps particularly in the royal court, to highlight God's commitments, not the equally important obligations and duties of the king and his court. Why else would Isaiah feel compelled to characterize God's judgment against Jerusalem as Yahweh's "strange" work (28:21-22)?

It is striking, however, that Isaiah has far less to say to the royal court of his day about a false, uncritical trust in the Zion Tradition than the later Jeremiah did (Jer 7:1-15). Isaiah is far more inclined to attack the royal advisors of his day, whether those of Ahaz or those of Hezekiah, with the charge that they did not believe their own theology. If they trusted the promises of Yahweh to David and Zion found in their own theological tradition, they would not in sheer terror be running with tribute to Assyria or to Nubian Egypt for help against whatever foe currently threatened them. Instead, they would stand in awe of Yahweh and by faith wait in quiet confidence for his deliverance (Isa 7:9; 8:11-15; 14:32; 18). Isaiah's opponents at court were not the fanatical religious upholders of a purely positive Zion Tradition but pragmatic statesmen who were more concerned with the number of cavalry, chariots, and infantry that they and the allies they could buy could muster against the dangerous enemies who threatened them. They were not outwardly antireligious or even a-religious (see Isa 29:13), but their diplomatic and military plans paid little attention to the promises found in the dominant religious tradition, and far more to the size of their military and the strength of their defensive fortifications (Isa 22:8-11). To them Isaiah was an infantile religious fool and an irritating security threat. They tried to keep their plans secret from him (Isa 29:15-16; 30:1-2; 31:1), though they were only partially successful, and Isaiah was as bitterly critical of them as they had been of him, accusing them of being drunken, scoffing idiots (Isa 28:7-8). The bitterness of this debate was probably exacerbated by the fact that Isaiah was one of them, a member of the Jerusalem elite, educated in the same wisdom tradition as the royal counselors he opposed. Isaiah's strong emphasis on God's plan, work, deed, and wisdom is probably a reflection of the influence of this wisdom tradition on his religious thought. Isaiah's own profound religious and prophetic experiences, however, had reshaped his outlook so that he took the promises in the religious tradition far more seriously than any of his opponents.

The Zion Tradition was the main theological influence on Isaiah's thought, but one also finds traces of a secondary influence of the Deuteronomistic Mosaic covenant theology. Isaiah 1:2-20 contains an elaborately developed covenant lawsuit, and traces of the same form are found in Isa 3:13-15. It is fashionable in some circles to date the Deuteronomistic covenant theology quite late,[9] and hence for those who adopt this dating, there is a tendency either to deny the obvious covenant lawsuit elements in these Isaianic passages or to date these Isaianic passages late as well.[10] Neither move is necessary in my opinion. Covenant theology connected with written laws, with the mention of both בְּרִית (bĕrît, "covenant") and תּוֹרָה (tôrâ, "law"), is already found in the late-eighth-century northern prophet Hosea (Hos 4:6; 6:7; 8:1, 12; 10:4), and it is likely that this "Deuteronomistic" theology came south with northern refugees after the collapse of most of the northern state in 732 BCE. It is even possible that an early prototype of Deuteronomy came south with the northern refugees as well.[11] It is striking that Hezekiah's religious reform in 715 BCE seems to have followed Deuteronomistic concerns (2 Kgs 18:3-6), and the Chronicler suggests that Hezekiah's reform involved an attempt to bring the north back under Davidic hegemony (2 Chronicles 29–31). It may even be that the old scroll of the law found in the temple in the time of Josiah (2 Kgs 22:8-13), which provoked a second religious reform similar to Hezekiah's (2 Kgs 23:1-25), had served a similar function under Hezekiah and had been deposited in the temple during his reign, only to fall into oblivion in the reign of the reprobate Manasseh. That such covenant theology, important to Hezekiah's reform activity, would have had some influence on Isaiah in the latter half of his ministry is not at all surprising, particularly since he seemed to share the same animosity as the Deuteronomist toward many of the same external cult objects, such as sacred trees, asherim, and the altars and incense altars that marked the numerous high places (Isa 1:29-31; 17:7-8, 10-11).

Text

The sheer number (more than twenty) of Hebrew scrolls of Isaiah that have turned up at Qumran, whether in more complete or very fragmentary condition, place Isaiah alongside the pentateuchal books Genesis, Exodus, and especially Deuteronomy, and the book of Psalms as one of the most popular biblical books at Qumran.[12]

---

9   Lothar Perlitt, *Bundestheologie im Alten Testament* (WMANT 36; Neukirchen-Vluyn: Neukirchener Verlag, 1969); Dennis J. McCarthy, *Treaty and Covenant: A Study in Form in the Ancient Oriental Documents and in the Old Testament* (AnBib 21; Rome: Pontifical Biblical Institute, 1963; rev. ed., 1978); Ernest W. Nicholson, *God and His People: Covenant and Theology in the Old Testament* (Oxford: Clarendon, 1986) 56–117.

10   For the latter view, see Vermeylen, *Du prophète Isaïe*, 1:70–71.

11   The debate over the compositional history of both Deuteronomy (see S. Dean McBride, "Polity of the Covenant People: The Book of Deuteronomy," in John T. Strong and Steven S. Tull, eds., *Constituting the Community: Studies on the Polity of Ancient Israel in Honor of S. Dean McBride Jr.* [Winona Lake, IN: Eisenbrauns, 2005] 17–33) and the Deuteronomistic History (see Gary N. Knoppers and J. Gordon McConville, eds., *Reconsidering Israel and Judah: Recent Studies on the Deuteronomistic History* [Sources for Biblical and Theological Study 8; Winona Lake, IN: Eisenbrauns, 2003]) remains very controversial and unsettled, though views similar to those presented here involving an early Hezekian edition of the Deuteronomistic History have been suggested in a number of Robert R. Wilson's works (*Prophecy and Society in Ancient Israel* [Philadelphia: Fortress Press, 1980] 157; "Introduction" and "Notes" on 1–2 Kings in *The HarperCollins Study Bible*, ed. Wayne A. Meeks et al. [New York: HarperCollins, 1993] 590; and "The Former Prophets: Reading the Books of Kings," in James Luther Mays, David L. Petersen, and Kent Harold Richards, eds., *Old Testament Interpretation: Past, Present, and Future. Essays in Honor of Gene M. Tucker* [Nashville: Abingdon, 1995] 91).

12   J. J. M. Roberts, "The Importance of Isaiah at Qumran," in James H. Charlesworth, ed., *The Bible and the Dead Sea Scrolls: The Princeton Symposium on the Dead Sea Scrolls* (Scripture and the Scrolls 1; Waco, TX: Baylor University Press, 2006) 273–86. There is the very famous, relatively complete 1QIsaᵃ (Millar Burrows, *The Dead Sea Scrolls of St. Mark's Monastery*, vol. 1, *The Isaiah Manuscript and the Habakkuk Commentary* [New Haven: ASOR, 1950]), the more fragmentary 1QIsaᵇ (1Q8), originally published by E. L. Sukenik (*The Dead Sea Scrolls of the Hebrew University* [Jerusalem: Magnes Press, Hebrew University, 1955]) and supplemented by additional fragments published later (D. Barthélemy and J. T. Milik, *Qumran Cave 1* [DJD 1; Oxford: Clarendon, 1955] 66-68). One also has the small fragment 5QIsa (5Q3) from cave 5 (M. Baillet, J. T. Milik, and R. de Vaux, eds., *Les "petites grottes" de Qumrân* [DJD 3; Oxford: Clarendon, 1962] 173) and the fragment from Murabbaᶜat (P. Benoit, J. T. Milik, and R. de Vaux, eds., *Les grottes de Murabbaᶜat* [DJD 2; Oxford: Clarendon, 1961] 79–80. Finally, from cave

This abundance of new Isaiah scrolls far earlier than any of the texts of Isaiah known before the discovery of the Qumran material is quite welcome; but despite this wealth of new textual evidence, its payoff for the textual criticism of the book of Isaiah is more limited than one would have hoped. Unlike the situation with regard to the book of Samuel or the book of Jeremiah, where Qumran manuscripts reflecting a textual family distinct from the proto-Masoretic text tradition appeared, all of the Isaiah manuscripts from Qumran appear to belong to the proto-Masoretic family. There are interesting variants to be sure, but these variants are by and large quite minor and hardly differ in kind from the type of variants found in medieval manuscripts.[13]

Compounding this disappointment is the fact that the Greek translation of Isaiah in the LXX is quite free compared to the literal word-for-word rendering characteristic of the Greek translator of Jeremiah. The Greek translator of Isaiah does not impress this commentator as very competent. It is clear that he often had no idea what the Hebrew text meant, and he constantly took refuge in loose paraphrases or summaries. Hebrew parallelism was apparently a bore to him, so he often omits lines he regards as redundant, reducing his workload. Some of these omissions may be accidental haplographies, since the poetry of Isaiah has many parallel lines that repeat the structure and much of the vocabulary of previous lines, setting up a careless scribe with the ideal conditions for accidental haplographies by homoioarcton or homoioteleuton. Indeed, the Hebrew text of Isaiah has suffered a number of such haplographies that may reasonably be restored (see the commentary at 7:8-9; 8:12; 28:12), and the Greek text is even more defective.

Nonetheless, the Greek translation, as by far our earliest translation of the Hebrew, occasionally offers some help in understanding a Hebrew idiom or in suggesting a possible emendation of a difficult Hebrew text.

The Vulgate, in contrast, tends to follow the MT rather slavishly, except where it shows a different understanding of Hebrew syntax from what is common among modern scholars. Both the LXX and the Vulgate seem more sensitive to the phenomenon of direct address and the need to mark that in translation with second person forms even where the Hebrew predominantly uses syntactically conditioned third person forms. Syriac often follows the lead of the LXX, but it usually remains closer to the Hebrew because, like Hebrew, it is a Semitic language. The Targum is far looser and more interpretive or homiletical in its renderings, so it is the least helpful of the translations for text criticism Even so, it is sometimes helpful in getting at the original meaning of the Hebrew text. The lack of non–proto-Masoretic Hebrew textual witnesses, the looseness of the LXX translation, and the relative lateness of the other ancient translations do mean, however, that critical work on the Hebrew text of Isaiah must depend far more on creative conjectural emendation than would be the case in New Testament studies, where the abundance of early textual material from competing textual families allows far more reliance on preserved textual evidence. To dismiss all conjectural emendation would be to settle for a clearly corrupt and defective text. There is no virtue in teasing a bogus meaning out of an obviously corrupt text.

---

4 come fragments of some eighteen or so additional scrolls of Isaiah, 4QIsa[a–r] (4Q55–69b), one of which, pap4QIsa[p] (4Q69), was written on papyrus (P. W. Skehan and E. Ulrich, "Isaiah," in E. Ulrich et al., eds., *Qumran Cave 4.X: The Prophets* [DJD 15; Oxford: Clarendon, 1997] 7–144.) In addition to these scrolls or fragments of scrolls from Isaiah, the Qumran literature also contains a large number of citations from Isaiah in other literature from Qumran (Roberts, "Importance of Isaiah," 275; Francis J. Morrow Jr., "The Text of Isaiah at Qumran" [PhD diss., The Catholic University of America, 1973] 205–13) as well as commentaries on Isaiah (Maurya P. Horgan, *Pesharim: Qumran Interpretations of Biblical Books*

[CBQMS 8; Washington, DC: Catholic Biblical Association of Amerca, 1979]; Horgan, "Pesharim," in James H. Charlesworth et al., eds., *The Dead Sea Scrolls: Hebrew, Aramaic and Greek Texts with English Translations*, vol. 6B, *Pesharim, Other Commentaries, and Related Documents* [PTSDSSP 6B; Tübingen: Mohr Siebeck; Louisville: Westminster John Knox, 2002] 1–193).

13 Patrick Skehan's judgment still rings true: "There remains only a single channel of transmission of this book, narrowly controlled from 300 B.C.E. until much later" ("IV. Littérature de Qumran: A. Textes biblique," *DBSup*, 9 [1978] 813).

Commentaries

There is no end to commentaries on the book of Isaiah,[14] and over the years I have read most of those written in English, German, Dutch, and French, while dabbling in the earlier works in Greek, Latin, and Hebrew, and only occasionally dipping into those in languages less familiar to me. I have learned from all of them, though in many ways the magisterial Biblischer Kommentar of Hans Wildberger has probably been the most influential on my own thought. As any reader of Wildberger's commentary and my present work will soon discover, I often disagree with Wildberger, but even where I disagree, I have been informed by his work. I was also profoundly influenced by William L. Holladay's little book, *Isaiah: Scroll of a Prophetic Heritage* (Grand Rapids: Eerdmans, 1978). I served on the NRSV revision committee with Holladay for several years during which, among other books, we revised the translation of Isaiah, and his contributions to that work and to my own thoughts on Isaiah were significant. John H. Hayes and Stuart A. Irvine's small Abingdon commentary on Isaiah, *Isaiah, the Eighth-Century Prophet: His Times and His Preaching*, should be mentioned as well. John is a longtime friend and adversary. Though I very often disagree with the conclusions he reaches, I almost always agree with the questions he insists on raising, and his arguments, even when I ultimately reject them, force me to rethink and refine my own arguments. I mention these three scholars, not because they were the only influences on my thought but simply to indicate that I am thoroughly aware how much my work has been influenced by other students of Isaiah, the Bible, and the ancient Near East, including my teachers and colleagues, my contemporaries and my predecessors, my supporters and my opponents. Any reader of this commentary thoroughly at home with the literature on Isaiah will quickly recognize my dependence on others, these and many unnamed, simply by reading what I have written, even when I do not specifically cite the views of earlier scholars with whom I agree. As a longtime reader of commentaries, perhaps not the most scintillating genre of literature ever devised, I confess that I am not fond of commentaries that insist on summarizing every contrasting opinion on every disputed point in the text. I often discover, after wading through such seemingly interminable discussions that, while I might now have some sense of the wide variety of viewpoints on the particular text being discussed, I have no clear sense of the commentator's own interpretation of the text in question, or how it coherently flows in his or her understanding from the preceding text and leads into the following text. If I want to know what everyone else thinks about the text, I prefer to read their works for myself. I am more interested in the commentator's coherent explanation of the text in question. As a result of my own preferences, readers will find that I often provide no detailed and annotated summary of all the other interpretations offered in the literature. I am more interested in clearly articulating the interpretation that I find the most compelling. For some this will appear a fault; for others, on the assumption that I am not a minority of one, this may appear a virtue. In any case, it is the choice I have made.

With regard to this commentary, I should also note that I write unapologetically as a Christian interpreter of the text. My primary exegetical interest lies in the historical-critical meanings that the text would have had to its first, clearly pre-Christian, audiences contemporary with Isaiah and his earliest disciples. Hence, I believe that, despite my Christian commitments, Jewish and other non-Christian readers interested in the earliest meanings of the text may profit from my exegetical observations. As a Christian interpreter, however, I have also addressed questions as to possible meanings of the text for contemporary Christian believers when I felt that the text called for such reflection. Not every text raised such issues for me, and I have made no attempt to gloss every text with such theological reflections. Such reflections, when they do not arise integrally from the preceding exegetical discussion but are simply tacked on at the end to satisfy an editorial or stylistic demand, often come across, at least to me, as superficial and ad hoc. No doubt some readers will regard my theological reflections as equally superficial or wrong, but I hope that at least these reflections, where they occur, will not appear to be a disappointing or irritating addendum, added only because the editors expected a "theological application."

---

14   See the section "Commentaries" in the Reference Codes in the front matter of this book.

Commentary

1

1/ The vision of[a] Isaiah, son of Amoz, which he saw concerning Judah and Jerusalem in the days of Uzziah,[b] Jotham, and Hezekiah,[c] kings of Judah.

Textual Notes

a   LXX differs from MT in having two relative clauses: "The vision which Isaiah son of Amoz saw, which he saw . . . ." This is clearly secondary.

b   For MT's וּעֻזִּיָּהוּ (ʿuzzîyāhû), 1QIsaᵃ has עוזיה with a plene writing of the initial short vowel and the shortened form of the theophoric ending.

c   MT has יְחִזְקִיָּהוּ (yĕḥizqîyāhû), while 1QIsaᵃ has חזקיה (ḥizqîyâ) corrected to יחזקיה (yĕḥizqîyâ). Elsewhere in MT this king's name is spelled four different ways: יחזקיהו (as here, 2 Kgs 20:10; Jer 15:4; 1 Chr 4:4; 2 Chr 28:27; 29:1, 20, 30-31, 36; 30:1, 18, 20, 22; 31:2, 8, 13, 20; 32:2, 8-9, 11-12, 16, 17, 20, 22-27, 30, 32-33; 33:3), יחזקיה (yĕḥizqîyâ, Hos 1:1; Mic 1:1), חזקיהו (ḥizqîyāhû, 2 Kgs 16:20; 18:9, 17, 19, 22, 29, 30-32, 37; 19:1, 3, 5, 9-10, 14-15, 20; 20:1, 3, 5, 8, 12-16, 19-21; 21:3; Isa 36:1, 2, 4, 7, 14-16, 18, 22; 37:1, 3, 5, 9-10, 14-15, 21; 38:1-3, 5, 9, 22; 39:1-5, 8; Jer 26:18-19; 1 Chr 3:13; 2 Chr 29:18, 27; 30:24; 32:15), and חזקיה (ḥizqîyâ, 2 Kgs 18:1, 10, 13-16; Zeph 1:1; Prov 15:1).

Commentary

By analogy to the superscriptions at the beginning of a number of other prophetic books (Jer 1:1-3; Hos 1:1; Joel 1:1; Amos 1:1; Obad 1:1; Mic 1:1; Nah 1:1; Hab 1:1; Zeph 1:1), the superscription in Isa 1:1 is probably intended as a heading for the whole book, or at least as much of the book as existed at the time the superscription was added. It seems clear that it was added after the time of Isaiah. Not only would the information contained in the heading be more important for a later audience than for Isaiah's contemporaries, but the diction is not that of Isaiah. Here, in the superscription in 2:1, and in the prose material in 36:7, the word order "Judah and Jerusalem" is found. Elsewhere in the genuine Isaianic oracles the order is always "Jerusalem and Judah" (3:1, 8; 5:3; 22:21). As the preceding reference to 2:1 indicates, the heading in 1:1 is only one of a number of superscriptions found in the book. In contrast to 1:1, however, these other superscriptions (2:1; 13:1; 14:28; 15:1; 17:1; 19:1; 21:1, 11, 13; 22:1; 23:1; 30:6) serve only as introductions to single oracles or, at most, to small groups of closely related oracles. Though assigning even relative dates to redactional work involves highly subjective and hypothetical reconstruction of an essentially private process, it would appear that these other superscriptions, attached as they are to individual units incorporated in the final collection, existed prior to the creation of 1:1.

In fact, one may argue that the superscription in 2:1 provided the model for the creation of 1:1.[1] Starting with הַדָּבָר אֲשֶׁר חָזָה יְשַׁעְיָהוּ בֶּן־אָמוֹץ עַל־יְהוּדָה וִירוּשָׁלָ͏ִם (haddābār ʾăšer ḥāzâ yĕšaʿyāhû ben-ʾāmôṣ ʿal-yĕhûdâ wîrûšālāim), "The word which Isaiah son of Amoz saw concerning Judah and Jerusalem," the redactor replaced הַדָּבָר (haddābār) "the word," with חָזוֹן (ḥāzôn) "vision," to go with the verb חָזָה (ḥāzâ), "to see." He then shifted the prophet's name and patronym immediately after the noun חָזוֹן to create a construct chain before the relative clause with the verb. Finally, he added the temporal element with the list of kings at the end of the superscription on the analogy of Hos 1:1 and Amos 1:1. The editor was able to create the list of kings by the references to three of these kings in the Isaiah corpus with which he was working: Uzziah (Isa 6:1), Ahaz (Isa 7:1, 10; 14:28), and Hezekiah (repeatedly in Isaiah 36–39). To fill out the list he only needed to insert Jotham between Uzziah and Ahaz, following the sequence he would have known from 2 Kgs 15:32-38.

Such a process behind the creation of Isa 1:1 might explain some of the peculiarities of this heading and its general inadequacy as a superscription even for all of chaps. 1–39, much less the whole of the present book of Isaiah. The heading suggests that Isaiah's ministry was

---

1   See the discussion in Vermeylen, *Du prophète Isaïe,* 1:38–41.

directed to Judah and Jerusalem, not to the northern kingdom, which may explain why none of the kings of Israel are listed, as they are in the superscriptions to Amos (1:1) and Hosea (1:1).[2] Nonetheless, the northern kingdom Israel figures prominently in a number of Isaiah's oracles (9:7-20; 10:10-11; 17:1-6; 28:1). Moreover, there is a whole series of oracles against foreign nations (chaps. 13–23). One would never guess this from the heading in Isa 1:1. This odd limitation of Isaiah's proclamation to Judah and Jerusalem may be the result of the redactor's using the older superscription in 2:1 as his model. Unlike Isa 1:1, the superscription in 2:1 was never intended as a superscription to the whole collection; it was apparently attached to a much shorter collection of oracles primarily concerning Judah and Jerusalem, that is, the major portion of the material in chaps. 1–5. One may question, however, whether the superscription in 2:1 is in its original position. It is possible that, when the redactor created the superscription for the book in 1:1, he moved the superscription for chaps. 1–5 to its present position at 2:1. He might have dropped this now-repetitive superscription entirely, but the insertion of 1:29-31 created a disjunction between the material about Jerusalem and Judah in 1:2-28 and its continuation in 3:1. Moreover, the same editor may have been responsible for inserting 2:2-22 before 3:1. Since, as I will argue in my treatment of 2:2-22, this material is addressed, at least fictively, to a northern Israelite audience, it creates a similar disjunction to Jerusalem and Judah in 3:1. Thus, placing the heading before this insertion was a way of recontextualizing this material so that it would be relevant to the Judean audience of the redactor's day. The redactor may also have wanted to claim 2:2-4 for Isaiah, since he was probably aware that the same oracle occurs in Mic 4:1-4.[3]

As a heading to the whole book, Isa 1:1 makes the theological claim that the message contained in this book came to Isaiah by divine revelation. It also purports to give us information about the prophet, the people to whom he prophesied, and the period of his prophetic ministry. Unfortunately, the information about Isaiah's family is not very helpful to the modern reader; all we know about this Amoz is that he was Isaiah's father. Moreover, I have already noted the inadequacy of the heading's information about the people to whom Isaiah prophesied. Finally, the information about the period of Isaiah's ministry does not seem to reflect any independent knowledge of the redactor that a modern reader could not obtain just by reading the book and its parallels in 2 Kings.

Nevertheless, it does serve as a healthy reminder of a very important fact. Isaiah's ministry began during the reign of Uzziah (c. 790–738 BCE), probably in the year of his death (6:1), and extended into the reign of Hezekiah (c. 715–687/686 BCE), how far we are not told, but at least through 701 BCE and the Sennacherib campaign. Thus, Isaiah's ministry spanned almost forty years and possibly another decade. This must be remembered when dealing with the Isaianic material. One cannot expect the same homogeneity in the literary deposit of a forty-year ministry as one might in that of a much shorter ministry such as that of Amos.

Bibliography

Freedman, David Noel, "Headings in the Books of the Eighth Century Prophets," in J. R. Huddleston, ed., *Divine Commitment and Human Obligation: Selected Writings of David Noel Freedman*, vol. 1, *History and Religion* (Grand Rapids: Eerdmans, 1997) 367–82.

Tucker, Gene M., "Prophetic Superscriptions and the Growth of the Canon," in George M. Coats and Burke O. Long, eds., *Canon and Authority: Essays in Old Testament Religion and Theology* (Philadelphia: Fortress Press, 1977), 56–70.

2   One should note, however, that Hosea does not list any contemporary Israelite king after Jeroboam II, which may suggest that the redactors of Hosea and Isaiah did not consider any of the later final six kings of Israel to be legitimate. See Francis I. Andersen and David Noel Freedman, *Hosea: A New Translation with Introduction and Commentary* (AB 24; Garden City, NY: Doubleday, 1980) 148–49; see also C. van Gelderin and W. H. Gispen, *Het Boek Hosea* (COuT; Kampen: J. H. Kok, 1953) 19; and Hellmuth Frey, *Das Buch des Werbens Gottes um seine Kirche: Der Prophet Hosea* (BAT 23/2; Stuttgart: Calwer, 1957) 8.

3   See also P. R. Ackroyd, "A Note on Isaiah 2:1," *ZAW* 75 (1963) 320–21.

1

2/   Hear, O heavens, and listen, O earth,
     for Yahweh has spoken:
  "Sons I have begotten[a] and reared,
     but they have rebelled against me.

3/   An ox knows its owner,[b]
     and an ass the trough of its lord,[c]
  But Israel does not know,[d]
     my people does not perceive."[d]

4/   Hey,[e] nation who keeps sinning![f]
     People heavy with iniquity!
  Offspring who do evil![g]
     Children who behave corruptly!
  Who have abandoned[h] Yahweh,
     Have spurned[h] the Holy One of Israel,
       Have become thoroughly[i] estranged![h]

5/   Why[j] would you be beaten any longer?
     Why do you continue to rebel?
  The whole head has become a wound,
     The whole heart faint.

6/   From the sole of the foot to the head
     There is no soundness in it;
  Just a bruise and a welt,
     And a bleeding wound—[k]
  They[k] have not been drained nor bound up,
     And it[k] has not been softened by oil.

7/   Your country is a desolation,
     Your cities are burned with fire.
  Your land—in your very presence
     Foreigners devour it,
  And it is a desolation[l] like the overthrow of Sodom![m]

8/   And daughter Zion is left
     like a booth in a vineyard,
     like a hut in a cucumber patch,
     like a blockaded city.[n]

9/   Had not Yahweh of hosts left a remnant for us,
     soon[o] we would have become like Sodom,
     we would have resembled Gomorrah.

10/   Hear the word of Yahweh,
     O rulers of Sodom,
  Listen to the word of our God,
     O people of Gomorrah.

11/   "What use do I have for the multitude of your sacrifices?"
     says Yahweh.
  "I am sated with burnt offerings of rams
     and the suet of fattened cattle;
  The blood of bulls and lambs[p] and goats
     I do not desire.

12/   When you come to see[q] my face,
     who sought this from your hand?

13/   Do not continue trampling my courts.[r]
  Bringing offerings is futile,[s]
     Incense is an abomination to me.
  New moon and sabbath, the calling of an assembly
     I cannot endure.
  Fast[t] and solemn assembly,[u] 14/ your festivals[v] and fixed seasons
     My soul hates.
  They[w] have become a burden to me
     I am tired of bearing.[x]

15/   When you spread out your hands,[y]
     I will hide my eyes from you;

Even if you pray at length,
    I will not listen.
    Your hands are full of blood.ᶻ

16/ Wash, cleanse yourself,
    Remove the evil of your deeds*ᵃ
    From before my eyes.
    Cease to do evil;

17/ Learn to do good.
    Seek justice;
    Right the wronged.*ᵇ
    Render judgment for the orphan,
    Plead the case of the widow.

18/ Come, let us reach an agreement,"
    says Yahweh.
    "Though your sins are like scarlet,*ᶜ
    They*ᵈ can be white as snow;
    Though they are red as crimson,
    They*ᵈ can be like wool.

19/ If you are willing and will listen,*ᵉ
    You will eat the good of the land;

20/ But if you refuse and rebel,*ᶠ
    You will be eaten by the sword,*ᵍ
    For the mouth of Yahweh has spoken."

Textual Notes

a   MT, supported by 1QIsaᵃ and by the traces in 4QIsaᵃ, has גִּדַּלְתִּי וְרוֹמַמְתִּי (*giddaltî wĕrômamtî*), "I reared and brought up." Despite the occurrence of the same two verbs as parallel terms in Isa 23:4, this usage seems curiously redundant here. The LXX has ἐγέννησα, "I begat," for the first verb, a reading that presupposes only a very slight change in the Hebrew text, יָלַדְתִּי (*yāladtî*) instead of גִּדַּלְתִּי (*giddaltî*).[1] This may be original. Deuteronomy 32:18 uses the same Hebrew verb, ילד (*yālad*, "to beget"), to describe Yahweh's creation of his people, and the LXX of Deut 32:18 translates the Hebrew verb with the same Greek verb used in Isa 1:2, γεννάω. The usage is a little unusual, since Hebrew normally uses the *hiphil* הוֹלִד (*hôlēd*) to refer to the father's role in childbearing, while the *qal* ילד (*yālad*) normally designates the mother's role. The use of the *qal* to express the father's role is well attested, however. See Gen 4:18; 10:8, 13, 15, 24, 26 (= 1 Chr 1:10, 11, 13, 18, 20); 22:23; 25:3; Prov 17:21; 23:22, 24. Nonetheless, the unusual character of this usage may explain the corruption in the MT. The change from ילדתי, "I begat," more normally, "I gave birth," to גדלתי, "I reared," could be a tendentious attempt to avoid using what was perceived, rightly or wrongly, to be feminine imagery for Yahweh.[2]

b   MT's singular noun קֹנֵהוּ (*qōnēhû*), "his owner," 1QIsaᵃ corrects to the plural קונ֯הו (*qônᵉhû*), "his owners" (with *yod* written above the word) to agree with the following plural בְּעָלָיו (*bĕʿālāyw*), "his lords."

c   The reason for the grammatical plural בְּעָלָיו (*bĕʿālāyw*), "his lords," is not clear. Because the lord in the metaphor clearly refers to God, this could be a plural of majesty similar to the use of the plural *ʾĕlōhîm* to refer to God, but the noun בַּעַל (*baʿal*) in the sense of a human owner is sometimes written as a plural before a singular suffix even when the context shows that a single human owner is meant (see Exod 22:10-14), so the plural here may be no more than a grammatical oddity.

d   The LXX was bothered by the lack of the direct object and supplies με, "me," thus making God the object of the verbs

---

1   Contra Wildberger, 1:8, the LXX reading does not presuppose the *hiphil*, הולדתי. As noted above, Deut 32:18 uses the *qal*, ילד, with Yahweh as the subject, and the LXX translates the term with γεννάω, just as it does here. Given the close literary ties between Isa 1:2-20 and Deuteronomy 32, one might well expect the same usage in Isaiah. Both texts begin with an appeal to heaven and earth to listen (Deut 32:1; Isa 1:2); both refer to Israel as God's rebellious and foolish children (Deut 32:5; Isa 1:2-6); both may use birth imagery of God (Deut 32:18; Isa 1:2 [see above]); both mention Sodom and Gomorrah (Deut 32: 32; Isa 1:9); and both present a choice between life and death (Deut 32:39; Isa 1:18-20)—to mention only the most obvious parallels.

2   It is dubious that Isaiah was concerned about the use of feminine imagery for God; Second Isaiah certainly made use of blatantly feminine imagery for God (Isa 42:14; see Katheryn Pfisterer Darr, *Isaiah's Vision and the Family of God* [Literary Currents in Biblical Interpretation; Louisville: Westminster John Knox, 1994] 104–10), but that is no guarantee that later tradents would be as comfortable with such imagery.

"to know" and "to perceive": "but Israel did not know me, my people did not recognize me." The Targum also supplies direct objects, but the MT is to be preferred. The ambiguity created by its lack of an explicit object appears to be intentional. See the commentary.

e   The particle הוֹי (hôy) does not mean "Woe!" It is a vocative particle used to get the attention of the party or parties being addressed. It typically introduces direct address and is followed by nouns or participles in the vocative identifying the addressee(s). Thus, it is often followed by forms in the second person, as one sees in the following verse. See the excursus on the hôy-oracles at Isa 5:8.

f   The form חֹטֵא (ḥōṭēʾ), "who keeps sinning," is a participle and thus characterizes the addressees by their continual behavior just like the following מְרֵעִים (mĕrēʿîm), "who do evil," and מַשְׁחִיתִים (mašḥîtîm), "who behave corruptly."

g   The singular noun זֶרַע (zeraʿ), "seed, offspring," is not in construct with the following participle and should not be rendered "offspring of evildoers." As a collective noun, זֶרַע can be modified by a plural adjective or participle, and that is the case here as the parallelism with בָּנִים מַשְׁחִיתִים (bānîm mašḥîtîm), "children who behave corruptly," shows quite clearly. It is not the parentage that is being attacked—God is the father (v. 2)—but the behavior of the children.

h   The final three verbs in the verse are all third person plurals, but they stand in unmarked relative clauses and in no way interrupt the direct address. The LXX, which lacks the last clause, and the Syriac, which has all three, actually translate these verb forms with the second person plural in order to make the direct address even clearer.

i   "Thoroughly" is an attempt to capture the sense of the Hebrew אָחוֹר (ʾāḥôr), "(to be estranged) behind."

j   The phrase עַל מֶה (ʿal meh) normally means "Why?" (see esp. Num 22:32), but in a couple of passages it has the sense "upon what" (Job 38:6; 2 Chr 32:10). Isaiah may be exploiting that ambiguity here. The obvious meaning is, "Why be beaten any further?," but one may hear overtones of, "Upon what/where would you be beaten further," since there is no longer a single sound spot to strike.

k   I have tried to maintain the poetic parallelism of the original in my translation. The three different nouns signifying types of wounds are all in the singular, despite the normal English translation of them as plural. The first two nouns, a masculine followed by a feminine, פֶּצַע וְחַבּוּרָה (pesaʿ wĕḥabbûrâ), "a bruise and a welt," are taken as a unit, so the verbs in the parallel line that refer to them are placed in the masculine plural, לֹא־זֹרוּ וְלֹא חֻבָּשׁוּ (lōʾ-zōrû wĕlōʾ ḥubbāšû), "they are not drained nor bound up." The third noun, a feminine singular, forms a unit with its modifying adjective, וּמַכָּה טְרִיָּה (ûmakkâ ṭĕriyâ), "and a bleeding wound," so the verb in the parallel line that refers

to it is placed in the feminine singular, וְלֹא רֻכְּכָה בַּשָּׁמֶן (wĕlōʾ rukkĕkâ baššāmen), "and it is not softened by oil."

l   For MT's וּשְׁמָמָה (ûšĕmāmâ), "and it is a desolation," 1QIsaᵃ has ושממו עליה (wĕšāmĕmû ʿālêhā), "and they will be appalled over it" (for the idiom, see Isa 52:14; Lev 26:32; Jer 2:12; et passim), but the Qumran reading has no other support in the textual tradition.

m   Reading כְּמַהְפֵּכַת סְדֹם (kĕmahpēkat sĕdôm), "like the overthrow of Sodom," for MT's כְּמַהְפֵּכַת זָרִים (kĕmahpēkat zārîm), "like the overthrow of foreigners." The versions all support the MT, but the repetition of זרים from the preceding line is harsh, and in the four other occurrences of כמהפכת, the construction is either כמהפכת סדום, "like the overthrow of Sodom" (Deut 29:22; Jer 49:18), or כְּמַהְפֵּכַת אֱלֹהִים אֶת־סְדֹם (kĕmahpēkat ʾĕlōhîm ʾet-sĕdōm), "like God's overthrow of Sodom" (Isa 13:19; Jer 50:40). The word סדם occurs twice in the context in vv. 9-10, so a comparison of Jerusalem's fate with the fate of that city is clearly present in this passage. Since ו (w) and י (y) are often confused, as are ד (d) and ר (r), the corruption is relatively easy to explain. The confusion between ס (s) and ז (z) is a little more difficult, at least in the square script, but if the writing were slightly damaged, it is possible. If one assumes that the offending scribe was coping from a manuscript with a plene orthography, סדום was misread as זרים by homoioteleuton due to the influence of the preceding זרים. Note, however, that 1QIsaᵃ has the plene writing סודם for the city name Sodom.[3]

n   This translation of כְּעִיר נְצוּרָה (kĕʿîr nĕṣûrâ), "like a blockaded city," tries to maintain the normal meaning of the verb נצר (nāṣar), "to guard" or "to watch," assuming the enemy's hostile guarding of a blockaded city (see Ezek 6:12; Jer 4:16), but this rendering is uncertain. The versions are consistent in translating the expression as "like a besieged city"; thus, commentators often suggest the emendation of נְצוּרָה (nĕṣûrâ) to נְצוֹרָה (nĕṣôrâ) from צור (ṣûr), "to besiege," but צור is not otherwise attested in the niphal conjugation. Moreover, either of these translations would seem to mean abandoning the metaphorical formulation of the two parallel lines for reality, since at the time of Sennacherib's invasion, Jerusalem was, in fact, a blockaded or besieged city, but see below. It would also mean abandoning the syntactic and poetic pattern of the two parallel lines, "like a . . . in a . . . ." To avoid these problems Wildberger adopts the emendation of כְּעִיר נְצוּרָה (kĕʿîr nĕṣûrâ) to כְּעַיִר בְּצִירָה (kĕʿayir bĕṣîrâ), "like a donkey in a pen" (Wildberger, 1:19). The emendation of נצורה to בצירה is plausible, as is the meaning "pen" or "sheepfold" for צירה, based on the Arabic cognate and the parallel in Mic 2:12.[4] But the introduction of a donkey, where the two parallel lines have a structure of some sort, is awkward. Sennacherib speaks of shutting up Hezekiah "like a bird in a cage," but the expression "like a donkey in a sheepfold" is otherwise unknown to me. Sheep growers in Texas sometimes put

---

3   See the discussion of this writing for *sodom* in E. Y. Kutscher, *The Language and Linguistic Background of the Isaiah Scroll (1QIsaᵃ)* (STDJ 6; Leiden: Brill, 1974) 109–10, 504.

4   See Delbert R. Hillers, *Micah: A Commentary on the Book of the Prophet Micah* (Hermeneia; Philadelphia: Fortress Press, 1984) 38.

an isolated donkey with a flock of sheep to ward off predators, but I am aware of no evidence that this practice was known in ancient Israel. The text may be corrupt, but none of the emendations so far suggested seems convincing. On the other hand, if the text dates to the time after Sennacherib's withdrawal, when Jerusalem was no longer under blockade, one could easily compare the isolated position of this surviving city in Hezekiah's decimated state of ruined cities with a besieged or blockaded city. Jerusalem's isolation remained just as palpable as when she was surrounded by Assyrian forts.

o The *athnach* is under כִּמְעָט (kimʿāṭ), which indicates that the MT read it with the preceding line, "Had not Yahweh of hosts left a remnant for us, just a little bit, we would. . . ." The syntactical parallel with Ps 94:17, however, suggests that כמעט begins a new line. The versions' failure to represent כמעט with a specific word in their translations is not sufficient textual evidence to delete the word.

p LXX omits וּכְבָשִׂים (ûkĕbāśîm), "and lambs," but, given LXX's tendency to shorten lists, this omission is hardly evidence that LXX was following a shorter Hebrew *Vorlage*.[5] Since the Greek translator had already used the word for lambs in the same verse to translate מְרִיאִים (mĕrîʾîm), "fattened cattle," he probably just opted not to repeat the word.[6]

q The idiom "to see the face of" is widely used of a supplicant gaining an audience with a superior—a king, high official, or God. When used of a human superior, the verb ראה (rāʾâ), "to see," in this idiom is always in the *qal* conjugation (Gen 43:3, 5; 44:23; Exod 10:28; 2 Sam 3:13; 2 Kgs 25:19; Jer 52:25). The same construction with the *qal* is also used when God tells Moses, "You cannot see my face, for no human can see me and live" (Exod 33:20). But in passages where a supplicant is seeking an audience with God, that is, visiting the sanctuary to worship, make offerings, and pray, the vast majority of MT manuscripts point the verb ראה as a *niphal* (Exod 23:15; 34:20, 24; Deut 31:11; Isa 1:12). This is clearly a secondary vocalization of the original idiom to avoid the notion that anyone could actually see God. In none of these texts does the consonantal form of ראה require that one analyze it as a *niphal*. In Isa 1:12, though the form is pointed as a *niphal* לֵרָאוֹת (lērāʾôt), "to appear, be seen," the consonantal form, לראות, suggests that the form should be analyzed as a *qal* infinitive construct, לִרְאֹת (lirʾōt), "to see." The pattern for the *niphal* infinitive construct is normally either לְהֵרָאֹ (lĕhērāʾô, Judg 12:21; 1 Sam 3:21) or לְהֵרָאוֹת (lĕhērāʾôt, 2 Sam 17:17; 1 Kgs 18:2; Ezek 21:29; Mal 3:2), not the anomalous לֵרָאוֹת (lērāʾôt) of the MT of Isa 1:12. It is possible that the initial *heh* of the *niphal* infinitive construct could be omitted by syncopation following a preposition, if בְּעֹטֵף in Lam 2:11 is correct, but it is possible that the *qal* infinitive, בַּעֲטֹף, "to languish," should be read even there. In any case, Syriac's *lmḥzʾ* supports the analysis of לראות as a *qal*, and even the LXX's ὀφθῆναί μοι may be taken that way, since the LXX

uses the same idiom in Exod 10:28 (ᾗ δ᾽ ἂν ἡμέρᾳ ὀφθῇς μοι ἀποθανῇ) to translate the *qal* construction בְּיוֹם רְאֹתְךָ פָנַי תָּמוּת (bĕyôm rĕʾōtĕkā pānay tāmût), "On the day you see my face you will die." When the LXX follows the exegetical tradition behind the MT in avoiding the notion of seeing God, it uses the idiom ὀφθήσῃ ἐνώπιον (Exod 23:15; 34:20; Deut 31:11) or ὀφθῆναι ἐναντίον (Exod 34:24), "to appear before."

r The line division here follows the LXX. The MT line division in vv. 12-13 produces awkward syntax and poor parallelism:

> When you come to see my face,
> who sought this from your hand—the trampling of my courts?
> Do not continue bringing a vain offering,
> Incense is an abomination to me. . . .

Wildberger wants to keep the MT line division, but "from your hand" does not fit very well if the demonstrative "this" is anticipating "the trampling of my courts." Thus, to save the MT's line division, he assumes that a whole line has been omitted between "face" and "who sought this," and he emends מִיֶּדְכֶם (miyyedkem), "from your hand," to מֵאִתְּכֶם (mēʾittĕkem), "from you":

> When you come to see my face,
> . . . . .
> Who demanded such from you,
> so that one tramples my courts? (Wildberger, 1:32–33)

Such radical textual surgery is too high a price to pay to preserve the MT's line division. With the line division suggested in my translation, "this" refers back to the multitude of animal sacrifices mentioned in v. 11, with which Yahweh was sated and which he did not desire.

s The LXX suggests reading this line as a nominal clause, which requires only the minor change of deleting the *maqqep*, which 1QIsaᵃ does not have, and repointing מנחת as a defectively written plural, which Syr. seems to have read—that is, correcting MT's מִנְחַת־שָׁוְא (minhat-šāwʾ), "vain offering," to מִנְחֹת שָׁוְא (minhōt šāwʾ), "bringing offerings is futile."

t MT's אָוֶן וַעֲצָרָה (ʾāwen waʿăṣārâ), "iniquity and solemn assembly," offers an odd parallelism that seems strangely out of place in a long list of cultic gatherings and activities. One could understand the phrase to mean that God cannot abide the mixture of cult and iniquity, but such an understanding anticipates too soon the explanation for Yahweh's disgust with the cult, which should be given only at the end of v. 15. Though the versions, apart from the LXX, support the MT's reading, the oddity of the MT's parallelism is reflected in the Syriac's mistranslation of the final term of the phrase, *dᶜtʾ wdḥ bwšʾy*, "depravity and imprisonment." The LXX has νηστείαν for the first term, a reading that presupposes צוֹם (ṣôm), "fast," in its Hebrew *Vorlage*. This offers better parallelism, since צוֹם, "fast," and עֲצָרָה, "solemn assembly," are paired elsewhere (Joel 1:14; 2:15), and it keeps the first term in line with the other cultic terminology in the series.

---

5 H. G. M. Williamson, "Isaiah 1.11 and the Septuagint of Isaiah," in A. Graeme Auld, ed., *Understanding Poets and Prophets: Essays in Honour of George* *Wishart Anderson* (JSOTSup 152; Sheffield: JSOT Press, 1993) 401–12.

6 Ibid., 408.

u The MT takes אָוֶן וַעֲצָרָה as the concluding phrase of the preceding sentence, but that creates a very awkward construction with objects both before and after the verb, which would appear to require an anacoluthon: "New moon and sabbath, the calling of an assembly—I cannot endure iniquity (or fast) and solemn assembly." The LXX, by contrast, allows the predicate לֹא־אוּכַל (lōʾ-ʾûkal), "I cannot endure," to conclude the sentence, and then begins the next sentence with צוֹם וַעֲצָרָה. This avoids the anacoluthon and allows the last sentence of v. 13 and both sentences of v. 14 to end with two-word predicates:

לֹא־אוּכַל (lōʾ-ʾûkal), "I cannot endure"
שָׂנְאָה נַפְשִׁי (śānĕʾâ napšî), "My soul hates"
נִלְאֵיתִי נְשֹׂא (nilʾêtî nĕśōʾ), "I am tired of bearing"

This is certainly an improvement over the poetic structure of the MT.

v The MT and the versions all seem to presuppose חָדְשֵׁיכֶם (ḥodšêkem), "your new moons," but this is an awkward repetition of the same word from v. 13. Wildberger (1:34), following N. H. Tur-Sinai, suggests emending to חַגֵּיכֶם (ḥaggêkem), "your festivals." Since both words begin with the same letter, an early scribe could have miscopied the word due to the influence of the preceding חֹדֶשׁ. One should also consider the possibility that the difficulties in vv. 13-14 are the result of secondary expansion of an originally shorter list of cultic events.

w The antecedents that provide the third person plural subject of the verb הָיוּ (hāyû), "have become," are the fast, solemn assembly, festivals, and fixed seasons of the preceding sentence. It is these festivals that have become a burden to Yahweh. Because the LXX construes the following verb נשא (nĕśōʾ), "to bear, carry," as meaning, "to forgive," it has taken the subject of הָיוּ (hāyû) to be the second person, and to make the sense clear, it has introduced the second person and has added three words not in its *Vorlage*: ἐγενήθητέ μοι εἰς πλησμον ἣν οὐκέτι ἀνήσω τὰς ἁμαρτίας ὑμῶν, "You have become a surfeit to me; I will no longer forgive your sins." The Vulgate and the Syriac support the MT.

x MT's נִלְאֵיתִי נְשֹׂא (nilʾêtî nĕśōʾ) is an unmarked relative clause with its understood object the burden consisting, as already noted, of the various religious celebrations mentioned in the preceding sentence, that is, "your festivals . . . have become a burden to me (that) I am tired of bearing." Nonetheless, Isaiah may have chosen the verb נשא here because of a possible double entendre. Though, given the preceding subject, the primary

sense of the verb here seems to be "to bear" or "to carry," the same verb is often used in the sense "to carry away or forgive sins," and there may be undertones of the reading suggested by LXX and Tg.: if God is weary of Israel's rituals, God may also be weary of forgiving.

y LXX adds "to me" to make it clear that this is a gesture of entreaty and prayer to God.

z 1QIsaᵃ adds a parallel line, ואצבעותיכם בעאון (ʾeṣbĕʿôtêkem bĕʿāʾwōn), "your fingers with iniquity," but this seems to be a secondary expansion under the influence of Isa 59:3, where the verb is גאל and both דם and עון are construed with the preposition:

כִּי כַפֵּיכֶם נְגֹאֲלוּ בַדָּם (kî kappêkem nĕgōʾălû baddām), "Because your hands are polluted with blood," וְאֶצְבְּעוֹתֵיכֶם בֶּעָוֹן (wĕʾeṣbĕʿôtêkem beʿāwon), "and your fingers with iniquity."

*a Instead of "of your deeds," LXX has "from your souls."

*b MT has חָמוֹץ (ḥāmôṣ), which by form should either designate the action, "oppression," or perhaps the agent of the action, "the oppressor." The versions, however, are consistent in rendering this word with a passive, which suggests that one repoint the word to חָמוּץ (ḥāmûṣ), "the oppressed, the wronged." A rendering, "right the oppression," however, remains possible.

*c MT has שָׁנִים (šānîm), "scarlet," which is presumably the plural, though one might explain the final *mem* as the enclitic *mem* on a singular form. 1QIsaᵃ has the singular שני, and since LXX, Syr., and Vg. all reflect the singular, it is probably the better reading.

*d Instead of MT's two distinct third person plural verbs, LXX repeats the same first person singular verb with God as the subject: λευκανῶ, "I will make white."

*e LXX adds the first person pronoun for clarity: ἐὰν θέλητε καὶ εἰσακούσητέ μου, "if you are willing and will obey me."

*f LXX repeats the same verbs from the contrasting line in v. 19 and again attaches the pronoun: ἐὰν δὲ μὴ θέλητε μηδὲ εἰσακούσητέ μου, "but if you are not willing and will not obey me."

*g MT's חֶרֶב (ḥereb), "sword," is to be construed as an adverbial accusative and is probably original. 1QIsaᵃ adds the preposition, בחרב, "by the sword," and Syr. does the same, but the preposition is probably a later addition to clarify the sense of the more difficult accusative construction. Neither LXX nor Vg. had the preposition in their Hebrew *Vorlage*, since they make sword the subject of the verb, "the sword shall eat you."

Commentary

Many scholars divide this speech into as many as four separate units: (1) vv. 2-3; (2) vv. 4-9; (3) vv. 10-17; and (4) vv. 18-20.[7] Verses 4-9 may also have existed at one

time as a separate oracle independent of this context, since the introductory particle הוֹי (hôy), "Hey!" normally introduces a new unit. This is not always the case, however, as J. T. Willis points out with reference to Jer 47:6;

---

7 Wildberger, 1:9, 18–20, 32–37, 50–51; R. E. Clements, *Isaiah 1–39* (NCB; Grand Rapids: Eerdmans, 1980) 30–35; Joseph Jensen, *Isaiah 1–39* (Old Testament Message 8; Wilmington, DE: Michael Glazier, 1984) 39-47.

50:27; Zech 11:17; and Isa 1:24.[8] Verses 10-17 may also have once been an independent piece, but the case for vv. 2-3 and 18-20 ever existing as complete, independent oracles is not very strong. In the present context, vv. 2-20 form a literary unit; there are transitions at vv. 4, 10, and 18, but these transitions are better explained as rhetorical shifts within a single speech. There are numerous indications of literary unity in the passage. Verses 4-9 are linked to vv. 2-3 by the shared motif of disobedient "sons" (1:2, 4) and to vv. 10-17 by the repetition of "Sodom" and "Gomorrah" (1:9,10). Verses 18-20 are linked to vv. 10-17 by the continuation of the series of imperatives in vv. 16-17 (1:18), and the theme of ritual purification. They are connected to vv. 4-9 by the motif of eating the good of the land (1:7, 19), and they are tied to vv. 2-3 by a striking literary and ideological *inclusio*, since both v. 2 and v. 20 have the phrase יהוה דבר (פי) כי (*kî [pî] YHWH dibbēr*), "for (the mouth of) Yahweh has spoken," and v. 2 opens with a typical lawsuit formula (see below) while vv. 19-20, with their choice of life or death, the blessing or the curse, conclude on the same note.

Moreover, the parallels with Deuteronomy 32, Mic 6:1-8, and Psalm 50 support the analysis of Isa 1:2-20 as a single speech. All of these texts involve a lawsuit between God and the people, and all of them call on heaven and earth, or other personified elements of the natural world, to listen to the case. Following this appeal in each of these texts, the prophet, or God, or both in turn, address God's people directly. This address is characterized by direct questions to Israel. It may concentrate on Yahweh's gracious treatment of Israel in the past, on Israel's disobedience, or on both, Yahweh's graciousness serving as a foil to make Israel's sin even more heinous. Just as in Isa 1:11-15, Psalm 50 and Micah 6 play down sacrifice in discussing what Yahweh really demands of his people. The recognition of the lawsuit in 1:2-20 clarifies the way in which these verses fit together as a coherent structure, in which the narrative moves logically from v. 2 to v. 20.

Even when one allows for individual variation in formulation, the striking similarities in thought and structure between this group of texts suggest that they represent a single genre rooted in the same ideological background. Psalm 50:5, 16 explicitly connect God's lawsuit to the covenant, so if one is willing to recognize the commonality of these texts, it is difficult to fault the designation of the genre as a "covenant lawsuit."[9] All these texts are presented as lawsuits filed by God against the people based on the conception that lies behind Deut 4:23-26; 30:19; and 31:24-30, where heaven and earth are called upon to be witnesses to the covenant between Yahweh and his people. The covenant established between Yahweh and Israel by Moses was in many ways analogous to ancient political treaties made between great kings and their vassals.[10] Those treaties typically contain a long

8   J. T. Willis, "The First Pericope in the Book of Isaiah," *VT* 34 (1984) 63–77.

9   Julien Harvey, *Le plaidoyer prophétique contre Israël après la rupture de l'alliance* (Bruges: Desclée de Brouwer, 1962); Harvey, "Le 'Rib-Pattern': Réquisitoire prophétique sur la rupture de l'alliance," *Bib* 43 (1962) 172–96; H. B. Huffmon, "The Covenant Lawsuit in the Prophets," *JBL* 78 (1959) 285–95; J. J. M. Roberts, "Zion in the Theology of the Davidic and Solomonic Empire," in Tomoo Ishida, ed., *Studies in the Period of David and Solomon and Other Essays: Papers Read at the International Symposium for Biblical Studies, Tokyo, 5–7 December 1979* (Tokyo: Yamakawa-Shuppansha; Winona Lake, IN: Eisenbrauns, 1982) 93–108; G. Ernest Wright, "The Lawsuit of God: A Form-Critical Study of Deuteronomy 32, in Bernhard W. Anderson and Walter Harrelson, eds., *Israel's Prophetic Heritage: Essays in Honor of James Muilenburg* (New York: Harper, 1962).

10   There are scores of such treaties extant from second-millennium BCE Mesopotamia (Dominique Charpin, "Une alliance contre l'Elam et le rituel du *lipit napištim*," in François Vallat, ed., *Contribution à l'histoire de l'Iran: Mélanges offerts à Jean Perrot* [Paris: Editions Recherche sur les civilisations, 1990] 109–18; Dominique Charpin, "Un traité entre Zimri-Lim de Mari et Ibâl-pî-El II d'Ešnunna," in Dominique Charpin and Francis Joannès, eds., *Marchands, diplomates et empereurs: Études sur la civilisation mésopotamienne offertes à Paul Garelil* [Paris: Editions Recherche sur les civilisations, 1991] 139–66, 7 plates; J.-M. Durand, "Fragments rejoints pour une histoire élamite," in L. de Meyer, H. Gasche, and F. Vallat, eds., *Fragmenta Historiae Elamicae: Mélanges offerts à M. J. Stève* [Paris: Editions Recherche sur les civilisations, 1986] 111–28; J. Eidem, "An Old Assyrian Treaty from Tell Leilan," in Charpin and Joannès, *Marchands, diplomates et empereurs,* 185–207; and, in the same volume, F. Joannès, "Le traité de vassalité d'Atamrum d'Andarig envers Zimri-Lim de Mari," 167–77) and from the region controlled by the Hittites (Gary Beckman, *Hittite Diplomatic Texts* [WAW

list of the gods of both states as well as personified elements of the natural world that were to serve as witnesses and guarantors of the treaty. If either party broke the treaty, the divine witnesses were to give their judgment against the guilty party. Given Yahweh's demand for sole allegiance, his treaty with Israel could hardly invoke other gods as witnesses and guarantors of this legal contract, but apparently the invocation of personified elements of the natural world such as heaven and earth, hills and mountains, did not create the same theological problems. Since these elements of nature had witnessed Israel's acceptance of the covenant, Yahweh could summon them, when Israel broke the covenant, to testify in his legal process against Israel. Nature was not only a witness to the covenant, however; it was also a guarantor. According to the prophets, human rebellion led to convulsions in nature—drought, famine, and plague (Jer 4:19-26; Hos 4:1-3; Amos 4:6-11), some of the curses for breach of covenant listed in Leviticus 26 and Deuteronomy 27–28.

The covenant lawsuit in Isa 1:2-20 has the following structure. It begins with the prophet's appeal to heaven and earth to hear God's complaint about his foolish children, which the prophet quotes (vv. 2-3). Then the prophet appeals directly to those children, berating

them and pointing out the consequences of their foolish behavior (vv. 4-9). The speaker in this whole section must be the prophet, since he identifies himself with his people in v. 9. In v. 10 the prophet again calls for the attention of the people, and especially of the leaders, since he is about to give another direct quotation from Yahweh. The import of Yahweh's word is to reject sacrificial ritual as an inappropriate response to Israel's sin; obedience is what is demanded (vv. 10-17). Yahweh's speech continues with an invitation to Israel to think over the divine terms; their response will determine whether they live or die. That is Yahweh's final word (vv. 18-20).

Isa 1:2-3

The reason for the appeal to heaven and earth is that, as already noted, heaven and earth were invoked as witnesses when God made his covenant with Israel (Deut 4:26; 30:19; 31:28; 32:1; Ps 50:4; cf. Mic 6:1-2).[11] Now they are invoked as witnesses to Israel's breach of that same covenant. The formula is part of the old traditional language inherited from the realm of international treaty making,[12] the political model early Israel adapted to express its relationship to Yahweh, but the theologically significant point is that Israel's behavior is sinful precisely

---

7; Atlanta: Scholars Press, 1996]). For a treatment of the these earlier known treaties, see Guy Kestemont, *Diplomatique et droit international en Asie occidentale: 1600–1200 av. J. C.* (Publications de l'Institut Orientaliste de Louvain 9; Louvain-la-Neuve: Université Catholique de Louvain, 1974). There are also numerous Assyrian treaties from the first millennium BCE (Simo Parpola and Kazuko Watanabe, *Neo-Assyrian Treaties and Loyalty Oaths* [SAA 2; Helsinki: Helsinki University Press, 1988]). Though there are parallels between the Israelite material and the Assyrian treaties, particularly with regard to the covenant curses, the closest parallels to the Israelite material are the earlier Hittite treaties, which contained not just curses but both a blessing if one kept the treaty and curses if one did not, and which rooted the vassal's obedience in his gratitude for the prior graciousness of the suzerain, not in the sheer terror that was the motivating factor in the Assyrian treaties. The Hittite treaties typically contain a historical narrative or prologue detailing the previous gracious actions of the suzerain to his vassal, and this element is conspicuously lacking in the preserved Assyrian treaties. In addition to the extant treaties, there are references

in extrabiblical texts to lawsuits decided by the gods due to the breach of treaty on the part of one of the parties to the treaty (see esp. Harvey, *Le plaidoyer prophétique*).

11 Despite claims to the contrary (Clements, 30), there is not the slightest evidence for the appeal to heaven and earth in ordinary legal practice at the village gates. One called human witnesses to testify to the truth or falsity of competing claims in ordinary village law. The appeal to the gods and deified elements of the universe comes from international law, where a dispute between two nations can be settled only by a decision of the gods who witnessed the prior agreement between the nations.

12 As an example of summoning the gods as witnesses to the breach of treaty, note the language of the treaty between Suppiluliuma of Hatti and Shattiwaza of Mittanni: "Whoever . . . alters this tablet, or sets it in a secret location—if he breaks it, if he changes the words of the text of the tablet—we have summoned the gods of secrets and the gods who are guarantors of the oath. They shall stand and listen and be witnesses" (Beckman, *Hittite Diplomatic Texts,* 42–44). There follows then a long list of gods, including

because it involves a breach of contract. It is not the behavior God could legitimately expect of his people.

This is elaborated in the following lines about the rebellious sons. The shift to familial imagery has suggested to some scholars that Isaiah's imagery is rooted in the language of family law (Deut 21:18-21), not covenantal law,[13] but the shift does not represent a real shift in thought. Familial imagery was widely used in covenant language. A great king was typically referred to as his subordinate's "father" (*CAD* A1, *abu* 2.b, 71) while his subordinate vassal was typically referred to as the great king's "son" (*CAD* M1, *māru* 3.a, 314). Moreover, the designation of Israel as Yahweh's "son" or "sons" in the earlier literature is closely tied in with the exodus and covenant that created the people Israel (Exod 4:22-23; Hos 1:10; 11:1-5; Deut 32:5-18). The parallels with the old poem in Deuteronomy 32 are particularly striking.[14] Both texts begin with an appeal to heaven and earth (Deut 32:1//Isa 1:2); both refer to Israel as God's rebellious and foolish children (Deut 32:5-6//Isa 1:2-6); both use birth or child-rearing imagery of God (Deut 32:18//Isa 1:2); both mention Sodom and Gomorrah (Deut 32:32// Isa 1:9); and both present a choice between life and death (Deut 32:39//Isa 1:18-20).

Just as children should obey their parents or vassals their overlord, so Israel should have obeyed Yahweh, but instead they rebelled against him. "Rebelled" is primarily a political term and shows again that the prophet is thinking in legal categories derived from international law.

The invidious comparison of Israel to dumb animals in v. 3 is intended to underscore how foolish the people's rebellion against God is. Even oxen and asses show more sense; they at least recognize their owner and the source of their food. A similar use of animal imagery involving the verb "to know" is found in Jer 8:7. Both texts underscore the biblical conception that righteousness and wisdom go together, that wickedness is folly. This is a favorite theme of the wisdom literature (Prov 1:20-33; 2:1-22), and Isaiah's almost proverbial reference to the ox and the ass may reflect the influence of that tradition on Isaiah.[15]

Isaiah, however, seems to be playing with different meanings of the verb "to know." The ambiguity in his use of the verb is underlined by the lack of an explicit object in v. 3b. What does Israel not know? What do the people not perceive? The LXX was bothered by the omission of the object and supplied the word "me." Israel did not "know" God. That would correspond to the ox "knowing" its owner, but it also comes close to the technical use of "to know" in treaty texts where the verb has the meaning "acknowledge" or "recognize someone as overlord or vassal," that is, to protect a vassal or obey an overlord.[16] Israel's problem was not religious ignorance in the sense that they failed to acknowledge God with the confession of their lips—they honored God with their lips

---

among the specifically named gods of Hatti, Mittanni, and the wider region, the deified mountains Nanni and Hazzi, the mountains, the rivers, the sea, the Euphrates, heaven and earth, the winds, and the clouds. The text then continues, "They shall stand and listen and be witnesses to these words of the treaty. If you, Prince Shattiwaza, and you Hurrians do not observe the words of the treaty, the gods, lords of the oath, shall destroy you [and] you Hurrians, together with your land, your wives, and your possessions. . . . If you, Prince Shattiwaza, and you Hurrians observe this treaty and oath, these gods shall protect you, Shattiwaza, together with your wife, [daughter of the King] of Hatti, her sons and grandsons, and you Hurrians. . . ."

13 Clements, 30; Jensen, 39; Hayes and Irvine, 71.

14 Paul Sanders notes the "remarkable correspondences" between Deuteronomy 32 and Isaiah 1:2-20, and comments that "if there is a direct relationship Deut. 32 would probably have the priority," though

Sanders thinks the relationship is indirect (*The Provenance of Deuteronomy 32* [OTS 37; Leiden: Brill, 1996] 355. He is arguing against H. Louis Ginsberg, who argued that Deuteronomy 32 was itself largely inspired by Isaiah (*The Israelian Heritage of Judaism* [Texts and Studies of the Jewish Theological Seminary of America 24; New York: Jewish Theological Seminary of America, 1982] 93). In contrast, I think the relationship between Deuteronomy 32 and Isaiah 1:2-20 is direct, and that Isaiah was influenced by the Deuteronomic text. See also L. G. Rignell, "Isaiah Chapter I: Some Exegetical Remarks with Special Reference to the Relationship between the Text and the Book of Deuteronomy," *ST* 11 (1957) 140–58.

15 The wisdom tradition delighted in speaking of the animal world in comparisons relevant for instructing humans in wise behavior (1 Kgs 5:13 [Eng. 4:33]; Prov 6:6; 7:22; 14:4; 15:16; 26:2-3; 30:25-28; Sir 33:25; cf. Wildberger, 1:14–15).

16 H. B. Huffmon, "The Treaty Background of Hebrew

(Isa 29:13)—their problem was the failure to acknowledge God by the obedience of their lives. The same point is expressed very well by Jesus in Luke 6:46: "Why do you call me, 'Lord, Lord,' and not do what I tell you?" This concept that knowing God involved obedient submission to the divine will was a major theme of Hosea's message as well (Hos 4:1-2).

One could also supply an object on the analogy of the ass knowing "its master's crib." The ass knows where it is fed, but Israel does not recognize the source of its blessings. Like the faithless wife in Hos 2:10, Israel does not know that it was Yahweh who gave it its grain, wine, oil, silver, and gold. Hosea and Isaiah both speak of the people perishing "for lack of knowledge" (Hos 4:6; Isa 5:13), but, although they deal with the same problem and Isaiah was probably influenced by Hosea,[17] the source of the problem is different in the two cases. Hosea's northern audience falsely attributed their blessings to the pagan deity Baal. Isaiah's southern audience, at least as envisioned by the final shape of this text, does not appear to have consisted of idolaters of quite the same sort. Their selfish indulgence in God's gifts had simply obscured their vision of the giver and his purpose for the gifts (Isa 5:12). A socially oppressive materialism rather than simple idolatry was the source of their willful ignorance (Isa 30:9-11).

Finally, one could supply an object for the verb "to know" in terms of the following context, particularly vv. 5-9. Israel does not perceive the predicament it is in. Like Ephraim in Hos 7:9, Israel has not recognized the precariousness of its position.[18] Israel is unwilling to face up to the unpleasant reality and persists in living in a fool's paradise (cf. Isa 9:9).

One need not decide among these candidates for the object of the verb. Isaiah's omission of the object with the resulting ambiguity is probably intentional; it invites the reader to reflect on each of these ways in which Israel has not understood and to ask the question whether we too may not be characterized by similar willful ignorance.

Isa 1:4-9

The vocative particle הוי (*hôy*) has its closest English correspondence in the colloquial interjection, "Hey!" It normally introduces a new oracle, except when it occurs in a series, but in Isa 1:4, as in 1:24, it simply calls attention, perhaps in a spoken context, to a logical shift in the larger composition. The oracle began with an address to heaven and earth as witnesses. Now the prophet turns and directly addresses God's people, the accused, as in the parallels Deut 32:6; Mic 6:3; Ps 50:7. Since v. 4 opens with a vocative particle and leads up to the second person address in v. 5, everything in between should be read as direct address, as the NEB and TEV have correctly seen.

The series of epithets that Isaiah hurls upon his audience underscores both the enormity and the ongoing character of their rebellion. Moreover, if Isaiah's horrible epithets for Israel underscore their alienation from God, the prophet's epithet for God, "the Holy One of Israel," expands that gulf while pointing to the relationship that should exist between God and his people. This epithet occurs twelve times in First Isaiah (1:4; 5:19, 24; 10:20; 12:6; 17:7; 29:19; 30:11-12, 15; 31:1; 37:23) and thirteen times in the later Isaianic tradition (41:14, 16, 20; 43:3, 14; 45:11; 47:4; 48:17; 49:7; 54:5; 55:5; 60:9, 14), but otherwise its occurrence is limited to one passage in Kings (2 Kgs 19:22), a couple of passages in Jeremiah (Jer 50:29; 51:5) and three times in the Psalms (Pss 71:22; 78:41; 89:19). It is one of Isaiah's favorite epithets for God, and if Isaiah did not coin the epithet, it nonetheless reflects the impression his inaugural vision of Yahweh's holiness (Isa 6:1-5) had on the prophet's understanding of God. For Isaiah, Yahweh alone was exalted, unapproachable in his majesty and sanctity; yet he had condescended to bring Israel into his awesome fellowship (cf. Exod 24:9-11) and had made his abode in Israel (Isa 12:6). How shocking, then, that Israel had deserted, despised, and turned its back on such a God.

Yādaʿ," *BASOR* 181 (1966) 31–37; S. B. Parker, "A Further Note on the Treaty Background of Hebrew *Yādaʿ*," *BASOR* 181 (1966) 36–38. Contrast Dennis J. McCarthy, *Old Testament Covenant: A Survey of Current Opinions* (Richmond: John Knox, 1972) 78.

17   There are several points of contact between the two books on the theme of knowledge in this section (see below), and one will find additional points of contact between Isa 1:21-26 and Hos 4:15-19 and 9:15.

18   Note that in both Hos 7:9 and Isa 1:7 the verb *ʾākal* ("devour") is used with the subject *zārîm* ("foreigners") to describe the destruction of God's people.

Such foolish behavior brings its appropriate punishment, and this provokes Isaiah's question why Israel persists in behavior that can only lead to more suffering. Verse 5, which finally introduces the main clause following the vocative epithets and relative clauses in v. 4, actually contains a double question, "Hey, sinful nation . . . , why should you be beaten anymore? Why do you continue to rebel?" The folly of continuing this behavior is spelled out by describing God's people under the metaphor of a body that is just covered with a mass of untreated wounds and bruises. Enough is enough. It is time Israel learned from their punishments.

In v. 7, the body metaphor is dropped for a realistic description of a land devastated by war. The description in its present form appears to reflect and show dependence on the common rhetoric of Neo-Assyrian royal inscriptions—*āla appul aqqur ina išati ašrup ākulšu*, "The city I devastated, destroyed, burned with fire, consumed it,"[19] but at the same time it probably reflects the actual desolation caused by Sennacherib's campaign against Hezekiah in 701 BCE, when Sennacherib took forty-six of Judah's walled cities, exiled 200,150 of its citizens, and shut Hezekiah up in Jerusalem "like a bird in a cage."[20] Sennacherib also took away part of Hezekiah's territory and imposed a heavy tribute. Zion, a poetic name for Jerusalem, was actually left standing as the only significant unconquered city in Judah.

Against this background of military defeat, Isaiah's designation of God in v. 9 as Yahweh of hosts sounds polemical. The original meaning of the epithet is still debated,[21] but "hosts" probably refers to Yahweh's heavenly army of royal attendants (1 Kgs 22:19),[22] and the epithet points to Yahweh's great imperial power. It was closely associated with the cherubim throne on the ark of the covenant at Shiloh (1 Sam 1:3, 11; 2 Sam 6:2). Later, when the ark was moved to Jerusalem, the epithet came to figure prominently in the imperial theology of Jerusalem (Pss 24:10; 46:8, 12; 48:9; 84:2, 4, 9, 13; 89:9). It is one of Isaiah's favorite designations for God, occurring some fifty-six times in Isaiah 1–39, but its occurrence here is hardly by chance. Judah's devastating defeat could have been seen as Yahweh's defeat at the hand of more powerful Assyrian gods, but Isaiah suggests instead that it was Yahweh's own might that was behind Judah's defeat.

---

19 Peter Machinist, "Assyria and Its Image in the First Isaiah," *JAOS* 103 (1983) 719–37, here 724–25.

20 *ANET*, 288; Daniel David Luckenbill, *The Annals of Sennacherib* (OIP 2; Chicago: University of Chicago Press, 1924) 32–34; A. Kirk Grayson and Jaime Novotny, *The Royal Inscriptions of Sennacherib, King of Assyria (704–681 BC)*, Part 1 (RINAP 3/1; Winona Lake, IN: Eisenbrauns, 2012).

21 The most promising suggestion is that of Frank Moore Cross, who argued that *yahweh ṣĕbāʾôt* originated as a verbal epithet for the god El, *ʾēl dū yahwī ṣĕbāʾôt*, "El who creates the heavenly armies" (*Canaanite Myth and Hebrew Epic: Essays in the History of the Religion of Israel* [Cambridge, MA: Harvard University Press, 1973] 68–72). For other views, see Wildberger, 1:28–29. Once the epithet had become an independent divine name for the deity, and *yahweh*, without the following expression, had become the most common name for Israel's deity, the meaning of the original verbal expression, especially as late as the late eighth century, was probably forgotten, and *yahweh ṣĕbāʾôt* was probably understood, however anomalously from the standpoint of ordinary Hebrew grammar, simply as a proper name in construct with the following noun, "Yahweh of hosts." One might compare the similarly anomalous, but inscriptionally attested construct chains, "Yahweh of Samaria" and "Yahweh of Teman," or more directly, *ršp ṣbi*, "Resheph of the Host" (F. W. Dobbs-Allsopp, J. J. M. Roberts, C. L. Seow, and R. E. Whitaker, *Hebrew Inscriptions: Texts from the Biblical Period of the Monarchy with Concordance* [New Haven: Yale University Press, 2005] 285, 290–92).

22 It is true that 1 Kgs 22:19 uses the singular *ṣĕbāʾ*, "host," not the plural *ṣĕbāʾôt*, "hosts," and that only the singular is attested in the twenty-two or so references to the "host of heaven," but I doubt that much significance should be attached to that observation. Apart from the divine epithet, the singular form is far more common in general, but where variation between the singular and plural is attested, it does not appear to alter the meaning. Note the variation in reference to Abner and Amasa, the commanders of the hosts (*śārê ṣibʾôt*) of Israel (1 Kgs 2:5), versus Abner, the commander of the host (*śar-ṣĕbāʾ*) of Israel, and Amasa, the commander of the host (*śar-ṣĕbāʾ*) of Judah (1 Kgs 2:34). One should also note the variation between the singular and the plural when referring to the host or hosts of the tribes of Israel (Num 1:45, 52; 2:3-4; et passim). See also Cross, *Canaanite Myth*, 70–71; and Wildberger, 1:28–29.

Had it not been for the grace of the divine ruler of the heavenly hosts, the destruction of Jerusalem would have been as complete as the proverbial destruction of Sodom and Gomorrah.

Isa 1:10-17

In v. 10 the prophet again calls for attention before quoting Yahweh's words in vv. 11-20. This time, however, he narrows in on the leaders as well as the people of Judah. He calls them "rulers of Sodom" and "people of Gomorrah," thus creating a link with v. 9; but in doing so the prophet picks up another undertone in this ancient parallel to the Jerusalem of his day. The rulers and people were citizens of a devastated state, but that state had been destroyed because of its wickedness, a wickedness that, like its desolation, rivaled that of Sodom and Gomorrah.

The ritual activity described in vv. 11-15 is probably to be seen as Judah's reaction to the disaster. Such disasters normally led to public fasts and additional sacrifices, as well as more punctilious observance of the regular rituals in an attempt to placate the anger of God and so prevent further losses (Hos 5:6; 5:15—6:3; Jer 14:1-12). In the context of such public assemblies, prophets would arise to give Yahweh's response (Jer 14:10-12; 15:1-4; Hos 6:4-6), and Isaiah's words are best understood as such a response. In God's lawsuit against Israel, he not only points up Israel's rebellion as the cause of its troubles; he also rejects the sacrificial ritual as an adequate remedy for the situation. Yahweh, who ordained the cult, is tired of church services. Sacrifices, regular festivals like sabbaths and new moons, special assemblies for fasting and public lamentation, and even the great yearly festivals had become a burden to God.

The purpose of the sacrificial ritual was to maintain the relationship with the deity, and that involved, among other things, seeking forgiveness for any sins that might rupture the relationship. As long as the relationship was maintained, one could hope and expect that the deity would respond to the people's needs and desires. But God threatens to refuse to look when the Israelites spread out their hands in prayer and to refuse to listen even if they persist in their supplications. God's refusal to hear prayer underscores, as nothing else would, the failure of the cult, but it also shows that Isaiah's criticism was not a rejection of the sacrificial cult per se; he was hardly against prayer. Why had the cult and prayer failed? The answer is graphically given in v. 15. The hands stretched forth in prayer were full of דָּמִים (dāmîm), "blood." This is not the דָּם (dām), "blood," of the sacrificial animals mentioned in v. 11, since the plural דָּמִים has a more precise meaning. It refers primarily to human blood shed by violence, particularly unjustified violence, and the blood guilt that splatters on the one guilty of such bloodshed. Thus, if one kills a burglar in the act of breaking in, presumably at night, there is no דָּמִים, but if one kills the thief the next day, presumably after the thief has left one's home and is therefore no longer a threat to one's person, there is דָּמִים (Exod 22:1-2).[23] As the following verses show, Isaiah was thinking primarily of acts of violence perpetrated against the weakest members of Israelite society.

The relationship with God sustained by the cult had been shattered by the people's mistreatment of the powerless. Ritual was meaningless until that relationship was restored by a dramatic change in the people's behavior. Ritualistic language is used in v. 16, "wash, cleanse yourself," but the following imperatives show that this language is metaphorical. They are to cleanse themselves not by ritual ablutions and bloody sacrifices but by turning away from their evil deeds and learning to do good, by saving the oppressed and seeing justice done for the powerless. The call for repentance here is a call to reverse the pattern of rebellious behavior attacked in vv. 2-4.

The formulations in v. 17 are very terse and require some comment. There is considerable uncertainty about the correct translation of אַשְּׁרוּ חָמוֹץ (ʾaššěrû ḥāmôṣ), "right the wronged." In addition to the problem discussed in the textual notes whether to take חמוץ as the action, the agent, or the passive recipient of the action, there is debate about the meaning of the verb אשר. G. R.

---

23   Or, perhaps, if the incident happened at night, the thief may be killed, because the owner could not be sure whether it was a thief or a potential murderer, whereas in the daylight it should have been clear that it was merely a thief, and thus not deserving of death. For a discussion of the passage and the sources, see Samuel Greengus, *Laws in the Bible and in Early Rabbinic Collections: The Legal Legacy of the Ancient Near East* (Eugene, OR: Cascade, 2011) 215–18.

Driver, on the basis of the Aramaic root, renders it as "strengthen,"[24] though looking to the Aramaic or the Syriac root, as Rignell's "be good to the oppressed" does, is rightly criticized by Wildberger.[25] The versions give widely varying translations. The LXX translates the term with ῥύσασθε, "deliver, save, rescue"; Vg. has *subvenite*, "come to the assistence of"; Syr. ʾṭ*bw*, "treat well"; and the Tg. זכ, "acquit." The Hebrew verb sometimes has the meaning "proceed, go on, advance" (Prov 4:14), and it sometimes means "to lead on" (Prov 23:19; Isa 3:12; 9:15). The last meaning has overtones of leading in the right direction, as is clear from its ironic juxtaposition with its opposite in the two Isaiah passages, that is, Israel's leaders (מְאַשְּׁרִים, *mĕʾaššĕrîm*) are misleaders (מתעים, *matʿîm*) who lead Israel astray from the right path (Isa 3:12; 9:15). Since injustice is often portrayed as turning someone aside (*hiphil* of נטה, *nāṭâ*) from justice, the way, or into ruin (Isa 10:2; 29:21; Amos 5:12; Mal 3:5; Job 24:4; Prov 18:5), one should probably understand the verb אשר in Isa 1:17 as the corrective to such action, that is, "to set the mistreated back on the road to justice."

A similar background lies behind the usage of the following two verbs. While the verb שפט (*šāpaṭ*) can mean simply "to render judgment," and ריב (*rîb*), "to plead or conduct a legal case," it is clear from the context that this action is for the benefit of the widow and the orphan (cf. Ps 82:2-3). Part of the reason for this usage is that the major obstacle in the way of the widow or the orphan getting justice was the difficulty of ever getting one's case heard in court. Even today, the wealthy and powerful can delay cases brought against them by the poor until most give up in despair, and in ancient Israel the situation was even worse. Unless the widow or orphan had an influential advocate, they had little hope of even having their case heard, much less decided in their favor.

Isa 1:18-20

Verse 18 continues the preceding sequence of imperatives, but there is a slight transition, as Yahweh now invites Israel to consider the alternatives. The word וְנִוָּכְחָה (*wĕniwwākĕḥâ*), translated "(and) let us reach an agreement," has a legal background and refers to the arbitration of legal disputes (Job 23:7). Yahweh offers to resolve his dispute with Israel on the basis of the change of behavior demanded above. No matter how red their sins—an allusion to the blood-stained hands of v. 15—they can become clean, if the people will respond in obedience. If they obey, God will hear their prayers and cure their distress. They, rather than the foreign oppressor (1:7), will eat the good of the land. If they refuse, however, the present distress will reach its climax, and they themselves will be eaten—by the sword. This is a clear, powerful metaphor, and there is no justification for correcting the text.

The choice is clear: life or death, the blessing or the curse. It is the choice of living in covenant with Yahweh or rejecting that fellowship (Deut 30:15-20). With this offer, the covenant lawsuit concludes almost as it began (1:2), "for the mouth of Yahweh has spoken."

This passage has been characterized as a summary of Isaiah's message used to introduce the whole following collection of his oracles, and, correctly understood, this characterization is appropriate.[26] It invites God's people today to reflect on their own relationship to the deity. In light of God's prior graciousness and acceptance of us, he could legitimately expect the grateful response of obedient lives. When we fail to acknowledge God in this way, we are choosing the foolish way of the man who built his house upon the sand (Matt 7:24-27). Not every sorrow that afflicts us can be attributed to our rebellion, and Isaiah's condemnation of Israel should not be twisted in this

24 G. R. Driver, "Linguistic and Textual Problems: Isaiah I–XXXIX," *JTS* 38 (1937) 37.

25 Rignell, "Isaiah Chapter I," 151; Wildberger, 1:34.

26 This characterization has become a scholarly commonplace for Isa 1:2-31 since G. Fohrer's "Jesaja 1 als Zusammenfassung der Verkündigung Jesaja," *ZAW* 74 (1962) 251–68, though John Willis ("First Pericope," 77) has made some necessary corrections to the way this view is often understood. Willis restricts the passage to vv. 2-20, rejects the notion

that this is the summarizing rearrangement of a later redactor, and notes, "[I]t may be that vv. 2-20 appear to be a summary of the prophet's message because he delivered this oracle near the end of his long career, when the various major emphases of his earlier oracles were paramount in his mind and seemed to be appropriate to the new situation with which the people were faced, a situation strikingly similar to several former ones experienced during his lifetime."

false and harmful way; but often we do destroy our own lives, our churches, and even our nation by our refusal to give up sinful, self-destructive behavior. Nor does church and religious activity provide an easy fix. Ritual is not a substitute for ethical and moral transformation but, properly understood, an enabler of such change. God calls us to a hard choice. We may choose life by paradoxically surrendering our autonomy in obedience to God as suzerain, or choose death by refusing to give up the foolish illusion that we are masters of our own lives (Matt 10:39; Gal 2:20). These are the narrow and broad ways of which Jesus also spoke (Matt 7:13-14).

Bibliography

Barbiero, G., "'Venite discutiamo!' Lettrua militaria di Is 1,2-20," *Salesianum* 51 (1989) 11–21, 89–100.

Begrich, Joachim, "Der Satzstil in Fünfer," *Zeitschrift für Semitistik* 9 (1933–34) 204–9. Reprinted in Begrich, *Gesammelte Studien zum Alten Testament* (ed. Walther Zimmerli; TB 21; Munich: Kaiser, 1964) 1:162–67.

Ben Zvi, Ehud, "Isaiah 1:4-9: Isaiah and the Events of 701 B.C.E. in Judah. A Question of Premise and Evidence," *JSOT* 9 (1991) 95–111.

Björndalen, Anders Jørgen, *Untersuchungen zur allegorischen Rede der Propheten Amos und Jesaja* (BZAW 165; Berlin: de Gruyter, 1986) 177–85.

——, "Zur Frage der Echtheit von Jesaja 1,2-3; 1,4-7," *NTT* 83 (1982) 89–100.

Condamin, A., "Les Chapitres I et II du Livre d'Isaïe," *RB* 13 (1904) 7–26.

Culver, R. D., "Is 1:18: Declaration Exclamation or Interrogation?" *JETS* 12 (1969) 133–41.

Dahood, Mitchell, "Hebrew-Ugaritic Lexicography X," *Bib* 53 (1972) 386–403 [אבוס, 386].

——, "Hebrew-Ugaritic Lexicography XI," *Bib* 54 (1973) 351–66 [שני, 362].

Darr, Katheryn Pfisterer, "Child Imagery and the Rhetoric of Rebellion." In Darr, *Isaiah's Vision and the Family of God* (Louisville: Westminster John Knox, 1994) 46–84.

Davies, Eryl W., *Prophecy and Ethics: Isaiah and the Ethical Traditions of Israel* (JSOTSup 16; Sheffield: JSOT Press, 1981).

Delcor, M., "Les attaches littéraires, l'origine et la signification de l'expression biblique 'Prendre à témoin le ciel et la terre,'" *VT* 16 (1966) 8–25.

Dobbie, R., "Sacrifice and Morality in the Old Testament," *ExpTim* 70 (1958) 297–300.

Driver, G. R., "Linguistic and Textual Problems: Isaiah I–XXXIX," *JTS* 38 (1937) 37.

Fensham, F. C., "Widow, Orphan, and the Poor in Ancient Near Eastern Legal and Wisdom Literature," *JNES* 21 (1962) 129–39.

Fohrer, G., "Jesaja 1 als Zusammenfassung der Verkündigung Jesajas," *ZAW* 74 (1962) 251–68.

Fuhs, Hans F., "Der Reichtum der Armen: Eine Betrachtung im Anschluss an Jes 1,10-17." *TGl* (1987) 218–24.

Fullerton, K., "The Rhythmical Analysis of Is 1,10-20," *JBL* 38 (1919) 53–63.

Gates, O. H., "Notes on Isaiah 1,18b and 7,14b-16," *AJSL* 17 (1900) 16–21.

Gitay, Yehoshua, "The Effectiveness of Isaiah's Speech," *JQR* 75 (1984) 162–72.

——, "Reflections on the Study of the Prophetic Discourse: The Question of Isaiah I 2-20," *VT* 33 (1983) 207–21.

Goldingay, John, "If Your Sins Are Like Scarlet . . . (Isaiah 1:18)," *ST* 35 (1981) 137–44.

Haag, Ernst, "Sündenvergebung und neuer Anfang: Zur Übersetzung und Auslegung von Jes 1,18," in Johannes Joachim Degenhardt, ed., *Die Freude an Gott, unsere Kraft: Festschrift für Otto Bernhard Knoch zum 65. Geburtstag* (Stuttgart: Katholisches Bibelwerk, 1991) 68–80.

Hammershaimb, E., "On the Ethics of the Old Testament Prophets," in *Congress Volume: Oxford 1959* (VTSup 7; Leiden: Brill, 1960) 75–101.

——. *Some Aspects of Old Testament Prophecy from Isaiah to Malachi* (Det Laerde Selskab Skrifter, Teologiske Skrifter 4; Copenhagen: Rosenkilde & Bagger, 1966).

Harvey, Julien, *Le plaidoyer prophétique contre Israël après la rupture de l'alliance*. Bruges: Desclée de Brouwer, 1967.

——. "Le 'Rib-Pattern': Réquisitoire prophétique sur la rupture de l'alliance," *Bib* 43 (1962) 172–96.

Hasel, Gerhard F., "New Moon and Sabbath in Eighth Century Israelite Prophetic Writings (Isa 1,13; Hos 2,13; Amos 8,5)," in Matthias Augustin and Klaus-Dietrich Schunck, eds., *Wünschet Jerusalem Frieden: Collected Communications to the XIIth Congress of the International Organization for the Study of the Old Testament, Jerusalem 1986* (BEATAJ 13; Frankfurt am Main: P. Lang, 1988) 37–64.

Hentschke, Richard, *Die Stellung der vorexilischen Schriftpropheten zum Kultus* (BZAW 75; Berlin: A. Töpelmann, 1957).

Hertzberg, H. W., "Die Nachgeschichte alttestamentlicher Texte innerhalb des Alten Testaments." In *Werden und Wesen des Alten Testaments: Vorträge gehalten auf der Internationalen Tagung Alttestamentlicher Forscher zu Göttingen vom 4.–10. September 1935* (BZAW 66; Berlin: A. Töpelmann, 1936) 110–21.

———, "Die prophetische Kritik am Kultus," *TLZ* 75 (1950) 219–26.

Hoffman, Hans Werner, *Die Intention der Verkündigung Jesajas* (BZAW 136; Berlin: de Gruyter, 1974).

Holladay, William L., "A New Suggestion for the Crux in Isaiah 1:4b," *VT* 33 (1983) 235–37.

Huffmon, H. B., "The Covenant Lawsuit in the Prophets," *JBL* 78 (1959) 285–95.

Jeffrey, David L., "How to Read the Hebrew Prophets," in Vincent L. Tollers and John Maier, eds., *Mappings of the Biblical Terrain: The Bible as Text* (Bucknell Review 33.2; Lewisburg, PA: Bucknell University Press, 1990) 282–98.

Jensen, Joseph, *The Use of Tôrâ by Isaiah: His Debate with the Wisdom Tradition* (CBQMS 3; Washington, DC: Catholic Biblical Association of America, 1973).

Jones, Douglas R., "Exposition of Isaiah 1,10-17," *SJT* 18 (1965) 457–71.

———, "Exposition of Isaiah 1, Verses 18-20," *SJT* 19 (1966) 319–27.

———, "Exposition of Isaiah Chapter One, Verses One to Nine," *SJT* 17 (1964) 463–77.

Koch, K., "Damnation and Salvation: Prophetic Metahistory and the Rise of Eschatology in the Book of Isaiah," *ExAu* 6 (1990) 5–13.

Lattey, C., "The Prophets and Sacrifice, a Study in Biblical Relativity," *JTS* 42 (1941) 155–65.

Lescow, Th., "Die dreistufige Tora: Beobachtungen zu einer Form," *ZAW* 82 (1970) 362–79.

Ley, J., "Metrische Analyse von Jesaja Kp. 1," *ZAW* 22 (1902) 229–37.

Loewenclau, I. von, "Zur Auslegung von Jesaja 1,2-3," *EvT* 26 (1966) 294–308.

Löhr, Max, *Das Räucheropfer im Alten Testament: Eine archäologische Untersuchung* (Schriften der königsberger gelehrten Gesellschaft, Geisteswissenschaftliche Klasse 4.4; Halle: Max Niemeyer, 1927).

Loretz, Oswald, "Die Twrh-Stellen in Jes 1," *UF* 8 (1976) 450–51.

Losoncy, Thomas A., "Will in St Anselm: An Examination of His Biblical and Augustinian Origins," in Raymonde Foreville, ed., *Les mutations socio-culturelles au tournant des XIe–XIIe siècles: Études anselmiennes (IVe session). Abbaye Notre-Dame du Bec, Le Bec-Helloin, 11–16 juillet 1982* (Spicilegium Beccense 2; Paris: Editions du Centre national de la recherche scientifique, 1984) 701–10.

Luc, A., "Isaiah I as Structural Introduction," *ZAW* 101 (1989) 115.

Mattioli, A., "Due schemi letterari negli oracoli d'interoduzione al libro di Isaia," *RivB* 14 (1966) 345–64.

Mayer Modena, Maria L., "'Ayl, El- 'L'animale e l'albero forte': Un'antica isoglossa Mediterranea," *Acme* 27 (1974) 99–301.

Melugin, Roy F., "Figurative Speech and the Reading of Isaiah 1 as Scripture," in Roy F. Melugin and Marvin A. Sweeney, eds., *New Visions of Isaiah* (JSOTSup 214; Sheffield: Sheffield Academic Press, 1996) 282–305.

Mendenhall, George E., "Ancient Oriental and Biblical Law," *BA* 17 (1954) 26–46.

———, "Covenant Forms in Israelite Tradition," *BA* 17 (1954) 50–76.

Milgrom, Jacob, "Concerning Jeremiah's Repudiation of Sacrifice," *ZAW* 89 (1977) 273–75.

———, "Did Isaiah Prophesy during the Reign of Uzziah?" *VT* 14 (1964) 164–82.

Niditch, Susan, "The Composition of Isaiah 1," *Bib* 61 (1980) 509–29.

Nielsen, E., "Ass and Ox in the Old Testament," in *Studia orientalia Ioanni Pedersen dicata* (Hauniae: E. Munksgaard, 1953) 263–74.

North, C. R., "Sacrifice in the Old Testament," *ExpTim* 47 (1935) 250–54.

Padilla, C. René, "The Fruit of Justice Will Be Peace," *Transformation* 2 (1985) 2–4.

Porteous, N. W., "Prophet and Priest in Israel," *ExpTim* 62 (1950) 4–9.

Rendtorff, Rolf, "Priesterliche Kulttheologie und prophetische Kultpolemik," *TLZ* 81 (1956) 339–42.

Reventlow, H. Graf, "Prophetenamt und Mittleramt," *ZTK* 58 (1961) 269–84.

Rignell, L. G., "Isaiah Chapter I: Some Exegetical Remarks with Special Reference to the Relationship between the Text and the Book of Deuteronomy," *ST* 11 (1957) 140–58.

Roberts, J. J. M., "Form, Syntax and Redaction in Isaiah 1:2-20," *PSB* 3 (1982) 293–306.

Robertson, E., "Isaiah Chapter 1," *ZAW* 52 (1934) 231–36.

Rowley, H. H., "The Prophets and Sacrifice," *ExpTim* 58 (1946) 305–7.

———, *Worship in Ancient Israel: Its Form and Meaning* (Edward Cadbury Lectures 1965; Philadelphia: Fortress Press, 1967).

Ruffenach, F., "Malitia et remissio peccati (Is 1:1-20)," *VD* 7 (1927) 145–49, 165–68.

Schoneveld, Jacobus, "Jesaia 1:18-20," *VT* 13 (1963) 342–44.

Seitz, Christopher, "'The Divine Council': Temporal Transition and New Prophecy in the Book of Isaiah," *JBL* 109 (1990) 229–47.

Snaith, N. H., "The Prophets and Sacrifice and Salvation," *ExpTim* 58 (1946) 152–53.

Speier, S., "Zu drei Jesajastellen (1,7; 5,24; 10,7)," *TZ* 21 (1965) 310–13.

Stachowiak, L., "Grzech Naradu Wybranego I Mozliowasc Rutunku wedlug Iz 1:2-17," *RocTK* 24,1 (1977) 5–19.

Steinberg, Theodore L., "Isaiah the Poet," in Vincent L. Tollers and John Maier, eds., *Mappings of the Biblical Terrain: The Bible as Text* (Bucknell Review 33.2; Lewisburg, PA: Bucknell University Press, 1990) 299–310.

Surburg, Raymond F., "Justification as a Doctrine of the Old Testament: A Comparative Study in Confessional and Biblical Theology," *CTQ* 46 (1982) 129–46.

Sweeney, Marvin A., *Isaiah 1–4 and the Post-Exilic Understanding of the Isaianic Tradition* (BZAW 171; Berlin: de Gruyter, 1988) 101–31.

Tucker, Gene M., "Sin and 'Judgment' in the Prophets," in Henry R. C. Sun et al., eds., *Problems in Biblical Theology: Essays in Honor of Rolf Knierim* (Grand Rapids: Eerdmans, 1997) 373–88.

Uchelen, N. A. van, "Isaiah I 9: Text and Context," in Bertil Albrektson, ed., *Remembering All the Way: A Collection of Old Testament Studies* (OTS 21; Leiden: Brill, 1981) 154–63.

Volz, P., "Die radikale Ablehnung der Kultreligion durch die alttestamentlichen Propheten," *ZST* 14 (1937) 63–86.

Vriezen, Th. C., *An Outline of Old Testament Theology* (Newton, MA: C. T. Branford, 1961).

Watts, J. Wash, A *Survey of Syntax in the Hebrew Old Testament* (Grand Rapids: Eerdmans, 1964).

Welch, Adam C., *Prophet and Priest in Old Israel* (New York: Macmillan, 1953).

Werner, Wolfgang, *Eschatologische Texte in Jesaja 1–39: Messias, Heiliger Rest, Volker* (2nd ed.; FB 46; Würzburg: Echter, 1986) 118–33.

——, "Israel in der Entscheidung: Überlegungen zur Datierung und zur theologischen Aussage von Jes 1:4-9," in Rudolf Kilian, Klemens Funk, and Peter Fassl, eds., *Eschatologie: Bibeltheologische und philosophische Studien zum Verhältnis von Erlösungswelt und Wirklichkeitsbewältigung. Festschrift Engelbert Neuhäusler zur Emeritierung gewidmet von Kollegen, Freunden und Schülern* (St. Ottilien: Eos, 1981) 59–72.

Westermann, Claus, "The Role of the Lament in the Theology of the Old Testament," *Int* 28 (1974) 20–38.

Williamson, H. G. M., "Isaiah 1.11 and the Septuagint of Isaiah," in A. Graeme Auld, ed., *Understanding Poets and Prophets: Essays in Honour of George Wishart Anderson* (JSOTSup 152; Sheffield: JSOT Press, 1993) 401–12.

Willis, John T., "The First Pericope in the Book of Isaiah," *VT* 34 (1984) 63–77.

——, "An Important Passage for Determining the Historical Setting of a Prophetic Oracle—Isaiah 1.7-8," *ST* 39 (1985) 151–69.

Wright, G. Ernest, "The Lawsuit of God: A Form Critical Study of Deuteronomy 32," in Bernhard W. Anderson and Walter Harrelson, eds., *Israel's Prophetic Heritage: Essays in Honor of James Muilenburg* (New York: Harper, 1962) 26–67.

Würthwein, Ernst, "Kultpolemik oder Kultbescheid?" in Ernst Würthwein and Otto Kaiser, eds., *Tradition und Situation: Studien zur alttestamentlichen Prophetie. Artur Weiser zum 70. Geburtstag am 18. 11. 1963 dargebracht von Kollegen, Freunden und Schülern* (Göttingen: Vandenhoeck & Ruprecht, 1963) 115–31.

Zawiszewski, E., "Synowie Niewzieẙchzni (Iz 1,1-20)," *Studia Warminskie* 12 (1975) 419–21.

Ziegler, J., "Ochs und Esel an der Krippe: Biblisch-patristische Erwägungen zu Is 1,3 und Hab 3,2 LXX," *MTZ* 3 (1952) 385–402.

Zorell, F., "Is C. 1," *VD* 6 (1926) 65–70.

1

21/ How she has become a whore!
   The faithful city,[a]
   That was full of justice,
   Where righteousness dwelled—
   But now murderers!
22/ Your silver has become dross,
   Your beer[b] is diluted[c] with water.
23/ Your royal officials are rebels
   And companions of thieves;
   Everyone loves a bribe
   And runs after gifts.
   They do not render judgment for the orphan,
   And the widow's lawsuit never reaches them.
24/ Therefore says the Lord, Yahweh of Hosts,
   the Mighty Bull of Israel:[d]
   "Hey! I will console myself against my foes,
   I will avenge myself on my enemies!
25/ I will turn my hand against you,
   And smelt your dross like a furnace,[e]
   And remove all your slag.
26/ I will restore your judges as at the first,
   And your counselors as in the beginning.
   After that you will be called
   The city of righteousness, faithful city."
27/ Zion will be redeemed by justice,
   And those in her who repent[f] by righteousness;
28/ But rebels and sinners will be shattered[g] together,
   and those who forsake Yahweh will perish.

Textual Notes

a   The Hebrew noun *qiryâ* and the participle modifying it *neˀĕmānâ*, "the faithful city," lack the article, but the absence of the article is common in Hebrew poetry. It is clear that the text is referring to the particular city Jerusalem; the LXX even adds Σιων, "Zion," to identify explicitly the city in question as Jerusalem. Thus, a translation with the indefinite article such as "a faithful city" can hardly be correct.

b   LXX (οἱ κάπηλοί σου) and Syr. (ḥnwyyky) appear to take MT's סָבְאֵךְ (sobˀēk) not as a suffixed word for a drink but as a suffixed word for the dispensers of the drink, "your tavern keepers." The Syriac has no word for the drink, "Your tavern keepers mix (drinks) with water." The LXX has τὸν οἶνον for the drink, "Your tavern keepers mix the wine with water." Hebrew סֹבֶא (sōbeˀ), however, clearly means the drink, not its dispensers, though there is debate whether it designates a kind of beer or a kind of wine. The JPS and the NRSV translations follow the LXX and the Vg. in rendering the word as "wine." The Akkadian cognates, however, suggest a beer, perhaps even a distinctive kind of beer sold in taverns. See Akk. *sību, sābu* (beer); *bīt sībi* (house of beer, tavern); *sābu, sābītu* (innkeeper, beer merchant); *sabû* (to draw beer) (*CAD* S, 5), to brew beer (*AHw*, 1000a). The word *sību* is probably to be identified with the *ši-kar si-bi-ˀi* beer served in a tavern, and this "tavern beer" must have had a distinctive flavor; compare modern draught

beer (M. Stol, "Beer in Neo-Babylonian Times," in Lucio Milano, ed., *Drinking in Ancient Societies: History and Culture of Drinks in the Ancient Near East. Papers of a Symposium Held in Rome, May 17–19, 1990* [HANE/S 6; Padua: Sargon, 1994] 164–65). Regardless of whether there is any linguistic connection, one should note that in Jerome's day there was a beer drunk in Illyria with a very similar name, *sabaium* (Hieronymus *Comm. Isa.* 7.19.10, lines 48–51; see also Ammianus Marcellinus 26.8.2).

c   The form מָהוּל (māhûl) is the *qal* passive participle from a very rare verb meaning "to dilute." It may be a biform of the verb מול (mûl), "to circumcise," with the semantic development "to cut something with water," hence "to dilute." See the discussion in H. G. M. Williamson, *A Critical and Exegetical Commentary on Isaiah 1–27* (3 vols.; ICC 23; London: T&T Clark, 2006–) 1:121, 138.

d   The LXX mistakenly construes the following הוֹי (hôy) as addressing the preceding אֲבִיר יִשְׂרָאֵל (ˀābîr yiśrāˀēl) and translates, οὐαὶ οἱ ἰσχύοντες Ισραηλ, "Ah, O strong ones of Israel," apparently misreading the expression אֲבִיר יִשְׂרָאֵל as a plural form אבירי ישראל (ˀābîrê yiśrāˀēl) and taking it as a designation for God's enemies. In fact, it is an epithet for God. Normally the divine epithet is אֲבִיר יַעֲקֹב (ˀābîr yaˁqōb, Gen 49:24; Isa 49:26; 60:16; Ps 132:2, 5); this is the only occurrence of אֲבִיר יִשְׂרָאֵל. The epithet אֲבִיר underscores God's strength, but it appears to do that by comparing God to a mighty bull. The words אַבִּיר (ʾabbîr) and אָבִיר (ʾābîr) appear to be artificially distinguished by the later scribes to avoid this animal imagery for God, since, in contrast to אָבִיר, used only as an epithet of God, אַבִּיר is often used of powerful bulls (Isa 10:13; 34:7; Pss 22:13; 50:13; 68:31; 78:25) and sometimes of stallions (Judg 5:22; Jer 8:16; 47:3; 50:11).

e   Reading כְּכוּר (kĕkûr), "like a furnace," in place of MT's כַּבֹּר (kabbōr), "like the lye." Another possibility is בְּכוּר (bĕkûr), "in a furnace;" a reading that occurs in Isa 48:10, where the later writer is apparently developing the thought he found in Isa 1:25. The versions all appear to have MT's reading, though apart from the Tg., which renders "with lye," they tend to take בֹּר (bōr) as the word meaning "purity" and translate the expression as "unto purity." While lye or potash was used for washing hands (Job 9:30), there is a serious question whether it was ever used in the ancient smelting process and, if it was, how important an element it was in the process. L. Köhler ("Miszellen: Alttestamentliche Wortforschung. *Sîg, sîgîm* = Bleiglätte," TZ 3 [1947] 232–33) argues that it was used as a flux in removing lead oxide from silver in the smelting process. Robert J. Forbes does not mention lye or potash, but he does refer to the role of bone ash in separating silver from lead. The crude lead produced by primitive smelting was put in a crucible or furnace dressed or lined with bone ash and melted; then a blast of air was introduced to oxidize the lead and other metal impurities. The porous bone ash resists corrosion by the oxides of the baser metals formed during this process of cupellation and absorbs these oxides, "and a cake of silver . . . remains behind in the furnace" (*Studies in Ancient Technology VIII* [Leiden: Brill, 1964] 238).

f   For MT's וְשָׁבֶיהָ (wĕšābêhā), "and her (people) who repent," LXX has ἡ αἰχμαλωσία αὐτῆς, "her captivity," which presupposes שִׁבְיָה (šibyāh), and Syr. appears to follow LXX in this reading. This would appear to imply an exilic date, and one could arrive at the same conclusion were one to take the MT to refer to a physical return to Jerusalem, "and her returnees." As Wildberger (1:56) has keenly observed, however, since v. 27 stands in negative parallel to v. 28, the interpretation "those in her who repent" is required as a contrast to the פֹּשְׁעִים וְחַטָּאִים (pōšĕʿîm wĕḥaṭṭāʾîm), "rebels and sinners" of v. 28.

g   The construct noun וְשֶׁבֶר (wĕšeber) at the beginning of v. 28, in a construction without any verb (lit., "and the shattering of rebels and sinners together"), is jarring, and most critics, following the translations of the versions, emend the noun to a passive verbal form.

Commentary

A new unit begins in v. 21. It opens with a lament over the terrible change in character that has turned Jerusalem into a city of sin. The nature of her sin is spelled out, and then, in vv. 24-28, Yahweh declares how he will correct the situation and restore Jerusalem to her original sanctity. Though these verses make up a separate prophetic composition, their placement in the present context is appropriate. It was suggested by the image of the desolate Zion in 1:8 and the comparison to Sodom and Gomorrah in vv. 9-10. Moreover, the references to orphans and widows in v. 23 provides a nice catchword reference back to v. 17. The end of the oracle is more difficult to determine. Some scholars regard vv. 27-28 as a later expansion (see further below).[1] There may also be some connection between this oracle, with or without vv. 27-28, and the famous passage in 2:2-5; Isa 1:29-31 is clearly a later intrusion, awkwardly connected to 1:28 by the common theme of the total destruction of the wicked. These issues will be discussed separately, under units 1:29-31 and 2:1-5.

The background to 1:21-28 is to be sought in the Zion Tradition's (see introduction) glorification of Jerusalem as the city of God. As the place where God dwelled, it was a place of righteousness and security, a place where evildoers were not tolerated (Pss 101:8; 132:13-18; Isa 33:14-16). What the tradition claimed for Jerusalem, however, Isaiah laments as no longer true. The faithful city of tradition had become a whore. Here Isaiah, like his contemporary Hosea, uses sexual imagery to characterize the city's fall, but his use of that imagery does not imply that the sins of Zion were the same as those Hosea attacked in the north or that Isaiah was necessarily dependent on Hosea for this imagery.[2] The specific accusations leveled in the following verses are concerned with social

---

1   Wildberger is among those who see these verses as a later expansion, and though he argues that the language could be Isaianic, he says, "But it is improbable that Isaiah himself would have expanded an earlier word through a supplement in this fashion, so that one must indeed see in the two verses the

hand of a disciple at work" (1:57). In contrast, I would argue the Isaiah often did supplement his earlier oracles in similar fashion (see especially the expansion and redirection of 28:1-6 by the later supplement in 28:7-15).

2   Hosea 4:15-19 uses the masculine term *zōneh*,

justice. They do not mention idolatry or cultic prostitution, the targets of much of Hosea's preaching and the source of his imagery. Isaiah simply uses the sexual metaphor alongside the metaphors of impure silver and watered down beer to suggest that Jerusalem is no longer the genuine article. What had been honorable, precious, and delicious has lost its honor, worth, and taste. Concretely, the traditional city of justice now houses evildoers, even murderers. Its high officials are scoundrels who associate with crooks and allow bribes and gifts to dictate government policy. The idiom "to run after gifts" vividly expresses how eagerly they court corruption. In such a climate the poor and powerless, the proverbial orphans and widows, cannot obtain justice.

It is worth noting that Isaiah attacks the high officials but not the king. These officials might be members of the royal family, "princes" as the RSV renders, but they need not be. The word שַׂר (śar) simply means officer, commander, or official. Isaiah, here perhaps influenced by Hosea (9:15), calls them סוֹרְרִים (sôrĕrîm), "rebels." The term was no doubt chosen partly for its alliteration with the word for "official," but its precise meaning in this context is important to specify. The term is used religiously to describe Israel as rebellious against God, but this is secondary religious usage and is probably not what the prophet has in mind. On a more primary level it is used of a disobedient child who rejects parental authority and goes his own way (Deut 21:18-20; Isa 30:1), of a faithless wife who refuses to stay at home in her husband's bed (Prov 7:11), and of a stubborn heifer that refuses to be herded (Hos 4:16). In each of these cases the rebel is one who subverts legitimate human authority by going his or her own way. Used of a government official in a monarchical system, therefore, it designates one who acts on his own, subverting the stated policies of the king. The prophet's failure to mention the king implies that he saw the problem not in the royal office but in the corrupt

bureaucracy that stood between the king and the people and subverted the good intentions of the king. That might suggest a date for the oracle in the reign of Hezekiah, who, unlike Ahaz, was respected by Isaiah, though the prophet criticized his officials severely and even singled one out as the subject for a whole oracle (22:15-25). The problem in the corrupt bureaucracy clearly does suggest an analogy to the contemporary disdain in which the institutional church is held. The problem is not with the teachings of Christ, the royal head of the church, but with his clerical officials, enough of whom have self-seekingly subverted Christ's instructions so as to bring the whole church into disrepute.

Yahweh's response to this situation is violent. As already explained in the textual notes, the epithet "Mighty Bull of Israel" occurs only in this passage. It appears to be a simple variant of the more common "Mighty Bull of Jacob," which occurs in texts associated with the early monarchy (Gen 49:24; Ps 132:2, 5) and in the later Isaianic tradition (49:26; 60:16). The epithet portrays God as a warrior, and his opening remark in v. 24 is that of a warrior. God's statement, "I will console myself," is a unique use of the *niphal* of the root *nḥm*; the closest parallels are in passages where the subject finds consolation after the death of a loved one (Gen 24:67; 2 Sam 13:39), finds new hope after severe suffering (Ezek 14:22), or, following death, is consoled by the death of those who afflicted him (Ezek 31:16; 32:31). The parallelism with *wĕʾinnāqĕmâ mēʾôyĕbāy*, "and I will avenge myself from my enemies," makes clear that here *ʾennāḥēm miṣṣāray*, "I will console myself from my enemies," means that God will relieve his rage and frustration by taking them out on the enemy who caused them. One should note that the enemy against whom the divine warrior is declaring war is his own people.

This military imagery is dropped in v. 25, however, for the imagery of metal refining, no doubt suggested by the

---

"fornicator, lecher," to refer to Israel, characterizes Israel as rebels using the verb *sārar* (see also Hos 9:15), and mentions *sobām*, "their beer." These resemblances with Isa 1:21-26 leads Vermeylen (*Du prophète Isaïe*, 101) to posit that the Isaiah passage is dependent on Hos 4:15-19 and 9:14-17. Vermeylen sees a late Deuteronomic influence on Hosea. Therefore, if Isa 1:21-26 is dependent on Hosea, then the Isaiah passage must be even later, and certainly not

from the eighth-century Isaiah of Jerusalem. The argument is not compelling, even assuming a clear influence of Hosea's vocabulary on Isaiah. It would not be surprising if the eighth-century Isaiah knew the work of his northern contemporary, who probably came south after the collapse of the northern kingdom. Certainly Hosea's work was preserved in the south, so such contact between Isaiah and Hosea by no means requires a late dating of Isa 1:21-26.

earlier metaphor of impure silver. When God is the subject, the idiom *ḥāšēb yād ʿal,* "to turn the hand against," is a general expression for divine judgment (Zech 13:7; Ps 81:15; cf. Isa 5:25; 9:11, 16, 20; 10:4 for the related idiom, *wĕʿôd yādô nĕṭûyâ,* "and his hand is still stretched out"), but the two following verbs specifically relate to the smelting process. The reading "as with lye" is problematic (see the textual note), since the evidence that it was used in the refining process for silver is disputed. Many scholars, therefore, correct the reading to "in a furnace" or "like a furnace." Either emendation is orthographically easy, and the first is perhaps supported by the occurrence of that expression in Isa 48:10, where Second Isaiah is apparently commenting on the earlier passage from First Isaiah. The smelting imagery, as Second Isaiah correctly saw, is a metaphor for God's refining judgment on his city, and it implies both punishment and a remnant who will survive the ordeal.

To solve the problem of rebellious, self-willed officials, Yahweh will restore the kind of judges and counselors that Jerusalem had in the beginning, that is, in the glory days of David and perhaps Solomon. There is a certain idealization of the past here—David's era was not without its problems in the administration of justice (2 Sam. 15:1-6)—but such idealization can serve a useful function as a goal to actualize, even if, as a historical portrayal of the past, it is inaccurate. Isaiah presents a similar vision of the future in 32:1, where he envisions both a king reigning in righteousness and officials ruling in justice. After the refining process, after the restoring of just officials, Jerusalem will once more be known as a city of righteousness. Her reputation, now besmirched, will again be above reproach.

The final "faithful city" of v. 26 forms a nice *inclusio* with the opening "faithful city" of v. 21 and suggests that the oracle originally ended at v. 26. Verses 27-28 appear to be an expansion, but whether by Isaiah himself or by

a disciple is impossible to say. The direct quotation of Yahweh ends in v. 26, since in v. 28 Yahweh is referred to in the third person, "those who forsake Yahweh," not "those who forsake me." This suggests that the expansion could be by the prophet himself, further interpreting the words of Yahweh. The verses are certainly compatible with Isaiah and correctly interpret the preceding text as proclaiming a purifying judgment on Zion in which the righteous would be saved while the wicked perished.

The precise meaning of "by justice" and "by righteousness" in v. 27 is debated; do "justice" and "righteousness" refer to God's justice and righteousness, or to the justice and righteousness of the inhabitants of Jerusalem?[3] Some scholars think it means that Zion will be saved by or in God's refining judgment, but it is more likely that the terms *justice* and *righteousness* refer primarily to the justice and righteousness of Zion's inhabitants. Isaiah 33:14-16, which specifies who can live in Zion with Yahweh, the devouring fire, provides the best commentary on this passage. It proclaims that only the repentant ones in Zion, those characterized by justice and righteousness, will be saved. The rest—the rebels, the sinners, and those who forsake Yahweh—will utterly perish.

Our present passage, 1:21-28, offers significant material for further reflection. First, with regard to Isaiah's theology, it indicates the importance of the Zion Tradition and Jerusalem in the prophet's thought. It also provides a standard for comparison for the many other passages in Isaiah where the prophet returns to the theme of God's plan for Jerusalem, a plan that involves both judgment and the salvation of a remnant. The extent and/or authenticity of many of these passages are disputed, and in evaluating that debate it is helpful to keep in mind this oracle, which, apart from vv. 27-28, is almost unanimously considered genuine.[4]

Second, the implications of the passage for the modern believer are numerous. Isaiah's condemnation of

---

3   See the discussion in Wildberger, 1:67; and John Oswalt's thoughtful comments (*The Book of Isaiah, Chapters 1–39* [NICOT; Grand Rapids: Eerdmans, 1986] 110).

4   A notable exception is Vermeylen, who dates the passage late, claiming that it is dependent on passages in Hosea, Jeremiah, and Ezekiel (*Du prophète Isaïe,* 100–105), but his analysis is not very compel-

ling. As already noted, any influence of Hosea on Isaiah says nothing about the date of the Isaianic passage, and Vermeylen's argument that Isa 1:21-26 is dependent on Jeremiah and Ezekiel, in contrast to the common view that the influence flows in the other direction, is highly subjective and totally unconvincing.

governmental corruption touches on a recurrent evil in human society. His idealization of Zion, however, rooted as it is in the Zion Tradition's identification of Jerusalem as the city of God, is difficult to accord with any contemporary secular government. If Israel's notion of Zion as the city of God has any continuity in the Christian faith, it is in terms of the community of the new covenant, the church (Heb 12:22-24), and Isaiah's oracle raises the issue of that community's responsibility to maintain its character as God's holy abode (1 Pet 2:4-10). Does it, like the Jerusalem of Isaiah's day, require the purging fire of judgment to restore it to its visionary ideal? Finally, if one speaks of restoring such an ideal, does it matter that the ideal never existed except in vision and in the nostalgic or didactic recasting of history?

Bibliography

Blum, E., "Jesajas prophetisches Testament: Beobachtungen zu Jes 1-11," *ZAW* 108 (1996) 562–68.

Dahood, Mitchell, "'Weaker Than Water': Comparative Beth in Isaiah," *Bib* 59 (1978) 91–92.

Hardmeier, C., "Jesajaforschung im Umbruch," *VF* 31 (1986) 3–31.

Hermisson, H. J., "Zukunftserwartung und Gegenwartskritik in der Verkündigung Jesajas," *EvT* 33 (1973) 54–77.

Jahnow, Hedwig, *Das hebräische Leichenlied im Rahmen der Völkerdictung* (BZAW 36; Giessen: A. Töpelmann, 1923) 239–53.

Jones, D. R., "Exposition of Isaiah Chapter One Verses Twenty-One to the End," *SJT* 21 (1968) 320–27.

Köhler, L., "Miszellen: Alttestamentliche Wortforschung. *Sĭg sĭgīm* = Bleiglätte," *TZ* 3 (1947) 232–34.

Lack, Rémi, *La symbolique du livre d'Isaïe: Essai sur l'image littéraire comme élément de structuration* (AnBib 59; Rome: Biblical Institute Press, 1973) 164–71.

Melugin, Roy F., "The Typical versus the Unique among the Hebrew Prophets," in Lane C. McGaughy, ed., *SBL 1972 Seminar Papers* (Missoula, MT: Scholars Press, 1972) 2:331–42.

Porteous, N. W., "Jerusalem-Zion: The Growth of a Symbol," in Arnulf Kuschke, ed., *Verbannung und Heimkehr: Beiträge zur Geschichte und Theologie Israels im 6. und 5. Jahrhundert v. Chr. Wilhelm Rudolph zum 70. Geburtstage dargebracht von Kollegen, Freunden und Schülern* (Tübingen: Mohr, 1961) 235–52.

Stolz, Fritz, *Strukturen und Figuren im Kult von Jerusalem* (BZAW 118; Berlin: de Gruyter, 1970).

Williamson, H. G. M., "Judgment and Hope in Isaiah 1:21-26," in J. Cheryl Exum and H. G. M. Williamson, eds., *Reading from Right to Left: Essays on the Hebrew Bible in Honour of David J. A. Clines* (JSOTSup 373; London: Sheffield Academic Press, 2003) 423–34.

Willis, John T., "Lament Reversed: Isaiah 1:21ff.," *ZAW* 98 (1986) 236–48.

1

29/ For you[a] shall be ashamed of the strong trees[b]
which you desired,
And you shall be embarrassed by the gardens
which you chose.
30/ For you shall be like a terebinth
whose leaf wilts,
And like a garden for which
there is no water.
31/ The strongest[c] will become tow,
and his work[d] a spark,
And both of them shall burn together,
with none to quench.

Textual Notes

a   The third person form יבשו (yēbōšû, "they will be ashamed"; MT 1QIsa[a] [plene] 4QIsa[f]) followed by a series of second person forms is difficult. Some Hebrew manuscripts have the second person תבשו (tēbōšû), "you will be ashamed," and the Tg. follows this tradition. By contrast, LXX and Syr. change all the verb forms in vv. 29-30 to third person to avoid the difficulty, while the Vg. limits this change to the immediately following verb. The original oracle must have had the second person; the change to the third person was an attempt to ease the connection between vv. 28 and 29, perhaps from the time when this oracle was inserted in its present context.

b   For MT's אילים (ʾêlîm), the plural of אַיִל (ʾayil), "strong tree," 1QIsa[a] has אלים, which is probably just a defective orthography, not the word "gods." LXX, Syr., and Vg. translate the word as "idols," but that is probably because they considered worship associated with these trees to be idolatrous. The Tg. has "the oaks of the idols."

c   For MT's הֶחָסֹן (heḥāsōn), "the strong one, the strongest," supported by 4QIsa[f], 1QIsa[a] has החסנכם (haḥāsōnkem), "your strong one," with the oddity of suffixed noun with the article. The Vg. seems to be following this reading with its *fortitudo vestra*, "your strength," though it misconstrues the nominalized adjective as an abstract noun. The LXX, Syr., and Tg. make the same mistake with the slightly different reading, "their strength." The addition of a pronominal suffix is a secondary development to ease the translation.

d   For MT's ופעלו (ûpōʿālô), lit., either "and his maker" or "and his work," 1QIsa[a] has ופעלכם, "and your work," which Vg. follows. The LXX and Syr. have "their works."

Commentary

Verses 29-31 disturb the context. Both the preceding and following verses deal with the theme of Zion as the city of God. This related material is split apart, however, by the insertion of the present pericope, which introduces a totally unrelated condemnation of sacred groves. The secondary character of this insertion is indicated also by the harsh stylistic feature of a sudden shift to the second person. These verses probably represent a floating oracle that was secondarily inserted here by the catchword principle. Verses 28 and 31 both pronounce judgment on certain parties "together," and the "burning" in v. 31 picks up on the judgment by fire in the smelting imagery in v. 25. When the floating oracle was inserted, its original second person address, as noted above, was slightly altered by the change of the first verb to the third person, apparently to ease its link to v. 28, which ends with a third person verb form.

The "terebinths" probably refer to the sacred groves usually associated with the cultic installations at the high places (cf. Isa 17:8), while the gardens may refer to the so-called Adonis gardens (cf. Isa 17:10-11). The sacred groves are often referred to in connection with idolatrous worship and probably have some relationship, if not identity, with the Asherim, which were cult symbols of the Canaanite goddess Athirat (1 Kgs 14:23; 2 Kgs 17:10). Hezekiah cut down such symbols during his reform (2 Kgs 18:4), so they were a religious issue during Isaiah's ministry, and that historical information suggests that this oracle dates prior to Hezekiah's reform. Isaiah condemns the people's devotion to these pagan symbols and, by implication, their participation in the cultic activities associated with these symbols.

Verse 31 is often treated as a crux, since it has been claimed that the usual reading of the nominalized adjective הֶחָסֹן (heḥāsōn) as referring to a powerful human, "the strong person," and the analysis of פֹּעֲלוֹ (pōʿălô) as the suffixed noun פֹּעַל (pōʿal), "his work," has the disadvantage of a rather abrupt introduction of a strong person into the context. The suggestion picked up by M. Tsevat[1] and modified and elaborated by S. E. Loewenstamm[2] that חסן means "semi-processed flax" is even less compelling. Loewenstamm admits that such an interpretation would totally isolate v. 31 from its context, destroying any original connection to the preceding verses.[3] The context is about sacred groves and gardens; this verse should have some connection to that topic.

The only other occurrence of the word חָסֹן (ḥāsōn), "strong," is in Amos 2:9, where it is used to compare men's strength to that of trees. In Isa 1:30 the prophet tells his audience that they will become like a dried-up terebinth. The continuation in v. 31 that "the strongest" (הֶחָסֹן) will become tow plays on the ambiguity of a double entendre: does the prophet mean the strongest tree in the grove, or does he mean the strongest person in his audience, who he has already said will become like a dried-up tree. NEB takes it as referring to "the strongest tree" and understands the form פֹּעֲלוֹ (pōʿălô) as "what is made of it," but it is more likely that the prophet is addressing "the strongest person" in his audience under the image of the dried-up tree. Like the dried-up terebinth, even the strongest, most oak-like person, will become like tow, and "his work" in constructing such pagan groves and gardens will become like a spark. Both the worshiper and his dried-up aids to worship will burn and perish together. For further discussion on Isaiah's attitude toward idolatry, see the treatment of Isa 17:7-11.

Bibliography

Klopfenstein, Martin A., *Scham und Schande nach dem Alten Testament: Eine begriffsgeschichtliche Untersuchung zu den hebräischen Wurzeln bôš, klm und ḥpr* (ATANT 62; Zurich: Theologischer Verlag, 1972).
Loewenstamm, S. E., "Isaiah I, 31," *VT* 22 (1972) 246–48.

Tsevat, M., "Isaiah I 31," *VT* 19 (1969) 261–63.
Williamson, H. G. M., "Isaiah 6:13 and 1:29-31," in J. van Ruiten and M. Vervenne, eds., *Studies in the Book of Isaiah: Festschrift Willem A. M. Beuken* (BETL 132; Louvain: Leuven University Press, 1997) 119–28.

1   M. Tsevat, "Isaiah I 31," *VT* 19 (1969) 261–63.
2   S. E. Loewenstamm, "Isaiah I 31," *VT* 22 (1972) 246–48.
3   Ibid., 248.

2

1/   The word which Isaiah son of Amoz saw[a] concerning Judah and Jerusalem.

Textual Notes

a   LXX's ὁ γενόμενος παρὰ κυρίου πρὸς, "(the word) which came to (Isaiah son of Amoz) from the Lord," presupposes the Hebrew הדבר אשר היה אל ישעיהו בן־אמוץ מאת יהוה (haddābār ʾăšer hāyâ ʾel yĕšaʿyāhû ben-ʾāmôṣ mēʾēt YHWH), but one may doubt whether the Greek translator had a Hebrew *Vorlage* with that text. It seems more likely that he misread חזה (ḥāzâ) as היה (hāyâ), and then substituted the formula so common in Jeremiah (7:1; 11:1; 18:1; 21:1; 36:1; 40:1).

Commentary

Unlike the heading in 1:1, the heading in 2:1 seems to serve as a superscription just for the immediately following oracle. Though it may have been the model for the superscription in 1:1, it appears to be a secondary editorial addition, and perhaps not in its original location. Like Isa 1:1 and 36:7, the latter part of the prose addition from 2 Kings, Isa 2:1 contains the word order "Judah and Jerusalem." Elsewhere in First Isaiah, the order is reversed; Jerusalem always comes first (3:1, 8; 5:3; 22:21). The heading was probably inserted here after the insertion of 1:29-31 broke the literary connection between 1:21-28 and 2:2-4, both of which deal with the new Zion of the future. The editor wanted to reassert that connection, and he may have wanted to claim 2:2-4 for Isaiah if he was aware that the same oracle also occurs in Mic 4:1-4.[1]

Bibliography

Ackroyd, P. R., "Isaiah I–XII: Presentation of a Prophet," in *Congress Volume: Göttingen 1977* (VTSup 29; Leiden: Brill, 1978) 16–48.
——, "A Note on Isaiah 2, 1," *ZAW* 75 (1963) 320–21.
Freedman, David Noel, "Headings in the Books of the Eighth-Century Prophets," *AUSS* 25 (1987) 9–26.
Goldingay, John, "Isaiah I 1 and II 1," *VT* 48 (1998) 325–32.
Sweeney, *Isaiah 1–4*, 30–32.
Tucker, Gene M., "Prophetic Superscriptions and the Growth of the Canon," in George M. Coats and Burke O. Long, eds., *Canon and Authority: Essays in Old Testament Religion and Theology* (Philadelphia: Fortress Press, 1977) 56–70.

---

1   See P. R. Ackroyd, "A Note on Isaiah 2, 1," *ZAW* 75 (1963) 320–21.

2

2/   And it will be at the end of days
        The mountain of the house of Yahweh[a] will be established[b]
    As the head of the mountains,[c]
        and it will be exalted above the hills,[d]
    And all the nations[e] will look to it[f] with joy.

3/   And many peoples[g] will come and say,
    "Come that we may go up to the mountain of Yahweh,[h]
        To[i] the house of the God of Jacob.
    That he[j] may teach us of his ways,[k]
        And that we may walk in his paths."[l]
    For from Zion will go forth instruction,
        And the word of Yahweh from Jerusalem.

4/   And he will judge between the nations,[m]
        And arbitrate for many peoples.[n]
    And they shall beat their swords[o] into plowshares,
        And their spears into pruning hooks.
    Nation[p] shall not lift[q] a sword against nation,
        And they shall no longer learn war.

5/   O house of Jacob, come that we may walk in the light of Yah-
        weh,

6/   For you[r] have forsaken your[r] people, O house of Jacob.
    For they[s] are full of . . .[t] from[u] the east,
        And soothsayers like the Philistines,
            And with[v] children of foreigners they clap.[w]

7/   And his[x] land is full of silver and gold,
        And there is no end[y] to his[x] treasures;
    And his[x] land is full of horses,
        And there is no end[y] to his[x] chariots.

8/   And his[x] land is full of idols,
        To[z] the work of his[x] hands they bow down,
            To what his[x] fingers have made.

9/   So the common folk have been humbled,
        And the gentry brought low,
        And you shall not forgive them.*[a]

10/   Enter into the rock,
        And hide yourself in the ground
    From before the terror of Yahweh,
        And from the splendor of his majesty.*[b]

11/   The commoner's haughty eyes shall be brought low,*[c]
        And the pride of the gentry shall be humbled,
    And Yahweh alone shall be exalted in that day.

12/   For there is a day to Yahweh of Hosts
        Against all that is proud and lofty,
        Against all that is lifted up and haughty.*[d]

13/   And against all the cedars of Lebanon,*[e]
        And against all the oaks of Bashan.

14/   And against all the high mountains,
        And against all the lofty hills.

15/   And against every high tower,
        And against every fortified wall,

16/   And against all the ships of Tarshish
        And against all the boats of Arabia.*[f]

17/   And the haughtiness of the commoner shall be humbled,
        And the loftiness of the gentry shall be brought low,
    And Yahweh alone shall be exalted in that day.

18/   And the idols shall totally pass away.*[g]

19/   And they shall enter*[h] into the caves of the rocks,
        And into the holes of the ground
    From before the terror of Yahweh,
        And from the splendor of his majesty,
    When he rises to terrify the land.

20/   On that day the commoner shall fling away
     His idols of silver and his idols of gold,
     Which his fingers made for himself*[i] to worship,
     To the shrews*[j] and the bats,
21/   In order to enter into the clefts of the rocks,
     And into the crevices of the crags,
     From before the terror of Yahweh,
      And from the splendor of his majesty
     When he rises to terrify the land.
22/   Cease from regarding mortals,
     in whose nostril is only breath,
     for of what account are they?

Textual Notes

a   The LXX, apparently influenced by v. 3, has τὸ ὄρος κυρίου καὶ ὁ οἶκος τοῦ θεοῦ, "the mountain of the Lord and the house of God," instead of MT's הַר בֵּית־יְהוָה (har bêt-YHWH), "the mountain of the house of Yahweh."

b   The MT has נָכוֹן יִהְיֶה הַר בֵּית־יְהוָה (nākôn yihyê har bêt-YHWH), while the parallel in Mic 4:1 moves נכון (nākôn) to the end of the clause. 4QIsa^a omits יהיה, but otherwise agrees with MT.

c   1QIsa^a omits the article on הֶהָרִים (hehārîm).

d   Micah 4:1 and 4QIsa^e insert the pronoun הוּא (hû') between MT's two words וְנִשָּׂא מִגְּבָעוֹת (wěniśśā' miggěbā'ôt), "and it will be exalted above the hills," though it does not change the meaning.

e   Micah 4:1 has עַמִּים ('ammîm), "peoples," for MT's כָּל־הַגּוֹיִם (kol-haggôyim), "all the nations." The parallelism with עַמִּים רַבִּים ('ammîm rabbîm, "many peoples") in v. 3 suggests that the כל is original, though whether gôyim or 'ammîm was the original a-word in the parallelism may be debatable.

f   For MT's אֵלָיו ('ēlāyw), "to it," Mic 4:1 has עָלָיו ('ālāyw), "upon it," and 1QIsa^a has the Aramaic-type suffix עלוהי ('ālôhî), "upon it."

g   Micah 4:2 has גּוֹיִם רַבִּים (gôyim rabbîm), "many nations."

h   1QIsa^a omits אֶל־הַר־יְהוָה ('el-har-YHWH), "to the mountain of Yahweh"; it is haplography due to homoioarcton with the following phrase.

i   Micah 4:2 and 4QIsa^e have ואל (wě'el), "and to," for the MT's אֶל ('el), "to."

j   1QIsa^a has וירונו, "that they may teach us."

k   LXX makes "way" singular.

l   LXX abbreviates to "in it."

m   Micah 4:3 has עַמִּים רַבִּים ('ammîm rabbîm), "many peoples."

n   Micah 4:3 has לְגוֹיִם עֲצֻמִים (lěgôyim 'ăṣūmîm), "for powerful nations," and then adds עַד־רָחוֹק ('ad-rāḥôq), "far away." Syr. has this final phrase in Isa 2:4.

o   1QIsa^a adds the prosaizing direct object marker את ('ēt) before חַרְבוֹתָם (ḥarbôtām), "their swords."

p   1QIsa^a adds the conjunction ו (wě), "and."

q   Micah 4:3 has the plural יִשְׂאוּ (yiśě'û), "they will not lift."

r   LXX corrects the second person forms of MT to the third person: ἀνῆκεν γὰρ τὸν λαὸν αὐτοῦ τὸν οἶκον τοῦ Ισραηλ, "for he has forsaken his people, the house of Israel." LXX makes the change because the Greek translator understood God as the subject and wanted the house of Israel to be the object. Vg. does not correct the text, but it does take *populum tuum domum Iacob*, "your people, the house of Jacob," as the object of God's forsaking. This is a common reading, but the second person forms following the vocative בֵּית יַעֲקֹב (bêt ya'ăqōb), "O house of Jacob," in the preceding verse make this reading very difficult, as the LXX correctly perceived. It is far more natural to take "your people" as the object, and the second בֵּית יַעֲקֹב (bêt ya'ăqōb) as another vocative and thus the understood subject of the verb. "Your people," then, would have to be distinct from the house of Jacob. This is the understanding of the Tg., though it may have missed the vocative in v. 5 (yymrwn byt y'qb 'ytw wnhk b'lpn 'wryt' dywy 'ry šbqtwn dḥlt tqyp' dhwh pryq lkwn dbyt y'qb 'ry 'tmly't 'r'kwn t'wn kyd mlqdmyn w'nnyn kplšt'y wbnmwsy 'mmy' 'zlyn, "They will say, 'O house of Jacob, come and let us walk in the teaching of the law of the Lord [or "Those of the house of Jacob will say, 'Come and let us walk in the teaching of the law of the Lord'"], for you have forsaken the fear of the strong one, who was your savior, you of the house of Jacob, because your land is filled with idols as from the east, and soothsayers like the Philistines, and they go in the customs of the Gentiles'").[1] Syr. should probably also be understood in this fashion (dbyt y'qwb tw n'zl bnwrh dmry' mtl dšbqtyhy l'mk dbyt y'qwb . . . , "O house of Jacob, come let us go in the light of the Lord, because you have forsaken your people, O house of Jacob . . ."). One should note that the first hand of Kennicott 96 has עמי ('ammî), "my people" (M. H. Goshen-Gottstein, *The Book of Isaiah* [Hebrew University Bible; Jerusalem: Magnes Press, Hebrew University, 1995] ז), which supports this understanding.

s   LXX has "their land is full," and Tg. has "your land is full," but both of these readings are influenced by v. 7, and neither can be judged original.

---

1   The second alternative is the translation of Bruce D. Chilton, *The Isaiah Targum* (Aramaic Bible 11; Wilmington, DE: Michael Glazier, 1987) 6–7.

t   It seems clear that a word has been lost by haplography, but it is difficult to decide what to restore. Kennicott 93 has ארם (Goshen-Gottstein, *Isaiah*, ז), which would suggest the rendering, "They are full of Aram(aeans) from the east (cf. Isa 9:11). One might also consider the plural אָרַמִּים (ʾărammîm). On the other hand, the missing word appears to be parallel with וְעֹנְנִים (wĕʿōnĕnîm), "and soothsayers," while מִקֶּדֶם (miqqedem), "from the east," balances כַּפְּלִשְׁתִּים (kappĕlištîm), "like the Philistines." That suggests a restoration such as קֹסְמִים (qōsĕmîm), "They are full of diviners from the east," that is, Aramean diviners.

u   MT has a simple מִקֶּדֶם (miqqedem), "from the east," but all the versions seem to indicate that a comparative כ stood before מִקֶּדֶם: LXX: ὡς τὸ ἀπ᾽ ἀρχῆς; Vg.: *ut olim*; Syr.: ʾyk dmn qdym; and Tg.: kyd mlqdmyn, "as from the beginning/east." The parallelism כמקדם//כפלשתים, "as from the east . . . like the Philistines," seems rather dubious, however. Either the versions introduce כ (kĕ) as an exegetical move, or the final ם (m) of the word that dropped out of the text was preserved and misread as a כ to be attached to the following word.

v   Some KR MSS. have וכילדי (wikyaldê), "and like children of," for MT's וּבְיַלְדֵי (ûbĕyaldê), "and with children of" (Goshen-Gottstein, *Isaiah*, ז).

w   For MT's יַשְׂפִּיקוּ (yaśpîqû) a number of MSS. have the biform יספיקו (yaspîqû, Goshen-Gottstein, *Isaiah*, ז). There are two verbs שפק/ספק: one means "to be numerous"; the other, "to strike (with the hand [with various connotations])." LXX and Syr. identify the verb as having the first meaning, "be numerous," while Vg. *et pueris alienis adheserunt*, "and with foreign children they stick together," presupposes the second verb, perhaps assuming a meaning like "to make an agreement." For further discussion of the meaning of the verb, see the following commentary.

x   LXX and Syr. have the plural suffix for MT's singular, but it is doubtful that this reflects a different Hebrew *Vorlage*.

y   1QIsaᵃ and 4QIsaᵇ have קץ (qēṣ), "end," for MT's קְצֵא (qēṣeʾ), "end." 4QIsaᵃ supports MT.

z   LXX appears to omit the preposition before מַעֲשֵׂה (maʿăśēh), "work," and misconstrues this construct as appositional with the preceding phrase, "And the land was filled with abominations, the works of their hands." It then takes the verb with the following clause, "And they bow down to what their fingers have made."

*a This line is very problematic. MT's וְאַל־תִּשָּׂא לָהֶם (wĕʾal-tiśśāʾ lāhem), "and may you not forgive them," suggests a negative prayer, but 4QIsaᵃ and 4QIsaᵇ have the negative ולא (wĕlōʾ), which suggests a simple statement of fact rather than a petition, and this is supported by LXX, Syr., and Vg. 1QIsaᵃ has a major haplography, omitting this whole line as well as all of v. 10. LXX changes the verb to the first person, "I will not forgive them." The second person in this line is unexpected

and abrupt and may suggest far deeper corruption, though no convincing emendation of the text has been offered.

*b LXX has the additional line found in the parallels at vv. 19 and 21, בְּקוּמוֹ לַעֲרֹץ הָאָרֶץ (bĕqûmô laʿărōṣ hāʾāreṣ, ὅταν ἀναστῇ θραῦσαι τὴν γῆν), "whenever he rises to terrorize/shatter the land."

*c MT's שָׁפֵל (šāpēl), "is low," disagrees with its subject in both gender and number and cannot be correct. 1QIsaᵃ has the imperfect third person feminine plural תשפלנה (tišpalnâ), "shall be lowered," which fits the context better and has the support of the Syr. and Tg. LXX had difficulty with this text and resolved it by inserting Yahweh into the first line: עני יהוה גבהות ואדם שפל (ʿēnê YHWH gabhût wĕʾādām šāpēl, οἱ γὰρ ὀφθαλμοὶ κυρίου ὑψηλοί, ὁ δὲ ἄνθρωπος ταπεινός), "for the eyes of the LORD are exalted, but man is humble."

*d MT, with support of most of the versions, has וְעַל כָּל־נִשָּׂא וְשָׁפֵל (wĕʿal kol-niśśāʾ wĕšāpēl), "against all that is lifted up, and it shall be lowered," but in the context one expects a parallel term to נִשָּׂא. LXX offers a double reading: ועל כל־נשא וגבה ושפל (wĕʿal kol-niśśāʾ wĕgābōah wĕšāpēl, καὶ ἐπὶ πάντα ὑψηλὸν καὶ μετέωρον, καὶ ταπεινωθήσονται), "and upon all that is exalted and haughty, and they shall be humbled." This suggests the correction to ועל כל־נשא וגבה (wĕʿal kol-niśśāʾ wĕgābōah), omitting ושפל.

*e MT's additional הָרָמִים וְהַנִּשָּׂאִים (hārāmîm wĕhanniśśāʾîm), "the high and lofty (cedars of Lebanon)," though supported by the versions, seems to be an expansion of the text. The pair of adjectives is drawn from v. 14, but they are inserted here in a way that disturbs the balance of the poetic parallelism.

*f The expression כָּל־שְׂכִיּוֹת הַחֶמְדָּה (kol-śĕkîyôt haḥemdâ), "boats of desire," has given both ancient and modern translators difficulty. It now appears that שכיה is a loanword from Egyptian *śk.tj*, "ship," also found in Ugaritic as *ṯkt* (*HALAT*, 1237). This fits the parallelism with אֳנִיּוֹת (ʾŏnîyôt), "ships," very nicely. Before the discovery of Ugaritic and the recognition of the Egyptian background to the word, it was normally derived from שכה/סכה, "to look out, view." Thus, Vg. has *omne quod visu pulchrum est*, "everything that is beautiful to view," and Syr. has klhwn dwqʾ drgtʾ, "all the glances of desire." LXX, while preserving this derivation, recognized that the context required boats and rendered ἐπὶ πᾶσαν θέαν πλοίων κάλλους, "upon every vision of beautiful boats." The vocalization הַחֶמְדָּה (haḥemdâ) may be questioned, since "desire" is a strange parallel to Tarshish. One might think of boats bringing luxury goods to Judea's rich, such goods replacing Yahweh in these consumers' affections and desires, but a place-name would be a better parallel to Tarshish. G. R. Driver vocalized החמדה as הַחֲמֻדָּה (haḥămuddâ) (and understood it as a place-name for Arabia, thus NEB's "dhows of Arabia."[2] While this reading remains uncertain, it is very suggestive.

*g Reading the plural יחלפו (yaḥălōpû), "they will pass away," with 1QIsaᵃ and the versions in place of MT's singular יַחֲלֹף (yaḥălōp),

2   G. R. Driver, "Difficult Words in the Hebrew Prophets," in H. H. Rowley, ed., *Studies in Old Testament Prophecy: Presented to Professor Theodore H. Robinson by the Society for Old Testament Study on His Sixty-fifth Birthday, August 9, 1946* (Edinburgh: T&T Clark, 1950) 52–53.

"it shall pass away." This reading takes כָּלִיל (kālîl) in an adverbial sense, "totally," but Peter Machinist (personal communication) has plausibly suggested that MT's singular is correct and that kālîl is to be understood as the singular subject, "The idols—the whole lot (of them)—shall pass away." The grammar differs, but the underlying sense remains the same.

*h   There is no compelling reason to emend the verb form here to match the imperative in v. 10. The same verb occurs in parallel expressions in vv. 10, 19, and 21, but in each case a different form of the verb is attested.

*i   MT's אֲשֶׁר עָשׂוּ־לוֹ (ʾăšer ʿāśû-lô), "which they made for himself," is grammatically very awkward, since it introduces a plural verb into a context in which the antecedent is singular and is resumed by a singular suffix. 1QIsaᵃ appears to have had אשר [עשו־לו אצב]עתיו (ʾăšer[ʿāśû-lô ʾeṣbē]ʿôtāyw), "which his [fin]gers [made for himself]." This reading resolves the grammatical problem, and the loss of אצבעותיו by haplography would explain the origin of the difficult MT reading. If one does not accept this reading, one must correct עשו (ʿāśû), "they made," to עשה (ʿāśâ), "he made."

*j   MT's פְּרוֹת לַחְפֹּר (laḥpōr pērôt) should probably be read with a few manuscripts as לחפרפרות (laḥăparpārôt) or with 1QIsaᵃ as לחפרפרים (laḥăparpārîm). Precisely what creature is designated by the term חפרפר (ḥăparpār) is disputed. It is usually identified either as a mole or shrew or as a variety of bat.

Commentary

Isa 2:2-4

The composition begins with a prophetic announcement of a future glorification of Jerusalem. This prediction, which is also found, but in a slightly variant form, in Mic 4:1-4, is one of the most moving and best-loved prophecies in all of the Old Testament. It is also one of the most disputed. The dispute begins with its authorship. Who wrote it? Did Isaiah borrow it from Micah? Did Micah borrow it from Isaiah? Did both borrow it from an earlier independent source? Or is it a secondary insertion in both books, the apocalyptic vision of an anonymous prophet of the postexilic period? Thus, the question of authorship feeds into the question of date. Can the oracle date from the eighth century BCE, the time of Micah and Isaiah? That question, in turn, involves the whole issue of interpretation. Is the vision "apocalyptic," or does it fit the general patterns of eighth-century prophecy?

The correct resolution of these questions depends on the insight that both eighth-century prophets were dependent on the Zion Tradition with its glorification of Jerusalem and concomitant attachment to the Davidic dynasty (see introduction). That Isaiah had a vision for the future Jerusalem is evident already from Isa 1:21-28, and that oracle also demonstrates that a terrible judgment on the contemporary city was not incompatible with the realization of this future ideal.

Moreover, once one has removed the later insertions in Isa 1:29-31 and 2:1, the literary context (our second level of interpretation) for the saying is much the same in both Isaiah and Micah. In Mic 3:9-12, Micah condemns the rulers and officials of Jerusalem for perverting judgment, for building Zion with blood and Jerusalem with iniquity. Building Jerusalem, of course, was the duty of the government officials, according to the Zion Tradition, but they had done it in the wrong way. Micah then illustrates his point by naming various officials in society such as rulers, priests, and prophets, who had exercised their legitimate functions, but in the wrong way—for bribery or personal gain. Yet these officials still trusted in the Zion Tradition's assertion that Yahweh was in their midst, protecting them from evil. Therefore, on their account, Zion would be utterly destroyed. Immediately following, then, Micah goes on to say how Jerusalem would be glorified in days to come. In this vision of the future, Yahweh takes over the governmental tasks botched by the officials in the preceding section. Yahweh teaches as a priest, gives his word as a prophet, and judges as a ruler (Mic 4:2 compared to 3:11).

In Isa 1:21-28 there is a similar condemnation of governmental officials for pursuing personal gain to the perversion of justice. It is for this reason that Yahweh will refine Jerusalem, utterly destroying his enemies. Isaiah is not as abrupt as Micah. He does not portray the destruction of Jerusalem as being quite as thorough as does Micah, and, unlike Micah, Isaiah does underscore the role of human agents in the purified city. But in both prophets the new vision of the glorified Zion follows an oracle of judgment in which the contemporary reality is condemned for the sake of the ideal symbolized by that reality. It is difficult to say which of the two prophets, if either, coined the announcement in Isa 2:4//Mic

4:1-4,[3] but that both used it, and that it fits in the eighth-century theology of both prophets, seems clear, as this commentator will seek to demonstrate in the following exposition.

"In the latter days" has an apocalyptic ring to it, particularly for Christians, who tend to read it in the light of Peter's misquotation of Joel's prophecy (Joel 3:1 [Eng. 2:28]) in his famous sermon on Pentecost (Acts 2:17). The Hebrew expression itself, however, does not necessarily convey such overtones. It can refer to some indefinite time in the future. In Gen 49:1 and Num 24:14, the expression is used in literary prophecies set in the time of Jacob and Moses to refer to the period of the Davidic monarchy. A more appropriate translation for the expression, therefore, following NEB, NAB, and TEV, would be, "In days to come. . . ."

The expression "the mountain of the house of Yahweh" is quite rare. Outside this passage and the parallel in Micah, it is found only in Mic 3:12, which is quoted in Jer 26:18, and in 2 Chr 33:15. Only the Chronicles passage is demonstrably late. Micah 3:12 is generally attributed to the eighth-century Micah and regarded as early, which explains why it could be quoted in Jeremiah. If this generally accepted judgment is correct, it indicates that the expression was current in Isaiah's time. The expression refers to the part of the eastern ridge just north of the old city of David on which Solomon's temple stood. Isaiah normally refers to it, or the eastern ridge as a whole, as "the mountain of (daughter) Zion" (Isa 4:5; 8:18; 10:12, 32; 16:1; 18:7; 29:8; 31:4), "the mountain of Yahweh" (2:3; 30:29), or "the mountain of my (God's) holiness" (11:9; cf. 27:13).

The prophecy promises that this mountain will become the tallest of all mountains. Such a promise is rooted in the Zion Tradition's mythological conceptions that associate the abode of deities with very high mountains. Isaiah may have believed that Mount Zion would actually experience a topographical transformation (cf. Zech 14:1-11, esp. v. 10); but even if he thought of that transformation as more than metaphorical, it remains a metaphor for Jerusalem's coming religiopolitical ascendancy. The theological implication of the topographical symbol is that Yahweh's abode will be exalted above all his rivals, so that even the foreign nations will acknowledge Yahweh's supremacy.

In response to the miraculous elevation of Yahweh's house, all the nations will gaze on God's temple with joy. The RSV, following the traditional understanding of the early versions, renders "shall flow to it," but this meaning for the Hebrew וְנָהֲרוּ אֵלָיו (wĕnāhărû ʾēlāyw) is problematic. It is based on the early versions and the assumed parallelism with the following verb "to go" and presupposes a denominative verb derived from the primitive noun נָהָר (nāhār) for "river." This meaning is attested in only one passage outside our oracle, however, and it is not clear there (Jer 51:44). Speaking of the Babylonian god Bel, Jeremiah says that the nations will no longer יִנְהֲרוּ אֵלָיו (yinhărû ʾēlāyw), "nhr to him," which could be rendered, "flow to him," but the context does not require that rendering, and one could as easily translate, "gaze upon him with joy," a translation that evokes the elaborate processionals in Babylon when the statue of Bel was paraded before the joyous gaze of huge crowds. One bilingual gives the following description of such a procession of Marduk (Bel):

> As his heart desired to go to Babylon, he came, and from the midst of wicked Elam he took a road of cheering, a way of joy, a path of homage and acceptance towards Babylon. The people of the land kept staring at his tall, majestic, lordly stature; acclaiming his brilliance, all of them stood at attention for him.[4]

The translation of the expression וְנָהֲרוּ אֵלָיו (wĕnāhărû ʾēlāyw) as "gaze on him/it with joy" follows the JPS and is based on a separate verbal root attested in Isa 60:5; Jer 31:12; and Ps 34:6 [Eng. 34:5]. In both the Isaiah and the Psalm passages the verb indicates a radiance of face that comes from looking upon something that brings joy. The Jeremiah passage is even more suggestive. It occurs in the so-called Book of Consolation, composed for the most part of oracles addressed to the remnants of the defunct northern kingdom during Josiah's reign. Jeremiah promises that they will be returned to their land to worship on Zion's height and rejoice over Yahweh's

---

3   From a text-critical point of view I am inclined to think that the Isaiah version is more pristine and original, but the element of subjectivity in such judgments is too high to truly resolve the issue.

4   Patrick D. Miller Jr. and J. J. M. Roberts, *The Hand of the Lord: A Reassessment of the "Ark Narrative" of 1 Samuel* [JHNES; Baltimore: Johns Hopkins University Press, 1977] 81, lines 12-16.

bounty. In developing this thought, however, Jeremiah uses a couple of phrases that suggest he may have known our oracle.

Thus, the cry of the Ephraimite watchmen in Jer 31:6: "Rise, and let us go up to Zion, to Yahweh our God!" is very similar to the cry of the foreigners in Isa 2:3: "Come, and let us go up to the mountain of Yahweh, to the house of the God of Jacob." This is followed in Jer 31:12 by the mention of a joyous pilgrimage and joyous shouting בִּמְרוֹם־צִיּוֹן (bimrom-ṣîyôn), "in/on the height of Zion," and then the same idiom (נהר אל) that is attested in Isa 2:2 occurs. Since the ideological context is the same, it is very difficult to separate the idiom in Jeremiah from the identical idiom in Isaiah, much less list them under two separate verbs. The idiom in Jeremiah, however, clearly belongs under the second נהר, as most translations and commentators agree. Thus, the RSV renders, "they shall be radiant over the goodness of the LORD." A similar rendering in Isa 2:2 has the merit of preserving the ideological connection between the two passages, but it also has exegetical advantages within the Isaiah context itself. Once God has elevated the Temple Mount above all the mountains of the world, thus making it clearly visible, the joyous gaze of the nations follows quite naturally. Moreover, it would motivate the decision to go to Zion in v. 3, rather than anticipating it in a logically awkward fashion. Nonetheless, one cannot rule out an intentional double entendre on the part of the prophet, intentionally playing with both meanings of these homonyms, since Isaiah has a penchant for double entendre.[5] Double entendres are almost impossible to translate into another language, but one can often get some sense of how they work. The elevation of the Temple Mount in v. 2 permits "all the nations" to look upon it with joy, suggesting that the verb be analyzed as נהר II, but then the quasi parallelism between "all the nations" (v. 2) and "many peoples" (v. 3) implies a kind of parallelism between the two verbs ונהרו (v. 2) and והלכו, "and *many peoples* will come" (v. 3), which forces the reader at least to consider the possibility that the author intended נהר I, "will flow," in v. 2. An author's such toying with his readers' minds is the essence of double entendre.

The nations decide to go up to this exalted temple of Yahweh that they also designate as "the house of the God of Jacob." Isaiah normally uses Jacob exclusively as a designation for the northern kingdom (see below), so while this seems to be a more inclusive use of the name, in the original historical setting of the Syro-Ephraimite war it may have functioned as a reminder to the north that the temple at Jerusalem was after all the house of *their* God, the ancient God of the Israelite league.

The reason the nations give for going up to Jerusalem is that they might learn how to walk in Yahweh's ways. It would be dangerous not to know how to serve the God who is so obviously supreme. Just as the pagan settlers in Samaria wanted to be taught the demands of Yahweh in whose land they had settled for the sake of their own self-preservation (2 Kgs 17:26-28), so in this glorious future, when Yahweh's imperial rank is recognized worldwide, the nations will desire to learn his ways.

Such instructions in the ordinances of the deity were normally given by priests or prophets, and the language used in v. 3 suggests the exercise of those offices. Thus, Yahweh "teaches" ירה (yōreh), just as the priest sent back to Samaria did (2 Kgs 17:27-28), and Yahweh's instruction תּוֹרָה (tôrâ) is issued from Jerusalem. "Law," though traditional, is not the best translation for תּוֹרָה (tôrâ). The noun is derived from the same root as the verb "to teach" (ירה) and is normally associated with the priest as the content of his teaching, over against the "word" (דָּבָר, dābār) of the prophet, or the "counsel" (עֵצָה, ʿēṣâ) of the wise (Jer 18:18). תּוֹרָה can be used for the instruction given by the prophet, however (Isa 30:9-10), and Isaiah uses the term in parallel with דָּבָר when referring to his own oracles (Isa 1:10; cf. 5:24). The expression "the word of the LORD" points to such prophetic instruction of these foreigners. On the other hand, "law" is not a totally misleading translation. While Yahweh's instruction of the nations is obtained by prophetic or priestly oracles, once issued it would have the force of imperial law.

The text makes no mention of the secondary human agents through whom this instruction in Yahweh's requirements will be carried out, but that need not imply that Yahweh does it directly without human mediation. In Micah, the human agents are omitted as part of the criticism of the contemporary holders of these offices,

---

5   See my "Double Entendre in First Isaiah," *CBQ* 54 (1992) 39–48.

but one cannot be certain that he envisioned an era when these offices would cease under a more direct rule of God. Since Isaiah assigns human agents an important role in his purged Jerusalem (1:26; 32:1-2), it is a safe assumption that he understood this instruction as mediated through human agency.

Moreover, as indicated by v. 4, the nature of this instruction is not merely or perhaps even primarily religious. The point of Yahweh's instruction is to settle disputes among the nations; "shall decide" in v. 4 could more clearly be rendered as "shall arbitrate" or "shall settle disputes" (cf. Gen 31:37, 42; Isa 29:21; Amos 5:10; Job 9:33). Yahweh's role here is clearly that of political suzerain. Just as the vassals of the Hittite state could not go to war with one another but had to submit their disputes to the Hittite overlord for settlement, so the nations, as Yahweh's vassals, will give up the right to make war and instead will submit their disputes to his arbitration. Thus, the pilgrimage of the nations to Jerusalem not only has religious implications but implies a political subservience to Zion as well. Jerusalem as the seat of the imperial God will have both religious and political preeminence.

Though our text is mute on this point, such political arbitration could again be carried out by Yahweh's human agents, perhaps even including the Davidic king (cf. Isa 9:5-6 [Eng. 9:6-7]; 11:3-10). At any rate, as a result of Yahweh's imperial arbitration, wars will cease. A new Jerusalemite peace will fulfill and surpass the ancient ideal of the Solomonic peace celebrated in the Zion Tradition (Ps 46:9-10 [Eng. 46:8-9]). The nations will turn their armaments into agricultural tools that promote life, and military training will become a thing of the past.

While this vision of the future obviously presents an ideal, the ideal has its roots in the early Zion Tradition; and despite the mythological background of much of its language, it envisions an earthly reality. Yahweh's new imperium is embodied in the reestablishment of Jerusalem's hegemony on a grander scale even than in the glory days of David and Solomon, but the Davidic-Solomonic empire, nevertheless, remains the model for this vision of the future. When the oracle is read in that imperial light,

there is nothing in it that is incompatible with a date in the late eighth century. Indeed, read in the light of the Davidic-Solomonic imperial ideology, the oracle enjoys a concreteness that gives coherence to its various elements. This concreteness is lost when a late dating forces a "spiritualized" interpretation on the text.[6]

But if this prophecy is understood so concretely, how does it continue to speak in a new context, to a new community of faith that does not share Isaiah's cultural presuppositions or his political aspirations for Israel? By New Testament times the concept of a heavenly Jerusalem as the real Jerusalem in contrast to the earthly Jerusalem in Palestine was sufficiently developed for Paul to use it in the defense of his gospel against his opponents, who demanded that gentile converts to Christianity keep the Law of Moses. In his allegory of Hagar and Sarah (see Gal 4:21—5:6 for the whole context) Paul clearly diminishes the importance of the earthly Jerusalem: "Now Hagar is Mount Sinai in Arabia and corresponds to the present Jerusalem, for she is in slavery with her children. But the other woman corresponds to the Jerusalem above; she is free, and she is our mother" (Gal 4:25-26). There is nothing in Paul or the other New Testament writers that provides justification for a Christian Zionism that awaits and tries to hasten a literal elevation of the earthly Jerusalem to the position of the political capital of a new world empire. Contemporary Christian Zionists who long for a literal rebuilding of the Jewish temple in Jerusalem as a sign of the end time à la Ezekiel 40–48 do so only by ignoring the rewriting of Ezekiel's vision, particularly of Ezekiel 47, in Revelation 21–22. John's vision of the heavenly Jerusalem, though heavily dependent on Ezekiel, nonetheless differs significantly in that there is no temple in the new Jerusalem (Rev 21:22). A temple is only a visible symbol of the invisible deity's divine presence, but when the deity's presence is immediate and visible, as it will be in the new, heavenly Jerusalem, the symbol is no longer needed. For the Christian, then, who tries to take both the Old Testament text and the New Testament reappropriation of it seriously, the question remains,

---

6   For a detailed defense and elaboration of these points, see my "The End of War in the Zion Tradition: The Imperialistic Background of an Old Testament Vision of Worldwide Peace," in M. Daniel Carroll R. and Jacqueline E. Lapsley, eds., *Character*

Ethics and the Old Testament: Moral Dimensions of Scripture (Louisville: Westminster John Knox, 2007) 119–28. A slightly shorter version of this article appeared earlier in *HBT* 26 (2004) 2–23.

"How can one remain true to the text and at the same time translate it into Christian categories?"

The text expresses the expectation that Yahweh's universal rule will one day become transparent to the whole world, and, as a result of this recognition of God's rule, an era of peace and well-being for all nations will begin, inaugurated from Jerusalem. Isaiah symbolizes the transparency of Yahweh's universal rule by the physical elevation of the Temple Mount, itself the symbol of God's presence in Israel. But if, for the Christian, Jesus or his body, the church, has replaced the temple as the symbol of God's presence and rule in the world, what would be an equivalent elevation of those symbols? Jesus's reference to his crucifixion in John 12:32 as a "lifting up" is suggestive. Indeed, that whole passage bears comparison with our text. Just as our text underscores the rule of God by the elevation of the Temple Mount and the subsequent pilgrimage of the people to that mount, so Jesus asserts God's rule by the casting out of the prince of this world (John 12:31) and then goes on to say, "and I, when I am lifted up (this is the same Greek verb ὑψόω, hypsoō, that is used in the LXX of Isa 2:2) from the earth, will draw all men to myself" (John 12:32). Since John elsewhere identifies Jesus as the temple (John 2:19-22), one may wonder whether John was already consciously translating the symbols of Isa 2:2.

Following this hint, to what extent can one speak of the reception of the gospel by the gentiles throughout the world as a pilgrimage to Jerusalem to learn the ways of the God of Israel? The structure of Luke's history of the church in Acts, beginning with the apostolic witness in Jerusalem and continuing with the proclamation of the gospel in all Judea, Samaria, and to the end of the earth (Acts 1:8), suggests that the word of the Lord did indeed go forth from Jerusalem. Moreover, Paul, in carrying out his great fund-raising campaign among the gentile churches for the poor saints in Jerusalem, seems to have regarded that ministry as in some sense a fulfillment of the related pilgrimage passage in Isa 60:1-7 (Rom 15:7-33).

Obviously, war has not yet been banished from the earth; that remains an unrealized ideal. But to what extent can one speak of the anticipation of that ideal in the church, in the community of faith that cuts across boundaries of nation, language, and race? The Ephesian letter speaks of Jesus as having broken down the dividing wall of hostility, thus establishing peace and reconciliation between people in the one new body, the church, the dwelling place of God in the Spirit (2:11-22).

As one reflects on Isaiah's prophecy in the light of the Christian faith, one can see something of the same tension that characterizes the whole New Testament outlook toward salvation. It is the tension between realized eschatology and future eschatology, between present participation in the life of the age to come and the full realization of that life in the final judgment, between the indicative description of life in the Spirit and the imperative demand to work out that description in everyday living. Even when Isaiah's prophecy has been translated into Christian symbols, it still stands as a hope for the future, a hope that is to some extent anticipated in Christian experience, but also a hope that calls for Christian effort toward its realization. It is worth noting that Isaiah's great vision of the nations' future decision to walk in God's ways is followed by an admonition to the house of Jacob to join the prophet and his people in setting the example. In other words, the promise is followed by the imperative.

Because I am a Christian, I have reflected on what this eighth-century BCE text might mean to a contemporary Christian audience that no longer shares the specific historical context and concomitant presuppositions of the historical Isaiah. I would not pretend to speak for my Jewish colleagues. Yet the problem of contemporary relevance is not a distinctly Christian issue. One does not need a profound knowledge of the wide variety of contemporary Jewish religious communities to realize that the future hope for many of them does not include the expectation of the restoration of a Davidic monarchy ruling the world for God from an imperial capital in Jerusalem. If Isaiah's words are to retain any relevance for such communities, they must address this issue of the gap between ancient expectations and contemporary application.

Isaiah 2:5-22

If the oracle in Isa 2:2-4 and Mic 4:1-4 ever existed independently of those two contexts, both prophets appended different though quite similar admonitions at the end of the unit (Isa 2:5; Mic 4:5). If one prophet borrowed from the other, the borrower intentionally altered the other's ending to suit his own purposes.

In Isaiah, "the house of Jacob" is addressed in the

vocative and, following an introductory imperative "come" (*lĕkû*), is urged with a first person plural cohortative (*wĕnēlĕku*, "that we may walk") to join with the prophet and his group in walking in the light of Yahweh. Note the parallel construction in v. 3, where the many peoples address one another with an introductory imperative "come" (*lĕkû*) and then follow that up with a first person plural cohortative (*wĕnaʿăleh*, "that we may go up"), urging one another to go up to the house of the God of Jacob. If v. 5 has ties back to v. 3, however, it also has ties to the following v. 6, where the designation "house of Jacob" occurs again, and again should be construed as a vocative. Verse 5 and the first line of v. 6 should be translated as follows:

O house of Jacob, come, that we may walk
  in the light of Yahweh,
For you have forsaken your people, O house
  of Jacob.

The RSV, along with most translations and commentators, makes God the subject of the verb "to forsake" and takes the second "house of Jacob" as appositional to the direct object "people," but this is difficult. The introduction of God as subject is quite abrupt in a context that begins with a vocative address to "the house of Jacob." Most commentators who take this approach, therefore, begin a new unit with v. 6. That still does not solve the problem, however, for it leaves the verse without any adequate introduction. One needs an antecedent reference to God before making God the understood subject of the verb. The alternate rendering suggested above has the support of the Targum; the Medieval Jewish commentator Rabbi Moshe Hakkohen, according to Ibn Ezra;[7] A. B. Ehrlich;[8] and the new JPS translation. It forces one to examine more carefully what is meant by the expression "house of Jacob."

The name Jacob occurs twelve times in First Isaiah (2:3, 5, 6; 8:17; 9:7; 10:20-21; 14:1; 17:4; 29:22-23), not counting the two occurrences in the Isaiah Apocalypse (27:6, 9), which cannot be cited for First Isaiah's usage. In several occurrences, Jacob clearly refers to the old northern kingdom (Isa 9:7; 17:4) or probably does (8:17; 10:20-21), and none of the passages in its original historical setting requires a general interpretation that would include Judah under the term Jacob. That being so, Isaiah's admonition in v. 5 is probably to be read as an invitation to the north to join in the service of their common God. The admonition is explained in v. 6 by the charge that the north had forsaken his own people, that is, Isaiah and his Judean compatriots in the southern kingdom, where the house of the God of Jacob had been since the time of Solomon. Such an invitation might have been offered to the north by a southern prophet any time after the north split away from Judah and its Davidic dynasty in the time of Jeroboam I, but the following lines suggest a more immediate context in the period of the Syro-Ephraimite war, when the northern kingdom Israel actually marched with the Arameans (Isa 7:1-6), Philistines (2 Chr 28:18), and perhaps Phoenicians against Judah in an attempt to replace Jerusalem's king, the Davidic Ahaz, with a foreigner.

If one adopts the translation of v. 6a suggested above, there is a somewhat abrupt shift from the second person vocative to the narrative third person in v. 6b. It may represent a shift in the prophet's attention from the fictive northern audience to the real southern audience for whom the oracle was actually intended. Oracles formally addressed to foreign nations are, in fact, usually spoken for the benefit of the prophet's own people. Isaiah's description of the north's alienation from their own heritage and therefore from the favor of Yahweh is one way of assuring Judah in the face of the northern threat (cf. 7:7-9).

The last part of v. 6 is marked by both textual corruption and translational difficulties. The textual corruption appears to require at minimum that one reconstruct a missing word, but there are two top candidates for that word, ארם or ארמים (*ʾărām* or *ʾărammîm*), "Arameans," or קסמים (*qōsĕmîm*), "diviners." Thus, one is left with a very tentative translation:

Because he is full of [Arameans/diviners . . .] from the east, And soothsayers like the Philistines, And with children of foreigners he claps in derision.

7   M. Friedländer, *The Commentary of Ibn Ezra on Isaiah*,
     3 vols. (London: N. Trübner, 1873) 2:4, 3:6.
8   Arnold B. Ehrlich, *Randglossen zur hebräischen Bibel:*
     Textkritisches, sprachliches, und sachliches (7 vols.;
     Leipzig: J. C. Hinrichs, 1908–14) 4:10.

The second hand of a late Hebrew manuscript has anticipated the emendation to Arameans, but "diviners" would provide a better parallel to "soothsayers." Even if the emendation to Arameans is not correct, however, the expression "from the east" should be understood as referring to the Arameans (Syria), since the same expression is used in 9:11, where the Arameans are put in parallel with the Philistines.

"Soothsayers" were a distinctive class of intermediaries between the divine and human realms, though we can no longer be sure how they obtained their oracles or how they differed from other classes of intermediaries. They were prohibited by the Deuteronomic law (Deut 18:10-14), perhaps because they were felt to be foreign in origin, but it is not clear whether the soothsayers mentioned here are actually foreign, or if they are Israelite imitators of the Philistine practice. Like other intermediaries such as prophets and diviners, soothsayers were involved in giving support to political decisions (Jer 27:9), and they are probably mentioned here because of their support for the Aramean–Israelite coalition against Judah.

The precise meaning of the verb that the RSV translates as "strike" and I translate as "clap" is a crux. As pointed out in the textual notes, there are two homophonous Hebrew verbs, one of which means "to be sufficient, numerous," the other "to slap, to strike." The second is used of clapping the hands together in anger or derision (Num 24:10; Job 27:23; Lam 2:15; cf. Ezek 21:22 [Eng. 21:17]) and of slapping the thigh as a sign of shame or lamentation (Jer 31:19; Ezek 21:17 [Eng. 21:12]). Despite the Vg.'s translation, there is no other evidence that the verb is ever used for shaking hands to seal an agreement, nor does hand clapping appear in any of these texts as a pagan rite for scaring off demonic powers. The use of the expression כף תקע (tāqaʿ kap, "to clap the hands") in Ps 47:2 in acclamation of Yahweh as king, suggests that hand clapping might also have marked the acclamation of a human king.[9] If so, one might think of the Israelites, prior to their attack on Jerusalem, joining their foreign allies in clapping to acclaim the son of Tabael, the new king they wanted to install in Jerusalem in place of Ahaz.[10] Nonetheless, in the absence of any other evidence for this practice in Israel, it is perhaps best to understand the verb as referring to the Israelites joining their foreign allies in making derisive gestures toward Jerusalem (cf. Isa. 10:32).

The RSV's "foreigners" depends on an emendation, because the Hebrew actually uses a compound term, "children of foreigners." The prophet may have used the compound term to emphasize the unnatural behavior of the house of Jacob. The house of Jacob, that is, the Israelites of the north, had forsaken Isaiah's own people, the Judeans of the south, and had joined the offspring of foreigners in deriding his own kinsmen.

The statement that the land of the house of Jacob is full of money and military equipment (v. 7) also underscores the political background of the oracle. The presence of horses and chariots in large numbers suggests mobilization for war, and it may indicate that Aramean contingents had already taken up forward positions in Israel in preparation for the attack on Jerusalem. Even the reference to large sums of money fits that context, as the money would be necessary for paying the troops, purchasing equipment, and procuring supplies—and, perhaps derisively in this verse, for bribing participants to join in the war against Judah. War was an expensive undertaking even in the ancient world, and without sufficient economic resources it was unlikely to succeed. There is no reason, therefore, to take the first part of v. 7 as referring to international trade. It continues the imagery of v. 6 and reflects Israel's continuing buildup for war in league with the foreign Arameans and Philistines.

Verse 8 might seem more difficult. How do idols fit in this assumed context? One must remember that the motivation behind the Syro-Ephraimite war was the desire on the part of Damascus and Israel to achieve a secure independence from Assyria.[11] When Ahaz of Judah refused to join their coalition, they marched against him to

9   See the more detailed discussion of J. S. Rogers, "An Allusion to Coronation in Isaiah 2:6," *CBQ* 51 (1989) 232–36.

10   See my detailed commentary on Isa 7:6.

11   See the detailed discussion in Stuart A. Irvine, *Isaiah, Ahaz, and the Syro-Ephraimitic Crisis* (SBLDS 123; Atlanta: Scholars Press, 1990) 101–4. Despite differences, on this point, Irvine is in basic agreement with Joachim Begrich (" Der syrisch-ephraimitische Krieg und seine weltpolitischen Zusammenhänge," *ZDMG* 83 [1929] 213–37; reprinted in *Gesammelte Studien zum Alten Testament* [Munich: C. Kaiser,

force Judah's support. At least as Isaiah saw it, the whole campaign—money, chariots, and all—was an attempt to achieve security by human means, even if it meant joining forces with foreigners against one's own people. There was a religious dimension to Israelite politics, however. Israel certainly did not go to war without consulting the deity, and even in the last days of Israel the official deity of the northern state was Yahweh. Isaiah, however, undercuts any claim that the north might make to be marching under the orders of Yahweh. According to him, the gods worshiped in the north were mere idols. Whatever the northerners may have thought of the worship carried out at Bethel, Dan, or Samaria, however they may have regarded the bull iconography of their sacred sites, Isaiah, with a Jerusalemite perspective, dismisses them as the work of human hands. For Isaiah, the Yahweh of Samaria, known now from the early-eighth-century Hebrew inscriptions of Kuntillet 'Ajrud,[12] was simply not Yahweh at all. The many cultic installations in the north, which were so popular in the last days of Israel (Hos 8:11), Isaiah dismisses as just another attempt to gain security by human means.

The result of this search for bogus security was its opposite. Because the house of Jacob bowed down to idols, everyone was brought low. Isaiah uses two different words for "man" in parallel here (v. 9): אָדָם (ʾādām) and אִישׁ (ʾîš). Sometimes the use of the two words implies a contrast between a person of standing (ʾîš) and an ordinary peasant (ʾādām, Ps 49:3), and Isaiah may have used the terms in parallel to indicate that both the rich and the poor were suffering as a result of Israel's unfortunate decision. This was a relatively new experience for the rich. Even in the wealthy days of Jeroboam II, the Israelite poor suffered severe exploitation from the cultic authorities (Amos 2:8), but not until the chaos of the ensuing period (2 Kgs 15:8-28) with the heavy tribute to Assyria (2 Kgs 15:19-20), the recurring civil strife, and then the disastrous attempt on Jerusalem, did the rich begin to experience

the pain. The financial burden imposed on the population to support the war against Judah and maintain the cult was enough to cripple the whole economic life of the country. The search for human security ended in the dust and ashes of destruction.

The final line of v. 9 is problematic. As the text stands, it is a prayer to God not to forgive the Israelites, but the prayer is so abrupt and unprepared for that one must suspect that the line is corrupt. Thus, as proposed in the textual notes, unless the corruption is far deeper and the original text simply unrecoverable, one should read the verse with the LXX as a statement of fact, not as a petition.

In v. 10 the prophet once again addresses the house of Jacob directly. He urges Israel to take refuge from the terror of Yahweh. The text calls to mind the passage in the Ugaritic Baal epic where Baal thunders from his mountain palace, and his enemies, who had been threatening his holy mountain, take flight in panic: "He opens a casement in the house, / A window within the pa[lace]. / Baal op[ens *rifts in* [the cloud]s. / Ba[al gives] forth his holy voice, / Baal discharges the *ut*[*terance of his li*]*ps*. / His h[oly] voice [convulses] the earth, . . . the mountains quake, / A-tremble are . . . / East and west, earth's high places reel. / Baal's enemies take to the woods, / Hadd's foes to the sides of the mountain" (*ANET*, 135 lines 25-36). Isaiah here seems to be using the Zion Tradition, which had incorporated many elements of the Canaanite Baal myth, to respond to the crisis of the Syro-Ephraimite war. The implication of his word is that Israel's plan against Jerusalem will come to naught, because Yahweh will intervene in a terror inspiring manner to save his city as the Zion Tradition asserted (Ps 48:4-9 [Eng. 48:3-8]; cf. elsewhere in Isaiah, 14:32; 28:5-8; 31:5-9; 33:10-16).

As a result, human pride will be abased, and Yahweh, the divine king, will alone be exalted (v. 11). This is a recurring theme of Isaiah's proclamation. It plays a fundamental role in his call experience (Isaiah 6), and

---

Begrich, 1964] 99–120); Herbert Donner (*Israel unter den Völkern: Die Stellung der klassischen Propheten des 8. Jahuhunderts v. Chr. zur Aussenpolitik der Könige von Israel und Juda* [VTSup 11; Leiden: Brill, 1964]), and Jesús María Asurmendi (*La guerra siro-efraimita: Historia y profetas* [Institución San Jerónimo 13; Valencia: Institución San Jerónimo para la Investigación Biblica, 1982]) against Bustenay Oded ("The

Historical Background of the Syro-Ephraimitic War Reconsidered," *CBQ* 34 [1972] 153–65), who sees the conflict as simply an inner-Syrian squabble.

12 See the final publication of Ze'ev Meshel, *Kuntillet 'Ajrud (Horvat Teman): An Iron Age II Religious Site on the Judah-Sinai Border* (Jerusalem: Israel Exploration Society, 2012), and the treatment of the texts in F. W. Dobbs-Allsopp et al., *Hebrew Inscriptions*, 277–98.

it appears as a constant feature in Isaiah's concern for God's "plan" for Jerusalem. In the various crises that threatened Jerusalem during Isaiah's ministry, he constantly called for God's people to look to God's plan, not to trust in military alliances and human devices (Isa 7:7-9; 22:8-11; 30:1-5; 31:1-3). Their security lay in trusting in Yahweh and his promises.

In v. 12 Isaiah picks up the theme of the day of Yahweh, a theme earlier developed by Amos as a day of judgment against God's people Israel (Amos 5:18-20). Isaiah treats it more generally as a day of God's judgment over anything that foolishly challenges Yahweh's supremacy, over anything so exalted that humans might be tempted to put their trust in these things rather than in Yahweh. The list (vv. 13-16) has an almost mythological character to it; the mention of cedars and oaks, mountains and hills, recalls those passages, such as the originally Canaanite Psalm 29, where the natural world is convulsed by the theophany of the deity or by his mighty roar (Amos 1:2; Hab 3:3-6; Ps 68:8-9 [Eng. 68:6-7]). The mention of high towers and fortified walls is a judgment against the human attempt to find security in military preparedness, and the mention of the ships may continue the military imagery, or it may refer to the search for security in trade and economic development.

Mention of the ships of Tarshish (v. 16) seems to be a traditional feature of the Zion Tradition. Psalm 48:8 [Eng. 48:7] refers to Yahweh's shattering of the ships of Tarshish in the context of his defeat of the enemy kings who marched against Jerusalem, and Isa 33:21-33 promises that the restored Jerusalem will never be threatened by enemy ships. Since ships were hardly a direct threat to Jerusalem, while Baal's Mount Zaphon, the modern Jebel al-Aqraᶜ, situated on a narrow coastal plain, near the mouth of the Orontes, was readily accessible to seaborne enemies, it may be that this motif derives from the Baal tradition, though there is no clear reference to a seaborne assault on Baal's mountain in the fragmentary Baal epic. Tarshish was a site in the western Mediterranean that gave its name to a particular type of oceangoing vessel. If Driver's identification (see textual note *f above) of החמדה as a place-name is correct, "craft of Hamuddah" or NEB's "dhows of Arabia" would give the same kind of parallelism as the "cedars of Lebanon" and the "oaks of Bashan" in v. 13. That rendering, with Tarshish in the west and Arabia in the east, might also suggest Yahweh's universal supremacy. Just as Baal's voice terrified both east and west (*ANET*, 135 line 34, though the interpretation of *qdm ym* remains disputed—other renderings include "before Yamm" and "the peoples of the east" [*qdmym*]),[13] so no human power, whatever its source, could threaten Yahweh's supremacy. Neither the ships of Tarshish nor the craft of Arabia were any threat to Yahweh. Whether their purpose was military, economic, or both, they were neither a threat to nor an adequate substitute for the security that could be found only in Yahweh.

Verse 17 repeats the refrain of v. 11 with slight variations in its wording (cf. also v. 9). The variation may be partly due to textual corruption (cf. 5:15), but the repetition, like the repetition in vv. 10, 19, and 21, may be a structuring device to tie vv. 5-22 together. In v. 18, Isaiah turns back to the fate of the idols first mentioned in v. 8. The context (see v. 20) suggests that these idols were objects small enough for a person to throw away while in flight. One might think, then, of the images and standards that accompanied an army into battle and which, along with the figurines belonging to individual soldiers, would be cast aside by troops fleeing the battlefield in panic. The best commentary on this passage is in 2 Sam 5:17-21, where the Philistines, thrown into a panic by Yahweh, left their gods to the victorious Israelites under David—a victory, moreover, that may have been a major ingredient in the development of the Zion Tradition.

The limestone rocks of Palestine are full of caves where refugees have fled from war over the centuries, and as the finds at Qumran and Wadi Daliyeh demonstrate, it is precisely in such places that such fugitives left their valuables when time gave them the opportunity. The word to be read חפרפרות (*ḥăpparpārôt*) or חפרפרים

---

13   See the discussion in André Caquot, Maurice Synycer, and Andrée Herdner, *Textes ougaritiques: Introduction, translation, commentaire,* vol. 1, *Mythes et légendes* (Littératures anciennes du Proche Orient 7; Paris: Cerf, 1974) 217, n. i′.

(*ḥăpparpārîm*), and translated "shrews," or "moles" in the RSV, occurs only here in the Bible. As noted above in the textual notes, its meaning is uncertain, but it may be another term for "bat." These caves were typically the home of bats[14]—many of the recent archaeological discoveries in these caves were found under a deep layer of bat dung[15]—so Isaiah's imagery was both powerful and true to the experience of his contemporaries.

The LXX omits v. 22, and it is generally regarded as a late gloss,[16] though it is preserved in the large Isaiah scroll from Qumran. If it is original, the shift to the plural imperative, last encountered in 2:5, raises the question of the implied subject. In 2:5 the subject was the collective "house of Jacob," who was urged to "come" (plural imperative) and join with Judah in walking ("let us walk" [plural cohortative]) in the light of Yahweh. The plural imperative in v. 22 could, as in v. 5, envision the house of Jacob as the implied subject, or, given the perhaps deliberate lack of an expressed subject here, it might envision both Israel and Judah. But even in v. 5 the house of Jacob, or Israel, was only Isaiah's fictive audience. The real audience was Judean, and it is even more likely in v. 22 that Isaiah's real audience is Judah and the inhabitants of Jerusalem. Isaiah orders them, just as he orders Ahaz in Isaiah 7, to cease worrying about the machinations of human foes. Of what concern are mere humans and their plots when Yahweh, the great suzerain of the whole earth, is directing the show? One need not fear the combined armies of Damascus and Israel if one only trusts in God and his promises. There is no need to turn to human pseudo-saviors like Assyria in this crisis.

If in the original historical context this fictive appeal to Israel to return to the house of Jacob's people and to their God actually functioned as reassurance to Judah, the judgment pronounced against Israel also stood as a warning to Judah not to make Israel's mistake of seeking security in false gods. That warning is then underscored by the secondary literary placement of this text, when Judah is now understood as being included in the appeal to the house of Jacob to return to Yahweh. The implication of this move is that Judah and its false sources of security are now in danger of suffering the same devastating judgment as befell Israel in the earlier period when the oracle was first formulated.

This warning against displacing God in the search for human security is a recurring theme in Isaiah, and it is a theme that remains relevant for the contemporary world. Reflection on the metaphors in which it is embodied, however, suggests the need for cautious thoughtfulness in its modern application. Yahweh's day of judgment is not only against every high tower, fortified wall, the ships of Tarshish, and the dhows of Arabia; it is also against the tall cedars, the exalted oaks, the high mountains, and the exalted hills. It is easy and faddish to assume a prophetic stance in railing against "the military-industrial complex," but the metaphorical character of Isaiah's language requires that one say both less and more than such posturing usually conveys. Unless one is prepared to say that God is against majestic trees and mountains as such, it is hard to argue that God is against military fortifications as such. The passage condemns the idolatrous elevation of any human work or natural phenomenon to the place of God. Only in walking in Yahweh's light is there true security. When the scramble for security alien-

---

14 Caves throughout Israel remain a primary nesting place for the some thirty-three species of bats found in Israel, where efforts are now being made to preserve them. See Benny Shalmon and Carmi Korine, "The Bats of Israel: Conservationists Make Steady Progress," *BATS Magazine* 21 (2003) 6–7. See also Yoram Yom-Tov and Ronen Kadmon, "Analysis of the Distribution of Insectivorous Bats in Israel," *Diversity and Distribution* 4 (1998) 63–70.

15 Frank Moore Cross mentions the host of bats that fluttered through the crevices of Qumran cave 11 at dawn and dusk, as well as the millennial deposits of bat guano that still sealed the Iron Age and Chalcolithic levels when the archaeologists halted the unauthorized excavation of the site by Taʿâmireh tribesmen (Cross, *The Ancient Library of Qumran and*

Modern Biblical Studies [Garden City, NY: Doubleday, 1961] 30). Precise information on the type of fill in each cave is hard to come by, since many of the caves were basically cleaned out before professional archaeologists reached them, but animal droppings by small wild animals, bats, or birds are mentioned in connection with several of the caves: see Barthélemy and Milik, *Qumran Cave I,* 6–7; Benoit et al., *Murabbaʿat,* 9–10. In Qumran cave 4, animal urine and an undefined meter of deposit built up over the Samuel scroll (F. M. Cross, D. W. Parry, R. J. Saley, and E. Ulrich, *Qumran Cave 4.XII: 1–2 Samuel* (DJD 17; Oxford: Clarendon, 2005] 2 n. 3, 3.

16 So Wildberger, 1:95; Otto Kaiser, *Der Prophet Jesaja: Kapital 1–12* (2nd ed.; ATD 17; Göttingen: Vandenhoeck & Ruprecht, 1963) 29; Jensen, 63.

ates one from God, when it takes precedence over God's commandments, one may be sure that an idol has been erected. Such idolatry may find expression in a campaign to promote a Star Wars military defense, but it may also find expression in an environmental campaign to save our forests from acid rain. It is not self-evident that it must be intrinsic to either.

Bibliography

Ackroyd, "Isaiah 2:1," 320–21.

Alonso Fontela, C., "Una breve nota marginal de Alphonsa de Smora sobre lahpor perot (Is 2,20)," *Sefarad* 52 (1992) 29–32.

Andersen, Francis I., and David Noel Freedman, "Excursus: The Relationship between Micah 4:1-5 and Isaiah 2:1-5," In *Micah: A New Translation with Introduction and Commentary* (AB 24E; New York: Doubleday, 2000) 413–27.

Asurmendi, Jesús María, *La guerra siro-efraimita: Historia y profetas* (Institución San Jerónimo 13; Valencia: Institución San Jerónimo para la Investigación Biblica, 1982).

Baker, D. W., "Tarshish (Place)," *ABD* 6:331–33.

Barré, Michael L., "A Rhetorical-Critical Study of Isaiah 2:12-17," *CBQ* 65 (2003) 503–21.

Barth, Hermann, *Die Jesaja-Worte in der Josiazeit: Israel und Asshur als Thema einer Produktiven Neuinterpretation des Jesajaüberlieferung* (WMANT 48; Neukirchen-Vluyn: Neukirchener Verlag, 1977) 191–92.

Becker, Joachim, *Isaias: Der Prophet und sein Buch* (SBS 30; Stuttgart: Katholisches Bibelwerk, 1968) 46.

Begrich, Joachim, "Der syrisch-ephraimitische Krieg und seine weltpolitischen Zusammenhänge," *ZDMG* 83 (1929) 213–37; reprinted in *Gesammelte Studien zum Alten Testament* (Munich: C. Kaiser, Begrich, 1964) 99–120.

Bertholet, Alfred, *Die Stellung der Israeliten und der Juden zu den Fremden* (Freiburg: J. C. B. Mohr [Paul Siebeck], 1896).

Bertram, G, "'Hochmut' und verwandte Begriffe im griechischen und hebräischen Alten Testament," *WO* 3 (1964) 32–43.

Blenkinsopp, Joseph, "Fragments of Ancient Exegesis in an Isaian Poem (Jes 2:6-22)," *ZAW* 93 (1981) 51–62.

Bourke, J., "Le jour de Yahvé dans Joel," *RB* 66 (1959) 5–31, 191–212.

Buchanan, G. W., "Eschatology and the 'End of Days,'" *JNES* 20 (1961) 188–93.

Budde, K., "Verfasser und Stelle von Mi. 4:1-4 (Jes 2:2-4)," *ZDMG* 81 (1927) 152–58.

Cannawurf, E., "The Authenticity of Micah IV 1-4," *VT* 13 (1963) 26–33.

Cannon, W., "The Disarmament Passage in Isaiah II and Micah IV," *Theology* 24 (1930) 2–8.

Cathcart, Kevin J., "Kingship and the 'Day of YHWH' in Isaiah 2:6-22," *Herm* 125 (1978) 48–59.

Causse, A., "Le mythe de la nouvelle Jérusalem," *RHPR* 18 (1938) 377–414.

Cazelles, H. "Qui aurait visé, à l'origine, Isaïe ii 2-5," *VT* 30 (1980) 409–20.

Černý, Ladislav, *The Day of Yahweh and Some Relevant Problems* (Práce z vedeckých ústavů 53; V Praze: Nákl. Filosofické Fakulty Univ. Karlovy, 1948).

Clifford, Richard J., *The Cosmic Mountain in Canaan and the Old Testament* (HSM 4; Cambridge, MA: Harvard University Press, 1972).

Cohen, Raymond, and Raymond Westbrook, eds., *Isaiah's Vision of Peace in Biblical and Modern International Relations: Swords into Plowshares* (Culture and Religion in International Relations; New York: Palgrave Macmillan, 2008).

Davidson, R., "The Interpretation of Isaiah II 6ff.," *VT* 16 (1966) 1–7.

Day, John, "Where Was Tarshish?" in *Let Us Go up to Zion: Essays in Honour of H. G. M. Williamson on the Occasion of His Sixty-Fifth Birthday* (ed. Iain Provan and Mark J. Boda; VTSup 153; Leiden: Brill, 2012) 359–70.

De Bruin, W. M., "De afbakening van Jesaja 2:5 in het licht van de oude tekstgestuigzen," *NedTT* 56 (2002) 280–98.

Deissler, A., "Die Völkerwallfahrt zum Zion, Meditation über Jesaja 2,2-4," *BibLeb* 11 (1970) 295–99.

Deist, F. E., "Notes on the Structure of Isa. 2:2-22," *Theologia Evangelica* [Pretoria] 10 (1977) 1–6.

Delcor, M., "Sion, centre universel, Is 2,1-5," *AsSeign* 2 (1960) 6–11.

Donner, Herbert, *Israel unter den Völkern: Die Stellung der klassischen Propheten des 8. Jahrhunderts v. Chr. zur Aussenpolitik der Könige von Israel und Juda* (VTSup 11; Leiden: Brill, 1964).

Eggebrecht, G., "Die früheste Bedeutung und der Ursprung der Konzeption vom 'Tage Jahwes,'" *Theologische Versuche* 13 (1983) 41–56.

Eichrodt, Walther, "Die Hoffnung des ewigen Friedens im alten Israel," *BFT* 25 (1920) 36–38, 69–74.

Feuerhahn, Ronald, et al., "Homilitical Helps on LW Series A—Old Testament Readings," *Concordia Journal* 12 (1986) 221–36.

Garbini, G., "Tarsis e Gen 10,4," *BeO* 7 (1965) 13–19.

Garrido Roiz, J. P., "El problema de Tartessos en relación con la región onobense," in *Ommagio a Fernand Benoit* (Rivista di studi liguri 33; Bordighera: Museo Bicknell, 1967) 1:354–60.

Gelin, A., "Jours de Yahvé et jour de Yahvé," *LumVie* 11 (1953) 39–52.

Gosse, B., "Michée 4,1-5 et Isaïe 2,1-5 et les rédacteurs finaux du livre d'Isaïe," *ZAW* 105 (1993) 98–102.

Gray, J., "The Day of Yahweh in Cultic Experience and Eschatological Prospect," *SEÅ* 39 (1974) 12–16.

Gross, H., *Die Idee des ewigen und allgemeinen Weltfriedens im Alten Orient und im Alten Testament* (TThSt 7; Trier: Paulinus-Verlag, 1956).

Hinson, E. Glenn, "Disarmament of the Heart," *Faith and Mission* 4 (1986) 3–12.

Hoffmann, Hans Werner, *Die Intention der Verkündigung Jesajas* (BZAW 136; Berlin: de Gruyter, 1974) 107.

Hoffmann, Y., "The Day of the Lord as a Concept and a Term in the Prophetic Literature," *ZAW* 93 (1981) 37–50.

Høgenhaven, Jesper, *Gott und Volk bei Jesaja: Eine Untersuchung zur biblischen Theologie* (ATDan 24; Leiden: Brill, 1988) 109–11.

Holmgren, F. C., "Isaiah 2:105," *Int* 51 (1997) 61–65.

Hubbard, Robert L., "Jai alai, hermeneutics, and Isaianic Peace," in Marl Lau Branson and C. Rene Padilla, eds., *Conflict and Context: Hermeneutics in the Americas. A Report on the Context and Hermeneutics in the Americas Conference Sponsored by Theological Students Fellowship and the Latin American Theological Fraternity, Tlayacapan, Mexico, November 24–29* (Grand Rapids: Eerdmans, 1986) 185–204.

Irvine, *Isaiah, Ahaz.*

James, F., "Is There Pacifism in the Old Testament?" *ATR* 11 (1928) 224–232.

Jensen, *Use of tôrâ.*

Junker, H., "Sancta Civitas, Jerusalem Nova: Eine formkritische und überlieferungsgeschichtliche Studie zu Is. 2," in H. Gross, ed., *Ekklesia: Festschrift für M. Wehr* (TThSt 15; Trier: Paulinus-Verlag, 1962) 17–33.

Kapelrud, A. S., "Eschatology in the Book of Micah," *VT* 11 (1961) 392–405.

Kosmala, H., "At the End of Days," *ASTI* 2 (1963) 27–37.

———, "Form and Structure in Ancient Hebrew Poetry," *VT* 14 (1964) 423–45 [includes 2:2-3].

Kselman, John S., "A Note on Is 2:2," *VT* 25 (1975) 225–27.

Lefèvre, A., "L'expression 'En ce jour-là' dans le livre d'Isaïe," in *Melanges bibliques rédiges en l'honneur de André Robert* (Travaux de l'institut catholique de Paris 4; Paris: Bloud & Gay, 1957) 174–79.

Limburg, James, "Swords to Ploughshares: Texts and Contexts," in C. C. Broyles and C. A. Evans, eds., *Writing and Reading the Scroll of Isaiah: Studies of an Interpretive Tradition* (2 vols.; VTSup 70; Leiden: Brill, 1997) 2:279–93.

Lipiński, E., "*B'hrjt hjmjm* dans les textes préexiliqus," *VT* 20 (1970) 445–50.

Lohfink, Gerhard, "Schwerter zu Pflugscharen: die Rezeption von Jes 2,1-5 par Mi 4,1-5 in der Alten Kirche und im Neuen Testament," *TQ* 166 (1986) 184–209.

Loretz, Oswald, *Der Prolog des Jesaja-Buches (1,1–2,5): Ugaritologische und kolometrische Studien zum Jesaja-Buch* (UBL 1; Altenberge: CIS-Verlag, 1984) 63–83.

Magonet, J., "Isaiah's Mountain or the Shape of Things to Come," *Proof* 11 (1991) 175–81.

Martin-Achard, R., "Israël, peuple sacerdotal," *VC* 18 (1964) 11–28.

Marx, Alfred, "Esaïe 2:20, une signature karaïte?" *VT* 40 (1990) 232–37.

Meek, T. J., "Some Emendations in the Old Testament," *JBL* 48 (1929) 162–68.

Middlemas, Jill, "Ships and Other Seafaring Vessels in the Old Testament," In I. Provan and M. J. Boda, eds., *Let Us Go up to Zion: Essays in Honour of H. G. M. Williamson on the Occasion of his Sixty-Fifth Birthday* (VTSup 153; Leiden: Brill, 2012) 407–22.

Milgrom, Jacob, "Did Isaiah Prophesy during the Reign of Uzziah?" *VT* 14 (1964) 164–82.

Miller, John W., "Can We Hope for a New World Order?" *Conrad Grebel Review* 9 (1991) 309–14.

Mowinckel, Sigmund, "Jahves Dag," *NTT* 59 (1958) 1–56, 209–29.

Müller, Werner, *Die Heilige Stadt: Roma quadrata, himmlisches Jerusalem und die Mythe vom Weltnabel* (Stuttgart: W. Kohlhammer, 1961).

Munch, P. A., *The Expression bajjôm hahu': Is It an Eschatological Terminus Technicus?* (Avhandlinger utgitt av det Norske videnskaps akademi i Oslo. II Hist.-filos. klasse 1936/2; Oslo: J. Dybwad, 1936).

Napier, B. D., "Isaiah and the Isaian," In *Volume du congrès: Genève 1965* (VTSup 15; Leiden: Brill, 1966) 240–51.

Navarra, L., "[Is 2,2s: 60,1] In margine a due citazioni di Isaia nell'Homilia in laudem Ecclesiae di Leandro di Siviglia," *SMSR* 53 (1987) 199–204.

Neveu, L., "Isaie 2,6-22: Le jour de Yhwh," In *La vie de la Parole: De l'Ancien au Nouveau Testament. Études de exégèse et d'herméneutique bibliques offertes à Pierre Grelot* (Paris: Desclée, 1987) 129–38.

Oded, B., "The Historical Background of the Syro-Ephraimitic War Reconsidered," *CBQ* 34 (1972) 153–65.

Ollenburger, Ben C., *Zion, the City of the Great King: A Theological Symbol of the Jerusalem Cult* (JSOTSup 41; Sheffield: JSOT Press, 1987) 110–12.

Pakozdy, L. M. von, "Jes. 2:2ff.: Geschichte–Utopie–Verkündigung," in K. Scharf, ed., *Vom Herrengeheimnis der Wahrheit: Festschrift für Heinrich Vogel* (Berlin: Lettner-Verlag, 1962) 416–26.

Pettinato, G., "Is. 2,7 e il culto del sole in Guida nel sec. VIII av. Cr," *OrAnt* 4 (1965) 1–30.

Rad, Gerhard von, "The Origin of the Concept of the Day of Yahweh," *JSS* 4 (1959) 97–108.

———, "Die Stadt auf dem Berge," *EvT* 8 (1948) 439–47. Eng. trans., "The City on a Hill," in *The Problem of the Hexateuch and Other Essays* (trans. E. W. Trueman Dicken; New York: McGraw-Hill, 1966) 232–42.

Rinaldi, G., "Il nome ʾaharît," *BeO* 7 (1965) 60.

Roberts, J. J. M., "Double Entendre in First Isaiah," *CBQ* 54 (1992) 39–48.

———, "The End of War in the Zion Tradition: The Imperialistic Background of an Old Testament Vision of Worldwide Peace," in M. Daniel Carroll R. and Jacqueline E. Lapsely, eds., *Character Ethics and the Old Testament: Moral Dimensions of Scripture* (Louisville: Westminster John Knox, 2007) 119–28.

———, "Isaiah 2 and the Prophet's Message to the North," *JQR* 75 (1985) 290–308.

Rogers, J. S., "An Allusion to Coronation in Isaiah 2:6," *CBQ* 51 (1989) 232–36.

Rohland, E., "Die Bedeutung der Erwählungstraditionen Israels für die Eschatologie der alttestamentlichen Propheten" (PhD diss., Heidelberg, 1956).

Rudman, D., "Zechariah 8:20-22 & Isaiah 2:2-4// Micah 4:2-3: A Study in Intertextuality," *BN* 107/108 (2001) 50–54.

Schmid, H. H., *Šalôm: Frieden im Alten Orient und im Alten Testament* (SBS 51; Stuttgart: KBW, 1971).

Schottroff, Luise, and Willy Schottroff, "Die Friedensfeier: Das Prophetenwort von der Umwandlung von Schwertern zu Pflugscharen (Jes 2:2-5/ Mic 4:1-5)," in Schottroff and Schottroff, *Die Parteilichkeit Gottes: Biblische Orientierung auf der Suche nach Frieden und Gerechtigkeit* (Munich: Kaiser, 1984) 78–102.

Schreiner, J., "Das Ende der Tage," *BibLeb* 5 (1964) 180–94.

———, *Sion–Jerusalem, Jahwes Königssitz: Theologie der heiligen Stadt im Alten Testament* (Munich: Kösel, 1963).

Schunck, K. D., "Strukturlinien in der Entwicklung der Vorstellung vom 'Tag Jahwes,'" *VT* 14 (1964) 319–30.

Seybold, Klaus, "Die anthropologischen Beiträge aus Jesaja 2," *ZTK* 74 (1977) 401–15.

Shazar, Z., "The Direction and Purpose of Time: Isaiah's Vision of the 'End of Days,'" *Dor leDor* 3 (1975) 7–9.

Sheppard, Gerald T., "The Anti-Assyrian Redaction and the Canonical Context of Isaiah 1–39," *JBL* 104 (1985) 193–216.

Staerk, W., "Der Gebrauch der Wendung הימים באחרית im at. Kanon," *ZAW* 11 (1891) 247–53.

Stamm, J. J., "Der Weltfriede im Alten Testament," in J. J. Stamm and H. Bietenhard, eds., *Der Weltfriede im Alten und Neuen Testament* (Zurich: Zwingli, 1959) 7–63.

Stampfer, J., "On Translating Biblical Poetry (Isaiah Chapters 1 and 2:1-4)," *Judaism* 14 (1965) 501–10.

Steck, O. H., *Friedensvorstellungen im alten Jerusalem: Psalmen, Jesaja, Deuterojesaja* (ThSt 111; Zurich: Theologischer Verlag, 1972).

———, "Jerusalemer Vorstellungen vom Frieden und ihre Abwandlungen in der Prophetie des Alten Israel," in Gerhard Liedke, ed., *Frieden–Bibel–Kirche* (Studien zur Friedensforschung 9; Munich: Kaiser, 1972) 75–95.

Stuhlmueller, Carroll, "The Prophetic Price for Peace," in John T. Pawlikowski and Donald Senior, eds., *Biblical and Theological Reflections on the Challenge of Peace* (Wilmington, DE: Glazier, 1984) 31–44.

Sweeney, *Isaiah 1–4*, 134–39.

———, "Micah's Debate with Isaiah," *JSOT* 93 (2001) 111–24.

Täckholm, U., "Neue Studien zum Taršiš-Tartessausproblem," *Opuscula Romana* 10 (1974) 41–58.

———, "Tarsis, Tartessos und die Säulen des Heracles," *Opuscula Romana* 5 (1965) 143–90.

Thomas, D. Winton, "Lost Hebrew Word in Isaiah 2:6," *JTS* 13 (1962) 323–24.

———, "Text of Jesaia 2:6 and the Word spq," *ZAW* 75 (1963) 88–90.

Vriezen, Th. C., *Jahwe en zijn stad: Rede gehouden in de Verenigde Vergadering van de beide Afdelingen der Koninklijke Nederlandse Akademie von Wetenschappen.* Amsterdam: Noord-Hollandsche Uitgeversmij, 1962.

Weiss, M., "The Origin of the 'Day of the Lord'— Reconsidered," *HUCA* 37 (1966) 29–72.

Wildberger, Hans, "Die Völkerwallfahrt zum Zion: Jes II 1-5," *VT* 7 (1957) 62–81.

———, "Jesaja 2:2-5," in G. Eichholz, ed., *Herr, tue meine Lippen auf* (2 vols.; Wuppertal: E. Müller, 1961) 2:97–105.

Willis, John T., "Isaiah 2:2-5 and the Psalms of Zion," in C. C. Boyles and C. A. Evans, eds., *Writing and Reading the Scroll of Isaiah: Studies of an Interpretive Tradition* (2 vols.; VTSup 70; Leiden: Brill, 1997) 1:295–316.

Wolff, Hans Walter, "Use of the Bible in Theology: A Case Study," *Evangelical Review of Theology* 11 (1987) 37–52.

———. "Schwerter zu Pflugscharen: Missbrauch eines prophetenwortes? Praktische Fragen und exegetische Klärungen zu Joel 4,9-12, Jes 2,2-5 und Mic 4,1-5," *EvT* 44 (1984) 280–92.

Zimmerli, Walther, "Jesaja 2,2-5," in *Festschrift L. Klein* (Jerusalem: Dormition Abbey, 1986) 49–54.

3

1/ For behold the Lord, Yahweh of hosts,
    Is about to remove from Jerusalem[a] and from Judah[a]
Stay and support,
    [Every[b] stay of bread and every[b] stay of water.][c]

2/ Strong man[d] and warrior,
    Judge[e] and prophet,
        And diviner and elder.

3/ Commander of fifty and dignitary,
    Counselor and skilled magician,[f] and expert enchanter.

4/ And I will make boys their officials,
    And the capricious[g] shall rule over them.

5/ So the people shall oppress each other,
    Every one against his neighbor;
The youth shall attack the elder,
    And the despised shall attack the honorable.

6/ If a man shall seize his brother,
    In the house of his father, (saying):
"You have a cloak. You shall be our leader,
    And this ruin[h] shall be under your hand,[i]"

7/ The other will cry out on that day saying:
"I will not be a bandager of wounds;
In my house there is neither food nor a cloak.[j]
    You will not make[k] me leader of the people."

8/ For Jerusalem has stumbled,
    And Judah has fallen,[l]
Because their tongue and their deeds are against[m] Yahweh,
    Rebelling before the eyes[n] of his glory.

9/ The acknowledgement on their face[o] testifies against them;
    They proclaim their sin[p] like Sodom, they do not hide it.
Woe to them!
    For they have brought evil upon themselves.

10/ Happy[q] the righteous person,[r] for it shall be good,
    For[s] the fruit of their deeds they shall eat.

11/ Woe to the wicked person, for[t] it shall be bad,
    For[u] what his hands have done shall be done[v] to him.

12/ O my people[w]—whose oppressor[x] is a child,[y]
    Over whom women[z] rule—
O my people, your leaders[*a] are misleaders;
    The course of your paths they have confused.

13/ Yahweh is about to rise[*b] for the lawsuit,
    He is about to stand[*b] to judge his people.[*c]

14/ Yahweh shall enter into judgment
    With the elders of his people and its officials:
"You are the ones who have devoured the vineyard;
    The goods stolen from the poor are in your houses.

15/ What is with you that you crush my people,
    That you grind the face of the poor?"
Says my Lord, Yahweh of Hosts.[*d]

Textual Notes

a   LXX reverses the order of Jerusalem and Judah to match the unusual order of these two terms in 1:1 and 2:1.

b   LXX omits the כל (kōl) "all."

c   For this line as a late gloss, see the commentary below.

d   LXX has a double translation of גבור (gibbôr), "strong man": γίγαντα καὶ ἰσχύοντα, "giant and strong man."

e   LXX adds the conjunction ו (wĕ), "and," before שׁפֵט (šôpēṭ), "judge."

f   The versions, followed by JPS, derive חֲרָשִׁים (ḥărāšîm) from חָרָשׁ (ḥārāš), "artisan," and translate in ways similar to JPS's "skilled artisan." Thus, LXX has σοφὸν ἀρχιτέκτονα; Syr. has wḥkym ngrʾ, "wisest of carpenters"; and Vg. has sapientem de architectis. The parallel with וּנְבוֹן לָחַשׁ (ûnĕbôn lāḥaš), "and expert enchanter," however, suggests that one derive חֲרָשִׁים (ḥărāšîm) from a noun חֶרֶשׁ (ḥereš), "magic art, magic potion," cognate with Aramaic חֲרָשׁ (ḥārāš), "sorcerer," חֶרְשִׁין (ḥeršîn) "sorcery"; with Syr. ḥaraš, "magician, enchanter, sorcerer," ḥaršāʾ or ḥeršāʾ, "enchantment, incantation, magic"; and with Ethiopic ḥaras, "magic."

g   The abstract noun תַּעֲלוּלִים (taʿălûlîm), "willfulness, capriciousness, wantonness," is being used here as an abstract for the concrete, which is common in Hebrew poetry when the abstract is in parallel with a concrete term (Isa 3:25; 60:17; Ps 36:12).[1] There seems to be a wordplay between this term and the noun עוֹלְלִים (ʿôlĕlîm), "children," the singular of which (עוֹלֵל, ʿôlēl, "child") probably should be read in v. 12. The thought seems to be that Judah's rulers will be as capricious as small children. Some modern translations actually render תַּעֲלוּלִים as "babes" (JPS, NRSV). As pointed out to me by Peter Machinist (private communication), there may also be a wordplay on נְעָרִים (nĕʿārîm), "boys" or "servants/officials," but the primary meaning here must stress the youth and inexperience of children as the contrast between hannaʿar, "the youth," and the hazzāqēn, "the old man, elder" in v. 5 indicates.

h   LXX has καὶ τὸ βρῶμά τὸ ἐμόν, "and let my food be under you," for MT's וְהַמַּכְשֵׁלָה הַזֹּאת (wĕhammakšēlâ hazzōʾt), "and this ruin." Wildberger (1:117) suggests that LXX's translation, "and let my food be under you," presupposes וּמַאֲכַלְתִּי (ûmaʾăkaltî), "and my food," but that it is just a misreading of the MT. I agree, though LXX may have been led to this misreading by the occurrence of לֶחֶם (leḥem), "food," in v. 7, which suggests that the man wanted his chosen, supposedly wealthy kinsman, to care for his needs.

i   1QIsaᵃ and some manuscripts read the plural ידיך (yādêkā), "your hands."

j   Wildberger (1:117) argues that וְאֵין שִׂמְלָה (wĕʾên śimlâ), "nor a cloak," is a "foolish addition" to the text, since it is already known from v. 6 that the man had a cloak. The expression does make for a rather long poetic line, but v. 6 tells us only what the man's kinsman claimed, not whether he was telling the truth. The denial is perfectly reasonable in the context and provides no independent reason for emending the text.

k   LXX mistakenly repeats the לֹא־אֶהְיֶה (lōʾ-ʾehyê, οὐκ ἔσομαι), "I will not be," of the first half of the verse in place of MT's לֹא תְשִׂימֵנִי (lōʾ tĕśîmēnî), "you will not place/make me."

l   1QIsaᵃ has the feminine נפלה (nāpĕlâ), "she fell," for MT's נָפַל (nāpāl), "he fell." The subject is יְהוּדָה (yĕhûdâ), "Judah," which is construed as masculine when it refers to the people of Judah (Hos. 4:15; Jer 2:28) but as feminine when it refers to the land or territory of Judah (Isa 7:6; Jer 23:6).

m   1QIsaᵃ has על (ʿal) "against," for MT אֶל (ʾel), "to," and the Qumran reading is probably original.

n   1QIsaᵃ has the normal orthography עיני (ʿênê), "eyes of," in place of the MT's defective עֲנֵי (ʿênê). The MT orthography could simply reflect the earlier orthographic practice that did not use matres lectionis for contracted diphthongs, or it might signal a textual corruption, particularly since the expression,

"eyes of his glory," is unique and unusual in meaning. The MT reading clearly lies behind the LXX and the Syriac, both of which had difficulty with this line. LXX apparently read ענו and understood it as a passive form of the verb ענה (ʿānâ), "to humble," but LXX butchers the text so badly that it cannot be taken seriously as the original reading: καὶ αἱ γλῶσσαι αὐτῶν μετὰ ἀνομίας, τὰ πρὸς κύριον ἀπειθοῦντες· διότι νῦν ἐταπεινώθη ἡ δόξα αὐτῶν, "and their tongues are with lawlessness, disobeying the matters relating to the Lord, therefore their glory has now been humbled." Syr. apparently read ענן כבודו (ʿānan kĕbôdô; wlʿnnʾ dʾyqrh), "and before the cloud of his glory." The radical solution of simply deleting עני has nothing to commend it, and even the more reasonable emendations such as פְּנֵי כְבוֹדוֹ (pĕnê kĕbôdô), "the face of his glory," פִּי כְבוֹדוֹ (pî kĕbôdô), "the mouth (word) of his glory," and עִם כְּבֹדוֹ (ʿim kĕbôdô), "against his glory," are ultimately not compelling. The phrase is unusual but understandable.

o   1QIsaᵃ has the feminine plural form הכרות (hakkārôt) in place of MT's feminine singular הַכָּרַת (hakkārat). The meaning of the idiom הַכָּרַת פְּנֵיהֶם (hakkārat pĕnêhem) is disputed. The verbal idiom הִכִּיר פָּנִים (hakkîr pānîm), in which פנים is the direct object, means "to show partiality to someone" in judgment (literally, "to recognize the face"; Deut 1:17; 16:19; Prov 24:23; 28:21), and that is the sense that the Syr. and Tg. give to this passage. But if "their face" is an objective genitive in the construct chain הַכָּרַת פְּנֵיהֶם (hakkārat pĕnêhem), "the recognition of their face," it cannot be the subject of the verbal action, "their recognition of someone else's face, that is, their showing of partiality." Thus, it is better to render "the acknowledgment on their face" or "the admission on their face," which fits the context very nicely, since the preceding verse speaks of their blatant rebellion against God, and the following line speaks of the openness with which they sin. Some such rendering is supported by LXX, which has ἡ αἰσχύνη τοῦ προσώπου αὐτῶν, "the shame of their face," and by Vg.'s agnitio vultus eorum, "the admission of their face."

p   Syr. and Tg. read the plural, "their sins."

q   Reading אַשְׁרֵי (ʾašrê), "blessed is," in place of MT's masculine plural imperative אִמְרוּ (ʾimrû), "speak!" The exclamation אַשְׁרֵי (ʾašrê) requires no preposition before the noun צַדִּיק (ṣaddîq), "the righteous one," unlike the verb, which usually requires the person addressed to be introduced by אל (ʾel), "to," or ל (lĕ) "to," which the corrector of 1QIsaᵃ adds above the line before צדיק. Syr. and Tg. both add the preposition in their translations. LXX has a double translation, which suggests a form of אסר (ʾāsar) "to bind," alongside אמרו, though it construes the beginning of v. 10 as a quotation of the wicked mentioned in v. 9: εἰπόντες Δήσωμεν τὸν δίκαιον, ὅτι δύσχρηστος ἡμῖν ἐστιν, "saying, 'Let us bind the righteous person, because he is useless to us.'"

---

1   See the discussion in Wilfred G. E. Watson, *Classical Hebrew Poetry: A Guide to Its Techniques* (corrected ed.; London: T&T Clark, 2005) 314, §11.10.

r The nominalized adjective צַדִּיק (ṣaddîq), "the righteous one," is masculine singular, though MT switches to the plural in the last half of the verse. Tg. pluralizes all the forms.

s MT and 1QIsaᵃ read the conjunction כִּי (kî), "because," here, and they are supported by the Syr., Tg., and Vg. LXX's rendering in v. 11 with κατά, "according to," does not justify emending these forms to the preposition כְּ (kě).

t It is likely that a כִּי (kî), "because," has dropped out of the text before רָע (rāᶜ), "it is bad." Given the number of times the word occurs in these two verses, the accidental loss of one כִּי would not be surprising. The missing word is not preserved in any of the versions, however, unless one assumes that the Vg.'s *in malum*, represents a reading בְּרָע (běrāᶜ), "into evil,"[2] corrupted from כְּרָע (kěrāᶜ) "as evil," itself corrupted from the original כִּי רָע (kî rāᶜ) "because it is bad."

u LXX rendering with κατά, "according to," does not justify emending this form to the preposition כְּ (kě).

v For MT כִּי־גְמוּל יָדָיו יֵעָשֶׂה לּוֹ (kî-gěmûl yādāyw yēᶜāśeh lô) "for the recompense of his hands/what his hands have done, will be done to him," 1QIsaᵃ has כיא גמול ידו ישוב לוא (kîᵃ gěmûl yādô yāšûb lô), "for the recompense of his hand/what his hand has done, will return to him."

w Reading עַמִּי (ᶜammî), "O my people," as a vocative like the following עַמִּי. The following third masculine singular suffixes are normal in unmarked relative clauses following a vocative, as Delbert Hillers has shown.[3]

x Reading either the singular participle with third masculine singular suffix followed by the enclitic *mem* נֹגְשׂוֹ־ם (nōgěśô-m), "his oppressor," or the singular participle with third masculine plural suffix נֹגְשָׂם (nōgěśām), "their oppressor." This presupposes that the initial *mem* on the following מְעוֹלֵל (měᶜôlēl) originally went with the preceding word. MT's plural נֹגְשָׂיו (nōgěśāyw), "his oppressors," is supported by Syr., Tg., and Vg. LXX has the plural, but a second person plural suffix. 1QIsaᵃ has the singular נגשׂו (nōgěśô), "his oppressor."

y MT's מְעוֹלֵל (měᶜôlēl) is a crux. The versions take it as a denominative verb in the *polel* meaning "to glean," but this is syntactically difficult following the plural subject that they read. G. R. Driver analyzes the verb as a *polel* from עוּל (ᶜāwal), "to deviate from justice," but to solve the syntactical problem he attaches the initial *mem* to the preceding word and adds a plural ending to the verb: either נֹגְשֵׂימוֹ עֹלֵלוּ (nōgěśêmô ᶜōlēlû) "their oppressors perverted justice," or נֹגְשִׂים עֹלֵלוּ (nōgěśîm ᶜōlēlû), "the oppressors perverted justice."[4] Wildberger (1:129) is also compelled to add a plural ending to the verb, reading either נגשׂיו מעוללים (nōgěśāyw měᶜōlělîm) or נגשׂיו עוללו (nōgěśāyw ᶜōlělû), "his oppressors are slave drivers." BDB took the form as a denominative verb from עוֹלֵל (ᶜôlēl), "child," meaning "to act like a child," but it is easier simply to remove the initial *mem* and then read the word as the noun עוֹלֵל (ᶜôlēl), "child." The thought is similar to that of v. 4, and it may be an allusion to Ahaz, who may have been only sixteen when he came to the throne.[5]

z The ancient versions and the modern commentators who derive מעולל from a verb meaning "to glean" or "to oppress" repoint MT's נָשִׁים (nāšîm), "women," to נֹשִׁים (nōšîm), "creditors." If the reading עוֹלֵל, "child," is correct, however, then the MT's "women" should be retained.

*a The versions erroneously derive this participle from אשׁר II, "to pronounce happy." Cf. the parallel in 9:15. 1QIsaᵃ's משׁריך is simply a mistake for מְאַשְּׁרֶיךָ (měᵃššěrêkā), "your leaders."

*b Both of these participles indicate God's imminent action in the near future.

*c MT has עַמִּים (ᶜammîm), "peoples," but LXX has τὸν λαὸν αὐτοῦ, "his people," and Syr. follows LXX. The context deals with God's judgment of his own people, not of the foreign nations, so the simple plural is awkward. Either one should read עַמֹּ־ם (ᶜammô-m), "his people," assuming an enclitic *mem* on the suffixed noun,[6] or simply correct to עַמּוֹ (ᶜammô), "his people."

*d LXX omits this whole line, but it is probably original. Syr. seems to be lacking אדני (ᵃdōnāy), "my Lord," and the corrector of 1QIsaᵃ has inserted it above the line, but it is reflected in Vg. and Tg., and it is as easy to explain the secondary loss of אדני as it is to explain its secondary insertion. Since by the time of the versions, יהוה and אדני were treated as equivalent terms, the presence of both terms together created a problem for the translator. Syr. renders both terms in Isa 7:7; 22:12, 14; 25:8; 28:16 but omits one in Isa 10:23, 24; 22:15; 28:22.

---

2 This accusative rendering (*in malum*) of בְּרָע (běrāᶜ) is found in the Vg. of Prov 13:17, and for בְּרָעָה (běrāᶜâ) in Prov 17:20; 24:16; 28:14.

3 Delbert R. Hillers, "Hoy and Hoy Oracles: A Neglected Syntactic Aspect," in Carol L. Meyers and M. O'Connor, eds., *The Word of the Lord Shall Go Forth: Essays in Honor of David Noel Freedman in Celebration of His Sixtieth Birthday* (ASOR Special Volumes Series 1; Winona Lake, IN: Eisenbrauns, 1983) 185–88.

4 Driver, "Linguistic and Textual Problems," 38.

5 According to 2 Kgs 16:2, Ahaz was twenty years old when he became king, and he ruled sixteen years in Jerusalem. Since Ahaz became king in 735 and ruled until 715 (2 Kgs 18:13), however, it is clear that Ahaz ruled for twenty years, not sixteen, so there is a good possibility that these numbers have simply been reversed in textual transmission. For the complicated and disputed chronological issues involved, see Edwin R. Thiele, *The Mysterious Numbers of the Hebrew Kings* (Grand Rapids: Eerdmans, 1965) 127–40, and my detailed discussion in this commentary at Isa 14:28-32 and the earlier literature cited there.

6 H. D. Hummel, "Enclitic *Mem* in Early Northwest Semitic, Especially Hebrew," *JBL* 76 (1957) 100.

Commentary

This oracle may be divided into three parts: (1) the break-down of Judean society (vv. 1-9); (2) a wisdom saying (vv. 10-11); and (3) an indictment of Judah's leadership (vv. 12-15). Many scholars break the section into several different oracles, either following these subdivisions or suggesting alternate divisions (Wildberger, 1:116–34: 3:1-11; 3:12; 3:13-15; Duhm, 22–26: 3:1-12; 3:13-15; Blenkinsopp, 198–200: 3:1-5; 3:6-7; 3:8-12; 3:13-15; Kaiser, *Jesaja 1–12*, 31–36: 3:1-9; 3:9b-11; 3:12-15), but while there are transitions in thought, there are no clearcut breaks that demand the beginning of a new prophetic speech (so also Marti, 35–42; and Hayes and Irvine, 87–93). If several different oracles have been fused in the process of literary composition, it has been done so well that the seams are largely obscured. It is difficult to date the material; a date early in the reign of Ahaz would fit, but a date late in the reign of Hezekiah might also be possible.

The opening "for" links this oracle with the preceding 2:22. Do not put your trust in men, because God is about to remove all those classes of men that one traditionally relied on in ancient Israelite society. The thought is consistent with the main theme of the preceding oracle, and it makes 2:22 a nice hinge, fitting equally with both the preceding and following material. Nonetheless, this "for" is probably an editorial link added in the process of literary composition to connect two originally separate oracles.

The epithets applied to God in this verse, literally, "the Lord, Yahweh of hosts," underscore his rulership. He is in charge, and he will soon remove from Jerusalem and Judah those human props necessary to a functional society. The phrase "the whole stay of bread and the whole stay of water" suggests that Yahweh will strip Jerusalem of food and water, a judgment that may imply the deprivation of siege, but this appears to be a late gloss, as noted above, influenced by Ezekiel's related use of a synonymous word meaning "staff" (Ezek 4:16). It appears

to misinterpret the original point of the oracle, since the list beginning in v. 2 identifies the stay and prop of Jerusalem and Judah not with bread and water but with their human leaders. Isaiah's point is not that Jerusalem will suffer famine and thirst but that the traditional supports for an ordered society provided by different classes of social leadership will soon be gone. One should note that the list contains perfectly respectable professions as well as some of the various types of practitioners of magic proscribed by Deuteronomistic law.

In place of this well-ordered society, Yahweh threatens Jerusalem and Judah with social chaos, symbolized by his giving them mere children for rulers. The result will be a bitter internal struggle to get ahead in which respected elders will suffer the arrogant abuse of young scoundrels, a horrifying prospect for any traditional society. Verses 6-7 continue the picture of social chaos begun in the preceding verses. Things will become so bad that no one will willingly accept a leadership role in his clan. The process envisioned shows how desperate the situation will become. One will be chosen to head the clan simply because he is the only one left with a mantle, but the nominee will deny the claim and refuse the office. A clan leader had certain responsibilities to the clan,[7] and in the imminent social chaos that would soon strip the position of its privileges when the economic collapse would leave everyone struggling just to survive, no one will want the added burden of "healing" the clan's wounds.

Both verbs that describe the nation's collapse in v. 8 are in the perfect tense, but this is probably the so-called prophetic perfect, the past tense used to underscore the certainty of the judgment proclaimed for the near future. It is not until the last half of v. 8 that the prophet finally begins to explain why Yahweh is going to do this to Judah. It is because they have rebelled against Yahweh in both speech and deeds. "The eyes of his glory" is a difficult phrase, but the meaning seems to be that they impudently defy God to his face. Their impudent, impenitent look when confronted with their sin testifies

---

7   See Philip J. King and Lawrence E. Stager, *Life in Biblical Israel* (Library of Ancient Israel; Louisville: Westminster John Knox, 2001) 36–61; H. Reviv, *The Elders in Ancient Israel: A Study of a Biblical Institution* (Jerusalem: Magnes Press, 1989); Timothy M. Willis, *The Elders of the City: A Study of the Elders-Laws in Deuteronomy* (SBLMS 55; Atlanta: Society of Biblical Literature, 2001); and my "Bearers of the Polity: Isaiah of Jerusalem's View of the Eight-Century Judean Society," in John T. Strong and Steven S. Tuell, eds., *Constituting the Community: Studies on the Polity of Ancient Israel in Honor of S. Dean McBride, Jr.* (Winona Lake, IN: Eisenbrauns, 2005) 145–52.

against them, since they make no attempt to cover up or deny their actions. Like Sodom, they openly boast of their wickedness. Thus, the coming judgment is something they have brought on themselves. The implication is that Judah is on trial and too arrogant to humor God by putting up a defense.

Verses 10-11 represent a slight correction to v. 9. The indiscriminate condemnation of all the inhabitants of Jerusalem and Judah in v. 9 is nuanced in these verses by drawing a sharp distinction between the righteous and the wicked. This is done in language that is at home in the wisdom tradition, and many scholars regard these verses as a later intrusion by a wisdom writer (Wildberger, 1:126–27; Kaiser, 17, 34). Isaiah was influenced by the wisdom tradition, however, and since he had spoken of the impending judgment as evil that the people had brought on themselves, he may have felt it necessary to separate the righteous, whose deeds did not deserve punishment, from the wicked. Isaiah's view of Yahweh's refining judgment on Jerusalem presupposes the deliverance of the righteous remnant, so these verses are not incompatible with the prophet's theology. As in Isa 1:19-20, both the righteous and the wicked will be rewarded according to their deeds, but it will be good for the righteous and bad for the wicked.

Verse 12 directly addresses the people as a whole. The first "my people" should be read as a vocative, just as the second. Isaiah's first remark is a parenthetical comment specifying in a disparaging way those who were actually governing Judah already. In v. 4 Isaiah had threatened Judah with infantile rule. Now he points out that this is not just a threat for the future; the judgment has already begun. The comment might be taken to indicate a date early in the reign of Ahaz; as we have seen, when possibly only a teenager, he was still heavily influenced by the queen mother and the royal counselors. At any rate, it disparages the king as not behaving in a manly fashion and assuming his responsibilities. The choice of the word "oppressor" for "ruler" underscores his rule as misrule, but the text goes on to denigrate the king's manhood by implying that his harem rules the country, that the king is not even lord in his own house. Such a comment would cut to the quick in an ancient society as patriarchal as Judah's, and it must have infuriated the king.

Nonetheless, Isaiah, seemingly unperturbed by the impact of his sharp words, broadens his attack in the second half of v. 12 to include the real powers behind the throne. Judah's leaders lead astray. There may be a double entendre in the word בִּלֵּעוּ (billēʿû), translated "have confused." The verb, perhaps from a separate root, also means "to swallow up," and it might suggest the character of the leaders' misrule as involving economic exploitation of the people. That would fit what is said in vv. 14-15. Those verses identify the culprits as the elders and high government officials, and their crime, whether through oppressive taxation, unjust expropriation, or the insistent demand for bribes (1:23), is the oppression of the poor. Note Isaiah's use of "vineyard" here as a metaphor for God's people, a metaphor that will recur several times in Isaiah (5:1-7; 27:2). The leaders who should have kept the vineyard have devastated it instead.

The unusual placement of the judgment scene in vv. 13-15, which portrays Yahweh as standing to render judgment (Isa 3:13-14a; cf. Ps 82:1), after the announcement of judgment has already been given (Isa 3:1-8), requires some comment. This peculiar order might be the result of editorial rearrangement when the material was fitted into the larger literary context. The secondary link with 2:22 has already been mentioned, and one should also note the way v. 15, which questions the arrogant and oppressive male leadership, leads into and is nicely balanced by the following judgment on the privileged women of Zion (3:16—4:1). On the other hand, Isaiah may have wanted to get the threatened judgment in first so that he could end with a question (v. 15)—a question that would force Judah's leaders to reflect on the folly of their behavior. Why were they crushing God's people and grinding the face of the poor? This foolish abuse of their offices would destroy the society that gave meaning to those offices and thus undercut their own basis for elevated status (cf. Isa 5:8). Any appetite, if not held in check, may destroy the very possibility for its own fulfillment, and if Isaiah could force Judah's leaders to reflect on that fact, perhaps, just perhaps, they might repent.

Bibliography

Bahbout, S., "Sull' interpretazione des vv. 10-11 del cap III di Isaia," *AnnStEbr* 1 (1963) 23–26.

Boer, P. A. H. de, "The Counselor," in M. Noth and D. Winton Thomas, eds., *Wisdom in Israel and the Ancient Near East: Presented to Professor Harold Henry Rowley by the Society for Old Testament Study in Association with the Editorial Board of Vetus Testamentum, in Celebration of His Sixty-fifth Birthday, 24 March 1955* (VTSup 3; Leiden: Brill, 1960) 42–71.

Borowski, W., "Ciemiţiehţzay zostanaţ. ukarani (Iz 3,1-15) [Les oppresseurs seront punis]." *Ruch Biblijny i Liturgiczny* 25 (1972) 242–48.

Chaney, M. L., "Class, Gender, and Age in the Composition and Textual Transmission of Isaiah 3:12-15," in *SBL Abstracts* (Atlanta: Society of Biblical Literature, 1994) 227.

Dearman, J. Andrew, *Property Rights in the Eighth-Century Prophets: The Conflict and Its Background* (SBLDS 106; Atlanta: Scholars Press, 1981).

DeRoche, Michel, "Yahweh's *rib* against Israel: A Reassessment of the So-Called 'Prophetic Lawsuit' in the Preexilic Prophets," *JBL* 102 (1983) 563–74.

Gamoran, H., "The Biblical Law against Loans on Interest," *JNES* 30 (1971) 127–34.

Gemser, B., "The *rib*- or Controversy-Pattern in Hebrew Mentality," in M. Noth and D. Winton Thomas, eds., *Wisdom in Israel and the Ancient Near East: Presented to Professor Harold Henry Rowley by the Society for Old Testament Study in Association with the Editorial Board of Vetus Testamentum, in Celebration of His Sixty-fifth Birthday, 24 March 1955* (VTSup 3; Leiden: Brill, 1960) 120–37.

Gnuse, R., *You Shall Not Steal: Community and Property in the Biblical Tradition* (Maryknoll, NY: Orbis Books, 1985).

Hesse, F., "Wurzelt die prophetische Gerichtsrede im israelitischen Kult?" *ZAW* 65 (1953) 45–53.

Hoffmann, Hans Werner, *Die Intention der Verkündigung Jesajas* (BZAW 136; Berlin: de Gruyter, 1974).

Holladay, William L., "Isa. III 10-11: An Archaic Wisdom Passage," *VT* 18 (1968) 481–87.

Horst, Friedrich. *Gottes Recht: Gesammelte Studien zum Recht im Alten Testament* (TB 12; Munich: C. Kaiser, 1961) 130 n. 315.

Köhler, Ludwig, "Der Stab des Brotes," in *Kleine Lichter: Fünfzig Bibelstellen erklärt* (Zwingli-Bücherei 47; Zurich: Zwingli, 1945) 25–27.

McKenzie, John L., "The Elders of the Old Testament," *Bib* 40 (1959) 522–40.

Neufeld, E., "The Prohibitions against Loans at Interest in Ancient Hebrew Laws," *HUCA* 26 (1955) 355–412.

Nielsen, Kirsten, *Yahweh as Prosecutor and Judge: An Investigation of the Prophetic Lawsuit (Rîb-Pattern)* (JSOTSup 9; Sheffield: Department of Biblical Studies, University of Sheffield, 1978) 29–32.

Platt, E. E., "Jewelry in Bible Times and the Catalog of Isa 3:18-23," *AUSS* 17 (1979) 71–81, 189–201.

Ploeg, J. van der, "Les anciens dans l'Ancien Testament," in Heinrich Gross and Franz Mussner, eds., *Lex tua veritas: Festschrift für Hubert Junker zur Vollendung des siebzigsten Lebensjahres am 8. August 1961, dargeboten von Kollegen, Freunden und Schülern* (Trier: Paulinus-Verlag, 1961) 175–91.

Saggs, H. W. F. "'External Souls' in the Old Testament," *JSS* 19 (1974) 1–12.

Schedl, C., "Rufer des Heils in heilloser Zeit (Is 3,1-12)," *TGl* 16 (1972) 92–98.

Stade, B., "Zu Jes 3:1,17,24. 5:1,8,12-14,16. 9:7-20. 10:26," *ZAW* 26 (1906) 129–41.

Stegmüller, F., "Prudentem eloquii mystici: Zur Geschichte der Auslegung von Is 3,3," in Leo Scheffczyk, Werner Dettloff, and Richard Heinzmann, eds., *Wahrheit und Verkündigung: Michael Schmaus zum 70. Geburtstag* (Munich: Paderborn; Vienna: Schöningh, 1967) 599–618.

Vaux, Roland de, *Ancient Israel: Its Life and Institutions* (trans. John McHugh; London: Darton, Longman & Todd, 1961).

Weil, H. M., "Exégèse d'Isaïe III,1-15," *RB* 49 (1940) 76–85.

Yalon, C. H., "Zu Jes 3,12 und 4,5," *BetM* 12 (1966) 3–5.

3

16/ Yahweh said,[a]
"Because the daughters of Zion are haughty
And walk with outstretched[b] necks,
Eyes ogling suggestively,
And trip along with mincing[c] steps,
Skipping with their feet"—

17/ My Lord[d] will thin (the hair on) the scalps[e] of the daughters of Zion,
And Yahweh[f] will lay bare their foreheads.

18/ On that day Yahweh[g] will remove the beauty of the anklets,[h] and the sun-
discs,[i] and the crescents;

19/ the pendants,[j] and the bracelets, and the veils;

20/ the turbans,[k] and the armlets, and the breastbands,[l] and the charm-cases,
and the charms;

21/ the signet rings, and the nose rings;

22/ the festal robes, and the mantles, and the wraps,[m] and the handbags;

23/ and the diaphanous garments,[n] and the linen shirts, and the turbans, and
the shawls.

24/ And instead of perfume[o] there will be[p] festering decay;
and instead[q] of a belt,[r] a rope;
And instead[q] of elaborate braidwork, baldness;
and instead of a rich robe, a girding of sackcloth;
For instead of beauty, (there will be) shame.[s]

25/ Your men shall fall by the sword,
and your warriors[t] in battle.

26/ And her gates shall lament and mourn,
and cleaned out, she will sit on the ground.

4:1/ And seven women will take hold[u]
of one man in that day saying,
"Our own food we will eat,
and our own clothes we will wear;
Just let us be called by your name;
Take away our reproach."

Textual Notes

a Syr. omits וַיֹּאמֶר יְהוָה (wayyōᵓmer YHWH), "and Yahweh said," probably because of the speech formula at the end of the immediately preceding verse.

b 1QIsaᵃ has נטיות in place of MT's kĕtîb נְטוֹוֹת (nĕṭûwōt), "out-stretched." Both forms are defective over against MT's qĕrēᵓ נְטוּיֹת (nĕṭûyôt).

c 1QIsaᵃ appears to read the participle וטופפ (wĕṭôpēp) in place of MT's infinitive absolute וְטָפֹף (wĕṭāpōp), "and mincing/taking short steps."

d 1QIsaᵃ has אדוני for MT's אֲדֹנָי (ᵓădōnāy) "my Lord," but the corrector has put dots under it and above, making the correction to יהוה (YHWH). Since 1QIsaᵃ has ואדוני in the second line for MT's ויהוה, that would give the normal word order of the parallel terms: Yahweh//My Lord. Thus, it is tempting to follow the corrector of 1QIsaᵃ, but 4QIsaᵇ supports MT, and the textual transmission of the divine name and its substitutes is too confused to allow certainty in the matter. LXX reads ὁ θεός, "God."

e Following normal Hebrew syntax, קָדְקֹד (qodqōd), "scalp, crown of the head, head," is singular. LXX mistook the term as a designation for a leader, ἀρχούσας θυγατέρας Σιων, "the ruling daughters of Zion," and Tg. takes the same tack.

f See preceding note d.

g Reading with 1QIsaᵃ against MT's אֲדֹנָי (ᵓădōnāy), though the corrector of 1QIsaᵃ marks יהוה with dots underneath and adds the correction אדוני above the line.

h 1QIsaᵃ has העכיסים (hāᶜākîsîm), but 4QIsaᵇ has MT's העכסים (hāᶜăkāsîm), "anklets."

i 1QIsaᵃ has והשבישים for MT's וְהַשְּׁבִיסִים (wĕhaššĕbîsîm), "and sun discs," while 4QIsaᵇ has והשבשים.

j 1QIsaᵃ has והנטפות, "and the pendants," for MT's הַנְּטִיפוֹת (hannĕṭîpôt), "the pendants."

k 1QIsaᵃ adds the conjunction והפארים, "and the turbans," against MT's simple הַפְּאֵרִים (happĕᵓērîm), "the turbans."

l 1QIsaᵃ omits the article.

m For MT's וְהַמִּטְפָּחוֹת (wĕhammiṭpāḥôt), "and the wraps," 4QIsaᵇ has the word written defectively והמטפחת (wĕhammiṭpāḥōt).

n 1QIsaᵃ has the plene spelling והגליונים (wĕhaggilyônîm) "and the diaphanous garments," for MT's וְהַגִּלְיֹנִים (wĕhaggilyōnîm).

o 1QIsaᵃ הבשם (habbōśem, with medial mem), "the perfume," adds the article to MT's בֹּשֶׂם (bōśem), "perfume."

p MT has two verbs in this line, וְהָיָה תַחַת בֹּשֶׂם מַק יִהְיֶה (wĕhāyâ *tahat bōśem maq yihyeh*), "And it will come to pass (that) instead of perfume there will be rottenness," but one of them is redundant. 1QIsaᵃ omits the second verb at the end of the line, and reads the first as a masculine plural, ויהיו (*wĕyihyû*), "and there will be," because of the series of subjects that follow. The versions also translate only one verb. The initial וְהָיָה was probably inserted as a linking device after the introduction of vv. 18-23 broke the smooth connection with v. 17. Originally the line began without a verb and perhaps without the conjunction, "(and) instead of perfume there will be rottenness."

q 1QIsaᵃ has the unusual spelling ותחות for MT's וְתַחַת (*wĕtahat*), "and instead of."

r 1QIsaᵃ misspells חֲגוֹרָה (*hăgôrâ*), "a belt," as הגורה (*hăgôra*).

s Reading כי תחת יפי בשת (*kî tahat yōpî bōśet*), "for instead of beauty there will be shame," with 1QIsaᵃ. MT has only

כִּי־תַחַת יֹפִי (*ki-tahat yōpî*), which has traditionally been rendered as "a burn mark instead of beauty," but MT seems clearly defective.

t 1QIsaᵃ has וגבוריך (*wĕgibbôrayik*), "and your warriors," for MT's וּגְבוּרָתֵךְ (*ûgĕbûrātēk*), lit., "and your strength," though a corrector has tried to bring 1QIsaᵃ into line with MT by a correction above the line. The different readings do not require different translations. If MT's text is correct, it would simply be another example of the use of an abstract noun for a concrete when in parallel with a preceding concrete noun.

u 1QIsaᵃ has והזיקה corrected to the third feminine singular והחזיקה (*wĕheḥĕzîqâ*), "and she will take hold" for MT's third common plural וְהֶחֱזִיקוּ (*wĕheḥĕzîkû*), "and *seven women* will take hold."

Commentary

It is clear that this oracle against the daughters of Zion was once an independent oracle. The previous oracle against the male leaders has a closing formula (v. 15), which marks it off from the following oracle against the women, and the judgment against the two groups is portrayed differently—internal collapse of a society versus collapse as a result of foreign conquest—suggesting different historical backgrounds for the two oracles. They have been combined only in the editorial process of arranging the Isaiah oracles, perhaps because of the mention of the women ruling in Judah in v. 12. Nevertheless, this present arrangement of the oracles works well thematically, implicating both the men and women responsible for Judah's collapse.

There is some question about the unity of this oracle against the women, however. Verses 18-23 are generally regarded as a secondary expansion (Wildberger, 1:140–45; Dumn, 27–28; Kaiser, *Jesaja 1–12*, 36, 38–39; Childs, 34), and Wildberger has also detached 3:25—4:1 from the preceding as a fragment of an originally independent oracle (1:146–47). If it were ever independent of its present context, it is certainly only a fragment, since it has no proper beginning. In contrast to the preceding verses, which discuss the women in the third person plural, v. 25 shifts to a direct address of the city Zion with second person feminine singular suffixes. Since Zion was mentioned in the expression בְּנוֹת צִיּוֹן (*bĕnôt ṣîyôn*), "the daughters of Zion," in vv. 16-17, however, this address to Mother Zion with regard to her daughters is not as abrupt as Wildberger implies. Isaiah quickly reverts to

the third feminine singular in referring to the city (v. 26), and women become the subject again in v. 27. Despite the shift in suffixes, therefore, these verses fit well with the preceding material and provide the clear statement of the coming military disaster that lies behind the threat in vv. 17-24. I see no reason to regard them as secondary in their present context.

In his condemnation of the leaders of Judean society, Isaiah did not overlook the prominent women. Here and again in Isa 32:9-14 he attacks them for their part in the corruption of Jerusalem's character. Like Amos (4:1-3), Isaiah recognized that the mothers, wives, and daughters of the society's comfortable upper class wielded a tremendous influence on the shape of that society. They wielded it both by the pressure they put on their men to provide them with the symbols of success and by the definition of success their own lifestyle helped to portray to the society as a whole. It was not a positive influence. In their complacent security, these women were blind to the human need around them. Their chief concerns were their own pleasure and the arrogant display of their own ostentatious luxury. In the best of times that is a selfish and trivial model for life, but in the face of the pervasive oppression of the poor that was characteristic of the time, it was a lifestyle that called for judgment.

Isaiah refers to these women in v. 16 as בְּנוֹת צִיּוֹן (*bĕnôt ṣîyôn*), "the daughters of Zion." This appears to be a general term for the society women of Jerusalem, young and old alike (cf. 3:17; 4:4; Song 3:11). The description of the behavior of these women in the verse contains several elements. To begin with, they are characterized by the verb גָּבַהּ (gābōah) as "haughty and arrogant." The expression נְטֻיוֹת גָּרוֹן (nĕṭûyôt gārôn), "(and walk) with outstretched necks," is unattested elsewhere, and its precise sense is disputed. The versions all suggest a head held erect, and, despite Wildberger's assertion (1:138), supported by Watts (p. 45), that נָטָה (nāṭâ) indicates not an "upward" stretching but "a turning or stretching to the side," there is no evidence to support this assertion other than the assumed synonymous parallelism with the following phrase. The head held erect probably continues the image of the women's pride, but, as Wildberger has correctly seen, more is involved than mere pride. It is not that the women have "their noses in the air" or "are looking down their noses at others." The following lines suggest that the posture of the outstretched neck has a brazen, coquettish aspect to it. While the precise sense of וּמְשַׂקְּרוֹת עֵינָיִם (umeśaqqĕrôt ʿênāyim) is also disputed,[1] the versions all take the expression to mean "to wink, make signs with the eyes." The verb שׁקר (śqr) seems to be cognate with Aramaic סקר (sqr), "to look at," so the sense of the expression seems to be "to ogle" or "to look at another in a seductive or inviting manner."[2] If that is correct, the "outstretched neck" probably refers to a lack of modesty and decorum in the presence of men other than their husbands. These women have the shameless brow of the prostitute (Jer 3:3).

Rather than modestly averting their eyes, these women hold their heads erect, fix their faces on men (Prov 7:13), and suggestively communicate to them with their eyes. At this point, the prophet moves from the women's heads to their feet, to describe their gait, but his description still seems to focus on the women's attempts at sexual seductiveness. The verb טָפַף (ṭāpap) suggests short, tottering steps, like that of young children טַף. There is more dispute about the meaning of the verb עכס (ʿākas). Traditionally it has been regarded as denominative from the noun עֶכֶס (ʿekes), "anklet" (v. 18) and given the mean-

ing "to shake or rattle the anklets." G. R. Driver, however, has convincingly shown that the verb means something like "to skip, prance, gambol."[3] See the corrected text of Prov 7:22, וּכְעֶכֶס אֶל־מוּסַר אֱוִיל (ûkĕʿakkēs ʾel-môsēr ʿayyāl),[4] "and like the stag bounds into the snare," and 11QPsᵃ, col. 22, lines 4-6:

זיז כבודך יינקו (zîz kĕbôdēk yînāqû)
The breast of your glory they will suckle,
וברחובות תפארתך יעכסו (ûbirḥôbôt tipʾartēk yĕʿakkĕsû)
And in the squares of your splendor they will skip.[5]

Thus, the two verbs טפף and עכס suggest a skipping, prancing, dancelike gait that would call attention to the women's female charms.

In response to this haughty and overtly sexual display of female beauty, the prophet announces God's punishment in v. 17. As so often in the prophetic literature, God's judgment on these women strikes them at the point of their sins. The things they put their pride in, their beauty and the elaborate attire that highlighted it, are stripped away. The first thing to go is their hair. As v. 24 indicates, their elaborate coiffures (מַעֲשֶׂה מִקְשֶׁה, maʿăśeh miqšeh, "elaborate braidwork") are replaced with baldness קָרְחָה (qorḥâ). Verse 17 indicates how. Traditionally the verb שִׂפַּח (śippaḥ) has been explained as a byform of a verb ספח (spḥ), related to the nouns סַפַּחַת (sappaḥat), "scab, skin disease, psoriasis," and מִסְפַּחַת (mispaḥat), "skin rash, skin disease," and translated as "strike with scabs."[6] But skin disease is hardly an apt parallel for the following line, and the wider context points to foreign conquest as God's tool for this judgment. With this in mind, Wildberger (1:139), following G. R. Driver,[7] connects the root of this Hebrew verb to Akkadian suppuḫu. The D-stem of the Akkadian verb sapāḫu, "to scatter," is attested at least once with regard to hair—šumma šārat qaqqadišu suppuḫ,

---

1 See the discussion in *HALOT*, 1350, s.v. שׁקר; and Wildberger, 1:138.

2 The other suggestion for the meaning of שׁקר is to connect it with the later Hebrew סקר, "to paint (the eyes)," but the lack of versional support for this rendering makes this interpretation dubious. This verbal meaning appears to be a much later development.

3 G. R. Driver, "Hebrew Notes," 241–50, with references to earlier scholarly literature.

4 Cf. the textual notes in *BHS* and the discussion in Jan de Ward, *Proverbs* (BHQ 17; Stuttgart: Deutsche Bibelgesellschaft, 2008).

5 See J. A. Sanders, *The Psalms Scroll of Qumrân Cave 11 (11QPs a)* (DJD 4; Oxford: Clarendon, 1965) 86–87.

6 See BDB, 705, s.v. ספח; *HALOT*, 1348, s.v. שפח.

7 Driver, "Hebrew Notes," 241.

"if the hair of his head is sparse."[8] The meaning that Driver and Wildberger posit for the Hebrew verb would assume that "head" is used for "hair," the proper object of the verb, by metonymy: *suppuḥ (śarat) qaqqadi*, "to scatter (the hair) of the head," > שִׂפַּח קדקד (*śappēaḥ qodqōd*), "to make the head bald." The Vulgate's *decalvabit*, "he makes bald," can be cited in support of Driver's suggestion, and the parallelism with יְעָרֶה (*yěʿārê*), "he will lay bare," also supports this meaning. Hebrew פָּתְהֵן (*pothēn*), which stands in parallelism to קָדְקֹד (*qodqōd*), "head," has traditionally been rendered "their secret parts,"[9] but the newer lexicography, following a suggestion of Driver,[10] connects it to the Akkadian *pūtu*, "forehead," a meaning that fits nicely in the context. The Vulgate's *crinem earum*, "their hair," is not far off. The LXX's τὸ σχῆμα αὐτῶν, "their clothing, figure, form," which Syr. follows with its *ʾskmhyn*, "their form, attire," understands the text in the traditional sense of stripping the clothing from someone to leave them naked. Contrary to this traditional rendering, the sense of the two parallel lines seems to be that Yahweh will shave off the women's locks, leaving them largely bald. What lies behind the image seems to be the expectation that women prisoners of war would be shorn, either to be marked as slaves according to a well-known Mesopotamian practice or as a purification ritual prior to marriage to their captors (cf. Deut 21:10-14).

Verses 18-23 appear to be a secondary expansion of the text, since these verses interrupt the connection between v. 17 and v. 24 with a long list of women's finery.[11] It is not self-evident that the list is to be read as poetry,[12] though that cannot be entirely ruled out. Poets can turn mere lists into poetry, even if it is not great poetry. One need only think of the American country-western song "I've Been Everywhere, Man," which con-

sists almost entirely of long lists of place-names bracketed by a short refrain. There is no convincing basis for dating the expansion. It need not be post-Isaianic, and one could entertain the possibility that Isaiah himself added this list, but it is certainly not necessary to date the list that early or to attribute it to Isaiah. The list consists of some twenty-one articles of women's clothing and accessories, and, as to be expected in such a list of specialized vocabulary, the precise identification of many of the articles is quite dubious. It is clear that the ancient versions are often guessing at the meaning of the words. The LXX begins the list with a summarizing generic expression not found in the MT: "In that day the Lord will also take away the glory of *their clothing and their jewelry*" (τοῦ ἱματισμοῦ αὐτῶν καὶ τοὺς κόσμους αὐτῶν, Isa 3:18).

1. Despite LXX's rendering of הָעֲכָסִים (*hāʿăkāsîm*) as τὰ ἐμπλόκια, "the hair clasps," the Hebrew term clearly has something to do with feet or ankles. Vg., Tg., Aquila, and Theodotion have "sandals," while Symmachus has "anklets." The Arabic cognate *ʿikās*, "foot chain (for a camel)," suggests anklet or ankle chain.[13]

2. שָׁבִיס (*šābîs*) is a term, probably diminutive, for a small ornament in the shape of a sun-disc, possibly a loan word from Arabic, as A. van den Branden has argued,[14] though it may be that Arabic simply furnishes the best extant parallel. Note the variant pronunciation of the consonants in the cognate words for sun: Hebrew *šmš*, Ugaritic *špš*, and Arabic *šms* or dialectical *šbs*. In later Hebrew these ornaments were an integral part of a woman's headband or hairnet, which may explain why LXX renders the term with καὶ τοὺς κοσύμβους, "and the hairnets," and the preceding term with τὰ ἐμπλόκια, "the hair clasps"; but the Hebrew text does not make clear on which part of the body these ornaments were worn.

8   *CAD* S, 154 5a.
9   See *BDB*, 834; *HALOT*, 983.
10 Driver, "Linguistic and Textual Problems," 38.
11 There are several good discussions of these items (A. van den Branden, "I gioielli delle donne di Gerusalemme secondo Isaia 3, 18-21," *BeO* 5 [1963] 87-94; H. F. B. Compston, "Ladies' Finery in Isaiah III 18-23," *CQR* 103 [1926] 316-30; S. Daiches, "Der Schmuck der Tochter Zions und die Tracht Istars," *OLZ* 14 [1911] 390-91; E. E. Platt, "Jewelry of the Bible Times and the Catalog of Isa. 3:18-23," *AUSS* 17 [1979] 71-84. Platt not only discusses the various items; she also gives archaeological examples of par-

ticular pieces, but her attempt to treat this list as a non-gender-specific list of insignia of rank common to both men and women is not convincing. While some of the ornaments were worn by men as well as women, in its present context, which is the only context we have for this list, the list must refer to the apparel of the women who are the subject of the oracle in both the preceding and following verses.
12 Contrary to the claims of I. J. Peters, "A Hebrew Folksong," *JBL* 33 (1914) 158-59.
13 *HALOT*, 824, s.v. עכס.
14 Van den Branden, "I gioielli delle donne di Gerusalemme secondo Isaia 3,18-21," 87-94.

3. The שַׁהֲרֹנִים (śaharōnîm) were ornaments in the shape of the crescent moon, as is clear from the cognates in several Semitic languages meaning moon or new moon, and from the LXX's τοὺς μηνίσκους, "crescents," and Vg.'s *lunulas*, "little moons." Gideon is reported to have taken such ornaments off the necks of the camels of the kings of Midian and off the kings of Midian themselves (Judg 8:21, 26).

4. The נְטִפוֹת (nĕṭîpôt) in v. 19 are pendants or beads, literally "drops" from the verbal root meaning "to drip." They are mentioned also in Judg 8:26 as part of the plunder Gideon took from the kings of Midian. One could think of beads hung as pendants from the ear as the Arabic *naṭafat*, "earring," suggests, or one could think of beads strung around the neck to make necklaces as LXX, Vg., and Tg. suggest.

5. The שֵׁירוֹת (šērôt), cognate with and perhaps a loanword from Akkadian *semeru* (*šawiru, šaweru, šewiru, šiwiru, šameru, šemeru, samaru, sabirru, šabirru*), were bracelets or armbands.

6. Based on an Arabic cognate *raʿl*, which designates a two-part head covering and veil, the רְעָלוֹת (rĕʿālôt) are normally identified, probably correctly, as veils (Wildberger, 1:142).[15] The noun is derived from a verbal root (רעל I), meaning "to quiver, shake," and a denominative verb (רעל II) attested at Qumran means "to cover."[16] Other suggestions for the meaning of the noun are "bells," "dangling beads," or "necklaces."

7. Verse 20 begins with the פְּאֵרִים (pĕʾērîm), cloth head-dresses or turbans (Ezek 24:23; 44:18) that were "bound" or "wrapped" (חָבַשׁ, ḥābaš) on the head (Ezek 24:17). They were headgear characteristic of priests (Exod 39:28) and were worn by other men, such as bridegrooms on happy, festal occasions (Isa 61:3, 10), but were normally put aside in times of mourning. They were presumably festal attire for women as well.

8. The meaning of צְעָדוֹת (ṣĕʿādôt) is less clear. It appears to be derived from the verb צעד, "to stride," so it has been interpreted to mean ankle-chains, a piece of jewelry intended to help women keep their stride short.[17] But the form אֶצְעָדָה (ʾeṣʿādâ), which differs from צְעָדָה

(ṣĕʿādâ) only in having the prosthetic *aleph*, is probably a variant pronunciation for the same word, and it clearly means "armlet" or "armband" (2 Sam 1:10). It is listed among the booty taken from the Midianites in the time of Moses (Num 31:50).

9. The קִשֻּׁרִים (qiššūrîm) were articles of clothing typical of a bride that one bound on (קָשַׁר, qiššēr; Jer 2:32; Isa 49:18). The LXX and Vg. of Jer 2:32 translate the word as "a woman's breastbands" (στηθοδεσμίδα, *pectoralis*). If the ancient translators of Jeremiah are correct, the term would refer to an article of clothing analogous to the Akkadian *dudinātu ša irtīša*, "the pectorals of her breast." Like the Hebrew term, the Akkadian term designates an article of clothing closely associated with brides.[18]

10. The meaning of בָּתֵּי הַנֶּפֶשׁ (bottê hannepeš), lit. "houses of the life/appetite," is very disputed. Vg.'s *olfactoriola*, "scent-bottle," has led many interpreters to identify these objects with small perfume containers worn on the person (Marti, 44; Kaiser, 36, 39; Watts, 44), but this identification remains uncertain. E. E. Platt, following A. Wilkinson, suggests that they were slim charm cases like those sometimes found in Egypt containing little papyrus scrolls with spells written on them.[19] Since the following word in the list refers to a charm or amulet of some kind, Platt's suggestion seems preferable to the perfume flask.

11. While the לְחָשִׁים (lĕḥāšîm) were charms or amulets of some kind, precisely what kind is not clear. The word is used of charms or incantations to avoid snakebite (Jer 8:17; Qoh 10:11), which were apparently spoken aloud by snake incantation specialists (מְלַחֲשִׁים, mĕlaḥăšîm, Ps 58:6). While the *piel* participle of the verb לחש is used to designate the snake incantation specialist, the *hithpael* of the same root is used of people whispering back and forth to one another (2 Sam 12:19; Ps 41:8). Since the verb indicates some kind of whispering noise, it has been suggested that the לְחָשִׁים (lĕḥāšîm) may have been amulets made out of a material that made a similar noise such as "humming mussel-shells."[20] One could also think of written incantations on little scrolls carried in the charm cases (בָּתֵּי הַנֶּפֶשׁ, bottê hannepeš), or little tablets with spells inscribed on them worn as both jewelry and amulets.

---

15 *HALOT*, 1266, s.v. רְעָלָה.

16 *HALOT*, 1266, s.v. רעל.

17 Gustaf Dalman, *Arbeit und Sitte in Palästina* (7 vols.; Gütersloh: C. Bertelsmann, 1928) 4:350–51.

18 *CAD* D, 168–70, esp. 170.

19 Platt, "Jewelry of the Bible Times," 198.

20 *HAL*, 501; cf. *HALOT*, 527, s.v. לחש: "string of conch shells."

12. The טַבָּעוֹת (ṭabbāʿôt) of v. 21 were signet rings worn on the finger and used by officials to seal documents (Gen 41:42; Esth 3:10-12; 8:2, 8, 10), but their use was not restricted to high officials. They are mentioned as both booty (Num 31:50) and freewill offerings brought by men and women (Exod 35:22). Whether all these had seals on them is doubtful; some may have been simple finger rings, as Wildberger suggests (1:143). One would expect an individual to wear only one ring for sealing documents, but Judith is said to have put on a number of finger rings (τοὺς δακτυλίους, Jdt 10:4). The same word could be used to designate other ring-shaped objects that have nothing to do with signets, such as attachments used for holding or carrying things (Exod 25:12, 14-15, 26-27; 26:24-29; 27:4-7; 28:23-24, 26, 28; 30:4; 36:29-34; 37:3, 5, 13-14, 27; 38:5-7; 39:16-17, 19, 21).

13. The נִזְמֵי הָאָף (nizmê hāʾāp) were nose rings. The word נֶזֶם (nezem) simply designates a ring-shaped ornament that could be worn on the ears (Gen 35:4; Exod 32:2-3; cf. Prov 25:12) or the nose (Gen 24:47; Ezek 16:12; Prov 11:22), but in construct with אָף (ʾāp), "nose," the expression is quite specific.

14. The מַחֲלָצוֹת (maḥălāṣôt) appear to be clean, white, or festive attire, marking the switch at v. 22 from jewelry to articles of clothing. The word is in contrast to הַבְּגָדִים הַצֹּאִים (habbĕgādîm haṣṣōʾîm), "the dirty garments," in Zech 3:4, the only other place the word occurs in the Bible. Cf. Akkadian ḫalāṣu, "to clean by combing," ḫalṣu, "combed (flax)," and Arabic ḫalaṣa, "to be clean, white."

15. The מַעֲטָפוֹת (maʿăṭāpôt) are mantles or outer garments. The cognate verb עָטַף (ʿāṭap) means "to dress, clothe, wrap, or cover oneself" (Pss 65:14; 73:6).

16. The מִטְפָּחוֹת (miṭpāḥôt) are also outerwear, probably large shawls or wraps. The noun is derived from a verb (טָפַח, ṭāpaḥ) that means "to spread out." Ruth was wearing one when she visited Boaz at the threshing floor, and Boaz and she each held one end of it while he measured out six measures of barley for her to carry home in it (Ruth 3:16).

17. The חֲרִיטִים (ḥărîṭîm) are normally identified as purses or handbags on the basis of 2 Kgs 5:23, where money is put into them. Note also Arabic ḫarîṭat, "sack."

18. The identification of the גִּלְיֹנִים (gilyōnîm) in v. 23 is quite disputed. In the only other occurrence of the word in the Bible, it appears to designate a writing tablet or papyrus sheet. Vg. and Tg., perhaps thinking of polished metal tablets, render the word as "mirrors," and this understanding still has its defenders.[21] The MT vocalization of the word in Isa 3:23 may have conflated two separate words, however. One might connect the word here with the Akkadian gulēnu garment, which is a kind of overgarment. On the other hand, the LXX's rendering, τὰ διαφανῆ Λακωνικά, "diaphanous garments of Sparta," suggests a very thin, revealing, gauzelike summer garment. The identification remains uncertain.

19. The סְדִינִים (sĕdînîm), to be identified with Akkadian saddinnu, which is both a cloth and a garment, are probably linen undergarments, perhaps shirts. In Akkadian the garments normally seem to be made of linen, though there are a few occurrences where they seem to be made of wool (TÚG šá-din SIG₅.meš).[22] Samson included thirty of these in his wager with the Philistines at his wedding (Judg 14:12-13), and the ideal woman of Proverbs makes them to sell at the market (Prov 31:24).

20. The צְנִיפוֹת (ṣĕnîpôt) are headware or turbans made by wrapping (צָנַף, ṣānap) cloth around. The high priest wore them on his head (Zech 3:5; Sir 40:4), and Zion in the figure of a woman is said to be a "crown of glory" (עֲטֶרֶת תִּפְאֶרֶת, ʿăṭeret tipʾeret) and a "royal turban" (צְנִיף מְלוּכָה, ṣĕnîp mĕlûkâ) in God's hand (Isa 62:3; cf. Sir 11:5; 47:6). The מִצְנֶפֶת (miṣnepet), which seems to be a synonymous term from the same root for the same article of clothing, was also worn by the king (Ezek 21:31) and the high priest (Exod 28:4, 37, 39; 29:6; 39:28, 31; Lev 8:9; 16:4; Sir 45:12). It is not clear how the צְנִיפוֹת (ṣĕnîpôt) differed from the פְּאָרִים (pĕʾērîm), if they differed at all.

21. The רְדִידִים (rĕdîdîm) were some kind of overgarments, as Song 5:7 indicates. Since the verbal root רָדַד (rādad) means "to beat out," one should probably think of a thin, lightweight covering, and LXX and Vg. treatment of רְדִידִים (rĕdîdîm) as summer garments supports this. Perhaps one should identify them as thin shawls or wraps that covered the head and the upper body.

Verse 24 continues the judgment begun in v. 17. The

---

21 This translation is preserved in Blenkinsopp, 200; and Watts, 44.

22 CAD S, 17.

things that enhanced these women's beauty and in which these women took pride will be replaced by things that detract from their beauty, things that embarrass and shame them. While בֹּשֶׂם (bōśem) can refer to the balsam bush or the oil extracted from it (Song 5:1; 5:13; 6:2; 8:14), it often functions generically for any sweet-smelling substance used to enhance the smell of incense or anointing oil (Exod 25:6; 30:23; 35:8). Here it appears to mean perfume, as in Esth 2:12. Instead of the attractive aroma of perfume, the women will soon give off the stench of decay (מַק, maq). One might think specifically of the foul odor of festering wounds (cf. Ps 38:6). The term חֲגוֹרָה (ḥăgôrâ) can designate a kind of apron or loincloth (Gen 3:7), or it can refer to a belt or sash worn on the outside of one's robe to tighten it around the waist (2 Sam 18:11; 1 Kgs 2:5; 2 Kgs 3:21). Its replacement with a mere cord or rope (נִקְפָּה, niqpâ) suggests that the second meaning is intended here. This is the only occurrence of נִקְפָּה in Biblical Hebrew, but it is derived from a verb meaning "to go around," and the LXX, Vg., and Syr. all support the rendering "cord" or "rope."[23] It is unclear whether the prophet was referring to ropes tied around the women by their foreign captors or whether he was simply indicating that their festive attire would be replaced by the cheapest goods imaginable. The precise meaning of מַעֲשֶׂה מִקְשֶׂה (maʿăśeh miqšeh), translated here as "elaborate braidwork," is disputed, and the construction is unusual. Normally when the noun מעשה, "work," precedes a noun qualifying the type of work, מעשה is pointed as a construct noun (maʿăśēh), "the work of . . ." (Gen 40:17; Exod 24:10; 26:1; 26:36; 28:15, 32; 30:25; Num 8:4; 31:51; 1 Kgs 7:8, 17, 19, 22, 26; Jer 32:30; Hab 3:17; Song 7:2; 1 Chr 9:31; 2 Chr 3:10; passim). Here the noun is pointed in the absolute state (maʿăśeh) and simply juxtaposed to the following noun, a construction otherwise unattested with this noun as far as I am aware. The noun miqšeh with which it is juxtaposed is attested only here, but the presumably related noun מִקְשָׁה (miqšâ) refers to "turned or beaten work" of various metals. One could think of an elaborate hair decoration of precious metal, as LXX

does, or one could think of the elaborate braiding and curling of the hair itself as the Vg. does (cf. 1 Tim 2:9; 1 Pet 3:3). In either case, the long, elaborately set hair, the glory of the ancient woman (cf. 1 Cor 11:15), would be replaced with baldness. The precise meaning of פְּתִיגִיל (pĕtîgîl), "rich robe," is also unclear, but the contrast with sackcloth suggests that it was an attractive and expensive article of attire. The final statement in this v. 24 is a summary of all that has preceded. The transformation of perfume to stench, elaborate hairdos to baldness, riches to rags—all of these simply illustrate how Yahweh will turn these women's beauty into their shame.

This change in fate reflects the women's change of status from society women in a stratified society to mere survivors in a city destroyed by war. Verse 25 underscores this point when the prophet slides from the image of the humiliated women of Jerusalem to a personification of the city itself as a woman. Zion will see her men slain in battle, and the emptied city, her gates hanging ajar in defeat, will sit on the ground—an inappropriate resting place for a noblewoman (Isa 47:l)—in lamentation. The shift from the second person feminine singular suffixes in v. 25 to the third feminine singular suffixes in v. 26 is awkward in English, but this shift from second to third person in direct address is not that unusual in Hebrew (Isa 1:2, 4, 5; 5:8; 22:16; 29:3-5, 7). It requires no emendation.

In that day of judgment, when the war has swept away most of the men, a woman's pride will have to be satisfied with merely having a husband in name, even if she has to share him with six other women and must provide her own food and clothing. The expression נִקְרָא שֵׁם עַל (niqrāʾ šēm ʿāl), lit., "to have one's name called over someone or something," implies that someone or something belongs to the one whose name is called over it (Deut 28:10; 2 Sam 6:2; 1 Kgs 8:43; Isa 63:19; Jer 7:10, 11, 14, 30; 14:9; 15:16; 25:29; 32:34; 34:15; Amos 9:12). To have no husband, to belong to no one, was a source of reproach and shame for an Israelite woman in Isaiah's day, as it had been throughout Israelite history.[24]

---

23 The Tg. connects the noun to a different verb meaning "to smite" and translates the term as רוּשְׁמִין דְּמַחָא (rûšmîn dĕmaḥaʾ), "marks of smiting," but that provides a very poor parallel to "belt."

24 Note the extremes to which Tamar went, if not to

get the expected husband, at least to get an heir (Gen 38:1-30), and the portrayal of Hagar and Ishmael's plight when they were forced from Abraham's household indicates the difficulty faced by a husbandless woman (Gen 16:3-15; 21:8-19).

Bibliography

Branden, A. van den, "I gioielli delle donne di Gerusalemme secondo Isaia 3,18-21," *BeO* 5 (1963) 87–94.

Chaney, M. L., "Class, Gender, and Age in the Composition and Textual Transmission of Isaiah 3:12-15," in *SBL Abstracts* (Atlanta: Society of Biblical Literature, 1994) 227.

Compston, H. F. B., "Ladies' Finery in Isaiah III 18-23," *CQR* 103 (1926) 316–30.

Daiches, S., "Der Schmuck der Töchter Zions und die Tracht Ištars," *OLZ* 14 (1911) 390–91.

Driver, "Hebrew Notes," 241–50.

Edwards, D. R., "Dress and Ornamentation," *ABD* 2:232–38.

Galling, K., "Die Ausrufung des Namens als Rechtsakt in Israel," *TLZ* 81 (1956) 65–70.

Greger, Barbara, "Petigil in Jes 3:24," *BN* 61 (1992) 15–16.

Hönig, H. W., "Die Bekleidung des Hebräer" (PhD diss., Zürich, 1957).

Loretz, Oswald, "Kj 'Brandmal' in Jes 3,24," *UF* 8 (1976) 448.

Maloney, R. P., "Usury and Restrictions on Interest-Taking in the Ancient Near East," *CBQ* 36 (1974) 1–20.

Meyers, J. M., "Dress and Ornaments," *IDB* 1:869–71.

Peters, I. J. P., "A Hebrew Folksong," *JBL* 33 (1914) 158–59.

Platt, E. E., "Jewelry of the Bible Times and the Catalog of Isa. 3:18-23," *AUSS* 17 (1979) 71–84.

Plautz, W., "Monogamie und Polygamie im Alten Testament," *ZAW* 75 (1963) 3–27.

Stade, B., "Zu Jes 3:1,17,24. 5:1,8,12-14,16. 9:7-20. 10:26," *ZAW* 26 (1906) 129–41.

Yalon, C. H., "Erklärung einiger Schriftstellen," *BetM* 11 (1965) 17–20.

Zeron, A., "Das Wort *niqpa*, zum Sturz der Zionstöchter (Is iii 24)," *VT* 31 (1901) 95–97.

Ziegler, Joseph, *Untersuchungen zur Septuaginta des Buches Isaias* (ATA 12.3; Münster: Aschendorff, 1934).

4

2/   **On that day**
    the sprout of Yahweh shall become a splendor and a glory,
        and the fruit of the land an object of pride and fame
    to the remnant of Israel.ᵃ

3/   **And whoever remains in Zion and is left in Jerusalem**
        shallᵇ be calledᶜ holy,
    Everyone who is written downᶜ for life in Jerusalem.

4/   **When the Lord washes away the filth of the daughters of Zion**
        And rinses the bloodshed of Jerusalem from its midst
        By a spirit of judgment and by a spirit of burning,ᵈ

5/   **Yahweh will createᵉ over the whole site of Mount Zion and**
        over her assembly a cloud by day,ᶠ and smoke and the bright-
        ness of flaming fire by night.ᵍ
    Indeed over everything gloryʰ will be a canopy 6/ and a pavil-
        ion as a shade by dayᶠ from the heat and as a protection and
        a shelter from the storm and rain.

Textual Notes

a   1QIsaᵃ adds ויהודה (wîhûdâ), "and Judah," but that appears to be a secondary expansion, since the versions all support MT's shorter reading. LXX's ἐπιλάμψει ὁ θεὸς ἐν βουλῇ μετὰ δόξης ἐπὶ τῆς γῆς τοῦ ὑψῶσαι καὶ δοξάσαι τὸ καταλειφθὲν τοῦ Ισραηλ, "God shall gloriously shine over the land with counsel to exalt and to glorify the remnant of Israel," is a very loose translation, but does not appear to reflect a different Hebrew *Vorlage*. Aquila, Symmachus, and Theodotion all correct LXX to a more literal rendering. Tg. is interpretive, but keeps the syntax of the Hebrew: בעידנא ההוא יהי משיחא דיהוה וליקר ועבדי אוריתא לרבו ולתושבחא לשיזבת ישראל, "At that time the messiah of Yahweh shall become a source of joy and glory, and those who do the law a source of majesty and praise for those of Israel who escape."

b   1QIsaᵃ has ויהיה (wĕyihyeh) for MT's וְהָיָה (wĕhāyâ).

c   LXX pluralizes both these verbs, which are singular in Hebrew.

d   1QIsaᵃ has mistakenly read סער (saʿar), "storm," for MT's more original בָּעֵר (bāʿēr), "burning."

e   1QIsaᵃ has וברא (wĕyibrāʾ) for MT's וּבָרָא (ûbārāʾ), both meaning "he will create." LXX's translation, καὶ ἥξει, "and he shall come," seems to presuppose the reading ויבוא (wĕyābôʾ), but this is hardly original.

f   1QIsaᵃ has omitted everything after יוֹמָם (yômām), "by day," in v. 5 through the יוֹמָם (yômām), "by day," in v. 6 by haplography, when the scribe's eye skipped to the second יוֹמָם.

g   4QIsaᵃ has xxזוlfor MT's לַיְלָה (lāylâ), "by night," which may represent לזהר (lĕzōhar), "for brightness" (so Skehan and Ulrich, "Isaiah," 10).

h   The text is normally rendered, according to the Masoretic marking, "Over all (the) glory there will be a canopy. . . ." On the other hand, the traditional imagery of the pillar of cloud and fire that offered Israel a protective buffer against the pursuing Egyptians in the exodus and that both revealed and hid God's presence (Exod 14:19-20, 24; Ps 105:39; cf. Exod 19:11-18; 40:34-38; Hab 3:3-4; Zech 2:8-9) leads one to expect the glory itself, which signals God's presence, to be the protective canopy and pavilion. One might consider the emendation to כְּבוֹדוֹ (kĕbôdô), "his glory," or כְּבוֹד יהוה (kĕbôd YHWH), "the glory of Yahweh" (see LXX A′), but even without emendation, "glory" is more likely what provides protection to Zion and its inhabitants than being itself in need of a tent to protect it from the heat and the rain. It is Yahweh who is the shelter from the rainstorm and the shade from the heat (Isa 24:4).

Commentary

Unlike the two preceding oracles, which are relatively independent units only loosely tied to their present literary contexts, Isa 4:2-6 seems dependent on the preceding context for its meaning. This oracle has clearly been inserted here to show that the awful judgment announced against Jerusalem in 3:1-8 and 3:17—4:1 is not Yahweh's last word. Yahweh may remove every mainstay of Jerusalem's social structure (3:1-2), but there will be a holy remnant (4:3). Yahweh may remove the "finery" (תִּפְאָרֶת, tipʾeret) of the haughty women of Jerusalem (3:18) and replace it with filthy rags (3:24), but after this judgment he will wash away their filth (4:4), and there will once more be "fame" or "glory" (תִּפְאָרֶת, tipʾeret) for the survivors of Israel (4:2).

This dependence on the preceding context and the difficulty of analyzing the oracle as poetry have led many scholars to treat the oracle as a postexilic insertion (e.g., Gray, 77; Wildberger, 1:152–54; Kaiser, 41–42), but one should note that the theology of the piece hardly differs from that found in 1:21-28. God's purpose for Jerusalem is to purify it, not destroy it. Moreover, there are enough traces of parallelism in the unit to posit an originally poetic text that has been corrupted into prose in the course of its textual transmission. Note the parallelism between "sprout of Yahweh" and "the fruit of the land," between "a splendor and a glory" and "an object of pride and fame," between "to the remnant of Israel," "whoever remains in Zion," and "is left in Jerusalem," between "shall be called holy" and "everyone who is written down for life," between "washes away the filth of the daughter of Zion" and "rinses the bloodshed of Jerusalem from its midst." The original could be Isaianic.[1]

Scholars disagree widely on the meaning of the expression צֶמַח יְהוָה (*semaḥ YHWH*), "the sprout of the Lord." The term צֶמַח (*semaḥ*), "sprout," often translated as "branch," serves as a messianic title in a number of later prophecies (Jer 23:5; 33:15; Zech 6:12); the Tg. translates the expression in our passage as "the Messiah of the Lord"; and some scholars still defend some form of this traditional messianic interpretation (Hayes and Irvine, 96; Childs, 36). Others argue that the parallelism with "the fruit of the land," which is not elsewhere attested as a messianic title, rules out the messianic interpretation (Wildberger, 1:154; Gray, 78). Arguing from this parallelism, many scholars understand "the sprout/branch of the Lord" to refer to the miraculously abundant crops that Yahweh will cause to grow in Judah in the eschatological future (cf. Amos 9:13-15) (Wildberger, 1:154; Gray, 78; Watts, 50). Such an interpretation is problematic, however, because neither of the preceding oracles of judgment (3:1-15; 3:16—4:1), to which Isa 4:2-6 is responding, explicitly mentions crop shortages. The shortage announced in the judgment (3:1-2; 3:25; 4:1) is a shortage of men! Moreover, Isaiah often employs plant imagery to refer to humans, especially in oracles threatening the decimation of the human population (5:7; 10:16-19; 17:4-6). Thus, both the context and Isaianic usage suggest that one understand "the fruit of the land" to refer to the human population that remains in Jerusalem and Judah.

The parallel term צֶמַח (*semaḥ*), "sprout," need not have an identical meaning, however. Parallel terms are often complementary rather than identical, as the parallelism in Isa 9:16 between "those who lead" and "those who are led" shows. In Isa 11:1 the prophet uses several synonyms of "sprout" to refer to the ideal king who would arise after God had hacked down the arrogant forest of his enemies who threatened Jerusalem, and in 11:10 this messianic figure is mentioned in parallel to his "resting place," which will be glorious. In the light of these passages, one could understand "the sprout of Yahweh" to be the ideal king of Isa 11:1 and "the fruit of the land" to be his purified subjects in Jerusalem. The survivors from the northern kingdom Israel will see their glory (4:2) and presumably join them in the purged and glorified city of God (cf. 2:2-6; 11:10).

The remnant who remain in Zion on that day will once again be called holy. Note that this idiom is the same as in 1:26; it implies a real change in character, not just a forensic designation. These survivors will be the righteous whose names were written in God's book of life (Exod 32:32) and therefore did not perish in God's refining judgment on Jerusalem. When God has purged his city of the women's filth and the officials' oppression through that judgment, this righteous remnant will once again experience Yahweh's protecting presence in Zion. Isaiah elaborates this traditional motif of the Zion Tradition with the cloud and fire imagery originally at home in the exodus tradition (Exod 13:21-22).

---

1   Some contemporary commentators as different as Hayes and Irvine (pp. 96–97) and Oswalt (pp. 143–49) still defend the authenticity of this passage. Many older scholars such as B. Stade, K. Budde, A. Dillmann, and O. Procksch held that at least parts of the passage could be attributed to the eighth-century Isaiah (see the discussion in Wildberger, 1:153). Otto Eissfeldt leaves open the possibility that Isa 4:2-6 may be a secondarily expanded passage of Isaiah in his comment on the passage: "... if the passage as a whole is non-genuine and is not merely a saying of Isaiah which has been secondarily expanded" (*The Old Testament: An Introduction* [New York: Harper & Row, 1965] 317).

Bibliography

Baldwin, Joyce G., "*Tsemach* as a Technical Term in the Prophets," *VT* 14 (1964) 93–97.

Búda, J., "ṣemaḥ Jahweh: Investigationes ad Christologiam Isaianam spectantes," *Bib* 20 (1939) 10–26.

Cazelles, Henri, "Qui aurait visé, à l'orgine, Isaïe II 2-5," *VT* 30 (1980) 409–20.

Fohrer, Georg, "Σιών," *TDNT* 7:292–319.

Herrmann, W., "Das Buch des Lebens," *Das Altertum* 20 (1974) 3–10.

Lipiński, E., "De la réforme d'Esdras au règne eschatologique de Dieu (Is 4,3-5a)," *Bib* 51 (1970) 533–37.

Mauchline, J., "Implicit Signs of a Persistent Belief in the Davidic Empire," *VT* 20 (1970) 287–303.

Prager, M., "Durch Gericht zum Heil—durch Tod zum Leben (Is 4,3-5a)," *BibLeb* (1964) 250–53.

Roberts, J. J. M., "The Meaning of ṣemaḥ hʾ in Isaiah 4:2," in Joshua J. Adler, ed., *Haim M. I. Gevaryahu Memorial Volume* (Jerusalem: World Jewish Bible Center, 1990) 110–18.

Yalon, H., "מקראות בישעיהו (Lectures in Isaiah) כבוד חופת .חופה כבוד.ב (Is 4,6) כיסוי לשון בלע.א." *BetM* 12.30 (1967) 3–5.

5

1/ Let me sing[a] for my friend my love song[b] for his[c] vineyard:
My friend had a vineyard on a fertile spur.[d]

2/ He dug it,[e] cleared it of stones,[f] and planted it[g] with choice vines.
He built[h] a watch-tower inside it and even hewed out[i] a wine press in it.
Then he waited[j] for it to produce grapes, but it produced sour grapes.

3/ And now, inhabitants[k] of Jerusalem and men of Judah,
Judge[l] between me and my vineyard:

4/ What more was there to do for[m] my vineyard
That I had not already done in it?
Why, when I waited for it to produce grapes,
Did it produce[n] sour grapes?

5/ And now[o] I will inform[p] you[q]
What I am about to do[r] to my vineyard:
I will remove[s] its hedge,[t]
That it may be left[u] for grazing;[v]
I will break down its wall,
That it may become[u] a trampled place.

6/ I will turn it into a wasteland;
It will not[w] be pruned, and it will not be hoed,
But it will grow up in thorns and thistles.[x]
And upon the clouds I will give command,
So that they will not drop rain upon it.

7/ For the vineyard of Yahweh of Hosts is the house of Israel,
And the men of Judah are the planting of his delight;[y]
But he waited[z] for justice,[*a] and there was only bloodshed;[*b]
For righteousness,[*c] but there was only the cry of the oppressed.

Textual Notes

a 1QIsaᵃ omits the particle נא (nāʾ).

b The MT reading דּוֹדִי (dôdî), "my friend," though supported by 1QIsaᵃ and the versions, produces an awkward threefold reference to the friend. The slight emendation of the vocalization to דּוֹדַי (dôday), "my (song of) love," avoids that redundancy. One could also consider the emendation to דּוֹדִים (dôdîm), "(song) of love."

c LXX has "for my vineyard."

d LXX and Syr. have "on a spur (horn) in a fertile place."

e LXX's καὶ φραγμὸν περιέθηκα, "and I put a hedge around it," assumes a first person verb form (cf. Tg.) and understands the verb עזק (ʿizzēq) to mean "to put a hedge around"; Vg., while preserving the third person, also understands the verb as "to hedge in."

f Again LXX's καὶ ἐχαράκωσα, "and I staked it," reads the first person against MT and 1QIsaᵃ's third person. LXX apparently misunderstood the verb סקל (siqqēl), "to clear of stones," to mean "to provide individual stakes to support the vines." Syr. has "he surrounded it with a hedge."

g LXX maintains the first person.

h For MT וַיִּבֶן (wayyiben) and 1QIsaᵃ ויבנא, "and he built," LXX has the first person καὶ ᾠκοδόμησα, "and I built."

i Again LXX has the first person.

j LXX has "I waited."

k For MT's singular יֹשֵׁב (yôšēb), "inhabitant" (cf. Vg.), 1QIsaᵃ has the plural יֹשְׁבֵי (yôšēbê), "inhabitants of" (cf. LXX, Syr., and Tg.).

l For MT's שִׁפְטוּ־נָא (šipṭû-nāʾ), "judge," 1QIsaᵃ has the variant spelling שפוטו נה (šipôtû nâ).

m MT has לְכַרְמִי (lĕkarmî), "for my vineyard," but 1QIsaᵃ, influenced by the following בּוֹ (bô), "in it," at the end of the clause, has בכרמי (bĕkarmî), "in my vineyard."

n For MT's וַיַּעַשׂ (wayyaʿaś), "and it made," 1QIsaᵃ has the defective וישה for וין[ע]שה (wayyaʿaśeh). Wildberger (1:164) thinks that the scribe may be deriving the form from נשא (nāśāʾ), "to bear fruit," but it is more likely that the ayin was simply elided because its pronunciation tended to fall together with aleph in late Hebrew and was quiescent at the end of a syllable. See Rudolf Meyer, Hebräische Grammatik (Berlin: de Gruyter, 1966), vol. 1, §22.3e.

o For MT's וְעַתָּה (wĕʿattâ), "and now," 1QIsaᵃ has the auditory error ואתה (wĕʾattâ), "and you."

p For MT אוֹדִיעָה־נָּא (ʾôdîʿâ-nnā), "I will inform," 1QIsaᵃ has the orthographic variant נא אודיע.

q For MT אֶתְכֶם (ʾetkem), "you," 1QIsaᵃ has the longer form אתכמה.

r 1QIsaᵃ has עושא (ʿôśeʾ) for MT's עֹשֶׂה (ʿōśeh), "I am about to do."

s The MT has the hiphil infinitive absolute הָסֵר (hāsēr), which is supported by the following infinitive absolute פָּרֹץ (pārōs); 1QIsaᵃ has the first person imperfect for the first verb אסיר (ʾāsîr), "I will remove," but it preserves the infinitive absolute for the second. LXX and Vg. have first person verb forms for both, but that is the way the infinitive absolutes must be rendered in the context (cf. Syr., which has the participle followed by the first person subject pronoun for both forms), so the ancient translations do not unambiguously support

1QIsaᵃ's reading. As Peter Machinist suggested to me (personal communication), 1QIsaᵃ's reading is probably not a witness to a different *Vorlage*, but an interpretive updating by the scribe, whose audience might not easily have understood the infinitive absolute here. Following this first person form, his readers could probably infer that *pārōṣ* was also to be understood in that fashion.

t For MT's מְשׂוּכָתוֹ (*mĕsûkkātô*), "its hedge," 1QIsaᵃ has the orthographic variant מסוכתו (*mĕsûkkātô*), which LXX and Vg. render as "its hedge." Syr. reads *mgdlw*, "its tower."

u MT's וְהָיָה (*wĕhāyâ*), "and it will become," is preferable to 1QIsaᵃ's ויהיה (*wĕyihyeh*).

v MT's לְבָעֵר (*lĕbāʿēr*), "for grazing," is supported by the versions against 1QIsaᵃ's בער (*bāʿēr*).

w For MT's לֹא (*lōʾ*), 1QIsaᵃ has ולוא (*wĕlōʾ*).

x LXX's καὶ ἀναβήσεται εἰς αὐτὸν ὡς εἰς χέρσον ἄκανθα, "and thorns shall grow up in it as in a dry place," is interpretive.

y MT has שַׁעֲשׁוּעָיו (*šaʿăšûʿāyw*), a plural intensive, "his delight," while 1QIsaᵃ has either an unexpected singular form שעשועו (*šaʿăšûʿô*) or a defectively written plural (*šaʿăšûʿāw*).

z MT and 1QIsaᵃ have וְיְקַו (*wayqaw*), "and he waited," the third person shortened form of the verb; LXX, Vg., Syr., and Tg. have the first person form.

*a MT, 1QIsaᵃ, and Syr. have simple לְמִשְׁפָּט (*lĕmišpāṭ*), "for justice"; the other versions are periphrastic, e.g., LXX τοῦ ποιῆσαι κρίσιν, "to do justice."

*b 1QIsaᵃ's למשפח (*lĕmišpāḥ*) "for bloodshed," is an obvious error, influenced by the preceding לְמִשְׁפָּט, for MT's correct מִשְׂפָּח (*miśpāḥ*), "bloodshed."

*c For MT and 1QIsaᵃ's לִצְדָקָה (*liṣdāqâ*), "for righteousness," LXX apparently had ולצדקה (*wĕliṣdāqâ*), "and for righteousness," which the translator misread as containing the negative, resulting in the odd translation καὶ οὐ δικαιοσύνην, "and not righteousness."

Commentary

There has been very intensive discussion of the genre of the Song of the Vineyard. Much of that discussion has been based on the simplistic assumption that the genre must be univocal, that if the genre is this, it cannot be that. If the genre is that of a love song, it cannot be a judicial parable, or vice versa. Good poetry is not that univocal, and most scholars would consider the Song of the Vineyard good poetry. One must be open, therefore, to the possibility that the poem operates on several different levels and participates in several different genres. On the literal level, it is a song about a man's vineyard, but since "vineyard" is a standard metaphor for one's "beloved" in Israelite love poetry (Song 1:6, 14; 2:3, 15; 4:12-16; 7:6-13; 8:12), the song was probably heard metaphorically as a love song (שירת דודי [*šîrat dôday*] "my love song" or שירת דודים [*šîrat dôdîm*] "a love song," Isa 5:1) of unrequited love. Lyrics about plants are not unheard-of even in modern love songs. Some years ago there was a popular song entitled "Lemon Tree" that commented on the beauty of the lemon tree, but judged that the fruit of the poor lemon was impossible to eat. Everyone with any sense understood that the song was not really about an actual lemon tree, but about a human beloved that was unresponsive to the singer, and the singer tried to convince his audience by plant metaphor that the fault lay with the beloved, not with the singer.

In a similar way, Isaiah sings his love song about his friend's vineyard on behalf of his friend. The word יָדִיד (*yādîd*) is most often used of individuals specially favored or loved by God (Deut 33:12; Pss 60:7; 108:7; 127:2; Jer 11:15). Here it is used of Isaiah's favorite or friend (לִידִידִי [*lîdîdî*] "for my friend"). It seems obvious that דודי and ידידי have different referents, though the MT's erroneous pointing of דודי (*dôdî*) as a singular noun may be due to the influence of the singular יְדִידִי (*yĕdîdî*), "my friend." Isaiah sings his love song for his friend, trying to convince the audience by the extended vineyard metaphor that it was through no fault of his friend that his friend's beloved did not reciprocate his love. Isaiah's friend chose a fertile spur of the hill country as the location for his vineyard. He did the necessary work of preparing the ground by digging it up to rid it of weeds and by removing the large stones that would impede growth. He planted the prepared vineyard with choice vine stock, built a tower within it to protect it from animal and human depredations, and hued out a wine vat in anticipation of the harvest. Then he waited for the well-tended vineyard to produce an abundance of grapes, but all it produced were sour, unripe, diseased berries.

Isaiah's audience could no doubt identify with both the experience of a disappointing grape harvest and the disappointing experience of unreciprocated love, and thus they are progressively led into total sympathy with the friend against his "vineyard." By v. 3 Isaiah is no longer speaking of his friend in the third person, but the friend himself speaks through Isaiah in the first person. This shift in the speaker's level of identification with his friend probably marks the point at which Isaiah's audience is hooked. Now, speaking as his friend, he invites them to judge between him and his "vineyard." Such judgment is still within the realm of a love song about unrequited love. The friend asks rhetorically if there was anything more he could have done for his vineyard, with the firm expectation that the audience will agree with him that he had already done all that could be reasonably expected. As a result, the audience is prepared for and sympathetic to the friend's violent reaction. He threatens to remove the hedge and wall around the vineyard so that the animals may graze and trample the unfruitful vineyard. He will no longer cultivate and prune the vineyard but will let it grow up in thorns and thistles like uncultivated wasteland. He will even command the clouds not to rain on it. Some scholars take this last statement of v. 6 as an unmistakable giveaway of the real speaker (Wildberger, 1:171; Kaiser, *Jesaja 1–12*, 48; Watts, 56), but one should note that love songs have always been noted for unrealistic hyperbole. If the highest mountain, the widest ocean, and the distant moon are no match for love in love songs, it is not clear that a disappointed lover's cosmic curse on his beloved transcends the genre's bounds.

Only after Isaiah has pronounced his judgment, a judgment with which his audience has already concurred, does he reveal the third and deepest level of meaning—Yahweh is the friend, and the vineyard is the house of Israel and the men of Judah. Note how this revelation is stylistically expressed in a return to speaking about the "friend" (= Yahweh) in the third person. So vv. 1-2 are balanced by v. 7, and together they form an envelope around the friend's/Yahweh's speech in the first person in vv. 3-5. Thus, the love song is not just an ordinary love song, seeking the sympathy and approval of the audience for the singer's friend, but a theological love song and judicial parable rolled into one. It is intended to entrap the audience into condemning themselves, presumably with the hope of changing their behavior. Just as Nathan trapped David into pronouncing judgment on himself by his judicial parable (2 Sam 12:1-7), so Isaiah entraps his audience with his multilevel love song/judicial parable, though apparently without the same positive results.

There is a striking play on words in v. 7 that cannot be duplicated in English. As the friend looked for a harvest of choice grapes only to be disappointed by diseased, unripe grapes, so Yahweh looked for justice (מִשְׁפָּט, *mišpāṭ*) only to see bloodshed (מִשְׂפָּח, *miśpāḥ*), for righteousness (צְדָקָה, *ṣĕdāqâ*) only to hear the cry (צְעָקָה, *ṣĕʿāqâ*) of the oppressed.

Bibliography

Anderson, Bernhard W., "'God with Us'—In Judgement and in Mercy: The Editorial Structure of Isaiah 5-10(11)," in Gene M. Tucker, David L. Petersen, and Robert R. Wilson, eds., *Canon, Theology and Old Testament Interpretation: Essays in Honor of Brevard S. Childs* (Philadelphia: Fortress, 1988) 230–45.

Bartelmus, R., "Beobachtungen zur literarischer Struktur des sog. Weinbergliedes (Jes. 5:1-7)," *ZAW* 110 (1998) 50–66.

Baumgarten, Joseph M., "4Q500 and the Ancient Conception of the Lord's Vineyard," *JJS* 40 (1989) 1–6.

Bentzen, A., "Zur Erläuterung von Jes 5:1-7," *AfO* 4 (1927) 209–10.

Berger, P. R., "Ein unerklärtes Wort in dem Weinberglied Jesajas (Jes 5,6)," *ZAW* 82 (1970) 116–17.

Boadt, Lawrence, "The Poetry of Prophetic Persuasion: Preserving the Prophet's Persona," *CBQ* 59 (1987) 12–16.

Brooke, George J., "4Q500 1 and the Use of Scripture in the Parable of the Vineyard," *DSD* 2 (1995) 286–94.

Cersoy, M., "L'apologue de la vigne au chapitre V d'Isaïe (versets 1-7)," *RB* 8 (1899) 40–49.

Dalman, *Arbeit und Sitte*, vol. 4.

Driver, "Linguistic and Textual Problems," 38 (chaps. 3, 5), 39 (chap. 10), 40 (chap. 15).

Emerton, J. A., "The Translation of Isaiah 5:1," in Florentino García Martínez et al., eds., *The Scriptures and the Scrolls: Studies in Honour of A. S. van der Woude on the Occasion of His 65th Birthday* (VTSup 49; Leiden: Brill, 1992) 18–30.

Fang Chih-Yung, M., "Yī shǒu hányì shēnzhàn de gǔshī" ["A Profoundly Meaningful Poem: Song of the Vineyard"], *Collectanea theologica Universitatis Fugen* 6 (1970) 541–55.

Feliks, Yehuda, "The Song of the Vineyard: The Allegory and Its Agricultural Background," in *Proceedings of the Tenth World Congress of Jewish Studies, Jerusalem, August 16–24, 1989: Division A,*

The Bible and Its World (Jerusalem: World Union of Jewish Studies, 1990) *19-*24.

Graffy, A., "The Literary Genre of Isaiah 5,1-7," *Bib* 60 (1979) 400-409.

Graham, W. C., "Notes on the Interpretation of Isaiah 5:1-14," *AJSL* 45 (1928) 167-78.

Haelewyck, J.-C., "Le cantique de la vigne: Histoire du texte vieux latin d'Is 5,1-7(9a)," *ETL* 65 (1998) 257-79.

Haupt, P., "Isaiah's Parable of the Vineyard," *AJSL* 19 (1902) 193-202.

Hewitt, T. Furman, "The Parable of the Vineyard: An Exegesis of Isaiah 5:1-8," *Faith and Mission* 9 (1991) 64-70.

Höffken, P., "Probleme in Jesaja 5,1-7," *ZTK* 79 (1982) 394-410.

Huber, K., "Vom 'Weinberglied' zum 'Winzergleichnis': Zu einem Beispiel innerbiblischer Relecture," *PzB* 5 (1996) 71-94.

Irsigler, H., "Speech Acts and Intention in 'The Song of the Vineyard' Isaiah 5:1-7," *OTE* 10 (1997) 39-68.

Jüngling, Hans-Winfrid, "Der heilige Israels: Der erste Jesaja zum Thema 'Gott,'" in E. Haag, ed., *Gott, der einzige: Zur Entstehung des Monotheismus in Israel* (QD 104; Freiburg im Breisgau: Herder, 1985) 91-114.

Junker, H., "Die literarische Art von Is 5:1-7," *Bib* 40 (1959) 259-66.

Kellermann, D., "Frevelstricke und Wagenseil: Bemerkungen zu Jesaja V 18," *VT* 37 (1987) 90-97.

Korpel, Marjo C. A., "The Literary Genre of the Song of the Vineyard (Isa 5:1-7)," in Willem van der Meer and Johannes C. de Moor, eds., *The Structural Analysis of Biblical and Canaanite Poetry* (JSOTSup 74; Sheffield: JSOT Press, 1988) 119-55.

Kosmala, H., "Form and Structure in Ancient Hebrew Poetry (Continued)," *VT* 16 (1966) 152-80.

L'Heureux, Conrad E. "The Redactional History of Isaiah 5:1-10:4," in W. Boyd Barrick and John R. Spencer, eds., *In the Shelter of Elyon: Essays in Ancient Palestinian Life and Literature in Honor of G. W. Ahlström.* (JSOTSup 31; Sheffield: JSOT Press, 1984) 99-119.

Loretz, Oswald, "Weinberglied und prophetische Deutung im Protest-Song Jes 5,1-7," *UF* 7 (1975) 573-76.

Luria, B. Z., "What Is the Vineyard in Isaiah's Proverb?" *BetM* 31.107 (1985) 289-92.

Lys, D., "La vigne et le double Je: Exercice de style sur Esaïe V 1-7," in *Studies on Prophecy: A Collection of Twelve Papers* (VTSup 26; Leiden: Brill, 1974) 1-16.

Margaretha, L., "A Literary Analysis of the 'Song of the Vineyard' (Is. 5:1-7)," *JEOL* 29 (1985) 106-23.

Marmorstein, A., "A Greek Lyric Poet and a Hebrew Prophet (Isaiah)," *JQR* 37 (1946-47) 169-73.

Neveu, L., "Le chant de la vigne (Is 5)," *AsSeign* 58 (1974) 4-10.

Niehr, Herbert, "Zur Gattung von Jes 5,1-7," *BZ* n.s. 30 no. 1 (1986) 99-104.

Nielsen, Kirsten. "Reinterpretation of Metaphors: Tree Metaphors in Isa 1-39," in Matthias Augustin and Klaus-Dietrich Schunck, eds., *Wünschet Jerusalem Frieden: Collected Communications to the XIIth Congress of the International Organization for the Study of the Old Testament, Jerusalem 1986* (BEATAJ 13; Frankfurt am Main: P. Lang, 1988) 425-29.

Olivier, Hannes, "God as Friendly Patron: Reflections on Isaiah 5:1-7," *IDS* 30 (1996) 293-304; reprinted in *"Feet on Level Ground"* (Festschrift G. Hassel; Berrien Center, MI: Hester, 1996) 301-28.

Olivier, J. P. J., "Rendering *dyd* as Benevolent Patron in Isaiah 5:1," *JNSL* 22 (1996) 59-65.

Orbiso, Teófilo de, "El cantico a la viña del amado (Is. 5:1-7)," *EstEcl* 34 (1960) 715-31.

Padilla, C. Ren, "The Fruit of Justice Will Be Peace," *Transformation* 2, no. 1 (1985) 2-4.

Pezzella, S., "La parabola della vigna Is 5:1-7," *BeO* 5 (1963) 5-8.

Premnath, D. N., "Latifundialization and Isaiah 5:8-10," *JSOT* 40 (1988) 49-60.

Rast, W. E., "Disappointed Expectation in the Old Testament," *Perspectiva* 12 (1971) 135-52.

Ringgren, Helmer, "The Marriage Motif in Israelite Religion," in Patrick D. Miller Jr., Paul Hanson, and S. Dean McBride, eds., *Ancient Israelite Religion: Essays in Honor of Frank Moore Cross* (Philadelphia: Fortress, 1987) 421-28.

Ross, J. F., "Vine, Vineyard," *IDB* 4:784-86.

Sanmartín-Ascaso, J., "*dôdh*," *TDOT* 3:143-46.

Schottroff, Willy, "Das Weinberglied Jesajas (Jes 5,1-7): Ein Beitrag zur Geschichte der Parable," *ZAW* 82 (1970) 68-91.

Scippa, V., "Il canto alla vigna (Is 5,1-7): Studio esegetico secondo il metodo dell'analisi strutturale," in C. Marcheselli-Casale, ed., *Oltre il racconto* (Naples: D'Auria, 1994) 49-68.

Sheppard, G. T., "More on Isaiah 5:1-7 as a Juridical Parable," *CBQ* 44 (1982) 45-47.

Sweeney, Marvin A., "New Gleanings from an Old Vineyard: Isaiah 27 Reconsidered," in Craig A. Evans and William F. Stinespring, eds., *Early Jewish and Christian Exegesis: Studies in Memory of William Hugh Brownlee* (Scholars Press Homage Series 10; Atlanta: Scholars Press, 1987) 51-66.

Tromp, N. J., "Un démasquage graduel: Lecture immanente d'Is 5,1-7," in J. Vermeylen, ed., *Book of Isaiah = Le livre d'Isaïe: les oracles et leur relectures unité et complexité de l'ouvrage* (BETL 81; Leuven: University Press/Peeters, 1989) 197–202.

Walsh, C. E., *The Fruit of the Vine: Viticulture in Ancient Israel* (Winona Lake, IN: Eisenbrauns, 2000).

——, "God's Vineyard: Isaiah's Prophecy as Vintner's Textbook," *BRev* 14.4 (1998) 42–49, 52–53.

Weren, M. C., "The Use of Isaiah 5,1-7 in the Parable of the Tenants (Mark 12,1-12; Matthew 21,33-46," *Bib* 79 (1998) 1–26.

Whedbee, J. W., *Isaiah and Wisdom* (Nashville: Abingdon, 1971) 43–51.

Williams, Gary R., "Frustrated Expectations in Isaiah 5:1-7: A Literary Interpretation," *VT* 35 (1985) 459–65.

Willis, John T., "The Genre of Isaiah 5:1-7," *JBL* 96 (1977) 337–62.

Yee, Gale A., "A Form Critical Study of Isaiah 5:1-7 as a Song and a Juridical Parable," *CBQ* 43 (1981) 30–40.

Zobel, H.-J., "*yadîd*," *TDOT* 5:444–48.

5

8/ Hey! You who join house to house,[a]
Who bring field near to field,
Until there is no more place,[b]
And you are left to dwell[c] by yourselves in the midst of the land—

9/ Yahweh of Hosts has sworn[d] in my ears,[e]
"Surely many houses shall become desolate,
Great and fine houses[f] without inhabitant.

10/ For ten acres of vineyard will produce but one[g] bath,
And a homer of seed will produce but an ephah."

11/ Hey! You who rise early[h] in the morning
That beer they may pursue,
Who tarry late[i] in the evening,
That wine may chase them.[j]

12/ And their banquets[k] have lyre and harp, timbrel and flute and wine,
But the action[l] of Yahweh they do not observe,[m]
And the work of his hands they do not perceive.[n]

13/ Therefore my people will go into exile for lack of knowledge;[o]
Its nobility shriveled[p] by hunger,
And its multitudes[q] parched by thirst.

14/ Therefore Sheol will open wide her maw,
And spread open her mouth in a measureless gape,
And her eminences and her multitudes will go down,
Her boisterous din and the exultant within her.[r]

15/ Yes, humans are bowed down,[s]
And man is brought low,
And the eyes of the haughty are brought low.

16/ And Yahweh of Hosts is exalted by judgment,
And the Holy God is sanctified by righteousness.

17/ And the lambs[t] will graze as (in) their pasture,[u]
And (among) the ruins of the fatlings[v] the kids[w] will eat.

18/ Hey! You who drag inequity with the cords of vanity,[x]
Or sin as with the ropes of a cart.[y]

19/ Who say, "Let him hurry,[z]
Let him rush*[a] his work*[b]
That we may see;
Let draw near*[c] and come*[d]
The plan of the Holy One of Israel
That we may know."*[e]

20/ Hey! You who call evil good,
And good evil;
Who make darkness into light,
And light into darkness;
Who make bitter into sweet,
And sweet into bitter.

21/ Hey! You who are so wise in their own eyes,*[f]
And in their*[f] own estimation so clever.

22/ Hey! You*[g] who are mighty to drink wine,
Who are valiant to mix beer.

23/ Who justify the wicked for a bribe,
And turn aside the vindication of the righteous from him.*[h]

24/ Therefore as a tongue of fire devours the stubble,
And chaff sinks in the flame,*[i]
Their root will become like decay,
And their flower will go up like dust,
For they have rejected the teaching of Yahweh of Hosts,
And the word of the Holy One of Israel they have spurned.

Textual Notes

a MT has בְּבַיִת (*bĕbayit*); 1QIsaᵃ omits the preposition here (בית) but keeps it on בְּשָׂדֶה (*bĕśādeh*) in the parallel line.

b MT, 1QIsaᵃ, and Vg. have עַד אֶפֶס מָקוֹם (*ʿad ʾepes māqôm*), "until there is no place"; LXX is periphrastic: ἵνα τοῦ πλησίον ἀφέλωνταί τι, "so that they may take something from their neighbor." Syr. has ܕܢܐܚܕܘܢ ܐܬܪܐ (*dtʾḥdwn ʾtrʾ*), "that they might seize the place."

c MT has the unusual *hophal* וְהוּשַׁבְתֶּם (*wĕhûšabtem*); 1QIsaᵃ has וישתם, an error for the *qal* וישבתם (*wîšabtem*), "and you will dwell." The *hophal* of *yāšab* is otherwise attested only in Isa 44:26 and conjectured in Ezek 35:9, in both places with a city or cities, not people, as the subject and having the sense "to be settled" or "to be inhabited."

d Reading נִשְׁבַּע (*nišbaʿ*), "he swore," by conjecture. A verb has to be supplied at the beginning of the verse, either נִשְׁבַּע, "Yahweh swore in my ears," נִגְלָה (*niglâ*), "Yahweh revealed in my ears," or נִשְׁמַע (*nišmaʿ*), "Yahweh was heard in my ears." The expression וְנִגְלָה בְּאָזְנַי יְהוָה צְבָאוֹת (*wĕniglâ bĕʾoznay YHWH ṣĕbāʾôt*), "and Yahweh of Hosts revealed in my ears," is found in Isa 22:14 introducing an oath formula, but LXX (ἠκούσθη), "it was heard," Syr. (ܐܫܬܡܥ, *ʾštmʿ*), "it was heard," and Tg. (באודני הויתי שמע), "in my ears I was hearing," suggest the verb נִשְׁמַע or נִשְׁבַּע, which could be easily mistaken for it. The word נִשְׁבַּע (*nišbaʿ*), "he swore," is preferable, since it is used to introduce an oath formula in Isa 14:24, while נִשְׁמַע (*nišmaʿ*), "it was heard," is never used to introduce an oath formula, either in Isaiah or in the rest of the OT.

e LXX misreads MT's בְּאָזְנַי יְהוָה (*bĕʾoznay YHWH*), "in my ears Yahweh" as בְּאָזְנֵי יְהוָה (*bĕʾoznê YHWH*), "in the ears of Yahweh" (εἰς τὰ ὦτα κυρίου); 1QIsaᵃ's באזני יהוה, "in my ears Yahweh," and Vg.'s *in auribus meis*, "in my ears," support MT.

f Syr. omits גְּדֹלִים וְטֹבִים (*gĕdōlim wĕṭôbîm*), "great and good," which is found in MT, 1QIsaᵃ, Vg., and Tg.; while LXX has the phrase, it misdivides the lines ἐὰν γὰρ γένωνται οἰκίαι πολλαί, εἰς ἔρημον ἔσονται μεγάλαι καὶ καλαί, καὶ οὐκ ἔσονται οἱ ἐνοικοῦντες ἐν αὐταῖς, "for if houses become many, great and beautiful ones will become desolate, and there will be none living in them."

g MT has the feminine numeral אַחַת (*ʾeḥāt*), "one," modifying בַּת (*bat*), "bath," while 1QIsaᵃ has the masculine אחד (*ʾeḥād*).

h Vg. renders MT's *hiphil* masculine plural construct participle מַשְׁכִּימֵי (*maškîmê*), "who rise early," with a second person plural verb form (*qui consurgitis*, "you who rise up").

i MT's מְאַחֲרֵי (*mĕʾaḥărê*), "who stay late," is supported by LXX and Syr.; 1QIsaᵃ has מאחזי (*mĕʾaḥăzê*), "who hold on *in the evening.*"

j Vg. renders MT and 1QIsaᵃ's יַיִן יַדְלִיקֵם (*yayin yadlîqēm*), "that wine may chase them," with the second person plural (*ut vino aestuetis*, "that you may be inflamed by wine").

k MT and 1QIsaᵃ have מִשְׁתֵּיהֶם (*mištêhem*), "their banquets"; Vg. has the second plural (*in conviviis vestris*, "in your banquets"), while LXX (πίνουσιν, "they drink") and Syr. (ܫܬܝܢ, *štyn*) appear to read שׁתים (*šōtîm*), "they are drinking."

l MT has the masculine construct פֹּעַל (*pōʿal*), "action of," while 1QIsaᵃ has the feminine construct פעלת, presumably *pĕʿullat*, with no discernible difference in meaning.

m MT has the imperfect יַבִּיטוּ (*yabbîṭû*), "they do (*not*) observe," while 1QIsaᵃ has the perfect הביטו (*hibbîṭû*); Vg. renders with the second person plural (*respicitis*), "you do (*not*) regard."

n Vg. renders MT's third person plural רָאוּ (*rāʾû*), "they do (*not*) perceive," with a second person plural form (*consideratis*), "you do (*not*) consider." Vg.'s second person forms are probably an interpretative attempt to make clear that this is still direct address as in v. 8.

o LXX adds an object (διὰ τὸ μὴ εἰδέναι αὐτοὺς τὸν κύριον, "because they did not know the Lord").

p Reading the conjectural מְזֵי רְעָב (*mĕzê rāʿāb*), "shriveled by hunger" (cf. Deut 32:24), based on the parallel with צִחֵה צָמָא (*ṣiḥēh ṣāmāʾ*), "parched by thirst." 1QIsaᵃ, LXX, Vg., Syr., and Tg. all follow MT's מְתֵי רְעָב (*mĕtê rāʿāb*), but they derive מְתֵי from מֵת, "dead," rather than from מְתִים, "men."

q LXX shortens the verse by omitting וַהֲמוֹנוֹ (*wahămônô*), "and its multitudes," but MT is supported by 1QIsaᵃ, Vg., and Tg.

r Syr. seems to omit the last term in the list.

s MT has וַיִּשַּׁח (*wayyiššaḥ*), "he is bowed down," while 1QIsaᵃ has ישח (*yiššaḥ*), "he will be bowed down"; all the versions translate with a future.

t MT has כְּבָשִׂים (*kĕbāśîm*), "lambs," supported by Vg. and Syr.; 1QIsaᵃ has כבושים, apparently the *qal* passive participle of כבש, "to subdue," that is, (*kĕbûśîm*), "the oppressed." LXX's translation, οἱ διηρπασμένοι, "those who have been plundered," appears to be based on this reading.

u MT and 1QIsaᵃ have כְּדָבְרָם (*kĕdobrām*), and this reading is apparently reflected in all the versions, despite their variations in rendering, with the possible exception of LXX. LXX's ὡς ταῦροι, "as bulls," confirms the initial preposition as כ, but the rendering "as bulls" suggests the translator was reading either כפר[י]ם (*kĕpārîm*) or כשור[י]ם (*kĕšôrîm*).

v For MT's מֵחִים (*mēḥîm*), "fatling sheep," 1QIsaᵃ has מיחים (*mêḥîm*). LXX apparently takes the form as a passive participle from מחה, "to wipe out, annihilate" (καὶ τὰς ἐρήμους τῶν ἀπηλειμμένων, "and the ruins of those who have been wiped out"). Vg. (*et deserta in ubertatem versa*, "and deserta turned into fruitfulness") and Syr. (ܘܚܪܒܬܐ ܕܐܬܒܢܝ, *wḥrbtʾ dʾtbny*, "and the ruins which have been rebuilt") both have odd but similar renderings.

w Reading גְּדָיִם (*gĕdāyîm*), "kids," based on the parallelism between כבש and גדי in Isa 11:6. MT, 1QIsaᵃ, and 4QIsaᵇ read גָּרִים (*gārîm*), "sojourners, foreigners," and this reading is supported by Vg. and Syr. LXX, however, reads an animal name (ἄρνες, "lambs") in parallel to its "bulls" in the first line. The notes to *BHS* suggest גְּרָיִם (*gĕrāyîm*), "lambs," based on an assumed Akkadian word *gurū* meaning "lamb." Unfortunately neither *CAD* nor *AHw* lists such a word, and I am unaware of any evidence for its existence.

x For MT's הַשָּׁוְא (*haššāwʾ*), "vanity," 1QIsaᵃ has השי, which appears to just be a scribal error of writing *yod* for *waw*, and the elision of the quiescent *aleph*. Vg. supports MT, but LXX and Syr. have "as with a long cord/rope."

y   MT's וְכַעֲבוֹת הָעֲגָלָה (wĕkaʿăbôt hāʿăgālâ), "as with the ropes of a cart," is supported by 1QIsaᵃ, Vg., and Syr., but LXX takes העגלה as hāʿeglâ meaning "heifer" (καὶ ὡς ζυγοῦ ἱμάντι δαμάλεως, "and as the thongs of the yoke of a heifer").

z   LXX (τὸ τάχος, to tachos, "quickly") and Syr. (bʿgl, "quickly") simplify by translating the first verb with an adverbial expression.

*a MT has the long form יָחִישָׁה (yāḥîšâ), "let him rush (his work)," while 1QIsaᵃ has the short form יחיש (yāḥîš); 4QIsaᵇ adds the conjunction ו[י]חישה (wĕyāḥîšâ), "and let him rush."

*b MT and 4QIsaᵇ have מַעֲשֵׂהוּ (maʿăśēhû), "his work," but with its correction above the line 1QIsaᵃ suggests the plural מעשׂהו, "his works."

*c MT has וְתִקְרַב (wĕtiqrab), "let the plan draw near," while 1QIsaᵃ and 4QIsaᵇ have the long form ותקרבה (wĕtiqrābâ). LXX apparently omits this verb, though it seems to have influenced the translation of yāḥîšâ in the preceding line: "quickly let him bring near [ἐγγισάτω] the things he will do."

*d MT and 1QIsaᵃ have the long form וְתָבוֹאָה (wĕtābôʾâ), "and let it come," while 4QIsaᵇ has the short form ותבוא (wĕtābôʾ). LXX renders καὶ ἐλθάτω, "and let the plan of the Holy One of Israel come."

*e MT has the long form וְנֵדָעָה (wĕnēdāʿâ), "that we may know," while 1QIsaᵃ has the short form ונדע (wĕnēdāʿ). Vg., Syr., and Tg. add a suffix, "that we may know it."

*f MT, 1QIsaᵃ, 4QIsaᵇ, and most of the versions have third person plural suffixes, but Vg. has second plural forms (vae qui sapientes estis in oculis vestris et coram vobismet ipsis prudentes, "woe you who are wise in your own eyes and in your own view prudent"). It is possible that Vg. went with the second person because it understood the passage as involving direct address, not necessarily because its Hebrew Vorlage had second person forms here.

*g Both LXX (οὐαὶ οἱ ἰσχύοντες ὑμῶν οἱ τὸν οἶνον πίνοντες καὶ οἱ δυνάσται οἱ κεραννύντες τὸ σικερα, "Ah, your strong ones who drink wine and your powerful ones who mix beer"), and Vg. (vae qui potentes estis ad bibendum vinum et viri fortes ad miscendam ebrietatem, "Woe, you who are powerful to drink wine, and are strong to mix an intoxicating drink") indicate direct address by their use of second person forms here.

*h Syr. and Tg. have the third person masculine plural suffix.

*i For MT and 4QIsaᵇ's וחשש להבה (wahăšaš lehābâ, "and chaff sinks in the flame"), 1QIsaᵃ has the far inferior and probably garbled reading ואש לוהבת (waʾēš lôhebet, "and a flaming fire sinks").

Commentary

Isaiah 5:8-24 is composed of a series of sayings introduced by the particle הוי (hôy). These sayings may originally have been independent of one another, but the arrangement of such sayings in a series has parallels (Isa 28:1; 29:1, 15; 30:1; 31:1; 33:1; Hab 2:6, 9, 12, 15, 19). The structure of these so-called woe oracles requires comment. The introductory particle הוי in such oracles has been traditionally rendered as "Woe to . . . ," but though traditional and appropriate for the related particle אוי (ʾôy) followed by the preposition ל (lĕ), it is hardly correct for הוי. The particle הוי is used primarily as an exclamation to gain the hearer's attention, and it is thus often followed by a vocative designating the hearer. The particle was used in funerary laments in the direct address of the dead (1 Kgs 13:30; Jer 22:18; 34:5), and in appropriate prophetic contexts it may carry some of the threatening overtones of the funerary lament. But the particle was by no means limited to such contexts, and my suspicion is that the context, not the inherent meaning of the exclamation, is responsible for this negative overtone. In Zech 2:10-11 (Eng. 2:6-7) the particle is used as an exclamation to get the attention of God's people, who are then called upon to flee Babylon and the land of the north. In the context, this is a salvation oracle, calling upon the people to return from exile. In Isa 55:1 the particle is similarly used to invite God's people to a free banquet. In both of these passages the exclamatory particle introduces good news. These are salvation oracles, and it is hard to see how הוי in either of these passages can be assigned a negative connotation. In prophetic oracles the particle normally functions structurally as a vocative exclamation to summon the attention of the prophet's audience, who are then designated and characterized by a following noun, adjective, or participial construction that may be extended with a relative clause. Whether the oracle is negative or positive depends not on the inherent meaning of הוי but on the following characterization of the audience and the admonition given to the audience. Most of the preserved preexilic הוי oracles are negative, at least for the sometimes "fictive" audience addressed (see Isa 10:1; 28:1), but in the exilic and postexilic period there are the positive examples mentioned above (Isa 55:1; Zech 2:10-11 [Eng. 2:6-7]).

To return specifically to the series of הוי oracles in Isa 5:8-24, the vocative exclamation is followed with the designation and/or characterization of the audience by a following noun, adjective, or participial construction sometimes extended with a relative clause. In Hebrew syntax, the relative clause following a participial construction is normally put in the third person, even though the construction actually involves direct address. That one is dealing with direct address is clear from v. 8, where the prophet uses a second person verb form and second person pronominal suffix to refer back to the party designated by the opening participial construction with its following third person plural imperfect. In the complete form represented by vv. 8-10, this vocative address and characterization of the audience's sins are followed by Yahweh's word of judgment, but many of the sayings in this chapter reflect an incomplete form without any explicit word of judgment. While this incomplete form seems to be attested only here, it is analogous to the incomplete oath formula in Hebrew where the standard form, "If I am lying, may Yahweh kill me!" (meaning, "I swear I am not lying!") is shortened by the omission of the apodosis: "If I am lying . . . !" This shortened, more common form of the oath formula also means, "I swear I am not lying!" Just as the apodosis is implicit in the incomplete oath formula, so the judgment expressed in the full form of the הוי oracle is implicit in the incomplete הוי oracle. Structurally it is comparable to the utterance of someone today who sees some boys vandalizing a store front and shouts, "Hey! You boys who are spray painting. . . ." One may add a specific threat, but often there is no need, since the mere characterization of the boys' actions as vandalism carries an implicit threat of intervention and may already have caused the culprits to flee. It should be evident, then, that the הוי oracle is not an impersonal form of address but a very personal one. With it the prophet seizes his audience's attention, accuses them of specific wrongdoing, and then either pronounces judgment on them explicitly or implies it by the very use of the incomplete form.

The audience and culprits in v. 8 are identified as those who constantly expand and consolidate their far-flung property holdings at the expense of others. "To join house to house and bring field near to field" suggests such amassing of property that the small landowners are squeezed out and absorbed by the expanding properties of the landed aristocracy.[1] Isaiah's contemporary, Micah, has a similar הוי oracle against the same people (Mic 2:1-6). It appears that the wealthy were taking advantage of the poor to seize their fields and houses. Exactly how they did this is not specified. They may have foreclosed on mortgages when the poor could not pay off their loans; they may have expropriated the property when the poor failed to pay their taxes or fines levied against them; or they may have simply seized the property without any justifiable legal claim, because they knew the poor had little hope of vindication in court as long as the royal officials were so open to bribery (cf. Isa 1:23). Whether technically legal or not—Isa 10:1-2 speaks of laws enacted to help despoil the poor—Isaiah and Micah both regarded such practices as a grave sin against God. Such amassing of land was apparently profitable because of an abundant pool of cheap farm labor, caused in part by the mass of now landless refugees from Israel seeking refuge in Judah after the dislocations of the Syro-Ephraimitic War (735–732 BCE) and the following disastrous revolts of Samaria in 725–722 BCE and again in concert with Hamath and Gaza in 720 BCE.[2]

---

1   Note the excellent work of J. Andrew Dearman, *Property Rights in the Eighth-Century Prophets: The Conflict and Its Background* (SBLDS 106; Atlanta: Scholars Press, 1988).

2   See Magen Broshi, "The Expansion of Jerusalem in the Reign of Hezekiah and Manasseh," *IEJ* 24 (1974) 21–26. For the ongoing dispute about the reasons for the rapid increase in Jerusalem's population during the last half of the eighth century BCE, see H. Geva, "Western Jerusalem at the End of the First Temple Period in Light of the Excavations in the Jewish Quarter," in A. G. Vaughn and A. E. Killebrew, eds., *Jerusalem in Bible and Archaeology: The First Temple Period* (SBLSymS 18; Atlanta: Society of Biblical Literature, 2003) 183–208; and, in the same volume, R. Reich and E. Shukron, "The Urban Development of Jerusalem in the Late Eighth Century B.C.E.," 209–18; and W. M. Schniedewind, "Jerusalem, the Late Judaean Monarchy, and the Composition of Biblical Texts," 375–93, and the literature cited in these articles. N. Na'aman has rejected the proposed role of northern refugees in

Note the second person forms in the last half of v. 8: והושבתם (wĕhûšabtem) "and you [pl.] are left to dwell" לבדכם (lĕbadkem) "by yourselves." This makes crystal clear that the oracle is to be understood as direct address. This comment indicates that, already in the description of their sin, Isaiah includes an implicit judgment. What good is all this property if the final result is to find oneself isolated and without community? To live alone by oneself in the midst of the land was not a good thing. Nonetheless, explicit judgment follows in v. 9.

Part of the opening of v. 9 has been lost in transmission. As it stands, the MT has simply, "In my ears Yahweh of Hosts [. . .]." A verb has fallen out and should be restored. For reasons given in the textual notes, I restore נשבע (nišbaʿ), "Yahweh of Hosts swore in my ears." What follows is an incomplete oath formula. Literally, "If many houses do not become desolate, great and fine houses without inhabitant . . . ," with some such apodosis as "may God do so to me and more also" understood. With the negative in the protasis, the meaning of the incomplete oath formula is positive, that is, "Surely many houses will become desolate, great and fine houses without inhabitant!" Yahweh swears that the large and beautiful houses the rich have obtained by oppression will be left vacant ruins.

The reason for this is given in v. 10. Ten acres of vineyard is an approximate translation for עשרת צמדי כרם (ʿăśeret ṣimdê kerem), which literally means "the area of vineyard that may be cultivated by ten yoke of oxen." A bath was a liquid measure that equaled about five and a half gallons, a grotesquely small yield for ten acres of vineyard.[3] The ephah was a dry measure that equaled only one-tenth of a homer, roughly 3.8 bushels, which means they would sow ten times more seed grain than they would reap at the harvest. A farmer cannot afford to lose ninety percent of his annual investment on a yearly basis for very long. Such losses over an extended period will inevitably lead to the abandonment of the land, and vacant, decaying houses, even once elegant houses, will stand as mute witnesses to such economic collapse.

Verses 11-13 present another complete הוי oracle. The vocative address expanded by relative clauses extends through v. 12, and the explicit judgment follows in v. 13. There are no explicit second person forms in these verses, but direct address is probably to be assumed with the Vulgate. The initial third person forms following the participles have probably influenced the author to remain with the third person despite the direct address. Here Isaiah singles out those in his audience who have given their lives over to drink and debauchery. From morning until evening their concern is for the next glass of wine, the next mug of beer. The alcoholic drink designated by שכר (šēkār) has been traditionally rendered in English as "strong drink," but the primary meaning of the Akkadian cognate šikaru is beer. It was long thought that the process for the distillation of alcoholic beverages was not yet known in the eighth century BCE, at least in the Near East,[4] ruling out the meaning "distilled liquor" and by implication "strong drink," but recent archaeological discoveries in Cyprus and the Philistine area suggest

---

the expansion of Jerusalem's population ("When and How Did Jerusalem Become a Great City? The Rise of Jerusalem as Judah's Premier City in the Eighth–Seventh Centuries B.C.E.," *BASOR* 347 [2007] 21–56), but whatever one thinks of the larger thesis of Israel Finkelstein, "The Settlement History of Jerusalem in the Eighth and Seventh Centuries BC," *RB* (2008) 499–515, on this point he seems to have the better of the argument.

3 For Israelite weights and measures, see M. A. Powell, "Weights and Measures," *ABD* 6:897–908; or R. Kletter, "Weights and Measures," *NIDB* 5:831–41.

4 E. Hyams thought that the Chinese discovered the process as early as the eighth century BCE (*Dionysus: A Social History of the Wine Vine* [New York: Macmillan, 1965] 226). R. J. Forbes attributed the discovery to the Greeks closer to the beginning of the Common Era (*A Short History of the Art of Distillation* [Leiden: Brill, 1948] 6). C. H. Patrick attributed the discovery to the Arabs much later (*Alcohol, Culture, and Society* [Durham, NC: Duke University Press, 1952] 29), while J. Doxat suggested that the process was independently discovered in a variety of places (*The World of Drinks and Drinking* [New York: Drake, 1971] 80). Nonetheless, it was generally held that distilled alcohol was not widely available in the Near East and Europe prior to the twelfth century CE. See also H. F. Lutz, *Viticulture and Brewing in the Ancient Orient* (New York: G. E. Stechert, 1922); S. P. Lucia, "The Antiquity of Alcohol in Diet and Medicine," in S. P. Lucia, ed., *Alcohol and Civilization* (New York: McGraw-Hill, 1963) 151–66; and L. Milano, ed., *Drinking in Ancient Societies: History and Culture of Drinks in the Ancient Near East. Papers of a Symposium Held in Rome, May 17–19, 1990* (HANE 6; Padua: Sargon, 1994).

that primitive methods for making distilled grape brandy were in fact known.[5] The Harvard archaeologist Lawrence Stager, who initially argued that שכר referred to a type of date wine, now believes that it refers to a distilled grape brandy or grappa.[6] In contrast, I think it is more likely that it normally refers to beer. Beer was the basic drink in both Egypt and Mesopotamia, while viticulture made grape wine the dominant alcoholic drink in Israel. Nonetheless, as a rich barley-producing region and the land bridge between Egypt and Mesopotamia, both of which exercised enormous cultural and often political influence on Palestine, it would be odd if the Israelites never made beer and even odder if they had no word for beer, as Stager claims. The paired use of the ordinary word for wine, *yayin*, and the word *šēkār* (Gen 9:21; Lev 10:9; Num 6:3; Isa 5:11, 22, passim) suggests that the two terms refer to two different alcoholic drinks. The latter is derived from the verbal root *šākar*, "to get drunk," but this does not imply that *šēkār* had a higher alcohol content than wine. The Akkadian cognate *šikarum* from the same verbal root means beer, and there is no evidence that Mesopotamian beer had an unusually high alcohol content. Though the Hebrew word *šēkār* may occasionally have been used as a generic term for any alcoholic drink (Jerome, letter to Nepotian), including grappa, the cognate evidence suggests that beer was its normal meaning. The LXX translator of Isa 19:10, who read *šēkār* for MT's *śeker*, understood the noun to mean beer, since he translates it as ζῦθον, a type of Egyptian beer (Jerome, *Comm. Isa.*). The common pairing with יין (*yayin*) "wine" suggests that *šēkār* was a very ordinary drink, which favors the translation "beer" over "brandy," since it would probably be available in much greater quantities than brandy, which required a more difficult process of production. Moreover, *šēkār* is not the only word for beer in Hebrew, since, as pointed out in the textual note on 1:22 above, the rare noun *sobeʾ* (Isa 1:22; Hos 4:8; Nah 1:10) probably refers to a specialty beer associated with taverns. Stager has made much of the fact that the inscription at Ashkelon mentioning quantities of *yn ʾdm* and *škr*, "red wine" and "brandy?/beer?," was found near a shop with objects that may have been used in distillation, but the find spot was also close to a building where grain was stored for grinding into flour.[7]

Verse 11 is very cleverly structured with a striking play on words to surprise the audience. Following the initial הוי, one has the masculine plural participle in construct, followed by the temporal expression introduced by the preposition, "in the morning," then the name of an alcoholic beverage which serves as the object of the following third masculine plural imperfect: "Hey you who rise early in the morning that beer they may pursue." The second line, minus the introductory הוי, appears to be following the identical structure—masculine plural participle in construct, followed by the temporal expression introduced by the same preposition, "in the evening," then the name of another alcoholic beverage, and finally the imperfect verb. Until the very last syllable of the line one expects the structure to be identical, but with the very last syllable Isaiah pulls a switch. Instead of third masculine plural imperfect, Isaiah uses a third masculine singular with a third masculine plural suffix, thus shifting the grammatical function of the second alcoholic beverage from object to subject: "who tarry late in the evening that wine may chase them." The verb דלק (*dālaq*) normally means "to burn" or "to set on fire," in the *hiphil* conjugation used here, but if one may judge from the usage of the *qal* conjugation, it can also mean "to pursue hotly" (Gen 31:36; 1 Sam 17:53; Ps 10:2; Lam 4:19). With his clever structuring of these two lines, Isaiah suggests that these people chase after wine and beer until they are enflamed or, given the equally clever double entendre, until the beer and wine begin chasing them. In short, the people are no longer in control; the alcohol is. Isaiah's last-minute shift of structural expectations is so surprising that even some normally brilliant scholars reveal a prosaizing pedantry in emending the text to preserve the expected structure. No less a figure than A. B. Ehrlich (p. 21) suggested an emendation of ידליקם (*yadlîqēm*, "that *wine* may pursue them") to ידליקו (*yadlîqû*, "that they may pursue *wine*").

Verse 12 indicates that the problem is not just alcoholism but a lifestyle of partying unconcern for the deep

5   L. E. Stager et al., eds., *Ashkelon 1: Introduction and Overview (1985–2006)* (Leon Levy Expedition to Ashkelon; Winona Lake, IN: Eisenbrauns, 2008) 271, 309, 341.

6   Ibid.; and King and Stager, *Life in Biblical Israel*, 101–3.

7   Stager, *Ashkelon 1*, 309.

issues facing the society. The situation is similar to that scored by Amos in Amos 6:1-7. Isaiah's contemporaries are condemned because their attention is so fixed on their own pleasure and entertainment that they pay no regard to what Yahweh is doing. The motif of Yahweh's deed, work, or plan is central in Isaiah's theology (Isa 5:19; 10:12; 14:24-27; 19:12, 17; 23:9; 28:21; 30:1). One should pay attention to God's work, but to see it requires that one look at what is going on in the world through eyes and minds informed and shaped by Israel's traditional religious heritage. To understand this passage is to raise the question whether we contemporary believers listen to the news of our day through ears informed by our religious faith. Do we allow our faith to inform our perception of the "real" world, or do we exclude politics, business, recreation, and the rest of our secular pursuits from what God is doing?

Because Judah's leaders in their intoxication with pleasure have lost the ability to discern God's work, because they can no longer creatively apply the insights of their religious tradition to the political and social problems of their day, Yahweh's people will go into exile for lack of this knowledge. The verb in v. 13 is probably to be understood as a prophetic perfect, so the verbal and nominal clauses in the verse should all be understood as announcing future judgment—though, depending on the date of the oracle, the similar destruction of the north may already be in the past. One should note the similarity of Isaiah's word here to that of Hos 4:6. The whole context of Hos 4:4-12 is similar, and Isaiah may have been influenced by his northern contemporary. In both cases the judgment fits the crime. In Isaiah the partying nobility will be emaciated (see the textual notes) by hunger, and the drunken crowd will be parched by thirst.

Something seems to be missing between v. 13 and v. 14. Verse 14 introduces another explicit judgment with the same conjunction לכן (lākēn) that introduced the judgment in v. 13, and it cannot be a simple continuation of the preceding judgment because of a change in pronominal suffixes. In v. 13 the two occurrences of the pronoun "its" translate Hebrew third masculine singular suffixes referring back to עמי (ʿammî), "my people," which is a masculine singular noun in Hebrew. In v. 14 the suffixes are third feminine singular, presumably referring back to Jerusalem, which, like all cities, is treated as a feminine singular in Hebrew, but Jerusalem is not in the text.

The RSV and NRSV add the city name without warrant, thereby obscuring the real difficulty in the text. It is probable that the beginning of the new הוי oracle mentioning Jerusalem has fallen out between v. 13 and v. 14. It was omitted because the ancient copyist's eye skipped from the לכן of v. 13 to the לכן of v. 14.

Thus, we do not know exactly what sins were charged to the group castigated here, though one could suggest something on the order of הוי בני ציון בדמים וירושלם בעולה (hôy bōnê ṣiyôn bĕdāmîm wîrûšālaim bĕʿawlâ), "Hey! You who build Zion with bloodshed and Jerusalem with iniquity!" (cf. Mic 3:9-12). The threatened punishment, however, is all too explicit. Again one should read the verbs in v. 14 as prophetic perfects or future tenses. Sheol, a personification of death and the underworld, will open her voracious jaws, and all Jerusalem's nobility and crowds, her boisterous din and the exultant crowds who make the din will go down into the underworld. One could debate whether the abstract terms הדרה (hădārāh), "her splendor," and המונה (hămônāh), "her turmoil, wealth, multitude," should be rendered as the concrete "her eminences" and "her multitudes," but the parallel between ושאונה ועלז בה (ûšĕʾônāh wĕʿālēz bāh), "and her boisterous din and the exultant within her," and Isa 24:8's שאון עליזים (šĕʾôn ʿallîzîm), "the noise of the exultant ones," seems to point in that direction. The imagery of Sheol's gaping mouth seems to be borrowed from Canaanite mythology about Mot, the god of death; the passage has a close parallel in the Baal epic, where Mot opens his gaping mouth to swallow Baal—"one lip to earth, one lip to heaven, his tongue to the stars that Baal might enter his stomach and go down into his mouth" (KTU 1.5 ii 2-4=ANET 138, g. I* AB, ii). Isaiah uses similar imagery in 29:4 about sinking into the underworld to express God's purging judgment on Jerusalem.

Verses 15-17 appear syntactically to be an extension of the announcement of judgment, but they present a number of difficulties. Verse 15 is a slight variation of the refrain found in 2:9, 17, and some scholars delete it and the following v. 16 as a secondary insertion here (Wildberger, 1:190–91; Gray, 92–93; Kaiser, *Jesaja 1–12*, 51). Though they may be read as futures by analogy with the prophetic perfect, most of the verbs in both v. 15 and v. 16 are in the past tense, and the verses seem to interrupt the logical connection between v. 14 and v. 17. If vv. 15-16 are not a late insertion, they are at least an editorial aside. They assert that God's righteous judgment will result in the humbling of human pride and the exaltation and sanctification of Yahweh of Hosts. Verse 17, then, resumes the thought of v. 14. When Jerusalem has slipped into the underworld, sheep and goats will graze among her ruins. This is a common topos in the description of ruined cities (Isa 27:10; Zeph 2:6-7, 13-14; cf. Isa 7:23-25). The verse is full of textual difficulties, however, and another interpretation is possible. In view of Hebrew's use of animal names to designate nobility, one might emend כדברם (kĕdobrām), "as (in) their pasture," to כר בראים (kar bĕrīʾîm), "the pasture of the fat [rams]," and וחרבות (wĕḥārbôt), "and the ruins," to רחבות (rĕḥābôt), "the broad [ranges]," and translate "Lambs shall graze on the pasture of the fat [rams], and on the broad ranges of the fatlings (mēḥîm) kids (gĕdāyîm) shall eat." The lambs and kids would be the righteous poor, and the fat rams and fatlings would be the rich oppressors (cf. Ezek 34:17-22). If this interpretation is followed, the judgment on Jerusalem is a purifying judgment which leaves a righteous remnant, as elsewhere in Isaiah.

Verses 18-19 present an incomplete הוי oracle. It is lacking any explicit word of judgment. On the other hand, it is possible that here and through v. 23, we have a quickening of the poetic rhythm: a piling up of protases of condemnation leading to a grand judgment on all of them in v. 24. The precise meaning of v. 18 is not entirely obvious. It appears to suggest that Isaiah's audience puts more strenuous effort into sinning than most people put into honest work. People do not normally take the role of oxen in pulling an ox cart, but Isaiah suggests that his audience is in harness, working like oxen to drag sin behind them. Whether this is simply the prophet's angry reaction to his audience's scoffing that is mentioned in v. 19, or whether he has some other sin in mind is not clear. What is clear is that his audience did not believe Isaiah's message. It may be that their lack of faith in his message simply reflected a deeper lack of faith in the religious traditions on which Isaiah based his message. Perhaps Isaiah was characterizing his audience as people who struggle and strain, making strenuous and sinful attempts to amass wealth, sate their desires for status and pleasure, and buy their own security, because they do not trust God enough to relax, relieve the oppressed, and enjoy the more modest fruits of righteousness (cf. Isa 28:12; 30:15; 32:17). In any case, in v. 19, apparently in response to Isaiah's earlier comment in v. 12, some scoffers in the crowd urged Yahweh to hurry up with his plans so someone other than the prophet could discern them and thus determine whether Yahweh would really act as the prophet claims. One might compare Elijah at Mount Carmel taunting the prophets of Baal to make their God act (1 Kgs 18:27). Here in Isaiah we would have a similar taunt, but now applied to Yahweh and his prophet! Jeremiah faced a similar response (Jer 17:15), which eventually led Jeremiah to cease praying for God's forbearance toward his adversaries and motivated him instead to pray for their utter destruction (Jer 18:19-23; cf. Jer 15:15). In contrast, Isaiah simply leaves God's judgment on these scoffers implicit, inherent in their characterization as those who scoff at the prophetic word, unless of course, as suggested above, v. 24 expresses the judgment on the whole series of hôy oracles in vv. 18-23.

Verse 20 is another apparently incomplete הוי oracle, addressed to those who call everything by a false name. What is ultimately involved in this false naming is the perversion of justice. Isaiah touches on the same theme in 32:4, when in his vision for the future he says, "The fool will no more be called noble, nor the knave said to be honorable." This problem of justification of sin by redefinition is still with us today. When a one-party dictatorship can be called "democratic," sexual promiscuity an "alternate lifestyle," bribery "lobbying," secret closed-door political wheeling and dealing "transparency in government," and the like, doublespeak is still with us.

Again an incomplete הוי oracle, v. 21 is perhaps aimed at the royal counselors whose policies Isaiah opposed. They belonged to the circle of the חכמים (ḥăkāmîm "the wise"), but Isaiah designates them as wise only in their own eyes. In taking this tack Isaiah turns one of the wisdom tradition's own themes against these early representatives of that tradition (see Prov 3:7; 26:5, 12, 16; 28:11). Compare Jeremiah's charge and threat against the ḥăkāmîm, "the wise" (Jer 8:8-10).

Verses 22-23 introduce the final oracle in the section, which is concluded by an explicit word of judgment in v. 24. Isaiah brings two charges against his hearers. They are valiant only as drinkers, and they pervert justice for the sake of a bribe. The connection between the two charges would seem to be that these officials are interested only in their own pleasure, not justice. They have no courage when it means rendering a judgment against the rich and powerful. Their cowardly approach is that it is better to accept the bribe than to try to buck the system. The wisdom tradition also notes an unfortunate connection between a ruler's overindulgence in drink and the miscarriage of justice (Prov 31:4-5).

Since all the incomplete הוי oracles are so short and at least several of them concern the matter of justice, it is tempting to take v. 24 as the explicit judgment for the whole group. An analogous situation exists in Job 31, however, where in a long list of oaths, complete and incomplete oath formulas are mixed together indiscriminately, and there it is clear from their specificity that the apodoses of the complete formulas cannot serve as single apodoses for a whole series of protases; for example, Job 31:22 serves as the apodosis only for 31:21. The same may be true in Isaiah's הוי oracles, which would make v. 24 the explicit judgment only for the parties designated in vv. 22-23. On the other hand, Isaiah's concluding rationale for the judgment, "For they have rejected the teaching of Yahweh of Hosts / And the word of the Holy One of Israel they have spurned," would be particularly appropriate as a characterization of those who made fun

of Isaiah's prophetic oracles in v. 19. The issue is hard to settle, but v. 24 seems general enough to apply to all of vv. 18-23. Moreover, the quickening of the poetic rhythm, which ramps up the dramatic tension, does look deliberate. If not, perhaps v. 24a is the explicit judgment following vv. 22-23, while v. 24b beginning with "for they have rejected" represents a summarizing statement intended as a closure for the whole collection of הוי oracles. The judgment is expressed in the third person rather than in the second person one might expect following the vocative address—the second person does occur elsewhere in judgments at the end of הוי oracles (see especially 10:3, since 10:1-4 was probably originally a part of the series of הוי oracles in 5:8-24 [see below]; and cf. 5:8)—but the third person is probably by attraction to the syntactically determined third person of the relative clause, "who turn aside the vindication of the righteous from him" (v. 23). The judgment announced on these evildoers is that their root and fruit, that is, their future in its totality, the future they had hoped to secure by their wickedness, will disappear in the fire like chaff or straw, vanishing like dried-up rot or a puff of dust.

Bibliography

Albrektson, Bertil, "The Divine Plan in History," in Albrektson, *History and the Gods : An Essay on the Idea of Historical Events as Divine Manifestations in the Ancient Near East and in Israel* (ConBOT 1; Lund: Gleerup, 1967) 68–97.

Alt, Albrecht, "Der Anteil des Königtums an der sozialen Entwicklung in den Reichen Israel und Juda," in Alt, *Kleine Schriften zur Geschichte des Volkes Israel* (3 vols.; Munich: C. H. Beck, 1953–59) 3:348–72.

Anderson, Bernhard W., "'God with Us'—In Judgement and in Mercy: The Editorial Structure of Isaiah 5-10(11)," in Gene M. Tucker, David L. Petersen, and Robert R. Wilson, eds., *Canon, Theology and Old Testament Interpretation: Essays in Honor of Brevard S. Childs* (Philadelphia: Fortress, 1988) 230–45.

Bardtke, Hans, "Die Latifundien in Juda während der zweiten Hälfte des achten Jahrhunderts v. Chr.," in *Hommages à André Dupont-Sommer* (Paris: Adrien-Maisonneuve, 1971) 235–54.

Bartelt, *Book around Immanuel.*

———, "Isaiah 5 and 9: In or Interdependence?" in Astrid B. Beck et al., eds., *Fortunate the Eyes That See: Essays in Honor of David Noel Freedman in Celebration of His Seventieth Birthday* (Grand Rapids: Eerdmanns, 1995) 157–74.

Blum, Erhard, "Jesajas prophetisches Testament: Beobachtungen zu Jes 1–11," *ZAW* 108 (1996) 547–68; 109 (1997) 12–29.

———, "Jesaja und der DBR des Amos: Unzeitgemässe Überlegungen zu Jes 5:25; 9:7-20; 10:1-4," *DBAT* 28 (1992–93) 75–95.

Boadt, Lawrence, "The Poetry of Prophetic Persuasion: Preserving the Prophet's Persona," *CBQ* 59 (1997) 1–21.

Brown, W. P., "The So-Called Refrain in Isaiah 5:25-30 and 9:7–10:4," *CBQ* 62 (1990) 432–43.

Chisholm, Robert B., Jr., "Structure, Style, and the Prophetic Message: An Analysis of Isaiah 5:8-30," *BSac* 143 (1986) 46–60.

Clifford, Richard J., "The Use of Hoy in the Prophets," *CBQ* 28 (1966) 458–64.

Davies, Eryl W., *Prophecy and Ethics: Isaiah and the Ethical Traditions of Israel* (JSOTSup 16; Sheffield: JSOT Press, 1981).

Dobberahn, F. E., "O texto nos envia para a rua: Sobre o papel da arqueologia na hermeneutica da America Latina [Isa 5:8-10]," *EstTeo* 32 (1992) 138–54.

Donner, Herbert, "Die soziale Botschaft der Propheten im Lichte der Gesellschaftsordnung in Israel," *OrAnt* 2 (1963) 229–45.

Emerton, J. A., "A Phrase in a Phoenician Papyrus and a Problem in Isaiah 5:14," in J. Cheryl Exum and H. G. M. Williamson, eds., *Reading from Right to Left: Essays on the Hebrew Bible in Honour of David J. A. Clines* (JSOTSup 373; London: Sheffield Academic Press, 2003) 121–27.

———, "The Textual Problems of Isaiah V 14," *VT* 17 (1967) 135–42.

Fichtner, J., "Jahwes Plan in der Botschaft des Jesaja," *ZAW* 63 (1951) 16–33.

Forbes, R. J., *A Short History of the Art of Distillation* (Leiden: Brill, 1948).

Fröhlich, I., "CD2:2—3:12; 4Q252; and the *Genesis Apocryphon*," in M. E. Stone and E. G. Chazon, eds., *Biblical Perspectives: The Early Use and Interpretation of the Bible in Light of the Dead Sea Scrolls* (STDJ 28; Leiden: Brill, 1998) 98–99.

Gerstenberger, Erhard S., "The Woe-Oracles of the Prophets," *JBL* 81 (1962) 249–63.

Graham, W. C., "Notes on the Interpretation of Isaiah 5:1–14," *AJSL* 45 (1928) 167–78.

Hardmeier, C., *Texttheorie und biblische Exegese: Zur rhetorischen Funktion der Trauermetaphorik in der Prophetie* (BEvT, Theologische Abhandlungen 79; Munich: Kaiser, 1978).

Hillers, Delbert R., "Hoy and Hoy Oracles: A Neglected Syntactic Aspect," in Carol L. Meyers and M. O'Connor, eds., *The Word of the Lord Shall Go Forth: Essays in Honor of David Noel Freedman in Celebration of His Sixtieth Birthday* (ASOR Special Volumes Series 1; Winona Lake, IN: Eisenbrauns, 1983) 185–88.

Hoffman, H. W., *Die Intention,* 105–7.

Horst, F., "Das Eigentum nach dem Alten Testament," in Horst, *Gottes Recht: Gesammelte Studien zum Recht im Alten Testament* (Munich: C. Kaiser, 1961) 203–21.

Horst, P. W. van der, "A Classical Parallel to Isaiah 5,8," *ExpTim* 89 (1978) 119–20.

Janzen, Waldemar, *Mourning Cry and Woe Oracle* (BZAW 125; Berlin: de Gruyter, 1972).

Kellerman, Diether, "Frevelstricke und Wagenseil: Bemerkungen zu Jesaja 5:18," *VT* 37 (1987) 90–97.

King and Stager, *Life in Biblical Israel.*

Korpel, Marjo C. A., "Structural Analysis as a Tool in Redaction Criticism: The Example of Isaiah 5 and 10:1–6," *JSOT* 69 (1996) 53–71.

Kossen, Henk B., "The Peace Church in a World of Conflict," *Conrad Grebel Review* 2, no. 1 (1984) 1–9.

Krause, H. J., "Hoj als prophetische Leichenklage über das eigene Volk im 8 Jahrhundert," *ZAW* 85 (1973) 15–46.

Lutz, H. F., *Viticulture and Brewing in the Ancient Orient* (New York: G. E. Stechert, 1922).

March, W. E., "Basic Types of Prophetic Speech," in John H. Hayes, ed., *Old Testament Form Criticism* (San Antonio, TX: Trinity University Press, 1974) 164–65.

Marshall, R. J., "The Unity of Isaiah 1–12," *LQ* 14 (1962) 21–38.

McKane, William, *Prophets and Wise Men* (SBT 44; London: SCM, 1965).

Milano, L., ed., *Drinking in Ancient Societies: History and Culture of Drinks in the Ancient Near East. Papers of a Symposium Held in Rome, May 17–19, 1990* (HANE 6; Padua: Sargon, 1994).

Mirsky, A., "The Third Benediction of the 'Amida and the Passage 'the Lord of Hosts Is Exalted' (Is 5,16)," *Tarbiz* 38, no. 3 (1969) 297–300.

Okoye, J., Review of *Exile: Old Testament, Jewish and Christian Conceptions,* ed. J. M. Scott, *CBQ* 61 (1999) 410–11.

Premnath, D. N., "Latifundialization and Isaiah 5:8–10," *JSOT* 40 (1988) 49–60.

Rad, Gerhard von, "Verheissenes Land und Jahwes Land im Hexateuch," *ZDPV* 66 (1943) 191–204.

———, "Das Werk Jahwes," in *Studia Biblica et Semitica Theodoro Christiano Vriezen qui munere professoris theologiae per XXV annos functus est . . . dedicata* (Wageningen: H. Veenman & Zonen, 1966) 290–98.

Roberts, J. J. M., "Double Entendre."

Speier, S., "Zu drei Jesajastellen (1,7; 5,24; 10,7)," *TZ* 21 (1965) 310–13.

Stager, Lawrence E., et al., eds., *Ashkelon 1: Introduction and Overview (1985–2006)* (Leon Levy Expedition to Ashkelon; Winona Lake, IN: Eisenbrauns, 2008).

Wanke, G., "'אוי' und 'הוי,'" *ZAW* 78 (1966) 215–17.

Westermann, Claus, *Basic Forms of Prophetic Speech* (trans. H. C. White; Philadelphia: Westminster, 1967; repr., Louisville: Westminster John Knox, 1991).

Whedbee, *Isaiah and Wisdom.*

Wildberger, Hans, "Israel und sein Land," *EvT* 16 (1956) 404–22.

Williams, J. G., "The Alas-Oracles of the Eighth Century Prophets," *HUCA* 38 (1967) 75–91.

Wolff, Hans Walter, *Amos' Geistige Heimat* (WMANT 18; Neukirchen-Vluyn: Neukirchener Verlag, 1964) 12–23.

In the present text, Isa 5:25-30 is connected to the preceding verse by the conjunction עַל־כֵּן (ʿal kēn), "therefore," in the sense of "that is why." The sin of rejecting God's word mentioned in v. 24c has provoked God's anger (v. 25). But v. 24c also goes with the preceding, and there are a number of indications that the connection between v. 24 and v. 25 is secondary. Verse 24 is part of the series of הוי oracles beginning in 5:8, a series that has a close parallel in 10:1-4a. Isaiah 5:25, however, is marked by the same structure and refrain that one finds in 9:7-20; 10:4b. Israel's past behavior and its consequent punishment are narrated only to be qualified by the following statement, "For all this his anger is not turned away and his hand is stretched out still." In terms of form, it would appear that 10:1-4a goes with 5:8-24, and 5:25-30 goes with 9:7-20, probably as its conclusion. This process was apparently disturbed in the process of editing the book.

Although the exact course of that process is not recoverable at this point, it may have taken place when the separate literary collection, 6:1—9:6, was inserted into the larger collection (for discussion see ahead). The editor apparently wanted to lead into the הוי oracle against Aššur introduced at 10:5 with another הוי oracle, so he transposed one of the הוי oracles originally belonging in the series in 5:8-24, maybe one of the last in that series, here (10:1-4a). In the process, however, he also took 5:25-30, the original conclusion to 9:7-20, which also originally introduced the oracle against Assyria in 10:5, and transposed it to the end of the הוי series (5:8-24). In so doing he linked together the material before and after the new insertion, 6:1—9:6, but at the high price of confusing both pericopes. In my opinion, it is highly unlikely that Isaiah himself would have so mutilated his own oracles. Assuming that the general lines of this hypothetical reconstruction are correct, therefore, I will treat 10:1-4a here, and 5:25-30 after 9:20, where the two pericopes originally belonged.

10:1-4a

1/   Hey, you who decree decrees[a] of iniquity,
    Who write writs[b] of oppression,
2/   To turn aside the needy from judgment,
    To snatch away justice from the poor of my people,
    So that widows may become their plunder,
    And orphans they may despoil!
3/   What will you[c] do in response to the day of punishment,
    To the storm when it comes from afar?
    To whom will you flee for help,
    And where will you abandon your wealth,
4/   So as not to cower[d] in the place of the captive,[e]
    Or fall[f] among the slain?
    [Yet in all this his anger has not turned back,
    And his hand is stretched out still.]

Textual Notes

a 1QIsaᵃ has חוקקי (ḥûqĕqê) for MT's חֹקְקֵי (ḥiqĕqê), "decrees of," though this is probably just a difference in pronunciation, not in meaning. LXX omits the word in its translation.

b Despite the apparent support of the versions apart from the Tg., MT's *piel* participle וּמְכַתְּבִים (ûmĕkattĕbîm), "and who keep writing," should probably be corrected to the plural construct noun with the enclitic *mem* וּמִכְתְּבֵם (wĕmiktĕbēm), "and writs of." It would be very odd to have both a finite verb and a participle in this construction, and the noun וּמִכְתְּבֵם makes a far better parallel to the noun חֹקְקֵי (ḥiqĕqê), "decrees," than the participle would.

c All the versions except LXX support MT's second person here, and even LXX has the second person in the rest of the verse.

d MT's third person masculine singular *qal* perfect כָּרַע (kāraʿ), "he bowed, cowered," seems odd following the negative בִּלְתִּי (biltî), which is normally used with infinitives. It is true that the following third plural finite verb יִפֹּלוּ (yippōlû) also seems to be governed by בִּלְתִּי (biltî), and that the related לְבִלְתִּי (lĕbiltî) sometimes governs finite verbs (Exod 20:20; 2 Sam 14:14). Nonetheless, the third masculine singular כָּרַע (kāraʿ) is also odd in that it follows three second person masculine plural verb forms in v. 3 that seem to have the same implied subject. Thus, I would correct to the infinitive כְּרֹעַ (kĕrōaʿ), "to bow, to cower," which would continue the second person plural address. Vg., Tg., and Syr. all render with a second person plural verb.

e LXX omits this whole line. The noun אַסִּיר (ʾassîr) is singular, thus the translation "in the place of the captive," but it could also be rendered as a collective, "among the captives."

f MT's qal imperfect third person plural יִפֹּלוּ (yippōlû), "or fall," is rendered with a second plural form by Vg., Tg., and Syr., while LXX renders with the infinitive. The versions recognize the continuation of the direct address. The switch to the third plural finite verb form following the infinitive, assuming my correction is accepted, may be due to the influence of the plural noun hărûgîm, "the slain," that precedes it, but the switch maintains the plural of the addressees of v. 3. The switch from second person to third person in direct address is not uncommon (Isa 5:8-10; 22:16-17; 33:1), but a switch from plural to singular or singular to plural would be uncommon.

Commentary

This oracle is a complete הוי saying with a theme similar to that found in the הוי sayings treated above (see esp. 5:23). The hearers are addressed in the second person, as is clear from v. 3, and they are characterized as "You who decree decrees of iniquity and write writs of oppression." Apparently the royal officials were promulgating legislation that made it easier for them to take the property of the poor and deprive them of legal redress. "To turn aside the needy from judgment" (דִּין, dîn) means that the unjust laws enabled the oppressors to prevent the oppressed from having their cases actually adjudicated in court (cf., e.g., Amos 2:7). "To snatch away justice (מִשְׁפַּט, mišpaṭ) from the poor," literally "the justice of the poor," simply underlines the same point. The oppressors stole the opportunity for judicial redress from the innocent poor. Thus, widows and orphans had no defense against being plundered by the wealthy and powerful of their own people. It is noteworthy that Isaiah uses the noun שָׁלָל (šālāl), "plunder," and the verb בָּזַז (bāzaz), "to take booty," both of which normally describe how an army plunders its foreign enemies, to describe the elite's treatment of their own people (cf. 3:9-13). In Israel's monarchical system, unless the king was both responsive to Yahweh's demands for justice and in clear control of the activities of his subordinates, the structure of the system left it open to serious abuse with little recourse for the oppressed. Ultimately, if the royal officials, either with the king's blessing or his neglect, rejected their task of seeing justice done, the only sanction left was divine judgment.

It is that sanction to which Isaiah turns in v. 3 with his questions to these royal bureaucrats. The first pair of questions asks the oppressors what preparation they will make for the coming day of punishment, for the storm that will come from afar. The word שׁוֹאָה (šōʾâ) has a range of meanings focused around the sense of "devastation, ruin." Used together with מְשׁוֹאָה (mĕšôʾâ) the noun sometimes designates a desolate desert wasteland (Job 30:3; 38:27), though the same expression in Zeph 1:15, given the cloud imagery of its immediate context, suggests the devastation of a violent storm. In Job 30:14, where šōʾâ is used alone, the word has been translated as "tempest" or "ruin, rubble."[1] In both Ezek 38:9 and Prov 1:27 the parallelism suggests strongly that šōʾâ means "a devastating storm." Though the occurrences in Isa 10:3 and 47:11 are less clear, I am convinced that at least in Isa 10:3 the translation "storm" is appropriate. The agents of the coming "devastation" are undoubtedly the Assyrians, whom Isaiah often portrays using storm imagery (5:28b-30; 8:7-8a; 28:17b-19), and the expression מִמֶּרְחָק (mimmerḥāq) "from afar" points in the same direction (cf. 5:26).

The second set of questions asks "to whom these oppressors will flee for help." The language of help (עֶזְרָה ʿezrâ) suggests they will search for a military ally that would protect them from the Assyrian menace (Isa 30:5, 7; 31:1, 3). The question, "Where will you abandon your wealth?" in this context most likely means, "to whom will you send your wealth in order to buy their military assistance against the Assyrians?" Verse 4a then states the reasons for these actions, "so as not to cower in the place of the captive or fall among the slain." It is clear from Isa 30:1-5, 6; 31:1-3 that Judah's court eventually chose to pay the Nubian rulers of Egypt for assistance against the Assyrians. Isaiah's questions are rhetorical, however. He is quite clear that the flight to Egypt and its Nubian

---

1 See Marvin H. Pope, *Job: Introduction, Translation, and Notes* (3rd ed.; AB 15; Garden City, NY: Doubleday, 1973) 221.

rulers for military assistance, however large the payment one sends to them, will be totally useless. As he puts it in 31:3, "The helper will stumble, the helped will fall, and together all of them will perish." In short, Judah's elite, who have amassed enormous wealth by plundering the poor of their own people, will see their wealth disappear into a foreign country, and its loss will not prevent them from cowering among the captives or falling among the slain.

Verse 4b, "For all this . . . stretched out still," is a fragment left over from the editing process and did not originally belong with this passage, where it disrupts the conclusion of the *hôy* oracle. Such a refrain belongs in the extended oracle against the northern kingdom in 9:7-20 + 5:25-30 prior to final judgment at the conclusion of this extended oracle.

Bibliography

Blum, Erhard, "Jesaja und der DBR des Amos: Unzeitgemässe Überlegungen zu Jes 5:25; 9:7-20; 10:1-4," *DBAT* 28 (1992–93) 75–95.

Brown, W. P., "The So-Called Refrain in Isaiah 5:25-30 and 9:7–10:4," *CBQ* 52 (1990) 432–43.

Crenshaw, James L., "A Liturgy of Wasted Opportunity (Isa 9,7–10,4)," *Semitics* 1 (1970) 27–37.

Crüsemann, F., *Studien zur Formgeschichte vom Hymnus und Danklied in Israel* (WMANT 32; Neukirchen-Vluyn: Neukirchener Verlag, 1969) 50–56, 227–29.

Goshen Gottstein, M. H., "Hebrew Syntax and the History of the Bible Text: A Pesher in the MT of Isaiah," *Textus* 8 (1973) 100–106.

Korpel, Marjo C. A., "Structural Analysis as a Tool for Redaction Criticism: The Example of Isaiah 5 and 10.1-6," *JSOT* 69 (1996) 53–71.

It appears that 6:1—9:7 once circulated as an independent collection. These chapters form a literary block that seems to have been inserted between chap. 5 and 9:8 with resulting disruptions in the text. Unlike the preceding and following material, almost all of 6:1—9:7 appears to date from a relatively restricted time period. Most of the material may be dated to the period of the Syro-Ephraimitic War (c. 735–732 BCE). The major exception is 9:1-7 (8:23—9:6 Heb.). It must date after 732, perhaps as late as 715, depending on the disputed question of the date of Hezekiah's accession to the throne (see the detailed discussion at 14:28-32).

Embedded in this literary block are several units narrated in the first person singular (6:1-13; 8:1-18). That suggests that this material once existed as first person memoirs of Isaiah. Since 7:1-17 has very close connections to 8:1-3, it is possible that this material also originally existed as first person memoirs, but has been secondarily turned into a third person account about the author. Possible parallels to this phenomenon may be seen in Amos 7:10-17, where an unusual third person narrative about the prophet's call interrupts a series of visionary experiences related in the first person, and in Hos 1:2-9, where a third person account about Hosea's relationship to his wife contrasts with a first person account, perhaps dealing with subsequent events, in 3:1-3. In both of these cases we may assume that original first person accounts going back to Amos and Hosea themselves have been transformed into third person narratives by their later editors. The importance of this observation arises in connection with the interpretation of 8:1 and 8:16. What was written on the tablet, and what was the content of the "testimony" and "teaching" sealed among Isaiah's disciples?

One might also argue that the original first person account of Isaiah showed a more logical development than the present form of this collection. However that may be, the present form simply juxtaposes oracles from the general period, following neither a strict chronological nor a logical development.

6

1/ In the year of the death of King Uzziah I saw[a] the Lord sitting on a high and lofty throne, and his skirts[b] filled the temple. 2/ Seraphim were in attendance above[c] him, each with six wings.[d] With two each would cover[e] his face, with two each would cover[e] his feet, and with two each would fly.[e] 3/ And one would call[f] to the other and say,[g] "Holy, holy, holy, is Yahweh of Hosts! His glory is the fullness of all the earth!" 4/ And the tangs (of the doorposts) in the threshold pivot stones shook[h] at the voice of the one calling, and the house began to fill[i] with smoke. 5/ And I said, "Woe to me![j] Surely I am silenced/destroyed! For I am a man of unclean[k] lips, and I live in the midst of a people of unclean lips, for my eyes have seen[l] the king, Yahweh of Hosts!" 6/ Then one of the seraphim flew[m] to me, having in his hand a live coal that he had taken from upon the altar with tongs. 7/ He touched (it) to my mouth and said, "Now that this has touched your lips, your iniquity will turn aside[n] and your sin[o] will be atoned.[n]" 8/ Then I heard the voice of the Lord saying, "Whom shall I send, and who will go for us?[p]" I said,[q] "Here am I, send me." 9/ He said, "Go and say to this people, 'Keep listening, but do not[r] understand. Keep looking[s], but do not[r] perceive.' 10/ Fatten[t] the mind of this people, and its ears make heavy, and its eyes smear over, lest it should see with its eyes, and with its ears hear, and its mind[u] should understand, and it turn and there be healing[v] for it." 11/ Then I said, "For how long, O Lord[w]?" He said, "Until cities crash into ruins without inhabitant, and houses without a man, and the land is left[x] a desolation. 12/ (Until) Yahweh removes the man far away, and abandonment[y] becomes abundant in the midst of the land."[z] 13/ If there is still in it a tenth, it will again be for grazing/burning. Like the terebinth or the oak whose*[a] *root-stock remains* in them*[b] when *felled*, its *root-stock* is the seed of holiness.*[c]

Textual Notes:

a   1QIsa[a] lacks the copulative on וָאֶרְאֶה (wā'er'eh), "I saw," but normal narrative tense sequence would require it.

b   LXX avoids the anthropomorphism of MT by rendering שׁוּלָיו (šûlāyw), "his skirts," as τῆς δόξης αὐτοῦ, "his glory." LXX also changes the construction of the clause to "and the house was full of his glory." Vg. has "and that which was under him was filling the temple."

c   LXX has κύκλῳ αὐτοῦ, "around him," perhaps to avoid placing the seraphim above God.

d   1QIsa[a] has lost the second שֵׁשׁ כְּנָפִים (šēš kĕnāpayim), "six wings,"

by haplography, but traces of the לְ (lĕ) before אֶחָד ('eḥād), "to each one," are present despite the failure of the original modern editor of this manuscript to note them.

e   Where the Hebrew has singular verbs, LXX, followed by Vg. and Syr., has plural verbs, which implies that they understood the seraphim to be covering God's face and feet, not their own, but this is unlikely. Tg. catches the sense of the passage much better: "Holy attendants were in the height before him, each having six wings. With two each covered his face that he might not see, with two each covered his body that he might not be seen, and with two each ministered." "Feet" here is probably a euphemism for genitalia as in Exod 4:25; Isa 7:20 (cf. Judg 3:24; 1 Sam 24:4).

f 1QIsaᵃ has the masculine plural participle וקראים (wĕqōrĕʾîm), "and they were calling," for MT's masculine singular converted perfect וְקָרָא (wĕqārāʾ), "and one would call." The participle is a secondary accommodation to the later language; both Syr. and Tg. have it. LXX and Vulg have finite verbs, but they do put them in the plural.

g 1QIsaᵃ omits וְאָמַר (wĕʾāmar), "and he would say," and the first קָדוֹשׁ (qādôš), "holy," but the versions support MT. They have a plural verb, but that is just to translate the reciprocal sense of the passage.

h LXX has ἐπήρθη τὸ ὑπέρθυρον, "the lintel of the door was lifted up," apparently influenced by the imagery of LXX Ps 23:7, 9, where the eternal gates are commanded to be lifted up (ἐπάρθητε) that the king of glory may come in. But the verb נוע (nûaʿ) means "to shake," not "lift up." The אַמּוֹת (ʾammôt) are the joints at the ends of the doorposts that fit into and turn in the socket hollowed out in the pivot stones (הַסִּפִּים, hassippîm) of the threshold.

i 1QIsaᵃ has נמלא (nimlāʾ), "was (being) filled," probably the participle though it could be the perfect, for MT's imperfect יִמָּלֵא (yimmālēʾ), "began to fill," but MT is to be preferred.

j 1QIsaᵃ has the peculiar spelling אילי for MT's אוֹי־לִי (ʾôy-lî), "woe to me," but it appears to be a mechanical haplographic mistake. 4QIsaᶠ follows MT.

k 1QIsaᵃ has the nonhistorical spelling טמה in the first occurrence of טְמֵא־שְׂפָתַיִם (ṭĕmēʾ śĕpātayim), "unclean of lips," but it follows MT in using the historical spelling in the second.

l LXX and Vg. have "I have seen with my eyes" for MT's "my eyes have seen," but this is stylistic; 1QIsaᵃ, Syr., and Tg. all support MT.

m LXX has ἀπεστάλη, "was sent," for MT's "flew," apparently to avoid any implication that the seraph acted on his own initiative. A similar motivation lies behind Tg.'s ואשתוי לותי, "and (one of the ministers) was sent/placed/given to me. . . ." Interestingly, Tg. puts a speech in the mouth of the minister, rather than a coal in his hand. 1QIsaᵃ's ויעוף is just a variant spelling of MT's וַיָּעָף (wayyāʿop), "and he flew."

n LXX makes iniquity and sins the object of the verbs, but this is just an example of the freedom LXX exercised in its translation.

o 1QIsaᵃ has the plural וחטאותיך (wĕḥaṭṭĕʾôtêkā), "your sins."

p LXX replaces "for us" with "to this people"; Syr. simply omits it, and Tg. replaces it with "to teach." This appears to be a doctrinal alteration to avoid God using the first person plural phrase.

q 1QIsaᵃ has the longer form ואמרה (wāʾōmĕrâ), "and I said."

r 1QIsaᵃ has ועל for MT's וְאַל (wĕʾal), "and not," which must be regarded as a simple auditory error, since syntactically ועל (wĕʾāl), "and upon," makes no sense.

s 1QIsaᵃ omits the copulative on וּרְאוּ (ûrĕʾû), "and keep looking," but the versions support retaining it.

t 1QIsaᵃ has השם, presumably the hiphil imperative (hāšēm) of שמם, "stupify," for MT's הַשְׁמֵן (hašmēn), "fatten." LXX eases the theological harshness of the passage by introducing a causal particle, changing the imperatives to finite verbs, and making the people the subject of the action: "For the mind of this people was fattened, and with their ears they heard with difficulty and they covered their eyes."

u 4QIsaᶠ has ובלבבו יבין (ûbilbābô yābîn), "and understand with its mind," and that is probably the *Vorlage* behind 1QIsaᵃ's awkward ישמעו בלבבו יבין (yišmĕʿû bilbābô yābîn), "and with its ears they will hear, with his mind he will understand"; the copyist has simply mistakenly attached the copulative to the preceding singular verb ישמע (yišmaʿ), "he will hear." The reading ובלבבו (ûbilbābô), "and with his mind," could be original.

v The verb וְרָפָא (wĕrāpāʾ), "and there be healing (for it)," is construed impersonally, but LXX makes God the subject, καὶ ἰάσομαι αὐτούς, "and I should heal them."

w 1QIsaᵃ has יהוה "Yahweh," for MT's אֲדֹנָי (ʾădōnāy), "my Lord," and that may be original.

x LXX has καταλειφθήσεται, "shall be left," which suggests the emendation of MT's תִּשָּׁאֶה (tiššāʾeh), "(and the land) be ruined (into a desolation)," to תִּשָּׁאֵר (tiššāʾēr), "(and the land) be left (a desolation)," though Syr. and Tg. support MT.

y 1QIsaᵃ lacks the article on הָעֲזוּבָה (hāʿăzûbâ), "abandonment."

z LXX may construe the final part of this verse positively, "and after these things God will remove men far away, and those left behind will be multiplied on the land."

*a 1QIsaᵃ has משלכת for MT's בְּשַׁלֶּכֶת (bĕšalleket).

*b 1QIsaᵃ has במה for MT's בָּם (bām), "in them."

*c The textual integrity and meaning of the relative clause in v. 13 are disputed and uncertain; see the commentary.

Commentary

Chapter 6 reports Isaiah's inaugural vision through which God called him to his prophetic office and commissioned him with his particular message. The reference to King Uzziah's death dates this experience and hence the beginning of Isaiah's prophetic ministry to about 738 BCE. The date of the death of Uzziah, also known as Azariah (2 Kgs 15:1-7, 13; 2 Chr 26:1-23), is disputed and often assumed to be earlier, in the late 740s,[1] but if the Azriyahu mentioned in Tiglath-pileser III's annals as the leader of the rebellious south Syrian league just prior to Tiglath-pileser's conquest of Kullani in 738 BCE was Azariah of Judah, as Hayim Tadmor and others have suggested,[2] Uzziah could not have died much before the fall of Kullani in 738 BCE. Moreover, the dramatic impact that the fall of Kullani obviously had on the Israelite and Judean public—both Amos 6:2 (Calneh) and Isa 10:9 (Calno) refer to this event—would make more sense if these publics had a vested interest in the outcome of this battle, something they would certainly have had if Uzziah had been the leader of the southern anti-Assyrian league encouraging Kullani's revolt against Assyria.

In contrast to Isaiah's actual visionary experience, however, it is not clear when this report of the experience was first shared publicly. The date formula would not have been necessary had Isaiah given this report orally immediately after his vision. Its inclusion suggests that Isaiah composed the report some years after the experience. Why? The prophetic books show very little interest in providing general biographical details about the prophets, yet several prophetic books provide details on the prophet's call (Jer 1:4-10; Ezek 1-3:9; Amos 7:12-15).

While by no means identical, these passages are similar enough in structure to Isaiah's report to suggest the existence of a relatively standardized pattern in Israelite society for the experience of a prophetic call. The prophet has a vision of Yahweh in which the deity gives him a message and commissions him to proclaim that message to a particular audience. Jeremiah does not emphasize the visionary element, but it is presupposed by his mention of Yahweh's hand (Jer 1:7), and though Amos 7:15 does not mention a vision, Amos 7:1-9, which immediately precedes Amos's brief reference to his call, shows the importance of the visionary experience to Amos's ministry. Usually there is an element of divine compulsion; though the prophet does not choose the job, he can hardly refuse it. The prophet may resist the task, but Yahweh overcomes that resistance through reassurance and by equipping the prophet for his task. Isaiah lacks the element of compulsion (cf., however, Isa 8:11), but before he can volunteer for the prophetic task, Yahweh must prepare him by the purification of his lips.

Isaiah's account of his call should also be compared to the vision of Micaiah son of Imlah in 2 Kgs 22:19-23. Though Micaiah's vision hardly marks his call to the prophetic office—he was already a well-known prophet at the time—it is in other respects the closest parallel to Isaiah's vision. One may legitimately ask whether it served a similar function. The function of Micaiah's report is clearly polemical. Because the king did not like his message (2 Kgs 22:17-18), the prophet recounts his vision to legitimate it (22:19-23). This was all the more necessary, since all the other prophets had given a favorable message (22:6, 11-13, 24). To justify his dissent, Micaiah must explain the reason for the other prophets' false prophecy.

Amos's call narrative occurs in a similar polemical setting and appears to serve a similar function. When ordered by Amaziah, the priest, to go elsewhere to prophesy (Amos 7:12-13), Amos justifies his refusal to obey the royal authority by pointing to the commission given him by a higher authority. God, who appointed him a prophet, also told him where to prophesy; Amos had no choice in the matter. When Amaziah tried to stop him, the priest was actually opposing God and would be punished accordingly.

---

1   In his dissertation (1943) Edwin R. Thiele originally dated Uzziah's death to 740/739 then revised it back to 743 BCE ("The Chronology of the Kings of Judah and Israel," *JNES* 3 [1944] 155–63; see *The Mysterious Numbers of the Hebrew Kings* [Chicago: University of Chicago Press, 1951], 205; *MNHK²*, 90–119; *MNHK³*, 139–62).

2   See Hayim Tadmor, *The Inscriptions of Tiglath-pileser III King of Assyria: Critical Edition, with Introductions, Translations, and Commentary* (Jerusalem: Israel Academy of Sciences and Humanities, 1994), 273–76.

The call narratives in Jeremiah and Ezekiel do not occur in the same kind of narrative setting, but their function seems very similar. The placement of these call narratives at the beginning of their respective prophetic books appears to be a secondary literary device by which the prophet or his editor claims divine authority for the written prophetic word that follows. It is unlikely that this purely literary context represents the original setting in which these call accounts functioned. Jeremiah, like Amos, appealed to his divine commission to justify himself in the face of fierce public opposition (Jer 26:12-15), and both Jeremiah and Ezekiel had to legitimate their message against the contradictory message of other prophets. They did this by claiming that their opponents were not speaking God's word; they had not stood in Yahweh's council, and he had not sent them (Jer 23:16-32; Ezek 13:1-6). The obverse of this claim is that Jeremiah and Ezekiel had stood in Yahweh's council, that Yahweh had sent them, and the accounts of their call probably originally functioned to make this positive claim in just such polemical settings.

Isaiah also faced bitter opposition. There were those who wanted to silence the prophetic word, or at least make it more palatable (Isa 30:8-11). Isaiah had to face both disbelief and hostile scoffing (28:9-10, 14). Some even jokingly urged God to hurry up with his plans so they could see what the prophet was talking about (5:18-19). In the face of such opposition, Isaiah's call narrative probably functioned polemically. Just as Micaiah had to explain the divergence of his message from that of the other prophets, so Isaiah had to explain why the people rejected his message, why the salvation he offered had not materialized, and why God's work was so slow in being realized. Though one cannot be certain, it is likely that the call narrative was placed here at the beginning of the sealed scroll of Isaiah's proclamations during the Syro-Ephraimitic War as a polemical justification for Isaiah, when Isaiah temporarily withdrew from public activity, after his message was rejected by both Ahaz's royal court and the larger public (see the discussion on Isa 8:1-18).

One should note, however, that neither the call narratives nor the report of Micaiah's vision is exhausted by their polemical function. The visionary experiences reported in these narratives contain a far richer message about God and reflect a more profound impact on the prophet's theological outlook than is required by their polemical function. Thus, we are justified in examining this account for its view of God and its impact on Isaiah. Nevertheless, one must remember the polemical function of the passage in the setting of the prophet's ministry before one can resolve the theological issues that the call narrative raises.

View of God

Isaiah saw Yahweh sitting enthroned as king, surrounded by his heavenly ministers. The conceptualization of God found here is very similar to that in Micaiah's vision. In both cases, Yahweh is portrayed in political categories as a great suzerain surrounded by his heavenly court of angelic courtiers. This conception is rooted in the ancient Jerusalemite tradition according to which the Davidic monarch was simply God's regent on earth (Psalm 2). The true king was the divine monarch who chose to reside in Zion (Ps 132:13-14). The majesty of this vision depends, however, on clarifying a number of details that are often glossed over.

To begin with, it is clear that the locus of this vision is in the temple. The prophet explicitly mentions the temple הַהֵיכָל (hahêkāl, v. 1), the tangs of the doorpost in the threshold pivot stones (אַמּוֹת הַסִּפִּים, ʾammôt hassippîm, v. 4), the house (הַבַּיִת, habbayit, v. 4, a common expression for temple), and the altar (הַמִּזְבֵּחַ, hammizbēaḥ, v. 6). That suggests that one explore the visual elements in this vision with close attention to what we know of the Yahwistic temple in Jerusalem where Isaiah lived.

A High and Lofty Throne

Most standard English translations curiously attempt to make the antecedent of the masculine singular adjectives רָם וְנִשָּׂא (rām wĕniśśāʾ), "high and lofty," Yahweh, but the adjectives immediately follow כִּסֵּא (kissēʾ), "throne," the nearest masculine singular antecedent, and there is no grammatical reason to prefer the more remote antecedent. But if this more natural translation is correct, what high and exalted throne might Isaiah have been viewing? One should note that one of the most common cultic epithets for Yahweh was יֹשֵׁב הַכְּרֻבִים (yōšēb hakkĕrūbîm), "who sits enthroned upon the cherubim" (1 Sam 4:4; 2 Sam

6:2; 2 Kgs 19:15; Isa 37:16; Pss 80:2; 99:1).[3] In material dealing with the premonarchic period, this epithet is associated with the ark, but after Solomon's construction of the temple, the epithet seems to be associated with the giant cherubim throne found in the inner sanctum of the temple. According to 1 Kgs 6:22-29, Solomon constructed two fifteen-foot tall cherubim out of gold-plated olive wood. These cherubim appear to have been mounted on wheels, since 1 Chr 28:18 refers to them as having the shape of a chariot, and Ezekiel, who was familiar with the temple before his deportation to Babylon, describes the wheels beneath the cherubim in his vision of God.

More significant for our purposes, the two cherubim appear to have been placed side by side in the דְּבִיר (děbîr), the innermost sanctuary, the most holy place, the throne room of the deity, facing outward toward the הֵיכָל (hêkāl), the nave or holy place, and beyond that toward the entrance of the temple. Their wings, stretching out to either side of their faces at right angles, the outer ones touching the side walls of the holy of holies, the inner ones touching the inner wing of their fellow cherub, formed a continuous platform, presumably at that fifteen-foot height, stretching across the whole thirty-foot breadth of the holy of holies (1 Kgs 6:23-28). This platform appears to have served as either the seat or the base for the seat of Yahweh's throne. Note that Ezekiel indicates that the cherubim formed the base of Yahweh's throne (Ezek 10:1-2; cf. 1:22-28; explicitly identified as a cherub in Ezek 10:20-21).

In ancient Syro-Palestinian iconography, cherubim are normally represented as winged sphinxes, winged creatures with a human head and the body of a lion. Less commonly one finds a representation of a similar creature with the body of a bull. The bull-bodied creature becomes more common farther east in Mesopotamia, though both are attested in Assyria.[4] The association of a pair of winged sphinxes with a throne is quite common in the iconography of ancient Near Eastern Syria-Palestine. One finds a representation of a throne with a winged sphinx forming its armrest on the eleventh century BCE sarcophagus of Ahiram of Byblos[5] and a similar representation on an ivory comb from Megiddo.[6] Because of the perspective in these representations, only one winged-sphinx cherub is visible, but the representation presupposes that both armrests were so constructed, so one must assume a throne with two cherubim forming the armrests on either side of the seat of the throne. This assumption is confirmed by a whole series of approximately one-half to one meter high model limestone thrones dating from the seventh to the second century BCE found in various places in Lebanon and Syria that preserve the winged sphinxes that form the armrests on either side of the seat of the throne.[7] One should note that the thrones represented on the sarcophagus of Ahiram and the ivory comb from Megiddo both have footrests for the seated figure occupying the throne, and the same may be said for some of the better-preserved limestone models. According to 1 Kgs 8:6-7, the ark of the covenant was deposited in the inner sanctum of the temple under the outspread wings of the cherubim, presumably between the two cherubim, and this sacred box apparently served as the footstool for the deity. Three or perhaps four times the expression הֲדֹם רַגְלָיו (hădōm raglāyw), "the footstool of his feet," is used in reference to the ark (1 Chr 28:2; Pss 99:5; 132:7; Lam 2:1—this last reference, however, might refer to the city of Jerusalem; cf. Jer 3:16-17). Thus, Yahweh was envisioned as invisibly seated upon the wings of the giant cherubim above the ark with his legs hanging down and his feet resting on the ark.

Anyone entering the inner sanctum to approach Yahweh, as Hezekiah apparently did when he spread out the letters of Sennacherib before Yahweh and prayed for

---

3   In early poetry, Yahweh is also portrayed as "mounted" (רכב) and "flying" (עוף) upon a cherub (1 Sam 22:11; Ps 18:11).

4   James B. Pritchard, *The Ancient Near East in Pictures Relating to the Old Testament* (2nd ed.; Princeton, NJ: Princeton University Press, 1969) 180 no. 534; 212 no. 647.

5   *ANEP*, 157–58 nos. 456–58; Martin Metzger, *Königsthron und Gottesthron: Thronformen und Throndarstellungen im Ägypten und im Vorderen Orient im dritten*

und zweiten Jahrtausend vor Christus und deren Bedeutung für das Verständnis von Aussagen über den Thron im Alten Testament (2 vols.; AOAT 15.1–2; Kevelaer: Butzon & Bercker; Neukirchen-Vluyn: Neukirchener Verlag, 1985) 2:237 no. 1183.

6   *ANEP*, 111 no. 332; Metzger, *Königsthron*, 2:237 no. 1181; King and Stager, *Life in Biblical Israel*, 264.

7   Metzger, *Königsthron*, 2:239–47.

deliverance (2 Kgs 19:14-15), would have been impressed with the height of Yahweh's cherubim throne.[8] The inner sanctum was only a thirty-foot cube, much of it occupied by the giant cherubim; with such limited space in the room, anyone entering it would have had to crane his neck back to see the platform formed by the wings of the cherubim. To put it in perspective, that platform, forming the seat of Yahweh's throne, stood one and a half times as high as a modern American NBA basketball hoop.

His Skirts

Not only did Isaiah see Yahweh seated on this exalted throne, however; he also saw "Yahweh's skirts filling the temple." The precise significance of this detail depends on how one translates שׁוּלָיו (šûlāyw). This suffixed noun, which is attested only in the construct plural or in the plural with a pronominal suffix, is usually understood as referring to parts of Yahweh's clothing. G. R. Driver understood it as referring to God's lower extremities,[9] but Driver's view is not supported by other occurrences of the word. The other biblical occurrences of this noun refer to parts of the high priest's robe, which was decorated with embroidery (Exod 28:33, 34; 39:24, 25, 26) or to parts of a female's article of clothing that could be soiled with uncleanness (Lam 1:9) or pulled up over the woman's face to expose the woman's nakedness (Jer 13:26; Nah 3:5), this public exposure of the woman's person being part of a public punishment that could also involve sexual violation of the woman (Jer 13:22). These references suggest that the word refers to the skirts or ends of a robe where there might be an embroidered border.

Some of the older English translations rendered the word as "his train," which conjures up the image of a wedding gown with a loose piece of fabric trailing the ground behind the bride, but the contemporaneous portrayals of Israelite robes in ancient Near Eastern iconography do not support this image. What evidence we have suggests that Israelite and Judean robes came down to around the ankles, and show no signs of any fabric dragging on the ground behind the wearer. The only Judean or Israelite king clearly represented in a contemporaneous visual portrayal, as far as I know, is the figure of Jehu prostrate in obeisance before Shalmaneser III on the Black Obelisk,[10] and his robe appears to come only to his ankles. That is a century before Isaiah's vision, however, and the fashionable length of robes could conceivably change in a century. There is no evidence, however, that they did. The evidence from Tiglath-pileser III's reliefs,[11] basically contemporary with Isaiah's vision, suggests that the customary length of robes at the time, from Assyria through Syria and down to Palestine, was still ankle-length. Soldiers wore a much shorter tunic that came to just above the knees, no doubt for mobility, but the robes portrayed on other men are usually ankle-length. That is the length of Tiglath-pileser III's robe wherever he is portrayed; it is the length of the robes of the men of Ashtaroth in the Transjordan portrayed carrying sacks over their backs to go into exile,[12] and it is the length of the robes of a number of vassals portrayed as submitting to the Assyrian king.[13] Unfortunately, the relief showing the capure of Gezer does not show the bottom of the robes of the defenders of Gezer,[14] since they are standing behind a wall. One might argue that divine robes could have been fuller and longer than human robes, but the

---

8   In the P material, only the high priest was permitted in the *dĕbîr*, or inner sanctum, but such restrictions do not appear to have been in effect during the period of the monarchy. Hezekiah clearly had access to the inner sanctum, and the elements of Isaiah's vision, apparently rooted in the actual visual experience of the sacred furniture of the inner sanctum, suggests that Isaiah had also been in this room.

9   G. R. Driver, "Isaiah 6:1: 'His Train Filled the Temple,'" in Hans Goedicke, ed., *Near Eastern Studies in Honor of William Foxwell Albright* (Baltimore: Johns Hopkins Press, 1971) 87–96.

10   *ANEP*, 120–22 nos. 351–55.

11   Hayim Tadmor, *The Inscriptions of Tiglath-Pileser III,*

King of Assyria: Critical Edition, with Introductions, Translations and Commentary (Jerusalem: Israel Academy of Sciences and Humanities, 1994) 241–56, figs. 11–12; R. D. Barnett, *The Sculptures of Aššur-nasir-apli II, 883–859 B.C., Tiglath-pileser III, 745–727 B.C., [and] Esarhaddon, 681–669 B.C., From the Central and South-West Palaces at Nimrud* (London: Trustees of the British Museum, 1962).

12   Barnett, *Sculptures of Aššur-nasir-apli II,* 120, pl. LXX; *ANEP*, 128 no. 366.

13   Ibid., 135, pl. LXXXV; 139, pl. LXXXIX.

14   Ibid., 112, pl. LXII; *ANEP*, 129 no. 369.

robes on the divine statues seated on thrones that the soldiers of Tiglath-pileser III are portrayed as carrying away from the city of Kullani in North Syria are basically the same ankle-length as the robes on contemporaneous humans.[15] If one skips down about thirty-eight years to Sennacherib's portrayal of the conquest of Lachish in 701 BCE, the robes on the male exiles leaving Lachish with bundles on their backs are again about ankle-length, and the same is true of those portrayed as bowing in submission before Sennacherib.[16] In short, "train" is a misleading translation. Since Yahweh is portrayed as seated, the word in question presumably refers to the skirts, bottoms, or possibly even borders of Yahweh's robe that hung down from his knees to his ankles.

But if the skirts of Yahweh's robe filled the whole temple, the implication is that the figure of Yahweh is gigantic. As a modern analogy one might think of the oversized statues of Buddha often found in East Asian temples, but there are plenty of ancient analogies. The motif of the divine ruler being gigantic in size is well attested in both the literature and the iconography of the ancient Near East. The gigantic size of Marduk is stressed in the Akkadian creation epic Enuma elish,[17] and the gigantic size of Baal in the Ugaritic texts is underscored by the notice that the god Athtar cannot take Baal's throne, because when Athtar tries to sit on it, his feet do not reach the footstool, and his head does not reach its top.[18] A similar motif is reflected in the physical remains of the Iron Age temple from ʿAin Dara in North Syria. At the entrance to the temple, two one-meter-long footprints are imprinted side by side on the paving stone, and as one enters the temple, about two meters farther on there is a single left footprint, and then ten meters farther into the temple a single right footprint. The approximately thirty-foot stride of the deity symbolized by these footprints suggests a deity at least sixty-five feet tall.[19] Isaiah's vision of a similarly gigantic Yahweh stands within this

same Near Eastern stream of tradition about the size of deities, and it eventually leads to the further theological judgment in both the later Deuteronomistic tradition (1 Kgs 8:27) and the later Isaianic tradition (Isa 66:1-2) that no temple built by human hands is really able to house the God who made both heaven and earth.

The Seraphim

As if this shocking vision of the gigantic divine king were not terrifying enough, Isaiah sees yet other creatures called "seraphim" standing in midair above Yahweh. But what are seraphim? The form is clearly a masculine plural of *śārāp*, which occurs six other times in the OT, of which two are in First Isaiah (14:29; 30:6). These Isaiah passages describe the *śārāp* as a flying *śārāp* (שָׂרָף מְעוֹפֵף, *śārāp mᵉʿôpēp*) and mention this creature in collocation with three other terms for deadly serpents. נָחָשׁ (*nāḥāš*, Isa 14:29) is the most common word for snake; צֶפַע (*sepaʿ*, Isa 14:29) is a *hapax legomenon* but presumably a synonym for the well-attested related term צִפְעוֹנִי (*sipʿônî*, Isa 11:8; 59:5; Jer 8:17; Ps 23:32), and both nouns appear to designate the viper. Finally, אֶפְעֶה (*ʾepʿê*, Isa 30:6) is clearly a poisonous snake (Isa 59:5; Job 20:16). Given this collocation of terms elsewhere in the same author, it seems certain that the seraphim of Isaiah's vision were winged serpents of some sort. The other occurrences of the term in Num 21:6, 8 and Deut 8:15 add further support to this identification. In Num 21:6 and Deut 8:15 שָׂרָף (*śārāp*) is placed behind נָחָשׁ (*nāḥāš*) to further characterize the nature of the serpents that were biting the rebellious Israelites in the wilderness. In Num 21:8 שָׂרָף (*śārāp*) is used without נָחָשׁ (*nāḥāš*) to designate the serpent that Moses was commanded to make and set up on a pole in the middle of the camp, but the following verse, which records the carrying out of the command, refers to the same bronze object as a נָחָשׁ (*nāḥāš*, v. 9). One should note that, according to 2 Kgs 18:4, this bronze, pole-

15   Barnett, *Sculptures of Aššur-nasir-apli II*, 142, pl. XCII.
16   *ANEP*, 129–31 nos. 371–73.
17   W. G. Lambert, *Enuma eliš: The Babylonian Epic of Creation, The Cuneiform Text* (Oxford: Clarendon, 1966) I, 90–100; Pritchard, *ANET* (3rd ed.; Princeton, NJ: Princeton University Press, 1969) 62.
18   *KTU* 1.6 i 54–64; *ANET*, 140.
19   J. Monson, "The New ʿAin Dara Temple, Closest Solomonic Parallel," *BAR* 26.3 (2000) 23, 26–27; A.

Abou-Assaf, *Der Tempel von ʿAin Dara* (Damaszener Forschungen 3; Mainz am Rhein: P. von Zabern, 1990) Abb. 13–14, 18 and Tafel 11; Lawrence E. Stager, "Jerusalem and the Garden of Eden," *ErIsr* 26 (1999) 186*; Stager, "Jerusalem as Eden," *BAR* 26.3 (2000) 46.

mounted serpent was still in the temple until the time of Hezekiah's reform, some years after Isaiah's visionary experience, and one must at least raise the question whether the presence of such an object in the Jerusalem temple at the time of Isaiah's vision may have influenced the shape of the vision. None of the passages that mention the bronze serpent provide enough descriptive detail to answer the question whether it was a winged serpent, but the portrayal of a couple of pole-mounted serpents embossed on a bronze bowl from Syria-Palestine contemporary with Isaiah suggest that it was. This bowl was part of the hoard of bronze objects taken back to Assyria by Tiglath-pileser III from his campaigns to Palestine—some of the bowls are inscribed with Hebrew inscriptions—and stacked away in a storeroom in the palace at Nimrud. A sketch of the bowl was made at the time of the discovery of the hoard in the 1850s, but as far as I know, no photograph of the bowl was ever published. The sketch of the bowl shows, among other embossed cultic figures, two two-winged serpents mounted on poles.[20] More recently I photographed another bowl from the same collection which also shows pole-mounted serpents acting as protective deities on either side of a stylized tree of life.[21]

Despite the unjustified reluctance of some commentators to accept the serpentine nature of the seraphim,[22] the identification of Isaiah's six-winged seraphim as flying serpents seems certain. The origin of this icono-

graphic motif seems to be clearly Egyptian, as even the association of the bronze serpent with the Egyptian-born Moses and the wilderness period following the exodus from Egypt would suggest. In Egyptian iconography, the serpent, especially the cobra or ureus, often appears as a protective spirit to ward off evil. Rows of cobra heads appear on friezes; two ureuses are a part of the Egyptian crown, and they often appear on either side of a symbol of kingship or divinity.[23] Even more to the point, the winged cobra is sometimes portrayed above and slightly behind the symbol of kingship with its wings stretched out in a protective gesture.[24] One should also note that these winged cobras are often associated with thrones. The armrests of the throne of Tutankhamon each consist of a crowned cobra facing forward with outstretched wings and a coiled tail, and the back of the throne has a row of puffed-up cobra heads to ward off evil approaching the king from the back.[25] A limestone model of a Phoenician sanctuary from Sidon has a frieze of Egyptian-style cobra heads at the top. Set within the representation of the sanctuary is the frontal view of a throne with two cherubim forming the sides of the throne and a niche between them for mounting the statue of the deity, but above the heads of each of the cherubim there appears to be the head of a cobra wearing the same kind of Egyptian crown as worn by the two winged cobras on the throne of Tutankhamon.[26]

---

20 A. H. Layard, *A Second Series of the Monuments of Nineveh, Including Bas-reliefs from the Palace of Sennacherib and Bronzes from the Ruins of Nimroud, From Drawings Made on the Spot, during a Second Expedition to Assyria* (London: John Murray, 1853) pl. 68, top row, 2nd drawing; R. D. Barnett, "Layard's Nimrud Bronzes and Their Inscriptions," *ErIsr* 8 (1967) 1*–7*. The drawing is reproduced in my article, "The Visual Elements in Isaiah's Vision," in Joyce Rilett Wood, John E. Harvey, and Mark Leuchter, eds., *From Babel to Babylon: Essays on Biblical History and Literature in Honour of Brian Peckham* (LHBOTS 455; London: T&T Clark, 2006) 205, fig. 1.

21 See my "The Rod That Smote Philistia," in David S. Vanderhooft and Abraham Winitzer, eds., *Literature as Politics, Politics as Literature: Essays on the Ancient Near East in Honor of Peter Machinist* (Winona Lake, IN: Eisenbrauns, 2013) 381–95, esp. 393.

22 Jensen (p. 86) rejected the identification because these "creatures have hands, faces, and sexual parts

. . . and so are basically human in form," but in the ancient iconographic tradition, serpents were portrayed with human hands, faces, legs, and feet; see Othmar Keel, *Jahwe-Visionen und Siegelkunst: Eine neue Deutung der Majestätsschilderungen in Jes 6, Ez 1 und Sach 5* (SBS 84/85; Stuttgart: Katholisches Bibelwerk, 1977) 77–78, Abb. 31–35.

23 Keel, *Jahwe-Visionen*, 85–90.

24 Ibid., 89–90, Abb. 48–49.

25 Metzger, *Königsthron*, 2:70, no. 253; Hugo Gressmann, *Altorientalische Bilder zum Alten Testament* (2nd ed.; Berlin: de Gruyter, 1927) 83; *ANEP*, 416–17.

26 It is hard to be absolutely sure of this point because of the poor quality either of the photographs or of the preservation of the original monument (*AOB* fig. 520; Metzger, *Königsthron*, 2:239, no. 1193; Sabatino Moscati, *The World of the Phoenicians* (New York: Praeger, 1968) 124, fig. 2.

As the last example shows, even if the motif of the winged cobra as a protective genius is Egyptian in origin, it spread to Phoenicia and Palestine. It is attested on Palestinian seals as early as the Late Bronze Age, and it is very common on inscribed Hebrew stamp seals from the eighth and very early seventh century BCE.[27] One can find nice photographs of a number of these seals in N. Avigad and B. Sass, *Corpus of West Semitic Stamp Seals* (Jerusalem: Israel Academy of Sciences and Humanities; Israel Exploration Society; Institute of Archaeology, the Hebrew University of Jerusalem, 1997) nos. 11, 104, 127, 194, 206, 284, 381, 385. Two- and four-winged cobras appear quite often on these seals, but, to my knowledge, no example of six-winged cobras has yet been published. It should also be noted that this motif disappears from Hebrew stamp seals after the early seventh century and never reappears. By the exilic period and later it is even questionable if there remained any very clear memory of what seraphim actually were. Apart from the Greek text of *1 Enoch* 20:7, which apparently refers to the seraphim as δράκονες, "serpents" (cf. 61:10; 71:7, where seraphim are listed instead), and a reference to "serpent-like angels, called Seraphim" in the Gnostic text "On the Origin of the World" from the Nag Hammadi Library, I have found no evidence that the later Jewish exegetical tradition preserved any knowledge of the original iconographic background of the seraphim. In the later tradition the seraphim have become simply an order of angels, and any attempt in the later tradition to explain the name appeals to the association with burning or fire, based on the verbal root שׂרף (*śārap*), "to burn," not to the serpentine form of these creatures, despite the collocation of the noun with other nouns referring to snakes in the biblical sources. This observation, in and of itself, is sufficient to demolish the absurd suggestion that the account of this vision does not come from the eighth century prophet but is a late composition of the exilic period.[28] It is precisely in the eighth and very early seventh centuries, at the time of Isaiah, that the presence of such flying snakes is best represented in Judean iconography, and it is the last period when such a creature was actually present in the temple as a part of the cultic paraphernalia of the inner sanctum.

One should note that the position of Isaiah's seraphim above Yahweh is precisely the position taken by the winged cobras in a number of Egyptian portrayals where such creatures clearly function as protective genii.[29] Moreover, Isaiah's portrayal of these winged serpents as six-winged, a type not attested on Hebrew seals from the period, suggests that Isaiah's seraphim are "souped up," a more high-powered variety than normal seraphim, a detail that would add to their terror-inspiring quality. Yet the use the seraphim make of their wings radically alters the role of these creatures from their function in the Hebrew glyptic art of the period and in the Egyptian sources that lie behind that art. In this Hebrew iconography and its Egyptian background, the winged cobras stretch out their wings to protect the divine king or deity from evil. In Isaiah's vision, however, the seraphim use one pair of wings to cover their faces, one pair to cover their feet—probably a euphemism for genitalia here (see the textual note)—and with one pair they fly. Nothing is said of any attempt of these creatures to protect the enthroned king Yahweh. Instead, they seem to be protecting themselves from Yahweh's glory. They cover their faces, because even for seraphim it is dangerous to look upon the glory of God, and they cover their "feet," because even seraphim must cover up their private parts in the presence of this holy deity. The other pair of wings functions only to keep the seraphim aloft, not to ward off evil from Yahweh. In a very real sense, the seraphim have lost their original function; the only role left for them is to point to the sole majesty of Yahweh, which they do by calling back and forth to one another in a thunderous voice, "Holy, holy, holy is Yahweh of Hosts. The whole earth is full of his glory." The sound is very loud and terrifying, its volume strong enough to cause the doorposts of the temple to shake in the pivot stones of the threshhold as smoke fills the temple. (The oral and visual details here call to mind the highly amplified sound

---

27 Keel, *Jahwe-Visionen*, 92–109.

28 So C. F. Whitley, "The Call and Mission of Isaiah," *JNES* 18 (1959) 38–48; and Kaiser, *Isaiah 1–12*, 121. Even Jacques Vermeylen, who dismisses much of Isaiah as late and non-Isaianic, rejects this late dating

of Isaiah's vision (*Du prophète Isaïe à l'apocalyptique*, 1:188–89.

29 Cf. n. 23.

and special visual effects of a modern rock concert.) But while the convulsion of the temple seems to be a direct result of the booming voice of the seraphim, underscoring their traditional terror-inspiring quality, the seraphim ultimately serve only to highlight the exalted figure of the divine king.

How many seraphim Isaiah saw in his vision is not entirely clear, but nothing in the account of the vision requires more than two. The only other occurrence of the idiom in v. 3, verb + זֶה אֶל־זֶה (zê ʾel-zê), "one would call to the other," deals with only two entities, the camp of the Hebrews and the camp of the Egyptians, "and one did not approach the other all night" (Exod 14:20). Moreover, the association of winged cobras with thrones, where they occur precisely in pairs as on the throne of Tutankhamon and probably on the throne in the model sanctuary from Sidon, suggests that one would be satisfied with a pair of seraphim.

But if Isaiah saw a pair of seraphim, and if seraphim associated with thrones typically come in pairs, that raises the question whether, despite the tradition reflected in Num 21:6-9 and 2 Kgs 18:4, there were actually a pair of pole-mounted winged serpents in the inner sanctum of the temple in Isaiah's time. The source of much of the imagery for Isaiah's vision appears to have come from physical realities that Isaiah regularly saw in the temple. Yahweh's exalted throne appears to reflect the fifteen-foot-tall cherub throne that actually stood in the temple, the cloud of smoke probably reflects the smoke of incense that periodically filled the inner sanctum, and the seraphim may well reflect the pole-mounted, or perhaps more likely, a pair of pole-mounted winged serpents that stood in the inner sanctum and supposedly went back to Moses. According to 2 Kgs 18:4, until the time of Hezekiah, the Israelites burned incense to the pole-mounted serpent, and Hezekiah destroyed it in his reform as an idolatrous object. Isaiah's vision does not characterize the seraphim as idols, but by stripping them of their original protective function, he does depotentize them and elevate Yahweh at their expense. They become mere heralds pointing to the matchless glory of Yahweh, and, as such, one could hardly continue to justify offering incense to them. It is probably no accident that the bronze serpent (or serpents) was (were) removed from the temple only a few years after Isaiah's vision and destroyed as (an)

object(s) of illegitimate worship. Curiously enough, the winged sphinxes of Yahweh's Judean throne, which also originally functioned as protective genii, were never tainted with the same suspicion, though the analogous bull pedestals of Yahweh in the northern kingdom were roundly condemned by even the northern prophet Hosea as idolatrous (8:5-6; 10:5-8; 13:2).

To summarize, the details of Isaiah's vision discussed above—the high and exalted throne, the oversized divine figure enthroned upon it, the mere skirts of whose robe totally filled the temple, the thundering and fearsome seraphim who nevertheless must cover and protect themselves from the overwhelming glory of this divine king to whose holiness they unceasingly point in their temple-shaking cry—make two related points: (1) Yahweh is a divine suzerain who will brook no rival, who alone will be exalted; and (2) Yahweh's exaltedness is linked to his holiness—to his total separation from all that is profane or unclean.

Impact on Isaiah

The enduring impact this experience had on Isaiah is reflected in the way these two points form two fundamental aspects of his message: (1) Yahweh alone must be exalted; anything that attempts to set itself up as God's rival must be lopped off, cast down, and abased (Isa 2:8-22; 10:5-19, 32-34; 14:4-23; 17:12-14; 28:1-4). It is Yahweh's imperial plans, not the machinations of mere humans, no matter how clever, devious, or seemingly powerful, that will ultimately be realized (Isa 7:4-9; 14:24-27; 28:14-22; 29:14-16; 30:27-33; 31:8-9). (2) Yahweh, for whom Isaiah's second favorite epithet, after the ubiquitous יְהוָה צְבָאוֹת (YHWH ṣĕbāʾôt), "Yahweh of Hosts," is קְדוֹשׁ יִשְׂרָאֵל (qĕdôš yiśrāʾēl), "the Holy One of Israel" (Isa 1:4; 5:19, 24; 10:20; 12:6; 17:7; 29:19; 30:11; 31:1; 37:23), is exalted precisely in terms of his holiness, in terms of his fierce intolerance of injustice (Isa 5:16). Therefore, the imperial Yahweh of Hosts should be the only source of one's fear and terror, but that terrified awe should sanctify and honor Yahweh as a potential sanctuary (מִקְדָּשׁ, miqdāš; see ahead to Isa 8:13-15). A sanctuary, however, only to those who allow God to transform their lives to reflect God's own holy מִשְׁפָּט (mišpāṭ), "justice," and צְדָקָה (ṣĕdāqâ), "righteousness" (Isa 28:16-17; 29:22-24; 33:14-16).

Woe is me! I am silenced.

The immediate impact of this vision on Isaiah, however, appears to have been one of sheer terror. According to Israelite tradition, no one could see God and live (Exod 33:20). The biblical text preserves no examples that prove that rule; it only cites the exceptions to the rule (Gen 16:13; 32:31; Exod 3:6; 24:11; Judg 6:22; 13:22), but the normal human response to such a theophany is the fear that one will die. Isaiah apparently shared that normal human response to the vision of God. His cry, "Woe is me!" implies such a fear and suggests that one render the following verb נִדְמֵיתִי (nidmêtî) as "I am destroyed" or the like. This initial impression is reinforced by the closing line of the verse, which refers directly to the old tradition about seeing God, "for my eyes have seen the king, Yahweh of Hosts." Yet the verb itself is ambiguous. There is a דמה (dāmâ), which in the niphal means "to be destroyed," but there is another דמה (dāmâ), a biform of דמם (dāmam), which in the niphal means "to be silent" or "to be silenced." Moreover, the two interior lines, with their repeated emphasis on the prophet's and his people's "unclean lips," seem to shift the emphasis away from destruction and point it toward silence. This is probably another example of the prophet's penchant for creative ambiguity, an intentional double entendre that forces the reader to take account of both possible meanings. On the one hand, Isaiah feared for his life. With his recognition of the character of this God came the recognition that neither he nor his people were fit to live in Yahweh's presence. The knowledge of God leads to a better knowledge of oneself. On the other hand, Isaiah lamented his inability to give voice to the glory of the vision that had been granted to him.

Isaiah puts emphasis on the uncleanness of lips for two reasons. In the first place, it underscores the shallowness of both Isaiah's and his people's commitment to Yahweh. If Isaiah's vision occurred during communal worship in the temple as we have suggested, both the future prophet and his people were involved in an outward display of devotion to Yahweh, but Isaiah's vision enabled him to see that display for what it really was. As he says of Yahweh in a later oracle, "This people draw near to me with their mouth and with their lips they honor me, but their heart is far from me" (Isa 29:13). Public worship that does not lead on to a transformed life and the everyday pursuit of God's will for justice is an abomination to God (Isa 1:10-17) and leaves one with lips stained unclean by hypocrisy (Isa 6:5). Isaiah's contemporaries had allowed their attention to traditional ritual detail—Isaiah's "commandment of men" (29:13)—to block their vision of God and his central demands. This was a major concern in the OT prophets (e.g., Amos 4:4-5; 5:21-24; Jer 7:1-15), and as both Jesus (Matt 15:1-11; Mark 7:1-13) and Paul (Col 2:20-23) in the New Testament point out, the danger is a recurring one. God's people must constantly strive for a renewed vision of God to prevent custom from stifling obedience.

The second reason for Isaiah's emphasis on the lips is that they are the organs used by the prophet as God's spokesman. While they remain unclean, Isaiah cannot take up the prophetic task. In Jeremiah's call narrative, Jeremiah is equipped for his task by God putting forth his hand, touching Jeremiah's mouth, and placing his word in the prophet's mouth (Jer 1:9). In Ezekiel's call narrative, Ezekiel is equipped for his task when God sets before him a scroll inscribed with God's message that the prophet must eat and digest. In an analogous way, Isaiah is equipped for his prophetic task by the purification of his unclean lips.

The Live Coal from the Altar

There still remains one visual detail to discuss. When Isaiah reacts in terror to his vision, apparently afraid that he will die because he has seen God, but with an interesting focus on the uncleanness of both his own lips and those of his people, one of the seraphim flies to him with a live coal in his hand that the sārāp had taken off the altar with a pair of tongs, touches it to Isaiah's mouth, and says, "Now that this has touched your lips, your iniquity will turn aside and your sin will be atoned." The amount of circumstantial detail heaped up in these two verses is remarkable and suggests that such details may carry theological weight.

The first thing to note is that the object whose contact with Isaiah's unclean lips removes his sin, thus purifying his lips and preparing him to be Yahweh's messenger, comes from the altar. Isaiah was very critical of Judah's sacrificial cultus and of the superficiality of her public worship in general (Isa 1:10-15; 29:13), but this detail in Isaiah's account of his own purification should make one skeptical of the widespread claim that Isaiah totally rejected the sacrificial cultus.[30] If Isaiah linked the purification of his own unclean lips to the altar, it is hard to believe that he denied any role to the altar in the purification of the people's unclean lips.

Yet the peculiar manner in which the altar served to purify Isaiah should be noted. It is not what he puts on the altar that purifies him but what is taken from it. What is taken from it is a hot coal. This is emphasized by the way the expression "having in his hand a live coal" is further explicated by the following unmarked relative clause, "that he had taken from upon the altar with a pair of tongs." The explanatory clause implies that the coal was too hot to touch even for a *sārāp*, and thus the phrase "in his hand" means that the *sārāp* was carrying the coal not in his bare hand but in the tongs he held in his hand. Imagine, then, how it must have felt on Isaiah's lips. The implication is that Isaiah's cleansing was painful, that his sin was burned out; and if Isaiah experienced the purging of his own unclean lips as a purging by fire, one may suspect that he saw no way for the purging of his people's unclean lips apart from a similar ordeal by fire. Indeed, the purification or attempted purification of God's people through the fire of judgment is a recurring motif in Isaiah's oracles (Isa 1:2-9, 25-28; 9:7-20; 29:1-8), and Isaiah sometimes refers to Yahweh himself as a "devouring fire" (Isa 33:14; cf. 10:17; 30:27-33; 31:9).

The Commission

Once Isaiah's lips have been purified by the burning coal, like Micaiah ben Imlah (1 Kgs 22:19-22), Isaiah overhears the divine king consulting with his heavenly council. The question, "Whom will I send?" is different from the question addressed to the heavenly court in the Micaiah narrative, "Who will entice Ahab so that he will go up and fall at Ramoth-Gilead?" (1 Kgs 22:20), but it is formulated in a very similar fashion. In both cases the question presupposes that Yahweh has rendered a judgment; all that is left to consider is how to implement that judgment. In

the Micaiah incident, the judgment is made explicit in Yahweh's question. In Isaiah 6 it is not. Apparently Isaiah was unaware of the decision that had been made. One may assume that he caught just the tail end of Yahweh's deliberations; a decision had been made before Isaiah tuned in. He heard only the final question and volunteered without knowing the purpose for being sent or the message he was to carry. Thus, he is surprised by the message Yahweh gives him.

The message is a perplexing one: "Keep listening, but do not understand. Keep looking, but do not perceive." Then God gives even stranger instructions to Isaiah: "Fatten the heart of this people, and make its ears heavy, and its eyes smear over, lest it should see with its eyes, and with its ears hear, and its mind should understand, and it turn and there be healing for it." Faced with such a commission we would surely ask, "Why? Does not God want to heal his people?" We might even ask, "How? What do I do to dull their mind?" Isaiah, however, asks, "How long?" The question sounds odd to most modern readers, but it would probably not have surprised Isaiah's contemporaries.

This question is very common in lament Psalms, where the psalmist asks God how long his anger or punishment will last or how long God will allow the enemy to triumph (Pss 6:4; 74:10; 80:5; 90:13; 94:3). When an ancient Israelite or Mesopotamian consulted a deity because sickness or some other disaster had overtaken him, he or she wanted to know three things—why did the disaster befall him, would he survive, and how long would it be before he recovered. This is not fundamentally different from what a modern individual wants to know from his physician—what is the name of my illness, will I recover, and how long before I feel better. The concern for a time limit is reflected in a number of texts. In the Akkadian *Ludlul bēl nēmeqi*, the righteous sufferer complains that the time limit passed, but he got no better (line 1), and then that the diviner could put no time limit on his illness (line 111).[31] A similar motif occurs in Ps 74:9, where the psalmist complains that "we have not seen (the fulfill-

---

30   See the commentaries of Duhm, Marti, Gray, and Eichrodt on Isa 1:10-17, and note especially Richard Hentschke, *Die Stellung der vorexilischen Schriftpropheten zum Kultus* (BZAW 75; Berlin: A. Töpelmann, 1957) 94–110.

31   W. G. Lambert, *Babylonian Wisdom Literature* (Oxford: Clarendon, 1960) 21–62, esp. 39, 45.

ment) of our signs, there is no longer a prophet, and there is no one with us who knows how long (עַד־מָה, ʿad-mâ)." Time limits were often the signs that prophets gave to confirm the legitimacy of their oracles (cf. Isa 7:8-9, 14-16; 8:3-4; 37:30-32). Isaiah simply wants to know how long this period of divine judgment will last.

The Answer

Unfortunately, the answer is not immediately reassuring, since it asserts that the period of divine judgment will last until the land lies in ruins, the population far removed, with numerous abandoned villages and empty houses throughout the land. What comes after this judgment and its time limit is not immediately clear because of the textual difficulties in v. 13. The first part of v. 13 does not explicitly offer hope for the future. A remnant of one tenth (עֲשִׂרִיָּה, ʿăśîrîyâ) seems to be traditional (cf. Amos 5:3), but Isaiah seems to say that even if a tenth remains, it will again be grazed or burned over—the verb can be derived from either of two homonymous roots, both of which are used to express God's judgment (Isa 5:5, "graze, devour"; Isa 4:4, "burn"). Understood in this way, the preceding verb וְשָׁבָה (wĕšābâ) means to "do again, repeat," and not "repent." JPS translates the verb as "it shall repent," but to do that the JPS translators have to detach the following phrase וְהָיְתָה לְבָעֵר (wĕhāyĕtâ lĕbāʿēr) and read it with the next line, which runs against the Masoretic punctuation. The thought appears similar to that in Amos 6:9—even if ten men are left in one house, they will die.

Nonetheless, the final part of v. 13, unless it is hopelessly corrupt, seems to include an element of hope for the time beyond the judgment. There is no lack of creative emendations and rewritings, particularly of the difficult relative clause, but none of them seems compelling. The text may be too corrupt to recover the original meaning without new textual evidence, but if the preserved text is correct, the metaphor concerning the trees seems to be a variant on that found in Job 14:7-9, "For there is hope for a tree, if it is cut down, that it might again flourish and its shoots not cease. Though its root (שָׁרְשׁוֹ, šoršô) grow old in the ground, and its stock (גִּזְעוֹ, gizʿô) die in the dust, at the smell of water it will sprout, and it will make branches as though newly planted." Assuming that מַצֶּבֶת (maṣṣebet) in Isa 6:13 is a synonym of šōreš and gezaʿ in Job 14:8, the sense of Isa 6:13b seems to be, "Like

a terebinth or an oak, whose root-stock remains in them when felled, its root-stock מַצַּבְתָּה (maṣṣabtāh) is the seed of holiness. The feminine singular suffix on maṣṣabtāh refers back to the land (הָאָרֶץ, hāʾāreṣ) of v. 12, just as the feminine singular suffix on בָּהּ (bāh, "in it") at the beginning of v. 13 does. The text does not explicitly promise renewal, but if the stock remains, and if the stock is the seed of holiness or holy seed, the source for new growth and renewed fertility for the human population of the land, the implication would seem to be that there is hope for renewal beyond the judgment. Even if the oracle does not explicitly address the issue of what comes after judgment, it does not deny such a future.

It is true that the transition between v. 13a, which speaks of additional judgment, and v. 13b, which, assuming the text is correct, offers hope beyond judgment, is quite abrupt. This has led many scholars to dismiss at least part of v. 13b as a late correction to Isaiah's bleaker outlook (so, for example, Marti, 69; Duhm, 46; Gray, 111). Yet neither the hope for new life after extreme judgment nor a somewhat abrupt introduction of that hope is lacking elsewhere in Isaiah. Isaiah promises Zion new life as a righteous city with just judges after a refining judgment of fire (1:25-26); after a devastating defeat that leaves too few men to provide husbands for the few surviving women (3:25—4:1), he promises a renewed fertility for Zion's human remnant (4:2-4); after a judgment by fire that terrifies the wicked in Jerusalem (33:10-14), he promises a glorious renewal of unshakable security for the city (33:17-24), and he promises a renewed fertility for the land after the devastation of Israel (7:20-25). Here Isaiah simply ignores the issue of the future, or only alludes to it implicitly, because to mention it explicitly would detract attention from the message of judgment.

In this regard, the parallel with the Micaiah narrative is quite striking in several respects. It too ignores what comes after the judgment; the oracle concentrates almost exclusively on the death of Ahab. It also throws an interesting light on our question, "How?" In the Micaiah narrative, the divine council explicitly discusses how to get Ahab into battle so that Yahweh can have him killed. Isaiah's commission is to perform a similar function of bringing his audience into judgment, but exactly how he is to dull the people's mind is not explained. There is no indication that Isaiah was to lie to the people, that he was to lull them into a stupor by a message of peace when there was no peace. Micaiah initially joined the other prophets in lying to Ahab, and one might conclude that he was reluctant to warn Ahab lest the Israelite king escape the predetermined judgment, but nothing even remotely similar is reported of Isaiah.

Apparently Isaiah was to dull the people's mind simply by the constant repetition of his message of trust in God, relief for the oppressed, and judgment on the disobedient (Isa 29:9-13). Isaiah spoke a true message that, if heeded, would have brought life and healing, but because the people refused to hear, rejected trust in God, and chose to rely on oppression, the spurned message simply heightened the judgment (Isa 30:8-17). Thereby a message of life brought death, a message of great insight greater blindness. The thought is very similar to and actually lies behind that found in the Synoptic Gospels' explanation for Jesus's parables. According to Matt 13:10-17 (= Mark 4:10-12; Luke 8:9-10), Jesus spoke to the crowds in parables so that the crowds could not understand. That is a very strange use of parables! One normally thinks of parables as a way of aiding understanding. For some they had this positive function. For some they revealed the secrets of the kingdom of heaven (Matt 13:11-12, 16-17), while for the many they veiled the message in obscurity. Such has always been the case with the divine word (2 Cor 2:14-16; 3:15). It all depends on one's willingness to hear. A refusal to hear turns the clearest warning into a sealed scroll, and God will reward such self-stupefaction with an even greater loss of understanding (Isa 29:9-14). As Jesus said,

"Take heed then how you hear; for to him who has will more be given, and from him who has not, even what he thinks that he has will be taken away" (Luke 8:18).

This point brings us to the final question, "Why?" Why does God want the prophet's message to dull the people's understanding? The parallel with the Micaiah narrative is again suggestive. Yahweh wanted to kill Ahab because of his repeated transgressions; God's patience had reached its limits. Yet even at this point God is gracious enough to warn Ahab again through Micaiah. In the same way, Yahweh reveals to Isaiah that his patience with Israel has run out, yet even so he still sends his prophet with a gracious if futile warning. There is irony in both passages. The God who decides to kill Ahab and purge Jerusalem takes pleasure in neither decision; his real desire is for the transformation of the wicked (Ezek 33:11). Even the bitter and apparently hopeless oracles of both Micaiah and Isaiah represent, ironically enough, a last ditch effort to break through their audiences's willful blindness.[32] Both attempt to justify the divine authenticity of the prophet's message by a bitterly polemical explanation of phenomena that might throw doubt on the message, but it is an explanation still addressed to those under the judgment. Like Paul's remark to the Jews in Rome (Acts 28:25-29), Isaiah's report of his call is aimed at those he calls blind, deaf, and without understanding. It has not yet become just an in-group explanation of why others have rejected the message as happens elsewhere (John 12:40; Rom 11:8).

Bibliography

Ahlström, G. W., "Isaiah VI.13," *JSS* 19 (1974): 169–72.

Albright, W. F., "The High Place in Ancient Palestine," in *Volume de Congrès: Strasbourg, 1956* (VTSup 4; Leiden: Brill, 1957) 242–58, esp. 254–55.

Alonso Díaz, José, "La ceguera espiritual del pueblo en Is 6:9-10 en relación con la acción de Dios," *EstEcl* 34 (1960) 129–53.

Alt, Albrecht, "Gedanken über das Königtum Jahwes," in *Kleine Schriften zur Geschichte des Volkes Israel* (3 vols.; Munich: C. H. Beck, 1953) 1:345–57.

Ambrose, A. A., "(Is. 6,9) 'Höre, ohne zu hören' zu Koran 4,46(48)," *ZDMG* 136 (1986) 15–22.

32   There is also an obvious parallel to the "hardening of Pharaoh's heart" in the plagues narrative in Exodus. Some texts speak of God hardening Pharaoh's heart (Exod 4:21; 7:3; 9:12; 10:1, 20, 27; 11:10; 14:4, 8, 17), some of Pharaoh hardening his own heart (Exod 8:11, 28; 9:34), and others more neutrally of Pharaoh's heart becoming hard (Exod 7:13-14; 8:15; 9:7, 35), though the composite narrative makes no clear attempt to explain the apparent conflict, whether by the ordering of the occurrences or by any extended reflection on the contrasting statements. As a result, despite the obviousness of these Mosaic parallels, their citation adds little clarity to the theological meaning of the oracles of either Micaiah ben Imlah or Isaiah.

Arida, Robert M., "Hearing, Receiving and Entering TO MYSTHRION/TA MYSTHRIA: Patristic Insights Unvieling the Crux Interpretum (Isaiah 6:9-10) of the Sower Parable," *St. Vladimir's Theological Quarterly* 38 (1994) 211–34.

Auret, A., "Jesaja 6:1aa meer as 'n historiese nota'?" *NGTT* 32 (1991) 368–77.

Bakon, S., "Kedusha–Holiness," *Dor leDor* 16 (1987) 2–9.

Baltzer, Klaus, "Considerations Regarding the Office and Calling of the Prophet," *HTR* 61 (1968) 567–81.

Barker, M., "Beyond the Veil of the Temple: The High Priestly Origins of the Apocalypses," *SJT* 51 (1998) 1–21.

Barth, Hermann, *Die Jesaja-Worte in der Josiazeit: Israel und Asshur als Thema einer Produktiven Neuinterpretation des Jesajaüberlieferung* (WMANT 48; Neukirchen-Vluyn: Neukirchener Verlag, 1977) 277–300.

Barthel, J., *Prophetenwort und Geschichte: Die Jesajaüberlieferung in Jes 6–8 und 28–31* (FAT 19; Tübingen: Mohr Siebeck, 1998).

Beale, Gregory K., "Isaiah 6:9-13: A Retributive Taunt against Idolatry," *VT* 41 (1991) 257–78.

Béguerie, P., "La vocation d'Isaïe," in P. Béguerie et al., eds., *Études sur les prophètes d'Israël* (LD 14; Paris: Cerf, 1954) 11–51.

Brettler, Marc Zvi, *God Is King: Understanding an Israelite Metaphor* (JSOTSup 76; Sheffield: Sheffield Academic Press, 1989).

Brock, Sebastian P., "The Thrice-Holy Hymn in the Liturgy," *Sobornost* n.s. 7 (1985) 24–34.

Brodie, Thomas L., "The Children and the Prince: The Structure, Nature and Date of Isaiah 6–12," *BTB* 9 (1979) 27–31.

Brownlee, W. H., "The Text of Isaiah VI 13 in the Light of DSIa," *VT* 1 (1951) 296–98.

Budde, K., *Jesaja's Erleben: Eine gemeinverständliche Auslegung der Denkschrift des Propheten (Kap 6, 1–9, 6)* (Gotha: Klotz, 1928).

Caspari, W., "Um ein vorhellenistisches Verständnis des Trisagion," *Theologische Bücherei* 4 (1925) 86–89.

Cate, Robert L., "We Need to Be Saved," *RevExp* 88 (1991) 137–51.

Cazelles, Henri, "La vocation d'Isaïe (ch 6) et les rites royaux," in L. Alvarez Verdes and E. J. Alonso Hernández, eds., *Homenaje a Juan Prado: Miscelánea de estudios bíblicos y hebráicos* (Madrid: Consejo Superior de Investigaciones Científicios, 1975) 89–108.

Chilton, Bruce, "The Temple in the Targum of Isaiah," in Chilton, *Targumic Approaches to the Gospels: Essays in the Mutual Definition of Judaism and* *Christianity* (Studies in Judaism; Lanham, MD: University Press of America, 1986) 51–61.

Clements, Ronald E., "Beyond Tradition History: Deutero-Isaianic Development of First Isaiah's Themes," *JSOT* 31 (1985) 95–113.

Crabtree, T. T., "The Prophetic Call—A Dialogue with God," *Southwestern Journal of Theology* 4 (1961) 33–35.

Crouzel, Henri, "Die Spiritualität des Origenes: Ihre Bedeutung für die Gegenwart," *TQ* 165 (1985) 132–42.

Driver, G. R., "Isaiah 6:1: 'His Train Filled the Temple,'" in Hans Goedicke, ed., *Near Eastern Studies in Honor of William Foxwell Albright* (Baltimore: Johns Hopkins Press, 1971) 87–96.

Dumbrell, W. J., "Worship and Isaiah 6," *RTR* 43 (1984) 1–8.

Eaton, J. H., *Vision in Worship* (London: SPCK, 1981).

Edward, J., "Prophetic Paradox: Isaiah 6:9-10," *Studia Biblica et Theologica* 6 (1976) 48–61.

Eissfeldt, Otto, "Jahwe als König," *ZAW* 46 (1928) 81–105.

Emerton, J. A., "The Translation and Interpretation of Isaiah vi.13," in J. A. Emerton and S. C. Reif, eds., *Interpreting the Hebrew Bible: Essays in Honour of E. I. J. Rosenthal* (Cambridge: Cambridge University Press, 1982) 85–118.

Engnell, Ivan, *The Call of Isaiah: An Exegetical and Comparative Study* (Uppsala universitets Årsskrift 1949:4; Uppsala: Lundequistska, 1949).

Eslinger, L., "The Infinite in a Finite Organical Perception (Isaiah vi 1-5)," *VT* 60 (1990) 145–73.

Evans, Craig A., "1QIsaiah and the Absence of Prophetic Critique at Qumran," *Revue de Qumran* 11 (1984) 537–42.

———, "Isa 6:9-13 in the Context of Isaiah's Theology," *JETS* 29 (1986) 139–46.

———, "The Text of Isaiah 6:9-10," *ZAW* 94 (1982) 415–18.

———, *To See and Not Perceive: Isaiah 6:9-10 in Early Jewish and Christian Interpretation* (JSOTSup 64; Sheffield: Sheffield Academic Press, 1989).

Flusser, David, "Jewish Roots of the Liturgical Trishagion (Is 6:3; Yannai's piyyutim)," *Immanuel* 3 (1973) 37–43.

Franklyn, Paul N., "Preaching on the Call to Prophecy in Epiphany [bibliog]," *Quarterly Review* 11 (1991) 96–107.

Fruhstorfer, K., "Isaias' Berufungsvision," *TPQ* 91 (1938) 414–24.

Gnilka, Joachim, *Die Verstockung Israels: Isaias 6:9-10 in der Theologie der Synoptiker* (SANT 3; Munich: Kösel, 1961).

Gouders, K., "Die Berufung des Propheten Jesaja (Jes 6,1-13)," *BibLeb* 13 (1972) 89–106, 172–84.

——, "Zu einer Theologie der prophetischen Berufung," *BibLeb* 12 (1971) 79–93.

Görg, M., "Die Funktion der Serafen bei Jesaja," *BN* 5 (1978) 28–39.

Gosse, B., "Isaïe vi et la tradition isaïenne," *VT* 42 (1992) 340–49.

——, "Isaïe 52:13–53:12 et Isaïe 6," *RB* 98 (1991) 537–43.

Gowan, Donald E., "Isaiah 6:1-8 [Expository article]," *Int* 45 (1991) 172–76.

Gray, J., "The Kingship of God in the Prophets and the Psalms," *VT* 11 (1961) 1–29.

Greenfield, Jonas C., "Baal's Throne and Isa 6:1," in A. Caquot, S. Legasse, and M. Tardieu, eds., *Mélanges bibliques et orientaux en l'honneur de M. Mathias Delcor* (AOAT 215; Kevelaer: Butzon & Bercker; Neukirchen-Vluyn: Neukirchener Verlag, 1985) 193–98.

Habel, Norman C., "The Form and Significance of the Call Narratives," *ZAW* 77 (1965) 297–323.

Hardmeier, Christof, "Jesajas Verkündigungsansicht in Jes 6," in Jörg Jeremias and Lothar Perlitt, eds., *Die Botschaft und die Boten: Festschrift für Hans Walter Wolff zum 70. Geburtstag* (Neukirchen-Vluyn: Neukirchener Verlag, 1981) 235–51.

Hartenstein, F., *Die Unzugänglichkeit Gottes im Heiligtum: Jesaja 6 und der Wohnort JHWHs in der Jerusalemer Kulttradition* (WMANT 75; Neukirchen-Vluyn: Neukirchener Verlag, 1997).

Hayward, R., "The Chant of the Seraphim and the Worship of the Second Temple," *PIBA* 20 (1997) 62–80.

Herntrich, V., "Die Berufung des Jesajas," *MPT* 35 (1939) 158–78.

Hesse, F., *Das Verstockungsproblem im Alten Testament* (BZAW 74; Berlin: A. Töpelmann, 1955).

Hirth, T., "Überlegungen zu den Seraphim," *BN* 77 (1995) 17–19.

Hollenbach, B., "Lest They Should Turn and Be Forgiven: Irony," *BT* 34 (1983) 312–21.

Horst, F., "Die Visionsschilderungen der alttestamentlichen Propheten," *EvT* 20 (1960) 193–205.

House, P. R., "Isaiah's Call and Its Context in Isaiah 1–6," *CTR* 62 (1993) 207–22.

Hubmann, F. D., "Der Bote des Heiligen Geistes: Jesaja 6,1-13 im Kontext von Berufung," *TPQ* 135 (1987) 228–39.

Hurley, R., "Le Seigneur endurcit le coeur d'Israel? L'ironie d'Isaïe 6,9-10," *Theoforum* 32 (2001) 23–43.

Hurowitz, V. A., "Isaiah's Impure Lips and Their Purification in Light of Mouth Purification and Mouth Purity in Akkadian Sources," *HUCA* 60 (1989) 39–89.

Hvidberg, F., "The Masseba and the Holy Seed," *NorTT* 56 (1955) 97–99.

Irsigler, Hubert, "Gott als König in Berufung und Verkündigung Jesajas," in F. Reiterer, ed., *Ein Gott, eine Offenbarung: Beiträge zur biblischen Exegese, Theologie, und Spiritualität: Festschrift für Notker Füglister* (Würzburg: Echter, 1991) 127–54.

Iwry, S., "*Maṣṣēbāh* and *Bāmāh* in 1Q Isaiah^A 6:13," *JBL* 76 (1957) 225–32.

Jenni, E., "Jesajas Berufung in der neueren Forschung," *TZ* 15 (1959) 321–39.

Jones, K. R., *Serpent Symbolism in the OT: A Linguistical, Archaeological and Literary Study* (Haddonfield, NJ: Haddonfield House, 1974).

——, "Winged Serpents in Isaiah's Inaugural Vision," *JBL* 86 (1967) 410–15.

Joosten, J., "La prosopopée, les pseudo-citations et la vocation d'Isaïe (Is 6:9-10)," *Bib* 82 (2001) 232–43.

Kaplan, M. M., "Isaiah 6:1-11," *JBL* 45 (1926) 251–59.

Keel, Othmar, *Jahwe-Visionen und Siegelkunst: Eine neue Deutung der Majestätsschilderungen in Jes 6, Ez 1 und Sach 5* (SBS 84/85; Stuttgart: Katholisches Bibelwerk, 1977).

Kellenberger, E., "Heil und Verstockung: Zu Jes 6,9f bei Jesaja und im Neuen Testament," *TZ* 48 (1992) 268–75.

Key, A. F., "The Magical Background of Isaiah 6:9-13," *JBL* 86 (1967) 198–204.

Kilian, Rudolf, "Die prophetischen Berufungsberichte." In *Theologie im Wandel: Festschrift zum 150 jährigen Bestehen der Katholisch-Theologischen Fakultät an der Universität Tübingen 1817–1967* (Munich: Wewel, 1967) 356–76.

——, "Der Verstockungsauftrag Jesajas," in H.-J. Fabry, ed., *Bausteine biblischer Theologie: Festgabe für G. Johannes Botterweck* (Bonn: Hanstein, 1977).

Kingsbury, E. C., "The Prophets and the Council of Yahweh," *JBL* 83 (1964) 279–86.

Klijn, A. F. J., "Jérome, Isaïe 6 et l'Evangile des Nazoréens," *VC* 40 (1986) 245–50.

Knierim, Rolf, "The Vocation of Isaiah," *VT* 18 (1968) 47–68.

Lacheman, E., "The Seraphim of Isaiah 6," *JQR* 59 (1968) 71–72.

Landy, F., "Strategies of Concentration and Diffusion in Isaiah 6," *BibInt* 7 (1999) 58–86.

Laridon, V., "Isaiae ad munus propheticum vocatio," *Collationes Brugenses* 45 (1949) 3–8, 29–33.

Lehnert, Volker A., *Die Provokation Israels: Die paradoxe Funktion von Jes 6,9-10 bei Markus und Lukas. Ein textpragmatischer Versuch im Kontext gegenwärtiger Rezeptionsästhetik und Lesetheorie* (Neukirchener theologische Dissertationen und Habilitationen 25; Neukirchen-Vluyn: Neukirchener Verlag, 1999).

Leiser, B. M., "The Trisagion of Isaiah's Vision," *NTS* 6 (1959) 261–63.

Lescow, Th., "Jesajas Denkschrift aus der Zeit des syrisch-ephraimitischen Krieges," *ZAW* 85 (1973) 315–31.

Liebreich, L. J., "The Position of Chapter Six in the Book of Isaiah," *HUCA* 25 (1954) 37–40.

Lind, M. C., "Political Implications of Isaiah 6," in C. C. Broyles and C. A. Evans, eds., *Writing and Reading the Scroll of Isaiah: Studies of an Interpretive Tradition* (2 vols.; VTSup 70; Leiden: Brill, 1997) 1:317–38.

Long, Burke O., "Reports of Visions among the Prophets," *JBL* 95 (1976) 353–65.

Love, J. P., "The Call of Isaiah," *Int* 11 (1957) 282–96.

Magonet, J., "The Structure of Isaiah 6," in *Proceedings of the Ninth World Congress of Jewish Studies: Jerusalem, August 4–12, 1985* (Jerusalem: Hebrew University, 1986) 91–97.

Marti, Karl, "Der jesajanische Kern in Jes 6:1–9:6," in *Beiträge zur alttestamentlichen Wissenschaft, Karl Budde zum siebzigsten Geburtstag am 13. April 1920* (BZAW 34; Giessen: A. Töpelmann, 1920) 113–21.

McLaughlin, J. L., "Their Hearts Were Hardened: The Use of Isaiah 6,9-10 in the Book of Isaiah," *Bib* 75 (1994) 1–25.

Menken, Martinus J. J., "Die Form des Zitates aus Jes 6:10 in Joh 12:40: Ein Beitrag zum Schriftgebrauch des vierten Evangelisten," *BZ* n.s. 32 (1988) 189–209.

Metzger, W., "Der Horizont der Gnade in der Berufungsvision Jesajas," *ZAW* 93 (1981) 281–84.

Milgrom, Jacob, "Did Isaiah Prophesy during the Reign of Uzziah?" *VT* 14 (1964) 164–82.

Montagnini, F., "La vocazione di Isaia," *BeO* 6 (1964) 163–72.

Moore, Carey A., "Mark 4:12: More like the Irony of Micah than Isaiah," in Howard N. Bream, Ralph D. Heim, and Carey A. Moore, eds., *A Light unto My Path: Old Testament Studies in Honor of Jacob M. Myers* (Gettysburg Theological Studies 4; Philadelphia: Temple University Press, 1974) 335–44.

Mowinckel, Sigmund, *Die Erkenntnis Gottes bei den alttestamentlichen Propheten* (Oslo: Grøndahl, 1941).

Müller, H. P., "Glauben und Bleiben: Zur Denkschrift Jesajas Kapitel VI.1–VIII.18," in *Studies on Prophecy: A Collection of Twelve Papers* (VTSup 26; Leiden: Brill, 1974) 25–54.

———, "Die himmlische Ratsversammlung," *ZNW* 54 (1963) 254–67.

Nicol, G. G., "Isaiah's Vision and the Visions of Daniel," *VT* 29 (1979) 501–4.

Niehr, H., "Zur Intention von Jes 6,1-9," *BN* 21 (1983) 59–65.

Nielsen, Kirsten, "I skal høre eg høre, men intet fatte; I skal se og se, men intet fortsta. Jesajas kaldelsesberetning set I lyset af de senere ars profet-

forskning," in B. Rosendal, ed., *Studier i Jesajabogen* (Aarhus: Universitetsforlag, 1989) 9–29.

———, "Is 6:1–8:18 as Dramatic Writing," *ST* 40 (1986) 1–16.

Nobile, M., "Jes 6 und Ezek 1,1–3,15: Vergleich und Funktion im Jeweiligen Redactionellen Kontext," in J. Vermeylen, ed., *Book of Isaiah = Le livre d'Isaïe: les oracles et leur relectures unité et complexité de l'ouvrage* (BETL 82; Leuven: Leuven University Press/Peeters, 1989) 211–26.

Peterson, E. H., "The Holy Stump," *Crux* 32 (1996) 2–11.

Rendtorff, Rolf, "Isaiah 6 in the Framework of the Composition of the Book of Isaiah," in J. Vermeylen, ed., *Book of Isaiah = Le livre d'Isaïe: les oracles et leur relectures unité et complexité de l'ouvrage* (BETL 81; Leuven: Leuven University Press/Peeters, 1989) 73–83. Reprinted in Rendtorff, *Canon and Theology: Overtures to an Old Testament Theology* (Minneapolis: Fortress Press, 1993) 170–80.

Reventlow, Henning Graf, "Das Ende der sogenannten 'Denkschrift' Jesajas [6:1–9:6]," *BN* 38–39 (1987) 62–67.

Roberts, J. J. M., "The Visual Elements in Isaiah's Vision in Light of Judean and Near Eastern Sources," in Joyce Rilett Wood, John E. Harvey, and Mark Leuchter, eds., *From Babel to Babylon: Essays on Biblical History and Literature in Honour of Brian Peckham* (LHBOTS 455; New York: T&T Clark, 2006) 197–213.

Robinson, G. D., "The Motif of Deafness and Blindness in Isaiah 6:9-10: A Contextual, Literary, and Theological Analysis," *BBR* 8 (1998) 167–86.

Ruben, P., "A Proposed New Method of Textual Criticism in the Old Testament," *AJSL* 51 (1934) 30–45.

Rüthy, A. E., "Das prophetische Berufungserlebnis," *Internationale Kirchliche Zeitschrift* 31 (1941) 97–114.

Sacchi, P., "Isaia 6 e la concezione di impurità nel medio giudaismo," *VH* 13 (2002) 55–77.

Savignac, J. de, "Les 'Seraphim,'" *VT* 22 (1972) 320–35.

Sawyer, J., "The Qumran Reading of Isaiah 6:13," *ASTI* 3 (1964) 111–13.

Schmidt, H., "Kerubenthron und Lade," in H. Schmidt, ed., *Eucharistérion: Studien zur Religion und Literatur des Alten und Neuen Testaments: Hermann Gunkel zum 60. Geburtstage* (Göttingen: Vandenhoeck & Ruprecht, 1923) 120–44.

Schmidt, J. H., "Gedanken zum Verstockungsauftrag Jesajas (Is 6)," *VT* 21 (1971) 68–90.

Schmidt, W., "Jerusalemer El-Traditionen bei Jesaja," *ZRGG* 16 (1964) 302–13.

———, "Wo hat die Aussage: Jahwe 'der Heilige' ihren Ursprung?" *ZAW* 74 (1962) 62–66.

Schoors, Anttoon, "Isaiah, the Minister of Royal Anointment," *OTS* 20 (1977) 85–107.

Schreiner, J., "Zur Textgestalt von Jes 6 und 7,1-17," *BZ* n.F. 22 (1978) 92–97.

Sonnet, J.-P., "Le motif de l'endurcissement (Is 6,9-10) et la lecture d'Isaïe," *Bib* 73 (1992) 208–39.

Spieckermann, Hermann, "Die ganze Erde ist seiner Herrlichkeit voll: Pantheismus im Alten Testament?" *ZTK* 87 (1990) 415–36.

Steck, Odil Hannes, "Bemerkungen zu Jesaja 6," *BZ* 16 (1972) 188–206.

———, "Rettung und Verstockung: Exegetische Bemerkungen zu Jesaja 7, 3-9," *EvT* 33 (1973) 77–90.

Steinmetz, D. C., "John Calvin on Isaiah 6: A Problem in the History of Exegesis," *Int* 36 (1982) 156–70.

Tidwell, N. L. A., "wā'ōmār (Zech 3:5) and the Genre of Zechariahs's Fourth Vision," *JBL* 94 (1975) 343–55.

Tsevat, M., "ישעיהו (Isa 6)," in B. Z. Luria, ed., *The Zalman Shazar Jubilee Volume* (Jerusalem: Kiryath Sepher, 1973) 161–72.

Tyler, Ronald L., "The Source and Function of Isaiah 6:9-10 in John 12:40," in James E. Priest, ed., *Johannine Studies: Essays in Honor of Frank Pack* (Malibu, CA: Pepperdine University Press, 1989) 205–20.

Uffenheimer, B., "The Consecration of Is. in Rabbinic Exegesis," *Scripta Hierosolymitana* 22 (1977) 233–46.

Vaccari, A., "Visio Isaiae (6)," *VD* 10 (1930) 100–106.

Vaux, Roland de, "Les chérubins et l'arche d'alliance, les sphinx gardiens et les thrones divins dans l'ancien Orient," *MUSJ* 37 (1961) 93–124.

Vieweger, Dieter, "Die Spezifik der Berufungsberichte Jeremias und Ezechiels im Umfeld ähnlicher Einheiten des Alten Testaments," *TLZ* 112 (1987) 860–62.

Vogels, W., "Les récits de vocation des prophètes," *NRT* 95 (1973) 3–24.

Wagner, Renate, *Textexegese als Strukturanalyse: Sprachwissenschaftliche Methode zur Erschliessung althebräischer Texte am Beispiel des Visionsberichtes Jes 6, 1-11* (ATSAT 32; St. Ottilien: EOS, 1989).

Walker, N., "Disagion versus Trisagion: A Copyist Defended," *NTS* 7 (1960) 170–71.

———, "The Origin of the 'Trice-Holy,'" *NTS* 5 (1958) 132–33.

Werner, Wolfgang, "Vom Prophetenwort zur Prophetentheologie: Ein redaktionskritischer Versuch zu Jes 6:1–8:18," *BZ* n.s. 29 (1985) 1–30.

Whitley, C. F., "The Call and Mission of Isaiah," *JNES* 18 (1959) 38–48.

Wieringen, A. L. H. M. van, *The Implied Reader in Isaiah 6–12* (BIS 34; Leiden: Brill, 1999).

———, "Jesaja 6: Aankondiging van noodlot of oproep tot heil? Een communicatieve lezing," in P. van Tongeren, ed., *Het lot in eigen hand? Reflecties op de betekenis van het (noodlot) in once cultuur* (Baarn: Gooi & Sticht, 1994) 109–25.

———, "Jes 6:13: Een structuuronderzoek," *Bijdragen* 48 (1987) 32–40.

Wildberger, Hans, "Jesaja 6:1-8," in G. Eichholz, ed., *Herr, tue meine Lippen auf* (Wuppertal: E. Müller, 1961) 346–55.

Williamson, H. G. M., "Isaiah 6:13 and 1:29-31," in J. Van Ruiten and M. Vervenne, eds., *Studies in the Book of Isaiah: Festschrift Willem A. M. Beuken* (BETL 132; Leuven: Leuven University Press/Peeters, 1997) 119–28.

Worschech, U. F. C., "The Problem of Isaiah 6," *AUSS* 12 (1974) 126–38.

Zeron, A., "Die Anmassung des Königs Usia im Lichte von Jesajas Berufung," *TZ* 33 (1977) 65–68.

Isaiah 7:1—8:18 contains a series of oracles all closely connected to the Syro-Ephraimitic war of 735–732 BCE. Several of these oracles give prominence to three children who bear symbolic names: Shear-jashub (7:1-9), Immanuel (7:10-17), and Maher-shalal-hush-baz (8:1-4). Given the similarity among these oracles, the common prophetic practice of giving their children symbolic names (cf. Hos 1:3-8), and the fact that Isaiah refers to the children whom God gave him as signs and portents in Israel (8:18), it is probable that all these children with symbolic names were Isaiah's children. The message of all these children oracles is basically the same. Judah and its Davidic dynasty should trust God's promises and not be afraid of the combined armies of Israel and Damascus, because within a very short time these two enemy states will be destroyed. The oracles follow one another in temporal progression just as the children are born in temporal progression, and one can sense something of the passage of time in the way in which the prophet progressively shortens the time until the expected destruction of the enemy. In the Shear-jashub oracle the prophet expects the destruction of Israel and Damascus within five to six years (Isa 7:8; see the textual emendation discussed below). The Immanuel oracle expects their demise in two to three years (7:15-16), and the Maher-shalal-hush-baz oracle looks for their destruction in one to two years (8:4).

The interpretation of these children oracles will draw on other material that has been displaced from its original historical setting. Thus, the explanation of the name Shear-jashub found in Isa 10:20-22, though it is now found in a much later context, can aid in the interpretation of 7:1-9. Isaiah 8:5-10 also seems to have been displaced from its original context, though not as far. Since it provides an explanation for the name Immanuel, historically it should have preceded the oracle about Maher-shalal-hush-baz in 8:1-4. In any case, it will contribute to the interpretation of the famous Immanuel passage in 7:10-17. Finally, 8:16-18, which has close ties to 8:1-4 and refers to Isaiah's children as signs and portents, will be taken as the original conclusion of this material.

That leaves two major pericopes in this block of material to be discussed: 7:18-25 and 8:11-15. Both of these pericopes appear to come from the same general period of the Syro-Epraimitic War, but their literary placement creates certain ambiguities in the message that may suggest later editing. These texts will be treated together with the question why Isa 8:5-10 has been placed after the Maher-shalal-hush-baz oracle.

7:1-7 The Shear-jashub Oracle; The Original Context

The historical setting for the prophetic confrontations narrated in the following verses was the Syro-Ephraimitic War. Rezin, the Aramean king of Damascus, and Pekah, the king of Israel, probably with Philistine and Phoenician support, were trying to create a new coalition to resist Assyrian expansion, modeled on the relatively successful Aramean coalitions of the preceding century. To succeed, however, they had to persuade Judah to join, and this Ahaz was reluctant to do. Thus, the allies decided to attack Jerusalem, overthrow Ahaz, and replace him with the more compliant son of Tabeel. The identity of this Tabeel is uncertain, and the name itself may be garbled. One suggestion is that the allies' candidate for the throne was a son of king Ittobaal of Tyre.[1] At any rate, faced with this threat from his northern neighbors, Ahaz was in a quandary. Could he resist an attack of the allies on his own, or should be appeal to Assyria to save him? How problematic Ahaz's position was is reflected in the panic that seized the king and his people when news of the Aramean-Israelite plans reached Jerusalem.

---

1   See my "The Context, Text, and Logic of Isaiah 7.7-9," in John Kaltner and Louis Stulman, eds., *Inspired Speech: Prophecy in the Ancient Near East. Essays in Honor of Herbert B. Huffmon* (JSOTSup 378; London: T&T Clark, 2004) 164; and the earlier works by A. Vanel, "Tâbe²él en Is VII 6 et le roi Tubail de Tyr," in *Studies on Prophecy* (VTSup 26; Leiden: Brill, 1974) 17–24; and Asurmendi, *La guerra siro-efraimita,* 54.

7

1/ In the days[a] of Ahaz son of Jotham son of Uzziah, king of Judah, Rezin, king of Aram, and Pekah son of Remaliah, king of Israel, went up to Jerusalem for war against it, but they[b] were unable to fight against it. 2/ In the meantime it was reported to the house of David, "Aram has turned aside[c] upon Ephraim." And his heart and[d] the heart of his people shook as the trees of a[e] forest shake before a wind. 3/ Then Yahweh said to Isaiah, "Go to meet Ahaz, you and Shear-jashub, your son, to the end of the conduit of the upper pool, to the road of the laundryman's field. 4/ And say to him, 'Be careful and be calm! Do not be afraid[f] and let your heart not be faint because of these two stumps of smoking firebrands, at the burning anger[g] of Rezin and Aram and the son of Remaliah. 5/ Because Aram—with Ephraim and the son of Remaliah[h]—has plotted[i] evil against you, saying: 6/ "Let us go up into Judah, and let us cut it[j] off,[k] and let us breach[l] it[j] for ourselves,[m] and let us install as king within it[j] the son of Ittobaal.[n]"'" 7/ Thus says the Lord Yahweh: "It[o] will not stand and it[o] will not happen. 8-9/ For the head of Aram is Damascus[p] and the head of Damascus[p] is Rezin;[q] [r]and the head of Ephraim is Samaria, and the head of Samaria is the son of Remaliah. And within only five years Ephraim will be destroyed as a people,[r] and within six years Damascus will be removed as a city.[s] If you do not believe, you will not be established."

Textual Notes

a The parallel in 2 Kgs 16:5 has, "Then Rezin, king of Aram, and Pekah son of Remaliah, king of Israel, went up to Jerusalem to fight, and they laid siege against Ahaz, but they were unable to fight."

b Reading the plural יָכֵלוּ (yākēlû), "they were unable," with 2 Kgs 16:5, 1QIsaᵃ, LXX, Vg., and Syr. against the singular יָכֹל (yākōl), "he was unable," of MT and Tg.

c The derivation and meaning of נָחָה (nāḥâ) is disputed. LXX, Syr., and Tg. understand it as meaning "to make an agreement with." This has led to the suggestion that it is a niphal of a denominative verb אחה (נחה > נאחה), "to become a brother." Vg. derives it from נוח, "to rest," but the subject "Aram" requires a third masculine form, not נָחָה, which is third feminine if derived from נוח. Another possibility, followed here, is to connect it to Arabic naḥā, "to wend one's way, go, walk, turn," and Akkadian nêʾu, "to turn away, turn back." I take the sense to be that the Aramean army has turned back from a more northerly defensive position facing Assyria and has moved into a forward offensive position in Ephraim in preparation for an attack on Jerusalem.

d 1QIsaᵃ omits לְבָבוֹ (lēbābô), "his heart," and the copulative on the following וּלְבַב (ûlēbab), "and the heart of," but this is a clear haplography because of the repetition of the same word; MT is supported by the versions.

e 1QIsaᵃ has the definite article before יַעַר (yaʿar), "forest," but this is a secondary prosaizing change.

f 1QIsaᵃ has ואל (wēʾal), "and not," for MT's אַל (ʾal), "not."

g 1QIsaᵃ adds כי (kî), "because," before בְּחֲרִי (boḥŏrî), "at the burning (anger)," and LXX apparently has it as well, though it has an odd rendering of the whole end of the verse: ὅταν γὰρ ὀργὴ τοῦ θυμοῦ μου γένηται πάλιν ἰάσομαι, "for when the anger of my wrath has passed, again I will heal." For the first part of this reading LXX seems to be following the same text as 1QIsaᵃ. It takes בחרי אף (boḥŏrî ʾap) as God's anger, adds a pronoun to make that clear (as the LXX translator in Lam 2:3 also does), and renders the sense of the preposition ב as temporal, a use it often has when followed by an infinitive. At this point it appears that LXX read ארפא (ʾerpāʾ) "I will heal," in his Vorlage, but it does not seem original; it may have arisen from a dittography of אף (ʾap), "anger," and a garbling of רצין (rēṣîn), "Rezin," that led to the following reading ארפא ובן ארם ובן־רמליהו. Once the verb ארפא (ʾerpāʾ) had been created by the corruption, the following names no longer fit syntactically, so they were attached as a pendens to the following verse, "As for

h   LXX omits the subjects אֲרָם ... אֶפְרַיִם וּבֶן־רְמַלְיָהוּ (ʾārām ... ʾeprayim ûben-rĕmalyāhû), "Aram . . . Ephraim and the son of Remaliah," in this verse, because it already supplied subjects from the names left over from the corruption of the previous verse.

i   LXX reads a plural verb as a result of the previous corruption that gave it a plural subject before the verb.

j   The object suffixes on the verbs and the suffix on בְּתוֹכָהּ (bĕtôkāh), "within it," are all feminine singular in the MT, which creates a grammatical difficulty with the apparent antecedent יְהוּדָה (yĕhûdâ), "Judah," since the name of the country is normally construed as masculine, though a few occurrences of yĕhûdâ as feminine are attested (Jer 23:6; Ps 114:2; Song 1:3). Syr. follows MT. LXX and Tg. translate the two object suffixes on the verbs as masculine plurals referring to the people, but even they translate the suffix on בְּתוֹכָהּ (bĕtôkāh), "within it," as a feminine singular, which suggests that their rendering of the object suffixes on the verbs is free translation and not evidence of a different *Vorlage*.

k   The meaning of וּנְקִיצֶנָּה (ûnĕqîṣennâ) is disputed; I assume a byform of the root קצץ (qāṣaṣ), "to cut off." LXX translates the verb as συλλαλήσαντες αὐτοῖς, "and having consulted with them. . . ."

l   LXX renders וְנַבְקִעֶנָּה אֵלֵינוּ (wĕnabqiʿennâ ʾēlênû), "and let us breach it for ourselves," as ἀποστρέψομεν αὐτοὺς πρὸς ἡμᾶς, "let us turn them aside to us," but the normal meaning of בקע (bāqaʿ) is "to breach."

m   Syr. omits the אֵלֵינוּ (ʾēlênû), "for ourselves."

n   The personal name appears to be garbled, perhaps intentionally (see the commentary). Tg. simply renders it with interpretive freedom as "the one who is pleasing to us."

o   The feminine singular subject of the verbs תָקוּם (tāqûm), "it will (not) stand," and תִהְיֶה (tihyê), "it will (not) happen," is either the nominalized feminine adjective רָעָה (rāʿâ) "evil," or more likely the implicit antecedent עֵצָה רָעָה (ʿēṣâ rāʿâ), "the evil plan" (7:5). For a parallel use of ʿēṣâ, compare 8:10.

p   1QIsaᵃ spells Damascus as דרמשק.

q   וְראֹשׁ דַּמֶּשֶׂק רְצִין (wĕrōʾš dammeśeq rĕṣîn), "and the head of Damascus is Rezin," has dropped out of LXX by haplography because of homoioarcton with the preceding ראֹשׁ.

r   Reading after רצין with a transposition and reconstruction of a half line:

בעוד חמש שנה יחת אפרים מעם
ובעוד שש מוסר דמשק מעיר

For details on the transposition and reconstruction see the commentary.

s   LXX adds ἡ βασιλεία before Ephraim, "the kingdom of Ephraim," as an explanatory expansion, and Tg. offers a similar explanatory translation, "the house of Israel will cease to be a kingdom."

Commentary

Verse 1, beginning with "Rezin, king of Aram," is taken from 2 Kgs 16:5 and probably represents a considerable expansion of Isaiah's original account by the later collector. Isaiah would have had little reason to provide detailed historical background information for his contemporaries, who were as familiar with the events as he. If Isa 6:1 provides a model, Isaiah's account probably began more modestly: "In the days of King Ahaz, the house of David was told. . . ." The later collector, however, needed to include background information so that later readers could understand the context. His quotation from 2 Kings provides that information, but it also confuses the issue by indicating the outcome of the crisis at the very beginning of the account. At the time Isaiah met Ahaz inspecting Jerusalem's water supply, the city was not yet under siege. The Davidic house had just become aware of the plans of the Aramean-Israelite coalition. It was certainly not yet clear that the coalition's assault on Jerusalem would fail.

In this context of Jerusalem's panic, uncertainty, and feverish preparation to resist a siege, Yahweh sent Isaiah together with his son, Shear-jashub, to meet King Ahaz. The reason for the presence of Isaiah's son is undoubtedly that Isaiah, like Hosea before him, had given his son a symbolic name. Unfortunately, this passage neither gives us the age of the child at this encounter nor interprets his symbolic name for us. If the child had been given this symbolic name at some earlier point, as seems likely from the wording of the command to Isaiah (7:3), the presence of the child was probably intended to remind Ahaz of an earlier oracle associated with the naming of the child in which his symbolic name was explained. On the other hand, if, despite the wording of the text, the child was actually named on this occasion, it is likely that the naming was accompanied by an oracle explaining the name.

In either case, such an explanatory oracle may be preserved in a pericope from this period that was reused in the later Assyrian crisis. Isaiah 10:21-22 interprets Shear-jashub, A-Remnant-Will-Return, to suggest that only a remnant of the northern kingdom, called "Jacob" and "your people Israel" (10:20-22) in contrast to Judah, called "my people who dwell in Zion" (10:24), would survive the Syro-Ephraimitic War. They would return to Yahweh and to El-gibbor, "Mighty God," a title for the Davidic king of Judah (Isa 9:6 [Heb. 9:5]). In other words, the surviving northerners would return to the kingdom of Judah. This explanation of the name is very closely tied to the Syro-Ephraimitic War, so either the child was given this name a relatively short time before Isaiah's meeting with Ahaz, or the name was reinterpreted at this time with specific reference to this war. At any rate, the presence at the meeting of this child with his symbolic name was intended to underscore Isaiah's message of salvation.

Isaiah's actual oracle to Ahaz begins in v. 4 with an admonition to Ahaz to be careful, to be calm, not to fear, and not to let his heart grow fearful. This is holy war language, as can be seen by a comparison with Deut 20:3, which contains the same idiom with רכך (rākak), "be faint," and also includes the synonyms ירא (yārēʾ), "to fear," חפז (ḥāpaz), "to be alarmed," and ערץ (ʿāraṣ), "to tremble, stand in awe." Isaiah also uses ירא and ערץ in a similar manner in 8:12. Given the parallels with Deut 30:2 and Isa 8:12, one should not overinterpret הִשָּׁמֵר וְהַשְׁקֵט (hiššāmēr wĕhašqēṭ), "be careful and be calm," as commands demanding quietism and a lack of preparation for war. Ahaz is admonished not to act foolishly in panic, but that does not require that he do nothing at all. Unfortunately, the text does not make clear what particular course of action Isaiah is warning Ahaz not to take. There are several possibilities. He could be warning him against joining the coalition. Contra G. Wong,[2] we do not know if this was a possibility, but since the coalition did not have immediate success, Ahaz may very well have had some room to bargain. Moreover, one could conceive of the young Ahaz as being more concerned to save his own skin than to save his throne—kings often fled their cities to save their own lives. Finally, he could have been considering appealing to the Assyrians, as he eventually did.

Whether Isaiah had any particular one of these scenarios primarily in mind is simply not clear from the text. Ahaz and his court were terrified at the plans of Aram and Israel, but Isaiah plays down this danger from Rezin king of Aram and the king of Israel, whose name he treats as unworthy of mention, referring to him merely as the son of Remaliah. These two enemies of whom Ahaz was in terror Yahweh dismisses as nothing more than the smoking stubs of two burned-out sticks, absolutely nothing of which to be afraid.

In v. 5 Yahweh then refers to the evil plan of these two states, and in v. 6 God specifies what that plan was by giving a direct quotation of the enemy. Literarily this has a close parallel in Ps 2:1-3, where again the enemies' evil plan is spelled out in a direct quotation put in the mouth of the enemies. According to v. 6, Aram and Israel planned to go up against Judah, cut her off, breach her for themselves, and install as king within her the son of a certain Tab'al. The "her" of the object suffixes on the two verbs and the preposition is more likely to be the remote antecedent, the city Jerusalem (7:1), than the country Judah. While the country may be grammatically construed as feminine (see textual notes), it is normally construed as masculine. Even more important than grammatical considerations, however, the strategy, involving a surprise attack specifically on Jerusalem (7:1), and the normal meaning of the verbs used—"to cut off" and "to breach," fit better with a city as the object than with a country. Jerusalem lay to the north of the Judean homeland not far from the border with Israel, in the former Jebusite enclave between Judah and Israel, and a rapid surprise attack from the north (the line of march is probably reflected in Isa 10:27d-34) offered the anti-Assyrian coalition the prospect of cutting Jerusalem off from southern Judean reinforcements long enough for the attackers to breach Jerusalem's walls and capture the city. Once they had succeeded in capturing Jerusalem, the coalition hoped, perhaps naively, that Judah would submit to the new Judean king installed by the coalition. The identity of this son of Tab'al is uncertain, partly because the name טָבְאַל (ṭābʾal), "Good for Nothing," appears to have been intentionally skewed. A number of suggestions have been made, but one of the most attractive is

---

2   G. Wong, "A Cuckoo in the Textual Nest at Isaiah 7:9b?" *JTS* n.s. 47 (1996) 123–24.

A. Vanel's suggestion, followed by J. M. Asurmendi, that Aram's candidate for the throne was a son of the Tubail (= Ittobaʿl) of Tyre mentioned in Tiglath-pileser III's tribute list from 737 BCE.[3] It is clear from Tiglath-pileser's campaign that Phoenicia along with the Philistines supported Rezin's anti-Assyrian coalition, so a king chosen from this ally would have made sense to the coalition. At any rate, nothing in the text suggests that the candidate was a Davidide from a secondary line of the royal Judean family. It is worth noting that the law of the king in Deut 17:15 specifically forbids the Israelites from installing a foreigner as a king over them. Since in Israel's recorded history, apart from this possible instance, there is no reference to any attempt to install a foreigner as king over either Judah or Israel, one must consider the possibility that this Deuteronomic prohibition arose as a specific response to this attempt during the Syro-Ephraimitic War.

After citing the enemy plan, God then reassures Ahaz in v. 7 that the plan will neither stand nor come to pass. Then vv. 8a-9a are introduced with the causal conjunction כי (kî), "because," and appear to give the reason why Ahaz and his court can trust the promise God gave in v. 7.

v. 8a   כי ראש ארם דמשק וראש דמשק רצין (kî rōʾš ʾărām dammeśeq wěrōʾš dammeśeq rĕṣîn)

v. 8b   ובעוד ששים וחמש שנה יחת אפרים מעם (ûběʿôd šiššîm wěḥāmēš šānâ yēḥat ʾeprayim mēʿām)

v. 9a   וראש אפרים שמרון וראש שמרון בן־רמליהו (wěrōʾš ʾeprayim šōmĕrôn wěrōʾš šōmĕrôn ben-rĕmalyāhû)

For the head of Aram is Damascus, and the head of Damascus is Rezin;
And within sixty-five years Ephraim will be shattered from being a people,
And the head of Ephraim is Samaria, and the head of Samaria is the son of Remaliah.

Needless to say, the logic of this formulation is not crystal clear. Some of the lack of clarity may stem from textual corruption, as there are clear signs of a disturbed text. The order of the three lines is quite odd. Verse

8b intrudes between and disrupts the clear parallelism between vv. 8a and 9a. In v. 8b an impending judgment is announced on Ephraim, but in v. 8a only Damascus has been mentioned; Ephraim is not mentioned until v. 9a, after the announcement of judgment. The temporal phrase in v. 8b, "within sixty-five years," gives too long a time period to fit the context as a reassurance to Ahaz. Faced with more immediate problems, Ahaz could hardly be particularly concerned with what would happen sixty-five years later. He could not expect to be around to see a judgment on his enemies that was delayed that long. Moreover, the time limits involved in the following oracles involving the other children with symbolic names are much shorter. With Immanuel in 7:16 the promise is that before the child can choose his own food, that is, before he is weaned (about three years after birth), the land of these two kings will be deserted; and with Maher-shalal-hush-baz in 8:4 the promise is that before the child can say, "Mommy," or "Daddy" (about a year after birth), the booty of these two enemy countries will be carried away to Assyria. One might expect a time limit of five to six years, since that would correspond to time limits of three to four and one to two, but a time limit of sixty-five years falls completely out of any meaningful sequence.

For these reasons it is fairly common for scholars to bracket out v. 8b as a later intrusive gloss. This move gets rid of the problem of the interruption of the parallelism between vv. 8a and 9a, but it has its own difficulties. Why would any later interpreter introduce such a gloss in so awkward a manner? Why would a glossator intentionally disrupt a clear parallelism in the text, mentioning only the weaker of Judah's two enemies and inserting his comment in the text prior to its reference to that enemy? Unless one assumes that ancient glossators were by definition stupid, it is hard to explain the disrupted text as the result of a simple misplaced gloss. There is no known historical event that transpired sixty-five years after 735 BCE, that is, c. 670 BCE, involving the destruction of Ephraim that could reasonably provoke such a gloss. Moreover, if one deletes this whole line as a gloss, one removes the only clear announcement of judgment on Judah's enemies found in the whole Shear-jashub

3   Vanel, "Tâbeʾél en Is VII 6," 18; Asurmendi, *La guerra siro-efraimita*, 54. For the identification of the name, see Vanel, 23 n. 3.

oracle, though the parallel Immanuel oracle (7:17) and Maher-shalal-hush-baz oracle (8:4) both have clear announcements of judgment on Aram and Israel. Finally, the vocabulary and syntax of this supposed gloss are distinctly Isaianic. Despite Wildberger's assertions to the contrary (Wildberger, *Isaiah 1–12*, 285), it is not at all clear that the use of חתת (*ḥātat*) in 7:8, "to be shattered," is different from its use in 8:9. The translation "be shattered" is just as appropriate there as the translation "be terrified." The sense "to be shattered" fits Isa 7:8; 8:9; 9:3; 30:31, while a greater emphasis on fear fits 20:5; 31:4, 9; 37:27; but the two usages are simply two poles of an external–internal continuum and do not suggest two different writers. One should also note that the idiom—verb of destruction + PN + מן + noun, "PN will be destroyed from being something"—is extremely rare in the OT. It is found only here, in the genuine Isaianic oracle from the period of the Syro-Ephraimitic War in 17:1, perhaps in a slightly altered form in Isa 25:2, and in Jer 48:42. It is hard to believe that a late glossator came up with such a rare idiom.

These observations suggest that one should try a different approach at solving the textual problem, which has been touched on in the textual notes above. One should note that the significant amount of repetition in vv. 8-9 invites textual corruption by haplography. Indeed, if one looks at the textual traditions for all of 7:1-9, one finds a significant number of haplographies in them. In v. 2, MT's לְבָבוֹ וּלְבַב עַמּוֹ (*lēbābô ûlēbab ʿammô*), "his heart and the heart of his people," is reduced by haplography in 1QIsaᵃ to לבב עמו (*lēbab ʿammô*), "the heart of his people." In v. 4, a major corruption in the LXX's *Vorlage* leads to a significantly different reading from MT's בַּחֳרִי־אַף רְצִין וַאֲרָם וּבֶן־רְמַלְיָהוּ (*boḥŏrî-ʾap rĕṣîn waʾărām ûben-rĕmalyāyû*), "at the fierce anger of Rezin and Aram and the son of Remaliah." LXX appears to read כי בחרי־אף ארפא ובן ארם ובן־רמליהו (*kî boḥŏrî-ʾap ʾerpāʾ ûben ʾărām ûben-rĕmalyāyû*), "for when my (God's) fierce anger has passed, I will again heal. And as for the son of Aram and the son of Remaliah. . . ." This LXX corruption in v. 4, because it has removed the syntactical connection between the concluding proper names and the earlier part of the verse, leads to a major omission by the LXX of all the proper names in v. 5, since the leftover names in v. 4 have now become the subject of the now plural verb in v. 5:

MT: יַעַן כִּי־יָעַץ עָלֶיךָ אֲרָם רָעָה אֶפְרַיִם וּבֶן־רְמַלְיָהוּ לֵאמֹר (*yaʿan kî-yāʿaṣ ʿālêkā ʾărām rāʿâ ʾeprayim ûben-rĕmalyāhû lēʾmōr*), "because Aram counseled evil against you (along) with Ephraim and the son of Remaliah, saying . . ."

LXX: לאמר [   ] רעה [   ] עליך כי־יעצו כי יען (*yaʿan kî-yāʿaṣ ʿālêkā rāʿâ lēʾmōr*), ("And as for the son of Aram and the son of Remaliah [v. 4]—because they counseled evil against you, saying . . ."

Finally, and most telling of all, one should note that the LXX has omitted the last half of v. 8a by a haplography caused by the recurring repetition of phrases:

MT: כי ראש ארם דמשק וראש דמשק רצין (*kî rōʾš ʾărām dammeśeq wĕrōʾš dammeśeq rĕṣîn*), "because the head of Aram is Damascus and the head of Damascus is Rezin"

LXX: [   ] כי ראש ארם דמשק (*kî rōʾš ʾărām dammeśeq*), "because the head of Aram is Damascus"

This pattern of haplographies in the text suggests that one look for the disruption in vv. 8a-9a as the result not of the awkward insertion of an incomprehensible gloss but of a major haplography and its attendant corruptions. Working from these presuppositions, I will suggest a plausible reconstruction of the original text and then explain how it was corrupted into the present text of the MT. The original text, presumably written in the script and orthography of preexilic Hebrew, ran something like the following:

8a כי ראש ארם דמשק וראש דמשק רצין (*kî rōʾš ʾărām dammeśeq wĕrōʾš dammeśeq rĕṣîn*)

9a וראש אפרים שמרן וראש שמרן בן־רמליהו (*wĕrōʾš ʾeprayim šōmĕrôn wĕrōʾš šōmĕrôn ben-rĕmalyāhû*)

8b בעוד חמש שנה יחת אפרים מעם (*bĕʿôd ḥāmēš šānâ yēḥat ʾeprayim mēʿām*)

8c בעוד שש מסר דמשק מעיר (*bĕʿôd šēš mūsār dammeśeq mēʿîr*)

For the head of Aram is Damascus and the head of Damascus is Rezin,
And the head of Ephraim is Samaria and the head of Samaria is the son of Remaliah;
Within five years Ephraim will be shattered from being a people,

And within six Damascus will be removed from being a city.

The restoration of the numbers assumes the common stylistic motif in which a number is cited and then that number plus one is mentioned (see esp. Prov 6:16; Job 5:19; Amos 1:3, 6, 9, 11, 13; 2:1, 4, 6; but cf. also Exod 20:5; 34:7; Num 14:18; Deut 5:9; 2 Kgs 13:19).[4] That Isaiah made use of this pattern is clear from two occurrences of it in 17:6: שְׁנַיִם שְׁלֹשָׁה (šĕnayim šĕlōšâ), "two or three," . . . אַרְבָּעָה חֲמִשָּׁה (ʾarbāʿâ ḥămiššâ), "four or five." The restoration of מסר דמשק מעיר in the reconstructed line is based on the occurrence of the similar expression הִנֵּה דַמֶּשֶׂק מוּסָר מֵעִיר (hinnê dammeśeq mûsār mēʿîr), "Damascus is about to be removed from being a city," in 17:1, another oracle against Damascus and Ephraim coming from the same period of the Syro-Ephraimitic War.

If one begins with this as the original text, it is easy to see how it could have been corrupted into the present MT. The scribe copied the first line without any problem, but when he looked back to his *Vorlage*, because of the repetitive nature of the lines, his eyes skipped over the second line and landed on the second ובעוד. The scribe then copied the first few words of v. 8c—ובעוד ששמ, mistakenly taking the initial מ on מסר as the final letter of the numeral. At this point he looked back to his *Vorlage* and saw the numeral חמש following the first ובעוד, so he continued writing, thus conflating the beginning of v. 8c with the end of v. 8b: ובעוד ששמ חמש שנה יחת אפרים מעמ, thus omitting entirely the end of v. 8c, just as the LXX omitted the end of v. 8a. At this point, however, the scribe looked back to his *Vorlage* and noted that he had omitted v. 9a, so he added it at the end. Thus, with the perhaps subsequent addition of final consonant forms, internal *matres*, and a stylistic ו before חמש, one finally arrives at what is essentially the present MT. All the posited errors are plausible and reflective of the kind of mistakes actually attested in the textual traditions for this section of First Isaiah.

Logic

If one accepts my reconstruction of the original text, the logic of the oracle is at least clearer, and an attempt to grasp the deeper significance of the repetitive mention of the various "heads" becomes possible. I have already alluded to a certain literary parallelism between Isa. 7:5-9 and Psalm 2, but the parallelism between these two passages reaches much deeper: they share a common theology. In Psalm 2, the foreign enemies are portrayed as restive vassals plotting to throw off the hegemony of Yahweh and his anointed, that is, the Davidic king in Jerusalem (Ps 2:1-3). But the divine suzerain laughs at their plans and scoffs at them (Ps 2:4), much as Yahweh belittles Rezin and the son of Remaliah in Isa 7:4. Then God speaks to these enemies and terrifies them with the assertion, "I have set my king on Zion my holy mountain" (Ps 2:5-6). The Davidic king then goes on to cite God's covenantal promise to him, "You are my son, today I have given birth to you. Ask of me, and I will give you the nations as your inheritance, the ends of the earth as your possession. You will shepherd/shatter [double entendre] them with a staff of iron; you will smash them like a potter's vessel" (Ps 2:7-9). In view of these promises, the king warns the rebellious vassals, "Now, O kings, be wise; be warned, O rulers of the earth. Serve Yahweh with fear and kiss his feet with trembling, lest he grow angry and you perish from the way; for his anger is very close to flaring up" (Ps 2:10-12). In short, the machinations of these enemy kings in Psalm 2 will come to naught precisely because God has chosen the Davidic king as his anointed and legitimate representative on earth, and he has chosen Zion/Jerusalem as his holy abode on earth. The same tradition of this double election of the Davidic line and the city Jerusalem is reflected also in Ps 132:10-18, and it was a fundamental part of the Zion theology cultivated at the royal court in Jerusalem and in which Isaiah also was steeped.[5]

Once one begins to think in Zion Tradition categories, however, the logic of the oracle becomes clear. The threat from Aram is not serious because the head of Aram is Damascus and the head of Damascus is merely Rezin. Damascus is not Yahweh's chosen city Jerusalem, and Rezin is not Yahweh's anointed Davidide. In the same way, Samaria is not God's chosen city, and the

4 See the detailed study of this pattern by Yair Zakovitch, *ha-Degem ha-sifruti sheloshah-arbaʿah ba-Miḳra* ['For three . . . and for four': the pattern of the numerical sequence three–four in the Bible]

(PhD diss., The Hebrew University, 1978; Jerusalem: Makor, 1979 [in Hebrew with English summary], pp. 628 + xxxi).

5 See my discussion in J. J. M. Roberts, "Isaiah in Old

son of Remaliah is certainly not Yahweh's anointed. Since Yahweh has chosen Jerusalem and David, Aram's presumptuous plan to seize Jerusalem and replace the Davidic line is contrary to the will of the divine suzerain and doomed to failure. Moreover, its failure will have disastrous consequences for the two ringleaders of the plan. Within the relatively short time span of five to six years Ephraim will cease to exist as a people, and Damascus will be destroyed as a city. In effect, Isaiah is urging Ahaz and the Davidic court to take seriously their own royal theology, and as a sign that the promise is reliable, Isaiah assures Ahaz that, if he will only stand firm, he will see the promise fulfilled within six years.

Isaiah concludes this oracle with a warning, however, that is also rooted in the same royal Zion theology. Playing on the root אמן ('āman), a root used in the promises made to David that Yahweh would build him a firm house בַּיִת נֶאֱמָן (bayit neʾĕmān, 1 Sam 25:28; 2 Sam 7:16) and keep for him "my firm covenant," בְרִיתִי נֶאֱמֶנֶת (bĕrîtî neʾĕmenet, Ps 89:29; cf. Isa 55:3), Isaiah warns Ahaz and his court אִם לֹא תַאֲמִינוּ כִּי לֹא תֵאָמֵנוּ (ʾim lōʾ taʾămînû kî lōʾ tēʾāmēnû), "If you do not believe, you will not be established." The best commentary on this phrase is found in an admonition King Jehoshaphat gives to the people of Judah and Jerusalem just prior to an expected battle with a far more numerous enemy in 2 Chr 20:20: הַאֲמִינוּ בַּיהוָה אֱלֹהֵיכֶם וְתֵאָמֵנוּ הַאֲמִינוּ בִנְבִיאָיו וְהַצְלִיחוּ (haʾămînû bĕYHWH ʾĕlōhêkem wĕtēʾāmēnû haʾămînû binbîʾāyw wĕhaṣĕlîḥû), "Believe in Yahweh your God and be established; believe in his prophets and succeed." The admonition is in response to an earlier prophetic oracle by Jahaziel in which God urged the people not to be afraid but to go forth to meet the enemy in the confidence that God was with them, because God promised that he would personally defeat the enemy and that the people need only to stand and observe the salvation of Yahweh (vv. 14–17). It is clear that the belief spoken of in 2 Chr 20:20 is quite particular: it is the belief in the promise God had just given through his prophet. In the same way, the belief Isaiah speaks of in Isa 7:9 is quite particular: it is belief in the promised deliverance from the threat of Aram and Ephraim that God has just given through Isaiah, based on the long-standing promises made to the Davidic house and Jerusalem so emphasized in the royal Zion theology. Just as in Isa 28:16–17, the implication seems to be that Yahweh's foundational commitments will remain firm and unmovable, providing security for the one who trusts Yahweh, but the one who attempts to find security on some other foundation will be washed away (Isa 28:17–19). Whether Isaiah intended this as a threat to the continuance of the whole Davidic line may be doubted. Given his fundamental commitment to the Zion theology, it is more likely that the threat was more particular and more limited, directed only to Ahaz, the reigning Davidide, and his advisors.

Bibliography

Achard, Martin R., "Esaïe et Jérémie aux prises avec les problèmes politiques," *RHPR* 47 (1967) 208–24.

Ackroyd, Peter, "The Bibical Interpretation of the Reigns of Ahaz and Hezekiah," in *In the Shelter of Elyon: Essays on Ancient Palestinian Life and Literature in Honor of G. W. Ahlström* (JSOTSup 31; Sheffield: JSOT Press, 1984).

Albright, W. F., "The Son of Tabeel (Isaiah 7:6)," *BASOR* 140 (1955) 34–35.

Althann, Robert, "Yôm, "Time" and Some Texts in Isaiah," *JNSL* 11 (1983) 3–8.

Asurmendi, *La guerra siro-efraimita.*

Barr, James, "Did Isaiah Know about Hebrew Root Meanings? [Isa 7:8; Reply to N.W. Porteous]." *ExpTim* 75 (1964) 242.

Begrich, J., "Der syrisch-ephraimitische Krieg und seine weltpolitischen Zusammenhänge," *ZDMG* 83 (1929) 213–37. Reprinted in Begrich, *Gesammelte Studien zum Alten Testament* (Munich: C. Kaiser, 1964) 99–120.

Blank, S. H., "The Current Misunderstanding of Isaiah's She'ar Yashub," *JBL* 67 (1948) 211–15.

Boehmer, J., "Der Glaube und Jesaja," *ZAW* 41 (1923) 84–93.

Bouzon, E., "A Mesagem Triologico do Immanuel," *Revista Eclesiástica Brasileira* 32 (1972) 826–41.

Testament Theology," *Int* 36 (1982) 130–43, esp. 136–38.

Brodie, L., "The Children and the Prince: The Structure, Nature, and Date of Isaiah 6–12," *BTB* 9 (1979) 27–31.

Brunet, G., *Essai sur l'Isaïe de l'histoire: Études de quelques textes, notamment dans Is 7,8 et 22 (I. l'Emmanuel: II. le Siloé)* (Paris: A. & J. Picard, 1975).

——, "Le terrain aux foulons," *RB* 71 (1964) 230–39.

Brux, A., "Is 7,6," *AJSL* 39 (1922) 68–71.

Budde, K., "Isaiah VII.1 and 2 Kings XVI.5," *ExpTim* 11 (1899) 327–30.

——, "Jesaja und Ahaz," *ZDMG* 84 (1931) 125–38.

Burrows, Millar, "The Conduit of the Upper Pool," *ZAW* 70 (1958) 221–27.

Christensen, Duane L. *Transformations of the War Oracle in Old Testament Prophecy: Studies in the Oracles against the Nations* (HDR 3; Missoula, MT: Scholars Press, 1975).

Clines, David J. A., "X, X Ben Y, Ben Y: Personal Names in Hebrew Narrative Style," *VT* 22 (1972) 266–67.

Day, John, "Shear-jashub (Isaiah VII 3) and the Remnant of Wrath (Ps 76:11)," *VT* 31 (1981) 76–78.

Dearman, J. Andrew, "The Son of Tabeel (Isa 7:6)," in Stephen B. Reid, ed., *Prophets and Paradigms: Essays in Honor of Gene M. Tucker* (JSOTSup 229; Sheffield: Sheffield Academic Press, 1996) 33–47.

Dietrich, W., *Jesaja und die Politik* (Munich: C. Kaiser, 1976).

Dohmen, Christoph, "Verstockungsvollzug und prophetische Legitimation: Literarkritische Beobachtungen zu Jes 7,1-17," *BN* 31 (1986) 37–56.

Donner, *Israel unter den Völkern.*

Evans, Craig A., "On Isaiah's Use of Israel's Sacred Tradition," *BZ* n.s. 30 (1986) 92–99.

Fensham, F. Charles, "A Fresh Look at Isaiah 7:7-9," in E. Conrad and E. Newing, eds., *Perspectives on Language and Text: Essays and Poems in Honor of Francis I. Andersen's Sixtieth Birthday, July 28, 1985* (Winona Lake, IN: Eisenbrauns, 1987) 11–17.

Fichtner, J., "Zu Jes. 7:5-7," *ZAW* 56 (1938) 176.

Fischer, Danièle, "Jalons pour une compréhension judaïsante du Christianisme," *Foi et Vie* 84.1-2 (1985) 79–87.

Frankena, R., "'Dit zij u een teken,'" in *Studies B.A. Brongers.* Theol Inst, 1974. 28-36.

Gamper, A., "La foi d'Esaïe," *RTP* n.s. 10 (1922) 263–91.

Gitay, Yehoshua, "Isaiah and the Syro-Ephraimite War," in J. Vermeylen et al., eds., *Le livre d'Isaïe: Les oracles et leurs relectures. Unité et complexité de l'ouvrage* (BETL 81; Leuven: Leuven University Press, 1989) 217–30.

Graham, W. C., "Isaiah's Part in the Syro-Ephraimitic Crisis," *AJSL* 50 (1934) 201–16.

Gunneweg, A. H. J., "Heils- und Unheilsverkündigung in Jes VII," *VT* 15 (1965) 27–34.

Hadley, Judith M., "2 Chronicles 32:30 and the Water Systems of Pre-Exilic Jerusalem," in Iain Provan and Mark J. Boda, eds., *Let Us Go Up to Zion: Essays in Honour of H. G. M. Williamson on the Occasion of His Sixty-Fifth Birthday* (VTSup 153; Leiden: Brill, 2012) 273–84.

Hardmeier, Christof, "Gesichtspunkte pragmatischer Erzähltextanalyse: 'Glaubt Ihr nicht, so bleibt Ihr nicht'—ein Glaubensappell an schwankende Anhänger Jesajas," *WD* 15 (1979) 33–54.

Hasel, Gerhard F., "Linguistic Considerations Regarding the Translation of Isaiah's Shear-Jashub: A Reassessment," *AUSS* 9 (1971) 36–46.

——, *The Remnant: The History and Theology of the Remnant Idea from Genesis to Isaiah* (Andrews University Monographs 5; Berrien Springs, MI: Andrews University Press, 1972).

Höffken, Peter, "Grundfragen von Jesaja 7:1-17 im Spiegel neuerer Literatur," *BZ* n.s. 33 (1989) 25–42.

——, "Notizen zum Textcharakter von Jes. 7:1-17," *TZ* 36 (1980) 321–37.

Hoffman, H. W., *Die Intention der Verkündigung Jesajas* (BZAW 136; Berlin: de Gruyter, 1974).

Hogenhaven, Jesper, "Die symbolischen Namen in Jesaja 7 und 8 im Rahmen der sogenannten 'Denkschrift' des Propheten," in J. Vermeylen et al., eds., *Le livre d'Isaïe: Les oracles et leurs relectures. Unité et complexité de l'ouvrage* (BETL 81; Leuven: Leuven University Press, 1989) 231–35.

Huber, F., *Jahwe, Juda und die anderen Völker beim Propheten Jesaja* (BZAW 137; Berlin: de Gruyter, 1976) 10–34.

Irvine, Stuart, "Isaiah's She'ar Yashub and the Davidic House," *BZ* n.s. 37 (1993) 78–88.

Jenni, Ernst, *Die politischen Voraussagen der Propheten* (ATANT 29; Zurich: Zwingli, 1956).

Kaminka, A., "Die fünfundsechzig Jahre in der Weissagung über Ephraim Jes 7,7-9," *MGWJ* 73 (1929) 471–72.

Keller, C. A., "Das quietistische Element in der Botschaft des Jesaja," *TZ* 11 (1955) 81–97.

Kraus, Hans-Joachim, *Prophetie und Politik* (Theologische Existenz heute n.F. 36; Munich: C. Kaiser, 1952).

Lescow, T., "Jesajas Denkschrift aus der Zeit des syrisch-ephraimitischen Krieges," *ZAW* 85 (1973) 315–31.

Linder, J., "Zu Isaiah 7:8f. und 7:16," *ZKT* 64 (1940) 101–4.

Lipiński, E., "Le S'r Yswb d'Isaïe VII 3," *VT* 23 (1973) 245–46.

Mittmann, S., "Das südliche Ostjordanland im Lichte eines neuassyrischen Keilschriftbriefes aus Nimrüd," *ZDPV* 89 (1973) 15–45.

Müller, W. E., *Die Vorstellung von Rest* (Leipzig: W. Hoppe, 1939).

Oded, B., "The Historical Background of the Syro-Ephraimitic War Reconsidered," *CBQ* 34 (1972) 153–65.

Ridderbos, N. H., "Enkele beschouwingen naar annleiding van ta'aminú in Jes 7,9," in *Schrift en uitleg: Studies van oud-leerlingen, collega's en vrienden aangeboden aan Prof. Dr. W. H. Gispen* (Kampen: Kok, 1970) 167–78.

Roberts, J. J. M., "The Context, Text, and Logic of Isaiah 7.7-9," in John Kaltner and Louis Stulman, eds., *Inspired Speech: Prophecy in the Ancient Near East. Essays in Honor of Herbert B. Huffmon* (JSOTSup 378; London: T&T Clark, 2004) 161–70.

———, "Isaiah and His Children," in A. Kort and S. Morschauser, eds., *Biblical and Related Studies Presented to Samuel Iwry* (Winona Lake, IN: Eisenbrauns, 1985) 193–203.

Saebø, Magne, "Formgeschichtliche Erwägungen zu Jes 7:3-9," *ST* 14 (1960) 54–69.

Schedl, C., "Textkritische Bemerkungen zu den Synchronismen der Könige von Israel und Juda," *VT* 12 (1962) 80–119.

Smend, R., "Zur Geschichte von *h'myn*," in *Hebräische Wortforschung: Festschrift zum 80. Geburtstag von Walter Baumgartner* (VTSup 16; Leiden: Brill, 1967) 284–90.

Steck, O. H., "Rettung und Verstockung: Exegetische Bemerkungen zu Jesaja 7,3-9," *EvT* 33 (1973) 77–90.

Stegemann, U., "Der Restgedanke bei Isaias," *BZ* 13 (1969) 161–86.

Stuhlmueller, Carroll, "Psalm 46 and the Prophecy of Isaiah," in J. Knight and L. Sinclair, eds., *The Psalms and Other Studies* (Cincinnatti: Forward Movement, 1990) 18–27.

Thompson, Michael E. W., *Situation and Theology: Old Testament Interpretations of the Syro-Ephraimite War* (Prophets and Historians 1; Sheffield: Almond, 1982).

Vanel, "Tâbe'él en Is VII 6," 17–24.

Vasholz, Robert Ivan, "Isaiah and Ahaz: A Brief History of Crisis in Isaiah 7 and 8," *Presbyterion* 13 (1987) 79–84.

Virgulin, S., "La 'Fede' nel profeta Isaia," *Bib* 31 (1950) 346–64.

———, *La 'Fede' nella profezia d'Isaia* (Quaderni della rivista "Bibbia e Oriente" 2; Milan: Piazza XXV, 1961).

Vogt, E., "Filius Tab'el (Isa. 7:6)," *Bib* 37 (1956) 263–64.

Wagner, N. E., "Note on Isaiah 7:4," *VT* 8 (1958) 438.

Wildberger, Hans, "'Glauben': Erwägungen zu האמן," in *Hebräische Wortforschung: Festschrift zum 80. Geburtstag von Walter Baumgartner* (VTSup 16; Leiden: Brill, 1967) 372–86.

———, "'Glauben' im Alten Testament," *ZTK* 65 (1968) 129–59.

Wolff, Hans Walter, *Frieden ohne Ende: Eine Auslegung von Jes. 7:1-7 und 9:1-16* (BibS[N] 35; Neukirchen Kreis Moers: Neukirchener Verlag, 1962).

———, *Immanuel: Das Zeichen, dem widersprochen wird. Eine Auslegung von Jesaja 7.1-17* (BibS[N] 23; Neukirchen: Neukirchener Verlag, 1959).

Wong, G., "A Cuckoo in the Textual Nest at Isaiah 7:9b?" *JTS* n.s. 47 (1996) 123–24.

Würthwein, E., "Jesaja 7,1-9: Ein Beitrag zu dem Thema: Prophetie und Politik," in *Theologie als Glaubenswagnis: Festschrift für Karl Heim zum 80. Geburtstag* (Hamburg: Furche, 1954) 47–63. Reprinted in Würthwein, *Wort und Existenz: Studien zum Alten Testament* (Göttingen: Vandenhoeck & Ruprecht, 1970) 127–43.

Zerafa, P., "Il resto di Israele nei profeti preesilici," *Ang* 49 (1972) 3–29.

7

The present narrative construes the following verses as a continuation of the preceding scene, but it is historically uncertain whether this oracle was given at the same location on precisely the same occasion. The difference between the two oracles in the time limit given for the fall of Judah's enemies might suggest that this oracle was actually given on a somewhat later occasion, but in any case it was a follow-up to the preceding prophecy.

10/ Yahweh again spoke to Ahaz saying,11/ "Ask a sign for yourself from Yahweh your God. Make it as deep as Sheol[a] or as high as the sky!" 12/ But Ahaz said, "I will not ask, and I will not test Yahweh."[b] 13/Then he [Isaiah] said, "Hear, O house of David, is it so insignificant for you to exhaust humans that you must also exhaust my God?14/ Therefore my Lord[c] himself will give you a sign. Look, the young woman is pregnant[d] and about to give birth to a son, and she[e] will name him Immanuel. 15/ Curds and honey he will eat by the time he learns to reject the bad and choose the good. 16/ For before the child knows to reject the bad and choose the good, the land before whose two kings you are in dread will be deserted. 17/Yahweh will bring[f] upon you, and upon your people, and upon the house of your father days that have not come since the day that Ephraim turned aside from Judah—the king of Assyria.

Textual Notes

a MT and Syr. read שְׁאָלָה (šĕʾālâ), "make the request deep," but LXX and Vg. read שְׁאֹלָה (šĕʾōlāh), "to Sheol," and this reading is supported by the parallelism with לְמַעְלָה (lĕmaʿĕlāh).

b Syr. adds "my God," perhaps influenced by the following verse.

c Syr. adds "God."

d The verbal adjective הָרָה (hārâ) can be translated either as a present tense (Gen 16:11; 38:24-25; 1 Sam 4:19; 2 Sam 11:5; Jer 31:8) or a future (Judg 13:5, 7).

e MT's וְקָרָאת (wĕqārāʾt) could be parsed formally as either second person feminine singular (cf. Gen 16:11) or third person feminine singular, but only the latter parsing fits contextually. Though third feminine singular forms with final ת are relatively rare, compare Deut 31:29. 1QIsaᵃ reads the indefinite third masculine singular וקרא (wĕqārāʾ), "and one will name him," which is probably reflected in Syriac's ܘܢܬܩܪܐ (wntqrʾ), "and he will be named." The LXX reads the form as a second masculine singular, as does the Old Latin, and the Vg., influenced by the preceding plural imperatives, translates the form as a second masculine plural.

f 1QIsaᵃ has ויביא (wĕyābîʾ) for MT יָבִיא (yābîʾ), but the versions support MT.

Commentary

By the terms of the preceding oracle, a failure to respond in faith would cast serious doubt on the continuing stability of the dynasty. The promise was contingent (cf. Isa 28:12-13; 30:15-17); therefore it was important, both for the dynasty and for the nation as a whole, to persuade Ahaz to choose the faithful course of action. Apparently Ahaz's response to the first oracle was less than encouraging, for Isaiah either continues or resumes the confrontation by offering Ahaz a sign from God as an inducement to faith. This move was not at all unusual. According to Israelite tradition God had often offered signs to overcome the doubts of his human agents (so Moses, Exod 3:11-12; 4:1-9; Gideon, Judg 6:15-18, 36-40; Saul, 1 Sam 10:1-7), and Isaiah later did the same for Hezekiah (2 Kgs 19:29), even to the extent of offering him a choice of signs (2 Kgs 20:8-11). The scope of the choice offered

Ahaz is unusual, however, and it underscores the importance Isaiah attached to the king's decision at this critical juncture. Yahweh was willing to pull out all the stops to secure Ahaz's faith.

Ahaz, however, refused to play by the rules. Hiding behind a false piety, he declined the invitation to ask for a sign. From Isaiah's response it is clear that the prophet regarded Ahaz's refusal to ask for a sign as a pious smokescreen. The king's real concern was not about testing God but about preserving his own freedom of choice in the situation. If he accepted the prophet's offer of a sign, and it was forthcoming, Ahaz would be locked into a quietistic policy of waiting out the expected siege. Without the confirmatory sign the king would have more freedom to go against the prophet's advice in considering other political choices such as an appeal to Assyria. Ahaz did not believe, and he did not want to be forced into a belief that would limit his freedom.

Apparently Ahaz's response reflected the views of the royal court, because Isaiah's retort is addressed to the whole Davidic house, not just to the king. The royal court had gone too far with this refusal. It was bad enough to exhaust the prophet's patience by their refusal to believe, but when one refused the offer of a sign from God himself, that was to exhaust the patience of Isaiah's God. The expression "my God" (v. 13) suggests the close relationship between the prophet and Yahweh, but it also contains a note of judgment. By the choice of this expression rather than "our God" or "your God," Isaiah pointedly excludes the Davidic house from that relationship of intimacy with God. It was a relationship sustained only by faith, and by their lack of faith the Davidic house had forfeited it. Nevertheless, even the court's faithlessness does not prevent God from trying again. Though Ahaz had refused to ask for a sign, God gives him one anyway, though now God chooses it, not Ahaz.

There is a lively debate among exegetes of this text about the nature of that sign, and to cut through to the heart of the matter four principles need to be observed: (1) the passage cannot be taken in isolation; it must be explained with attention to its context in Isa 7:10-17; (2) the passage must be correctly translated; (3) nothing should be deleted without very good reason; and (4) one should pay close attention to the remarkable parallel in Isa 8:1-4.

Matthew 1:23 cites Isa 7:14 as a prophecy fulfilled in the virgin birth of Jesus, and this reading, reinforced by later Christian works and popularized in Handel's *Messiah*, has dominated the popular Christian understanding of Isaiah 7. This interpretation fails to do justice to the context in Isaiah, however. One should note that Matthew was more interested in finding prophecies about Jesus than in explaining the Old Testament. This Gospel writer has a habit of citing Old Testament texts in ways that ignore their original significance. He cites Hos 11:1, for example, as a prophecy concerning Jesus's sojourn in Egypt (Matt 2:15), yet a quick check of the context of Hos 11:1 will show that the passage in Hosea is not a prophecy at all but a historical reference back to Israel's exodus from Egypt. One may excuse Matthew, since his exegetical method was the common practice of his day, as a comparison with the ancient commentaries of the Dead Sea Scrolls community shows, but this method can hardly be the model for contemporary believers. The Christian interpreter may well note that, whereas Isaiah's child with his symbolic name pointed to God's continuing presence in Jerusalem and Judah, Jesus, without the symbolic name Immanuel, embodies God's presence with us in a far more profound way, but though this understanding of Christian interpretation may be true, even this observation is not particularly helpful for understanding the message of Isaiah. If one wishes to understand Isaiah rather than Matthew's use of Isaiah, the contemporary interpreter must show how Isa 7:14 fits into the larger context of Isa 7:10-17.

The crucial line in 7:14 should be rendered, "Look, the young woman is pregnant and will soon bear a son, and she will name him Immanuel." One is dealing here with a traditional announcement formula by which the birth of a child is promised to particular individuals (Gen 16:11; Judg 13:3—the same basic construction is even found in an earlier Ugaritic text, *CTA* 24:7 = *KTU* 1.24.7), and that together with the definite article indicates that Isaiah is speaking of a particular woman. He does not call her a virgin; עַלְמָה (ʿalmâ) does not have that meaning in Hebrew. Like its masculine counterpart עֶלֶם (ʿelem, "young man," 1 Sam 17:56; 20:22), עַלְמָה (ʿalmâ) simply points to the youth, not the lack of sexual experience of the young woman (Gen 24:43; Exod 2:8; Ps 68:26; Prov

30:19; Song 1:3; 6:8).[1] Moreover, the parallel with the announcement to Hagar in Gen 16:11 suggests that the woman was already pregnant at the time Isaiah called attention to her. Nothing in the Hebrew text suggests that the conception lay in the future. In fact, the use of the participle יֹלֶדֶת (wĕyōledet) implies that the birth itself was imminent. The woman was "about" or "soon" to give birth. Unfortunately, one cannot translate this so-called *futurum instans* use of the participle into a specific time frame. It might be as easily said of a woman a few months into her term as of a woman nearing the end of her term.

Precisely who this woman was is a subject of debate, but two suggestions seem most probable. Either Isaiah was referring to a wife of Ahaz or to his own wife. The close parallel with the prophetic oracle in 8:1-4, where Isaiah's wife is probably the mother of the child (see the discussion there)—the prophet is clearly the father—suggests that Isaiah is also referring to his own wife here. Though we do not know exactly how old Shear-jashub was at the time of Isaiah's encounter with Ahaz, he could not have been very old. The fact that Isaiah gave him a symbolic name presupposes that he was born after Isaiah's call to be a prophet, hence after the death of Uzziah. If the symbolic name was given specifically for this encounter, Shear-jashub may have been just an infant, and in any case he could not have been over three or four years old. Apparently Shear-jashub was Isaiah's firstborn, and since Israelite women married quite early and had children as soon as possible, Isaiah's wife could still have been in her teens. Thus, he could still refer to her as a "young woman." The presence of the young child at the outdoor meeting might also explain Isaiah's reference to the young woman. This is particularly true if the events of 7:1-9 and 7:10-17 took place on the same occasion. It is unlikely that any pregnant woman from the royal court would have been present at this meeting by the aqueduct, and had Isaiah's wife been present, it is strange that she is not mentioned along with her son. But with Shear-jashub present, Isaiah might have referred to the boy's young mother, who was presumably well known to Ahaz, as the young woman who was again pregnant. Isaiah does not say "my wife," but neither does he use that unequivocal expression in 8:3, where it is probably his wife who is meant.

If one is correct in identifying the young woman in Isa 7:14 as Isaiah's wife who was pregnant with her second child, in what does the sign actually consist? It does not consist in a miraculous birth. Does it consist in the symbolic name alone, or is there more to it? At this point it would be helpful to look at 8:1-4 before continuing with 7:14-17. The oracle in 8:1-4 also records the birth of a son who is given a symbolic name, presumably the third son, and the significance of that name is explicated by reference to a time limit. By the time Isaiah's son Maher-sha-lal-hush-baz is old enough to say, "Daddy!" or "Mommy!", that is, within one to two years, the wealth of Damascus and the booty of Samaria will have been rushed off to Assyria. In other words, the threat to Ahaz from Aram and Israel will be over in less than a couple of years. For more details, see the discussion of that passage.

Returning to 7:14-17, one notes that the symbolic name Immanuel is also explicated by reference to a time limit. Note that in both 8:4 and 7:15-16 the verb יָדַע (yādaʿ, "to know") is used of the child's ability to act on its own, and this ability provides the framework for a time limit. According to 7:15-16, by the time this child is old enough to choose the good and reject the bad, the territory of the two kings whom the Judean court so feared would be abandoned and left desolate. Verse 15 defines what is meant by choosing the good and is necessary for a correct understanding of the time limit. When the child is old enough to choose between various foods, that is, when the child is weaned from the breast and begins eating other food, the danger from the northern kingdom and its Aramean allies will be past, and the child will be able to choose from the richest foods appropriate to its age. Since Israelite children were normally weaned around the age of three (2 Macc 7:27; cf. 1 Sam 1:22-28; 2:11, where the weaned Samuel is old enough to be left to live with and serve the priest Eli), the remaining gesta-

---

1 The Hebrew word for a female virgin is בְּתוּלָה (bĕtûlâ, Gen 24:16; Exod 22:15-16; Lev 21:14; Deut 22:19), and the masculine plural abstract from the same root, בְּתוּלִים (bĕtûlîm), is used for "virginity" (Lev 21:13; Deut 22:14) and for the wedding cloth kept by the parents of the bride after her wedding night as the proof of the bride's virginity at the time of her wedding (Deut 22:15, 17).

tion period and the period of nursing after birth would suggest a time limit of three to four years. The word חֶמְאָה (ḥemʾâ), translated "curds," refers to a liquid milk product similar to modern ghee or Arabic *leben*. It occurs in contexts that suggest it was a choice food (Gen 18:8; Deut 32:14; Judg 5:25; Job 20:17; 29:6) just as milk and honey, which served as a proverbial pair for referring to abundance (Exod 3:8, 17; 33:3; Lev 20:24; passim). Thus, there is no justification for taking the mention of these foods as a sign of scarcity. Even the reference in Isa 7:22 suggests that the surviving remnant will have rich and abundant fare, though the vineyards are ruined. Moreover, these foods would probably be choice foods for a newly weaned child, since the milk product maintains some continuity with the child's earlier nursing food, and honey would appeal to the child's sweet tooth.

On the surface, therefore, the oracle would appear to be positive. By the time the child is weaned—that is, within three to four years—he will be able to choose the richest foods appropriate for his age. Milk products and honey are not readily available in an ancient city under siege, but Isaiah promises that whatever food shortages have resulted or will result from Aram's and Israel's attempts to besiege Jerusalem will have been made good within three years of the birth of Immanuel. Accord-

ingly, v. 17 should be taken in a positive sense. Yahweh will bring upon Judah days of abundance such as she had not known since the northern tribes split off from Judah under Solomon's successor. The final words of v. 17, "the king of Assyria," give the verse a negative slant, but these words, which are quite abrupt in the context, are generally considered a late gloss, even by those scholars who understand the oracle as a threat.[2]

A positive interpretation of the Immanuel oracle is also supported by the meaning of the symbolic name itself. The name means "God is with us." It appears to be a name that reflects the Jerusalemite theology of the Zion Tradition. Note the very similar expression that recurs as a refrain in one of the songs of Zion where the security of Jerusalem is based on the fact that "Yahweh of hosts is with us" (Ps 46:7, 11 [Heb. 46:8, 12]). Unlike the oracle in Isa 8:1-4, which provides an explanation of the symbolic name Maher-shalal-hush-baz, Isaiah 7 offers no explanation of the symbolic name Immanuel, just as it offers no explanation of the name Shear-jashub. But there is another oracle that does provide an explanation for Immanuel, just as there was in the case of Shear-jashub. The other Immanuel oracle is found in Isa 8:5-10, so for details, check the discussion there.

Bibliography

Abschlag, W., "Jungfrau oder junge Frau? Zu Jes. 7,14," *Anzeiger für die katholische Geistlichkeit* 83 (1974) 290–92.

Bartelmus, R., "Jes 7:1-17 und das Stilprinzip des Kontrastes: Syntaktisch-stilistische und traditionsgeschichtliche Anmerkungen zur 'Immanuel-Perikope,'" *ZAW* 96 (1984) 50–66.

Becker, *Isaias*.

Beecher, Willis J., "The Prophecy of the Virgin Mother," in Walter C. Kaiser, ed., *Classical Evangelical Essays in Old Testament Interpretation* (Grand Rapids: Baker, 1973) 179–85.

Benson, G. P., "Virgin Birth, Virgin Conception [Reply to G. Bostock, ExpTim 97 (1986) 260–63]." *ExpTim* 98 (1987) 139–40.

Berg, W., "Die Identität der 'jungen Frau' in Jes 7:14, 16," *BN* 13 (1980) 7–13.

Bird, T. E., "Who Is the Boy in Isaiah 7:16?" *CBQ* 6 (1944) 435–43.

Bjornard, Reidar B., "Isaiah 7 Once More," *Foundations* 3 (1960) 70–73.

Blank, S. H., "Immanuel and Which Isaiah?" *JNES* 13 (1954) 83–86.

Bouzon, E., "A mensagem teológica do Immanuel (Is 7,1-17)," *REB* 32, no. 128 (1972) 826–41.

Brennan, J. P., "Virgin and Child in Is. 7:14," *TBT* 1 (1964) 968–74.

Brunec, M., "De sensu 'signi' in Is 7,14," *VD* 33 (1955) 257–66, 321–30.

Brunet, G., "La vierge d'Isaïe," *Cahier Renan* 22, no. 86 (1974) 1–16.

2   See the discussion in Wildberger, 1:268, 297–98. The gloss may have been added by a reader vainly attempting to forge a closer connection with the material in 7:18-25.

Buchanan, G. W., "The Old Testament Meaning of the Knowledge of Good and Evil," *JBL* 75 (1956) 114–20.

Budde, K., "Das Immanuelzeichen und die Ahaz-Begegnung Jesaja 7," *JBL* 52 (1933) 22–54.

——, "Noch Einmal, Dank an Karl Thieme," *TBl* 12 (1933) 36–38.

Bulmerincq, A. von, "Die Immanuelweissagung im Lichte der neueren Forschung," *Acta et Commentationes Universitatis Tartuensis (Dorpatensis) B 37* 1 (1935) 1–17.

Carreira das Neves, J., "Is 7,14: Da exegese à hermenéutica," *Theol* 4 (1969) 399–414.

——, "Isaias 7:14 no texto massoretico e no texto Grego: A obra de Joachim Becker," *Did* 2 (1972) 79–112.

Cazelles, Henri, and Franz D. Hubmann, "La Septante d'Is 7, 17," in A. Triacca and A. Pistoia, eds., *La mère de Jésus-Christ et la communion des saints dans la liturgie* (Rome: CLV Edizione Liturgiche, 1986) 45–54.

Clements, Ronald E., "The Immanuel Prophecy of Isa 7:10-17 and Its Messianic Interpretation," in Erhard Blum et al., eds., *Die Hebräische Bibel und ihre zweifache Nachgeschichte: Festschrift für Rolf Rendtorff zum 65. Geburtstag* (Neukirchen-Vluyn: Neukirchener Verlag, 1990) 225–40.

Coppens, J., "L'interpretation d'Is. VII, 14 à la lumière des études les plus récentes," in Heinrich Gross, ed., *Lex tua veritas: Festschrift für Herbert Junker zur Vollendung des siebzigsten Lebensjahres am 8 August 1961 dargeboten von Kollegen, Freunden und Schülern* (Trier: Paulinus-Verlag, 1961) 31–45.

——, "Le messianisme royal," *NRT* 90 (1968) 30–49, 82–85, 225–51, 479–512, 622–50, 834–63, 936–75.

——, "Un nouvel essai d'interprétation d'Is 7,14-17," *Salm* 23 (1976) 85–88.

——, "La prophétie de la ʿalmah," *ETL* 28 (1952) 648–78.

——, "Le prophétie d'Emmanuel," in L. Cerfaux et al., *L'attente du messie* (Recherches bibliques 1; Paris: Desclée de Brouwer, 1954) 39–50.

Creager, H. L., "Immanuel Passage as Messianic Prophecy," *LQ* 7 (1955) 339–43.

Criado, R., "El valor de laken (Vg "propter") en Is. 7:14: Contribution al estudio del Emmanuel," *EstEcl* 34 (1960) 741–51.

Delling, Gerhard, "*Parthenos B 1*," *TDNT* 5:831–32.

Dequeker, Luc, "Isaie 7:14: wqrʾt shmw ʿmnwʾl," *VT* 12 (1962) 331–35.

Dohmen, Christoph, "Das Immanuelzeichen: Ein jesajanisches Drohwort und seine inneralttestamentliche Rezeption," *Bib* 68 (1987) 305–29.

Duncker, P. G., "Ut sciat reprobare malum et eligere bonum, Is VII 15b," *SP* 1 (1959) 408–12.

Fahlgren, K. H., "*ha ʿalma*: En undersokning till Jes. 7," *SEÅ* 4 (1939) 13–24.

Feinberg, Charles L., "The Virgin Birth in the Old Testament and Isaiah 7:14," *BSac* 119 (1962) 251–58.

Feuillet, A., "Le signe propose a Achaz el l'Emmanuel (Isaie 7:10-25)," *RSR* 30 (1940) 129–51.

Fohrer, G., "Zu Jes 7:14 im Zusammenhang von Jes 7:10-22," *ZAW* 68 (1956) 54–56.

Gates, O. H., "Notes on Isaiah 1,18b and 7,14b-16," *AJSL* 17 (1900) 16–21.

Gese, Hartmut, "Natus ex virgine," in Hans Walter Wolff, ed., *Probleme biblischer Theologie: Gerhard von Rad zum 70. Geburtstag* (Munich: C. Kaiser, 1971) 73–89.

Ginsberg, H. L., "Der Davidsbund und die Zionserwählung Immanuel (Is 7,14)," *ZTK* n.F. 61 (1964) 10–26.

——, "Immanuel (Is. 7:14)," *EncJud* 8 (1971) 1293–95.

Gordon, C. H., "ʿAlmah in Isaiah 7:14," *JBR* 21 (1953) 106.

Gottwald, Norman K., "Immanuel as the Prophet's Son," *VT* 8 (1958) 36–47.

Gressmann, Hugo, *Der Messias* (FRLANT 43; Göttingen: Vandenhoeck & Ruprecht, 1929).

Guthe, H., "Zeichen und Weissagung in Jes 7:14-17," in Karl Marti, ed., *Studien zur semitischen Philologie und Religionsgeschichte: Julius Wellhausen zum siebzigsten Geburtstag am 17. Mai 1914* (Giessen: A. Töpelmann, 1914) 177–90.

Haag, H., "Is. 7:14 als alttest. Grundstelle der Lehre von virginitas Mariae," in Hermann Josef Brosch and Josef Hasenfuss, eds., *Jungfrauengeburt gestern und heute* (Mariologische Studien 4; Essen: Driewer, 1969) 137–43.

Hammershaimb, E., "The Immanuel Sign: Some Aspects of Old Testament Prophecy from Isaiah to Malachi," *ST* 3 (1951) 124–42.

——, "Immanuelstegnet (Jes. 7:10ff)," *DTT* 8 (1945) 223–44.

——, *Some Aspects of Old Testament Prophecy from Isaiah to Malachi* (Copenhagen: Rosenkilde & Bagger, 1966).

Hartmann, K. C., "More about the RSV and Isaiah 7:14," *LQ* 7 (1955) 344–47.

Hempel, J., "Chronik," *ZAW* 49 (1931) 150–60.

Herrmann, S., *Die Prophetischen Heilserwartungen im Alten Testament* (BWANT 85; Stuttgart: Kohlhammer, 1965).

Hindson, E. E., "Development of the Interpretation of Isaiah 7:14: A Tribute to E. J. Young," *Grace Journal* 10 (1969) 19–25.

——, "Isaiah's Immanuel," *Grace Journal* 10 (1969) 3–15.

Höffken, Peter, "Grundfragen von Jesaja 7:1-17 im Spiegel neuerer Literatur," *BZ* n.s. 33, no. 1 (1989) 25–42.

——, "Notizen zum Textcharakter von Jesaja 7,1-17," *TZ* 36 (1980) 321–37.

Homerski, J., "Piesni izajasza o Emmanuelu," *Theologica Varsaviensia* 14, no. 2 (1976) 13–46.

Irsigler, Hubert, "Zeichen und Bezeichnetes in Jes 7:1-17: Notizen zum Immanueltext," *BN* 29 (1985) 75–114.

Jenni, E., "Immanuel," *RGG³*, 677–78.

Jensen, J., "The Age of Immanuel," *CBQ* 41 (1979) 220–39.

Johnson, A. R., *Sacral Kingship in Ancient Israel* (Cardiff: Wales University Press, 1967).

Johnson, Elliott E., "Dual Authorship and the Single Intended Meaning of Scripture," *BSac* 143 (1986) 218–27.

Jones, B. E., "Immanuel: A Historical and Critical Study" (PhD diss., University of Wales, Aberystwyth, 1966–67).

Jüngling, Hans, "The Religious Ambiguity of the Davidic-Solomonic State," in S. Freyne, W. Beuken, and A. Weiler, *Truth and Its Victims* (Concilium 200; Edinburgh: T&T Clark, 1988) 21–34.

Junker, H., "Ursprung und Grundzüge des Messiasbildes bei Isajas," in *Volume du Congrès: Strasbourg 1956* (VTSup 4; Leiden: Brill, 1957) 181–96.

Kaiser, Walter C., Jr., "The Promise of Isaiah 7:14 and the Single-Meaning Hermeneutic," *Evangelical Journal* 6 (1988) 55–70.

Kamesar, Adam, "The Virgin of Isaiah 7:14: The Philological Argument from the Second to the Fifth Century," *JTS* 41 (1990) 51–75.

Kida, T., "Immanuel-yogen (Immanuel Prophecy—A Study of Is. 7:1-16)," in N. Tajima, ed., *Festschrift I. Takayanagi* (Tokyo: Sobunsha, 1967) 275–93.

Kilian, Rudolf, "Die Geburt des Immanuel aus der Jungfrau, Jes 7:14," in Karl Suso Frank, ed., *Zum Thema Jungfrauengeburt* (Stuttgart: Katholisches Bibelwerk, 1970) 9–35.

——, "Prolegomena zur Auslegung der Immanuelverheissung," in J. Schreiner, ed., *Wort, Lied und Gottesspruch: Festschrift für Joseph Ziegler* (2 vols.; FB 1–2; Würzburg: Echter; Katholisches Bibelwerk, 1972) 2:207–15.

——, *Die Verheissung Immanuels, Jes 7,14* (SBS 35; Stuttgart: Katholisches Bibelwerk, 1968).

Kipper, B., "O problema da ʿAlmah nos estudos recentes," *RCB* 7, no. 25/26 (1963) 80–92; n.s. 1 (1964) 180–95.

Kissane, E. J., "Butter and Honey Shall He Eat (Isaiah 7:15)," *Orientalia et Biblica Louvaniensia* 1 (1957) 169–73.

Köhler, L., "Zum Verständnis von Jes 7:14," *ZAW* 55 (1967) 249–58.

Kosmala, H., "Form and Structure in Ancient Hebrew Poetry," *VT* 14 (1964) 423–45.

Kraeling, E. G., "The Immanuel Prophecy," *JBL* 50 (1931) 277–97.

Kruse, H., "Alma redemptoris mater: Eine Auslegung der Immanuel-Weissagung Is 7:14," *TTZ* 74 (1965) 15–36.

Laato, Antti, "Immanuel—Who Is with Us? Hezekiah or Messiah?" in M. Augustin, ed., *"Wünschet Jerusalem Frieden": Collected Communications to the XIIth Congress of the International Organization for the Study of the Old Testament, Jerusalem 1986* (Frankfurt am Main: P. Lang, 1988) 313–22.

Lacheman, E. R., "A propos of Isaiah 7:14," *JBR* 22 (1954) 43.

Lagarde, Paul de, "Kritische Anmerkungen zum Buche Isaias," *Sem* 1 (1878) 1–23.

Lattey, C., "The Emmanuel Prophecy: Is 7:14," *CBQ* 8 (1946) 369–76.

——, "The Term ʿAlmah in Is. 7:14," *CBQ* 9 (1947) 89–95.

——, "Various Interpretations of Isaiah 7:14," *CBQ* 9 (1947) 147–54.

Lawlor, George L., *ʿAlmah–Virgin or Young Woman?* (Des Plaines, IL: Regular Baptist Press, 1973).

Lehnhard, H., "'Jungfrau' oder 'Junge Frau' in Jesaja 7,14-17," *TBei* 7 (1976) 264–67.

Lescow, T., "Das Geburtsmotiv in den messianischen Weissagungen bei Jesaja und Micha," *ZAW* 79 (1967) 172–207.

Lindblom, Johannes, *A Study on the Immanuel Section in Isaiah: Isa. vii, 1–ix, 6* (Scripta Minora Regiae Societatis Humaniorum Litterarum Lundensis 4; Lund: Gleerup, 1957).

Lohfink, Norbert, *Bibelauslegung im Wandel: Ein Exeget ortet seine Wissenschaft* (Frankfurt am Main: Knecht, 1967).

——, "On Interpreting the OT (Is 7:14)," *TD* 15 (1967) 228–29.

Loss, N. M., "'Ecce Virgo concipiet': Reflexoes sobre a relacao entre Sinai e significacao em Is. 7:14-16," in S. Voigt et al., eds., *Actualidades Biblicas* (Petropolis, 1971) 309–20.

Lust, J., "The Immanuel Figure: A Charismatic Judge-Leader. A Suggestion Towards the Understanding of Is 7,10-17 (8:23–9:6; 11:1-9)," *ETL* 47 (1971) 464–70.

Madl, H., "Die Gottesbefragung mit dem Verb šāʾal," in Heinz-Josef Fabry, ed., *Bausteine biblischer Theologie: Festgabe für G. Johannes Botterweck zum 60. Geburtstag, dargebr. von seinen Schülern* (BBB 50; Cologne: Hanstein, 1977) 37–70.

McKane, William, "The Interpretation of Isaiah VII 14-25," *VT* 17 (1967) 208–19.

McNamara, Martin, "The Immanuel Prophecy in Its Context," *Scr* 14 (1962) 118–25; 15 (1963) 19–23.

Mejía, J., "Contribución a la exégesis de un texto difícil," *EstBíb* 24 (1965) 107–21.

Messerschmidt, H., "Se, jomfruen skal undfange of fode en son (Is. 7:14...)," *Lumen* 6 (1962) 160–69.

Montagnini, F., "L'interpretazione di Is 7,14 di J.L. Isenbiehl (1744–1818)," in *Il messianismo: Atti della Xviii Settimana Biblica* (Brescia: Paideia, 1966) 95–104.

Moody, D., "Isaiah 7:14 in the Revised Standard Version," *RevExp* 50 (1953) 61–68.

Moriarty, F. L., "The Immanuel Prophecies," *CBQ* 19 (1957) 226–33.

Motyer, J. A., "Context and Content in the Interpretation of Is 7:14," *TynBul* 21 (1970) 118–25.

Mowinckel, Sigmund, *He That Cometh: The Messiah Concept in the Old Testament and Later Judaism* (Nashville: Abingdon, 1956).

Mueller, W., "Virgin Shall Conceive," *EvQ* 32 (1960) 203–7.

Myers, A. E., "Use of ʿalmah in the Old Testament," *LQ* 7 (1955) 137–40.

Neff, R. W., "The Announcement in Old Testament Birth Stories" (PhD diss., Yale University, 1969).

Nestle, E., "Miszelle," *ZAW* 25 (1905) 213–15.

Oberweis, Michael, "Beobachtungen zum AT-Gebrauch in der matthäischen Kindheitsgeschichte," *NTS* 35 (1989) 131–49.

Olmo Lete, Gregorio del, "La profecía del Emmanuel (Is. 7:10-17): Estado actual de la interpretacíon," *Ephemerides Mariologicae* 22 (1972) 357–85.

Owens, J. J., "The Meaning of ʿalmah in the Old Testament," *RevExp* 50 (1953) 56–60.

Patterson, Richard D., "A Virgin Shall Conceive [Isa 7:14; Treasures from the Text]," *Fundamentalist Journal* 4, no. 11 (1985) 64.

Porúbcan, Stefan, "The Word ʾôt in Isaiah 7:14," *CBQ* 22 (1960) 144–59.

Prado, J., "La madre del Emmanuel: Is 7,14 (Reseña del estado de las cuestiones)," *Sef* 21 (1961) 85–114.

Preuss, H. D., "'Ich will mit dir sein!'" *ZAW* 80 (1968) 139–73.

Price, Charles Philip, "Immanuel: God with Us [Isa 7:14]," *Christianity and Crisis* 23 (1963) 222–23.

Räsel, Martin, "Die Jungfrauengeburt des endzeitlichen Immanuel: Jesaja 7 in der Übersetzung der Septuaginta," in I. Baldermann et al., eds., *Altes Testament und christlicher Glaube* (Jahrbuch für biblische Theologie 6; Neukirchen-Vluyn: Neukirchener Verlag, 1991) 135–51.

Reese, J. M., "The Gifts of Immanuel," *TBT* 27 (1966) 1880–85.

Rehm, Martin, *Der königliche Messias im Licht der Immanuel-Weissagungen des Buches Jesaja* (Eichstätter Studien n.F. 1; . Kevelaer: Buzton & Bercker, 1968.

——, "Das Wort ʿAlmah in Is 7:14," *BZ* n.s. 8 (1964) 89–101.

Rengstorf, K. H., "Semeion" *TDNT* 7:200–269, esp. 209–19.

Reymond, Robert L., "Who Is the ʿlmh of Isaiah 7:14?" *Presb* 15 (1989) 1–15.

Rice, G., "The Interpretation of Isaiah 7:15-17," *JBL* 96 (1977) 363–69.

——, "A Neglected Interpretation of the Immanuel Prophecy," *ZAW* 90 (1978) 220–27.

Rignell, L. G., "Das Immanuelszeichen: Einige Gesichtspunkte zu Jes. 7," *ST* 11 (1957) 99–119.

Ringgren, Helmer, *The Messiah in the Old Testament* (SBT 18; London: SCM, 1957).

Rösel, Martin, "Die Jungfrauengeburt des endzeitlichen Immanuel," in I. Baldermann et al., eds., *Altes Testament und christlicher Glaube* (Jahrbuch für biblische Theologie 6; Neukirchen-Vluyn: Neukirchener Verlag, 1991) 135–51.

Salvoni, F., "La profezia di Isaia sulla 'vergine' partoriente (Is 7,14)," *Ricerche Bibliche e Religiose* 1 (1966) 19–40.

Sancho-Gili, J., "Sobre el sentido mesiánico de Is 7,14: Interpretaciones biblicas y magisterales," *CB* 27 (1970) 67–89.

Sanneh, Lamin, "Dreams and Letting God Be God [Isa 7:10-17]," *ChrCent* 106 (1989) 1195.

Savoca, G. M., "L'Emmanuele al centro della storia, segno di salvezze e di rovina," *Palestro del Clero* 33 (1954) 753–61.

Scharbert, J., "Was versteht das Alte Testament unter Wunder?" *BK* 22 (1967) 37–42.

Schildenberger, J., "Die jungfräuliche Mutter des Emmanuel," *Sein und Sendung* 30 (1965) 339–53.

Schmidt, Hans, *Der Mythos vom wiederkehrenden König im Alten Testament: Festrede gehalten am 17. Januar 1925 zur Feier des Tages der Reichsgründung* (Schriften der Hessischen Hochschulen, Universität Giessen, 1925, 1; Giessen: A. Töpelmann, 1925).

Schoors, Antoon, "The Immanuel of Isaiah 7,14," *OLP* 18 (1987) 67–77.

Schulz, A., "ʿAlmah," *BZ* 23 (1935) 229–41.

Scullion, J. J., "An Approach to the Understanding of Isaiah 7:10-17," *JBL* 87 (1968) 288–300.

Severino Croatto, J., "El 'Enmanuel' de Isaias 7:14

como signo de juicio: Análisis de Isaías 7:1-25," *RevistB* 50 (1988) 135–42.

Seybold, K., *Das davidische Königtum im Zeugnis der Propheten* (FRLANT 107; Göttingen: Vandenhoeck & Ruprecht, 1972).

Shupak, Nili, "Stylistic and Terminological Traits Common to Biblical and Egyptian Literature," *WO* 14 (1983) 216–30.

Skemp, Annie E., "'Immanuel' and 'the Suffering Servant of Jahweh,'" *ExpTim* 44 (1932) 94–95.

Smith, George D., Jr., "Isaiah Updated," *Dialogue (Mormon)* 16 (1983) 37–51.

Speier, S., "Notes," *JBL* 72 (1953) xiv.

Stacey, W. D., "Prophetic Signs: A Re-Examination of the Symbolic Actions of the Prophets of the OT" (PhD diss., Bristol, 1971).

Stamm, J. J., "Die Immanuel-Perikope: Eine Nachlese," *TZ* 30 (1974) 11–22.

——, "Die Immanuel-Perikope im Lichte neuerer Veröffentlichungen," in Wolfgang Voigt, ed., *XVII Deutscher Orientalistentag* (ZDMGSup 1; Wiesbaden: F. Steiner, 1969) 281–90.

——, "Die Immanuelweissagung: Ein Gespräch mit E. Hammershaimb," *VT* 4 (1954) 20–33.

——, "Die Immanuel-Weissagung und die Eschatologie des Jesaja," *TZ* 16 (1960) 439–55.

——, "Neuere Arbeiten zum Immanuel-Problem," *ZAW* 68 (1956) 46–53.

——, "La prophétie d'Emmanuel," *RTP* n.s. 32 (1944) 97–123.

——, "La propheties d'Immanuel," *RHPR* 23 (1943) 1–26.

Steck, O. H., "Beiträge zum Verständnis von Jes 7,10-17 und 8,1-4," *TZ* 29 (1973) 161–78.

Steinmueller, J. E., "Etymology and Biblical Usage of ʿAlmah," *CBQ* 2 (1940) 28–43.

Stern, S., "The Knowledge of Good and Evil," *VT* 8 (1958) 405–18.

Stolz, F., "Zeichen und Wunder," *ZTK* 60 (1972) 125–44.

Stuhlmueller, Carroll, "The Mother of the Immanuel," *Marian Studies* 12 (1961) 165–204.

Surburg, R. F., "Interpretation of Isaiah 7:14," *Springfielder* 38 (1974) 110–18.

Sutcliffe, E. F., "The Emmanuel Prophecy of Is. 7:14," *EstEcl* 34 (1960) 737–65.

Testa, E., "L'Emmanuele e la santa Sion," *SBFLA* 25 (1975) 171–92.

Thieme, K., "Vierzigjahrfeier der eisenacher Erklärung und Jungfrauengeburt," *TBl* 11 (1932) 300–310.

Vawter, Bruce, "The Ugaritic Use of *Glmt*," *CBQ* 14 (1952) 319–22.

Vella, G., "Isaia 7,14 e il parto verginale del Messia," in *Il messianismo: Atti della Xviii Settimana Biblica* (Brescia: Paideia, 1966) 85–93.

Vendrame, C., "Sentido coletivo da ʿAlmah (Is 7, 14)," *RCB* 7 (1963) 10–16.

Vischer, W., *Die Immanuel-Botschaft im Rahmen des königlichen Zionsfestes* (ThSt 45; Zurich: Evangelischer Verlag, 1955; originally, "La prophétie d'Emmanuel et la fête royale de Sion," *ETR* 3 [1954] 55–97).

Wagner, N. E., "A Note on Isaiah Vii 4," *VT* 8 (1958) 438.

Watson, W., "Shared Consonants in Northwest Semitic," *Bib* 50 (1969) 525–33.

Weren, W., "Quotations from Isaiah and Matthew's Christology," in J. van Ruiten and M. Vervenne, eds., *Studies in the Book of Isaiah: Festschrift Willem A. M. Beuken* (BETL 132; Leuven: Leuven University Press, 1997) 447–65.

Werlitz, J., "Noch einmal Immanuel—Gleich zweimal! Rudolf Kilian in Dankbarkeit zugeeignet," *BZ* n.s. 40 (1996) 254–63.

Willis, John T., "The Meaning of Isaiah 7:14 and Its Application in Matthew 1:23," *ResQ* 21 (1978) 1–18.

Wolf, H. M., "A Solution to the Immanuel Prophecy in Isaiah 7:14—8:22," *JBL* 91 (1972) 449–56.

Wolff, Hans Walter. *Immanuel: Das Zeichen, dem widersprochen wird* (BibS[N] 23; Neukirchen-Vluyn: Neukirchener Verlag, 1959).

Wolverton, W. I., "Judgment in Advent: Notes on Isaiah 8:5-15 and 7:14," *ATR* 37 (1955) 284–91.

Young, Edward J., "The Immanuel Prophecy: Isaiah 7:14-16," in Edward J. Young, ed., *Studies in Isaiah* (London: Tyndale, 1955) 143–98.

Yubero, D., "El 'Emmanuel' o 'Dios con nosotros,'" *CB* 252 (1973) 295–98.

Zimmermann, F., "Immanuel Prophecy," *JQR* 52 (1961) 154–59.

Zwieten, J. W. M. van, "Jewish Exegesis within Christian Bounds: Richard of St Victor's De Emmanuele and Victorine Hermeneutics," *Bijdragen* 48 (1987) 327–35.

The material in these verses appears to be a loose collection of four sayings, each of which is introduced by the phrase "on that day." The sayings do not all appear to be from the same period, and they may have suffered extensive glossing.

18/ **On that day Yahweh will whistle for the fly that is[a] at the end of the streams of Egypt and for the bee that is in the land of Assyria. 19/ And they will all come and settle in the ravines of the cliffs and in the clefts of the rocks[b] and in all the thornbushes and in all the watering places.[c] 20/ On that day my Lord will shave with a razor[d] that is hired[e] in the regions beyond the Euphrates—with the king of Assyria—the head, and the pubic hair,[f] and it will remove the beard as well. 21/ On that day a man will keep alive a heifer of the herd and two sheep, 22/ and because of the abundance of milk they produce, he will eat curds, for everyone who is left in the land will eat curds and honey.[g] 23/ On that day every place where there used to be a thousand vines worth a thousand shekels of silver will become[h] thorns and thistles. 24/ With bow[i] and arrows one will go there, for the whole land will become thorns and thistles. 25/ But as for all the hills that used to be tilled with a hoe, the fear of thorns[j] and thistles will not go there;[k] this area[l] will become a place where cattle are released and sheep and goats tramp about.**

Textual Notes

a   LXX's "that rules" is expansive and not indicative of a different Hebrew *Vorlage*.

b   LXX's καὶ ἐν ταῖς τρώγλαις τῶν πετρῶν καὶ εἰς τὰ σπήλαια, "and in the clefts of the rocks and into the caves," appears to be a double translation of וּבִנְקִיקֵי הַסְּלָעִים (*ûbinqîqê hassĕlā'îm*), "and in the clefts of the rocks."

c   Syr. omits one of the final two phrases.

d   LXX has "with a great razor."

e   LXX and Syr. misunderstand הַשְּׂכִירָה (*haśśĕkîrâ*), "that is hired," as השכירה (*haššĕkîrâ*), "that is drunken."

f   הָרַגְלָיִם (*hāraglāyim*), "the feet," is a euphemism for genitals (cf. Exod 4:25; 2 Kgs 18:27; Isa 36:12).

g   LXX shortens the Hebrew by omitting the first יֹאכַל (*yō'kal*), "he will eat," and כִּי־חֶמְאָה (*kî-ḥem'â*), "because curds."

h   1QIsa[a] omits the first יִהְיֶה (*yihyê*), "it will be," which may be correct, because one of the two in MT seems redundant.

i   1QIsa[a], Syr., and Tg. have the plural "bows."

j   1QIsa[a] inserts ברזל, "iron," above the line before "thorns," but the correction seems out of place and secondary.

k   NRSV renders לֹא־תָבוֹא שָׁמָּה (*lō'-tābô' šāmmâ*) in the second person, "you will not go there," though the second person is not otherwise used in the context. I follow all the ancient translations and JPS in taking the subject of *tābô'* as the feminine construct noun יִרְאַת (*yir'at*), "the fear of thorns and thistles will not go there."

l   The text literally has the singular verb "it will become," though the antecedent is plural, "all the hills. . . ."

Commentary

In vv. 18-19 God threatens to summon both the Assyrian bee and the Egyptian fly to come and take up abode in the Israelite heartland simultaneously. Historically, Egypt and the major Anatolian, North Syrian, or Mesopotamian powers vied for control of Palestine, and Palestine tried to play one off against the other for its own benefit. In the late eighth century BCE, Israel and Judah appealed to either Assyria or Egypt as an ally against the other, flitting from one to the other in pursuit of what the Israelite and Judean royal advisors perceived to be their own self-interest. Wildberger (p. 1:303) argues that the reference to Egypt is a later addition to the text, since Egypt was no threat in 735 BCE, but that argument represents historical hindsight, not the views of the participants in the historical moment. Hanun of Gaza, one of the participants in the revolt against Assyria, fled to Egypt for refuge from the Assyrians, and then in turn quite abruptly fled Egypt and returned to Gaza to pay homage to Tiglath-pileser.[1] Hanun's flight to Egypt suggests that he considered Egypt a support against Assyria, and it is possible that the motivation for his precipitous return from Egypt was Piye's (Piankhi's) Nubian campaign against Tefnakht of Sais and his Delta allies in 734 BCE—better the enemy he knew than the unknown Nubian.[2] Nubian contact with Assyria is clearly attested by 732 BCE, when both Nubians and Egyptians were among those receiving rations of wine at the Assyrian capital Calah.[3] In 725 BCE, Hosea sent messengers to an Egyptian king, which provoked Shalmaneser V's attack on Samaria (2 Kgs 17:4), and in 720 BCE, when Hanun of Gaza along with Hamath and Samaria again revolted against Assyria, the Nubian rulers of Egypt sent an army under a commander named Reu to relieve Sargon's siege of Gaza,[4] and reliefs from Sargon's palace at Dur-sharukken show Nubian soldiers defending the walls of Raphia and Gabbatuna.[5] One could also argue that Isa 7:18-25 dates a few years later than 735–732 BCE, when Israel's flitting between Assyria and Egypt is clearly attested by Hosea (9:3, 6; 11:5; 12:2). Whatever the precise date of the original oracle, the implication is that God will use the erstwhile allies of Israel or Judah as his agents to punish his people. I see no reason to delete either Egypt or Assyria from the original oracle.

The reference to flies from Egypt, given the abundance of insects along the Nile, requires no comment, but the reference to bees from the land of Assryia is more striking. The cultivation of bees was apparently practiced by the Habhu people in the mountains to the north and northeast of Assyria, and whatever the practice in Assyria proper, sometime in the second quarter of the eighth century, prior to Isaiah, a certain Shamash-resha-uṣur, governor of the land of Sūhu on the middle Euphrates, boasts of introducing the practice into his country, an area that had been controlled by Assyria and was again incorporated into Assyria by Tiglath-pileser III.[6] For whistling to attract bees, see the discussion in Wildberger (p. 304). Whether humans ever whistled to attract flies is irrelevant; God may summon any creature by his command. Neither an encounter with swarms of biting flies nor one with stinging bees would be a particularly welcome experience for God's people, and they will discover the major powers to whom they had appealed for help,

---

1   Tadmor, *Inscriptions of Tiglath-pileser III*, Summ. 4, 8′-14′; Summ. 8, 14′-19′; see now Hayim Tadmor and Shigeo Yamada, *The Royal Inscriptions of Tiglath-pileser III (744–727 BC) and Shalmaneser V (726–722 BC), Kings of Assyria* (RINAP 1; Winona Lake, IN: Eisenbrauns, 2011) pp. 105–6, 42:8′-14′; p. 127, 48:14′-19′.

2   See my "Isaiah's Egyptian and Nubian Oracles," in Brad E. Kelle and Megan Bishop Moore, eds., *Israel's Prophets and Israel's Past: Essays on the Relationship of Prophetic Texts and Israelite History in Honor of John H. Hayes* (LHBOTS 446; New York: T&T Clark, 2006) 201–9, esp. 202 nn. 3-5, and the literature cited there, especially the work of D. Kahn.

3   J. V. Kinnier-Wilson, *The Nimrud Wine Lists: A Study of Men and Administration at the Assyrian Capital in the Eighth Century B.C.* (Cuneiform Texts from Nimrud 1; London: British School of Archaeology in Iraq, 1972) 91–92.

4   Roberts, "Isaiah's Egyptian and Nubian Oracles," 203.

5   N. Franklin, "The Room V Reliefs at Dur-Sharruken and Sargon II's Western Campaigns," *TA* 21 (1994) 255–75, esp. 264–68, figs. 3–7.

6   Grant Frame, *Rulers of Babylonia from the Second Dynasty of Isin to the End of Assyrian Domination (1157–612 BC)* (RIMB 2; Toronto: University of Toronto Press, 1995) 275–77, 281–87; S.0.1001.1.iv 13-v 6; S.0.1001.4.A1-6.

whether Egyptian or Assyrian, to be just as unpleasant a presence in their land.

Verse 20 speaks only of Assyria as Yahweh's hired razor that will shave away all the body hair of his people. The imagery suggests the abusive and shameful treatment accorded prisoners of war. Shaved locks, leaving only the *abbuttu*-lock, were a way of marking slaves in Mesopotamia,[7] and Israel was familiar with the humiliation imposed on women captives when their heads were shaved (Deut 21:12) or on men when their beards were removed (2 Sam 10:4), and the unparalleled mention of the hair of the feet, a euphemism for pubic hair, could only heighten this sense of humiliation. The implication is that God will use the Assyrian king as his agent to punish his people, but the adjective "hired" is ambiguous. It could simply mean that Yahweh had employed the Assyrians to punish Israel, but if one heard the oracle after Ahaz had paid the Assyrians to save him, it could be taken to mean that Yahweh would punish Judah (as well as Israel) with their own hired help.

Verses 21-22 contain both a threat and a promise. They suggest that only a small remnant with a few animals will survive the judgment, but these animals will produce so much that the surviving remnant will have no shortage of rich food. This combination of threat, followed by a promise to the surviving remnant, is a recurring feature in Isaiah (1:21-28; 29:1-8; 31:4-9). Isaiah 7:21-22 seem dependent on 7:15, but they probably date to a slightly later period when Isaiah expected Judah to be devastated alongside Israel.

Verses 23-25 continue this portrayal of the devastated countryside with its ruined vineyards overgrown with thorns and thistles. Much of the countryside, once covered with expensive vineyards, will be too wild and overgrown to venture into without being well armed with bow and arrows. This motif suggests the increased danger of wild predators, a phenomenon that often follows a drastic reduction in the human population of an area.[8] Only the presumably steeper hills that were cultivated exclusively with a hoe will be relatively free of these thorns and thistles, and there the survivors will be able to pasture their cattle and sheep. As Hayes and Irvine noted (p. 140), the imagery of these verses has close ties to the imagery of Isaiah's oracle about Yahweh's vineyard (Isa 5:1-7), which includes both Israel and Judah, and these parallels suggests again that the judgment will strike Judah as well as Israel.

Whatever the original date and intent of these separate sayings, the effect of their juxtaposition in their present context is to give a negative slant to the earlier positive promise to Ahaz. Judah's enemies, Israel and Damascus, will indeed be destroyed, but because Ahaz did not respond to this promise with faith, Judah will also be submerged in this judgment, and even in Judah only a small remnant will escape to eat the rich food promised to the child Immanuel.

Bibliography

Childs, *Assyrian Crisis*.
Margulies, H., "Das Rätsel der Biene im AT," *VT* 24 (1974) 56–76.

---

7   *CAD* A1, 49–50, s.v. *abbuttu*.
8   For Isaiah's views on the drastic reduction in population produced by God's judgment, see Isa 3:25—4:1; 6:12-13a.

8

1/ And Yahweh said to me, "Get you a large[a] piece of scroll[b] and write on it with an ordinary stylus[c] 'Belonging to Maher-shalal-hush-baz,[d]'" 2/ So I summoned[e] for myself reliable witnesses, Uriah the priest, and Zechariah, the son of Jeberechiah. 3/ Then I approached the prophetess,[f] and she conceived and bore a son. Yahweh said to me,[g] "Name him Maher-shalal-hush-baz,[h] 4/ for before the lad knows to call out, 'Daddy!'[i] and 'Mommy!'[i] one will carry off the wealth of Damascus and the booty of Samaria into the presence of the king of Assyria."

Textual Notes

a LXX has τόμον καινοῦ μεγάλου, "a sheet of a big new (scroll)." The last two words appear to be a double translation of גָּדוֹל (gādôl), "large," but perhaps they are just an interpretation of גִּלָּיוֹן (gillāyôn). *BHS* suggests that instead of *gādôl*, "large," the original reading was גּוֹרָל (gôrāl), "lot," and that the LXX reading is an inner-Greek corruption of κλῆρου, "lot," to καινοῦ, "new." That would yield a reading, "an inheritance scroll," but it does not explain the double translation in the present LXX text. I do not find the suggestion persuasive.

b The meaning of גִּלָּיוֹן (gillāyôn) is hotly debated. Some scholars suggest a writing tablet, whether of metal, wood, or leather.[1] I take it to be a large piece, perhaps several sheets, of papyrus or leather scroll that could be rolled up and sealed.

c The precise meaning of בְּחֶרֶט אֱנוֹשׁ (bĕḥereṭ ʾĕnôš) remains uncertain. The word חֶרֶט (ḥereṭ) normally means a stylus or writing instrument of some sort, but it might also refer to the ductus or style of writing produced by the instrument. LXX, Vg., and Syr. all understand אֱנוֹשׁ (ʾĕnôš) in the sense of "man," but "the stylus of a man" is an odd expression. From what other kind of stylus or ductus would the addition of this modifier serve to distinguish it? It is possible that אֱנוֹשׁ (ʾĕnôš) here is a rare word with a completely different meaning. Tg. interprets the expression to mean "in clear writing" (כתב מפרש, kĕtāb mĕpāraš).

d MT has לְמַהֵר שָׁלָל חָשׁ בַּז (lĕmahēr šālāl ḥāš baz), and its reading is supported by 1QIsaᵃ, but 4QIsaᵉ, where it is preserved in v. 2, gives the name as מהר שלל חוש בז (mahēr šālāl ḥûš baz), which is probably a superior reading. Maher-shalal-hush-baz, as the continuation of the text shows, is a symbolic proper name containing two verbal elements, each followed by a noun referring to plunder taken after successful conquest. As vocalized by MT, מהר (mahēr) appears to be a *piel* imperative or infinitive, while חש (ḥāš) appears to be a *qal* participle, but the variation in the verbal form in the two halves is odd. For the sake of consistency, some analyze מהר as a *piel* participle lacking the initial *mem* (Wildberger, 313), but it is easier, following the reading

of 4QIsaᵉ, to revocalize the name as Maher-shalal-hush-baz and analyze both verb forms as imperatives, "Hurry-plunder!-Hasten-booty!" So analyzed, the name is comparable to the similarly symbolic Akkadian name for the ferryman of the underworld Ḫumuṭ-tabal, "Hurry-take-away!"

e MT supported by Tg. reads וְאָעִידָה (wĕʾāʿîdâ), but the simple *waw* before the cohortative does not fit here. Following the preceding imperatives "get" and "write" in v. 1, that construction would imply purpose or result, "that I might summon. . . ." I prefer to revocalize to the *waw*-consecutive וָאָעִידָה (wāʾāʿîdâ) with Vg., "then I summoned." 4QIsaᵉ has the same consonantal text as MT, but without vocalization it is unclear how the scribe understood the text. 1QIsaᵃ followed by LXX and Syr. reads the imperative והעד (wĕhāʿēd), "then summon." One might consider the possibility that the present text is a conflated text due to haplography and that the original text was fuller: "'. . . and summon for me reliable witnesses.' So I summoned Uriah the priest and Zechariah the son of Jeberechiah." The logic of the context, following the normal practice of sealing contracts and important documents (cf. Jer 32:9-15), suggests that God commanded Isaiah to prepare a scroll and write on its outside a tagline indicating what the contents of the scroll were about. In order to carry out the command, whether God specifically demanded witnesses or not, required that Isaiah summon witnesses to attach their signatures so that in the future they could verify that Isaiah had indeed written this material in the said scroll and sealed it on a particular date.

f 1QIsaᵃ either omits the final *mater* on הַנְּבִיאָה (hannĕbîʾâ), "the prophetess," or the ink has faded. 4QIsaᵉ preserves it.

g 4QIsaᵉ omits אֵלַי (ʾēlay), "to me," but MT is supported by 1QIsaᵃ, LXX, Syr., Vg., and Tg.

h Reading with 4QIsaᵉ מהר שלל חוש בז (mahēr šālāl ḥûš baz).

i MT has the first person suffix, "my father or my mother," but 1QIsaᵃ has the third person אביו ואמו (ʾābāyw wĕʾimmô), "his father or his mother," and it is followed by Vg. It is difficult to tell from the traces in 4QIsaᵉ and 4QIsaᶠ whether to read the first or third person suffix, since the *yod* and *waw* are so similar

---

1 See Wildberger, 312, and the sources cited there, for example.

in this script. LXX has no suffix on the forms, and both Tg. and Syr. omit any pronominal suffix, but this may represent a translation by sense rather than a different text. I follow the MT, but the sense is readily conveyed in English without translating the suffixes. The reference is to the child's first efforts to say, "Daddy!" and "Mommy!"[2]

Commentary

The incident in 8:1-4 apparently took place sometime after the events in 7:1-17, but still during the crisis of the Syro-Ephraimitic War. If the first took place early in 735 BCE, the second could have taken place late in 735 or early in 734, depending on how far along in her pregnancy Isaiah's wife was at the time the oracle in 7:14 was uttered. There is no logical reason why she could not have conceived again shortly after the birth of Immanuel. Apparently Ahaz had not yet sent an embassy to Tiglath-pileser, because the oracle appears to be another attempt to assuage the king's fears by promising the destruction of his enemies. The oracle is clearly prior to Tiglath-pileser's invasion of the Israelite heartland in 733 BCE, when its truth would have been obvious to everyone, and it may even be prior to the Assyrian conquest of Philistia in 734 BCE, though by the time of this oracle Isaiah is certain that Assyria will be the agent for God's destruction of Israel and Damascus.

The text begins with a symbolic act that is unfortunately obscure because of the uncertainty about the meaning of a couple of key words. Isaiah is told to take a large *gillāyôn* and write on it "belonging to" or "with regard to Maher-shalal-hush-baz." There is a debate whether *gillāyôn* refers to a writing tablet made of an inflexible material such as wood, stone, or metal, or whether it refers to a piece of papyrus or leather that could be rolled up as a scroll. In the present state of research, the issue cannot be settled by lexicographical evidence alone, as it is ambiguous, but I am inclined to the latter. That would fit better with the idea that the document was sealed and witnessed. The witnesses are specifically mentioned, and a notice about the sealing of

Isaiah's testimony of the time is found in 8:16, a notice that is probably associated with the symbolic act in 8:1-4. The writing is to be done with a certain kind of stylus or ductus. The RSV's rendering "in common characters" is just a guess at the meaning, but other suggestions are no more convincing. The writing is apparently meant to be visible, so if the sheet consisted of material that could be rolled up, the writing was on the outside. Though there is some debate on the correct grammatical analysis of the name, it is clearly symbolic, and its general import is clear. It either means "Hurry-plunder!-Hasten-booty!," or less likely "Plunder-hurries-booty-hastens."

In order to carry out God's command, Isaiah summoned two reliable witnesses to witness his actions. Both appear to have been important men at the court, but as far as we know, neither was a particularly close friend to Isaiah. Uriah was the high priest who made a copy of the foreign altar for Ahaz (2 Kgs 16:11), and Zechariah may have been the maternal grandfather of Hezekiah, and so the father-in-law of Ahaz (2 Kgs 18:2). Yet due to the highly elliptical nature of the narrative, two questions remain to be answered. What precisely were the two men to witness? And what was the purpose of having them witness whatever they witnessed? Despite the flow of the narrative as it now stands, where immediately after summoning the witnesses, Isaiah has intercourse with the prophetess (קרב, *qārab*, "to draw near," often has the sense of sexual intimacy [Gen 20:4; Lev 18:6, 14, 19; 20:16; Deut 22:14; Ezek 18:6]), it is highly unlikely that these two witnesses observed the act of intercourse. Not only would such behavior be extremely odd in Israel, but the prophetic significance of having such witnesses would

2   The Bible preserves very little of children's speech, but the possibility that the use of the first person suffix has a caritative significance is suggested by the exchange between Abraham and Isaac in Gen 22:7, in a context where Abraham's love for Isaac has been emphasized (v. 2), though Isaac is clearly much older in this story than the child who is just learning to speak in Isaiah 8.

be totally opaque. Following intercourse, the woman conceived and bore a son, but that was at least a nine-month process, and the legal act of witnessing is a punctiliar event, so it could hardly be her pregnancy and subsequent birth that the witnesses witnessed. One may even question whether the intercourse with the prophetess followed the act of witnessing. This may have preceded the affair with the witnesses; the chronological sequence in this narrative is not at all clear.

What is clear is that Isaiah summoned the witnesses after he was told to write something on a scroll. In Israel witnesses customarily served to verify that the content of a contract or important document was genuine and was actually written at the time the document claimed to be written. Witnesses normally added their name and seal to the bottom of the written document, and if later there was a dispute about the document, they could be called to testify to its genuineness (see Jer 32:12). But if that is the case here, something must have been written on the inside of the rolled up scroll. The simple phrase "concerning Maher-shalal-hush-baz" could hardly be more than a tag written on the outside of the sealed scroll to identify the contents of the scroll should one need to open it at some point in the future. Presumably the contents of the scroll included a prophecy along the lines of vv. 3-4, that is, that Isaiah would have a son named Maher-shalal-hush-baz and that before he was old enough to say, "Daddy" or "Mommy," both Damascus and Samaria would be plundered by Assyria. The writing down, calling witnesses, and sealing the scroll with the enclosed prophecy was intended to confirm that this prophetic symbolic act and its interpretation had been performed and announced prior to the resolution of the Syro-Ephraimitic crisis. Thus, it was intended to protect Isaiah from the charge of fudging prophecy after the event (cf. 30:8-9). Whether the large piece of scroll contained more than just the prophecy about Maher-shalal-hush-baz is uncertain, but Isa 8:16-18 might suggest that the oracles connected to Isaiah's earlier children, Shear-jashub and Immanuel, were also included in the scroll. In that case the tag line is simply derived from the latest oracle in the group.

In any case, Isaiah had intercourse with the prophetess, and she conceived. The significance of the term "the prophetess" is ambiguous. Most scholars assume that the term refers to Isaiah's wife (Wildberger, 317).[3] If this is correct, she may have been a prophetess in her own right, but it is also possible that she is referred to as "the prophetess" simply because she was married to a prophet. We do not know enough about ancient Judean conventions of referring to wives to rule out that possibility, and there is no evidence that Isaiah consciously rejected the term "prophet" (נביא, *nābî'*) as an inappropriate designation for his function (contra Wildberger, 318).

Nine months later, when Isaiah's wife bore their son, God commanded the prophet to give him the symbolic name previously announced. One could take the tense sequence to imply that the meaning of the name was clearly articulated to Isaiah only after the birth of the child, but that seems quite dubious. Unless the name of the child were already interpreted in the sealed and witnessed document before the birth of the child, it is hard to understand the need for witnesses at all. The interpretation of the name is quite clear. Most children learn to say "Daddy" and "Mommy" by the age of one. Thus, counting the nine-month gestation period and the first year of life up to a point before the child begins speaking his first words, means that within less than two years or so, both Damascus and Samaria will be plundered by the Assyrians. Note that the symbolic name gains its full significance only when explicated and tied to a time limit. The point is that the Davidic court need not fear Aram and Israel, because within less than two years their power will be broken by Assyria. If the court would only trust the prophetic word, there would be no need to rush into a defensive alliance that required submission to another power.

---

3   See my discussion on Isa 7:14-15.

Bibliography

Ahlström, G. W., "Oral and Written Transmission: Some Considerations," *HTR* 59 (1966) 69–81.

Anderson, R. T., "Was Isaiah a Scribe?" *JBL* 79 (1960) 57–58.

Galling, Kurt, "Ein Stück judäischen Bodenrechts in Jesaja 8," *ZDPV* 56 (1933) 209–18.

Jepsen, Alfred, "Die *Nebiah* in Jes 8:3," *ZAW* 72 (1960) 267–68.

Jirku, A., "Zu 'Eilebeute' in Jes. 8, 1.3," *TLZ* 75 (1950) 118.

Katz, P., "Notes on the Septuagint: I. Isaiah Viii 1a," *JTS* 47 (1946) 30–31.

Loiser, M. A., "Witness in Israel of the Hebrew Scriptures in the Context of Ancient Near East" (PhD diss., University of Notre Dame, 1973).

Morenz, S., "'Eilebeute,'" *TLZ* 74 (1949) 697–99.

Rignell, G., "'Das Orakel' *Maher-salal Has-bas*," *ST* 10 (1956) 40–52.

Stade, B., "Zu Jes. 8,1f.," *ZAW* 26 (1906) 1325–37.

Steck, O. H., "Beiträge zum Verständnis von Jes 7,10-17 und 8,1-4," *TZ* 29 (1973) 161–78.

Talmage, F., "חרט אנוש in Isaiah 8:1," *HTR* 60 (1967) 465–68.

Vogt, E., "'Eilig tun' als adverbielles Verb und der Name des Sohnes Isaias' in Is 8,1," *Bib* 48 (1967) 63–69.

8

5/ And Yahweh spoke to me again saying:
6/ "Because this people have rejected the waters of the canal[a] that flow gently and rejoice with[b] Rezin and the[c] son of Remaliah,"

7/ therefore[d] my Lord[e] is about to bring up upon them[f] the powerful[g] and massive[g] waters of the Euphrates, the king of Assyria and all[h] his glory. And it will rise over all its[i] stream beds and go up over all its[i] banks.[j] 8/ And it will pass on[k] into Judah, flooding[l] and overflowing,[l] it will reach to the neck.[m] But the spreading of his wings will fill the breadth of your land, O Immanuel.[n] 9/ Unite[o] yourselves, O peoples, and be shattered; and give ear, all distant parts of the earth. Gird yourself and be shattered. [p]Gird yourself and be shattered.[p] 10/ Take counsel, but it will be frustrated. Speak a word, but[q] it will not stand, for God is with us.

Textual Notes

a For MT's הַשִּׁלֹחַ (haššilōaḥ) 1QIsa[a] has השולח (haššôlēaḥ) and 4QIsa[e] השילה (haššilōh), both probably from an original השילח (haššilaḥ). The Hebrew appears to be a variant of שֶׁלַח (šelaḥ), "canal" (Neh 3:15); cf. Akk. šiliḫtu—part of a canal. The reference is presumably to a canal that took the water from the Gihon Spring south down the Kidron Valley prior to Hezekiah's construction of the tunnel to redirect those waters. This canal has been identified with canal II that emptied into the old reservoir now called *birket el-ḥamra* (J. Simons, *Jerusalem in the Old Testament: Researches and Theories* [Leiden: Brill, 1952] 176–77). The fall of level of this canal has been calculated as "4 millimetres per metre for the first 230 metres and 5 for the next 100 metres. Only in the last stretch along the hill-slope, for about 10 metres, the fall increases to 5 centimetres per metre, diminishing to 3 centimetres under the *Point Sud* itself" (ibid., 178). This was indeed a gently flowing canal.

b MT's וּמְשׂוֹשׂ (ûmĕśôś) is supported by 4QIsa[e] and 4QIsa[f]. 1QIsa[a] reads משיש (māśîś), perhaps the *hiphil* participle, though the *hiphil* is otherwise unattested for this verb, and the reading is probably secondary. The expression וּמְשׂוֹשׂ אֶת־רְצִין (ûmĕśôś ʾet-rĕṣîn), literally, "and the joy (is) with Rezin," is a long-standing crux. The versions all appear to have that reading, though they finesse the translation in various ways: LXX has ἀλλὰ βούλεσθαι ἔχειν τὸν Ρααςςων καὶ τὸν υἱὸν Ρομελιου βασιλέα ἐφ᾽ ὑμῶν, "but wishes to have Rezin and the son of Remaliah as king over you"; Vg. has *et adsumpsit magis Rasin et filium Romeliae*, "and he has chosen rather Rezin and the son of Remaliah"; Syr. has "they have rejoiced in Rezin and the son of Remaliah." Tg. is particularly interesting: "Because this people despised the kingdom of the house of David which leads them gently as the waters of Shiloah that flow gently and desired Rezin and the son of Remaliah." The grammatical awkwardness of the nominal phrase or clause has led modern scholars to suggest any number of emendations. The most common is to correct מְשׂוֹשׂ (mĕśôś) to מָסוֹס (māsôs), the infinitive absolute of מסס (māsas), "to melt." The verb occurs numerous times in the *niphal* with לבב (lēbāb) in the sense, "to lose heart, to despair out of fear," including two occurrences in Isaiah (13:17; 19:1). It occurs once in the *qal* in the sense "to waste away" (כִּמְסֹס נֹסֵס, kimsôs nōsēs), "like a sick man who wastes away" (Isa 10:18), unless one also wants to give this passage the sense of despair: "like a sick man who despairs." In Isa 8:6 it is assumed to mean, "and they melted in fear." The verb is never construed as transitive, however, so this emendation requires that one also emend the את (ʾet) before Rezin. Some suggest לפני (lipnê), "before Rezin," but Wildberger reconstructs מסוס משאת רצין (māsôs miśśĕʾēt rĕṣîn), "but they melted before the haughtiness of Rezin." The emendation is suggestive and possible, but it has no support in the versions. In contrast to מסס, the root שׂושׂ is clearly attested construed with אֵת (ʾet), שׂישׂו אִתָּה מָשׂושׂ (śîśû ʾittāh māśôś) "rejoice with her [Jerusalem] in joy" (Isa 66:10). In Isa 8:6 the construction is perhaps due either to haplography or to a poetic ellipsis for וּמָשׂושׂ [שׂושׂו] את־רצין (ûmāśôś)[śāśû][ʾet-rĕṣîn), "and in joy they rejoiced with Rezin." An alternative is to take the nominal form וּמְשׂוֹשׂ (ûmĕśôś) as being used in place of the infinitive absolute as a substitute for the finite verb or the participle, either "and they rejoiced with Rezin" or "rejoicing *instead* with Rezin."

c For MT's וּבֶן (ûben), 1QIsa[a] has ואת בן (wĕʾet ben), but MT is supported by 4QIsa[e] and 4QIsa[f].

d The initial *waw* on MT and 1QIsa[a] וְלָכֵן (wĕlākēn), "and therefore," is the *waw* of apodosis and may be original even if not reflected in the translations of the versions other than the Tg.

e 1QIsa[a] reads יהוה (YHWH) for MT's אדני (ʾădōnāy), "my Lord," but then inserts the supralinear correction אדוני (ʾădônāy).

f LXX reads עליכם (ʿălêkem), "against you," but the other versions and 1QIsa[a], 4QIsa[e], and 4QIsa[f] all support the MT.

g 4QIsa[f] reverses the order of הָעֲצוּמִים וְהָרַבִּים (hāʿăṣûmîm wĕhārabbîm), "the powerful and massive."

h   LXX omits כל (*kol*), "all," but all the other versions and 1QIsa^a, 4QIsa^e, and 4QIsa^f have it.

i   LXX has the second person plural suffix "your."

j   For MT's גְּדוֹתָיו (*gĕdôtāyw*), "its banks," 4QIsa^e has גדיותיו (*gedyôtāyw*), "its kids." It is hard to tell whether 1QIsa^a has גדיותיו (*gedyôtāyw*) or גדוותיו (*gedwôtāyw*), and the unclearly written third letter could even be confused for a *resh* (ר), which may partially explain the LXX reading גדרתיכם (*gidrôtêkem*), περιπατήσει ἐπὶ πᾶν τεῖχος ὑμῶν, "and he will walk on your every wall," and Syr.'s "their walls."

k   LXX's καὶ ἀφελεῖ ἀπὸ τῆς Ἰουδαίας ἄνθρωπον ὃς δυνήσεται κεφαλὴν ἆραι ἢ δυνατὸν συντελέσασθαί τι, "and he will take away from Judah (every) man who is able to raise (his) head or is able to do anything," may simply be a loose interpretation of the received text that the translator did not understand, but even if it is based on a totally different text, that text is hardly original.

l   MT, 1QIsa^a, and 1QIsa^f share the same consonantal text שטף ועבר (*šāṭap wĕ ʿābar*), against a number of later manuscripts, which have ושטף ועבר (*wĕšāṭap wĕ ʾābar*), though if both verbs are perfects, as the MT points them, one would expect ושטף (*wĕšāṭap*) to express the future. The consonantal text is correct, but both verbs should probably be pointed as infinitive absolutes (*šāṭôp wĕ ʿābôr*) as suggested by the Vg.'s *inundans et transiens*, "inundating and passing through."

m   4QIsa^e has צער (*ṣ ʿr*), presumably the place-name Zoar, for MT, 1QIsa^a, and 4QIsa^f's צַוָּאר (*ṣawwā ʾr*), "neck." This must be an oral mistake. Vg. and Syr. follow MT.

n   Tg. is alone in having ישראל (*yiśrā ʾēl*), "Israel," for עמנואל (*ʿimmānû ʾēl*), "Immanuel"; it is clearly a secondary reading.

o   LXX's γνῶτε, "know," suggests that it was reading דעו (*dĕ ʿû*). MT's רעו (*r ʿw*) is supported by 1QIsa^a, 4QIsa^e, 4QIsa^f, and the other versions. Vg.'s *congregamini*, "assemble," and Tg.'s אתחברו (*ʾithabarû*), "join together," appear to be analyzing the Hebrew verb as רעו (*rĕ ʿû*), "unite yourselves," from רעה II (*rā ʿâ*), "to associate with," while Syr. ܙܘܥܘ (*zw ʿw*), "quake," appears to follow MT's pointing in reading it as רעו (*rō ʿû*), "be shattered," from רעע II (*rā ʿa ʿ*), "to shatter." The derivation from רעה II (*rā ʿâ*), "to associate with," better fits the parallelism with התאזרו (*hit ʾazzĕrû*), "gird yourself." This is a Zion Tradition motif about the march of foreign enemies against Yahweh, his king, and his city Jerusalem, found also in similar formulations in Pss 2:2 and 48:5, where the foreign enemies of Jerusalem *yityaṣṣĕbû . . . nôssĕdû-yaḥad*, "set themselves . . . and took counsel together," or *nô ʿādû ʿābĕrû yaḥdāw*, "assembled and came on together."

p   This repetition of the previous line in the MT is supported by LXX—though its translation is very loose—the Vg., and Tg., but it is lacking in 1QIsa^a, Syr., and, despite the break, apparently in 4QIsa^e and 4QIsa^f, since there is not sufficient space in either manuscript to include the repeated line (Skehan and Ulrich, "Isaiah," 93, 105).

q   4QIsa^e omits the *waw* on ולא (*wĕlō ʾ*), "and not," but MT is supported by 1QIsa^a, Vg., Syr., and Tg.

Commentary

The original historical setting for Isa 8:5-10 must have been prior to the Maher-shalal-hush-baz oracle in 8:1-4, and is probably the same time period as the Immanuel oracle in 7:10-17, since the symbolic name Immanuel is central to them both. Moreover, both may have been given either on the same occasion when Isaiah met Ahaz as the king was inspecting Jerusalem's water supplies (7:1-9) or shortly after, when the memory of that meeting was still quite fresh. Note how the oracle in 8:6 refers to Jerusalem's gently flowing canal stream as a metaphor for the rule of the Davidic house. This metaphorical language would be particularly fitting if the oracle was given to Ahaz either during or shortly after his inspection of this stream. One should also note the very close parallel in language between 7:1-9 and 8:5-10. Both speak of plans against Jerusalem that will not stand (7:5, 7; 8:10), and both identify the enemy as Rezin and the son of Remaliah (7:4; 8:6).

Isaiah sometimes uses the expression "this people" to refer to the northern kingdom, Israel (9:15), sometimes to refer to Judah, the southern kingdom (28:14), and sometimes perhaps to refer to the whole people, including both the northern and southern kingdoms (6:10), so one can identify the intended referent in 8:6 only by close attention to the context. "This people" are accused of doing two things: they rejected the gently flowing waters of the canal, and they "rejoiced with" or "in" Rezin and the son of Remaliah. The second point is obscured in the RSV, which emends the Hebrew text to get the reading "and melt in fear before Rezin." The text is difficult, but, as indicated above, the LXX, Syriac, Vulgate, and Targum all support the MT, which may be translated as "and they rejoice with or in Rezin." The implication of this phrase is that "this people" delight in or desire the rule of Rezin and Pekah. Since there is no clear evidence that Judah revolted against Ahaz or desired to join the Syro-Ephraimite coalition under these non-Davidide rulers, "this people" must refer to Israel, the northern kingdom. In support of this understanding, note the striking contrast between the עֲלֵיהֶם (ʿălêhem), "against them," of v. 7 and the אַרְצֶךָ (ʾarṣĕkā), "your land," of v. 8b. When addressing Ahaz and his court, Isaiah uses the second person. Note עָלֶיךָ וְעַל־עַמְּךָ וְעַל־בֵּית אָבִיךָ (ʿālêkā wĕʿal-ʿammĕkā wĕʿal-bêt ʾābîkā), "against you, and against your people, and against the house of your father," of 7:17.

The waters of the canal presumably refers to canal II, a canal fed by the Gihon Spring on the southeastern slope of Jerusalem (cf. Neh 3:15). On one metaphorical level the expression could refer to the Davidic monarch, perhaps because of the role that this spring appears to have played in the Judean enthronement ceremony (1 Kgs 1:32-40; cf. Ps 110:7). The north's delight in Rezin and Pekah certainly implied the rejection of the Davidic claims to hegemony over the north, but on a deeper level it also implied a rejection of Yahweh, for it was Yahweh who had chosen both David and Jerusalem. Because the north had rejected these gentle waters, God was going to bring over them the violent floodwaters of the Euphrates, a metaphor for the Assyrian armies. This flood would completely submerge the north and pass on into Judah, where it would reach up to the neck, but at this point a contrast is drawn between the north and the south. One could question whether the mention of Judah here is original, or whether it represents a secondary expansion of the text by Isaiah after Ahaz ignored all three of the oracles of promise directly connected to the children with symbolic names.

The RSV translates 8:8b as "and its outspread wings will fill the breadth of your land, O Immanuel." This translation understands the antecedent of "its" to be the mighty waters of the Euphrates. "Wings" are never used in reference to rivers, however, so this pronoun should probably be translated "his" and its antecedent understood as "the Lord" of v. 7 (cf. JPS and the comments in Hayes and Irvine): "but his (the Lord's) outspread wings will fill the breadth of your land, O Immanuel." Yahweh is often portrayed metaphorically as a bird with wings outstretched to protect or care for his worshipers (Deut 32:11; Pss 17:8; 36:8; 57:2; 61:5; 63:8; 91:4). This imagery is probably dependent on Solomon's temple in Jerusalem, both because of its function as a place of asylum and because of the iconography in its inner sanctum,

where the outspread wings of two giant cherubim formed the seat of God's throne and overshadowed the ark of the covenant, his footstool (1 Kgs 6:23-28). Isaiah uses the imagery elsewhere to refer to Yahweh's protection of Jerusalem (31:5). The statement in 8:8b is ostensibly addressed to the child Immanuel, but that is only a rhetorical device to emphasize the meaning of the child's symbolic name to Isaiah's real audience, the Judean royal court. Although the Assyrian flood will overwhelm the north and, if Judah is original, seriously threaten the south, Judah can take comfort in God's promise of protection, for God is with us.

This is made quite explicit in vv. 9-10. The foreign nations hostile to Judah are called upon to make their plans against Judah, but they should realize beforehand that their plans will come to naught, because, as the repetition of the child's name Immanuel proclaims, "God is with us." Just as the Zion Tradition promised, Yahweh would protect his city Jerusalem from the onslaught of the enemy kings. Thus, the Davidic court need not fear the plot of Rezin, Pekah, and their allies. They need only fear Yahweh and trust in his promises.

Secondary Reading

As noted above, the original context for these verses would have been in connection with the Immanuel oracle in 7:10-17, prior to the later oracle concerning Maher-shalal-hush-baz. The present literary placement of these verses after the Maher-shalal-hush-baz oracle, however, suggests that they now, perhaps with some updating and recasting, represent Isaiah's second thoughts after Ahaz had demonstrated his refusal to trust in God by sending for Assyrian help. In such a context, the refusal of the gentle waters of the canal could also refer to the Davidic house's refusal to trust Yahweh, and the threat of being overrun by the mighty waters of the Euphrates could also be seen as God's poetic justice in punishing Judah through Assyria, the very false savior that Ahaz had chosen in preference to Yahweh. But even so, God would spare a remnant of Judah. When the flood had reached the neck, at the last moment, God would save his remnant, for the promise of Immanuel had not been revoked.

Bibliography

Bauer, J., "Altsumerische Beiträge 1-3," *WO* 6 (1970) 143-52.

Budde, K., "Jes 8:6b," *ZAW* 44 (1926) 65-67.

———, "Zu Jesaja 8, Vers 9 und 10," *JBL* 49 (1930) 423-28.

Driver, G. R., "Isaiah 1-39: Textual and Linguistic Problems," *JSS* 13 (1968) 36-57.

Fullerton, K., "The Interpretation of Isaiah 8:5-10," *JBL* 43 (1924) 253-89.

Hadley, Judith M., "2 Chronicles 32:30 and the Water Systems of Pre-Exilic Jerusalem," in Iain Provan and Mark J. Boda, eds., *Let Us Go Up to Zion: Essays in Honour of H. G. M. Williamson on the Occasion of His Sixty-Fifth Birthday* (VTSup 153; Leiden: Brill, 2012) 273-84.

Honeyman, A. M., "Traces of an Early Diakritic Sign in Isa 8:6b," *JBL* 63 (1944) 45-50.

Kaiser, Otto, *Die mythische Bedeutung des Meeres in Ägypten, Ugarit und Israel* (BZAW 78; Berlin: A. Töpelmann, 1959).

Klein, H., "Freude an Rezin," *VT* 30 (1980) 229-34.

———, "Freude an Rezin: Ein Versuch, mit dem Text Jes. 8.6 ohne Konjectur auszukommen," *ZAW* 72 (1960) 267-68.

Lutz, H. M., *Jahwe, Jerusalem und die Völker* (WMANT 27; Neukirchen-Vluyn: Neukirchener Verlag, 1968).

May, H. G., "Some Cosmic Connotations of *mayim rabbîm*, 'Many Waters,'" *JBL* 74 (1954) 9-21.

Poe, Harry L., "Isaiah 8:5-15 [Expository Article]," *RevExp* 88 (1991) 189-93.

Sæbø, M., "Zur Traditionsgeschichte von Jesaja 8:9-10," *ZAW* 76 (1964) 132-43.

Schmidt, H., "Jesaja 8:9-10," in Georg Bertram, ed., *Stromata: Festgabe des Akademisch-Theologischen Vereins zu Giessen im Schmalkaldener Kartell anlässlich seines 50. Stiftungstages* (Leipzig: Hinrichs, 1930) 3-10.

Schroeder, O., "2. Jes 8[6b]; ומשוש eine Glosse zu רְצִון," *ZAW* 32 (1912) 301-2.

Simons, Jan Jozef, *Jerusalem in the Old Testament: Researches and Theories* (Studia Francisci Scholten memoriae dicata 1; Leiden: Brill, 1952).

Wolverton, W. I., "Judgment in Advent: Notes on Isaiah 8:5-15 and 7:14," *ATR* 37 (1955) 284-91.

8

11/ **For thus said Yahweh to me during a prophetic seizure,[a] turning me aside[b] from going in the way of this people, saying, 12/ "Do not call conspiracy everything[c] that this people calls conspiracy, and what it fears do not fear nor dread <what it dreads>.[d] 13/ Yahweh of Hosts— him you will sanctify; he will be what you fear, [e]and he will be what you dread.[e] 14/ And he will be[f] for a sanctuary, or for a stone to strike against, or for a rock to stumble over to the two[g] houses[h] of Israel,[i] for a trap and for a snare to the inhabitant/ruler of Jerusalem. 15/ And[j] many will stumble over them, and they will fall and be broken, and they will be snared[k] and captured."[l]**

Textual Notes

a It is hard to decide between MT's כְּחֶזְקַת הַיָּד (kĕḥezqat hayyād), lit., "as the hand seized (me)," and 1QIsaᵃ's כחזקת יד kĕḥezqat yād) without the article). The expression is a technical expression for the onset of prophetic inspiration as Tg. recognized, כְּמִתְקַף נְבוּאְתָא (kĕmitqap nĕbûʾĕtāʾ), "when the prophecy was strong." It is the hand of Yahweh that seizes the prophet. Cf. Ezek 1:3; 3:14, 22; 8:1; 33:22; 37:1; 1 Kgs 18:46; 2 Kgs 3:15; Jer 15:17 and my discussion of the background of these expressions in "The Hand of Yahweh," *VT* 21 (1971) 244–51.

b MT's וְיִסְּרֵנִי (wĕyissĕrēnî) is pointed in such a way as to suggest a choice of readings between וְיִסְּרֵנִי (wĕyissĕranî), "and he rebuked me," the *piel* perfect third person masculine singular with the first common singular suffix of יסר (yāsar), "to teach, rebuke," and וַיְסִרֵנִי (wayyĕsîrēnî), "and he turned me aside," the *hiphil* converted imperfect third person masculine singular with the first common singular suffix of סור (sûr), "to turn." Vg. and Tg. support the former reading, but Syr. supports the latter, and so does 1QIsaᵃ, which has יסירני (yĕsîrēnî), the *hiphil* imperfect of סור (sûr), though without the copula. The LXX has completely misunderstood the passage, τῇ ἰσχυρᾷ χειρὶ ἀπειθοῦσιν τῇ πορείᾳ τῆς ὁδοῦ τοῦ λαοῦ τούτου "with a strong hand they disobey in the course of the way of this people."

c For MT's לְכֹל אֲשֶׁר־יֹאמַר (lĕkōl ʾăšer-yōʾmar), "everything that this people calls," Syr.'s ܐܝܟ ܕܐܡܪ (ʾyk dʾmr) seems to read כאשר יאמר (kaʾăšer yōʾmar), "as this people says."

d LXX's haplography of וְהוּא מַעֲרִצְכֶם (wĕhûʾ maʿărîṣĕkem), "he will be your object of dread/what you dread," in v. 13 raises the question whether all the textual traditions except Tg. have

suffered a haplography of את מערצו (ʾet-maʿărîṣô), "his object of dread/what he dreads," in v. 12. Tg. retains an object in the line: wĕʿal tûqpêyh lāʾ têymĕrûn taqîp, "and concerning his strength you will not say, 'It is strong.'"

e LXX omits וְהוּא מַעֲרִצְכֶם (wĕhûʾ maʿărîṣĕkem), "he will be what you dread," by haplography. It is present in MT, 1QIsaᵃ, 4QIsaˡ, Vg., Tg., and Syr.

f MT's וְהָיָה (wĕhāyâ), "and he will be," is supported by 4QIsaˡ; 1QIsaᵃ has והיא corrected to והיה (wĕyihyê), "and he will be." Vg. adds "to you" (et erit vobis, "and he will be to you"). LXX has an interpretive expansion, καὶ ἐὰν ἐπ' αὐτῷ πεποιθὼς ᾖς ἔσται σοι εἰς ἁγίασμα καὶ οὐχ ὡς λίθου προσκόμματι συναντήσεσθε αὐτῷ οὐδὲ ὡς πέτρας πτώματι, "and if you trust upon him, he will be to you for a sanctuary, and you will not come upon him as a stumbling over a stone nor as a falling over a rock," and Tg. has a slightly different interpretive expansion.

g LXX omits לִשְׁנֵי (lišnê), "to both;" but MT is supported by 1QIsaᵃ, Vg., Syr., and Tg.

h LXX has the singular.

i Instead of MT's יִשְׂרָאֵל (yiśrāʾēl), "Israel," LXX has יעקב (yaʿăqōb), "Jacob."

j LXX adds διὰ τοῦτο, "because of this," at the beginning of the verse, but this appears to be an interpretive expansion.

k LXX appears to misread וְנוֹקְשׁוּ (wĕnôqĕšû), "and they will be snared," as ונגשו (wĕniggĕšû), "and they drew near" (καὶ ἐγγιοῦσιν).

l LXX ends the verse with another interpretive expansion, ἄνθρωποι ἐν ἀσφαλείᾳ ὄντες, "(and) men (will be caught) when (they thought) they were safe."

Commentary

It is very difficult to assign a precise date to this oracle, but its present literary placement and the mention of the two houses of Israel (8:14), if this refers to Israel and Judah, suggests a late stage in the Syro-Ephraimitic War,

when it was obvious to Isaiah that neither Israel or Judah would listen to his prophetic word. In this critical context, Yahweh, through prophetic inspiration, instructed Isaiah or turned him aside so that he would not behave in the same manner as "this people." The idiom translated by the RSV as "with his strong hand upon me" (כחזקת היד,

kĕḥezqat hayyād) is a technical expression for the onset of prophetic inspiration, and the word translated "warn" (וְיִסְּרֵנִי) contains a textual problem that could be resolved by a derivation from either a verb meaning "to rebuke" or, more probably, a verb meaning "to turn aside." Just who is designated by "this people" is ambiguous at first, and that ambiguity is not cleared up by the two following verses.

Yahweh's instruction to Isaiah in vv. 12-13 is intended for a larger audience than just the prophet, for he is addressed with the second person plural. Isaiah and this larger circle are not to shout, "Treason!" every time "this people" shout, "Treason!" Nor are they to fear what this people fear. Scholars have been puzzled by these references and have suggested all sorts of contradictory theories about who was crying out, what caused them to cry out, who was frightened, and what they were frightened about. Was it Judah, fearful of Israel and claiming that Israel had betrayed his own kin?[1] Was it Ahaz and the Davidic court, fearful of Israelite sympathizers among their own Judean subjects?[2] Was it Israel, fearing Assyrian expansion, who felt betrayed by Judah's refusal to join their defensive coalition against Assyria? All of these parties were in fact frightened, and in their fear a sense of having been betrayed was quite understandable. The present text does not offer enough concrete detail to decide among these various possibilities, and the various textual emendations that have been suggested to bring more clarity or consistency to the text do not carry conviction. Assuming that the mention of the two houses of Israel in v. 14 refers to both Judah and Israel, this inclusive definition of "this people" suggests that the present text may be equally inclusive of all these explanations for the charge of treason. That is, in a crisis situation characterized by fear on all sides, every party was castigating their opponents as traitors. Everyone was so mesmerized by their own particular fears for the future, fears that were in one sense quite reasonable, that no one was willing to look to God and so put those fears in perspective. They all acted as though God did not enter into the picture at all. Their religious traditions, including even

the particular divine promises made to Jerusalem and the Davidic dynasty, were simply forgotten in the face of this overpowering fear.

Unfortunately, such crippling fear is not just an ancient phenomenon. Even today one can observe how fear can blind one to well-known ethical and religious obligations. An obsessive concern with even legitimate fears can cause one to lose sight of God's demands in any sphere of life—politics, business, religion, or everyday relationships. Isaiah's solution to that threat is to sanctify God as the one whom one respects and fears above all else. If God is the ultimate object of one's fear, one can remain honest in politics and business, faithful in religion, and considerate and loving in everyday situations, even when those situations are fraught with real danger.

Indeed, in such situations, Isaiah says, God will become our sanctuary (8:14a). Many commentators emend away the word sanctuary in this verse[3] because it clashes so sharply with what is said of God in the rest of the verse, but there is no strong textual evidence for such a change, and one may explain the harsh juxtaposition as intentional. Ancient temples were places of asylum or safety, so to refer to God as a sanctuary is equivalent to calling him a place of refuge. The same could be said of the use of "rock" as a metaphor for God in Israel's traditional religious language. One spoke of God as a צוּר (*ṣûr*), "rock," of refuge or the like (Deut 32:2, 15, 18, 30, 31, 37; Isa 17:10; 30:29; Pss 18:3, 32, 47; 19:15; 27:5; 62:8; 89:27; see Gen 49:24 for a similar use of the synonym אֶבֶן, *'eben*, "stone"). One could also speak of Yahweh's protection of his servants so that they would not even stub their toe against a stone (פֶּן־תִּגֹּף בָּאֶבֶן רַגְלֶךָ, *pen-tiggōp bā'eben raglekā*, "lest you stub your foot against a stone," Ps 91:12). Isaiah abruptly reverses that traditional imagery here, however. Yahweh may become a sanctuary, but he may also become not a rock of refuge but a stone to stub the toe against and a rock to fall over, and many from both houses of Israel, including the inhabitants of Jerusalem, will fall over him and be broken, snared, and captured. Yahweh remains a rock, but what sort of rock depends on the human response to him. If one sanctifies him as one's

---

1   So L. G. Rignell, "Das Orakel '*Maher-salal Has-bas*,'" *ST* 10 (1956) 45; see my commentary on Isa 2:5-6.

2   This is apparently the view of Hayes and Irvine, 149. See also Wildberger, 337.

3   See Wildberger, 335, and the literature cited there.

ultimate fear, he can be the unshakable foundation for one's life, the rock of refuge that puts all other fears in perspective (Isa 28:16). If, however, one takes one's eye off of God by concentrating on other fears, he will not be one's refuge, but the stone over which one stumbles, the hidden factor that confounds all one's plans, the rejected stone that simply will not be ignored (Ps 118:22).

In the crisis of the Syro-Ephraimitic War, few were ultimately willing to fear God above all else and to seek their refuge in God's promises. Both Israel and Judah sought other pseudo sanctuaries, and as a result Isaiah threatened both with impending judgment. This per-spective seems later than that found in 8:1-4 and 8:16-18, where Isaiah still draws a sharp distinction between Israel and Judah. Once 8:11-15 is inserted between these oracles, however, its inclusive use of Israel forces one to reread 8:18 in much the same way. Its impact is similar to that of the other insertions and rearrangements discussed above. Thus, the secondary editing produces a picture of Isaiah disappointed with both Israel and Judah, who has temporarily withdrawn from further prophesying until his words are realized, and whose hope for the future is now focused on only a small remnant.

Bibliography

Arnold, Bill T., "The Love-Fear Antinomy in Deuteronomy 5–11," *VT* 61 (2011) 551–69.

Driver, G. R., "Two Misunderstood Passages of the Old Testament," *JTS* 6 (1955) 82–87.

Evans, Craig A., "An Interpretation of Isa 8:11-15 Unemended," *ZAW* 97 (1985) 112–13.

Ford, J. M., "Jewel of Discernment: A Study of Stone Symbolism," *BZ* 11 (1967) 109–16.

Häusserman, F., *Wortempfang und Symbol in der alt-testamentlichen Prophetie* (BZAW 58; Giessen: A. Töpelmann, 1932).

Kooij, Arie van der, "1QIsaᵃ Col. Viii, 4-11 (Isa 8:11-18): A Contextual Approach of Its Variants," *RevQ* 13 (1988) 569–81.

——, "Septuagint of Isaiah," 127–33.

Kratz, Reinhard G., "The Two Houses of Israel," in Iain Provan and Mark J. Boda, eds., *Let Us Go Up to Zion: Essays in Honour of H. G. M. Williamson on the Occasion of His Sixty-Fifth Birthday* (VTSup 153; Leiden: Brill, 2012) 167–80.

Lohfink, Norbert, "Isaias 8:12-14," *BZ* 7 (1963) 98–104.

Rignell, L. G., "Das Orakel '*Maher-salal Has-bas*,'" *ST* 10 (1956) 40–52.

Stählin, Gustav, *Skandalon: Untersuchung zur Geschichte eines biblischen Begriffs* (BFCT: 2nd Series, Sammlung wissenschaftlicher Monographien 24; Gütersloh: C. Bertelsmann, 1930).

Wolverton, W. I., "Judgment in Advent: Notes on Isaiah 8:5-15 and 7:14," *ATR* 37 (1955) 284–91.

8

16/ Bind up[a] the testimony, seal[a] the instructions with my disciples.[b] 17/ And[c] I will wait for Yahweh who is hiding his face[d] from the house of Jacob, and I will look to him. 18/ Here[e] am I and the children that Yahweh has given me as signs and portents in/against Israel from Yahweh of Hosts who dwells in Mount Zion.

Textual Notes

a Syr. reads both imperatives as plural, but MT is supported by 1QIsa[a], Vg., and Tg. Wildberger suggests reading both forms as infinitive absolutes in order to make an easier transition to the first person verb form in v. 17: "I will bind up the testimony and seal the instructions with my disciples, then I will wait."

b LXX has a peculiar interpretive translation of the verse, τότε φανεροὶ ἔσονται οἱ σφραγιζόμενοι τὸν νόμον τοῦ μὴ μαθεῖν, "then those who are sealed so as not to learn the law will be manifest."

c LXX adds ואמר (wĕʾāmar, καὶ ἐρεῖ), "and one will say."

d 1QIsa[a] inserts the direct object marker as a supralinear correction above פָּנָיו (pānāyw), "his face."

e 1QIsa[a] has אנה for MT's הִנֵּה (hinnê), "behold."

Commentary

If the Immanuel material in 8:5-10 originally preceded the Maher-shalal-hush-baz material in 8:1-4, 8:16-18 must have been the original continuation of 8:1-4. Both 8:5-10 and 8:11-15 represent secondary insertions in the context. The testimony mentioned in 8:16 probably refers back to the witnesses mentioned in v. 2, and the binding and sealing probably referred originally to the document mentioned in 8:1. Having given the last of his prophecies connected with his children's names, and having protected himself by the use of impartial witnesses from the charge of later fudging of the prophecies, Isaiah prepared to wait out the fulfillment of his prophetic word. He and his children would stand as signs and portents to Israel. The contrast between the house of Jacob, from whom Yahweh was hiding his face, and Yahweh, who dwells on Mount Zion, suggests again that the oracles connected to the names of Isaiah's children were primarily aimed against the north and offered a word of hope to the south.

The Secondary Editing

This pro-Judean and anti-Israel interpretation of the preceding oracles (7:1-9, 10-17; 8:1-4, 5-10, 16-18), however, is an interpretation of these oracles as they would have been heard in their original historical setting. They now stand in a literary setting where the originally positive import of these words for Judah has been considerably dampened. As noted in the earlier discussion, scholars normally consider the final words of 7:17—"the king of Assyria"—a gloss, but once that gloss has entered the text, the promise to Judah found in v. 17 begins to sound as much like a threat as like a promise. The expansion of 7:10-17 by the collection of related sayings in 7:18-25, the placement of 8:5-10 after 8:1-4, and the insertion of 8:11-15 produce a similar effect. All these editorial moves tend to make the judgment threatened against Israel a threat against Jerusalem and Judah as well. This negative editing of his earlier oracles by rearrangement should probably be attributed, at least in part, to Isaiah himself. Just as he extended an early oracle against the north in 28:1-6 to include Judah in the judgment (28:7-15), so by the rearrangement of these oracles Isaiah brings Judah at least partially under the earlier judgment announced against Israel.

Bibliography

Boehmer, J., "'Jahwes Lehrlinge' im Buch Jesaja," *AR* 33 (1936) 171–75.

Driver, G. R., "Hebrew Notes on Prophets and Proverbs," *JTS* 41 (1940) 162–75.

———, "Isaianic Problems," in G. Wiesner, ed., *Festschrift für Wilhelm Eilers* (Wiesbaden: Harrassowitz, 1967) 43–57.

Ginsberg, H. L., "An Unrecognized Allusion to Kings Pekah and Hoshea of Israel," *ErIsr* 5 (1958) 61*–65*.

Gozzo, S., "Isaia profeta e i suoi figli 'segni e presagi in Israele,'" *Anton* 31 (1956) 215–46, 355–82.

Guillaume, A., "Paronomasia in the Old Testament," *JSS* 9 (1964) 282–90.

Oudenrijn, F. M. Avanden, "L'expression 'fils des prophètes' et ses analogies," *Bib* 6 (1925) 165–71.

Rost, L., "Gruppenbildungen im Alten Testament," *TLZ* 80 (1955) 1–8.

Skehan, Patrick W., "Some Textual Problems in Isaia," *CBQ* 22 (1960) 47–55.

Thompson, J. A., "A Proposed Translation of Isaiah 8:17," *ExpTim* 83 (1971–72) 376.

Whitley, C. F., "The Language and Exegesis of Isaiah 8:16-23," *ZAW* 90 (1978) 28–43.

Wong, Gordon C. I., "Faith in the Present Form of Isaiah vii 1-17," *VT* 51 (2001) 535–47.

8

These very difficult verses are often treated as isolated fragments.[1] One cannot rule out that possibility, but vv. 19-20 clearly represent an oracle directed against the practice of necromancy, and vv. 21-23a may be interpreted as the continuation of that oracle. Verse 20b announces a judgment on those who promote necromancy, and vv. 21-23a elaborate on that judgment. The oracle is placed here probably due to the catchword principle. Isaiah or a later editor apparently saw the appeal to necromancy as an alternative to seeking "instruction" (תּוֹרָה *tôrâ*) and "testimony" (תְּעוּדָה *tĕʿûdâ*) from the prophetic word, perhaps because that prophetic word was now sealed (8:16).

19/ **Now should they say**[a] **to you,**[b] **"Consult the ghosts**[c] **and the familiar spirits**[d] **who chirp and moan. Should not a people consult**[e] **its gods,**[f] **the dead**[g] **on behalf of the living**[h] **20/ for instruction and testimony?"**[i] **Surely those who speak**[j] **according to this word will be the people**[k] **for whom there is no dawn! 21/ He**[l] **will pass through it**[m] **dejected**[n] **and hungry, and it will be that when**[o] **he becomes hungry and falls into a rage,**[p] **then he will curse his king and his God.**[q] **He will turn his face upward 22/ and look to the ground,**[r] **and behold there will be affliction and darkness,**[s] **without daybreak,**[t] **distress and gloom without dawn.**[u] **23/ Surely**[v] **it will be without daybreak**[w] **to the one distressed by it.**[x]

Textual Notes

a   1QIsaᵃ has the orthographic variant יואמרו for MT יֹאמְרוּ (*yōʾmĕrû*), "should they say."

b   1QIsaᵃ has the orthographic variant אליכמה for MT אֲלֵיכֶם (*ʾălêkem*), "to you."

c   For MT הָאֹבוֹת (*hāʾōbôt*), "the ghosts," 1QIsaᵃ has the orthographic variant האבות.

d   For MT הַיִּדְּעֹנִים (*hayyiddĕʿōnîm*), "the familiar spirits," 1QIsaᵃ has the orthographic variant הידעונים.

e   1QIsaᵃ has the orthographic variant ידרוש for MT יִדְרֹשׁ (*yidrōš*), "let him consult."

f   For MT אֱלֹהָיו (*ʾĕlōhāyw*), "its gods," 1QIsaᵃ appears to read the singular, אלוהו (*ʾĕlôhô*), "its God" (cf. Hab 1:11), which is also found in LXX and Vg.

g   For MT הַמֵּתִים (*hammētîm*), "the dead," 1QIsaᵃ has the orthographic variant המיתים.

h   MT's הַחַיִּים (*haḥayyîm*), "the living," has the article, 1QIsaᵃ omits it (חיים).

i   One should construe לְתוֹרָה וְלִתְעוּדָה (*lĕtôrâ wĕlitʿûdâ*), "for instruction and for testimony," as the conclusion of v. 19 and as the concluding words of those who recommend necromancy as a good source of oracular knowledge. MT and the versions misconstrue the phrase as the beginning of a new statement, which would require a positive translation such as "To the law and to the testimony!" and would imply a shift of speakers. The following censure of the preceding quotation, however, leaves no room for either a change of speakers or for a positive interpretation of this phrase. To maintain it, the versions have to resort to a torturous translation of either the preceding or following statements or both, so LXX: οὐκ ἔθνος πρὸς θεὸν αὐτοῦ; τί ἐκζητοῦσιν περὶ τῶν ζώντων τοὺς νεκρούς; νόμον γὰρ εἰς βοήθειαν ἔδωκεν, ἵνα εἴπωσιν οὐχ ὡς τὸ ῥῆμα τοῦτο, περὶ οὗ οὐκ ἔστιν δῶρα δοῦναι περὶ αὐτοῦ; "should not a nation be with its God? Why do they consult the dead concerning the living? For he has given a law as a help so that they may not speak a word such as this one, concerning which there are no gifts to give." The Vg. is not much better: *ad legem magis et ad testimonium quod si non dixerint iuxta verbum hoc non erit eis matutina lux*, "Rather to the law and to the testimony, for if they do not speak according to this word, there will be no morning light to them." Neither version renders the oath formula correctly. The mistake is due to the very common use of the Hebrew terms תּוֹרָה (*tôrâ*), "instruction," and תְּעוּדָה (*tĕʿûdâ*), "testimony," to refer positively to an oracle from the true God.

j   For MT's אִם־לֹא יֹאמְרוּ (*ʾim-lōʾ yōʾmĕrû*), "surely those who speak," 1QIsaᵃ has the orthographic variants אם לוא יואמרו.

k   There is a shift from the preceding plural here to the singular. Since the last singular antecedent was the masculine singular noun עַם (*ʿam*), "people," in v. 19, that is probably the implied

---

1   So Wildberger, 343, 356, and literature cited there.

subject here, and in the following verses. This is a judgment not on isolated individuals but on a people that turns from its God to seek direction from the underworld powers.

l   "He," that is, "the people" ("people" is often construed with a singular verb in Hebrew).

m   The feminine singular antecedent of בָּהּ (bāh), "through it," is not expressed, but since there is no dawn for this people, one may probably assume that the understood antecedent is חשכה (ḥăšēkâ), "darkness," or one of its feminine singular synonyms mentioned in v. 22. BHS suggests inserting בארץ (bāʾāreṣ), "through the land," but apart from a very periphrastic Tg., there is no textual support for this emendation, and it does not give a superior meaning.

n   MT's reading נִקְשֶׁה (niqšê), "dejected, hard pressed," supported by Vg., is preferable to 1QIsaᵃ's נקשה, supported by Syr.

o   For כִּי (kî), "because," 1QIsaᵃ has the orthographic variant כיא.

p   For MT וְהִתְקַצַּף (wĕhitqaṣṣap), "and falls into a rage," 1QIsaᵃ has יתקצף (yitqaṣṣēp, "he will fall into a rage").

q   For MT אֱלֹהָיו (ʾĕlōhāyw), "his gods," 1QIsaᵃ appears to read the singular אלוהו, (ʾĕlōhô), "his God."

r   1QIsaᵃ has the article הארץ; MT אֶרֶץ (ʾereṣ), "the ground," does not.

s   For MT וַחֲשֵׁכָה (waḥăšēkâ), "darkness," 1QIsaᵃ has חשוכה.

t   Reading מֵעִיף (mēʿîp) with 1QIsaᵃ against MT's מְעוּף (mēʿûp), and analyzing it as the privative מִן plus the noun עיף, "brightness, glimmer, light." For this noun and its verbal root, see H. L. Ginsberg, "An Unrecognized Allusion to Kings Pekah and Hoshea of Israel," ErIsr 5 (1958) *63–*64.

u   Reading מִנֹּגַהּ (minnōgah), "without dawn, light," for MT's מְנֻדָּח (mĕnuddāḥ), "scattered, driven." LXX's ὥστε μὴ βλέπειν, "so that they cannot see," is little help in establishing the original text, since it seems to be a loose translation for sense.

v   Reading כי לו (kî lû, "for surely") with 1QIsaᵃ instead of MT's כִּי לֹא (kî lōʾ), "for not."

w   Reading מֵעִיף (mēʿîp) again for MT's מוּעָף (mûʿāp) and 1QIsaᵃ's מעופף (mᶜwpp).

x   The feminine singular antecedent for לָהּ (lāh), "by it," is either צוּקָה (ṣûqâ, "distress") or one of its feminine singular synonyms in v. 22.

Commentary

Verse 19 suggests that some unnamed persons may say to Isaiah's audience, referred to by the second person plural suffix and the plural imperative, "consult the ghosts and familiar spirits." The precise meaning of אוֹב (ʾôb) and יִדְּעֹנִי (yiddĕʿōnî) is disputed, but the former appears to refer to the ghost of a dead person and the latter either to the knowing ghost or to a practitioner of necromancy skilled in the art of calling up the ghosts of the dead.[2] For a detailed literary account of such necromancy, see 1 Sam 28:3-25. The reference to chirping and moaning appears to be Isaiah's snide characterization of the sound of the ghost and its handler inserted into the recommendation of the proponents of necromancy. A similar characterization of the sound of the dead is found in Isa 29:4. Apparently the practitioners of necromancy were accustomed to moan and chirp like birds (cf. Isa 10:14) in their séances. The conclusion of v. 19 is a continuation of the recommendation of these proponents of necromancy. By itself the phrase אֶל־אֱלֹהָיו יִדְרֹשׁ (ʾel ʾĕlōhāyw yidrōš) could either mean, "consult its God [Yahweh]," or "consult its gods [the ghosts of the dead]," but the continuation

with אֶל־הַמֵּתִים (ʾel-hammētîm), "the dead," makes it clear that אֱלֹהִים (ʾĕlōhîm), "gods," here refers to the ghosts of the dead just as it refers to the ghost of the dead Samuel in 1 Sam 28:13. According to the proponents of necromancy, it is only appropriate that a people should consult its dead for the sake of the living. Why it is assumed that the dead have special knowledge about the future not available to the living is not at all clear. The first phrase of v. 20 should actually be taken as the concluding words of the sentence in v. 19 uttered by Isaiah's opponents. According to them, if you want "instruction" and "testimony," forget the prophet, consult the ghosts of the dead instead. Thus, necromancy is recommended as a rival to prophecy for the knowledge one needs to live.

Isaiah, however, swears a somewhat elliptical oath that those who recommend necromancy in this fashion, and by implication those who accept their recommendation, will become like a people for whom there is no dawn, that is, like a people that has no future (v. 20b). Such a people will pass through it—the feminine singular antecedent of "it" is unexpressed, but presumably it refers to the darkness (no dawn) mentioned with several feminine singular synonymns in v. 22—dejected and hungry. The

---

2   See my "Necromancy," in Joel B. Green, Jacqueline E. Lapsley, Rebekah Miles, and Allen Verhey, eds., *Dictionary of Scripture and Ethics* (Grand Rapids: Baker Academic, 2011) 545–46, and the literature cited there.

"instruction and testimony" of the dead will prove useless advice in dealing with the affliction, darkness, distress, and gloom that befall such a people, and eventually in his hopeless hunger and anger, such a people will curse both his king and his God. There will be no help from political leaders or from God. Whether such a people looks to heaven or to the underworld, there will be only affliction and darkness without any hope of daybreak or a light at the end of the tunnel. The implication seems to be that such a people will be consigned to the same unbroken gloom of death as the useless ghosts whom he called up for advice.

Bibliography

Carroll, R. P., "Translation and Attribution in Isaiah 8.19f.," *BT* 31 (1980) 126–34.
Dietrich, M., O. Loretz, and J. Sanmartin, "Ugaritisch *Ilib* und hebräisch ʾ(W)B 'Totengeist,'" *UF* 6 (1974) 450–51.
Driver, "Prophets and Proverbs," 162–75.
Hoffner, H. A., Jr., "Second Millennium Antecedents to the Hebrew ʾŌ*B*," *JBL* 86 (1967) 385–401.
Jepsen, K., "Call and Frustration: A New Understanding of Isaiah VIII 21-22," *VT* 32 (1982) 145–57.
Jirku, A., *Die Dämonen und ihre Abwehr im Alten Testament* (Leipzig: A. Deichert, 1912).
Lindblom, *Immanuel Section*.
Müller, H. P., "Das Wort von den Totengeistern, Jes 8,19f.," *WO* 8 (1975) 65–76.
Schmidt, H., "Swb," in *Vom Alten Testament: Karl Marti zum siebzigsten Geburtstage gewidmet von Freunden, Fachgenossen und Schülern in ihrem Namen* (Giessen: A. Töpelman, 1925) 253–61.
Schmidtke, F., "Träume, Orakel und Totengeister als Künder der Zukunft in Israel und Babylonien," *BZ* n.F. 11 (1967) 240–46.
Schwarz, G., "Zugunsten der Lebenden an die Toten,'" *ZAW* 86 (1974) 218–20.
Skehan, "Textual Problems," 47–55.
Trencsényi-Waldapfel, I., "Die Hexe von Endore und die griechisch-römische Welt," *AcOr* 12 (1961) 201–22.
Vattioni, F., "La necromanzia nell' Antico Testamento," *Aug* 3 (1963) 461–81.
Vieyra, M., "Les noms du 'mundus' en Hittite et en Assyrien et la pythonisse d'Endor," *RHA* 19 (1961) 47–55.
Whitley, C. F., "The Language and Exegesis of Isaiah 8:16-23," *ZAW* 90 (1978) 28–43.
Wohlstein, H., "Zu den israelitischen Vorstellungen von Toten- und Ahnengeistern," *BZ* n.F. 5 (1961) 30–38.
Wohlstein, H., "Zu einigen altisraelitischen Volksvorstellungen von Toten- und Ahnengeistern in biblischer Überlieferung," *ZRGG* 19 (1967) 348–55.
Woude, A. S. van der, "Jesaja 8,19-23a als literarische Einheit," in J. van Ruiten and M. Vervenne, eds., *Studies in the Book of Isaiah: Festschrift Willem A. M. Beuken* (BETL 132; Leuven: Leuven University Press, 1997) 129–36.

8/9

8:23b/ **As at the former**[a] **time**[b] **he treated with contempt**[c]
     <The Sharon and the land of Gilead,>[d]
     The land[e] **of Zebulon and the land**[f] **of Naphtali,**
     So at the latter time he has honored[g] **the way of the sea,**
     Trans-Jordan, Galilee of the nations.[h]

9:1/ **The people who were walking in darkness**
     Have seen[i] **a great light;**
     Those who were dwelling in a land of gloom,[j]
     On them[k] **a light has shone.**

2/ **You have multiplied**[l] **the joy,**[m]
     You have made great[n] **the rejoicing;**
     They rejoice before you as with the rejoicing of the harvest,
     Like the joy they have when they divide the spoil.

3/ **For the yoke**[o] **of his burden**[p]
     And the bar[q] **across his shoulder,**
     The staff of his oppressor[r]
     You[s] **have smashed as on the day of Midian.**[t]

4/ **For every**[u] **sandal that tramped along**[v] **raising a din,**
     And the garment splattered with blood[w]
     Shall be for burning, as food for the fire.

5/ **For a child has been born**[x] **to us,**
     A son has been given to us,
     And the rule[y] **has fallen**[z] **upon his shoulder,**
     And one has named[*a] **his name:**
     Wonderful counselor, Mighty god,
     Father of eternity, Prince of peace,[*b]

6/ **. . . Great**[*c] **will be (his)**[*d] **rule**[*e]
     And to peace[*d] **there will be no end,**
     On the throne[*f] **of David,**[*g]
     And over his kingdom,
     To establish it,[*h]
     And to maintain it,[*h]
     With justice and righteousness
     From now and unto eternity.
     The zeal of Yahweh of Hosts shall accomplish this.[*i]

Textual Notes

a   For MT's הָרִאשׁוֹן (hārī'šôn), "former," 1QIsa[a] has the merely orthographic variant הרישון.

b   MT's construal of כָּעֵת (kā'ēt), "as at the (former) time," with the following is supported by 1QIsa[a] and Vg.; LXX and Syr. misconstrue it with the preceding line.

c   MT's הֵקַל (hēqal), "he treated with contempt," is supported by 1QIsa[a]'s הקל, but Vg. translates as a passive, *adleviata est*, "was treated lightly (that is, with contempt)." LXX (ταχὺ ποίει) and Syr. (ܣܪܗܒܐ, *srhbt*) understand the verb as an imperative, "do swiftly"; Tg.'s גְּלוֹ (gĕlô), "(the people of the land) went into exile" is interpretive. The subject of the verb is disputed. Albrecht Alt restored יהוה, "Yahweh," as the subject.[1] Wildberger (pp. 363–

64) understands the subject as the masculine singular noun עֵת ('ēt), "time,"—"as the earlier time brought into contempt . . . so the future (time) brings to honor." I think it is more likely that the implied subject is God, unexpressed at first in order to heighten the initial suspense of the oracle. Even Wildberger admits that the "theological" subject of the sentence is Yahweh.

d   Alt brilliantly recognized that something was missing in the text here, since "the land of Zebulon and the land of Naphtali" is echoed by the following "Galilee of the nations," but neither "the way of the sea" nor "Trans-Jordan" is paralleled in the first part of the verse. Based on his metrical analysis following his restoration of "Yahweh" as the subject of the first line, Alt restored עֵמֶק הַשָּׁרוֹן וְהַר גִּלְעָד ('ēmeq haššārôn wĕhar gil'ād), "the valley of Sharon / and Mount Gilead."[2] Despite the brilliance of

1   Albrecht Alt, "Jesaja 8,23–9,6: Befreiungsnacht und Krönungstag," in *Kleine Schriften zur Geschichte des Volkes Israel*, vol. 2 (3rd ed.; Munich: C. H. Beck, 1964) 211; originally published in Walter Baumgart-ner, ed., *Festschrift Alfred Bertholet zum 80. Geburtstag gewidmet von Kollegen und Freunden* (Tübingen: J. C. B. Mohr, 1950) 29–49.

2   Ibid., 211.

his insight, however, there are problems with this restoration. Metrics is a weak reed on which to base an emendation, and while *šārôn* occurs seven times in the OT, all but once with the article (Josh 12:18; Isa 33:9; 35:2; 65:10; Song 2:1; 1 Chr 5:16; 27:29), the expression *ʿēmeq haššārôn*, "the valley of Sharon," is not attested. Moreover, based on Alt's restoration it is hard to see what would trigger such a major haplography. Any restoration is problematic, given the lack of evidence, but my restoration הַשָּׁרוֹן וְאֶרֶץ הַגִּלְעָד (*haššārôn wěʾereṣ haggilʿād*), "the Sharon and the land of Gilead," stays with attested expressions (for "the land of Gilead," see Num 32:1, 29; Josh 17:5, 6; 22:9, 13, 15, 32; Judg 10:4; 20:1; 2 Sam 17:26; 1 Kgs 4:19; 2 Kgs 10:33; Zech 10:10; 1 Chr 2:22; 5:9), and the repetition of ʾrṣh could have led an early scribe's eye to jump to the second ʾrṣh, "the land (of Zebulon)," thus helping to explain the haplography.

e For MT's אַרְצָה (*ʾarṣāh*), "the land," 1QIsaᵃ has ארץ. The MT form here and in the following note may preserve an archaic accusative ending,[3] or perhaps simply an otiose *heh*-directive. In any case, it is doubtful that it preserves any discernible syntactical significance.

f For MT's וְאַרְצָה (*wěʾarṣāh*), "and the land," 1QIsaᵃ has וארץ.

g 1QIsaᵃ and Vg. support MT's וְהָאַחֲרוֹן הִכְבִּיד (*wěhāʾaḥărôn hikbîd*), "so in the latter he has honored," though Vg. again translates the verb as a passive, *adgravata est*, "was treated with weight [that is, with honor]." LXX appears to omit the phrase, though after דֶּרֶךְ הַיָּם (*derek hayyām*), "the way of the sea," it has a line that may represent a translation of this phrase and an alternate translation of דֶּרֶךְ הַיָּם (*derek hayyām*), "the way of the sea": καὶ οἱ λοιποὶ οἱ τὴν παραλίαν κατοικοῦντες, "and the remnant of those dwelling by the seashore"; cf. Tg., which renders וְהָאַחֲרוֹן as "their remnant" (ושאהרון); Syr. renders as ܐܚܝܢܐ ܥܫܢܐ (*w'ḥdn' ʿšn*), "a strong possession"; cf. Tg.'s "their remnant a strong king [מלך תקיף] will take into exile [יגלי] because they did not remember the strength of the sea."

h For MT's הַגּוֹיִם (*haggôyim*), "of the nations," 1QIsaᵃ has the orthographic variant הגואים; LXX adds an additional phrase at the end of the verse τὰ μέρη τῆς Ιουδαίας, "the regions of Judah."

i MT's רָאוּ (*rāʾû*), "they have seen," is supported by 1QIsaᵃ, Vg., Syr., and Tg.; LXX reads the verb as a plural imperative ἴδετε, "see!"

j For MT's בְּאֶרֶץ צַלְמָוֶת (*běʾereṣ ṣalmāwet*), "in a land of gloom," supported by 1QIsaᵃ, Vg., Syr., and Tg., LXX, ἐν χώρᾳ καὶ σκιᾷ θανάτου, "in the land and shadow of death," appears to read בארץ וצלמות (*běʾereṣ wěṣalmāwet*). The vocalization צַלְמָוֶת (*ṣalmāwet*) may be a secondary vocalization based on folk etymology, "the shadow of death," for an original צַלְמוּת (*ṣalmût*), "gloom."[4]

k For MT's עֲלֵיהֶם (*ʿălêhem*), "upon them," supported by 1QIsaᵃ,

Vg., Syr., Tg., LXX reads the second person plural suffix עליכם (ἐφ' ὑμᾶς, "upon you").

l For MT's הִרְבִּיתָ (*hirbîtā*), "you made great," 1QIsaᵃ has the orthographic variant הרביתה; LXX appears to read the construct nominalized adjective רַבַּת (τὸ πλεῖστον τοῦ λαοῦ, "most of the people").

m Reading הַגִּילָה (*haggîlâ*), "the joy," based on the parallelism in the verse between the verbs שָׂמַח (*śāmaḥ*), "to rejoice," and גִּיל (*gîl*), "to exult, have joy," and their cognate nouns שִׂמְחָה (*śimḥâ*), "rejoicing," and גִּילָה (*gîlâ*), "joy." What is written (the *kĕtîb*) in the MT, supported by 1QIsaᵃ, is הִרְבִּיתָ הַגּוֹי לֹא הִגְדַּלְתָּ הַשִּׂמְחָה (*hirbîtā haggôy lōʾ higdaltā haśśimḥâ*), "You multiplied the nation; you did not make great the rejoicing." Vg. translates this text quite literally, and the old KJV followed suit, but it is obvious from this rendering that there is a problem with the text. The parallelism is strangely contradictory, and construing the negative לֹא with the following as required by grammar results in two very unequal parallel lines. The ancients knew something was wrong with the text, and to fix it they read (MT's *qĕrē*) לוֹ (*lô*, "for him") instead of the negative לֹא. This permitted the translation, "You multiplied the nation for him you increased the joy," though the ambiguous לוֹ still seems best construed with the following, thus leaving the parallel lines unbalanced. This is presumably the reading behind Tg.'s, "You have increased the people, the house of Israel; for them you have increased the joy," and Syr.'s, "You have increased the people and for him you have increased the joy." Better to assume the relatively easy corruption of הגילה > הגי לה > הגי לו > הגי לא >, and read הִרְבִּיתָ הַגִּילָה (*hirbîtā haggîlâ*), "you multiplied the joy," which restores balanced parallelism and the clear play on the two synonymous verbs and their cognate nouns.

n 1QIsaᵃ has the orthographic variant הגדלתה for MT's הִגְדַּלְתָּ (*higdaltā*), "you made great." LXX misunderstands the whole line as ὃ κατήγαγες ἐν εὐφροσύνῃ σου, "whom you brought back in your joy."

o For MT עֹל (*ʿōl*), "yoke," 1QIsaᵃ has עול; LXX adds the verb ἀφῄρηται, "is taken away"; cf. Tg. אַעֲדִיתָא (*ʾaʿdîtāʾ*), "you removed."

p For MT סֻבֳּלוֹ (*subbŏlô*), "his burden," 1QIsaᵃ has סבלו; LXX paraphrases ὁ ἐπ' αὐτῶν κείμενος, "which lies upon them."

q Reading מֹטַת (*môṭat*), the construct of מֹטָה (*môṭâ*), "carry pole, cross bar of the yoke," by conjecture. MT, supported by 1QIsaᵃ, LXX, Vg., and Syr., has מַטֵּה (*maṭṭēh*), the construct of מַטֶּה (*maṭṭê*), "stick, staff." The traditional reading מַטֶּה (*maṭṭê*), "stick," provides a good parallel to the following שֵׁבֶט (*šēbet*), "staff, scepter," which might explain the reading, but the expression "the stick of his shoulder" is an odd expression for a stick an oppressor uses to beat on the shoulder of his servant. The expression "the cross bar of his shoulder" presents no dif-

---

3 E. Kautzsch and A. E. Cowley, eds., *Gesenius' Hebrew Grammar* (2nd ed.; Oxford: Clarendon Press, 1910; repr., 1988) 250, §90f.

4 See H. Niehr, "צַלְמָוֶת *ṣalmāwet*," *TDOT* 12:391–99;

and W. Gesenius, *Hebräisches und aramäisches Handwörterbuch über das Alte Testament* (18th ed.; Berlin: Springer, 2013) 1120a.

ficulties since the cross bar of the yoke rested on the shoulder of the yoked animal.

r   For MT הַנֹּגֵשׂ (hannōgēs), "of his oppressor," 1QIsaᵃ has הנוגש.

s   MT has הַחִתֹּתָ (haḥittōtā), "you smashed," which seems to be supported by the Vg. and Syr.; 1QIsaᵃ adds the copulative והחתת, "and you smashed"; 4QIsaᶜ appears to read the first person [הח]תותי, "and I smashed"; and LXX switches to the third person and inserts a subject, διεσκέδασεν κύριος "the Lord broke."

t   MT has מִדְיָן (midyān), "Midian," and is followed by Vg., Syr., and Tg.; 1QIsaᵃ has מדים (mdym) and is followed by LXX's Μαδιαμ (Madiam).

u   For MT כָּל (kol), "every," 1QIsaᵃ has the orthographic variant כול.

v   The ancient translations did not understand סְאוֹן סֹאֵן (sěʾôn sōʾēn), "sandal that tramped": LXX has "every garment acquired by deceit"; Vg. "every violent depredation with tumult"; Syr. "every sound heard in quaking"; Tg. "all their taking and bringing home in wickedness." The noun סְאוֹן (sěʾôn), "sandal," is a loanword from Assyrian šēnu, "sandal," like Syriac sěʾûnāʾ, "sandal, shoe," and the participle סֹאֵן (sōʾēn) is from a denominative verb, "to tramp," like Assyrian šēnu, "to put on shoes," and Syriac seʾn, "to put on sandals, shoes." Official Aramaic has the noun as šʾn, "shoe, sandal," which, if a loanword, must come from Babylonian rather than Assyrian. Assyrian mešēnu, "shoe," passes into Official Aramaic as msn, into Hatra as mšn, into Palestinian Aramaic as מסן (msn), "shoe," into Syriac as měsanāʾ, "shoe, sandal."

w   LXX misunderstands מְגוֹלָלָה בְדָמִים (měgôlālâ bědāmîm), "splattered with blood," because of the late use of דָּמִים (dāmîm) in the sense of "price, payment." LXX gives the odd rendering ὅτι πᾶσαν στολὴν ἐπισυνηγμένην δόλῳ καὶ ἱμάτιον μετὰ καταλλαγῆς ἀποτείσουσιν καὶ θελήσουσιν εἰ ἐγενήθησαν πυρίκαυστοι, "because every cloak and garment acquired by deceit they will repay by reconciliation, and they will be willing to do so even if they were burned by fire."

x   For MT יֻלַּד (yullad), 1QIsaᵃ has the variant orthography יולד.

y   MT has הַמִּשְׂרָה (hammiśrâ), "the rule," but 1QIsaᵃ has המשורה.

z   For MT וַתֵּהִי (wattēhî), "has fallen, has come," 1QIsaᵃ has ותהי.

*a   MT and 4QIsaᶜ have וַיִּקְרָא (wayyiqrāʾ), "one has named," but 1QIsaᵃ has וקרא (wěqārāʾ), "and one will name."

*b   MT has שַׂר־שָׁלוֹם (śar-šālôm), "prince of peace," while 1QIsaᵃ has the definite article שר השלום (śar haššālôm), but the definite article here probably only indicates a generalized abstraction, so there is no essential difference in meaning from MT.

*c   MT's kětîb has לְסַרְבֵּה (lěmarbê) with an odd internal final mem that suggests the manuscript tradition divided the letters into two words, לם רבה (lm rbh), though their pointing suggests the qěrēʾ reading לְמַרְבֵּה (lěmarbēh), "to the increase." If the kětîb is the older reading, as I believe, the initial לם is either a dittography of the final letters of the preceding word written defectively (<šā>lōm), or, in my opinion more likely, the remnant of an expanded fifth name that has been mostly lost or deleted, and the remaining word should be read as רַבָּה (rabbâ) "will be great." 1QIsaᵃ has the qěrēʾ, למרבה (lěmarbēh), and this reading is supported by Syr. However, LXX and perhaps Vg. support the kětîb.

*d   LXX and Syr. have the third person masculine singular suffix after both "rule" and "peace," while Vg. has it after "rule," but this is translational, not evidence of a variant text.

*e   For MT's הַמִּשְׂרָה (hammiśrâ), "the rule," 1QIsaᵃ has the corrected form המשׂרה.

*f   For MT's כִּסֵּא (kissēʾ), "throne," 1QIsaᵃ has the orthographic variant כסה (kissê), "throne"; and 4QIsaᶜ has כסיא (kissê).

*g   For MT דָּוִד (dāwīd), "David," 1QIsaᵃ has the orthographic variant דויד (dāwîd).

*h   For MT's feminine suffixes אֹתָהּ וּלְסַעֲדָהּ (ʾōtāh ûlěsaʿădāh), "(to establish) it and to maintain it," that refer back to the feminine noun מַמְלַכְתּוֹ (mamlaktô), "his kingdom," as their antecedent, 1QIsaᵃ has the masculine suffixes אותו ולסעדו (ʾôtô ûlěsaʿădô), "(to establish) it and to maintain it," which would appear to refer back to the masculine noun כִּסֵּא (kissēʾ), "throne." LXX supports MT, but the original reading may very well have been a combination of the two variants—אֹתוֹ וּלְסַעֲדָהּ (ʾōtô ûlěsaʿădāh), "(to establish) it [the throne], and to sustain it [the kingdom]." That is, the initial masculine suffix on the direct object marker referred back to the masculine noun כִּסֵּא (kissēʾ), "throne," and the feminine suffix on the following infinitive referred back to the parallel feminine noun מַמְלֵכָה (mamlěkâ), "the kingdom." Isaiah is known to use such precise shifts in gender or number when referring back to nouns in parallelism, as the example of Isa 1:6 demonstrates. The misunderstanding resulting in the uniform reading either of MT or of 1QIsaᵃ was due to the ambiguity of ה as vowel letter or mater in the preexilic script. It could stand for either â or ô. MT's textual tradition read it consistently one way; 1QIsaᵃ's tradition read it consistently the other way. Both oversimplified the originally more complex poetry.

*i   For MT זֹאת (zōʾt), "this," 1QIsaᵃ has the orthographic variant זאות.

Commentary

Isaiah 8:23b—9:6 celebrates the rise of a new Davidic king as promising salvation not only to his Judean subjects but to the Israelite inhabitants of the former northern territories as well. Numerous scholars have interpreted this text as a postexilic "messianic" prophecy (so Marti, 94–95; Kaiser, *Isaiah 1–12*, 205–18; less clear are Gray, 168; Duhm, 68), but the text contains no hint that it is concerned with the restoration of a presently defunct Davidic monarchy, and the specific details of geography, royal names, and expected imperial power are far more easily explained in the context of the preexilic period. The passage is best explained as an oracle composed by Isaiah for the coronation ceremony of Hezekiah. It may have been reread to refer to Josiah in the Josianic era, but nothing in the oracle points to the time of Josiah as its original date of composition. It could hardly refer to Ahaz's coronation, since it presupposes events that took place after his accession.

The territories listed in 8:23b correspond to the Israelite territories devastated during the Syro-Ephraimitic War (735–732 BCE) and annexed as Assyrian provinces by the Assyrian king Tiglath-pileser III at the conclusion of that war (732 BCE).[5] "The way of the sea" is not identical to the much later Via Maris of the Christian era, but refers to the coastal area south of Mount Carmel that became the Assyrian province of Dūʾru (biblical Dōʾr/Dôr—Josh 11:2; 12:23; 17:11; Judg 1:27; 1 Kgs 4:11; 1 Chr 7:29; 1 Macc 15:11).[6] The expression עֵבֶר הַיַּרְדֵּן (ʿēber hayyardēn, "Trans-Jordan") can refer to the territory in both the Bashan and Gilead, claimed and sometimes controlled by Israel (Josh 9:10; 12:4-6; 13:7-13, 24-32; 17:1, 5; Judg 5:17; 10:8). In the late ninth century, Hazael the Aramean king of Damascus took much of this territory away from Israel (2 Kgs 10:33), but in the early eighth century first Joash of Israel (2 Kgs 13:25) and then Jeroboam II reclaimed much of Israel's lost territory (2 Kgs 14:25, 28). These victories clearly involved recapturing not only Gilead but important areas in the Bashan as well, since Amos mentions Israelite boasting over their conquest of two major cities there, Lo-debar and Qarnaim (Amos 6:13). Qarnaim eventually became the provincial capital of the Assyrian province of Qarnini (see below). After Jeroboam II's death, in the years between 745 and 735 BCE, Rezin of Damascus may have recaptured much of the Bashan for the Arameans and obviously did put heavy pressure on Gilead—Pekah, the son of Remaliah, presumably a Gileadite (2 Kgs 15:25), was clearly a vassal of Rezin (2 Kgs 15:37; Isa 7:1-9). Nonetheless, whoever may have ruled and occupied the Bashan in the late eighth century, Israel still regarded both it and Gilead as Israelite territory and looked forward to again pasturing their animals there (Mic 7:14). That might suggest restoring both geographical names in the assumed haplography here, but only Gilead is specifically mentioned in the reference to Tiglath-pileser's annexation of Israelite territory in 2 Kgs 15:29. Gilead was certainly incorporated into the Assyrian provincial system, though whether it was made a separate province or, as increasingly appears more likely, was absorbed as part of the province of Qarnini in the Bashan[7] remains uncertain.[8] "Galilee of the nations,"

---

5   Tiglath-pileser III's inscriptions are very fragmentary, but his conquest of Galilee is narrated in Tadmor, *Inscriptions of Tiglath-pileser III*, 81–83:3′-7′; Tadmor and Yamada, RINAP 1, 44:17′-18′; 49:rev 9; and his annexation of Gilead at 139:6′-8′; 187:3-4; Tadmor and Yamada, RINAP 1, 42:5′-7′; 49:rev 3-4; 50:rev 3-4. Cf. 2 Kgs 15:29.

6   Dūʾru is mentioned in a couple of lists of provinces, see F. M. Fales and J. N. Postgate, *Imperial Administrative Records, Part II* (SAS 11; Helsinki: Helsinki University Press, 1995) 1 rev. I 11′; 2 II 3. Karen Radner ("Provinz: Assyrien," *RlA* 11:42–68) denies that Dūʾru was a separate province, saying that this area south of Mount Carmel was part of the province of Megiddo (p. 66), but there is no basis for this claim, and it is just hypercriticism in view of the attestation of Dūʾru in a list of provinces. One should note that already in Solomon's administrative districts Dôr and the area south of Carmel had its own governor separate from the governor of Megiddo and the area of the Esdraelon valley north of Carmel (1 Kgs 4:11-12).

7   Qarnini is mentioned in a list of provinces, Fales and Postgate, 1 rev I 7′.

8   Alt, based on the earlier work of E. Forrer (*Die Provinzeinteilung des assyrischen Reiches* [Leipzig: Hinrichs, 1920]), thought it was a separate province ("Das System der assyrischen Provinzen auf dem Boden des Reiches Israel," in *Kleine Schriften*, 2: 188–205), though he admitted that the name of the east Jordanian province was still uncertain ("Jesaja 8, 23–9, 6," in *Kleine Schriften*, 2:211 n. 1.). In contrast, Nadav Naʾaman in two articles originally published in 1995, argued that there was no province of Gilead and that in fact Gilead was not even Israelite territory at the time of Tiglath-pileser's conquests ("Rezin of Damascus and the Land of Gilead," *ZDPV* 111 [1995] 105–17; "Province System and Settlement Pattern in the Neo-Assyrian Period," originally in Mario Liverani, ed., *Neo-Assyrian Geography* [Quaderni di geografia storica 5; Rome: Università di Roma, 1995] 103–15; reprinted in *Ancient Israel and Its Neighbors: Interaction and Counteraction* [Collected Essays 1; Winona Lake, IN: Eisenbrauns, 2005] 220–37). Naʾaman, however, too easily dismisses the biblical evidence for Israelite Gilead (2 Kings 15:29) as a late gloss.

which includes the territories of Naphtali and Zebulon, was incorporated in the Assyrian province of Magidû (Megiddo).[9] Since this oracle looks back at the conquest and annexation as events lying some time in the past, and Ahaz's accession took place several years prior to the Assyrian conquest and annexation of this territory, Ahaz cannot be the new king envisioned in the oracle.

The RSV translation of the verbs in 8:23b as "he brought into contempt" and "he will make glorious" has been challenged by a number of scholars, including Ronald E. Clements, John H. Hayes, and especially J. A. Emerton.[10] Both verbs are Hebrew perfects, so there is no justification, they argue, for translating the second as though it were a future tense. Moreover, they claim that both verbs designate a negative action, that is, "he brought into contempt" and "he made harsh."

The latter claim is most improbable. The Hebrew verb הַכְבֵּד (hakbēd), literally "to make heavy," can be used in either a negative sense, "to make burdensome," or a positive sense, "to give weight to, to honor." Its parallel term, the verb הֵקֵל (hāqēl), literally "to make light," can also be used in either a negative sense, "to make light of, treat with contempt," or a positive sense, "to lighten" one's burden. *Hiphil* verbal forms of the roots כבד and קלל do not occur often enough in the Bible to make a judgment about their possible distribution based on these forms alone, but the roots כבד and קלל (and its byform קלה) do occur in other verbal and nominal forms often enough to be fairly certain of their meaning when the two roots are juxtaposed. When the two roots are used together, they are always contrasted with one another; they are never used as synonyms. Thus, if כבד carries a negative sense, קלל in the same context will carry a positive sense (1 Kgs 12:10; 2 Chr 10:10), but if קלל or its byform קלה carries a negative sense, כבד in the same context will carry a positive sense (Isa 3:5; 16:14; 23:9; and cf. Ezek 22:7 and Deut 27:16, both of which use קלל or קלה to designate behavior that is implicitly contrasted with the behavior demanded by the command to honor [כבד] one's parents). Given this pattern of contrast, well attested elsewhere in Isaiah, it would be totally arbitrary to translate the verbs here in Isa 9:1 as synonyms. Even Emerton's attempt to create a slight contrast in meaning while preserving a basic synonymity between the two verbs remains arbitrary and in conflict with the normal pattern of usage.[11] The RSV is correct with regard to the sense of the verbs.

The RSV's treatment of the tense of the second verb as a prophetic perfect, however, needs some slight adjustment. Since the two verbs express contrasting actions, the temporal contrast between "former" and "latter" cannot be collapsed into an idiom referring to a single event, as Emerton and Clements argue. On the other hand, a future translation for the second verb also creates an inappropriate contrast between the second verb and the following series of five perfects that the RSV translates with the past tense (9:2-3). The second verb, like those following verbs, should actually be treated as a perfect describing an action that is happening even as the prophet speaks, similar to the epistolary aorist in Greek. God is the understood subject of the first two verbs. He treated Israel with contempt at the time of the Syro-Ephraimitic War (735–732 BCE), using his Assyrian agent to punish and humiliate them, but now some years later God has done something to bring honor to this region. The inhabitants of this conquered region who had dwelt in darkness of Assyrian domination since their humiliating defeat have now seen a great light.

Darkness is used here as a metaphor for political oppression and injustice, and light is the contrasting metaphor for political release from such oppression. This imagery was traditional in the ancient Near East, where kings often employed it to contrast their just rule to the oppression characteristic of the preceding era. To cite only one example, the Babylonian king Hammurabi in the prologue to his lawcode described the purpose for which the gods made him king as follows:

9   Magidû is mentioned in a list of provinces (Fales and Postgate, 2 II 4), and Issi-Adad-anenu, the governor of Megiddo, was the *limmu* official or eponym for the year 679 BCE; see Alan Millard, *The Eponyms of the Assyrian Empire 910–612 B.C.* (SAAS 2; Helsinki: Neo-Assyrian Text Corpus Project, 1994) 61.

10   Clements, 104; Hayes and Irvine, 176–78; J. A. Emerton, "Some Linguistic and Historical Problems in Isaiah VIII. 23," *JSS* 14 [1969] 151–75.

11   Emerton translates, "Now has everyone, from first to last, treated with contempt and harshness the land of Zebulun and the land of Naphtali, the way of the sea, the region beyond Jordan, Galilee of the nations" ("Linguistic and Historical Problems," 170).

to cause justice to prevail in the land, to destroy the wicked and the evil, that the strong might not oppress the weak, to rise like the sun over the black-headed (people), and to light up the land.[12]

In the same text, Hammurabi also describes himself as "the sun of Babylon who caused light to go forth over the lands of Sumer and Akkad."[13]

Thus, this traditional use of light imagery and Isaiah's coronation language in 9:6-7 suggest that the great new light seen by these oppressed Israelites is connected with the inauguration of a new Judean king, most likely Hezekiah, who made overtures to the north to join him in his nationalistic religious reform (2 Chr 30:1-11). Of course this glorious characterization of the inauguration of his reign is written from a Judean standpoint, just as Hammurabi's characterization of his reign reflected the viewpoint of the Babylonian royal court; many Israelites actually scoffed at Hezekiah's attempt to "restore" the north (2 Chr 30:10).

The NRSV's translation of the opening line of v. 2, "you have multiplied the nation," following the earlier RSV, is the result of a strained effort to make sense of a textual corruption. Even defenders of this translation on the NRSV committee admitted in the debate over this passage that the text was corrupt and did not represent Isaiah's words.[14] The far better reading defended in the textual notes restores the clear play on the nominal and verbal roots גיל/גִילָה (gîl/gîlâ) and שמח/שִׂמְחָה (śāmaḥ/śimḥâ) running through the verse, and there is no difficulty in explaining the corruption of הגילה (haggîlâ) to הגוי לא (haggôy lōʾ). Moreover, the resulting translation has no awkward or problematic syntax or seriously unbalanced lines:

You have multiplied the joy,
You have made great the rejoicing;
They rejoice before you as with the rejoicing of the harvest;

Like the joy they have when they divide the spoil. There is some ambiguity, however, in the identification of "you" in the passage. Does "you" refer to God or to the new Davidic king? It is difficult to decide, since either answer makes sense in the passage. Such rejoicing characterized coronation ceremonies, and the rejoicing at such ceremonies was done before both the new human king and Yahweh, the divine king, who fathered and installed the new Davidide as his human regent. Perhaps the ambiguity is purposeful, with both intended.

Nevertheless, as v. 2 intimates by its language of "dividing the spoil," and as v. 3 makes explicit, the reason for the rejoicing at this coronation ceremony may go much deeper than that of the typical accession ritual. At least from the perspective of this oracle, the inauguration of Hezekiah's rule means the end of Assyrian oppression. The Assyrians spoke of their vassals as bearing their yoke,[15] so Isaiah uses the same imagery to describe the end of Israel's vassalage. With the elevation of his new king, Isaiah proclaims that Yahweh and/or his new king have broken the burdensome yoke, the heavy bar across their shoulder, and the stick[16] with which their Assyrian oppressor beat and goaded them on. This has happened as on the day of Midian; that is, as Yahweh and his human leader Gideon once broke the oppressive power of Midian over the northern tribes (Judg 6:33—8:28), so now Yahweh and/or his new king Hezekiah have broken the Assyrian yoke. Again "you" remains perhaps intentionally ambiguous, because the human leader, and especially the king, participates in the work of God. In any case, soon the last vestiges of the frightening enemy will be gone; Assyrian battle sandals and blood-splattered cloaks left behind in the imminent Assyrian retreat will be burned as fuel for the fire.

Much of the imagery of vv. 2-4 is traditional, stereotyped "court language" that treated every new king as the ideal who would end the oppression of the past and inaugurate an era of peace. The destruction of the military equipment of the enemy, for example, is an element

---

12 Trans. T. J. Meek, *ANET*, 3rd ed., 164.
13 Ibid., 165.
14 I was present at this debate of the NRSV subcommittee that revised the translation of Isaiah as the scholar responsible for preparing the agenda on Isaiah. A summary account of the debate is found in my "An Evaluation of the NRSV: Demystifying Bible Translation," *Insights: A Journal of the Faculty of Austin Seminary* (1993) 25–36.
15 "*nīru A*," *CAD* N2, 262–63: 2, 2ʹ.
16 One should note that Isaiah uses the same word שֵׁבֶט, "stick, rod," in 10:5 to describe Assyria as the "stick" that God used to punish Israel.

of the motif of the "conflict with the nations," which formed a part of the royal Zion theology (Pss 46:10; 76:4). Nonetheless, Assyria seems clearly envisioned as the oppressive power in Isa 9:2-5. Contra Clements (p. 106), the application of this imagery to refer to Assyrian oppression (Isa 10:24, 26, 27; 14:25) is hardly secondary reinterpretation. The proclamation of Israel's deliverance from oppressive rule at the time of Hezekiah's inauguration, if it were not dismissed as empty noise signifying nothing, could only refer to deliverance from Assyria. Nor does such direct historical application force one to date the original prophecy to the time of Josiah. I date Hezekiah's accession to 715 BCE,[17] but whether Hezekiah's accession date was 729 BCE or 715 BCE, the historical situation in either period left open the possibility of hope for a real change. After 731 BCE Tiglath-pileser III was occupied in the east, and shortly after the accession of his successor, Shalmaneser V, in 727 BCE, Samaria actually revolted. After 720 BCE, Sargon II, the next Assyrian king, lost Babylon to Merodach-baladan and was not able to regain control of Babylonia until 710 BCE. Sargon was also under heavy pressure from the kingdom of Urartu to his north, and he did not intervene in Palestine again, apart from a brief intervention into Ashdod's affairs in 716 or 715 BCE,[18] until his campaign of conquest against Ashdod in 711 BCE. Thus, whether in 729 BCE or 715 BCE, the Judean court, supported by the prophet Isaiah, could have greeted Hezekiah's accession as the opportunity for both Israel and Judah to be free of Assyrian domination. The fact that the expectations expressed in this oracle did not find fulfillment in the reign of Hezekiah is no argument against the view that Isaiah held and proclaimed

such views. Prophetic expectations even of the canonical prophets were often disappointed, as Ezekiel's prophecies concerning Nebuchadnezzar's conquest of Tyre make abundantly clear (see esp. Ezek 29:17-20).[19]

The reference to the birth of a child in v. 5 has been variously interpreted, but despite attempts to connect the child Immanuel (Isa 7:14) with the child mentioned here and to interpret Isa 9:5 as an actual birth announcement of a new male baby just born to the royal family,[20] such an interpretation is highly unlikely (so also Clements, 107). Immanuel is closely related to Shear-jashub and Maher-shalal-hush-baz, but has no original connection to the child mentioned here. Moreover, the parallels to Isa 9:5, both biblical and nonbiblical, suggest that it is better to take the birth imagery in the verse as the metaphorical language of the coronation service. The best biblical parallel is Ps 2:7, where the new Davidic king quotes the promise God made to him on his coronation day: "You are my son; today I have given birth to you." A similar divine pronouncement should probably be reconstructed behind the corrupt Hebrew text of Ps 110:3b: "From the womb of Dawn I gave birth to you like the dew."[21]

As demonstrated by Gerhard von Rad, followed by his teacher Albrecht Alt, the ultimate source for such highly mythological language is probably Egypt, which was a major influence on Israel and Judah in the formative days of the Judean monarchy under David and Solomon and which became a major influence again in Hezekiah's time.[22] In the Egyptian coronation service, the divine birth of the new pharaoh was also proclaimed. In Egypt the birth actually referred to the physical birth of the king, which took place long before the coronation, but it

---

17 See the detailed discussion at Isa 14:28.
18 Assyria's brief intervention in Ashdod to replace the rebellious Azuri with his more compliant brother Ahimeti had no long-term effect in Ashdod, since the people of Ashdod promptly removed Ahimeti as soon as the Assyrians withdrew, replaced him with the nonroyal Yamani/Yadna, and continued their attempt to stir up revolt against Assyria (see my "Egypt, Assyria, Isaiah, and the Ashdod Affair: An Alternative Proposal," in Andrew G. Vaughn and Ann E. Killebrew, *Jerusalem in Bible and Archaeology: The First Temple Period* [SBLSymS 18; Atlanta: Society of Biblical Literature, 2003] 273). If Assyria's brief intervention in Ashdod created no more fear there than this, it is doubtful that it had any long-

term restraining impact on either the nationalists or the pro-Egyptian rebellion party in Judah.
19 Note the discussion in Walther Zimmerli, *Ezechiel* (2 vols.; BKAT 13; Neukirchen/Vluyn: Neukirchener Verlag, 1969) 2:720–23.
20 So Lindblom, *Immanuel Section*. Wildberger also tries to see Isa 9:5 as an actual birth announcement unconnected to the enthronement ceremony of a new king (pp. 377–81), but his treatment of the parallel Egyptian material is totally unconvincing.
21 Correcting MT's מרחם משחר לך טל ילדתיך to מֵרֶחֶם שַׁחַר כְּטַל יְלִדְתִּיךָ.
22 Gerhard von Rad, "Das judäische Königsritual," *TLZ* 72 (1947) 211–16; reprinted in *Gesammelte Studien zum Alten Testament* (TB 8; Munich: C. Kaiser, 1961)

was announced at the king's coronation, as the enthronement texts concerning Hatshepsut, Amenhotep III, and Haremhab demonstrate.[23] In a Memphis text, the god Amon says to Haremhab, just prior to taking him into the divine assembly to be acclaimed king, "You are my son and my heir, who has come out of my members." The Egyptian coronation ritual, however, does not only have Amon making the proclamation of the king's divine sonship directly to the new pharaoh. Amon or Thoth speaking for him also addresses the divine council, using third person pronouns to present the human king to them as Amon's son, and the assembly of the gods responds to the presentation, in turn, by referring to the king in the third person. In a Judean royal ritual dependent on this Egyptian model, it would thus not be surprising to find references to the king's divine birth in both direct address to the king and third person announcements, with either Yahweh as the speaker or another member of his divine council as the speaker. There is no reason to expect such announcements to be formulated only in the active voice. Furthermore, while the Egyptian texts may identify the onset of the king's divine sonship with the physical birth of the king, the actual public announcement of that divine birth comes only at his accession and coronation, that is, at the time of the promulgation of the royal titulary. That a Judean adaptation of this ceremony should take the form of a traditional birth announcement and accordingly should use vocabulary referring to a young child is not at all surprising. It does not suggest a recent birth of a new royal baby any more than the parallel birth narratives in the Egyptian enthronement texts do. Finally, the Egyptian parallels suggest that the speaking voice in the whole passage is either that of Yahweh or that of an angelic member of Yahweh's divine council speaking for the entire council. If the second person references in vv. 2-3 are addressed to the human king, Yahweh may be the speaker throughout. In this case, the first person plural pronouns in v. 5 would be Yahweh's reference to himself and his surrounding divine council, just as in Isa 6:8. If the second person references in vv. 2-3 are addressed to Yahweh, the speaker should be identified with another member of the divine council. On either reading there is no need to see a change of speakers at v. 5, and on either reading the first person plural pronouns in v. 5 refer at least to the members of Yahweh's divine court. It should be noted that Isaiah had no qualms about attributing such speech to the divine council, since he explicitly quotes the words of the seraphim in 6:3, and the later Isaianic tradition continued to put important words in the mouth of members of the divine council (see Isa 40:3). Thus, one may read Isa 9:5 as reflecting the joyous assent of the divine council to the new king as a child of Yahweh born to us, a son of Yahweh given to us, that is, to the divine council. Moreover, the assent continues with the announcement that the royal rule would rest upon the shoulders of this new king.

This Egyptian influence can be detected also in the marvelous names given to this new Davidic ruler. In the Egyptian enthronement ceremony following the announcement of the divine birth of the king the royal titulary of the new king was announced. This was a series of five names, four of which were crown names composed for the occasion and one of which was the name given the king at birth. These names had particular designations and were given in a certain order, but they were different for each king, even when two separate pharaohs (Hatshepsut and Amenhotep III) used the same story to describe their divine birth. The names Isaiah gives to the new Judean king are roughly comparable in type to these Egyptian crown names. "Wonderful counselor" stresses the new king's wisdom in counsel and may be compared to such Egyptian crown names as "ready in plans," "establisher of laws," and "great in marvels." "Mighty God" (cf. 10:21) expresses the new king's power and is paralleled by such Egyptian names as "good god," "mighty bull," and "great in strength." "Everlasting father" points to a long

---

205–13; Albrecht Alt, "Jesaja 8,23—9,6: Befreiungsmacht und Krönungstag," in Walter Baumgartner, ed., *Festschrift Alfred Bertholet zum 80. Geburtstag gewidmet von Kollegen und Freunden* (Tübingen: J. C. B. Mohr, 1950) 29–40; reprinted in Albrecht Alt, *Kleine Schriften zur Geschichte des Volkes Israel* (3 vols.; Munich: C. H. Beck, 1953–59) 2:206–25. For my detailed response to the critics of von Rad and

Alt with reference to the Egyptian sources, see my "Whose Child Is This? Reflections on the Speaking Voice in Isaiah 9:5," *HTR* 90 (1997) 115–29.

23 For Hatshepsut and Amenhotep III, see J. H. Breasted, ed., *ARE* 2:75–100, 334; for Haremhab, see *ARE* 3:12–19, and Alan H. Gardiner, "The Coronation of King Haremhab," *JEA* 39 (1953) 13–31.

reign for the king as the father and protector of his people. It may be compared to the Egyptian "goodly in years," or "living forever and ever." "Prince of peace" points to the security and peace that this king's reign will bring. It may be compared to the Egyptian "who gives life."

Isaiah gives only four names compared to the five names always found in the Egyptian royal titulary, but there is some textual evidence to suggest that a fifth name has dropped out of the text. As discussed in the textual notes, MT's *kĕtîb* suggests that the original reading at the beginning of v. 6 was לם רבה.... Since the first two letters would constitute only a fragment of a word, the possibility exists that the scribal tradition preserves the memory of a textual omission at this point. The fifth name in the Egyptian titulary was the name given the king at birth plus some epithet or blessing, so if there was an original correspondence here, one might have expected the name Hezekiah plus an epithet or blessing, perhaps ending in the word for eternity, עוֹלָם (*ʿôlām*). Since in the orthography of the Isaianic period both שָׁלֹם (*šālōm*), "peace," and עֹלָם (*ʿōlām*), "eternity," end with the letters לם (*lm*), the fifth name could have dropped out accidentally by homoioteleuton. It is also possible that the name was deliberately deleted in order to adapt the oracle for use by Josiah in the seventh century or to make it more open to an indefinite messianic interpretation.

In any case, the prophet proclaims that this new Davidic ruler will enjoy a great and long-lasting rule of unending peace upon the throne of David and his kingdom, which he, presumably the Davidic king, will establish and sustain with justice and righteousness. The whole oracle is marked by typically hyperbolic coronation language, though the announcement that the king will establish and sustain his throne and kingdom by justice and righteousness may contain at least a trace of an implicit prophetic criticism of the rule of Ahaz, the previous king. The final statement, "The zeal of Yahweh of Hosts shall accomplish this," underscores the certainty of what has been proclaimed as present fact, while at the same time the imperfect or future tense verb form unmasks the oracle as actually prophetic prediction. It is a prediction that, like Psalm 2, has propaganda value for the new Judean ruler. On one level, it could be read as an invitation to the inhabitants of the old northern kingdom to seek refuge under the royal protection of the new Judean king. At the same time, however, it ultimately undercuts excessive Judean pride in this expected deliverance of Israel, because it attributes this marvelous salvation, not to human strength, not even to the strength of the powerful new Davidic king, but to the "zeal of the Yahweh of hosts."

If, as I have argued, this oracle was originally composed for the coronation of Hezekiah, Isaiah's expectations for this king were sadly disappointed. Despite the influx of population into Jerusalem and Judah from the north,[24] the northern territories did not accept Hezekiah's Davidic rule, and the respite from Assryian domination was brief in the extreme. The author of 2 Kings gave Hezekiah much higher marks than Ahaz, but Isaiah learned that ultimately Hezekiah was no more willing to trust in God's promises than Ahaz had been. He, like Ahaz, sought for security in foreign alliances; the only difference was the choice of allies. Ahaz looked to Assyria; Hezekiah to Babylon and Egypt.

These disappointed expectations were reawakened about a hundred years later in the days of the Judean king Josiah. Just as Hezekiah had done, he instituted a religiopolitical reform, one purpose of which was to regain control over the north for the Davidic throne. He was partially successful for a period, and in his days Judah did see the final collapse of the Assyrian empire, but in the long run he also failed to realize the ideal expressed in this oracle. Josiah was killed, and Assyrian domination was simply replaced, first by Egyptian, then by Babylonian domination. Moreover, within twenty-five years after Josiah's death there was no longer a Judean, much less a scion of David, on the throne of Judah.

The ideal and hopes expressed in this oracle did not die, however. The surviving religious community continued to read the prophecy as offering hope in their changed situation. The particularity of the original historical situation behind the oracle was forgotten or ignored, and the oracle was read in a typological fashion that allowed it to be applied to new situations. The commu-

---

24 Nadav Na'aman continues to deny any such influx ("Dismissing the Myth of a Flood of Israelite Refugees in the Late Eighth Century BCE," *ZAW* 126 [2014] 1–14), but I continue to find his arguments totally unconvincing. See my note on the earlier literature in my commentary on 5:8.

nity awaited the coming of God's chosen Davidic king in whose reign God would deliver them from their enemies of the moment, whether Persian, Seleucid, or later the Romans. With this loss of the original historical particularity, the possibility of a remythologization of some of the ideas in the oracle developed. Though the Judean royal ideology was heavily influenced by Egyptian ideas, the Judean concept of the divine birth of the Davidic king may have differed significantly from Egyptian conceptions. In Judah neither the king nor the office of king was considered ontologically divine.[25] Once this oracle was freed from its original connection to the coronation of a particular human king and attached to the ideal figure of a coming Messiah of the future, however, the mythological background of both the claim to divine sonship and many of these enthronement names opened the way for speculation about the nature of the Messiah. Christians, in particular, when they apply this oracle to Christ, claim that the Egyptian mythological language used as a metaphor in the Judean enthronement ceremony is literally true in the case of Jesus. He was and is, not just metaphorically but essentially, God.

To juxtapose my earlier historical reading of the oracle to this later Christian reading or to trace the historical development of this later reading is not to reject this later development of the exegetical tradition as illegitimate. If my reconstruction of the original meaning of this oracle has any validity, it harbors a finite limitation that the prophet Isaiah never addressed. If Hezekiah was the new king idealized in this oracle, how could Isaiah claim he would reign for ever? How could Isaiah so ignore Israel's long historical experience as to expect that no new source of oppression would ever arise? The language, as is typical of royal ideology, is hyperbolic, and perhaps neither Isaiah nor his original audience would have pushed it to its limits, beyond its conventional frames of reference, but the language itself invites such exploitation. If one accepts God's providential direction of history, it is hard to complain about the exegetical development this exploitation produced. The new readings preserve the fundamental ideals of the royal theology that informed the original oracle, and God remains the ultimate source

of the awaited salvation. Moreover, the new Christian reading, like other secondary readings that preceded it, allows the old symbols to continue to function powerfully for a continuing religious community dealing with new problems and new sources of oppression. Finally, one cannot object that the Christian claims for Jesus grew out of a misconstrual of the original meaning of such prophetic oracles, because such an objection represents a serious misapprehension of the relationship between prophecy and Christian faith. A misreading of Old Testament prophecy did not lead the early disciples to belief in Jesus; rather it was the encounter of these early disciples with Jesus, with his life, his teachings, his death, and his resurrection that led them to read the Old Testament prophecies in this new way.

If the original prophecy constituted not only a promise but an invitation to the oppressed of Israel to seek refuge under the rule of God's chosen king, the new Christian reading also contains an invitation to the oppressed to accept the salvation offered by God's anointed. The Christmas message of Luke's angel, confirmed by the angelic choir (Luke 2:10-14), contains an implicit invitation:

"Be not afraid; for behold, I bring you good news of a great joy which will come to all the people; for to you is born this day in the city of David a Savior, who is Christ the Lord. And this will be a sign for you: you will find a babe wrapped in swaddling cloths and lying in a manger." And suddenly there was with the angel a multitude of the heavenly host praising God and saying, "Glory to God in the highest, and on earth peace among men with whom he is pleased!"

If one refuses that invitation, as Israel refused Hezekiah's appeal, can one hope to be among those with whom God is pleased? Jesus's lament over Jerusalem forms a sorrowful and threatening counterpart to the angels' happy message:

O Jerusalem, Jerusalem, killing the prophets and stoning those who are sent to you! How often would I

---

25 There is, of course, an ongoing debate in Egyptological circles on the status of the Egyptian king as divine. See, for example, the essays in David O'Connor and David P. Silverman, eds., *Ancient Egyptian Kingship* (Probleme der Ägyptologie 9; Leiden: Brill, 1995).

have gathered your children together as a hen gathers her brood under her wings, and you would not! (Luke 13:34).

Thus, the prophecy still stands as a promise and an invitation, and, if refused, ultimately as a threat.

Bibliography

Alonso Schökel, L. "Dos poemas a la paz," *EstBib* 18 (1959) 149–69.

Alt, Albrecht, "Jesaja 8,23–9,6: Befreiungsmacht und Krönungstag," in Walter Baumgartner, ed., *Festschrift Alfred Bertholet zum 80. Geburtstag gewidmet von Kollegen und Freunden* (Tübingen: J. C. B. Mohr, 1950) 29–40; reprinted in Albrecht Alt, *Kleine Schriften zur Geschichte des Volkes Israel* (3 vols.; Munich: C. H. Beck, 1953–59) 2:206–25.

Barnes, W. E., "A Study of the First Lesson for Christmas Day," *JTS* 4 (1903) 17–27.

Barth, *Die Jesaja-Worte*.

Becker, Joachim, *Messianic Expectation in the Old Testament* (Philadelphia: Fortress Press, 1980).

Bentzen, Aage, *King and Messiah* (2nd ed.; Oxford: Blackwell, 1970).

Brongers, H. A., "Der Eifer des Herrn Zebaoth," *VT* 13 (1963) 269–84.

Brunner-Traut, E., "Die Geburtsgeschichte der Evangelien im Lichte der ägyptologischen Forschungen," *ZRGG* 12 (1960) 97–111.

———, "Pharao und Jesus als Söhne Gottes," *Antaios* 2 (1960) 266–84.

Brunner, Hellmut, *Die Geburt des Gottkönigs: Studien zur Überlieferung eines altägyptischen Mythos* (ÄgAbh 10; Wiesbaden: Harrassowitz, 1964).

Burney, C. F., "The 'Boot' of Isaiah IX 4," *JTS* 11 (1910) 438–43.

Carlson, R. A., "The Anti-Assyrian Character of the Oracle in Is 9:1-6," *VT* 24 (1974) 130–35.

Caspari, W., "Echtheit, Hauptbegriff und Gedankengang der messianischen Weissagung Jes. 9,1-6," BFCT 12 (1908) 280–320.

Cazelles, Henri, "De l'idéologie royale," *JANESCU* 5 (1973) 59–73.

Coppens, Joseph, *Le messianisme et sa relève prophétique: Les anticipations vétérotestamentaires. Leur accomplissement dans le Christ* (BETL 38; Leuven: Leuven University Press, 1974).

———, "Le messianisme royal."

———, "Le roi idéal d'Is. IX 5-6 et XI 1-5, est-il une figure messianique?" in *A la rencontre de Dieu: Mémorial Albert Gelin* (Bibliothèque de la Faculté Catholique de théologie de Lyon 8; Paris: Mappus, 1961) 85–108.

Crook, M. B., "Did Amos and Micah Know Isaiah 9:2-7 and 11:1-9?" *JBL* 73 (1954) 144–51.

———, "A Suggested Occasion for Isaiah 9:2-7 and 11:1-9," *JBL* 68 (1949) 213–24.

Dietze, K., "Manasse, eine chronologische Untersuchung zu Jesaja 9:1-6," in *Festschrift des Bremer Gymnasiums* (1925) 245–81.

Driver, "Isaianic Problems," 43–49.

Emerton, J. A., "Some Linguistic and Historical Problems in Isaiah VIII 23," *JSS* 14 (1969) 151–75.

Erbt, W. E., "Zu F.E. Peisers 'Jesaja Kap. 9,'" *OLZ* 20 (1917) 78–81.

Eshel, Hanan, "Isaiah 8:23: An Historical-Geographical Analogy," *VT* 40 (1990) 105–9.

Grelot, P., "L'interpretation d'Isaïe IX 5 dans le Targoum des prophètes," in M. Carrez et al., eds., *De la Tôrah au Messie: Études d'exégèse et d'herméneutique bibliques offertes à Henri Cazelles pour ses 25 années d'enseignement à l'Institut catholique de Paris, octobre 1979* (Paris: Desclée, 1981) 535–43.

Gressmann, Hugo, *Der Messias* (FRLANT 43; Göttingen: Vandenhoeck & Ruprecht, 1929).

Harrelson, Walter, "Nonroyal Motifs in the Royal Eschatology," in Bernhard W. Anderson and Walter Harrelson, eds., *Israel's Prophetic Heritage: Essays in Honor of James Muilenburg* (New York: Harper & Row, 1962) 149–53.

Jagt, Krijn A. van der, "Wonderful Counsellor (Isaiah 9:6)," *BT* 40 (1989) 441–45.

Jarick, John, "Shalom Reaffirmed: A Response to [Gillis] Gerleman's Theory ['Die Wurzel Šlm,' *ZAW* 85 (1973)1–14]." *Lutheran Theological Journal* 20 (1986) 2–9.

Johnson, A. R., *Sacral Kingship in Ancient Israel* (Cardiff: Wales University Press, 1967).

Kennett, R. H., "The Prophecy in Isaiah IX 1-7," *JTS* 7 (1906) 321–42.

Kraus, H. J., "Jesaja 9,5-6 (6-7)," in G. Eichholz, ed., *Herr tue meine Lippen auf* (Wuppertal: E. Müller, 1961) 43–53.

LaSor, W. S., "The Messiah: An Evangelical Christian View," in M. Tannenbaum et al., eds., *Evangelicals and Jews in Conversation on Scripture, Theology, and History* (Grand Rapids: Eerdmans, 1973) 76–95.

Lescow, Th., "Das Geburtsmotiv in den messianischen Weissagungen bei Jesaja und Micha," *ZAW* 79 (1967) 172–207.

Lindblom, *Immanuel Section.*

Lipiński, E., "Etudes sur des textes 'messianiques' de l'Ancien Testament,"*Sem* 20 (1970) 41–58.

——, "An Israelite King of Hamat?" *VT* 21 (1971) 371–73.

Luke, K., "The Names in Is 9:5b," *LW* (1973) 169–82.

Lust, J., "The Immanuel Figure: A Charismatic Judge-Leader. A Suggestion Towards the Understanding of Is 7,10-17 (8:23—9:6; 11:1-9)," *ETL* 47 (1971) 464–70.

Machinist, Peter, "Assyria and Its Image in the First Isaiah," *JAOS* 103 (1982) 719–37.

Mauchline, J., "Implicit Signs of a Persistent Belief in the Davidic Empire," *VT* 20 (1970) 287–303.

McClellan, W. H., "El Gibbor," *CBQ* 6 (1944) 276–88.

McKenzie, J. L., "Royal Messianism," *CBQ* 19 (1957) 25–52.

Meshel, Z., "Was There a 'Via Maris'? (Is 8:23; Ez 41:12.)," *IEJ* 23 (1973) 162–66.

Mettinger, Tryggve N. D., *King and Messiah: The Civil and Sacral Legitimation of the Israelite Kings* (ConBOT 8; Lund: Gleerup, 1976).

Michel, Walter L., "*slmwt,* 'Deep Darkness' or 'Shadow of Death'?" *BR* 29 (1984) 5–20.

Morenz, S., "Ägyptische und davidische Königstitulatur," *AZ* 49 (1954) 73–74.

Mowinckel, Sigmund, *He That Cometh.*

——, "Urmensch und 'Königsideologie,'" *ST* 2 (1948) 71–89.

Müller, Hans Peter, "Uns ist ein Kind geboren . . . : Jes 9:1-6 in traditionsgeschichtlicher Sicht," *EvT* 21, no. 9 (1961) 408–19.

Olivier, J. P. J., "The Day of Midian and Isaiah 9:3b," *JNSL* 9 (1981) 143–49.

Olmo Lete, Gregorio del, "Los titulos mesianicos de Is. 9:5," *EstBib* 24 (1965) 239–43.

Oswalt, John N., "God's Determination to Redeem His People (Isaiah 9:1-7; 11:1-11; 26:1-9; 35:1-10)," *RevExp* 88 (1991) 153–65.

Peiser, F. E., "Jesaja Kap. 9," *OLZ* 20 (1917) 129–39.

Rad, G. von, "Das judäische Königsritual," *TLZ* 72 (1947) 211–16; reprinted in *Gesammelte Studien zum Alten Testament* (TB 8; Munich: C. Kaiser, 1961) 205–13.

Rehm, M., *Der königliche Messias im Lichte der Immanuel-Weissagungen des Buches Jesaja* (Eichstätter Studien 1; Kevelaer: Butzon & Bercker, 1968) 145–66.

Renaud, Bernard, "La forme poétique d'Is 9,1-6," in A. Caquot, S. Legasse, et al., eds., *Mélanges bibliques et orientaux en l'honneur de M. Mathias Delcor* (AOAT 215; Kevelaer: Butzon & Bercker; Neukirchen-Vluyn: Neukirchener Verlag, 1985) 331–48.

Reventlow, Henning Graf, "A Syncretistic Enthronement-Hymn in Is 9:1-6," *UF* 3 (1971) 321–25.

Ringgren, Helmer, "König und Messias," *ZAW* 64 (1952) 120–47.

——, *The Messiah in the Old Testament* (SBT 18; Chicago: A. R. Allenson, 1956).

Roberts, J. J. M., "Whose Child Is This? Reflections on the Speaking Voice in Isaiah 9:5," *HTR* 90 (1997) 115–29.

Scharbert, Josef, *Heilsmittler im Alten Testament und im Alten Orient* (QD 23/24; Freiburg: Herder, 1964).

——, "Der Messias im Alten Testament und im Judentum," in H. Gross, ed., *Die religiöse und theologische Bedeutung des Alten Testaments* (Bayern: Katholischen Akademie,1967) 47–78.

Schildenberger, J., "Durch Nacht zum Licht (Jes 8,1–9,6)," *Sein und Sendung* 30 (1965) 387–401.

Schmidt, W. H., "Die Ohnmacht des Messias," *KD* 15 (1969) 18–34.

Schunck, K. D., "Der fünfte Thronname des Messias (Jes. IX 5-6)," *VT* 23 (1973) 108–10.

Scipione, G., "The Wonderful Counselor, the Other Counselor, and Christian Counseling (Is 9:6)," *WTJ* 36 (1973) 174–97.

Selwyn, William, *Horae Hebraicae: Critical Observations on the Prophecy of Messiah in Isaiah, Chapter IX, and on Other Passages of the Holy Scriptures* (Cambridge: University Press, 1848).

Seybold, K., *Das davidische Königtum im Zeugnis der Propheten* (FRLANT 107; Göttingen: Vandenhoeck & Ruprecht, 1972).

Snaith, N. H., "The Interpretation of El Gibbor in Isaiah IX.5," *ExpTim* 52 (1940) 36–37.

Soggin, J. Alberto, *Das Königtum in Israel: Ursprünge, Spannungen, Entwicklung* (Berlin: A. Töpelmann, 1967).

Stuhlmueller, Carroll, "The Prophetic Price for Peace," in John T. Pawlikowski and Donald Senior, eds., *Biblical and Theological Reflections on the Challenge of Peace* (Wilmington, DE: Glazier, 1984) 31–44.

Thompson, M. E. W., "Isaiah's Ideal King," *JSOT* 24 (1982) 79–88.

Torczyner, H., "Ein vierter Sohn des Jesaja," *MGWJ* 74 (1930) 257–59.

Treves, M., "Little Prince Pele-Joez," *VT* 17 (1967) 464–77.

Vieweger, Dieter, "Das Volk, das durch das Dunkel zieht: Neue Überlegungen zu Jes (8:23abb) 9:1-6," *BZ* n.s. 36 (1992) 77–86.

Vischer, W., *Die Immanuel-Botschaft im Rahmen des königlichen Zionsfestes* (ThSt 45; Zurich: Evangelischer Verlag, 1955; originally, "La prophétie d'Emmanuel et la fête royale de Sion," *ETR* 3 (1954).

Vollmer, J., "Zur Sprache von Jesaja 9:1-6," *ZAW* 80 (1968) 343–50.

Wegner, Paul D., "Another Look at Isaiah 8:23b," *VT* 41 (1991) 481–84.

——, "A Re-Examination of Isaiah IX 1-6," *VT* 42 (1992) 103–12.

Wildberger, Hans, "Die Thronnamen des Messias: Jes. 9,5b," *TZ* 16 (1960) 314–32.

Wolff, Hans Walter, *Frieden ohne Ende; Jesaja 7,1-17 und 9,1-6 ausgelegt* (Neukirchen Kreis Moers: Neukirchener Verlag, 1962).

Zimmerli, Walther, "Jes 8,23*—9,6," *Göttinger Predigt-Meditationen* 16 (1961) 64–69.

——, "Vier oder fünf Thronnamen des messianischen Herrschers von Jes 9,5b.6?" *VT* 22 (1972) 249–52.

Zorell, F., "Vaticinium messianicum Isaiae 9,1-6 Hebr. = 9,2-7 Vulg.," *Bib* 2 (1921) 215–18.

Isaiah 9:7-20 describes a series of judgments that God sent against the northern kingdom Israel because of its sins. The purpose of these judgments was, as v. 12 shows, to get Israel to return to God, which for Isaiah meant, among other things, to return to the fold of the Davidic monarchy. The literary placement of the oracle immediately following the coronation oracle of the new Davidic king was probably intended to remind the north of the consequences of not accepting the implicit invitation of that royal oracle. Unfortunately, Israel had not responded favorably to these earlier attempts of God to get their attention. Despite the judgments, Israel had remained adamant in its sinful rebellion, and God's anger remained unabated. This point is made by the refrain, "For all this his anger is not turned away and his hand is stretched out still," which is repeated three times in this material (9:11 [Eng. 12], 16 [Eng. 17], 20 [Eng. 21]), once in 10:4, and once in 5:25, each time following an account of judgment. The refrain ties Isa 9:7-20 together as a unit,

but 9:20 is far too abrupt to be the original conclusion to the oracle. The oracle, with its series of past judgments and repeated refrain, seems to be modeled on Amos 4:6-12, to which Isa 9:7 may refer (see below), and by analogy with that model one expects a conclusion in which the prophet turns from the narration of past judgments to the announcement of a future judgment. Isaiah 10:1-4, which some scholars have proposed as the conclusion because of the refrain at the end of v. 4 (Watts, *Isaiah 1–33*, 177–83), does not provide an appropriate conclusion, and probably belongs with the *hôy*-oracles of 5:8-24 (Clements, 60–62). Isaiah 10:4, or at least the final refrain, appears to be just a misplaced fragment that confuses because it is out of context (Wildberger, 180). In contrast, Isa 5:25-30 fits the pattern found in 9:7-20 and provides a suitable and probably the original conclusion for the whole oracle. It was presumably detached from this position in the editorial work that accompanied the insertion of 6:1—9:6 (see the discussion on chap. 5).

9:7-20 (Eng. 9:8-21)

7/   Yahweh[a] sent a word[b] against Jacob;
        And it fell[c] against Israel

8/   And all the people knew[d]—
        Ephraim and the inhabitants[e] of Samaria—
        Saying in pride and haughtiness of heart,

9/   "The bricks have fallen,[f]
        But we will rebuild with ashlars;
        The sycamores[g] have been cut down,[h]
        But with cedars we will replace them.[i]"

10/   And Yahweh raised up oppressors from Rezin[j] against him
        And his enemies he provoked.

11/   Aram[k] from the east and the Philistines from the west,
        And they devoured Israel with the whole mouth;
        Yet in all this[l] his anger has not turned back,
        And his hand[m] is stretched out still.

12/   And the people did not return to the one who smote them,[n]
        And Yahweh of Hosts[o] they did not seek.

13/   Yahweh cut off from Israel head and tail,
        Palm frond and reed in one day.[p]

14/   The elder and the dignitary—he is the head,
        And the prophet who teaches lies—he is the tail.

15/   Those leading[q] this people have become misleaders,
        And those being led[q] are being led astray.

16/   That is why the Lord does not rejoice[r] over its young men,
        And for its orphans and its widows he has no pity;
        For everyone is profane and an evildoer,
        And every mouth speaks folly;
        Yet in all this his anger has not turned back,
        And his hand is stretched out still.

17/   For wickedness burned like fire,

It devoured thorn and thistle,
And it caught in the thickets of the forest,
And they billowed up in a column of smoke.

18/ By the wrath[s] of Yahweh of Hosts the earth shook,[t]
And the people became as food for the fire.
A man showed no compassion[u] for his brother.

19/ One devoured[v] on the right, and was hungry;
He ate on the left,[w] and he was not sated.[x]
Each one was eating[y] the flesh of his own arm;

20/ Manasseh[z] Ephraim and Ephraim Manasseh,
Together they were against*[a] Judah,
Yet in all this his anger has not turned back,
And his hand is stretched out still.

Isa 5:25-30

25/ Therefore the anger of Yahweh burned against his people,
And he stretched his hand out against him and smote him,
And the mountains shook, and their corpses became*[b]
Like garbage in the midst of the streets.
Yet in all this his anger did not turn back;
His hand*[c] is still stretched out.

26/ He will raise a signal flag for a nation*[d] from afar,
And he will whistle for him*[e] from the end of the earth,
And surely he*[f] will come very swiftly.

27/ There is no straggler*[g] and no stumbler in his*[h] ranks;
He does not slumber and does not sleep.
The belt of his loins is never loosened,
And the thong of his sandals never breaks.

28/ His arrows are sharpened,
And all his*[i] bows are strung.
The hooves of his*[i] horses are like flint,
And his*[i] wheels are like a storm wind.

29/ His roaring is like the lion,
He roars*[j] like the young lions;*[k]
He growls*[l] and seizes prey,
He carries it off, and there is no one to save (it).

30/ He will growl*[m] over it on that day
Like the growling of the sea,
And one will look*[n] to the earth,
But there will be nothing but the darkness of affliction,
And the light will be darkened by clouds.*[o]

Textual Notes

a   Reading יהוה (YHWH), "Yahweh," with 1QIsaᵃ and Tg.; MT's אֲדֹנָי (ʾădōnāy), "my Lord," is a secondary change due to the later practice of not pronouncing the divine name when reading the text.

b   MT's דָּבָר (dābār), "word," is supported by Vg., Tg., and Syr.; LXX's Θάνατον, "death," suggests that it has mistakenly vocalized the Hebrew word as דֶּבֶר (deber), "plague."

c   MT's וְנָפַל, "and it fell," is a simple past tense following the perfect שָׁלַח (šālaḥ), "he sent." This rendering is supported by

1QIsaᵃ, Vg., and Syr. LXX's ἦλθεν, "it came," and Tg.'s וְאִשְׁתְּמַע (wĕʾištĕmaʿ), "it was heard," are just interpretive attempts to ease the harshness of the original.

d   MT's וַיְדְעוּ (wĕyādĕʿû), "and they knew," if it is the correct reading, is to be understood like the preceding וְנָפַל (wĕnāpal), "and it fell," as a simple past tense. This is not a converted tense sequence, though LXX, Vg., and Syr. all translate the verb as a future. 1QIsaᵃ has וירעו, which could be read as וַיָּרֵעוּ (wayyārēʿû), "and they did evil," the converted hiphil imperfect of rʿʿ, or as וַיָּרִיעוּ (wayyārîʿû), "they shouted out," the converted hiphil imperfect of rwʿ. Either reading would make a somewhat smoother transition than MT, since the movement from "knowing" to "saying" is a bit abrupt. Tg. also reads a different verb, וְאִתְרַרְבוּ (wě'itrārabû), "and *all this people* boasted," but whether this is evidence of a different text or simply an attempt to relieve the roughness in the MT remains debatable.

e   The singular יוֹשֵׁב (yôšēb) may be understood either as the ruler of (that is, the one who sits enthroned in) Samaria (cf. Amos 1:5, 8), or as a collective "the inhabitants of Samaria." LXX, Vg., and Syr. all opt for the latter interpretation, which makes for a somewhat better parallel to Ephraim.

f   Syr. reads a first person plural, "let us make bricks," for MT's לְבֵנִים נָפָלוּ (lěbēnîm nāpālû), "the bricks have fallen."

g   For MT's and 1QIsaᵃ's שִׁקְמִים (šiqmîm), "sycamores," 4QIsaᶜ has שׁוקמין]ם.

h   For MT's passive גֻּדָּעוּ (guddāʿû), "were cut down," 1QIsaᵃ and Vg. have the active גדעו, (giddēʿû), "they cut down," but MT's passive fits better as a parallel to the intransitive nāpālû, "have fallen."

i   LXX misses the contrast between the two inexpensive building materials and their two expensive replacements with its free translation, "The bricks have fallen, but come let us hew out stones and let us cut sycamores and cedars and build a tower for ourselves." Tg. interprets the metaphor but keeps the contrast: "The leaders have gone into exile, but we will appoint better ones than them; the possessions have been plundered, but we will buy nicer ones than them."

j   MT, supported by 1QIsaᵃ, 4QIsaᵇ, Vg., and Syr., has the reading אֶת־צָרֵי רְצִין (ʾet-ṣārê rěṣîn), "the enemies of Rezin," but this makes no sense in a reference to past judgments against Israel, since Rezin was the enemy of Israel. Tg. expands to clarify the sense: וְתַקֵּף יוי יָת סַנְאֵיהּ דְיִשְׂרָאֵל רְצִין עֲלוֹהִי (wětaqēp YWY yāt sānĕ'êh děyiśrā'ēl rěṣîn ʿělôhî), "Yahweh strengthened the enemy of Israel, Rezin, against him." I read צֹרְרֵי רְצִין (ṣōrěrê rěṣîn), "oppressors from Rezin," a subjective genitive as in Isa 11:13. Two other corrections are also possible, though they assume more serious textual corruption. One could either read צָרָיו (ṣārāyw), "his foes," and delete רְצִין, "Rezin," as an interpretive gloss, or one could read רְצִין, "Rezin," and delete צָרָיו (ṣārāyw), "his foes," as an interpretive gloss. The versions appear to understand the passage as a future judgment against Rezin, but that does not fit the context. Aram (v. 11) was Rezin's country, and the Philistines were his allies against Israel until Israel joined their defensive alliance against Assyria. LXX is even stranger. It reads: καὶ ῥάξει ὁ θεὸς τοὺς ἐπανιστανομένους ἐπ᾽ ὄρος Σιων ἐπ᾽ αὐτοὺς καὶ τοὺς ἐχθροὺς αὐτῶν διασκεδάσει, "and God will smite those who rise up on Mount Zion (apparently reading something like צרי הר ציון, ṣārê har ṣîyôn, "the enemies of Mount Zion") against them and he will scatter their enemies." In the context, the antecedent of the masculine pronominal suffixes should be Jacob, Israel, or Ephraim, that is, the northern kingdom.

k   MT, 1QIsaᵃ, LXX, Vg., and Tg. all have ארם (ʾărām), "Aram" or "Syria"; Syr.'s אדום (ʾĕdôm), "Edom," is clearly a mistake.

l   MT, LXX, Vg., and Tg. have בכל־זאת (běkol-zōʾt), "in all this";

1QIsaᵃ, 4QIsaᵃ, and Syr. add the copulative, "and in all this." For the same refrain in v. 16, MT, 1QIsaᵃ, LXX, Vg., and Tg. have בכל־זאת (běkol-zōʾt), "in all this," and only Syr. adds the copulative, "and in all this." In v. 20 both 1QIsaᵃ and Syr. have the copulative.

m   For MT's singular יָדוֹ (yādô), "his hand," 1QIsaᵃ has the plural form ידיו (yādāyw), "his hands," though it is construed with the same feminine singular qal passive participle נְטוּיָה (nĕṭûyâ), "is stretched out," and the same is true in vv. 16 and 20.

n   For MT's עַד־הַמַּכֵּהוּ (ʿad-hammakkēhû), "the one who smote him," 1QIsaᵃ has על ימכהו (ʿl ᵈmkhw), though there is little difference in meaning.

o   LXX shortens MT's וְאֶת־יְהוָה צְבָאוֹת (wě'et-YHWH ṣěbā'ôt), "and Yahweh of Hosts," to καὶ τὸν κύριον, "and the Lord."

p   For MT's accusative of time יוֹם אֶחָד (yôm 'eḥād) "in one day," 1QIsaᵃ has the prepositional phrase ביום אחד (běyôm 'eḥād) with no difference in meaning.

q   The versions misunderstand the verb אשר (ʾaššēr) in this verse as the verb, "to call happy or blessed," but while a homonym, the verb here as well as in Isa 3:12 means, "to lead."

r   For MT's יִשְׂמַח (yiśmaḥ), "he rejoices," 1QIsaᵃ has יחמל (yaḥmōl), "he has compassion." 1QIsaᵃ's reading may provide a closer parallel to יְרַחֵם (yěraḥēm), "he takes pity," but all the versions support MT. 1QIsaᵃ's secondary correction may have been influenced by the occurrence of the verb יחמלו (yaḥmōlû) in v. 18.

s   For MT's בְּעֶבְרַת (bě'ebrat), "by the wrath," 1QIsaᵃ has מעברת (mē'ebrat), "from the wrath." The two expressions are equivalent in meaning.

t   The meaning and derivation of נֶעְתַּם (neʿtam) is disputed. Vg. (conturbata est terra), "the earth is convulsed," Syr. (zˁt ʾrˁ), "the earth shook," and Tg. (חֲרוֹבַת אַרְעָא, ḥĕrôbat ʾarʿā), "the earth was devastated," may all suggest a derivation from נוע (nûaʿ), "to quake," analyzing the form as a qal perfect third feminine singular with enclitic mem—נָעַת־ם (nāʿat-m), "the earth shook." On the other hand, the context is dominated by fire imagery, and the LXX renders the phrase as συγκέκαυται ἡ γῆ ὅλη, "the whole earth is burned." There is an old lexicographical tradition that analyzes the verb as a niphal third masculine singular perfect from a root עתם (ʿtm), attested in Arabic with the meaning "to blacken" (BDB, 801). This is an attractive possibility, but the lack of agreement between the feminine subject אֶרֶץ (ʾāreṣ), "earth," and the masculine verb form נֶעְתַּם (neʿtam) would remain troubling.

u   Despite the plural in MT יחמלו (yaḥmōlû) and 1QIsaᵃ יחמולו (yaḥmôlû), supported by Tg., the other versions (LXX, Vg., and Syr.) have the singular, which grammatically is more appropriate with the singular subject איש (ʾîš), "man, each." The use of the plural in Hebrew, here and selectively in v. 19, original or not, is probably due to the sense that multiple individuals were so acting.

v   LXX and Vg. both render this verb as "turn aside," while Syr. uses the same verb in Syriac as the Hebrew, but with the meaning "cut off." In light of the parallelism, the sense seems to be "to cut off" or "to tear off" for the purpose of eating. The cognate root *jazara* is used in Arabic for "slaughtering" or "butchering."[1]

w   For MT's ויאכל על שמאול (*wayyōʾkal ʿal-śĕmôʾl*), "he ate on the left," 1QIsaᵃ has ויאכל ועל שמאול, "and he ate and on the left," which may simply be an issue of poor spacing, indicating that the Qumran text originally had the plural verb, "and they ate on the left."

x   MT, 1QIsaᵃ, 4QIsaᶜ, supported by Syr., have the plural שבעו (*śābēʿû*), "they were not sated"; LXX, Vg., and even Tg. preserve the singular.

y   For MT's יאכלו (*yōʾkēlû*), "they were eating," supported by 4QIsaᵉ and Tg., 1QIsaᵃ has ויאכל (*wayyōʾkal*), "and he ate," which it construes with the following verse. LXX, Vg., and Syr. also have the singular. LXX apparently reads the verb twice, construing it both with v. 19 and then with v. 20. Vg. construes the verb with v. 19, and Syr. is more ambiguous. Grammatically the singular is to be preferred.

z   1QIsaᵃ and LXX have a verb here, "Manasseh devours Ephraim, and Ephraim Manasseh."

*a   LXX supplies the verb πολιορκήσουσιν, "together they besiege Judah."

*b   1QIsaᵃ and 4QIsaᶠ have the long form ותהיה for MT's וַתְּהִי (*wattĕhî*), "and it became."

*c   1QIsaᵃ has ידיו (*yādāyw*) for MT's singular ידו (*yādô*).

*d   The mimmation on MT לגוים (*laggôyim*) and 1QIsaᵃ לגואים is probably to be understood as an enclitic *mem* (*laggôy-m*), not as the masculine plural ending, since the following references to this nation indicated by the pronominal suffix on the preposition לו (*lô*), "for him," and by the subject of the verb יבוא (*yābôʾ*), "he will come," are both masculine singular (cf. Jer 5:15). The versions take the form as a plural.

*e   Despite the singular in MT (לו) and 1QIsaᵃ (לוא), followed by Vg., LXX and Syr. translate this form as a plural to agree with their understanding of its antecedent לגוים as a plural.

*f   LXX and Syr. render the verb as a plural against MT, 1QIsaᵃ, and Vg.

*g   For MT עָיֵף (*ʿāyēp*), "weary, faint, straggler," 1QIsaᵃ has יעף (*yāʿēp*), "weary, faint," but 4QIsaᵇ supports MT.

*h   Literally, "in him" (בו, *bô*). Vg. closely follows MT, but LXX and Syr. turn everything into plurals following their understanding of "nations."

*i   LXX and Syr continue with their consistent plurals.

*j   Reading יִשְׁאַג (*yišʾag*), "he roars," with MT's *qĕrēʾ*, 1QIsaᵃ, and pap4QIsaᵖ.

*k   Reading כַּכְּפִרִים (*kakkĕpirîm*), "like the young lions," with MT and pap4QIsaᵖ. 1QIsaᵃ has וככפירים (*wĕkakkĕpirîm*), "and like the young lions."

*l   Reading וְיִנְהֹם (*wĕyinhōm*), "and he growls," with MT; 1QIsaᵃ has ינהם (*yinhōm*), "he growls."

*m   MT and pap4QIsaᵖ have וְיִנְהֹם (*wĕyinhōm*), "and he growls"; 1QIsaᵃ has ינהם (*yinhōm*), "he growls."

*n   MT and 1QIsaᵃ have וְנִבַּט (*wĕnibbat*), "and one will look"; pap4QIsaᵖ has והביט (*wĕhēbît*), "and one will look." Vg. reads the verb form as a first person plural (*aspiciemus*, "we will look").

*o   MT's בַּעֲרִיפֶהָ (*baʿărîpêhā*) is a crux. The word is probably cognate with Akkadian *erpetu* and Ugaritic *ʿrpt*, "clouds," but MT's pointing with a feminine suffix is odd, since the only feminine antecedent is ארץ, "earth." Perhaps one should point the word as בַּעֲרִיפִיָּא (*baʿărîpiyyâ*), "by clouds," or emend to בַּעֲרִיפִים (*baʿărîpîm*), "by clouds."

Commentary

Both verbs in 9:7 should be translated as past tenses with the LXX and Vg. Isaiah is describing something that has already happened to Israel. Jacob and Israel are used here specifically of the northern kingdom as the parallel usage of Ephraim and Samaria in the next verse shows. The reference to the "word" that God sent against Israel probably refers to an earlier prophetic message that has come to pass. It may refer specifically to the message of Amos, since this whole unit with its repeated refrain seems to be modeled on Amos 4:6-12, where the failure of a series of past punishments to accomplish their purpose is marked by the repeated refrain, "yet you did not return to me, says Yahweh" (Amos 4:6, 8, 9, 10, 11), ultimately leading to the announcement of a climactic future judgment (Amos 4:12). The LXX reading of דֶּבֶר (*deber*), "plague," for MT's דָּבָר (*dābār*), "word," is hardly original, but it does accurately characterize this word as a word of judgment.

The first verb in v. 8 should also be translated as a past tense, because Isaiah is describing the past actions of the Israelites. God's word of judgment had fallen upon the people, and, if the reading וְיָדְעוּ (*wĕyādĕʿû*) is correct, all of them had known or experienced it. The phrase "Ephraim and the inhabitants of Samaria" spells

1   Hans Wehr, *A Dictionary of Modern Written Arabic* (ed. J. M. Cowan; Ithaca, NY: Cornell University Press, 1961) 123.

out what is meant by all of the people. Samaria lay within the territory of Manasseh, and Ephraim and Manasseh were the two dominant sectional units in the northern kingdom during its decline in the eighth century after the death of Jeroboam II. As v. 20 indicates, juxtaposed as it is with the preceding vv. 18-19, these two territories, though composed of kinsmen who should be compassionate toward one another, were often virulently hostile to one another during this period because of sectional jealousy over who would control the throne. Thus, Isaiah makes a point of indicating that both of these parts of the northern kingdom had experienced God's prophetic word of judgment. Yet despite this experience, they had learned nothing from it. They still continued in their arrogant optimism. If the reading וַיְרַעוּ (wayyārīʿû) is correct, however, one could simply translate, "But all the people shouted out—Ephraim and the inhabitants of Samaria—saying in pride and haughtiness of heart. . . ." In any case, despite the judgment that had fallen upon them, all the people boasted that they would rebuild with even better and far more costly material than that which had fallen. Mud bricks were cheap building material; ashlars were the large, expensive hewn stones used only in palaces, temples, and very expensive buildings. Sycamores were very common and a source of cheap, poor-quality lumber, while the expensive cedar was normally imported from Lebanon only for very costly buildings. From the metaphorical language used here it is difficult to know precisely to what historical events Isaiah may be referring. If one understands the building material in a literal fashion, one might think of the earthquake in the days of Uzziah (Amos 1:1; Zech 14:5). If one understands the language as more general metaphorical references to political leaders or the political stability of the country, one might think of the destruction and political chaos that followed on the collapse of Jeroboam II's dynastic line, which Amos predicted (Amos 7:9; 2 Kgs 15:8-16).

Since Israel had not learned from this experience of judgment, God then stirred up the Arameans and the Philistines against them, and they gobbled up former Israelite territory. Again, all the verbs in vv. 10-11, following the initial converted imperfect, should be translated in the past tense. The MT of v. 10 mentions Rezin, the king of Damascus, who must be counted as one of the enemies God stirred up against Israel, but the MT's "Yahweh raised up the enemies of Rezin against him"

is clearly garbled and must be corrected to make sense. See the textual notes. I prefer the correction to צֹרְרֵי רְצִין (sōrĕrê rĕsîn), "the oppressors from Rezin," reading the construction as a subjective genitive (cf. Isa 11:13). Two other corrections are also possible, but even if the proper name "Rezin" is deleted as a gloss, that gloss should be regarded as an accurate interpretation, since Rezin was the leader of Israel's Aramean enemies. Isaiah is referring to the Aramean and Philistine response to the Israelite weakness that resulted from the political chaos in the north. The Arameans and Philistines took advantage of Israelite weakness to expand their own territory, but part of the reason for their interference in Israelite affairs grew out of Aramean and Philistine interest in forcing Israel and eventually Judah into their anti-Assyrian defensive alliance. Cf. Isa 2:6; 11:13-14; 2 Kgs 15:37; 16:5-6; 2 Chr 28:5-7, 18. Even this additional judgment of foreign oppression did not bring Israel to its senses, however, so God's anger did not abate, and his hand remained stretched out to discipline the north.

The people did not return to or inquire of Yahweh who smote them, so he continued to punish them. Isaiah's view of what was involved in returning to or inquiring of Yahweh probably involved the north's acceptance of Davidic rule and pilgrimage to the temple in Jerusalem. See Isa 2:1-6 and note also in 10:21 Isaiah's comment associated with the name Shear-yashub (שְׁאָר יָשׁוּב, šĕʾār yāšûb) that "a remnant of Jacob" (שְׁאָר יַעֲקֹב, šĕʾār yaʿăqōb) will return to Mighty God (אֵל גִּבּוֹר, ʾēl gibbôr)." It is hardly coincidental that Mighty God is one of the coronation names he gave to Hezekiah (9:5).

The continued punishment took the form of the amputation of Israel's leadership. Both metaphors in 9:13-14, lumping the top with the bottom, have in mind public officials, not ordinary citizens. It is not until 9:15b-16 that the prophet spells out the implications of this judgment for the ordinary citizens. There is no justification for deleting 9:15 as a gloss. Both elders and prophets were public officials, and it is not surprising that Isaiah would particularly disparage religious figures that supported any northern rival to the Davidic king in Jerusalem, since in Isaiah's view the Davidic monarch was the only legitimate ruler of Israel. The "cutting off" probably refers to the decimation of all levels of Israel's civil service, religious as well as purely political, as a consequence of the overthrow of Jeroboam II's dynasty, the resulting civil war, and the continuing pressure from Aram and Philistia. It was not a safe time to be a government official. The situation reflected in these verses corresponds to that reflected in Hosea 7:1-7; 8:4; 10:3-4; 13:9-11.

The loss of qualified leaders resulted in the people being led by misleaders, and so the led were led astray. Corruption in the government produced corruption in the populace (cf. Hosea's comments on the effects of priestly corruption, Hos 4:4-9), so Yahweh took no delight or joy in the young men, and even on the orphans and widows, traditionally oppressed classes who deserved special consideration, he had no compassion. Everyone, including the oppressed classes, had become such godless evildoers as to be punished without mercy. The first verb in v. 16 has a variant reading in the Qumran scroll that would provide closer parallelism to the second verb, "to have pity," but the slight contrast between "rejoicing in the young men" and "taking pity" on the orphans and widows may be an intentional contrast, reflecting a more complex parallelism, based on the quite normal human attitudes that differed for different groups within the society. Both verbs should be construed as indicating continuous action in the past.

Despite this harsh judgment, God still did not relent, because Israel's wickedness went on unabated. Isaiah describes the spread of that wickedness and its devastating effect with the metaphor of a brush fire. The development of Isaiah's argument here resembles that of Paul in Romans 1. God punishes the wickedness of his people by giving them up to the results of their own behavior. Thus, the fate of the land can be described as due to the wrath of God and, at the same time, to the wickedness of humans. Because of the wrath of God the land burned or shook (v. 18)—the derivation and precise meaning of the Hebrew word are debated—and the people in their unnatural hostility devoured their own kin, brother against brother without mercy. In the middle of v. 18 Isaiah switches from fire imagery to that of cannibalism, which becomes quite graphic in v. 19. The last line of that verse in the uncorrected Hebrew text actually says, "Each one devoured the flesh of his own arm." This may be the correct text; all the emendations are an attempt to tone down the harshness of the metaphor, but Isaiah was perfectly capable of describing an attack on fellow Israelites, one's kin, as self-mutilation.

It is only with v. 20 that the political events behind these metaphors become evident. The conflict between Ephraim and Manasseh refers to the sectional struggle for the northern throne following the fall of Jeroboam II's dynasty. Menahem seized the throne from Shallum son of Jabesh in a bloody campaign, but his control over the throne was never more than shaky, and his son was murdered and replaced by Pekah with strong support from Gilead (2 Kgs 15:8-25). The tribal affiliations of these various pretenders to the throne is not as clear as one would like, but Ephraim and Manasseh were the two dominant elements of the northern population, and any claimant to the throne would have to have one of these groups as a major base of support. Pekah's Gileadite supporters certainly included the Trans-Jordanian clans of Manasseh. The joint attack of Ephraim and Manasseh against Judah presumably refers to the Israelite and Aramean surprise attack on Jerusalem early in the Syro-Ephraimitic War, shortly after Pekah had united the north under his rule (2 Kgs 15:37; 16:5). Isaiah characterized this internecine strife as an expression of cannibalistic greed and saw it as God's judgment on his people. Yet, even this self-destruction did not turn aside God's anger.

It is obvious that v. 20 cannot be the original conclusion of this extended oracle. The judgments so far narrated all stand in the past, and the refrain indicating that God's hand is still stretched out in anger suggests that the sequence should end with an announcement of an impending and climactic future judgment, just as in the similarly constructed sequence in Amos 4:6-12. One might read 10:1-4 as this continuation, since the judgment announced in these verses appears to be future, but the introduction of these verses with the particle הוי makes that dubious, and the addition of the refrain at the end of 10:4 would prevent the reading of these verses as the conclusion of the series. Verses 10:1-4, minus the concluding refrain in v. 4b, were probably originally a part of the sequence of הוי oracles in Isa 5:8-24. See the discussion there. Isaiah 10:4b, with the repetition of the refrain, is a secondary effort to connect 10:1-4a to 9:7-20. But that means one is still lacking the original conclusion to the sequence of judgments in 9:7-20. The best candidate for that missing conclusion is 5:25-30, which begins by listing another judgment in the past, followed by the same refrain (v. 25), and then ends with the announcement of a climactic future judgment (vv. 26-30).

5:25-30

Isaiah 5:25 portrays another preliminary judgment in the series before the final threat, and it may be out of sequence. If one takes the imagery of quaking mountains literally, the imagery suggests the devastation of a massive earthquake, which makes one think of the earlier disaster in Uzziah's day. Of course, one could take the imagery metaphorically as a description of the tumult of battle followed by a graphic portrayal of the corpse-littered streets of fallen cities. In that case, this judgment would fit almost anywhere in the series, including its present position just before the conclusion. In support of this reading and its present placement, one might cite the allusion to the refrain in the idiom ויט ידו עליו (*wayyēṭ yādô ʿālāyw*), "and he stretched out his hand against him."

The conclusion to the series begins in Isa 5:26, where Isaiah switches from the past tense to the future. Because none of God's earlier judgments had brought the north to its senses, God is about to summon a powerful enemy from a distant land to come and destroy Israel. The reference is clearly to Assyria, though the images used to portray the speed, unrelenting preparedness, and fierceness of this enemy could be used of any foreign power. At the end of v. 30, the prophet turns from the frightening description of the Assyrian advance to portray the despair it will evoke in its victims. Thus, the oracle ends on a rather bleak note.

The original composition of the oracle would appear to date during the Syro-Ephraimitic War prior to the final intervention of Assyria that devastated the north in 733 BCE. Less likely is a slightly later date wherein the conclusion points forward, not to Tiglath-pileser III's attack in 733, but to Shalmaneser V's destruction of Israel in 725–722 BCE. The removal of 5:25-30 from its original connection with 9:7-20 and its attachment to the material in chap. 5, however, clearly suggests that this older material was reused some years later as a threat of judgment against Judah. In its present position in chap. 5 it serves as a warning to the Judean oppressors targeted in the preceding *hoy* oracles that they too, like the greedy, voracious Israelites before them, would face God's judgment at the hand of his hired Assyrians.

Bibliography

Crenshaw, James L., "A Liturgy of Wasted Opportunity (Am 4,6-12; Isa 9,7—10,4; 5:25-29)," *Semitics* 1 (1970) 27–37.

Donner, *Israel unter den Völker*, 64–75.

Goshen-Gottstein, M. H., "Hebrew Syntax and the History of the Bible Text: A Pesher in the MT of Isaiah," *Textus* 8 (1973) 100–106.

Fey, *Amos und Jesaja*.

Honeyman, A. M., "An Unnoticed Euphemism in Isaiah IX 19-20?" *VT* 1 (1951) 221–23.

Kruger, Paul A., "Another Look at Isa 9:7-20 [Bibliog]," *JNSL* 15 (1989) 127–41.

Ockinga, B. S., "*rās wĕzānāb kippah wĕʾagmôn* in Isa 9:13 and 9:15," *BN* 10 (1979) 31–34.

Thomas, D. W., "A Note on the Meaning of *jada* in Hosea 9:9 and Isaiah 9:8," *JTS* 41 (1940) 43–44.

Wallenstein, M., "An Unnoticed Euphemism in Isaiah IX 19-20?" *VT* 2 (1952) 179–80.

Wohlmann, H., "The Bricks Are Fallen, but We Will Build with Hewn Stones," *BetM* 1 (1956) 37–43.

10

Isaiah 10:5-34 contains a series of oracles that, in their present literary arrangement, are directed against Assyria. This material has a complex prehistory, however. Despite the clear anti-Assyrian intent of the present text, some of the material incorporated in it appears to be material originally directed against Israel and Syria at the time of the Syro-Ephraimitic War. Some of these older Isaianic oracles have been adapted and reused in the new situation, perhaps by Isaiah himself, but others of them appear to have been inappropriately inserted unchanged in an alien context by later redactors. Such blatant insertions tend to leave clear traces, but even an original author's adaptation of old material for new situations often fails to obscure all the signs of the original situation to which the material referred, as any one who has ever reused old sermons knows. Even within Isaiah's later material composed specifically to address Assyria, there are some traces of later adaptation.

10:5-15 Assyria Nothing but God's Tool

5/   Hey! Assyria is the rod of my anger;
     And (he) is[a] the staff in the hand[b] of my wrath.[c]
6/   Against a godless nation I keep sending him,[d]
     And against the people[e] of my fury[f] I keep ordering him.[g]
     To plunder (its) plunder,
     And to take (its) booty;
     And to make it[h] a thing trampled,
     Like the mire of the streets.
7/   But he does not so intend,
     And his heart does not so consider;
     For it is in his heart to destroy,
     And to cut off nations not a few.
8/   For he says,[i] "Are not my officers all kings,
9/   Was not Calno like Carchemish?
     Or was not Hamath like Arpad?
     Or was not Samaria like Damascus?
10/   As my hand reached to the kingdoms of the idols[j]—
     And their images were (more) than (those) of Jerusalem and Samaria . . .
11/   As I have done to Samaria and its idols,
     Shall I not do the same to Jerusalem and its images?"
12/   But it will be when my Lord has finished all his work on Mount Zion and in
        Jerusalem, I will punish the fruit of the haughtiness of heart of the king
        of Assyria and the pride of his exalted eyes.
13/   For he said, "By the strength of my hand I did (it),
     And by my wisdom, for I am clever;
     I removed[k] the boundaries of the peoples,
     I plundered their treasures,
     And like a bull I brought down[k] (their) rulers.
14/   And my hand reached the wealth of the peoples like a bird's nest,
     And as one gathers abandoned eggs, I gathered the whole earth;
     There was no one flapping a wing, or opening the mouth and chirping."
15/   Does the ax boast over the one who hews with it?
     Or does the saw exalt itself over the one who saws with it?[l]
     As if the rod waved[m] the one[n] who lifts it,[op]
     As if the staff lifted the one who is not wood![q]

Textual Notes

a   The pronoun הוּא (hûʾ), "he," serves as a copulative and indicates that both lines are to be read as nominal clauses, so also the Syriac.

b   MT's בְּיָדָם supported by 1QIsaᵃ and all the versions, is probably to be analyzed as a noun in construct followed by the enclitic mem (bĕyad-m), "in the hand of," rather than as a noun followed by the third person masculine plural suffix (bĕyādām), "in their hand," as it is pointed.

c LXX has a double translation of זַעְמִי—"the rod of my anger and **wrath** is in their hands; (v. 6) my **wrath** I will send against a lawless nation." Syr. has "in their hand of my smiting."

d LXX omits the suffix on "send" because it took "my wrath" from the previous verse as the object of the verb.

e LXX renders "to my people."

f LXX omits "of my fury," and Syr. simply omits the suffix.

g LXX omits the object suffix.

h MT וּלְשִׂימוֹ (ûlĕsîmô), "and to make it," with qĕrē' ולשומו (ûlĕsûmô), "and to make it," is supported by 4QIsaᵉ; 1QIsaᵃ ולשום lacks the suffix.

i LXX's very loose translation of vv. 8-9—"And if they say to him, 'You alone are ruler,' then he will say, 'Did I not take the country above Babylon and Chalanne, where the tower was built? And I took Arabia and Damascus and Samaria'"—is not indicative of a variant text.

j For MT's הָאֱלִיל (hā'ĕlîl), "worthless idol," 1QIsaᵃ has האלילים (hā'ĕlîlîm), "worthless idols."

k MT's simple imperfects וְאָסִיר (wĕ'āsîr), "and I will remove," and וְאוֹרִיד (wĕ'ôrîd), "and I will bring down," do not fit with the parallel perfects עָשִׂיתִי ('āśîtî), "I did," and שׁוֹשֵׂתִי (šôśētî), "I plundered." They should be repointed to the past tense waw-consecutives—וָאָסִיר (wā'āsîr) and וָאוֹרִיד (wā'ôrîd)—with Vg. and Syr.

l MT מְנִיפוֹ (mĕnîpô), "the one who saws with it"; 1QIsaᵃ מניפיו (mĕnîpāyw), "those who saw with it."

m Syr. renders MT's כְּהָנִיף (kĕhānîp), "as if the *rod* waved," as, "or does the rod exalt itself over the one who raises it."

n Read את ('et) with 1QIsaᵃ in preference to MT's וְאֶת (wĕ'et).

o Read the singular מרימו (mĕrîmô), "the one lifting it," with LXX, Vg., Syr., in preference to מְרִימָיו (mĕrîmāyw), "those lifting it," of MT and 1QIsaᵃ.

p LXX omits the whole phrase כהניף שבט את-מרימו (kĕhānîp šēbeṭ 'et-mĕrîmô), "as though the rod waved the one who lifts it."

q LXX renders the final phrase as though it had כהרים מטה או-עץ (kĕhārîm maṭṭê 'ô-ʿēṣ, ὡσαύτως ἐάν τις ἄρῃ ῥάβδον ἢ ξύλον) "as if someone should lift a rod or tree"; Syr. omits the last phrase. Thus, both LXX and Syr. show haplography of one unit; they just differ in which one.

Commentary

Isaiah 10:5-15 characterizes Assyria as merely the tool God used to punish any nation with which he was angry. Assyria, however, misunderstood its role, assumed that its successes resulted from its own power, grew proud and boastful, and even vaunted itself against the LORD whose tool it was. Thus, when God has finished the work for which this tool is needed, Assyria itself will receive its punishment in turn. The purpose of the oracle was apparently to reassure Judah that the LORD remained in control of history and that it was God's work, albeit his strange work (28:21), that was being realized in the frightening events taking place around them. Thus, they could still trust in God's promises.

The oracle begins with the vocative exclamation הוֹי (hôy), but since Isaiah's real audience is Judah, not Assyria, the fiction of a direct address to Assyria is quickly dropped in favor of third person references, apart from the direct quotations of Assyria's boasting in the first person in vv. 8-11, 13-14. Assyria is merely the staff God in his anger uses to administer punishment. The metaphor is clarified in v. 6, where God asserts that he sends Assyria to plunder and conquer any nation or people who provoke his anger by their profane, ungodly behavior. Israel and Judah are included in this general class, but there is no reason to take "the profane nation" as a specific and exclusive reference to Israel, as the reference to many nations in v. 7 indicates. Assyria carried out its task, but with a basic misunderstanding. Its plan exceeded God's commission. Assyria was not content to plunder the nations against which God was angry; its lust for conquest was unbridled. Success had made it overconfident.

The boast of Assyria or its king is quoted in vv. 8-11. A mere royal official (שַׂר, śar) of the Assyrian king is equal to the kings (מְלָכִים, mĕlākîm) of other countries. There is obviously a clever wordplay here on Assyrian and Hebrew cognates, indicating some knowledge of Assyrian, since Hebrew śar, "royal official," is cognate with Akkadian šarru (pronounced śarru in Assyrian), "king."[1] Moreover, Assyria boasts that future conquests will be as easy as past ones have been. These references to past conquests raise some historical problems, however, due to the peculiarity of the order in which they are cited. The

---

1 For other plays on Assyria and Assyrian royal inscriptions in this passage, see the extended discussion in Machinist, "Assyria and Its Image," 719–37; and Michael Chan, "Rhetorical Reversal and Usurpation: Isaiah 10:5-34 and the Use of Neo-Assyrian Royal Idiom in the Construction of an Anti-Assyrian Theology," *JBL* 128 (2009) 717–33.

grammatical structure of the question, "Is not Calno like Carchemish?" suggests that Calno will be as easy to take as Carchemish, implying that Carchemish was captured first. Actually, however, Calno, Assyrian Kullani in North Syria (cf. Amos 6:2), fell to Tiglath-pileser III in 738 BCE, while Carchemish was conquered by Sargon II later in 717 BCE. Carchemish was obviously allied to Tiglath-pileser when he campaigned west of the Euphrates in 743–738 BCE, but there is no record of his conquering the city. Arpad and Hamath come in the right order, but it is not entirely clear to what events the text refers. Tiglath-pileser captured Arpad in 740 after a three-year siege, and Hamath fell to Sargon II in 720 BCE. Sargon may have reasserted his authority over Arpad in 720 before taking Hamath, and Tiglath-pileser in 738 clearly regained control of the regions of Hamath that had joined Kullani's rebellion against him, but which of these events does the prophet have in mind? Damascus fell to Tiglath-pileser in 732 BCE; Samaria was captured by Shalmaneser V in 722; and both were sacked again by Sargon II in 720. If one could be certain of the precise events to which the prophet was referring, it would help immensely in dating the oracle.

The nature of the problem is indicated by a comparison of vv. 10-11. Isaiah 10:10 is an incomplete sentence that presupposes that Samaria has not yet been taken:

As my hand has reached to the kingdoms of the idols,
And their images were (more numerous) than (those) of Jerusalem and Samaria . . .

One expects a concluding apodosis such as "thus I will do to Jerusalem and Samaria." Verse 11 cannot be that apodosis, because it is a complete sentence that presupposes that Samaria has already fallen:

As I have done to Samaria and its idols,
Shall I not do the same to Jerusalem and its images?"

Verse 10 is only a fragment, and perhaps a reworked fragment at that. Something has fallen out of the text, and

what remains may have been touched up when v. 11 was added.

It is not necessary to dismiss 10:11-12 as exilic additions to the text, however (Wildberger, Gray, Duhm, and others). The original form of v. 10 may suggest that this oracle was first composed prior to the fall of Samaria in 722 and then later adapted by Isaiah to deal with the threat to Jerusalem in 701 BCE. Verses 11-12 would be part of the later adaptation. The reference to Jerusalem's idols in v. 11 is not to be understood as a genuine charge of idolatry against Jerusalem leveled by the prophet or a later glossator.[2] The Assyrian king is speaking, and his comment, like his comment on Samaria and Jerusalem's relative lack of images in v. 10, simply betrays his basic misunderstanding of the religious situation in Jerusalem (cf. Isa 36:7-10). It is part and parcel of Assyria's total failure to recognize what was really taking place, namely, that it was only a tool in the LORD's hand. Jerusalem's God, far from being a mere image, was directing the show, and even Assyria's victories were the LORD's doing. Because of Assyria's arrogant misunderstanding of the real situation, God will put it in its place as soon as he has finished using it in his work on Mount Zion. Verse 12's mention of God's work on Mount Zion and in Jerusalem parallels the reference to his "strange work" in Isa 28:21 and should be understood as referring to his purging of the city by judgment (Isa 1:21-28). It is a "strange work," because it seems to go against the Zion Tradition's promises that God founded (Ps 78:68-69; Isa 14:32) and lived in Jerusalem (Psalms 46; 48; 132; Isa 8:18), and so would protect it and its inhabitants from their enemies, but Isaiah claimed that God must purge Jerusalem before it could be saved (Isa 1:21-28). Assyria was to be the tool in this work, but before Jerusalem was utterly destroyed, the LORD would intervene to save a remnant and, in the process, destroy Assyria, Jerusalem's oppressor (Isa 29:1-8; 31:4-9; cf. 14:24-27).

The reason for this threatened judgment on Assyria is further elaborated in vv. 13-15, where the prophet first quotes the Assyrian king's arrogant boasting and then concludes with a question reminiscent of proverbial

---

2   Isaiah has relatively little to say in criticism of idolatry (Isa 1:29-31; 2:8, 18, 20; 17:7-8, 10-11; 31:6), particularly with regard to Jerusalem. His criticism of Jerusalem's leaders is about governmental corruption, unjust oppression, and a refusal in foreign policy to trust in God's promises to the Davidic house and Jerusalem (Isa 3:12-15; 5:1-24; 10:1-4; 7:1–8:18; 30:1-5; 31:1-5).

literature. Note the whole series of first person references in the Assyrian's boast. Isaiah has obviously put this speech in the Assyrian's mouth, but it is a reasonably fair portrayal of the typical claims of the Assyrian kings to enormous power, almost endless military success, and great wisdom, as a comparison with the royal inscriptions of Sargon II or Sennacherib will show.[3] Sargon describes himself in his clay cylinder inscription as,

The king (*šarru*) for whom, since the (first) day of his rule [*bēlūtīšu*], there has been no prince [*malku*] who was an equal opponent for him [*gabarâšu*], and who in battle and war saw no one who could defeat him. Who smashed all the enemy lands to pieces like pottery sherds, and put nose ropes on the rebels of the four world regions. Who opened up the difficult passages into numerous high mountains and saw their remote regions, who again and again crossed over inaccessible, difficult paths whose location was terrifying, and who again and again crossed all the swamps. Who ruled everything from the land of Rashi on the border of Elam, the tribes of Puqudu and Damumu, the cities Dur-Kurigalzu and Rapiqu and the whole steppe, as far as the Brook of Egypt, the wide land of Amurru, and the land of Hatti in its entirety. Whose great hand conquered from the land of Hashmar to the land of Simash on the border of the land of the distant Medes of the sunrise, the land of Namri, the land of Ellibi, and the land of Bit-Hamban, and from the lands of Parsua, Mannaya, Urartu, Kasku, and Tabalum, as far as the land of Musku. Who appointed his eunuchs over them as governors and imposed tax and tribute upon them like that of the Assyrians.[4]

Just as Isaiah's boasting Assyrian, who compares himself to a wild ox (*'abbîr*) that brings down the rulers of the foreign lands he conquers (v. 13), so several times Sennacherib compares himself to a wild ox (*rīmu*).[5] Moreover, both Sargon and Sennacherib refer to their terrified enemies as abandoning their habitations or removing their gods and fleeing away like frightened birds.[6] Isaiah underscores the folly of such arrogant Assyrian pride by comparing Assyria to an inanimate tool like an ax or a saw which boasts against the animate workman who wields them.

Bibliography

Ahlström, Gösta W., "Prophetical Echoes of Assyrian Growth and Decline," in H. Behrens, ed., *Dumu-e2-dub-ba-a: Studies in Honor of Åke W. Sjöberg* (Occasional papers of the Samuel Noah Kramer Fund 11; Philadelphia: University Museum, 1989) 1–6.
Barth, *Die Jesaja-Worte.*
Chan, "Rhetorical Reversal."
Childs, *Assyrian Crisis.*
Driver, "Isaiah 1–39: Problems."
Fichtner, J., "Jahwes Plan in der Botschaft des Jesaja," *ZAW* 63 (1951) 16–33.
Fohrer, G., "Wandlungen Jesajas," in G. Wiesner, ed., *Festschrift für Wilhelm Eilers* (Wiesbaden: Harrassowitz, 1967) 67–70.
Freedman, David Noel, "The Broken Construct Chain," *Bib* 53 (1972) 534–76.
Fullerton, K., "The Problem of Isaiah, Chapter 10," *AJSL* 34 (1917–18) 170–84.
Haag, E., "Prophet und Politik im AT," *TTZ* 80 (1971) 222–46.
Huber, Friedrich, "Die Worte Jesajas gegen Assur," in Huber, *Jahwe, Juda und die anderen Völker beim Propheten Jesaja* (BZAW 137; Berlin: de Gruyter, 1976) 35–76.

3 A limited selection of these inscriptions is available in A. Leo Oppenheim's English translation in *ANET* 3rd ed. (1969), 284–88; a German translation of Sargon II's inscriptions from Khorsabad is available in Andreas Fuchs, *Die Inschriften Sargons II. aus Khorsabad* (Göttingen: Cuvillier, 1994); and a convenient, if dated, English translation of Sennacherib's inscriptions is found in Daniel David Luckenbill, *The Annals of Sennacherib* (OIP 2; Chicago: University of Chicago Press, 1924). See now A. Kirk Grayson and Jamie Novotny, *The Royal Inscriptions of Sennacherib, King of Assyria (704–681), Part 1* (RINAP 3.1; Winona Lake, IN: Eisenbrauns, 2012), for an up-to-date and excellent edition and translation.
4 Fuchs, *Die Inschriften Sargons II*, pp. 32–34, 289–90, lines 8-16.
5 Luckenbill, *Annals of Sennacherib*, 36 iv 2; 50:19; 71:39; Grayson and Novotny, RINAP 3/1, p. 33, 1:19; p. 177, 16:iv 82.
6 Fuchs, *Die Inschriften Sargons II*, pp. 206, 346, line 50; Luckenbill, *Annals of Sennacherib*, 35 iii 65; Grayson and Novotny, RINAP 3/1, p. 98, 14:iv 33'-34'.

Kilian, Rudolf, "Jesaja und Assur," in Kilian, *Jesaja 1–39*, 98–111.

Machinist, "Assyria and Its Image."

Mittmann, Siegfried, "Wehe! Assur, Stab meines Zorns (Jes 10,5-9.13ab-15)," in Volkmar Fritz, Karl-Friedrich Pohlmann, and Hans-Christof Schmitt, eds., *Prophet und Prophetenbuch: Festschrift für Otto Kaiser zum 65. Geburtstag* (BZAW 185; Berlin: de Gruyter, 1983) 111–32.

Robertson, E., "Some Obscure Passages in Isaiah," *AJSL* 49 (1932–33) 320–22.

Sander, O., "Leib–Seele–Dualismus im Alten Testament," *ZAW* 77 (1965) 329–32.

Schildenberger, J., "Das 'Wehe' über den stolzen Weltherrscher Assur," *Sein und Sendung* 30 (1965) 483–89.

Skehan, Patrick W. "A Note on Is 10:11b-12a," *CBQ* 14 (1952) 236.

Speier, S., "Zu drei Jesajastellen (1,7; 5,24; 10,7)," *TZ* 21 (1965) 310–13.

Tadmor, H., "The Campaigns of Sargon II of Assur: A Chronological-Historical Study," *JCS* 12 (1958) 33–40, 77–100.

10:16-19 An Early Oracle against Israel

16/ Therefore[a] the Lord Yahweh[b] of Hosts will send leanness into his[c] stout ones,[d] and instead of his[c] glory there will burn a burning like the burning of fire. 17/ And the light of Israel will become a fire, and his holy one[e] a flame, and it will burn and consume his thorn and his thistle[f] in one day.[g] 18/ And the glory of his woods and his orchard[h] from spirit to flesh he will bring to an end,[i] and he will become like the melting of a sick man.[j] 19/ And the remnant of the trees of his woods[k] will be so few in number that even a lad will be able to write them down.

Textual Notes

a LXX misreads לָכֵן (lākēn), "therefore," as ולא כן (wĕlōʾ kēn, καὶ οὐχ οὕτως), "and not so, rather"; 1QIsaᵃ supports MT.

b LXX has only one κύριος for הָאָדוֹן יְהוָה (hāʾādôn YHWH), "the Lord Yahweh"; 1QIsaᵃ supports MT.

c LXX has the second person singular.

d For MT's בְּמִשְׁמַנָּיו רָזוֹן (bĕmišmannāyw rāzôn), "leanness into his stout ones," LXX has εἰς τὴν σὴν τιμὴν ἀτιμίαν, "unto your honor dishonor," a very prosaic effort to interpret what is in the MT. 1QIsaᵃ, Vg., and Syr. follow MT. LXX does not seem to know the meaning of רזה (rāzâ); cf. 17:4, where it translates the verb from this root as σεισθήσεται, "shall be shaken." There it renders וּמִשְׁמַן בְּשָׂרוֹ (ûmišman bĕśārô), "the fatness of his flesh," as καὶ τὰ πίονα τῆς δόξης αὐτοῦ, "and the fat/rich ones of his glory."

e 1QIsaᵃ, Vg., and Syr. agree with MT; LXX misunderstands the epithet "his holy one" and translates that part of the verse as καὶ ἁγιάσει αὐτὸν ἐν πυρὶ καιομένῳ, "and he shall sanctify him in burning fire."

f LXX renders "his thorn and his thistle" [thorny undergrowth and thorn bushes] as ὡσεὶ χόρτον τὴν ὕλην, "(he will devour) the forest like grass"; Syr. has "his forest and his thorns."

g For בְּיוֹם אֶחָד (bĕyôm ʾeḥād), "in one day," LXX has τῇ ἡμέρα ἐκείνῃ "in that day"; 1QIsaᵃ, Vg., and Syr. follow MT.

h 1QIsaᵃ, Vg., and Syr. follow MT. LXX has an odd plus, ἀποσβεσθήσεται τὰ ὄρη καὶ οἱ βουνοὶ καὶ οἱ δρυμοί, "The mountains and the hills and the woods will be extinguished."

i LXX, Syr., and Vg. read the verb יכלה (yĕkallê), "he will finish," as a passive.

j All the versions had difficulty with כְּמְסס נֹסֵס (kimsōs nōsēs), "like the melting of a sick man." LXX and Vg. both saw here the root נוס (nûs), "to flee." LXX has καὶ ἔσται ὁ φεύγων ὡς ὁ φεύγων ἀπὸ φλογὸς καιομένης, "and the one fleeing shall be like the one fleeing from a burning flame," and Vg. has *terrore profugus*, "he will be a fugitive from terror." Syr. has ܘܢܗܘܐ ܐܝܟ ܕܠܐ ܗܘܐ (wnhwʾ ʾyk dlʾ hwʾ), "and it will become as if it had not been."

k 1QIsaᵃ and Syr. follow MT, as does Vg. with a slight paraphrase for sense: *et reliquiae ligni saltus eius pro paucitate nerabuntur et puer scribet eos*, "and the remnants of the wood of his forest will be able to be numbered because of scarcity so that even a lad may write them down." LXX has "those left of them" without specifically mentioning either trees or forest.

Commentary

Isaiah 10:16-19 is linked to the preceding material with a "therefore" that introduces an explicit judgment in response to Assyria's foolish pride, but there is reason to suspect that this placement of 10:16-19 is secondary, since the unit does not continue any of the imagery of the preceding verses. If one may judge from the continuity and consistency of imagery, the original conclusion to Isa 10:5-15 is to be found in 10:24*-27a. Isaiah 10:16-23* is a secondary insertion in this original unit. Isaiah 10:16-19 may have been inserted here by Josianic editors well after the time of Isaiah, but it is very improbable that the verses were composed by any one other than Isaiah. Far from being a late redactional composition, they are more likely part of an earlier Isaianic oracle against Israel from the time of the Syro-Ephraimitic War, which has been secondarily inserted here to make God's judgment on Assyria explicit. The imagery in these verses has its closest parallels in the oracle against Damascus and Ephraim in Isa 17:1-6. There as here Isaiah speaks of a wasting away (רָזוֹן//יֵרָזֶה *rāzôn//yērāzeh*) of the enemy's fatness (מִשְׁמַנָּיו *mišmannāyw//*מִשְׁמַן *mišman*; 10:16//17:4), a loss of his glory (10:18//17:4), and a destruction expressed in terms of arboreal or horticultural imagery. The description of

the destruction of a people under the image of a brush fire is found also in the oracle against Israel in 9:17-18.

In 10:17, however, the source of that fire is said to be God himself. There is a clever wordplay in Isaiah's choice of "Light of Israel" as an epithet to designate the LORD, particularly if this word was originally directed against Israel. The word "light" (אוֹר *'ôr*) differs only in its vowel from a word meaning flame or fire (אוּר *'ûr*; see Isa 31:9), implying that the God, who once provided Israel light (*'ôr*), has now become instead the flame (*'ûr*) that burns Israel. Of course, in the present literary context, it is Assyria, not Israel, that God burns. In the course of Isaiah's prophetic career, the object of God's judgment changed, but the prophet never seemed to tire of fire imagery as an appropriate metaphor to convey God's holy rage for righteousness.

The extent of the destruction of the enemy, under the figure of the forest, is graphically portrayed by the imagery of v. 19. There will be so few trees left after this brush fire that even a young lad will know the correct numerals for recording their number in writing. Since Israelite scribes made use of Egyptian hieratic numerals in recording numbers,[7] a lad with limited scribal training would be unlikely to know how to write more than a few of the basic numbers.

10:20-23 A Shear-jashub Oracle

20/ In that day the remnant of Israel and the survivors of the house of Jacob will no longer lean[a] upon the one who smote him,[a] but he will lean[a] upon[b] Yahweh, the holy one of Israel, in truth. 21/ Only a remnant will return,[c] a remnant of Jacob to[d] Mighty God. 22/ For even if your people, O Israel,[e] are like the sand of the sea, only a remnant in it[f] will return;[g] destruction is decreed overflowing with righteousness. 23/ For my Lord, Yahweh of Hosts,[h] is about to make a decreed destruction[i] in the midst of the whole land.

---

7 Hieratic numerals are quite common in Hebrew inscriptions; note particularly the inscriptions from Arad (F. W. Dobbs-Allsopp, J. J. M. Roberts, C. L. Seow, and R. E. Whitaker, *Hebrew Inscriptions: Texts from the Biblical Period of the Monarchy with Concor-* dance [New Haven: Yale University Press, 2005] 5–108), and cf. William M. Schniedewind, *A Social History of Hebrew: Its Origins through the Rabbinic Period* (AYBRL; New Haven: Yale University Press, 2013) 36, 58, 68–69, 101–2, 125.

a   In MT and 1QIsaᵃ the verbs יוֹסִיף (yôsîp), "will no longer (lean)," וְנִשְׁעַן (wěniš'an), "but will lean," and the suffix on מַכֵּהוּ (makkēhû), "the one who smote him," are all third person masculine singular, with שְׁאָר (šě'ār), "remnant," as the presumed subject and antecedent. LXX and Syr. take the first verb as singular, but the second verb and the suffix they translate with the plural. Vg. reads only the suffix as plural, while Tg. reads all the forms as plural.

b   1QIsaᵃ has the aural mistake of אֶל ('el), "to," for MT's עַל ('al), "upon."

c   LXX omits שְׁאָר יָשׁוּב (šě'ār yāšûb), "a remnant will return," by haplography; it is present in 1QIsaᵃ, Vg., and Syr.

d   LXX has ἐπί, apparently reading עַל ('al), "upon," for אֶל- ('el-), "to."

e   LXX has "the people Israel" instead of "your people, O Israel," but 1QIsaᵃ, Vg., and Syr. support MT.

f   LXX may be misreading בוֹ (bô), "in it," as כִּי (kî), "for," and construing it with the following, which it renders as λόγον γὰρ συντελῶν καὶ συντέμνων ἐν δικαιοσύνῃ, "for he is bringing to an end and cutting short a word in righteousness."

g   For שְׁאָר יָשׁוּב (šě'ār yāšûb), "a remnant will return," LXX has τὸ κατάλειμμα αὐτῶν σωθήσεται, "their remnant shall be saved."

h   For "Lord Yahweh of Hosts," LXX has only ὁ θεός; Syr. has "Lord Almighty" omitting either אֲדֹנָי or יְהוָה, but 1QIsaᵃ and Vg. support MT.

i   For כָּלָה וְנֶחֱרָצָה (kālâ wěneḥěrāṣâ), lit. "a destruction and decreed," that is, "decreed destruction," LXX has λόγον συντετμημένον "a decisive word."

Commentary

This block of material also appears to be older material from the Syro-Ephraimitic War that was inserted here together with 10:16-19. There is no trace of editorial adaptation that would identify the enemy as Assyria. Verses 20-23 can be read as the original continuation of vv. 16-19, both of which envision Israel as the enemy of Judah under discussion and should be dated to the Syro-Ephraimitic War. Following the judgment on the northern kingdom portrayed in vv. 16-19, the surviving remnant of Israel would no longer lean on the one who smote it, Rezin of Damascus (see Isa 9:11-12), but would truly lean on the LORD, the Holy One of Israel. Note the use of the same epithet that occurs in 10:17. Verse 21 begins with an expression that is identical to the symbolic name of Isaiah's first son—Shear-jashub, "a remnant will return." Since that son played his symbolic role at the beginning of the Syro-Ephraimitic War (Isa 7:3), this is another indication that this oracle, which provides the otherwise missing explanation of the symbolic name, had its original setting in that earlier period.

The intended referent of the expression "mighty God" is unclear. This is one of the coronation names given to the Judean king in Isa 9:6, but if the king under discussion there was Hezekiah, as seems probable, the giving of this name to the Judean king dates from some years later than the reference to "mighty God" in Isa 10:21. The expression could simply be another epithet for the LORD, simply repeating the comment of v. 20 that the remnant of Israel would truly return to God. It may be, however,

that the epithet was a traditional royal epithet in the south even before Hezekiah, and that it equates Israel's return to God to Israel's return to the hegemony of the Davidic monarchy.

Verses 22-23 pick up the motif of judgment again in a graphic reversal of the ancient patriarchal promise that Israel's descendants would be as numerous as the sand of the seashore (Gen 22:17; 32:13; cf. Hos 1:10 [Heb. 1:9—2:1]). Even if they should be that numerous, only a small remnant from the northern kingdom will return. Note, moreover, that in Isa 10:22 God pointedly refuses to call Israel "my people," but addressing Israel directly, refers to the northern population as "your people, O Israel." "Israel" here is clearly vocative, as the JPS translation makes clear but which the RSV and NRSV's, "your people Israel," leave ambiguous. This refusal to acknowledge Israel, while counter to the promise in Hosea, has a counterpart in Hosea's earlier word of judgment (Hos 1:9). There is hope for no more than a remnant from the north, for the LORD has decided on a thorough, though just, destruction of Israel. Verse 23 characterizes that decision as irrevocable, but the RSV's "in the midst of all the earth" should probably be rendered as "in the midst of the whole land" and be taken as a reference to the northern territory. The decreed destruction is the same as that announced in Isa 7:16 and 8:4.

As in 7:16 and 8:4, the real audience for this announcement of judgment on the north is Judean. The purpose of the oracle is to reassure the Judeans in the face of the threat from the north that they can continue to trust in God's promises to protect the Davidic throne and his holy city Jerusalem. That would be even clearer if this oracle, with the reassuring promise found in v. 24: אל תירא עמי ישב ציון (ʾal tîrāʾ ʿammî yōšēb ṣîyôn), "Do not fear, O my people, who dwell in Zion," had a slightly different ending. This explicit acknowledgment of Judah as God's people would provide a sharp contrast to God's refusal to acknowledge Israel, if the continuation of the verse, instead of naming Assyria as the object of the fear of God's people in Zion, had named Israel, its king, or its Syrian allies as the object of Judah's fear, similar to the related promise given to Ahaz in Isa 7:4. Nonethe-

less, when this promise was later revised to address the now more pressing fear that Judah felt toward the more powerful Assyrian enemy, who smote them with a rod and raised his staff over them as Egypt had done, this alteration led to the insertion of all of Isa 10:16-24a into the anti-Assyrian oracle found in 10:24b-27a. What had been an oracle against Israel in the Syro-Ephraimitic War was thus turned into an expanded oracle against Judah's later enemy Assyria, though at the expense of a number of rough edges and inconsistencies in the updated oracle.

Bibliography

Binns, L. E., "Midianite Elements in Hebrew Religion," *JTS* 31 (1930) 337–54.

Hasel, Gerhard F., *The Remnant: The History and Theology of the Remnant Idea from Genesis to Isaiah* (Andrews University Monographs 5; Berrien Springs, MI: Andrews University Press, 1972).

Schwarz, G. ". . . das Licht Israels? Eine Emendation (Isa 10:17a)," *ZAW* 82 (1970) 447–48.

Stegemann, U., "Der Restgedanke bei Isaias," *BZ* n.F. 13 (1969) 161–86.

Widengren, G., "Yahweh's Gathering of the Dispersed," in W. Boyd Barrick and John R. Spencer, eds., *In the Shelter of Elyon: Essays on Ancient Palestinian Life and Literature in Honor of G.W. Ahlström* (JSOTSup 31; Sheffield: JSOT Press, 1984) 227–45.

10:24-27a An Oracle against Assyria

24/   Therefore thus says my Lord Yahweh of Hosts, "Do not fear, O my people, who live in Zion, from Assyria, at[a] the rod which smote you and his staff[b] which he raised against you[c] in the manner of Egypt. 25/ For in just a little while and the wrath will be complete, and my anger upon their destruction.[d] 26/ And Yahweh of Hosts[e] is about to swing[f] a whip[g] against him as he smote Midian at the rock of Oreb,[h] and his staff he will raise against him,[i] and he will raise it in the manner of Egypt. 27/ And on that day his weight[j] will turn aside from upon your shoulder,[k] and his yoke from upon your neck[l] will be destroyed.[m]

Textual Notes

a   MT בַּשֵּׁבֶט (baššēbeṭ), "at the rod," is supported by the versions against משבט (miššēbeṭ), "from the rod," of 1QIsaᵃ.

b   MT וּמַטֵּהוּ (ûmaṭṭēhû), "and his staff"; so 4QIsaᶜ; ומטו (ûmaṭṭô), 1QIsaᵃ.

c   LXX has πληγὴν γὰρ ἐγὼ ἐπάγω ἐπὶ σὲ τοῦ ἰδεῖν ὁδὸν Αἰγύπτου, "for I will bring a blow upon you so that you may see

the way of Egypt." Here LXX must be reading אשא (ʾeśśāʾ), "I will raise, bring," for MT ישא (yiśśāʾ), "he will raise, bring."

d   תַּבְלִיתָם (tablîtām) is a crux; some reconstruct תכליתם (taklîtām), "their end, destruction." LXX has ὁ δὲ θυμός μου ἐπὶ τὴν βουλὴν αὐτῶν, "and my wrath will be upon their will"; Vg. *et furor meus super scelus eorum*, "and my fury over their wickedness"; Syr. "my wrath will be upon their destruction." Possible reconstruction: וְאַפִּי עַל תֶּכֶל יִתֹּם (wĕʾappî ʿal tekel yittōm), "and my anger will be completely ended."

e LXX has only "(the) God."

f For MT's וְעֹרֵר (wĕʿôrēr), "is about to swing," 1QIsaᵃ has ויעיר (wĕyāʿîr), "and he will swing."

g LXX omits שׁוֹט (šôṭ), "whip," in its translation, but its translation is so garbled—καὶ ἐπεγερεῖ ὁ θεὸς ἐπ' αὐτοὺς κατὰ τὴν πληγὴν τὴν Μαδιαμ ἐν τόπῳ θλίψεως, καὶ ὁ θυμὸς αὐτοῦ τῇ ὁδῷ τῇ κατὰ θάλασσαν εἰς τὴν ὁδὸν τὴν κατ' Αἴγυπτον, "and God will stir up against them like the stroke of Madiam at the place of affliction, and his wrath will be by the way of the sea, on the way toward Egypt"— there is no guarantee it was reading a different text.

h For עֹרֵב בְּצוּר (bĕṣûr ʿôrēb), "rock of Oreb," Syr. has ܘܒܠܐ ܕܒܛܘܪ ܕܚܘܪܝܒ (dbṭwrʾ dḥwryb), "which was in the mountain of Horeb." Isaiah here is referring to the incident in Judg 7:25 about the death of the two leaders of Midian.

i Emending the text to ומטהו עליו ירים (ûmaṭṭēhû ʿalāyw yārîm), "and his staff he will raise against him." Though MT's וּמַטֵּהוּ עַל־הַיָּם (ûmaṭṭēhû ʿal-hayyām), "and his staff against the sea," is supported by 1QIsaᵃ, Vg., and Syr., it is very awkward and probably not original.

j LXX has "his fear," but MT סֻבֳּלוֹ (subbŏlô), "his weight, burden," is supported by 1QIsaᵃ, Vg., and Syr.

k LXX has "from you" for MT מֵעַל שִׁכְמֶךָ (mēʿal šikmekā), "from upon your shoulder."

l LXX has "from upon your shoulder" for MT מֵעַל צַוָּארֶךָ (mēʿal ṣawwāʾrekā), "from upon your neck."

m Read יְחֻבַּל (yĕḥubbal), "will be destroyed," for MT וְחֻבַּל (wĕḥubbal), "and will be destroyed." LXX has a dittography, καὶ καταφθαρήσεται ὁ ζυγὸς ἀπὸ τῶν ὤμων ὑμῶν, "and the yoke will be destroyed from your shoulders," that has led to a corruption of the following line.

Commentary

Isaiah 10:24-27a forms the original conclusion to 10:5-15. Like 10:16-23, it begins with the typical "therefore" (לָכֵן lākēn) that announces the prophetic judgment against a party following the statement of charges, but, unlike 10:16-23, 10:24-27a continues the imagery and motifs found in vv. 5-15 and clearly portrays Assyria as the enemy envisioned. One could easily delete 10:16-23 from its present context, and 10:5-15 + 24-27a would read smoothly as a continuous unit. In fact, the passage would be far clearer, because the presence of 10:16-23 in the context creates numerous anomalies and difficulties (see below).

After expressing the folly of Assyria's pride under the humorous figure of a tool that boasts against the workman who uses it (10:15), God urges the inhabitants of Zion not to be afraid of this staff that the Lord had used to punish them (10:24). The comparison of Assyria's oppression to that of the earlier Egyptian oppression is perhaps intended to call up memories of the exodus deliverance. At any rate, Judah need not fear Assyria, for God promises that the period of his anger toward his people will soon be over, and then God will turn his wrath against Assyria. He will raise up a scourge against it just as he once smote Midian in the days of Gideon (Judg 7:25), and he will wield his staff against it as he once wielded his staff against Egypt in the days of the exodus. When that happens, the Assyrian yoke will finally be broken and removed from the neck of God's people in Jerusalem (10:27a)

The Secondary Reading of 10:16-23

The present, though secondary, literary context of 10:16-23, resulting from its redactional insertion in the middle of an oracle against Assyria, has imposed a new reading on this material with varying degrees of success. The transformation of the first part of this materiel, that is, vv. 16-19, from a judgment against Israel into a judgment against Assyria presents no major difficulties, since these verses contain no explicit mention of Israel. The recovery of the original target of 10:16-19 is possible only because of very similar material elsewhere in Isaiah, where it is specifically directed against Israel (17:4-6; 9:17-18).

The situation is quite different in the case of 10:20-23, however. The transformation of this material into an oracle against Assyria has created real havoc in the understanding of Isaiah's message, because it means that one must invent ad hoc reinterpretations of specific allusions to conditions at the time of the Syro-Ephraimitic War. If one reads this as an oracle against Assyria from late in Hezekiah's reign when Sennacherib was threatening Judah, then Israel must be understood as a generic term to include and, in fact, refer primarily to Judah. But then the concept of the remnant is turned into an insoluble riddle. Its obvious connection to Isaiah's early message concerning the conflict between Judah and Israel, reflected in the identity of the name of his son Shear-jashub and the expression used twice in Isa 10:21-

22, is obscured and usually ignored,[8] and the import of the concept becomes highly ambiguous. Is it positive or negative? It can remain a positive concept that gives hope to Judah only by an exegetical tour de force. How can the promise that a mere remnant of Judah would survive God's decisive judgment provide the logical basis for the appeal to the inhabitants of Zion not to be afraid of Assyria?

In my judgment, Isaiah could not be responsible for the present placement of Isa 10:16-23, and the redactors who are responsible have not provided a context that permits a coherent reading of vv. 20-23. A coherent reading of these verses requires that one interpret them together with vv. 16-19 in isolation from the larger literary context in which they are presently placed.

Bibliography

Binns, L. E., "Midianite Elements in Hebrew Religion," *JTS* 31 (1930) 337–54.

Soggin, J. Alberto, "*Tablîtām* in Isaiah 10:25b," *BeO* 13 (1971) 232.

10:27d-34 An Early Oracle about the Syro-Ephraimite Attack on Jerusalem

27d/ He has gone up from before Samaria.[a] 28/ He has gone upon Ayath,[b] he has crossed over by Migron.[c] At Michmash he deposited his baggage. 29/ They[d] have crossed over the pass.[e] At Geba they spent the night.[f] Ramah became alarmed; Gibeah of Saul has fled. 30/ Give a shrill cry,[g] O Daughter Gallim. Pay attention, O Laishah.[h] Answer her,[i] O Anathoth. 31/ Madmenah[j] has taken flight. The inhabitants of Gebim[k] sought refuge. 32/ Yet today he will stand at Nob and shake[l] his hand[m] against the mount of daughter[n] Zion, the hill of Jerusalem.[o] 33/ Now the Lord Yahweh of Hosts is about to lop off branches with terrifying power,[p] and the towering ones[q] will be felled, and the high ones will be brought low. 34/ And he will strike off the thickets of the woods with iron, and the Lebanon will fall in its majesty.

Textual Notes

a Read עלה מפני־שמרן (ʿālâ mippĕnê-šōmĕrōn), "he has gone up from before Samaria," for MT's corrupt עֹל מִפְּנֵי־שָׁמֶן (ʿōl mippĕnê-šāmen), "yoke from before fatness."

b MT עַיַּת (ʿayyat), "Ayath," Vg., Tg.; 1QIsaᵃ עייה (ʿayyatah); 4QIsaᶜ עיות (ʿayyôt); Syr. ענת (ʿnt); LXX πόλιν Αγγαι, "city of Aggai."

c MT מִגְרוֹן (migrôn), "Migron," so Vg., Tg.; Μαγεδω, "Magedo," LXX, Syr.

d עָבְרוּ (ʿābĕrû), "they crossed over," MT, Vg.; עבר (ʿābar), "he crossed over," 1QIsaᵃ, LXX, Syr.

e מַעְבְּרָה (maʿbārâ), "the pass," MT, LXX, Vg.; במעברה (bĕmaʿbārâ), "through the pass," 1QIsaᵃ.

f For גֶּבַע מָלוֹן לָנוּ (gebaʿ mālôn lānû), "At Geba they spent the night"; LXX has καὶ ἥξει εἰς Αγγαι, "and will come to Aggai," which looks as though he miscopied a preceding line; Vg. has *Gabee sedes nostra* "Geba was our camp," having misread לָנוּ (lānû), the *qal* perfect third person masculine plural of לוּן (lûn),

---

8 Wildberger (pp. 412–16) does not even mention the name of Isaiah's son, and, while they mention it, neither Gray (pp. 202–4) nor Kaiser (*Isaiah 1–12*, 240–42) considers the possibility that an older oracle from the Syro-Ephraimitic period may be embedded here.

"to spend the night," as the prefixed preposition לְ (lĕ) + נו (nû), the first person plural pronominal suffix.

g   צַהֲלִי קוֹלֵךְ (sahălî qôlēk), "give a shrill cry," MT, 1QIsaᵃ, Syr; LXX omits.

h   לַיְשָׁה (layšāh) MT, LXX, Vg.; ליש (layiš) 1QIsaᵃ, Syr.

i   Read עֲנִיהָ (ʿănîhā), "answer her O Anathoth" for עֲנִיָּה (ʿăniyâ) MT, 1QIsaᵃ; עני Syr.; LXX repeats the translation of הַקְשִׁיבִי (haqšîbî), ἐπακούσεται, "she shall hear."

j   מַדְמֵנָה (madmēnâ), "Madmenah," MT, Vg.; מרמנה (marmēnâ) 1QIsaᵃ, Syr.; מ*מנה 4QIsaᶜ; Μαδεβηνα LXX.

k   הַגֵּבִים (haggēbîm), "Gebim," MT; גבים 1QIsaᵃ; Γιββιρ LXX.

l   יְנֹפֵף (yĕnōpēp), "he will shake," MT; ינוף (yānûp) 1QIsaᵃ.

m   יָדוֹ (yādô), "his hand," MT, Syr., Vg.; ידיו (yādāyw), "his hands," 1QIsaᵃ.

n   בֵּית (bêt), "house," MT kĕtîb; the qĕrē' has the correct בַּת (bat), "daughter," 1QIsaᵃ, 4QIsaᶜ, Syr., Vg., LXX.

o   LXX misunderstands the whole verse: "Today, O mountain and O hills which are in Jerusalem, exhort daughter Zion with the hand to remain in the way."

p   בְּמַעֲרָצָה (bĕmaʿărāṣâ), "with terrifying power," MT, 1QIsaᵃ; LXX μετὰ ἰσχύος, "with strength," followed by Syr.; Vg. in terrore, "with terror."

q   הַקּוֹמָה (haqqômâ), "the towering one," MT; קומה 1QIsaᵃ.

Commentary

Isaiah 10:27b-32 describes the march of an enemy army against Jerusalem until it stops just before the walls of Jerusalem and the enemy waves his hand in a gesture of derision against the city. Given the preceding context, the natural assumption is to identify this enemy with the Assyrian foe mentioned in 10:24-27a. There are serious difficulties with that identification, however. No known Assyrian advance against Jerusalem took the route outlined in these verses. Sennacherib's well-documented third campaign in 701 BCE took the normal invasion route for Assyrian and later Babylonian armies in first marching down the coast through Philistine territory in order to secure the Assyrian's southern flank from the threat of any possible Egyptian relief force. Then once this flank was secured, the Assyrian force systematically reduced the outlying fortresses in the Judean Shepelah to open its way for an attack on Jerusalem. Sennacherib's approach to Jerusalem, therefore, came from the west or the southwest, not from the north, as Isa 10:27b-32 portrays. Because of this difficulty, scholars have postulated an unrecorded Assyrian advance against Jerusalem in 715 or 711 BCE,[9] but there is no evidence that such an advance even took place, much less that it followed the route described in Isaiah 10. Nor is there any reason to believe that this description simply adapts an old pilgrimage route in an imaginative portrayal of God's threat to Jerusalem.[10]

There is only one historically verifiable march of an enemy army against Jerusalem that took place during Isaiah's lifetime, and for which the line of march portrayed in this account is probable—Syria and Israel's joint attack on Jerusalem during the Syro-Ephraimitic War (Isa 7:1-9; 2 Kgs 16:5). The natural road for such an attack was the north–south road from Shechem to Jerusalem that followed the spine of the central ridge, and where this account deviates from that road, tactical considerations uniquely appropriate to the Syrian-Israelite strategic objectives in that war account for the deviation. Since we have already found significant material from the period of the Syro-Ephraimitic War inserted in this chapter (10:16-23), it is no surprise that a description of this Syrian-Israelite attack on Jerusalem should also be inserted in an Assyrian context. Unless one wants to resort to manufacturing history, there is good reason to follow Herbert Donner in dating this original oracle to the period of the Syrian-Israelite attack on Jerusalem and in identifying the campaign reflected in this oracle with that event.[11] Against Donner, however, I would date the attack at least a year earlier, to 734 or perhaps even 735 BCE, since this attack apparently preceded Tiglath-pileser III's campaign through Philistia.

The beginning of the account in 10:27b is garbled, but a better restoration than that underlying the RSV's reading would give, "He has gone up from before Samaria." Such an emendation involves the restoration of only two letters: על]ה[מפני שמ]ר[ן (ʿl<h> mpny šm<r>n), and it

---

9   See the discussion in Wildberger, 427–28.
10 So Duane L. Christensen, "The March of Conquest in Isaiah X 27c-34," VT 26 (1976) 385–99.
11 Herbert Donner, "Der Feind aus dem Norden: Topographische und archäologische Erwägungen zu Jes 10:27b-34," ZDPV 84 (1968) 46–54.

fits the historical situation. A joint Syrian and Israelite army operating from Israelite territory would be likely to muster in the neighborhood of the Israelite capital.

Aiath is probably to be identified with the Ai of Josh 7:22–8:29, and Migron with modern Makrun north of Michmash. At Michmash the enemy made final preparations for battle before crossing over the pass at Michmash and making camp for the night at Geba. Since these four sites—Aiath, Migron, Michmash, and Geba—are all significantly east of the main north–south road,[12] the route described here suggests that the attacking army made a wide swing to the east of that road somewhere in the vicinity of Bethel and did not rejoin it until somewhere south of Ramah. The purpose for the choice of this unusual and more difficult route was apparently to avoid the Judean border fortress at Mizpeh. This would fit the Syrian-Israelite strategy in their attempt on Jerusalem. They were interested in a surprise attack against Jerusalem that would enable them to isolate the city, quickly breach its defenses, capture Ahaz, and replace him with a king of their own choosing. All of this had to be accomplished in time to regroup their forces and redeploy to the north in order to meet the threat of an Assyrian invasion. Syria and Israel could not afford to become bogged down in long, drawn-out siege warfare with Judah's major border fortifications on the main road, so a flanking move to bypass the border stongpoints was in order, and that seems to be what is reflected in crossing the pass between Michmash and Geba.

Verses 29b-31 reflect the terrifying effect that the sudden appearance of this enemy army in Judean territory at Geba had on the towns in its possible path just north of Jerusalem. Ramah and Gibeah, two major towns that represented possible points of attack on the main north–south road, were in absolute panic, and the smaller villages lying east of that road along the three possible approaches to Jerusalem scurried for safety in terror. Bath-Gallim has been identified with Khirbet Kaʿkūl or Khirbet Erḥa, both just north of Jerusalem.[13] Laishah has

been identified with el-ʿIsāwīje or Khirbet Rās et-Tāwil, farther north, near and to the east of Gibeah (Tell el-Fūl).[14] The precise identifications of Madmenah[15] and Gebim[16] remain uncertain. The Hebrew contains some poetic play on the similarity in sound between the village names and what is said about them,[17] but it is difficult to capture it in English translation except by accident, as in "Answer her, Anathoth!"

The climax of this description, but not the end of the oracle, is reached in 10:32, when the enemy stops at Nob just north of Jerusalem, perhaps to be located on the present Mount Scopus, and shakes his fist at Jerusalem. As I have demonstrated elsewhere, this gesture, whether it is actually "shaking the fist" or some other movement of the hand, is clearly an expression of contempt for Mount Zion.[18] That makes it impossible to accept the attempt of Clements and other scholars to find the original conclusion of the oracle here (Clements, 120; Duhm, 80; Gray, 211). Given Isaiah's view that Yahweh lived on Mount Zion (8:18), one would hardly expect an Isaianic oracle to end with a foreign enemy disparaging God's city with apparent impunity, and if that foreign enemy were the leader of the Syro-Ephraimitic coalition, then it is simply out of the question. Isaiah's well-known attitude toward those two powers excludes such an ending.

The ending, which gives God's response to the arrogant presumption of this enemy, is found in 10:33-34. It portrays the enemy under the image of a forest of tall, majestic trees which God violently cuts down with an iron tool. The word translated "axe" by the RSV is not the same word used in 10:15, so there does not appear to be a direct connection between 10:33-34 and the Assyrian oracle in 10:5-15 + 24-27a, though the theme of God's humiliation of a foolishly arrogant enemy is the same. One should note that the description of the enemy's destruction through the metaphor of destroying a forest is similar to the one used for the destruction of Israel in 9:17 and 10:16-19, and for the haughty enemy in 2:12-13. Thus, 10:34a recalls 9:17c, and 10:33a in a less direct way

---

12 See the useful map in Wildberger, 431.
13 See Jeffries M. Hamilton, "Gallim," *ABD* 2:901.
14 See Rüdiger Liwak, "Laishah," *ABD* 4:131.
15 See Gary A. Herion, "Madmenah," *ABD* 4:462.
16 See Gary A. Herion, "Gebim," *ABD* 2:923.
17 So ṣahălî qôlēk bat-gallim, "Give a shrill cry with your voice, O daughter Gallim"; haqšîbî layšâ, "Pay attention, O Laishah"; ʿănîhā ʿănātôt, "Answer her, O Anathoth"; nādĕdâ madmēnâ, "Madmenah has taken flight"; and yôšĕbê haggēbîm hēʿîzû, "The inhabitants of Gebim sought refuge."
18 J. J. M. Roberts, "Isaiah 2 and the Prophet's Message to the North," *JQR* 75 (1985) 290–308, esp. n. 29.

echoes 9:17d and 2:12-13. The reference to the Lebanon, which may also include the Anti-Lebanon here, probably alludes to the Syrian element in this enemy coalition, since Syria controlled the Anti-Lebanon and apparently exercised some political influence in the Lebanon region as well, since some of the Phoenician cities were part of their anti-Assyrian front.

In many ways Sennacherib's attitude toward Jerusalem was similar to that exhibited by Rezin and Pekah, so it is possible that this oracle from the period of the Syro-Ephraimitic War was heard in a new way at the time of Sennacherib's campaign in 701 BCE, possibly with Isaiah's blessings. Its placement in chap. 10 directly following a threat against Assyria shows that the final editors of the book of Isaiah understood it in that fashion, though this obscures some of its original historical particularity and leaves many details unexplained and unexplainable. The theological point of the oracle remains clear, however, and can be applied to analogous situations in the life of God's people over and over again. Despite appearances to the contrary, the boasting disparagement of God by the powerful enemies of God's people is not the last word. Those who lift themselves up against God will in time be cut down, and God's people can continue to trust in God as the source of their security.

Bibliography

Albright, W. F., "The Assyrian March on Jerusalem, Isa X, 28-32," *AASOR* 4 (1924) 134–40.

Alonso Schökel, L., "Is 10,28-32: Análisis estilístico," *Bib* 40 (1959) 230–36.

Christensen, Duane L., "The March of Conquest in Isaiah X 27c-34," *VT* 26 (1976) 385–99.

Dalman, Gustaf, "Palästinische Wege und die Bedrohung Jerusalem nach Jesaja 10," *PJ* 12 (1916) 37–57.

Donner, Herbert, "Der Feind aus dem Norden: Topographische und archäologische Erwägungen zu Jes 10:27b-34," *ZDPV* 84 (1968) 46–54.

Féderlin, L., "A propos d'Isaïe X, 29-31," *RB* n.s. 3 (1906) 266–73.

Ginsberg, H. L., "Reflexes of Sargon in Isaiah after 715 B.C.E.," *JAOS* 88 (1968) 47–53.

Gordon, Robert P., "The Interpretation of 'Lebanon' and 4Q285," *JJS* 43 (1992) 92–94.

Jirku, A., "Die Zwölfzahl der Städte in Jes 10, 28-32," *ZAW* 48 (1930) 230.

Roberts, J. J. M., "Isaiah 2 and the Prophet's Message to the North," *JQR* 75 (1985) 290–308.

Tadmor, Hayim, "The Campaigns of Sargon II of Assur: A Chronological-Historical Study," *JCS* 12 (1958) 22–40, 77–100.

Vermes, Geza, "The Symbolical Interpretation of Lebanon in the Targums," *JTS* n.s. 9 (1958) 1–12.

Walker, H. H., "Where Were Madmenah and the Gebim?" *JPOS* 13 (1933) 90–93.

Younger, K., "Sargon's Campaign against Jerusalem: A Further Note," *Bib* 77 (1996) 108–10.

11

In its original historical context, Isa 10:33-34 promises that God will destroy the Aramean and Israelite hosts threatening Jerusalem; Isa 11:1-9 promises that God will raise up a new Davidic king who will bring justice, well-being, and peace to Judah; and Isa 11:10 expands on that vision by promising that this king will also be the focal point for the extension of that imperial peace to all the nations. Isaiah 11:11-16, then, further expands on these slightly earlier prophecies by returning to the fate of Israel and its relationship to Judah. The destruction of

Israel announced in 10:33-34 and in many other of Isaiah's oracles from the time of the Syro-Ephraimitic War (7:16; 8:4; 9:8-21 + 5:25-30; 10:16-23; 17:1-6, 12-14; 28:1-6) is not Yahweh's last word concerning Israel. His rejection of his people is not permanent; a remnant of Israel will return, they will be reconciled to Judah, and together they will exercise hegemony over the surrounding region as they once did in the days of the united kingdom under David and Solomon.

11:1-10

1/   **But there will go forth a shoot from the stump of Jesse,**
    And a sprout from his root[a] will shoot up.[b]

2/   **And the spirit of Yahweh will rest upon him;**
    The spirit of wisdom and understanding,
    The spirit of counsel and strength,
    The spirit of knowledge and the fear of Yahweh.

3/   **And his sense (for justice) comes from the fear of Yahweh:[c]**
    And not[d] by the sight of his eyes[e] will he judge,
    And not[d] by the hearing of his ears[f] will he arbitrate;

4/   **But he will judge the poor in righteousness,**
    And arbitrate in equity for the humble of the land.
    He will smite the violent[g] by the rod[h] of his mouth,
    And by the breath of his lips he will slay[i] the wicked.

5/   **Righteousness will be the girdle of his hips,**
    And faithfulness[j] will be the belt[k] of his loins.

6/   **The wolf will dwell with the young ram,**
    And the leopard will lie down with the kid;
    The young bull and the young lion will graze[l] together,
    And a young child will lead them.

7/   **And a heifer and a bear will graze**
    Together[m] their young will lie down;[n]
    And the lion will eat hay like an ox.

8/   **A nursing child will play[o] on the hole[p] of the viper,**
    And on the cave[q] of the adder[r] the weaned child will place[s] his hand.

9/   **They will not[t] hurt and they will not[t] destroy**
    In all[u] my holy[v] mountain,
    For[w] the earth will be as full[x] of the knowledge of Yahweh[y]
    As waters cover the sea.

10/   **And on that day the root of Jesse**
    Which remains standing
    Shall become a signal flag for the peoples;
    To him the nations[z] will go for consultation,*[a]
    And his resting place*[b] will be*[c] glorious.

Textual Notes

a   1QIsaᵃ has the orthographic variant משורשיו for MT מִשָּׁרָשָׁיו (*miššorāšāyw*), "from his root."

b   Reading יִפְרַח (*yiprah*), "to shoot up, to sprout," with LXX, Vg., and Syr., in place of MT and 1QIsaᵃ's יִפְרֶה (*yipreh*), "to bear fruit."

c   The line וַהֲרִיחוֹ בְּיִרְאַת יְהוָה (*wahărîhô běyir'at YHWH*), "and his insight comes from the fear of Yahweh," is a crux. The problem lies in the *hiphil* infinitive וַהֲרִיחוֹ, literally "and his sense of smell." The verb is sometimes used of God being soothed by the smell of sacrifice (1 Sam 26:19; Gen 8:21; Lev 26:31), and sometimes of a human taking pleasure in the smell of something that reminds him of a favorite memory (Gen 27:27). It is also used of "sensing" something without actually coming into contact with it—a horse sensing battle (Job 39:25) or tow sensing fire (Judg 16:9). Because the meaning in this passage is not immediately transparent and the phrase has many similarities with the last line of the preceding verse, many scholars delete it entirely as a corrupt dittography of that line (Duhm, 82; Marti, 111; Gray, 211; and Clements, 121, to name only a few of the many who hold this opinion). If so, it would have to be a very early corruption, since it is found in 1QIsa[a] and in all the versions, though the versions clearly do not understand the line. LXX and Vg. render it, "the spirit of the fear of God/the Lord fills him," while Syr. has, "he will shine forth in the fear of the Lord." If the line is original, it may mean something like "he sniffs out the truth by the fear of Yahweh," that is, his sense for true justice comes from his piety. Compare JPS's rendering, "He shall sense the truth by his reverence for the LORD."

d   1QIsa[a] has the orthographic variant ולוא for MT וְלֹא (wĕlōʾ), "and not."

e   1QIsa[a] has the orthographic variant עניו for MT עֵינָיו (ʿênāyw), "his eyes."

f   1QIsa[a] has the orthographic variant אוזנו for MT אָזְנָיו (ʾoznāyw), "his ears."

g   Reading עָרִיץ (ʿārîṣ), "the violent," by conjecture, since עָרִיץ provides a better parallel to the following רָשָׁע (rāšāʿ), "the wicked" (cf. Isa 13:11), than אֶרֶץ (ʾereṣ), "the land, earth." MT has אֶרֶץ (ʾereṣ), "the earth"; 1QIsa[a] adds the article הארץ (hāʾereṣ), "the earth," and the versions all support this reading, but it was probably introduced as an aural mistake early due to the influence of the preceding ארץ in the expression לְעַנְוֵי־אָרֶץ (lĕʿanwê ʾāreṣ), "for the humble of the land." Note that a similar aural mistake may be present in v. 8c.

h   1QIsa[a] has a supralinear correction בשט to MT's בְּשֵׁבֶט (bĕšēbeṭ), "with the rod."

i   MT's יָמִית (yāmît), "he will slay," is supported by the versions. 4QIsa[c] appears to read ימות (yāmût), "(the wicked) will die," while 1QIsa[a] has the passive יומת (yûmat), "will be slain." 1QIsa[a] also has the expression יומת רשע (yûmat rāšāʿ), "the wicked will be slain," both preceding and following וברוח שפתיו (ûbĕrûaḥ śĕpātāyw), "and with the breath of his lips," but it has circled its first occurrence before וברוח שפתי with little dots, suggesting this placement was a mistake.

j   1QIsa[a]'s ואמונה (weʾĕmûnâ), which omits the article, is probably more original than MT וְהָאֱמוּנָה (wĕhāʾĕmûnâ), "and faithfulness," since the article is often a secondary prosaic element in poetry.

k   The repetition of the same word for girdle (אֵזוֹר, ʾēzôr) in both the a and b lines of poetic parallelism is unusual, though not entirely unique, in Hebrew poetry.[1] Nonetheless, one may suspect that either the a or b line originally had another, synonymous term for girdle, perhaps אֵסוּר (ʾēsûr), "belt," or less likely חֲגוֹרָה (ḥăgôrâ), "belt." The similarity in both appearance and sound of ʾēzôr and ʾēsûr could easily have led to the present repetitive text. LXX, Vg., Syr., and Tg., though quite different, all render the term in the two lines with two different words.

l   Reading יִמְרְאוּ (yimrĕʾû), "they will graze," following the suggestion of 1QIsa[a]'s defective spelling ימרו (yimrû), "they will graze." MT's וּמְרִיא (ûmĕrîʾ), "and fatling, stall-fed calf," is problematic, since it would introduce a third animal in the third line and omit the verb, while the preceding two lines have only two animals and either begin or end with a verb.

m   The word יַחְדָּו (yaḥdāw), "together," functions equally well as the end of the first line "the heifer and the bear graze together," and as the beginning of the second line, "together their young lie down," so probably should be understood as an apokoinu construction.[2] Both LXX and Syr. repeat the word in their translations.

n   The reading of MT and 4QIsa[a] יִרְבְּצוּ (yirbĕṣû), "they will lie down," is clearly superior to 1QIsa[a]'s ורבצו, (wĕrābĕṣû), "and they will lie down."

o   1QIsa[a] has וישעשע (wîšaʿăšaʿ), "and he will play," the imperfect with a simple waw, for MT's more original converted perfect וְשִׁעֲשַׁע (wĕšiʿăšaʿ), "and he will play."

p   1QIsa[a] has the orthographic variant חור for MT חֻר (ḥur), "hole."

q   1QIsa[a] has the plural מאורות (mĕʾûrôt), for MT's singular מְאוּרַת (mĕʾûrat). The meaning of the word is disputed. Gesenius and BDB derived it from the root אור (ʾwr), "to give light," and understood it as meaning "light hole," hence secondarily "den." HALOT takes it as an aural mistake for מְעָרַת (mĕʿārat), "hole, cave."

r   1QIsa[a] has the plural צפעונים (ṣipʿônîm), "vipers," for MT's singular צִפְעוֹנִי (ṣipʿônî), "viper, adder."

s   4QIsa[c] has the imperfect יהדה (yehdê), "he will put, stretch," for the perfect of MT, 1QIsa[a], and 4QIsa[b], הָדָה (hādâ, "he put"), which is grammatically easier, since one expects a future tense.

t   1QIsa[a] has the orthographic variant לוא for MT's לֹא (lōʾ), "not."

u   1QIsa[a] omits כָל, "all," in MT's בְּכָל־הַר קָדְשִׁי (bĕkol har qodšî), "in all my holy mountain."

v   4QIsa[c] has the orthographic variant קודשי for MT's קָדְשִׁי.

w   4QIsa[c] has the orthographic variant כיא for MT's כִּי (kî), "for."

x   For MT מָלְאָה (mālĕʾâ), "will be filled," 1QIsa[a] has the peculiar long form of the third person feminine imperfect תמלאה (timlĕʾâ), "will be full." 4QIsa[c] supports MT.

y   For MT's דֵעָה אֶת־יְהוָה (dēʿâ ʾet YHWH), "the knowledge of Yahweh," supported by 1QIsa[a], 4QIsa[c] has לדעה את כבוד יהוה, (lēdēʿâ ʾet kĕbôd YHWH), "with the knowledge of the glory of Yahweh." For the explanation of this construction with אֶת

---

1   Oswalt (p. 282 n. 23) cites Isa 15:8; 16:7; 17:12, 13; 51:8; 54:13; 59:10 as examples of this, but these are not all that clearly parallel, and one may certainly question the text in a number of these examples.

2   Wilfred G. E. Watson, *Classical Hebrew Poetry: A Guide to Its Techniques* (corrected ed.; London: T&T Clark, 2005) is one of the standard works on the techniques of classical Hebrew poetry, but he does not discuss this device under that term.

('ēt), the direct object marker, see P. Jouon and T. Muraoka, *A Grammar of Biblical Hebrew* (SubBib 14; Rome: Pontifical Biblical Institute, 1993) 2:435, §124j.

z 1QIsaᵃ has the orthographic variant גואים for MT's גּוֹיִם (*gôyīm*), "nations."

*a 1QIsaᵃ and 4QIsaᶜ have the orthographic variant ידרוש for MT's יִדְרֹשׁוּ (*yidrōšû*), "they will go to consult."

*b 1QIsaᵃ and 4QIsaᶜ have the orthographic variant מנוחתו for MT's מְנֻחָתוֹ (*měnūḥātô*), "his resting place."

*c MT's reading וְהָיְתָה (*wěhāyětâ*), "and it will be," is supported by 4QIsaᶜ and is clearly superior to 1QIsaᵃ's odd reading והיא.

Commentary

The oracle in Isa 11:1-10 follows nicely on the conclusion of the oracle in 10:27d-34. In vv. 33-34 Yahweh threatens to chop down the lofty forests of the original Syro-Ephraimitic foes. As already noted, a similar motif, except using fire, is also found in 10:17-19, and one should also compare 9:17 and 2:13. Then in contrast to the negative judgment proclaimed against the lofty forests of Aram and Ephraim, Yahweh promises that new growth will sprout from the stump or root of Jesse. The mention of stump or root suggests that Judah had been at least temporarily humbled by its Syro-Ephraimitic enemies, but the promise of new growth suggests that Judah will recover while its Syro-Ephraimitic enemies will not. The mention of Jesse, the father of David, rather than David, just as the mention of Bethlehem rather than Jerusalem in Mic 5:1, is probably to be understood as an implicit critique of the current Davidic king, presumably the disappointing and faithless Ahaz (Isa 7:9, 13), and a promise that the new David would revert to the original stock and again incorporate the ancient ideals of Davidic kingship.

Just as the spirit of Yahweh had come upon and remained with David (1 Sam 15:13), so the spirit of Yahweh will rest on this new son of Jesse (Isa 11:2). This spirit is further characterized as the source of this future king's wisdom and understanding, of his ability to make wise plans and perform feats of military strength (cf. the language of Isa 28:6). The spirit is also the source of the new king's piety. Knowledge and the fear of Yahweh are probably to be understood as synonymous. Knowledge here does not refer to knowledge in general, but to knowing Yahweh, what v. 9 calls דֵּעָה אֶת־יְהוָה (*děʿâ ʾet YHWH*), "the knowledge of Yahweh," and Hosea refers to as דַּעַת אֱלֹהִים (*daʿat ʾělōhîm*), "the knowledge of God" (Hos 4:1; 6:6; and cf. Jer 9:23; 22:16). In the Old Testament, "the fear of Yahweh/God," like synonymous expressions in Akkadian[3] and other Semitic languages,[4] is the mark of the pious person, that is, the person whose socially responsible behavior is rooted in awe and respect for the deity.

Verse 3, if the text is correct, suggests that it is this awe and respect for the deity that allows the new David to penetrate beyond surface appearances of innocence and guilt and render true justice. He will get beyond the mere oral testimony and visual appearance of the witnesses, since conflicting oral testimony and lying appearances often obscure the truth. Like the wise Solomon of 1 Kgs 3:16-28, he will be able to discern who is lying and who is telling the truth, and render judgment accordingly. As a result, he will be able to render just judgments and offer equitable settlements for the poor and humble of the land. Verse 4 singles out the poor and the humble, not because they are given preferential treatment even when they are in the wrong, but because they are the ones most likely to suffer injustice in the Israelite judicial system. The Israelite legal codes specifically prohibited showing partiality to the poor or deference to the great (Lev 19:15; Exod 23:2-3); showing partiality and the taking of bribes were equally prohibited, so that justice and only justice would be rendered (Deut 16:18-20). In Isa 11:4, the parties contrasted to the poor and humble are not the rich and powerful but the "wicked" or "guilty" and, if the emendation is correct, the "violent oppressor." The Davidic king will smite and slay these guilty parties by the

---

3 See *palāḫu* (*CAD* P, meaning 4, pp. 41–45).

4 In Syriac and the Aramaic of the Targum the root *dḥl*, "to fear," has a similar range of meaning.

judicial decision issuing like a sword from his mouth and lips. Such righteousness and faithfulness will be so integral to the reign of this king that the prophet describes them as the girdle or belt with which he girds his waist (v. 5).

Such evenhanded justice and quick punishment of the violent and wicked will result in an idyllic situation in which young wild carnivores adopt the eating habits of young tame herbivores, so that the two may live together in harmony and peace. Both classes of animals will be so tame and harmless that a small child may lead them. Even grown bears and lions will graze and eat straw like cows and oxen, while their young will lie down together in the same meadow. Little children will be able to play outdoors near the den of a serpent unsupervised without fear of being bitten by the snake, for nothing will hurt or destroy in all God's holy mountain.

The language in vv. 6-9 is certainly dependent on the myth of the peaceable kingdom in primordial times before the fall and perhaps on the hope of its restoration at the end-times. In the Yahwist's (J) story of the garden of Eden in Genesis 2–3 there is no hint of mortal hostility between humans and wild animals until after the transgression of Adam and Eve. God creates the wild animals and birds in an attempt to find a suitable companion for Adam, brings them before Adam without incident, and Adam names them, though none of them qualify as an appropriate companion for him (Gen 2:18-21). The serpent and Eve carry on a conversation with each other without any hint of fear or danger (Gen 3:1-5). It is only after Adam and Eve's transgression that enduring and deadly hostility between humans and snakes becomes the norm (Gen 3:15), and life becomes difficult and harsh (Gen 3:16-19). Moreover, in the Priestly (P) account of origins, humans, animals, birds, and creeping things are originally given only plants for food (Gen 1:29-30). It is only after the flood that God puts the fear of humankind on the animals, birds, creeping things, and fish, when he assigns them, like the plants, to humans as food (Gen 9:2-3). Despite obvious conflicts with other primeval stories—the animal-skin clothes (Gen 3:21), animal sacrifice (Gen 4:4; 8:20-21), and the pre-flood violence (Gen 4:8, 23-25; 6:5-7, 11-12)—this suggests the belief, at least in certain Israelite circles, that humans and animals should have been vegetarian before God eased dietary restrictions after the flood. Thus, the expectation of a return to that mythological golden age of peace and security between humans and animals under the messianic rule of God's ideal king is not surprising. Such an idealized covenant of peace between humans and the animal world is also envisioned in Hosea's portrayal of Israel's future salvation (Hos 2:20). The parallel covenant in Ezekiel (34:25-26) and the similar promise in Lev 26:6 at least will cause the חַיָּה רָעָה (ḥayyâ rāʿâ), "the evil wild beast," to cease from the land. As in Isa 35:9, the redeemed will encounter no lion or violent wild beast on their pathway.

Nonetheless, one must ask whether this language is functioning metaphorically in this passage to refer to more mundane realities. It is not uncommon in Hebrew poetry to compare the wicked, whether foreign enemies (Isa 5:29; Jer 2:15; 5:6; 51:38; Hab 1:8), greedy native rulers (Ezek 22:27; Zeph 3:3), or personal foes (Ps 22:13-14, 17), to lions, wolves, bears, wild oxen, and other dangerous creatures. It would be an obvious mistake to read most of these texts literally, and it is probably just as much a mistake to read the same kind of language in Isaiah 11 with a full-fledged mythological literalness. Such a literal reading is often used as a argument for a very late, postexilic dating of this passage, but the parallel in Isa 65:25 is probably dependent on chap. 11, not the other way around. The point is that the new king's just rule will put an end to the abusive force inflicted by the violent and evil on the innocent and harmless.

This emphasis on justice, good order, security, and the well-being of the weakest members of society under the reign of the coming king is, along with fertility and prosperity (cf. Hos 2:21-25; Ezek 34:26-31; Amos 9:11-15), a common feature in Near Eastern royal ideology, as is clear from Egyptian accession hymns and from Mesopotamian texts that characterize the wonderful blessings that accompanied a particular king's rule. To cite only a few examples, note the accession hymn for Merneptah:

Be glad of heart, the entire land! The goodly times are come! A lord—life, prosperity, health—is given in all lands, and normality has come down (again) into its place: the King of Upper and Lower Egypt, the lord of millions of years, great of kingship like Horus: Ba-en-Re Meri-Amon—life, prosperity, health!—he who crushes Egypt with festivity, the Son of Re, (most) serviceable of any king: Mer-en-Ptah Hotep-hir-Maat—life, prosperity, health! All ye righteous, come that ye may see! Right has banished wrong. Evildoers have fallen (upon) their faces. All the rapacious are ignored. The water stands and is not dried up; the Nile lifts high. Days are long, nights have hours, and the moon comes normally. The gods are satisfied and content of heart. [One] lives in laughter and wonder.[5]

Another accession hymn for Ramses IV states,

A happy day! Heaven and earth are in joy, for thou art the great lord of Egypt. Those who were fled have come (back) to their towns; they who were hidden have come forth (again). They who were hungry are sated and gay; they who were thirsty are drunken. They who were naked are clothed in fine linen; they who were dirty are clad in white. They who were in prison are set free; they who were fettered are in joy. The troublemakers in this land have become peaceful. High Niles have come forth from their caverns, that they may refresh the hearts of the common people. The homes of the widows are open (again), so that they may let wanderers come in. The womenfolk rejoice and repeat their songs of jubilation . . . , saying: "Male children are born (again) for good times, for he brings into being generation upon generation. Thou ruler—life, prosperity, health!—thou art for eternity!" The ships, they rejoice upon the deep. They have no (need of) ropes, for they come to land with wind and oars. They are sated with joy, when it is said: "The king of Upper and Lower Egypt: Heqa-maat-Re Setep-en-Amon—life, prosperity, health!—wears the White Crown again; the Son of Re: Ramses Heqa-maat—life, prosperity, health!—has taken over the office of his father!" All lands say to him: "Gracious is the Horus upon the throne of his father Amon-Re, the god who sent him forth, the protector of the prince who carries off every land!"

To move to Mesopotamia, a letter to the new Assyrian king, Aššur-banipal, from a supplicant named Adad-šum-uṣur, before mentioning his request for his son, flatteringly characterizes the new king's rule in this fashion:

Ash[ur, the king of the go]ds has pronounced the name of the [king] my lord for the kingship over the land of Aššur. In their reliable oracle Shamash and Adad have established for the king my lord, for his kingship over the lands, a happy reign: days of justice, years of equity, heavy rains, waters in full flood, a thriving commerce. The gods are reconciled, divine worship is wide-spread, the temples are enriched. (This) the great gods of heaven and earth have brought about in the time of the king my lord. The old men dance, young men sing, women and maidens are gl[ad (and) ma]ke merry. Wives they take, deck with ear-[ri]ngs, Beget sons and daughters—the offspring are instructed. Whom his crime had condemned to death, the king my lord has let live; [who] was held prisoner many [ye]ars, is set free; [who] were sick many days, have recovered. The hungry have been sated; the lice-infested have been anointed; the naked have been clad in garments.[6]

Retrospectively Aššur-banipal himself in his annals makes very similar claims for his rule:

Since Aššur, Sin, Šamaš, Adad, Bel, Nabu, Ištar of Nineveh, the queen of Kidmuri, Ištar of Arbela, Ninurta, Nergal, and Nusku had graciously allowed me to take my place on the throne of my father who begot me, Adad released his rain, Ea opened his springs, the grain grew 5 ells high in its head, the heads were 5/6 of an ell long, the fruits of the field prospered, the wheat was abundant, the Giparu-tree was continually covered with green, the fruit trees brought the fruit to maturity in abundance, the cattle succeeded in calving. During my reign abundance came, during my years surplus was piled up.[7]

---

5 The translation of this and the following hymn is that of John A. Wilson in *ANET* 3rd ed., 378–79.

6 Translated by W. Moran in *ANET* 3rd ed., 626–27.

7 For the Akkadian text and a German translation, see Maximilian Streck, *Assurbanipal und die letzten assyrischen Könige bis zum Untergange Niniveh's* (3 vols.; VAB 7; Leipzig: Hinrichs, 1916) 2:6–7, col. 1, 41–51.

For a much later period, many scholars have noted Virgil's *Fourth Ecologue*, which appears to celebrate Octavian's rise to imperial power in semi-mythological terms (Wildberger, 1:440–41). In the light of such royal ideology, not unknown in Israel (see Psalm 72), contemporary with the kings they celebrate, it is not difficult to assume that the language in Isa 11:1-9 comes from the time of Isaiah in the late eighth century BCE, when Judah's Davidic kingship still existed, and such expectations for the rule of a new shoot from that line would be current.

To return to Isa 11:9-10, the focus of such future peace is God's holy mountain, Mount Zion in Jerusalem, Yahweh's chosen dwelling place (Isa 2:2-3; 8:18; 14:32; cf. Ps 132:13-14), but it will spread far beyond the sacred mountain, because the recognition and acknowledgment of Yahweh will extend to the whole earth, as universal as the waters that cover the sea. Verse 10 elaborates this thought in language that recalls the oracle in Isa 2:2-5. In the earlier oracle it is the elevation of the sacred mountain itself that provokes the nations to go up to the mountain of Yahweh to receive instruction and have their disputes arbitrated by the imperial deity. In Isa 11:10, it is the root of Jesse that remains standing, when the forests of Zion's enemies have been cut down, that serves as the signal flag to draw the peoples to Zion. The nations will come to the new David to inquire of the deity. The verb דְּרַשׁ (*dāraš*) is used as a technical term for seeking a divine oracle, so the action of the nations here is parallel to that of the nations in Isa 2:2-5, though *dāraš* is not used there. In both cases the nations are coming to Jerusalem to receive instruction from the imperial God Yahweh, but while Isa 2:2-5 does not mention any human agent through whom such instruction is mediated, 11:10 focuses on the new David as the mediator of Yahweh's imperial edicts. Nonetheless, Isa 11:10 also highlights the future glorification of Zion just as 2:2-5 does. The new David's resting place, that is, Zion—the same term מְנוּחָה (*měnûḥâ*), "resting place," used here to describe the abode of the root of Jesse, is used in Ps 132:13-14 to characterize Zion as God's chosen abode—will be glorious.

Bibliography

Aharoni, I., "On Some Animals Mentioned in the Bible," *Osiris* 5 (1938) 461–78.

Alonso-Díaz, J., "Mito o coloración mitológica en la figura del Mesías," *EstBíb* 27 (1968) 233–45.

Alonso Schökel, L., "Dos poemas a la paz," *EstBíb* 18 (1959) 149–69.

Balz, H. R., "Furcht vor Gott?" *EvT* 29 (1969) 626–44.

Barrois, G., "Critical Exegesis and Traditional Hermeneutics: A Methodological Inquiry on the Basis of the Book of Isaiah," *St. Vladimir's Theological Quarterly* 16 (1972) 107–27.

Bartelmus, Rüdiger, "Die Tierwelt in der Bibel II: Tiersymbolik im Alten Testament: Exemplarisch dargestellt am Beispiel von Dan 7, Ez 1, 10 und Jes 11, 6-8," in Bernd Janowski et al., eds., *Gefährten und Feinde des Menschen: Das Tier in der Lebenswelt des alten Israel* (Neukirchen-Vluyn: Neukirchener Verlag, 1993) 283–306.

Beer, G., "Bermerkungen zu Jes. 11,1-8," *ZAW* 18 (1898) 345–47.

Becker, Joachim, *Gottesfurcht im Alten Testament* (AnBib 25; Rome: Pontifical Biblical Institute, 1965) 258–59.

Bodenheimer, F. S., *Animal and Man in Bible Lands* (2 vols.; Leiden: Brill, 1960–72).

Brown, Raymond E., "The Messianism of Qumran," *CBQ* 19 (1957) 53–82.

Buchheit, Vinzenz, "Tierfriede bei Hieronymus und seinen Vorgängern," *JAC* 33 (1992) 21–35.

Caspari, W., "Die Anfänge der alttestamentlichen messianischen Weissagung," *NKZ* 31 (1920) 455–81.

Celada, B., "Una profecía altamente espiritual, y una manera general de entender todas las profecías del AT (Is 11,9)," *CB* 24 (1967) 158–62.

Childs, Brevard S., *Myth and Reality in the Old Testament* (London: SCM, 1960) 65–69.

Coppens, J., "Les espérances messianiques du Proto-Isaïe et leurs prétendues relectures," *ETL* 44 (1968) 491–97.

——, "Le messianisme royal."

Corley, D. H., "Messianic Prophecy in First Isaiah," *AJSL* 19 (1922) 220–24.

Crook, M. B., "Did Amos and Micah Know Isaiah 9:2-7 and 11:1-9?" *JBL* 73 (1954) 144–51.

——, "A Suggested Occasion for Isaiah 9:2-7 and 11:1-9," *JBL* 68 (1949) 213–24.

DeGuglielmo, A., "The Fertility of the Land in the Messianic Prophecies," *CBQ* 19 (1957) 306–11.

Deist, F., "Jes 11,3a: Eine Glosse?" *ZAW* 85 (1973) 351–55.

Delord, R., "Les charismes de l'ancienne alliance commandment: la paix du mond nouveau, Esaie 11:1-10," *ETR* 52 (1977) 555–56.

Freedman, David Noel, "Is Justice Blind? (Is 11:3f.)," *Bib* 52 (1971) 536.

García del Moral, A., "Sentido trinitario de la expresión "Espíritu de Yavé" de Is XI,2 en I Pdr.IV,14," *EstBíb* 20 (1961) 169–206.

——, "Sobre el significado del verbo Nuah en Is 11,2," *MEAH* 10, no. 2 (1961) 33–63.

Gray, G. B., "The Strophic Division of Isaiah 21:1-10 and 11:1-8," *ZAW* 32 (1912) 190–98.

Gressmann, *Der Messias.*

Gross, Heinrich, *Die Idee des ewigen und allgemeinen Weltfriedens im alten Orient und im Alten Testament* (TThSt 7; Trier: Paulinus-Verlag, 1967).

Gryson, Roger, "Les six dons du Saint-Esprit: La version hiéronymienne d'Isaïe 11,2-3," *Bib* 71 (1990) 395–400.

Haag, Ernst, "Der neue David und die Offenbarung der lebensfülle Gottes nach Jesaja 11:1-9," in Michael Böhnke and Hanspeter Heinz, eds., *Im Gespräch mit dem dreieinen Gott: Elemente einer trinitarischen Theologie: Festschrift zum 65. Geburtstag von Wilhelm Breuning* (Düsseldorf: Patmos, 1985) 97–114.

Harrelson, Walter, "Nonroyal Motifs in the Royal Eschatology," in Bernhard W. Anderson and Walter Harrelson, eds., *Israel's Prophetic Heritage: Essays in Honor of James Muilenburg* (New York: Harper, 1962) 147–65.

Hermisson, H. J., "Zukunfterwartung und Gegenwartskritik in der Verkündigung Jesajas," *EvT* 33 (1973) 54–77.

Jenny, M., "'Es ist ein Ros entsprungen': Ein katholisches Weihnachtslied?" *Neue Zürcher Zeitung* 791 (1968) 49–50.

Koch, R., "Der Gottesgeist und der Messias," *Bib* 27 (1946) 241–68.

Koppers, W., "Prophetismus und Messianismus als völkerkundliches und universalgeschichtliches Problem," *Saeculum* 10 (1959) 38–47.

Lange, F., "Exegetische Probleme zu Jes 11," *LRb* 23 (1975) 115–27.

Lanternari, V., "Messianism: Its Origin and Morphology," *HR* 2 (1962) 52–72.

Montagnini, F., "Le roi-messie attendu, Is 11:1-10," *AsSeign* 2, no. 6 (1969) 6–12.

Oesterley, W. O. E., "Messianic Prophecy and Extra-Israelite Beliefs," *CQR* 119 (1934) 1–11.

Oswalt, John N., "God's Determination to Redeem His People (Isaiah 9:1-7; 11:1-11; 26:1-9; 35:1-10)," *RevExp* 88 (1991) 153–65.

Plath, Siegfried, *Furcht Gottes: Der Begriff yāra'im im Alten Testament* (AzTh 2/2; Stuttgart: Calwer, 1963) 83–84.

Rehm, M., *Der königliche Messias im Licht der Immanuel-Weissagungen des Buches Jesaja* (Kevelaer: Buzton & Bercker, 1968).

Roberts, J. J. M., "The Translation of Isa 11:10 and the Syntax of the Temporal Expression '*whyh bywm hhw*'," in M. Mori et al., eds., *Near Eastern Studies: Dedicated to H. I. H. Prince Takahito Mikasa on the Occasion of his Seventy-fifth Birthday* (Wiesbaden: Harrassowitz, 1991) 363–70.

Ruiten, Jacques T. A. G. M. van, "The Intertextual Relationship between Isa 11,6-9 and Isa 65,25," in F. García Martínez, A. Hilhorst, and C. J. Labuschagne, eds., *The Scriptures and the Scrolls: Studies in Honour of A. S. van der Woude on the Occasion of His 65th Birthday* (VTSup 49; Leiden: Brill, 1992) 31–42.

Schmid, Hans Heinrich, *Sālôm: Frieden im Alten Orient und im Alten Testament* (SBS 51; Stuttgart: KBW, 1971).

Schmidt, W. H., "Die Ohnmacht des Messias," *KD* 15 (1969) 18–34.

Stamm, J. J., and H. Bietenhard, *Der Weltfriede im Alten und Neuen Testament* (Zurich: Zwingli, 1959).

Steck, Odil Hannes, "Ein kleiner Knabe kann sie leiten: Beobachtungen zum Tierfrieden in Jesaja 11,6-8 und 65,25," in J. Hausman et al., eds., *Alttestamentlicher Glaube und Biblische Theologie: Festschrift für Horst Dietrich Preuss zum 65. Geburtstag* (Stuttgart: Kohlhammer, 1992) 104–13.

Stuhlmueller, Carroll, "The Prophetic Price for Peace," in John T. Pawlikowski and Donald Senior, eds., *Biblical and Theological Reflections on the Challenge of Peace* (Wilmington, DE: Glazier, 1984) 31–44.

Sweeney, Marvin A., "Jesse's New Shoot in Isa 11: A Josianic Reading of the Prophet Isaiah," in Richard D. Weis and David M. Carr, eds., *A Gift of God in Due Season: Essays on Scripture and Community in Honor of James A. Sanders* (JSOTSup 225; Sheffield: Sheffield Academic Press, 1996) 103–18.

Unterman, Jeremiah, "The (Non)Sense of Smell in Isaiah 11:3," *HS* 33 (1992) 17–23.

Wildberger, Hans, "Jesaja 11,1-5, 9," in G. Eichholz and A. Falkenroth, eds., *Hören und Fragen: Eine Predigthilfe* (Neukirchen-Vluyn: Neukirchener Verlag, 1967) 58–67.

——, "Die Völkerwallfahrt zum Zion, Jes. 11:1-5," *VT* 7 (1957) 62–81.

Zenger, Erich, "Die Verheissung Jesaja 11,1-10: Universal oder partikular?" in J. van Ruiten and M. Vervenne, eds., *Studies in the Book of Isaiah: Festschrift Willem A. M. Beuken* (BETL 132; Leuven: Leuven University Press, 1997) 137–47.

11

11/ And in that day the Lord[a] will again lift up[b] his hand (a second time)
To acquire[c] the remnant[d] of his people
Who are left from Assyria
And from Egypt and from Patros
And from Cush and from Elam[e]
And from Shinar and from Hamath
And from the islands of the sea.[e]

12/ He will lift[f] a signal flag for the nations,[g]
And he will gather those driven away from Israel,
And those dispersed[h] from Judah he will collect
From the four wings[i] of the earth.

13/ And the jealousy of Ephraim will depart
And the harassers[j] from Judah will be cut off;
Ephraim will not be[k] jealous of Judah
And Judah will not[k] harass Ephraim.

14/ But with (one) shoulder[l] they will fly[m] against the Philistines[n] to the west,
Together they will plunder[o] the children of the east.
Edom and Moab shall be under their hand,
And the Ammonites will be subject to them.

15/ Yahweh will dry up[p] the tongue[q] of the sea of Egypt[r]
And he will wave his hand[s] over the River with the power[t] of his wind[u]
And he will smite it into seven[v] wadis so that one may cross[w] (it) in sandals.

16/ And there will be[x] a road for the remnant of his[y] people
Who remain from Ashur[z]
As there was*[a] for Israel
In the day he went up from the land of Egypt.

Textual Notes

a   1QIsaᵃ has the orthographic variant אדוני for MT אֲדֹנָי (ʾădōnāy), "my Lord."

b   Following the verb יֹסִיף (yôsîp), "to do again," one expects an infinitive expressing the action that is done again. Since "his hand" is the object of this action, a verb of lifting, waving, or stretching forth the hand is expected, but any such verb is missing in the Hebrew textual tradition. LXX supplies the infinitive τοῦ δεῖξαι, "to show," but whether the translator's Hebrew *Vorlage* had any corresponding Hebrew verb is dubious. A number of emendations have been suggested to supply the missing infinitive. Some have emended שֵׁנִית (šēnît), "a second time," to שְׁאֵת (śĕʾēt, the *qal* infinitive from נשא, "to lift up"), or to שַׁנּוֹת (šannôt, the *piel* infinitive from שנה III, "to be high"). In favor of such an emendation is that שֵׁנִית (šēnît) seems an unnecessary redundancy of יסף, "to do something again." This is the only occurrence of *šēnît* following *yôsîp*, and the only vaguely similar redundancy with *šēnît* that I could find was וישלח עוד שנית (wayyišlaḥ ʿôd šēnît), "And he sent again a second time" (2 Sam 14:29). If *šēnît* is original despite the redundancy, another possibility is to consider a haplography from an original שַׁנּוֹת שֵׁנִית (šannôt šēnît) or שְׁאֵת שֵׁנִית (śĕʾēt šēnît), either meaning, "to lift a second time." Some such verbal element must be supplied for sense, even if the text is correct and simply elliptical.

c   LXX's ζηλῶσαι, "to show zeal for," misreads לִקְנוֹת (liqnôt), "to acquire" (MT, 1QIsaᵃ, Vg., Syr.) as though it were from the root קנא (qānāʾ), "to be jealous."

d   For MT אֶת־שְׁאָר (ʾet-šĕʾār), "the remnant," 1QIsaᵃ originally omitted the direct object marker, but then added it in a supralinear correction שאר ﬞאﬞת; LXX has a double translation, τὸ καταλειφθὲν ὑπόλοιπον, "the remnant that is left."

e   LXX has a different order of places in the last two lines: καὶ Βαβυλωνίας καὶ Αἰθιοπίας καὶ ἀπὸ Αιλαμιτῶν καὶ ἀπὸ ἡλίου ἀνατολῶν καὶ ἐξ Ἀραβίας, "and Babylonia and Ethiopia and from the Ailamites and from where the sun rises and out of Arabia."

f   1QIsaᵃ has the orthographic variant ונשה (wĕnāśâ) for MT וְנָשָׂא (wĕnāsāʾ), "and he will raise."

g   1QIsaᵃ has the orthographic variant לגואים for MT לַגּוֹיִם (laggôyīm), "for the nations."

h   1QIsaᵃ has the orthographic variant ונפצות for MT וּנְפֻצוֹת (ûnĕpūṣôt), "and the dispersed."

i   MT מֵאַרְבַּע כַּנְפוֹת (mēʾarbaʿ kanpôt), "from the four wings," is supported by 4QIsaᵃ (fragmentary but probable), LXX, Vg., Syr., Tg.; 1QIsaᵃ has only מכנפות (mikkanpôt), "from the wings."

j   1QIsaᵃ has the orthographic variant וצוררי יהודה for MT וְצֹרְרֵי יְהוּדָה (wĕṣōrĕrê yĕhûdâ), "and the harassers from Judah." The construction is a subjective genitive as the parallel lines make clear. The harassers do not harass Judah; they come from Judah to harass Ephraim. LXX (καὶ οἱ ἐχθροὶ Ιουδα) and Vg. appear to read וצרי יהודה (wĕṣārê yĕhûdâ), "and the enemies of Judah."

k   1QIsaᵃ has the orthographic variant לוא for MT לֹא (lōʾ), "not."

l   Most modern translations render MT's בְּכָתֵף פְּלִשְׁתִּים (bĕkātēp pĕlištîm) as "upon the shoulder of the Philistines," or some-

184

thing similar, but that would require repointing the first word as a construct בְּכֶתֶף (běketep). I would rather keep the MT's pointing and see the expression as elliptical, similar to שְׁכֶם אֶחָד (šĕkem ʾeḥād), "with one shoulder, one accord," in Zeph 3:9. Thus the expression would be parallel to the following יַחְדָּו (yaḥdāw), "together." Cf. Tg. וְיִתְחַבְּרוּן כְּתַף חַד לְמִמְחֵי יָת פְּלִשְׁתָּאֵי דבמערבא, "and they will join together with one shoulder to smite the Philistines who are in the west." LXX's reading is strange: ἐν πλοίοις ἀλλοφύλων, "in boats of the Philistines."

m For MT וְעָפוּ (wĕʿāpû), "and they will fly," supported by 1QIsaᵃ, LXX, and Vg., 4QIsaᵃ has ועפף, probably due to the misreading of a final ו as a final ף.

n 1QIsaᵃ has the orthographic variant פלשתיים for MT פְּלִשְׁתִּים (pĕlištîm), "the Philistines."

o For MT יָבֹזּוּ (yābōzzû), "they shall plunder," 1QIsaᵃ has the erroneous ובבזזו (wĕbābĕzĕzû), "and they shall plunder," because it mistakenly construes יחדו (yaḥdāw), "together," with the preceding clause.

p MT's וְהַחֲרִים (wĕheḥĕrîm), "and he will devote to the ban," though supported by 1QIsaᵃ, seems inappropriate in the passage. HALOT (p. 353), following G. R. Driver (JTS 32 [1931] 251), has listed a חרם II with the meaning "to divide," that would fit here, but the clear attestation of this root in Hebrew is quite problematic. The versions seem to be reading וְהֶחֱרִיב (wĕheḥĕrîb), "and he will dry up." LXX's ἐρημώσει, "he shall make waste," and Vg. et desolabit, "and he will make desolate," are not entirely clear, but Syr.'s wnḥrb, using the cognate root, and Tg.'s וייבש (wîyabēš), both of which mean "he will dry up," strongly support emending the Hebrew text to וְהֶחֱרִיב.

q LXX omits לְשׁוֹן (lĕšôn), "tongue," but MT, 1QIsaᵃ, 4QIsaᵃ, and the other versions support it.

r For possible emendations of this phrase, see the commentary.

s The singular יָדוֹ (yādô), "his hand" (MT, LXX, Vg., Syr.) is preferable to 1QIsaᵃ's ידיו (yādāyw), "his hands."

t For MT בַּיָּם (baʿyām) 1QIsaᵃ has בעיים, but the meaning of עָיָם (ʿāyām) is disputed. Some[1] connect it to Arabic ġāma or ġamma, "to be overcast, to be intensely hot," hence the NRSV rendering of the larger phrase, "with a scorching wind." None of the ancient versions rendered the expression in that fashion, however. LXX has πνεύματι βιαίῳ, "by a powerful wind"; Vg. has in fortitudine spiritus sui, "by his strong wind"; and Syr. has bʾwḥdnʾ drwḥḥ, "by the power of his wind." This has led to the common emendation of the form to בְעֹצֶם (bĕʿōṣem), "by the might (of his wind)"; so JPS.

u The suffix on רוּחוֹ (rûḥô), "his wind," is omitted by 1QIsaᵃ and LXX.

v 1QIsaᵃ has the construct form of the noun לשבעת (lĕšibʿat) for MT's absolute state לְשִׁבְעָה (lĕšibʿâ), "into seven."

w Though the final letter is faded, 1QIsaᵃ appears to have the plural והדריכו (wĕhidrîkû) for MT's singular וְהִדְרִיךְ (wĕhidrîk), "so that one may cross."

x 1QIsaᵃ has the orthographic variant והיתה for MT וְהָיְתָה (wĕhāyĕtâ), "and there will be."

y LXX and Vg. have "my people."

z LXX reads במצרים (bĕmiṣrāyim), "in Egypt," rather than מֵאַשּׁוּר (mēʾaššûr), "from Aššur or Assyria," with MT, 1QIsaᵃ, 4QIsaᶜ, Vg., Syr., Tg.

*a 1QIsaᵃ has the orthographic variant היתה for MT הָיְתָה (hāyĕtâ), "as there was."

Commentary

Isaiah 11:11 describes God's reacquisition of this remnant of Israel as a new exodus, analogous to the time God first acquired Israel when he brought them out of the land of Egypt with a mighty hand. One expects an infinitive after the initial verb, so, as discussed in the textual notes, one should probably either assume a haplography and restore either the *piel* infinitive שַׂנּוֹת (śannôt), "to lift," or the *qal* infinitive שְׂאֵת (śĕʾēt), "to lift," before שֵׁנִית (šānît), "a second time," or alternatively, simply correct שֵׁנִית to one of these two forms. The lifting of the hand recalls God's "mighty hand," which he "stretched out" against the Egyptians in the story of the exodus, and לִקְנוֹת

(liqnôt), "to acquire," is the same verb used in Exod 15:16 to describe God's original acquisition of his people Israel: "Terror and dread fell upon them; at the majesty of your arm [בִּגְדֹל זְרוֹעֲךָ, bigdōl zĕrôʿăkā] they became as silent as a stone, until your people passed by, O Yahweh, until the people whom you acquired [קָנִיתָ, qānîtā] passed by."

In contrast to the first exodus, however, this new exodus of the remnant of his people will be primarily from Assyria, not from Egypt. Note the poetic use of sound in the Hebrew: לִקְנוֹת אֶת־שְׁאָר עַמּוֹ אֲשֶׁר יִשָּׁאֵר מֵאַשּׁוּר (liqnôt ʾet-šĕʾār ʿammô ʾăšer yiššāʾēr mēʾaššûr), "to acquire the remnant of his people who remain from Assyria." The rest of v. 11, beginning with "from Egypt," appears to be a secondary expansion. In v. 16, where most of the phrase

---

1   Duhm (p. 86) took this position; it is listed as a possibility in HALOT, 817; and discussed in Wildberger, 1:464.

about Assyria is repeated, Egypt is mentioned, but Egypt in v. 16 simply refers back to the first exodus; it is not another place alongside Assyria from which the remnant of God's people will return in the new exodus. Nonetheless, Egypt was probably introduced into v. 11 from v. 16, and the insertion of Egypt into the verse then led to a further elaboration of the list of places from which the exiles would return. I will discuss these place-names and the possible date of this expansion below. The emphasis in this verse, and again in v. 16 on the remnant (שְׁאָר, šĕ'ār) of his people, connects this oracle with the expectations associated with the Syro-Ephraimitic War, Isaiah's child with the symbolic name שְׁאָר יָשׁוּב (šĕ'ār yāšûb, "A-Remnant-Will-Return"), and the prophet's hope that at least a remnant of the northern kingdom would return to Yahweh and Judah's Davidic king (see 10:20-23; cf. 2:5-6). That suggests that the oracle, without the expansion of place-names, may originally date to not long after the Syro-Ephraimitic War.

Verse 12 picks up the imagery of the signal flag found in v. 10, though it may be using it in a slightly different way. God raises the flag, but here it serves not as a signal for the nations to come to the new king to have their disputes settled but as a signal for the return of those who had been driven away or deported from Israel and Judah. The reference to the scattered of Israel and Judah does not require a late date. The Syro-Ephraimitic War resulted in a significant dislocation of the population of both states. In the early stages of the war, the Arameans, Israelites, and Philistines appear to have captured and enslaved many Judeans as prisoners of war (2 Chr 28:5-18), and in the nature of such events it is more than doubtful, despite the Chronicler's piously positive spin (2 Chr 28:9-15), that many of these unfortunate people made their way back home when the tide of war turned. Some may have been sold and shipped to more distant areas as a part of the international slave trade (cf. Amos 1:6, 9) prior to Assyria's intervention in the conflict, and one may probably assume that some of the Judean captives were mixed in with the Aramean, Israelite (2 Kgs 15:29), and Philistine populations that Tiglath-pileser III deported during and immediately following the Syro-Ephraimitic War of 734–732 BCE. The historical conditions for such a promise, then, were already in place any time after 732 BCE.

According to v. 13, when these exiles return, the strife between Judah and Israel that reached such a high point in the Syro-Ephraimitic War, but which had simmered ever since the division of the monarchy under Solomon's successor, will finally be resolved. Ephraim will no longer be jealous of Judah, and Judah will no longer harass Ephraim. This final statement of v. 13 shows that the construct expressions in the earlier statement, "the jealousy of Ephraim and the harassers of Judah," are both to be understood as subjective genitives, contrary to the RSV, which mistakenly takes the second as an objective genitive: "those who harass Judah." The correct sense is "the jealousy that Ephraim harbors against Judah and the harassers who come out of Judah to attack Ephraim." The reference to "the harassers from Judah" probably alludes to Judean attacks against Israel waged in concert with the Assyrian campaign in the north. Hosea 5:10-11 probably implies that Judah took this opportunity to extend its border northward at Israel's expense. There is certainly no basis for deleting the second half of the verse as a secondary expansion. It is obviously not needless repetition, but necessary for the correct understanding of the first half of the verse. The scholars who omit it uniformly misunderstand the genitives in the preceding half of the verse as objective genitives, and thus must delete the second half of the verse in order to maintain their misreading of the first half. A clearer case of turning truth on its head cannot be found than Clements's statement: "The context shows that the adversaries . . . of Judah are from Ephraim" (p. 126). Such a judgment is possible only if one first deletes the prophet's own epexegetical comment.

Once Judah and Israel are reconciled, they will again establish their hegemony over the surrounding states, thus restoring the ancient ideal of the Davidic monarchy (v. 14). Scholars normally take "the shoulder of the Philistines" to refer either to the western slope of the Judean highlands overlooking the Philistine coastal plain (Duhm, 86; Wildberger, 1:472; Gray, 227), or the coastal plain itself (Clements, 126), but the expression בְכָתֵף (bĕkātēp) may actually not be part of a construct chain but an elliptical adverbial idiom meaning "with one shoulder" (cf. Zeph 3:9). Thus, the translation, "But with (one) shoulder they will fly against the Philistines to the west." The parallel line, "Together they will plunder the children of the east," in this Isaiah context most likely refers to the Arameans. The expression בְּנֵי קֶדֶם (bĕnê *qedem*), "children of the east," occurs numerous times (Gen 29:1; Judg 6:3, 33; 7:12; 8:10; 1 Kgs 5:10; Isa 11:14; Jer 49:28; Ezek 25:4, 10) and can refer to other peoples living to the east of Israel, but in the account of Jacob's flight to the "land of the children of the east (Gen 29:1)," it is clear that the "land of the children of the east" refers to a North Syrian area—Haran (Gen 29:4), or in P, Padan-Aram, "the road of Aram" (Gen 28:2)—settled by Aramaic-speaking peoples. On his return to Palestine, Jacob makes a treaty at Mount Gilead in the Transjordan with his Aramean kinsmen in which both promise not to cross this border to harm the other (Gen 31:44-54), an indication that this story functioned at some historical time period as an etiological basis for the border between Aram and Israel being at Mount Gilead. The expression "children of the east" occurs only here in Isaiah, but elsewhere the prophet uses the term קֶדֶם (*qedem*), "east," in passages referring to the Arameans—ארם מקדם ופלשתים מאחור (*ʾărām miqqedem upĕlištîm mēʾāḥôr*), "Aram from the east and Philistines from the west" (Isa 9:11); and cf. כי מלאו מקדם ועננים כפלשתים (*kî mālĕʾû miqqedem wĕʿōnĕnîm kappĕlištîm*), "for they are full of . . . from the east and soothsayers like the Philistines" (Isa 2:6, see the discussion at that passage). In all three of these passages, the easterners are linked with the Philistines to the west, and in one passage it is absolutely clear that the easterners are the Arameans. The Arameans from the east and the Philistines from the west were the enemies who pressured Israel into the anti-Assyrian defensive alliance and then, together with the subdued Israel, attacked Judah in the beginning of the Syro-Ephraimitic War. Thus, the reconstituted Davidic kingdom of Judah and Israel will have its revenge on its two main enemies of that war. In contrast, Edom, Moab, and Ammon were not directly involved in the Syro-Ephraimitic War, so their subjugation cannot be understood as punishment for their involvement in that affair; they are included simply because they were part of the ideal Davidic empire. For this Judean ideal, compare the language of Ps 60:8-10: "God has spoken in his sanctuary, 'I will exult. I will divide up Shechem, and apportion the valley of Succoth. Gilead is mine; Manasseh is mine. Ephraim is my helmet; Judah is my scepter. Moab is my washbasin; on Edom I hurl my shoe; over Philistia I shout in triumph.'"

The reference to God destroying the tongue of the sea of Egypt in v. 15 is puzzling, since the continuation in v. 16 has exiles returning only from Assyria. This led Hayes and Irvine (p. 217) to delete the whole first line of v. 15 as a secondary addition to the text. That is improbable, since the line introduces Yahweh as the subject that is presupposed by the rest of the verse. Verse 16 would lead one to expect a comparison in v. 15 in which Yahweh's earlier drying up of the sea of Egypt will be repeated by the drying up of "the River." The word הַנָּהָר (*hannāhār*, "the river") here refers, as often in Hebrew, specifically to the Euphrates (Gen 31:21; Exod 23:31; Num 22:5; Josh 24:2-3, 14-15; Isa 7:20; 8:7;[2] 27:12; Jer 2:18; Mic 7:12; Zech 9:10; Ps 72:8). One might think of a restoration such as: "As Yahweh dried up the tongue of the sea of Egypt, So he will wave his hand over the River with the power of his wind; And he will smite it into seven wadis, So that one may cross it in sandals." It is difficult, however, to explain how such a text could be corrupted into the present text. Perhaps, therefore, one should reconstruct the original text of the first line with the idiom בְּדֶרֶךְ מִצְרָיִם (*bĕderek miṣrāyîm*), "in the manner of Egypt," which occurs twice in the preceding chapter (Isa 10:24, 26). Thus, one might read והחריב יהוה את לשון ים בדרך מצרים (*wĕheḥĕrîb YHWH ʾēt lĕšôn yām bĕderek miṣrāyim*), "And Yahweh will dry up the tongue of the sea in the manner of Egypt." Because of the close association of the word יָם (*yām*), "sea," with Egypt, בְּדֶרֶךְ (*bĕderek*, "in the manner of") could easily have dropped out of the text by haplography, perhaps partially due to the similarity with the verb והדריך (*wĕhidrîk*), "and he caused (one) to walk," later in the verse. One might also consider the possibility of a longer haplography of what was originally a poetic couplet, such as והחריב יהוה את לשון ים ובקעהו בדרך מצרים (*wĕheḥĕrîb YHWH ʾēt lĕšôn yām ûbĕqāʿāhû bĕderek miṣrāyim*), "And Yahweh will dry up the tongue of the sea, And split it in the manner of Egypt."[3]

The two other major textual difficulties in the verse have already been adequately discussed in the textual notes, where I adopted the common emendations of

---

2   Here this meaning allows the mighty floodwaters of the Euphrates to serve as a metaphor for the overflowing and overpowering might of Assyria.

3   For this use of the verb *bāqaʿ* see Exod 14:6; Ps 78:13; Neh 9:11; Isa 63:12.

וְהֶחֱרִים (wĕheḥĕrîm), "to put under the ban," to וְהֶחֱרִיב (wĕheḥĕrîb), "to dry up," and of בְּעֺצֶם (ba'yām), "?," to בְעֺצֶם (bĕ'oṣem), "with the might of," following the versions. The result of God's drying up of the Euphrates as he once dried up the sea at the original exodus is that his people can again march home to Palestine, crossing over the major water barrier without getting their sandals wet. Indeed, there will be a veritable highway for his people who remain over from Assyria just as there once was for Israel when God brought them up out of Egypt at the original exodus (v. 16). This clearly anticipates Second Isaiah's highway imagery in Isa 40:3 and his larger second exodus theme (see below). Note the repetition of the same phrase in v. 16 that occurred in v. 11 and the limitation of the remnant here to those from Assyria.

But what is one to make of the expansion of place-names mentioned in v. 11b from which the exiles are to return? How late must this secondary expansion be dated? The places mentioned are Egypt, Patros, which was the territory along the border between Egypt and Cush, Cush or Nubia (modern Sudan), Elam (the western area of modern Iran), Shinar (a term for Mesopotamia, including Babylonia, of disputed origin), Hamath (a city in central Syria on the Orontes river north of the Anti-Lebanon range), and the islands of the Mediterranean Sea.[4] When would Israelites and Judeans have been exiled to these places? According to both 2 Kgs 15:29 and Tiglath-pileser III's inscriptions,[5] this Assyrian king exiled Israelites to Assyria in 732 BCE. Ten years later Shalmaneser V deported more Israelites to Assyria from Samaria, and their place of exile is further defined as in

Halah, on the Habor, the river of Gozan, all of which are Assyrian areas in northwestern Mesopotamia, and in the cities of the Medes (2 Kgs 17:6), which would normally be located to the north and east of Elam. When Sargon II put down the Hamath-Gaza-Samaria revolt in 720 BCE, he again deported Israelites from Samaria and resettled the area of Samaria with exiles from other parts of the Assyrian empire, including Babylon and Cutha in central Babylonia and Hamath (2 Kgs 17:24). It may be that some of the Israelites were resettled in Hamath and central Babylonia, though the texts are not specific on that point. Then in 701 BCE, Sennacherib claims to have deported 200,150 inhabitants of Judah,[6] though their place of exile is not specified. There is no Assyrian claim to have exiled Israelites or Judeans to the islands of the Mediterranean, but the slave trade in captives of war may have resulted in Israelites and Judean captives being sold by Philistine or Phoenician middlemen to Greek or Cypriot merchants for use in the Mediterranean islands.

The Assyrians in the eighth century certainly did not exile Israelites or Judeans to Egypt, Patros, or Cush, but it may very well be that some Israelites and Judeans fled to these areas to avoid the Assyrian depredations in their own countries. Egypt and Cush were often allied with the southern Palestinian states against Assyria in the late eighth century, probably as early as 734 BCE and certainly by 720, and we know that Yamani, the ruler of Philistine Ashdod, sought asylum in the region of Patros on the border of Cush when he fled the Assyrian attack on Ashdod in 711 BCE.[7] Hezekiah apparently engaged in very serious negotiations with the Cushite rulers of Egypt dur-

---

4   The precise expression איי הים ('iyê hayyām), "the islands/coastlands of the sea," occurs only here, in Isa 24:15, and in Esth 10:1, but both the singular אי ('î), "island/coastland" (Isa 20:6; 23:2, 6; Jer 25:22; 47:4) and the plural in both construct (Jer 2:10; Zeph 2:11) and absolute forms (Isa 40:15; 41:1, 5; 42:4, 10, 12, 15; 49:1; 51:5; 59:18; 60:9; 66:19; Jer 31:10; Ezek 26:15, 18; 27:3, 6-7, 15, 35; 39:6; Pss 72:10; 97:1) are widely attested elsewhere. Depending on context, the reference may point to the coastal area of Palestine (Isa 20:6), to more distant islands like Cyprus (Jer 2:10; 31:10; Ezek 27:6-7) and Crete or the coastland of Cilicia (Jer 47:4), or even to areas in the western Mediterranean (Ps 72:10).

5   Tadmor and Yamada, RINAP 1, p. 106, no. 42:15'-19'; p. 112, no. 44:17'-18'; pp. 131-32, no. 49:9-12.

6   Grayson and Novotny, RINAP 3/1, pp. 65-66, no.

4:48-58; pp. 96-97, no. 15:iv 1-25, 1'-14'; pp. 114-16, no. 16: iii 69b-iv 37; pp. 132-33, no. 17: iii 33-81; p. 151, no. 18: iii 10b-31; pp. 176-77, no. 22: iii 14b-49; pp. 193-94, no. 23:iii 12b-42.

7   See Andreas Fuchs, *Die Annalen des Jahres 711 v. Chr. nach Prismenfragmenten aus Ninive und Assur* (SAAS 8; Helsinki: Neo-Assyrian Test Corpus Project, 1998) 81-96; Fuchs, *Die Inschriften Sargons II*, pp. 76, 307, Small Display 2.2, lines 11-13; pp. 219-21, 348, Large Display 2.4, lines 90-108; pp. 132-35, 326, Annals, lines 241-54; Grant Frame, "The Inscription of Sargon II at Tang-i Var," *Or* 68 (1999) 31-57; and my discussion in "Egypt, Assyria, Isaiah," 265-83.

ing his revolt against Assyria in 705–701 BCE. This would have involved Judean diplomats and military officials traveling to Egypt to deliver money and bring back horses (Isa 30:1-7; 31:1-3), and, given the thoroughness of Sennacherib's devastation of the Judean homeland, it would be surprising if some Judean refugees did not seek safety by fleeing to Egypt, just as others did a century later when fleeing from the Babylonian conquest (Jeremiah 42–44). By the end of 701 BCE, following all these Assyrian attacks on Israel and Judah, the number of Israelites and Judeans living in exile probably exceeded or at least equaled a significant percentage of the remaining population of the homeland. One certainly need not await the Babylonian exile of 586 BCE to find the historical conditions presupposed by v. 11. Even the secondary expansion of the verse can be attributed to Isaiah of Jerusalem as a later expansion of his own oracle.

But if Isa 11:1-16 is substantially from Isaiah of Jerusalem, these verses anticipate by almost two hundred years Deutero-Isaiah's use of the second exodus motif. For this motif in Deutero-Isaiah, in addition to Isa 40:3, cited above, see Isa 43:16-21; 44:26-28; 48:17-21; 49:8-13; 51:9-11; 52:7-12. One might legitimately expect, therefore, that there would be some trace of this motif in the intervening literature, and this expectation is not disappointed. Jeremiah predicted the return of a remnant of the former citizens of the northern kingdom from their exile in the land of the north, and he did so in language that seems dependent on both this passage and the pilgrimage to Jerusalem passage in Isa 2:2-4.

Jeremiah 31:1-14, which probably dates from early in Jeremiah's ministry, looks back to the first wilderness wandering in promising a resettlement of Israel in Samaria and the hill country of Ephraim (vv. 5-6). In language strikingly similar to that of the nations in Isa 2:3, the people of Israel will call upon one another to go up to Zion, to Yahweh their God (Jer 31:6), and they will go up to the height of Zion, where they will be radiant (וְנָהֲרוּ, wĕnāhărû) over the goodness of God (Jer 31:12) just as the nations in Isaiah will look with radiance (וְנָהֲרוּ, wĕnāhărû) upon Jerusalem (Isa 2:2). God will save the remnant of Israel (שְׁאֵרִית יִשְׂרָאֵל, šĕʾērît yıśrāʾēl) from the land of the north and bring them back on a level road by streams of water (Jer 31:7-9). One should note that Isaiah speaks of Assyria, and Jeremiah of the northland, as the place of exile; neither mentions Babylon as such, which is very peculiar if either text really dated to the period of the Babylonian exile.

Jeremiah 23:1-8, while it dates later, probably to the last days of Judah under Zedekiah, also appears dependent on Isaiah 11. Jeremiah speaks of God's gathering up the remnant of his people whom he had scattered (Jer 23:2-3), using vocabulary very similar to that found in Isa 11:12.[8] Jeremiah also speaks of God's raising up a righteous sprout for David who will rule justly and wisely (Jer 23:5), language and motifs similar to Isa 11:1-10. In this king's days, both Judah and Israel will dwell securely (Jer 23:6), a motif comparable to the reconciliation of the two people in Isa 11:13-14. Finally, this new salvation promised by God will be so impressive that the exodus of Israel from the north country and from all the lands where God had scattered them will replace the exodus from Egypt as the major paradigm for God's salvation (Jer 23:7-9), a thought that represents a clear development of Isa 11:11,16. Deutero-Isaiah had his forerunners, and any attempt to date all this material to the time of the anonymous, late-exilic prophet simply confuses the actual development of the prophetic traditions.

Secondary Interpretations

The original context of all of Isaiah 11 was the Syro-Ephraimitic War. Isaiah 11:1-10 was the direct continuation of the preceding material in 10:27b-34 and was given in the context of that joint Aramean-Israelite threat to Jerusalem and the Davidic throne. Isaiah 11:11-16 probably dates from a couple of years later, after Israel had been crushed by the Assyrian invasion and tormented by Judean annexation of territory on its southern border. If this is correct, Isa 11:1-10 was actually given earlier than the coronation oracle for Hezekiah in Isa 9:1-7. Unlike 9:1-7, the prophecy in 11:1-10 does not seem to have had a particular royal prince in mind; it appears to be a more general prediction that a new king will arise to fulfill the ancient ideal.

---

8   Note the common use of forms of נדח (ndḥ), "to be driven away, drive away"; פוץ (pwṣ), "to be scattered, to scatter"; and קבץ (qbṣ), "to gather."

Either Isaiah or the later editors of the book of Isaiah have imposed a new reading on chap. 11, however. The explicit identification of the enemy in chap. 10 as Assyria forces one to think of the army threatening Jerusalem in 10:32 as the Assyrian army of Sennacherib. The ideal king of 11:1-10 must then refer to some king to come after Hezekiah. This new reading of the older oracles undoubtedly reflects the impact of the disaster of 701 BCE on the editors of the book, and Isaiah himself may have played a part in this reinterpretation by a reuse of these oracles in the later situation. In this context, any reader of Isa 11:12 must have thought of the thousands of Judean exiles that Sennacherib deported during his devastating campaign in Judah, and the expansion of place-names in 11:11b may derive from this same context.

After the fall of Jerusalem and the Davidic dynasty at the time of the Babylonian exile near the beginning of the sixth century BCE, the oracles in Isaiah 11 would have been read as a promise of the restoration of the monarchy and a return from Babylonian exile, but this change in reading introduced few if any actual textual changes.

Even the expansions in 11:11b and possibly in 11:15 do not require an exilic dating. Babylon is introduced only obliquely under the term Shinar, and both the enemy and the place of exile from which Israel and Judah would return remain Assyria and Assyrian controlled territories, or a few areas outside her control where slaves may have been sold or where refugees may have fled in the late eighth century.

As in the case of Isa 9:1-7, Isaiah's expectations for Jerusalem's deliverance and for the deliverance and reconciliation of Judah and Israel under the reign of an ideal king were not fully realized. Jerusalem survived the siege by the Syro-Ephraimitic army, and it also survived Sennacherib's campaign against Judah; but restoration and reunification did not take place, and no subsequent king really measured up to the ideal. Nonetheless, the secondary readings of these oracles, the first of which may go back to Isaiah himself, suggest the continuing typological power of these particular prophetic words to express the hope for God's ultimate salvation and vindication of his people.

Bibliography

Erlandsson, S., "Jesaja 11,10-16 och dess historiska Bakgrund," *SEÅ* 36 (1971) 24–44.

Luria, B. Z., "The Prophecy in Isa 11:11-16 on the Gathering of the Exiles" (in Hebrew), *BetM* 26 (1981) 108–14.

Vajda, G., "Fragments d'un commentaire judeo-arabe sur le livre d'Isaie (Isaie 11:10–13:14)," *VT* 13 (1963) 208–24.

Volmer, J., *Geschichtliche Rückblicke und Motive in der Prophetie des Amos, Hosea, und Jesaja* (BZAW 119; Berlin: de Gruyter, 1971).

Widengren, Geo, "Yahweh's Gathering of the Dispersed," in W. Boyd Barrick and John R. Spencer, eds., *In the Shelter of Elyon: Essays on Ancient Palestinian Life and Literature in Honor of G.W. Ahlström* (JSOTSup 31; Sheffield: JSOT Press, 1984) 227–45.

Williamson, H. G. M., "Isaiah xi 11-16 and the Redaction of Isaiah i–xii," in J. A. Emerton, ed., *Congress Volume: Paris 1992* (VTSup 61; Leiden: Brill, 1995) 343–57.

12

Isaiah 12:1-6 is a hymn of praise for salvation either composed or inserted in response to the preceding promise of salvation in chap. 11. The date and authorship of the hymn are debated, and little certainty on either question is possible. Both the theology and the vocabulary of the hymn are compatible with Isaiah of Jerusalem. One thinks especially of the epithet "the Holy One of Israel" and the motif of the triumphant deity being "great in the midst of enthroned Zion." But this theology and much of the vocabulary are continued in the ongoing Isaianic tradition of Second and Third Isaiah,[1] and the motif of making Yahweh's glorious deeds known among the peoples and in all the earth cannot help but make the reader think of Second Isaiah (Isa 42:10-12; 43:21; 44:23; 45:25; 48:20; 49:1-6; 52:7-10). Despite the uncertainty, it is to this later period that I am inclined to date the composition.

1/   And you will say[a] in that day,
       "I will praise you,[b] Yahweh!
       Although you have been angry[c] with me,
       May your anger turn,[d] and may you comfort me.
2/   Behold the God of my salvation![e]
       I will trust and not[f] be afraid,
       For my strength and my might are Yah,[g]
       And he has become my salvation."[h]
3/   And you will draw[i] water with joy
       from the springs of salvation.
4/   And you will say[j] in that day,
       "Praise[k] Yahweh! Call upon his name!
       Make known his deeds[l] among the peoples!
       Proclaim that his name is exalted![m]
5/   Praise Yahweh in song[n] for he has done gloriously,
       Let this be made known[o] in all the earth.[p]
6/   Cry aloud and shout for joy, O enthroned Zion,[q]
       For[r] great in your midst is the Holy One of Israel.

Textual Notes

a   MT וְאָמַרְתָּ (wĕʾāmartā, "and you will say"); 1QIsaᵃ has the final *mater* ואמרתה. Tg. has second person plural.

b   MT אוֹדְךָ (ʾôdĕkā, "I will praise you"); 1QIsaᵃ אודכה.

c   MT אָנַפְתָּ (ʾānaptā, "you have been angry"); 1QIsaᵃ אנפתה.

d   MT יָשֹׁב אַפְּךָ (yāšōb ʾappĕkā, "May your anger turn"); note that the verb form is the jussive, not יָשׁוּב (yāšûb), the imperfect; 1QIsaᵃ has the converted perfect and final *mater* ושב אפכה; LXX and Syr. render the verb as a second person singular in the simple past tense with "your anger" as the object.

e   MT, followed by Vg., has only one word for God in this line הִנֵּה אֵל יְשׁוּעָתִי (hinnê ʾēl yĕšûʿātî, "Behold the God of my salvation!"), but 1QIsaᵃ has two הנה אל אל ישועתי, "Behold El (or God) is the God of my salvation." LXX's odd reading ἰδοὺ ὁ θεός μου σωτήρ μου κύριος, "Behold the Lord is my God, my Savior," might suggest restoring the line to הנה יהוה אל ישעתי,

"Behold Yahweh is the God of my salvation," but both Syr. and Tg. apparently read the preposition על before אל, "Behold upon God, my salvation, I trust." That could easily result from a misreading or correction of the initial אל, and the repetition of the same word אל would be a nice poetic counterpart to the repetition later in the verse of יה יהוה, "Yah Yahweh," were that reading correct, but see note g. It is probable that 1QIsaᵃ has a simple dittography.

f   MT וְלֹא (wĕlōʾ, "and not"); 1QIsaᵃ ולוא.

g   MT כִּי־עָזִּי וְזִמְרָת יָהּ יְהוָה (kî-ʿozzî wĕzimrat Yāh YHWH, "for my strength and my might are Yah Yahweh"); 1QIsaᵃ has עוזי כיא וזמרתי יהוה. This suggests that the scribe initially read, "for my strength and might are Yahweh," but then realizing that he had omitted a ה, he inserted it above the line. The correction supports MT, though one could argue for an original כי עזי וזמרתי יה יהוה, with a suffix on both עזי and וזמרתי. The MT reading is odd, however. The parallel expression in Exod 15:2 has only

1   See my discussion in "Isaiah in Old Testament Theology," *Int* 36 (1982) 130–43.

יָהּ (*yāh*), which suggests that the extra יהוה in Isa 12:2 may have originated as a gloss to explain the archaic shorter form.

h MT וַיְהִי־לִי לִישׁוּעָה (*wayhî-lî lîšû'â*, "and he has become for me salvation"); 1QIsaᵃ reads the perfect היה לי לישועה, "he has become for me salvation."

i MT וּשְׁאַבְתֶּם (*ûšĕ'abtem*, "and you will draw"); 1QIsaᵃ ושאבתמה. The switch to the plural here will be discussed in the commentary below.

j MT וַאֲמַרְתֶּם (*wa'ămartem*, "and you will say"); 1QIsaᵃ ואמרתה, "and you [sg.] will say." The versions support MT's plural.

k MT הוֹדוּ (*hôdû*, "praise!"); 1QIsaᵃ has the *aphel* form אודו, "praise!"

l MT עֲלִילֹתָיו (*'ălîlōtāyw*, "his deeds"); 1QIsaᵃ עלילותיו.

m MT נִשְׂגָּב (*niśgāb*, "is exalted"); 1QIsaᵃ נˢגב.

n MT זַמְּרוּ יְהוָה (*zammĕrû YHWH*, "praise Yahweh in song"); 1QIsaᵃ זמרו ליהוה, "sing hymns to Yahweh."

o MT מְיֻדַּעַת זֹאת (*mĕyuddaʻat zō't*, "let this be made known" [the *kĕtîb*, the *pual* feminine singular participle]) or מוּדַעַת (*mûdaʻat*, "let this be made known" [the *qĕrē'*, the *hophal* feminine singular participle]); 1QIsaᵃ מודעות זאת. The plural ending in 1QIsaᵃ seems an obvious mistake.

p MT בְּכָל־הָאָרֶץ (*bĕkol-hā'āreṣ*, "in all the earth"); 1QIsaᵃ בכול הארץ.

q MT יוֹשֶׁבֶת צִיּוֹן (*yôšebet ṣiyyôn*, "O enthroned Zion"); 1QIsaᵃ בת ישבת ציון, "daughter ᵉⁿᵗʰʳᵒⁿᵉᵈ Zion." The word בת, "daughter," was crossed through before "enthroned" was inserted above the line. MT is the better reading; 1QIsaᵃ initially made a natural mistake because בת ציון is the more common expression.

r MT כִּי (*kî*, "for"); 1QIsaᵃ כיא.

Commentary

The opening expression in the second masculine singular, "And you will say in that day," seems to envision the personified people of God as the singular subject. It ties the following statement of God's people to the preceding prophecy of future salvation in chap. 11. It introduces the thanksgiving of Yahweh's personified people in anticipation of this announced salvation. The hymn of thanksgiving begins with a first person singular speaker, presumably the personified nation, directly addressing the deity. The vow or promise "I will praise you!" is often found in psalms of supplication (Pss 35:18; 43:5; 57:10; 71:22; 86:12) and, when such supplications are answered, sometimes in the responsive thanksgiving psalms (Pss 108:4; 118:21, 28; 138:1-2), which is what this text seems to be patterned on. Although Yahweh has been angry with him, the speaker petitions God to let his anger turn aside and so offer comfort to the speaker. Yahweh's anger is a reference back to the implied judgment of the mere stump or root of Jesse (11:1, 10) and the remnant of God's people (11:11), and to the fuller and more explicit portrayal of that anger and judgment in chaps. 6–10. The petition for the turning aside of that anger to comfort Israel stands in expectant anticipation of the promise of the new ideal king in 11:1-10, and the restoration of the remnant and victorious reunification of Judah and Ephraim in 11:11-16.

These promises move the speaker to praise the God of his salvation (12:2). El is probably used here simply as a generic name for God, but it is also the proper name of an ancient high God, the head of the Canaanite pan-theon. If the repetition of the designation in 1QIsaᵃ were original (see textual notes), it would suggest that the first El is the proper name and the second is the generic usage functioning as the predicate of the nominal sentence. The antiquity of Israel's worship of El is evident from the fact that the theophoric element in the name Isra-el is the divine name El, but it is also clear that the Israelites identified El with Yahweh, the God of the exodus, well before the monarchical period. Israel's earliest poetry, the ancient Song of the Sea (Exod 15:1-18) and the Song of Deborah (Judg 5:1-31), identifies Yahweh as the God of Israel, and the archaic Oracles of Balaam explicitly put Yahweh and El in poetic parallelism (Num 23:8, 21-23). Because of God's promises of salvation, the speaker affirms that he will trust and not be afraid *while he awaits the fulfillment of those promises*. The italicized continuation of the speaker's statement is unexpressed, but clearly implied (cf. Hab 2:3). That trust is rooted in the speaker's reliance on Yah (an archaic, shortened form of Yahweh) as his strength and might, the source of his salvation. This end of the verse is clearly derived from the opening lines of Exod 15:2. The allusion to the Song of the Sea, celebrating the exodus from Egypt, is appropriate in a text celebrating in anticipation the new exodus of Israel's remnant from Assyrian captivity (Isa 11:11-16).

In v. 3 the writer switches from the second masculine singular in addressing the personified people to the second masculine plural: "You (all) will draw water with joy from the springs of salvation." The use of "water" and "springs" as metaphors for life and salvation is a common biblical trope (Jer 2:13; 17:13; Ps 87:7; Prov 4:23; John 4:10-11) and easily understandable in an environment where life-threatening droughts were a common occurrence.

Verse 4 repeats the opening statement of v. 1, but this time in the second masculine plural: "And you (all) will say in that day . . . ." The following invocation of praise is also altered from a first singular cohortative to a plural imperative: "Praise Yahweh! Call upon his name! Make known his deeds among the peoples! Proclaim that his name is exalted!" The reiterated command to praise God is a standard feature of hymns and psalms of thanksgiving, as is the proclamation of his deeds and greatness to the peoples and regions beyond Israel's national borders (Pss 18:50; 57:10; 96:3, 10; 108:4; 126:2). The people of God, then, call upon one another to praise Yahweh in song for his glorious acts of salvation, to make known in all the earth these mighty acts that Yahweh has done for his people (v. 5).

Finally, the thanksgiving song ends with a feminine singular imperative addressed to enthroned city Zion urging her to cry aloud and shout with joy, for "the Holy One of Israel is great in your midst" (v. 6). The use of the epithet יוֹשֶׁבֶת (yôšebet, "enthroned") suggests that Zion was about to regain her imperial status (see Mic 4:6-8; and cf. Isa 47:1-5, where Virgin Babylon's loss of imperial status is marked by her loss of a throne and the necessity of her sitting on the ground). The NRSV tries to capture the sense of the expression by translating, "O royal Zion." The final thought suggests that Yahweh, who had been angry with Zion and therefore punished her (cf. Isa 1:21-28; 29:1-4; 31:4), perhaps even abandoning her for this purpose (Jer 8:18—9:2; Ezek 10:1—11:25), was about to return (Isa 40:9-11; 52:7-10) and again take up his majestic, protective abode within her (cf. Pss 46:2, 8, 12; 48:2-4; 76:2-3). It is not that this salvation was actually a past event for the poet in Isaiah 12 any more than it was for Second Isaiah, but rather the poet's fervent hope for its coming "in that day" allows him to concretize its realization in expectation.

Bibliography

Ackroyd, P. R., "Isaiah I–XII: Presentation of a Prophet," *VT* 29 (1978) 16–48.

Alonso Schökel, L., "De duabus methodis pericopam explicandi," *VD* 34 (1956) 154–60.

Craigie, P. C., "Psalm XXIX in the Hebrew Poetic Tradition," *VT* 22 (1972) 143–51.

Crüsemann, Frank, *Studien zur Formgeschichte von Hymnus und Danklied in Israel* (WMANT 32; Neukirchen-Vluyn: Neukirchener Verlag, 1969) 227–28.

Ehrlich, E. L., *Die Kultsymbolik im Alten Testament und im nachbiblischen Judentum* (Symbolik der Religionen 3; Stuttgart: A. Hiersemann, 1959) 54–58.

Feuchtwang, D., "Das Wasseropfer und die damit verbundenen Zeremonien," *MGWJ* 54 (1910) 535–52, 713–29.

Good, E. M., "Exodus XV 2," *VT* 20 (1970) 358–59.

Gottlieb, H., "Jesaja, Kapitel 12," *DTT* 37 (1974) 29–32.

Loewenstamm, S. E., "The Lord Is My Strength and My Glory," *VT* 19 (1969) 464–70.

Marshall, R. J., "The Structure of Is 1–12," *BR* 7 (1962) 19–32.

——, "The Unity of Is 1–12," *LQ* 14 (1962) 21–38.

Parker, Simon B., "Exodus XV 2 Again," *VT* 21 (1971) 373–79.

Prinsloo, Willem S., "Isaiah 12: One, Two or Three Songs?" in Klaus-Dietrich Schunck and Matthias Augustin, eds., *Goldene Äpfel in silbernen Schalen: Collected Communications to the XIIIth Congress of the International Organization for the Study of the Old Testament, Leuven, 1989* (BEATAJ 20; Frankfurt am Main: P. Lang, 1992) 25–33.

Seydl, E., "Zur Strophik von Jesaja 12," *TQ* 82 (1900) 390–95.

Spence, R. M., "Yah, Yahve," *ExpTim* 11 (1899) 94–95.

Tur-Sinai, N. H., "A Contribution to the Understanding of Isaiah I–XII," in Chaim Rabin, ed., *Studies in the Bible* (ScrHier 8; Jerusalem: Magnes Press, Hebrew University, 1961) 154–88.

Wieringen, A., "Isaiah 12,1-6: A Domain and Communication Analysis," in J. van Ruiten and M. Vervenne, eds., *Studies in the Book of Isaiah: Festschrift Willem A. M. Beuken* (BETL 132; Leuven: Leuven University Press, 1997) 149–72.

Zolli, J., "Note esegetiche," In *Giornale della Società Asiatica Italiana* (1935) 290–92.

13

Isaiah 13 appears to be a unified composition directed against Babylon (vv. 1, 19) and involving the Medes (v. 17) as God's army of judgment. While the text sees this as a paradigm of worldwide judgment of the wicked (vv. 5, 10-11), the focus is on Babylon, and the reference to everyone returning to his own land (v. 14) suggests that with the destruction of Babylon, the exiles of its far-flung conquests will be free to return to their own lands. Despite the heading, then, it is difficult to attribute this oracle to Isaiah, son of Amoz, in the late eighth or early seventh century BCE. The focus on Babylon as the enemy from which exiles may return suggests the period of the Babylonian exile, and the focus on the Medes as the agent of judgment suggests a period early in the Babylo-nian exile before the rise of Cyrus and the replacement of the Median empire with the Persian empire (cf. Jer 51:11, 28), thus sometime early in the period between 597 and 545 BCE.[1] The description of the merciless Medes is probably rooted in the reports of the earlier Median conquest of Aššur (615 BCE) and participation in the fall of Nineveh (612 BCE) and thus points again to the first half of the sixth century. The author is clearly familiar with the earlier work of Isaiah of Jerusalem, but he reuses his motifs, such as the signal flag on the mountain, much as the author of Isaiah 24–27 reuses motifs from Isaiah of Jerusalem. One should probably consider the possibility that the author of chap. 13 and chaps. 24–27 are one and the same disciple.

1/	The oracle concerning Babylon which Isaiah[a] the son of Amoz saw.[b]
2/	Upon the bare mountain lift a signal flag, Raise the voice to them, Wave the hand, That they may enter[c] the gates of the nobles.
3/	I have commanded my sanctified ones; I have also summoned my warriors for my anger, The exultant ones of my pride.[d]
4/	The sound of a multitude on the mountains, Like that of many people, The sound of the noise of kingdoms, Of nations being gathered;[e] Yahweh of Hosts is mustering[f] A host for battle.
5/	The are coming from a distant land, From the end of the heavens, Yahweh and the weapons of his wrath, To destroy the whole earth.
6/	Wail for the day of Yahweh is near, Like shattering from Shaddai it comes.
7/	Therefore all hands grow limp,[g] And every human heart sinks.[h]
8/	They will be terrified with pains[i] And birth pangs will seize (them);[j] They will writhe like a woman in travail, Each will look in horror to his neighbor, Their faces pale with fright.[k]
9/	Behold the day of Yahweh is coming, Cruel,[l] with wrath and burning anger, To turn the earth[m] into a desolation, And its sinners[n] it will destroy from it.

---

1   It is true that "Mede" continues to be used in the very late period to refer to a Persian ruler long after the arrival and defeat of the Achaemenids (Dan 6:1), but given the existence of Isaiah scrolls containing Isaiah 13 from the second century BCE, one can hardly date the composition of this chapter as late as Daniel in the mid-second century BCE. It is also difficult to attribute to its author the historical confusion so blatantly characteristic of the last tradents of the Daniel tradition.

10/ For the stars of heaven
And their constellations° will not shine^p their light;
The sun will grow dark when it goes forth,
And the moon will not^q shine its light.

11/ And I will punish the world for evil,
And the wicked for their sin;^r
And I will bring to an end the pride of the insolent,
And the haughtiness of the violent I will humble.

12/ I will make humans more rare^s than refined gold,
And mankind than the gold of Ophir.

13/ That is why I will shake^t the heavens,
So that the earth trembles from its place,^u
At the wrath of Yahweh of Hosts,
On the day of his burning anger.

14/ And they will be^v like a gazelle driven away,
And like sheep^w with no one to gather them;
They will turn each to his own people,
They will flee each to his own land.

15/ Every one^x who is found will be pierced,
And every one^x who is caught will fall by the sword.

16/ Their children will be smashed^y before their eyes,
Their houses plundered,^z their wives raped.*a

17/ I am about to stir up against them the Medes
Who do not*b consider*c silver
And who take no*b pleasure in gold.

18/ And the bows of the young men are smashed,*d
And for the fruit of the womb*e they show no pity,*f
Their eye does not*f spare the children.

19/ And Babylon the glory of kingdoms,*g
The beauty of the pride of the Chaldeans,*h
Will be like God's overthrow*i
Of Sodom and Gomorrah.*j

20/ It will not*k be inhabited for ever,
Nor*k dwelt*l in for generation to generation;
And an Arab will not*k camp*m there,*n
And shepherds*o will not*k rest their flocks*p there.

21/ But desert animals will lie down there,
And their houses will be full of howling creatures,
And ostriches will dwell there,*q
And satyrs will dance there.

22/ Hyenas will dwell*r in its towers,*s
And jackals in the pleasant palaces;*t
And its time is near to coming,*u
And its days will not*v be drawn out.

Textual Notes

a   MT יְשַׁעְיָהוּ (yĕšaʿyāhû), "Isaiah"; 1QIsaᵃ has the shorter form ישעיה.

b   MT חָזָה (ḥāzâ), "he saw"; 1QIsaᵃ has the participle חוזה (ḥôzê), "he was seeing," but MT is supported by LXX, Vg., and Syr.

c   MT וְיָבֹאוּ (wĕyābōʾû), "that they may enter"; 1QIsaᵃ has יבוא, "let him enter." Vg., Syr., and Tg. all have the plural. LXX goes its own way with μὴ φοβεῖσθε, παρακαλεῖτε τῇ χειρί, Ἀνοίξατε, οἱ ἄρχοντες, "Do not be afraid, encourage with the hand, 'Open, O rulers!'"

d   LXX has a very periphrastic translation of this verse: ἐγὼ συντάσσω, καὶ ἐγὼ ἄγω αὐτούς· ἡγιασμένοι εἰσίν, καὶ ἐγὼ ἄγω αὐτούς· γίγαντες ἔρχονται πληρῶσαι τὸν θυμόν μου χαίροντες ἅμα καὶ ὑβρίζοντες, "I organize and I lead them; they are sanctified, and I lead them. Mighty ones come to fulfill my wrath, at the same time rejoicing and reviling."

e MT גּוֹיִם נֶאֱסָפִים (gôyim neʾĕsāpîm), "of nations being gathered"; 1QIsaᵃ גואים נספים. The syllable-closing aleph (neʾsāpîm) is sometimes elided in the late period,[2] and the spelling of gôʾyīm, "nations," with an aleph is common in Qumran Hebrew.

f MT מְפַקֵּד (mĕpaqqēd), "is mustering," with piel participle; so also 1QIsaᵃ; 4QIsaᵇ has the hiphil participle מפקיד (mapqîd).

g MT כָּל-יָדַיִם תִּרְפֶּינָה (kol-yādayim tirpênâ), "all hands grow limp"; 1QIsaᵃ כול ידין תרפינה with an internal mater is a feature of Qumran Hebrew, and the unusual nunation instead of mimation for the dual is probably due to the Aramaizing influence in second temple Hebrew; 4QIsaᵃ כל ידים תרפיניה.

h MT יִמָּס (yimmās), "sinks, melts"; so 1QIsaᵃ; but 4QIsaᵇ has ימאס, which nonetheless is probably just a graphic variant, not an indication that the scribe was reading a different verb.

i LXX misunderstands צִירִים (ṣîrîm, "pains") for its homonym, "messengers, ambassadors."

j LXX misdivides the lines as καὶ ὠδῖνες αὐτοὺς ἕξουσιν ὡς γυναικὸς τικτούσης· καὶ συμφοράσουσιν ἕτερος πρὸς τὸν ἕτερον καὶ ἐκστήσονται, "and birth pangs will seize them like a woman giving birth; and they shall wail each to the other and they shall be amazed."

k MT פְּנֵי לְהָבִים פְּנֵיהֶם (pĕnê lĕhābîm pĕnêhem), "their faces faces of flame," that is, "their faces pale with fright"); 1QIsaᵃ ופני להבים פניהם, "and their faces faces of flame." LXX has καὶ τὸ πρόσωπον αὐτῶν ὡς φλὸξ μεταβαλοῦσιν, "and they will change their face like a flame."

l MT אַכְזָרִי (ʾakzārî), "cruel"; 1QIsaᵃ אגזרי.

m MT הָאָרֶץ (hāʾāreṣ), "the earth"; 1QIsaᵃ ארץ, "earth."

n MT וְחַטָּאֶיהָ (wĕḥaṭṭāʾêhā), "and its sinners," supported by 4QIsaᵃ and 4QIsaᵇ, Vg., Tg., Syr.; the suffix is lacking in 1QIsaᵃ (וחטאים, "and sinners,") and LXX.

o MT וּכְסִילֵיהֶם (ûkĕsîlêhem), "and their constellations"; 1QIsaᵃ וכסליהם; LXX has καὶ ὁ Ὠρίων καὶ πᾶς ὁ κόσμος τοῦ οὐρανοῦ, "and Orion and all the world of heaven."

p MT לֹא יָהֵלּוּ אוֹרָם (lōʾ yāhēllû ʾôrām), "will not shine their light"; 1QIsaᵃ לוא יאירו אורם, "will not shine their light," apparently substituting a more common word for the very rare הלל I (hll), which is attested only here, in Job (29:3; 31:26; 41:10), and in Ben Sira 36:27.

q MT לֹא (lōʾ), "not"; 1QIsaᵃ לוא.

r MT עֲוֹנָם (ʿăwōnām), "their iniquity"; 1QIsaᵃ עוונם.

s MT אוֹקִיר (ʾôqîr), "I will make rare"; 1QIsaᵃ אוקיר.

t MT אַרְגִּיז (ʾargîz), "I will shake," so 1QIsaᵃ, 4QIsaᵃ, 4QIsaᵇ, Vg., Syr., Tg.; LXX has ὁ γὰρ οὐρανὸς θυμωθήσεται, "for heaven will be enraged."

u MT מִמְּקוֹמָהּ (mimmĕqômāh), "from its place," so 1QIsaᵃ and the versions; 4QIsaᵇ ממקוה, which involves the simple omission of a letter.

v MT וְהָיָה (wĕhāyâ), "and it will be"; 1QIsaᵃ והיו, "and they will be." MT's singular is due to the singular noun "gazelle" that immediately follows, but the subject of the verb is not "gazelle" but the people who are compared to a gazelle and sheep. Read the plural with 1QIsaᵃ to agree with the other verbs in the verse, which are all plural.

w MT וּכְצֹאן (ûkĕṣōʾn), "and like sheep"; 1QIsaᵃ וכצאן.

x For MT's כל (kol), "everyone," 1QIsaᵃ has the fuller orthography כול.

y MT וְעֹלְלֵיהֶם יְרֻטְּשׁוּ (wĕʿōlĕlêhem yĕruṭṭĕšû), "and their children will be smashed"; 1QIsaᵃ ועילוליהמה ירוטשו.

z MT יִשַּׁסּוּ (yiššassû), "will be plundered"; 1QIsaᵃ adds an erroneous conjunction וישסו.

*a MT וּנְשֵׁיהֶם תִּשָּׁגַלְנָה (ûnĕšêhem tiššāgalnâ), "and their wives raped." The verb שגל was considered so crude, analogous to English "fucked," that it was replaced in public reading with the qĕrēʾ (tiššākabnâ) תִּשָּׁכַבְנָה, "slept with."[3] 1QIsaᵃ adopts this reading along with a longer suffix on the noun ונשיהמה תשכבנה.

*b For MT's לֹא (lōʾ), "not," 1QIsaᵃ has the fuller orthography לוא.

*c MT יַחְשֹׁבוּ (yaḥšōbû), "they consider," is the pausal form; 1QIsaᵃ יחשוב has the fuller orthography characteristic of Qumran Hebrew.

*d Reading תְּרֻטַּשְׁנָה (tĕruṭṭašnâ), "will be smashed," with Wildberger for MT תְּרַטַּשְׁנָה (tĕraṭṭašnâ), "the bows will shatter." LXX has τοξεύματα νεανίσκων συντρίψουσιν, "the bows of the young men will shatter." If the conjectural reading is correct, there is a double entendre here; "bows" refers not only to the weapons of war but to a young man's sexual potency. If the bows of the young men are smashed, there could be a reference here to castration or sexual mutilation.

*e MT וּפְרִי-בֶטֶן (ûpĕrî-beṭen), "and for the fruit of the womb"; 1QIsaᵃ ועל פרי בטן (wĕʿal pĕrî beṭen), "and upon the fruit of the womb."

*f MT (lōʾ), "not"; 1QIsaᵃ לוא.

*g MT מַמְלָכוֹת (mamlākôt), "kingdoms"; 1QIsaᵃ ממלכת.

*h MT כַּשְׂדִּים (kaśdîm), "Chaldeans"; 1QIsaᵃ כשדיים.

*i MT כְּמַהְפֵּכַת אֱלֹהִים (kĕmahpēkat ʾĕlōhîm), "like God's overthrow"; 1QIsaᵃ כמאפכת אלוהים.

*j MT אֶת-סְדֹם וְאֶת-עֲמֹרָה (ʾet-sĕdōm wĕʾet-ʿămōrâ), "of Sodom and Gomorrah"; 1QIsaᵃ את סודם ואת עומרה.

*k MT לֹא (lōʾ), "not"; 1QIsaᵃ לוא.

*l MT תִּשְׁכֹּן (tiškōn), "dwelt in"; 1QIsaᵃ תשכון.

*m The verb יַהֵל (yahēl) < יַאֲהֵל (yĕʾahēl) appears to be a piel imperfect, denominative from the noun אֹהֶל (ʾōhel), "tent," meaning "to tent, to camp."

*n MT שָׁם (šām), "there"; 1QIsaᵃ שמה, "thither."

*o MT וְרֹעִים (wĕrōʿîm), "and shepherds"; 1QIsaᵃ ורועים.

2 Joüon and Muraoka, Grammar, 92 §24 fa.
3 See Wilhelm Gesenius, Hebräisches und aramäisches Handwörterbuch über das Alte Testament (18th ed.; Berlin: Springer, 1987) 1323b; R. Borger, BO 18 (1961) 151–52; and B. Landsberger, "Akkadisch-hebräische Wortgleichungen," in Hebräische Wortforschung: Festschrift zum 80. Geburtstag von Walter Baumgartner (VTSup 16; Leiden: Brill, 1967) 176–204, esp. 198–200.

*p   MT יַרְבִּצוּ (*yarbîṣû*), "they will cause to rest"; 1QIsaᵃ inserts a supralinear *yod* as a *mater*: ירבצו.

*q   MT שָׁם (*šām*), "there"; 1QIsaᵃ שמה, "thither."

*r   The NRSV takes וְעָנָה (*wĕ'ānâ*) as ענה IV, "to sing, cry," but the third person masculine singular form does not agree with the plural subject אִיִּים ('*îyîm*), "hyenas"—1QIsaᵃ has the *yod* inserted as a correction above the line אם ('*m*). It seems more likely that the verb form should be understood as a third person feminine plural from the verb עון III ('*wn*), "to dwell," just as the verbs in the preceding v. 21 stress the idea of wild animals lying down, filling, and dwelling in the abandoned houses. See the discussion in *HALOT*, 799, and Wildberger, 2:504–5.

*s   MT בְּאַלְמְנוֹתָיו (*bĕ'almnôtāyw*), "in its towers"; 1QIsaᵃ באלמנותו (*b'lmnwtw*). The noun '*almān* appears to be a simple by-form of אַרְמוֹן ('*armôn*), "tower, palace," as the parallel with the following "in the palaces of pleasure" suggests.

*t   MT בְּהֵיכְלֵי עֹנֶג (*bĕhêkĕlê 'ōneg*), "in the palaces of pleasure"; 1QIsaᵃ בהיכלו ענוגו.

*u   MT וְקָרוֹב לָבוֹא עִתָּהּ (*wĕqārôb lābô' 'ittāh*), "and its time is near to coming"; 1QIsaᵃ קרוב לבוא עתה.

*v   MT לֹא (*lō'*), "not"; 1QIsaᵃ לוא.

Commentary

While Babylon is mentioned (Isa 11:11 [Shinar]; 14:4, 22 [this verse could represent later editing]; 21:9) or alluded to (22:2-3) in oracles that I attribute to Isaiah of Jerusalem, this is the only place where an oracle focuses solely on Babylon. The attribution to Isaiah, son of Amoz, is apparently to give the oracle the authority of the great eighth-century prophet, though the contents of the following oracle seem to reflect the concerns of a period a century later than the time of Isaiah of Jerusalem. The motif of raising a signal flag for Yahweh to summon humans is common in Isaiah of Jerusalem (5:26; 11:10, 12; 18:3; 30:17; 31:9), but while Yahweh may whistle (שרק, *šāraq*) for his agents to come (5:26; 7:18), nowhere else in First Isaiah does he raise his voice or wave his hand to summon them. These are probably common expressions, however, and one should be hesitant to assign much significance to this observation. God's agents are summoned to "enter the gates of the nobles (v. 2)," but it is not yet entirely clear what these gates are or the purpose for this gathering and entrance into the gates.

With v. 3 this uncertainty is erased. Those summoned are Yahweh's sanctified warriors, the mighty ones to carry out his wrath. Sanctifying warriors in preparation for war was a common practice in the ancient Near East (1 Sam 21:6), and thus one could speak of "sanctifying war" against someone (Jer 6:4; Joel 4:9; Mic 3:5), or refer as here to one's warriors as "one's sanctified ones." For the closest parallel, compare Jer 51:27-28. It is clear now that those summoned are to enter the gates with hostile intent. Verse 4's description of the sound of this vast host on the mountains picks up the ancient motif of the rebel nations gathered against Jerusalem on the mountains of

Israel (Ps 48:5-8; Isa 14:24-27; 17:12-13; 29:5-8; Joel 4:9-14; Zech 14:1-19; Ezekiel 38–39), but here the gathering for battle is not against Jerusalem but against Babylon as the symbol of worldwide injustice. Nonetheless, it is Yahweh who is mustering this great army for battle. Just as he summoned his agents or tools for punishing Israel and Jerusalem from the far corners of the earth (Isa 5:26; 7:18; 10:5-6), so now the weapons of his wrath are again coming from afar, from the end of the heavens (v. 5), to destroy the whole earth.

Verse 5 calls upon his fictive audience, presumably the inhabitants of Babylon, to wail because the day of Yahweh is near, coming upon them swiftly like a sudden shattering from Shaddai. The choice of the divine name Shaddai is dictated by the assonance and alliteration with the noun שד (*šōd*, "disaster," rendered "shattering" here to try to capture the sound play). The suddenness of the disaster will leave the Babylonians in shock, with limp hands and demoralized hearts (v. 7). It will come upon them as suddenly and sharply as birth pangs, and they will look to one another in hopeless confusion (v. 8). This cruel and fierce day of Yahweh is coming in great wrath to turn the earth into a desolation and to destroy its sinners from it (v. 9). In typical fashion, this judgment is described as blacking out the light of the heavenly bodies (v. 10; cf. Amos 5:18-20; Joel 4:14-15). The shift of the destruction from Babylon to the whole earth is probably simply a reflection of the fact that, for inhabitants of the Babylonian empire, Babylon was the center of the whole world, providing the framework certainly for its political and economic coherence, and probably for its coherence on many other levels as well.

This judgment is directed against the world's evil, against the wicked for their sin, against the pride of the insolent and the haughtiness of the violent (v. 11), but the result will be to leave a very small, rarified human remnant (v. 12), which suggests how few righteous the prophet envisioned. The very heavens and earth will be shaken by the anger of Yahweh of Hosts in this day of his fierce anger (v. 13; cf. 24:1-2, 21-23; 26:21). With this destruction, the remnant will be like driven gazelles or sheep without one to gather them (v. 14). In the absence of their foreign overlords, they will simply turn and flee, each to his own country (cf. 27:12-13; Jer 51:6, 9, 45).

Verses 15-16 turn from the fate of the exiles to that of the Babylonian survivors. Any who are found or caught will be pierced and will fall by the sword. They will find no mercy from their conquerors. Their children will be smashed before their eyes, their houses plundered, their wives raped. As the textual note indicates, the language used for "rape" here is intentionally crude and vulgar, to indicate the horrific character of this judgment on the Babylonians.

The judgment is so horrific and merciless, because the enemy that Yahweh is stirring up against the Babylonians is not a civilized people that shares the Babylonian cultural norms but the fierce Medes, who have no regard for silver and gold (v. 17). They cannot be bought off, and they show no pity on the young (v. 18). If the MT is correct, bows shatter the young men; if the conjectural emendation is correct, the bows of the young men are smashed. That is, not only are they defeated, but they lose their sexual potency by castration or mutilation. One should note that in the rhetoric of war claims of the uniqueness of the enemy's barbarism are not to be taken at face value. In World War II a defeated Germany complained about the savage barbarism of the Russians, but, even admitting the savagery, the Russians hardly did anything to the Germans that the Germans had not already done to the Russians in the early years of the war, when the Germans were winning. Here the prophet por-

trays the Babylonians' coming perception of their enemy, but nothing portrayed as done to the Babylonians goes beyond what other texts portray as the treatment meted out by the Babylonians to those they conquered (see Lam 5:11-14).

The result of God's judgment will be the complete overthrow of Babylon, the pride of the Chaldean tribes and the glory of kingdoms (v. 19). Though Babylon was the greatest city in the world at the time, the prophet claims that it will become as desolate and abandoned as the proverbial twin cities of Sodom and Gomorrah. It will never again be inhabited, even by a nomadic Arab camping in a tent or a shepherd with his flock (v. 20).[4] It will be inhabited only by wild animals and desert creatures, leaving it a lonely, frightening, and desolate place (vv. 21-22). Moreover, the time for its judgment is near, and its days will not be prolonged.

A modern visitor to the ancient site of Babylon might see the ruins there as confirmation of this prophecy of the destruction of Babylon,[5] but one should note that neither this prophet's nor Jeremiah's prophecy (Jeremiah 51) of the fall of Babylon at the hand of the Medes came to pass in precisely the way predicted. If one takes "Medes" here literally, there was *no* Median conquest of Babylon(ia) at all. If "Medes" here means the Median-Persian ruler Cyrus II, there was a conquest, but not, it appears, with the destruction described here in Isaiah. Despite the power of the Medes that contributed to the fall of Assyria between 615 and 609 BCE, and the Medes' potential threat to Babylon, their former ally, which became particularly acute in the early years of Nabonidus (556–539 BCE), the last Neo-Babylonian ruler, the Medes never took Babylon. It was not until the rise of the Persians[6] that Babylonia fell to Cyrus II (539 BCE), and the city of Babylon, far from being destroyed in battle, opened its gates to Cyrus as a deliverer from what the priests of Marduk regarded as the misrule of Nabonidus.

---

4   The Arabs continued a nomadic or semi-nomadic lifestyle long after Israel and its more sedentary neighbors had largely given up dwelling in tents for more permanent structures. See Israel Eph'al, *The Ancient Arabs: Nomads on the Borders of the Fertile Crescent, 9th–5th Century B.C.* (Jerusalem: Magnes Press; Leiden: Brill, 1982).

5   See, e.g., the work of a major excavator of Babylon, Robert Koldewey, *Das wieder erstehende Babylon* (5th ed.; Munich: C. H. Beck, 1990), with an English translation published from an earlier edition, *The Excavations at Babylon* (trans. Agnes Sophia Johns; London: Macmillan, 1914).

6   Cyrus II's defeat of his Median overlord Astyages took place c. 546 BCE.

Even then, Babylon remained an important provincial capital for a significant period of time. It was only centuries later, after the death of Alexander the Great, that the city of Babylon was abandoned and left an uninhabited ruin.[7] Nonetheless, a significant portion of those Jewish exiles who returned from Babylonian captivity to their homeland after 539 BCE must have regarded the prophecies of Isaiah 13, Jeremiah 51, and Isaiah 46–47; 52:11-12 as essentially fulfilled by the restoration of Jewish life and worship in Judea.

Bibliography

Ahlström, G. W., *Joel and the Temple Cult of Jerusalem* (VTSup 21; Leiden: Brill, 1971) 62–97.

Alonso Schökel, L., "Traducción de textos poéticos Hebreos I (Is 13)," *CB* 17 (1960) 170–76.

Bach, Robert, *Die Aufforderungen zur Flucht und zum Kampf in alttestamentlichen Prophetenspruch* (WMANT 9; Neukirchen: Neukircherner Verlag, 1962).

Boer, P. A. H. de, "An Inquiry into the Meaning of the Term *mś²*," *OTS* 5 (1948) 197–214.

Boutflower, C., *The Book of Isaiah Chapters [I–XXXIX] in the Light of the Assyrian Monuments* (London: SPCK, 1930).

Brinkman, J. A., "Merodach Baladan II," in *Studies Presented to A. Leo Oppenheim, June 7, 1964* (Chicago: Oriental Institute of the University of Chicago, 1964) 6–53.

———, *A Political History of Post-Kassite Babylonia* (AnOr 43; Rome: Pontifical Biblical Institute, 1968).

Brueggemann, Walter, "2 Kings 18–19: The Legitimacy of a Sectarian Hermeneutic," *HBT* 7 (1985) 1–42.

Buccellati, G., "Enthronement of the King," in *Studies Presented to A. Leo Oppenheim, June 7, 1964* (Chicago: Oriental Institute of the University of Chicago, 1964) 54–61.

Budde, K., "Jesaja 13," in Wilhelm Frankenberg and Friedrich Küchler, eds., *Abhandlungen zur semitischen Religionskunde und Sprachwissenschaft, Wolf Wilhelm Grafen von Baudissin zum 26. September 1917* (BZAW 33; Giessen: A. Töpelmann, 1918) 55–70.

Carniti, C., "L'espressione 'Il giorno di Jhwh': Origine ed evoluzione semantica," *BeO* 12 (1970) 11–25.

Christensen, Duane L., *Prophecy and War in Ancient Israel: Studies in the Oracles against the Nations in Old Testament Prophecy* (Berkeley, CA: Bibal, 1989).

———, *Transformations of the War Oracle in Old Testament Prophecy. Studies in the Oracles against the Nations* (HDR 3; Missoula, MT: Scholars Press, 1975).

Eaton, J. H., "The Origin of the Book of Isaiah," *VT* 9 (1959) 138–57.

Eggebrecht, G., "Die früheste Bedeutung und der Ursprung der Konzeption vom 'Tag Jahwes,'" *TLZ* 93 (1968): 631–32.

Erlandsson, Seth, *The Burden of Babylon: A Study of Isaiah 13:2–14:23* (ConBOT 4; Lund: Gleerup, 1970).

Fensham, F. C., "Common Trends in Curses of the Near-Eastern Treaties and *kudurru*-Inscriptions compared with Maledictions of Amos and Isaiah," *ZAW* 75 (1963) 144–75.

Fohrer, Georg, "Entstehung, Komposition und Überlieferung von Jesaja 1–39," in Fohrer, *Studien zur alttestamentlichen Prophetie, 1949–1965* (BZAW 99; Berlin: A. Töpelmann, 1967) 113–47.

Gehman, H. S., "The 'Burden' of the Prophets," *JQR* 31 (1940) 107–21.

Geyer, J. B., "Twisting Tiamat's Tail: A Mythological Interpretation of Isaiah 13:5 and 8," *VT* 37 (1987) 164–79.

Gosse, Bernard, "Isaïe 13:1–14:23 dans la tradition littéraire du livre d'Isaïe et dans la Tradition des oracles contre les nations," *ETR* 67 (1992) 270.

———, "Un texte pré-apocalyptique du règne de Darius: Isaïe 13:1–14:23," *RB* 92 (1985) 200–222.

Görg, Manfred, "Dämonen statt 'Eulen' in Jes 13:21," *BN* 62 (1992) 16–17.

Gottwald, Norman K., *All the Kingdoms of the Earth: Israelite Prophecy and International Relations in the Ancient near East* (New York: Harper & Row, 1964).

Grimme, H., "Ein übersehenes Orakel gegen Assur (Isaias 13)," *TQ* 85 (1903) 1–11.

Hayes, John H., "The Oracles against the Nations in the Old Testament" (Th.D. thesis, Princeton Theological Seminary, 1964).

———, "The Usage of Oracles against Foreign Nations in Ancient Israel," *JBL* 87 (1968) 81–92.

7 For easily accessible treatments of Babylon's history, see A. Kirk Grayson, "Mesopotamia, History of (Babylonia)," *ABD* 4:755–77, and the earlier work by H. W. F. Saggs, *The Greatness That Was Babylon: A Survey of the Ancient Civilization of the Tigris-Euphrates Valley* (2nd ed.; London: Sidgwick & Jackson, 1988).

Heintz, J. G., "Aux origines d'une expression biblique: *ūmūšu qerbū* in A.R.M. X 6,8," *VT* 21 (1971) 528–40.

Hillers, Delbert R., "Convention in Hebrew Literature: The Reaction to Bad News," *ZAW* 77 (1965) 86–90.

——, *Treaty Curses and the Old Testament Prophets* (BibOr 16; Rome: Pontifical Biblical Institute, 1964).

Jenkins, Allan K., "The Development of the Isaiah Tradition in Is 13–23," in J. Vermeylen et al., eds., *Le livre d'Isaïe: Les oracles et leurs relectures. Unité et complexité de l'ouvrage* (BETL 81; Leuven: Leuven University Press, 1989) 237–51.

Klein, R. W., "The Day of the Lord," *Concordia Theological Monthly* 39 (1968) 517–25.

Koch, J., "Der Finsternisbericht Jesaja 13,10," *UF* 25 (1993) 201–17.

Krause, Alfred E., "Historical Selectivity: Prophetic Prerogative or Typological Imperative?" in E. Gileadi, ed., *Israel's Apostasy and Restoration: Essays in Honor of Roland K. Harrison* (Grand Rapids: Baker, 1988) 175–212.

Krumwiede, Hans Walter, "*Usus Legis* und *Usus Historiarum*: Die Hermeneutik der Theologia Crucis nach Luthers Auslegung von Jesaja 13," *KD* 8 (1962) 238–64.

Lambert, W. G., "The Babylonians and Chaldaeans," in D. J. Wiseman, ed., *Peoples of Old Testament Times* (Oxford: Clarendon, 1973) 179–96.

Liebreich, L. J., "The Compilation of the Book of Isaiah," *JQR* 46 (1955) 259–77; 47 (1956) 114–38.

Margulis, Barry Baruch, "Studies in the Oracles against the Nations" (Ph.D. diss., Brandeis University, 1967).

Miller, Patrick D., "The Divine Council and the Prophetic Call to War," *VT* 18 (1968) 100–107.

Müller, H. P., *Ursprünge und Strukturen alttestamentlicher Eschatologie* (BZAW 109; Berlin: A. Töpelmann, 1969) 72–85.

Reid, D. G., "The Burden of Babylon: A Study of Isaiah 13" (research paper, Fuller Theological Seminary, 1979).

Saggs, H. W. F., *The Greatness That Was Babylon: A Survey of the Ancient Civilization of the Tigris-Euphrates Valley* (2nd ed.; London: Sidgwick & Jackson, 1988).

——, "The Nimrud Letters, 1952: Part I, The Ukin-Zer Rebellion and Related Texts," *Iraq* 17 (1955) 21–56.

Schunk, K. D., "Der 'Tag Jahwes' in der Verkündigung der Propheten," *Kairos* 11 (1969) 14–21.

Schwarz, G., "Jesaja 13:7-8a: Eine Emendation," *ZAW* 89 (1977) 119.

Scott, R. B. Y., "The Meaning of *maśśā'* as an Oracle Title," *JBL* 67 (1948) 5–6.

Smith, S., "The Supremacy of Assyria," in I. E. S. Edwards et al., eds., *The Cambridge Ancient History*, vol. 1.1, *Prolegomena and Prehistory* (Cambridge: Cambridge University Press, 1970) 39–62.

Stolz, Fritz, "Jahwes und Israels Kriege," in Stolz, *Jahwes und Israels Kriege: Kriegstheorien und Kriegserfahrungen im Glauben des alten Israel* (ATANT 60; Zurich: Theologischer Verlag, 1972) 158–61.

Torrey, C. C., "Some Important Editorial Operations in the Book of Isaiah," *JBL* 57 (1938) 109–39.

Weis, Richard D., *A Definition of the Genre Massa' in the Hebrew Bible* (Ann Arbor, MI: University Microfilms, 1985).

Weiss, M., "The Origin of the 'Day of the Lord'—Reconsidered," *HUCA* 37 (1966) 29–72.

Witt, Douglas A., "The Houses Plundered, the Women Raped: The Use of Isaiah 13 in Zechariah 14:1-11," in Terrance Callan, ed., *Proceedings, Eastern Great Lakes & Midwest Biblical Society*, vol. 11 (1991) 66–74.

14

The introduction in vv. 1-4a to the following taunt song against the king of Babylon in vv. 4b-21 is generally dated to the postexilic period (Marti, 122; Duhm, 92–93; Gray, 233; Clements, 138, 140).[1] There are certain similarities in language and style to Second and Third Isaiah, and even Zechariah (note the use of *bāḥar* for God's choosing his people again, Zech 1:17; 2:16), so this generally accepted dating may be correct. Nonetheless, this dating is by no means certain. The people addressed in this introduction are Israel, Jacob, and the house of Jacob, not Judah, or Jerusalem as in Zechariah; and in the language of First Isaiah, the terms Israel, Jacob, and the house of Jacob would refer specifically to the northern kingdom. The eighth-century Isaiah of Jerusalem did, in fact, harbor hopes for the restoration of at least a remnant of the northern kingdom as a number of passages indicate (8:23b—9:6; 10:20-23; 11:11-16). When Hezekiah came to the throne of Judah in 715 BCE, he made overtures to the inhabitants of the former northern kingdom (2 Chr 30:1–31:1), and, while the response may not have been as enthusiastic as the Judean court hoped, it does indicate the hope and expectation in the southern kingdom that the northerners would again acknowledge Davidic hegemony over the north. Such hopes are reflected in the Judean editing of Hosea (Hos 3:5), and they are given strong expression in the time of Josiah in Jeremiah (Jer 31:1-14) and a bit later in Ezekiel (Ezek 37:15-27). It is possible that the surprising death of Sargon II of Assyria in 705 BCE led Isaiah of Jerusalem to give this expression to these hopes at the end of the eighth century. The mention of the king of Babylon in v. 4 does not rule out this possibility, because Sargon II finally recaptured Babylon and had himself crowned king of Babylon in 709 BCE, just four years before his defeat and death at the hands of mountain tribesmen in 705.

1/	For[a] Yahweh will have compassion for Jacob[b] And he will again choose Israel And he will set them[c] upon their land And the sojourner will join himself[d] to them And they will attach themselves[e] to[f] the house of Jacob.[b]
2/	And peoples[g] will take them And bring them to their place;[h] And the house of Israel[i] will inherit them On[j] the land of Yahweh[k] As slaves and maidservants, And they will become captors to their captors,[l] And they will rule[m] over their oppressors.
3/	On the day[n] Yahweh[o] gives you rest From your pain and from your turmoil[p] And from the hard labor[q] which they imposed[r] on you,
4a/	You will take up[s] this taunt[t] against[u] the king of Babylon And you will say:[vw]

Textual Notes

a כִּי (*kî*), "for," MT, 1QIsa[a], 4QIsa[c] (א[כי]), Vg., Tg., Syr.; LXX καί, "and"; Vg. reads the last half of 13:22 as part of 14:1: *prope est ut veniat tempus eius et dies eius non elongabuntur miserebitur enim Dominus Jacob et eliget adhuc de Israel*, "Its time is near to come and its day will not be long delayed, for the Lord will take pity on Jacob and choose Israel again."

b 1QIsa[a] has the orthographic variant יעקוב for MT יַעֲקֹב (*Yaʿăqōb*), "Jacob."

---

1 Wildberger (2:525, 538–39) split vv. 1-2 from 3-4a and thinks that vv. 1-2 could come from the exilic period. Hayes and Irvine (p. 227) are rather unique in dating this material to 729–727 BCE.

c וְהִנִּיחָם (wĕhinnîḥām), "he will set them" or "he will give them rest," MT, 1QIsaᵃ, Vg., Tg., Syr.; LXX ἀναπαύσονται, "they shall rest."

d וְנִלְוָה הַגֵּר (wĕnilwâ haggēr), "and the sojourner will join himself," MT, 1QIsaᵃ (ונלוא הגר orthographic variant); LXX, Vg.; Tg. and Syr. have the plural.

e וְנִסְפְּחוּ (wĕnispĕḥû), "and they will attach themselves," MT, 1QIsaᵃ, Syr, Tg.; LXX and Vg. have the singular.

f עַל־בֵּית (ʿal-bêt), "to the house," MT, LXX, Tg., Syr.; 1QIsaᵃ either omits על, or the ink has faded.

g עַמִּים (ʿammîm), "peoples," MT, LXX, Vg., Syr., Tg.; 1QIsaᵃ has עמים רבים, "many peoples."

h אֶל־מְקוֹמָם (ʾel mĕqômām), "to their place," MT, 4QIsaᶜ (frag.), LXX, Vg., Tg.; אל אדמתם ואל מקומם, "to their land and to their place" 1QIsaᵃ; ܠܐܪܥܗܘܢ (lʾrᶜhwn), "to their land" Syr.

i בֵית־יִשְׂרָאֵל (bêt yiśrāʾēl), "house of Israel," MT, 1QIsaᵃ, 4QIsaᶜ (frag), Vg., Syr., Tg.; omitted by LXX, which has καὶ πληθυνθήσονται, "and they shall be multiplied."

j עַל (ʿal), "against," MT, LXX, Vg., Tg.; אל (ʾel, "to") 1QIsaᵃ.

k יְהוָה MT, Vg., Tg., Syr.; τοῦ θεοῦ LXX.

l וְהָיוּ שֹׁבִים לְשֹׁבֵיהֶם (wĕhāyû šōbîm lĕšōbêhem), "and they will be captors to their captors," MT, 1QIsaᵃ, Vg., Syr.; καὶ ἔσονται αἰχμάλωτοι οἱ αἰχμαλωτεύσαντες αὐτούς, "and those who captured them will become captives" LXX.

m וְרָדוּ (wĕrādû), "and they will rule," MT, 4QIsaᶜ, Vg., Syr. Tg.; 1QIsaᵃ has the participle ורדים (wĕrōdîm); LXX has the passive: καὶ κυριευθήσονται οἱ κυριεύσαντες αὐτῶν, "and those who lorded over them will be lorded over."

n בְּיוֹם (bĕyôm) "in the day," MT, 1QIsaᵃ, 4QIsaᶜ, Vg. (in die illa cum), Syr., Tg.; LXX has ἐν τῇ ἡμέρᾳ ἐκείνῃ, "in that day," followed by the main clause rather than the temporal clause of the other texts.

o יְהוָה MT, 1QIsaᵃ, 4QIsaᶜ, Syr., Tg.; LXX ὁ θεός; Vg. Deus.

p 1QIsaᵃ has the orthographic variant ומרוגזך for MT וּמֵרָגְזֶךָ (ûmērogzekā), "and from your turmoil."

q 1QIsaᵃ has the orthographic variant העבודה for MT הָעֲבֹדָה (hāʿăbōdâ), "the labor."

r עבדו (ʿābĕdû), "they imposed, forced to do," 1QIsaᵃ, 4QIsaᶜ; cf. Exod 1:14. MT's עֻבַּד־בָּךְ (ʿubbad bāk), "which was done by you," is awkward, because the masculine verb does not agree in gender with the feminine implied subject הָעֲבֹדָה (hāʿăbōdâ), "the labor"; LXX, Vg., and Syr. have the verb in the second person.

s וְנָשָׂאתָ (wĕnāśāʾtā), "and you will take up," MT, 4QIsaᶜ, 1QIsaᵃ (ונשאתה, wĕnāśāʾtâ); 4QIsaᶜ follows 1QIsaᵃ but omits the א.

t הַמָּשָׁל (hammāšāl), "the taunt," MT, 4QIsaᶜ, 1QIsaᵃ (adds the prosaizing את before הַמָּשָׁל) Vg., Tg., Syr.; LXX has τὸν θρῆνον τοῦτον, "this lament."

u עַל (ʿal), "against," MT, 1QIsaᵃ, LXX, Vg., Tg., Syr. אל (ʾel), "toward"; 4QIsaᶜ.

v 1QIsaᵃ has the orthographic variant ואמרתה for MT וְאָמַרְתָּ (wĕʾāmārtā), "and you will say."

w LXX adds ἐν τῇ ἡμέρᾳ ἐκείνῃ, "in that day."

Commentary

The promise that Yahweh will have compassion (רחם) on Jacob is a reversal of the judgment God announced on the northern kingdom in Isa 9:16, and it may be a play on the symbolic name of Hosea's second child Lo-ruhamah (Hos 1:6; 2:6 [Eng. 2:4]), which announced a similar judgment on the northern kingdom, though not on Judah (Hos 1:7), only to retract it after the time of judgment had passed (Hos 2:3 [Eng. 2:1]; 2:25 [Eng. 2:23]). This compassion is expressed by again choosing (בחר) Israel. First Isaiah uses this verb (Isa 1:29; 7:15-16), but of humans choosing, not God, and the usage here is strikingly similar to the use of this verb in Second Isaiah (Isa 41:8-9; 43:10; 44:1-2; 49:7), where God is the subject and Israel, Jacob, or the house of Jacob is the object of the choosing. The parallel usage is one of the strongest arguments for attributing this introduction to Second Isaiah or a disciple of his.

Moreover, Yahweh will either set or give Jacob/Israel rest on their land. Both meanings are attested for the

hiphil of נוח in First Isaiah (28:2, 12; 30:32). Second Isaiah uses it once only in the first sense (46:7). When Israel has been restored to its land, the sojourner or foreigners will join and attach themselves to the house of Jacob. The niphal of לוה is not otherwise attested in First Isaiah—or Second Isaiah for that matter—but it is attested in a somewhat similar sense of "joining oneself to Yahweh" in Third Isaiah (56:3, 6). The niphal of ספח is not attested elsewhere in Isaiah at all.

According to v. 2, it will be these foreign peoples who take Israel and bring them back to their own place. When that happens, the house of Israel will receive these foreigners as their inheritance on the land of Yahweh. These foreigners will be Israel's male and female slaves, so that Israel will end up as the captors of their former captors, and they will now rule over their former oppressors. This motif of the foreign nations bringing God's people back to their own land and serving them there is found in Second Isaiah (49:22-26) and in Third Isaiah (60:9-16; 61:5), but there is little continuity in the vocabulary used here and the vocabulary in those passages. Third Isaiah uses the *qal* passive participle of שבה in the sense of captive (61:2), and he uses the active participle of נגש in the sense of "overseer, oppressive ruler" (60:17), but that is as far as it goes. Second Isaiah uses neither term. Isaiah of Jerusalem employs the participle of נגש in this sense several times (3:12; 9:3; 14:4), and he also uses the verb רדה, "to rule over," in 14:6. It is unattested in Second and Third Isaiah. The basic idea expressed in 14:2 is also expressed in Second and Third Isaiah, but the vocabulary used to express this idea is not very similar.

The promise that Israel will take up this taunt against the king of Babylon on the day that God gives them rest from their pain and turmoil and hard labor that their captors imposed upon them suggests that the deliverance of Israel will follow closely upon the death of this king. If the taunt song is Isaiah's response to the death of Sargon II, as I will argue, then it suggests that Isaiah expected the deliverance of the north in the near future. That is already implied by his earlier coronation oracle for Hezekiah in 8:23—9:6, where their deliverance is seen as like the day of Midian. In Isa 10:26 God's deliverance of Israel from the yoke of bondage is compared to the defeat of Midian and to God's deliverance of Israel from Egypt at the sea, and in 11:11-16 the deliverance of Israel is seen as a second exodus. Here in Isa 14:3, Isaiah's choice of vocabulary, particularly "the hard labor they imposed upon you," links this present suffering of Israel to the paradigm of Israel's suffering in Egypt (Exod 1:14) and suggests a deliverance like that from Egypt.

14

4b/ How[a] the oppressor[b] has ceased!
The onslaught[c] has stopped!

5/ Yahweh[d] has broken the staff[e] of the wicked,
The rod[e] of rulers.[f]

6/ Who smote the peoples in wrath
With a smiting that never stopped;
Who oppressed[g] the nations[h] in anger
With a persecution that never relented.

7-8/ The whole[i] world is at rest and quiet;
Even the junipers[j] break forth into singing,[k]
The cedars of Lebanon[l] rejoice over you:
"Since you have lain down,[m]
No[n] cutter[o] has come up against us."

9/ Sheol from below stirs itself for you[p] to meet[q] you when you come,
It rouses[r] the Rephaim for you,[p] all the leaders of the earth,
It raises[s] all[t] the kings of the nations[u] from their thrones.

10/ All of them[v] answer and say to you,
Even you have become weak[w] like us,
To us you have become equal.[x]

11/ Your pride[y] is brought down to Sheol,
To Death[z] your corpse,[*a]
Beneath you worms are spread out,
And maggots are your covering.[*b]

12/ How[*c] you have fallen[*d] from the heavens,[*e]
O Helel,[*f] son of the dawn;
You have been cut down[*g] to earth,
Lying prostrate[*h] upon (your) back.[*i]

13/ You said[*j] in your heart,[*k]
I will ascend the heavens,
Above[*l] the stars of El[*m] I will raise my throne,
I will sit[*n] on the mount of assembly,
On the heights of Zaphon.

14/ I will go up on the backs[*o] of the cloud,
I will be like Elyon (The Most High).

15/ But to Sheol you were brought down,
To the depths of the pit.

16/ Those who see you[*p] will stare at you,
They will gaze at you;[*q]
"Is this the man who troubled[*r] the earth,[*s]
Who caused kingdoms to shake?[*t]

17/ Who[*u] made the earth like a desert,
And[*v] its cities he destroyed;
Who did not[*w] let his prisoners go home?"

18/ All[*x] the kings of the nations,[*y] all of them[*z]
Lie in glory, each in his house,

19/ But you are cast out[†a] from your grave[†b]
Like a loathsome miscarriage,[†c]
Clothed[†d] with the slain,[†e]
Those pierced by the sword,
Who go down[†f] to the stones of the pit,[†g]
Like a trampled corpse.

20/ You were not[†h] united[†i] with them[†j] in the grave,
Because your land[†k] you destroyed,[†l] your people[†k] you killed.[†m]
May the seed of evildoers not[†h] be mentioned[†n] forever.

21/ Prepare slaughter for his sons,[†o]
Because of the iniquity[†p] of their fathers.[†q]
May they not rise up[†r] and possess the earth,
And fill[†s] the face of the world with cities.[†t]

204

Textual Notes

a   אֵיךְ (ʾêk) "how" MT; 1QIsaᵃ איכה [(ʾêkâ).

b   MT נֹגֵשׂ (nōgēś), "the oppressor"; 1QIsaᵃ has the orthographic variant נוגש.

c   מַדְהֵבָה (madhēbâ) MT מרהבה [(mrhbh) 1QIsaᵃ. Though the correct reading here is disputed, 1QIsaᵃ's מרהבה is to be preferred. The *qal* of the root רהב (rāhab) is actually attested in Isa 3:5 in the sense "to storm, assault, press," and the *hiphil* in Song of Songs 6:5, "to overwhelm." This root probably lies behind the LXX and Syr.'s rendering here, "the one who compels or exhorts." The verbal root is attested also in Ps 138:3; Prov 6:3; and Sir 13:8, though all of these passages are of disputed interpretation. If one adopts the reading מרהבה, one must still decide whether to understand the form as expressing the action *marhēbâ*, "the onslaught," or whether to make the slight emendation to the *hiphil* מַרְהִיב *marhîb* or *piel* מְרַהֵב *mĕraheb*) participle as expressing the agent, "the attacker." It is hard to defend the reading מדהבה (madhēbâ), since the evidence for a credible Hebrew root דהב (dāhab) is problematic. The appeal to Arabic *ḏahaba*, giving the noun the meaning "the destroyer" or the like, is dubious, because proto-Semitic *ḏ* normally becomes *z* in Hebrew. Orlinsky's derivation from the root דבא (dābaʾ) is equally problematic.[1]

d   יְהוָה MT, 1QIsaᵃ, 4QIsaᵉ, Vg., Tg., Syr. ὁ θεὸς LXX.

e   LXX mistranslates both מַטֶּה (maṭṭēh) and שֵׁבֶט (šēbeṭ), synonyms meaning "staff" or "rod," as τὸν ζυγὸν, "the yoke."

f   1QIsaᵃ has the orthographic variant מושלים for MT מֹשְׁלִים (mōšĕlîm), "rulers."

g   MT רֹדֶה (rōdeh);1 QIsaᵃ רודה.

h   MT גּוֹיִם (gôyīm); 1QIsaᵃ גואים.

i   MT כָּל (kol), "the whole"; 1QIsaᵃ כול.

j   Reading against the MT verse division. MT's verse division requires that one construe פָּצְחוּ רִנָּה (pāṣĕḥû rinnâ), "they break forth in singing," with the preceding, כָּל־הָאָרֶץ (kol-hāʾāreṣ), "the whole earth," but that creates a grammatical problem of agreement in gender and number between the subject and the verb. The noun אֶרֶץ (ʾereṣ, "earth") is a feminine singular and should take a feminine singular verb, as is the case with the initial verbs נָחָה (nāḥâ), "she is at rest," and שָׁקְטָה (šāqĕṭâ), "she is quiet." The verb פָּצְחוּ is a masculine plural, possibly generic plural, but no plural noun stands in the text. The problem is illustrated by a comparison of the JPS translation: "All the earth is calm, untroubled; Loudly *it* cheers" over against the NRSV: "The whole earth is at rest and quiet; *they* break forth into singing." The NRSV preserves the grammar, but who are "they"? One must either assume an ellipsis of the subject, perhaps יֹשְׁבֶהָ (yōšĕbêhâ), "its inhabitants," or take the following גַם־בְּרוֹשִׁים (gam bĕrôšîm), "even the junipers," as the subject, which would leave "the cedars of Lebanon" as the subject of the parallel verb שָׂמְחוּ (śāmĕḥû), "they rejoiced."

k   MT רִנָּה (rinnâ), "singing, shout of joy"; 1QIsaᵃ has רונה, implying an odd vocalization *ronnâ*.

l   MT לְבָנוֹן (lĕbānôn), "Lebanon"; 1QIsaᵃ הלבנון (hallĕbānôn), "the Lebanon."

m   MT שָׁכַבְתָּ (šākabtā), "you have lain down"; 1QIsaᵃ שכבתה.

n   MT לֹא (lōʾ), "no"; 1QIsaᵃ ולוא, "and no".

o   MT הַכֹּרֵת (hakkōrēt), "the cutter"; 1QIsaᵃ הכורת.

p   1QIsaᵃ לכה is only an orthographic variant of MT לָךְ (lĕkā) "for you."

q   MT לִקְרַאת (liqraʾt), "to meet"; 1QIsaᵃ לקרת, an orthographic variant.

r   MT עוֹרֵר (ʿôrēr), "rousing," is the *polel* infinitive absolute. 1QIsaᵃ corrects to the third person feminine singular perfect עו[ר]רה; there is no difference in meaning, and the infinitive as the continuation of the preceding finite verb is probably more original.

s   MT הֵקִים (hēqîm), "he raised," the third person masculine singular *hiphil* perfect, cannot be correct. 1QIsa has the third person feminine singular perfect הקימה, which is grammatically correct, but the original was probably the *hiphil* infinitive absolute הָקֵם (hāqēm).

t   MT כֹּל (kol), "all"; 1QIsaᵃ כול.

u   MT גוֹיִם (gôyīm), "nations"; 1QIsaᵃ גואים.

v   MT כֻּלָּם (kullām), "all of them"; 1QIsaᵃ כ[ו]לם, LXX, Vg., Tg.; 4QIsaᵉ and Syr. omit.

w   MT חֻלֵּיתָ (hullêtā), "you have become weak"; 1QIsaᵃ חליתה may be a mere orthographic variant, or it may suggest the *qal* perfect rather than the *pual*. LXX renders as καὶ σὺ ἑάλως ὥσπερ καὶ ἡμεῖς, "and you were taken even as we were."

x   MT נִמְשַׁלְתָּ (nimšāltā), "you have become like"; 1QIsaᵃ נמשלתה. LXX has ἐν ἡμῖν δὲ κατελογίσθης, "you were counted among us."

y   MT גְּאוֹנֶךָ (gĕʾôneka), "your pride," 1QIsaᵃ, 4QIsaᵉ, versions. A similar use of this noun with the *hophal* of ירד is found in Zech 10:11: וְהוּרַד גְּאוֹן אַשּׁוּר (wĕhûrad gĕʾôn ʾaššûr), "and the pride of Assyria will be laid low." Nonetheless, it is not the king's glory and music that will be covered with worms, but his corpse, and that suggests at least a play on a similar appearing word like גְּוִיָתְךָ (gĕwîyatkā), "your corpse," or better, preserving the agreement in gender with the masculine verb, its masculine counterpart, attested as גֵּוֶךָ (gēwĕkā) or גַּוְּךָ (gawwĕkā), "your back, trunk, body." By analogy with other feminine/masculine nouns of similar formation אֳנִיָּה (ʾŏnîyâ)/אֳנִי (ʾŏnî), "ship," שִׁבְיָה (šibyâ)/שְׁבִי (šĕbî), "captive, captivity," Raymond Van Leeuwen suggests that the original form of the masculine noun may have been גֵּוִי (gēwî), "back."[2]

z   MT הֶמְיַת (hemyat), "noise, sound," is supported by Tg. (תֻּשְׁבְּחַת זְמָרָך, *tušbĕḥat zĕmārāk*, "the praise of your music") and obliquely by LXX (ἡ πολλή σου εὐφροσύνη, "your abundant joy"), but 1QIsaᵃ המות suggests either a passive verbal form from מות, "to die," perhaps הוּמַת (hûmat, "your corpse was

1   H. M. Orlinsky, "Madhebah in Isaiah XIV 4," *VT* 7 (1957) 202–3.

2   R. C. Van Leeuwen, "Isa 14:12, hôlēš ʿal GWYM and Gilgamesh XI, 6," *JBL* 99 (1980) 173–84.

slain"), or the noun מות (*māwet*), "Death," as a parallel with Sheol. Symmachus has ἐθανατώθη το πτωμα σου, "your corpse was put to death," while Theodotion has ο θανατος κατερρηξεν σε, "death broke you down." Vg. renders the form as a verb *concidit cadaver tuum*, "your corpse collapsed."

*a MT נְבָלֶיךָ (*nĕbālêkā*), "your harps," is the traditional reading with הֲמוֹן שָׁרֶיךָ וְזִמְרַת נְבָלֶיךָ (*hămôn šīrêkā wĕzimrat nĕbālêkā*), "the noise of your songs and the music of your harps" (Amos 5:23) often cited as a parallel expression (so Wildberger, 2:550). But 1QIsaᵃ has נבלתך (*niblātĕkā*), "your corpse," and this reading seems to be supported by 4QIsaᶜ, though the final letter is unreadable, and by Vg.'s *cadaver*, "corpse," as well as by Symmachus το πτωμα σου, "your corpse."

*b MT וּמְכַסֶּךָ (*ûmĕkassêkā*, "and your covering"); 1QIsaᵃ has the orthographic variant ומכסך.

*c MT אֵיךְ (*ʾêk*), "how"; 1QIsaᵃ היכה is only an orthographic variant.

*d MT נָפַלְתָּ (*nāpaltā*), "you have fallen"; 1QIsaᵃ נפלתה.

*e MT מִשָּׁמַיִם (*miššāmayim*), "from the heavens"; 1QIsaᵃ explicitly adds the article מהשמים, "from the heavens."

*f MT הֵילֵל (*hêlēl*, probably the name of a star); 1QIsaᵃ has the orthographic variant היליל.

*g MT נִגְדַּעְתָּ (*nigdaʿtā*), "you have been cut down"; 1QIsaᵃ נגדעתה.

*h As Van Leeuwen has demonstrated,[3] חוֹלֵשׁ (*ḥôlēš*) is probably to be understood in the usual sense of the verb as "to lie weak" or "prostrate." Cf. Job 14:10: וְגֶבֶר יָמוּת וַיֶּחֱלָשׁ וַיִּגְוַע אָדָם וְאַיּוֹ (*wĕgeber yāmût wayyeḥĕlāš wayyigwaʿ ʾādām wĕʾayyô*), "a man dies and lies prostrate, a human perishes and is no more."

*i MT עַל־גּוֹיִם (*ʿal gôyīm*), "upon nations." 1QIsaᵃ על גוי. "Upon nation(s)" makes little sense, even when one takes the verb חלש as a transitive verb with the sense to crush, עַל, "upon," is often emended to כָּל (*kol*), "all," "who crushed all the nations." It is better to follow Van Leeuwen in understanding the noun as גֵּו (*gēwî*), "back," followed by an energic *mem*, which 1QIsaᵃ did not understand and so omitted.

*j MT אָמַרְתָּ (*ʾāmartā*), "you said"; 1QIsaᵃ אמרתה.

*k MT בִּלְבָבְךָ (*bilbābĕkā*), "in your heart"; 1QIsaᵃ בלבבכה.

*l MT מִמַּעַל (*mimmaʿal*), "above"; 1QIsaᵃ ממעלה.

*m MT לְכוֹכְבֵי־אֵל (*lĕkôkĕbê ʾēl*), "the stars of El," 1QIsaᵃ, Vg., Syr.; LXX has τῶν ἄστρων τοῦ οὐρανοῦ, "the stars of heaven."

*n MT וְאֵשֵׁב (*wĕʾēšēb*), "and I will sit"; 1QIsaᵃ אשב lacks the copulative with LXX, Vg., Syr., Tg.

*o MT בָּמֳתֵי (*bomŏtê*), "backs"; 1QIsaᵃ בומתי.

*p MT רֹאֶיךָ (*rōʾêkā*), "those who see you"; 1QIsaᵃ רואיך.

*q MT אֵלֶיךָ (*ʾēlêkā*), "at you"; 1QIsaᵃ אליכה.

*r MT מַרְגִּיז (*margîz*), "who troubled"; 1QIsaᵃ has the article המרגיז.

*s MT הָאָרֶץ (*hāʾāreṣ*), "the earth"; 1QIsaᵃ ארץ.

*t MT מַרְעִישׁ (*marʿîš*), "who shook"; 1QIsaᵃ המרעיש.

*u LXX erroneously introduces God (ὁ θεός) to make clear the subject of this verse.

*v MT וְעָרָיו (*wĕʿārāyw*), "and his cities," LXX, Vg., Tg., Syr.; 1QIsaᵃ עריו omits the conjunction.

*w MT לֹא (*lōʾ*), "not"; 1QIsaᵃ לוא.

*x MT כָּל (*kol*), "all"; 1QIsaᵃ כול.

*y MT גּוֹיִם (*gôyīm*), "nations"; 1QIsaᵃ גואים.

*z MT כֻּלָּם (*kullām*), "all of them," Vg., Tg.; 1QIsaᵃ, LXX, Syr. omit. The reading should be retained for emphasis.

†a MT הָשְׁלַכְתָּ (*hošlaktā*), "you are cast out"; 1QIsaᵃ הושלכתה.

†b MT מִקִּבְרֶךָ (*miqqibrĕkā*), "from your grave"; 1QIsaᵃ מקוברך. LXX has ἐν τοῖς ὄρεσιν, "in the mountains."

†c MT כְּנֵצֶר (*kĕnēṣer*), "like a shoot," 1QIsaᵃ, Vg., Syr.; LXX has ὡς νεκρὸς ἐβδελυγμένος, "like a detestable dead one"; and Tg., "like a hidden miscarriage." Plant imagery of a "shoot" seems totally inappropriate here. One should probably emend to a word designating an abandoned corpse of some kind, perhaps נֵצֶל (*nēsel*), which in Mishnaic Hebrew can refer to a decaying corpse,[4] or נֵפֶל (*nēpel*), meaning "miscarriage."

†d MT לְבוּשׁ (*lĕbûš*), "clothed"; 1QIsaᵃ לבש.

†e MT הֲרֻגִים (*hărugîm*), "the slain"; 1QIsaᵃ הרוגים.

†f MT יוֹרְדֵי (*yôrĕdê*), "who go down" the erroneous 1QIsaᵃ יורדו.

†g MT אֶל־אַבְנֵי־בוֹר (*ʾel ʾabnê bôr*), "to the stones of the pit"; 1QIsaᵃ אל בור, with "stones" inserted above the line as a correction.

†h MT לֹא (*lōʾ*), "not"; 1QIsaᵃ לוא.

†i MT תֵּחַד (*tēḥad*), "you will (*not*) be united," from יחד, Vg., Syr., Tg.; 1QIsaᵃ תחת ("you will [*not*] go down," from נחת). LXX has the odd reading οὕτως οὐδὲ σὺ ἔσῃ καθαρός, "thus you will not be pure."

†j MT אִתָּם (*ʾittām*), "with them," Vg., Syr., Tg.; 1QIsaᵃ אותם apparently has the same meaning. LXX appears to omit the whole expression, "with them in the grave."

†k For אַרְצֶךָ (*ʾarṣĕkā*), "your land," and עַמֶּךָ (*ʿammĕkā*), "your people," MT, 1QIsaᵃ, Syr., Tg., LXX has "my land" and "my people."

†l MT שִׁחַתָּ (*šiḥattā*), "you destroyed; 1QIsaᵃ שחתה.

†m MT הָרַגְתָּ (*hārāgtā*), "you killed"; 1QIsaᵃ הרגתה.

†n MT יִקָּרֵא (*yiqqārēʾ*), "be mentioned," is singular agreeing with its subject זֶרַע (*zeraʿ*), "seed," Vg., Tg.; 1QIsaᵃ יקראו is plural, either by the plural sense of "seed," or as an active verb with "seed" as the object: "may they never mention the seed of evildoers for ever." Syr. has "the wicked seed will not remain forever," while LXX has οὐ μὴ μείνῃς εἰς τὸν αἰῶνα χρόνον, σπέρμα πονηρόν, "you will not remain forever, you wicked seed."

†o MT לְבָנָיו (*lĕbānāyw*), "for his sons", 1QIsaᵃ, Vg., Syr.; Tg. has "for their sons," and LXX has "your children."

†p MT בַּעֲוֺן (*baʿăwōn*), "for the iniquity"; 1QIsaᵃ בעוון.

†q MT אֲבוֹתָם (*ʾăbôtām*), "of their fathers," 1QIsaᵃ, Vg., Tg.; LXX has τοῦ πατρός σου, "of your father."

†r MT בַּל־יָקֻמוּ (*bal yāqūmû*), "may they not rise up"; 1QIsaᵃ בל יקומו[ן].

†s MT וּמָלְאוּ (*ûmālĕʾû*), "and fill"; 1QIsaᵃ ומלו.

3   Ibid., 173–84.
4   Jastrow, 2:929.

†t MT's עָרִים (ʿārîm), "cities," is supported by 1QIsaᵃ and Vg. LXX, followed by Syr., has πολέμων, "wars," but this is probably an inner-Greek corruption of πόλεων, "cities," which some texts, including the later translations of Aquila, Theodotion, Symmachus have.[5] Tg., however, has בעלי דבב (baʿĕlê dĕbāb), "enemies." See the commentary.

Commentary

The taunt song opens with a surprised exclamation commenting on the sudden end of the oppressor and his onslaughts against others. It is Yahweh who has broken the staff of the wicked and the rod of rulers. The use of the plural here for both "wicked" and "rulers" is interesting. The particular king whose death is being celebrated in this taunt song is presumably the Assyrian Sargon II, since he is the only king of Babylon[6] during the relevant periods known to have died in the manner reflected in the poem.[7]

Excursus: The Death of Sargon II and Unburied Babylonian Kings

According to the Eponym Chronicle, in 705 BCE, while Sargon was on campaign "against Qurdi the Kulummaean, the king was killed, and the camp of the king of Assyria [was overrun?/plundered?], and on the 12th of Ab (roughly midsummer), Sennacherib [became] king."[8] Chronicle 1 mentions a campaign of Sargon to Tabalu in the same year, but it is badly broken after the initial line and any account of Sargon's death is lost in the break.[9] For more details on the death of Sargon, we are dependent on the text K. 4730, supplemented by the fragment Sm. 1876, a transliteration and translation of which appeared as text 33. "The Sin of Sargon," in Alasdair Livingstone, *Court Poetry and Literary Miscellanea* (SAA 3; Helsinki: Helsinki University Press, 1989) 77–79,[10] but which has now been given a thorough new edition by Hayim Tadmor, Benno Landsberger, and Simo Parpola, "The Sin of Sargon and Sennacherib's Last Will," *State Archives of Assyria Bulletin* 3 (1989) 3–51. This text purports to give an account of an extispicy that Sennacherib, the son and successor of Sargon II, had performed in order to learn what sin his father, Sargon, had committed against the gods to suffer such an ignominious end. With reference to the details of Sargon's death, the key lines are found on obv. 7-20, in the translation of Tadmor, Landsberger, and Parpola's edition:

> While thus [reverently] pondering [in my heart] over the deeds of the gods, the death of Sargon, [my father, who was killed in the enemy country] and who was not interred in his house, oc[curred] to my mind, [and I said to myself]: "[Let me examine] by means of extispicy the sin of Sargon, my father, let me then determine [the circumstances] and le[arn the . . .; let me make] the sin he committed against the god an abom[ination to

---

5 See Ziegler, 2nd ed., 176–77.

6 For Sargon as "king of Babylon," see Grant Frame, *Rulers of Babylonia: From the Second Dynasty of Isin to the End of Assyrian Domination (1157–612 BC)* (RIMBP 2; Toronto: University of Toronto Press, 1995) 143–52; note esp. 152, 6:4-6–ᵈLUGAL-*ú-kin . . .* lugal KÁ.DINGIR.RA.KI, "Sargon . . . king of Babylon." Sargon ascended the throne in Babylon and took the hand of Bel (Marduk) in the Babylonian new year's festival (A. Kirk Grayson, *Assyrian and Babylonian Chronicles* [Texts from Cuneiform Sources 5; Locust Valley, NY: J. J. Augustin, 1975] 75 ii 5-1').

7 Already Hugo Winckler, who published K. 4730 in his *Sammlung von Keilschriftentexten* (3 vols.; Leipzig: E. Pfeiffer, 1893–95) vol. 2, no. 52, and offered an interpretation in his *Altorientalische Forschungen* (3 vols; Leipzig: E. Pfeiffer, 1893–1906) 1:410ff., saw the connection between the surprising death of Sargon on the battlefield and the unburied king of Isa 14:4-20a. W. von Soden also made this connection in his *Herrscher im alten Orient* (Berlin: Springer, 1954) 103–5. Other scholars making such a connection include H. L. Ginsberg, "Reflexes of Sargon in Isaiah after 715 B.C.E.," *JAOS* 88 (1968) 47–53; H. Tadmor, "The Sin of Sargon" (in Hebrew), *ErIsr* 5 (1958) 150–62; and E. Frahm, "Nabu-zukup-kenu, das Gilgameš-Epos und der Tod Sargons II.," *JCS* 51 (1999) 73–90, who suggested that the last tablet of the Gilgamesh epic dealing with the underworld was added in response to the shocking death of Sargon. For a detailed treatment of the death of Sargon see the following excursus.

8 Millard, *Eponyms*, 48, 60.

9 Grayson, *Assyrian and Babylonian Chronicles*, 76, 6'-18'.

10 In this volume the supplementary fragment is given as Sm. 1816, but in the fuller edition it is normally given as Sm. 1876 (pp. 5, 10, 16, 17, 18, 19, 45), once as Sm. 1870 (p. 6), and on plates 1 and 2 as Sm. 1816. I am not clear why this variation in the numbering of the fragment exists.

myself], and with god's help let me save myself,"
I w[ent and collected the haruspices], who guard
the secret of god and king, the courtiers of my
palace, divided them [into several (lit., three or
four) groups] so that they could not ap[proach or
speak to one another], and [investigated] the sin
of Sargon, my father, by extispicy, [inquiring of
Šamaš and Adad] as follows: "Was it because [he
honored] the gods o[f Assyria too much, placing
them] above the gods of Babylonia [. . . , and was it
because] he did not [keep] the treaty of the king of
the gods [that Sargon, my father,] was killed [in the
enemy country and] was not b[uried] in his house?"

In the light of this text and the entry in the eponym
list noted above, it is clear that Sargon died in battle
on a foreign campaign, that his camp was overrun,
and that Sargon's body was not recovered to receive
proper burial back in Assyria. It would not be surprising had Sennacherib reacted to this shocking demise
of Sargon by submitting such oracular questions to
the deity—that would be in line with the oracular
practices of the Neo-Assyrian kings—but this particular
text was actually composed in the time of Esarhaddon
as a clever piece of religious propaganda to justify
Esarhaddon's renewed pro-Babylonian policy after
the virulently anti-Babylonian policy of Sennacherib.
The text has Sennacherib, or the ghost of Sennacherib, encouraging his heirs not to make his mistake
in offending Marduk, and thus provoking a punishment such as befell Sargon and even to a lesser extent
Sennacherib himself. Sennacherib was murdered by a
son in a rebellion on the 20th of Tebet (c. January 22,
681 BCE), and the rebellion continued until the 2nd of
Adar (c. March 4, 681 BCE), a little less than a month
and a half later, and his son Esarhaddon ascended
the throne on the 18th/28th of Adar.[11] As far as I am
aware, we have no reliable evidence on the burial or
lack of burial of Sennacherib, but while Sennacherib
ruled directly over Babylonia for two separate periods,
unlike his father, Sargon, Sennacherib never seems to
have assumed the titles "king of Babylon," "viceroy of
Babylon," or "king of the land of Sumer and Akkad";

in his single Babylonian inscription and in three
Babylonian economic texts dated by his regnal years,
Sennacherib is referred to as "king of Assyria."[12]

There is even less evidence to tie the poem in
Isaiah 14 to any other Assyrian ruler of the period.
Both Tiglath-pileser III and Shalmaneser V apparently
died natural deaths and received normal burials.[13]
Both Esarhaddon and Ashurbanipal appear to have
died natural deaths,[14] and there is no evidence that
either of them was left unburied. Nor is there any evidence to suggest that the actual deaths of any of the
Neo-Babylonian kings provided the concrete imagery
for the graphic portrayal of the death of this tyrant
in Isaiah 14. The only real evidence for a Babylonian
king who died in battle and did not receive proper
burial concerns Sargon II, an event that occurred during the ministry of the eighth-century prophet Isaiah
of Jerusalem and must have been quickly known in
Judah, since the death of Sargon was the proximate
occasion for Hezekiah's joining in the rebellion
against Sargon's successor, Sennacherib.

Sargon, however, is seen as representative of a class
of wicked rulers. He was simply one in a series of Assyrian rulers who had wielded the rod of oppression against
Assyria's neighbors. According to Isa 10:5, Assyria was
the "rod" and "staff" Yahweh used to punish any nation
with which God was angry, though Assyria erroneously
assumed that it conquered others through its own power,
not realizing it was a mere tool in the hand of God
(Isa 10:7-15). Here the rod is specifically Sargon, who
never relented in his constant campaigns against other
peoples. Isaiah's portrayal of Sargon's unrelenting military campaigns against the surrounding states, though
it would also be true of a number of other Assyrian
kings, is confirmed for Sargon by his own inscriptions,
where hardly a year goes by without military campaigning on one front or another.[15] The prophet is obviously
speaking from the viewpoint of those who were on the

---

11 For these details, see Grayson, *Assyrian and Babylo-
    nian Chronicles*, Chronicle 1, iii 34-38; in Esarhad-
    don's own inscriptions he claims to have entered
    Nineveh on the 8th of Adar and to have sat happily
    on his father's throne (Erle Leichty, *The Royal Inscrip-
    tions of Esarhaddon, King of Assyria [680–669 BC]*
    [RINAP 4; Winona Lake, IN: Eisenbrauns, 2011] 14,
    text 1, i 87–ii 11). For more details on the murder
    of Sennacherib, apparently by an older half-brother
    of Esarhaddon, Arda-Mulissi, see S. Parpola, "The

    Murder of Sennacherib," in Bendt Alster, *Death in
    Mesopotamia: Papers Read at the XXVIe Rencontre assyri-
    ologique internationale* (Mesopotamia 8; Copenhagen:
    Akademisk, 1980) 171–82.
12 Frame, *Rulers of Babylonia*, 153–54.
13 See Grayson, *Assyrian and Babylonian Chronicles*,
    72–73, Chronicle 1, i 24-30; cf. Frame, *Rulers of Baby-
    lonia*, 133–34.
14 Cf. Frame, *Rulers of Babylonia*, 194.
15 See esp. Fuchs, *Die Inschriften Sargons II.*

receiving end of Assyria's military actions, not from the viewpoint of Assyria or its loyal allies. For those attacked by Assyria, Assyria's actions were seen as unrelenting persecution, permitting no rest or quiet. But now that Yahweh has broken Sargon, this staff, the whole world is at rest and quiet (vv. 7-8). Even the trees of the forest break forth into singing and rejoice over the death of the Assyrian king, because since his death the lumbermen have ceased going up in the Lebanon to cut trees down. This is poetry, so one must be careful about seeing too much correspondence between the claims of the text and historical reality. Nonetheless, in his last years Sargon was involved in the major building project of constructing his new capital Dur-Sharrukin ("Fortress of Sargon," modern day Khorsabad), and with his death work on the unfinished city stopped and the new capital was soon abandoned.[16] Lumbering activity in the Lebanon and the Amanus must have been impacted by this sudden end to Sargon's demand for massive amounts of lumber to satisfy his very ambitious building activities.

At v. 9 the image shifts from the mountains of Lebanon to the underworld. Sheol, the underworld abode of the dead, stirs itself to greet this newcomer to its world. It rouses its inhabitants as a welcoming committee, particularly the Rephaim,[17] the famous dead of the past, the dead leaders of the earth, and the former kings of the nations,[18] who are portrayed as still seated on thrones, even in the underworld. This host of the notable dead will address the now dead Sargon in palpable amazement. "Even you have become as weak as we are!" (v. 10). One could debate how far the quotation of these dead extends, but I would see it ending in v. 10, and the primary voice of the prophet resuming in v. 11, since the first person plural of these dead speakers is not

repeated. There is another brief quotation of those who see the dead Sargon in vv. 16-17, which is clearly ended there, since v. 18 refers to these foreign kings in the third person. That suggests that both of these quotations are relatively short.

There are a number of cruxes in v. 11. The first half of the traditional Hebrew text of the MT could be rendered, "Your pride is brought down to Sheol, the sound of your harps," but the continuation of the text speaks of worms being spread out beneath and maggots as a covering, and this maggot imagery suggests that what is being covered top and bottom is neither "pride" nor "music" but a dead corpse. See the textual notes for variants that indirectly support the reading, "to death your corpse" in place of "the sound of your harps." Indeed, despite the lack of textual variants, the imagery suggests an emendation of גְּאוֹנֶךָ (gĕʾôneka), "your pride," to גֵּוֶךָ (gawweka), "your body is brought down to Sheol," and הֶמְיַת נְבָלֶיךָ (hemyat nĕbālêka), "the sound of your harps," to הַמָּוֶת נִבְלָתְךָ (hammāwet niblātĕka), "to Death your corpse." Of course, the rather gruesome imagery of a maggot-enveloped corpse is the very antithesis of any royal pomp and ceremony.

Verse 12 shifts the attention back to the great height from which this enemy king has fallen. He has fallen from the very heavens. To underscore this point, the king is addressed as Helel the son of Shahar, or the dawn. Mark Shipp has made a good case for identifying Helel as the name of "a star in the constellation Šinūnūtu, in visual proximity to the constellation Annunītu, associated with Ištar and through which passes Venus/Dilibat, likewise the star of Ištar,"[19] but that provides limited help in interpreting the passage. Once the enemy king occupied the starry heights like Helel, but now he has been cut down to earth. Whether there was a narrative myth known

16   See ibid., 4-11, and the earlier works detailing the archaeology of the site listed there. In addition, note Annie Caubet, *Khorsabad, le palais de Sargon II, roi d'Assyrie: Acts du colloque organisé au musée du Louvre par le Services culturel les 21 et 22 janvier 1994* (Louvre conférences et colloques; Paris: La Documentation française, 1995).

17   For the Rephaim, see the discussions in Theodore J. Lewis, *Cults of the Dead in Ancient Israel and Ugarit* (HSM 39; Atlanta: Scholars Press, 1989); Brian B. Schmidt, *Israel's Beneficent Dead: Ancestor Cult and Necromancy in Ancient Israelite Religion and Tradition* (FAT 11; Tübingen: Mohr Siebeck, 1994); and M. S. Smith, "Rephaim," *ABD*, 5:674–76.

18   Cf. Ezek 32:17-32, where Pharaoh and his host, soon to fall, are spoken of by the dead hordes of former great nations already slain and consigned to the shame of Sheol.

19   R. Mark Shipp, *Of Dead Kings and Dirges: Myth and Meaning in Isaiah 14:4b-21* (Academia Biblica 11; Atlanta: Society of Biblical Literature, 2002) 79.

to Isaiah and his audience in which a similar fate befell Helel remains unknown. The motif of a human ascending to the heavens, only to be eventually cast down for over-reaching is certainly known in Mesopotamian literature, as the badly broken and incomplete Etana myth attests,[20] but Helel and Dawn play no role in that myth as we have it. In the absence of any compelling textual evidence for such an explanatory narrative myth, it seems pointless to reconstruct it with the characters in this verse, and then use the phantom reconstruction to interpret the text we actually have. Moreover, one must ask whether the assumed background myth was really about an overreaching human or rather about a god seeking the supreme position in the heavens among the gods—one may think of the god ʿAṭṭar's futile attempt in the Ugaritic Baal cycle (*KTU* 1.6 i 56-61) to ascend the heights of Zaphon (*yʿl . bṣrrt . ṣpn*) and occupy the exalted throne of Baal (*yṯb . lkḥt . aliyn bʿl*) only to discover that his feet would not reach the footstool (*pʿnh . ltmǵyn hdm*) and that his head would not reach the top of the throne (*rišh . lymǵy apsh*)—which is then here adapted to a human attempting to ascend to the heights of Zaphon (*yrkty ṣpwn*) to exalt his throne (*ʾrym ksʾy*) as the equal or superior to the Most High God (*ʾdmh lʿlywn*). If even a powerful but lesser god could not succeed in replacing the king of the gods, how much more presumptuous and foolish for a mere human, as powerful as he might temporarily be, to harbor such illusions of grandeur. In any case, this human king, once ensconced on high like the star Helel, has now been cut down to earth, where he lies prostrate and helpless on his back.

This fate was far from what the enemy king had envisioned. He had planned (v. 13) to ascend the heavens and place his throne above the stars of the high god El, the head of the pantheon in Canaanite mythology. His goal was to sit enthroned on the mountain where the assembly of the gods met, on the heights of Mount Zaphon, in effect as the king of the gods. Some translations render the Hebrew expression בְּיַרְכְּתֵי צָפוֹן (*bĕyarkĕtê ṣāpôn*), "on the heights of Zaphon," as "in the far north" (RSV) or "in the sides of the north" (KJV, Douay), but a number of observations undercut this traditional rendering. Mount Zaphon was the sacred mountain of Baal in Canaanite mythology, and the original Zaphon is to be identified with the Jebel el-Aqra north of Ugarit on the Syrian coast of the Mediterranean. This lookout point and landmark on the Mediterranean was sacred to the Hittites as Mount Hazizi and later to the Greeks as Mount Casius.[21] The Semitic name is from the final weak root צפה (*ṣpy*), "to watch, look out," with an ending that suggests the meaning "lookout point, watchplace" for צָפוֹן. The term comes to be used ordinarily in Hebrew as a directional designation for north, but the directional designation is secondary, as is true of most directional terms in Hebrew. Just as the common use of יָם (*yām*), "sea," for "west" is clearly secondary to the original meaning "sea," and is based on the geographical fact that the sea was to the west, so the use of צָפוֹן (*ṣāpôn*), "Mount Zaphon," for "north" is clearly secondary to the original meaning "Mount Zaphon," and is based on the geographical fact that Mount Zaphon was to the north of Ugarit and certainly of Palestine. In our passage, the understanding of the term as the name of the sacred mountain is secured by the parallelism with the expression בְּהַר־מוֹעֵד (*bĕhar môʿēd*), "in the mount of assembly." Zaphon is identified as the name of the mount of assembly. The expression יַרְכְּתֵי (*yarkĕtê*) refers to the most distant points on a plane, and the appropriate translation depends on whether that plane is vertical or horizontal. In our context, the plane is vertical, as the contrast between בְּיַרְכְּתֵי צָפוֹן (*bĕyarkĕtê ṣāpôn*), "on the heights of Zaphon," and אֶל־יַרְכְּתֵי־בוֹר (*ʾel-yarkĕtê-bôr*), "to the depths of the pit" (v. 15) demonstrates. It is true that in Ugaritic mythology Zaphon, the mountain of Baal, is not the mount of assembly—that honor being reserved

---

20 J. V. Kinnier Wilson, *The Legend of Etana* (new ed.; Warminster: Aris & Phillips, 1985), and cf. the treatment in Stephanie Dalley, *Myths from Mesopotamia: Creation, the Flood, Gilgamesh, and Others* (rev. ed.; Oxford World's Classics; Oxford: Oxford University Press, 2000).

21 See Otto Eissfeldt, *Baal Zaphon, Zeus Kasios und der Durchzug der Israeliten durchs Meer* (Beiträge zur Religionsgeschichte des Altertums 1; Halle: Niemeyer, 1932) 5–9; Eissfeldt, "Die Wohnsitze der Götter von Ras Schamra," *Forschungen und Fortschritte* 20 (1944) 25 (= *Kleine Schriften* [Tübingen: Mohr, 1963] 2:503); Hatice Gonnet, "Les montagnes d'Asie Mineure d'après les testes hittites," *Revue hittite et asianique* 26 (1968) 146–47; and my "The Davidic Origin of the Zion Tradition," *JBL* 92 (1973) 329–44, and the extensive literature cited there.

for the mountain abode of El,[22] but the situation appears to be different in the Canaanite theology known in Judah much farther south and almost a thousand years later. Moreover, it should be noted that the distant "north" in neither Ugaritic nor Mesopotamian texts carries the mythological freight that defenders of this traditional rendering assign to "the far north" in this Hebrew phrase.[23]

Three other OT texts seem to preserve this original meaning of Zaphon as the name of the sacred mountain. I would translate Ps 48:2-3 as "Great is Yahweh and greatly to be praised in the city of our God. His holy mountain, beautiful in elevation, is the joy of the whole earth. Mount Zion is the heights of Zaphon [הַר־צִיּוֹן יַרְכְּתֵי צָפוֹן, har-ṣîyôn yarkĕtê ṣāpôn], the city of the great king." The psalmist is identifying his Mount Zion with the far older and famous mountain of Baal, Mount Zaphon, thus claiming the prestige of the older mountain of Baal for the Yahwistic sanctuary on Mount Zion. It is part of the general Israelite pilfering of Baal's epithets, mythological victories, and the like, for their own glorification of Yahweh. Psalm 89:13 also seems to use Zaphon as the name of the mountain, though this is obscured in many translations. The last half of the verse clearly mentions two sacred mountains: תָּבוֹר וְחֶרְמוֹן בְּשִׁמְךָ יְרַנֵּנוּ (tābôr wĕḥermôn bĕšimkā yĕrannēnû), "Tabor and Hermon praise your name." Given the parallelism, I would render the first half of the verse: "Zaphon and Ammana(na) (the Anti-Lebanon), you have created them" (צָפוֹן וְיָמִין אַתָּה בְרָאתָם, ṣāpôn wĕyāmîn ʾattâ bĕrāʾtām). This rendering would require the emendation of וְיָמִין (wĕyāmîn, lit., "the right hand," but often used for "south") to a consonantal text something like ואמן. Others suggest the reading אֲמָנָה (ʾămānâ), the Amanus.[24] The textual corruption to "south" would have resulted from the rare name in Hebrew for the Anti-Lebanon or Amanus Mountains, and the common use of Zapon to mean "north" in Hebrew, but the occurrence of these two terms next to Tabor and Hermon suggests that they too refer to sacred mountains. The last occurrence is in Job 26:7 נֹטֶה צָפוֹן עַל־תֹּהוּ תֹּלֶה אֶרֶץ עַל־בְּלִי־מָה (nōṭeh ṣāpôn ʿal tōhû tōleh ʾereṣ ʿal bĕlî mâ), "who stretches out Zaphon over the void, who hangs the earth over nothing." I understand the imagery here as reflecting the visual phenomenon of observing mountains at a distance when haze obscures their base, resulting in the appearance of the mountains as if they were floating in the air. As my editor, Peter Machinist, pointed out to me, there may also be something theological here, God's stretching out and hanging up of his created Zaphon and earth to fill up and order primeval chaos and nothingness.

---

22 In *KTU* 1.2 i 14, 20, ǵr . ll, "Mount La/e/il," associated with the abode of El, is the site where the pḫr . mʿd, "divine assembly," meets. See my discussion of various attempts to equate ǵr . ll with Mount Zaphon in "Davidic Origin," 335 and n. 39.

23 See my detailed discussion of this point and the literature cited there in my "ṣāpôn in Job 26, 7," *Bib* 56 (1975) 554–57.

24 See O. Mowan, "Quator montes sacri in Ps. 89 13?" *VD* 41 (1965) 11–20, esp. 15. The emendation to ʾmnh could be correct (see Cant 4:8), but the identification with Mount Amanus is problematic for the reasons I noted in "Davidic Origin," 334 n. 37. The name for Mount Amanus is normally written in Akkadian sources with an initial ḫ, which would not correspond to a West Semitic aleph (Simo Parpola, *Neo-Assyrian Toponymns* [AOAT 6; Neukirchen: Neukirchener Verlag; Kevelaer: Butzon & Bercker, 1970] 145). It is easier to identify ʾmnh with Mount Ammana(na), apparently a different mountain (ibid., 16). It occurs in one text along with Mount Amanus and Mount Lebanon: KURḪa-[m]a-na KURLab-na-na u₃ KURAm-ma-na-na (Tadmor and Yamada, RINAP 1,

text 47 rev. 26; cf. texts 13:6; 30:2; 46:23). Mount Ammana(na) is probably to be identified with a part of the Anti-Lebanon range (J. Simons, *The Geographical and Topographical Texts of the Old Testament* [Studia Francisci Scholten memoriae dicata 2; Leiden: Brill, 1959] 2; cf. Gonnet, "Les montagnes," 116–17, and literature cited there. So still Siegfried Mittmann and Götz Schmitt's, *Tübinger Bibelatlas* (Stuttgart: Deutsche Bibelgesellschaft, 2001), map B IV 5. Michael Astour, however, identifies Mount Ammanana with the Jebel Quṣeir, a low range just southeast of Atakya, where boxwood grows ("History of Ebla," in Cyrus H. Gordon, Gary Rendsburg, Nathan H. Winter, eds., *Eblaitica: Essays on the Ebla Archives and Eblaite Language* (Publications of the Center for Ebla Research at New York University; Winona Lake, IN: Eisenbrauns, 2002) 105–6, and n. 295. Simo Parpola and Michael Porter prefer the identification with the Jebel an-Nuṣairiya, farther south and west (*The Helsinki Atlas of the Near East in the Neo-Assyrian Period* [Helsinki: Casco Bay Assyriological Institute, Neo-Assyrian Text Corpus Project, 2001] 5), though they list Jebel Quṣeir as an alternate location.

In Isaiah 14:14, Sargon continues to reflect on his arrogant plan to ascend to the heights. He will go up on the backs of the clouds and be as exalted as the god Elyon (the Most High). Here again the theological viewpoint reflected is different from that of the Ugaritic texts, where, as far as I am aware, the divine name Elyon (ʿlyn) is not even attested. It is not found on the pantheon list (*Ugaritica* V [Mission de Ras Shamra 16; Paris: Imprimerie Nationale, 1968] 42–64) and no occurrence of the name is listed in Richard E. Whitaker's *A Concordance of the Ugaritic Literature* (Cambridge, MA: Harvard University Press, 1972). The name occurs in the mid-eighth-century BCE. Aramaic treaty from Sfire southeast of Aleppo between Bargaʾya, king of *Ktk*, and Mattiʿil, King of Arpad, at the end of the group of named gods listed as guarantors of the treaty, "before El and ʿElyon" (ʾl w ʿlyn), and before the group of deified natural phenomena, "before Heaven [and Earth, before A]byss and Source, and before Day and Night," which completed the list of guarantors of the treaty.[25] Otherwise I am unaware of any other early mention of the divine name ʿElyon outside the biblical text. Apparently Elyon, if known, was not that prominent a figure of devotion in the early Canaanite pantheon north of Phoenicia. Farther south in Palestine and later in the first millennium, at least in Israelite sources, Elyon becomes important as a designation for the highest God, and the identification of Yahweh with Elyon is a way of claiming imperial supremacy for Yahweh. In Canaanite religion, at least in the Phoenician version, even as late as Sakunyathon's account of Phoenician religion, Elioun identified as Hypsistos, "the most high," remained merely one of the primeval deities of the theogony, more ancient but far less important than El (Kronos) and Baal and the other gods actively worshiped in the cult.[26] It is possible that both the elevation of Elyon and the identification with Yahweh are an Israelite innovation, analogous to the Assyrian theologians' identification of their national deity Aššur with the primeval deity

Anšar.[27] In both cases, it would be a way of giving the national deity greater authority by virtue of greater age than their thus younger rivals Baal and Marduk.

Nonetheless, Sargon's quest for the imperial authority of the highest god came to naught. Instead of sitting as head of the gods on the mount of assembly, on the heights of Zaphon, above the clouds, he was brought down to Sheol, to the bottoms of the pit (v. 15). Thus, those prominent dead who rose to greet him will stare at Sargon, gaping in amazement at the dead king's unpretentious appearance, decaying and covered as he now is with maggots. In astonishment they ask, "Could this really be the man who troubled the earth and caused kingdoms to shake? Who turned the earth into a desert, destroyed its cities, and refused to allow his prisoners to go home." The last statement is a reference to the Assyrian practice of the forced deportation of a defeated population to a different part of the Assyrian empire.

In contrast to the dead and unburied Sargon, the prophet notes that the other dead kings of the nations, all of them, lie in glory, each buried in his own proper burial place ("his house") with the honors customarily accorded to dead kings (v. 18). Sargon, however, who was killed and his camp overrun in an ambush by mountain tribesmen, remained unburied, because his body was never recovered by the Assyrians.[28] The prophet graphically describes his fate as being "cast out from your grave like a loathsome miscarriage," and then continues with imagery that well captures the picture of the dead king covered with the fallen corpses of his trampled and pierced body guards that littered the ground above and around the king's own corpse, all of these mutilated dead going down to the bottom stones of the pit with the corpse of Sargon. This last image may suggest that the mountain tribesmen who defeated Sargon disposed of his body and those of his troops by throwing them into a common pit and covering it so that no Assyrian relief force could ever recover the bodies. Thus, Sargon was not united with

---

25   See the translation by Franz Rosenthal in *ANET*, 3rd ed., 659–61, and the earlier editions and studies cited there.

26   Eusebius, *Praep. evang.* 1.10; Carl Clemen, *Die phönikische Religion nach Philo von Byblos, MVAG* 42/3 (Leipzig: Hinrichs, 1939) 29; Harold W. Attridge and Robert A. Oden Jr., *Philo of Byblos, The Phoenician History: Intro., critical text, translation, notes* (CBQMS

9; Washington, DC: Catholic Biblical Association of America, 1981) pp. 46-47, PE 1.10.15; pp. 50-55, PE 1.10.20-32.

27   See my discussion in "Davidic Origin," 340–42; and see Tadmor, Landsberger, and Parpola, "Sin of Sargon," 3–51.

28   See the excursus above.

the other kings of the nations, or even of Assyria, in the grave, since Sargon was never properly buried (v. 20). According to the prophet, the reason for this frightening judgment was that Sargon had destroyed his own land and killed his own people (v. 20). Sargon did come to the Assyrian throne in a coup, but since the text characterizes him as a king of Babylon, it is more likely that the reference is to his vigorous campaigning against Merodach-baladan in Babylonia that eventually led to Sargon's assuming the crown of Babylon. Despite Sargon's claim that Merodach-baladan had broken a treaty made in the name of the gods of Assyria and Babylon, it is historically more probable that Sargon was the party breaking the treaty, perhaps at the instigation of priests of Marduk in Babylon who were not enthralled by the Chaldean Merodach-baladan.[29]

The prophet then moves from a description of past events to a wish or prayer for the future. He asks that the offspring of evildoers never be mentioned. The plural "evildoers" presumably refers not only to Sargon but also to the Assyrian (and Babylonian) kings Tiglath-pileser III and Shalmaneser V, who preceded Sargon. An unnamed plural is called upon to prepare slaughter for his sons, because of the iniquity of their fathers (v. 21). The plural "fathers" after the singular "his" is a bit odd, but it seems to focus on the children of Sargon while attributing the iniquity not just to Sargon but to the whole line of previous Assyrian kings. The prayer is that Sargon's descendants not rise up and possess the earth as Sargon had, and fill the face of the earth with cities. This last statement seems a little odd, and the LXX and Syriac's, "wars" or "war," and the Targum's, "enemies,"[30] have led some critics to emend the word עָרִים (ʿārîm), "cities." Hayes and Irvine (p. 34) suggest the emendation to רָעִים (rāʿîm), "evils," while Marti, Duhm, and Gray simply omit the word, though mentioning earlier expla-

nations such as an Aramaism for צָרִים (ṣārîm), "enemies, oppressors," a corruption of an original עָרְצִים (ʿārîṣîm), "tyrants," or an error for עִיִּים (ʿîyîm), "ruins." (Marti, 127; Duhm, 98; Gray, 261). If Sargon is the butt of this taunt song, however, this emendation is unnecessary. In his last years, Sargon was heavily involved in the construction of his new capital city Dur-Sharrukin on previously rural, undeveloped land, and his building activities were widely heralded throughout the empire. In a world where cities were normally built in favored localities, usually on the ruins of earlier cities, it must have seemed to many observers in the empire that Sargon intended "to fill the face of the earth with cities." It may also reflect the pleased awareness that Dur-Sharrukin, at least, was abandoned as the Assyrian capital shortly after Sargon's death, and perhaps harbors the hope that the rest of Assyria's great imperial cities would soon meet the same fate.

14:22-23 An Exilic Addition

The taunt song actually ends with the wish or prayer in vv. 20b-21. God's response in vv. 22-23 appears to be a later addition (Marti, 129–30; Duhm, 98; Gray, 262; Clements, 144–45).[31] The dating of these verses varies considerably, though the majority of scholars date them to the exilic or postexilic period. The verses have strong literary connections to the description of Edom's fate in Isa 34:11-17, which I attribute to Second Isaiah or at least to the exilic period of Second Isaiah, and with some similarities to the judgments announced against Babylon in Jeremiah 50–51, particularly Jer 50:39-40 and 51:37, 43, all of which presuppose Nebuchadnezzar's conquest of Jerusalem and thus must date at the earliest to the early exilic period.

---

29 See Tadmor et al., "Sin of Sargon," 23–28.
30 See the textual notes.
31 Hayes and Irvine (p. 234) are among the minority of scholars who regard the verses as integral to the preceding poem and attribute them to the eighth-century Isaiah of Jerusalem.

22/ And I will rise up against them,[a] says[b] Yahweh of Hosts,
And I will cut off from Babylon[c] name and remnant,[d]
Offspring[e] and posterity, says[b] Yahweh.
23/ And I will make it[f] a possession[g] of the owl[h]
And pools[i] of water;
And I will sweep it[j] with a broom of destruction,
Says[k] Yahweh of Hosts.

Textual Notes

a   MT עֲלֵיהֶם (ʿălêhem), "against them"; 1QIsaᵃ עליהמה.

b   MT נְאֻם (nĕʾūm), lit., "oracle of" but traditionally rendered "says"; 1QIsaᵃ נואם.

c   MT לְבָבֶל (lĕbābel), "from Babylon"; 1QIsaᵃ לבב.

d   MT וּשְׁאָר (ûšĕʾār), "and remnant"; 1QIsaᵃ has the feminine ושארית (wišʾērît).

e   MT וְנִין (wĕnîn), "and offspring,"; Vg., Syr., Tg.; 1QIsaᵃ נין omits the conjunction. LXX translates the pair וְנִין וָנֶכֶד (wĕnîn wāneked), "offpring and posterity," with a single word καὶ σπέρμα, "and offspring."

f   MT וְשַׂמְתִּיהָ (wĕśamtîha), "and I will make it," Vg., Syr., Tg.;

1QIsaᵃ ושמתי omits the suffix; LXX clarifies the suffix, καὶ θήσω τὴν Βαβυλωνίαν ἔρημον, "and I will make Babylonia desolate."

g   MT לְמוֹרָשׁ (lĕmôraš), "to a possession"; 1QIsaᵃ למירש.

h   MT קִפֹּד (qippōd), "hedgehog" or "owl"; the versions all have "hedgehog"; 1QIsaᵃ קפז, probably "owl" or some type of desert bird.

i   MT וְאַגְמֵי־מָיִם (wĕʾagmê māyîm), "and pools of water," Vg., Syr.; 1QIsaᵃ אגמי מים omits the conjunction.

j   MT וְטֵאטֵאתִיהָ (wĕṭēʾṭēʾtîhā), "and I will sweep it," Vg., Syr., Tg.; 1QIsaᵃ וטאטאתי omits the suffix.

k   MT נְאֻם (nĕʾūm); 1QIsaᵃ נואם.

Commentary

In answer to the preceding prayer, Yahweh promises to rise up against the descendants of the king of Babylon and cut off from Babylon "name and remnant, offspring and posterity" (v. 22). Babylon will be left a swampy desolation, inhabited only by owls and such creatures, having been swept clear of human inhabitants and their domesticated animals by a thorough broom of destruction. Both

the *pilpel* verb טֵאטֵא (ṭēʾṭēʾ), "to sweep," and the cognate noun מַטְאֲטֵא (maṭʾăṭēʾ), "broom," occur only here in the Old Testament, and this precise image does not seem to occur elsewhere in the Old Testament despite the English translations of other verbs that are not clearly associated with the action of a broom (see the NRSV in Gen 18:23-24; Pss 26:9; 58:9; 69:15; 90:5; Prov 21:7; Isa 8:8; 21:1; 28:17; Hab 1:11; Zeph 1:2-3).

Bibliography for Isa 14:1-23

Alfrink, B., "Der Versammlungsberg im äussersten Norden (Is.14)," *Bib* 14 (1933) 41–67.

Alonso Schökel, L., "Traducción de textos poéticos hebreos II (Is 14)," *CB* 17 (1960) 257–65.

Anderson, Gary A., *A Time to Mourn, A Time to Dance: The Expression of Grief and Joy in Israelite Religion* (University Park: Pennsylvania State University Press, 1991) 60–82.

Avishur, Y., "'Atudei eretz' (Is 14,9)," in Moshe Weinfeld and Jonas C. Greenfield, eds., *Shnaton: An Annual for Biblical and Ancient Near Eastern Studies*, vol. 9 (Jerusalem: Israel Bible Co., 1985) 159–64.

Bost, H., "Le chant sur la chute d'un tyran en Ésaïe," *ETR* 59 (1984) 3–14.

Burns, John Barclay, "Does Helel 'Go to Hell?' Isaiah 14:12-15," *Proceedings, Eastern Great Lakes & Midwest Biblical Society* 9 (1989) 89–97.

———, "*Hôlesh ʾal* in Isaiah 14:12: A New Proposal," *ZAH* 2 (1989) 199–204.

Carmignac, Jean, "Six passages d'Isaïe eclaires par Qumran," in S. Wagner, ed., *Bibel und Qumran: Beiträge zur Erforschung der Beziehungen zwischen Bibel- und Qumranwissenschaft* (Berlin: Evangelische Haupt-Bibelgesellschaft, 1968) 37–46.

Clifford, Richard J., *The Cosmic Mountain in Canaan and the Old Testament* (HSM 4; Cambridge, MA: Harvard University Press, 1972), 160–68.

Cobb, W. H., "The Ode in Isaiah XIV," *JBL* 15 (1896) 18–35.

Craigie, P. C., "Helel, Athtar and Phaethon (Jes 14:12-15)," *ZAW* 85 (1973) 223–25.

Dahood, M., "Punic *bkkbm 'l* and Isa 14 13," *Or* n.s. 34 (1965) 170–72.

Dupont-Sommer, A., "Note exégétique sur Isaïe 14:16-21," *RHR* 134 (1948) 72–80.

Erlandsson, L., *The Burden of Babylon: A Study of Isaiah 13:2–14:23* (ConBOT 4; Lund: Gleerup, 1970).

Etz, Donald V., "Is Isaiah 14:12-15 a Reference to Comet Halley?" *VT* 3 (1986) 289–301.

Franke, C. A., "The Function of the Oracles against Babylon in Isaiah 14 and 47," in *SBLSP* (Atlanta: Scholars Press, 1993) 250–59; reprinted as "Reversals of Fortune in the Ancient Near East: A Study of the Babylonian Oracles in the Book of Isaiah," in Roy F. Melugin and Marvin A. Sweeney, eds., *New Visions of Isaiah* (JSOTSup 214; Sheffield: Sheffield Academic Press, 1996) 104–23.

Gallagher, W., "On the Identity of *Helel Ben Shaher* in Is. 4:12-15," *UF* 26 (1994) 131–46.

Ginsberg, H. L., "Reflexes of Sargon in Isaiah after 715 B.C.E.," *JAOS* 88 (1968) 47–53.

Gorman, F. H., "A Study of Isaiah 14:4*b*-23" (research paper, Fuller Theological Seminary, 1979).

Gosse, Bernard, "Un texte pré-apocalyptique du règne de Darius: Isaïe 13:1–14:23," *RB* 92 (1985) 200–222.

Grelot, Pierre, "Isaïe XIV 12-15 et son arrière-plan mythologique," *RHR* 149 (1956) 18–48.

——, "Sur la vocalisation de *hyll* (Is.XIV 12)," *VT* 6 (1956) 303–4.

Heiser, M. S., "The Mythological Provenance of Isa xiv 12-15: A Reconsideration of the Ugaritic Material," *VT* 51 (2001) 354–69.

Hirsch, S. A., "Isaiah 14:12," *JQR* n.s. 11 (1920) 197–99.

Holladay, William L., "Text Structure and Irony in the Poem on the Fall of the Tyrant, Isaiah 14," *CBQ* 61 (1999) 633–45.

Hudson, J. T., "Isaiah XIV.19," *ExpTim* 40 (1928) 93.

Jahnow, Hedwig, *Das hebräische Leichenlied im Rahmen der Völkerdichtung* (BZAW 36; Giessen: A. Töpelmann, 1923) 239–53.

Jensen, Hans J. L., "The Fall of the King," *SJOT* 5 (1991) 121–47.

Jensen, J., "Helel Ben Shahar in Bible and Tradition," in C. Broyles and C. Evans, eds., *Writing and Reading the Scroll of Isaiah: Studies of an Interpretive Tradition* (2 vols.; VTSup 70; Leiden: Brill, 1997) 1:339–56.

Johnson, H., and S. Holm-Nielsen, "Comments on Two Possible References to Comets in the Old Testament," *SJOT* 7 (1993) 99–107.

Keown, G., "A History of the Interpretation of Isaiah 14:12-15" (PhD diss., Southern Baptist Theological Seminary, 1979).

Khoo, J., "Isaiah 14:12-14 and Satan: A Canonical Approach," *Stulos Theological Journal* 2 (1994) 67–77.

Koenig, N. A., "Lucifer," *ExpTim* 17 (1906) 479.

Köhler, L., "Isaiah XIV.19," *ExpTim* 39 (1928) 236.

Köszegby, Miklós, "Hybris und Prophetie: Erwägungen zum Hintergrund von Jesaja XIV 12-15," *VT* 44 (1994) 549–54.

Lang, Bernhard, "Afterlife: Ancient Israel's Changing Vision of the World Beyond," *BRev* 4 (1988) 12–23.

Langdon, S. H., "The Star Hêlel, Jupiter?" *ExpTim* 42 (1930) 172–74.

Levine, Baruch A., and Jean M. Tarragon, "Dead Kings and Rephaim: The Patrons of the Ugaritic Dynasty," *JSOT* 104 (1984) 649–59.

Lohmann, P., "Die anonymen Prophetien gegen Babel aus der Zeit des Exils" (diss., Rostock, 1910).

——, "Zu Text und Metrum einiger Stellen aus Jesaja," *ZAW* 33 (1913) 251–56.

Loretz, Oswald, "Der kanaanäische Mythos vom Sturz des Sahar-Sohnes Hêlel (Jes 14,12-15)," *UF* 8 (1976) 133–36.

Martin-Achard, Robert, "Esaie et Jérémie aux prises avec les problèmes politiques: Contribution á l'étude du thème, prophétie et politique," *Cahiers de la Revue de Théologie et de Philosophie* 11 (1984) 306–22.

——, *From Death to Life: A Study of the Development of the Doctrine of the Resurrection in the Old Testament* (Edinburgh: Oliver & Boyd, 1960).

McKay, J. W., "Helel and the Dawn-Goddess: A Re-Examination of the Myth of Isaiah XIV 12-15," *VT* 20 (1970) 451–64.

Mowinckel, Sigmund, "Die Sternnamen im AT," *NTT* 29 (1928) 1–74.

O'Connell, Robert H., "Isaiah 14:4b-23: Ironic Reversal through Concentric Structure and Mythic Allusion," *VT* 38 (1988) 406–18.

Ohler, A., *Mythologische Elemente im Alten Testament: Eine motivgeschichtliche Untersuchung* (Düsseldorf: Patmos, 1969).

Oldenburg, U., "Above the Stars of El: El in Ancient South Arabic Religion," *ZAW* 82 (1970) 187–208.

Orlinsky, H. M., "Madhebah in Isaiah XIV 4," *VT* 7 (1957) 202–3.

Pope, Marvin H., *El in the Ugaritic Texts* (VTSup 2; Leiden: Brill, 1955).

Prinsloo, W. S., "Isaiah 14:12-15: Humiliation, Hubris, Humiliation," *ZAW* 93 (1981) 432–38.

Quell, G., "Jesaja 14:1-23," in Johannes Herrmann and Leonhard Rost, eds., *Festschrift Friedrich Baumgärtel zum 70. Geburtstag, 17 Januar 1958* (Erlanger Forschungen A10; Erlangen: Universitätsbund, 1959) 131–57.

Savignac, J. de, "Note sur le sens du terme Saphón dans quelques passages de la Bible," *VT* 3 (1953) 95–96.

Schiffer, S., "Un chant de triomphe méconnu sur la mort de Sanchérib," *REJ* 76 (1923) 176–82.

Schmidt, K. L., "Lucifer als gefallene Engelmacht," *TZ* 7 (1951) 161–79.

Sen, F., "Variantes de algunos textos de Isaias con respecto al texto Masoretico." *CB* 33 (1976) 223–25.

Shipp, R. Mark, *Of Dead Kings and Dirges: Myth and Meaning in Isaiah 14:4b-21* (Academia Biblica 11; Atlanta: Society of Biblical Literature, 2002).

Smith, M. S., "Rephaim," *ABD* 5:675–76.

Staerk, Willy, *Das assyrische Weltreich im Urteil der Propheten* (Göttingen: Vandenhoeck & Ruprecht, 1908).

Stolz, F., "Die Baüme des Gottesgartens auf dem Libanon," *ZAW* 84 (1972) 141–56.

———, *Strukturen und Figuren im Kult von Jerusalem* (BZAW 118; Berlin: A. Töpelmann, 1970).

Talmon, S., "Biblical *repaim* and Ugaritic *rpu/i(m)*," *HAR* 7 (1983) 235–49.

Tate, Marvin E., "Satan in the Old Testament," *RevExp* 89 (1992) 461–74.

Tromp, Nicholas J., *Primitive Conceptions of Death and the Nether World in the Old Testament* (BibOr 21; Rome: Pontifical Biblical Institute, 1969).

Tsumura, David Toshio, "Tohû in Isaiah xiv 19," *VT* 38 (1988) 361–64.

Vanderburgh, F. A., "The Ode on the King of Babylon, Isaiah XIV, 4b-21," *AJSL* 29 (1912) 111–21.

Van Leeuwen, Raymond C., "Isa 14:12 *hôlēs ʿl goyim* and Gilgamesh XI.6," *JBL* 99 (1980) 173–84.

Yee, Gale A., "The Anatomy of Biblical Parody: The Dirge Form in 2 Samuel 1 and Isaiah 14," *CBQ* 50 (1988) 565–86.

Youngblood, R. F., "Fallen Star: The Evolution of Lucifer," *BRev* 14 (1998) 547–55.

14

In contrast to the preceding two verses, Isa 14:24-27 appears to be from the eighth-century Isaiah of Jerusalem. The theme of God's plan is a major theme in Isaiah of Jerusalem, and both the vocabulary and the theology of these verses are familiar Isaianic features. The judgment against Assyria corresponds to God's comments about Assyria in Isa 10:12-15 and to the announcement of the removal of the Assyrian yoke in the coronation oracle for Hezekiah in Isa 8:23b—9:6. Its placement here suggests that the editor, whether Isaiah himself or one of his disciples, was fully aware that the preceding taunt song, minus the later exilic addition in vv. 22-23, was really about an Assyrian tyrant. Thus, it makes an appropriate divine response to the concluding prayer of the taunt song in 14:20b-21.

24/ Yahweh of Hosts has sworn,[a] saying,
   "Surely as I have designed,[b]
   So will it be;[c]
   As I have planned,
   So will it come to pass.
25/ To break Assyria in my land,
   And upon my mountains I will trample[d] him,
   And his yoke will turn aside from upon them,[e]
   And his burden shall turn aside from on his shoulder.[f]"
26/ This is the plan that is planned[g] against the whole earth,
   And this is the hand that is outstretched against all the nations.
27/ For Yahweh of Hosts[h] has planned,
   And who can annul?
   His hand is stretched out,
   And who can turn it back?

Textual Notes

a   נִשְׁבַּע (nišbaʿ), "he swore," MT, 1QIsaᵃ, Vg., Syr., Tg.; LXX τάδε λέγει, "thus he says," is either a very loose translation or presupposes כה אמר (kōh ʾāmar).

b   דִּמִּיתִי (dimmîtî), "I planned," MT, 1QIsaᵃ ,Vg., Tg., Syr.; LXX εἴρηκα, "I spoke," appears to have either דברתי (dibbartî) or אמרתי (ʾāmartî), clearly a secondary reading.

c   MT's הָיָתָה (hāyātâ), if original, would have to be a prophetic perfect, not a genuine past tense; 1QIsaᵃ has the easier תהיה (tihyê), and all the versions translate the verb as future tense.

d   LXX καὶ ἔσονται εἰς καταπάτημα, "and they shall become a trampled thing," is a very loose translation of אֲבוּסֶנּוּ (ʾăbûsennû), "I will trample him"; it renders the text as though it had והיו למרמס (wĕhāyû lĕmirmās); cf. 5:5. 1QIsaᵃ and the other versions support MT.

e   מֵעֲלֵיהֶם (mēʿălêhem), "from upon them," MT; מעליכמה (mēʿălêkēmâ), "from upon you," 1QIsaᵃ; none of the versions supports the Qumran reading.

f   שִׁכְמוֹ (šikmô), "his shoulder," MT; 1QIsaᵃ שכמכה (šikmĕkâ), "your shoulder." The versions, if they reflect a pronominal suffix, have the third person masculine plural, "their shoulder," but that could be a mere translation of the third masculine singular referring to the people as a collective.

g   הַיְעוּצָה (hayyĕʿûṣâ), "that is planned," MT, 1QIsaᵃ, Syr., Tg.; neither LXX's ἣν βεβούλευται κύριος, "which the LORD planned," nor Vg.'s quod cogitavi, "which I planned," appears more original.

h   יְהוָה צְבָאוֹת (YHWH ṣĕbāʾôt), MT, 1QIsaᵃ, Vg., Syr., Tg.; LXX has the peculiar translation ὁ θεὸς ὁ ἅγιος, "the holy God."

Commentary

Yahweh of Hosts has sworn that he will carry out his judgment on Assyria precisely according to his divine plan, thus reassuring his people of the certainty of his promise. Isaiah of Jerusalem puts oath formulas in the mouth of Yahweh of Hosts on other occasions (5:9; 22:14), and the same verb for swearing used in 14:24 (נשבע) should probably be restored in 5:9, so this usage is typically Isaianic. The content of the oath is also typically Isaianic. The verbs used for Yahweh's designing and planning here, the *piel* of דמה (*dāmâ*) and the *qal* of יעץ (*yāʿaṣ*), are used similarly elsewhere in First Isaiah. The verb דמה is used in 10:7 for Assyria's rival design, and the verb יעץ is used both for the plans of Yahweh's enemies Aram and Ephraim (7:5) and for Yahweh's plans against his enemies Egypt (9:12, 17) and Tyre (23:8-9). Moreover, the verbs used for the fulfillment of the plans, the *qal* of היה (*hāyâ*) and קום (*qûm*), are also used in the same way elsewhere in Isaiah. Both are used together in 7:7, and קום is used in a similar context in 8:10.

Verse 25 then reveals God's plan as "breaking" Assyria in God's land, "trampling" him on God's mountain, and "turning aside" Assyria's yoke and burden from his people. The verb used for "breaking" Assyria (שבר, *šābar*) is the same verb used for breaking the evil staff in the taunt song (14:5). The verb used for "trampling" Assyria (בוס, *bûs*) is the same verb used in the taunt song, though in the passive *hophal* participle, for the trampled corpse of the Assyrian king and his bodyguard (14:19). The verb used for "turning aside" Assyria's yoke and burden (סור, *sûr*) is the same verb used in a very similar context in 10:27. While the verb is different, the removal of Assyria's yoke and burden is also mentioned with similar vocabulary in Isa 9:3. Thus, the vocabulary of v. 25 links it both to the taunt song and to other passages in First Isaiah. Yahweh's plan is not only to crush Assyria, but to do it in Yahweh's land and on Yahweh's mountain. This clearly echoes the motif in the Zion Tradition that celebrates Yahweh's victory over the enemy nations who march against his city Zion (see Psalms 2; 46; 48; 76).

According to v. 26, the plan mentioned in v. 25 is a divine plan that touches on the whole earth and reveals Yahweh's hand that is stretched out against all the nations. The theme of Yahweh's stretched-out hand occurs as a repeated refrain in the litany-like oracle of judgment against the northern kingdom Israel in Isa 9:11, 16, 20; 5:25. It also occurs in an oracle against Judah and their Egyptian ally in Isa 31:3, and together with the motif of God's plan in an oracle against Tyre in Isa 23:8, 9, 11. See also 10:13-14, where "hand" is used by the Assyrian king in his boast about conquest, which may suggest that here in 14:26 one has a deliberate reversal of Assyria's boastful plan. Isaiah 14:25-26 does not explain how Yah-weh's plan to crush Assyria in Yahweh's land on Yahweh's mountains impacts all the other nations, but if one looks at these texts in the light of Isaiah's firm commitment to the Zion Tradition, the answer seems obvious. When Aram and Israel marched against Zion in the Syro-Ephraimitic war, Isaiah proclaimed that their plan would fail, for Yahweh had chosen Zion as his city and David's dynasty as his kings (Isa 7:1-17; 8:1-4, 8b-10; 10:20-23, 27d-34; 17:1-14). Isaiah had seen the divine king in the prophet's inaugural vision, and Isaiah was concerned that Yahweh's imperial claims and his choice of Zion and the Davidic dynasty be recognized by the whole world (chap. 2). What better way to do that than to crush the Assyrian oppressor on Yahweh's chosen Mount Zion precisely as the Zion Tradition hymns claimed that God did to the hostile nations who marched against Zion? In the coronation oracle for Hezekiah, the expectation is expressed that the Assyrian domination would be broken in the reign of this new David and that his kingdom would be established in justice forever (8:23b—9:6). In the perhaps earlier prediction of a new Davidic king (11:1-10), the ideal reign of this new king leads to the pilgrimage of the nations to him and Jerusalem (11:10), much as the elevation of Jerusalem in 2:2-4 leads to the same result. But one should note that this ideal reign follows on the defeat of the enemy threatening Jerusalem (10:27d-34) much as the ideal reign of the Davidic king in 8:23b—9:6 begins with the defeat of Assyria. Yahweh's defeat of Assyria, then, would be paradigmatic of what would happen to any nation that did not recognize Yahweh's imperial status. Assyria had been used to punish Israel and even Judah (8:5-8a), Jerusalem, and its Davidic king (10:12), because of Ahaz's refusal to trust in God's promises (7:9), but Isaiah apparently expected that Hezekiah would avoid this failure of faith, perhaps because he had earlier convinced the king (cf. Isaiah 20) not to join the Nubian-supported Ashdod revolt. When Hezekiah flunked this test by turning to Egypt and her Nubian rulers for assistance rather than trusting in God (Isa 31:3), Isaiah apparently felt that Yahweh still had some use for Assyria as God's rod for punishing Jerusalem, though the ultimate outcome, after the successful punishment, remained the destruction of the foreign hosts besieging the city (29:1-8). Isaiah 14:24-27, however, seems to date soon after the knowledge of Sargon's death reached Judah and probably before Hezekiah's renewed diplomatic negotiations with

Nubia and Egypt, or at least before the prophet Isaiah became aware of them.

Isaiah ends the oracle in v. 27 with a couple of rhetorical questions obviously demanding a negative answer. Yahweh of Hosts has made this plan, so who is able to annul (יָפֵר, yāpēr, hiphil third person masculine singular imperfect of פרר) it? The plan made against Zion and its Davidic king by the nations would be annulled (וְתֻפַר, wĕtūpār, hophal second person feminine singular imperfect of פרר, Isa 8:10), but no one can annul God's plan. It is Yahweh's hand that is stretched out, so who is able to turn it back. The expected answer, of course, is no one.

The use of יְשִׁיבֶנָּה (yĕšîbennâ), "can turn it back," here is similar to Amos's use of the same verb for averting punishment (לֹא אֲשִׁיבֶנּוּ, lōʾ ʾăšîbennû, "I will not turn it back," Amos 1:3, 6, 9, 11, 13; 2:1, 4, 6), though the antecedent of the masculine suffix in Amos is not expressed and cannot refer to Yahweh's hand, which would require a feminine suffix as in Isa 14:27. Despite this slight difference in construction, the possibility of an influence of Amos on Isaiah's formulation should not be discounted. No one can annul God's plan or turn back his hand from carrying out the planned punishment on Assyria.

Bibliography

Bailey, L. R., "Isaiah 14:24-27," *Int* 36 (1982) 171–76.

Barth, *Die Jesaja-Worte,* 103–19.

Childs, *Assyrian Crisis,* 38–39.

Clements, Ronald E., "Isaiah 14,22-27: A Central Passage Reconsidered," in J. Vermeylen, ed., *Le livre d'Isaïe: Les oracles et leurs relectures unité et complexité de l'ouvrage* (BETL 81; Leuven: Leuven University Press, 1989) 254–62.

Dietrich, *Jesaja und die Politik,* 120–21.

Donner, *Israel unter den Völkern,* 145–46.

Eareckson, V. O., "The Originality of Isaiah XIV 27," *VT* 20 (1970) 490–91.

Fichtner, J., "Jahwes Plan in der Botschaft des Jesaja," *ZAW* 63 (1951) 16–33.

Gonçalves, Francolino J., *L'expédition de Sennachérib en Palestine dans la littérature hébraïque ancienne* (Publications de l'Institut orientaliste de Louvain 34; Louvain-la-Neuve: Université catholique de Louvain, 1986) 33–36, 307–9.

Gosse, Bernard, "Isaïe 14:24-27 et les oracles contre les nations du livre d'Isaïe," *BN* 56 (1991) 17–21.

Høgenhaven, *Gott und Volk,* 126–27.

Jenkins, A. K., "The Development of the Isaiah Tradition in Is 13–23," in J. Vermeylen, ed., *Le livre d'Isaïa: Les oracles et leurs relectures unité et complexité de l'ouvrage* (BETL 81; Leuven: Leuven University Press, 1989) 249–51.

Skehan, "Textual Problems," 47–55.

Vermeylen, *Du prophète Isaïe,* 1:252–62, 296–97.

Werner, W., *Studien zur alttestamentlichen Vorstellung vom Plan Yahves* (BZAW 173; Berlin: de Gruyter, 1988).

14

28/ [a]In the year of the death of the king[b] Ahaz this oracle
came.
29/ Do not rejoice, O Philistia, all of you,
That the rod[c] that smote you is broken,
For from the root of the serpent
Shall go forth an adder;
And his fruit will be a flying cobra.[d]
30/ And the firstborn of the poor will graze,
And the needy will lie down in security,
But I[e] will kill your root with famine,
And your remnant he/it[f] will slay.
31/ Wail, O gate! Cry out, O city!
Melt in fear, O Philistia, all of you,[g]
For from the north comes smoke,
And there is no straggler[h] in his ranks.[i]
32/ And what will one answer[j] the messengers[k] of the nation?
That Yahweh has founded Zion,
And in it[l] the poor of his people will find refuge.

Textual Notes

a At the beginning of the verse, Syr. has "an oracle concerning Philistia" (ܡܫܩܠܐ ܕܦܠܫܬ, *mšqlᵓ dplšt*), but the heading is not found in any other textual tradition.

b 1QIsaᵃ omitted the final letter of הַמֶּלֶךְ (*hammelek*), "king," but then inserted it above the line.

c LXX ὁ ζυγὸς reads עֹל (*ᶜōl*), "yoke," but MT is supported by 1QIsaᵃ and the other versions.

d The versions all seem to reflect the text of MT, though their renderings of the text vary. LXX and Syr. are fairly literal; Vg. has "a devouring flying creature" (*absorbens volucrem*), while Tg. interprets the text as a reference to the Messiah: אֲרֵי מִבְּנֵי בְנוֹהִי דְּיִשַׁי יִפּוֹק מְשִׁיחָא וִיהוֹן עוֹבָדוֹהִי בְּכוֹן כְּחִוֵּי מַפְרִית: "for from the sons of the sons of Jesse the Messiah will come forth, and his deeds will be among you as a biting serpent."

e LXX and Tg. read the third person, "he will kill," probably to make it agree with the parallel verb; MT is supported by 1QIsaᵃ 4QIsaᵒ ,Vg., and Syr..

f MT's יַהֲרֹג (*yahărōg*), "he/it will kill," is supported by LXX, Tg., and probably Syr., which translates with a passive, "your remnant will be slain." 1QIsaᵃ has אהרוג (*ᵓehĕrōg*), "I will kill," which is supported by Vg. The variation in the versions suggests different attempts to create consistency of person, and the same concern may be behind the text of 1QIsaᵃ. The easier reading would be to follow 1QIsaᵃ, but the more difficult reading of MT may be the more original. It better explains the confusion in the versions. The subject of יַהֲרֹג (*yahărōg*), "he/it will kill,"

g could either be the flying cobra of v. 29 or the famine (רָעָב, *rāᶜāb*) of v. 30.

LXX, Vg., and Syr. ignore the second person suffix on כֻּלֵּךְ (*kullēk*), "all of you," and that permits them to translate the infinite absolute נָמוֹג (*nāmôg*), "melt in fear," as a finite verb rather than as an imperative, but MT is supported by 1QIsaᵃ and Tg.

h MT's בּוֹדֵד (*bôdēd*), "straggler," is supported by 4QIsaᵒ, Vg., Syr., and Tg. 1QIsaᵃ's מוֹדֵד (*môdēd*) is an obvious transcription error. LXX has omitted the end of the verse.

i MT's בְּמוֹעָדָיו (*bĕmôᶜādāyw*), "in his ranks," is supported by Vg., Syr., and Tg. 1QIsaᵃ's במודעיו (*bmwdᶜyw*) and 4QIsaᵒ's במידעיו (*bmydᶜyw*) are both obvious transcription errors.

j MT has the singular יַעֲנֶה (*yaᶜănê*), "will he answer," supported by Syr.; but 1QIsaᵃ has the plural יענו (*yaᶜănû*), "will they answer," and it is followed by LXX and Tg., while Vg. reads a passive singular that could translate either reading.

k MT, Vg., Tg., and some Syr. texts have מַלְאֲכֵי (*malᵓăkê*), "messengers of," but 1QIsaᵃ, LXX, and some Syr. texts have מלכי (*malkê*), "kings of." Either reading makes sense, but "messengers" is more probable. The answer would be given to messengers who had traveled to Jerusalem, and they in turn would report it to the king or kings who had sent them.

l The reading וּבָהּ (*ûbāh*), "and in it" (referring to Zion), MT, 4QIsaᵒ ,Vg., Syr., Tg., is superior to ובו (*ûbô*), "and in him," referring to Yahweh (1QIsaᵃ, LXX), though eventually they amount to the same thing. Yahweh has founded Zion, and within it, protected by Yahweh's promises and sure foundation, his people will find refuge.

Commentary

Isaiah 14:28-32 begins with a historical notice that dates the following oracle in the year of the death of King Ahaz. The oracle then follows with an admonition to the Philistines not to rejoice that the rod that smote them has been broken, for from the root of the serpent will come forth an even more dangerous flying cobra. The juxtaposition of the historical notice and the following verse leads quite logically to the conclusion that Ahaz was the rod that smote the Philistines, that the Philistines were rejoicing over the news of Ahaz's demise, and that Isaiah was warning them that Hezekiah, Ahaz's successor, would become an even more dangerous opponent of the Philistines than Ahaz had been. Yet, despite the apparent logic of these conclusions, very few modern scholars identify the serpent or the rod that smote Philistia with Ahaz.[1] For those scholars who do not simply dismiss the historical notice,[2] it is far more common to identify this enemy of Philistia as one or another of the Assyrian kings of the period contemporary with Ahaz—Tiglath-pileser III, Shalmaneser V, or Sargon II.[3]

The reasons for this quick dismissal of the internal logic of the passage are summarized nicely by Gray (p. 266): (1) Gray assumes that the smoke that comes from the north mentioned in v. 31 must refer to the army of this new opponent of the Philistines, and since an attack from Judah would come from the east, not the north, this threatening army and the new opponent of Philistia must both be Assyrian, not Judean. (2) The oracle states that the former opponent of Philistia had inflicted injury on the Philistines in the past, which means Ahaz could not be that opponent, "for Ahaz did not smite the Philistines, but was smitten by them (2 Ch 28:18)." The further argument is sometimes made that it would be strange for the prophet to use serpent imagery of a Judean king (Blenkinsopp, 292; Watts, *Isaiah 1–33*, 277). But if one preserves the historical notice and denies that the dead Ahaz is the broken rod, then one is forced to look for an Assyrian ruler whose own demise took place at roughly the same chronological period as Ahaz's death—a search that has yielded no satisfactory results. Tiglath-pileser III died in 727, Shalmaneser V in 722, and Sargon II in 705, and none of those dates can be closely linked to the date of the death of Ahaz, as I will show.

In this commentary, I want to suggest that the internal logic of the passage has been dismissed too quickly, that Ahaz was indeed the rod that smote Philistia. In order to sustain this argument, I will review the evidence for the date of Ahaz's death, examine the possibility that Ahaz did in fact inflict injury upon the Philistines, consider the snake imagery used to characterize the opponents of Philistia, consider whether it is really necessary to identify the smoke from the north as identical with the rod and serpent, and point to a very concrete historical situation, reflected in other Isaianic texts, in which the details of this oracle make perfect sense.[4]

The Date of Ahaz's Death

The biblical evidence for the date of Ahaz's reign and death is contradictory. According to the regnal formula in 2 Kgs 16:1-2, Ahaz was twenty years old when he came to the throne of Judah in the seventeenth year of the Israelite king Pekah, son of Remaliah, and Ahaz remained on the throne for sixteen years. According to 2 Kgs 16:20, Ahaz died and was replaced by his son Hezekiah, and the regnal formula in 2 Kgs 18:1 dates the accession of Hezekiah to the third year of the Israelite king Hoshea son of Elah. Since Tiglath-pileser III's inscriptions indicate that Hoshea seized the throne of Israel in 732,[5] his third

---

1 The conservative scholar John N. Oswalt (p. 331) recognizes that this is "the most obvious interpretation of the *broken staff*," but he does not follow it because, "the biblical accounts make it plain that the Philistines had not suffered at Ahaz's hand."

2 Many authors dismiss the notice about Ahaz's death as the work of a later redactor and therefore worthless for purposes of dating the oracle; so Clements, 148; Marti, 130; Kaiser, *Jesaja 13–39*, 44; Duhm, 100. Others, for example, Vermeylen (*Du prophète Isaïe*, 300, and n. 1), follow J. A. Brewer, "The Date in Isa. 14:28," *AJSL* 54 (1937) 62, in emending away the name Ahaz.

3 So Childs, 128; Gray, 265; Hayes and Irvine, 237; Herbert, 106; Jensen, 151; Oswalt, 332; Watts, *Isaiah 1–33*, 277; Wildberger, *Isaiah 13–27*, 92; Seitz, 136–38.

4 I have alluded to this viewpoint in earlier articles, especially in my "Isaiah's Egyptian and Nubian Oracles," in Brad E. Kelle and Megan Bishop Moore, eds., *Israel's Prophets and Israel's Past: Essays on the Relationship of Prophetic Texts and Israelite History in Honor of John H. Hayes* (LHBOTS 446; New York: T&T Clark, 2006) 201–9, but my first full defense of this interpretation is in "The Rod That Smote Philistia: Isaiah 14:28-32," in David S. Vanderhooft and Abraham Winitzer, eds., *Literature as Politics, Politics as Literature: Essays on the Ancient Near East in Honor of Peter Machinist* (Winona Lake, IN: Eisenbrauns, 2013) 381–95.

5 See Tadmor and Yamada, RINAP 1, 42:15′b-19′a; 44:17′-18′; 49:rev 9-11.

year and Hezekiah's accession year would be 729. The synchronistic notice in 2 Kgs 18:9-10, based on the regnal formula, likewise links Hoshea's seventh year and Hezekiah's fourth year to Shalmaneser V's campaign against Samaria in 725, again underscoring Hezekiah's accession year as 729. In contrast, the synchronistic notice in 2 Kgs 18:13, which is clearly independent of the regnal formulae, dates Sennacherib's campaign against Jerusalem to Hezekiah's fourteenth year. Since Assyrian sources clearly date Sennacherib's third campaign to 701,[6] that synchronism would date Hezekiah's accession to 715, not 729. Both dates cannot be correct, so the question is which synchronism is more probable.

When compared to Assyrian sources, the regnal formulae in 2 Kgs do not seem very reliable for this period. According to Tiglath-pileser III's inscriptions, Menahem was still king of Israel in 738 and probably part of 737.[7] According to 2 Kgs 15:23, Menahem's son Pekahiah succeeded his father and ruled two years in Samaria. That would bring one to 735 as the earliest date possible for Pekah the son of Remaliah to have seized the Israelite throne, and since he was killed in 732 according to Assyrian records, there is no way to give him a twenty-year reign over Israel in Samaria as 2 Kgs 15:27 does. Since 2 Kgs 15:25 identifies Pekah the son of Remaliah, the murderer of Pekahiah son of Menahem, as an officer in the service of Pekahiah, his "third man" (שָׁלִישׁוֹ, šālîšô), one cannot even assume that he was ruling as a rival to Pekahiah elsewhere in Israelite territory. There is simply no room for more than a three-year reign for Pekah the son of Remaliah. At best one might argue that he had been governing Israelite territory in the Transjordan for Pekahiah, since he is accompanied by fifty Gileadites when he murders his sovereign, and that he claimed his years as governor as part of his reign, but this is mere speculation.

Moreover, Ahaz appears to have assumed the throne of Judah at about the same time as Pekah son of Rema-liah seized the throne of Samaria, that is, in 735. The notice in 2 Kgs 17:1 that Hoshea came to the throne in the twelfth year of Ahaz makes no sense, since that would date the beginning of Ahaz's reign in 744, which is clearly too early, if Pekah the son of Remaliah campaigned with Rezin of Damascus against Ahaz's predecessor, Jotham, as 2 Kgs 15:37 claims. According to 2 Kgs 15:37, God began to send Rezin of Damascus and Pekah son of Remaliah against Judah in the days of Jotham, and 2 Kgs 16:5 dates the campaign of Rezin and Pekah against Jerusalem to the time of Ahaz. Since Pekah did not seize the throne of Samaria until 735, Rezin and Pekah's incursions into Judah can hardly date before that year, which suggests that Jotham died in 735 and was succeeded by his son Ahaz in the same year. But if Ahaz became king in 735 and ruled for sixteen years as the regnal formula in 2 Kgs 16:2 states, then Hezekiah's accession year should be 719, not 729 or 715. All these difficulties suggest that one take the figures in the regnal formulae with a big grain of salt.

Back in the early 1990s a student of mine, Jeffrey S. Rogers, wrote a Princeton Theological Seminary dissertation on the synchronisms and literary structure in 1–2 Kings.[8] He studied the synchronisms in 1–2 Kings in the light of such Mesopotamian parallels as the Synchronic Chronicle. He began with the assumption that the regnal formulae in the books of Kings derived from ancient sources, perhaps early royal chronicles, and that they were an ancient and reliable chronological framework on which to hang the narratives. This was an assumption he thought I wanted him to demonstrate in the dissertation. As his worked progressed, however, he came to doubt this assumption. He discovered that the numbers cited in the regnal formulae varied considerably in the different textual traditions. In contrast, he found that the numbers in the synchronisms standing outside the regnal formulae were far more fixed across the textual traditions. With some trepidation he suggested that, far from being an

---

6   See Grayson and Novotny, RINAP 3/1, pp. 10–11, texts 4:32-58; 6:1'-14'; 15:iii 1–iv 14'; 16: ii 76–iv 37; 17: ii 58–iii 81; 18:ii 1''–iii 36; and note also texts 19, 21, 22, 23, 26, and 34.

7   See Tadmor and Yamada, RINAP 1, p. 44, text 14:10; p. 69, text 27:3; p. 76, text 32:2; p. 79, text 35:iii 5.

8   Jeffrey S. Rogers, "Synchronism and Structure in 1–2 Kings and Mesopotamian Chronographic Literature" (PhD thesis, Princeton Theological Seminary, 1992).

ancient framework on which the narratives could be confidently hung, the regnal formulae were actually shaped by the surrounding narratives, the numbers dependent on the arrangement of the narratives in the different textual traditions. In any case, his work suggested that, when faced with a choice between a synchronism in the regnal formulae versus a synchronism standing outside the regnal formulae, the independent synchronism was apt to be more reliable, and certainly less subject to secondary editorial revision.

In the light of his study, and since the synchronisms for Ahaz in the regnal formulae have been shown to be unreliable on other grounds, I suggest that we take the independent synchronism in 2 Kgs 18:13 as a preferable point of departure. According to this synchronism, the accession of Hezekiah and thus the death of his predecessor, Ahaz, took place in 715. Assuming that Ahaz came to the throne in 735, that would give Ahaz a reign of twenty years. The regnal formula in 2 Kgs 16:2 says that Ahaz was twenty years old when he came to the throne and that he reigned sixteen years, but if those numbers were reversed, if Ahaz were sixteen when he came to the throne and he ruled twenty years, then those twenty years would agree with the time span 735–715 established on other grounds. Nor is this suggestion being too casual with numbers. There are a number of indications that Ahaz was just a youth when he came to the throne. In Isa 3:4, Isaiah threatens Judah with the rule of boys and women:

וְנָתַתִּי נְעָרִים שָׂרֵיהֶם וְתַעֲלוּלִים יִמְשְׁלוּ־בָם׃
(wĕnātattî nĕʿārîm śārêhem wĕtaʿălûlîm yimšĕlû-bām)
I will make boys their rulers,
and babes will rule over them.

But in Isa 3:12 that threatened judgment is stated as a current reality:

עַמִּי נֹגְשׂוֹ־ם עוֹלֵל וְנָשִׁים מָשְׁלוּ בוֹ
(ʿammî nōgĕśô-m ʿôlēl wĕnāšîm māšĕlû bô)
עַמִּי מְאַשְּׁרֶיךָ מַתְעִים וְדֶרֶךְ אֹרְחֹתֶיךָ בִּלֵּעוּ׃
(ʿammî mĕʾaššĕrêkā matʿîm wĕderek ʾōrḥōtêkā billēʿû)
O my people—whose oppressor is a child,
Over whom women rule—
O my people, your leaders are misleaders;
The course of your paths they have confused.

For this text and translation, see the commentary and textual notes at 3:12.

Of the Judean kings who came to the throne during Isaiah's ministry, Ahaz was clearly the youngest. The regnal formulae give the age of Jotham at accession as twenty-five (2 Kgs 15:33), Hezekiah as twenty-five (2 Kgs 18:2), and Manasseh as twenty-two (2 Kgs 21:2). Moreover, when Isaiah confronts Ahaz during the beginning stages of the Syro-Ephraimitic conflict shortly after Ahaz had come to the throne, it is interesting to note Isaiah's mode of address to the king. In his first oracle, Isaiah addresses Ahaz personally, using the singular imperative (7:4), before switching to the plural at the end of the oracle (7:9), when there seems to be some hint that the king and his counselors did not believe God's promise. In the second oracle, Isaiah again addresses Ahaz personally using the singular imperative (7:11), but when Ahaz rejects God's command by refusing to ask for the sign, Isaiah then switches to the plural imperative (7:13), apparently addressing the whole royal court, and he does not revert to the singular until the very end of the oracle in vv. 16-17. It is as if Isaiah had decided that it was not the young Ahaz, but his royal counselors, perhaps including prominent women such as the queen mother, who were calling the shots. If Ahaz was only sixteen at the time, rather than twenty, that might provide a better explanation for Isaiah's direct address to the royal court and his sarcastic dismissal of Judah's rulers as mere babes. Given the problem with the reliability of the information in the regnal formulae, perhaps one should not give these numbers credence even as garbled figures, but, in any case, I am working on the hypothesis that Ahaz's reign lasted twenty years, from 735 to 715, and that correspondingly the oracle in Isa 14:28-32 should be assigned to the year 715.

But what is one to make of the claim that Ahaz never smote the Philistines, was only smitten by them? It seems odd to me that critical scholars can be quite skeptical and are willing to dismiss a dating notice as a late secondary addition if it creates problems for their reconstruction, and yet at the same time are willing to swallow the Deuteronomistic Historian's and Chronicler's accounts of Ahaz's reign as the whole truth. One would have thought that the example of Ahab would have made them more skeptical. The Deuteronomistic Historian had a theological bias against Ahab and his whole dynasty, and he

223

constantly refers to evil kings as walking in the way of the house of Ahab (1 Kgs 16:30; 21:20-26; 2 Kgs 8:18, 27; 9:7-9; 10:10-11; 21:3). He has very little good to say about Ahab, and if the Deuteronomistic Historian was our only source for Ahab, we would never have guessed that Ahab was one of the most powerful kings of Syria-Palestine in the mid-ninth century, capable of sending the largest chariot force to the coalition's campaign against Shalmaneser III in 854 BCE. One finds a similar animosity toward Ahaz on the part of both the Deuteronomistic Historian and the Chronicler. Both regarded Ahaz as an evil king for religious reasons (2 Kgs 16:2-4, 7-18; 2 Chr 28:1-4, 16-25), and, given that bias, one should not be surprised that neither records any military successes of Ahaz. Had Ahaz had any military successes against Philistia, there would be no reason to expect the Deuteronomistic Historian to record them. The Chronicler, while dependent on the Deuteronomistic History, is even more hostile to Ahaz, and his claim that Ahaz's submission to Tiglath-pileser III was of no benefit to Ahaz (2 Chr 28:20-21) is patently false, disagreeing even with his source in 2 Kgs 16:7-10. Ahaz and Judah survived, while its enemies, the Arameans of Damascus and Israel, were destroyed, and the Phoenicians and the Philistines were beaten into submission. Contrary to the Chronicler's claim (2 Chr 28:20), there is no evidence that the Assyrians attacked Judah. 2 Kings 16:6 and 2 Chr 28:5-15 claim that the Arameans and Israelites inflicted serious losses on Judah during the early stages of the Syro-Ephraimitic War, and, despite the semilegendary nature of the Chronicler's account, there is no reason to doubt the general claim. Isaiah 7:1-9 and the account of the enemy army's surprise march on Jerusalem in Isa 10:27d-34, an account originally about the Aramean and Israelite attack on Jerusalem, indicate that the Arameans and Israelites achieved an initial success against Judah, and that Judean towns as far south as Jerusalem were in an absolute panic.[9] 2 Kings mentions no Philistine incursions against Ahaz, but 2 Chr 28:18 does, and there is no reason to doubt that such incursions took place, though the date of these incursions is not so clear. One can think of two possible occasions. At the time of the Syro-Ephraimitic War, the Philistines may have made incursions into the Shephelah to distract Judah from the main attack, which was to be launched against Jerusalem by Aram and Israel. All three states were obviously interested in forcing Judah into their anti-Assyrian defensive alliance. Moreover, the Philistines and Arameans appear to have cooperated in putting the pressure on Israel that eventually resulted in Pekah the son of Remaliah, an ally and vassal of Rezin, replacing the pro-Assyrian dynasty of Menahem. Isaiah 9:10-11 speaks of Aramean attacks on Israel from the east and Philistine attacks from the west before speaking of intertribal warfare in Israel between Ephraim and Manasseh (Isa 9:20). It is also possible, maybe even probable, that the Philistines made incursions into Judean territory early in the major revolt against Sargon II in 720. This revolt led by Hamath and supported by Samaria and the Philistines, indeed by almost all the Syria-Palestinian states except Judah, put the pro-Assyrian Ahaz in a very precarious position, and it would not be surprising if the surrounding states had again tried to pressure him into joining the revolt, though it appears that he remained loyal to Assyria despite his difficult predicament.

Nonetheless, even if Philistia struck Ahaz some serious blows in the beginning of the Syro-Ephraimitic War in 735 and again in the beginning of the Hamath revolt in 720, that is not the whole story. One has to ask how Ahaz responded once the Assyrian army arrived and the Philistines had to pull their forces from the Judean front to face the Assyrians. Hosea 10:5, which characterizes the rulers of Judah as those who move boundary markers, suggests that once the Assyrians forced the Israelites to abandon their assault on Jerusalem in order to defend their own territory, the Judean army moved north to expand their border at Israel's expense. Such actions would be consonant with Judah's alliance with Assyria, since loyal vassals were expected to assist Assyria in its military campaigns against its enemies. Despite the lack of explicit sources, it is also probable that Ahaz would have joined in the attack on Philistia, especially in 720, and especially along his border, when the Assyrian attack into the Philistine heartland drew their forces from Judah's border. Ahaz would almost certainly have

9   See my article, "Isaiah and His Children," in Ann Kort and Scott Morschauser, eds., *Biblical and Related Studies Presented to Samuel Iwry* (Winona Lake, IN: Eisenbrauns, 1985) 193–203, esp. 201, and the earlier literature cited there.

attempted to regain the territory he had lost to the Philistines, and in retaliation for the Philistine attacks on his territory, it is doubtful that he would have shown the isolated Philistine outposts any mercy. One should not expect the hostile Deuteronomistic Historian, much less the even more hostile Chronicler, to preserve any such positive notice of Ahaz's victories, and the Assyrian annals seldom mention the contribution of their vassals to Assyrian conquests. In short, there is no substantive basis to deny categorically that Ahaz ever smote the Philistines.

Before addressing the assumed identity of the serpent and the smoke from the north, let us turn to the historical circumstances of 715 that may have provoked this oracle.[10] Sometime after Sargon II put down the general rebellion in Philistia in 720, Azuri, the Philistine king of Ashdod began writing letters to the surrounding states trying to reignite rebellion against Assyria in the west. The Assyrians got word of his actions and removed him from his throne, replacing him with his brother Ahimeti. This action presupposes the presence of an Assyrian force in Philistia sufficient to impose an unpopular action on the populace. We know from Sargon's annals that such a force was present along the border with Egypt in 716–715, so one should probably date Azuri's removal to 716–715. Sometime after the Assyrian army withdrew, however, the populace drove Ahimeti, the Assyrian puppet, out of town and replaced him with a commoner, perhaps a Greek or Cypriot adventurer,[11] named Yamani or Yadna. Yamani then resumed the correspondence with the surrounding states, trying to get them to join him in a revolt against Assyria. As Sargon says in one of his inscriptions,

> To the kings of the land of the Philistines, the land of Judah, the land of Edom, the land of Moab, and those who dwell by the sea, all of whom were responsible for tribute and presents to Aššur, my lord, they sent lies

and seditious words in order to make them enemies with me. To Pharaoh king of Egypt, a ruler who could not save them, they carried their present, and they kept asking him for military help.[12]

Sargon eventually responded to this seditious activity, sending an army commanded by his *turtannu*, who sacked Ashdod in 711. According to Isaiah 20, however, Isaiah spent three years demonstrating in Jerusalem against joining this Ashdod-led alliance against Assyria, which means that the diplomatic contact between Ashdod and Jerusalem had been going on since as early as 714. Moreover, Isaiah 20 suggests that Nubia and its Egyptian vassals were seen as the real force behind this planned revolt. A combined Nubian and Egyptian army had already fought against Assyria in Philistine territory in the failed revolt of 720, so it was not unthinkable that the Nubians might intervene again. In fact, Isaiah 18 suggests that Nubian messengers had actually appeared in Jerusalem to encourage Judah to join in the Ashdod-led revolt, but whose success was clearly dependent on major Nubian and Egyptian military assistance.

Unfortunately, we do not know whether Azuri's seditious activity began while Ahaz was still alive, or whether it started immediately after his death, perhaps emboldened by the death of this longtime pro-Assyrian Judean. It is also possible that it started during the last years of Ahaz's reign, and that Ahaz is the one who reported Azuri to the Assyrians. If so, the death of Ahaz in 715 and the accession of Hezekiah, a king whose coronation service may have suggested a more anti-Assyrian bent,[13] could have led to rejoicing in Philistia and could have encouraged the Ashdodites to throw out Ahimeti and resume plotting revolt. Isaiah, who was certainly not pro-Assyrian, was nonetheless adamantly opposed to Judah's joining in these defensive alliances, and, as Isaiah 20 indicates, he actively opposed the alliance with Ashdod and their Nubian and Egyptian allies. In contrast, he

---

10 For a fuller discussion of these events and the sources for them, see my "Egypt, Assyria, Isaiah," 265–83; and my "Egyptian and Nubian Oracles," 201–9.

11 See the discussion of this point in the articles mentioned in the preceding note.

12 Sargon's Annals of year 711: K1668b + D.T. 6 VII.b, lines 25-33; see Andreas Fuchs, *Die Annalen des Jahres* *711 v. Chr. nach Prismenfragmenten aus Ninive und Assur* (SAAS 8; Helsinki: Neo-Assyrian Text Corpus Project, 1998); cf. Fuchs, *Die Inscriften Sargons II*; and Grant Frame, "The Inscription of Sargon II at Tang-i Var," *Or* 68 (1999) 31–37.

13 For this reading of Isa 8:23b–9:6, see my "Whose Child Is This?" 115–29.

urged a quiet faith in the promises God had made to the Davidic dynasty and God's city Zion. Isaiah's response to the messengers from Ashdod and Nubia in Isaiah 18 and 20 is essentially the same as that to the messengers of the nation in 14:32: "Yahweh has founded Zion, and in it the poor of his people will find refuge." The similarity is so striking, partly because all three oracles come out of the same historical context.

The serpent symbolism for these two enemies of Philistia, the dead king and his successor, is quite striking, and far from being an argument against the identity of these kings as Judean, it actually lends weight to that identity and undercuts the attempt to identify them as Assyrian. Snake symbolism, clearly borrowed from Egypt, is well attested in Judean stamp seals from the late eighth century.[14] The seals often show cobras in a protective stance above and on either side of the sundisk, presumably a symbol of kingship. A number of Judean seals from this period also contain two-winged or four-winged cobras, the winged or flying seraphs of Isa 6:2; 14:29; and 30:6. On these seals the sundisk is absent, and the winged seraph alone seems to symbolize Judean kingship. These winged seraphs also appear on at least two of the bronze bowls taken as booty or tribute from Palestine by Tiglath-pileser III during his campaigns in 734–732. On one, preserved in a watercolor from the 1850s, a two-winged seraph mounted on a pole stands facing outward in a protective gesture on either side of a winged dung beetle mounted on a pole.[15] Another bowl, which I actually photographed in a glass display case in either the British Museum or while it was on loan in the Berlin Museum,[16] has a dung beetle embossed in the center of the bowl, and on the two outside registers, among some other figures, are a series of two-winged pole-mounted seraphs facing outward in a protective gesture standing on either side of a stylized tree, perhaps an asherah. It is widely accepted that the dung beetle was a symbol of Judean kingship in the late eighth century, particularly under Hezekiah, though whether this was for religious or political reasons is still debated,[17] and it is clear both from the presence of the pole-mounted seraph in the royal Jerusalem temple and from Isaiah's vision of the winged seraphim in attendance on Yahweh, the divine king, that the winged seraphs were protective spirits closely associated with Judah's imperial god, and hence protectors of his chosen Davidic kings.

There is no comparable evidence to link serpents, winged or not, with Assyrian kingship. Winged serpents are relatively rare in Assyrian art, and while Assyrian kings often describe themselves with metaphors involving lions or wild bulls, Assyrian royal inscriptions using metaphors comparing Assyrian kings to serpents are rare, if they exist at all. Moreover, Isaiah uses lion (5:29) and bull imagery (10:13) to refer to Assyrian kings, and it is likely that his usage is simply mirroring Assyrian royal propaganda. Why then would he choose the unusual snake imagery, if he wanted to characterize an Assyrian king? It is far more likely that he chose this serpentine imagery precisely because it was so closely associated with Judean royal theology, and thus the use of this imagery supports the identification of the two rulers as the Judean kings Ahaz and Hezekiah.

---

14   See Keel, *Jahwe-Visionen*; N. Avigad and B. Sass, *Corpus of West Semitic Stamp Seals* (Jerusalem: Israel Academy of Sciences and Humanities, 1997); and see my articles listed in the following two notes.

15   A reproduction of this drawing is found in my "The Visual Elements in Isaiah's Vision in Light of Judean and Near Eastern Sources," in Joyce Rilett Wood, John E. Harvey, and Mark Leuchter, eds., *From Babel to Babylon: Essays on Biblical History and Literature in Honour of Brian Peckham* (LHBOTS 455; New York: T&T Clark, 2006) 197–213, fig. 1, p. 205.

16   See fig. 1 in my "The Rod That Smote Philistia: Isaiah 14:28-32," in David S. Vanderhooft and Abraham Winitzer, eds., *Literature as Politics, Politics as Literature: Essays on the Ancient Near East in Honor of Peter Machinist* (Winona Lake, IN: Eisenbrauns, 2013) 393.

17   See already Yigael Yadin, "A Note on the Nimrud Bronze Bowls," *ErIsr* 8 (1967) 6; for the continuing discussion, see F. M. Cross, "King Hezekiah's Seal Bears Phoenician Imagery," *BAR* 25, no. 2 (1999) 42–45, 60; Meir Lubetski, "King Hezekiah's Seal Revisited: Small Object Reflects Big Geopolitics," *BAR* 27, no. 4 (2001) 44–51, 59; Robert Deutsch, *Messages from the Past: Hebrew Bullae from the Time of Isaiah through the Destruction of the First Temple* (Tel Aviv: Archaeological Center Publications, 1999) 51; and the online publication by Daniel Sarlo, "Winged Scarab Imagery in Judah: Yahweh as Khepri," http://www.academia.edu/5562359/Winged_Scarab_Imagery_in_Judah_Yahweh_as_Kephri (2014) 1–16.

The "smoke coming from the north," however, could hardly refer to either Judean king, since a Judean campaign against Philistia would come from the west, not the north. Moreover, the imagery in v. 31 that describes this smoke as an enemy army that has no straggler in its ranks has its closest parallel in Isa 5:26b-28, which describes the swift approach of a presumably Assyrian army that is thoroughly professional, fully manned, and totally prepared. Nonetheless, there is no need to identify the future threat of an enemy army "from the north" with the "rod that smote Philistia" in the past.

If this oracle was given in 715 after the death of Ahaz and the accession of Hezekiah in response to Philistine diplomatic messages to Hezekiah urging him to join with Ashdod and their Nubian and Egyptian supporters in a planned revolt against Assyria, then there is no compelling reason to identify the smoke from the north with the rod that smote Philistia. The Philistines were happy that the pro-Assyrian Ahaz was dead, because they expected the more nationalistic Hezekiah to be more amenable to joining their coalition. Isaiah's response to the Philistines' diplomatic maneuver is to pour cold water on their hopes. He claims that Hezekiah will be an even more dangerous opponent than Ahaz had been. The oracle, while ostensibly addressed to the Philistines, is actually intended primarily for Hezekiah and his royal advisors. The whole point of the oracle is to influence the answer that the Judean court gives to the Philistine initiative, as v. 32 makes perfectly clear. The same is true in both Isaiah 18 and 20. Oracles ostensibly addressed to Nubian and Egyptian messengers and their Philistine allies are really intended primarily for the Judean court. If Hezekiah and his court heed the warnings against the Philistines and their Nubian-Egyptian allies and instead rely on the promises God made to Zion, they will, in effect, refuse to join the Philistine alliance and continue Ahaz's hostile stance toward Philistia. One should note that Hezekiah did, in fact, wage war against Philistia. According to the Deuteronomistic Historian, Hezekiah "attacked the Philistines as far as Gaza and its territory, from watchtower to fortified city" (2 Kgs 18:8). Precisely when these attacks took place is not indicated, but it is possible they came early in Hezekiah's reign, perhaps in the Ashdod conflict of 711 BCE, when Hezekiah remained a loyal vassal of the Assyrians and as a loyal vassal took advantage of the Philistine disaster to expand his borders. From the Assyrian records, we know that, after he rebelled against Sennacherib in 705 BCE, Hezekiah continued to bully the Philistines, imprisoning in Jerusalem Padi, the Philistine ruler of Ekron, who had remained loyal to Assyria, but there is no reason to limit Hezekiah's depredations against Philistia to this late period of his rebellion against Assyria. Nonetheless, in the Ashdod conflict of 714–711 BCE, the primary threat to Philistia would come not from Judah but from Assyria, against whom Philistia was revolting. This is explicitly stated in Isa 20:4, clearly alluded to by the reference to "the smoke from the north" in 14:31, and implicitly, as the agent of God's judgment on Nubia, in Isa 18:5-6.

Bibliography

Beck, B. L., "The International Role of the Philistines during the Biblical Period" (PhD diss., Southern Baptist Theological Seminary, 1980) 146–50.

Begrich, J., "Jesaja 14, 28-32: Ein Beitrag zur Chronologie der Israelitisch-judäischen Königszeit," *ZDMG* 86 (1932) 66–79; reprinted in Begrich, *Gesammelte Studien zum alten Testament* (TB 21; Munich: C. Kaiser, 1964) 121–31.

Brunet, G., *Essai sur l'Isaïe de l'histoire* (Paris: A. & J. Picard, 1975) 154–57.

Childs, *Assyrian Crisis,* 59–61.

Fullerton, K., "Isaiah 14:28-32," *AJSL* 42 (1925) 80–109.

Gitin, S., "The Philistines in the Prophetic Texts: An Archaeological Perspective," in Jodi Magness and Seymour Gitin, eds., *Hesed ve-emet: Studies in Honor of Ernest S.* Frerichs (BJS 320; Atlanta: Scholars Press, 1998) 273–90.

Gosse, Bernard, "Isaïe 14:28-32 et les traditions sur Isaïe d'Isaïe 36–39 et Isaïe 20:1-6," *BZ* n.s. 35 (1991) 97–98.

Haak, R. D., "The Philistines in the Prophetic Texts," in Jodi Magness and Seymour Gitin, eds., *Hesed ve-emet: Studies in Honor of Ernest S.* Frerichs (BJS 320; Atlanta: Scholars Press, 1998) 37–51.

Irwin, W. A., "The Exposition of Isaiah 14:28-32," *AJSL* 44 (1927) 73–87.

Jenkins, A. K., "Isaiah 14, 28-32: An Issue of Life and Death," *FO* 21 (1980) 47–63.

Kedar-Kopfstein, B. A., "A Note on Isaiah 14:31," *Textus* 2 (1962) 143–45.

Onwurah, E., "Isaiah 14: Its Bearing on African Life and Thought," *BiBh* 13 (1987) 29–41.

Roberts, J. J. M., "The Rod That Smote Philistia: Isaiah 14:28-32," in David S. Vanderhooft and Abraham Winitzer, eds., *Literature as Politics, Politics as Literature: Essays on the Ancient Near East in Honor of Peter Machinist* (Winona Lake, IN: Eisenbrauns, 2013) 381–95.

Savignac, J. de, "Les 'Seraphim,'" *VT* 22 (1972) 320–25.

Tadmor, Hayim, "The Campaigns of Sargon II of Assur: A Chronological-Historical Study," *JCS* 12 (1958) 22–40, 77–100.

——, "Philistia under Assyrian Rule," *BA* 29 (1966) 86–102.

Wiseman, D. J., "Flying Serpents?" *TynBul* 23 (1972) 108–10.

Wyatt, Nicholas, "The Hollow Crown: Ambivalent Elements in West Semitic Royal Ideology," *UF* 18 (1986) 421–36.

15

Isaiah 15–16 appears to represent a single, coherent oracle against Moab, but it apparently incorporates an older oracle (see 16:13), and one may wonder how much Moabite poetry about her key sites, or Moabite lament literature for that matter, may have influenced the Israelite prophet. Jeremiah's presumably later oracle against Moab (Jeremiah 48) seems influenced by this text, though opinions may differ on the direction of influence.[1] The text is quite difficult, and the difficulty is increased both by our insufficient knowledge of Moabite geography and by our lack of detailed knowledge of Moabite history in the late eighth century on into the early sixth century. The text seems to presuppose a major enemy attack on Moab which threatens its national existence, but the identity of the attacker is never given, a point irrelevant to the contemporaries of the prophet, who would not have needed this information from him, but which makes the task of the modern interpreter quite difficult. One could think of the invasion of any number of Assyrian monarchs, but it is equally possible that the disaster involved Arab tribes from the desert steppe expanding their zone of occupation at the expense of the Moabite settlements. I interpret the text as Isaianic, but only because it is in the Isaiah collection and because nothing in the text, in my opinion, compels a later date. The prophet sees this attack as the beginning of the end for Moab as an influential power, an end that will occur within three years. This expectation was certainly not realized in Isaiah's lifetime, but many of Isaiah's expectations were not realized in his time frame (his expectations for the end of Assyrian rule over Judah; Isa 8:23b—9:6; 10:12-19; 14:24-27; 30:27-33; 33:13-24), and the lack of fulfillment of a prophetic word is an insufficient basis for denying the word to a particular prophet.

1/   An Oracle concerning Moab:
        Because in the night[a] Ar[b] was plundered,[c]
        Moab was destroyed;[d]
        Because in the night[a] Kir[e] was plundered,[c]
        Moab was destroyed;

2/   He went up to the temple,[f] and Dibon[g] to the high places[h] to weep,
        Over Nebo and over Medeba[i] Moab is wailing;[j]
        On every head[k] there is baldness,
        Every beard[l] is trimmed.

3/   In its streets[m] they have girded[n] on sackcloth,
        Upon its roofs and in its squares[o] everyone wails,[p]
        Streaming down[q] with weeping.

4/   Heshbon and Elealeh cried out;
        Their voice was heard as far as Jahaz.
        That is why the armed men[r] of Moab shout in alarm,[s]
        His soul quivers[t] within him.

5/   My heart cries out for Moab,[u]
        Her fugitives[v] are as far as Zoar,[w]
        To Eglath-Shelishiyyah;[x]
        Indeed in the ascent of Luhith[y] he goes up weeping,
        Indeed on the way of Horonaim[z] they raise a shout of destruction.[*a]

6/   Indeed the waters of Nimrim are become desolate,
        For the grass has dried up,
        The new growth has failed,
        There is no verdure.[*b]

7/   That is why the increase he made
        And their stored supplies,[*c]
        They carry away across the Wadi of the Willows.[*d]

8/   For the cry has circled the border of Moab,
        As far as Eglaim its wailing,[*e]
        And to Beer-elim its wailing.

1   Wildberger has a long discussion of the various possibilities and their defenders, though he opts for the priority of Isaiah (2:605).

9/	For the waters of Dimon*[f] are full of blood,
	Yet I will place upon Dimon*[f] even more;*[g]
	I will give a thorough drenching*[h] to those of Moab who escape,
	Even to the remnant of the land.
16:1/	Send young rams to the ruler of the land*[i]
	From Sela*[j] in the desert
	To the mountain of daughter Zion.
2/	And it will come to pass*[k] that like a fluttering bird,
	Like an outcast nestling,
	So will be*[l] the daughters of Moab
	By the fords of the Arnon.*[m]
3/	Bring counsel,*[n]
	Make judgment,*[o]
	Place your shade like the night
	In the middle of noontime,
	Hide those driven away,
	Do not reveal the fugitive.*[p]
4/	Let the outcasts of Moab*[q] sojourn in you,
	Be a shelter for them*[r] from before the plunderer.
	When the oppressor*[s] has ceased,
	The destruction*[t] has ended,
	And tramplers have vanished*[u] from the land,
5/	There will be established in steadfast love a throne,
	And there will sit upon it in faithfulness in the tent of David*[v]
	A ruler and seeker*[w] of justice
	And zealous for righteousness.
6/	We have heard of the pride of Moab—
	He is very proud*[x]—
	Of his arrogance,*[y] and his pride, and his rage;*[z]
	His boasting is dishonest.[ta]
7/	Therefore Moab will wail,[tb]
	For Moab let everyone wail,
	For the raisin-cakes of Kir-hareset
	You will moan, yes stricken.[tc]
8/	For the vineyard[td] of Heshbon languishes,[te]
	The vine of Sibmah,[tf]
	Whose clusters once made drunk the lords of the nations,[tg]
	To Jazer they reached,
	They strayed to the desert;
	Whose shoots were rampant,
	They crossed the sea.[th]
9/	That is why I weep with the weeping of Jazer
	For the vine of Sibmah;
	I drench you with my tears,[ti]
	O Heshbon and Elealeh,
	For over[tj] your fruit harvest,
	And over your grain harvest,
	The shout has ceased.[tk]
10/	And joy and rejoicing are removed[tl] from the farmland,
	And in the vineyards there is no shouting or cheering;[tm]
	The treader no longer treads[tn] wine in the winepresses,
	The shout you have brought to an end.[to]
11/	That is why my bowels moan for Moab like a lyre,
	And my insides for Kir-hares.[tp]
12/	And it will be[tq] when it is seen that Moab has failed[tr] on the high place,
	Then he will go to his sanctuary[ts] to pray,
	But he will not succeed.[tt]
13/	This is the word which Yahweh has spoken to Moab long ago.
14/	And now Yahweh has spoken saying,[tu]
	In three[tv] years according to the years of a hired man,

230

The weight of Moab will become light
In spite of all[tw] the large multitude,[tx]
And the remnant will be very few,[ty]
Of no consequence.[tz]

Textual Notes

a MT בְּלֵיל (bĕlêl), "in the night"; 1QIsaᵃ and 4QIsaᵒ בלילה.

b MT עָר (ʿār), Ar; 1QIsaᵃ עיר מואב, "the city of Moab." LXX omits the word.

c MT שֻׁדַּד (šuddad), "was plundered"; 1QIsaᵃ שודד. LXX omits either this or the following verb.

d MT נִדְמָה (nidmâ), "was destroyed"; 1QIsaᵃ ונדמה, "and was destroyed"; the copulative means that 1QIsaᵃ misconstrued the line as "for the city of Moab was plundered in the night, and was destroyed."

e MT קִיר־מוֹאָב (qîr-môʾāb), "Kir (the city of) Moab"; 1QIsaᵃ עיר מואב, "the city of Moab." 4QIsaᵒ קיר סו]אב, "Kir, Moab.". One could also read 4QIsaᵒ as a construct chain with MT and presumably 1QIsaᵃ, but I reject that syntactical analysis and see the line and clause division between Kir and Moab, "Kir was plundered, Moab was destroyed." The versions all interpret as a construct chain, "the wall of the Moab/Moabites" (LXX, Vg., Syr.) or "the city of Moab" (Tg.), though this leads LXX to omit either the initial or the final verb, Syr. and Tg. to insert a copulative before the final verb, and Vg. to leave it hanging in a somewhat indeterminate syntactical relationship to the preceding clause. Both Ar and Kir, however, are to be understood as the proper names of particular and distinct cities in Moab, though the two names are put in parallel precisely because both names are derived from synonymous terms, both meaning "city".

f MT עָלָה הַבַּיִת (ʿālâ habbayit), "he went up to the temple"; so also 1QIsaᵃ. This clause gave the versions difficulty. Syr. and Tg. attached the following proper noun and read "they went up to the temple/s of Dibon"; Vg. has "the house (palace?) went up and Dibon to the heights"; and LXX has the odd reading λυπεῖσθε ἐφ᾽ ἑαυτοῖς, ἀπολεῖται γὰρ καὶ Λεβηδων, "Grieve for yourselves, for also Lebedon will perish."

g MT וְדִיבֹן (wĕdîbôn), "and Dibon"; 1QIsaᵃ ודיבון. As observed in the preceding note, Syr. and Tg. lack the copulative.

h MT הַבָּמוֹת (habbāmôt), "the high places"; 1QIsaᵃ הב’מות, "the high places"; LXX renders with a second person plural verb: οὗ ὁ βωμὸς ὑμῶν, ἐκεῖ ἀναβήσεσθε κλαίειν, "where your altar is, there you will go up to weep."

i MT מֵידְבָא (mêdĕbāʾ), "Medeba"; 1QIsaᵃ מידבה (a variant orthography of the same name). LXX may omit this word with its ἐπὶ Ναβαυ τῆς Μωαβίτιδος, "over Nebo of the Moabite."

j MT יְיֵלִיל (yĕyēlîl), "he wails, will wail"; 1QIsaᵃ יליל. LXX has the second person plural imperative ὀλολύζετε, "wail!"

k MT בְּכָל־רֹאשָׁיו (bĕkol-rōʾšāyw), "upon all his heads"; 1QIsaᵃ בכול ראושו.

l MT כָּל־זָקָן (kol-zāqān), "every beard"; 1QIsaᵃ וכל זקן, "and every beard." LXX has πάντες βραχίονες κατατετμημένοι, "all arms will be gashed." The other versions stay with MT.

m MT בְּחוּצֹתָיו (bĕḥûṣōtāyw), "in his streets"; 1QIsaᵃ בחוצותיה, "in her streets." The masculine singular suffix in MT is odd, since the other suffixes with the same reference in the verse are feminine singular. There is a masculine singular suffix in v. 2, so one might argue that the antecedent shifts back and forth here between Moab (m.) and one of its cities (f.), but I am inclined to think the masculine singular suffix here is simply an error due to attraction to v. 2. Read the feminine singular suffix with 1QIsaᵃ and LXX.

n MT חָגְרוּ (ḥāgĕrû), "they girded on"; 1QIsaᵃ חגרו, "they girded on." LXX continues with its plural imperative, but it inserts an additional verb: ἐν ταῖς πλατείαις αὐτῆς περιζώσασθε σάκκους καὶ κόπτεσθε, "in her wide streets gird yourself with sackcloth and mourn."

o MT וּבִרְחֹבֹתֶיהָ (ûbirḥōbōtêhā), "and in its squares"; 1QIsaᵃ וברחובתיה.

p MT כֻּלֹּה יְיֵלִיל (kullōh yĕyēlîl), "everyone wails"; 1QIsaᵃ כלה יהליל, preserving the internal heh of the hiphil imperfect. LXX maintains the plural imperative.

q MT יֹרֵד (yōrēd), "streaming, going down"; the reference is to the flowing of tears (cf. Ps 119:136; Lam 1:16; 3:38; Jer 9:17; 13:17; 14:17); 1QIsaᵃ וירד. The insertion of the conjunction in 1QIsaᵃ is secondary.

r For MT's חֲלֻצֵי מוֹאָב (ḥălūṣê môʾab), "the armed men of Moab," the unpointed 1QIsaᵃ has חלצי מואב, which could be vocalized as ḥălāṣê môʾab, "the loins of Moab," which apparently lies behind LXX's ἡ ὀσφὺς τῆς Μωαβίτιδος, "the waist of Moab." The other versions support MT.

s MT יָרִיעוּ (yārîʿû), "they are shouting"; 1QIsaᵃ ירע. The versions all understand this verb in the sense of "crying out" or "wailing," but the hiphil of the verb רוע normally means "to raise a war cry," while here the sense would seem to be some sort of response of fear or terror to the outcry from Heshbon and Elealeh. One suggestion is to read ירעו (yārĕʿû), "they quivered, trembled, were apprehensive," from the verb ירע (so Gray, 280, 282), but the parallel verb in the next line also seems to be from ירע, and the repetition of the same word in poetic parallelism, while attested, does not produce very elegant poetry. Another suggestion is to read רעדו (rāʿādû), "they trembled" (so Kaiser, *Jesaja 13–39*, 49 n. 6), which would make a good parallel to ירע, "to quiver," but that would require a major emendation.

t MT יְרֵעָה (yārĕʿâ), "she quivered"; 1QIsaᵃ ירע. The attentive reader will note a constant shifting back and forth between singular and plural forms. This is because in Hebrew a people is often personified as an individual, though the actual individuals who make up the people can also be referred to as a group in the plural.

u LXX has "the heart of Moabitis cries aloud within her."

v MT בְּרִיחֶהָ (bĕrîḥehā), "her fugitives"; 1QIsaᵃ ברחוה. LXX and Syr. apparently read ברוחה, "within her, in her spirit." Vg. understands בְּרִיחֶהָ as "her bars," that is, the bars locking her city gates.

w MT עַד־צֹעַר ('ad-ṣōʿar), "as far as Zoar"; 1QIsaᵃ עד צוער. LXX and Vg. vocalize the place-name as Σηγωρ or Segor.

x MT עֶגְלַת שְׁלִשִׁיָּה ('eglat šĕlišîyâ), Eglath-Shelishiyyah, perhaps "The-Third-Heifer," referring to a third town in the same general area; 1QIsaᵃ עגלת שלישיה. The versions do not appear to take Eglath-Shelishiyyah as a place-name; LXX renders δάμαλις γάρ ἐστιν τριετής, "for she is a three-year-old heifer," and Vg., Syr., and Tg. have similar renderings that appear to take the expression as appositional, modifying Zoar.

y MT הַלּוּחִית (hallûḥît), "of the shelf, of Luhith"; 1QIsaᵃ הלוחות.

z MT חֹרֹנָיִם (ḥôrōnayim), "Horonaim"; 1QIsaᵃ חורונים.

*a MT זַעֲקַת־שֶׁבֶר יְעֹעֵרוּ (zaʿăqat-šeber yĕʿōʿērû), "a cry of destruction they raise"; 1QIsaᵃ זעקת שברי ערו, but the last two words are at the very end of the line, which may have led to a confusing spacing of the letters. LXX has βοᾷ σύντριμμα καὶ σεισμός, "she cries aloud, 'Destruction and an earthquake!'"

*b MT יֶרֶק לֹא הָיָה (yereq lōʾ hāyâ), "there is no verdure"; 1QIsaᵃ ירוק לוא אהיא. LXX reduces the last three lines to two: καὶ ὁ χόρτος αὐτῆς ἐκλείψει· χόρτος γὰρ χλωρὸς οὐκ ἔσται, "and its grass will fail, for there will be no green grass."

*c MT וּפְקֻדָּתָם (ûpĕquddātām), "their stored supplies"; 1QIsaᵃ ופק דתם; there are ink blobs marking apparent erasures before and after the ד and after the ת.

*d MT עַל נַחַל הָעֲרָבִים יִשָּׂאוּם ('al naḥal hāʿărābîm yiśśāʾûm), "across the Wadi of the Willows they carry them"; 1QIsaᵃ על נחל ערבי תישאום, "across the Arabian wadi they carry them"; the ת prefix on the verb is probably a misread final mem that belongs on the end of the preceding word. MT's reading is far superior, and is supported by 1QIsaᵇ. LXX garbles the verse very badly, μὴ καὶ οὕτως μέλλει σωθῆναι; ἐπάξω γὰρ ἐπὶ τὴν φάραγγα Ἄραβας, καὶ λήμψονται αὐτήν, "Even so, will she be saved? For I will bring Arabs to the ravine, and they will take her." All the versions struggled with the meaning of the verse, which will be discussed below.

*e LXX simplifies and abbreviates by omitting the first יְלָלָתָה (yilēlātāh), "her wailing": συνῆψεν γὰρ ἡ βοὴ τὸ ὅριον τῆς Μωαβίτιδος τῆς Αγαλλιμ, καὶ ὀλολυγμὸς αὐτῆς ἕως τοῦ φρέατος τοῦ Αιλιμ, "for her cry has reached the border of Moabitis of Agallim, and her wailing as far as the well of Ailim." Vg. is much closer to the Hebrew.

*f MT דִּימוֹן (dîmôn), Dimon; 1QIsaᵃ has דיבון (dîbôn), Dibon; LXX has Ρεμμων (Rimmon), misreading the dalet as a resh. Vg. has Dibon. Tg. and 1QIsaᵇ appear to follow MT, while Syr. agrees with 1QIsaᵃ and Vg. I read with MT, because the text does not otherwise repeat place-names that have already been mentioned. The same place-name may be hidden under the corrupt reading גַּם־מַדְמֵן תִּדֹּמִּי (gam-madmēn tiddommî), "you also will

be silenced, O Madmen [Dung Heap]," Jer 48:2); the original reading was probably "you also will be silenced, O Dimon." It is dubious that the Moabites actually named any of their towns "Dungheap"!

*g MT כִּי אָשִׁית עַל דִּימוֹן נוֹסָפֹת (kî ʾāšît ʿal dîmôn nôsāpōt), "yet I will place on Dimon even more," similarly Vg. and Syr.; LXX goes its own way, ἐπάξω γὰρ ἐπὶ Ρεμμων Ἄραβας καὶ ἀρῶ τὸ σπέρμα Μωαβ καὶ Αριηλ καὶ τὸ κατάλοιπον Αδαμα, "for I will bring Arabs upon Rimmon, and I will take away the seed of Moab and Ariel and the remnant of Adama."

*h Reading אֲרַוֶּה ('arweh), "I will water," with 1QIsaᵃ; MT has אַרְיֵה ('aryê), "lion"; Vg. follows MT. LXX reads אריאל ("Ariel," the hearth of an altar, cultic official, or possibly some sort of warrior; see the Mesha stela, line 12, and cf. 2 Sam 23:20; Isa 29:1; Ezek 43:15-16) rather than "lion." The introduction of a lion in this context seems very abrupt, whereas the idea that Yahweh would add to the blood in the water by drenching the survivors with more of the same seems less disruptive.

*i MT שִׁלְחוּ־כַר מֹשֵׁל־אֶרֶץ (šilḥû-kar mōšēl-ʾereṣ), "send a young ram to the ruler of the land"); 1QIsaᵃ שלחו כרמשל ארץ involves a simple failure to divide the words correctly. LXX's Ἀποστελῶ ὡς ἑρπετὰ ἐπὶ τὴν γῆν, "I will send as though it were creeping things upon the land," appears to be reading שלח כרמשל לארץ with the initial verb either a participle or an infinitive used in place of a first person finite verb. The singular kar is quite odd as any sort of desperate offering, so it is likely it should be emended to the plural karîm, an easy emendation, since the final mem of the plural could easily be lost by haplography before the initial mem of mōšel. One might take "ruler of the land" as a vocative and thus the subject of the imperative, but "ruler" is singular, and the imperative is plural, so the rendering as an adverbial accusative is more likely. Another possible emendation is to read שלחו כרם ממשל ארץ, "send young rams from the ruler of the land."

*j MT מִסֶּלַע (misselaʿ), "from Sela"; 1QIsaᵃ מסלה.

*k MT וְהָיָה (wĕhāyâ), "and it will come to pass that"; 1QIsaᵃ והיא with an erasure between the י and the א. LXX omits this verb.

*l MT תִּהְיֶינָה (tihyênâ), "so will be (the daughters of Moab)"; 1QIsaᵃ תהינה. LXX reads the verb as a second person singular and takes "daughter Moab," which it reads as singular, as a vocative, ἔσῃ γὰρ ὡς πετεινοῦ ἀνιπταμένου νεοσσὸς ἀφῃρημένος, θύγατερ Μωαβ, "For you will be like a nestling taken away from a flying bird, O daughter Moab."

*m LXX totally misconstrues this last line and takes it with the following verse, ἔπειτα δέ, Αρνων, πλείονα βουλεύου, "And then, O Arnon, take further counsel."

*n MT kĕtîb הָבִיאוּ (hābîʾû), "bring," is a masculine plural imperative, but read with the qĕrēʾ הָבִיאִי (hābîʾî), "bring," a feminine singular imperative. This agrees with all the feminine singular forms at the end of the verse—שִׁיתִי (šîtî), "put"; צִלֵּךְ (ṣillēk), "your (f. sg.) shade"; סַתְּרִי (sattĕrî), "hide"; אַל־תְּגַלִּי ('al-tĕgallî), "do not reveal"—and it agrees with feminine Zion as the subject of these verbs and the referent of the pronominal suffix. 1QIsaᵃ has הביו, though the final letter could easily be read as י. Tg.

and Syr. both read feminine forms consistently through the verse.

*o MT עָשׂוּ (ʿāśû), "make"; so also 1QIsaᵃ, but correct to the feminine singular imperative עֲשִׂי (ʿāśî), "make," for the reasons mentioned in the previous note.

*p MT נֹדֵד (nôdēd), "fugitive"; 1QIsaᵃ נודד. There appears to be a wordplay here with the same word in v. 2, where the Moabites are compared to birds fleeing their nest. LXX makes hash of the whole verse: πλείονα βουλεύου, ποιεῖτε σκέπην πένθους αὐτῇ διὰ παντός· ἐν μεσημβρινῇ σκοτίᾳ φεύγουσιν, ἐξέστησαν, μὴ ἀπαχθῇς, "take further counsel, and make for her a shelter for mourning for all time. They flee in darkness at noon; they were astonished; do not be taken away."

*q MT נִדְּחַי מוֹאָב (niddāḥay môʾāb), "my scattered ones from Moab"; so Vg. (profugi mei Moab, "my fugitives from Moab") involves an unusual suffix in the middle of a construct chain or an unusual vocalization of the masculine plural construct; correct to niddĕḥê môʾāb, "the fugitives of Moab."

*r MT הֱוִי־סֵתֶר לָמוֹ (hĕwî-sēter lāmô), "be a shelter to them"; so also 1QIsaᵃ. LXX mistakenly reads a plural form and misconstrues the clause as ἔσονται σκέπη ὑμῖν ἀπὸ προσώπου διώκοντος, "they shall be a shelter to you from the face of the pursuer."

*s MT הַמֵּץ (hammēṣ), "the oppressor," an uncertain word from the possible root מיץ (myṣ), "to squeeze"; 1QIsaᵃ המוץ (perhaps hammôṣ, "the chaff, dust"; so Vg., Syr.); but read חמוץ (ḥāmôṣ), "oppressor"; so Tg., and cf. Isa 1:17. LXX has ἡ συμμαχία σου, "your alliance."

*t MT שֹׁד (šōd), "destruction"; so 1QIsaᵃ; Syr. and Tg. have "the plunderer," and Vg. reads it as a passive (miser, "the afflicted"); LXX apparently read שַׂר (śar, "prince, ruler"), since it has ὁ ἄρχων ἀπώλετο, "the ruler perished."

*u MT תַּמּוּ רֹמֵס (tammû rōmēs), "the trampler have vanished"—note the lack of agreement between the masculine plural verb and the masculine singular participle!); 1QIsaᵃ makes both sg תמ רומס (tam rōmēs), "the trampler has vanished"; LXX, Vg., and Syr. read a singular, while Tg. has the plural. Either read the singular with 1QIsaᵃ or emend the participle to the plural תמו רמסים (tammû rōmĕsîm), "the tramplers have vanished." The loss of the plural mimation before the following preposition min would be easy to explain. The singular reading could have been introduced when the singular šōd, "destruction," was misunderstood as the agent of destruction rather than the destruction itself, and a singular rōmēs, "trampler," was then preferable in apposition to it.

*v MT בְּאֹהֶל דָּוִד (bĕʾōhel dāwid), "in the tent of David"; 1QIsaᵃ באוהל דויד.

*w MT שֹׁפֵט וְדֹרֵשׁ (šōpēṭ wĕdōrēš), "a ruler and seeker of"; 1QIsaᵃ שופט ודורש.

*x MT גֵּא מְאֹד (gēʾ mĕʾōd), "he is very proud"; 1QIsaᵃ גאה מואד (gēʾeh mĕʾōd), "he is very proud."

*y MT גַּאֲוָתוֹ (gaʾăwātô), "his arrogance"; 1QIsaᵃ גאתו.

*z MT וְעֶבְרָתוֹ (wĕʿebrātô), "and of his rage"; so 1QIsaᵃ and Vg. LXX appears to read this as a second person singular verb form: τὴν ὑπερηφανίαν ἐξῆρας, "you have removed his arrogance."

†a MT לֹא־כֵן בַּדָּיו (lōʾ-kēn baddāyw), "not so is his boasting"; 1QIsaᵃ

לכן בדיו. LXX renders baddāyw as ἡ μαντεία σου, "your divination," while Vg. has fortitudo eius, "his strength."

†b MT לָכֵן יְיֵלִיל מוֹאָב (lākēn yĕyĕlîl môʾāb), "therefore Moab will wail"; so Syr. and Vg.; 1QIsaᵃ ולכן לא יליל מואב ("and therefore will not Moab wail?"); LXX also seems to have the negative here.

†c For the last two lines LXX has τοῖς κατοικοῦσιν Δεσεθ μελετήσεις καὶ οὐκ ἐντραπήσῃ, "you will take care of those who dwell in Deseth, and you will not be ashamed." Vg. has the equally odd, his qui laetantur super muro cocti lateris loquimini plagas suas, "to those who rejoice over a wall of baked brick, you will tell their blows."

†d The form שַׁדְמוֹת (šadmôt) appears to be a plural form, but the only two times it is construed with a verb, the verb form is singular (here and in Hab 3:17). It seems to refer to a vineyard (note the parallelism) or field constructed by terracing (Wildberger, 2:627; HALOT, 1423).

†e MT אֻמְלָל (ʾumlāl), "languished"; 1QIsaᵃ אמללה.

†f 1QIsaᵃ has suffered a major haplography, omitting everything after the שִׂבְמָה (sibmâ), "Sibmah," of v. 8 through "Sibmah" of v. 9.

†g MT בַּעֲלֵי גוֹיִם הָלְמוּ שְׂרוּקֶּיהָ (baʿălê gôyim hālĕmû śĕrûqqêhā), "whose clusters made drunk the lords of the nations"; LXX apparently reads בלע (blʿ), "to swallow," for בַּעֲלֵי (baʿălê), "lords of": καταπίνοντες τὰ ἔθνη καταπατήσατε τὰς ἀμπέλους αὐτῆς ἕως Ιαζηρ, "as you swallow the nations trample her vineyards as far as Yazer." Vg. makes "lords" the subject of the verb: domini gentium exciderunt flagella eius, "the lords of the nations cut its shoots"; so also Syr.

†h LXX garbles the end of the verse: οὐ μὴ συνάψητε, πλανήθητε τὴν ἔρημον· οἱ ἀπεσταλμένοι ἐγκατελείφθησαν, διέβησαν γὰρ τὴν ἔρημον, "you will not come together, you will wander in the wilderness; those who were sent have been forsaken, for they crossed the wilderness."

†i MT אֲרַיָּוֶךְ דִּמְעָתִי (ʾărayyāwek dimʿātî); one should correct the reading of the first word to ארויך (ʾărawwāyēk dimʿātî), "I drench you with my tears"; Vg. "I make you drunk with my tears"; Syr. "I will drench you with your tears"; 1QIsaᵃ misreads the first word as ארזיך (ʾarzêk), "your cedars," which appears to be the source of LXX τὰ δένδρα σου κατέβαλεν, "your trees he cut down."

†j MT כִּי עַל (kî ʿal), "for upon"; 1QIsaᵃ על <<ל>> כיא (there is an erased lamed before ʿal).

†k Most of the versions take הֵידָד (hêdād), "shout," either as the shout of or a figure for the oppressing or trampling enemy; so Vg., Tg., Syr.; LXX has ὅτι ἐπὶ τῷ θερισμῷ καὶ ἐπὶ τῷ τρυγήτῳ σου καταπατήσω, καὶ πάντα πεσοῦνται, "because upon your harvest and upon your vintage I will trample, and all will fall." Nonetheless, the noun normally refers to the joyous shout of workers bringing in the harvest, and the following verse suggests that such shouting has ceased. For that reason, it is best to take the verb נפל (nāpal), "to fall," here in the sense of "cease, stop."

†l MT וְנֶאֱסַף (wĕneʾĕsap), "and is gathered up, taken away" (the

latter sense corresponds to *HALOT* meaning 4 of the *qal* [p. 74]); 1QIsaᵃ וגסף.

†m MT לֹא־יְרֻנָּן לֹא יְרֹעָע (*lōʾ-yĕrunnān lōʾ yĕrōʿāʿ*), "there is no shout-ing, no cheering"; 1QIsaᵃ לוא ירננו ולוא ירועע, "they do not shout, and there is no cheering."

†n MT לֹא־יִדְרֹךְ הַדֹּרֵךְ (*lōʾ-yidrōk haddōrēk*), "the treader no longer treads"; 1QIsaᵃ לוא ידרוך הדורך.

†o MT הֵידָד הִשְׁבַּתִּי (*hêdād hišbattî*), "I/you brought the shout to an end"—*hišbattî* could be analyzed as either as the first person common singular *hiphil* perfect of *šabat*, "to stop," or as the archaic second person feminine singular of the same form. Since the references in the first person seem to be sympathetic to Moab, the second person feminine singular may be correct, suggesting that just as "the shouts of joy over *your* harvest have ceased" so "*you* have brought to an end your shouts of joy." LXX has simply πέπαυται γάρ, "for it has ceased," which has led some scholars to emend the verb to הֻשְׁבַּת (*hošbāt*), "is brought to an end," the third person feminine singular *hophal* perfect (so Clements, 156), but the subject of this passive verb would be הֵידָד (*hêdād*), "shout of joy," which is masculine singular. For that reason Gray (p. 293) suggests reading the third person masculine singular stative verb שָׁבַת (*šābat*), "the shouting has ceased."

†p LXX apparently read לְקִיר חָרֶשׂ (*lĕqîr ḥāreś*), "for Qir-hares," as לקיר חדש, which it renders ὡσεὶ τεῖχος, ὃ ἐνεκαίνισας, "as a wall, which you renewed"; Vg. maintains its earlier rendering, *ad murum cocti lateris*, "for a wall of baked brick."

†q MT וְהָיָה (*wĕhāyâ*), "and it will be"; 1QIsaᵃ יהיה, "it will be." The versions support MT. 1QIsaᵃ's reading appears to be a linguistic updating to the (vernacular) state of Second Temple Hebrew, where the *waw*-consecutive was dying out.

†r MT כִּי־נִלְאָה (*kî-nilʾâ*), "that (*Moab*) has failed"; 1QIsaᵃ כי בא, "that (*Moab*) has entered." The versions support MT.

†s MT אֶל־מִקְדָּשׁוֹ (*ʾel-miqdāšô*), "to his sanctuary"; 1QIsaᵃ אל מקדשו.

†t MT וְלֹא יוּכָל (*wĕlōʾ yûkāl*), "but he will not succeed"; 1QIsaᵃ ולוא יכל.

†u MT לֵאמֹר (*lēʾmōr*), "saying"; 1QIsaᵃ לאמור.

†v MT בְּשָׁלֹשׁ (*bĕšālōš*), "in three"; 1QIsaᵃ בשלוש.

†w MT בְּכֹל (*bĕkōl*), "in all"; 1QIsaᵃ בכול.

†x MT הֶהָמוֹן הָרָב (*hehāmôn hārāb*), "the large multitude"; 1QIsaᵃ המון הרב.

†y MT מְעַט מִזְעָר (*mĕʿaṭ mizʿār*), "very few"; 1QIsaᵃ מעט מצער (for the second word the scribe originally wrote *mṣr*, then marked through the *ṣ* and wrote *z* above the erased letter.

†z MT לֹוא כַּבִּיר (*lôʾ kabbîr*), "of no strength, consequence"; 1QIsaᵃ ולוא כבוד, "and no weight, glory." LXX seems to support 1QIsaᵃ, while Vg. follows MT.

Commentary

The oracle against Moab begins with the announcement that Moab was destroyed, because in the night the cities of Ar and Kir, both names meaning "city," were plundered (v. 1). One could take the two synonymous names as mere poetic parallelism referring to one and the same city, but that seems unlikely in the context. Ar was a city marking the traditional northern border of Moab near but just south of the Arnon (Num 21:5; Deut 2:18-19), and Kir is probably the same as Kir-Hareseth, an important Moabite city, perhaps the capital, on the central plateau (2 Kgs 3:25), farther south of the border. Ar is often identified with Rabbah, and Kir is traditionally identified with *el-Kerak*, a bit farther south, though neither of these identifications is absolutely certain. The Moabite response to this disaster is to go up to the temple or high places to lament (v. 2). Three new sites are mentioned, all north of the plundered cities. Dibon, located three miles north of the Arnon next to the modern town of Dhiban, had been a Reubenite inheritance (Josh 13:9, 17), before it was taken by Moab. The great Moabite king Mesha in his famous stela claimed to be from Dibon and mentions several construction projects in his royal quarters there (see also Jer 48:18, 22).[2] Nebo, farther north, usually identified as *Kh. el-Muḥayyit* on the southeastern slopes of Mount Nebo, some seven kilometers northwest of Medeba, had also been a Reubenite city (Num 32:2-3, 38), but had been retaken by Mesha (Mesha Stela; Jer 48:1, 22). Medeba, modern Madaba thirty kilometers south of Amman, had also been an Israelite city before being recaptured by Mesha (Mesha Stela, lines 7-9). There is

---

2 For a convenient English translation of the Moabite Stone, see *ANET*, 320–21. There is a more recent translation by K. A. D. Smelik in William W. Hallo and K. Lawson Younger, eds., *The Context of Scripture* (3 vols.; Leiden: Brill, 2003) 2:137–38, but even it is lacking André Lemaire's convincing restoration of the reading *bt[d]wd*, "the house of [D]avid," in line 31 of the text. See "'House of David' Restored in Moabite Inscription: A new restoration of a famous inscription reveals another mention of the 'House of David' in the ninth century B.C.E.," *BAR* 20, no. 3 (1994) 30–37.

poetic ambiguity in the phrasing. Do the Moabites wail upon the high places in Nebo and Medeba, or do they wail over Nebo and Medeba for the fate that is threatening them? Probably the poet intended both. All the people have shaved their heads and beards as a sign of mourning; they dress in sackcloth, and on the housetops and in the squares they all wail and their tears of weeping stream down their faces (v. 3; cf. Jer 48:37-38).

Then Heshbon and Elealeh cry out so loudly that their voice is heard as far away as Jahaz (cf. Jer 48:34). Heshbon, identified with *Ḥesbān*, located on the western edge of the plateau six miles north of Medeba, had been taken by the Amorite Sihon from the Moabites, then from him by the Israelites (Num 21:21-34; Deut 1:4; 2:24; 3:2, 6; 4:46; 29:7; Num 32:37-38; Josh 12:2; 13:15-23; 21:38-39; Judg 11:19-26), before being retaken by the Moabites (Jer 48:2, 34-35), and it was later claimed by the Ammonites (Jer 49:3). Elealeh, usually identified with *Khirbet el-ʿÂl*, some 1.5 miles northeast of Heshbon, had also been alloted to Reuben (Num 32:3, 37) before being retaken by the Moabites (see Isa 16:9; Jer 48:34). Jahaz (Num 21:23; Deut 2:32; Josh 13:18; 21:36; Judg 11:20; Moabite Stela 15-20) must be located southeast of Heshbon and north of Dibon, though the precise identification with a modern site is still uncertain. It is often identified with modern Khirbet el-Medeiyineh, but Khirbet Libb and Khirbet Iskander have also been suggested.[3] This loud, penetrating outcry has apparently demoralized the troops of Moab with terror (v. 4), though there is textual uncertainty here (see the textual notes).

In response to Moab's disaster, the prophet's heart cries out for Moab (v. 5). Her fugitives flee as far as Zoar, usually identified with *Ġōr eṣ-ṣāfiye* in the plain at the southeastern end of the Dead Sea,[4] though some scholars defend a location north of the Dead Sea,[5] and Eglath-Shelishiyyah, whose identification is uncertain. The fugitives go up the ascent of Luhith weeping (cf. Jer 48:5), and on the way to Horonaim (cf. Jer 48:3, 5, 34) they raise a cry about their destruction. The ascent of Luhith is probably to be located in the southwest portion of the Moabite plateau on a road leading up to the escarpment before descending the plateau to circle around the southern end of the Dead Sea, and Horonaim is probably to be located along the same road. The modern sites of Kathrabba, southwest of Kerak, and Ai, a town just east of Kathrabba, make good candidates for these ancient sites, though the identifications are by no means certain. The uncertainty about the precise location of these sites leaves the geographical plotting of the flight of the Moabite refugees uncertain, though they certainly fled south from the affected area of Ar and Kir. The precise location of the waters of Nimrim (cf. Jer 48:34) is uncertain,[6] but most scholars identify them with the Wadi *en-Numeirah*,[7] a small stream flowing into the Dead Sea just above the Wadi *el-Ḥesā*, about eight to ten miles above its southern end. The drying up of these waters and the resulting loss of pasture land (v. 6) forces these refugees to carry the goods they have saved farther south, across the Wadi of the Willows, which is to be identified with the Wadi *el-Ḥesā* at the southern end of the Dead Sea (v. 7).

The cry has reached all of Moab's borders (v. 8). The wailing has reached as far as Eglaim, which is sometimes

---

3   Most of the proposed locations for the sites mentioned in these two chapters may be found in Siegfried Mittmann and Götz Schmitt's *Tübinger Bibelatlas* (Stuttgart: Deutsche Bibelgesellschaft, 2001) map B IV 6, or on the excellent maps in J. M. Miller's "Moab and the Moabites," in J. Andrew Dearman, ed., *Studies in the Mesha Inscription and Moab* (Archaeology and Biblical Studies 2; Atlanta: Scholars Press, 1989) 1–40. Some may also be located on the online topographical maps found on Google Earth, but one must be prepared for a dizzying array of variant spellings in the different sources. See also the maps of north and south Moab included here as figs. A and B.

4   So M. C. Astour, "Zoar," *ABD* 6:1107.

5   So Simons, *Geographical and Topographical Texts;* and apparently Brian C. Jones, "Zoar," *IDB* 5, 990–91.

6   Nelson Glueck identified it with the modern wādi nimrīn (= wādi šuʿēb), opposite Jericho (*Explorations in Eastern Palestine* [4 vols. in 5; AASOR 14, 15, 18-19, 25/28; New Haven: American Schools of Oriental Research, 1934–51] vol. 18–19, 213; vol. 25/28, 367 n. 1048); Glueck, "Some Ancient Towns in the Plains of Moab," *BASOR* 91 (1943) 11–13.

7   See already A. Musil, *Moab: Topographischer Reisebericht,* vol. 1 of *Arabia Petraea* (3 vols.; Vienna: A. H. Holder, 1907–08) 157, 170; and note the discussion in Wildberger, 2:616.

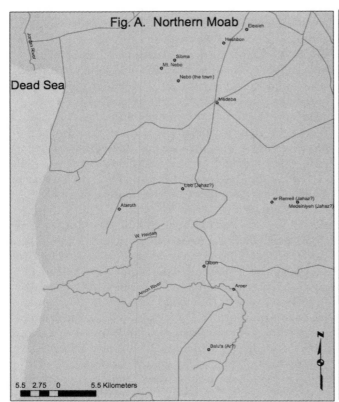

Fig. A. Northern Moab

Jordan River
Dead Sea
Elealeh
Heshbon
Sibma
Mt. Nebo
Nebo (the town)
Mādeba
Iahaz (Jahaz?)
Ataroth
er Remeil (Jahaz?)
Medeiniyeh (Jahaz?)
W. Heidan
Dibon
Arnon River
Aroer
Balu'a (Ar?)

5.5 2.75 0   5.5 Kilometers

Fig. B. Southern Moab

Arnon River
Aroer
Dead Sea
Balu'a (Ar?)
Waters of Dimon
Dimon
Rabba (Ar?)
Wadi el-Kerak
Wadi 'Isal
Kir
Luhith
Horonaim
Waters of Nimrim
Zoar
Wadi al-Hasa

5.5 2.75 0   5.5 Kilometers

N

Map was created by Timothy Evans and Alexandra Locher, Grand Valley State University (Feb. 12, 2015) using ArcGIS software version 10.1 (Environmental Systems Research Institute, Redlands, California). Projected coordinate system was Universal Transverse Mercator Zone 36 North.

Map was created by Timothy Evans and Alexandra Locher, Grand Valley State University (Feb. 12, 2015) using ArcGIS software version 10.1 (Environmental Systems Research Institute, Redlands, California). Projected coordinate system was Universal Transverse Mercator Zone 36 North.

identified with *rujm el-Jilīme*, southeast of Kerak,[8] and to Beer-elim, perhaps a site on the Wadi *eth-Themed*, north of the River Arnon,[9] but this identification is disputed, and the site may also be south of the Arnon.[10] In short, the uncertainty in the identification of either site makes it impossible to be certain of the geographical extent of the area affected by this lament, except to say that it spread throughout the Moabite homeland. Verse 9 describes the waters of Dimon as filled with blood, presumably the blood of slain Moabites, and the speaker, apparently the deity Yahweh, goes on to say that he will impose yet more of the same on the Moabites who escaped, inundating

the remnant of the land. Dimon, if the reading is correct (see the textual notes), is probably to be identified with *Khirbet Dimneh*, about two and a half miles northwest of Rabba, overlooking the Wadi *Ibn Hammād*, a major wadi system that could explain the expression "the waters of Dimon." The imagery suggests that significant bloodshed has taken place among the Moabite inhabitants south of the Arnon and threatens that far more is expected to overtake the fleeing Moabite survivors.

At this point the text suggests that a major disaster has overtaken the center of Moabite settlements on the plateau south of the Arnon. The bloody fall of Ar and Kir

---

8   Simons, *Geographical and Topographical Texts,* §1259.

9   So Félix Marie Abel, *Géographie de la Palestine* (2 vols.; Paris: Gabalda, 1967) 1:461; Simons, *Geographical and Topographical Texts,* §441.

10   Wildberger (2:617) points out the extreme uncertainty of the proposed locations.

has resulted in a flood of refugees with their cries of woe fleeing both north and south, north across the Arnon toward the major cities there, and southwest across the Wadi *el-Ḥesā* and off the plateau toward the plains at the southern end of the Dead Sea.

Isaiah 16:1 is plagued by a number of textual and syntactic uncertainties, but it appears to contain a command to the Moabites to send an offering of young rams from Sela in the wilderness to the Judean ruler in Mount Zion, presumably to gain permission for the fleeing Moabite refugees in the south to find asylum in Judean territory. Verse 2 then switches to the north, to the fords of the Arnon, where the daughters of Moab, the pathetic Moabite refugees, are described as fluttering birds driven from their nests. Then v. 3 picks up on v. 1, and offers a series of feminine singular imperatives (see textual notes) addressed to Zion, urging her to take counsel, probably in response to the official Moabite entreaty (v. 1), and to provide shelter and protection for the refugees from Moab. She is to let the fugitives from Moab sojourn in her as resident aliens and to offer them protection from the enemy plundering Moab. When the oppressor has ceased, the destruction has ended, and the tramplers have vanished from the land of Moab, then a throne will be firmly established in steadfast love and there will sit on it faithfully in the tent of David a ruler who seeks justice and is zealous for righteousness (v. 5). This is a remarkable passage that ties the fulfillment of the promised ideal Davidide to the present merciful treatment of Judah's Moabite enemies in their hour of disaster and desperate need, and it is certainly congenial to the theology of the eighth-century Isaiah of Jerusalem.

But the appeal to be merciful does not ignore Moab's past arrogance. The Judeans, who now speak in the first person plural, acknowledge the great arrogance and false boasting of their Moabite enemies (v. 6). Therefore Moab will wail, and everyone will wail for Moab, and switching to the second person plural with the Moabites as the presumed subject, the prophet announces (v. 7), you will moan, crushed, for the lost raisin cakes of the destroyed Kir-hareset (presumably a fuller name for the plundered

Kir already mentioned). But the lament extends north of the Arnon, for the languishing vineyard of Heshbon and the vine of Sibmah (v. 8), whose clusters once inebriated the lords of the nations—perhaps a testimony to the international wine trade—and whose incredibly fruitful shoots once reached Jazer, strayed into the desert, and in hyperbole crossed the Dead Sea (cf. Jer 48:32). Sibmah (Num 32:3, 38; Josh 13:19; Jer 48:32-33) was obviously a famous wine-producing town near Heshbon. It is sometimes identified with Khirbet Qarn al-Qibsh about five kilometers southwest of Heshbon, but in the absence of Iron Age ruins there, other scholars have suggested a location farther south.[11] Jazer (Num 21:31-32; 32:1-5, 35; Josh 13:25; 2 Sam 24:5; 1 Chr 26:31; Jer 48:32) is probably to be identified with Kh. Jazzir, west of Amman, and about thirteen to fourteen miles north of Heshbon. The disaster that has spread from south of the Arnon is now afflicting the area to the north. In response, the prophet weeps like Jazer over the vines of Sibmah and drenches Heshbon and Elealeh, which he addresses in the vocative, with his tears, for the joyous shout of the harvesters has ceased and fallen silent over your (feminine singular, presumably referring to Heshbon) fruit and grain harvest (v. 9). The rejoicing and joy are removed from the farmland, and in the vineyards there is no shouting and cheering; no one treads out the grapes in the wine vats, for you (feminine singular, presumably still referring to Heshbon, which personifies Moab as a woman) have brought the joyous shout to an end (v. 10). If chap. 16 is correctly read as a continuation of chap. 15, the reason for this failure of the harvest is presumably the fear of an imminent enemy attack north of the Arnon following the disaster in the south. If the chapter is isolated from the preceding one, however, one might also consider drought or other causes as the source of the crop failures. Nonetheless, the prophet's following lament over Kir-hares (v. 11), presumably the same as Kir (15:1) and Kir-hareset (16:7), supports the unity of the two chapters and the military interpretation. The prophet's bowels moan for Moab like a lyre, and his innards growl for Kir-hares. Yet Moab's intercessions on the high place, and his

---

11   So M. Wüst, *Untersuchungen zu den siedlungsgeographischen Texten des Alten Testaments*, vol. 1, *Ostjordanland* (Beihefte zum Tübinger Atlas des Vorderen Orients, Reihe B 9; Wiesbaden: Reichert, 1975) 160; and Zecharia Kallai, *Historical Geography of the Bible: The Tribal Territories of Israel* (Jerusalem: Magnes Press; Leiden: Brill, 1986) 441.

prayers in the sanctuary will not succeed (v. 12). Yahweh has decreed this word of judgment on Moab long ago (v. 13), and within three years the glory of Moab and his great multitude will be left a small remnant of no significance (v. 14).

Bibliography

Abel, Félix-Marie, *Géographie de la Palestine* (2 vols.; Paris: J. Gabalda, 1967).

Alonso Schökel, L., *Estudios de poética hebrea* (Barcelona: J. Flors, 1963).

———, "Traducción de textos poéticos III. Isa. 15-16," *CB* 18 (1961) 336–46.

Bardtke, H., "Jeremia der Fremdvölkerprophet," *ZAW* 54 (1936) 240–62.

Barrick, W. Boyd, "The Bamoth of Moab," *Maarav* 7 (1991) 67–89.

Bartlett, J. R., "Edom," *ABD* 2:287–95.

———, "The Moabites and the Edomites," in D. J. Wiseman, ed., *Peoples of Old Testament Times* (Oxford: Clarendon, 1973) 229–58.

Bernhardt, K. H., "Beobachtungen zur Identifizierung moabitischer Ortslagen," *ZDPV* 76 (1960) 136–58.

Bonnet, C., "Echos d'un rituel de type adonidien dans l'oracle contre moab d'Isaïe (15)," *Studi Epigrafici e Linguistici* 4 (1987) 101–19.

Boraas, Roger S., and Siegfried H. Horn, *Heshbon 1971: The Second Campaign at Tell Ḥesbân. A Preliminary Report* (Andrews University Monographs 6; Berrien Springs, MI: Andrews University Press, 1973).

Carroll, Robert P., *Jeremiah: A Commentary* (OTL; Philadelphia: Westminster, 1986) 778–97.

Christiansen, Duane L., "Zephaniah 2:4-15: A Theological Basis for Josiah's Program of Political Expansion," *CBQ* 46 (1984) 669–82.

Cross, Frank Moore, and David Noel Freedman, *Early Hebrew Orthography: A Study of the Epigraphic Evidence* (New Haven: American Oriental Society, 1952).

Dearman, J. Andrew, "The Moabite Sites of Horonaim and Lulith," *PEQ* 122 (1990) 41–46.

———, ed., *Studies in the Mesha Inscription and Moab* (Archaeology and Biblical Studies 2; Atlanta: Scholars Press, 1989).

Dimant, Devorah, "Targum Jonathan to Isa XVI.6 and Jer XLVIII.29f.," *JSS* 18 (1973) 55–56.

Donner, Herbert, "Neue Quellen zur Geschichte des Staates Moab in der 2 Hälfte des 8. Jahrhunderts v.Chr.," *MIO* 5 (1957) 155–84.

Donner, Herbert, and H. Cäppers, "Die Restauration und Konservierung der Mosaikkarte von Madeba," *ZDPV* 83 (1967) 1–33.

Driver, G. R., "Notes on Isaiah," in Johannes Hempel and Leonhard Rost, eds., *Von Ugarit nach Qumran: Beiträge zur alttestamentlichen und altorientalischen Forschung. Otto Eissfeldt zum 1 September 1957* (BZAW 77; Berlin: A. Töpelmann, 1958) 42–48.

———, "Textual Problems," 38–40.

Easterly, Ellis, "Is Mesha's *qrḥḥ* Mentioned in Isaiah 15:2?" *VT* 41 (1991) 215–19.

Fohrer, Georg, "Vollmacht über Völker und Königreiche: Beobachtungen zu den prophetischen Fremdvölkersprüchen Anhand von Jer 46–51," in Josef Schreiner, ed., *Wort, Lied und Gottesspruch: Festschrift für Joseph Ziegler* (2 vols.; FB 1–2; Würzburg: Echter, 1972) 2:145–53.

Glueck, Nelson, *Explorations in Eastern Palestine* (4 vols. in 5; AASOR 14, 15, 18/19, 25/28; New Haven: American Schools of Oriental Research, 1934–51).

———, "Some Ancient Towns in the Plains of Moab," *BASOR* 91 (1943) 7–20.

Gosse, Bernard, "La nouvelle alliance et les promesses d'avenir se référant à David dans les livres de Jérémie, Ezéchiel et Isaïe," *VT* 41 (1991) 419–28.

Guillaume, A., "A Note on the Root ירע, ריע, and רעע in Hebrew," *JTS* 15 (1964) 293–95.

Hitzig, F., *Des Propheten Jonas Orakel über Moab kritisch vindicirt und durch Übersetzung nebst Anmerkungen erläutert* (Heidelberg: Mohr, 1831).

Hookermann, J., "[Is 15,5 *horonim*] Etymological theories 5," *BetM* 32, no.109 (1986) 124–34.

Jones, Brian C., *Howling over Moab: Irony and Rhetoric in Isaiah 15–16* (SBLDS 157; Atlanta: Scholars Press, 1996).

Kallai, Zecharia, *Historical Geography of the Bible* (Jerusalem: Magnes Press; Leiden: Brill, 1986).

Knauf, Ernst Axel, "Jeremiah xlix 1-5: Ein zweites Moab-Orakel im Jeremia-Buch," *VT* 42 (1992) 124–28.

Kuschke, A., "Historisch-topographische Beiträge zum Buche Josua," in Henning Graf Reventlow, ed., *Gottes Wort und Gottes Land: Hans-Wilhelm Hertzberg zum 70. Geburtstag am 16. Januar 1965 dargebracht von Kollegen, Freunden und Schülern* (Göttingen: Vandenhoeck & Ruprecht, 1965) 90–109.

———, "Horonaim and Qiryathaim: Remarks on a

Recent Contribution to the Topography of Moab," *PEQ* 99 (1967) 104–5.

——, "Jeremia 48 1-8: Zugleich ein Beitrag zur historischen Topographie Moabs," in A. Kuschke, ed., *Verbannung und Heimkehr: Beiträge zur Geschichte und Theologie Israels im 6. und 5. Jahrhundert v. Chr. Wilhelm Rudolph zum 70. Geburtstage dargebracht von Kollegen, Freunden und Schülern* (Tübingen: Mohr, 1961) 181–96.

Landes, G., "The Fountain at Jazer," *BASOR* 144 (1956) 30–37.

Miller, J. M., "Moab and the Moabites," in J. Andrew Dearman, ed., *Studies in the Mesha Inscription and Moab* (Archaeology and Biblical Studies 2; Atlanta: Scholars Press, 1989) 1–40.

Mittmann, S., "The Ascent of Luhith," in A. Hadidi, ed., *Studies in the History and Archaeology of Jordan I* (Amman: Department of Antiquities, 1982) 175–80.

——, "Das südliche Ostjordanland im Lichte eines neuassyrischen Keilschriftbriefes aus Nimrud," *ZDPV* 89 (1973) 15–25.

Musil, A., *Moab: Topographischer Reisebericht,* vol. 1 of *Arabia Petraea* (3 vols.; Vienna: A. H. Holder, 1907–8).

Nötscher, F., "Entbehrliche Hapaxlegomena in Jesaja," *VT* 1 (1951) 299–302.

Nyberg, H. S., "Studien zum Religionskampf im Alten Testament," *AR* 35 (1938) 329–87.

Olivier, H., "Archaeological Evidence Pertaining to a Possible Identification of Ar-Moab and Er-Rabbah," *NedTT* 30 (1989) 179–89.

Rabin, Ch., "Hebrew *Baddim* 'Power,'" *JSS* 18 (1973) 57–58.

Reider, J., "Contributions to the Scriptural Text," *HUCA* 24 (1952) 85–106.

Rendtorff, Rolf, "Zur Lage von Jaeser," *ZDPV* 76 (1960) 124–35; 82 (1966) 163–208.

Rudolph, W., "Jesaja XV–XVI," in D. Winton Thomas and W. D. McHardy, eds., *Hebrew and Semitic Studies Presented to Godfrey Rolles Driver in Celebration of His Seventieth Birthday, 20 August 1962* (Oxford: Clarendon, 1963) 130–43.

Saggs, H. W. F., "The Nimrud Letters, 1952: Part II, Relations with the West," *Iraq* 17 (1955) 126–60.

Sawyer, John F. A., and David J. A. Clines, eds., *Midian, Moab, and Edom: The History and Archaeology of Late Bronze and Iron Age Jordan and North-west Arabia* (JSOTSup 24; Sheffield: JSOT Press, 1983).

Schottroff, W., "Horonaim, Nimrim, Luhith und der Westrand des 'Landes Astaroth': Ein Beitrag zur historischen Topographie des Landes," *ZDPV* 82 (1966) 163–208.

Schwally, F., "Die Reden des Buches Jeremia gegen die Heiden: XXV.XLVI–LI," *ZAW* 5 (1888) 177–217.

Schwarzenbach, A., "Die geographische Terminologie im Hebräischen des Alten Testaments" (Diss., University of Zürich, 1954).

Segert, S., "Die Sprache der moabitischen Königsinschrift," *ArOr* 29 (1961) 197–267.

Simons, J., *Geographical and Topographical Texts.*

——, *Handbook for the Study of Egyptian Topographical Lists Relating to Western Asia* (Leiden: Brill, 1937).

Smothers, T., "Isaiah 15–16," in James W. Watts and Paul R. House, eds., *Forming Prophetic Literature: Essays on Isaiah and the Twelve in Honor of John D. W. Watts* (JSOTSup 235; Sheffield: Sheffield Academic Press, 1996) 70–85.

Timm, Stefan, *Moab zwischen den Mächten: Studien zu historischen Denkmälern und Texten* (Ägypten und Altes Testament 17; Wiesbaden: Harrassowitz, 1989).

Tushingham, A. D. T., "The Excavations at Dibon (Dhîbân) in Moab," *AASOR* 40 (1972) 1–172.

Ullendorff, E., "The Contribution of South Semitics to Hebrew Lexicography," *VT* 6 (1956) 190–98.

Van Zyl, A. H., *The Moabites* (Pretoria Oriental Series 3; Leiden: Brill, 1960).

Vaux, R. de, "Notes d'histoire et de topographie transjordaniennes," *Vivre et penser 1* (1941; replaced *RB* 1940–45 [*RB* 50–52]) 16–47.

Vera Chamaza, Galo W., *Die Rolle Moabs in der neuassyrischen Expansionspolitik* (AOAT 321; Münster: Ugarit-Verlag, 2005).

Vogel, E. K., "Bibliography of Holy Land Cities," *HUCA* 42 (1971) 1–96.

Winnet, Fred V., and William L. Reed, *The Excavations at Dibon (Dhîbân) in Moab* (AASOR 36–37; New Haven: American Schools of Oriental Research, 1957).

Woods, Julie, *Jeremiah 48 as Christian Scripture* (Princeton Theological Monographs 144; Eugene, OR: Pickwick, 2011).

Worschech, Udo, and Ernst Axel Knauf, "Dimon und Horonaim," *BN* 31 (1986) 70–95.

Worschech, Udo, *Die Beziehungen Moabs zu Israel und Ägypten in der Eisenzeit: Siedlungsarchäologische und siedlungshistorische Untersuchungen im Kernland Moabs (Arḍ el-Kerak)* (Ägypten und Altes Testament 18; Wiesbaden: Harrassowitz, 1990).

Wüst, Manfried, *Untersuchungen zu den siedlungsgeographischen Texten des Alten Testaments, 1: Ostjordanland* (Beihefte zum Tübinger Atlas des Vorderen Orients, Reihe B 9; Wiesbaden: Reichert, 1975).

Yalon, C. H., "Erklärung einiger Schriftstellen," *BetM* 11 (1965) 17–20.

17:1-14 Oracles against Damascus and Ephraim

17

1/ **Oracle concerning Damascus.[a]**
Damascus[a] is about to be removed from being a city,
And it shall become[b] a heap[c] of ruins.
2/ **Abandoned forever shall be the city;[d]**
It[e] will be for flocks,
And they will lie down, and there will be no one to drive them away.
3/ **And the fortress will cease from Ephraim,**
And the kingdom from Damascus;[f]
And the remnant of Aram[g] will be[h] like the glory of the sons of Israel,
Says[i] Yahweh of Hosts.
4/ **And it will come to pass on that day**
That the glory of Jacob[j] will become poor,[k]
And the fatness of his flesh[l] will become lean.[m]
5/ **And it will be as when one gathers the harvest of standing grain,[n]**
And his arm[o] harvests[p] the ears of grain;
And it will be as when one gleans ears in the valley of Rephaim.[q]
6/ **And there will be left in it a gleaning,[r]**
As in the shaking of an olive tree;
Two or three[s] berries[t] in the topmost[u] bough,
Four or five in the branches[v] of the fruit tree,
Says[w] Yahweh, the God[x] of Israel.
7/ **On that day man will gaze upon his maker,[y]**
And his eyes will look to the Holy One of Israel.
8/ **And he will not[z] gaze upon[*a] the altars,**
The work of his hands,[*b]
And what[*c] his fingers have made he will not regard,[*d]
Neither the asherim nor the incense stands.[*e]
9/ **On that day his fortified cities[*f] shall be**
Like the abandoned sites[*g] of the Amorites and the Hivites[*h]
Which they abandoned before the sons of Israel,
And there will be[*i] desolation.
10/ **For you have forgotten[*j] the God[*k] of your salvation,[*l]**
And the rock[*m] of your stronghold[*n] you have not remembered;
That is why, though you plant plantings for Naaman,[*o]
And (with) the shoot for a strange god[*p] you sow it,[*q]
11/ **Though on the day of your planting you cause it to grow,[*r]**
And on the morning of your sowing you cause it to bud,
The harvest vanishes[*s] on a day of sickness[*t] and mortal anguish.[*u]
12/ **Hey! Tumult of many nations,**
Who roar like the roaring of the seas,
And the noise of the peoples,[*v]
Who make a din[*w] like the noise of mighty[*x] waters—
13/ **The peoples[*y] make a din like the noise of many waters,[*z]**
But he will rebuke[†a] him, and he will flee far away,
He will be chased like the chaff of the mountains before the wind,
And like the tumbleweed before the storm.
14/ **At the time of evening there is terror,**
But before morning[†b] it is no longer;[†c]
This is the portion of those who would despoil us,
And the lot for those who would plunder us.[†d]

Textual Notes

a For MT's דמשק (*Dammā/eśeq*) 1QIsa^a has דרמשק (*Darmeśek*).
b MT וְהָיְתָה (*wĕhāyĕtâ*); 1QIsa^a והיית.
c MT's מְעִי מַפָּלָה (*mĕʿî mappālâ*), though supported by 1QIsa^a מעי מפלה, is problematic. While the noun עִי (*ʿî*), "ruin, pile of stones," is known, the noun מְעִי is otherwise unattested. LXX has only εἰς πτῶσιν, "unto a fallen ruin," which might suggest a reading לעי מפלה or even למפלה. In the latter case, מעי may simply be a partial dittography of the preceding מעיר. The double construction, though supported by Vg.'s *sicut acervus lapidum in ruina* ("like a stone heap in ruins") and Syr.'s *lḥwrbʾ wlmpwltʾ* ("to a ruin and to a collapsed ruin") is unusual. Cf. 23:13; 25:2.

d MT's עֲזֻבוֹת עָרֵי עֲרֹעֵר (ʿăzūbôt ʿārê ʿărōʿēr), "forsaken are the cities of Aroer," though supported by 1QIsaᵃ עזבות ערי עורערו, and Vg.'s *derelictae civitates Aroer*, is a longtime crux. Aroer on the Arnon, a Moabite city (Num 32:34; Deut 2:36; 3:12; passim), can hardly be correct, and neither the Aroer in Gad opposite Rabbat Ammon (Josh 13:25; Judg 11:33) nor the Judean Aroer (1 Sam 30:28) works any better. Apart from this dubious passage in Isa 17:2, there is no other evidence for an Aroer in Aramean territory. Moreover, one hardly expects the mention of a group of cities belonging to Aroer right after the mention of the single city, Damascus. Syr.'s "the cities of Adoer" (ʾdwʿyr) suggests the possibility of a confusion between the letters *resh* and *dalet*, and the same is suggested by LXX's καταλελειμμένη εἰς τὸν αἰῶνα ("it shall be abandoned for ever"). The original reading probably contained the expression עֲדֵי עַד (ʿădê ʿad), "forever" (Pss 83:18; 92:8; 132:12, 14; Isa 26:4; 65:18), which leaves possible several reconstructions: עזובה עיר עדי עד (ʿăzūbâ ʿîr ʿădê ʿad), "the city will be abandoned forever; עזובה עדי עד עיר (ʿăzūbâ ʿădê ʿad ʿîr), "abandoned forever will be the city"; or even עזובות עריה עדי עד (ʿăzūbôt ʿārêhā ʿădê ʿad), "abandoned will be its cities [referring to the cities ruled over by Damascus, the Aramean capital] forever."

e MT תִּהְיֶינָה (tihyeynâ) and 1QIsaᵃ תהינה are plural forms ("they will be"); the correction of עָרֵי (ʿārê), "the cities of," to עיר (ʿîr), "the city," would require the correction of תהיינה to תהיה (tihyê), "it will be."

f 1QIsaᵃ and Syr. have דרמשק for MT דַּמֶּשֶׂק (Dammeśeq), "Damascus."

g MT וּשְׁאָר אֲרָם (ûšĕʾār ʾărām), "and the remnant of Aram," 1QIsaᵃ, LXX, Vg.; Syr. has wšrkʾ dʾprym, "and the remnant of Ephraim."

h MT's plural יִהְיוּ (yihyû), "they will be," is supported by Vg. and Syr., but 1QIsaᵃ has the singular יהיה ("it will be"). LXX's translation is very loose: καὶ τὸ λοιπὸν τῶν Σύρων ἀπολεῖται· οὐ γὰρ σὺ βελτίων εἶ τῶν υἱῶν Ισραηλ καὶ τῆς δόξης αὐτῶν, "and the remnant of Syria will perish, for you are not better than the sons of Israel and their glory."

i MT נְאֻם (nĕʾūm), lit., "oracle of"; 1QIsaᵃ נואם.

j MT יַעֲקֹב (Yaʿăqōb); 1QIsaᵃ יקוב.

k MT יִדַּל (yiddal), "become poor," 1QIsaᵃ, Vg., Syr., Tg.; LXX has the noun ἔκλειψις, "a failing of the glory of Jacob."

l MT בְּשָׂרוֹ (bĕśārô), "his flesh," 1QIsaᵃ, Vg., Syr.; LXX (τῆς δόξης αὐτοῦ) and Tg. have "of his glory."

m MT יֵרָזֶה (yērāzeh), "will become lean," 1QIsaᵃ; LXX has σεισθήσεται, "will be shaken," apparently reading a form of זוע (zûaʿ).

n MT קָמָה (qāmâ), "standing grain," 1QIsaᵃ, LXX, Syr., Tg.; Vg. is interpretive *quod restiterit*, "what remains (standing)," but in some ways this catches the sense of the passage quite well, as the last half of the verse indicates. It is a picture of gleaning, not of a full harvest. Cf. esp. Deut 23:26; Ruth 2:15-17.

o MT וּזְרֹעוֹ (ûzĕrōʿô), "and his arm," 1QIsaᵃ, Vg., Syr., Tg.; LXX reads זֶרַע (zeraʿ), "seed," σπέρμα, though the Lucianic texts later corrected toward MT with a double reading: καὶ σπέρμα

σταχύων ἐν τῷ βραχίονι αὐτοῦ ἀμήσῃ, "and he shall reap the seed of the ears of grain in his arm."

p MT יִקְצוֹר (yiqṣôr), "he shall harvest," LXX, Vg., Syr., Tg.; 1QIsaᵃ has וקציר, "and the harvest," which is an error due to the preceding קציר.

q MT רְפָאִים (Rĕpāʾîm), "Rephaim," 1QIsaᵃ, Vg., Syr., have it as a proper name. Tg. translates it appropriately enough, "Valley of Giants," but LXX fails to recognize it as a proper name and renders it as "firm" (ἐν φάραγγι στερεᾷ, "in a firm ravine").

r MT עוֹלֵלֹת (ʿôlēlōt), "gleaning," 1QIsaᵃ (עוללות), Syr., Tg.; LXX has καλάμη, "straw," understanding it as the leftover from the grain harvest, while Vg. has *racemus*, "cluster."

s MT שְׁלֹשָׁה (šĕlōšâ), "three," 1QIsaᵃ שלושה.

t MT גַּרְגְּרִים (gargĕrîm), "berries," LXX, Tg.; 1QIsaᵃ has a copyist's error גדרים.

u MT בְּרֹאשׁ (bĕrōʾš), "in the topmost," 1QIsaᵃ ברואש.

v MT בִּסְעִפֶיהָ פֹּרִיָּה (bisʿîpeyhā pōrîyâ), "on its boughs the fruit tree," though perhaps supported by Vg. *in cacuminibus eius fructus eius*, "in its tops its fruit," cannot be correct. Either detach the suffix from the first word and read it as the article on the second word (בסעפי הפריה, "on the boughs of the fruit tree") or follow 1QIsaᵃ in simply omitting this suffix פריה, בסעפי, "on the boughs of (the) fruit tree." LXX and Syr. omit פריה.

w MT נְאֻם (nĕʾum), 1QIsaᵃ נואם.

x MT אֱלֹהֵי (ʾĕlōhê), "God of," 1QIsaᵃ אלוהי.

y MT עֹשֵׂהוּ (ʿōśēhû), "his maker," 1QIsaᵃ עושיהי (miscopied for עושיהו).

z MT וְלֹא (wĕlōʾ), "and not," 1QIsaᵃ ולוא.

*a MT יִשְׁעֶה אֶל (yišʿeh ʾel), "look to"; 1QIsaᵃ ישעה על ("gaze upon"), LXX, Vg., Syr., Tg. The 1QIsaᵃ reading with על is probably original (cf. 31:1). One should note, however, that אֶל (ʾel) and עַל (ʿal) are often interchanged, especially in Jeremiah and Ezekiel (so Gesenius, *Handwörterbuch*, 18th ed.), so the MT reading may be the result of Aramaizing influence.

*b MT מַעֲשֵׂה יָדָיו (maʿăśēh yādāyw), "the work of his hands," LXX, Vg., Syr., Tg.; 1QIsaᵃ מעשיו, "his works."

*c MT וַאֲשֶׁר (waʾăšer), "and what," Vg., Tg.; 1QIsaᵃ אשר, "what," LXX.

*d MT לֹא יִרְאֶה (lōʾ yirʾeh), "he will not regard," Vg., Tg.; 1QIsaᵃ ולוא יראה, "and he will not regard," LXX, Syr.

*e MT וְהָאֲשֵׁרִים וְהָחַמָּנִים (wĕhāʾăšērîm wĕhāḥammānîm), lit., "and the asherim and the incense stands," Tg.; 1QIsaᵃ האשרים והחמנים ("the asherim and the incense stands"), LXX δένδρα αὐτῶν οὐδὲ τὰ βδελύγματα αὐτῶν ("their trees nor their abominations"), Vg. *lucos et delubra* ("groves and temples"), Syr. "their idols and false gods."

*f MT עָרֵי מָעֻזּוֹ (ʿārê māʿuzzô), lit., "the cities of his stronghold," that is, "his fortified cities," 1QIsaᵃ (ערי מעוזו), Vg., Syr., Tg.; LXX αἱ πόλεις σου, "your cities."

*g MT כַּעֲזוּבַת (kaʿăzûbat), "like the abandoned site," Tg. ("like the fortress"); 1QIsaᵃ כעזובות ("like the abandoned sites"), LXX, Vg. Read the plural with 1QIsaᵃ.

*h MT הַחֹרֶשׁ וְהָאָמִיר (haḥoreš wĕhāʾāmîr), "of the Horesh and the Amir," 1QIsaᵃ החרש והאמיר is a long-standing crux. One

241

expects the names of peoples, but neither Horesh nor Amir is attested in that sense. LXX has οἱ Ἀμορραῖοι καὶ οἱ Εὑαῖοι, "the Amorites and the Hivvites," and, while in reverse order, suggests a possible emendation. The other versions seem to be attempting to make sense of the received but obscure Hebrew text: Vg. *sicut aratra et segetes*, "like the plows and the harvests," Syr. *ʾyk gwbʾ dḥrš wdʾmyr*, "like the pit of a sorcerer and of a commander," Tg. כְּכֶרֶךְ דְּחָרוּב וְאִתְחֲמַר, "like a fortress which is ruined and destroyed." Read הָאֱמֹרִי וְהַחִוִּי, "of the Amorites and the Hivites."

*i MT וְהָיְתָה (wĕhāyĕtâ), "and there will be," 1QIsaᵃ והייתה.

*j MT שָׁכַחַתְּ (šākaḥat), "you have forgotten," 1QIsaᵃ שכחתי, but it does not preserve this old second person feminine singular ending for the next verb זכרת.

*k MT אֱלֹהֵי (ʾĕlōhê), "the God of," 1QIsaᵃ אלוהי.

*l MT יִשְׁעֵךְ (yišʿēk), "of your salvation," 1QIsaᵃ, Tg.; LXX, Vg., Syr. have "God your Savior."

*m MT וְצוּר (wĕṣûr), "and the rock," 1QIsaᵃ; the versions all interpret the figure: LXX καὶ κυρίου, "and the Lord"; Vg., Syr. "and the strong one"; Tg. "and the fear of the strong one whose word."

*n MT מָעֻזֵּךְ (māʿuzzēk), "your stronghold," 1QIsaᵃ מעוזך; LXX, Vg. "your helper"; Syr. "your defender"; Tg. "your help."

*o MT נִטְעֵי נַעֲמָנִים (niṭʿê naʿămānîm), "plantings of/for Naaman," 1QIsaᵃ נטעי נעמונים; LXX has φύτευμα ἄπιστον, "an unfaithful planting"; Vg. *plantationem fidelem*, "a faithful planting"; Syr. "a comely planting"; Tg. "a select plant." Naaman was the name of a pagan god, Adonis, though the apparently plural form *naʿămānîm* is odd. One could explain it as a misunderstanding of *naʿmān + ma*—the singular plus mimation (so A. Jirku, "NIṬʿĒ NAʿAMANIM [Jes xvii 10 c] = NIṬʿĒ NAʿAMAN-MA," *VT* 7 [1957] 201–2), or one could see the construction as similar to the plurals *bĕʿālîm* and *ʿaštārôt* to designate the pagan "gods" and "goddesses," or the plural *ʾăšērîm* to designate the "sacred poles." If so, one might translate the phrase in Isaiah, "plantings for the pagan gods."

*p MT וּזְמֹרַת זָר (ûzĕmōrat zār), "and the shoot of/for a strange god," 1QIsaᵃ וזמורת זר; LXX καὶ σπέρμα ἄπιστον, "and a faithless seed"; Vg. *et germen alienum*, "and an alien seed"; Syr. "with alien shoots."

*q MT תִּזְרָעֶנּוּ (tizrāʿennû), "you sow it," 1QIsaᵃ תזרענו, Syr.; Vg. omits the suffix, and LXX omits the word entirely.

*r MT תְּשַׂגְשֵׂגִי (tĕśagśēgî), "you cause to grow"; 1QIsaᵃ went wild

with an extra consonant תשגגשגי (tĕśagśagśî), 4QIsaᵃ תשתגשגי (tištagśēgî); Syr. "a blossom will go forth"; Vg. renders the unusual verb as *labrusca*, "wild grape"; LXX misunderstands the verb as שגג (πλανηθήσῃ, "you will be led astray/deceived").

*s MT נֵד קָצִיר (nēd qāṣîr), "heap of harvest," gives no usable sense, 1QIsaᵃ נד קציר. Repoint נֵד to נַד (nad), the qal perfect of נדד, and one can render, "the harvest has fled." Cf. Vg. *ablata est messis*, "the harvest is taken away." LXX may read עַד instead of נַד, εἰς ἀμητόν, "unto/for harvest."

*t MT בְּיוֹם נַחֲלָה (bĕyôm naḥălâ), "on a day of sickness," 1QIsaᵃ; LXX and Vg. misunderstand נחלה as "inheritance."

*u MT וּכְאֵב אָנוּשׁ (ûkĕʾēb ʾānûš), "and mortal anguish," 1QIsaᵃ וכאוב אנוש. LXX misunderstands both words and then expands: καὶ ὡς πατὴρ ἀνθρώπου κληρώσῃ τοῖς υἱοῖς σου, "and like the father of a man you will take possession of it for your sons." This verse was very difficult for the versions.

*v MT לְאֻמִּים (lĕʾummîm), "peoples," 1QIsaᵃ לאומים.

*w MT יִשָּׁאוּן (yiššāʾûn), "they make a din"; 1QIsaᵃ has erroneously copied this final word in the verse not as a verb but as the noun with the copulative ושאון—influenced no doubt by two occurrences of the noun earlier in the verse. That would depart from the clear poetic structure of the verse, however, which plays on the repetitive sounds between the verbs המה (hāmâ, "roar,") and שאה (šāʾâ, "make a din," and their cognate nouns המון (hāmôn, "tumult,") and שאון (šĕʾôn, "noise.")

*x MT כַּבִּירִים (kabbîrîm), "mighty"; 1QIsaᵃ has the erroneous כבדים, "heavy," due to the confusion of ר and ד.

*y MT לְאֻמִּים (lĕʾummîm), "peoples," 1QIsaᵃ לאומים.

*z The first line in v. 13a לְאֻמִּים כִּשְׁאוֹן מַיִם רַבִּים יִשָּׁאוּן, "the peoples make a din like the noise of many waters," is repetitive of v. 12b and is omitted by Syr., but it is present in 1QIsaᵃ, the traces in 4QIsaᵃ and 4QIsaᵇ, and in LXX and Vg.

†a MT וְגָעַר (wĕgāʿar), "and he will rebuke," 4QIsaᵇ; 1QIsaᵃ has ויגער, which is the inferior reading.

†b MT בֹּקֶר (boqer), "morning," 1QIsaᵃ; 4QIsaᵇ omitted it, and then inserted it above the line.

†c MT אֵינֶנּוּ (ʾênennû), "it is no longer"; 1QIsaᵃ and 4QIsaᵇ ואיננו, "and it is no longer," which seems to be supported by LXX, Vg., and Syr.

†d MT לְבֹזְזֵנוּ (lĕbōzĕzēnû), "for those who plunder us," 1QIsaᵃ לבוזזינו.

Commentary

Isaiah 17 contains a number of probably originally independent short oracles. Verses 1-3 are an oracle against Damascus, which also contains a judgment against Ephraim. The linkage of the two suggests that it comes out of the context of the Syro-Ephraimitic War in 735–732 BCE, when the Arameans of Damascus and Israel were allied against Judah and its Davidic king. Verses 4-6 contain another oracle against Israel, the northern kingdom, designated as Jacob in v. 4, introduced by the clause, וְהָיָה בַּיּוֹם הַהוּא (wĕhāyâ bayyôm hahûʾ), "and it will come to pass on that day." The first oracle ends with the phrase, נְאֻם יְהוָה צְבָאוֹת (nĕʾum YHWH ṣĕbāʾôt), "says Yahweh of Hosts," and the second ends in a similar manner with, נְאֻם־יְהוָה אֱלֹהֵי יִשְׂרָאֵל (nĕʾum YHWH ʾĕlōhê *yiśrāʾēl*), "says Yahweh the God of Israel." The next two oracles begin with the expression, בַּיּוֹם הַהוּא, "on that day" (vv. 7-8 and 9-11), though there is no distinctive conclusion for either. The final oracle (vv. 12-14) is a *hôy*-oracle introduced by the particle הוֹי, "Hey!" These oracles have apparently been strung together in this chapter because they were all originally directed against the northern kingdom Ephraim/Israel and its Aramean overlords during the Syro-Ephraimitic crisis of 735–732 BCE. For that reason, I will treat them as a single literary compositional unit in my commentary.

Following the brief heading, Damascus is threatened with being removed as a city, to be left nothing more than a pile of ruins. Then, in v. 2, if one adopts the emendation suggested in the notes, the city would be abandoned forever, a place where flocks would lie down to rest with no one around to frighten them away. Tiglath-pileser III did destroy Damascus during the Syro-Ephraimitic War, but the city was soon rebuilt and restored, albeit as an Assyrian provincial center, and it continues as a vibrant city to this day. In the long run, Isaiah's expectations for the permanent destruction of Damascus were not fulfilled. Despite the heading, v. 3 makes clear that the oracle involves more than Damascus. Damascus's kingdom will come to an end, which it did, but the prophet also threatens that the fortress—presumably Samaria with its massive walls—will cease from Ephraim. Ephraim, or Israel the northern kingdom, was allied with Damascus, and, according to the prophet, Israel will share in the judgment directed against Damascus. What is left of the Arameans will be as weak as the faded glory of the Israelites. Both will perish before the Assyrians. Cf. Isa 7:4-9, 16; 8:4.

Verses 4-6 then expand on the departure of glory from the northern kingdom. On that day of judgment, the glory of Jacob will become poor and the fatness of his flesh emaciated. The imagery of economic decline and starvation is further elaborated by agricultural imagery that implies a massive loss of population. Israel will become like a grain field that is harvested and gleaned (v. 5), but not just any field, one in the valley of Rephaim near Jerusalem. The mention of this particular valley near Jerusalem is probably to suggest a field that is thoroughly stripped by the harvesting and gleaning, because it is so convenient to a large and poor urban population. The implication is that the remaining population of the north-

ern kingdom would be like the few grains of barley or wheat left in a harvested and gleaned field near an overpopulated urban center. This is underscored by v. 6 and its additional agricultural imagery. Israel will be like a harvested olive tree in which only two or three olives remain in the highest and thus most inaccessible branches, four or five in the tree all together. This imagery for the radical reduction of the population of the northern kingdom should be compared to Isa 6:11-13; 10:16-23; 28:4.

On that day, presumably in response to the preceding judgment, one will look to one's maker and fix one's eyes on the Holy One of Israel rather than putting one's trust in the work of one's own hands (vv. 7-8). Note the similar reaction to judgment in 10:20, where Israel will no longer rely on human enemies that smote him, but on Yahweh the Holy One of Israel. Here the work of one's own hands is defined as the local altars, asherahs (sacred trees or the stylized poles set up to represent sacred trees), and incense stands, all of which, along with the stone stela, were important accouterments of worship at the local high places, but which had come under increasing criticism in the nascent Deuteronomistic movement of the last half of the eighth century (Deut 7:5; 12:3; 16:21). The northern prophet Hosea complains about the numerous altars in the north (Hos 8:11; 10:1-2; 12:12) and speaks of a time of judgment during which Israel would live without sacrifice and stone stelas (Hos 3:4). Micah (5:12-13) and Isaiah (17:8; cf. 1:29-31) both mention such cultic equipment in a negative light, and the Judean king Hezekiah in his Deuteronomistically influenced reform early in his reign (ca. 715 BCE) made a point of destroying such objects in Judah (2 Kgs 18:4).

On that day of judgment, Israel's fortified cities will be abandoned just as the Hivites and the Amorites abandoned their cities before Israel during Israel's conquest of the land (v. 9—these two ethnic groups often occur in lists of the peoples displaced by Israel [see Exod 3:8, 17; 13:5; 23:23, 28; 33:2; 34:11; Deut 7:1; 20:17; Josh 3:10; 9:1; 12:8; 24:11]), and desolation will dominate the landscape. All of this will happen because Israel, personified now as a woman, has forgotten the God of her salvation and has not remembered the rock of her stronghold (v. 10; cf. the similar language addressed to the house of Jacob in 2:6). Rather than trusting in Yahweh, who drove out the Hivites and Amorites before them and gave them their land (cf. the similar argument in Amos 2:9), Israel has turned to cultic activity addressed to other divine powers. The reason for the shift to the feminine gender is not explicit in the text, but it may be because the cultic activity discussed next in the text was an activity in which women played a major role, just as they played a major role in making offerings to the Queen of Heaven in Jeremiah's time (Jer 44:15-19). It appears they were setting out quick-growing Adonis gardens to stimulate fertility. These were basically platters with a thin layer of soil in which seeds were planted, watered, and set out in the sun so that they would quickly germinate, though they would soon wither and die before reaching maturity because of the shallow root system. The purpose was not to produce food or herbs, but either to celebrate brief, transitory pleasure or, as some have argued, to promote fertility by a type of sympathetic magic.[1] In any case, the ritual was associated with a foreign deity, the Semitic Naaman, identified with the later Greek Adonis.[2] Isaiah takes the fate of these little pagan gardens as emblematic for what is about to happen to Israel. Even though they set out these plants to a foreign god and cause them to grow on the very day that they plant them, the plants soon wither and die, and that is the judgment awaiting Israel—no harvest, but an early death on a day of mortal anguish and sickness (vv. 10-11).

Verse 12 then addresses the many peoples who have come up against Jerusalem, presumably the Aramean, Israelite, and perhaps Philistine and Phoenician troops, at the time of the Aramean-Israelite surprise attack on the city at the beginning of the Syro-Ephraimitic War (Isa 7:1-9). There is a similar direct address of these peoples in 8:9-10, and 28:1-6 contains a similar *hôy*-oracle against the king of Israel. The noise of this host is compared to the noise of the sea and the sound of mighty waters (vv. 12-13), a motif that suggests Yahweh's cosmogonic battle against the primeval sea (Ps 95:3-4), and Yahweh's defense of Zion against mythologized foreign enemies in the Songs of Zion (Pss 46:2-4, 6-12; 48:4-8). As in the Zion Tradition (Pss 2:5; 46:7; 76:7), Yahweh will utter his rebuke, and this enemy host will quickly vanish (v. 13), chased away like chaff on the mountains before a wind, or tumbleweeds before a storm. The disappearance of the enemy army is so sudden, it is as though in the evening the inhabitants of Jerusalem were in terror of the enemy, but before morning the terror is gone (v. 14). That is the allotted portion of those who would despoil and plunder Jerusalem. The oracle itself never mentions Jerusalem by name, but the mention of those who despoil and plunder *us*, and the parallels with the Zion Songs make it clear that Isaiah is speaking from a Zion perspective, as he clearly did during the Syro-Ephraimitic War (see Isa 8:18). For a similar Isaianic portrayal of the transitoriness of a mortal threat against Jerusalem, this time from the period of Sennacherib's impending attack on Jerusalem, see Isa 29:5-8 and 31:4-5. One should note that while *hôy*-oracles tend to be direct address, the enemy host here, as in Isa 8:9-10, is only the fictive audience of this oracle. The real audience for whom this and the preceding series of short oracles are intended is a Judean audience that the prophet was reassuring in the face of a terrifying threat from the north.

In my view, the original context for this collection of interrelated oracles was the Syro-Ephraimitic War of 735–732 BCE, but for its intended Judean audience it would certainly have been relevant again in the Assyrian crisis of Sennacherib's invasion in 701 BCE, and I do not doubt that it was heard again in that period. On the other hand, I am unable to find any clear traces in this material of an obvious reediting for the Assyrian crisis.

---

1   See the extensive discussion in Wildberger, 2:657–60. For the later practice, continuing into modern times, see W. Baumgartner, "Das Nachleben der Adonisgärtchen auf Sardinien und im übrigen Mittelmeergebiet," in Baumgartner, *Zum Alten Testament und seiner Umwelt: Ausgewälte Aufsätze* (Leiden: Brill, 1959) 247–73.

2   W. W. Baudissin, *Adonis und Esmun: Eine Untersuchung zur Geschichte des Glaubens an Auferstehungsgötter und an Heilgötter* (Leipzig: Hinrichs, 1911) 88–89.

Bibliography

Barth, *Die Jesaja-Worte.*

Baudissin, W. W., *Adonis und Esmun: Eine Untersuchung zur Geschichte des Glaubens an Auferstehungsgötter und an Heilgötter* (Leipzig: Hinrichs, 1911).

Baumgartner, W., "Das Nachleben der Adonisgärtchen auf Sardinien und im übrigen Mittelmeergebiet," in Baumgartner, *Zum Alten Testament und seiner Umwelt: Ausgewälte Aufsätze* (Leiden: Brill, 1959) 247–73.

Bernhardt, K. H., "Aschera in Ugarit und im Alten Testament," *MIO* 13 (1967) 163–71.

Day, John, "Asherah in the Hebrew Bible and Northwest Semitic Literature," *JBL* 105 (1986) 385–408.

Delcor, M., "Le problème des jardins d'Adonis dans Isaïe 17,9-11," *Syria* 54 (1977) 371–94.

Eissfeldt, Otto, "Die Wanderungen palästinisch-syrischer Götter nach Ost und West im zweiten vorchristlichen Jahrtausend," in Eissfeldt, *Kleine Schriften* (6 vols.; Tübingen: J. C. B. Mohr, 1962–79) 2:58.

Elliger, K., "Chammanim = Masseben?" *ZAW* 57 (1939) 256–65.

——, "Der Sinn des Wortes Chamman," *ZDPV* 66 (1943) 129–39.

Fohrer, Georg, "*Sion,*" *ThWNT* 7 (1964) 291–318.

Galling, K., "Baʿal Ḥammon in Kition und die *ḥammanîm,*" in Hartmut Gese and Hans Peter Rüger, eds., *Wort und Geschichte: Festschrift für Karl Elliger zum 70. Geburtstag* (AOAT 18; Kevelaer: Butzon & Bercker, 1973) 65–70.

Gerleman, G., "Die lärmende Menge," in Hartmut Gese and Hans Peter Rüger, eds., *Wort und Geschichte: Festschrift für Karl Elliger zum 70. Geburtstag* (AOAT 18; Kevelaer: Butzon & Bercker, 1973) 71–75.

Gosse, Bernard, "Isaïe 17:12-14 dans la redaction du livre d'Isaïe," *BN* 58 (1991) 20–23.

Hayes, John H., "The Tradition of Zion's Inviolability," *JBL* 82 (1963) 419–26.

Ingholt, H., "Le sens du mot *ḥammān,*" in *Mélanges syriens offerts à monsieur René Dussaud* (2 vols.; Paris: P. Geuthner, 1939) 2:795–802.

Jirku, A., "NIṬʿĒ NAʿAMANIM (Jes xvii 10 c) = NIṬʿĒ NAʿAMAN-MA," *VT* 7 (1957) 201–2.

Katzenstein, H. J., *The History of Tyre: From the Beginning of the Second Millennium B.C.E. until the Fall of the Neo-Babylonian Empire in 538 B.C.E.* (Jerusalem: Schocken Institute for Jewish Research of the Jewish Theological Seminary of America, 1973; 2nd rev. ed., Beersheva: Ben-Gurion University of the Negev Press, 1997).

Kenyon, K., *Amorites and Canaanites* (London: Oxford University Press, 1966).

Kuschke, A., "Hiwwiter in Ha-Fai?" in Hartmut Gese and Hans Peter Rüger, eds., *Wort und Geschichte: Festschrift für Karl Elliger zum 70. Geburtstag* (AOAT 18; Kevelaer: Butzon & Bercker, 1973) 115–19.

Lutz, Hanns-Martin, *Jahwe, Jerusalem und die Völker: Zur Vorgeschichte von Sach. 12, 1-8, und 14, 1-5* (WMANT 27; Neukirchen-Vluyn: Neukirchener Verlag, 1968).

Malamat, A., "The Arameans," in D. J. Wiseman, ed., *People of Old Testament Times* (Oxford: Clarendon, 1973) 134–55.

North, R., "The Hivites," *Bib* 54 (1973) 43–62.

Noth, Martin, "Die syrisch-palästinische Bevölkerung des zweiten Jahrtausends v. Chr. im Lichte neuer Quellen," *ZDPV* 65 (1942) 9–67.

Patai, R., "The Goddess Ashera," *JNES* 24 (1965) 37–52.

Reed, William L., *The Asherah in the Old Testament* (Fort Worth: Texas Christian University Press, 1949).

Rinaldi, G., "*Lqt* 'raccogliere,'" *BeO* 13 (1971) 210.

Rohland, E., "Die Bedeutung der Erwählungstraditionen Israels für die Eschatologie der alttestamentlichen Propheten" (Diss., Heidelberg, 1956).

Scharbert, J., "Besprechung von G. Wanke, Zionstheologie," *BZ* 12 (1968) 274–75.

Scharff, A., "Frühe Vorstufen zum 'Kornosiris,'" *FF* 21 (1947) 38–39.

Schmidt, H., *Das Gebet des Angeklagten im Alten Testament* (BZAW 49; Giessen: A. Töpelmann, 1928).

——, "Israel, Zion, und die Völker: Eine motivgeschichtliche Untersuchung zum Verständnis des Universalismus im Alten Testament" (Diss., Zürich, 1966).

Schreiner, J., *Sion-Jerusalem: Jahwes Königssitz* (Munich: Kösel, 1963).

Smend, R., "Altar," *BHH* 1:63–65.

Snijders, L. A., "The Meaning of *Zr* in the Old Testament: An Exegetical Study," *OTS* 10 (1954) 1–21.

Speiser, E. A., "Ethnic Movements in the Near East in the Second Millennium B.C.: The Hurrians and Their Connection with the Habiru and the Hyksos," *AASOR* 13 (1931) 13–54.

Stolz, F., *Strukturen und Figuren im Kult von Jerusalem* (BZAW 118; Berlin: A. Töpelmann, 1970).

Sulze, H., "*Adonidos Khpoi* I. Die Kultischen Adonisgärtchen," *Angelos* 3 (1928) 72–91.

Unger, Merrill F., *Israel and the Arameans of Damascus: A Study in Archaeological Illumination of Bible History* (London: J. Clarke, 1957).

Vaux, Roland de, "Jérusalem et les prophètes," *RB* 73 (1966) 481–509.

Vellay, Ch., *Le culte et les fêtes d'Adônis-Thammouz dans l'Orient antique* (Paris: E. Leroux, 1904).

Vogt, E., "Jesaja und die drohende Eroberung Palästinas durch Tiglatpilesar," in Hartmut Gese and Hans Peter Rüger, eds., *Wort und Geschichte: Festschrift für Karl Elliger zum 70. Geburtstag* (AOAT 18; Kevelaer: Butzon & Bercker, 1973) 249–55.

Wanke, G., *Die Zionstheologie der Korachiten in ihrem traditionsgeschichtlichen Zusammenhang* (BZAW 97; Berlin: A. Töpelmann, 1966).

Ziegler, J., "Die Hilfe Gottes 'Am Morgen,'" in Herbert Junker and Johannes Botterweck, eds., *Alttestamentliche Studien: Friedrich Nötscher zum sechzigsten Geburtstag, 19. Juli 1950, gewidmet von Kollegen, Freunden und Schülern* (BBB 1; Bonn: P. Hanstein, 1950) 281–88.

Zobel, H. J., "*Yhwdh*," in Helmer Ringgren and G. Johannes Botterweck, eds., *Theologisches Wörterbuch zum Alten Testament* (2 vols.; Stuttgart: Kohlhammer, 1973–77) vol. 2, cols. 520–22.

18

1/	Hey, land of winged skiff,[a]
	Which is beyond the rivers of Kush,[b]
2/	Who sends[c] messengers[d] by sea,
	And in vessels of papyrus[e] upon the waters,
	Go,[f] swift messengers,
	To[g] a nation tall[h] and smooth,[i]
	To a people feared from its beginning onwards,[j]
	A nation of strength[k] and trampling[l]
	Whose land the rivers sweep away.[m]
3/	All you inhabitants[n] of the world,
	And you dwellers[o] of the earth,
	As one raises a standard on the mountain, you will see;
	As one blows[p] the trumpet, you will hear.[q]
4/	For[r] thus said Yahweh to me:
	I will be quiet and watch from my dais[s]
	Like shimmering heat upon the light,
	Like a cloud of dew in the heat of harvest.
5/	For before the harvest when the budding is finished,
	And the bloom is becoming a ripening grape,[t]
	He will cut off the tendrils with pruning knives
	And the twigs he will remove, he will strike off.
6/	They will be left[u] together for the bird of prey of the mountains
	And for the beast[v] of the earth,
	And the bird of prey will summer[w] on it,
	And every beast[x] of the earth will winter[y] on it.
7/	At that time[z] a present will be brought to Yahweh of Hosts
	From a people tall[*a] and smooth[*b]
	And from a people feared from its beginning[*c] onwards,
	A nation of strength[*d] and trampling[*e]
	Whose land the rivers sweep away[*f]
	To the place of the name of Yahweh of Hosts,[*g] Mount Zion.

Textual Notes

a   The meaning of MT's צְלְצַל (ṣilṣal [1QIsaᵃ divides the two syllables צל צל]) is disputed. The LXX (Οὐαὶ γῆς πλοίων πτέρυγες, "Woe, O wings of the land of boats"), Theodotion (naves, "boats"), and Tg. ("Ah, O land, to whom they come in boats from a distant land and their sails are spread like the eagle which hovers with its wings") understand the word as designating boats of wings," and Vg. (vae terrae cymbalo alarum, "Woe to the land with the sound/cymbal of wings") takes the word as meaning "sound" or "cymbal." Syr. takes the word as meaning shade, "the shade of wings." Certain classical Arabic dictionaries list a noun zulzul as meaning sufun (plural of safine), "boats, skiffs." E. W. Lane dismisses this entry as a mistranscription of suʿne, "awning," since f and ʿ differ only in the dot over f, and zul is associated with shade,[1] but awnings on roofs and sails on boats have a certain resemblance, and it is quite possible the Arabic zulzul could have been used both for "awning" and for "sailing skiff." In any case, the evidence of LXX and Tg. support the rendering of צְלְצַל כְּנָפַיִם as "skiff of wings, winged skiff, sailboat."

b   MT כוש (kûš), so also 1QIsaᵃ and Syr., is rendered by LXX and Vg. as Ethiopia, and by Tg. as הֹודוּ (hôdû), "India," but the later Ethiopia is too far to the east. Ancient Kush corresponded to later Nubia, the northern area of modern Sudan and southern Egypt.

c   MT הַשֹּׁלֵחַ (haššōlēaḥ), "who sends"; 1QIsaᵃ השולח.

d   MT צִירִים (ṣîrîm), "messengers," 1QIsaᵃ, Tg., V. (legatos, "envoys"); LXX has ὅμηρα, which normally means "hostages," but Syr. ḥmyrʾ, which follows the Greek, may have the broader meaning of "envoys." As first Hayim Tadmor and then Peter Machinist have pointed out, the Akkadian cognate ṣīru can also mean "envoy" in Neo-Assyrian texts.[2]

e   MT וּבִכְלֵי־גֹמֶא (ûbiklê gōmeʾ), "and in vessels of papyrus," 1QIsaᵃ, Vg., Syr., Tg. (וּבְדגֹוגִין, "and in skiffs"); LXX has καὶ ἐπιστολὰς βυβλίνας, "and papyrus letters."

f   MT לְכוּ (lĕkû), "go!", 1QIsaᵃ, Vg., Tg., Syr.; LXX apparently read כי ילכו (πορεύσονται γὰρ, "for swift messengers will go").

1   Edward William Lane, Arabic-English Lexicon (2 vols.; Cambridge: Islamic Texts Society, 1984) 2:1917.

2   Machinist, "Assyria and Its Image," 730 n. 65.

g MT has אֶל (ʾel), "to," while 1QIsaᵃ has the synonym לְ (lĕ), "to."

h MT גּוֹי מְמֻשָּׁךְ (gôy mĕmuššāk), "a nation tall," lit., "stretched out," 1QIsaᵃ, LXX; Vg. "torn" (convulsam), Syr. "despoiled" (mlyg), Tg. "robbed" (ʾnys).

i MT וּמוֹרָט (ûmôrāṭ), "and smooth," that is, "hairless," "without beards"; 1QIsaᵃ וממורט (the *pual* participle instead of MT's *qal* passive). LXX may omit this word, since καὶ ξένον λαὸν καὶ χαλεπόν, "and a foreign and fierce people," appears to be an expanded translation of the following אֶל־עַם נוֹרָא (ʾel ʿam nôrā), "to a people feared"; Vg. has "torn" (dilaceratum), Syr. "uprooted" (wʿqyr), Tg. "plundered" (bzyz).

j MT מִן־הוּא (min-hûʾ), "from its beginning," lit. "from it."

k MT גּוֹי קַו־קָו (gôy qaw-qāw), "a nation of strength"; 1QIsaᵃ is probably correct in reading qawqāw as a single word (גוי קוקו). Others, such as Hayes and Irvine (p. 255) and Clements (p. 165), following Donner,[3] have suggested that is onomatopoetic babble to denote an unintelligible language. The versions did not understand the expression; LXX and Vg. connected it to the verb קוה, "to await, hope," thus LXX ἔθνος ἀνέλπιστον, "a nation without hope," and Vg. *gentem expectantem expectantem*, "a nation awaiting, awaiting." Syr. has "disfigured" (mškr), and Tg. has "robbed" (ʾnys).

l MT וּמְבוּסָה (ûmĕbûsâ), "and trampling," 1QIsaᵃ; all the versions understood the word as passive, indicating that this nation was oppressed.

m MT בָּזְאוּ (bāzĕʾû), "sweep away, wash away"; 1QIsaᵃ has mistakenly copied בזאי. Vg. renders the verb as "tear apart" (diripuerunt); Syr. and Tg. as "spoil" or "plunder" (bzw); LXX either misunderstood or misread the verb and so corrupted the beginning of the following verse: νῦν οἱ ποταμοὶ τῆς γῆς πάντες ὡς χώρα κατοικουμένη, "now all the rivers of the land will be like an inhabited country."

n MT כָּל־יֹשְׁבֵי (kol-yōšĕbê), "all the inhabitants of," 1QIsaᵃ כול יושבי.

o MT וְשֹׁכְנֵי (wĕšōkĕnê), "and dwellers of," 1QIsaᵃ ושוכני.

p MT וְכִתְקֹע (wĕkitqōʿ), "and as one blows," 1QIsaᵃ וכתקוע.

q Because of its misunderstanding of the end of the preceding verse and the beginning of this verse, LXX also garbles the end of this verse badly: κατοικηθήσεται ἡ χώρα αὐτῶν ὡσεὶ σημεῖον ἀπὸ ὄρους ἀρθῇ, ὡς σάλπιγγος φωνὴ ἀκουστὸν ἔσται, "their land shall be inhabited as if a sign were lifted from the mountains, like the sound of a trumpet it shall be heard."

r MT כִּי (kî), "for"; 1QIsaᵃ כיא.

s MT אֶשְׁקוֹטָה וְאַבִּיטָה בִמְכוֹנִי (ʾešqôṭâ wĕʾabbîṭâ bimkônî), "I will be quiet and watch from my dais"), 1QIsaᵃ, Vg., Syr.; LXX has Ἀσφάλεια ἔσται ἐν τῇ ἐμῇ πόλει, "there will be safety in my city."

t MT וּבֹסֶר גֹּמֵל (ûboser gōmēl), "and a ripening grape"; 1QIsaᵃ has ובסור גמול.

u MT יֵעָזְבוּ (yēʿāzĕbû), "they will be left," 4QIsaᵇ; 1QIsaᵃ has erroneously copied ועזבו.

v MT וּלְבֶהֱמַת (ûlĕbehĕmat), "and for the beast of"; 1QIsaᵃ has the plural ולבהמות, "and for the beasts of"; 4QIsaᵇ has ולבממת, a simple error with an attempted correction. Eugene Ulrich thought the original scribe corrected the fifth letter, writing *mem* over *taw*, or vice versa,[4] but I think the scribe may have written *heh* over the second *mem*, though he should have written it over the first *mem*, the fourth letter.

w MT וְקָץ (wĕqāṣ), "and will summer," 1QIsaᵃ, 4QIsaᵇ, Vg.; LXX συναχθήσεται ("will be gathered"); Syr. tknš ("will gather").

x MT וְכָל־בֶּהֱמַת (wĕkol-behĕmat), "and every beast of"; 1QIsaᵃ has וכול בהמות, "and all the beasts of," but the singular verb supports MT.

y MT תֶּחֱרָף (teḥĕrāp), "shall winter," 1QIsaᵃ, 4QIsaᵇ, Vg.; LXX ἥξει ("will come"); Syr. trgz ("will rage, be angry").

z MT בָּעֵת הַהִיא (bāʿēt hahîʾ), "at that time," 4QIsaᵇ; 1QIsaᵃ בעתה ההיא.

*a MT עַם מְמֻשָּׁךְ (ʿam mĕmuššāk), "from a people tall," supported by 4QIsaᵇ's עם ממשך, is apparently an accusative of source; 1QIsaᵃ clarifies the sense by adding the preposition מעם ממשך, "from a people tall," as in the parallel line in all the texts.

*b MT וּמוֹרָט (ûmôrāṭ), "and smooth," that is, "hairless," "without beards," 4QIsaᵇ; 1QIsaᵃ וממרט.

*c MT מִן־הוּא (min-hûʾ), "from its beginning," lit., "from it"; 1QIsaᵃ has מהוא, and 4QIsaᵇ has suffered a haplography, omitting הוא altogether.

*d See note j above.

*e See note k above; here, however, 1QIsaᵃ has the variant spelling ומבוסא.

*f See note l above.

*g 1QIsaᵃ omits צְבָאוֹת (sĕbāʾôt), "of Hosts," but 4QIsaᵇ, LXX, Vg., Syr., and Tg. all support MT.

Commentary

The historical context for the oracle in Isaiah 18 is probably the Ashdod crisis of 716–711 BCE. In other words, it probably dates to the same general period as the material in Isaiah 20 and 14:28-32. This was the period of several years after Hezekiah came to the throne in 715, when Philistine Ashdod and its Nubian and Egyptian supporters were trying to persuade the Judean royal court and a number of other states in the area to join in Ashdod's revolt against Assyria. We know from Sargon's inscriptions that first Azuri, before he was removed by the

---

3 Donner, *Israel unter den Völkern*, 122–24.

4 Skehan and Ulrich, "Isaiah," 30.

Assyrians, and then, after the people of Ashdod drove out Ahimeti, Azuri's brother and Assyria's appointee, and replaced him with Yamani, that Yamani had sent letters to the surrounding states urging them to join the revolt. Sargon specifically mentions Yamani's letters to the king of Judah:

a-na lu[gal^mes-*ni*] *ša* kur *Pi-liš-te* kur *Ya-ú-di* kur *Ú-d*[*u-me/ mu*] kur *Ma-a-bi a-ši-bu-ut tam-tim na-áš bil-*[*ti u*] [*t*]*a-mar-ti ša* ^d*A-šur₄ be-lí-y*[*a*] *da-bab sa-ar-ra-a-ti at-me-e nu-ul-la-a-te ša it-ti-ya a-na šum-ku-ri*

To the kings of the land of the Philistines, the land of Judah (*Ya-ú-di*), the land of Edom, the land of Moab, and those who dwell by the sea, all of whom were responsible for tribute and presents to Ashur, my lord, <they sent> lies and seditious words in order to make them enemies with me. (Annals of Year 711: K.1668b + D.T. 6 VII.b lines 25-30).[5]

Sargon also mentions Ashdod's sending tribute to Egypt in an attempt to enlist their support for the revolt (lines 30-33), but he does not mention messengers from Nubia showing up in the various Palestinian royal courts to encourage this revolt. Nonetheless, Isaiah's response to this situation in Isa 14:28-32; 18; and 20, suggests that the new Nubian rulers of Egypt were actively encouraging this revolt by sending messengers from the distant Nubian court to their potential vassals in Philistia, Judah, Edom, and Moab. Isaiah, in turn, did his best to dissuade Hezekiah from being drawn into the revolt. Instead, Hezekiah should trust in God's promises to Zion and the Davidic dynasty and simply watch from the sidelines.

The present *hôy* oracle begins with a direct address to the land of Kush (Nubia). It is characterized as the "land of winged skiffs" or sailboats beyond the rivers of Kush. The first expression is disputed. Some scholars understand the expression as referring to the buzzing of swarms of insects,[6] the "land of whirring of wings," but the lexical evidence, as discussed above, gives stronger support to the understanding of the expression as refer-

ring to sailboats, and that fits better the larger context, which goes on to speak of sending messengers by water. For an ancient wooden model of an Egyptian sailboat, see *ANEP*, 33, fig. 110. The second expression, "beyond the rivers of Kush," is also a source of some discussion.[7] What river besides the Nile did the prophet have in mind? The heartland of ancient Kush was north of modern Khartoum, where the Blue Nile joins the Nile, so it is unlikely that the prophet was thinking of the Blue Nile. Perhaps he was thinking of the Nile and the Atbarah, which come together north of Meroe. On the other hand, one may well question how precise the prophet's or his audience's knowledge of the geography of Kush actually was, and it is doubtful that Isaiah was trying to specify a very precise area within, much less beyond, the Nubian heartland. The language is probably just a way of expressing again how distant this remote land was from Jerusalem.

Verse 2 further characterizes the land of Kush as the one who sends messengers by sea, by papyrus boats on the face of the waters. For an ancient model of Egyptian papyrus fishing boats, see *ANEP*, 33, fig. 109. "Sea" here clearly refers to the Nile as in Isa 19:5. The Nile, of course, provided both the quickest and the cheapest method of transportation from Nubia through Egypt. Whether the messengers continued their travel from the Delta to the Philistine coast by boat on the Mediterranean, which would probably have been both quicker and safer, or whether they traveled overland via the coastal road to Palestine, is not clear. At any rate, these swift messengers are then commanded to go to a tall and smooth-skinned nation. The צִירִים (*ṣîrîm*), "messengers," and מַלְאָכִים קַלִּים (*malʾākîm qallîm*), "swift messengers," refer to the same people. Isaiah is commanding these swift messengers from Kush to go to a nation that he characterizes as tall and smooth-skinned. This characterization fits the ancient artistic portrayals of the black Nubian warriors, who are typically portrayed as both tall and beardless (see *ANEP*, 55, fig. 179). In contrast, the Assyrian warriors as well as those of Palestine, Syria, and almost all the Asiatic countries are typically portrayed with beards, the only major exception being certain

---

5   Fuchs, *Die Annalen*. The annals from Khorsabad present a similar picture but are far less detailed and specific; see Fuchs, *Die Inschriften Sargons II*, pp. 132 and 326, lines 241-54.

6   So Gray, 309, and the NRSV, among many others.

7   See esp. the measured discussion of Gray, 309–11.

high officials who were eunuchs. There is no compelling reason to introduce the Assyrians into the oracle at this point. In effect, Isaiah is urging these Nubian messengers to Jerusalem to return to their Nubian rulers who sent them. Why would Isaiah command them to go anywhere else but home after they had delivered their message to Hezekiah? The focus remains on the Nubians. They are the people feared from its beginning onward. The expression מִן־הוּא וָהָלְאָה (min-hûʾ wāhālĕʾâ), "from here and beyond," is a bit ambiguous; it could be taken either temporally or locally, "from its beginning onward," or "far and wide." This characterization of the Nubians following their conquest of Egypt makes perfectly good sense. As the conquerors of Egypt, they were a people "of strength and trampling." Alternatively, if קַו־קָו וּמְבוּסָה (qaw-qāw ûmĕbûsâ) refers to the unintelligibility of their speech to ordinary Judeans, it would fit the Nubians quite as well or even better than it would fit the Assyrians, since the Assyrians, after all, spoke a Semitic language related to Hebrew, even if the ordinary Hebrew speaker could not understand Assyrian (cf. Isa 28:11; 33:19; Deut 28:49). The meaning of the verb בָּזְאוּ (bāzĕʾû) is disputed, but it probably refers to the waters of the Nile and Atbarah sweeping away the soil of the highlands of Sudan rather than to these rivers dividing the country of Kush.

At v. 3 the prophet turns from the Nubians to address all the inhabitants of the world, whom he calls to watch and listen as people watch the raising of a signal flag on a mountain or listen to the blowing of a trumpet. In effect, the peoples of the world are called upon to witness Yahweh's reaction to the current international crisis over Ashdod's revolt against Assyria. Despite the feverish diplomatic activity involving messages from Ashdod and swift messengers from as far away as the court of the Nubian pharaoh, Yahweh declares (v. 4) that he will quietly rest and watch from his dais, which in Isaiah's Zion theology would be from Mount Zion in Jerusalem, uninvolved and elevated above the fray, like shimmering heat upon the light, or like a cloud of dew in the heat of summer. The expression כְּחֹם צַח עֲלֵי־אוֹר (kĕḥōm ṣaḥ ʿălê-ʾôr),

"like shimmering heat upon the light," probably refers to the visual phenomenon of light being refracted in the summer heat and shimmering in wavelike fashion.

Then unhurried, like a wise farmer, in due time before the harvest, when the bud has finished and the bloom has become a ripening grape, Yahweh will prune the vine, leaving the tendrils and twigs for the beasts of the field and the birds of the mountains to feast upon for the rest of the summer and winter. This agricultural pruning imagery, as so often in the Old Testament, suggests the cutting down of Yahweh's human enemies, leaving their fallen bodies for the beasts and birds to feed upon. In the present context, as a comparison with Isa 20:3-6 suggests, those human enemies are the Nubians, the Egyptians, and their Philistine clients. In response to this judgment (v. 7), the Nubians will recognize that the true imperial power is Yahweh's, and rather than Judah sending tribute to Nubia, as Hezekiah later did in the crisis of 701 BCE (see Isa 30:1-7), Nubia would send tribute to Yahweh of Hosts, to the place of Yahweh of Hosts, that is, to Mount Zion in Jerusalem.

In Isaiah 20, and at least obliquely in 14:28-32 under the imagery of "smoke from the north (v. 31)," the prophet mentions Assyria as the agent Yahweh uses to punish the Nubians or their Philistine clients, but nothing in chap. 18 specifically refers to the Assyrians. The emphasis here is simply on Yahweh's calm mastery of the situation. One could debate whether this oracle was actually given in the Judean court in the presence of the foreign Nubian messengers, but though one cannot rule out that possibility, in a deeper sense both the Nubian messengers and the inhabitants of the world called upon to witness the scene are really a fictive audience; the real audience is the Judean royal court and, perhaps more broadly, the Judean populace. As in Isa 14:32 and chap. 20, the intent is to convince the Judean court and the broader populace to trust calmly in God's promises to Zion and its Davidic king, not to seek their security in treaties with Nubian Egypt and their Philistine vassals.

Bibliography

Barth, H., "Israel und das Assyrerreich in den nicht-jesajanischen Texten des Protojesajabuches" (diss., Hamburg, 1974).

———, *Die Jesaja-Worte*.

Baumann, E., "Zwei Einzelbemerkungen: I. Jes 18,4," *ZAW* 21 (1901) 266–88.

Borger, R., "Das Ende des ägyptischen Feldherrn Sibʾe = Swʾ," *JNES* 19 (1960) 49–53.

Donner, *Israel unter den Völkern*, 122–24.

Elat, M., "The Economic Relations of the Neo-Assyrian Empire with Egypt," *JAOS* 98 (1978) 20–34.

Erman, A., and H. Ranke, *Ägypten und ägyptisches Leben im Altertum* (Tübingen: H. Laupp, 1923).

Frame, "Inscription of Sargon II," 31–57.

Frankenstein, S., "The Phoenicians in the Far West: A Function of Neo-Assyrian Imperialism," in Mogens Trolle Larsen, ed., *Power and Propaganda: A Symposium of Ancient Empires* (Mesopotamia 7; Copenhagen: Akademisk Forlag, 1979) 263–94.

Franklin, N., "The Room V Reliefs at Dur-Sharruken and Sargon II's Western Campaigns," *TA* 21 (1994) 255–75, esp. 264–68, figs. 3–7.

Fuchs, *Die Annalen*.

———, *Die Inschriften Sargons II.*

Gonzáles, A., "El Rocío del Cielo," *EstBíb* 22 (1963) 109–39.

James, T. G. H., "The Twenty-Fifth and Twenty-Sixth Dynasties," in *The Cambridge Ancient History*, vol. 3.2, 677–747.

Janzen, Waldemar, *Mourning Cry and Woe Oracle* (BZAW 125; Berlin: de Gruyter, 1972) 60–61.

Jenkins, A. K., "The Development of the Isaiah Tradition in Is 13–23," in J. Vermeylen, ed., *Le livre d'Isaïe: Les oracles et leurs relectures. Unité et complexité de l'ouvrage* (BETL 81; Leuven: Leuven University Press, 1989) 244–45.

Kahn, D., "The Inscription of Sargon II at Tang-I Var and the Chronology of Dynasty 25," *Or* n.s. 70 (2001) 1–18.

Kitchen, K. A., *The Third Intermediate Period in Egypt, 1100–650 B.C.* (2nd ed. with suppl.; Warminster: Aris & Phillips, 1986).

Köhler, L., "Bāzaʾ," *TZ* 6 (1950) 316–17.

Lemaire, A., "Note épigraphique sur la pseudo-attestation du mois 'SHS,'" *VT* 23 (1973) 243–45.

Lichtheim, Miriam, *Ancient Egyptian Literature: A Book of Readings*, vol. 3, *The Late Period* (Berkeley: University of California Press, 1980).

Lubetski, Meir, and Claire Gottlieb, "Isaiah 18 in the Egyptian Nexus," in Meir Lubetski, Clair Gottlieb, and Sharon Keller, eds., *Boundaries of the Ancient Near Eastern World: A Tribute to Cyrus H. Gordon* (JSOTSup 273; Sheffield: Sheffield Academic Press, 1998) 364–83.

Montagnini, F., "Come caldo sereno al brillar della luce? (Is 18,4)," *RivB* 11 (1963) 92–95.

Naʾaman, N., "The Brook of Egypt and Assyrian Policy on the Border of Egypt," *TA* 6 (1979) 68–90.

Niccacci, Alviero, "Isaiah XVIII–XX from an Egyptological Perspective," *VT* 48 (1998) 214–38.

Oded, B., "The Phoenician Cities and the Assyrian Empire in the Time of Tiglath-Pileser III," *ZDPV* 90 (1974) 38–49.

Otto, Eberhard, *Ägypten: Der Weg des Pharaonenreiches* (Stuttgart: Kohlhammer, 1966).

Rainey, Anson F., and R. Steven Notley, *The Sacred Bridge: Carta's Atlas of the Biblical World* (Jerusalem: Carta, 2006).

Redford, D. B., "Studies in Relations between Palestine and Egypt during the First Millenium B.C. to the Twenty-Second Dynasty," *JAOS* 93 (1973) 3–17.

Roberts, J. J. M., "Egypt, Assyria, Isaiah."

———, "Egyptian and Nubian Oracles."

———, "Rod That Smote," 381–95.

Soggin, J. Alberto, "Zum wiederentdeckten altkanaanäischen Monat *Zḥ*," *ZAW* 77 (1965) 83–86 [und Nachtrag 326].

Tadmor, "Campaigns of Sargon II," 22–40, 77–100.

Toivanen, Aarne, "A Bible Translation as the Communicator of Alien Culture," *Temenos: Studies in Comparative Religion* 26 (1991) 129–37.

Török, László, *The Kingdom of Kush: Handbook of the Nabatan-Meriotic Civilization* (HO 1: Der Nahe und Mittlere Osten 31; Leiden: Brill, 1977).

Vogt, E., "'Eber Hayyarden," *BZ* 34 (1953) 118–19.

Weippert, M., "Archäologischer Jahresbericht," *ZDPV* 80 (1964) 155 (chap. 20), 82–83 (chap. 18).

Winckler, H., "Das Land Kus und Jes. 18," in *Alttestamentlicher Untersuchungen* (Leipzig: Pfeiffer, 1892) 146–56.

Wolf, Walther, *Die Welt der Ägypter* (Zurich: Fretz & Wasmuth, 1955).

Wutz, A., "Abweichende Vokalisationsüberlieferungen im hebräischen Text," *BZ* 21 (1933) 7–21.

Zeissl, Helene von, *Äthiopen und Assyrer in Ägypten* (ÄF 14; Glückstadt: J. J. Augustin, 1944).

Unlike the previous oracle in chap. 18 or the following oracle in chap. 20, both of which seem to date to the period of the Ashdod affair, roughly 715–711 BCE, the material in Isaiah 19 is far more difficult to date precisely.[1] Part of the difficulty is the uncertainties involved in the Egyptian royal chronology for the late eighth century, and another difficulty is the ambiguously allusive quality of the historical referents in the text that leaves open multiple possibilities in the search for the most likely historical context or contexts for the material in Isaiah 19.

In the earlier chronology laid out by K. A. Kitchen, elaborated by László Török, and still followed by J. K. Hoffmeier,[2] Kashta, the founder of the Egyptian Twenty-Fifth or Nubian dynasty, is dated to 760–747 BCE, Pi(ankh)y to 747–716, Shabako to 716–702, and Shebitku to 702–690. Hoffmeier dates Pi(ankh)y's military conquest of Upper and Middle Egypt to c. 727 BCE, but, according to him, Pi(ankh)y soon returned to Nubia, and Tefnakht of Sais (727–720) regained control of the Delta and even moved south again to Memphis. The Nubians, according to Hoffmeier, did not regain control of the Delta until early in Shabako's reign (716–702), when he killed Bakenranef (720–715), the son of Tefnakht, and reinstituted a more peaceful policy toward Assyria than the hostile one followed by the kings of Sais. There are serious difficulties with this reconstruction, however. Sargon II's inscription at Tang-i Var, dating from 706 BCE, specifically names Shebitku, not Shabako, as the Nubian king who extradited Yamani, the leader of the Ashdod revolt (715–711), from Nubia to Assyria.[3] Unless one assumes a co-regency between Shabako and Shebitku,[4] Shebitku must have succeeded Shabako by 706, not 702 or 701, and that would require adjustments in the dates

assigned to the earlier members of the dynasty. D. Kahn and Anson Rainey,[5] who follows him, date the end of Kashta's reign to 753 BCE, Pi(ankh)y to 753–721, Shabako to 721–706, and Shebitku to 706–690. Moreover, according to Kahn, Pi(ankh)y's campaign against Tefnakht of Sais and his Delta allies was launched in 734 and was the reason why Hanun of Gaza, who had sought asylum with his Egyptian supporters, now threatened by the Nubians, did not remain in Egypt but returned home to submit to Tiglath-pileser III. Nubian contacts with Assyria are clearly attested by 732 BCE, when both Nubians and Egyptians are listed as among those receiving rations of wine at the Assyrian capital, Calah.[6] Both chronologies agree that Tefnakht soon reasserted control over the Delta, and both agree that it was either to Tefnakht directly or to him through his vassal Osorkon IV of Tanis that Hoshea of Israel sent tribute to secure Egyptian aid for his revolt against Shalmaneser V. But, according to Kahn, Tefnakht (734–725) was succeeded by his son Bakenranef (725–720) five years earlier than in Hoffmeier's chronology. This has a bearing on who was responsible for sending the Egyptian army under Reu to relieve Sargon's siege of Gaza during the Hamath-Gaza-Samaria revolt of 720 BCE. Hoffmeier apparently thinks this was a force sent by Tefnakht or Bakenranef or their Delta vassals, but there is strong evidence that Nubian troops made up a significant part of this relief force. Reliefs from Sargon's palace at Dur-Sharruken show Nubian soldiers defending the walls of Raphia and Gabbatuna.[7] That would be easier to explain, if one saw this relief force as sent by a Nubian ruler, either Pi(ankh)y, following Hoffmeier's chronology, or more likely Shabako after his disposal of Bakenranef, following Kahn's chronology. The supposedly moderately peaceful policy of Shabako toward Assyria is

---

1   See my "Egyptian and Nubian Oracles," 201–9, from which much of the following discussion is taken.

2   Kitchen, *Third Intermediate*, 3rd ed.; Török, *The Kingdom of Kush: Handbook of the Napatan-Meroitic Civilization* (HO 31; Leiden: Brill, 1997); J. K. Hoffmeier, "Egypt's Role in the Events of 701 B.C. in Jerusalem: A Rejoinder to J. J. M. Roberts," in Andrew G. Vaughn and Ann E. Killebrew, eds., *Jerusalem in Bible and Archaeology: The First Temple Period* (SBLSymS 18; Atlanta: Society of Biblical Literature, 2003) 219–34.

3   Frame, "Inscription of Sargon II," 31–57; D. Kahn, "The Inscription of Sargon II at Tang-I Var and the Chronology of Dynasty 25," *Or* n.s. 70 (2001) 1–8.

4   See Hoffmeier, "Egypt's Role," 285–89.

5   Kahn, "Inscription of Sargon II," 1–8; Rainey and Notley, *Sacred Bridge*, 233.

6   J. V. Kinnier Wilson, *The Nimrud Wine Lists: A Study of Men and Administration at the Assyrian Capital in the Eighth Century B.C.* (Cuneiform Texts from Nimrud 1; London: British School of Archaeology in Iraq, 1972) 91–92.

7   N. Franklin, "The Room V Reliefs at Dur-Sharruken and Sargon II's Western Campaigns," *TA* 21 (1994) 255–75, esp. 267, fig. 5.

difficult to justify in any case. After the defeat of Reu's Egyptian/Nubian army in 720, there does appear to have followed a brief period of detente between Assyria and Egypt. Sargon claims to have opened trade with Egypt,[8] a claim that is usually dated to the period between the suppression of the Hamath-Gaza-Samaria revolt in 720 and the renewed difficulties with Ashdod c. 715. Osorkon IV of Tanis even sent a gift of horses to Sargon in 716 or 715.[9] According to Hoffmeier's chronology, this period of peace would largely fall in the reign of Bakenranef of Sais, before Shabako's conquest of the Delta, and thus would reflect the policy of the Delta rulers, not that of the Nubians. By 715 BCE such a temporary peace is clearly on the way out. Azuri of Ashdod's attempt to recruit other small Palestinian and south Syrian states to join in his anti-Assyrian rebellion appears to have had encouragement from the Nubian court. When an Assyrian force removed him from office and replaced him with his pro-Assyrian brother Ahimeti, the inhabitants of Ashdod soon removed this Assyrian puppet and replaced him with the adventurer Yamani, who again began writing letters to the surrounding states urging a united revolt against Assyria. It seems clear that the real power behind this anti-Assyrian agitation was the Nubians and their Egyptian vassals, whose ambassadors were promising military assistance to the small Palestinian states who would join this revolt. On either chronology, the Nubian ruler of Egypt during this period was Shabako. When Sargon's military commander (*turtānu*) put down the Ashdod revolt in 711 BCE, no Nubian-Egyptian relief force came to the assistance of Ashdod as it had to Gaza in 720, but Shabako's continuing hostility toward Assyria is indicated by the fact that he gave Yamani political asylum in upper Egypt near Nubia for some four to five years. It was only in 707 or 706 that (following Hoffmeier) Shabako had his co-regent Shebitku extradite Yamani to Assyria, or (following Kahn) that Shebitku at his accession to the Nubian throne in 706 decided to extradite Yamani to Assyria. In either case, that action need not suggest a new Nubian desire for a genuine long-term peace with Assyria. Shabako, or the supposedly more hostile Shebitku, may have wanted to avoid any immediate outbreak of hostilities with Assyria. But it is also true that, by 706 BCE, Yamani would have lost any political value his continued asylum might have had for Nubia, and his extradition would not only appease Assyria for the moment but would also allow the Nubian agents who escorted him to Assyria to gain useful intelligence about Assyria.

To indicate how both the uncertainty about the Egyptian chronology for this period and the allusive quality of the historical references in Isaiah 19 contribute to the difficulty of a clear, historically contextual interpretation of this material, one need cite only one example. The threat that Yahweh would stir up internecine warfare within Egypt (19:2) and then deliver the Egyptians into the hand of a harsh master (19:4), could reasonably be interpreted to refer to the forcible unification of the Delta rulers under Tefnakht of Sais and his campaign to take Memphis, or to his successor Bakenranef's renewed attempt to achieve the same goal. In the same way, the harsh master into whose hand Yahweh would deliver the Egyptians could be interpreted to refer to Pi(ankh)y and his famous conquest of Middle Egypt and his temporary subjugation of the Delta rulers, including Tefnakht of Sais, who, while refusing to appear before Pi(ankh)y, nonetheless paid tribute to the officers of Pi(ankh)y at Sais. Or the harsh master could be interpreted to refer to Pi(ankh)y's successor Shabako, who resubjugated the Delta rulers, and, according to Manetho, burned Bakenranef, Tefnakht's successor in Sais, to death. But if the references are to Tefnakht's campaign and Pi(ankhy)'s response, are the events to be dated to approximately 734–733, the period of the Syro-Ephraimitic War, following Kahn's chronology, or to around 727, following Hoffmeier's chronology? And if the references are to Bakenranef's campaign and Shabako's response, are the events to be dated around 720, the period of the Hamath-Gaza-Samaria revolt, according to Kahn's chronology, or to 715, near the beginning of the Ashdod affair, according to Hoffmeier's chronology? One may have strong preferences for one interpretation over another, but, given the state of the evidence, real certainty is impossible.

---

8   Fuchs, *Die Inschriften Sargons II,* pp. 88 and 314, lines 17-18.
9   See the references and discussion in my "Egypt, Assyria, Isaiah," 265–83, esp. 269.

Another major difficulty in interpreting the text is the issue of the extent of the literary units. Isaiah 19:1-4 could easily be read as a complete, independent prophetic oracle, since it has a clearly marked beginning and end and it expresses a complete thought. Isaiah 19:5-15 could also be taken as an independent oracle, but neither its beginning nor its end is as clearly marked as 19:1-4, and, whatever its oral prehistory, Isa 19:5-15 appears to have been attached to 19:1-4 as its literary extension, thereby allowing vv. 1-4 to influence the interpretation of the following verses. The fivefold repetition of "in that day"

to introduce vv. 16-17; v. 18; vv. 19-22; v. 23; and v. 24 has usually been seen as a means of attaching five brief additions of later writers of much later date, but the actual historical setting of these sayings is quite uncertain, and in their present literary setting they represent a literary extension of 19:1-4, 5-15. In the commentary, I will treat this material as three units: vv. 1-4; vv. 5-15; and vv. 16-24, though recognizing that these units now constitute a single literary whole, and thus the bibliography will be given only at the end of the commentary on the third unit.

19:1-4

1/ Oracle concerning Egypt:
 Yahweh is about to ride[a] upon a swift cloud,
 And he will enter Egypt,
 And the idols of Egypt will quake before him,
 And the heart of Egypt[b] will melt in its midst.[c]
2/ And I will stir up[d] Egyptian against Egyptian,[e]
 And they will fight each against his brother and each against his neighbor.
 City against city,[f] kingdom against kingdom;
3/ And the spirit of Egypt will be emptied in its midst,
 And his counsel I will swallow up/confuse,
 And to inquire they will go to the idols and to the ghosts,
 And to the necromancers[g] and to the mediums.
4/ And I will deliver the Egyptians into the hand of a harsh master,[h]
 And a strong king will rule[i] among them,
 Says[j] the Lord Yahweh[k] of Hosts.

Textual Notes

a MT has רֹכֵב (*rōkēb*), "is about to ride, mount"; 1QIsaᵃ רוכב; LXX has κάθηται, "is sitting."

b MT וּלְבַב מִצְרַיִם (*ûlĕbab miṣrayim*), "and the heart of Egypt/the Egyptians," 1QIsaᵃ, Vg., Syr., Tg.; LXX καὶ ἡ καρδία αὐτῶν, "and their heart."

c MT בְּקִרְבּוֹ (*bĕqirbô*), "in its midst"; 1QIsaᵃ ברבו.

d MT וְסִכְסַכְתִּי (*wĕsiksaktî*), "and I will stir up, incite, provoke"; 1QIsaᵃ וס'סכתי; active first person also in Vg., Tg., Syr.; 4QIsaᵇ, though the last letter is missing in a break, apparently has the shortened form וסכתי. LXX turns the verb into a plural passive καὶ ἐπεγερθήσονται, "and (Egyptians) will be raised up against (Egyptians)."

e MT מִצְרַיִם בְּמִצְרַיִם (*miṣrayim bĕmiṣrayim*), "Egyptian against Egyptian," so 1QIsaᵃ and the versions; 4QIsaᵇ has an obviously corrupt במצרים במצרֹם.

f MT עִיר בְּעִיר (*ʿîr bĕ ʿîr*), "city against city," so also the versions; 1QIsaᵃ adds the copulative ועיר בעיר, "and city against city."

g MT וְאֶל־הָאֹבֹות (*wĕ ʾel-hā ʾōbôt*), "and to the necromancers"; 1QIsaᵃ ואל האיבות.

h MT בְּיַד אֲדֹנִים קָשֶׁה (*bĕyad ʾădōnîm qāšeh*), "into the hand of a harsh master"; 1QIsaᵃ ביד אדונים קשה; *ʾădōnîm* is a plural form, perhaps a plural of majesty, but is intended to refer to a single master, as the following singular adjective *qāšeh* shows.[10] Tg. gets it right, but LXX, Vg., and Syr. all read a plural.

i MT וּמֶלֶךְ עַז יִמְשָׁל (*ûmelek ʿaz yimšol*), "and a strong king will rule," so 1QIsaᵃ, Vg., Syr., Tg.; LXX has the plural καὶ βασιλεῖς σκληροὶ κυριεύσουσιν αὐτῶν, "and cruel kings will lord it over them."

j MT נְאֻם (*nĕ ʾum*), "says," "oracle of"; 1QIsaᵃ נואם.

k MT הָאָדֹון יְהֹוָה (*hā ʾādôn YHWH*), "the Lord Yahweh," so 1QIsaᵃ; LXX, Vg., and Syr. omit one of the two words.

10 See 1 Kgs 16:24; Gen 40:7; Exod 21:4, 6, 8, 32; passim; BDB, 11, s.v. אָדֹון, col. 1, 2.a-g.

Commentary

The oracle is introduced with the term מַשָּׂא (*maśśā*), "oracle," followed by a country name indicating whom the oracle concerns, as in 13:1 and 15:1. A similar construction followed by a city name is found in 17:1; 21:11; and 23:1. The term is also used to introduce oracles followed by less specific place-names in 21:1, 13; 22:1, and by a reference to animals in 30:6. Here Egypt is the target of the oracle, though the real audience for the oracle is not Egyptians but the prophet's Judean contemporaries, especially the Judean royal court. The oracle against Egypt is a warning to the Judean court not to trust Egypt as a potential ally against the Assyrian threat, as the Philistines, Israel, Hamath, and other south Syrian states were repeatedly tempted to do in the last three decades of the eighth century BCE.

Yahweh threatens to invade Egypt, riding on a swift cloud. The imagery is derived from that of the storm god Baal, one of whose standard epithets was *rkb ʿrpt*, "rider of the clouds,"[11] an epithet apparently appropriated for Yahweh in Ps 68:5's סֹלּוּ לָרֹכֵב בָּעֲרָבוֹת (*sōllû lārōkēb bāʿărābôt*), "lift up a song to the one who rides upon the clouds." In 2 Sam 22:11 and Ps 18:11 the poet says of Yahweh, וַיִּרְכַּב עַל־כְּרוּב וַיָּעֹף וַיֵּדֶא עַל־כַּנְפֵי־רוּחַ (*wayyirkab ʿal-kĕrûb wayyāʿōp wayyēde*[12] *ʿal-kanpê-rûaḥ*), "and he rode upon a cherub and flew, and glided on the wings of the wind." Both expressions are connected to the ancient tradition of Yahweh's theophanic appearance in the clouds of a violent thunderstorm (Exod 15:8-10; Judg 5:4-5; 2 Sam 22:8-16; Pss 18:8-16; 68:8-10; Hab 3:3-15). The association between the clouds and storm winds and the cherub as Yahweh's chariot mount is probably also indicated by the iconography of the giant cherubim throne with their wings outstretched in the inner sanctum of the Jerusalem temple and the common epithet for Yahweh יֹשֵׁב הַכְּרוּבִים (*yōšēb hakkĕrûbîm*), "who sits enthroned upon the cherubim" (1 Sam 4:4; 2 Sam 6:2; 2 Kgs 19:15; Isa 37:16; Pss 80:2; 99:1; 1 Chr 13:6). The imagery suggests that Yahweh will swoop down on the Egyptians with unexpected suddenness and frightening speed, and the impact on the unsuspecting Egyptians and their idols will be sheer terror, leaving the idols quaking and the Egyptians without heart or courage.

Verse 1 describes the action as Yahweh's action, the heavenly or divine reality behind what is about to happen on earth, but v. 2 indicates the human agents or earthly actors by which this divine action will be accomplished. Yahweh will stir up Egyptians against Egyptians, and Egypt will be racked by civil war. The description fits very well the impact on the Delta region that the military campaigns Tefnakht and Bakenranef of Sais waged to unite all the kinglets of lower Egypt under their rule.[13] Under the Libyan dynasts of the eighth century, Egypt was split up among a host of independent or semi-independent kingdoms until Tefnakht forcibly subjected them in his campaign to subdue all of Egypt. His march south alarmed the Nubian rulers of upper Egypt, however, and the Nubian Pi(ankh)y soon marched north, driving Tefnakht from Memphis and forcing all the Delta dynasts to acknowledge the Nubian as their overlord. Even Tefnakht grudgingly paid tribute, though refusing to appear before Pi(ankh)y. After Pi(ankh)y's withdrawal from middle Egypt, however, Tefnakht again began to assert control over the dynasts of lower Egypt, and his successor, Bakenranef, continued this policy, eventually feeling strong enough to march against upper Egypt. He in turn was defeated by Pi(ankh)y's successor, Shabako, who killed Bakenranef and imposed stronger Nubian controls on the delta region.

In v. 3 the prophet characterizes Egyptian behavior during this period of civil war as abject folly. The "emptying of Egypt's spirit" is the equivalent of saying they will lose their senses, but their foolish behavior has a deeper root—it is Yahweh himself who will confuse their counsel. In this confusion and folly, the Egyptians will resort to idols, ghosts, necromancers, and mediums, all of which underscores the Egyptians' lack of sense. The first term in the list normally refers to pagan gods as vain and useless, but the last three terms all refer to the practice of

---

11 Richard E. Whitaker's *A Concordance of the Ugaritic Literature* (Cambridge, MA: Harvard University Press, 1972) 573, lists sixteen occurrences of the epithet.

12 2 Samuel 22:11 reads וַיֵּרָא (*wayyērā*), "and was seen," but this is probably an error involving the common misreading of *dalet* as *resh*.

13 See the discussion and the sources mentioned in the introduction to this section.

consulting the ghosts of the dead for information about the future. One wonders whether Isaiah's highlighting of necromancy reflects its actual importance in contemporary Egyptian practice, or whether it is more of a dig against Isaiah's Judean contemporaries, who also engaged in and defended this practice (Isa 8:19-20). In any case, Isaiah's word lumps together all who rely on ghosts for advice, whether Egyptian or Judean, as bereft of sense.

Yahweh's ultimate judgment of Egypt's folly is to hand them over to a harsh master and a strong king who will rule over them. Attempts to identify this harsh master have suggested many possibilities, including the Egyptian Tefnakht, the Nubians Pi(ankh)y and Shabako, a number of Assyrian kings, and, for those who date the passage quite late, even Persian and later kings. In my judgment, the passage fits an eighth-century date quite well, and neither the content nor the vocabulary of the oracle offers any compelling reason to deny it to Isaiah of Jerusalem. Assuming it is by Isaiah in the eighth century, I doubt he intended to identify any of the Delta dynasts, even one of the vigorous rulers of Sais, as the harsh master.

Tefnakht or Bakenranef may have been more powerful than any of their Delta colleagues, but they were still part of the group. The same could not be said of Pi(ankh)y or Shabako, who imposed imperial Nubian rule on the Delta rulers either for the first time or, in the case of Shabako, more thoroughly than his predecessor. Thus, one of these two Nubian rulers was probably the harsh master originally intended by Isaiah. In the course of time, as Assyria became more of a threat to Egypt, first under Sargon II (721–705 BCE); then especially under Sennacherib (704–681); Esarhaddon (680–669), who invaded Egypt; and Ashurbanipal (668–626), who conquered Egypt, one could see how the oracle could be reread as referring to an Assyrian king as the harsh ruler. But by the time any of these Assyrian kings seriously threatened Egypt, Egypt was already under Nubian rule, and, had that been the original sense, one might have expected the description of Egyptian civil war to include both Egyptians and Nubians, not just Egyptians. The oracle closes with a formula whose epithets for Yahweh—the Lord Yahweh of Hosts—highlight his imperial and military might.

19:5-15

5/   And the waters will dry up[a] from the sea (Nile),
    And the river will become dry[b] and parched,

6/   And the canals[c] will stink,[d]
    The water courses of Egypt[e] will become low and dry;[f]
    The canes and reeds will wilt,[g]

7/   The rushes[h] beside the Nile, by the mouth of the Nile,[i]
    And everything[j] sown by the Nile will dry up,[k] be blown away,[l] and be no more.[m]

8/   And the fishermen[n] will lament,
    And all[o] who cast a hook into the Nile[p] will mourn,
    And those who spread a net[q] upon the surface of the waters[r] will languish.

9/   And those who work[s] with flax[t] will be ashamed,[u]
    The combers[v] and weavers[w] will grow pale[x]

10/   And those who drink wine[y] will be crushed,
    And all who make beer[z] will be sad of soul.*[a]

11/   Yes, the princes of Tanis are fools,
    The wisest*[b] counselors of Pharaoh (give)*[c] foolish counsel.
    How can you say to Pharaoh,
    "I*[d] am the son*[d] of wise men,*[e] the son*[d] of kings of old?

12/   Where then are your wise men?
    Let them tell you, let them know*[f]
    What Yahweh of Hosts*[g] has planned against Egypt.

13/   The princes of Tanis have become fools,*[h]
    The princes of Memphis are deceived,*[i]
    The cornerstones*[j] of its tribes have made Egypt stagger.

14/   Yahweh has mixed*[k] into her midst a spirit of confusion,*[l]
    And they have caused Egypt to stagger in all its work,*[m]
    Like a drunk man staggers in his vomit.*[n]

15/   And there will not*[o] be for Egypt any work
    Which either head or tail, palm frond or reed,*[p] may accomplish.

Textual Notes

a   LXX misunderstands the verb וְנִשְּׁתוּ (wĕniššĕtû), "and they will dry up," the niphal perfect third person masculine plural of נשׁת, as though it were from שׁתה, "to drink," and thus renders καὶ πίονται οἱ Αἰγύπτιοι ὕδωρ τὸ παρὰ θάλασσαν, "and the Egyptians will drink the water which is by the sea."

b   MT יֶחֱרַב (yeḥĕrab), "will become dry"; 1QIsaᵃ has יחרוב with dots above and below the ו, suggesting the waw is a mistake.

c   MT נְהָרוֹת (nĕhārôt), "rivers," omits the article; 1QIsaᵃ has it (הנהרות, "the rivers").

d   Read והזניחו (wĕheznîḥû), "and they will stink," with 1QIsaᵃ. MT וְהֶאֱזְנִיחוּ (wĕheʾeznîḥû) is a conflation of the aphel and hiphil forms, even if the remnants of 4QIsaᵇ support MT; the versions understand the verb in the sense of "be lacking, dry up."

e   MT יְאֹרֵי מָצוֹר (yĕʾōrê māṣôr), "the water courses of Egypt"; 1QIsaᵃ יאורי מצור. The form מָצוֹר (māṣôr), "Egypt," is not the usual spelling for Egypt, though the form is also attested in Isa 37:25; 2 Kgs 19:24; and Mic 7:12, so it is not surprising that none of the versions translates it correctly. LXX renders the expression as πᾶσα συναγωγὴ ὕδατος, "every gathering of water"; Vg. has rivi aggerum, "rivers of the ramparts"; Syr. has "strong rivers"; and Tg. has "their deep rivers."

f   MT דָּלֲלוּ וְחָרֵבוּ (dālălû wĕḥārēbû), "will become low and dry"; 1QIsaᵃ has ודללו וחרבו. Vg. and Tg. seem to support MT's reading, while Syr. supports 1QIsaᵃ. LXX's translation is too free to help.

g   MT קָמֵלוּ (qāmēlû), "will wilt"; 1QIsaᵃ וקמלו. The waw-conversive is not expected when the verb follows the subject.

h   MT עָרוֹת (ʿārôt), "rushes," 1QIsaᵃ, 4QIsaᵇ; LXX καὶ τὸ ἄχι τὸ χλωρὸν πᾶν τὸ κύκλῳ τοῦ ποταμοῦ, "and the green marsh grass, all that is around the river"; Syr. "and pond weed that is by the river and by the mouth of the river." Vg. reads the form as a verb, nudabitur alveus rivi a fonte, "the channel of the river will be laid bare to the source."

i   MT עַל־יְאוֹר עַל־פִּי יְאוֹר (ʿal-yĕʾōr ʿal-pî yĕʾōr), "beside the Nile, by the mouth of the Nile"; 1QIsaᵃ על יאר על פי יאור; both 1QIsaᵇ and 4QIsaᵇ appear to have the variant spelling יאר, though otherwise the same text. One may wonder whether ʿal-yĕʾōr and ʿal-pî yĕʾōr were originally variant readings that were conflated.

j   MT וְכֹל (wĕkōl), "and all"; 1QIsaᵃ וכול.

k   MT יִיבַשׁ (yîbaš), "will dry up"; 1QIsaᵃ יבש.

l   MT and 4QIsaᵇ נִדַּף (niddap), "be blown away"; 1QIsaᵃ ונדף, "and be blown away."

m   MT and 4QIsaᵇ וְאֵינֶנּוּ (wĕʾênennû), "and it is not, will be no more"; 1QIsaᵃ ואין בו, "and it will not be in it." LXX omits the phrase.

n   MT and 4QIsaᵇ הַדַּיָּגִים (haddayyāgîm), "the fishermen"; 1QIsaᵃ הדגים.

o   MT כָּל (kol), 4QIsaᵃ כל; but 1QIsaᵃ כול.

p   MT and 1QIsaᵃ בַיְאוֹר (bayʾôr), "into the Nile"; 1QIsaᵇ ביאר.

q   LXX has a double translation for "those who spread the net": καὶ οἱ βάλλοντες σαγήνας καὶ οἱ ἀμφιβολεῖς, "and those throwing nets and those casting nets."

r   LXX omits the phrase "upon the surface of the waters."

s   MT and 4QIsaᵇ עֹבְדֵי (ʿōbĕdê), "the workers of"; 1QIsaᵃ עובדי.

t   MT פִּשְׁתִּים (pištîm), "flax"; 1QIsaᵃ originally wrote פשׁתיים, but blotted the second yod out with ink.

u   MT וּבֹשׁוּ (ûbōšû), "and they will be ashamed"; 1QIsaᵃ and 4QIsaᵇ יבשו.

v   MT, supported by 1QIsaᵃ, has שְׂרִיקוֹת (śĕrîqôt), "combed," and the MT accentuation places this word with the preceding line: "The workers of combed flax will be ashamed." LXX follows this reading with its τὸ λίνον τὸ σχιστὸν, "the split linen." The reading, whether with the LXX addition or not, is problematic, however, since it makes the first line of v. 9 about twice as long as the second line, and the adjective śĕrîqôt is a feminine plural while pištîm, the noun it supposedly modifies, is masculine plural. Vg., Syr., and Tg. all have an active masculine plural participle, but that leaves unclear how the corruption to the feminine plural form took place. I restore the feminine plural participle שׂרקות (śōrĕqôt), "those who comb," and assume that the combers at the time were typically women. The correction to the masculine plural in the versions is due to the masculine plural participles before and after this form, and it reflects the general tendency among scribes to shift to the masculine.

w   MT וְאֹרְגִים (wĕʾōrĕgîm), "and weavers"; 1QIsaᵃ ואורגים.

x   Reading חָוְרוּ (ḥāwĕrû), "they grow pale," with 1QIsaᵃ (חורו) and 4QIsaᵇ (חורו); MT's and 1QIsaᵇ's חֹרָי (ḥōrāy) is normally understood as "white cloth."[14] The verb fits the context better and is attested elsewhere in Isaiah in parallelism to בוש (Isa 29:22) as here, though none of the ancient versions reads the form as a verb.

y   With A. B. Ehrlich, I emend MT's שָׁתֹתֶיהָ (šātōteyhā), "its (fem.) . . . ," to שׁתי יין (šōtê yayin), "drinkers of wine"; cf. Joel 1:5).[15] Wine was produced in at least limited quantities in Egypt, as tomb reliefs (see ANEP 48, fig. 156) and other evidence demonstrate, though in contrast to beer, wine was a drink largely limited to the elite.[16] The MT reading, supported by 1QIsaᵇ,

---

14   So BDB, 301.

15   Arnold B. Ehrlich, *Randglossen zur hebräischen Bibel, textkritisches, sprachliches und sachliches*, vol. 4, *Jesaia, Jeremia* (Leipzig: Hinrichs, 1912) 70.

16   See Leonard H. Lesko, *King Tut's Wine Cellar* (Berkeley: B.C. Scribe Publications, 1977); H. F. Lutz, *Viticulture and Brewing in the Ancient Orient* (Leipzig: Hinrichs, 1922); P. E. McGovern, S. J. Fleming, and S. H. Katz, eds., *The Origins and Ancient History of Wine* (Food and Nutrition in History and Anthropology 11; Amsterdam: Gordon & Breach, 1996); Patrick E. McGovern, *Uncorking the Past: The Quest for Wine, Beer, and Other Alcoholic Beverages* (Berkeley: University of California Press, 2009);

and the reading of 1QIsaᵃ and 4QIsaᵇ (שׁותתיה), which suggests an active participle, are both difficult cruxes. To begin with, the meaning of the main word is disputed. One explanation is to see the form *šātōt* as a masculine plural of שֵׁת (*šēt*), "foundation, buttock"; see esp. Ps 11:3.[17] With this derivation one would get the translation, "And its foundations will be crushed." Other suggestions include שֹׁתֶיהָ (*šōtêhā*), "her weavers," from שׁתה I.[18] and שְׁתִיתֶיהָ (*šětîtêhā*), "her weavers," based on Coptic *štit*, "weaver."[19] A problem with all these suggestions is the final third person feminine singular suffix. Egypt is sometimes construed as a feminine singular, but the last mention of Egypt was back in v. 4, and there is no other feminine noun to serve as the antecedent for this pronoun in the immediately preceding verses. It is obviously an old crux, since the versions all struggled with the expression. LXX rendered καὶ ἔσονται οἱ διαζόμενοι αὐτὰ ἐν ὀδύνῃ, "and those who weave them will be in pain," turning the suffix into a plural and making it refer to "the split flax" and "linen" that LXX saw in the *pištîm śěrîqôt* and *ḥôrāy* of v. 9. Vg. obviously sees the root as שׁתה II, "to drink," with its rendering, *et erunt inrigua eius flaccentia*, "and its marshes (well-watered places) will be languishing." Tg.'s "and the place where one drinks its water will be crushed," and Syr. (see below) take a similar tack.

z   MT כָּל־עֹשֵׂי שֶׂכֶר (*kol-ʿōśê śeker*) and 1QIsaᵃ כל עושי שכר also constitute a crux. I correct שֶׂכֶר to שֵׁכָר (*šēkār*), "beer," and translate "all those who make beer" with the LXX: καὶ πάντες οἱ τὸν ζῦθον ποιοῦντες, "and all who make beer." Syr. appears to have the same reading with its simplified translation of the verse, "and all those who make beer to drink shall be crushed of soul [*wntmkkwn kl dʿbdyn škrʾ lmštyʾ dnpšʾ*]." Others see שכר as a byform of סכר and understand the word as "dam,"[20] which seems to lie behind Tg.'s "the place of those who make a dam and gather water," and Vg.'s *omnes qui faciebant lacunas ad capiendos pisces*, "all who make lakes for catching fish." Other modern scholars understand שֶׂכֶר (*śeker*) as "wage," and translate "all those who work for hire" (Watts, *Isaiah 1–33*, 305, 307; NRSV). Given the difficulty of the verse, any claim to certainty as to the correct interpretation and reading should be greeted with great skepticism. Nonetheless, despite the emendation in the first line of the verse, I think my reading makes the most sense of the text. The two parallel lines in the verse should deal with related ideas. The first line should not still be about working and weaving flax as in v. 9, if the second line of the verse is about some entirely different activity. Wine and beer are often in parallel (Isa 5:11, 22; 24:9; 28:7; 29:9; Lev 10:9; Num 6:3;

Deut 14:26; passim), and if the second line is about those who make beer, those who drink wine would fit well in the first line. Ehrlich argued that עֹשֵׂי שֵׁכָר, "those who make beer," was not a good Hebrew expression, that in Hebrew one would talk not about the maker but the consumer of beer; hence he corrected the expression in the second line to שׁתי שכר, "the drinkers of beer" (see n. 15 above). But the repetition of שׁתי in both lines of poetry would not be elegant, and Ehrlich's argument makes no sense. As the Syr. translator understood, one makes beer to drink it. The brewing of beer is more labor-intensive than the fermenting of wine, and the drying up of the water courses of the Nile would mean a shortage of the water necessary for the brewing process.

*a   LXX seems to have a double translation for אַגְמֵי־נָפֶשׁ (*ʾagmê nāpeš*), "those grieved of soul": λυπηθήσονται καὶ τὰς ψυχὰς πονέσουσιν, "they will be grieved and afflict their souls."

*b   MT and 1QIsaᵇ חַכְמֵי יֹעֲצֵי פַרְעֹה (*ḥakmê yōʿăṣê parʿōh*), "the wisest of the counselors of Pharaoh"; 4QIsaᵇ חכמי יועצי פרעה; but 1QIsaᵃ חכמיה יועצי פרעוה (*ḥakmêhā yōʿăṣê parʿōh*), "its wise men, the counselors of Pharaoh."

*c   The Hebrew text seems to be lacking a verb, which the versions supply in one fashion or another. LXX adds a suffix to the word for "counsel" to ease the translation: ἡ βουλὴ αὐτῶν μωρανθήσεται, "the wise counselors of the king—their counsel will become foolish"; Vg. (*dederunt consilium insipiens*, "they gave foolish counsel") and Syr (*mlkʾ mlkʾ šṭyʾ*, "they counsel foolish counsel") simply add a verb, while Tg. turns the construct participle יעצי (*yōʿăṣê*) into a finite verb (*ḥkymyʾ dmlkwhy lprʿh mylk dṭʿw*, "the wise men who counsel Pharaoh a deceitful counsel").

*d   The Hebrew texts MT, 1QIsaᵃ, and 4QIsaᵇ all have the singular forms אני, "I," and בן, "son," and Vg. follows suit. LXX, Tg., and Syr. turn these into plurals.

*e   MT and 4QIsaᵇ חֲכָמִים (*ḥăkāmîm*), "wise men"; 1QIsaᵃ accidentally omits a letter חמים.

*f   MT וְיֵדְעוּ (*wěyēděʿû*), "that they may know, let them know," is treated by LXX (καὶ εἰπάτωσαν, "and let them say") and Vg. (*et indicent*, "and declare") as though it meant "let them make known."

*g   1QIsaᵃ originally omitted צְבָאוֹת (*šěbāʾôt*), "of Hosts," but then inserted it above the line.

*h   MT נֹואֲלוּ (*nôʾālû*), "they have become fools"; 1QIsaᵃ נאלו. The two verbs יאל and אול are byforms of the same root. LXX has ἐξέλιπον οἱ ἄρχοντες Τάνεως, "the princes of Tanis failed."

M. A. Murray with N. Boulton and C. Heron, "Viticulture and Wine Production," in P. T. Nicholson and I. Shaw, eds., *Ancient Egyptian Materials and Technology* (Cambridge: Cambridge University Press, 2000) 577–608; Muzhou Pu (Mu-Chou Poo), *Wine and Wine Offering in the Religion of Ancient Egypt* (New York: Kegan Paul International/Columbia University Press, 1995).

17   So David Kimchi and Ibn Ezra according to Gray, 328.

18   So *HALOT*, 1667.

19   So I. Eitan, "An Egyptian Loan Word in Is 19," *JQR* 15 (1924–25) 419–22, followed by *BHS*.

20   So Rashi, Kimchi, and Ibn Ezra according to Gray, 328, and among modern translators, the JPS.

*i MT נִשְׁאוּ (niššĕʾû), "they are deceived," 1QIsaᵃ נש'או. LXX, followed by Syr., misreads the verb as though it were from *nāśāʾ*, "to lift up": καὶ ὑψώθησαν οἱ ἄρχοντες Μέμφεως, "and the princes of Memphis have been exalted"; Vg. has "the princes of Memphis have withered [*emarcuerunt*]."

*j MT פִּנַּת (pinnat), "cornerstone"; 1QIsaᵃ and 4QIsaᵇ פנת. Since the verb הִתְעוּ (hiteʿû), "they led astray," is plural, one should either correct the noun to the plural *pinnōt*, or assume that the singular was being treated as a collective. LXX has καὶ πλανήσουσιν Αἴγυπτον κατὰ φυλάς, "and they shall deceive Egypt tribe by tribe," while Vg. takes פנת as appositional to Egypt: *deceperunt Aegyptum angulum populorum eius*, "and they have deceived Egypt, the corner of his people."

*k MT and 1QIsaᵃ מָסַךְ (māsak), "he mixed"; 4QIsaᵇ נסך], "he poured"; LXX, Vg., and Syr. support MT.

*l MT עֹעֵעִים (ʿiwĕʿîm), "confusion"; 1QIsaᵃ עועיים.

*m MT בְּכָל־מַעֲשֵׂהוּ (bĕkol-maʿăśēhû), "in all his/its work"; 1QIsaᵃ בכול מעשהו. The switch to the masculine suffix here after the feminine suffix on בְּקִרְבָּהּ (bĕqirbâ), "in her midst," is confusing, though it may be provoked by the masculine metaphor about the drunk and his vomit which follows.

*n MT and 4QIsaᵇ בְּקִיאוֹ (bĕqîʾô, "in his vomit"); 1QIsaᵃ בקיאו. LXX and Vg. read a participle here, "and the one who vomits."

*o MT וְלֹא (wĕlōʾ, "and not"); 1QIsaᵃ ולוא.

*p MT רֹאשׁ וְזָנָב כִּפָּה וְאַגְמֹן (rōʾš wĕzānāb kippâ wĕʾagmôn, "head and tail, palm frond and reed"); 1QIsaᵃ ראוש וזנב כפה ואגמן. LXX, Vg., and Syr. all take these terms as objects of the verb, while the Hebrew apparently understands them as the subject.

Commentary

Whether Isa 19:5-15 ever existed as an independent oracle is open to debate, but in its present form it has no clear beginning or a sharply marked conclusion. If it was originally an independent oracle, it appears to have been edited to make it a simple literary continuation of the preceding oracle in vv. 1-4. It depends on the preceding verses for its setting, and its lack of a forceful closing makes it easy to extend by additional sayings. In its present form it reads as a natural continuation of Yahweh's judgment on Egypt, though it does switch from language of military conquest to the language of drought and nature-inspired disruption of Egypt's economic prosperity. In v. 11, however, the author reverts to the theme of Egypt's folly, and in vv. 12 and 14 the earlier theme of Yahweh's intervention to disrupt Egypt's wisdom or counsel (v. 3) is again sounded. The similarities in motifs and vocabulary make it at least possible that vv. 5-15 represent Isaiah's own expansion of his thoughts in vv. 1-4.

The author of vv. 5-10 seems to be intimately acquainted with Egyptian culture and customs. This has led Wildberger (2:707), who accepts vv. 1b-4 and 11-14 as Isaianic, to reject Isaiah as the possible author of vv. 5-10, since, in his opinion, Isaiah had not visited Egypt and could not have had that detailed a knowledge of Egyptian economic activities (2:704). But that judgment is hardly self-evident. Isaiah was clearly part of Jerusalem's elite, as his easy access to the Judean kings indicates, and he probably had the same educational background as the royal counselors, with some of whom he constantly clashed. We know very little about Isaiah's private life, but Judah neighbored on Egypt, and Egypt both was a major trading partner and exercised significant cultural influence on Judah. This cultural, economic, and political influence was particularly strong in the last half of the eighth century. As part of the cultured elite, Isaiah may very well have visited Egypt as he was growing up. He certainly seems to have had contacts with emissaries from both Egypt and Nubia during his prophetic ministry (Isa 14:32; 18:1-2; 20:1-6; 30:1-7; 31:1-3). Moreover, general Judean knowledge of Egypt and Egyptian economic practices, particularly among Judah's cultural elite, was probably more extensive than modern scholars sometimes imagine. It is not clear that the description of Egyptian economic life in vv. 5-10 is beyond the knowledge of any well-educated member of Jerusalem's elite, even if that individual had never personally visited Egypt.

The judgment announced in these verses begins with the drying up of the Nile, the backbone of the Egyptian economy and life itself in Egypt. The word pair יָם and נָהָר (yām and nāhār), "sea and river," is a traditional poetic pair going back to Ugaritic myth (see *KTU* 1.2 iii 16; 1.2 iv 27; 1.3 iii 39-40; *passim*; Pss 24:2; 66:6; 72:8; 80:12; 89:26; Isa 11:15; 50:2), but when used of Egypt, both terms refer to the Nile. Egyptian agriculture and economic life depend on the annual rising of the Nile, and when that does not happen or is less than expected due to drought along the headwaters of the river, the economic impact on Egypt can be quite severe. The resulting low waters in the many canals and channels in the Delta region mean that drying mud banks will begin to stink and the reeds along the banks will begin to wither (v. 6). This thought is furthered by the description of all the rushes and crops planted by the Nile drying up, being blown away, and disappearing (v. 7). The word עָרוֹת (ʿārôt), "rushes," is an Egyptian loanword (see *HALOT*) and helps to give this text its strong Egyptian color. The repetition "beside the Nile" "by the mouth of the Nile" may be an intentional poetic device, or it may be the result of the simple conflation of two poetic variants.

At v. 8 the prophet switches from the description of the impact of the low Nile on the vegetation around the Nile to the description of its impact on human economic activity dependent on the Nile flooding. The fishermen are the first to be mentioned. Whether they fish with hook or net, they will lament, mourn, and languish, presumably because the low Nile will seriously reduce their catch. The drying up of the canals and channels in the Delta region would certainly reduce the number of locations along the Nile where fishing remained possible. The second group of workers to be mentioned are those involved in the manufacture of linen. Without the water to grow flax, those who harvest and prepare the flax for further work, those who comb it, and finally those who spin it into linen will be without work. Thus, all these groups will be appalled and pale with worry (v. 9).

Verse 10 is an ancient crux and textually very difficult, but following the readings defended in the textual notes, it appears to address the negative impact of the dry Nile on the Egyptian production and therefore on the drinking of both wine and beer. Beer was a common drink of all classes, so beer brewing was a major industry in Egypt and required a good supply of water. Wine production was more limited, since the drinking of wine tended to be more restricted to the elite, but it was done, and the low Nile would make the necessary irrigation of vineyards more problematic. Everyone in Egypt, from the elite drinkers of wine to the more common producers and drinkers of beer, says the prophet, will suffer and be saddened by the severe shortage of their favorite drinks brought on by the drying up of their water supplies.

At v. 11 the prophet switches from his description of the drying up of the Nile and its impact on the Egyptian economy and returns to his earlier motif of Yahweh's confusion of the counsel of the Egyptians (v. 3). He characterizes the princes of Tanis as fools and asserts that the wisest of Pharaoh's counselors give foolish counsel. Tanis, or Zoan, in the eastern Delta would be the first of the Delta kingdoms that a visitor from Judah would encounter, and Judah's contact with other, more powerful Delta kingdoms like Sais or the even more powerful but more distant Nubian monarchs would require passage through the territory of and presumably permission and safe conduct from the Egyptian ruler of Tanis, here referred to as Pharaoh. The Egyptian counselors apparently claimed a distinguished ancestry, tracing their lineage back to ancient sages and even Egyptian royalty, but Isaiah challenges that claim based on the foolishness of their advice. If they were truly wise, they would be able to tell the ruler of Tanis what Yahweh was planning against Egypt (v. 12), the plan that the prophet announced in vv. 1-4.

In v. 13 the prophet expands his vision to include not only the princes of Tanis but the princes of Memphis and the cornerstones of its tribes as well. They have become fools, are deceived, and have misled Egypt. The reference to the tribes of Egypt expresses well the Libyan tribal roots of the local dynasts of the Delta region. The prophet characterizes the political policies of these local dynasts as foolish. Isaiah does not specify exactly what in their policies he regarded as foolish, but, as my discussion of v. 2 suggests, it may have had to do with Tefnakht or Bakenranef's attempts to unite or reunite all of Egypt under the rule of the kings of Sais. It is noteworthy, however, that the oracle does not specifically mention the princes of Sais.

In any case, Yahweh is responsible for Egypt's confusion. He has caused the country to stagger in all its work, just as a drunk staggers in his vomit (v. 14). The result will be the inability of the Egyptians to accomplish any work, whether the initiative is from the top or the bottom. This concluding verse seems to unite the judgment on the foolish Egyptian leaders (vv. 11-14) with the earlier judgment on the Nile and the tradesmen dependent on its largess (vv. 5-10). In effect, both the political and economic foundations of Egypt will collapse under Yahweh's judgment.

16/ In that day[a] Egypt shall be like women, and it will tremble and be afraid[b] of the waving of the hand of Yahweh of Hosts which he is about to wave over it.[c]

17/ And the land of Judah shall become[d] to Egypt a source of dread;[e] every one[f] to whom someone mentions it[g] shall be afraid of the plan[h] of Yahweh of Hosts which he is planning against it.

18/ In that day there will be five cities in the land of Egypt that speak the language of Canaan and that swear by Yahweh of Hosts;[i] one of these shall be called the city of the sun.[j]

19/ In that day there will be an altar to Yahweh[k] in the midst of the land of Egypt and a stela beside its border for Yahweh.

20/ And it will be[l] as a sign and witness[m] to Yahweh of Hosts[n] in the land of Egypt because they will cry to Yahweh on account of the oppressors[o] and he will send them a savior and defender[p] and he will deliver them.

21/ And Yahweh will make himself known to the Egyptians, and the Egyptians will know Yahweh in that day, and they will make a sacrifice and an offering and they will vow a vow to Yahweh and fulfill (it).

22/ And Yahweh will smite the Egyptians, smiting and healing,[q] and they will return to Yahweh, and he will be entreated by them and he will heal them.

23/ In that day there will be a highway from Egypt to Assyria, and Assyria shall enter[r] into Egypt and Egypt into Assyria, and the Egyptians[s] will serve Assyria.

24/ In that day Israel will be a third to Egypt and to Assyria, a blessing in the midst of the earth,

25/ which Yahweh of Hosts blessed him saying,[t] Blessed be my people Egypt, and the work of my hands Assyria,[u] and my inheritance Israel.

Textual Notes

a   MT בַּיּוֹם הַהוּא (bayyôm hahû᾽), "in that day"; 1QIsa[a] has mistakenly ommited the article on the demonstrative pronoun ביום הוא.

b   MT וְחָרַד וּפָחַד (wĕḥārad ûpāḥad) "and he/it will tremble and be afraid"—(note that Egypt here is construed as masculine singular), 1QIsa[b], 4QIsa[b], Syr.; 1QIsa[a] has the plural וחרדו ופחדו, so also Vg. and Tg. LXX renders ἐν φόβῳ καὶ ἐν τρόμῳ, "in fear and in trembling."

c   MT מֵנִיף עָלָיו (mēnîp ῾ālāyw), "which he is about to wave over him/it"; 1QIsa[a], מ'ניף ידו עליה, "who is about to wave his hand over her." 1QIsa[a] has repeated "his hand" redundantly and appears to be construing Egypt as a feminine, but the MT reading is to be preferred.

d   MT וְהָיְתָה (wĕhāyĕtâ), "and she will become," 4QIsa[b]; 1QIsa[a] והיית.

e   MT לְחָגָּא (lĕḥoggā᾽), "to become a source of dread"; 1QIsa[a] לחוגה. Vg. misunderstands it as in festivitatem, "to a feast, festival," apparently reading לחג (lĕḥag or lĕḥog).

f   MT כֹל (kol), "everyone"; 1QIsa[a] כול.

g   MT אֹתָהּ (᾽ōtāh), "it"; 1QIsa[a] אותה.

h   MT מִפְּנֵי עֲצַת (mippĕnê ῾ăṣat), "from before the plan of," 1QIsa[a] and the versions; 4QIsa[b] has מפני תנופת יד (mippĕnê tĕnûpat yad), "from before the waving of the hand of").

i   LXX omits "of Hosts."

j   MT עִיר הַהֶרֶס (῾îr haheres), "city of destruction"; Syr. just transliterates hrs; 1QIsa[a] and 4QIsa[b] עיר החרס (῾îr haḥeres), "the city of the sun," Vg.; Tg. combines the two readings, "Of the city, house of the sun, which is about to be destroyed, it shall be said, this is one of them." LXX's Πόλισ-ασεδεκ seems to reflect the reading עיר הצדק (῾îr haṣṣedeq), "the city of righteousness." The name ῾îr haḥeres, "the city of the sun," is Hebrew for Heliopolis, and is probably the original reading. Since the name suggests the possibility of idolatrous sun worship, the text was probably intentionally altered for religious reasons.

k   Though the text is broken, 4QIsa[b] appears to add the word צבֿ[אות (ṣĕbā[᾽ôt), "of Ho[sts]") here.

l   MT וְהָיָה (wĕhāyâ), "and it will be," 4QIsa[b]; 1QIsa[a] והייה.

m   MT וּלְעֵד (ûlĕ῾ēd), "and for a witness," 1QIsa[a], 4QIsa[b], Vg., Tg., Syr.; LXX reads לעד (lĕ῾ad), "forever," εἰς τὸν αἰῶνα).

n   LXX omits "of Hosts."

o   MT לֹחֲצִים (lōḥăṣîm), "oppressors"; 1QIsa[a] לוחצים.

p   MT וְרָב (wārāb), "and defender"; 1QIsa[a] וירד (wĕyārad), "and he will go down." The versions, with their different translations, read a participle of ריב here, "a defender, judge, champion," that is, "one who contends legally."

q MT וְרָפוֹא (wĕrāpôʾ), "and healing"; 1QIsaᵃ ונרפו (wĕnirpû), "and they will be healed."

r MT וּבָא־אַשּׁוּר (ûbāʾ-ʾaššûr), "and Assyria will enter"; Tg. is the only version to misunderstand this "entering" as "making war against."

s MT וְעָבְדוּ מִצְרַיִם (wĕʿābĕdû miṣrayim), "and the Egyptians will serve," so also 1QIsaᵇ, 4QIsaᵇ, and all the versions; 1QIsaᵃ omits miṣrayim.

t MT לֵאמֹר (lēʾmōr), "saying"; 1QIsaᵃ לאמור.

u MT עַמִּי מִצְרַיִם וּמַעֲשֵׂה יָדַי אַשּׁוּר (ʿammî miṣrayim ûmaʿăśēh yāday ʾaššûr), "my people Egypt and the work of my hands Assyria," so 1QIsaᵃ, Vulg; LXX has ὁ λαός μου ὁ ἐν Αἰγύπτῳ καὶ ὁ ἐν Ἀσσυρίοις, "my people who are in Egypt and who are in Assyria"; Syr. has "my people who are in Egypt and the work of my hands who are in Assyria." LXX and Syr. are obviously thinking not of Egyptians and Assyrians, but of Israelite exiles in these two countries as the slightly variant Tg. translation makes clear: "my people whom I brought forth from Egypt; because they sinned before me I exiled them to Assyria."

Commentary

Verses 16-17 state that in the day when Yahweh of Hosts waves his hand over Egypt, Egypt will become like women;[21] it will tremble and be afraid, and the land of Judah will become such a source of dread to the Egyptians that every Egyptian to whom another mentions Judah will fear because of the plan of Yahweh of Hosts against Egypt. These verses are clearly dependent on the preceding texts that describe Yahweh's assault on Egypt (vv. 1-4) and his plan against Egypt (vv. 5-15, esp. v. 12). Whether they represent a much later expansion of these texts or whether they go back to Isaiah himself is a subject of debate, but neither the vocabulary nor the thoughts expressed in the verses demand a rejection of Isaianic authorship. The "hand" of Yahweh figures prominently in Isaianic oracles of judgment (5:25; 9:11, 16, 20; 10:5), and Isaiah makes use of the *hiphil* of the verb נוף (nûp), "to wave, wield," in similar usage (10:15; cf. 30:32). The mention of Judah as Egypt's object of fear is a little unusual, though it is clear that Yahweh is the power behind Judah's actions that Egypt fears. The thought is not significantly different from Judah joining with Ephraim to swoop down on the Philistines, plunder the Arameans, and subjugate Edom, Moab, and Ammon (Isa 11:13-14). One could also compare the participation of Ahaz's successor as king of Judah in Yahweh's killing of the remnant of the Philistines (Isa 14:28-30). It would not be strange, then, for Isaiah to speak of Judah's participation in Yahweh's punishment of another enemy of Judah. And Egypt was an enemy. During Ahaz's reign, Egypt was the political enemy of Judah, since Ahaz followed a pro-Assyrian policy. While Hezekiah appears to have been tempted to join a Nubian-Egyptian–sponsored anti-Assyrian league during the Ashdod crisis of 715–711, and did actually join such a league after the death of Sargon II in 705 and before Sennacherib's invasion of Judah in 701 BCE, Isaiah remained adamantly opposed to such treaties with Egypt or Nubia-Egypt (Isa 14:32; 18:1-7; 20:1-6; 28:14-15; 30:1-7; 31:1-3). For the prophet, Judah's security lay in trusting in Yahweh and his promises to Jerusalem and the Davidic dynasty (Isa 7:1-15; 8:1-4; 14:32). Isaiah

---

21 Wildberger (2:732) finds this notice surprising, because the OT otherwise knows nothing about women being especially fearful, but the feminization of warriors is a standard feature in treaty curses in the ancient Near East, as a passage from the treaty between Ashurnirari V of Assyria and Matiʾilu of Arpad indicates: "If Matiʾilu sins against this treaty . . . may Matiʾilu become a prostitute, his soldiers women, . . . may Matiʾilu (seed) be that of a mule, his wives *barren*, may Ishtar, the goddess of men, the lady of women, take away their "bow," cause their [steri]lity . . .(*ANET*, 3rd ed., 533). Note also from Esarhaddon's treaty of succession: "May all the gods who are called by name in this treaty tablet spin you around like a spindle-whorl, may they make you like a woman before your enemy" (S. Parpola and K. Watanabe, *Neo-Assyrian Treaties and Loyalty Oaths* [SAA 2; Helsinki: Helsinki University Press, 1988] 56, lines 616-17). Moreover, the disparagement of warriors as fearful "women" is still present in the Middle East in contemporary Arab culture. As a graduate student during the 1967 Arab–Israeli Six-Day War, I remember a fellow student, a woman from Lebanon, contemptuously characterizing the Egyptian soldiers as "women," once the Egyptian front collapsed.

regarded both Assyria and Egypt as hostile powers (Isa 7:18-19) whom Yahweh would eventually judge (Isa 10:12; 14:24-27; 18:1-7; 20:1-6; 31:3; 31:8-9), and the Judean king had no business making treaties with either.

Verse 18 adds a new thought that is not clearly anticipated in either vv. 1-15 or vv. 16-17. In this coming day five cities in Egypt will speak the language of Canaan, that is, Hebrew, and will swear by the name of Yahweh of Hosts. Moreover, these cities will not be limited to insignificant settlements, but will include as important a city as Heliopolis. The author does not specify whether these speakers of Hebrew and worshipers of Yahweh are Judean settlers in Egypt or native Egyptian converts to Yahwism. In either case, this is a thought that seems problematic for the late eighth century, since there is little evidence for significant Judean settlement in Egypt or Judean religious influence on Egypt in the eighth century. By the early sixth century, with the collapse of Judah there was a significant Jewish refugee community in Egypt, and the beginning of Jewish settlements in Egypt may perhaps be traced back to the seventh century when the Egyptian campaigns of the Assyrian kings Esarhadon and Ashurbanipal probably made use of Judean auxiliaries and may have stationed some of these troops in Egypt as garrison troops when the main Assyrian armies returned home. Once such settlement had begun, it would be easy to see how a writer might make such a prophetic addition to the text. It seems more difficult to attribute such an expansion to the eighth-century Isaiah of Jerusalem.

Verses 19-22 form a long expansion, but it makes no specific reference to v. 18, and may be both independent of and earlier than the expansion in v. 18. There will be an altar for Yahweh in the midst of the land of Egypt and a stela for Yahweh beside its border. These will serve as historical monuments or signs in honor of Yahweh of Hosts bearing witness to what this deity has done in the land of Egypt, and these actions are now explained as transcending the judgment on Egypt that the earlier verses had announced. If v. 4 announced that Yahweh would hand the Egyptians over to a harsh master so that a strong king would rule over them, v. 20 says that the Egyptians would cry out to Yahweh because of their oppressors and that Yahweh would send to them a savior and a defender, and he would deliver them. By this response to the Egyptians' cry for help, Yahweh

would make himself known to the Egyptians, and the Egyptians would come to know or acknowledge Yahweh. In response, the Egyptians would offer a sacrifice and an offering to Yahweh, vow a vow to Yahweh, and fulfill it (v. 21). Thus, the altar mentioned in v. 19 would not be just an unused historical monument, as was the altar set up by the Reubenites, the Gadites, and the half-tribe of Manasseh east of the Jordan in Josh 22:10-34 (esp. vv. 22-29), at least according to the Deuteronomistic History. While both altars served as a witness, this Egyptian altar would actually be used to pay sacrificial homage to Yahweh, who would first punish and then deliver Egypt. Isaiah 19:22 spells this out. Yahweh would smite the Egyptians, smiting and healing, because they would turn to Yahweh, so God would allow himself to be entreated by them, and he would heal them. It is striking how closely these verses make the predicted Egyptian experience of sin, punishment, repentance, and deliverance parallel to the similar cyclic experience of the Israelites in the book of Judges (Judg 2:10-23), though the schema in this Isaiah passage lacks the repetitive quality that characterizes the Deuteronomistic schema of Judges.

It is very difficult to date these verses. They are generally dated much later than the time of Isaiah, though an attribution to Isaiah is not impossible. If composed by Isaiah, the promised deliverer of Egypt should probably be regarded as an undefined figure of the future who would drive out the Nubian overlords, but one cannot rule out the possibility that Isaiah envisioned this savior of Egypt as an Assyrian ruler. If the passage is later than Isaiah, any number of possibilities are opened up—by the second quarter of the seventh century it might be taken as a reference to Esarhaddon or Ashurbanipal, the Assyrian opponents of the Nubian pharaohs. In the later seventh century one could think of Psammetichus, the Egyptian ruler who successfully drove out the Assyrians, and, if one goes as late as the Persian period, one might think of the leader of one of the several Egyptian revolts against Persian rule. The difficulty with the later datings, however, is that the text does not mention the Persians or even the Babylonians. The writer seems to be fixated on the relations among Egypt, Assyria, and Israel.

Verse 23 adds the thought that there will be a highway from Egypt to Assyria, and that Assyria will go into Egypt, and the Egyptians will go into Assyria. At the very least, this suggests very active trade relations between Assyria and Egypt. Sargon II boasts of having opened a trading station with Egypt, a claim that is usually dated to the period immediately following Sargon's suppression of the Hamath revolt in 720 (see n. 8 above). The years between the suppression of that revolt and the revival of Philistine unrest in 715 appear to have been a brief period when Assyrian–Egyptian relations were relatively positive. Osorkon IV of Tanis even sent a gift of horses to Sargon in 716 or 715 (see n. 9 above). This would have been a period in which a peaceful Judah under Ahaz could enjoy and perhaps even participate in the profit from the free flow of trade moving back and forth between Assyria and the Delta region of Egypt, and that historical context could well have given rise to the prophetic images expressed in this verse. The last statement in v. 23 is lexically and grammatically ambiguous. It may be translated either as "And the Egyptians will serve Assyria," or "The Egyptians will serve (worship <Yahweh>) along with Assyria." I have opted for the first translation, because the second translation has to assume a major gap with the omission of the object "Yahweh," and the assumed use of עבד (ʿbd) in the sense of "worship" is not attested anywhere else in this passage. In the period under question, it was clear that an Egyptian Delta ruler like Osorkon IV, though not an Assyrian vassal, was subservient to the Assyrians.

Verses 24-25 add to this picture of the back-and-forth trade between Assyria and Egypt the thought that Israel will represent a third party in this relationship between Assyria and Egypt. Israel is clearly being used here in the collective sense of all Israel, not in the particular sense of the northern kingdom. The image of Israel as a virtual equivalent to Egypt and Assyria, like them a blessing in the midst of the earth, is quite striking, and the statement that Yahweh of Hosts will bless them all saying, "Blessed be my people Egypt, and the work of my hands Assyria, and my inheritance Israel," is unparalleled elsewhere in Scripture. Such a statement exaggerates the political importance of Israel in whatever ancient historical period one places it, but it is at least conceivable in the late eighth century in the thought of Isaiah of Jerusalem, who believed that Yahweh dwelt in Jerusalem and used both Assyria and Egypt as his agents however God pleased. Perhaps one could also attribute such a thought to a later disciple of Isaiah in the seventh century, when both Assyria and Egypt remained major powers and Judah, as the embodiment of the all-Israel ideal, still remained a national state. It is hard to believe, however, that anyone would create such a notion after the disappearance of Assyria as a nation between 612 and 609 BCE. If the text is dated even later, why does the author not speak of Babylon, or Persia, or the Greeks as composing one of the thirds with Egypt and Israel? I think such a late dating is highly improbable.

Bibliography

Abel, F.-M., "Les confins de la Palestine et de l'Égypte," *RB* 49 (1940) 224–39.

Badawi, A., *Memphis als zweite Landeshauptstadt im neuen Reich* (Cairo: Imprimerie de l'Institut français d'Archéologie Orientale, 1948).

Beek, M. A., "Relations entre Jérusalem et la diaspora égyptienne au 2e siècle avant J.-C.," *OTS* 2 (1943) 119–43.

Beckerath, Jürgen von, *Tanis und Theben: Historische Grundlagen der Ramessidenzeit in Ägypten* (ÄF 16; Glückstadt, NY: J. J. Augustin, 1951).

Bietak, M., "Die Hauptstadt der Hyksos und die Ramsesstadt," *Antike Welt* 6 (1975) 28–43.

Brueggemann, Walter, "2 Kings 18–19: The Legitimacy of a Sectarian Hermeneutic," *HBT* 7 (1985) 1–42.

Calderone, P. J., "The Rivers of 'Maṣor,'" *Bib* 42 (1961) 423–32.

Capart, J., and M. Werbrouck, *Memphis à l'ombre des pyramides* (Brussels: Vromant, 1930).

Causse, A., "Israël et la vision de l'humanité," *Etudes d'histoire et de philosophie religieuses publiées par la faculté de théologie protestante de l'université de Strasbourg* 8 (1924) 97–98.

———, "Les origines de la diaspora juive," *RHPR* 7 (1927) 97–128.

Cheyne, T. K., "The Nineteenth Chapter of Isaiah," *ZAW* 13 (1893) 125–28.

Condamin, A., "Interpolations ou transpositions accidentelles? (Michée, II,12,13; Osée, II,1-3,8,9; Isaïe, V,24,25; XIX 21,22)," *RB* 11 (1902) 379–97.

Cowley, A. E., *Aramaic Papyri of the Fifth Century B.C.* (Oxford: Clarendon, 1923).

Crocker, P., "Egypt in Biblical Prophecy," *BurH* 34 (1998) 105–10.

Croughs, M., "Intertextuality in the Septuagint: The Case of Isaiah 19," *BIOSCS* 34 (2001) 60–80.

Deissler, Alfons, "Der Volk und Land überschreitende Gottesbund der Endzeit nach Jes 19,16-25," in Ferdinand Hahn et al., eds., *Zion: Ort der Begegnung. Festschrift für Laurentius Klein zur Vollendung des 65. Lebensjahres* (BBB 90; Bodenheim: Athenäum Hain Hanstein, 1993) 7–18.

Delcor, M., "Le problème des jardins d'Adonis dans Isaïe 17,9-11," *Syria* 54 (1977) 371–94.

———, "Le temple d'Onias en Égypte," *RB* 75 (1968) 188–205.

Eitan, I., "An Egyptian Loan Word in Isaiah 19," *JQR* 15 (1924) 419–22.

Elat, M., "The Economic Relations of the Neo-Assyrian Empire with Egypt," *JAOS* 98 (1978) 20–34.

Erman, A., and H. Ranke, *Ägypten und ägyptisches Leben im Altertum* (Tübingen: H. Laupp, 1923).

Feuillet, A., "Un sommet religieux de l'Ancien Testament: L'oracle d'Isa 19:19-25 sur la conversion de l'Egypte," *RSR* 39 (1951) 65–87.

Fohrer, Georg, "Die Gattung der Berichte über symbolische Handlungen der Propheten," in Fohrer, *Studien zur alttestamentlichen Prophetie (1949–1965)* (BZAW 99; Berlin: A. Töpelmann, 1967) 65–80; reprinted from *ZAW* 64 (1952) 101–20.

———. *Die symbolischen Handlungen der Propheten* (2nd ed.; ATANT 14; Zurich: Zwingli, 1968).

Gadd, C. J., "Inscribed Prisms of Sargon II from Nimrud," *Iraq* 16 (1954) 173–201.

Gomaà, F., *Die libyschen Fürstentümer des Deltas: Vom Tod Osorkons II bis zur Wiedervereinigung Ägyptens durch Psametik I* (Beihefte zum Tübinger Atlas des Vorderen Orients, B 6; Wiesbaden: L. Reichert, 1974).

Gosse, B., "Isaïe 21,11-12, et Isaïe 60-62," *BN* 53 (1990) 21–22.

Gottwald, *All the Kingdoms*, 222–28.

Guillaume, Alfred, "Note on Isaiah 19:7," *JTS* n.s. 14 (1963) 382–83.

Haag, Ernst, "'Gesegnet sei mein Volk Ägypten' (Jes 19, 25): Ein Zeugnis alttestamentlicher Eschatologie," in Martina Minas et al., eds., *Aspekte spätägyptischer Kultur: Festschrift für Erich Winter zum 65. Geburtstag* (Mainz am Rhein: P. von Zabern, 1994) 139–47.

Harmatta, J., "Zur Geschichte des frühhellenistischen Judentums in Ägypten," *Acta Antiqua Academiae Scientiarum Hungaricae* 7 (1959) 337–409.

Hayward, R., "The Jewish Temple at Leontopolis: A Reconsideration," *JJS* 33 (1982) 429–43.

Helck, W., *Die altägyptischen Gaue* (Beihefte zum Tübinger Atlas des Vorderen Orients, B 5; Wiesbaden: L. Reichert, 1974).

Hengel, M. *Judentum und Hellenismus: Studien zu ihrer Begegnung unter besonderer Berücksichtigung Palästinas bis zur Mitte des 2. Jh. v. Chr.* (WUNT 10; Tübingen: J. C. B. Mohr, 1969).

Herz, N., "Isaiah 19,7," *OLZ* 15 (1912) 496–97.

Holladay, John S., Jr., "Judean (and Phoenicians) in Egypt in the Late Seventh to Sixth Centuries B.C.," in Gary N. Knoppers and Antoine Hirsch, eds., *Egypt, Israel, and the Ancient Mediterranean World: Studies in Honor of Donald B. Redford* (Probleme der Ägyptologie 20; Leiden: Brill, 2004) 405–38.

Hoonacker, A. van., "Deux passages obscurs dan le chapitre XIX d'Isaïe (versets 11,18)," *Revue Bénédictine* 36 (1924) 297–306.

Israelit-Groll, Sarah, "The Egyptian Background to Isaiah 19:18," in Meir Lubetski, Claire Gottlieb, and Sharon Keller, eds., *Boundaries of the Ancient Near Eastern World: A Tribute to Cyrus H. Gordon* (JSOTSup 273; Sheffield: Sheffield Academic Press, 1998) 300–303.

Jirku, A., "Die fünf Städte bei Jes 19,18 und die fünf Tore des Jahu-Tempels zu Elephantine," *OLZ* 15 (1912) 247–48.

Kaiser, Otto, "Der geknickte Rohrstab," in Hartmut Gese and Hans Peter Rüger, eds., *Wort und Geschichte: Festschrift für Karl Elliger zum 70. Geburtstag* (AOAT 18; Kevelaer: Butzon & Bercker, 1973) 99–106.

———, "Zwischen den Fronten," in Josef Schreiner, ed., *Wort, Lied und Gottesspruch: Festschrift für Joseph Ziegler* (2 vols.; FB 1–2; Würzburg: Echter, 1972) 2:197–206.

Kitchen, *Third Intermediate*, 362–80.

Keel, Othmar, and Christoph Uehlinger, *Gods, Goddesses, and Images of God in Ancient Israel* (trans. T. A. Trapp; Minneapolis: Fortress, 1998).

Kooij, Arie van der, "The Old Greek of Isaiah 19:16-25: Translation and Interpretation," in C. Cox, ed., *Sixth Congress of the International Organization for Septuagint and Cognate Studies, Jerusalem, 1986* (SCS 23; Atlanta: Scholars Press, 1987) 127–66.

Kraeling, E. G., *The Brooklyn Museum Aramaic Papyri* (New Haven: Yale University Press, 1953).

Krause, Alfred E., "Historical Selectivity: Prophetic Prerogative or Typological Imperative?" in A. Gileadi, ed., *Israel's Apostasy and Restoration: Essays in Honor of Roland K. Harrison* (Grand Rapids: Baker, 1988) 175–212.

Loretz, Oswald, "Der ugaritische Topos *b'l rkb* und die 'Sprache Kanaans' in Jes 19,1-25," *UF* 19 (1987) 101–12.

Lucas, A., *Ancient Egyptian Materials and Industries* (London: E. Arnold, 1962).

Martin-Achard, Robert, "De Jean 4:22 à Esaïe 19:23-25: À propos d'une décalaration de Karl Barth," *FoiVie* 84 (1985) 23–32.

Monsengwo-Pasinya, L., "Isaïe 19:16-25 et universal-isme dans la LXX," in J. A. Emerton, ed., *Congress Volume: Salamanca 1983* (VTSup 36; Leiden: Brill, 1985) 192–207.

Montet, P., *Tanis, douze années de fouilles dans une capitale oubliée du delta égyptien* (Paris: Payot, 1942).

Moret, Alexandre, *The Nile and Egyptian Civilization* (1927; repr., Mineola, NY: Dover, 2001).

Na'aman, N., "The Brook of Egypt and Assyrian Policy on the Border of Egypt," *Tel Aviv* 6 (1979) 68–90.

Naville, Edouard, *The Mound of the Jew and the City of Onias* (Memoir of the Egypt Exploration Fund 7; London: K. Paul, Trench, Trübner, 1890).

Niccacci, A., "Isaiah xviii–xx from an Egyptological Perspective," *VT* 48 (1998) 214–38.

Porten, B., "The Diaspora: The Jews in Egypt," in W. D. Davies and L. Finkelstein, eds., *The Cambridge History of Judaism*, vol. 1, *Introduction; The Persian Period* (Cambridge: Cambridge University Press, 1984) 372–400.

Randles, R. J., "The Interaction of Israel, Judah and Egypt: From Solomon to Josiah" (PhD diss., Southern Baptist Theological Seminary, 1980) 155–208.

Sacchi, P., "Nota a Is. 19,7," *RivB* 13 (1965) 169–70.

Sawyer, John F. A., "Blessed Be My People Egypt (Isaiah 19:25): The Context and Meaning of a Remarkable Passage," in James D. Martin and Philip R. Davies, eds., *A Word in Season: Essays in Honour of Willam McKane* (JSOTSup 42; Sheffield: JSOT Press, 1986).

——, "The Role of Jewish Studies in Biblical Semantics," in H. L. J. Vanstiphout et al., eds., *Scripta Signa Vocis: Studies about Scripts, Scriptures, Scribes, and Languages in the Near East Presented to J. H. Hospers by His Pupils, Colleagues, and Friends* (Groningen: E. Forsten, 1986) 201–8.

Schenker, A., "La fine dela storia di israeli recapitolera il suo inizio: Esegesi di Is 19,16-25," *RivB* 42 (1994) 321–29.

Schürer, Emil, *Geschichte des jüdischen Volkes im Zeitalter Jesu Christi* (3rd ed.; Leipzig: Hinrichs, 1902).

Schvindt, Claudio, "Análisis literario y de la relectura de las tradiciones en Isaías 19:16-25," *RevistB* 48 (1986) 51–59.

Smith, W. S., *Interconnections in the Ancient Near East: A Study of the Relationships between the Arts of Egypt, the Aegean, and Western Asia* (New Haven: Yale University Press, 1965).

Snaith, N. H., "*Ym-Swp*: The Sea of Reeds, The Red Sea," *VT* 15 (1965) 395–98.

Spalinger, A., "The Year 712 B.C.E. and Its Implications for Egyptian History," *JARCE* 10 (1973) 95–101.

Steuernagel, C., "Bemerkungen über die neuentdeckten jüdischen Papyrusurkunden aus Elephantine und ihre Bedeutung für das Alte Testament," *Theologische Studien und Kritiken* 22 (1909) 1–12.

Strange, John, "Some Notes on Biblical and Egyptian Theology," in Gary N. Knoppers and Antoine Hirsch, eds., *Egypt, Israel, and the Ancient Mediterranean World: Studies in Honor of Donald B. Redford* (Probleme der Ägyptologie 20; Leiden: Brill, 2004) 347.

Tadmor, "Campaigns of Sargon II," 22–40, 77–100.

Thacker, T. W., "A Note on Frwt (Is XIX 7)," *JTS* 34 (1933) 163–65.

Vandier, Jacques, *La famine dans l'Égypte ancienne* (Recherches d'archéologie, de philologie et d'histoire 7; Cairo: Institut français d'archéologie orientale, 1936).

Vervenne, M., "The Phraseology of 'Knowing Yhwh' in the Hebrew Bible: A Preliminary Study of Its Syntax and Function," in J. van Ruiten and M. Vervenne, eds., *Studies in the Book of Isaiah: Festschrift Willem A. M. Beuken* (BETL 132; Leuven: Leuven University Press, 1997) 467–92.

Vogels, W., "L'Egypte mon peuple—l'universalisme d'Is 19, 16-25," *Bib* 57 (1976) 494–514.

Ward, W. A., "The Semitic Biconsonantal Root Sp and the Common Origin of Egyptian Cwf and Hebrew Suf: 'Marsh(-Plant),'" *VT* 24 (1974) 339–99.

Wilson, Ian, "In That Day: From Text to Sermon on Isaiah 19:23-25," *Int* 21 (1967) 66–86.

Wodecki, B. S. V. D., "The Heights of the Religious Universalism in Is XIX: 16-25," in *"Lasset uns Brücken Bauen...": Collected Communication of the XVth Congress of the Organization for the Study of the Old Testament, Cambridge 1995* (BEATAJ 42; Bern: Lang, 1998) 117–91.

Wolf, Walther, *Kulturgeschichte des alten Ägypten* (Stuttgart: A. Kröner, 1962).

——, *Die Welt der Ägypter* (Zurich: Fretz & Wasmuth, 1955).

Wong, G. C. I., *Foolish Leaders and the Will of Yahweh: Editorial Effects in Isaiah 19* (Singapore: Insight, 2009).

Wreszinski, W., *Atlas zur ägyptischen Kulturgeschichte* (Geneva: Slatkine Reprints, 1923).

20

From Sargon II's inscriptions it is clear that the Assyrians conquered the Philistine city of Ashdod and the immediately surrounding area in 711 BCE,[1] but the background to this event extended farther back in time. The Philistines had been turned into vassals of Assyria by Tiglath-pileser III's campaigns into Palestine in 734–732 BCE,[2] and that status had been reconfirmed by Sargon II's crushing of the Hamath, Gaza, and Samaria revolt of 720. Despite this vassal status, however, the Philistine ruler of Ashdod, a certain Azuri, plotted a new revolt against Sargon II and wrote letters to the kings of the surrounding states trying to persuade them to join him in throwing off the Assyrian yoke. The Assyrians got wind of Azuri's activities, perhaps reported by a more loyal vassal like Ahaz of Judah, and an Assyrian detachment present on the border with Egypt, probably in 716 or early in 715, visited Ashdod and removed Azuri from the throne. The Assyrians replaced him with his brother Ahimeti, but Ahimeti was very unpopular, and sometime after the Assyrian detachment had withdrawn, the citizens of Ashdod drove Ahimeti from the city and replaced him with a nonroyal adventurer referred to in the texts as Yamani, or in one text as Yadna. Given the possible etymology of this name, the new ruler may have been Greek or Cypriot, but he quickly resumed Azuri's policy of writing letters to the rulers of the surrounding states, including Judah, Edom, Moab, and the Philistines and perhaps the Phoenicians of the coastal area, urging them to join him in his revolt against Assyria. In the meantime, Ahaz, the king of Judah, had died and been replaced by Hezekiah, and the Philistines apparently thought the new Judean king would be more receptive to their plans for revolt (Isa 14:28-32). The Philistines obviously sent messengers to the Judean court trying to persuade Hezekiah to join the revolt, and it is clear that they were promising support from the new Kushite or Nubian dynasty now ruling Egypt. From Isaiah 18 it is even likely that actual messengers from the distant Nubian court made their appearance in Jerusalem. Over against this feverish Philistine and Nubian courting of the Judean king to join the revolt, however, the prophet Isaiah mounted a major and very public campaign to dissuade Hezekiah from making any such agreement. In a shocking prophetic display guaranteed quickly to become the talk of the city and soon the countryside—here in chap. 20—Isaiah began appearing publicly in Jerusalem in front of the palace naked and barefoot, thus symbolizing the fate that awaited the promised and highly touted relief force of the combined Nubian and Egyptian army as Assyrian captives. Isaiah apparently continued this demonstration for a part of three years, at least from 714 to 712, and perhaps as late as early 711, when word of an approaching Assyrian army led Yamani to flee Ashdod and take refuge on the border between Egypt and Nubia. Once Yamani had fled in the face of Assyrian reprisals, there would be little enthusiasm left for joining the doomed revolt, and it appears that Isaiah was successful in frustrating the plans of those Judean royal advisors who were encouraging Hezekiah to join the rebels. Nonetheless, the enemies Isaiah made at court by his public and apparently very controversial actions would dog him through the rest of Hezekiah's reign. His opponents at court despised and distrusted him, and in the future crisis following the death of Sargon II, they did their best to cut Isaiah out of the loop and to keep their deliberations secret from the prophet, whom they considered, perhaps rightly, to be a dangerous security risk.

In the meantime, the Assyrian army besieged, captured, and plundered Ashdod and the neighboring cities, deported their population, and then resettled them with people taken from elsewhere in the Assyian empire. No Nubian-Egyptian relief force arrived to assist the rebels, so Isaiah's prediction of the fate of such a force was untested. Yamani remained an exile, presumably harbored by the Nubian court, for about four years, until around 707 BCE, when the Nubian king Shabataqa decided to extradite him in chains to Sargon II of Assyria. The reasons for the Nubian action are unclear, but the case can be made that this action was taken not because of any desire for a long-term peace with Assyria but in preparation for renewed hostilities. Yamani was

---

1   For the primary sources, see Fuchs, *Die Annalen,* 44–46, 73–74, and the extended discussion on 124–31; Fuchs, *Die Inschriften Sargons II,* 75, 308, lines 11–14; 132–35, 326, lines 241–54; 219–22, 348–49, lines 90–112; and Frame, "Inscription of Sargon II,"

31–57. For fuller discussion and secondary literature, see my "Egypt, Assyria, Isaiah," 265–83.

2   For Tiglath-pileser's inscriptions, see now Tadmor and Yamada, RINAP 1.

no longer of any political use to Nubia, since he was no longer a credible leader around whom to foment revolt in Philistia against the Assyrians, but extraditing him to Assyria would give the Nubian officials escorting him to Assyria a chance to obtain firsthand intelligence about the situation in Assyria. Extraditing him might also lull the Assyrian court into thinking that Nubia no longer constituted any threat on Assyria's frontier with Egypt. It would certainly give Nubia more time to prepare for what the Nubian court apparently considered an inevitable war with Assyria.

1/   **In the year that the field marshal[a] came to Ashdod, when Sargon[b] the king of Assyria sent him,[c] and he fought against Ashdod, and he took it,[d]**

2/   **at that time Yahweh spoke by the hand of Isaiah,[e] the son of Amoz, saying,[f] "Go and remove the sackcloth[g] from upon your loins and your sandals[h] you shall remove[i] from upon your feet." And he did so, walking[j] naked and barefoot for three years.[k]**

3/   **And Yahweh said,[l] "As my servant Isaiah[m] walked naked and barefoot[n] as a sign and portent[o] against Egypt and against Kush,**

4/   **thus[p] the king of Assyria will lead away the captives of Egypt and the exiles of Kush,[q] young men and old, naked and barefoot, with butts uncovered,[r] to the shame/nakedness of Egypt.**

5/   **And they will be dismayed and ashamed[s] of Kush to whom they looked,[t] and of Egypt[u] their boast.**

6/   **And the inhabitant of this seacoast[v] will say in that day, 'If this is the fate of the one to whom we looked, where we rushed[w] for help to be saved from the king of Assyria, then how can we escape?'"**

Textual Notes

a   MT תַּרְתָּן (*tartān*), "field marshal"; 1QIsaᵃ תורתן has a different vocalization, but both vocalizations, *tartānu* and *turtānu*, are attested in Akkadian for this high official.

b   MT סַרְגוֹן (*Sargôn*), 1QIsaᵃ, 4QIsaᵇ, Vg., Tg., Syr.; LXX has the garbled Σαρναν.

c   MT אתוֹ (*ʾōtô*), "him"; 1QIsaᵃ אותו.

d   MT וַיִּלְכְּדָה (*wayyilkĕdāh*), "and he took it"; 1QIsaᵃ וילכודה.

e   MT בְּיַד יְשַׁעְיָהוּ (*bĕyad yĕšaʿyāhû*), "by the hand of Isaiah"; 1QIsaᵃ and 4QIsaᵇ have the shortened form of the proper name ביד ישעיה), Vg., Tg., Syr.; LXX has simply τότε ἐλάλησεν κύριος πρὸς Ησαιαν, "then the Lord spoke to Isaiah." Syr. adds the word "the prophet" after Isaiah.

f   MT לֵאמֹר (*lēʾmōr*), "saying," 4QIsaᵇ; 1QIsaᵃ לאמור.

g   1QIsaᵃ initially omitted הַשָּׂק (*haśśaq*), "the sackcloth," but then inserted it above the line.

h   MT וְנַעַלְךָ (*wĕnaʿalkā*), "and your sandal," though it is followed by the dual, "from upon your feet"; Tg. has singular for both; 1QIsaᵃ has the more natural plural ונעליך, "and your sandals," and so do LXX, Vg., and Syr.

i   MT תַּחֲלֹץ (*taḥălōṣ*), "you shall remove"; 1QIsaᵃ has תחליץ.

j   MT הָלֹךְ (*hālōk*), "walking," 1QIsaᵃ הלוך.

k   I have transposed שָׁלֹשׁ שָׁנִים (*šālōš šānîm*), "for three years"; 1QIsaᵃ has the orthographic variant שלוש שנים from v. 3. I think the phrase was originally here and was accidentally transposed to v. 3 because of the repetition of the phrase עָרוֹם וְיָחֵף (*ʿārôm wĕyāḥēp*), "naked and barefoot." The phrase "for three years" makes sense here, but not in v. 3, as I will explain in the commentary.

l   MT וַיֹּאמֶר (*wayyōʾmer*), "and he said"; 1QIsaᵃ ויואמר.

m   MT יְשַׁעְיָהוּ (*yĕšaʿyāhû*), "Isaiah"; 1QIsaᵃ ישעיה.

n   See note k above.

o   MT וּמוֹפֵת (*ûmôpēt*), "and portent"; 1QIsaᵃ ומפת.

p   LXX inserts כִּי (*kî*), "because" ὅτι, before כֵּן (*kēn*), "thus."

q   MT וְאֶת־גָּלוּת כּוּשׁ (*wĕʾet-gālût kûš*), "and the captivity of Kush," 1QIsaᵃ ואת גולת כוש נערים, Vg., Tg., Syr.; LXX simplifies by omitting גָּלוּת (*gālût*).

r   MT וַחֲשׂוּפַי שֵׁת (*waḥăśûpay šēt*) should be corrected to וַחֲשׂוּפֵי שֵׁת (*waḥăśûpê šēt*), "and uncovered of buttock"; 1QIsaᵃ וחשופי שת, similarly though without the *mater*; 4QIsaᵃ חשפי שת[ו], Vg., Tg.; LXX and Syr. omit שֵׁת (*šēt*), "of buttock."

s   MT וָבֹשׁוּ (*wābōšû*), "and they will be ashamed"; 1QIsaᵃ ובושו.

t   MT מַבָּטָם (*mabbāṭām*), "their hope, to whom they looked";

1QIsaᵃ has מבטחם (mibṭeḥām), "their trust." Both MT and 1QIsaᵃ have מבטנו (mabbāṭēnû), "to whom we looked," in v. 6, which tends to confirm MT's reading here.

u MT וּמִן־מִצְרַיִם (ûmin-miṣrayim), "and from Egypt"; 1QIsaᵃ וממצרים. LXX construes the verse quite differently, making the Egyptians the subject: καὶ αἰσχυνθήσονται ἡττηθέντες οἱ Αἰγύπτιοι ἐπὶ τοῖς Αἰθίοψιν, ἐφ᾽ οἷς ἦσαν πεποιθότες οἱ Αἰγύπτιοι, ἦσαν γὰρ αὐτοῖς δόξα, "And the Egyptians, having been defeated, will be ashamed of the Ethiopians upon whom the Egyptians were trusting, for they were their glory."

v MT יֹשֵׁב הָאִי הַזֶּה (yōšēb hāʾî hazzeh), "the inhabitant of this seacoast"; 1QIsaᵃ יֹשׁב האי הזה.

w MT אֲשֶׁר־נַסְנוּ שָׁם לְעֶזְרָה (ʾăšer-nasnû šām lĕʿezrâ), "where we rushed for help," is superior to 1QIsaᵃ's אשר נסמד שם לעזרה ("where we leaned for help <?>"), since one would expect nissāmēk ʿālāyw, "upon whom we leaned," rather than nissāmēk šām. Again the LXX construes the verse differently: Ἰδοὺ ἡμεῖς ἦμεν πεποιθότες τοῦ φυγεῖν εἰς αὐτοὺς εἰς βοήθειαν, οἳ οὐκ ἐδύναντο σωθῆναι ἀπὸ βασιλέως Ἀσσυρίων· καὶ πῶς ἡμεῖς σωθησόμεθα; "See, we trusted to flee to them for help who were not able to be saved from the king of Assyria, so how can we be saved?"

Commentary

Verse 1 connects the following narrative to the year 711 BCE,[3] when Sargon II sent his field marshal (the *tartānu*) to Ashdod to put down the revolt there, and the field marshal attacked and took the city. Nonetheless, like similar datings in Isa 7:1 and 14:28, the dating fixes the general setting of the narrative, but it does not require that the events narrated in the subsequent verses all took place in that same year or even that they were historically subsequent to the field marshal's conquest of Ashdod. In fact, it is clear from the mention of Isaiah's activity over a three-year period that the narrative is dealing with a process that extended over a period of several years, and the logic of the actions suggests that this multiyear period preceded rather than followed the field marshal's conquest of Ashdod. After Ashdod had fallen without the appearance of any Nubian-Egyptian relief force, it is unlikely that anyone in the Judean court would have continued to promote joining the revolt against Assyria, or would have continued to tout the reliable support of the powerful Nubian-Egyptian army. The verse also provides a helpful corrective to Sargon's inscriptions in which Sargon claims to have personally led the campaign against Ashdod. The biblical account makes clear that an Assyrian general led the campaign against Ashdod and

---

3   The primary sources are confusing on the dating. The three sources that give information over the temporal sequence of events in his tenth (712) and eleventh (711) years do not agree (see Fuchs's discussion in *Die Inschriften Sargons II,* 381, and *Die Annalen,* 124–31). Prism a+b puts Ashdod in year 9 (= 10, since this text dates everything a year earlier) followed by the Marqasa campaign and the campaign to Kammanu, Til-Garimmu, and the bringing of the wealth of Hatti. The Annals, in contrast, put Kammanu, Til-Garimmu, and the bringing of the wealth of Hatti in year 10, and the Marqasa and Ashdod campaigns in year 11. But the Eponym Chronicle Cᵇ4 (Millard, *Eponyms,* 47, 60) has the king "in the land," that is, not on campaign, in year 10 (712 BCE) and the Marqasa campaign in year 11 (711). It does not mention the campaigning in Kammanu and Til-Garimmu and the resulting booty, but campaigning in those areas could not have taken place in 712, when the king remained home, and since they are geographically in proximity to Marqasa, those campaigns are probably combined in the Eponym Chronicle under the campaign to Marqasa. The Eponymn Chronicle Cᵇ4 omits any reference to Ashdod, which led E. Weidner to assume that the Eponymn Chronicle included only campaigns in which the king was personally involved ("Šilkan(he)ni, König von Muṣri, ein Zeitgenosse Sargons II: Nach einem neuen Bruchstück der Prisma-Inschrift des assyrischen Königs," *AfO* 14 [1941–44] 14, 53), opening up the possibility for dating the Ashdod campaign to 712 BCE, when the king stayed home. Fuchs convincingly demonstrates that such an assumption is false (*Die Annalen,* 86), however, since for the years 708 and 706, the Chronicle records campaigns in which the king did not participate. The omission in the Eponymn Chronicles apparently means no more than that the Chronicle simply lumped all the western campaigns of that year, whether in the northwest or much farther south, whether led by Sargon or by his high official, under the Marqasa campaign.

that Sargon II was not actually present. Since the Ashdod campaign took place in such close proximity to the Judean kingdom, Fuchs thinks the biblical information is more believable than Sargon's claim's for his personal involvement.[4] The Judeans would surely have known had Sargon been personally present. Moreover, the different Assyrian accounts differ considerably from one another. The Khorsabad Annals from 707 BCE, for instance, summarizes so blatantly that it makes it appear that Yamani, called Yadna only here, was captured along with his wives and family when Ashdod fell to the Assyrian siege in 711, not extradited by the Nubian ruler Shebitku some four years or so later. Indeed, as Fuchs makes clear, the inscriptions of Shalmaneser III, Tiglath-pileser III, and Sargon II all contain peculiarities, falsifications, and errors in dating, though the reasons for these anomalies probably differ from case to case and for the most part are unknown.[5]

In this general context, while the revolt was still alive and active in Ashdod, Yahweh spoke by means of his prophet Isaiah (20:2). God gave Isaiah the command to remove the sackcloth from his loins and the sandals from his feet, obviously as a symbolic act to underscore his message. Sackcloth, a heavy course cloth, was normally worn next to the skin as a sign of mourning, and to remove it from the loins suggests that the prophet stripped and appeared in public bare naked and barefoot. Such behavior would be shocking and shameful in Israelite society, as the many references to nakedness in the Bible clearly indicate, though shocking and shameful behavior is often associated with the symbolic acts of the prophets. One may think of Hosea's symbolic dealings with a woman or women of loose sexual morals or of the outrageous symbolic names that a Hosea or an Isaiah gave to their children. Moreover, since the symbolic uncovering of Isaiah's nakedness presages the coming nakedness of the Nubian and Egyptian men, a nakedness that explicitly mentions their exposed buttocks (v. 4), the symbolic act is far more likely to have involved total nakedness of the prophet's private parts than a more modest appearance in underwear. The strange yet widespread concern of modern scholars to save the prophet's

modesty is misguided and hard to fathom and has led to very odd arguments. One such argument is O. Kaiser's claim (*Jesaja 13–39*, 95), cited as "to be considered" by Wildberger (2:756), that the climate in Jerusalem was too harsh to allow Isaiah to go naked for three years. In addition to other gratuitous assumptions, the argument assumes that the prophet remained unclothed twenty-four hours a day every day for three years. This assumption ignores the fact that Isaiah's lack of clothing was intended as a very public display to underscore a public message; just as with modern political demonstrators, there would be no reason to maintain that appearance when the public had gone home or Isaiah had retired for the night. Isaiah's actions were intended to sway the opinion of the Judean royal court and perhaps the broader Judean public against joining Ashdod's revolt against Assyria. Given that intention, it is reasonable to assume that Isaiah appeared undressed each day in front of the royal palace to demonstrate against the proposed alliance with Ashdod and its Nubian and Egyptian backers. Nothing indicates how long each day he stayed there, or whether he took periodic breaks for meals or to warm himself, and he may very well have returned home each night to a warm bed. We are not told.

Isaiah did as he was commanded, going about naked and barefoot for three years. The MT and all the textual traditions preserve the phrase "for three years" in v. 3 as part of Yahweh's explanation of the prophet's symbolic act, "And Yahweh said, 'As my servant Isaiah walked naked and barefoot for three years as a sign and portent against Egypt and against Kush, thus the king of Assyria will lead away the captives of Egypt and the exiles of Kush, young men and old, naked and barefoot, with their butts uncovered, to the shame of Egypt.'" But the temporal phrase does not really fit in v. 3. Read literally, the verse would imply that Yahweh did not explain his prophet's shocking symbolic behavior until three years after it had begun. That is hardly likely, as it would undercut the persuasive power of the prophet's actions. The meaning of the symbolic action must have been publicly proclaimed early on, when the public was still interested in what the prophet's strange behavior meant,

4   Fuchs, *Die Annalen*, 86. This appears to be the common opinion among Assyriologists. There may be those who think Sargon was personally present at the

siege of Ashdod, but I have not come across them in my reading.
5   Fuchs, *Die Annalen*, 96.

and when it had a chance to sway the decision making in the royal court. It is far more likely that the original placement of the phrase was at the end of v. 2, where it simply expressed how long Isaiah's public demonstrations lasted: "And he did so, going about naked and barefoot for three years." An early and unintentional scribal error (see textual notes above) led to the transposition of the phrase "for three years" from behind the phrase "naked and barefoot" in v. 2, to the same position behind "naked and barefoot" in v. 3.

Verses 3-4 give the meaning of Isaiah's symbolic act, and this explanation must have accompanied the symbolic act almost from the first day, as soon as the curious public began to ask the prophet the meaning for his outrageous behavior. His behavior, Yahweh explains, was intended as a sign and portent against Egypt and Kush. Just as Isaiah had appeared in public naked and barefoot, so the king of Assyria would lead away the captives of Egypt and Kush, young men and old alike, naked and barefoot with their butts uncovered to the shame of Egypt (v. 4). That the threat is directed first against Egypt and Kush rather than Ashdod makes clear that the success of Ashdod's revolt was dependent on help from Nubia and its Egyptian vassals, and it is only the firm promise of such help that could entice the Judean court to consider joining the revolt. From Isaiah 18 it appears likely that actual messengers from the Nubian court had appeared in Jerusalem to underscore this promise of help. Thus, the reference to the captives of Egypt and Kush could only refer to the Egyptian and Kushite soldiers of a promised relief force sent to support Ashdod and its prospective allies against the expected Assyrian attack. A partial model for Isaiah's imagery may be the Egyptian army led by Re'e that came to the relief of Hanun of Gaza at Rapihu in 720 BCE. Sargon defeated that army in an open battle in full view of the defenders on the wall of Rapihu and then proceeded to conquer the city. It was not unknown for the Assyrians to lead away their military prisoners stripped naked (note Shalmaneser III's depiction of the bound and naked troops of Hazazu [*ANEP*, 2nd ed., p. 124 n. 358]), so the type of treatment threatened against these Nubian and Egyptian soldiers may actually have been observed by Isaiah's Judean audience in the wars of 734–732 and 720 BCE

Verses 5-6 express the reaction of the people watching from the walls of Ashdod to the fate of the Egyptian and Nubian relief force. They are crushed and ashamed of the Nubians to whom they looked and of the Egyptians in whose support they had boasted. Once the mighty relief force is defeated, there is no more hope for the inhabitants of the besieged Philistine cities. They simply resign themselves to their inevitable and unenviable fate with the plaintive question, "If this is the fate of the one to whom we looked, where we rushed[6] for help to be saved from the king of Assyria, then how can we escape?"

This oracle must have been repeated numerous times in the course of three years along with related oracles on the same topic (see Isa 14:28-32 and chap. 18), but it is also clear from this oracle that it was given prior to Sargon's conquest of Ashdod. The oracle expected a Nubian and Egyptian relief force to come to the aid of Ashdod, as the Philistines and Nubians were apparently promising, but in actual fact, no such army appeared. The inhabitants of Ashdod and its neighboring cities were crushed and ashamed, but without any temporary hope being raised by the appearance of such an army. In other words, the oracle was given and probably repeated during a period when Isaiah's audience still had the opportunity to decide on their course of action. That raises the question of Isaiah's real audience versus his fictive one. His real audience was not primarily the Nubian or Philistine messengers in Jerusalem; it was Hezekiah and the Judean court that Isaiah was trying to sway. The whole point of the oracle and others like it was to dissuade Hezekiah from accepting the Philistine and Nubian invitation to join the revolt, and in this case, Isaiah appears to have been successful. There is no indication that Judah joined the revolt or suffered Assyrian retaliation at the time.

---

6   The verb נוס, while it often means "to flee," can also mean "to move quickly" (Isa 30:16; 31:1). It does not imply that the people of Ashdod had fled to Egypt and now were threatened as an exiled community in Egypt by an Assyrian invasion of Egypt. The people of Ashdod had sent to Egypt and Nubia for help, but they had not moved their residence to Egypt.

Bibliography

Barstad, Hans M., "Who Destroyed Ashkelon? On Some Problems in Relating Text to Archaeology," in Iain Provan and Mark J. Boda, eds., *Let Us Go Up to Zion: Essays in Honour of H. G. M. Williamson on the Occasion of his Sixty-Fifth Birthday* (VTSup 153; Leiden: Brill, 2012) 345–58.

Baumgartner, W., "Beiträge zum hebräischen Lexikon," in *Gottes ist der Orient: Festschrift für Prof. D. Dr. Otto Eissfeldt DD zu seinem 70. Geburtstag am 1. September 1957* (Berlin: Evangelische Verlagsanstalt, 1959) 25–31.

Beck, B. L., "The International Roles of the Philistines during the Biblical Period" (PhD diss., Southern Baptist Theological Seminary, 1980) 151–53.

Beegle, D. M., "Proper Names in the New Isaiah Scroll," *BASOR* 123 (1951) 26–30.

Bonner, L., "Rethinking Isaiah 20," *OTWSA* 22–23 (1979) 32-52.

Born, Adrianus van den, *Profetie Metterdaad: Een Studie over de symbolische Handelingen der Profeten* (Bijbelsche Monographieën; Roermond-Maaseik: J. J. Romen & Zonen, 1947).

———. *De symbolische Handelingen der Oud-testamentische Profeten* (Utretch: Dekker & Van de Vegt, 1935).

Bright, John, *A History of Israel* (Philadelphia: Westminster, 1981).

Brunet, Gilbert, *Essai sur l'Isaïe de l'histoire* (Paris: A. & J. Picard, 1975) 145–53.

Burney, C. F., "The Interpretation of Isa XX 6," *JTS* 13 (1912) 417–23.

Criado, R., "Tienen alguna eficaria real las acciones simbolicas de los profetas?" *EstBíb* 7 (1948) 167–217.

Cross, Frank Moore, and David Noel Freedman, "The Name of Ashdod," *BASOR* 175 (1964) 48–50.

Dothan, M., "Ashdod: A City of the Philistine Pentapolis," *Archaeology* 20 (1967) 178–86.

———, *Ashdod II–III: The Second and Third Seasons of Excavation, 1963, 1965, Soundings in 1967* ('Atiqot 9-10; Jerusalem: Israel Department of Antiquities and Museums, 1971).

Dothan, M., and D. N. Freedman, *Ashdod I: The First Season of Excavations, 1962* ('Atiqot 7; Jerusalem: Israel Department of Antiquities and Museums, 1971).

Driver, G. R., "Notes and Studies: Hebrew Scrolls," *JTS* 2 (1951) 17–30.

Eph'al, Israel, "On Warfare and Military Control in the Ancient Near Eastern Empires: A Research Outline," in H. Tadmor and M. Weinfeld, eds., *History, Historiography and Interpretation: Studies in Biblical and Cuneiform Literatures* (Jerusalem: Magnes; Leiden: Brill, 1986) 88–106; first edition 1983.

Fohrer, Georg, "Die Gattung der Berichte über symbolische Handlungen der Propheten," *ZAW* 64 (1952) 101–20.

———, *Die symbolischen Handlungen der Propheten.* ATANT 25. Zurich: Zwingli-Verlag, 1953.

Frame, "Inscription of Sargon II," 31–57.

Franklin, N., "The Room V Reliefs at Dur-Sharruken and Sargon II's Western Campaigns," *TA* 21 (1994) 255–75, esp. 264–68, figs. 3–7.

Fuchs, *Die Annalen.*

———, *Die Inschriften Sargons II.*

Gottwald, *All the Kingdoms of the Earth,* 167–68.

Haran, M., "Isaiah the Prophet's Walking 'Naked and Barefoot for Three Years' (Isa 20)" (in Hebrew), in *Homage to Shmuel: Studies in the World of the Bible* (Festschrift S. Ahituv; Jerusalem: Bialik, 2001) 163–66.

Helfmeyer, F. J., "ʾwt," *ThWAT* 1:182–205.

Jenkens, A. K., "The Development of the Isaiah Tradition in Is 13–23," in J. Vermeylen, ed., *Le livre d'Isaïe: les oracles et leurs relectures unité et complexité de l'ouvrage* (BETL 81; Leuven: Leuven University Press, 1989) 245–46.

Kahn, D., "The Inscription of Sargon II at Tang-I Var and the Chronology of Dynasty 25," *Or* n.s. 70 (2001) 1–18.

Kaplan, J., "The Stronghold of Yamani at Ashdod-Yam," *IEJ* 19 (1969) 137–49.

Keller, C. A., "Das Wort *OTH*" (diss., Basel, 1946).

Kitchen, K. A., "Late Egyptian Chronology and the Hebrew Monarchy: Critical Studies in Old Testament Mythology, I," *JANES* 5 (1973) 225–33.

———, *Third Intermediate.*

Kleinert, P., "Bemerkungen zu Jes. 20–22 und 2 Kön. 18–20," *TSK* 50 (1877) 167–80.

Lang, Bernhard, "Prophecy, Symbolic Acts, and Politics: A Review of Recent Studies," in Lang, *Monotheism and the Prophetic Minority: An Essay in Biblical History and Sociology* (Social World of Biblical Antiquity 1; Sheffield: Almond, 1983) 83–91.

Martin-Achard, Robert, "Esaie et Jérémie aux prises avec les problèmes politiques: Contribution á l'étude du thème, Prophétie et politique," *Cahiers de la Revue de Théologie et de Philosophie* 11 (1984) 306–22.

Mattingly, G. L., "An Archaeological Analysis of Sargon's 712 Campaign against Ashdod," *NEASB* 17 (1981) 47–64.

Nötscher, F., "Entbehrliche Hapaxlegomena in Jesaja," *VT* 1 (1950) 301.

Rainey and Notley, *Sacred Bridge.*

Redford, D. W., "Quest for the Crown Jewel: The Centrality of Egypt in the Foreign Policy of Esarhaddon" (PhD. diss., Hebrew Union College, Cincinnati, 1998).

Roberts, J. J. M., "Egypt, Assyria, Isaiah," 265–83.
——, "Egyptian and Nubian Oracles," 201–9.
——, "Rod That Smote," 381–95.
Spalinger, A., "The Year 712 B.C. and Its Implications for Egyptian History," *JARCE* 10 (1973) 95–101.
Stolz, F., "ʾwt," *THAT* 1:91–95.
Suarez, L., "La realidad objectiva de las acciones simbolico-profeticas," *Illustración del clero* 36 (1943) 53–58, 132–36.
Tadmor, "Campaigns of Sargon II," 22–40, 77–100.
——, "Fragment of a Stele of Sargon II from the Excavations of Ashdod" (in Hebrew), *ErIsr* 8 (1967) 241–45.
——, "Philistia under Assyrian Rule," *BA* 29 (1966) 86–102.

Thompson, R. C., "An Assyrian Parallel to an Incident in the Story of Semiramis," *Iraq* 4 (1937) 35–43.
Weidner, E., "Šilkan(ḫe)ni, König von Muṣri, ein Zeitgenosse Sargons II. Nach einem neuen Bruchstück der Prisma-Inschrift des assyrischen Königs," *AfO* 14 (1941–44) 40–53.
Weippert, M., "Archäologischer Jahresbericht," *ZDPV* 80 (1964) 82 (chap. 18), 155 (chap. 20).
Wilhelm, G., "Ta/erdennu, Ta/urtannu, Ta/urtanu," *UF* 2 (1970) 277–82.
Wright, E. M., "The Eighth Campaign of Sargon II of Assyria (714 B.C.)," *JNES* 2 (1943) 173–86.

Though the dating of the three oracles in Isaiah 21 is disputed, with scholars like W. E. Barnes, E. Dhorme, and S. Erlandsson opting for a date or dates during Isaiah's lifetime, the more dominant view today tends to put the oracles later, usually in the period of the Babylonian exile (so Wildberger, 2:770–74, 794, 799, Clements, 176–80), though Vermeylen has suggested a slightly later date in the Persian period for vv. 1-10 (*Du prophète Isaïe*, 327), and Clements suggests a date as late as the third century for vv. 16-17 (p. 181). The dating to the period of the Babylonian exile is largely based on the mention of the fall of Babylon in v. 9 and the assumed role of the Medes and Elamites in this event. This move, however, too easily ignores the fact that Babylon was fought over and fell several times during the late eighth century and early seventh, thus in the lifetime of Isaiah of Jerusalem. The two most relevant of these conflicts for interpreting the present oracles are, in my opinion, Sennacherib's first campaign against Babylon in 703–702 BCE and his war against Elam and Babylon in 691–689 BCE and its aftermath.

In the first war, Sennacherib marched against Merodach-baladan and his Elamite, Aramean, Sutean, Arab, and Chaldean allies, who had retaken Babylon and Babylonia after the death of Sargon II in 705. Sennacherib sent one contingent of his army to Kish to keep watch on Merodach-baladan's main force, while Sennacherib himself attacked Kutha. The Assyrian army sent to Kish was defeated and besieged and sent urgent word to Sennacherib for assistance. Sennacherib was more successful at Kutha, capturing and plundering the city, before marching to the relief of his troops at Kish. According to Sennacherib, Merodach-baladan lost his nerve and fled the scene before the battle, but the Elamites, Chaldeans, Arameans, and Arabs put up a fight, though Sennacherib succeeded in defeating them. Sennacherib captured Baskanu, the brother of the queen of the Arabs, as well

as many chariots, wagons, horses, mules, asses, camels, and dromedaries that had been abandoned during the battle. Sennacherib then hastened to Babylon, which he captured and plundered without a significant battle, though there is no record that he smashed the Babylonian gods on this occasion. He then pursued Merodach-baladan but, being unable to find him, had to be satisfied with capturing many of the cities of Merodach-baladan's Aramean and Chaldean allies along with many Arabs, Arameans, and Chaldeans found in the cities of Uruk, Nippur, Kish, and Harsagkalamma.[1] Despite this initial success, however, Sennacherib continued to have trouble with Babylonia. He had appointed Bel-ibni the governor of Babylonia, but after three years he was removed and Sennacherib installed his own son Ashur-nadin-shumi on the throne of Babylon. Then, after a six-year reign of Ashur-nadin-shumi, the Elamite king Hallushu-Inshushinak I took him away as a prisoner to Elam and installed Nergal-ushezib on the throne of Babylon. Nergal-ushezib lasted only six months, but then Mushezib-Marduk took the throne of Babylon and was able to hold it for four years against the Assyrians.

That led to the second relevant war in 691–689. Despite Sennacherib's relatively successful campaigning against Elam, the Elamites sent a huge force to support Mushezib-Marduk against Sennacherib's attempts to recapture Babylon. This force included Elamite vassals from the lands of Parsuash, Anzan, Pasheru, Ellipi, and the tribal groups of Yazan, Lakabra, Harzunu, Dummuku, Sulai, and Samuna, as well as Aramean groups, and the battle was joined at Halule. The precise location of Halule is uncertain. The Helsinki Atlas places it on the Tigris well north of Babylon at 34°10'N latitude 43°52'E longitude.[2] Grayson places it on the Tigris farther south in the vicinity of the Diyala River, but still north of Babylon.[3] Though Sennacherib claimed a decisive victory,[4]

1 Luckenbill, *Annals*, 48-54:6-53. For this first campaign, see the modern edition in Grayson and Novotny, RINAP 3/1, no. 1, 5-62; no. 2, 5-19; no. 3, 5-19; no. 4, 5-17; no. 8, 5-16; no. 9, 5-13; no. 15, i 27-ii 5; no. 17, i 22-77; no. 18, i 1″-13″; no. 22, i 20-64; no. 23, i 18-58; no. 24, i 19-26; no. 26, i 1′-4′a; no. 34, 6b-8a; Grayson and Novotny, RINAP 3/2, no. 42, 3b-4,6; no. 44, 7b-11a, 13b-15a; no. 46, 3b-9a; 231, 7b-11; no. 135, 3b-5; no. 137, i 1′-22′; no. 165, i 29-64; no. 213, 5-61.

2 Simo Parpola and Michael Porter, *The Helsinki Atlas of the Near East in the Neo-Assyrian Period* (Helsinki: Neo-Assyrian Text Corpus Project, 2001) p. 9, map 10.

3 Grayson, *Assyrian and Babylonian Chronicles*, 255.

4 Luckenbill, *Annals*, 82-83:34-43; 88-89:44-55; 91-92:1-21. Grayson and Novotny, RINAP 3/1, no. 18, v 1′-vi 15′; no. 22, v 17-vi 35; no. 23, v 9-vi 30; no. 34, 44b-55a; no. 35, 29′b-52′; Grayson and Novotny, RINAP 3/2, no. 223, 34b-43a; no. 230, 11b-16a, 49b-112; no.

the Babylonian Chronicle indicates that the Elamite king forced an Assyrian retreat.[5] Despite his exaggerated claims of victory, Sennacherib's account does suggest that the battle was extremely costly for both sides. Both sides apparently suffered enormous losses, and despite a temporary tactical victory, it was a Pyrrhic victory for the Babylonians and their Elamite supporters. Soon after the Elamite king suffered a stroke,[6] which left the Elamites unable to regroup in time to successfully follow up on their victory, and in the meantime Sennacherib did regroup and put the city of Babylon under siege. When the city finally fell in 689 BCE after a prolonged siege, Sennacherib thoroughly sacked the city, allowed his soldiers to smash the Babylonian gods, and even went to the massive, labor-intensive trouble of diverting the irrigation canals through the city in an attempt to forever wipe out the ancient foundation trenches of Babylon and its temples so that the city and its temples could never be rebuilt.[7]

Sometime either during the siege of Babylon or possibly after the fall of Babylon in 689, Sennacherib or his generals also campaigned against Babylon's Arab supporters in the north Arabian desert. The text mentions the defeat of a queen of the Arabs, Telhunu, and a certain Hazael, and it also mentions the Arabs fleeing to or from Adummatu, an oasis in the desert, in an area of thirst where there were no pastures or drinking places.[8] This is the same site as Dumah in Isa 21:11 and is to be identified with Dumat al-Jundal in the Al Jawf province of modern Saudi Arabia. It was the capital of the Qedarite Arabs. It is certainly worth noting that the oracle about the fall of Babylon (Isa 21:1-10), is immediately followed by the oracle against Dumah (21:11-12), and another oracle against the Arabs of Qedar (21:13-17) that deals with fugitives of war facing thirst and hunger in the desert. The correspondence between this inscription of Sennacherib and the material in Isaiah 21 suggests that all these oracles date to the period around 691–689 BCE, and if not the work of Isaiah of Jerusalem, could be from a very early disciple of his.

21:1-10 Oracle on the Fall of Babylon

1/   Oracle concerning the wilderness of the sea.[a]
    Like storms passing through the Negeb
      it comes from the wilderness
        from a fearsome[b] land.
2/   A harsh vision was reported to me:
    "The treacherous one deals treacherously;[c]
    The plunderer plunders.[c]"
    Go up, O Elam! Besiege, O Medes!
    Put an end[d] to all his[e] groaning!
3/   Therefore my loins are full of writhing,
      Pangs have seized me, like the pangs of one giving birth;
    I am bent over in pain from hearing;
    I am terrified from seeing.[f]
4/   My heart[g] is bewildered/staggers,[h] shuddering terrifies me;
      The evening I desired[i] he has turned into trembling for me.
5/   Arrange the table, spread the tablecloth,[j] eat, drink;
      Rise up O officers, anoint the shield.
6/   For thus my Lord has said to me:
    "Go station the watchman;

143, ii 1'-4'; no. 144, i 1'-8'; no. 145, i 1-19'; no. 146, obv. 1-16; no. 147, obv. 1-14; no. 148, 1'-11'.

5 Grayson, *Assyrian and Babylonian Chronicles*, 80:16-18.
6 Ibid., 80:19-22.
7 Luckenbill, *Annals*, 83-84:43-54; Grayson and

Novotny, RINAP 3/1, no. 24 vi 1'-16'; Grayson and Novotny, RINAP 3/2, no. 223, 43b-54a.
8 Luckenbill, *Annals*, 92-93:22-27; Grayson and Novotny, RINAP 3/1, no. 35, 53'-9".

7/ What he sees let him report.[k]
    When he sees[l] chariotry with a yoke of horses,[m]
        donkey riders,[n] camel riders;[o]
    Then he shall pay attention, close attention.”

8/ And the seer[p] called out,[q]
    “Upon the watchpost, my Lord,[r] I[s] have been standing[t] continually by day,
        And upon my post I[s] have stationed myself all[u] the nights.

9/ And now this one is coming, a charioteer[v] with a yoke of horses;
    And he answered[w] and said,[x] 'Babylon has fallen, fallen,
        and all[y] the images of her gods[z] he has smashed[*a] to the ground!'

10/ My threshed one and the son of my threshing floor,[*b]
    What I have heard from Yahweh of Hosts,
        the God[*c] of Israel, I have reported to you.”[*d]

Textual Notes

a   The MT reading מִדְבַּר־יָם (*midbar yām*), “wilderness of the sea,” is supported by Syr. and Vg.; 1QIsaᵃ has דבר ים; LXX apparently simply read מדבר (τῆς ἐρήμου), “of the wilderness.”

b   MT, 1QIsaᵃ (in a correction above the line) and Vg. support נוֹרָאָה (*nôrāʾâ*), “fearsome”; LXX construes as modifying “vision” (φοβερὸν τὸ ὅραμα), “dreadful is the vision”; 1QIsaᵃ (written on line and then marked through) and Syr. have רחוקה (*rĕḥôqâ*), “from a distant land.”

c   The suggestion of Clements (pp. 177–78) to read MT's active participles בּוֹגֵד (*bôgēd*), “deals treacherously,” and שׁוֹדֵד (*šôdēd*), “plunders,” as qal passives, בּוּגַד (*bûgad*), “is treated treacherously,” and שׁוּדַד (*šûdad*), “is plundered,” is supported only by Tg., perhaps influenced by Isa 33:1; LXX, Syr., and Vg. have active forms.

d   Reading the feminine imperative הַשְׁבִּתִּי (*hašbittî*), “put an end to,” for MT's הִשְׁבַּתִּי (*hišbattî*), “I have brought to an end.” LXX, Vg., Syr., and Tg. all support MT, but the first person perfect is suspect following two feminine imperatives.

e   Reading אַנְחָתֹה (*ʾanḥātōh*), “his groaning,” for MT's אַנְחָתָהּ (*ʾanḥātâ*), “groaning.” A double feminine ending is otherwise unattested for this noun, so the final ה is probably a suffix (cf. Syr.), but the antecedent is masculine, which suggests the preexilic use of ה as a *mater* for the third person masculine singular suffix *ô* has been misread by the later scribes.

f   It is unclear whether the prophet is “too terrified to hear and see” (so LXX, Syr.; cf. Tg.) or “terrified because of what he hears and sees” (Vg.). Perhaps the sense is that his expectations are so high that he is afraid to look.

g   MT לְבָבִי (*lĕbābî*), “my heart,” LXX, Syr., Vg.; 1QIsaᵃ and 4QIsaᵃ have ולבבי, “and my heart.”

h   1QIsaᵃ has the participle תועה for the perfect תָּעָה (*tāʿâ*), “is bewildered,” MT, 4QIsaᵃ, Syr.

i   MT נֶשֶׁף חִשְׁקִי (*nešep ḥišqî*), “the evening I desired,” MT, 1QIsaᵃ, cf. Syr., Tg.; Vg. inserts Babylon interpretatively: *Babylon dilecta mea*, “Babylon, my delight”; LXX misreads נֶשֶׁף as נֶפֶשׁ (*nepeš*), “soul”: ἡ ψυχή μου ἐφέστηκεν εἰς φόβον, “my soul has turned to fear.”

j   MT has עָרֹךְ הַשֻּׁלְחָן צָפֹה הַצָּפִית (*ʿārōk haššulḥān ṣāpōh haṣṣāpît*), “arrange the table, spread the tablecloth,” and 1QIsaᵃ varies only slightly ערוך השלחן צופה הצפית, “arrange the table, spreading the tablecloth”; LXX compresses the two phrases (ἑτοίμασον τὴν τράπεζαν, “prepare the table”). For the second phrase Syr. “watch, O watchmen”; Tg. “set up watchmen”; and Vg., “observe on a high place,” all assume the verb is צפה I, “to watch,” but the root here is צפה II. The sense of the verb is to spread out or set in order, parallel to ערך. The noun צָפִית (*ṣāpît*) could be a covering for the table, a rug for the guests to recline on, or a cushion for the same purpose.

k   MT יַגִּיד (*yaggîd*), “let him report”; 1QIsaᵃ ויגיד, “and let him report”; LXX introduces the second person (καὶ ὃ ἂν ἴδῃς ἀνάγγειλον, “and whatever you see, report”). LXX thus seems to identify the watchman with the prophet.

l   MT וְרָאָה (*wĕrāʾâ*), “when he sees,” 1QIsaᵃ, Vg.; LXX (καὶ εἶδον, “and I saw”).

m   MT has רֶכֶב צֶמֶד פָּרָשִׁים (*rekeb ṣemed pārāšîm*), followed by Vg. (*currum duorum equitum*, “a chariot of two horses”); 1QIsaᵃ has רכב צמד איש פרשים (*rekeb ṣemed ʾîš pārāšîm*); 4QIsaᵃ איש [פרש]י[ם]; and LXX ἀναβάτας ἱππεῖς δύο, “two riding horsemen.”

n   MT רֶכֶב חֲמוֹר (*rekeb ḥămôr*), “rider(s) of donkeys”; 1QIsaᵃ ר[כב] חמור, “a donkey rider”; LXX ἀναβάτην ὄνου, “a rider on a donkey”; Vg. *ascensorem asini*, “a rider on a donkey,” Syr.

o   MT רֶכֶב גָּמָל (*rekeb gāmāl*), “rider(s) of camels”; 1QIsaᵃ רוכב גמל (*rôkēb gāmāl*), “a camel rider”; LXX ἀναβάτην καμήλου, “a rider on a camel”; Vg. *ascensorem cameli*, “a rider on a camel,” Syr.

p   Reading הראה (*hārōʾeh*), “the seer,” with 1QIsaᵃ and Syr. (“the observer”); MT has the obscure אַרְיֵה (*ʾaryēh*), “lion,” which Vg. follows but LXX takes as the proper name אוּרִיָּה (Uriah, Ουριαν; see Isa 8:2).

q   LXX misreads the verb as an imperative, καὶ κάλεσον Ουριαν εἰς τὴν σκοπιὰν κυρίου, “and call Uriah to the watchtower of the Lord.”

r   MT אֲדֹנָי (*ʾădōnāy*); 1QIsaᵃ אדוני.

s   MT אָנֹכִי (*ʾānōkî*), “I”; 1QIsaᵃ אנוכי.

t   MT עֹמֵד (*ʿōmēd*); 1QIsaᵃ עומד.

u   MT כָּל (*kol*); 1QIsaᵃ כול.

v   MT רֶכֶב אִישׁ (*rekeb ʾîš*); 1QIsaᵃ רוכב איש, “a man riding”; LXX

$\dot{\alpha}\nu\alpha\beta\dot{\alpha}\tau\eta\varsigma$ $\sigma\upsilon\nu\omega\rho\dot{\iota}\delta\sigma\varsigma$, "a rider of a pair of horses"; Syr. "behold there comes a man from the horsemen and says."

w   MT וַיַּעַן (wayya‘an), "and he answered"; 1QIsaᵃ ויעני.

x   MT וַיֹּאמֶר (wayyōʾmer), "and said"; 1QIsaᵃ ויואמר.

y   MT וְכָל (wěkol), "and all"; 1QIsaᵃ וכול.

z   MT אֱלֹהֶיהָ (ʾělōhêhā), "her gods"; 1QIsaᵃ אלוהיה.

*a MT שִׁבַּר (šibbar), "one smashed"; 1QIsaᵃ has the plural שברו (šibběrû), "they smashed," and this is supported by Tg.; LXX, Vg., and Syr. also have the plural, but in the passive "were smashed."

*b MT וּבֶן־גָּרְנִי (ûben-gornî), "and son of my threshing floor," Vg., Syr.; 1QIsaᵃ ובן גדרי (ûben gědērî) "and son of my wall."

*c MT אֱלֹהֵי (ʾělōhê), "God of"; 1QIsaᵃ אלוהי.

*d LXX has an expansive and loose translation of this verse: ἀκούσατε, οἱ καταλελειμμένοι καὶ οἱ ὀδυνώμενοι, ἀκούσατε ἃ ἤκουσα παρὰ κυρίου σαβαωθ· ὁ θεὸς τοῦ Ισραηλ ἀνήγγειλεν ἡμῖν, "Hear, you who have been left and who are in pain, hear what I heard from the Lord Sabaoth; the God of Israel has announced to us."

Commentary

The wilderness of the sea is probably a reference to the area in far southern Mesopotamia where the lower Tigris and the Uqnu flow into the reed marshes of the Aramean tribe of Bit-Yakin, the ancient Sealand (Māt Tâmti), along the border with Elam. It was in this area that Sennacherib had campaigned against the Arameans and Elam before Elam launched its counteroffensive. The military maneuvers in this area are compared to storm winds in the Negeb, and from the prophet's point of view, this was both a wilderness and a fearsome land.

In v. 2 the harsh vision reported to the prophet involves "the treacherous one dealing treacherously and the plunderer plundering." The language used here appears to be borrowed from Isa 33:1, where, at least in my opinion, "the treacherous one and the plunderer" refers to Sennacherib and his treatment of Hezekiah and Judah during his campaign of 701 BCE. In this context, it probably again refers to the hated Sennacherib, but this time in regard to his invasion of Elamite territory in Sennacherib's attempt to regain a lasting control of Babylon and Babylonia. The response, however, is a command to Elam and the Medes to attack and besiege and put an end to "his," presumably the treacherous plunderer's, that is, Sennacherib's, groaning. The mention of the Medes has led many scholars to interpret this text with reference to the later conflict between Babylon and the Medes and Persians, but Elam does not really fit in that context, and

it is not at all obvious that they are called upon to attack Babylon. Note that Elam is mentioned first; the Medes here could well represent tribal groups in vassalage to the Elamite empire. The command instead suggests a united attack of the Elamites and their allies on the Assyrian plunderer.

Verse 3 then reflects the prophet's response to the harsh vision, which seems to take a turn against the prophet's hopes and expectations. Either what he sees and hears contains bad news that terrifies him, or he is so afraid that it will be bad news that he cannot bear to see and hear. In any case, the prophet reacts to this real or anticipated bad news in stereotypical fashion, with writhing and anguish like a pregnant woman in birth pangs.[9] As v. 4 indicates, the "evening the prophet desired" has turned into a source of fear and trembling. The implication would seem to be that the prophet was looking for the good news of Babylon and Elam's defeat of the hated Assyrian, but instead the news is that, far from Assyria being put out of its misery by a final climactic defeat, the outcome has been indecisive and Assyria is regrouping and remains a threat. An Assyrian victory or prospective victory over Babylon and Elam would be regarded as bad news in Judah, for it would mean that Assyria's heavy yoke on restive Judah would remain in place.

In v. 5 the prophet calls upon the allied soldiers to eat their meal and anoint their shields, that is, prepare for battle. In the meantime, God has commanded the speaker, the prophet, to station the watchman (הַמְצַפֶּה,

---

9   For the convention of reaction to bad news, see D. R. Hillers, "Convention in Hebrew Literature: The Reaction to Bad News," *ZAW* 77 (1965) 86–90.

hammĕṣappeh) and have him report what he observes (v. 6). When he sees riders coming, he is to pay especially close attention (v. 7). The expression used for riders is ambiguous. Does רֶכֶב (*rekeb*) refer to a column or detachment of riders or to an individual rider? At least the expressions רֶכֶב חֲמוֹר (*rekeb ḥămôr*), "donkey riders," and רֶכֶב גָּמָל (*rekeb gāmāl*), "camel riders," refer to an individual or contingent of individuals mounted on donkeys and camels, since neither donkeys nor camels were normally used at this period to draw chariots. The expression רֶכֶב צֶמֶד פָּרָשִׁים (*rekeb ṣemed pārāšîm*) is more ambiguous. It could refer to a chariot or a detachment of chariots, each drawn by a span of horses, or it could refer to a detachment of cavalry, perhaps riding in a column of twos. In v. 9, however, the רֶכֶב אִישׁ צֶמֶד פָּרָשִׁים (*rekeb 'îš ṣemed pārāšîm*) is treated as a singular person who comes (זֶה בָא, *zeh bā'*), "this one is coming," replies (וַיַּעַן, *wayya'an*), "and he answered," and speaks (וַיֹּאמֶר, *wayyō'mer*), "and he said," as an individual. That is why I understand the expression as referring to a single charioteer driving a yoke or span of horses.

It is also unclear at this point what the actual relationship between the prophet and the watchman is. Is the watchman a separate individual whom the prophet sends out to watch for individuals fleeing from the war in Mesopotamia, or is the prophet referring to himself as he awaits visionary confirmation of the outcome of the war? The *piel* of צפה (*sph*) (v. 6) is used metaphorically of the prophet as God's watchman (Mic 7:7; Hab 2:1), and the passage from Habakkuk is particularly interesting, since a number of vocabulary items from that passage also appear here (עַל־מִשְׁמַרְתִּי, *'al mišmartî*, "upon my post," Isa 21:8; עמד, *'md*, "to station, stand," Isa 21:6, 8; ראה, *r'h*, "to see," Isa 21:6; נצב, *nṣb*, "to stand, station," Isa 21:8, a byform of יצב, *yṣb*, "to stand, station," Hab 2:1). The parallels between Isa 21:8 and Hab 2:1 provide a strong case for identifying the prophet with the watchman and seer. Apparently the seer, like Habakkuk in the parallel, stayed at his post day and night until he received the divine oracle concerning the outcome of the battle (v. 8).

On the other hand, is it likely that a prophetic announcement over the outcome of the war in Mesopotamia, particularly an outcome undesired by the prophet himself, would be announced in the absence of actual news arriving from the distant battlefield? Perhaps news had arrived in the ordinary way of such news, but in the prophetic vision this news is reported as the word of a man who had just arrived, having apparently escaped from the battle driving a chariot pulled by a team of horses (Isa 21:9). He responds to the prophetic watchman by announcing, "Babylon has fallen, and all the images of her gods he has smashed to the ground!" (v. 9). The "he" is not specifically identified, but the prophet probably has a specific individual in mind—the hated Assyrian king Sennacherib. This report of the fate of the images of the Babylonian gods corresponds to what Sennacherib said about them when he captured Babylon in 689 BCE. In contrast, there is no indication that the Babylonian images were destroyed in Sennacherib's earlier conquest of Babylon in 703–702, much less in the Persian Cyrus's rather bloodless occupation of the city in 539 BCE. The only relevant conquest of Babylon for which this announcement corresponds to explicit external historical evidence is that of 689 BCE.

In v. 10 the prophet declares that what he had heard from Yahweh of Hosts, the God of Israel, he had announced to his audience. His opening address of this audience as "my threshed one and the son of my threshing floor" is not crystal-clear, but its meaning is probably rather somber. "Threshing" is often a symbol for judgment and oppression (2 Kgs 13:7; Amos 1:3; Hab 3:12), and both the larger oracle and this final address suggest that Israel's threshing at the hands of its hated Assyrian enemy is, contrary to preliminary hopes, far from over. Their hopes that Babylon and its Elamite allies would put a final end to Sennacherib's Assyrian oppression were devastated by the collapse of the coalition and the fall of Babylon.

Bibliography

Ackroyd, P., *Exile and Redemption* (Philadelphia: Westminster, 1968) 223.

Barnes, W. E., "A Fresh Interpretation of Isaiah XXI 1-10," *JTS* 1 (1900) 583–92.

Benz, Ernst, *Die Vision: Erfahrungsformen und Bilderwelt* (Stuttgart: E. Klett, 1969).

Benzinger, I., *Hebräische Archäologie* (Tübingen: Mohr, 1907).

Bosshard-Nepustil, Erich, *Rezeptionen von Jesaja 1–39 im Zwölfprophetenbuch: Untersuchungen zur* literarischen Verbindung von Prophetenbüchern in babylonischer und persischer Zeit (OBO 154; Freiburg: Universitätsverlag; Göttingen: Vandenhoeck & Ruprecht, 1997) 23-42.

Boutflower, Ch., "Isaiah XXI in the Light of Assyrian History," *JTS* 14 (1913) 501–15.

Brinkmann, J. A., "Elamite Military Aid to Merodach-Baladan II," *JNES* 24 (1965) 161–66.

——, "Merodach-Baladan II," in R. D. Briggs and J. A. Brinkman, eds., *Studies Presented to A.Leo Oppenheim, June 7, 1964* (Chicago: Oriental Institute of the University of Chicago, 1964) 6–53.

Buhl, F., "Jesaja 21,6-10," *ZAW* 8 (1888) 157–64.

Carmignac, J., "Six passages d'Isaïe éclairés par Qumran," in Siegfried Wagner, ed., *Bibel und Qumran: Beiträge zur Erforschung der Beziehungen zwischen Bibel- und Qumranwissenschaft. Hans Bardtke zum 22. 9. 1966* (Berlin: Evangelische Haupt-Bibelgesellschaft, 1968) 37–46.

Cobb, W. H., "Isaiah XXI.1-10 Re-Examined," *JBL* 17 (1898) 40–61.

Dhorme, E., "Le désert de la mer (Isaïe, XXI)," *RB* 31 (1922) 403–6.

Droysen, H., *Heerwesen und Kriegführung der Griechen* (Freiburg: Mohr, 1889).

Eliade, Mircea, *Schamanismus und Archaische Ekstasetechnik* (Zurich: Rascher, 1957).

Erlandsson, *Burden of Babylon*, 95–97, 97–101 (chap. 23).

Galling, K., "Jesaja 21 im Lichte der neuen Nabonidtexte," in Ernst Würthwein and Otto Kaiser, eds., *Tradition und Situation: Studien zur alttestamentlichen Prophetie. Artur Weiser zum 70. Geburtstag am 18. 11. 1963* (Göttingen: Vandenoeck & Ruprecht, 1963) 49–62.

Geyer, J., "Mythology and Culture in the Oracles against the Nations," *VT* 34 (1986) 129–45.

Gosse, Bernard, *Isaïe 3,1–14,23 dans la tradition littéraire du livre d'Isaïe et dans la tradition des oracle contre les nations* (OBO 78; Freiburg: Universitätsverlag; Göttingen: Vandenhoeck & Ruprecht, 1988).

——, "Isaïe 21,11-12 et Isaïe 60–62," *BN* 53 (1990) 21–22.

——, "Le 'moi' prophétique de l'oracle contre Babylone d'Isaïe 21:1-10," *RB* 93 (1986) 70–84.

——, "Un texte pré-apocalyptique du règne de Darius: Isaïe 13:1–14:23," *RB* 92 (1985) 200–222.

Gray, G. B., "The Strophic Division of Isaiah 21:1-10 and 11:1-8," *ZAW* 32 (1912) 190–98.

Hänel, Johannes, *Das Erkennen Gottes bei den Schriftpropheten* (BWA[N]T n.F. 4; Leipzig: Kohlhammer, 1923).

Hillers, D. R., "Convention in Hebrew Literature: The Reaction to Bad News," *ZAW* 77 (1965) 86–90.

Hinz, W., *The Lost World of Elam: Re-creation of a Vanished Civilization* (New York: New York University Press, 1973).

Hölscher, G., *Die Profeten: Untersuchungen zur Religionsgeschichte Israels* (Leipzig: Hinrichs, 1914).

Grayson, and Novotny, RINAP 3/1.

——, RINAP 3/2.

Jenkins, A. K., "The Development of the Isaiah Tradition in Is 13–23," in J. Vermeylen, ed., *Le livre d'Isaïe: Les oracles et leurs relectures unité et complexité de l'ouvrage* (BETL 81; Leuven: Leuven University Press, 1989) 246–47.

Kleinert, P., "Bemerkungen zu Jes. 20–22," *TSK* 1 (1877) 174–79.

König, Friedrich Wilhelm, *Geschichte Elams* (Der alte Orient 29.4; Leipzig: Hinrichs, 1931).

Lohmann, P., "Die anonymen Prophetien gegen Babel aus der Zeit des Exils" (Diss., Rostock, 1910) 61.

——, "Zur strophischen Gliederung von Jes 21 1-10," *ZAW* 33 (1913) 262–64.

Macintosh, A. A., *Isaiah XXI: A Palimpsest* (Cambridge: Cambridge University Press, 1980).

Obermann J., "YHWH's Victory over the Babylonian Pantheon: The Archetype of Is 21 1-10," JBL 48 (1929) 301–28.

Osten, Hans Henning van der, *Die Welt der Perser* (Grosse Kulturen der Frühzeit 4; Stuttgart: G. Kilpper, 1956).

Salonen, E., *Die Waffen der alten Mesopotamier* (StOr 33; Helsinki: Suomalaisen Kirjallisuuden Kirjapaino, 1965).

Schmökel, H., *Keilschriftforschung und alte Geschichte Vorderasiens* (HO 3.2; Leiden: Brill, 1957).

Schüttler, G., "Das mystisch-ekstatische Erlebnis: Systematische Darstellung der Phänomenologie und des psychopathologischen Aufbaus," Inaugural-Dissertation zur Erlangung der Doktorwürde der Hohen Medizinischen Facultät der Rheinischen Friedrich-Wilghelms-Universität zu Bonn (Medical diss., Bonn, 1968).

Scott, R. B. Y., "Isaiah XXI 1-10: The Inside of a Prophet's Mind," *VT* 2 (1952) 278–82.

Seierstad, I., *Die Offenbarungserlebnisse der Propheten Amos, Jesaja und Jeremia* (Oslo: J. Dybwad, 1946).

Sen, F., "Variantes de algunos textos de Isaias con respecto al Texto Masoretico," *CB* 33 (1976) 223–25.

Sievers, E., "Zu Jesaja 21 1-10," in K. Budde, ed., *Vom Alten Testament: Karl Marti zum siebzigsten Geburtstage* (BZAW 41; Giessen: A. Töpelmann, 1925) 262–65.

Smith, S., *Babylonian Historical Texts Relating to the Capture and Downfall of Babylon* (London: Methuen, 1924; repr., Hildesheim: G. Olms, 1975).

Torczyner, H., "Biblische Kleinprobleme II.3: Ein verkannter Volksname in der Bibel," *MGWJ* 75 (1931) 15–17.

Uffenheimer, B., "'The Desert of the Sea' Pronouncement (Isaiah 21:1-10)," in David P. Wright, David Noel Freedman, and Avi Hurvitz, eds., *Pomegranates and Golden Bells: Studies in Biblical, Jewish, and Near Eastern Ritual, Law, and Literature in Honor of Jacob Milgrom* (Winona Lake, IN: Eisenbrauns, 1995) 677–88.

Wilhelmi, G., "Polster in Babel? Eine Überlegung zu Jesaja XXI 5+8," *VT* 25 (1975) 121–23.

Winckler, H., *Alttestamentliche Untersuchungen* (Leipzig: Pfeiffer, 1892) 120–25.

Wong, G. C. I., "Isaiah's Opposition to Egypt in Isaiah xxi 1-3," *VT* 46 (1996) 392–401.

21:11-12 The Dumah Oracle

11/ **Oracle concerning Dumah[a]**
To me one is calling from Seir,
"Watchman, what of the night?"[b]
Watchman, what of the night?"[c]

12/ **The watchman said,**
"The morning has come but also the night.
If you would inquire, inquire;
Return,[d] come again."

Textual Notes

a   דוּמָה (*Dûmâ*) MT, 1QIsaᵃ, 4QIsaᵇ ([דו]מה); LXX τῆς Ἰδουμαίας.

b   MT has שֹׁמֵר מַה־מִלַּיְלָה (*šōmēr mah millaylâ*), "watchman, what of the night?" 1QIsaᵃ has an orthographic variant שומר מה מליל; while LXX seems to read שמרו חילות (Φυλάσσετε ἔπαλξεις), "guard the battlements."

c   MT repeats the preceding phrase with the shortened form מִלֵּיל (*millêl*), "of the night," that 1QIsaᵃ uses in both lines. LXX has φυλάσσω τὸ πρωὶ καὶ τὴν νύκτα, "I will guard (them) in the morning and at night." Syr. omits the repetition.

d   MT's שֻׁבוּ (*šubû*), "return"; 1QIsaᵃ (שובו) is misread by LXX as שְׁבוּ (οἴκει), "dwell."

Commentary

This very short oracle seems purposely clouded in darkness and mystery. The heading identifies its concern with the oasis Dumah, or Adummatu of Sennacherib's inscription.[10] A probably fictive supplicant from Seir, presumably an Edomite trader or perhaps a Qedarite kinsman residing in Seir, cries out to the prophet for news from Dumah. The repetition of the question suggests the urgency of the request, while the question itself—"Watchman, what of the night?"—though mysterious, seems to imply, "What word have you received from the deity during the night about Dumah's fate?" But the answer is not reassuring. The morning has come, and night has returned, but there is still no answer from the deity. If you want to inquire of the deity, come back and try again. A deity's refusal to respond to an oracular request in such a fashion, even if it is simply to delay responding, has negative overtones and suggests that the oracle, if it ever comes, will not be good news (cf. 1 Sam 14:37; 28:6; Amos 8:11-12; Mic 3:6-7).

---

10   Grayson and Novotny, RINAP 3/1, no. 35, 53′-9″.

Bibliography

Bartlett, J. R., "Edom," *ABD* 2:287–95.

——, "From Edomites to Nabataeans: A Study in Continuity," *PEQ* 111 (1979) 53–66.

Galling, K. B., "Jes. 21 im Lichte der neuen Nabonidtexte," in Ernst Würthwein and Otto Kaiser, eds., *Tradition und Situation: Studien zur alttestamentlichen Prophetie. Artur Weiser zum 70. Geburtstag am 18. 11. 1963* (Göttingen: Vandenhoeck & Ruprecht, 1963) 49–62.

Geyer, John B., "The Night of Dumah (Isaiah XXI 11-12)," *VT* 42 (1992) 317–39.

Gosse, Bernard, "Isaïe 21,11-12 et Isaïe 60–62," *BN* 53 (1990) 21–25.

Grayson and Novotny, RINAP 3/1.

Lindsay, J., "The Babylonian Kings and Edom 605–550 B.C.," *PEQ* 108 (1978) 23–29.

Lohmann, P., "Das Wächterlied Jes 21 11,12," *ZAW* 33 (1913) 20–29.

Rabin, Ch., "An Arabic Phrase in Isaiah," in *Studi sull'Oriente e la Bibbia, Offerti al p. Giovanni Rinaldi nel 60° compleanno da allievi, colleghi, amici* (Genoa: Studio e vita, 1967) 303–9.

Schlossberg, E., "Who Is the Subject of the 'Burden of Dumah' Prophecy?" *Studies in Bible and Exegesis* 4 (1997) 273–77.

21:13-17 The End of Qedar

13/ The oracle "In the steppe":[a]
In the thicket in the steppe[b] you will lodge,
O caravans of Dedanites;[c]
  14/ To meet the thirsty bring water.[d]
O inhabitants of the land of Tema,[e]
With food[f] meet[g] the fugitive.[h]

15/ For they have fled[i] from before the swords,[j]
From before the drawn sword,[k]
  And from before the strung bow,
    And from before the weight[l] of war.

16/ For thus says my Lord[m] to me,
"In one more year,[n] according to the years of a hired laborer,
  All[o] the glory of Kedar will come to an end,[p]
  17/ And the remaining bows of the warriors of Kedar[q] will become few,"
For Yahweh the God[r] of Israel has spoken.

Textual Notes

a   MT's מַשָּׂא בַּעְרָב (*maśśā' ba'rāb*), "the oracle 'in the steppe,'" is supported by 1QIsaᵃ, the traces in 4QIsaᵃ and 4QIsaᵇ, Vg. (*onus in Arabia*, "the burden 'in Arabia'"), and Syr. ("the burden concerning Arabia"); LXX omits the heading.

b   MT's בַּיַּעַר בַּעְרָב תָּלִינוּ (*bayya'ar ba'rab tālînû*), "in the thicket in the steppe you will lodge," is supported by 1QIsaᵃ and the traces in 4QIsaᵃ and 4QIsaᵇ; LXX, Vg., and Syr. all read בערב as "in the evening"—"in the evening you will lie down/spend the night in the thicket." The MT is the superior reading, because it contains the expression behind the title of the oracle.

c   MT's אֹרְחוֹת דְּדָנִים ('*ōrĕḥôt dĕdānîm*), "caravans of the Dedanites," with the orthographic variant in 1QIsaᵃ אורחות דודנים is treated as a masculine plural as in Job 6:18-19. LXX misunderstands

the text as ἐν τῇ ὁδῷ Δαιδαν, "in the way of Dedan"; Vg. and Syr., as "in the way of the Dodanites."

d   MT's הֵתָיוּ (*hētāyû*), "bring," elides the initial *aleph* of the root אתה in the *hiphil* imperative, while 1QIsaᵃ and 4QIsaᵃ preserve it האתיו. I take the subject of this verb to be the preceding vocative, "O caravans of the Dedanites."

e   The following יֹשְׁבֵי אֶרֶץ תֵּימָא (*yōšĕbê 'ereṣ têmā'*) MT, 1QIsaᵃ (יושבי ארצ תימא) is also to be read as a vocative, "O inhabitants of the land of Tema," though the versions seem to read Teman rather than Tema.

f   The reading בְּלַחְמוֹ (*bĕlaḥmô*), "with his food,") found in MT and 4QIsaᵇ seems odd. 1QIsaᵃ omits the suffix as do LXX and Vg., while Syr. has the second person plural suffix, "your bread." If the singular suffix is original, it refers proleptically to the singular fugitive who needs the bread, not to the plural community providing the bread.

g MT's קִדְּמוּ (qiddĕmû), "they met," is pointed as a *piel* perfect; it should be corrected to קַדְּמוּ (qaddĕmû), "meet," the *piel* masculine plural imperative, with the versions.

h MT נֹדֵד (nōdēd), "fugitive"; 1QIsaᵃ נודד is singular like the earlier צָמֵא (sāmēʾ), "thirsty," because the fugitives escape as individuals, not as large groups. This supports the claim that "the caravans of the Dedanites" were not those needing help, but were called upon to offer help just as "the inhabitants of the land of Tema" were.

i MT switches to the plural verb נָדְדוּ (nādādû), "they fled," while 1QIsaᵃ keeps the singular נדד ("he fled"). Either reading could be original.

j For MT חֲרָבוֹת (ḥărābôt), "swords," 1QIsaᵃ has רבות".

k MT has חֶרֶב נְטוּשָׁה (ḥereb nĕṭûšâ), "drawn sword," 1QIsaᵃ חרב נטשה; but Syr. seems to read חרב לטושה (ḥereb lĕṭûšâ), "sharpened sword," and Vg. has "overhanging sword" (gladii inminentis). LXX just badly paraphrases this whole verse: διὰ τὸ πλῆθος τῶν φευγόντων καὶ διὰ τὸ πλῆθος τῶν πλανωμένων καὶ διὰ τὸ πλῆθος τῆς μαχαίρας καὶ διὰ τὸ πλῆθος τῶν τοξευμάτων τῶν διατεταμένων καὶ διὰ τὸ πλῆθος τῶν πεπτωκότων ἐν τῷ πολέμῳ, "because of the multitude of those fleeing, and because of the multitude of those wandering and because of the multitude of the short sword, and because of the multitude of the poised arrows and because of the multitude of those who had fallen in the war."

l MT has כֹּבֶד (kōbed), "weight, heaviness, vehemence," while 1QIsaᵃ has כבוד with no difference in meaning.

m MT and 4QIsaᵃ have אֲדֹנָי (ʾădōnāy, "my Lord"), but 1QIsaᵃ has יהוה, "Yahweh," which may be original.

n MT's שָׁנָה (šānâ), "year," is supported by LXX, Vg., Syr., and Tg.; 1QIsaᵃ has שלוש שנים ("three years").

o MT's כָּל (kol), "all," is supported by Vg., Syr., and Tg.; it is omitted by 1QIsaᵃ and LXX.

p MT וְכָלָה (wĕkālâ), "and will come to an end"; 1QIsaᵃ יכלה.

q MT בְּנֵי־קֵדָר (bĕnê qēdār), lit., "sons of Qedar"; 1QIsaᵃ בני־קדר.

r MT אֱלֹהֵי (ʾĕlōhê), "God of"; 1QIsaᵃ אלוהי.

Commentary

The title of the oracle, "In the steppe," is taken from the phrase in the first line of the oracle, "In the thicket *in the steppe* you will lodge." Since the title repeats this phrase, it confirms the MT reading over against the versions that understood בערב in the title correctly but misunderstood it in the first line as "in the evening." The direct address with the second person plural indicates that the addressees, the caravans of the Dedanites, will spend the night in the scrub brush of the steppe, but it does not immediately explain what they are doing there. This is remedied by the plural imperative in the first line of v. 14, "Bring water to meet the thirsty one." I understand the subject of this imperative to be the same "caravans of the Dedanites" that was also the subject of the preceding second plural, "you will lodge." In other words, the "caravans of the Dedanites" are not fugitives from the battle wandering around in the steppe, but they are called upon to go out into the steppe with water to assist such fugitives just as their neighbors, the inhabitants of the land of Tema, are commanded to bring food to them in the parallel lines. As noted in the textual notes, both the thirsty one (צָמֵא, sāmēʾ) to whom the helpers bring water and the fugitive (נֹדֵד, nōdēd) to whom they bring food are referred to in the singular. The helpers go out in groups, but the fugitives from the battle are encountered as isolated individuals trying to escape through the steppe.

Verse 15 characterizes these fugitives as those who have fled from the drawn sword, the strung bow, and the weight or crush of battle. Verses 16-17 then identify these fugitives as Qedarites, or "sons of Qedar," a north Arabian tribe associated with the oasis at Dumah. Apparently, then, this oracle is a continuation of the Dumah oracle of vv. 11-12 and refers to Sennacherib's campaign against the Arabs of Dumah or Adummatu. If so, the prophet characterizes Sennacherib's defeat of the Arabs of Dumah as the beginning of the end of the Qedarite Arabs. Within a year, proclaims the prophet, the glory of Qedar will come to an end, and the famous archers of the Qedarite Arabs will be reduced to a pitiful remnant, for Yahweh the God of Israel has spoken. No reason is given for this divine judgment on Qedar, but in the larger context of Isaiah one might hazard the guess that it was rooted in the false hopes that Judah placed upon these Arabs along with Babylon and Elam for deliverance from Assyria, just as they had earlier placed their hopes on Egypt and Nubia, rather than trusting in Yahweh for deliverance.

Bibliography

Abbott, N., "Pre-Islamic Arab Queens," *AJSL* 58 (1941) 1–22.

Borger, Riekele, *Die Inschriften Asarhaddons, Königs von Assyrien* (AfOB 9; Graz: E. Weidner, 1956).

Buhl, F., *Geschichte der Edomiter* (Leipzig: A. Edelmann, 1893).

Caskel, Werner, *Das altarabische Königreich Lihyan* (Krefeld: Scherpe, 1950).

Eph'al, Israel, *The Ancient Arabs: Nomads on the Borders of the Fertile Crescent, 9th–5th Century B.C.* (Jerusalem: Magnes Press, Hebrew University; Leiden: Brill, 1982).

Graf, G. F., "Dedan," *ABD* 2:121–23.

Grohmann, A., *Arabien* (Kulturgeschichte des Alten Orients 3.1.3.4; Munich: Beck, 1963).

Knauf, E. A., *Ismael: Untersuchungen zur Geschichte Palästinas und Nordarabiens im I. Jahrtausend v. Chr.* (2nd ed.; Wiesbaden: Harrassowitz, 1989).

——, "Kedar," *ABD* 4:9–10.

——, "Tema (Place)," *ABD* 6:346–47.

Leichty, RINAP 4.

Macintosh, A. A., *Isaiah XXI: A Palimpsest* (Cambridge: Cambridge University Press, 1980).

Philby, H. St., *The Land of Midian* (London: Benn, 1957).

Rabinowitz, I., "Aramaic Inscriptions of the Fifth Century B.C.E. from a North-Arab Shrine in Egypt," *JNES* 15 (1956) 1–9.

Streck, M., *Assurbanipal und die letzten assyrischen Könige bis zum Untergange Ninivehs* (3 vols.; VAB 7; Leipzig: Hinrichs, 1916).

Täubler, E., "Kharu, Horim, Dedanim," *HUCA* 1 (1924) 119–23.

1/   Oracle concerning the valley of vision[a]
      What is it with you[b] that you have gone up,[c]
        All of you,[d] to the rooftops?

2/   Why are you filled with shoutings,[e]
      O boisterous city, O exultant town?[f]
    Your slain are not those slain by the sword,
      And they are not those dead from war.

3/   All your officials fled together,
      Without the bow[g] they were captured;[h]
    All yours who were found[i] were taken prisoner,
      Together they fled far away.[j]

4/   Therefore I said, "Look away[k] from me;[l]
      I will be bitter[m] in my weeping.
    Do not press[n] to comfort me,
      Because of the destruction of the daughter of my people."

5/   For there is a day of tumult[o] and trampling and confusion
      To my Lord Yahweh of Hosts in the valley of vision.[p]
    Qir cried out a cry[q] and the Suteans a shout[r] to/on[s] the mountain;

6/   And Elam bore the quiver,[t]
      With the chariotry/riders of Aram[u] (and) horsemen,
        And Qir[v] uncovered the shield.

7/   And the choicest of your valleys were filled[w] with chariots,
      And the horsemen stationed themselves at the gate.[x]

8/   And he removed[y] the covering[z] of Judah,
      And you looked*[a] on that day
        To the armory of the house of the forest.*[b]

9/   And the breaches*[c] of the city of David,*[d]
      You saw*[e] that they were many;*[f]

10/   And the houses of Jerusalem you counted,
      And you tore down*[g] the houses to fortify*[h] the wall.*[i]

11/   And a reservoir you made between the two walls,*[i]
      For the waters of the old pool.

9b/   And you gathered the waters of the lower pool,*[j]

11b/   But you did not*[k] look*[l] to the one who is doing it;*[m]
      And the one who is fashioning it from distant times you did not*[n] consider.

12/   And my Lord*[o] Yahweh of Hosts called on that day
      For weeping and for lamentation,
    And for baldness and for girding*[p] on sackcloth;

13/   But (instead) there was jubilation and rejoicing,
      Killing oxen and slaughtering sheep,*[q]
        Eating*[r] meat and drinking wine;
    "Eat and drink, for tomorrow we die!"

14/   And Yahweh of Hosts revealed himself in my ears,*[s]
      "Surely this sin will never be atoned for you until you die!"*[t]
    Says my Lord*[u] Yahweh of Hosts.

Textual Notes

a   1QIsaᵃ has גי חזיון for MT's גֵּיא חִזָּיוֹן (gê᾿ ḥizzāyôn); LXX read גיא ציון (τῆς φάραγγος Σιων).

b   1QIsaᵃ has מלכי with assimilation of the ה and the older second person feminine singular suffix for MT's מַה־לָּךְ (mah-llāk).

c   1QIsaᵃ עליתי for MT עָלִית (ʿālît).

d   The Hebrew texts maintain the second person feminine singular with "city" as the understood subject, but LXX switches to the second person common plural due to the influence of "all."

e   LXX mistakenly construes תשאות (těšū᾿ôt), "shoutings," MT, 1QIsaᵃ, with the preceding verse ("vain roofs," δώματα μάταια). The direct address is continued as the second person feminine singular suffix on the following חֲלָלַיִךְ (ḥălālayik), "your slain," indicates.

f   LXX, in its typical manner, omits the second of the two synonymous phrases עִיר הוֹמִיָּה קִרְיָה עַלִּיזָה (ʿîr hômîyâ qiryâ ʿallîzâ), "O boisterous city, O exultant town," compressing the repetition into a single phrase (ἐνεπλήσθη ἡ πόλις βοώντων, "the city was filled with people shouting").

g   MT and 1QIsaᵃ have מקשת (*miqqešet*), "without the bow"; LXX (σκληρῶς) and Vg. (*dureque*) render as though from קשה (*qāšeh*), "and harshly they are bound."

h   Reading אֻסָּרוּ (*ʾussārû*) with MT; 1QIsaᵃ's אסורה (*ʾāsûrâ*) appears to be construed as an adjective modifying מקשת, "without bow tied on/strung (?)."

i   For MT כָּל־נִמְצָאַיִךְ (*kol-nimṣāʾayik*); 1QIsaᵃ כול נמצאיך; LXX apparently had a double reading: ונמצאיך (καὶ οἱ ἁλόντες, "those captured") and ואמיציך (καὶ οἱ ἰσχύοντες ἐν σοὶ, "and those who are strong in you").

j   The MT accentuation would suggest the translation "all yours who were found were taken prisoner together, they fled far away," but just as נָדְדוּ־יָחַד (*nādēdû yaḥad*), "they fled together," goes together in v. 3a, so יַחְדָּו מֵרָחוֹק בָּרָחוּ (*yaḥdāw mērāḥôq bārāḥû*), "together they fled far away," belongs together in v. 3d. Read against the MT accentuation because of the length of the lines and to preserve the chiastic parallelism with v. 3a; in both cases *yaḥad* or *yaḥdāw* underscores the flight of all the officials.

k   MT שְׁעוּ (*šēʿû*), "look away"; 1QIsaᵃ שועו; the versions all render by sense, "leave me alone."

l   MT מִנִּי (*minnî*), "from me"; 1QIsaᵃ ממני.

m   MT's אֲמָרֵר (*ʾămārēr*), "I will be bitter," is supported by the versions against 1QIsaᵃ's ואמרר.

n   For MT תָּאִיצוּ (*tāʾîṣû*), "do not press"; 1QIsaᵃ has the odd form תוצו.

o   For MT מְהוּמָה (*mēhûmâ*), "tumult," 1QIsaᵃ, Vg., Syr., and Tg.; LXX has a double translation (ταραχῆς καὶ ἀπωλείας, "of trouble and of destruction").

p   MT בְּגֵיא חִזָּיוֹן (*bēgêʾ ḥizzāyôn*), "in the valley of vision"; 1QIsaᵃ בגי חזיון; LXX apparently read בגיא ציון (ἐν φάραγγι Σιων).

q   The expression מְקַרְקַר קִר (*mēqarqar qir*), "Qir cried out a cry," is very difficult; the ancient versions all go their own way, indicating they did not understand the expression. 1QIsaᵃ has קדש for MT's קר וְשׁוֹעַ (*qir wēšôaʿ*), suggesting that the meaning of the expression was lost fairly early in the scribal tradition. I assume the prophet is using the *pilpel* participle of a verb קרר, "to cry out," with an intentional double entendre between the cognate accusative קר (*qir*), "cry," and the people or place-name קיר (*qîr*), "Qir," mentioned in the following verse.

r   The term וְשׁוֹעַ (*wēšôaʿ*) probably also contains an intentional double entendre, the noun שׁוֹעַ (*šôaʿ*), "shout," and the people name *šôaʿ*, "the Suteans."

s   MT has אֶל (*ʾel*), "to"; 1QIsaᵃ על (*ʿal*), "upon."

t   For MT's אַשְׁפָּה (*ʾašpâ*), "quiver"; 1QIsaᵃ has the variant spelling אשפא.

u   MT's בְּרֶכֶב אָדָם פָּרָשִׁים (*bērekeb ʾādām pārāšîm*) though supported by 1QIsaᵃ, is difficult to translate, as the variations in the versions indicate. One might take each of the three terms to indicate a different type of military unit: "with chariotry, infantry, (and) cavalry." I prefer to emend אדם (*ʾādām*), "man," to the people name ארם (*ʾārām*), "Aram," as a parallel to עילם and קיר.

v   For MT's וְקִיר (*wēqîr*), "and Qir"; 1QIsaᵃ has וקור. The versions seem to take the word to mean "wall," even if LXX understands this in a metaphorical sense of an unbroken battle line

(καὶ συναγωγὴ παρατάξεως, "and a gathering of the battle line"), but as a parallel with עילם, "Elam," the place or people name קיר seems more likely (cf. 2 Kgs 16:9; Amos 1:5; 9:7).

w   MT's וַיְהִי (*wayhî*), "and it came to pass that," suggests a past tense; 1QIsaᵃ has the future tense והיה, and the versions follow it, but MT is the superior reading.

x   MT's הַשַּׁעְרָה (*haššāʿērâ*), "at the gate," is supported by 1QIsaᵃ, Vg., Syr., and Tg.; LXX's τὰς πύλας σου, "your gates," is translational and does not require an alternate Hebrew *Vorlage*.

y   MT's וַיְגַל (*waygal*), "and he removed, uncovered," is third person masculine singular past tense; so also 1QIsaᵃ; LXX has third person masculine plural future tense (καὶ ἀνακαλύψουσιν, "and they will uncover").

z   LXX's τὰς πύλας Ιουδα, "the gates of Judah," for אֵת מָסַךְ יְהוּדָה (*ʾet māsak yēhûdâ*), "the covering of Judah," MT, 1QIsaᵃ, Vg., Syr., Tg. is just loose translation.

*a   MT's וַתַּבֵּט (*wattabbēṭ*), "and you looked," is supported by 1QIsaᵃ, Vg., and Syr. LXX maintains the third person masculine plural (καὶ ἐμβλέψονται, "and they will look").

*b   LXX misread הַיַּעַר (*hayyāʿar*), "of the forest," as העיר (*hāʿîr*; τῆς πόλεως, "of the city").

*c   LXX seems to repeat the וַיְגַל (*waygal*), "and he removed") of v. 8, at least by sense, before וְאֵת בְּקִיעֵי עִיר־דָּוִד (*wēʾēt bēqîʿê ʿîr-dāwid*), "and the breaches of the city of David," for which LXX offers the odd translation καὶ ἀνακαλύψουσιν τὰ κρυπτὰ τῶν οἴκων τῆς ἄκρας Δαυιδ, "and they shall uncover the hidden things of the houses of the acropolis of David."

*d   MT דָּוִד (*dāwīd*), "David," 1QIsaᵃ דויד.

*e   MT רְאִיתֶם (*rēʾîtem*), "you saw"; 1QIsaᵃ ראיתמה. LXX has καὶ εἴδοσαν, "and they saw."

*f   The line וַתְּקַבְּצוּ אֶת־מֵי הַבְּרֵכָה הַתַּחְתּוֹנָה (*wattēqabbēṣû ʾet-mê habbērēkâ hattaḥtônâ*), "and you gathered the waters of the lower pool," appears to have suffered an ancient transposition. It is out of place here, as it interrupts the description of the shoring up of the breaches in the defensive wall. It should go either at the beginning of v. 11 or immediately after the mention of the "old pool," where I have placed it in my translation.

*g   MT וַתִּתְּצוּ (*wattittēṣû*), "and you tore down"; 1QIsaᵃ ותתוצו.

*h   MT לְבַצֵּר (*lēbaṣṣēr*), "to fortify"; 1QIsaᵃ has the *qal* infinitive לבצור with the same meaning. LXX maintains its third person masculine plural and abbreviates the verse: καὶ ὅτι καθείλοσαν τοὺς οἴκους Ιερουσαλημ εἰς ὀχύρωμα τοῦ τείχους τῇ πόλει, "and that they had destroyed the houses of Jerusalem for the fortification of the walls in the city."

*i   MT has the dual הַחֹמָתַיִם (*haḥōmātayim*), "the two walls," and is supported by LXX and Vg.; 1QIsaᵃ has החומה.

*j   Transposed from v. 9, see n. *f above.

*k   MT וְלֹא (*wēlōʾ*); 1QIsaᵃ ולוא.

*l   MT הִבַּטְתֶּם (*hibbaṭtem*), "you looked"; 1QIsaᵃ and 4QIsaᶜ have the longer form הבתתמה.

*m   MT אֶל־עֹשֶׂיהָ (*ʾel-ʿōśêhā*), "to the one doing it"; 1QIsaᵃ על עושיה.

*n   MT לֹא (*lōʾ*); 1QIsaᵃ לוא.

*o   MT אֲדֹנָי (*ʾădōnāy*), "my Lord"; 1QIsaᵃ אדוני.

*p   MT וְלַחֲגֹר (*wēlaḥăgōr*), "and the girding on"; 1QIsaᵃ ולחגור.

*q   MT צֹאן (*ṣōʾn*), "sheep"; 1QIsaᵃ צאן.

*r   MT אָכֹל (ʾākōl), "eating"; 1QIsaᵃ אכול.

*s   MT וְנִגְלָה בְּאָזְנָי יְהוָה צְבָאוֹת (wĕniglâ bĕʾoznāy YHWH ṣĕbāʾôt), "and Yahweh of Hosts revealed himself in my ears"; 1QIsaᵃ ונגלה באוזני יהוה צבאות; LXX has καὶ ἀνακεκαλυμμένα ταῦτά ἐστιν ἐν τοῖς ὠσὶν κυρίου σαβαωθ, "and these things were revealed in the ears of the Lord Sabaoth," and Vg. has a similar *et revelata est in auribus meis Domini exercituum*, "and it was revealed in the ears of my Lord of Hosts."

*t   MT has the incomplete oath formula אִם־יְכֻפַּר הֶעָוֺן הַזֶּה לָכֶם עַד־תְּמֻתוּן (ʾim-yĕkuppar heʿāwōn hazzeh lākem ʿad-tĕmūtûn), lit., "If this sin is atoned for you until you die . . . ," but the sense is "I swear that this sin will not be atoned for you until you die." 1QIsaᵃ inserts an additional "for you" and includes some variant spellings: אם יכפר לכם העוון הזה לכמה עד תמותון.

*u   MT אֲדֹנָי (ʾădōnāy), "my Lord"; 1QIsaᵃ אדוני.

Commentary

The heading, "Oracle concerning the valley of vision," suggests that this oracle concerns a visionary experience about a valley that the prophet sees only in his vision, not a valley stretching out before the prophet's actual eyes. Verse 5 says that Yahweh of Hosts has a day of tumult, trampling, and confusion in this "valley of vision," where Qir raised a cry and the Suteans a shout to the mountains, where Elam bore the quiver and Qir uncovered the shield (v. 6). The mention of Qir, the homeland of the Arameans presumably in lower Mesopotamia (Amos 9:7); the Suteans, a Mesopotamian tribal group; and the Elamites, a powerful rival to Assyria located in the southwestern corner of modern Iran, suggests that these were major participants in the battle in this visionary valley, but that suggests a battle in far-away Mesopotamia, not in Palestine. Each of these groups is specifically mentioned as fighting against Assyria in 703 BCE, when Sennacherib marched against Babylon in his first campaign.

But if this visionary valley is located in distant Mesopotamia, that in turn has a bearing on the interpretation of the following direct address. Who is it that the prophet addresses as having gone up to their rooftops? Or, in the words of v. 2, what is the identity of the "boisterous city, the exultant town" that is "filled with shouting"? What appears to be the dominant view identifies the city with Jerusalem (e.g., Wildberger, 2:816), but that does not comport well with the idea that the valley is a distant site seen only in a vision, nor does it conform well with the thought that the city's slain were not slain with the sword nor killed in battle. Further, it is difficult to understand the claim in v. 3 that all the city's officials fled together and were captured without the bow, that all of them who were found were taken prisoner where they had fled far away. Nothing we actually know about Sennacherib's siege of Jerusalem in 701 BCE would explain this rather detailed imagery. In contrast, the imagery fits very well the behavior of Merodach-Baladan and his closest advisors and officers in Babylon during Sennacherib's first campaign against Babylon.[1] Despite the allies' initial success against the Assyrians at Kish, success that might explain the rejoicing in the city of Babylon, the war soon turned in the Assyrians' favor. When Sennacherib took Kutha and came to the aid of his besieged troops in Kish, Merodach-Baladan did not match Sennacherib's resolve. The Babylonian ruler panicked, deserted his troops and their Elamite, Sutean, Aramean, Chaldean, and Arab allies at Kish, abandoned his capital Babylon without a fight, and fled into the swamps of lower Mesopotamia to save his own life. Sennacherib defeated the suddenly unsupported allied army at Kish, scattering their troops and taking a number of prominent captives, including Adinu, son of the wife of Merodach-Baladan, and Baskanu, the brother of Yati'e, queen of the Arabs. Sennacherib then hurried to Babylon, which he captured without resistance, and proceeded to plunder it of its treasures, counting Merodach-Baladan's wife, harem, chamberlains, officials, courtiers, musicians, palace slaves, and artisans as spoil. After securing Babylon, Sennacherib pursued Merodach-Baladan south into the swamps, where the Assyrian soldiers searched for him for five days. While

---

1   For an easily accessible English translation of Sennacherib's earliest account of this first campaign, see Luckenbill, *Annals,* 48–55. See now Grayson and Novotny, RINAP 3/1, 1–72.

he was unable to find Merodach-Baladan, Sennacherib scooped up many allied soldiers across the steppes and highlands where they had fled far from the battle, because they had no place to take refuge. "Your slain are not those slain by the sword, and they are not those dead by war" fits perfectly as a plaintive description of the behavior of Merodach-Baladan, the king of Babylon, and his closest advisors (v. 2). Babylon's top officials did flee together, and those who were captured, were captured without the bow, that is, without a fight, and those who were found, were found far away where they had fled (v. 3). None of this fits what we know of Hezekiah and his top advisors during Sennacherib's third campaign against Judah.

Why, though, would Isaiah react so strongly to events in far-off Babylon? The answer is that the outcome of Assyria's attack on Babylon would have immediate ramifications for the fate of Judah. If Babylon defeated Assyria, Judah would have far less reason to fear a major Assyrian campaign against Judah. Assyria needed to secure its southern border against its close and very dangerous enemies in Babylon and their Elamite, Sutean, Aramean, Chaldean, and Arab allies before moving against the far more distant and less threatening rebels in its western provinces. An Assyrian victory of the magnitude that occurred would free up the Assyrian army for an immediate and major campaign against the western rebels, and Judah would feel the full force of the Assyrian might.

Thus, it is not surprising that the prophet is inconsolable. He urges his Judean audience to look away from him that he might weep bitterly, to make no attempt to console him for the destruction of the daughter of his people (v. 4). This is a prospective destruction that had not yet occurred, but which Isaiah saw coming with certainty, now that Judah's allies in the east had been defeated. Verses 5-6 give a further description of Isaiah's vision of these climactic events in the east. It was a day of "tumult, trampling, and confusion" for Isaiah's Lord, Yahweh of Hosts, in this far-off valley of vision. The terminology, "a day . . . to my Lord," suggests a connection to the theme of "the day of Yahweh." This was apparently a day on which the popular religious imagination expected Yahweh to intervene to punish Yahweh's

foreign enemies, but at least beginning with Amos (Amos 5:18-20), some of Israel's and Judah's prophets, including Isaiah (Isa 2:12; 10:3; 13:6, 9), began to proclaim this as a day on which Yahweh's own people could also face divine judgment.

The prophet then mentions some of the allied participants in the battles at Kutha and Kish. Isaiah perhaps chose the word קִיר (Qir), the name of the homeland of the Arameans (see Amos 9:7), over ארם (Aram, the Arameans), because that allowed an interesting play on words with double entendres so dear to Isaiah's poetic heart.[2] The expression מְקַרְקַר קִר (měqarqar qir) could be rendered either as "Qir cried out" or "One cried out a cry," and since the double entendre is probably intentional, I would render, "Qir cried out a cry." In the same way, the term וְשׁוֹעַ (wěšôaʿ) probably also contains an intentional double entendre, the noun שׁוֹעַ, (šôaʿ), "shout," and the people name, "the Suteans." Thus, I render, "and the Suteans a shout." The mentions of Qir, the Suteans, and the Elamites all point to these events in Mesopotamia. The widespread explanation of these names as simply referring to foreign auxiliary detachments in Sennacherib's Assyrian army (so Wildberger, 2:818) is lame in the extreme. If the prophet were speaking of Sennacherib's Assyrian campaign against Judah in 701 BCE, one would expect him to mention the Assyrians, not these enemies of Assyria.

The brief vignettes that Isaiah gives are more evocative than descriptive of the military maneuvering, noise, excitement, terror, chaos, and confusion of the major military engagement in which these allies were engaged. Verse 7, still speaking of the events in this distant area, mentions the assembly of the large allied force in Babylon's choicest valleys. The reference here is probably to the sending of some of the army to Kutha, and some to Kish. It is less clear which was the gate where the horsemen were stationed. Does it refer to a significant mobile reserve force stationed at the gates of Babylon or to calvary stationed in the field near the gates of Kish? Since Sennacherib seems to indicate that Merodach-Baladan was in the field at Kish, perhaps it refers to the gates of Kish,[3] but the Isaiah text is not as clear as one would like. One might question the source of Isaiah's knowledge of

2 See my "Double Entendre."

3 Grayson and Novotny, RINAP 3/1, text 1, 20-22.

this distant battle, as well as how detailed and accurate that knowledge was, but it is likely that this knowledge was not just visionary, that messengers had actually arrived from the Babylonian side or Assyrian, or both, bringing news of the outcome of this battle. Isaiah had opposed those advisors of Hezekiah who had promoted a policy of defensive alliances with Nubian Egypt and Babylon (Isaiah 28–32; 39:1-8), and, while those advisors had tried to keep their deliberations secret from the prophet by cutting the prophet out of the king's inner circle,[4] with the defeat of Babylon and the beginning of the unraveling of this foreign policy of defensive alliances, it is likely that the prophet's access to diplomatic news and court deliberations was beginning to improve.

At v. 8 the prophet shifts his attention to Judah. The statement that "he removed the covering of Judah" is probably a reference to the fall of Babylon. As long as Babylon held out, it would divert attention from Judah. It would remain the screen that protected Judah from Assyrian retaliation. With the fall of Babylon, however, everyone knew that the Assyrians would be coming west, and so it was necessary to prepare to meet that inevitable invasion. On that day, presumably the day that the news of Babylon's fall reached the palace in Jerusalem, Isaiah complains that the first move of the Judean king (note the second person masculine singular "you" in v. 8)[5] was to look to the weapons in the royal armory located in the part of the palace complex known as "the house of the forest." In other words, Hezekiah was taking stock of the military arsenal available to him to resist the expected Assyrian attack, but the prophet, as he will explicitly state in v. 11, felt that Hezekiah and his advisors should have

first looked to God rather than immediately moving to practical military measures. After checking on the royal arsenal, Hezekiah's officials inspected the state of Jerusalem's defensive fortification. What they found was not reassuring. According to v. 9, there were many breaches in the fortification walls of the city of David. These would have to be fixed and the walls strengthened, particularly on the north side of Jerusalem where the topography provided a more accessible attack point for a besieging army. The present text of v. 9 includes a line about gathering the waters of the lower pool, but that line appears to be out of place, interrupting as it does the material about fortifying the walls. It should probably be transposed to v. 11b, or possibly v. 11a, where the other material about the city's water supply is found. Its present position is probably due to an ancient transposition by an early but careless scribe.

In order to make the necessary and urgent repairs to the walls, the royal officials counted the houses of Jerusalem and tore down some of these houses, perhaps partly to gain quick access to the required building material to shore up old fortifications, and partly to clear the necessary space for the construction of new fortifications (v. 10). The archaeology of the northern wall of the city on the western hill has uncovered traces of this activity of Hezekiah.[6] The wall actually runs through the ruins of one of the houses torn down for this bolstering of Jerusalem's fortifications. One could perhaps understand some delay about undertaking this intensive work as long as hope remained that Babylon would keep Assyria occupied indefinitely, but one would hardly wait to make such preparations for war if Assyrian columns were already

4   See J. J. M. Roberts, "Blindfolding the Prophet: Political Resistance to First Isaiah's Oracles in the Light of Ancient Near Eastern Attitudes toward Oracles," in Roberts, *The Bible and the Ancient Near East: Collected Essays* (Winona Lake, IN: Eisenbrauns, 2002) 282–91; earlier published in Jean-Georges Heintz, ed., *Oracles et prophéties dans l'antiquité: Actes du Colloque de Strasbourg 15-17 juin 1995* (Travaux du Centre de recherche sur le Proche-Orient et las Grèce antiques 15; Strasbourg: De Boccard, 1997) 135–46.

5   The second person feminine singular in v. 7 presumably refers to the city Babylon. The second person masculine plurals in vv. 9-11 refer not just to the

Judean king but also to the Judean court, the king and his advisors. Cf. the similar usage in Isa 7:10-14.

6   H. Geva, "Western Jerusalem at the End of the First Temple Period in Light of the Excavations in the Jewish Quarter," in Andrew G. Vaughn and Ann E. Killebrew, eds., *Jerusalem in Bible and Archaeology: The First Temple Period* (SBLSymS 18; Atlanta: Society of Biblical Literature, 2003) 183–208, esp. 190-94. This is based on excavations in Jerusalem led by Nahman Avigad between 1969 and 1982, the final reports of which are found in H. Geva, ed., *Jewish Quarter Excavations in the Old City of Jerusalem Conducted by Nahman Avigad, 1969–1982* (2 vols.; Jerusalem: Israel Exploration Society, 2000).

operating in the Judean countryside. This makes it even more doubtful that "the covering of Judah" could refer to a site in Judah such as one of the outlying fortress cities like Lachish (v. 8),[7] or that the "boisterous, exultant city" of v. 1, could refer to Jerusalem. By then it would be far too late to make the necessary defensive preparations; waiting until news of the fall of Babylon reached Jerusalem, but perhaps still months before the arrival of the attacking Assyrian army, was already cutting the time available for defensive preparations perilously short.

Verse 11 continues with the Judean court's efforts to protect Jerusalem's water supply. There was an attempt to secure the water supply by making a reservoir for the old pool between the two defensive walls of the city, suggesting that prior to this time, the reservoir, whatever its precise location, lay outside the outer wall, and that whatever earlier defensive arrangements had been made, they were felt inadequate to a serious Assyrian siege. The transposed line from v. 9c then indicates that one also gathered the waters of the lower pool. The lower pool presumably refers to the pool of Siloam, and the reference possibly alludes to the underground tunnel Hezekiah dug to gather the waters of the Gihon Spring into the pool of Siloam, which lay within the defensive walls of the city.[8] It would be nice if one possessed an ancient map of Hezekiah's Jerusalem, but in the absence of such sources and with the limitations on the archaeology of the ancient city imposed by religious sensibilities and an extensive modern city sitting on the site, much about the ancient description of building activities in the city remains uncertain. Yet, again, these efforts to secure the city's water supplies must have been done before the Assyrian army showed up in Judah, and the Assyrian siege of Jerusalem prevented anyone from either going in or out of Jerusalem.

From the prophet's point of view, all these military preparations of Hezekiah's court and generals was inadequate and wrongheaded, because they had not first looked to Yahweh, the one who was directing these events and who had planned them long ago (v. 11). They had ignored God and rejected the admonitions of his prophet, and now they were paying the price for their rejection of the prophetic word. In this context of the dire threat from Assyria, Yahweh of Hosts was calling for weeping, lamentation, shaving of the sides of the head as a mark of sorrow, and for the wearing of sackcloth (v. 12). All these actions typically accompanied public repentance in the attempt to win back the favor and forgiveness of an angry deity (cf. Amos 8:10; Isa 3:34; 15:2). Such would have been the appropriate behavior of the leaders of Judah, but instead they were behaving in exactly the opposite fashion. What the prophet actually saw in Jerusalem was frantic partying (v. 13)—jubilation and rejoicing, the slaughtering of oxen and sheep, the eating of meat and drinking of wine as on days of joyous celebration. This strange behavior was justified by a saying that apparently was making the rounds among Jerusalem's upper class in those days, "Eat and drink, for tomorrow we die." In effect, many of the nobility were resigned to their own demise, so they might as well selfishly enjoy life while they still had the opportunity. Such behavior certainly cut against any serious effort to prepare the city for siege, since one of the first requirements to endure a long-term siege is to secure not only an adequate water supply but also an adequate food supply. Even in crisis, the rich elite of Jerusalem would not look beyond their own wants to the actual needs of the larger community dependent upon them.

In response to this obtuseness, Yahweh revealed his oath to the ears of Isaiah. The oath is formulated as an incomplete oath formula, as is common in Hebrew, so that literally it reads, "If this iniquity is ever atoned for you until you die." The full formula would include an apodosis, which, simply for the sake of understanding, might be completed as, "If this iniquity is ever atoned for you until you die, then my name is not Yahweh."

---

7   J. D. W. Watts speaks of "the line of fortress towns that protected" Jerusalem from invasion (*Isaiah 1-33*, rev. ed., 338). Wildberger (2:816, 821) specifically rejects this interpretation, claiming that the "covering of Judah" (v. 8) as well as the "boisterous, exultant city" (v. 1) must refer to Jerusalem itself.

8   2 Chronicles 32:3-5, 30 refers to this work of Hezekiah, and one should also consider the inscription inscribed in the wall of this Siloam water tunnel as well as the tunnel itself. See F. W. Dobbs-Allsopp, J. J. M. Roberts, C. L. Seow, and R. E. Whitaker, eds., *Hebrew Inscriptions: Texts from the Biblical Period of the Monarchy with Concordance* (New Haven: Yale University Press, 2005) 499–506, and the literature cited there.

Unfortunately, while incomplete oath formulas of this type are well attested for God (Num 32:10-11; Deut 1:34-35; 1 Sam 3:14; Amos 8:7; Ps 95:11), complete oath formulas are not attested for the deity. Such complete oath formulas, where humans are swearing, take different types of apodoses, such as, "If I have raised my hand against the orphan, . . . then let my shoulder blade fall from my shoulder, and let my arm be broken from its socket" (Job 31:21-22), or, "May Yahweh/God/the gods do so to me and more also, if . . ." (1 Sam 3:17; 25:22; 1 Kgs 20:10). In the oath that Yahweh revealed to Isaiah, the apodosis is simply understood though unspoken, giving the sense, "I swear that this iniquity will never be atoned for you until you die." One should note that "you" here is plural, designating a collective, the ruling elite of Jerusalem. The oracle ends, then, on this somber note of Yahweh's oath not to forgive the leaders of Jerusalem for their selfish, foolish, and totally inappropriate behavior. This somber note is highlighted by the bracketing references to Yahweh of Hosts as the one who revealed and spoke the oath. Yahweh of Hosts, found also in vv. 5 and 12, is one of Isaiah's favorite designations for the God of Israel, but it is particularly appropriate in this context of impending warfare, for it characterizes Yahweh as the leader, if not the creator, of the heavenly armies. Unfortunately for Jerusalem's elite, the oracle ends with no promise of a last-minute divine intervention of these heavenly armies. The death they had announced for themselves in v. 13 will come to this group without forgiveness or hope.

Bibliography

Amiran, R., "The Water Supply of Israelite Jerusalem," in Yigael Yadin, ed., *Jerusalem Revealed: Archaeology in the Holy City, 1968–1974* (New Haven: Yale University Press, 1976) 75–78.

Avigad, Nahman, "The Epitaph of a Royal Steward from Siloam Village," *IEJ* 3 (1953) 137–52.

Baumgartner, Walter, "Herodots babylonische und assyrische Nachrichten," in Baumgartner, *Zum Alten Testament und seiner Umwelt: Ausgewälte Aufsätze* (Leiden: Brill, 1959) 282–331.

Bosshard-Nepustil, Erich, *Rezeptionen von Jesaja 1–39 im Zwölfprophetenbuch: Untersuchungen zur literarischen Verbindung von Prophetenbüchern in babylonischer und persischer Zeit* (OBO 154; Freiburg: Universitätsverlag; Göttingen: Vandenhoeck & Ruprecht, 1997) 42–67.

Box, G. H., "Some Textual Suggestions on Two Passages in Isaiah," *ExpTim* 19 (1908) 563–64.

Brinkmann, J. A., "Elamite Military Aid to Merodach-Baladan II," *JNES* 24 (1965) 161–66.

Broshi, M., "The Expansion of Jerusalem in the Reigns of Hezekiah and Manasseh," *IEJ* 24 (1974) 21–26.

Brunet, *Essai sur l'Isaïe.*

Childs, *Assyrian Crisis.*

Clements, Ronald E., *Isaiah and the Deliverance.*

——, "The Prophecies of Isaiah and the Fall of Jerusalem in 587 B.C.," *VT* 30 (1980) 421–36.

Dahood, M., "בֵּין הַחֹמֹתַיִם (Isa 22:11 etc. nota discussionem sensus accurati)," *Bib* 42 (1961) 474–75.

Dietrich, *Jesaja und die Politik*, 193–95.

Donner, *Israel unter den Völkern*, 126–28.

Driver, "Isaiah 1–39: Problems," 36–57.

Eggebrecht, G., "Die früheste Bedeutung und der Ursprung der Konzeption vom 'Tage Jahwes,'" *Theologische Versuche* 13 (1983) 41–56.

Eissfeldt, O., "Ezechiel als Zeuge für Sanheribs Eingriff in Palästina," in Eissfeldt, *Kleine Schriften* (6 vols.; Tübingen: J. C. B. Mohr, 1962–79) 2:239–46.

Emerton, J. A., "Notes on the Text and Translation of Isaiah XXII 8–11 and LXV 5," *VT* 30 (1980) 437–51.

Erlandsson, *Burden of Babylon.*

Everson, A. J., "The Days of Yahweh," *JBL* 93 (1974) 329–37.

Fensham, F.C., "A Possible Origin of the Concept of the Day of the Lord," in *Proceedings of the Ninth Meeting of "Die Ou-Testamentiese Werkgemeenskap in Suid-Afrika"* (Stellenbosch: University of Stellenbosch, 1966) 90–97.

Gallagher, William R., *Sennacherib's Campaign to Judah: New Studies* (SHCANE 18; Leiden: Brill, 1999).

Gottwald, *All the Kingdoms of the Earth*, 193–96.

Guillaume, A., "A Note on the Meaning of Isaiah XXII. 5," *JTS* n.s. 14 (1963) 383–85.

Honor, L. L., *Sennacherib's Invasion of Palestine* (New York: Columbia University Press, 1926).

Jeremias, J., *Theophanie: Die Geschichte einer alttestamentlichen Gattung* (WMANT 10; Neukirchen-Vluyn: Neukirchener Verlag, 1965).

Kenyon, K., "Excavations in Jerusalem, 1962," *PEQ* 95 (1963) 7–21.

Preuss, H. D., *Jahweglaube und Zukunftserwartung* (BWA[N]T 87; Stuttgart: Kohlhammer, 1968).

Rudolph, W., "Sanherib in Palästina," *PJ* 25 (1929) 59–80.

Soden, W. von, "Sanherib vor Jerusalem 701 v. Chr,"
in *Antike und Universalgeschichte: Festschrift Hans
Erich Stier zum 70. Geburtstag am 25. May 1972*
(Fontes et commentationes, Supplement-band 1;
Münster: Aschendorff, 1972) 43–51; reprinted in
H.-P. Müller, ed., *Bibel und alter Orient: Altorien-
talische Beiträge zum Alten Testament* (BZAW 162;
Berlin: de Gruyter, 1985) 149–57.

Torczyner, H., "Dunkle Bibelstellen," in K. Budde,
ed., *Vom Alten Testament: Karl Marti zum siebzigsten
Geburtstage* (BZAW 41; Giessen: A. Töpelmann,
1925) 276, 563–64.

Tushingham, A. D., "The Western Hill under the
Monarchy," *ZDPV* 95 (1979) 39–55.

Vermeylen, *Du Prophète Isaïe*.

Weippert, M., "Mitteilungen zum Text von Ps 19,5
und Jes 22,5," *ZAW* 73 (1961) 97–99.

Wilkinson, J., "Ancient Jerusalem: Its Water Supply
and Population," *PEQ* 106 (1974) 33–51.

22

This oracle against Shebna probably dates from approximately the same time period as the preceding oracle. A clue to the date of the oracle may be seen in the prophetic proclamation that Eliakim would replace Shebna as the high royal official אֲשֶׁר עַל-הַבָּיִת (ʾăšer ʿal-habbāyit), "who was over the palace." By the time Sennacherib's army appeared in Palestine in 701 BCE, and his high officials, the tartān, the rab-sārîs, and the rab-šāqê, appeared before the walls of Jerusalem to parley with the Judean officials, Eliakim was already ʾăšer ʿal-habbāyit, and Shebna was only הַסֹּפֵר (hassōpēr, "the scribe"; 2 Kgs 18:18; cf. Isa 36:3). Given Isaiah's animosity to Shebna, it seems likely that Shebna was one of the royal advisors who had promoted the policy of defensive alliances that no longer seemed so attractive in the face of the conquering Assyrian army, and his demotion and the promotion of Eliakim to Shebna's former position may suggest that Eliakim was a royal official less tainted by this failed policy and more open to the political advice of Isaiah. This shift in their relative positions probably occurred after the news of Babylon's defeat reached Jerusalem, but apparently sometime before the Assyrian delegation appeared before the walls of Jerusalem. The oracle appears to have a later addendum in v. 25 or perhaps vv. 24-25 in which the prophet or his editor revises the earlier positive evaluation of Eliakim. Apparently Eliakim's growing nepotistic abuse of his office led to this negative change in appraisal.

15/   Thus says my Lord[a] Yahweh of Hosts,
         Go[b] now to this administrator,[c]
         Against[d] Shebna[e] who is over the palace.[f]
16/   What do you have[g] here?
         Or whom do you have here,
         That you have hewn out for yourself[h] a grave here,
         Hewing out on the height your grave,
         And inscribing[i] in the rock your tomb?
17/   Yahweh is about to hurl you away violently, fellow,[j]
         And he is about to wrap you up[k] tightly;
18/   Wadding you up, he will sling you away energetically[l]
         Like a ball into a wide land.
         There you will die and there (will remain) the chariots of your glory,
         O shame of your master's house.[m]
19/   And I will thrust you from your station,
         And from your position one will tear you away.[n]
20/   On that day I will summon[o] my servant, Eliakim the son of Hilkiah,[p]
21/   And I will dress him[q] in your tunic,[r]
         And with your linen sash[s] I will gird him,
         And your authority I will put in his hand,
         And he will become a father to the inhabitant of Jerusalem,
         And to the house of Judah.
22/   And I will put the key of the house of David[t] upon his shoulder,
         And he will open, and no one will close,[u]
         And he will close, and no one will open.[v]
23/   And I will fasten him as a peg in a firm place,[w]
         And he will become a throne of honor to his father's house.
24/   And they will hang upon him all[x] the weight[y] of his father's house,
         The offspring[z] and the issue, all[x] the small utensils,*[a]
         From the vessels of bowls and to all the vessels*[b] of jars.
25/   On that day, says*[c] Yahweh of Hosts,
         The peg fastened in a firm place will give way,
         And it will be cut off and fall,
         And the load that was on it will perish*[d]
         For Yahweh has spoken.

Textual Notes

a MT אֲדֹנָי (ʾădōnāy), "my Lord"; 1QIsaᵃ אדוני.

b MT לְדָ-בֹא (lek-bōʾ), "go enter"; 1QIsaᵃ לך בוא.

c MT אֶל-הַסֹּכֵן הַזֶּה (ʾel-hassōkēn hazzeh), "to this administrator"; 1QIsaᵃ אל הסוכן הזה; LXX's Πορεύου εἰς τὸ παστοφόριον, "go into the chamber," may be based on the reading אל-הלשכה (ʾel-halliškâ), "to the chamber" (cf. 1 Chr 9:26; 23:28; 28:12; 2 Chr 31:11; Ezek 40:17); Vg., however, appears to be reading אל השוכן (ʾel haššōkēn), ad eum qui habitat in tabernaculo, "to the one who lives in the tabernacle."

d MT עַל (ʿal), "against"; 1QIsaᵃ אל, "to."

e For שֶׁבְנָא (šebnāʾ), "Shebna," LXX has Σομναν, "Somnas."

f LXX adds the phrase καὶ εἰπὸν αὐτῷ, "and say to him," to make clear that the following verse is a quotation.

g MT מַה-לְּךָ (mah-llěkā), "what do you have"; 1QIsaᵃ מהלך.

h MT כִּי-חָצַבְתָּ לְּךָ (kî-ḥāṣabtā lělkā), "that you have hewn out for yourself"; 1QIsaᵃ כי חצבתה לכה.

i MT חֹקְקִי (ḥōqěqî), "inscribing," 1QIsaᵃ חוקקי.

j MT גֶּבֶר (gāber), "man, fellow," 1QIsaᵃ; 1QIsaᵇ has גבור.

k MT וְעֹטְךָ (wěʿōtěkā), "and is about to wrap you up"; 1QIsaᵃ has the imperfect יעוטך, but this is probably a scribal error, though both 4QIsaᵃ and 1QIsaᵇ, while damaged, seem to have ויעטך.

l MT צָנוֹף יִצְנָפְךָ צְנֵפָה (ṣānôp yiṣnopkā ṣěnēpâ), lit., "he will surely sling you a slinging," so also 4QIsaᵃ); 1QIsaᵃ צנוף וצנפכה צנפה, while 4QIsaᶠ has צנוף יצנוך צנפה. The phrase is a difficult crux, because there are two identical verbal roots, צנף I, meaning "to wrap, wind up"; צנף II, meaning "to sling, throw, hurl." LXX, Vg., and Tg. all seem to take the noun צנפה as from the first root, with the meaning "turban" or "crown."

m MT בֵּית אֲדֹנֶיךָ (bêt ʾădōnêkā), "your master's house"; 1QIsaᵃ בית אדוניך.

n MT יֶהֶרְסֶךָ (yehersekā), "one will tear you away"; 4QIsaᶠ has ויהסירד, but 1QIsaᵃ has הרסך, apparently a qal perfect third person masculine singular, "and from your office one has torn you away." Syr. and Vg. translate both verbs in the first person,

but LXX omits the second as redundant and turns the first into a second person singular passive: καὶ ἀφαιρεθήσῃ ἐκ τῆς οἰκονομίας σου καὶ ἐκ τῆς στάσεώς σου, "and you will be taken from your office and from your station." Tg. stays with MT.

o MT וְקָרָאתִי (wěqārāʾtî), "and I will summon"; 1QIsaᵃ וקרתי.

p MT חִלְקִיָּהוּ (ḥilqîyāhû), "Hilkiah"; 1QIsaᵃ has the shorter spelling חלקיה.

q MT וְהִלְבַּשְׁתִּיו (wěhilbaštîw), "and I will dress him"; 1QIsaᵃ והלבש-יו.

r MT כֻּתָּנְתֶּךָ (kuttontekā), "your tunic"; 1QIsaᵃ כתנותך.

s MT וְאַבְנֵטְךָ (wěʾabnētěkā), "your linen sash"; 1QIsaᵃ ואבניטך. LXX καὶ τὸν στέφανόν σου δώσω αὐτῷ ("and your crown I will give to him") misunderstands this word as "crown."

t MT דָּוִד (dāwîd), "David"; 1QIsaᵃ דויד.

u MT סֹגֵר (sōgēr), "one who closes"; 1QIsaᵃ סוגר.

v MT פֹּתֵחַ (pōtēaḥ), "one who opens"; 1QIsaᵃ פותח. LXX interprets rather than translates this verse: καὶ δώσω τὴν δόξαν Δαυιδ αὐτῷ, καὶ ἄρξει, καὶ οὐκ ἔσται ὁ ἀντιλέγων, "And I will give the glory of David to him, and he will rule, and there will be no one who resists."

w Again LXX gives a loose interpretation: καὶ στήσω αὐτὸν ἄρχοντα ἐν τόπῳ πιστῷ, "And I will make him a ruler in a secure place."

x MT כֹל (kol), "all"; 1QIsaᵃ כול.

y MT כְּבוֹד (kěbôd), "glory, weight of"; 1QIsaᵃ כביד.

z MT הַצֶּאֱצָאִים (haṣṣeʾěṣāʾîm), "offspring"; 1QIsaᵃ הצאצאים.

*a MT כְּלֵי הַקָּטָן (kělê haqqātān), "vessels of the small size," so also 4QIsaᵃ and 4QIsaᵇ; 1QIsaᵃ lacks the article כלי קטן.

*b MT כָּל-כְּלֵי (kol-kělê), "all the vessels of"; 1QIsaᵃ כול כלי.

*c MT נְאֻם (něʾūm), "oracle of," traditionally rendered "says"; 1QIsaᵃ נואם.

*d LXX remains interpretative: κινηθήσεται ὁ ἄνθρωπος ὁ ἐστηριγμένος ἐν τόπῳ πιστῷ καὶ πεσεῖται, καὶ ἀφαιρεθήσεται ἡ δόξα ἡ ἐπ᾽ αὐτόν, "the man who was fixed in a firm place will be moved and will fall, and the glory that was upon him will be taken away."

Commentary

The oracle begins with a command from Yahweh of Hosts to go confront this royal official, Shebna, ʾăšer ʿal-habbāyit, "who is over the palace," though the command does not specify where Shebna was to be found. Verse 16, however, implies that Shebna was out inspecting his new tomb cut in the rock cliff in the Kidron Valley, east of the City of David, in what is now the modern village of Silwan. This tomb was probably discovered in the remains of a necropolis there. The identification of it as Shebna's tomb is based on a late-eighth-century BCE Hebrew inscription cut into a panel over the entrance to the tomb in which the owner of the tomb is

identified as being ʾăšer ʿal-habbāyit, "who is over the palace." The inscription was finally deciphered by N. Avigad in 1953, long after its initial discovery, and his reading of the inscription is now universally accepted. The three-line text reads with the bracketed restoration: 1. zʾt [qbrt šbn]yhw ʾšr ʿl hbyt . ʾyn ph ksp . wzhb 2. [ky] ʾm [ʿṣmtw] wʿṣmt ʾmth ʾth . ʾrwr hʾdm ʾšr 3. yptḥ ʾt zʾt, "This is [the tomb of Shebna]yahu who is over the palace. There is no silver or gold here, [on]ly [his bones] and the bones of his female slave with him. Cursed be the man who opens this (tomb)!" The form שֶׁבְנָא (šebnāʾ) or שֶׁבְנָה (šebnâ), Shebna, is a hypocoristicon, or shortened form of the name שְׁבַנְיָהוּ (šěbanyāhû), Shebnayahu or Shebaniah. Other restorations of the broken name have been suggested, but all the circumstantial evidence points to Shebna as the most likely candidate for the owner of this tomb.[1]

Isaiah's questions to Shebna, "What right do you have here? Or whom do you have here that you have hewn out a grave for yourself here?," imply that Isaiah and Shebna are standing in close proximity to the tomb in question. The questions also suggest that Shebna did not have the ancestral connections to justify putting his family tomb here. The continuation of v. 16 describes Shebna as חֹצְבִי מָרוֹם קִבְרוֹ חֹקְקִי בַסֶּלַע מִשְׁכָּן לוֹ (ḥōṣĕbî mārôm qibrô ḥōqĕqî bas-selaʿ miškān lô), lit., "hewing out on the height his grave, and inscribing in the cliff a tomb for himself"). The third person masculine singular suffixes appear to be syntactically conditioned by the preceding participles, however, since the second person forms reappear in v. 17, making it clear that the direct address continues.[2] That is why I have translated with second person masculine singular suffixes, "hewing out on the height your grave, and inscribing in the cliff a tomb for yourself." The unusual final î on the end of the participles ḥōṣĕbî and ḥōqĕqî, the so-called hireq compaginis, has still not received an adequate explanation. Both verbs could simply refer to the carving out of the burial chamber, since the verbs are synonyms, but חקק is also used for inscribing an inscription (Isa 10:1; 30:8), so it might complement the meaning of the first verb by referring to the inscribing of the inscription on the panel at the entrance to the burial chamber. Some scholars (Marti, 174; Duhm, 138) have suggested that Shebna may have been a foreigner and that his type of burial chamber varied from the Judean norm, but if that is what irritated the prophet about Shebna and his actions, it is not very clearly expressed. Isaiah obviously did not think Shebna had any justification for excavating his tomb in this locality, but the reason is not stated. If the placement of the two oracles in the chapter is not accidental and both date to the same general time period, however, Isaiah's irritation with Shebna probably has deeper roots, perhaps including long-standing foreign policy differences between Shebna and the prophet. It

is interesting that Shebna's tomb construction follows shortly after the mention of the popular saying among Jerusalem's elite, "Eat and drink, for tomorrow we die" (v. 13). If Shebna was seeing to his burial spot soon after word had come of Babylon's defeat and before Sennacherib's Assyrian army had reached Judah, as I have suggested, Isaiah may have regarded Shebna as a classic narcissistic example of what was wrong with Jerusalem's ruling elite. At any rate, Yahweh's judgment on Shebna is just as harsh as the broader collective judgment on Jerusalem's elite in 22:14. He will never get to use the elaborate tomb that he went to such expense to provide for himself and his slave-wife.

Instead, Yahweh announces that he is about to hurl this fellow far away. The unusual pilpel participle of טול (twl) and its cognate accusative have the meaning "to hurl a hurling," that is, "to hurl violently," but the meaning of the following verb עטה (ʿth) is disputed. There is a cognate Arabic root that means "to seize, grasp," and Driver argued that the verb meant to "delouse" a garment (cf. Jer 43:12), that is, to pick it clean of lice.[3] If that is the sense of the verb, it implies that Yahweh regarded Shebna as being as worthless and annoying as a small, discomfort-producing insect. The imagery of hurling and throwing, however, which precedes and follows this verb, suggests that the verb conveys the sense of wrapping or wadding up a garment tightly so that one is able to throw it away. In this case, it would imply that Yahweh was discarding Shebna as a piece of used and useless old clothing. The ambiguity is compounded by the triple use of the root צנף (ṣnp) for the infinitive absolute, suffixed imperfect, and the cognate noun at the beginning of v. 18. There are two such roots, as noted above. One means "to wrap around" or "wind around," and its homonym means "to sling or throw." I think the prophet is making an intentional double entendre, playing off the meaning of both roots. Yahweh is about to wad or twist Shebna up like an old garment in a tight ball in order to sling him away like a ball, just as one would do to such

1   See Dobbs-Allsopp et al., *Hebrew Inscriptions*, 507–12.
2   See Delbert R. Hillers, "*Hôy* and *Hôy*-Oracles: A Neglected Syntactic Aspect," in Carol L. Meyers and M. O'Connor, eds., *The Word of the Lord Shall Go Forth: Essays in Honor of David Noel Freedman* (Winona Lake, IN: Eisenbrauns, 1981) 185–88; J. J. M. Roberts, "Form, Syntax," 293–306.
3   Driver, "Isaiah 1–39: Problems," 48–49.

rejected clothing. He will be thrown into a broad land, which is a rather clear allusion to exile somewhere in the broad expanse of the Assyrian empire, and there he would die, obviously far away from his fancy tomb just outside Jerusalem. The reference to the chariots of his glory is presumably to fancy chariots that marked their rider as very important, perhaps suggesting that Sheba promoted himself publicly with an elaborate entourage, much as Absalom and Adonijah had done (2 Sam 15:1; 1 Kgs 1:5; cf. also Joseph in Egypt, Gen 41:43). In any case, these fancy chariots would wind up in Assyrian exile just like Shebna, and, far from addressing Shebna with deference as important, Isaiah addresses him as "O shame of your master's [Hezekiah's] house."

The direct address of the oracle continues in v. 19 with Yahweh's threat to Shebna "to thrust you from your station and tear you away from your position." Moreover, Yahweh would promote a rival, Eliakim the son of Hilkiah, to Shebna's former office on that day (v. 20). As a sign of this transfer of office to Eliakim, Yahweh would dress Eliakim in Shebna's official tunic and gird Eliakim with Shebna's linen sash. Yahweh would give Shebna's former rule into the hand of Eliakim, and Eliakim would become the father figure to Jerusalem and Judah, second only to the king himself (v. 21).

This transfer of Shebna's former authority to Eliakim is further indicated by Yahweh's putting the key (מַפְתֵּחַ maptēaḥ) to the house of David on Eliakim's shoulder (v. 22). The reference is to a large key that locked and unlocked the lockable doors in the palace complex. Both the locks and the keys of the time were large, and the ʾăšer ʿal-habbāyit, "the one over the palace," wore the palace key, attached in some fashion, on his shoulder, probably both as a sign of authority and as a convenient way to keep track of the tool. As the keeper of the key, this official had the authority both to unlock and to lock doors, and there was no authority apart from the king to countermand him. Apparently they had not yet encountered the more modern problem of too many sets of duplicate keys.

Yahweh promises to set Eliakim firmly into this office like a peg driven into a secure place, so that Eliakim will become a throne of glory for his ancestral house (v. 23), but in the original context of Isaiah's confrontation with Shebna all these promises to Eliakim seem

to function more to heighten Shebna's judgment than to reassure Eliakim. Whether Eliakim was even present on the occasion seems doubtful. The real focus of the oracle was Shebna, whom Isaiah addressed with the second person of direct address. The prophet refers to Eliakim only in the third person. Nonetheless, Isaiah's more positive appraisal of Eliakim may suggest that Eliakim was more aligned with or at least more open to Isaiah's diplomatic and political views that Shebna had been. Whether Isaiah's prophecy of Shebna's exile and death in Assyria came to pass, we do not know. It is clear from 2 Kgs 18:18 (cf. Isa 36:3), however, that Shebna was demoted and that Eliakim replaced him in the office of ʾăšer ʿal-habbāyit, "the one over the palace."

Perhaps both v. 24 and v. 25, but certainly v. 25, appear to be an addendum to the Shebna oracle. It is unlikely that in an oracle of judgment against Shebna, Isaiah would promise his office to Eliakim and then, in the same oracle, announce the collapse of Eliakim's office. Expanding on the metaphor of Eliakim being a peg driven into a secure place, v. 24 suggests that they will hang on him all the glory of his ancestral house. That could be taken in a positive sense, but when the verse continues with the notice that all the descendants of his ancestral house, like so many bowls, jars, and other utensils, will hang on this one peg, the image becomes far more ambiguous. It sounds as though all Eliakim's kinfolk will obtain palace jobs through Eliakim's nepotism. They all hang on that one peg. But, as v. 25 makes clear, that one peg, though it was firmly driven into a secure place, cannot hold this excess weight. Eventually, overloaded as it is, the peg gives way and collapses with all this excess weight. It would appear that, sometime later than the original Shebna oracle, Isaiah updated his comments on Eliakim with a divine word explaining the subsequent fall of Eliakim from royal favor.

Bibliography

Albright, W. F., "The Seal of Eljakim and the Latest Preëxilic History of Judah, with Some Observations on Ezekiel," *JBL* 51 (1932) 77–106.

Alt, A., "Hohe Beamte in Ugarit," in Alt, *Kleine Schriften*, 3:186–97.

Auret, Adrian, "A Different Background for Isaiah 22:15-25 Presents an Alternative Paradigm: Disposing of Political and Religious Opposition?" *OTE* 6 (1993) 46–56.

Avigad, N., "The Epitaph of a Royal Steward from Siloam Village," *IEJ* 3 (1953) 137–52.

———, "Excavations in the Jewish Quarter of the Old City of Jerusalem, 1970," *IEJ* 20 (1970) 129–40.

———, *Hebrew Bullae from the Time of Jeremiah* (Jerusalem: Israel Exploration Society, 1986).

Brunet, *Essai sur l'Isaïe*.

Diringer, D., *Le Iscrizioni Antico-Ebraico Palestinesi* (Florence: F. Le Monnier, 1934).

Driver, "Isaiah 1–39: Problems," 36–57.

Emerton, J. A., "Binding and Loosing—Forgiving and Retaining [Mt. 14:19 and Isa. 22:22]," *JTS* n.s. 13 (1962) 325–31.

Fullerton, K., "A New Chapter out of the Life of Isaiah," *AJT* 9 (1905) 621–42.

———, "Shebna and Eliakim: A Reply," *AJT* 11 (1907) 503–9.

Gall, A. von, "Jeremia 43,12 und das Zeitwort עטה," *ZAW* 24 (1904) 105–21.

Ginsberg, H. L., "Some Emendations in Isaiah 22, 17-21, 17-18a," *JBL* 69 (1950) 55–56.

———, "Gleanings in First Isaiah: VI. The Shebna-Eliakim Pericope, 22:15-25," in M. Davis, ed., *Mordecai M. Kaplan: Jubilee Volume on the Occasion of His Seventieth Birthday* (2 vols.; New York: Jewish Theological Seminary, 1953) 1:245–59, esp. 252–57.

Jenni, Ernst, *Die politischen Voraussagen der Propheten* (ATANT 29; Zurich: Zwingli, 1956) 42.

Kamphausen, A., "Isaiah's Prophecy Concerning the Major-Domo of King Hezekiah," *AJT* 5 (1901) 43–74.

Katzenstein, H. J., "The Royal Steward (*Asher 'Al Ha-Bayith*)," *IEJ* 10 (1960) 149–54.

König, E., "Shebna and Eliakim," *AJT* 10 (1906) 675–86.

Lipiński, E., "Skn et Sgn dans le Sémitique Occidental du Nord," *UF* 5 (1973) 191–207.

Martin-Achard, R., "L'oracle contre Shebnâ et le Pouvoir des Clefs, Es. 22,15-22," *TZ* 24 (1968) 241–54.

Mettinger, Tryggve N. D., *Solomonic State Officials:* A Study of the Civil Government Officials of the Israelite Monarchy (ConBOT 5; Lund: Gleerup, 1971) 70–110.

Moscati, S., *L'epigrafia ebraica antica* (BibOr 15; Rome: Pontificio Istituto Biblico, 1951).

Mulder, M. J., "Versuch zur Deutung von *Sokenet* in 1. Kön. I 2, 4," *VT* 22 (1972) 43–54.

Rabin, C., "Etymological Miscellanea," in C. Rabin, ed., *Studies in the Bible* (ScrHier 8; Jerusalem: Magnes Press, Hebrew University, 1961) 395–96.

Ussishkin, D., "The Necropolis from the Time of the Kingdom of Judah at Silwan, Jerusalem," *BA* 33, no. 2 (1970) 34–46.

Vaux, Roland de, "Titres et fonctionnaires Égyptiens à la cour de David et Salomon," *RB* 48 (1939) 394–405.

Vogt, E., "Sepulcrum Praefecti Palatii Regum Iuda," *Bib* 35 (1954) 132–34.

Wahl, O., "Woher unsere Festigkeit kommt: Zur Botschaft von Jesaja 22,20-5 für uns heute," *Forum katholische Theologie* 3 (1987) 187–202.

Weis R. D., "A Definition of the Genre *Massa'* in the Hebrew Bible" (PhD diss., Claremont Graduate School, 1986).

Wessels, W. J., "Isaiah of Jerusalem and the Royal Court: Isaiah 22:15-25, a Paradigm for Restoring Just Officials," *OTE* 2.2 (1989) 1–13.

Willis, John T., "'ab as an Official Term," *SJOT* 10 (1996) 115–36.

———, "Historical Issues in Isaiah 22,15-25," *Bib* 74 (1993) 60–70.

———, "Textual and Linguistic Issues in Isaiah 22,15-25," *ZAW* 105 (1993) 377–99.

23

The oracle against Tyre is an extremely difficult oracle, as even a casual comparison of modern translations of the text will confirm. The audience to whom the prophet originally spoke the oracle presumably found the oracle easier to understand, because they knew the contemporary reports about what was going on in Tyre and were probably familiar with poetic references to Tyre. Modern interpreters are largely lacking such information, and we have the added disadvantage of having to date the oracle to a particular time period. Dates assigned by different commentators range from the late eighth century to the time of Nebuchadnezzar's siege of Tyre in the early sixth century, and some date it even later.[1] If it is the work of Isaiah of Jerusalem, the most likely date for the oracle would be during Sennacherib's third campaign of 701 BCE, and it is against that historical background that this commentator will try to explain the text.

From the inscriptions of Tiglath-pileser III, we know that the following kings of Tyre paid tribute to this Assyrian king: Tuba'il (Ethbaal II) 740 BCE (?), Hiram (Hiram II) 738–734 BCE, and Metenna (Mattan II) 728 BCE.[2] During this period, the king of the island city of Tyre also ruled over the Phoenician coast opposite Tyre, including the city of Sidon, for which a separate king is never mentioned. Even though Hiram joined with Rezin of Damascus, Pekah of Israel, and the Philistines in the anti-Assyrian alliance leading up to the Syro-Ephraimitic War, he apparently was able to submit and make amends to Tiglath-pileser, who doubtless judged that harsh treatment of the Phoenicians was not in Assyria's interest, without suffering the severe territorial losses inflicted on the other participants in the alliance. Apparently Hiram, Metenna (Mattan II), and even Luli (Eloulaios) in the beginning of his reign 729/728 BCE, remained kings of the Sidonians, ruling over Tyre and the Phoenician coast opposite it. Shalmaneser V of Assyria (727–722 BCE) changed that with his campaigns against Tyre, during which Sidon and the Phoenician coast joined Assyria in hostility to Tyre. When Sargon II came to the Assyrian throne, however, Luli apparently made peace with him, helped him in his sea campaign against Greek pirates, and by the end of Sargon's reign had regained his former control of Sidon and the Phoenician coast. Nonetheless, the death of Sargon in 705 BCE led Luli to join the large anti-Assyrian coalition of western states supported by Babylon and its allies in the east and by Nubian Egypt in the south. With the collapse of Babylon and the eastern allies as a result of Sennacherib's first two campaigns (703–702 BCE), the way was now open for the Assyrians to march against the western states, and Phoenicia was the first target in Sennacherib's third campaign against the west (701 BCE). According to Sennacherib, Luli, king of Sidon, fled to Cyprus in the midst of the sea and disappeared, and Sennacherib placed a certain Tuba'lu on his royal throne. Curiously, however, while Sennacherib mentions the submission of a host of the Phoenician cities on the mainland, he never mentions Tyre. It is likely that the submissive Tuba'lu was made vassal king in Sidon on the mainland, but that Tyre remained independent, though probably blockaded from access to the coast, with the seat of the Tyrian government transferred to Cyprus during this crisis.[3]

---

1 Among those who attribute the text to Isaiah from the eighth century are Hayes and Irvine, 289–90; W. Rudolph, "Jesaja 23,1-14," in *Festschrift Friedrich Baumgärtel zum 70. Geburtstag, 14. Januar 1958, gewidmet von den Mitarbeitern am Kommentar zum Alten Testament (KAT)* (Erlanger Forschungen A.10; Erlangen: Universitätsbund Erlangen, 1959) 166–74; Erlandsson, *Burden of Babylon*, 97–101. Wildberger (2:865) attributes vv. 1-14 to the time of Esarhaddon, and he is followed in this by Watts (p. 362). Marti (p. 181) and Duhm (p. 141) date the oracle to 348 BCE, to the time of Artaxerxes III Ochus. Because of the difficulty in dating the text, Gray (p. 386), Blenkinsopp (pp. 344–45), and Clements (pp. 191–92) discuss several proposed dates without definitely committing to any of them.

2 See Tadmor, *Inscriptions of Tiglath-Pileser III*, 267; cf. Katzenstein, *History of Tyre*, 349.

3 See the long discussion in Katzenstein, *History of Tyre*, 246–58.

1/ The Oracle concerning Tyre:
Wail[a] O ships of Tarshish,[b]
For it is plundered,[c] no longer a home.[d]
When they came[e] from the land of Kittim,[f]
It was revealed to them.[g]

2/ Moan,[h] O inhabitants[i] of the island,
O traders of Sidon,[j] you whom seafarers[k] thronged.[l]

3/ And over many waters the grain of Shihor,[m]
The harvest of the Nile,[n] was its revenue,
And it was from the trade of the nations.[o]

4/ Be ashamed, O Sidon,[p]
For the sea has spoken,[q]
The stronghold of the sea, saying,[r]
"I have not[s] been in labor,
And I have not[s] given birth.
I have not[s] raised young men,
Nor reared young women."

5/ When the report reaches Egypt,[t]
They will be in travail over the report about Tyre.

6/ Cross over[u] to Tarshish,[v]
Wail, O inhabitants[w] of the island!

7/ Is this[x] your[y] exultant city,[z]
Whose origin[*a] is from days of old?
Did her feet carry her[*b] to settle far away?[*c]

8/ Who planned this[*d] against Tyre, who wore the crown,[*e]
Whose traders[*f] were princes,
Her merchants the honored of the earth?[*g]

9/ Yahweh of Hosts planned it—
To defile the pride of all glory,[*h]
To dishonor all[*i] the honored of the earth.

10/ Cross over[*j] your land like the Nile,
O daughter Tarshish,[*k]
There is no longer a wharf.[*l]

11/ He stretched out his hand[*m] over the sea,
He shook up[*n] kingdoms.
Yahweh commanded concerning Canaan
To destroy[*o] its strongholds.[*p]

12/ And he said:[*q]
"You will exult no[*r] longer,
O oppressed[*s] virgin daughter Sidon;
To Kittim rise up, cross over[*t]—
Even there[*u] there will be no rest for you."

13/ Behold[*v] the land of the Chaldeans![*w]
This is the people which are not.[*x]
Assyria destined her for desert creatures.[*y]
They raised[*z] his siege towers,[†a]
They demolished[†b] her palaces,[†c]
He turned her into a ruin.[†d]

14/ Wail O ships of Tarshish,
For your stronghold[†e] is plundered![†f]

15/ And it will come to pass on that[†g] day
that Tyre[†h] will be forgotten for seventy years
like the days of one king.
At the end of seventy years it will be[†i] to Tyre[†j] as in the song about the prostitute:

16/ "Take a lyre, go about the city,
O forgotten prostitute,
Play well, make much music
that you may be remembered."

17/ And at the end of seventy[†k] years Yahweh will visit[†l] Tyre,[†m]
and she will return to her prostitute's pay,

and she will prostitute herself with all[n] the kingdoms of the earth
    upon the face of the earth.
18/ But her profit and her hire will be a holy thing[o] to Yahweh;
    It will not[p] be treasured up or stored,
    but[q] her profit will be for those who dwell[r] before Yahweh,
    That they may eat their fill[s] and may dress themselves elegantly.[t]

Textual Notes

a   MT, 4QIsaᵃ הֵילִ֫ילוּ (hêlîlû), "wail!"; 1QIsaᵃ has the later, Aramaic-influenced *aphel* imperative איליל (ʾêlîlû), "wail!"

b   MT אֳנִיּ֣וֹת תַּרְשִׁישׁ (ʾoniyôt taršîš), "ships of Tarshish," 1QIsaᵃ, 4QIsaᵃ; cf. Syr. which preserves Tarshish; LXX has πλοῖα Καρχηδόνος, "ships of Carthage," while both Vg. and Tg. have "ships of the sea."

c   MT, 1QIsaᵇ, 4QIsaᵃ שֻׁדַּד (šuddad), "was plundered"; 1QIsaᵃ שודד. The grammar is a bit awkward, since the understood subject of the masculine singular verb "was plundered" is presumably the feminine Tyre.

d   MT מִבַּיִת (mibbayit), lit., "from a house," is supported by 1QIsaᵃ, 1QIsaᵇ, 4QIsaᵃ, Vg., Syr., and probably Tg. מָחוֹזֵיהוֹן (māḥôzêhôn), "their harbors"; LXX, however, seems to omit the word, probably because of the similarity to the following מִבּוֹא (mibbôʾ), "from going." The meaning of the expression, however, is ambiguous. Does it mean that the place was devastated so badly that no house was left, as JPS ("not a house is left") seems to take it? Or does it mean that the place was so devastated that it could no longer be a home, house, or port for the ships of Tarshish? I am inclined to the latter understanding.

e   The meaning of מִבּוֹא (mibbôʾ), "from going," is also ambiguous. LXX καὶ οὐκέτι ἔρχονται ἐκ γῆς Κιτιαίων ("and they no longer come from the land of the Kitians") and perhaps Syr. and Tg. ("so that there is no entry") seem to take the preposition as a privative negation. Others take the preposition as having a temporal meaning, "in connection with the return home" (HALAT, 566), while still others emend to mābôʾ, "entrance, port" (Clements, 193; Wildberger 2:855).

f   MT כִּתִּים (kittîm), "Kittim"; 1QIsaᵃ כתיים; LXX Κιτιαίων (kitiaiōn), "of the Kitians," originally referred to the Phoenician settlement at Kition on Cyprus, but then came to refer to Cyprus as a whole.

g   MT נִגְלָה־לָמוֹ (niglâ-lāmô), "it was revealed to them"; cf. 1QIsaᵃ נגלה למו. LXX appears to read only the first word with this verse: ἥκται αἰχμάλωτος ("she has been led captive").

h   Reading MT דֹּמּוּ and 1QIsaᵃ דמו (dommû) as the *qal* masculine plural imperative of דמם II, "to wail, moan," because of the parallel with the masculine plural imperative in v. 1; Vg. and Syr. read the verb as from דמם I, "to keep silent," while Tg. seems to derive it from דמם III, "to perish, be destroyed." LXX's τίνι ὅμοιοι γεγόνασιν οἱ ἐνοικοῦντες ἐν τῇ νήσῳ ("to whom have those who dwell in the island become similar") seems to presuppose a reading למי דמו יושבי אי, perhaps growing out of a corrupt text like 4QIsaᵃ's למודמו יושבי אי (see Ulrich's comment in *Qumran Cave 4.X*, 17).

i   MT יֹשְׁבֵי אִי (yōšĕbê ʾî), "O inhabitants of the island"; 1QIsaᵃ ישבי אי; cf. 4QIsaᵃ.

j   I take the singular סֹחֵר צִידוֹן (sōḥēr ṣîdôn), "merchant of Sidon" (so MT, 1QIsaᵃ, and probably 4QIsaᵃ) as a collective "merchants of Sidon" and a vocative parallel to "inhabitants of the island."

k   MT עֹבֵר יָם (ʿōbēr yām), "the one crossing the sea, seafarer"; 1QIsaᵃ and 4QIsaᵃ appear to have עברו ים (ʿābĕrû yām), "they crossed the sea." The Qumran texts may suggest reading the plural ʿōbĕrê yām, "those crossing the sea." I take these seafarers as distinct from the merchants of Sidon.

l   MT מִלְאוּךְ (milĕʾûk), "they filled you [fem. sg.]"; cf. 4QIsaᵃ מלאך, which is supported by Vg., Tg., and Syr. 1QIsaᵃ has מלאכיך (malʾākayik), "your messengers [crossed the sea]"). The mixture of masculine plural and feminine singular vocatives makes the poetry syntactically awkward. I take the "inhabitants of the island" and the "merchants of Sidon" to be the citizens of Tyre, and Tyre is the feminine singular "you" whom those who cross the sea have filled.

m   MT שִׁחֹר (šîḥōr), "Shihor"—a designation for one of the branches of the Nile or a lake fed by it in the Delta from Egyptian š(y)-ḥr, "pond of Horus"; so also 1QIsaᵃ and 4QIsaᵃ and Vg. LXX, Tg., and Syr. appear to read סחר (sōḥēr), "merchant," or saḥar, "trade, business," here as at the end of the verse.

n   MT יְאוֹר (yĕʾôr, from Egyptian yrw, "the Nile," then any "river"); so also 1QIsaᵃ; 4QIsaᵃ has the variant spelling יואר.

o   MT גּוֹיִם (gôyīm), "nations"; 1QIsaᵃ גואים.

p   MT, 1QIsaᵇ, 4QIsaᵃ צִידוֹן (ṣîdôn), "Sidon"; 1QIsaᵃ צידן.

q   MT, 1QIsaᵇ, and 4QIsaᵃ have the expected third person masculine singular אָמַר (ʾāmar), "the [the article is missing as often in poetry] sea has spoken," since "sea" is masculine in Hebrew; 1QIsaᵃ has the third person feminine singular אמרה, which may derive from a mistaken division of an original אמר הים, "the [with the article expressed] sea has spoken."

r   MT and 4QIsaᵃ לֵאמֹר (lēʾmōr), "saying"; 1QIsaᵃ לאמור.

s   MT and 4QIsaᵃ write the negative לֹא (lōʾ), "not," without the *mater*; 1QIsaᵃ לוא uses it.

t   MT לְמִצְרַיִם (lĕmiṣrayim), "to Egypt"; 1QIsaᵃ מצרים.

u   MT and apparently 4QIsaᵃ עִבְרוּ (ʿibrû, "cross over" [masc. pl. imperative]); 1QIsaᵃ עוברי (ʿōbĕrê, "those who cross over" [qal masc. pl. participle]).

v MT תַּרְשִׁישָׁה (taršîšāh), "to Tarshish"; 1QIsaᵃ originally wrote תלשישה, then tried to erase ל and insert ר in its place above the line.

w MT יֹשְׁבֵי (yōšĕbê), "inhabitants of"; 1QIsaᵃ יושבי.

x MT הֲזֹאת (hăzōʾt), "is this?"; 1QIsaᵃ הזואת.

y MT לָכֶם (lākem), "to you, your"; 1QIsaᵃ לכמה.

z MT עַלִּיזָה (ʿallîzâ), "[the] exultant [city]"; 1QIsaᵃ העלוזה adds the article and misreads the form as a passive participle.

*a MT קַדְמָתָהּ (qadmātāh), "her origin"; 1QIsaᵃ קדמותה.

*b MT יֹבִלוּהָ (yōbīlûhā), "they carried her"; 1QIsa וביה is simply garbled.

*c MT מֵרָחוֹק (mērāḥôq), "far away, from afar"; 1QIsaᵃ מרחק.

*d MT זֹאת (zōʾt), "this"; 1QIsaᵃ זואת.

*e MT הַמַּעֲטִירָה (hammaʿăṭîrâ), "who wore the crown"; 1QIsaᵃ המעטרה. It is not clear what LXX was reading to justify its translation, μὴ ἥσσων ἐστὶν ἢ οὐκ ἰσχύει; ("Is she inferior or does she have no strength?").

*f MT סֹחֲרֶיהָ (sōḥărêh[ā]), "her traders"; cf. 4QIsaᵃ; 1QIsaᵃ סוחריה; cf. 4QIsaᶜ [סוחר]יה.

*g MT אֶרֶץ (ʾāreṣ), "of the earth"; 1QIsaᵃ had הארץ, but the initial article has been erased, leaving it in agreement with MT.

*h MT גְּאוֹן כָּל-צְבִי (gĕʾôn kol-ṣĕbî), "the pride of all glory"; 1QIsaᵃ כול גאון צבי, "all pride of glory."

*i MT כָּל- (kol-), "all of"; 1QIsaᵃ כול, but 4QIsaᵃ has כל.

*j MT עִבְרִי (ʿibrî), "cross over" (fem. sg. imperative); cf. 4QIsaᶜ עבורי; LXX's ἐργάζου ("work [your land]") follows 1QIsaᵃ עבדי, "work."

*k MT כְּיאֹר בַּת-תַּרְשִׁישׁ (kayʾōr bat-taršîš), "like the Nile, O daughter Tarshish," is supported by 1QIsaᵃ's כיאור בת תרשיש as well as by Vg., Tg., and Syr.; LXX's καὶ γὰρ πλοῖα οὐκέτι ἔρχεται ἐκ Καρχηδόνος, "for indeed the ships no longer come from Carthage," appears to be reading something like כי אניות מתרשיש for the beginning of the clause.

*l MT's מֵזַח (mēzaḥ) is supported by 1QIsaᵃ and Vg.'s cingulum, "girdle," but the meaning of the term is disputed. Mēzaḥ II, "girdle," doesn't fit the context, so some see a mēzaḥ I, another Egyptian loanword meaning "wharf, shipyard" from Egyptian mdḥ, "to construct the framework of a wooden ship," which would give the translation, "there is no longer a wharf" (so Wildberger 2:857). Others simply assume the accidental transposition of the second and third consonant and thus emend to מחז (māḥôz), "harbor," a word clearly attested in Ps 107:30 (so Clements, 194).

*m LXX has an odd reading with a second person suffix that sees the hand as Tyre's: ἡ δὲ χείρ σου οὐκέτι ἰσχύει κατὰ θάλασσαν, ἡ παροξύνουσα βασιλεῖς, "Your hand, which provoked kings, is no longer strong by sea," but there is no support for this reading in the other textual traditions.

*n MT, 1QIsaᵃ, 4QIsaᵃ, הִרְגִּיז (hirgîz), "he shook up"; 4QIsaᶜ להרגיז, "to shake up."

*o MT לַשְׁמִד (lašmīd), "to destroy"; 1QIsaᵃ להשמיד (fuller orthographic variant).

*p MT and probably 4QIsaᶜ have מָעֻזְנֶיהָ (māʿuznêhā), "her strongholds"; 1QIsaᵃ has the more common מעוזיה, "her strongholds." The MT reading is either corrupt, perhaps by confusion with

מעוניה, "her dwellings," or it represents a synonym of מעוז with an additional afformative -n, מעוזן (māʿôzen), "stronghold."

*q MT וַיֹּאמֶר (wayyōʾmer), "and he said"; 1QIsaᵃ and 4QIsaᶜ ויואמר. There is no support for LXX's plural, "and they will say."

*r MT לֹא (lōʾ), "no"; 1QIsaᵃ and 4QIsaᶜ לוא.

*s MT, 4QIsaᶜ הַמְעֻשָּׁקָה (hamʿuššāqâ), "O oppressed"; 1QIsaᵃ מעשקה omits the article; LXX and Tg. mistakenly read the form as active and thus make the subject someone other than Sidon who is inflicting wrong on Sidon.

*t MT, 1QIsaᵃ עִבְרִי (ʿābōrî), "cross over"; 4QIsaᶜ עבורי.

*u MT, 1QIsaᵃ שָׁם (šām), "there"; 4QIsaᶜ שמה, "to there."

*v MT הֵן (hēn), "behold"; 1QIsaᵃ הנה.

*w MT כַּשְׂדִּים (kaśdîm), "Chaldeans"; 1QIsaᵃ כשדיים.

*x MT לֹא (lōʾ), "not"; 1QIsaᵃ and 4QIsaᶜ לוא.

*y MT and 4QIsaᶜ לְצִיִּים (lĕṣiyîm), "for desert creatures"; 1QIsaᵃ has nunation לציין.

*z MT הֵקִימוּ (hēqîmû), "they raised"; 1QIsaᵃ הקימה, "they raised for/against her."

†a MT kĕtîb is בְּחִינָיו (bĕḥînāyw), "his siege towers"; qĕrēʾ בַחוּנָיו (baḥûnāyw), "his siege towers"; 1QIsaᵃ has בחינה.

†b MT עֹרְרוּ (ʿōrĕrû), "they demolished"; 1QIsaᵃ עוררו.

†c MT and 1QIsaᵃ אַרְמְנוֹתֶיהָ (ʾarmĕnôtêhā), "her palaces"; 4QIsaᶜ אר'מנותיו.

†d MT and 4QIsaᶜ לְמַפֵּלָה (lĕmappēlâ), "to a ruin"; 1QIsaᵃ למפלה.

†e MT and 4QIsaᶜ have מָעֻזְכֶן (māʿuzzĕken), "your [fem. pl.] stronghold"; 1QIsaᵃ מעוזך, "your [fem. sg.] stronghold."

†f MT and 4QIsaᶜ שֻׁדַּד (šuddad), "is plundered"; 1QIsaᵃ שודד.

†g MT and 1QIsaᵃ בַּיּוֹם הַהוּא (bayyôm hahûʾ), "on that day"; 1QIsaᵃ has ביום הוא, and 4QIsaᶜ has ביום ההוא.

†h MT צֹר (ṣōr), "Tyre"; 4QIsaᶜ צור. There is a long haplography in 1QIsaᵃ, which omits everything after "And it will come to pass on that day" down to לצר, "to Tyre as in the song about the prostitute."

†i MT יְהְיֶה (yihyeh), "it will be"; 4QIsaᶜ והיה, "and it will be."

†j MT and 1QIsaᵃ לְצֹר (lĕṣōr), "to Tyre"; 4QIsaᶜ לצור.

†k For MT שִׁבְעִים (šibʿîm), "seventy," 1QIsaᵃ again has nunation שבעין.

†l MT יִפְקֹד (yipqōd), "will visit"; 1QIsaᵃ and 4QIsaᵈ יפקוד.

†m MT and 1QIsaᵃ צֹר (ṣōr), "Tyre"; 4QIsaᶜ צור.

†n MT, supported by all the versions, has כָּל (kol), "all"; 1QIsaᵃ omits the word.

†o MT קֹדֶשׁ (qōdeš), "holiness, dedication," though the noun here is used as an adjective, "a thing dedicated or holy to Yahweh"; 1QIsaᵃ and 4QIsaᶜ קודש.

†p MT writes the negative without a mater לֹא (lōʾ), "not"; 1QIsaᵃ and 4QIsaᶜ have the mater לוא.

†q For MT and 1QIsaᵃ כִּי (kî), "but," 4QIsaᶜ has כיא.

†r MT לַיֹּשְׁבִים (layyōšĕbîm), "for those who dwell"; 1QIsaᵃ and 4QIsaᶜ ליושבים.

†s MT לֶאֱכֹל לְשָׂבְעָה (leʾĕkōl lĕsobʿâ), "to eat to satiety"; 1QIsaᵃ לאכול לשבעה.

†t MT and 1QIsaᵃ עָתִיק (ʿātîq), "elegantly"; 4QIsaᶜ עתק.

Commentary

The heading מַשָּׂא צֹר (*maśśāʾ ṣōr*), "the oracle concerning Tyre," is syntactically the same as "the oracle concerning Babylon" (13:1), "the oracle concerning Moab" (15:1), "the oracle concerning Damascus" (17:1), "the oracle concerning Egypt" (19:1), and "the oracle concerning Dumah" (21:11), and is similar to 21:1, 13; and 30:6, though these passages do not explicitly mention a state or city as the subject of the oracle. At the time of Sennacherib's third campaign against Palestine in 701 BCE, Tyre was the island capital of the Phoenician kingdom that also controlled the coastal mainland opposite it, including the cities of Great Sidon, Little Sidon, Bit-Zitti, Zaributu, Mahalliba, Ushu, Akzib, and Akko. Sennacherib refers to Luli as king of Sidon, and claims the capture of all these mainland cities, but he says nothing of Tyre itself, which suggests that he was unable to capture it. The loss of Tyre's mainland cities and their supplies of food, water, and other resources, however, was enough to place the island fortress in a difficult situation. Apparently the Tyrian king Luli felt it was the better part of valor to transfer his capital to Cyprus during this difficult time. In response, probably to reports of these events, the prophet calls upon the ships of Tarshish, the big commercial vessels that sailed the Mediterranean and frequented the double harbor at Tyre, to wail in mourning. With the Assyrian conquest of the sea coast, and the Phoenicians of the coast now allied with Assyria under Ethbaal (Tuba'lu), Tyre was no longer a secure home port for these vessels. When they arrived from Kition on Cyprus, they would clearly observe the now perilous predicament of the port of Tyre.

The precise identification of the inhabitants of the island whom the prophet calls upon to moan is a bit ambiguous (v. 2). The term אִי (*ʾî*), "island, coastland," can be used of an island or of the coastlands in general (Isa 11:11; 24:15; 40:15; 42:15; Jer 2:10; 25:22; Ezek 27:6), but I understand it here as referring to the inhabitants of Tyre. The phrase "trader of Sidon" is probably to be read as a collective, "O traders of Sidon," as a poetic parallel to "O inhabitants of the island," though one might read the singular as modifying "island" as a poetic designation for Tyre—"Moan, O inhabitants of the island, O trader of Sidon, whom seafarers thronged." In any case, the second feminine singular suffix on the verb "filled/thronged" shows that the opening plural address has shifted at some point from the plural "inhabitants" to the singular of the inhabited city itself. To refer to the inhabitants of Tyre as the traders of Sidon, or to Tyre itself as the trader of Sidon, probably arises out of the notion of the king of Tyre as the king of the Sidonians, Sidon functioning almost as later Phoenicia to designate the whole area.

Tyre's revenue that came in over many waters included the grain of Shihor from the Nile Delta, and the harvest of the Nile, and this revenue was derived from Tyre's trade with the nations (v. 3). But now Sidon is called upon to be ashamed, because of the utterance of the sea, or rather the stronghold of the sea (v. 4). The sea, or stronghold of the sea, is presumably referring to Tyre, whose situation as a well-fortified island in the sea off the Phoenician coast made it very difficult to capture or subdue. Nonetheless, the utterance of this stronghold suggests a new situation of desperate hopelessness. To be without birthpangs, not to give birth, to raise neither young men nor young women, suggests that the city, personified as a woman, has lost its future, is no longer growing and prosperous but is dwindling in population and facing the inevitable decline associated with such a precipitous drop in population. The specific background to this threat is probably Sennacherib's attack on the mainland, which has cut off the island Tyre from its mainland source of nourishment, without which it could not support a growing population. When the report concerning Tyre reaches Egypt, one of its main trading partners, Egypt will also be in travail and agony (v. 5).

Verse 6 calls for the inhabitants of the island not only to wail but to cross over to Tarshish. The sense seems to be that they are leaving Tyre for a point far to the west in the Mediterranean. Whether the reference is to Carthage, as the LXX understands it, or to a less precise destination in the west remains a debatable point. Given this exodus from Tyre, the prophet addresses a taunt to the former inhabitants of the island: "Is this your exultant city, whose origin is from days of old? Did her feet bring her to settle far away (v. 7)?" That in turn leads to the question, "Who planned this against Tyre (v. 8)?" The radical shift from Tyre as a royally crowned city, whose traders were princes and whose merchants were the honored of the earth, suggests that someone has plotted this astounding change in fate, and the prophet identifies the culprit as Yahweh of Hosts (v. 9). Yahweh has planned this against

Tyre in order to defile Tyre's pride in all her glory and beauty, and to humiliate all the honored of the earth. Both motifs, that of Yahweh's plan (Isa 5:19; 14:24-27; 19:12, 17; 28:29) and that of Yahweh's penchant to abase all that is high or exalted in competition with the deity (2:12-17), are favorite motifs of Isaiah of Jerusalem and point to his authorship.

In v. 10 the prophet calls for daughter Tarshish, the Tyrian settlement in the Mediterranean, to pass through her former homeland as the Nile passes through Egypt, and she will see that there is no longer a wharf or harbor there. Yahweh has stretched out his hand over the sea, he has shaken up kingdoms, he has commanded the destruction of the strongholds of Canaan (v. 11). The reference here is probably to the fall of the major cities of the coastland to Sennacherib. One should note that the motif of Yahweh's outstretched hand is another favorite of Isaiah of Jerusalem (see 5:25; 9:11, 16, 20; 14:26-27; 31:3).

In v. 12 he, presumably Yahweh, addresses the oppressed virgin daughter Sidon and warns her, "you will no longer exult; cross over to Kition, but even there you will find no rest." Again Sidon here appears to stand for the larger kingdom of which Tyre was the capital, rather than as a reference to the city Sidon in contrast to Tyre. The crossing over to Kition probably refers to the flight of Luli and his government from Tyre to the Tyrian colony at Kition on Cyprus. The verse certainly does not read as though the prophet were contrasting the fate of the city of Sidon with that of the city of Tyre.

Verse 13 has been translated in various ways, one of which I will note below. My translation assumes that the verse concerns the collapse of Babylonian resistance against Sennacherib during his first two campaigns in 703–702 BCE, a collapse that opened the way for Sennacherib to move west against Phoenicia in 701. The Phoenicians, like Judah (see the discussion above on Isa 22:1-8), were depending on Babylon in the east as a bulwark against an Assyrian invasion of the west, but Babylon as the land of the Chaldeans, the people of Merodachbaladan, has ceased to exist. Assyria has destined it for the desert creatures. The use of language here is quite striking. The verb יסד (yāsad), "to found," normally means to found or lay a foundation for a building, but the building Assyria "founds" in the land of the Chaldeans is not for people but for wild desert creatures that inhabit aban-

doned ruins. This is spelled out in the continuation of the verse, when the prophet describes Assyria's raising up of his (Assyria's) siege towers, and their (Assyria's troops) destruction of her (the land of the Chaldeans) palaces. He (Assyria) turned her (the land of the Chaldeans) into a ruin. The shift back and forth between masculine singular and masculine plural forms referring to Assyria or the Assyrian king and his troops seems awkward, even a bit confusing, and there may be some textual corruption here, but the contrast between these masculine suffixes and the feminine singular suffixes referring to the land of the Chaldeans seems consistent. The historical reference is to Sennacherib's defeat of Merodach-baladan at Kutha and Kish and his following decimation of the fortresses and settlements farther down river in Chaldea proper. In contrast to this translation and interpretation, which fits a late-eighth-century date, NRSV's translation, "Look at the land of the Chaldeans! This is the people; it was not Assyria. They destined Tyre for wild animals . . . ," must assume a secondary correction of the text, probably dating from the time of Nebuchadnezzar's siege against Tyre. The original text would have dealt with Assyria's defeat of Tyre, but a later redactor would have corrected the text by introducing Tyre, "Look to the land of the Chaldeans! This is the people who destroyed Tyre; it was not Assyria." One should note, however, that v. 13 never actually mentions Tyre; the NRSV imports that understanding by replacing a feminine singular suffix that could easily refer to the feminine singular antecedent "land of the Chaldeans" with the name Tyre. Secondary redactions and glosses do occur, but one should not introduce them unless they are necessary to explain the text, and that does not seem to be the case here.

In v. 14 the prophet shifts his attention back to the people of Tarshish, here commanding the ships of Tarshish to join in the wailing, for their stronghold has been plundered. The implication seems to be that trade with Tyre has been or soon will be cut off. From that day forward Tyre will be forgotten for seventy years (v. 15), the equivalent period of the lifetime of a single king. This statement is apparently rooted in the notion that an average lifetime was seventy years (Ps 90:10), though relatively few kings in antiquity actually lived that long, much less reigned that long, but the seventy-year period was a traditional round number signifying a long time (see Jer 25:11-12; 29:10; Zech 1:12; 7:5; and cf. Marduk's decision to leave Babylon for seventy years).[4] At the end of those seventy years Tyre will have been forgotten so long that she will have to make a real effort to be remembered, like the old, temporarily retired, and now forgotten prostitute in the popular ditty, which the prophet then quotes: "Take a lyre, go about the city, O forgotten prostitute; Play well, make much music that you may be remembered!" (v. 16).

At the end of the seventy years, then, Yahweh will visit Tyre, and she will return to her prostitute's pay—אתנן ('etnan), sometimes translated as "hire" or "trade" is actually "the pay given to a prostitute"—and once again work as a prostitute with all the kingdoms of the earth upon the face of the earth (v. 17). Whether the preceding ditty of the forgotten prostitute suggested this characterization of Tyre's trade as prostitution, or whether the prophet's view of Tyre's international trade as prostitution suggested the ditty of the forgotten prostitute, this characterization of international trade controlled by a major city as prostitution (cf. Nah 3:4) is later picked up and elaborated in Revelation's judgment on Rome, Babylon the great whore, in Revelation 17–18 (see esp. 18:3, 9-19, 23-24). When Tyre returns to her international trade, however, her trade income and her prostitute's pay will now be holy to Yahweh. It will not be treasured up or stored away for her own glory, but her income will be for those who dwell before Yahweh, so that those who faithfully serve him may eat their fill and cover themselves in fine apparel (v. 18).

To some extent, Isaiah's prophecy was fulfilled. Tyre did suffer at least a temporary decline due to Sennacherib's conquest of the Phoenician coastal cities, and Luli seems to have died without ever returning to Tyre, but Tyre's importance as a trading center was not forgotten for seventy years. Within about twenty years of Sennacherib's campaign, by the time Esarhaddon came to the Assyrian throne in 680 BCE, Tyre seems to have made a major recovery under its king Ba'lu.[5] Esarhaddon forced Ba'lu to submit and accept a treaty with Assyria, but even so, Tyre and its king Ba'lu fared much better than mainland Sidon and its king Abdi-milkutti. Esarhaddon had Abdi-milkutti beheaded, and turned his territory into an Assyrian province, while Ba'lu remained a vassal king in his island city of Tyre. During the great expansion of Assyrian power under Esarhaddon and Ashurbanipal, Tyre's freedom for independent action was severely limited, but the ongoing importance of Tyre in this period is indicated by the constant listing of Ba'lu, king of Tyre, at the head of the twenty-two kings of Hatti land.[6] Moreover, Tyre felt secure enough in its island fortress during Ashurbanipal's second campaign against Thebes to revolt, though when Ashurbanipal's third campaign was directed against Tyre and involved a strangling Assyrian blockade of the island, Ba'lu adroitly and successfully sued for peace and was allowed to continue his rule on Tyre.

Bibliography

Ackroyd, P. R., "Two Old Testament Historical Problems of the Early Persian Period," *JNES* 17 (1958) 23–27.

Albright, W. F., "New Light on the Early History of Phoenician Colonization," *BASOR* 83 (1941) 14–22.

Ap-Thomas, D. R., "The Phoenicians," in D. J. Wiseman, ed., *Peoples of Old Testament Times* (Oxford: Clarendon, 1973) 259–86.

Astour, M. C., "The Origin of the Terms 'Canaan,' 'Phoenicians' and 'Purple,'" *JNES* 24 (1965) 346–50.

Borger, R., "An Additional Remark on P.R. Ackroyd, *JNES* XVII, 23-27," *JNES* 18 (1959) 74.

Dahood, M., "Textual Problems in Isaiah," *CBQ* 22 (1960) 400–409.

——, "The Value of Ugaritic for Textual Criticism: Isa 23,9," *Bib* 40 (1959) 160–64.

Day, John, "Where Was Tarshish?" in Iain Provan and Mark J. Boda, eds., *Let Us Go Up to Zion: Essays in*

---

4   Borger, *Die Inschriften Asarhaddons,* 14–15, episodes 6–10. See now Leichty, RINAP 4, 104, i 34–ii 9a.
5   See Katzenstein, *History of Tyre,* 262–69.
6   See Leichty, RINAP 4, 1 v 55.

Honour of H. G. M. Williamson on the Occasion of His Sixty-Fifth Birthday (VTSup 153; Leiden: Brill, 2012) 359–70.

Ehrlich, E. L., "Der Aufenthalt des Königs Manasse in Babylon," TZ 21 (1965) 281–86.

Eissfeldt, O., "Phoiniker und Phoinikia," Pauly-W 20, no. 1 (1941) 350–80.

——, "Tyros," Pauly-W 7A, no. 2 (1948) 1876–1908.

Elat, M., "The Political Status of the Kingdom of Judah within the Assyrian Empire in the 7th Century B.C.E.," in Yohanan Aharoni, ed., Investigations at Lachish: The Sanctuary and the Residency (Lachish V) (Publications of the Institute of Archaeology 4; Tel Aviv: Gateway, 1975) 61–70.

Erlandsson, Burden of Babylon, 98–102.

Fischer, T., and U. Rütherswörden, "Aufruf zur Volks- lage in Kanaan (Jesaja 23)," WO 13 (1982) 36–49.

Flint, Peter W., "From Tarshish to Carthage: The Septuagint Translation of Tarsis in Isaiah 23," Proceedings, Eastern Great Lakes & Midwest Biblical Society 8 (1988) 127–33.

——, "The Septuagint Version of Isaiah 23:1-14 and the Massoretic Text," BIOSCS 21 (1988) 35–54.

Galling, K., "Der Weg der Phöniker nach Tarsis in literarischer und archäologischer Sicht," ZDPV 88 (1972) 1–18.

Gibson, C. L., "Observations on Some Important Ethnic Terms in the Pentateuch," JNES 20 (1961) 217–38.

Ginsburg, H. L., "Judah and the Transjordan States from 734 to 582 B.C.E.," in Alexander Marx: Jubilee Volume on the Occasion of His Seventieth Birthday (Philadelphia: Jewish Publication Society of America, 1950) 347–68.

Gray, Canaanites.

Grünberg, S., "Exegetische Beiträge: Jesaja 23,15," Jeschurun: Monatsschrift für Lehre und Leben im Juden- tum 13 (1926) 50–56.

Hagedorn, Anselm C., "Tyre and the Mediterranean in the Book of Isaiah," in Iain Provan and Mark J. Boda, eds., Let Us Go Up to Zion: Essays in Honour of H. G. M. Williamson on the Occasion of His Sixty-Fifth Birthday (VTSup 153; Leiden: Brill, 2012) 127–42.

Harden, D. B., The Phoenicians (London: Thames & Hudson, 1962).

Hill, G., A History of Cyprus (4 vols.; Cambridge: Uni- versity Press, 1940–52).

Høgenhaven, Gott und Volk, 157–61.

Honigmann, E., "Sidon," Pauly-W IIA (1923) 2216–29.

Katzenstein, History of Tyre.

Kooij, A. van der, The Oracle of Tyre: The Septuagint of Isaiah XXIII as Version and Vision (VTSup 71; Leiden: Brill, 1998).

——, "A Short Commentary on Some Verses of the Old Greek of Isaiah 23," BIOSCS 15 (1982) 36–50.

Lindblom, J., "Der Ausspruch über Tyrus in Jes. 23," ASTI 4 (1965) 56–73.

Linder, J., "Weissagung über Tyrus, Isaias Kap. 23," ZKT 65 (1941) 217–21.

Lipiński, E., "The Elegy on the Fall of Sidon in Isaiah 23," ErIsr 14 (1978) 79–88.

Maisler, B., "Canaan and the Canaanites," BASOR 102 (1946) 7–12.

Middlemas, Jill, "Ships and Other Seafaring Vessels in the Old Testament," in Iain Provan and Mark J. Boda, eds., Let Us Go Up to Zion: Essays in Honour of H. G. M. Williamson on the Occasion of His Sixty-Fifth Birthday (VTSup 153; Leiden: Brill, 2012) 407–22.

Moscati, S., "Sulla Storia del Nome Canaan," in Studia biblica et orientalia, vol. 3, Oriens antiquus (AnBib 12; Rome: Pontificio Istituto Biblico, 1959) 266–69.

Na'aman, N., "The Shihor of Egypt and Shur That Is before Egypt," TA 7 (1980) 95–109.

Noth, M., "Zum Ursprung der phönikischen Küsten- städte," WO 1 (1947) 21–28.

Orr, A., "The Seventy Years of Babylon," VT 6 (1956) 304–6.

Plöger, O., "'Siebzig Jahre,'" in Festschrift Friedrich Baumgärtel zum 70. Geburtstag, 14. Januar 1958, gewidmet von den Mitarbeitern am Kommentar zum Alten Testament (KAT) (Erlanger Forschungen A.10; Erlangen: Universitätsbund Erlangen, 1959) 124–30.

Postgate, J. N., "Assyrian Texts and Fragments," Iraq 35 (1973) 16–36.

Randles, R. J., "The Interaction of Israel, Judah, and Egypt from Solomon to Josiah" (PhD diss., South- ern Baptist Theological Seminary, 1980) 210–38.

Renz, T., "Proclaiming the Future: History and Theol- ogy in Prophecies against Tyre," TynBul 51 (2000) 17–58.

Reyes, A. Y., Archaic Cyprus (Oxford: Clarendon, 1994).

Rudolph, W., "Jesaja 23:1-14," in Festschrift Friedrich Baumgärtel zum 70. Geburtstag, 14. Januar 1958, gewidmet von den Mitarbeitern am Kommentar zum Alten Testament (KAT) (Erlanger Forschungen A.10; Erlangen: Universitätsbund Erlangen, 1959) 166–74.

Schulten, A., "Tartessos," Pauly-W IVA, 2 (1932) 2446–51.

Speiser, E. A., "The Name Phoinikes," in J. J. Finkel- stein and Moshe Greenberg, eds., Oriental and Biblical Studies: Collected Writings of E. A. Speiser (Philadelphia: University of Pennsylvania Press, 1967) 324–31.

Tsirkin, J. B., "The Hebrew Bible and the Origin of Tartessian Power," AuOr 4 (1986) 179–85.

Tuplin, C., Achaemenid Studies (Stuttgart: Steiner, 1996).

Watson, W. G. E., "Tribute to Tyre (Is. XXIII 7)," *VT* 26 (1976) 371–74.

Werner, W., *Studien zur alttestamentlichen Vorstellung vom Plan Yahves* (BZAW 173; Berlin: de Gruyter, 1988) 54–60.

Whitley, C. F., "The Term Seventy Years Captivity," *VT* 4 (1954) 60–72.

Wolff, H. W., "Der Aufruf zur Volksklage," *ZAW* 76 (1964) 48–56.

The so-called Little Isaiah Apocalypse, Isaiah 24–27, is one of the most difficult sections to interpret in the whole book of Isaiah. It is generally, though not universally, agreed that these four chapters are dependent on, but later than and not composed by, Isaiah of Jerusalem, who wrote in the late eighth and very early seventh century BCE. There is, however, no real agreement on how much later a date is to be assigned to this material. The dates given by different scholars range anywhere from the late seventh/early sixth centuries to the Hellenistic period after the breakup of Alexander's empire among his generals.[1] The reason for this vast range of assigned dates is the fact that this material is totally devoid of indisputable allusions to datable historical events. In contrast to such passages in Isaiah as 6:1; 7:1; 14:28; 20:1; 36:1, which date the following material to a particular year or a well-known event that then allows it to be dated to a particular year or limited range of years, there are no date formulas in chaps. 24–27. Moreover, with this datable framework, many other passages in First Isaiah may be assigned with confidence within a very limited time frame. Such is not the case in chaps. 24–27. There are historical allusions, but they are tantalizingly vague and open to multiple interpretations. For years I vacillated between different dates, frustrated and with little confidence that I had any real grasp of what was going on in these chapters. I much prefer interpreting material whose historical context is clearly known and which may provide some clues for understanding the argument in the text.

Nonetheless, a commentator is expected to comment even on those passages in his or her assigned text for which he has no new, brilliantly original interpretation to offer. In the course of time, I was struck by the similarity in the use of the resurrection motif in Isa 26:14, 17-19 (cf. also the end-of-death motif in Isa 25:7-8) and the use of the same motif in Ezek 37:11-14. It seemed probable, therefore, that Ezekiel and the author of Isaiah 24–27 came from the same general time period.

The author of Isaiah 24–27, however, speaks of an expected rebirth of the nation that ended in the disappointment of a stillbirth or even a false pregnancy, and that suggests that the author may have lived through the exciting optimism of the Josianic reform and national revival, only later to see those hopes collapse with Josiah's death and the imposition of Egyptian in place of Assyrian hegemony. The celebration over the ruined city of aliens (Isa 25:1-5; 26:5-6) would fit well with the destruction of Assyria in 615–610 BCE and would help explain the optimistic expectations of national revival. But the experienced disappointment of the collapse of Josiah's revival and the imposition of Egyptian hegemony would explain the hostility toward Egypt expressed in the mythological imagery in Isa 27:1-2, and the admonition to God to make his judgments once again obvious to the world, as he had done with Assyria (Isa 26:9-11).

This desire for Yahweh's renewed intervention in judgment ultimately leads to the picture of Yahweh's universal judgment of all nations and the divine principalities and powers behind their human rulers (chap. 24). Whether this prophet's ministry and life extended into the period of Babylonian hegemony after 605 BCE, or especially the period of the Babylonian conquest and exile with the capture of Jerusalem in 597 and again in 587 BCE, is uncertain. What is certain is that the author never once mentions Babylon in his whole corpus. When he speaks of a return from exile in 27:12-13, it is a return of those who were lost in the land of Assyria, and those who were driven out to the land of Egypt. The implication would seem to be that at the time this author was writing, the exiles of Israel and Judah were to be found primarily in Assyria and Egypt. That suggests this composition was written prior to 597 and certainly prior to 587 BCE. If somehow the author lived to experience the two Babylonian conquests of Jerusalem and the great Babylonian exile that followed and actually wrote his material after these events, that is, very curiously, not what he chose to write about. The conceit that Assyria is a code word for Babylon is

---

1   Hayes and Irvine (pp. 295–98) still attribute this material to Isaiah of Jerusalem in the late eighth century BCE. William R. Millar dates it between 587 BCE and the last half of the sixth century BCE (*Isaiah 24–27 and the Origin of Apocalyptic* [HSM 11; Missoula, MT: Scholars Press, 1976] 118–20). Clements (p. 199) puts it in the fifth-century Persian period; Blenkinsopp (p. 348) dates it after the fall of Babylon to Cyrus in 539 BCE, or roughly contemporaneous with Second Isaiah; Gray (pp. 400–401) suggests the postexilic period c. 400 BCE, while Duhm (pp. 147–48) dated it impossibly late, in the time of John Hyrcanus in the late second century BCE.

totally unconvincing.[2] Prophets who clearly experienced the Babylonian conquests like Jeremiah, Ezekiel, and Habakkuk had not the slightest hesitancy to call Babylon Babylon. Thus I would date the Little Isaiah Apocalypse to the late seventh and very early sixth century.

Bibliography

Amsler, Samuel, "Des visions de Zacharie à l'apocalypse d'Esaïe 24–27," in J. Vermeylen et al., eds., *Le livre d'Esaïe: Les oracles et leurs relectures unité et complexité de l'ouvrage* (BETL 81; Leuven: Leuven University Press, 1989) 263–73.

Anderson, G. W., "Isaiah XXIV–XXVII Reconsidered," in *Congress Volume: Bonn 1962* (VTSup 9; Leiden: Brill, 1963) 118–26.

Aubert, L., "Une première apocalypse (Esaïe 24–27)," *ETR* 11 (1936) 280–96.

Beek, M. A., "Ein Erdbeben wird zum prophetischen Erleben," *ArOr* 17 (1949) 31–40.

Biddle, M., "The City of Chaos and the New Jerusalem: Isaiah 24–27 in Context," *PRSt* 22 (1995) 5–12.

Bosman, H. J., "Annotated Translation of Isaiah 24–27," in H. J. Bosman, H. van Grol, et al., eds., *Studies in Isaiah 24–27: The Isaiah Workshop–de Jesaja Werkplaats* (OtSt 43; Leiden: Brill, 2000) 3–12.

——, "Syntactic Cohesion in Isaiah 24–27," in H. J. Bosman, H. van Grol, et al., eds., *Studies in Isaiah 24–27: The Isaiah Workshop–de Jesaja Werkplaats* (OtSt 43; Leiden: Brill, 2000).

Brockhaus, G., "Untersuchungen zu Stil und Form der sogenannten Jesaja-Apokalypse" (Master's thesis, Bonn, 1972).

Carroll, Robert P., "City of Chaos, City of Stone, City of Flesh: Urbanscapes in Prophetic Discourse," in Lester L. Grabbe and Robert D. Haak, eds., *"Every City Shall Be Forsaken": Urbanism and Prophecy in Ancient Israel and the Near East* (JSOTSup 330; Sheffield: Sheffield Academic Press, 2001) 45–61.

Coggins, R. J., "The Problem of Isaiah 24–27," *EvT* 90 (1979) 328–33.

Day, John, "A Case of Inner Scriptural Interpretation: The Dependence of Isaiah XXVI.13–XXVII.11 on Hosea XII 4–XIV.10 (Eng. 9) and Its Relevance to Some Theories of the Redaction of the 'Isaiah Apocalypse,'" *JTS* 31 (1980) 309–19.

Dempsey, C. J., *Isaiah: God's Poet of Light* (St. Louis: Chalice, 2010).

Domínguez, N., "Vaticinios sobre el fin del mundo," *CTom* 51 (1935) 125–46.

Doyle, Brian, *The Apocalypse of Isaiah Metaphorically Speaking: A Study of the Use, Function, and Significance of Metaphors in Isaiah 24–27* (BETL 151; Leuven: Leuven University Press, 2000).

Elder, W. H., "Theological-Historical Study of Isaiah 24–27" (PhD diss., Baylor University, 1974; Ann Arbor, MI: University Microfilms, 1974).

Fichtner, J., "Prophetismus und Apokalyptik in Protojesaja" (Inaug. diss., Breslau, 1929).

Fohrer, Georg, "Der Aufbau der Apokalypse des Jesajabuchs (Is 24–27)," *CBQ* 25 (1963) 34–45; reprinted in Fohrer *Studien zur alttestamentlichen Prophetie*, 170–81.

Gilse, J. von, "Jesaja XXIV–XXVII," *NedTT* 3 (1914) 167–93.

Grol, H. W. M. van, "An Analysis of the Verse Structure of Isaiah 24–27," in H. J. Bosman, H. van Grol, et al., eds., *Studies in Isaiah 24–27: The Isaiah Workshop–de Jesaja Werkplaats* (OtSt 43; Leiden: Brill, 2000) 51–80.

Hanson, Paul D., *The Dawn of Apocalyptic: The Historical and Sociological Roots of Jewish Apocalyptic Eschatology* (Philadelphia: Fortress Press, 1975).

——, "Jewish Apocalyptic against Its Near Eastern Environment," *RB* 78 (1971) 31–58.

——, "Old Testament Apocalyptic Reexamined," *Int* 25 (1971) 454–79.

Henry, M. L., *Glaubenskrise und Glaubensbewährung in den Dichtungen der Jesajaapokalypse* (BWANT 86; Stuttgart: Kohlhammer, 1966).

Hilgenfeld, A., "Das Judentum in dem persischen Zeitalter," *ZWT* 9 (1866) 398–488.

Hylmö, Gunnar, *De s.k. profetiska liturgiernas rytm, stil och komposition* (Lunds universitets årsskrift n.f., adv. 1, 25.5; Lund: Gleerup, 1929).

Jenner, K. D., "Petucha and Setuma: Tools for Interpretation or Simply a Matter of Lay-Out?" in H. J. Bosman, H. van Grol, et al., eds., *Studies in Isaiah*

---

2   Few scholars, apart from Gray (p. 463), who sees the term *Assyria* as a continuing designation for the same area after the fall of Assyria, even discuss the issue. Marti (p. 201) and Duhm (p. 168) simply translate Assyria as Syria. Wildberger (2:1023) states that v. 13 is "unambiguously about the return of diaspora Jews from Babylon and Egypt," though he does not bother to say why "Assyria" should be understood as "Babylon."

24–27: *The Isaiah Workshop–de Jesaja Werkplaats* (OtSt 43; Leiden: Brill, 2000) 81–117.

Johnson, D. G., "Devastation and Restoration: A Compositional Study of Isaiah 24–27" (PhD diss., Princeton Theological Seminary, 1985; Ann Arbor, MI: University Microfilms, 1986).

——, *From Chaos to Restoration: An Integrative Reading of Isaiah 24–27* (JSOTSup 61; Sheffield: JSOT Press, 1988).

Kaiser, W. C., *Preaching and Teaching the Last Things: Old Testament Eschatology for the Life of the Church* (Grand Rapids: Baker Academic, 2011).

Kessler, W., *Gott geht es um das Ganze: Jesaja 56–66 und Jesaja 24–27* (BAT 19; Stuttgart: Calwer, 1960).

Kline, Meredith G., "Death, Leviathan, and Martyrs: Isaiah 24:1–27:1," in Walter C. Kaiser Jr. and Ronald F. Youngblood, eds., *A Tribute to Gleason Archer* (Chicago: Moody, 1986) 229–49.

Koch, K., *Ratlos vor der Apokalyptik* (Gütersloh: Gütersloher Verlagshaus, 1970).

Lagrange, M. J., "L'apocalypse d'Isaïe (24–27)," *RB* 3 (1894) 200–231.

Liebmann, E., "Der Text zu Jesaja 24–27," *ZAW* 22 (1902) 285–304; 23 (1903) 209–86.

Lindblom, Johannes, *Die Jesaja-Apokalypse, Jes. 24–27* (Lunds universitets årsskrift n.f., adv. 2, 34.3; Lund: Gleerup, 1938).

——, "Die Jesaja-Apokalypse (Jes 24–27) in der neuen Jesaja-Handschrift," *K. Humaniska Vetenskaps-samsfundets i Lund Arsberattelse* 2 (1950–51) 79–144.

Lohmann, P., "Die selbständigen lyrischen Abschnitte in Jes 24–27," *ZAW* 37 (1917) 1–58.

Ludwig, O., *Die Stadt in der Jesaja-Apokalypse: Zur Datierung von Jesaja 24–27* (Cologne: Kleikamp, 1961).

March, W. E., "A Study of Two Prophetic Compositions in Is 24 1–27 1" (ThD thesis, Union Theological Seminary, 1966).

Martin-Achard, Robert, "Trois remarques sur la resurrection des morts dans l'Ancien Testament," *Cahiers de la Revue de Theologie et de Philosophie* 11 (1984) 170–84.

Millar, William R., *Isaiah 24–27 and the Origin of Apocalyptic* (HSM 11; Missoula, MT: Scholars Press, 1976).

Mulder, E. S., *Die Teologie van die Jesaja-Apokalipse* (Groningen/Djarkarta: J. B. Wolters, 1954).

Neves, J. C. M., *A teologia da tradução grega dos setenta no livro de Isaías (cap. 24 de Isaiás)* (Lisbon: Universidade Catolica Portuguesa, 1973).

Nitsche, S. A., *Jesaja 24–27, ein dramatischer Text: Die Frage nach den Genres prophetischer Literatur des Alten Testaments und die Textgraphik der grossen Jesajarolle aus Qumran* (BWANT 166; Stuttgart: Kohlhammer, 2006).

Otzen, B., "Traditions and Structures of Isaiah XXIV–XXVII," *VT* 24 (1974) 196–206.

Pagan, Samuel, "Apocalyptic Poetry: Isaiah 24–27," *BT* 43 (1992) 314–25.

Plöger, Otto, *Theokratie und Eschatologie* (WMANT 2; Neukirchen: Kreis Moers, Neukirchener Verlag, 1959) esp. 69–97. English trans., *Theocracy and Eschatology* (trans. S. Rudman; Richmond: John Knox, 1968).

Polaski, D. C., *Authorizing an End: The Isaiah Apocalypse and Intertextuality* (BIS 50; Leiden: Brill, 2001).

——, "Destruction, Construction, Argumentation: A Rhetorical Reading of Isaiah 24–27," in G. Carey and L. G. Bloomquist, eds., *Vision and Persuasion: Rhetorical Dimensions of Apocalyptic Discourse* (St. Louis: Chalice, 1999) 19–39.

Redditt, Paul L., "Isaiah 24–27: A Form Critical Analysis" (PhD thesis, Vanderbilt University, 1972).

——, "Once Again, the City in Isaiah 24–27," *HAR* 10 (1987) 317–35.

Ringgren, Helmer, "Some Observations on Style and Structure in the Isaiah Apocalypse," *ASTI* 9 (1973) 107–15.

Rochais, G., "Les origines de l'apocalyptique," *ScEs* 25 (1973) 15–50.

Rudolph, W., *Jesaja 24–27* (BWANT 62; Stuttgart: Kohlhammer, 1933).

Sawyer, John F. A., "'My Secret Is with Me': Some Semantic Links between Isaiah 24–27 and Daniel," in A. Graeme Auld, ed., *Understanding Poets and Prophets: Essays in Honour of George Wishart Anderson* (JSOTSup 152; Sheffield: JSOT Press, 1993) 307–17.

——, *Sacred Texts and Sacred Meanings: Studies in Biblical Language and Literature* (Hebrew Bible Monographs 28; Sheffield: Sheffield Phoenix, 2011).

Scholl, Reinhard, *Die Elenden in Gottes Thronrat: Stilistisch-kompositorische Untersuchungen zu Jesaja 24–27* (BZAW 274; Berlin: de Gruyter, 2000).

Seebass, Gottfried, "The Importance of Apocalyptic for the History of Protestantism," *Colloquium* 13, no. 1 (1980) 24–35.

Sievers, E., "Alttestamentliche Miscellen I: Jesaja 24–27," in *Berichte über die Verhandlungen der königlich sächsischen Gesellschaft des Wissenschaft zu Leipzig, Phil.-Hist. Kl.*, vol. 56 (1904) 151–88.

Smend, R., "Anmerkungen zu Jes. 24–27," *ZAW* 4 (1884) 161–224.

Sweeney, Marvin A., "Textual Citations in Isaiah 24–27: Toward an Understanding of the Redactional Function of Chapters 24–27 in the Book of Isaiah," *JBL* 107 (1988) 39–52.

Youngblood, Ronald, "A Holistic Typology of Prophecy and Apocalyptic," in A. Gileadi, ed., *Israel's Apostasy and Restoration: Essays in Honor of Ronald K. Harrison* (Grand Rapids: Baker Book House, 1988) 213–21.

Vermeylen, J., *La composition littéraire de l'apocalypse d'Isaïe: (Is., XXIV–XXVII)* (ALBO 5/14; Louvain: Ephemerides Theologicae Lovanienses, 1974).

Zyl, A. H. van, "Isaiah 24–27: Their Date of Origin," *OTWSA* 5 (1962) 44–57.

24

1/ Now Yahweh[a] is about to destroy the earth,[b] and devastate it, and he
will twist its surface, and scatter its inhabitants.[c]

2/ The same fate will befall the people and the priest,[d] the slave and his
master,[e] the maidservant and her mistress, the buyer[f] and the seller,
the lender and the borrower, the creditor[g] and his debtor.[h]

3/ The earth will surely be destroyed and plundered[i] because[j] Yahweh
has spoken this word.

4/ The earth has dried up, is withered,
The world languishes, is withered,
The heaven languishes[k] with[l] the earth.

5/ And the earth has become defiled under its inhabitants,[m] because[n]
they transgressed the laws,[o] overstepped[p] the statute,[q] broke[r] the
eternal covenant.

6/ That is why a curse devours the earth,[s]
And those living in it[t] pay the penalty;[u]
That is why the inhabitants of the earth[v] have dwindled,[w]
And only a few people are left.

7/ The new wine dries up,
The vine languishes,[x]
All[y] the merry-hearted groan.

8/ The mirth of the tambourines[z] has ceased,
The noise of the exultant[*a] has stopped,
The mirth of the lyre has ceased.

9/ They no longer[*b] drink wine with singing;[*c]
Beer has become bitter[*d] to its drinkers.[*e]

10/ The desolate city is broken;[*f]
Every[*g] house is shut[*h] so that no one can enter.

11/ There is an outcry[*i] in the streets over the wine;
All[*j] rejoicing has gone down,
The mirth of the earth has departed.

12/ Desolation is left in the city,[*k]
And in ruins[*l] the gate[*m] lies smashed.[*n]

13/ For thus[*o] it will be in the midst of the earth,
In the middle of the peoples like the shaking[*p] of an olive tree,
Like the gleanings[*q] when the vintage is over.

14/ They will lift up their voice,[*r]
They[*s] will exult[*t] in the majesty of Yahweh,
They will shout from the sea.[*u]

15/ That is why in the east[*v] they honor[*w] Yahweh,
In the islands of the sea the name of Yahweh, the God[*x] of Israel.

16/ From the end of the earth we hear singing:[*y]
Glory to the righteous one!
And I said,[*z] "I waste away!
I waste away! Woe is me!
The treacherous[ta] deal treacherously,
And with treachery the treacherous deal treacherously."

17/ Terror, pit, and snare are upon you, O inhabitant of the earth.

18/ And the one who flees from the sound of terror
Shall fall[tb] into the pit,
And the one who climbs up out of the pit
Shall be caught in the snare,
For the sluice gates are opened on high,
And the foundations of the earth are shaken.

19/ The earth is utterly broken,[tc]
The earth is split asunder,
The earth is violently shaken.[td]

20/ The earth will stagger[te] like the drunkard,
And it will sway like the hut;[tf]
And its transgression will lie heavy upon it,
And it will fall never again to rise.[tg]

21/   And it will be in that day that
    Yahweh will punish[th] the host of heaven in the heaven,
    And the kings of the earth upon the earth.

22/   And they shall be gathered like prisoners[ti] in a pit,
    And they will be locked in a dungeon,
    And after many[tj] days they will be punished.

23/   And the moon will be ashamed,
    And the sun abashed;[tk]
    For Yahweh of Hosts will reign in Mount Zion and in Jerusalem,
    And before his elders[tl] there will be glory.

Textual Notes

a   MT, 1QIsa^a יהוה, "Yahweh"; 4QIsa^c אדוני (ʾădōnāy), "my Lord."

b   MT, 4QIsa^c הָאָרֶץ (hāʾāreṣ), "the earth"; 1QIsa^a האדמה (hāʾădāmâ), "the land."

c   MT, 4QIsa^f יֹשְׁבֶיהָ (yōšĕbêhā), "its inhabitants"; 1QIsa^a, 4QIsa^c יושביה (yōšĕbêhā).

d   MT כַּכֹּהֵן (kakkōhēn), "as priest"; 1QIsa^a, 4QIsa^c כבוהן (kakkôhēn).

e   MT כַּאדֹנָיו (kaʾdōnāyw), "as his master"; lit., "as his masters," but the plural suffix, perhaps the plural of majesty, is sometimes used when referring to a singular "master" or "owner"; see Isa 1:3; Exod 22:13-14; 1QIsa^a, 4QIsa^c כאדוניו (kaʾdōnāyw).

f   MT, 1QIsa^a, 4QIsa^c כַּקּוֹנֶה (kaqqônê), "as the buyer"; 4QIsa^f כקנה (kaqqōnê).

g   MT כַּנֹּשֶׁה (kannōšê), "as the creditor"; 4QIsa^c כנושה (kannôšê), and 1QIsa^a corrects to that orthography כנושה.

h   MT, 1QIsa^a נֹשֶׁא בּוֹ (nōšēʾ bô), "the debtor," lit., "the one to whom he lends"; 4QIsa^c נושה בו (nōšê bô), "the debtor."

i   MT, 1QIsa^a וְהִבּוֹז תִּבּוֹז (wĕhibbôz tibbôz), "and surely be plundered"; 4QIsa^c והבוז תבוז; and 4QIsa^f appears to have תבז (wĕhibbōz tibbōz).

j   MT, 1QIsa^a כִּי (kî), "because"; 4QIsa^c כיא (kîʾ), "because."

k   MT אֻמְלְלוּ (ʾumlĕlû), "they languish," the plural, is supported by LXX, Tg.; 1QIsa^a, 4QIsa^c אמלל (ʾumlal), "he/it languishes," the singular, is supported by Vg., Syr. Since the grammatical subject מָרוֹם (mārôm), "heaven" is singular, one would expect the verb in the singular, but since "heaven" was languishing "with the earth," the plural may have been introduced because of the sense of a compound subject.

l   Repointing MT's עַם (ʿam), "people," as עִם (ʿim), "with." 4QIsa^c has basically the same consonantal text as MT, though without the maqqep, מרום עם הארץ (mrwm ʿm hʾrṣ), but the original text of 1QIsa^a omitted עם and then inserted it as a correction above the line מרום ^{עם} הארץ. Neither LXX (οἱ ὑψηλοὶ τῆς γῆς, "the exalted ones of the earth") nor Syr (rwmh dʾrʿ, "the height of the earth") reflects עם in their translations, so they may have been following a text like the uncorrected 1QIsa^a. Vg.'s altitudo populi terrae, "the height of the people of the earth," and Tg.'s tĕqôp ʿamāʾ dĕʾarʿāʾ, "the strength of the people of the earth," reflect MT's עם (ʿam), "people." The LXX translation has led many commentators and translations to stick with MT's pointing and to understand מָרוֹם (mārôm) in the sense of the "socially elevated," and thus מְרוֹם עַם־הָאָרֶץ (mĕrôm ʿam-hāʾāreṣ) as "the most exalted people of the earth." Job 5:11 and Eccl 10:6 give some support for the sense of "socially elevated" for mārôm, but the idiom mĕrôm ʿam, "the height/most exalted of the people," remains unique and unparalleled. The normal meaning of mārôm for this writer is "heaven" (Isa 24:18, 22; cf. 26:5).

m   MT יֹשְׁבֶיהָ (yōšĕbêhā), "its inhabitants"; 1QIsa^a, 4QIsa^c יושביה (yōšĕbêhā).

n   See note j above.

o   MT תּוֹרֹת (tôrōt), "laws"; 1QIsa^a תורות (tôrōt), Vg.; 4QIsa^c תורה (tôrâ), "the law"; LXX, Syr., and Tg. support the singular.

p   MT has the qal חָלְפוּ (ḥālĕpû), "they overstepped." Based on LXX καὶ ἤλλαξαν, "and they changed," and Vg. mutaverunt, "they changed," a number of critics emend to the piel ḥillĕpû, "they changed," but MT's pointing is probably correct; the qal makes a very close synonym of the preceding עברו (ʿābĕrû), "they transgressed."

q   MT חֹק (ḥōq), "statute"; 1QIsa^a, 4QIsa^c חוק (ḥôq); LXX and Tg. translate as a plural.

r   MT, 4QIsa^c הֵפֵרוּ (hēpērû), "they broke"; 1QIsa^a הפירו (hēpîrû). LXX omits this verb.

s   MT, 4QIsa^c אֶרֶץ (ʾereṣ), "the earth"; 1QIsa^a omits the word, but the versions have it.

t   MT יֹשְׁבֵי בָהּ (yōšĕbê bāh), "those living in it"; 1QIsa^a, 4QIsa^c יושבי בה (yōšĕbê bāh).

u   MT, 4QIsa^c וַיֶּאְשְׁמוּ (wayyeʾšĕmû), "and they pay the penalty"; 1QIsa^a וישמו could be analyzed as from שמם, "to be appalled, be desolate," but it probably is from אשם with the loss of the quiescent, syllable-closing א.

v   MT יֹשְׁבֵי אֶרֶץ (yōšĕbê ʾereṣ), "inhabitants of the earth"; 1QIsa^a יושבי ארץ (yôšĕbê ʾereṣ); 4QIsa^c appears to have had the article on the noun (yôšĕbê hā[ʾāreṣ]).

w   MT חָרוּ (ḥārû), "they dwindled, became few"); 1QIsa^a חורו (ḥorû). The root appears to be חור, cognate with Arabic ḥara/ḥwr, "to recede, decrease, diminish, be reduced" (see Hans Wehr, A Dictionary of Modern Written Arabic [Ithaca, NY: Cornell University Press, 1961], 212; and E. W. Lane, Arabic-English Lexicon [Cambridge: Islamic Texts Society, 1985; reproduction of 1863 original] 1:665), though Arabic would also allow the root to be חרה (ḥarāy), "to decrease"; see HALAT, 351; Gesenius, Handwörterbuch, 18th ed., 395a.

x   MT אֻמְלְלָה-גָפֶן (ʾumlĕlâ-gāpen), "the vine languishes"; 1QIsaᵃ אמללה גפן, while 4QIsaᶜ adds a word אמללה גפן יצהר (ʾumlĕlâ-gāpen yiṣhār) "the vine languishes, the oil" perhaps influenced by Joel 1:10, but the addition is not supported by the versions.

y   MT כָּל (kol), "all"; 1QIsaᵃ, 4QIsaᶜ כול (kôl).

z   MT, 1QIsaᵃ תֻּפִּים (tuppîm), "tambourines"; 4QIsaᶜ תופים.

*a MT, 1QIsaᵃ עַלִּיזִים (ʿallîzîm), "the exultant"; 4QIsaᶜ appears to have עלוזים. LXX renders this second clause as πέπαυται αὐθάδεια καὶ πλοῦτος ἀσεβῶν, "the self-will and wealth of the impious has ceased."

*b MT לֹא (lōʾ), "not, no longer"; 1QIsaᵃ and 4QIsaᶜ לוא.

*c MT בַּשִּׁיר (baššîr), "with singing, with the song," is supported by 1QIsaᵃ, 4QIsaᶜ, and all the versions except LXX. LXX has ᾐσχύνθησαν, "they were ashamed," apparently reading בשו (bōšû), "they were ashamed."

*d MT and 4QIsaᶜ יֵמַר (yēmar), "was bitter"; 1QIsaᵃ וימר, "and was bitter." The versions all support MT.

*e MT לְשֹׁתָיו (lĕšōtāyw), "to its drinkers"; 1QIsaᵃ לשותיו, but 4QIsaᶜ לשותיהו.

*f MT קִרְיַת-תֹהוּ (qiryat-tōhû), "the city of chaos/desolation," is supported by Vg.'s civitas vanitatis, "the city of vanity," but 1QIsaᵃ and 4QIsaᶜ have only קרית תהו, omitting the maqqēp. Tg. does not construe the expression as a construct chain, but renders, "their city is broken, left desolate." Neither LXX (ἠρημώθη πᾶσα πόλις, "every city was made desolate") nor Syr. (ʾtbzt qrytʾ, "the city was plundered") translates tōhû, and the JPS translation appears to follow Tg. in rendering, "Towns are broken, empty."

*g See note y above.

*h MT, 1QIsaᵃ סֻגַּר (suggar), "is shut, locked"; 4QIsaᶜ סוגר.

*i LXX reads the noun צְוָחָה (sĕwāḥâ), "outcry," as a plural imperative ὀλολύζετε, "wail." It also reduces and combines the second and third lines into a single line (ὀλολύζετε περὶ τοῦ οἴνου πανταχῇ ·πέπαυται πᾶσα εὐφροσύνη τῆς γῆς, "Wail everywhere for the wine; all the joy of the earth has ceased").

*j See note y above.

*k MT, 1QIsaᵃ, 4QIsaᶜ בָּעִיר (bāʿîr), "in the city," supported by the versions apart from LXX; LXX has καὶ καταλειφθήσονται πόλεις ἔρημοι, "and the cities shall be left desolate."

*l MT, 1QIsaᵃ וּשְׁאִיָּה (ûšĕʾîyâ), "and a ruin"; 4QIsaᶜ ושואה (wĕšôʾâ), "and a ruin."

*m MT, 1QIsaᵃ שָׁעַר (šāʿar), "gate"; 4QIsaᶜ שערה, "its gate." Vg., Syr., and Tg. have the plural "gates." LXX has καὶ οἶκοι ἐγκαταλελειμμένοι ἀπολοῦνται, "and abandoned houses will perish."

*n MT, 4QIsaᶜ יֻכַּת (yukkat), "is smashed"; 1QIsaᵃ יוכת.

*o MT, 1QIsaᵃ כִּי כֹה (kî kōh), "for thus"; 4QIsaᶜ כיא כוה.

*p MT, 1QIsaᵃ בְּנֹקֶף (kĕnōqep), "as the shaking"; 4QIsaᶜ כנקוף.

*q MT, 1QIsaᵃ כְּעוֹלֵלֹת (kĕʿôlēlōt), "like the gleanings"; 4QIsaᶜ כעוללות.

*r MT, 1QIsaᵃ קוֹלָם (qôlām), "their voice"; 4QIsaᶜ קולמ with a blank space at the end of the word where a ה appears to have been erased.

*s LXX adds οἱ δὲ καταλειφθέντες ἐπὶ τῆς γῆς, "but those who are left upon the earth."

*t MT יָרֹנּוּ (yāronnû), "they will exult"; 1QIsaᵃ ירונו; and 4QIsaᶜ ורננו. The Masoretes divide the verse after yāronnû, as their accent mark indicates, but in so doing, they destroy the parallelism in the verse.

*u MT, 1QIsaᵃ צָהֲלוּ מִיָּם (ṣāhălû miyyām), "they will shout from the sea"; so Vg. and Syr.; 4QIsaᶜ וצהלו מיום, "and they will shout from the day"; LXX appears to read מי ים, "the water of the sea will be troubled."

*v MT, 1QIsaᵃ בָּאֻרִים (bāʾūrîm) is a crux; it is normally rendered "in the east," from אוּר (ʾûr), "firelight, fire," with the plural אֻרִים (ʾūrîm) serving as an abstract meaning, "region of light, east" (see discussion in Wildberger, 2:932). That understanding is supported by the further gloss in 4QIsaᶜ בוארים בארם, "in the east, in Aram." JPS has "with lights," influenced apparently by Tg.'s, "when lights come to the righteous." LXX omits the expression, and Syr. has "with praise praise the Lord. Vg. in doctrinis, "in doctrine." "In the east" has the further advantage of creating a merismus with "the coastlands of the sea" in the west to incorporate the whole world in a song of praise to Yahweh. The expression is unique, found only here, however, and that and the orthographic similarity between בארים and the following באי הים ("in the coastlands/islands of the sea") suggest that the former could just be a variant of the latter found earlier in the verse in some manuscripts and then miswritten when the variant texts were conflated (cf. BHS). The nice parallelism, however, argues for preserving the longer text.

*w MT reads the piel imperative כַּבְּדוּ (kabbĕdû), "honor, glorify!," and is supported by Vg. and the later Syr. tradition with vowel points; 1QIsaᵃ has the same consonantal text as MT, but one cannot tell from the consonantal text whether it is an imperative or a perfect. Tg. has an imperfect, not the imperative. 4QIsaᶜ [ ] כבוד, "the glory [of Yahweh]"; cf. LXX ἡ δόξα κυρίου, "the glory of the Lord." Despite MT and its support in some of the versions, the imperative is problematic. Of the many occurrences of עַל-כֵּן (ʿal-kēn), "that is why," in the Old Testament, this would be the only case where it is followed by an imperative. In all the other occurrences it is followed by a perfect, imperfect, or participle. Moreover, כַּבְּדוּ (kabbĕdû), "honor, glorify!,") is the only imperative in the context in Isa 24:15; it is preceded by two imperfects and a perfect (v. 14) and is followed by another perfect (v. 16). Thus, I repoint to the perfect כִּבְּדוּ (kibbĕdû), "they honor, glorify."

*x MT אֱלֹהֵי (ʾĕlōhê), "the God of"; 1QIsaᵃ אלוהי.

*y MT, 1QIsaᵃ זְמִרֹת (zĕmīrōt), "songs, singing"; LXX has τέρατα, "wonders."

*z MT וָאֹמַר (wāʾōmar), "and I said"; so Vg., Syr.; 1QIsaᵃ ואמר is ambiguous; Tg., "the prophet said"; LXX has the third person plural with an ellipsis of the end of the verse: καὶ ἐροῦσιν Οὐαὶ τοῖς ἀθετοῦσιν, οἱ ἀθετοῦντες τὸν νόμον, "And those who reject the law will say, 'Woe to those who reject.'"

†a MT בֹּגְדִים (bōgĕdîm), "the treacherous"; 1QIsaᵃ בוגים. The repetition in MT could be treated as a partial dittography, but one should note the similar repetition with slight variation in the third and fourth lines of the verse, which supports staying with

MT over against LXX and its constant bias toward shortening the text.

†b MT יִפֹּל (yippōl), "he shall fall"; 1QIsaᵃ יפול.

†c MT רֹעָה הִתְרֹעֲעָה הָאָרֶץ (rōʿâ hitrōʿăʿâ hāʾāreṣ), "the earth is utterly broken"; 1QIsaᵃ רוע התרועעה הארץ; but 1QIsaᵇ רעה התרועעה הא[רע]ה אר]ץ.

†d LXX omits the third line.

†e MT נוֹעַ תָּנוּעַ אֶרֶץ (nôaʿ tānûaʿ ʾereṣ), "the earth will stagger"; 1QIsaᵃ ניע תנוע הארץ.

†f MT וְהִתְנוֹדְדָה כַּמְּלוּנָה (wĕhitnôdĕdâ kammĕlûnâ), "and it will sway like the hut"; 1QIsaᵃ והתנודדא וכמלונה, "and it will sway also like the hut."

†g MT וְנָפְלָה וְלֹא-תֹסִיף קוּם (wĕnāpĕlâ wĕlōʾ-tōsîp qûm), "and she [the earth] will fall never again to rise"; 1QIsaᵃ ונפל ולוא תיסיף קום, "and he [the gender is obviously incorrect, because it does not

agree with the following verb having the same subject] will fall never again to rise."

†h MT יִפְקֹד (yipqōd), "he will punish"; 1QIsaᵃ, 4QIsaᶜ יפקוד.

†i MT וְאֻסְּפוּ אֲסֵפָה אַסִּיר (wĕʾussĕpû ʾăsēpâ ʾassîr, "and they will be gathered together like prisoners"); 1QIsaᵃ אספה omits אסיר, "prisoner"; 4QIsaᶜ ואסף אסוף אס]יר.

†j MT וּמֵרֹב (ûmērōb), "and after many"; 1QIsaᵃ ומרוב.

†k LXX has καὶ τακήσεται ἡ πλίνθος, καὶ πεσεῖται τὸ τεῖχος, "and the brick will dissolve, and the wall will fall," apparently reading hallĕbēnâ, "the sun-baked brick" for hallĕbānâ, "the moon," and haḥômâ, "the city wall," for haḥammâ, "the sun." The other versions follow MT.

†l Syr. has "his saints" (wqdm qdyšwhy nštbḥ, "and before his saints he will be praised").

Commentary

Verse 1 begins with an announcement that Yahweh is about to lay waste (בּוֹקֵק, bôqēq) the earth or the land (הָאָרֶץ, hāʾāreṣ). The word hāʾāreṣ is ambiguous; it can mean either "the earth" or "the land," referring to a particular land (cf. Jer 51:2, where the same verb is used with respect to the land of Babylon). At this point it is unclear whether the announced judgment is against the land of Judah or against some other land, or whether it is a universal judgment against the earth in general; but when one reaches v. 13 and the verses that follow, it seems clear that the prophet is speaking of a worldwide judgment. God will devastate the earth, twist its surface, and scatter its inhabitants. Twisting the surface of the earth might suggest earthquake (see vv. 18-20), but scattering its inhabitants, while it could reflect the reaction to earthquake, might make one think more easily of the forced deportations of large populations following the military conquests of imperial powers like Assyria and Babylon (see v. 22).

At any rate, the whole population will suffer the same fate. There will be no distinction between the ordinary people and the priest, between the slave and his master, between the maidservant and her mistress, between the buyer and the seller, between the lender and the borrower, between the creditor and the one to whom he was lending. One should note that there is no consistent pat-

tern in placing the wealthier or more prominent figure either first or last in these comparisons. The series begins with the socially less elevated figure being mentioned first, but when one gets to buyer and seller it is unclear who is the more elevated, and the last two comparisons mention the lender and creditor, the wealthier figure, before his borrower and debtor. The sense seems to be that the powerful will not escape because of their former privileges, but the poor will not escape just because they are not the movers and shakers of society. Everyone will suffer the same disaster.

The land or earth will surely be destroyed and thoroughly plundered (וְהִבּוֹז תִּבּוֹז, wĕhibbôz tibbôz). The use here (v. 3) of the niphal of בזז (bāzaz), "to plunder, take booty," supports, because it presumes an agent, the understanding of the disaster as a military invasion of some sort, not just a natural disaster. The disaster will come, however, because Yahweh has spoken this word of judgment.

If vv. 1-3 seem to present the coming disaster as imminent, yet future, v. 4 switches tenses to the perfect as though to describe a situation that already exists in the land. This apparently past-tense narration continues through v. 12, but then v. 13 switches back to the future in a way that suggests that this past-tense narration, apart from the transgressions of v. 5, is actually describing a largely future situation after God's judgment has fallen.[1] The land has dried up and withered; the world (תֵּבֵל,

---

1   See the discussion of the "prophetic perfect" in GKC §106n.

tēbēl, "the mainland, dry land," perhaps even "inhabited and arable land" as opposed to "desert"; see Isa 14:17) languishes and withers. Even heaven languishes with the earth. For this reading and translation, see the textual notes. A similar thought is expressed in Jer 4:28, where the earth (הָאָרֶץ, *hāʾāreṣ*) and the heavens above (הַשָּׁמַיִם מִמַּעַל, *haššāmayim mimmaʿal*) are similarly linked in mourning.

The reason for this state of affairs is that the land has become defiled (חָנְפָה, *ḥānĕpâ*) under its inhabitants (v. 5). Those inhabitants transgressed (עָבְרוּ, *ʿābĕrû*) the laws (תוֹרֹת, *tôrōt*), overstepped (חָלְפוּ, *ḥālĕpû*) the statute (חֹק, *ḥōq*), and broke (הֵפֵרוּ, *hēpērû*) the eternal covenant (בְּרִית עוֹלָם, *bĕrît ʿôlām*). The primary sense of עָבַר (*ʿābar*) is "to cross over," hence with laws, "to transgress," and the *qal* of חָלַף (*ḥālap*), which is used several times as a parallel to עָבַר (Hab 1:11; Job 9:11; Song 2:11), means "to pass by, pass through, pierce" (Judg 5:26; Job 20:24), "pass on" (note the occurrences in Isa 2:18; 8:8; 21:1). Passing by or through a statute or ordinance would be the equivalent to crossing over a law. Both are idioms for transgressing limits set by God. Thus, there is no reason to emend the *qal* of חָלַף here to the *hiphil* or *piel* in order to get the meaning, "change." "Changing the statute" is not as good a parallel to "transgressing the law" as "overstepping or passing through the statute." The *hiphil* of פָּרַר (*pārar*) is commonly used with בְּרִית (*bĕrît*), "covenant," and parallel terms for "commandment," "law," and the like, in the sense of "break." Note, for example, the similar terminology in Isa 33:8. This breach of covenant, with the transgression of its laws and statutes, is why a curse devours the land and its inhabitants pay the penalty (v. 6). That is why the population has dwindled and so few people remain (וְנִשְׁאַר, *wĕnišʾar*). The repetition of עַל־כֵּן (*ʿal-kēn*), "that is why," is striking and poetically effective in underscoring how the curse for breaking the covenant (see Deut 27:11-26; 28:15-68; Lev 26:14-39) imposes the penalty of a vastly reduced human population. This is a standard punishment for serious sin in the prophets (e.g., Amos 5:3; 6:9-10; Isa 6:11-13), but the use of the verb שָׁאַר (*šāʾar*), "to remain," also ties it to the important theme of "remnant" in First Isaiah (Isa 4:3; 7:3; 10:19-22; 11:11, 16; 14:22; 16:14; 17:3, 6; 21:17; 28:5; 37:31). For a similar connection between breach of covenant and the languishing of both nature and the human population, see Hos 4:2-3 and cf. Jer 4:22-28. What is odd about the present passage, however, is that in the context of the chapter this breach of covenant is not restricted to Israel but is something in which the whole earth seems to be involved. This oddity, together with the odd use of tense, may suggest that the writer incorporated and reworked an older oracle of Isaiah directed against Israel (or Judah) to turn it into a threat of divine judgment against the whole world.

Part of the languishing of nature is the drying up of the new wine because of the withering of the grape vine (v. 7). New wine (תִּירוֹשׁ, *tîrôš*) was not unfermented grape juice, or at least not for long. It quickly fermented, and this newly fermented תִּירוֹשׁ was potent enough "to cheer both God(s) and men" (Judg 9:13), and, imbibed to excess, along with older and stronger wine (יַיִן, *yayin*), capable of intoxicating a person and taking away his sense (Hos 4:11). Ben Sira similarly points to the alcoholic nature of תִּירוֹשׁ, when he urges his audience not to prove their manliness by wine (היין, *hyyn*), for new wine (תירוש) has caused many to stumble (Sir 31:25). For Ben Sira, both *yyn*, "wine," and *tyrwš*, "new wine," were clearly alcoholic and a potential danger, though he argues that both, used wisely, were a blessing from God. He claims that wine (יין, *yyn*) drunk at the right time and in the right manner is gladness of heart and joy and merriment, and he questions the quality of life, if one lacks new wine (תירוש), since from the beginning it was apportioned to bring joy (Sir 31:28). The pleasantness or mildness of new wine (נועם תירוש, *nwʿm tyrwš*) is the perfect accompaniment to the sound of singing (Sir 32:6). The lack of this source of joy and merriment in Isa 24:7, then, results in all the merry-hearted (כָּל־שִׂמְחֵי־לֵב, *kol-śimḥê-lēb*) turning from song to groaning.

The mirth of the tambourines and lyres has ceased, and the noisy partying (שָׁאוֹן, *šĕʾôn*) of the exultant has come to a halt (v. 8). They no longer drink wine (יַיִן, *yayin*) with song or singing (בַּשִּׁיר, *baššîr*), and beer (שֵׁכָר, *šēkār*) has become bitter to those who drink it (v. 9). The party is over, and what alcoholic drinks are left are incapable of reproducing the former mirth. One should compare Isaiah's similar comments on the end of drinking parties and the failure of the vintage (Isa 5:11-14; 32:10-14).

The city is broken and empty, and every house is locked up so it cannot be entered (v. 10). There is a great deal of discussion as to the identity of the city in this verse, particularly on the part of those scholars who translate the MT's קִרְיַת־תֹּהוּ (qiryat-tōhû) following the Vulgate's *civitas vanitatis* as "city of vanity" or "city of chaos." The other versions do not treat the phrase as a construct chain, however. The LXX ignores *tōhû* altogether and treats *qiryat* almost as a collective: ἠρημώθη πᾶσα πόλις, "every city was made desolate." The Targum has "their city is broken down, devastated." The Syriac has simply "the city was plundered." The Hebrew *qiryat* does appear to be in the construct, but the meaning of *tōhû*, when used with "city," is not unambiguous. It could mean "empty" or "desolate," that is, "the city of desolation" or "the desolate city is broken." It remains ambiguous whether the prophet is speaking of a particular city or of cities in general. The image of a broken, empty city with locked houses suggests a prior conquest and a continuing lack of security. There are apparently a few people left (see vv. 6, 11), but not enough to provide security, and the locked houses imply that the survivors do not particularly trust one another. If there is an Isaianic oracle underlying this reworking, the original oracle may have had either Jerusalem (Isa 3:25-26) or the Judean cities in general (Isa 32:13-14) in view.

There is an outcry (צְוָחָה, *sĕwāḥâ*) or lament in the streets over the lack of wine (הַיָּיִן, *hayyayin*), so someone is left to lament (v. 11), but all rejoicing has gone down (עָרְבָה, *ʿārĕbâ*) like the setting sun, and the mirth of the land has departed (גָּלָה, *gālâ*) like an exile. Only desolation remains (נִשְׁאַר, *nišʾar*) in the city, and the gate lies smashed in ruins (v. 12). As in v. 6, the use of the verb שָׁאַר (*šāʾar*), "to remain," recalls Isaiah's vocabulary. One should also note that the description of the ruined city gate is quite parallel to the imagery in Isa 3:26.

Verse 13 with its future tense, "for thus it will be" (כִּי כֹה יִהְיֶה, *kî kōh yihyeh*), suddenly reveals that the situation described above is not a present situation but the result of a still future judgment—or, perhaps a present judgment about a future event. If the perfects in vv. 4-12 are prophetic perfects, as they seem to be, perhaps our author is playing with his audience. That is, vv. 4-12 look at first as if they describe a past event, but the clear future form in v. 13 suddenly forces the audience to realize that the earlier verses were describing a future, in prophetic perfects—a future, however, that being in prophetic perfects has already been decided upon and fixed. This odd shift may also indicate that, while vv. 4-12 may go back to an earlier oracle against Judah or Israel only

lightly edited, the following verses, even if dependent in places on earlier material, have been far more thoroughly reworked. One cannot render the phrase "for thus he will be" with perhaps Ephraim as the assumed antecedent, for in the present text there is no extant masculine singular antecedent. The expression "like the shaking of an olive tree" (כְּנֹקֶף זַיִת, *kĕnōqep zayit*) refers either to the process of beating or shaking an olive tree to harvest the last remaining olives or to the few olives so recovered, and the expression "like the gleanings" (כְּעוֹלֵלֹת, *kĕʿôlēlōt*) "when the vintage is over" (אִם־כָּלָה בָצִיר, *ʾim-kālâ bāṣîr*) refers to the last few grapes gathered after the main harvest was finished. It is an agricultural metaphor for the scarcity of human population based on Isaiah's earlier oracle against Ephraim in Isa 17:5-6. Here, however, this takes place in the midst of the earth (בְּקֶרֶב הָאָרֶץ, *bĕqereb hāʾāreṣ*), in the middle of the peoples (בְּתוֹךְ הָעַמִּים, *bĕtôk hāʿammîm*), implying that this is a worldwide judgment resulting in a reduction of the population of all peoples in the whole world, not just that of Ephraim or Judah.

Apparently this small remnant of the peoples of the world (vv. 6, 13)—there is no other antecedent for הֵמָּה (*hēmmâ*, "they")—will raise their voice, exult in the majesty of Yahweh, and shout from the sea or west (v. 14). For this reason they honor Yahweh in the east, and the name of Yahweh the God of Israel in the coastlands of the sea (v. 15). The whole world from the sunrise in the east to the coastlands of the Mediterranean in the west join in this praise of the God of Israel. See the textual notes for the justification of this understanding of the text. The logic behind the use of the expression עַל־כֵּן (*ʿal-kēn*), "for this reason, that is why," seems to be that the world's experience of God's worldwide judgment has persuaded the surviving remnant that Yahweh is indeed the God of the whole world. The prophet and his audience hear songs of praise coming from the end of the earth proclaiming splendor or glory to the righteous one. The referent of צַדִּיק (*saddîq*), "the righteous one," is a bit ambiguous. In the context of hymns of praise, it is natural to take it as referring to Yahweh, who is being praised not just for his awesome judgment but for his righteous judgment (Pss 7:10, 12; 11:7; 119:37; 129:4; 145:17). Nonetheless, the LXX with its Ἐλπὶς τῷ εὐσεβε ("Hope for the godly one") and the Targum with its plural ("the righteous ones") seem to take the term as referring to God's faithful human servant or servants. Isaiah 26:2, 7 apply the term to humans, which is the common usage in First Isaiah (3:10; 5:23; 29:21) and attested in Second and Third Isaiah (41:26[?]; 49:24; 53:11; 57:1; 60:21), though Second Isaiah also uses it of God (45:21). If one assumed our passage was as late as Second Isaiah, one might take this as the nations' praise of God's servant whose suffering made many righteous (see Isa 52:13–53:1, 11).

This praise to the righteous one, however, provokes a bitter response from the speaking voice, who laments, saying, "Woe is me!" The lament is provoked because those behaving treacherously are still behaving treacherously בֹּגְדִים בָּגָדוּ (bōgĕdîm bāgādû), and the speaker repeats his lament with an additional word for emphasis וּבֶגֶד בּוֹגְדִים בָּגָדוּ (ûbeged bôgĕdîm bāgādû), "and with treachery the treacherous are behaving treacherously." The motif of the treacherous one is taken from Isa 21:2 and 33:1 and suggests that the prophet, speaking for his people Israel, is complaining about continuing depredations of foreign powers. Introducing this lament, however, is a repeated expression whose meaning is still debated: "And I said, 'Rāzî to me! Rāzî to me!'" (רָזִי־לִי רָזִי־לִי, rāzî-lî rāzî-lî). Some take the disputed word as Aramaic rāz, "secret," which would result in a translation like, "I have a secret! I have a secret!" It is probably preferable to see the word as a nominal form רָזִי (rāzî), "diminution, vanishing," derived from רָזָה (rāzâ), "grow thin, waste away"; see Isa 10:16; 17:4. The sense would then be, "There is diminution to me!," that is, "I waste away! I waste away!" This could refer to the prophet's depression at the situation he sees, but since he speaks for his people and since the uses of the verb and related noun in 10:16 and 17:4 refer originally to the diminution of Ephraim and its army, it is probable that the cry also complains about the continuing decimating of his people by the depredations of the foreign enemy who continues his treacherous ways.

But the lament turns quickly to an announcement of judgment in direct address to those who continue to behave treacherously. Terror, pit, and snare are about to fall upon you, O inhabitant of the earth! (v. 17). There is no escaping this judgment (v. 18). Whoever flees from the sound of the terror will fall into the pit, and whoever climbs out of the pit will be caught in the snare. For other examples of this prophetic motif of the inescapability of divine judgment, see Amos 5:19; 9:1-4. One cannot escape the judgment announced in our passage, because it is a universal judgment. The windows or sluice gates of heaven are opened (אֲרֻבּוֹת מִמָּרוֹם נִפְתָּחוּ, ʾărubbôt mimmārôm niptāḥû) and the foundations of the earth are shaken. This is the language of the return to primeval chaos, as in the time of the universal flood, when the fountains of the great deep burst forth and the windows of the heavens were opened (וַאֲרֻבֹּת הַשָּׁמַיִם נִפְתָּחוּ, waʾărubbôt haššāmayim niptāḥû) to flood the living space of the whole world (Gen 6:11). Cf. the similar picture of judgment as a return to chaos in Jer 4:23-26.

In this cataclysmic judgment, the earth is utterly broken (רֹעָה הִתְרֹעֲעָה, rōʿâ hitrōʿăʿâ), split asunder (פּוֹר הִתְפּוֹרְרָה, pôr hitpôrĕrâ), and violently shaken (מוֹט הִתְמוֹטְטָה, môṭ hitmôṭĕṭâ, v. 19). The earth will stagger like the drunk man, and it will sway like a flimsy hut in a strong wind (v. 20). Again the imagery seems to be taken from the experience of a severe earthquake. The reason for this judgment is that the earth's transgression or rebellion (פִּשְׁעָה, pišʿāh) lies heavy upon it, and it will fall never to rise again (וְנָפְלָה וְלֹא־תֹסִיף קוּם, wĕnāpĕlâ wĕlōʾ-tōsîp qûm). Note that almost the identical idiom is used for the permanent fall of Virgin Israel in Amos 5:2, where the language refers to the Assyrian destruction and depopulation of Israel.

On that day Yahweh will punish the host of heaven (צְבָא הַמָּרוֹם, ṣĕbāʾ hammārôm) in heaven (בַּמָּרוֹם, bammārôm) and the kings of the earth (מַלְכֵי הָאֲדָמָה, malkê hāʾădāmâ) on the earth (עַל־הָאֲדָמָה, ʿal-hāʾădāmâ, v. 21). The host of heaven, normally expressed as כָּל־צְבָא הַשָּׁמַיִם (kol-ṣĕbāʾ haššāmayim, "all the host of heaven") refers to the sun, moon, stars, and planets, which Yahweh created (Gen 2:1; Isa 40:26; 45:12), but which were also seen as divine beings subservient to Yahweh, a part of his divine council (1 Kgs 22:19), and members of his heavenly army (see Judg 5:20). This notion of Yahweh as the creator and leader of the heavenly host lies behind the very popular epithet of Yahweh, יהוה צְבָאוֹת (YHWH ṣĕbāʾôt, "Yahweh of Hosts"). Nonetheless, Israel was sometimes tempted to worship the host of heaven (Deut 4:19; 17:3), and, as objects of worship, they were considered illegitimate foreign gods (2 Kgs 17:16; 21:3, 5; 23:4-5). Here, as in Isa 34:2, 4, this heavenly host is seen as the rebellious divine powers in heaven opposed to Yahweh and supporting the foreign earthly armies that were oppressing God's people. Thus, on the heavenly plane Yahweh must punish them, while on the earthly plane God must punish their human agents.

These defeated enemies, presumably both the heavenly and the earthly, will be gathered together like prisoners—the singular אָסִיר (ʾassîr) is used but with a collective sense—in a pit and locked up in a dungeon, where they will wait a long time before receiving their punishment (v. 22). For the notion of judging and punishing other gods, see Psalm 82, especially vv. 6-7. Cf. also the New Testament adaptation of this motif in Revelation, where Satan is imprisoned in the bottomless pit for a thousand years before his final punishment with his human followers (Rev 20:1-10).

This motif of war in heaven explains why the moon (הַלְּבָנָה, hallĕbānâ, lit., "the white one," that is, "the full moon") will be abashed and the sun (הַחַמָּה, haḥammâ, "the hot one, the sun") will be ashamed (v. 23). They were among the hostile host of divine beings in heaven vanquished by Yahweh. Just as in Gen 1:14-18, where the writer refers to the sun and moon as the big light and the little light as a way of demythologizing these former divine beings and belittling them as mere created objects, so our writer here avoids their normal names שֶׁמֶשׁ (šemeš, "sun") and יָרֵחַ (yārēaḥ, "moon"), thereby undercutting any residual religious awe still associated with these designations, which were proper divine names in the surrounding cultures, and sometimes even in Israel itself (Deut 4:19; 2 Kgs 23:5; Jer 8:2). The unusual names used for the moon and sun here may also suggest a change in color, that is, "going pale" and "blushing," as signs of the embarrassment of these heavenly bodies. They are abashed and ashamed because they have been defeated, and now Yahweh of Hosts (יהוה צְבָאוֹת, YHWH ṣĕbāʾôt)—the actual creator and true leader of the host of heaven—reigns openly as king on Mount Zion and in Jerusalem, and before his elders there will be glory. The last statement is a bit obscure. It is unclear whether "elders" refers to angelic beings, or more likely, in my opinion, the elders of Yahweh's redeemed human community. The glory before them, however, probably refers to the manifest glory of his chosen dwelling place in Zion (cf. Isa 4:5-6; 11:10).

Bibliography

Beek, M. A., "Ein Erdbeben wird zum prophetischen Erleben," *ArOr* 17 (1949) 31–40.

Ben David, Y., "Ugaritic Parallels to Isa 24:18-19" (in Hebrew), *Leš* 45 (1980) 56–59.

Charles, N. J., "A Prophetic (Fore) Word: 'A Curse Devouring the Earth' (Isa 24:6)," in Norman C. Habel, ed., *The Earth Story in the Psalms and the Prophets* (Earth Bible 4; Sheffield: Sheffield Academic Press, 2001) 123–28.

Chilton, Bruce D., *The Glory of Israel: The Theology and Provenience of the Isaiah Targum* (JSOTSup 23; Sheffield: JSOT Press, 1983) 49–50.

De Groot, J., "Alternatieflezingen in Jesaja 24," *NThSt* 22 (1939) 153–58.

Domínguez, N., "Vaticinios sobre el fin del mundo," *CTom* 51 (1935) 125–46.

Floss, J. P., "Die Wortstellung des Konjugationssystems in Jes 24: Ein Beitrag zur Formkritik poetischer Texte im Alten Testament," in Heinz-Josef Fabry, ed., *Bausteine biblischer Theologie: Festgabe für G. Johannes Botterweck zum 60. Geburtstag* (BBB 50; Cologne: Hanstein, 1977) 227–44.

Hayes, K. M., "'The Earth Mourns': Earth as Actor in a Prophetic Metaphor" (PhD diss., Catholic University of America, 1997).

Irwin, W. H., "The Punctuation of Isaiah 24:14-16*a* and 25:4-5," *CBQ* 46 (1984) 215–22.

Johnson, D. G., *From Chaos to Restoration: An Integrative Reading of Isaiah 24–27* (JSOTSup 61; Sheffield: JSOT Press, 1988).

Lewis, D. J., "A Rhetorical Critical Analysis of Isaiah 24–27" (Diss., Southern Baptist Theological Seminary, 1985).

Loete, J., "A Premature Hymn of Praise: The Meaning and Function of Isaiah 24:14-16*c* in Its Present Context," in H. J. Bosman, H. van Grol, et al., eds., *Studies in Isaiah 24–27: The Isaiah Workshop–de Jesaja Werkplaats* (OtSt 43; Leiden: Brill, 2000) 22–28.

Millar, W. R., "Isaiah Book of (Isaiah 24-27)," *ABD* 3:488–90.

Nevas, J. C. M., "A Teologia da Traducao Grega dos Setenta no Libro de Isias" (Diss., Lisbon, 1973).

Niehaus, J., "*raz-pešar* in Isaiah XXIV," *VT* 31 (1981) 376–78.

Noegel, S. B., "Dialect and Politics in Isaiah 24–27," *AcOr* 12 (1994) 177–92.

Oded, Bustenay, *Mass Deportations and Deportees in the Neo-Assyrian Empire* (Wiesbaden: Reichert, 1979).

Pagan, S., "Apocalyptic Poetry: Isaiah 24–27," *BT* 43 (1992) 314–25.

Polaski, D. C., "Reflections on a Mosaic Covenant: The Eternal Covenant (Isaiah 24) and Intertextuality," *JSOT* 7 (1998) 55–73.

Redditt, Paul L., "Once Again, the City in Isaiah 24–27," *HAR* 10 (1987) 317–35.

Sasson, Jack M., "The Worship of the Golden Calf," in Harry A. Hoffner, ed., *Orient and Occident: Essays Presented to Cyrus H. Gordon on the Occasion of His Sixty-Fifth Birthday* (AOAT 22; Kevelaer: Butzon & Bercker; Neukirchen-Vluyn: Neukirchener Verlag, 1973) 151–59.

Sawyer, John F. A., "The Role of Jewish Studies in Biblical Semantics," in H. L. J. Vanstiphout et al., eds., *Scripta Signa Vocis: Studies about Scripts, Scriptures, Scribes, and Languages in the Near East, Presented to J. H. Hospers by His Pupils, Colleagues, and Friends* (Groningen: Egbert Forsten, 1986) 201–8.

——, "'My Secret Is with Me' (Isaiah 24:16): Some Semantic Links between Isaiah 24–27 and Daniel," in A. Graeme Auld, ed., *Understanding Poets and Prophets: Essays in Honour of George Wishart Anderson* (JSOTSup 152; Sheffield: JSOT Press, 1993) 307–17.

Sweeney, Marvin A., "Textual Citations in Isaiah 24–27: Toward an Understanding of the Redactional Function of Chapters 24–27 in the Book of Isaiah," *JBL* 107 (1988) 39–52.

Todd, Virgil H., "Apocalyptic Eschatology," *Cumberland Seminarian* 52 (1987) 36–49.

Towner, W. Sibley, "Tribulation and Peace: The Fate of Shalom in Jewish Apocalyptic," *HBT* 6 (1984) 1–26.

Waard, Jan de, "The Interim and Final HOTTP Reports and the Translator: A Preliminary Investigation," in Gerard J. Norton and Stephen Pisano, eds., *Tradition of the Text: Studies Offered to Dominique Barthélemy in Celebration of His 70th Birthday* (OBO 109; Freiburg: Universitätsverlag; Göttingen: Vandenhoeck & Ruprecht, 1991) 277–84.

Willis, Timothy M., "Yahweh's Elders (Isa 24,23): Senior Officials of the Divine Court," *ZAW* 103 (1991) 375–85.

Yee, Gale A., "The Anatomy of Biblical Parody: The Dirge Form in 2 Samuel 1 and Isaiah 14," *CBQ* 50 (1988) 565–86.

25

1/   Yahweh, you are my God,[a]
    I will exalt you, I will praise your name,[b]
    For you have performed[c] marvels,
    Plans[d] made of old in steadfast faithfulness.[e]

2/   For you have turned[f] the city[g] to a stone heap,
    The fortified city to a pile of ruins,[g]
    The palace of strangers into rubble,[h]
    So that it will not[i] be rebuilt for ever.

3/   That is why strong peoples[j] will honor you,
    Cities of violent nations will fear you.

4/   For you have been[k] a refuge to the poor,
    A refuge to the needy in his affliction,
    A shelter[l] from the rainstorm,
    A shade from the heat.[m]
    When the wind of the violent
    was like a cold[n] rainstorm,

5/   The roar of strangers
    Like heat[o] in a dry land,[p]
    You suppressed the heat[q] with the shade of a cloud;
    The song[r] of the violent was vanquished.[s]

6/   And Yahweh of Hosts will make for all[t] peoples on this mountain
    A feast of rich foods, a feast of aged wines,
    Rich foods full of marrow, filtered[u] aged wines.[v]

7/   And he will swallow[w] on this mountain
    The face[x] of the shroud that is wrapped[y]
    Upon all[z] peoples,
    And the covering that is woven
    Upon all[z] nations.*[a]

8/   He will swallow up death for ever,*[b]
    And my Lord*[c] Yahweh will wipe away tears
    From upon every*[d] face,
    And he will remove the reproach of his people
    From upon the whole*[d] earth,
    For Yahweh has spoken.

9/   And one will say*[e] in that day,
    "Behold, this is our God;*[f]
    We waited for him, and he saved us.
    This is Yahweh,*[g] we waited for him;
    Let us rejoice and exult*[h] in his salvation!"*[i]

10/   For the hand of Yahweh*[j] will rest*[k] upon this mountain,
    But Moab will be trodden down*[l] in its place*[m]
    As straw is trodden down in dung.*[n]

11/   And he will spread his hands in its midst
    As the swimmer*[o] spreads*[p] (them) to swim;
    And he will sink his pride with the movements of his hands.

12/   And the high fortification of your walls*[q]
    He will throw down,*[r] humble, bring down*[s] to earth,
    To the very dust.

Textual Notes

a   MT אֱלֹהַי (ʾĕlōhay), "my God"; 1QIsaᵃ אלוהי (ʾĕlôhay).

b   MT, 1QIsaᵃ שִׁמְךָ (šimkā), "your name"; 4QIsaᶜ את שמכה (ʾet šimkâ), "your name."

c   MT עָשִׂיתָ (ʿāśîtā), "you performed"; 1QIsaᵃ עשיתה (ʿāśîtâ).

d   MT עֵצוֹת (ʿēṣôt), "plans"; 1QIsaᵃ אצית (ʾṣyt) involves a confusion of *yod* for *waw*, and a hearing error of *aleph* for *ayin* due to the loss of phonetic distinction between these two consonants in the late period.

e   LXX, Vg., and Syr. take final אֹמֶן (ʾomen), "steadfastness" (but used here adverbially), as the formula for concluding a prayer.

f   MT שַׂמְתָּ (śamtā), "you have placed, turned"; 1QIsaᵃ שמתה (śamtâ).

g   MT, 1QIsaᵃ מֵעִיר (mēʿîr), "from being a city," but none of the versions reflects the preposition מִן (min), "from." Read עיר (ʿîr),

319

"city," without the prefixed *mem*. The -*m* is either an enclitic *mem* that originally was at the end of the preceding verb—*śamtā-m*—or it is a simple error introduced from the following *mᵉʿyr* in the verse.

h MT, 1QIsaᵃ מֵעִיר (*mēʿîr*), "from being a city"; with the exception of LXX, which simply omits the phrase, all the versions reflect the Hebrew in this second occurrence of the expression. The phrase is attested in Isa 17:1, and Vg. gives a similar rendering of the expression here: *ut non sit civitas*, "that it should not be a city." Two main corrections have been suggested. One is to read מְעִי (*mᵉʿî*), analyzing it as a *mem*-prefix noun synonymous with ʿî, "ruin" (see Isa 17:1); the other is to read מֹעַר (*muʿār*), "is destroyed," the *hophal* participle of ערר (so J. A. Emerton, "A Textual Problem in Isaiah 25:2," *ZAW* 89 [1977] 64–73).

i MT לֹא (*lōʾ*), "not"; 1QIsaᵃ לוא (*lôʾ*).

j MT עַם־עָז (*ʿam-ʿāz*), "strong peoples"—both forms are singular, but the plural verb shows that the form is being used as a plural; 1QIsaᵃ עז עם, so also the versions apart from LXX. LXX has ὁ λαὸς ὁ πτωχός, "the poor people."

k MT כִּי־הָיִיתָ (*kî-hāyîtā*), "for you have been"; 1QIsaᵃ כי היתה (*kî hāyîtâ*).

l MT מַחְסֶה (*maḥsê*), "a shelter"; 1QIsaᵃ originally had ומחסה (*ûmaḥsê*), "and a shelter," but then erased the ו, "and."

m MT מֵחֹרֶב (*mēḥōreb*), "from the heat"; 1QIsaᵃ מחורב (*mēḥôreb*).

n Reading קוֹר (*qōr*), "cold," for MT and 1QIsaᵃ קיר (*qîr*), "wall." Vg., Syr., and Tg. support MT. LXX's translation is too loose to be helpful: ἐγένου γὰρ πάσῃ πόλει ταπεινῇ βοηθὸς καὶ τοῖς ἀθυμήσασιν διὰ ἔνδειαν σκέπη, καὶ ἀπὸ ἀνθρώπων πονηρῶν ῥύσῃ αὐτούς, σκέπη διψώντων καὶ πνεῦμα ἀνθρώπων ἀδικουμένων, "for you were a help to every humble city and a shelter to those dispirited because of poverty, you will deliver them from evil men, a shelter for the thirsty and breath for oppressed men."

o MT כְּחֹרֶב (*kᵉḥōreb*), "as heat"; 1QIsaᵃ כחורב (*kᵉḥôreb*).

p LXX misunderstood MT and 1QIsaᵃ בְּצָיוֹן (*bᵉṣāyôn*), "on dry land," as *bᵉṣîyôn*, "in Zion." One should consider the possibility, however, that the prophet was intentionally playing on the similarity in sound (see the commentary).

q MT and 1QIsaᵃ each have the same orthography as in note o, except that the preposition is omitted.

r Vg. misunderstood זְמִיר (*zᵉmîr*), "song, singing," as "branch" (זָמִיר II, "trimming").

s MT's *qal* is possible, but *BHS* corrects to the *niphal*, based on Syr. *ntmkk*, and others like Marti (p. 189) emend to the *hiphil*, "he humbles."

t MT לְכָל (*lᵉkol*), "for all"; 1QIsaᵃ לכול.

u MT מְזֻקָּקִים (*mᵉzuqqāqîm*), "filtered, purified,"; 1QIsaᵃ מזוקקים.

v For the last two lines, LXX has the loose translation πίονται εὐφροσύνην, πίονται οἶνον, χρίσονται μύρον, "they will drink joy, they will drink wine, they will anoint themselves with perfume."

w MT, 1QIsaᵃ וּבִלַּע (*ûbillaʿ*), "and he will swallow"; Vg. "and he will cast headlong"; Syr. and Tg. render with the passive; LXX has ἐν τῷ ὄρει τούτῳ παράδος ταῦτα πάντα τοῖς ἔθνεσιν, "and in this mountain deliver [sing. imperative] all these to the nations."

x MT פְּנֵי־הַלּוֹט (*pᵉnê-hallôṭ*), "the face of the shroud"; 1QIsaᵃ פנו הלוט; Syr., "the face of the ruler"; Tg., "the face of the great one"; Vg., "the face of the chain/bond." The expression seems odd, and one wonders if פְּנֵי (*pᵉnê*) has been misplaced. JPS's translation seems to imply an emendation to הַלּוֹט הַלּוֹט עַל־פְּנֵי־כָל־הָעַמִּים (*hallôṭ hallôṭ ʿal-pᵉnê-kol-hāʿammîm*), "the shroud that is drawn over the faces of all the peoples."

y MT's *qal* participle הַלּוֹט (*hallôṭ*), "that covers," should probably be repointed to the *qal* passive participle הַלּוּט (*hallûṭ*), "that is drawn over."

z MT כָּל (*kol*), "all"; 1QIsaᵃ כול.

*a MT הַגּוֹיִם (*haggôyīm*), "the nations"; 1QIsaᵃ הגואים. For the second half of the verse, LXX has only ἡ γὰρ βουλὴ αὕτη ἐπὶ πάντα τὰ ἔθνη, "for this counsel is against all the nations."

*b MT, 1QIsaᵃ בִּלַּע הַמָּוֶת לָנֶצַח (*billaʿ hammāwet lāneṣaḥ*), "he will swallow death for ever"; Vg., "he will cast down death for ever"; Syr., "and death will be swallowed up in victory for ever"; Tg., "they will forget death forever"; LXX κατέπιεν ὁ θάνατος ἰσχύσας, "death having prevailed swallowed (them)." The use of the simple perfect form in this line for the future, followed by the converted perfect in the next line, and the imperfect in the following line is either a case of the prophetic perfect or a reflection of the same freedom found in archaic poetry.

*c MT, 1QIsaᵃ אֲדֹנָי יְהוָה (*ʾădōnāy YHWH*), "my Lord Yahweh"; 1QIsaᵃ אדוני יהוה; LXX has only ὁ θεός, "God"; Vg. *Dominus Deus*, "Lord God"; Syr., "the Lord God Almighty"; Tg. יוי אֱלֹהִים (*YWY ʾᵉlōhîm*), "Yahweh God."

*d See note z above.

*e MT וְאָמַר (*wᵉʾāmar*), "and he/one will say," traces of 4QIsaᶜ, Vg., Tg.; 1QIsaᵃ ואמרת (*wᵉʾāmartā*), "and you will say," Syr.; LXX, "they will say."

*f MT אֱלֹהֵינוּ זֶה (*ʾᵉlōhênû zeh*), "this is our God," LXX, Vg., Tg.; 1QIsaᵃ יהוה אלוהינו זה, "this is Yahweh our God," Syr.

*g MT, 1QIsaᵃ זֶה יְהוָה (*zeh YHWH*), "this is Yahweh," Vg., Tg.; LXX omits and shortens the verse; Syr., "this is the Lord our God."

*h MT, 1QIsaᵃ וְנִשְׂמְחָה (*wᵉniśmᵉḥâ*), "and let us rejoice"; 1QIsaᵃ נשמח.

*i MT, 1QIsaᵃ בִּישׁוּעָתוֹ (*bîšûʿātô*), "in his salvation," Vg., Syr., Tg.; LXX, "our salvation."

*j MT, 1QIsaᵃ יַד־יְהוָה (*yad-YHWH*), "the hand of Yahweh," 1QIsaᵃ, Vg., Syr., Tg.; LXX has only ὁ θεὸς, "God," omitting the word "hand."

*k MT תָּנוּחַ (*tānûaḥ*), "shall rest," 1QIsaᵃ, Vg., Syr., Tg.; LXX apparently reads the *hiphil*, ὅτι ἀνάπαυσιν δώσει, "because *God* will give rest."

*l MT וְנָדֹשׁ (*wᵉnādōš*), "and *Moab* will be trodden down"; 1QIsaᵃ ונדש.

*m MT, 1QIsaᵃ תַּחְתָּיו (*taḥtāyw*), "in its/his [Moab's] place"; Tg., "in their place"; LXX does not translate; Vg. has *sub eo*, "under him." The masculine singular suffix should refer back to Moab, not God.

*n Reading with the *qᵉrēʾ* of MT בְּמוֹ מַדְמֵנָה (*bᵉmô madmēnâ*), "in a dungheap"; *kᵉtîb*, 1QIsaᵃ בְּמֵי מַדְמֵנָה (*bᵉmê madmēnâ*), "in the water of a dungheap"; LXX ἐν ἁμάξαις, "with wagons"; Vg., "with a cart"; Syr., "with a threshing sled"; Tg., "in the mud."

*o MT הַשֹּׂחֶה (*haśśōḥê*), "the swimmer"; 1QIsaᵃ השוחה.

*p MT יְפָרֵשׂ (yĕpārēś), "he spreads"; 1QIsaᵃ יפרש, but 4QIsaᶜ has the *qal* יפרוש. LXX makes little sense of this verse, apparently assuming that God is the subject of all the verbs in the passage: καὶ ἀνήσει τὰς χεῖρας αὐτοῦ, ὃν τρόπον καὶ αὐτὸς ἐταπείνωσεν τοῦ ἀπολέσαι, καὶ ταπεινώσει τὴν ὕβριν αὐτοῦ ἐφ᾽ ἃ τὰς χεῖρας ἐπέβαλεν, "and he will send forth his hands as he himself brought him low to destroy him, and he will bring low his pride, upon which he cast the hands."

*q MT חוֹמֹתֶיךָ (ḥômōtêkā), "your walls"; 1QIsaᵃ חומותיך, but 4QIsaᶜ חומותי[כה].

*r MT, 4QIsaᶜ הֵשַׁח (hēšaḥ), "he will throw down"; 1QIsaᵃ השח.

*s MT, 4QIsaᶜ הִגִּיעַ (higgîaᶜ), "he will bring down to"; 1QIsaᵃ יגיע (yaggîaᶜ), "he will bring down to."

Commentary

The text opens with an individual prayer or hymn of praise to God, "Yahweh you are my God, I will exalt you, I will praise your name!" In typical hymnic fashion, then, the following כִּי (kî), "because, for," introduces both the reason for and the content of the praise. In God's apparently recent actions, God has performed marvelous deeds (פֶּלֶא, pele᾽), executing plans made long ago (עֵצוֹת מֵרָחֹק, ᶜēṣôt mērāḥôq) in steadfast faithfulness (אֱמוּנָה אֹמֶן, ᾽ĕmûnâ ᾽ōmen). Those recent actions will be spelled out in the the verses that follow, beginning in v. 2. In the context of the present collection of the Isaiah Apocalypse one might think of the hymn as a natural response to the worldwide judgment described in the preceding chapter, but what follows in vv. 2-5 does not reflect quite the same picture as the judgment in chap. 24, and it is not at all certain that chap. 24 was written as early as the material in chap. 25. The theme of God's marvelous deeds is taken from First Isaiah (28:29; 29:14; cf. 9:5), where it is part of the same complex of ideas as God's work (מַעֲשֶׂה, maᶜăśeh), labor (עֲבֹדָה, ᶜăbōdâ), deed (פֹּעַל, pōᶜal), and plan (עֵצָה, ᶜēṣâ), often set in opposition to the plans or work of God's human adversaries (Isa 5:12, 19; 8:10; 10:7, 12; 14:24-27; 19:3, 11-12, 14-15, 17; 23:8-9; 28:21, 28; 29:15; 30:1). Following this older tradition, our writer describes God's plans (עֵצוֹת, ᶜēṣôt) as ancient, as being made a long time ago (מֵרָחֹק, mērāḥôq, "from a remote time"). The final expression (אֱמוּנָה אֹמֶן, ᾽ĕmûnâ ᾽ōmen) is grammatically a bit ambiguous. I take it as an adverbial accusative modifying God's behavior, in steadfast faithfulness carrying out his plans made long ago, even if to his people the delay has seemed interminable. Others take it almost as an interrupted construct chain modifying "plans," "plans made of old, of steadfast faithfulness" (see Wildberger, 2:955; Clements, 207). Ultimately the difference is quite slight.

The second כִּי (kî), "because, for," at the beginning of v. 2, explains, still addressing Yahweh in the second person, what God's marvelous deeds mentioned in v. 1 actually were. The statement of praise to Yahweh—"For you turned the city into a stone heap, the fortified city into a pile of ruins, the palace of strangers into rubble, so that it would never be rebuilt"—is both tantalizingly specific, yet frustratingly vague. The prophet is apparently celebrating the total destruction of an important city that was both fortified and the site of a palace of foreigners (אַרְמוֹן זָרִים, ᾽armôn zārîm), probably implying that the city itself was foreign, not a Judean or Israelite city. Yet the prophet does not name the city, which would have provided a firmer historical-geographical framework that would have helped place this material in a more specific historical context. The failure to name the city leaves open the possibility that the prophet is speaking of oppressive foreign cities in general, a possibility LXX seems to adopt when it reads the first two occurrences of the different words for city, both in the singular in Hebrew (עִיר, ᶜîr; קִרְיָה, qiryâ), as plurals, "cities." Nonetheless, if the prophet is speaking of the actual total destruction of a particular foreign city, or even a group of foreign cities, regarded as representative of Israel's oppressor, for the possible periods in which this material could have been written, the most likely candidate would be Nineveh (612 BCE) or Aššur (614 BCE), or, more generally, the fortified cities of Assyria's heartland (615–610 BCE). Babylon was not destroyed when it was captured by the Persians (539 BCE), and no other candidates seem very likely.

Verse 3 confesses to Yahweh that Yahweh's destruction of the fortified city is the reason why strong peoples (עַם־עָז, ᶜam-ᶜāz) and cities of violent nations (קִרְיַת גּוֹיִם עָרִיצִים, qiryat gôyîm ᶜārîṣîm) will honor and fear Yahweh. The governing noun in both phrases is singular, but since each takes a plural verb, they function as collective plurals. If one identifies the destroyed city as Aššur or

Nineveh, or even as a collective describing the destruction of all the fortified cities of the Assyrian heartland in the years 615–610 BCE, then the strong peoples and the cities of violent nations could be understood as the Medes and Babylonians and their allies. The description of the Medes in Isa 13:17-18 and that of the Babylonians in Hab 1:6-7, though not identical to the language used here, are comparable in meaning. Moreover, Ezekiel uses the expression עָרִיצֵי גוֹיִם (ʿarîṣê gôyīm, "the most terrible/violent of the nations") some four times to refer to Nebuchadnezzar's Babylonians (Ezek 28:7; 30:11; 31:12; 32:11-12). The prophet assumes that these foreign powers will recognize that their victory over Assyria was the gift of Yahweh and emblematic of his universal majesty, just as Second Isaiah assumes that Cyrus will come to realize that it was Yahweh who led him to victory over his enemies (Isa 44:28–45:7).

It is not just that Yahweh has permanently overthrown the powerful fortified city or cities of the enemy. "For (כִּי, kî) in so doing," the prophet says, "You, Yahweh, have proven to be a refuge to the poor and needy in their affliction, a shelter from the rainstorm (זֶרֶם, zerem) and a shade from the heat" (v. 4). The language of Yahweh as a refuge and shelter takes up a motif of the Zion tradition dear to Isaiah, the notion that the poor of Yahweh's people take refuge in Zion, which God has founded, in which he dwells, and which he will protect (see Isa 4:6; 8:18; 14:32; 18:4-7; 28:16; 29:8; 30:27-33; 31:5-9; 33:10-24). The second כִּי (kî) in v. 4 serves as a temporal conjunction to introduce two parallel temporal clauses against the MT's sentence division, accentuation, and the later verse division: "(v. 4) When the wind/blast of the violent was like a cold rainstorm, (v. 5) The roar of strangers like heat in a dry land. . . ." The word order of the translation is for clarity in English, but the poetic structure in Hebrew is more complicated and artistic:

When the wind/blast of the violent was like a cold rainstorm,
(When) like heat in a dry land was the roar of strangers . . .

This is followed by the parallel main clauses:

You suppressed the heat with the shade of a cloud,
The song of the violent was vanquished.

The metaphor of the enemy as a cold rainstorm (זֶרֶם קוֹר, zerem qôr) plays on a common motif in Isaiah, where the Assyrians are compared to an overflowing flood that would reach up to Judah's neck (8:7-8) or a violent rainstorm that would wash away the flimsy foundations of Judah and Jerusalem's false shelter in Egypt (28:2, 15, 17-19). It is also possible that the choice of בְּצָיוֹן (bĕṣāyôn, "in a dry land") was intended to evoke the similar-sounding בְּצִיּוֹן (bĕṣîyôn, "in Zion")—"when the roar of strangers was like heat in Zion"—suggesting the siege of Jerusalem. In chap. 25 it is Yahweh's work to be a shelter from the rainstorm and a shade from the heat for the poor, but in 32:2 the same imagery is used to portray how the ideal human king of the future and his royal officials will share in this divine work.

In v. 6 the direct address ceases, and Yahweh is referred to in the third person, which might suggest the beginning of a new oracle, but the future promises of vv. 6-10a follow naturally after the preceding praise, so the transition creates no disturbing literary jolt. In the present literary context, if not in the original oral context, Yahweh's preceding defeat of the powerful city or cities of his enemy leads to the promise that Yahweh of Hosts will make a great banquet for all peoples, presumably all those peoples who had suffered under the oppression of Yahweh's recently defeated enemy. The site of that banquet is specified by the phrase בָּהָר הַזֶּה (bāhār hazzeh), "in or on this mountain," which is repeated three times in the immediate context (vv. 6, 7, 10). While the mountain is not named, the mention of Yahweh's people (עַמּוֹ, ʿammô, "his people," v. 8) makes it crystal clear that the reference is to Mount Zion in Jerusalem. The banquet on the mountain is presumably a covenant-type banquet on Yahweh's sacred dwelling place in which the peoples participate to acknowledge Yahweh's rule over them (see Exod 24:9-11; 1 Kgs 18:41-42; Zech 14:9, 16; Isa 55:1-3; and cf. Isa 2:2-4; 11:10). Moreover, it is a sumptuous banquet befitting the king of the world, a banquet of rich foods (שְׁמָנִים, šĕmānîm) and well-aged wine (שְׁמָרִים, šĕmārîm). In the biblical world, rich foods (שְׁמָנִים, šĕmānîm) were foods served with plenty of oil in contrast to dry rations, while well-aged wine (שְׁמָרִים, šĕmārîm) referred to wines allowed to age on their lees, but these rich oily foods are also richly seasoned with marrow (מְמֻחָיִם, mĕmuḥāyīm) and the well-aged wines are filtered clear (מְזֻקָּקִים, mĕzuqqāqîm) of sediments.

Apparently while Yahweh's human guests are eating God's rich food and drinking his fine wine, on this same mountain Yahweh himself will swallow down (וּבִלַּע, *ûbillaʿ*, "and he will swallow") the face of the shroud (פְּנֵי־הַלּוֹט, *pĕnê-hallôṭ*) that is wrapped (הַלּוֹט, *hallôṭ*) upon all peoples, and the covering (וְהַמַּסֵּכָה, *wĕhammassēkâ*) that is woven (הַנְּסוּכָה, *hannĕsûkâ*) over all nations (v. 7). It is tempting to identify the הַלּוֹט (*hallôṭ*) as the smaller burial cloth that one wrapped around the face of the corpse, and the הַמַּסֵּכָה (*hammassēkâ*) as the larger burial cloth that was wrapped around the body of the corpse (for the distinction, see John 11:44; 20:5-7), but neither noun occurs often enough in our small corpus of texts for this distinction to be certain. At this point, the meaning of God's act is not yet completely clear, needing the further explanation in v. 8 for total clarity, and even then the translators of the ancient versions did not catch the mythological allusion and so wildly mistranslated the verb בָּלַע (*bālaʿ*, "to swallow").

Verse 8 explains, "He will swallow up death [הַמָּוֶת, *hammāwet*] for ever." In Canaanite myth death, personified as the god Mot, is described as having a ravenous appetite, and he swallows the storm god and god of fertility, Baal Hadad: (2) [*špt . l a*]*rṣ . špt . l šmm* (3) [*yšt .*] *lšn . l kbkbm . yʿrb* (4) *bʿl . b kbdh . b ph . yrd*, "[One lip to e]arth, one lip to heaven, (Mot) [places] his tongue to the stars. Baal must enter his innards, he must go down into his mouth" (*KTU* 1.5 ii 2-4). A similar description of the insatiable appetite of Death is found in Hab 2:5, where the plundering Babylonians are compared to Death and Sheol: אֲשֶׁר הִרְחִיב כִּשְׁאוֹל נַפְשׁוֹ וְהוּא כַמָּוֶת וְלֹא יִשְׂבָּע (*ʾăšer hirḥîb kišʾôl napšô wĕhûʾ kammāwet wĕlōʾ yiśbāʿ*, "who opens his throat wide like Sheol, and like Death he is never satisfied"). Similar language is used of Sheol, a synonym for Death, in Isa 5:14: "Therefore Sheol opens her throat wide and gapes open her mouth without measure, and her [Jerusalem's] nobility and her multitude and her throng and those who exult in her go down." Cf. also Prov 30:15-16. The shocking reversal in our passage is that instead of Death swallowing up Yahweh as he swallowed up Baal, Yahweh turns the table on Mot and swallows him. The use of the same verb (בִּלַּע, *billaʿ*, "he swallows") in v. 8 for "swallowing Death" as was used in v. 7 for swallowing the shroud and covering strongly supports the idea that these terms refer to burial clothes. Both verses are celebrating Yahweh's termination of Death and the

sorrow humans experience in connection with it. Thus, v. 8 continues with the thought, "And my Lord Yahweh will wipe away the tears from upon every face." But the end of Death and its sorrows for all peoples is also joined with a particular blessing for God's own people, "And the reproach of his people [וְחֶרְפַּת עַמּוֹ, *wĕḥerpat ʿammô*] he will remove from upon the whole earth." Reproach and disgrace came upon Israel because of Israel's rebellion against Yahweh and the ensuing judgment that left Israel a despised and reviled community in the larger world (Isa 4:1; 30:5; 47:3; 51:7; 54:4; Jer 23:40; 24:9; 29:18; 42:18; 44:8). The promise is for new life and a restoration of Israel's dignity among the nations, as well as for new life for the rest of the peoples of the world. Moreover, this outcome is certain, "for Yahweh has spoken."

In that day, when Yahweh has set this banquet and saved his people, it will be common for members of his people to say, "This is our God, we waited for him [קִוִּינוּ לוֹ, *qiwwînû lô*] and he saved us; this is Yahweh, we waited for him, let us be glad and rejoice in his salvation [בִּישׁוּעָתוֹ, *bîšûʿātô*]" (v. 9). While not using the same vocabulary, the confession and admonition pick up the note of praise found in v. 1. Isaiah spoke personally of "waiting" for God (8:17), and in 33:2 the community of Judah centered in Jerusalem implored God on the basis of their "waiting for him" to see his "salvation": "Yahweh be gracious to us, for you we wait [לְךָ קִוִּינוּ, *lĕkā qiwwînû*]; be our support in the morning, even our salvation [יְשׁוּעָתֵנוּ, *yĕšûʿātēnû*] in the time of stress." It is as though members of the community will confess "in that day" the fulfillment of the earlier supplications of the community.

The fulfillment will come, because Yahweh's hand will rest on this mountain (v. 10a). In Isaiah, the hand of Yahweh is usually the instrument of Yahweh's judgment (1:25; 5:12, 25; 9:11, 16, 20; 10:4, 5; 19:16; 23:11; 31:3), but sometimes that judgment, because directed against others, is a positive thing for Israel or Judah (11:11, 15; 14:26-27; 26:11). The usage here is different, in that the gesture seems to be one of protection. The closest semantic parallels may be in Isa 49:2 and 51:16, where Yahweh protects his servant by hiding him (הֶחְבִּיאָנִי, *heḥbîʾānî*, "he hid me"; כִּסִּיתִיךָ, *kissîtîkā*, "I have hidden you") in the shadow of his hand (בְּצֵל יָדוֹ, *bĕṣēl yādô*; בְּצֵל יָדִי, *bĕṣēl yādî*, "in the shadow of my hand"). Yahweh's hand here functions almost like the protective cover that Yahweh will create over Jerusalem in Isa 4:5-6.

Following this note of promise focused on God's people on Mount Zion, but including all the nations, the negative reference to Moab in vv. 10b-12 comes as something of a jolt. It is likely that these verses originally constituted a completely separate oracle, unconnected with the preceding. The background to the judgment announced against Moab is unknown, but apparently Moab had done something during the prophet's time that provoked this threat of future judgment, and it is a rather harsh and demeaning judgment. Moab will be trodden down in its place as straw is trodden down in a dung heap. Trying to escape this humiliating fate, Moab will spread his hands in the midst of this stinking liquid mess like a swimmer trying to swim, and with each stroke of his hands in this cesspool of dung and straw, he will sink the pride of Moab (v. 11). The subject of וְהִשְׁפִּיל (wĕhišpîl, "and he will sink, make low") is ambiguous; it could be Yahweh, who is apparently the subject of all the verbs in the following v. 12, including the repeated הִשְׁפִּיל

(hišpîl), or it could be Moab, who humiliates himself further by his attempts to escape his fate. If the subject is Yahweh, it suggests the image of the deity pushing the head of Moab, the frantic swimmer, under the muck. The repeated use of the expression יָדָיו (yādāyw, "his hands") in v. 11 may have been the catchword that led the editor to attach this oracle to v. 10a, thereby creating a contrast between the protective hand of Yahweh and the frantic hands of Moab.

Then, in a direct address to Moab, v. 12 leaves the metaphor for the expected historical reality behind it. The high fortifications of your walls Yahweh will throw down, humble, bring down to the ground, to the very dust. This fate is similar to that of the evil city in 24:10-12, but it is hard to imagine that any city of Moab could have been the background for the oracle in chap. 24. Moab shares the same fate as the other rebellious kings of the world (24:21), but it was hardly the original model for these oppressive foreign powers.

Bibliography

Bammel, Fritz, *Das heilige Mahl im Glauben der Völker: Eine religionsphänomenologische Untersuchung* (Gütersloh: C. Bertelsmann, 1950).

Beuken, W. A. M., "The Prophet Leads the Readers into Praise: Isaiah 25:1-10 in Connection with Isaiah 24:14-23," in H. J. Bosman, H. van Grol, et al., eds., *Studies in Isaiah 24–27: The Isaiah Workshop–de Jesaja Werkplaats* (OtSt 43; Leiden: Brill, 2000) 121–56.

Box, G. H., "Some Textual Suggestions on Two Passages in Isaiah," *ExpTim* 19 (1908) 563–64.

Caquot, André, "Remarques sur le 'banquet des nations' en Esaïe 25:6-8," *RHPR* 69 (1989) 109–19.

Choque, E., "Cano anticipado por la liberación final: Una exposición escatológica de Isaías 25," *Theologika* 14 (1999) 172–87.

Coste, J., "Le texte Grec d'Isaïe XXV 1-5," *RB* 61 (1954) 36–68.

Delcor, Mathias, "La festin d'immortalité sur la montagne de Sion à l'ère eschatologique en Is 25,6-9," in Delcor, *Études bibliques et orientales de religions comparées* (Leiden: Brill, 1979) 122–31.

Doyle, B., "A Literary Analysis of Isaiah 25,10a," in J. van Ruiten and M. Vervenne, eds., *Studies in the Book of Isaiah: Festschrift Willem A. M. Beuken* (BETL 132; Leuven: Leuven University Press/Peeters, 1997) 173–93.

Easterley, E., "Is Mesha's *qrhh* Mentioned in Isaiah xv 2?" *VT* 41 (1991) 215–19.

Ellington, J., "A Swimming Lesson," *BT* 47 (1996) 246–47.

Emerton, J. A., "A Textual Problem in Isaiah 25:2," *ZAW* 89 (1977) 64–73.

Gray, G. B., "Critical Discussions: Isaiah 26; 25 1-5; 34 12-14," *ZAW* 31 (1911) 111–27.

Harrelson, Walter, "Death and Victory in I Corinthians 15:51-57: The Transformation of a Prophetic Theme," in John T. Carroll, Charles H. Cosgrove, and E. Elizabeth Johnson, eds., *Faith and History: Essays in Honor of Paul W. Meyer* (Scholars Press Homage Series 18; Atlanta: Scholars Press, 1990) 149–59.

Herrmann, W., "Die Implikationen von Jes 25.8a," *BN* 104 (2000) 26–30.

Kooij, A. van der, "The Teacher Messiah and Worldwide Peace: Some Comments on Symmachus' Version of Isaiah 25:7-8," *JNSL* 24 (1998) 75–82.

Lobmann, P., "Die selbstständigen lyrischen Abschnitte in Jes 24–27," *ZAW* 37 (1917-18) 1–58.

——, "Zu Text und Metrum einiger Stellen aus Jesaja: II. Das Lied Jes 25 1-5," *ZAW* 33 (1913) 256–62.

Martin-Achard, Robert, *De la mort à la résurrection d'après l'Ancien Testament* (Neuchâtel: Delachaux & Niestlé, 1956). Eng. trans. *From Death to Life: A Study of the Development of the Docrine of the*

Resurrection in the Old Testament (trans. J. P. Smith; Edinburgh: Oliver & Boyd, 1960).

——, "Il engloutit la mort à jamais: Remarques sur Esaïe, 25, 8," in A. Caquot, S. Légasse, and M. Tardieu, eds., *Mélanges bibliques et orientaux en l'honneur de M. Mathias Delcor* (AOAT 215; Kevelaer: Butzon & Bercker; Neukirchen-Vluyn: Neukirchener Verlag, 1985) 283–96.

Miller, Glenn, "Isaiah 25:6-9," *Int* 49 (1995) 175–78.

Staudigel, Helgalinde, "Hermeneutische Überlegungen zu einer triumphalen Glosse in Jesaja 25,6-8," in J. Rogge and G. Schille, eds., *Theologische Versuche* (Berlin: Evangelische Verlagsanstalt, 1989) 9–13.

Van Zyl, A. H., *The Moabites* (Pretoria Oriental Series 3; Leiden: Brill, 1960) 158–59.

Vermeylen, J., *Du Prophète Isaïe,* 1:366–69.

——, "La composition littéraire de l'apocalypse d'Isaïe (Is., XXIV–XXVII)," *ETL* 50 (1974) 5–38.

Virgulin, S., "Il lauto literatur convito sul Sion," *BeO* 11 (1969) 57–64.

Wildberger, H., "Das Freudenmahl auf dem Zion: Erwägungen zu Jes 25,6-8," *TZ* 33 (1977) 373–83.

Wodecki, Bernard, "The Religious Universalism of the Pericope Is 25:6-9," in Klaus-Dietrich Schunck and Matthias Augustin, eds., *Goldene Äpfel in silbernen Schalen: Collected Communications to the XIIIth Congress of the International Organization for the Study of the Old Testament, Leuven, 1989* (BEATAJ 20; Frankfurt am Main: P. Lang, 1992) 35–47.

26

1/ On that day this song[a] will be sung[b] in the land of Judah,
We have a strong[c] city,
He makes salvation[d] (its) inner and outer walls.[e]

2/ Open the gates,[f]
So that a righteous nation
That keeps faith[g] may enter.[h]

3/ The firm mind[i] you keep in peace,[j]
In peace, because in you it trusts.[k]

4/ Trust in Yahweh[l] forever,[m]
For in Yah Yahweh there is an eternal rock.[n]

5/ For he[o] has thrown down[p] the inhabitants[q] of the height,
The exalted city, he has humbled it,
He has humbled it[r] to the ground,
He has brought it down to the dust.[s]

6/ The foot will trample it;[t]
The feet of the needy,[u]
The soles of the poor.

7/ The path[v] for the righteous person is level,[w]
You level[x] smooth a trail for the righteous person.[y]

8/ Indeed for the path[z] of your justice, O Yahweh,[*a] we wait for you,[*b]
The desire of (our) soul[*c] is for your name and your renown.[*d]

9/ With my soul I desire you[*e] in the night,
Yes, with my spirit within me I seek you,[*f]
For when your judgments are in the earth,[*g]
The inhabitants[*h] of the world learn righteousness.[*i]

10/ If the wicked is shown favor,[*j]
He does not learn righteousness;
In the land of uprightness[*k] he does wrong,[*l]
And does not see the glory of Yahweh.

11/ O Yahweh, your hand[*m] is lifted up,[*n]
but they do not see (it);
Let them see and be ashamed[*o] by (your) zeal for (your) people,[*p]
Yes, may the fire for your enemies devour them.[*q]

12/ O Yahweh,[*r] may you appoint[*s] peace for us,
For even all our accomplishments[*t] you have done[*u] for us.

13/ O Yahweh our God,[*v]
Lords[*w] other than you have ruled us,[*x]
But we will call[*y] upon your name alone.

14/ The dead[*z] do not live,
The shades[ta] do not rise,[tb]
Because you have punished and destroyed them,
And you have wiped out[tc] all[td] memory[te] of them.

15/ You have added to the nation, O Yahweh,
You have added[tf] to the nation, you are glorified,
You have extended all[tg] the ends of the land.[th]

16/ Yahweh, in affliction they sought you;[ti]
They poured out a whispered prayer,[tj]
When your chastening was upon them.[tk]

17/ Like a pregnant woman who draws near to give birth,
Who writhes and cries out in her travail,
Thus we were before you, O Yahweh.[tl]

18/ We were pregnant, we writhed,
But it is as though we gave birth only to wind;
We achieved no successes[tm] on earth,
And the inhabitants of the world were not born.[tn]

19/ Your dead[to] shall live!
(Your) corpses[tp] shall rise!
Awake, and shout for joy,[tq]
You who dwell in the dust![tr]

For your dew is a dew of light,[ts]
And the earth will give birth to the dead.[tt]

20/ Go my people,
Enter into your chambers,
And lock your doors[tu] behind you.
Hide[tv] for a little while,
Until the wrath[tw] passes.[tx]

21/ For behold[ty] Yahweh is coming forth from his place
To punish[tz] the iniquity[ta] of the inhabitant[tb] of the earth upon him,
And the earth will uncover her blood,
And she will no[tc] longer cover over her slain.

Textual Notes

a   MT, 4QIsa[c], הַשִּׁיר־הַזֶּה (haššîr-hazzeh), "this song"; 1QIsa[a] השיר הזואת; and 1QIsa[c] השירה הזאת.

b   MT, 4QIsa[c] יוּשַׁר (yûšar), "will be sung," Vg., Syr.; 1QIsa[a] ישיר (yāšîr), "he/one will sing"; LXX, Tg., "they will sing."

c   MT עָז (ʿoz), "strong"; 1QIsa[a] עוז.

d   LXX "our salvation."

e   MT, 1QIsa[a] חוֹמוֹת וָחֵל (ḥômôt wāḥēl), "(its) inner walls and outer wall"; 4QIsa[c] חומותיה וחילה (ḥômôtêhā wāḥêlâ), "its inner walls and its outer wall." For the meaning of these two words, cf. Nah 3:8 and 2 Sam 20:15.

f   MT, 1QIsa[b], LXX, Vg., Tg., Syr., שְׁעָרִים (šĕʿārîm), "the gates"; 1QIsa[a] שעריך, "your gates."

g   MT שֹׁמֵר אֱמֻנִים (šōmēr ʾĕmūnîm), "that keeps faith"; 1QIsa[a], 4QIsa[c] שומר אמונים. LXX has λαὸς φυλάσσων δικαιοσύνην καὶ φυλάσσων ἀλήθειαν, "a people guarding righteousness and guarding truth."

h   MT וְיָבֹא (wĕyābōʾ), "that he may enter"; 1QIsa[a] ויבוא; but 1QIsa[b] ויבאו, "that they may enter."

i   MT, 1QIsa[a] יֵצֶר סָמוּךְ (yēṣer sāmûk, "a firm mind, inclination"); εβρ' ιεσρο σαμωχ, which suggests יצרו סמוך, "the one whose mind is firm."[1] LXX, "that lays hold of truth"; Syr., "that keeps guard of truth"; Vg., vetus error abiit, "the old error is passed away"; Tg., "with a perfect heart."

j   MT, 1QIsa[a] תִּצֹּר שָׁלוֹם (tiṣṣōr šālôm), "you keep in peace"; LXX has καὶ φυλάσσων εἰρήνην, "and who guards peace"; Vg., "you will keep peace"; Tg., "they have kept peace"; Syr., "you will keep peace for us."

k   MT, 1QIsa[b] כִּי בְךָ בָּטוּחַ (kî bĕkā bāṭûaḥ), "because in you it trusts"; 1QIsa[a] כי בכה ("because in you," בטח has dropped out by haplography because of the following בטח); LXX also drops the word, using the piel perfect of the following verse as the verb for the concluding phrase of v. 3.; Vg. and Syr., "because in you we hoped"; Tg., "because in your word they trusted."

The passive participle is a bit unusual, but the same passive form with the same meaning is attested in Ps 112:7.

l   MT has the masculine plural imperative בִּטְחוּ בַיהוָה (biṭĕḥû bĕYHWH), "trust in Yahweh"), cf. Tg.; LXX read this as a perfect, "in you they trusted, O Lord"; Syr., "in you we trusted, O Lord"; Vg. has "you trusted in the Lord."

m   MT עֲדֵי־עַד (ʿădê-ʿad), "forever"); 1QIsa[a] עד עד.

n   MT, 1QIsa[a] כִּי בְּיָהּ יְהוָה צוּר עוֹלָמִים (kî bĕyāh YHWH ṣûr ʿôlāmîm), "for in Yah Yahweh there is an eternal rock"; 4QIsa[b] probably had כי ביה אדני, "for in Yah, the Lord . . . ." The versions had difficulty with this clause: LXX, "the great, everlasting God"; Vg., "in the Lord God strong forever"; Syr., "because the Lord God is strong forever"; Tg., "for then you will be saved by the word of the fearful one, the Lord is strong forever."

o   LXX reads all the verbs in this verse as second person.

p   MT כִּי הֵשַׁח (kî hēšaḥ), "for he has brought low"; 1QIsa[a] כי השת ("for he has placed," but this is a mistake because of the similarity of ת and ח in the late script; the hiphil of שית is not otherwise attested in Biblical Hebrew). MT is supported by 1QIsa[b], 4QIsa[b], and by 4QIsa[c] כיא השח.

q   MT, 1QIsa[b] יֹשְׁבֵי מָרוֹם (yōšĕbê mārôm), "the inhabitants of the height"; 1QIsa[a], 4QIsa[c] יושבי מרום.

r   MT יַשְׁפִּילֶנָּה יַשְׁפִּילָהּ עַד־אֶרֶץ (yašpîlennâ yašpîlāh ʿad-ʾereṣ), "he has humbled it, he has humbled it to the ground"; 1QIsa[a] has only one verb: ישפילנה עדי ארץ, "he has humbled it to the ground." 4QIsa[b-c] are both defective at this point, as is 1QIsa[b]. Vg. and Tg. support MT, while Syr. supports 1QIsa[a]. LXX shortens even further: πόλεις ὀχυρὰς καταβαλεῖς καὶ κατάξεις ἕως ἐδάφους, "strong cities you cast down and you bring down to the ground."

s   MT יַגִּיעֶנָּה עַד־עָפָר (yaggîʿennâ ʿad-ʿāpār), "he brought it down to the dust"; 1QIsa[a] יגיענה עדי עפר.

t   MT תִּרְמְסֶנָּה רָגֶל (tirmĕsennâ rāgel), "the foot will trample it"; 4QIsa[c] תרמסינה רגל seems to support MT, as does Vg., but 1QIsa[a] omits רגל and reads the verb as a feminine plural,

---

1   Joseph Ziegler, Isaias (Septuaginta Vetus Testamentum Graecum auctoritate Academiae Litterararum Gottingensis 14; Göttingen: Vandenhoeck & Ruprecht, 1967) 210.

תרמסנה רגלי עניים, "the feet of the needy . . . trample"; so also LXX.

u MT רַגְלֵי עָנִי (raglê ʿānî), "the feet of the needy"; 1QIsaᵃ רגלי עניים.

v MT אֹרַח (ʾōraḥ), "path"; 1QIsaᵃ אורח.

w MT, 1QIsaᵃ מֵישָׁרִים (mêšārîm), "level"; 4QIsaᶜ מיש[ר]ים.

x MT תְּפַלֵּס (tĕpallēs), "you level"; 1QIsaᵃ תפלט (tĕpallēṭ), "you save." LXX has "and the way of the godly has been prepared," while Tg. has "also the deeds of the way of the righteous you will establish." The other versions do not seem to read a verb here.

y MT יָשָׁר מַעְגַּל צַדִּיק (yāšār maʿgal ṣaddîq), "straight/smooth the path of the righteous"; 1QIsaᵃ ישר מעגל צדק; but 4QIsaᶜ ר[וי]ש מעגל צדק, "they ma]ke straight the path of the righteous."

z MT אֹרַח (ʾōraḥ), "path"; 1QIsaᵃ אורח.

*a MT מִשְׁפָּטֶיךָ יְהוָה (mišpāṭêkā YHWH), "your justice, O Yahweh," so Vg., Syr., and Tg.; 1QIsaᵃ has the same text with a blank space between mišpāṭêkā and YHWH. LXX has ὁδὸς κυρίου κρίσις, "the way of the Lord is judgment."

*b MT קִוִּינוּךָ (qiwwînûkā), "we wait for you"; 1QIsaᵃ קוינו (qiwwînû), "we wait"; so also Tg., Syr., and LXX, though LXX makes the following לְשִׁמְךָ (lĕšimkā), "for your name," the object of the verb, ἠλπίσαμεν ἐπὶ τῷ ὀνόματί σου, "we hoped upon your name."

*c MT תַּאֲוַת־נָפֶשׁ (taʾăwat-nāpeš), "the desire of the soul"; 1QIsaᵃ תאית נפש. LXX has ῆ ἐπιθυμεῖ ἡ ψυχὴ ἡμῶν, "that our soul desires." Tg. and Syr. are similar but without the relative pronoun.

*d MT וּלְזִכְרְךָ (ûlĕzikrĕkā), "and for your renown/memory," so LXX, Vg., Syr., Tg., and traces of 4QIsaᶜ; 1QIsaᵃ ולתורתך (ûlĕtôrātĕkā), "and for your law."

*e MT, 1QIsaᵃ נַפְשִׁי אִוִּיתִךָ (napšî ʾiwwîtîkā), "with my soul I desire you," Vg., Syr., Tg.; LXX omits.

*f MT אֲשַׁחֲרֶךָּ (ʾăšaḥărekkā), "I seek you"; 1QIsaᵃ אשחרכה. LXX adds ὁ θεός, "O God."

*g MT, 1QIsaᵃ כִּי כַּאֲשֶׁר מִשְׁפָּטֶיךָ לָאָרֶץ (kî kaʾăšer mišpāṭêkā lāʾāreṣ), "for when your judgments are in the earth"; LXX has διότι φῶς τὰ προστάγματά σου ἐπὶ τῆς γῆς, "because your ordinances are a light upon the earth."

*h MT יֹשְׁבֵי (yōšĕbê), "the inhabitants of"; 1QIsaᵃ יושבי.

*i MT צֶדֶק לָמְדוּ יֹשְׁבֵי תֵבֵל (ṣedeq lāmĕdû yōšĕbê tēbēl), "the inhabitants of the world learn righteousness"; LXX reads the imperative, "learn righteousness, you who live upon the earth" (δικαιοσύνην μάθετε, οἱ ἐνοικοῦντες ἐπὶ τῆς γῆς).

*j MT יֻחַן (yūhan), "is shown favor" (qal passive); 1QIsaᵃ יחון (yāḥôn), "if one shows favor" (qal). The versions differ widely: LXX πέπαυται γὰρ ὁ ἀσεβής, "for the impious one has come to an end"; Vg. misereamur impio, "if we show pity to the impious one"; Syr., "the evildoer fled afar"; Tg., "you gave respite to the wicked."

*k MT נְכֹחוֹת (nĕkōḥôt), "uprightness"; 1QIsaᵃ נכוחות.

*l MT and traces in 4QIsaᵇ יְעַוֵּל (yĕʿawwēl), "he does wrong"; 1QIsaᵃ יעיל (as written, a hiphil, but probably miswritten for יעול, since the hiphil is otherwise unattested).

*m MT, 4QIsaᵇ יָדְךָ (yādĕkā), "your hand"; 1QIsaᵃ ידכה.

*n MT, 1QIsaᵃ רָמָה (rāmâ), "is lifted up"; 4QIsaᵇ רומה. The MT

accentuation marks the form as the qal perfect third person feminine singular, but the feminine singular qal participle differs only in the accent, and there is little difference in meaning between the two forms for a stative verb.

*o MT יֶחֱזוּ וְיֵבֹשׁוּ (yeḥĕzû wĕyēbōšû), "let them see and let them be ashamed"; 1QIsaᵃ ויחזו ויבושו, "and let them see and let them be ashamed."

*p MT קִנְאַת־עָם (qinat-ʿām), "the zeal of/for the people"; 1QIsaᵃ קנאת העם.

*q MT, 1QIsaᵃ אַף־אֵשׁ צָרֶיךָ תֹאכְלֵם (ʾap-ʾēš ṣārêkā tōʾkĕlēm), "yes, may the fire for your enemies devour them"; LXX and Vg. ignore the suffix on the verb, and one could consider treating it as an enclitic mem, in which case one could simply render, "yes, may fire devour your enemies."

*r LXX adds "our God."

*s MT תִּשְׁפֹּת (tišpōt), "may you appoint, place"); 1QIsaᵃ תשפוט (tišpôt), "give a verdict"; 4QIsaᵇ תשפט. The versions support MT.

*t MT כָּל־מַעֲשֵׂנוּ (kol-maʿăśênû), "all our deeds/accomplishments"; 1QIsaᵃ כול מעשינו. LXX omits maʿăśênû.

*u MT פָּעַלְתָּ (pāʿaltā), "you have done"; 1QIsaᵃ פעלתה.

*v MT אֱלֹהֵינוּ (ʾĕlōhênû), "our God"; 1QIsaᵃ אלוהינו.

*w MT, 1QIsaᵃ אֲדֹנִים (ʾădōnîm), "lords"; 1QIsaᵃ אדנים; LXX takes this word as referring to God.

*x MT, 1QIsaᵃ בְּעָלוּנוּ (bĕʿālûnû), "have ruled us"; 4QIsaᵇ בעלנו. LXX reads the imperative, κύριε ὁ θεὸς ἡμῶν, κτῆσαι ἡμᾶς, "O Lord, our God, take possession of us."

*y MT, 4QIsaᵇ נַזְכִּיר (nazkîr), "we will call upon"; 1QIsaᵃ has the qal נזכור rather than the hiphil. LXX understands the last half of the verse quite differently, κύριε, ἐκτὸς σοῦ ἄλλον οὐκ οἴδαμεν, τὸ ὄνομά σου ὀνομάζομεν, "Lord, apart from you we have known no other, your name we name."

*z MT מֵתִים (mētîm), "the dead"; 1QIsaᵃ מיתים.

†a MT רְפָאִים (rĕpāʾîm), "the shades"; 1QIsaᵃ originally had ורפאים, but then the initial ו was erased.

†b MT בַּל־יָקֻמוּ (bal-yāqūmû), "they do not rise"; 1QIsaᵃ בל יקומו.

†c MT וַתְּאַבֵּד (wattĕʾabbēd), "and you have wiped out"; 1QIsaᵃ ותאסר, "and you imprisoned." The versions support MT.

†d MT כָּל (kol), "all"; 1QIsaᵃ כול.

†e MT, 1QIsaᵃ זֵכֶר לָמוֹ (zēker lāmô), "memory of them"; LXX misunderstands this as zākār, πᾶν ἄρσεν αὐτῶν, "every male of them." The other versions support MT.

†f MT יָסַפְתָּ (yāsaptā), "you have added"; 1QIsaᵃ יספתה.

†g See note †d above.

†h Vg. and Syr. stay fairly close to the Hebrew, but the other versions had difficulty with this verse. LXX has πρόσθες αὐτοῖς κακά, κύριε, πρόσθες κακὰ πᾶσιν τοῖς ἐνδόξοις τῆς γῆς, "Add evils to them, O Lord, add evils to all the glorious ones of the earth."

†i MT, 1QIsaᵃ בַּצַּר פְּקָדוּךָ (baṣṣar pĕqādûkā), "in affliction they sought you," so also Vg.; LXX ἐν θλίψει ἐμνήσθην σου, "in affliction I remembered you."

†j MT, 4QIsaᵇ צָקוּן לַחַשׁ (ṣāqûn laḥaš), "they poured out a whispered prayer"; 1QIsaᵃ צקון לחשו, "oppressed, they whispered a

prayer," cf. Syr. LXX ἐν θλίψει μικρᾷ, "in small affliction"; Vg. *in tribulatione murmuris*, "in tribulation of murmuring."

†k MT מוּסָרְךָ לָמוֹ (*mûsārĕkā lāmô*), "when your chastening was upon them"; 1QIsaᵃ מוסריך למו. LXX ἡ παιδεία σου ἡμῖν, "Your chastening was on us." Vg. *doctrina tua eis*, "your teaching was to them."

†l At the end of this verse, LXX has the odd rendering οὕτως ἐγενήθημεν τῷ ἀγαπητῷ σου διὰ τὸν φόβον σου, κύριε, "thus we became to your beloved because of the fear of you, O Lord."

†m MT יְשׁוּעֹת (*yĕšûʿōt*), "victories, salvation, successes," Vg.; 1QIsaᵃ ישועתך, "your salvation." LXX reads this as a positive statement: πνεῦμα σωτηρίας σου ἐποιήσαμεν ἐπὶ τῆς γῆς, "a wind of your salvation we accomplished on the earth."

†n MT וּבַל־יִפְּלוּ יֹשְׁבֵי תֵבֵל (*ûbal-yippĕlû yōšĕbê tēbēl*), "and the inhabitants of the world were not born (lit., did not drop)"; 1QIsaᵃ ובל יפולו יושבי תבל. LXX misunderstands this as ἀλλὰ πεσοῦνται οἱ ἐνοικοῦντες ἐπὶ τῆς γῆς, "but those who dwell upon the earth shall fall." Despite the objections of C. F. Whitley ("The Positive Force of בל," *ZAW* 84 [1972] 215–16) and the doubts expressed by J. D. W. Watts (*Isaiah 1–33*, 399), and others, the meaning "give birth" for the verb *nāpal* here and in the *hiphil* in v. 19 is hardly problematic (see Wildberger, 2:986).

†o MT מֵתֶיךָ (*mētêkā*), "your dead"; 1QIsaᵃ מיתיך; LXX omits any suffix, but Syr. and Vg. follow MT.

†p MT and 1QIsaᵃ נְבֵלָתִי (*nĕbēlātî*), "my corpses" (singular with collective sense)." LXX again omits the suffix; Vg. follows MT, but Syr. has "their corpses." The abrupt shift in the Hebrew text from the second person masculine singular suffix to the first person common singular on parallel terms, however, is troubling. Either the ending on *nĕbēlātî* is not a suffix, just a redundant final -*î* similar to the *hireq compaginis*, and the suffix

on *mētêkā* does double duty, as is often the case in parallel lines in poetry, or an original second person masculine singular suffix *nĕbēlātêkā* has been lost in textual transmission.

†q MT הָקִיצוּ וְרַנְּנוּ (*hāqîṣû wĕrannĕnû*), "awake and shout for joy!"; 1QIsaᵃ יקיצו וירננו, "let them awake and shout for joy!"

†r MT שֹׁכְנֵי עָפָר (*šōkĕnê ʿāpār*), "you who dwell in the dust"; 1QIsaᵃ שוכני עפר.

†s MT טַל אוֹרֹת (*ṭal ʾôrōt*), "a dew of light"; 1QIsaᵃ טל אורות.

†t LXX misunderstands the idiom and renders ἡ δὲ γῆ τῶν ἀσεβῶν πεσεῖται, "but the land of the ungodly will fall"; Vg. makes a similar mistake, *et terram gigantum detrahes in ruinam*, "and the land of the giants you will pull down in ruins," as does Syr.

†u MT *kĕtîb* and 1QIsaᵃ דְּלָתֶיךָ (*dĕlātêkā*), "your doors," Vg., Syr.; *qĕreʾ* דְּלָתְךָ (*dĕlātĕkā*), "your door," LXX.

†v MT חֲבִי (*ḥăbî*), "hide yourself," though the form seems odd for a couple of reasons: (1) it appears to be a *qal* feminine singular imperative of חבה, a byform of חבא, though it occurs in a series of masculine singular forms that would lead one to expect a masculine singular form; and (2) the root חבא never occurs in the *qal*; 1QIsaᵃ חבו (*ḥăbû*), "hide yourselves," masculine plural; Vg. translates with an infinitive, *abscondere*, "to hide," which may suggest it was reading the infinitive *ḥābô*.

†w MT, 1QIsaᵃ זַעַם (*zaʿam*), "wrath, indignation," so Vg.; LXX has "the wrath of the Lord," and Syr., "my wrath."

†x MT *kĕtîb* and 1QIsaᵃ יַעֲבוֹר (*yaʿăbôr*), "it passes"; *qĕreʾ* יַעֲבָר (*yaʿăbor*), "it passes."

†y MT הִנֵּה (*hinnê*), "behold," LXX, Vg., Syr., Tg.; 1QIsaᵃ omits.

†z MT לִפְקֹד (*lipqōd*), "to punish"; 1QIsaᵃ לפקוד.

‡a MT עָוֹן (*ʿāwōn*), "iniquity"; 1QIsaᵃ עוון.

‡b MT יֹשֵׁב (*yōšēb*), "inhabitant"; 1QIsaᵃ יושב; LXX has the plural.

‡c MT וְלֹא (*wĕlōʾ*), "and no (longer)"; 1QIsaᵃ ולוא.

Commentary

The "on that day" in v. 1 picks up the thought of 25:9, but here, when that day of salvation comes, this song will be sung (יוּשַׁר הַשִּׁיר־הַזֶּה, *yûšar haššîr-hazzeh*) in the land of Judah. What follows appears to be the words of the song. The strong city (עִיר עָז, *ʿîr ʿāz*) which Judah possesses is Jerusalem, but its inner and outer walls now consist of the salvation (יְשׁוּעָה, *yĕšûʿâ*) that God provides for it. The sense is that the city's real protection is the presence of Yahweh. This is an old motif in the Zion Tradition (Pss 46:5-8, 12; 48:4; 76:2-10), and it is reiterated in Isaiah (4:5-6; 33:20-22). Third Isaiah elaborates this motif when he speaks of the gates of this restored Jerusalem never being closed, day or night (60:11), and when he says the walls of Jerusalem will be named Salvation (יְשׁוּעָה, *yĕšûʿâ*)

and her gates Praise (תְּהִלָּה, *tĕhillâ*, 60:18). Similar motifs of the future security of Jerusalem are found in many of the prophets (see, e.g., Zeph 3:11-20; Joel 4:16-21; Zech 14:6-11).

As the song continues in v. 2, the singer(s) command the gates of the city to be opened that a righteous nation that keeps faith may enter. The language here is borrowed from the old entrance liturgies performed at the city gates when a returning cultic procession sought access into the city (see Ps 24:3-10; cf. Psalm 15; Isa 33:13-16). The righteous nation that keeps faith is the characterization of the refined and reformed remnant that will inhabit Jerusalem in the day of salvation. Such individuals who are committed to Yahweh with a firm mind or intent (יֵצֶר, *yēṣer*) God will keep in peace (תִּצֹּר שָׁלוֹם, *tiṣṣōr šālôm*, lit., "you will keep in peace"), because they trust in

Yahweh (כִּי בְךָ בָטוּחַ, *kî běkā bātûaḥ*, lit. "because in you it [the firm mind] trusts," v. 3). Note that the words of the song address God in the second person. For the poetic artistry of the prophet, observe the intentional sound play between *yēṣer* and *tiṣṣōr*.

At v. 4 the singer or singers turn from Yahweh to address the community with a command: "Trust in Yahweh forever, for in Yah Yahweh there is an eternal rock." The juxtaposition of the shortened form of the divine name just before the long form is a bit disconcerting and has led to numerous textual emendations,[2] but the same juxtaposition is also found in Isa 12:2, and note יָהּ אֱלֹהִים (*YH ʾĕlōhîm*, "Yah God") in Ps 68:19, in the Elohistic Psalter (Psalms 42–83), where *ʾĕlōhîm* is often a replacement for an original Yahweh (cf. also Isa 38:11). Since peace is to be found in a mind fixed on trusting in Yahweh, trust in Yahweh. The image of Yahweh as an "eternal rock" (צוּר עוֹלָמִים, *ṣûr ʿôlāmîm*) is rooted in the experience of the high, rocky cliff (צוּר, *ṣûr*) as an easily defendable refuge from one's enemies (Pss 27:5; 61:3; cf. Isa 2:10, 19, 21). It is an ancient and common metaphor applied to God (Deut 32:4, 18, 37; 1 Sam 2:2; 2 Sam 22:32/Ps 18:32; passim) and was well known to Isaiah (17:10; 30:29).

Yahweh has proven himself to be a refuge by bringing low the inhabitants of a rival height, by humbling the exalted city, by humbling it to the ground, bringing it down to the very dust, where the feet of the poor and needy may trample it (vv. 5-6). The humbled city probably refers back to the same city mentioned in 24:10 and 25:2. If this refers to a past event, as I think it does, it probably refers to the fall of the city of Nineveh or Aššur, or perhaps more generally, to the fortified cities of the Assyrian heartland, an event that gave great joy to Judah and many of the peoples who had suffered under Assyrian domination (see Nahum, especially the last verse, 3:19). The needy and poor here are the purified remnant of Judah and are equivalent to the righteous mentioned in the following verses.

Yahweh's action has reinforced Judah's belief in the promise that "the path [אֹרַח, *ʾōraḥ*] for the righteous person [צַדִּיק, *ṣaddîq*] is level" (v. 7). Because of God's actions in crushing Judah's oppressor, the singer(s) now confess

to Yahweh, "you level [תְּפַלֵּס, *tĕpallēs*] smooth or straight [יָשָׁר, *yāšār*] a trail [מַעְגַּל, *maʿgal*] for the righteous person." The righteous person here is the equivalent of the mind fixed in trust on God back in v. 3, and the metaphor of path and trail refers to the course of life made easier by God for those who trust in him. Their path in life is straight, level, and smooth, in its success as well as in its moral quality, rather than crooked, steep, and rocky. Yet, despite Yahweh's overthrow of the exalted city (v. 5), the community confesses that it still waits for God to open up or finish leveling the path of his justice (v. 8): "Indeed, for the path of your justice, O Yahweh, we wait for you [קִוִּינוּךָ, *qiwwînûkā*]." From the point of view of the community, God's work is not yet finished. As the community says, "The desire of (our) soul [תַּאֲוַת־נָפֶשׁ, *taʾăwat-nāpeš*] is for your name [לְשִׁמְךָ, *lĕšimkā*] and your fame [וּלְזִכְרְךָ, *ûlĕzikrĕkā*]." The implication seems to be that if Yahweh wants his name and renown to be acknowledged throughout the world, God still has more work to do.

In v. 9 the speaker reverts to the singular, while continuing the direct address to God. The language, "With my soul [נַפְשִׁי, *napšî*] I desire you [אִוִּיתִיךָ, *ʾiwwîtîkā*] in the night, yes, with my spirit within me [רוּחִי בְקִרְבִּי, *rûḥî bĕqirbî*] I seek you [אֲשַׁחֲרֶךָ, *ʾăšaḥărekkā*]," suggests diligent supplication on the part of the individual. For the verb שחר (*šḥr*), normally in the *piel*, see Hos 5:15; Pss 63:2; 78:34; Job 7:21; 8:5; 24:5; Prov 1:28; 7:15; 8:17; 11:27; 13:24. This diligent personal seeking after Yahweh, however, remains basically a supplication to God to make "your judgments" (מִשְׁפָּטֶיךָ, *mišpāṭêkā*) transparent to the world for the sake of the world, and ultimately for the sake of the speaker's particular national community. The reason for this supplication is that "when your judgments are in the earth"—that is, when your judgments are transparent, as in the case of the overthrow of the exalted city—"the inhabitants of the world learn [לָמְדוּ, *lāmĕdû*] righteousness [צֶדֶק, *ṣedeq*]." On the other hand, if the wicked person (רָשָׁע, *rāšāʿ*) is shown favor and left unpunished, he will not learn righteousness (בַּל־לָמַד צֶדֶק, *bal-lāmad ṣedeq*). In a land of uprightness, he will continue to act perversely (יְעַוֵּל, *yĕʿawwēl*) and fail to see or recognize the majesty of Yahweh (v. 10). It is clear that,

2   The most common is simply to delete בְיָהּ (*běyāh*), as the textual note in *BHS* does.

for the writer, despite Yahweh's overthrow of the exalted city of the oppressor, other oppressors and enemies of the speaker and his community are still around and in need of punishment by Yahweh, if Yahweh's fame is to be recognized and his community's salvation and security are to be realized.

The speaker confesses to Yahweh that "your hand is raised up," but unfortunately the enemy does not "see (it)," and therefore he prays, "Let them see and be ashamed by (your) zeal for (your) people; yes, may the fire for your enemies devour them" (v. 11). For this use of fire imagery that devours the enemies of God's people, compare Isa 30:27-33; 33:10-12. The prayer for the destruction of Judah's present enemies makes clear that some other oppressive power has replaced the exalted city that was overthrown, and both Yahweh's fame and Judah's salvation are dependent on God's intervention to deal with this new enemy as he had dealt with the former one.

Verse 12 is to be read as a communal prayer, "O Yahweh, may you appoint peace for us," but the reason given to bolster this prayer is less clear. The sense seems to be that the people are confessing their realization that even all their great works or accomplishments (גַּם כָּל־מַעֲשֵׂינוּ, gam kol-maʿăśênû, "even all our accomplishments") in the past, accomplishments for which the people could be tempted to be proud (see Amos 6:13), were actually performed for them by Yahweh (פָּעַלְתָּ לָּנוּ, pāʿaltā lānû, "you did for us"). That is, their accomplishments were not wrought by their own power, by chariots and horses and military strength and their own shrewd scheming, but through the power of God (see Ps 20:8; Zech 4:6). The versions, apart from the Targum, seem to take the passage in that sense. The Targum understands the passage as, "for in all times you were making with us a restraint from our sins," which is somewhat ambiguous—either God was showing mercy and not punishing them to the extent their sins deserved, or God was restraining them from sinning by severely punishing them. JPS seems to follow the Targum, while opting for the second possibility, "since you have also requited all our misdeeds." This is an interesting suggestion, but the interpretation found in the other versions and in most modern translations seems more likely.

The prayer continues in v. 13 with another invocation of the deity, "O Yahweh our God." The invocation expresses and stresses the relationship between the people and their God, Yahweh, though the continuation of the prayer admits that at times other lords (אֲדֹנִים זוּלָתֶךָ, ʾădōnîm zûlātekā, "lords other than you") ruled over them (בְּעָלוּנוּ, bĕʿālûnû, "ruled us"). There is a bit of ambiguity with respect to these other lords. They clearly are political powers such as Egypt and Assyria, to which Israel and Judah had submitted as vassals when they turned to them for help against other enemies, a foreign policy that prophets like Hosea (5:13; 7:11; 8:9-10; 11:5) and Isaiah (7:1-17; 8:5-8; 28:14-22; 30:1-7; 31:1-3) regarded as rebellion against Yahweh, their rightful suzerain. But given our author's penchant for seeing a two-tiered universe, for noting the powers in heaven behind earthly powers (Isa 24:21), it is likely that the prayer is also a confession of past idolatry. Nonetheless, the prayer continues, it is you alone, O Yahweh, upon whose name we will now call. The prayer promises a sole devotion to Yahweh that excludes the appeal to other political powers or to other gods for help (cf. Hos 14:4).

While v. 14 maintains the direct address to Yahweh, the logical connection between v. 14 and the preceding verse is not immediately apparent. The term רְפָאִים (rĕpāʾîm), "shades," in parallel with מֵתִים (mētîm), "the dead," refers to the disembodied spirits of the dead that continue a shadowy existence in the netherworld until they gradually fade away as the memory of them in the world above fades away (see Isa 14:9-11), but does the statement that "the dead do not live, the shades do not rise" (בַּל־יָקֻמוּ, bal-yāqūmû) refer to a specific group of the dead, or is it a general statement of fact about all human dead? The only qualification given is that they are dead and will not live again, because you (God) punished them, destroyed them, and wiped out all memory of them (כָּל־זֵכֶר לָמוֹ, kol-zēker lāmô). In some ways the language reminds one of the taunt song over the death of Sargon II and his reception by the shades in the underworld in Isa 14:4-21, and particularly of the prayer for Sargon's children: "May the seed of evildoers not be mentioned forever [לֹא־יִקָּרֵא לְעוֹלָם, lōʾ-yiqqārēʾ lĕʿôlām]; prepare slaughter for his sons because of the iniquity of their fathers, may they not rise up [בַּל־יָקֻמוּ, bal-yāqūmû] and possess the earth and fill the face of the world with cities" (Isa 14:20-21). If the fall of the fortified city in 25:2 is a reference to the fall of Assyrian cities in 615–610 BCE, it is possible that there is an allusion here to the fulfillment of Isaiah's prayer in 14:20-21, and that the reference to the dead whose very memory was destroyed by Yahweh includes, even if it is not restricted to, the hated Assyrians.

If there is an allusion to the fall of Assyria here, then v. 15 may refer to Josiah's expansion of Judean territory during the same general period prior to his shocking death in 609 BCE (see 2 Kgs 23:15-30; 2 Chr 34:6-7, 33; 35:1-27).[3] The repeated assertion, "you have added to the nation [יָסַפְתָּ לַגּוֹי, yāsaptā lagôy], O Yahweh," reminds one of the textual error in Hezekiah's enthronement oracle, הִרְבִּיתָ הַגּוֹי (hirbîtā haggôy), "you increased the nation" (Isa 9:2), and the resemblance may suggest that this textual corruption was very early and that this text was cited as fulfilled by Josiah during his reform movement. According to v. 15, Yahweh was glorified (נִכְבָּדְתָּ, nikbādtā, "you were glorified") when he added to the nation and extended (רִחַקְתָּ, riḥaqtā, "you made distant, extended") all the borders of the land.[4] This would fit very well with the heyday of the Josianic reform, when Yahweh was glorified over all his rivals, and Josiah's successes, combined with the rapid decline of Assyria, gave great hope for the renewal of Judah's golden age. Unfortunately, the euphoria did not last. The intervention first of Egypt, the resulting death of Josiah, and then the intervention of Babylon turned this Judean euphoria into a pervasive gloom.

The direct address to Yahweh continues in v. 16 with an account of how his people in affliction and under God's discipline sought Yahweh and poured out a whispered prayer to him. Presumably this reflects the situation after the frustrating and demoralizing death of Josiah. The use of the third person and the past tense—"in affliction they sought you" (בַּצַּר פְּקָדוּךָ, baṣṣar pĕqādûkā); "they poured out (צָקוּן, ṣāqûn) a whispered prayer when your chastening was upon them (מוּסָרְךָ לָמוֹ, mûsārĕkā lāmô)"—creates some distance between the speaker and the people he is describing. That suggests

that the speaker is looking back on this period from a later standpoint in time.

What follows in vv. 17-18, however, may very well be a quotation of the prayer that those earlier frustrated Judeans addressed to Yahweh: "Just as a pregnant woman who draws near to give birth, writhes and cries out in her birth pangs, so we were before you, O Yahweh. We were pregnant, we writhed, but it is as though we gave birth only to wind. . . ." One should compare this imagery to the imagery of daughter Zion being in labor and eventually giving birth in Mic 4:9-10; 5:3. With the collapse of Assyria and Josiah's expansion and reform, there was great hope for the rebirth of the Judean nation, but with his death and first Egyptian and then Babylonian domination those hopes were aborted. The speakers lament, "we achieved no successes on earth," because Josiah's successes were quite ephemeral and quickly lost after his death. The last statement, "and the inhabitants of the world were not born [lit., did not drop]," is birth imagery continuing the opening pregnancy imagery, but apart from completing the metaphor, it adds little clarity to the meaning of the metaphor.

The meaning of v. 19 is dependent on the identity of the speaker, whether it is a continuation of the prayer addressed to Yahweh or Yahweh's response to that prayer. I take it to be the prophet's oracular response to that prayer, in which God grants the people's desire for new life. The second person masculine singular suffixes, then, refer to God's people personified as a man, just as the second person masculine singular suffixes in v. 20 do, but the third person masculine plural verbs refer to the plurality that makes up the people. God promises his people, "Your dead shall live, (your) corpses shall rise." God then commands those who dwell in the dust, that is, the dead and buried, to wake up and shout for joy. The reason is that the dew that touches God's people (טַלְּךָ, ṭallekā, "your dew") is a dew of light. This imagery of dew as giving new life is rooted in the importance of dew in

3   Both Hezekiah and Josiah sponsored Deuteronomistic religious reform movements, and both appear to have attempted an expansion into Israelite territory (for Hezekiah, see 2 Chr 31:1; and Andrew G. Vaughn, *Theology, History, and Archaeology in the Chronicler's Account of Hezekiah* [Archaeology and Biblical Studies 4; Atlanta: Scholars Press, 1999]).

4   This usage of the verb in the sense of "to extend the borders of a land" is rare, but its correctness is supported by the related expression אֶרֶץ מַרְחַקִּים (ʾereṣ marḥaqqîm, "a land of wide extent," Isa 33:17).

Israel for the renewal of plant life, but Hosea had already anticipated our author in connecting Ephraim's failure to achieve birth, the threat of death, and God's gift, like dew, of new life (Hos 13:13-14; 14:5-9). The reference to light is probably to underscore the notion that the dead are no longer confined to the darkness and gloom of the dirt and the underworld, for the earth or the underworld will expel in birth (תַּפִּיל, *tappîl*, lit. "cause to drop") the shades of the dead (רְפָאִים, *rĕpā'îm*).

Precisely what this resurrection from the dead meant to the author is subject to debate. In Hosea in the late eighth century BCE the resurrection motif was a way of speaking about national revival or rebirth (Hos 6:1-3; 13:13-14; 14:5-9), and in Ezekiel at approximately the same date as here in the Isaiah Apocalypse, the motif was used in precisely the same way (Ezek 37:11-14). That is probably the main significance of this motif to our author, but the imagery in Isa 25:7, while it does stress national rebirth in the removal of the reproach of God's people, seems to transcend this limited sense of resurrection. It extends the blessing of the swallowing up of death to all peoples and suggests that the prophet may have expanded this metaphor in the direction it was later taken of a genuine, universal resurrection from the dead. At the very least, his work provided the base and the impetus for this later development reflected in Dan 12:2 (note the similar use of *'āpar*, "dust," and the *hiphil* of *qîṣ*, "to awake," which seems to echo our passage), in other late Jewish works from just before the common era, and in the New Testament.

Verse 20, however, qualifies this joyous announcement of resurrection and national rebirth with a command to be patient just a little longer. God, still addressing his people in the second person masculine singular, urges them to go into their chambers and lock the doors behind them and hide for just a little while until the wrath passes (עַד יַעֲבוֹר זָעַם, *'ad ya'ăbôr zā'am*). The imagery is suggestive of the passover story, when the Israelites were to remain in their houses until Yahweh had passed (עָבַר, *'ābar*) through the land of Egypt executing his wrath on his enemies (Exod 12:22-23). The motif of patiently waiting for Yahweh's certain intervention is found also in Hab 2:2-3, a passage that probably dates to about the same time period as the Isaiah Apocalypse.

In v. 21, the prophet, speaking now for Yahweh, who is mentioned in the third person, explains that Yahweh is about to come out from his place to impose the punishment for the sin of the inhabitant of the earth upon him. The idiom "to punish the sin upon its perpetrator" is a way of underscoring that the punishment fits the crime. The singular construction (יֹשֵׁב־הָאָרֶץ, *yōšēb-hā'āreṣ*, "the inhabitant of the earth") is probably just a collective for all the inhabitants of the earth, but it might point to the ruler of Babylon, the new world ruler who had replaced Assyria as Judah's oppressor. In any case, the earth will reveal the bloodshed in it and will no longer cover up those who have been slain in it. The hidden atrocities of the powerful and ruthless will no longer be hidden, and those who perpetrated them will receive their just punishment in the wrath of Yahweh's judgment.

Bibliography

Beeston, A. F. L., "The Hebrew Verb *špt*," *VT* 8 (1958) 216–17.

Birkeland, H., "The Belief in Resurrection of the Dead in the Old Testament," *ST* 3 (1950) 60–78.

Blenkinsopp, J., "Fragments of Ancient Exegesis in an Isaian Poem," *ZAW* 93 (1981) 51–62.

Botterweck, G. J., "Marginalien zum Atl. Auferstehungsglauben," *WZKM* 54 (1957) 1–8.

Bregman, Lucy, "Academic 'Immortality' and the Eschatological Destiny of the Dead," *Religion and Intellectual Life* 2, no. 3 (1985) 28–36.

Day, John, "A Case of Inner Scriptural Interpretation: The Dependence of Isaiah XXVI.13–XXVII.11 on Hosea XIII 4–XIV.10 (Eng. 9) and Its Relevance to Some Theories of the Redaction of the 'Isaiah Apocalypse,'" *JTS* 31 (1980) 309–19.

——, "The Dependence of Isaiah 26:13–27:11 on Hosea 13:4–14:10 and Its Relevance to Some Theories on the Redaction of the 'Isaiah Apocalypse,'" in C. C. Broyles and C. A. Evans, eds., *Writing and Reading the Scroll of Isaiah: Studies of an Interpretive Tradition* (2 vols.; VTSup 70; Leiden: Brill, 1997) 1:357–68.

——, "*ṭal ôrôt* in Isaiah 26,19," *ZAW* 90 (1978) 265–69.

Emerton, J. A., "Notes on Two Verses in Isaiah (26:16 and 66:17)," in J. A. Emerton, ed., *Prophecy: Essays Presented to Georg Fohrer on His Sixty-Fifth Birthday, 6 September 1980* (BZAW 150; Berlin: de Gruyter, 1980) 12–25.

Fabry, H.-J., "*nebela*," *TDOT* 9:156.

Fohrer, G., "Das Geschick des Menschen nach dem Tode im Alten Testament," *KD* 14 (1968) 249–62.

Fouts, David M., "A Suggestion for Isaiah 26:16," *VT* 41 (1991) 472–75.

Gordon, Cyrus H., "Hby, Possessor of Horns and Tail," *UF* 18 (1986) 129–32.

Gray, G. B., "Critical Discussions. Isaiah 26; 25 1-5; 34 12-14," *ZAW* 31 (1911) 111–27.

Gryson, R., "'Enfanter un esprit de salut': Histoire du texte d'Isaïe 26:17-18," *RTL* 27 (1996) 25–46.

Haenchen, E., "Auferstehung im Alten Testament," in Haenchen, *Die Bibel und Wir: Gesammelte Aufsätze*, Vol. 2 (Tübingen: J. C. B. Mohr, 1968) 73–90.

Hauge, Martin Ravndal, "Some Aspects of the Motif 'the City Facing Death' of Ps 68:21," *SJOT* 2 (1988) 1–29.

Helfmeyer, F. J., "'Deine Toten—Meine Leichen': Heilzusage und Annahme in Jes 29,19," in Heinz-Josef Fabry, ed., *Bausteine biblischer Theologie: Festgabe für G. Johannes Botterweck zum 60. Geburtstag* (BBB 50; Cologne: Hanstein, 1977) 245–58.

Humbert, P., "La rosée tombe en Israel," *TZ* 13 (1957) 487–93.

Irwin, W. H., "Syntax and Style in Isaiah 26," *CBQ* 41 (1979) 240–61.

Johnson, D. G., *From Chaos to Restoration: An Integrative Reading of Isaiah 24–27* (JSOTSup 61; Sheffield: JSOT Press, 1988).

Kaminka, A., "Le développement des idées du prophète Isaïe et l'unité de son livre VIII: L'authenticité des chapîtres xxiv à xxvii," *REJ* 81 (1925) 27–36.

König, Franz, *Zarathustras Jenseitsvorstellungen und das Alte Testament* (Vienna: Herder, 1964) esp. 214–40.

Martin-Achard, Robert, *De la mort à la résurrection, d'après l'Ancien Testament* (Bibliothèque théologique; Neuchâtel: Delachaux & Niestlé, 1956).

Nötscher, Friedrich, *Altorientalischer und alttestamentlicher Auferstehungsglauben* (Würzburg: C. J. Becker, 1926).

Oswalt, John N., "God's Determination to Redeem His People (Isaiah 9:1-7; 11:1-11; 26:1-9; 35:1-10)," *RevExp* 88 (1991) 153–65.

Ploeg, P. J. van der, "L'espérance dans l'Ancien Testament," *RB* 61 (1954) 481–507.

Preuss, H. D., "'Auferstehung' in Texten alttestamentlicher Apokalyptik (Jes 26,7-19; Dan 12,1-4)," *Linguistische Theologie* 3 (1972) 101–72.

Rost, Leonhard, "Alttestamentliche Wurzeln der ersten Auferstehung," in Werner Schmauch, ed., *In Memoriam Ernst Lohmeyer* (Stuttgart: Evangelisches Verlagswerk, 1951) 67–72.

Running, Leona, "Syriac Variants in Isaiah 26," *AUSS* 5 (1967) 46–58.

Savignac, J. de, "La rosée solaire de l'ancienne Égypte," *NC* 6 (1954) 345–53.

Sawyer, John F. A., "Hebrew Words for the Resurrection of the Dead," *VT* 23 (1973) 218–34.

Schmitz, P. C., "The Grammar of Resurrection in Isaiah 26:19a-c," *JBL* 122 (2003) 145–49.

Schwarz, G., "'. . . Tau der Lichter . . .'? Eine Emendation," *ZAW* 88 (1976) 280–81.

Snoek, J., "Discontinuity between Present and Future in Isaiah 26:7-21," in F. Postma et al., eds., *The New Things: Eschatology in Old Testament Prophecy. Festschrift for Henk Leene* (Amsterdamse cahiers voor exegese van de Bijbel en zijn traties 3; Maastricht: Shaker, 2002) 211–18.

Stemberger, G., "Das Problem der Auferstehung im Alten Testament," *Kairos* 14 (1972) 272–90.

Sysling, H., *Teḥiyyat Ha-Metim: The Resurrection of the Dead in the Palestinian Targums of the Pentateuch and Parallel Traditions in Classical Rabbinic Literature* (TSAJ 57; Tübingen: Mohr Siebeck, 1996) 72–73.

Vervenne, M., "The Phraseology of 'Knowing Yhwh' in the Hebrew Bible: A Preliminary Study of Its Syntax and Function," in J. van Ruiten and M. Vervenne, *Studies in the Book of Isaiah: Festschrift Willem A. M. Beuken* (BETL 132; Leuven: Leuven University Press/Peeters, 1997) 467–92.

Virgulin, S., "La risurrezione dei morti in Is 26,14-19," *BO* 14 (1972) 273–90.

Wahl, O., "Wir haben eine befestigte Stadt: Botschaft von Jes 26:1-6," in Friedrich Diedrich and Bernd Willmes, eds., *Ich bewirke das Heil und erschaffe das Unheil (Jesaja 45,7): Studien zur Botschaft der Propheten. Festschrift für Lothar Ruppert zum 65. Geburtstag* (FB 88; Würzburg: Echter, 1998) 459–81.

Whitley, C. F., "The Positive Force of בל," *ZAW* 84 (1972) 215–16.

Wieringen, A. L. H. M. van, "'I' and 'We' before 'Your' Face: A Communication Analysis of Isaiah 26:7-21," in H. J. Bosman, H. van Grol, et al., eds., *Studies in Isaiah 24–27: The Isaiah Workshop–de Jesaja Werkplaats* (OtSt 43; Leiden: Brill, 2000) 239–51.

Zolli, E., "Il canto dei morti risorti e il ms. DSS in Isa 26:18," *Sef* 12 (1952) 375–78.

1/ On that day Yahweh will punish[a]
 With his harsh,[b] and great, and strong sword
 Leviathan the fleeing[c] serpent,
 And Leviathan the twisting serpent,
 And he will kill the dragon which is in the sea.[d]

2/ On that day:
 A vineyard of beauty,[e]
 Sing of it![f]

3/ I, Yahweh, am its[g] guard;
 I will water it[g] constantly.
 Lest one harm[h] it,[g]
 I will guard[i] it[g] night and day.

4/ I have no wrath.
 If it gives[j] me thorns (and) thistles,[k]
 I will advance against it[j] in war,
 I will set it[j] on fire together.[l]

5/ Or if it holds fast to my refuge,[m]
 it makes peace with me,
 peace it makes with me.[n]

6/ In days to come[o] Jacob will take root,[p]
 Israel shall sprout and blossom,[q]
 And the face of the world will be filled with fruit.

7/ Has he beaten him as his beater was beaten?
 Or was he slain as his slayers[r] were slain?

8/ By expulsion[s] and sending him[t] away he contended[u] with him,[t]
 With his harsh wind he removed (him)[v] on the day of the east wind.

9/ Therefore by this[w] will the iniquity of Jacob[x] be atoned,
 And this will be the full[y] expression [of repentance] for the removal[z] of his sin;*[a]
 When he makes all[y] the altar stones like smashed limestones,*[b]
 (And) sacred poles and incense altars will not remain standing.*[c]

10/ For the fortified city lies alone,
 A dwelling*[d] deserted and abandoned like the wilderness;
 There the calf grazes,
 There it lies down and devours its twigs.

11/ When its branch is dry, they are broken;*[e]
 Women come*[f] and make a fire of it,*[g]
 Because he is not*[h] a people of understanding,
 That is why his maker*[i] does not*[h] show him pity,
 And his creator*[j] shows him no*[h] favor.*[k]

12/ And in that day
 Yahweh will beat out*[l] (grain) from the stream*[m] of the Euphrates
 To the Wadi of Egypt,
 And you*[n] will be picked up*[o] one by one,
 O sons of Israel.

13/ And on that day
 There will be blown on a great trumpet,
 And those lost*[p] in the land of Assyria will come,
 And those scattered in the land of Egypt,
 And they will worship Yahweh on the holy mountain, in Jerusalem.

Textual Notes

a MT יִפְקֹד (yipqōd) "will punish"; 1QIsaᵃ יפקוד.

b MT, 1QIsaᵃ הַקָּשָׁה (haqqāšâ), "the harsh," so Vg., Syr., Tg.; LXX τὴν ἁγίαν, "the holy," is apparently reading הקדשה.

c MT בָּרִחַ (bārîaḥ), "the fleeing"; 1QIsaᵃ בורח. Vg. understands the word as referring to the "bar" of a gate, "the bar serpent."

d MT, 1QIsaᵃ אֲשֶׁר בַּיָּם (ʾăšer bayyām), "which is in the sea," so also Vg., Syr., and Tg.; LXX omits, probably because of the orthographic similarity to the opening of the next verse, בַּיּוֹם (bayyôm), "on that day."

e MT כֶּרֶם חֶמֶד (kerem ḥemed), "a vineyard of beauty"; LXX follows MT, though it has a double translation of ḥemed, ἀμπελὼν καλός· ἐπιθύμημα ἐξάρχειν κατ᾽ αὐτῆς, "a *beautiful* vineyard, a *desire* to begin (singing) about it"; 1QIsaᵃ חוסר כרם (*kerem ḥomer*), "a vineyard of wine," so also Vg. and Syr.

f MT, 1QIsaᵃ עֲנוּ־לָהּ (*ʿannû-lāh*), "sing to her!", Tg., Syr.; Vg., "he will sing to her." The gender of the suffix is a bit disturbing. The word כֶּרֶם (*kerem*), "vineyard," is normally masculine, as consistently in the earlier Song of the Vineyard (Isa 5:1-7), not feminine as here and in Lev 25:3. One wonders whether the *mater* ה (*-h*), which could stand for a final *-ô*, "his," as well as a final *-â*, "her," in the preexilic script, has been consistently misread in this text. The suffix is pointed as feminine four times in v. 3 and twice in v. 4, but the feminine suffixes in v. 4 appear to refer back to the subject of the third person masculine singular verb in v. 4, viz., יִתְּנֵנִי (*yittĕnēnî*), "if it gives me," and the three parallel verbs in v. 5 are all third person masculine singular.

g Again, the suffixes referring back to כֶּרֶם (*kerem*), "vineyard," are all feminine where one would expect masculine suffixes. See note f above.

h MT יִפְקֹד (*yipqōd*), "he harms, punishes"; 1QIsaᵃ יפקוד.

i MT אֶצֳּרֶנָּה (*ʾeṣṣŏrennâ*), "I will guard it"; 1QIsaᵃ אצורנה. LXX makes hash of the verse: ἐγὼ πόλις ἰσχυρά, πόλις πολιορκουμένη, μάτην ποτιῶ αὐτήν· ἁλώσεται γὰρ νυκτός, ἡμέρας δὲ πεσεῖται τὸ τεῖχος, "I am a strong city, a besieged city; in vain do I water it, for it will be taken by night, and by day the wall will fall."

j The verb form in the expression מִי־יִתְּנֵנִי (*mî-yittĕnēnî*), "whoever gives me," is third person masculine singular, but the following pronominal suffixes on בָּהּ (*bāh*), "against it," and אֲצִיתֶנָּה (*ʾaṣîtennâ*), "I will set it on fire," are both third person feminine singular. There is no basis for this sudden shift in gender, so either it is a blatant error, or a careless error due, as noted above in note f, to misreading an ambiguous *mater* as a feminine marker.

k MT שָׁמִיר שַׁיִת (*šāmîr šayit*), "thorns (and) thistles"; 1QIsaᵃ שימיר ושית with an erasure of the first *yod* (*šāmîr wĕšayit*), "thorns and thistles."

l MT יַחַד (*yāḥad*, "together"); 1QIsaᵃ יחדו (*yaḥdāw*), "together." LXX again struggles with the verse: οὐκ ἔστιν ἣ οὐκ ἐπελάβετο αὐτῆς· τίς με θήσει φυλάσσειν καλάμην ἐν ἀγρῷ; διὰ τὴν πολεμίαν ταύτην ἠθέτηκα αὐτήν. τοίνυν διὰ τοῦτο ἐποίησεν κύριος ὁ θεὸς πάντα, ὅσα συνέταξεν. κατακέκαυμαι, "There is none who has not taken it. Who will set me to watch stubble in a field? Because of this enmity I set it aside. Therefore because of this the Lord God has done all these things which he ordained. I have been burned up."

m LXX has βοήσονται οἱ ἐνοικοῦντες ἐν αὐτῇ, "those who dwell in it will cry out."

n LXX has ποιήσωμεν εἰρήνην αὐτῷ, ποιήσωμεν εἰρήνην, "let us make peace with him, let us make peace"; and Syr. has "I will make peace with him, peace I will make with him."

o MT, 1QIsaᵃ הַבָּאִים (*habbāʾîm*), "the ones coming," though followed by the versions, is clearly defective. One should restore something like הנה ימים באים, "behold days are coming" (cf. Isa 39:6), or בימים הבאים, "in the coming days."

p MT יַשְׁרֵשׁ יַעֲקֹב (*yašrēš yaʿăqōb*), "Jacob will take root"; 1QIsaᵃ ישריש יעקוב.

q MT יָצִיץ וּפָרַח יִשְׂרָאֵל (*yāṣîṣ ûpāraḥ yiśrāʾēl*), "Israel will sprout and blossom"; 1QIsaᵃ ויציץ ופרח ישראל, "and Israel will sprout and blossom."

r Reading the active participle with 1QIsaᵃ הורגיו (*hôrĕgāyw*), "those slaying him," against MT's passive הֲרֻגָיו (*hărūgāyw*), "those slain by him," since this agrees with the preceding active participle מַכֵּהוּ (*makkēhû*), "the one who beat him." The question assumes a negative answer and implies that God's punishment of Israel was not as severe as the punishment meted out to those whom God used to punish Israel.

s The correct vocalization of the *palpel* or *pilpel* infinitive of סאסא and its precise meaning are open to discussion. The Leningrad Codex has the weird pointing בְּסַאסְּאָה (*bĕssaʾssĕʾâ*); the notes to *BHS* suggest either the reading בְּסַאסְּאָה (*bĕsaʾssĕʾâ*) or בְּסַסְּאָה (*bĕsassĕʾâ*). One should also consider בְּסַאסְּאָה (*bĕsaʾsĕʾāh*) with the feminine suffix. The general sense of the verb is perhaps supplied by the parallel *piel* infinitive of the verb שלח (*šālaḥ*), "to send away."

t The feminine suffixes on בְּשַׁלְּחָהּ (*bĕšalĕḥāh*), "in sending her away," and תְּרִיבֶנָּה (*tĕrîbennâ*), "you contented with her," and perhaps בסאסאה, "in expelling her," are problematic, since God's people are referred to in the preceding verse with the third person masculine singular suffix. It is probable that this is a mistaken pointing resulting from a misreading of the earlier usage of ה as a *mater lexionis* to indicate a final *-ô* vowel as well as a final *-â* vowel; see notes f and j above.

u MT, 1QIsaᵃ תְּרִיבֶנָּה (*tĕrîbennâ*), "you contended with her/him," with the second person verb form, is odd, since the following verb, also with God as the assumed subject, is in the third person. I accept the emendation to יריבנה, "he contended with her/him," though the versions seem to support the second person.

v MT הֵגָה (*hāgāh*), "he removed," should perhaps be emended to הֵגָהּ (*hāgāh*), "he removed her/him," assuming the same feminine misreading of the *mater* that originally served for both the third person masculine singular *-ô* and the third person feminine singular *-â*.

w MT בְּזֹאת (*bĕzōʾt*), "by this"; 1QIsaᵃ בזואת.

x MT עֲוֹן־יַעֲקֹב (*ʿăwōn yaʿăqōb*), "iniquity of Jacob"; 1QIsaᵃ עוון יעקוב.

y MT כָּל (*kol*), "all, the full"; 1QIsaᵃ כול.

z MT הָסֵר, the *hiphil* infinitive construct (*hāsîr*), "the removal"; 1QIsaᵃ הסיר.

*a MT חַטָּאתוֹ (*ḥaṭṭāʾtô*), "of his sin"; 1QIsaᵃ חטאוו, probably miswritten for חטאיו (*ḥăṭāʾāyw*), "of his sins."

*b MT כְּאַבְנֵי־גִר (*kĕʾabnê-gīr*), "like limestones"; 1QIsaᵃ כאבני גיר.

*c MT לֹא־יָקֻמוּ (*lōʾ-yāqūmû*), "will not remain standing"; 1QIsaᵃ לוא יקומו.

*d MT, 1QIsaᵃ נָוֶה (*nāweh*), "dwelling, habitation, pasture"; traces in 4QIsaᶠ נהוה. LXX and Vg. support MT.

*e MT תִּשָּׁבַרְנָה (*tiššābarnâ*), *niphal* imperfect third person feminine plural, "will be broken," has been questioned (see *BHS*), since its subject קְצִירָהּ (*qĕṣîrāh*), "its branch," is grammatically singular though a collective. Erhlich (*Randglossen* [1912] 97), cited with approval by Wildberger (2:1014), suggested emending to תִּשָּׁבֶרְנָה (*tišbĕrennâ*), *qal* imperfect third person feminine singular with third person feminine singular suffix) in order to take נָשִׁים (*nāšîm*), "women," as the subject: "When its branch is dry, women break (it); they come and set it afire." That is hardly an improvement, since there is still no agreement in number between the singular verb and the newly proposed plural subject, which is no longer a collective. The emendation does not seem necessary; it is easier to understand the singular collective *qĕṣîrāh*, "its branch," as the subject of the third person feminine plural *niphal* imperfect verb, since collectives are often rendered by sense.

*f MT בָּאוֹת (*bāʾôt*), "will come"; 1QIsaᵃ adds the word as a correction above the line בואת.

*g MT, 1QIsaᵃ מְאִירוֹת אוֹתָהּ (*mĕʾîrôt ʾôtāh*), "and light it, make a fire of it"; Vg., Syr., and Tg. took this verb in the sense of "enlighten" or "teach." LXX goes its own way: γυναῖκες ἐρχόμεναι ἀπὸ θέας, δεῦτε, "you women who come from a spectacle, come here!"

*h MT לֹא (*lōʾ*), "not, no"; 1QIsaᵃ לוא.

*i MT עֹשֵׂהוּ (*ʿōśēhû*), "his maker"; 1QIsaᵃ עושהו.

*j MT וְיֹצְרוֹ (*wĕyōṣĕrô*), "and his creator"; 1QIsaᵃ ויוצרו.

*k MT יְחֻנֶּנּוּ (*yĕḥunnennû*, "shows him (*no*) favor"); 1QIsaᵃ יחוננו.

*l MT יַחְבֹּט (*yaḥbōṭ*), "he will beat out (*grain*)"; 1QIsaᵃ יחבוט. The verb refers to beating out grain as part of the harvest after the grain is cut, but LXX and Tg. seem to misunderstand the imagery. LXX has συμφράξει κύριος, "the Lord will fence them in," and Tg. has "the slain will be cast before the Lord."

*m MT מִשִּׁבֹּלֶת הַנָּהָר (*miššibbōlet hannāhār*), "from the stream of the Euphrates"); 1QIsaᵃ משבל הנהר. There is an intentional double entendre here, for which see the commentary ahead.

*n MT וְאַתֶּם (*wĕʾattem*), "and you"; 1QIsaᵃ ואתמה.

*o MT, 1QIsaᵃ תְּלֻקְּטוּ (*tĕluqqĕṭû*), "you will be picked up"; LXX misreads the verb as an imperative, ὑμεῖς δὲ συναγάγετε τοὺς υἱοὺς Ισραηλ κατὰ ἕνα ἕνα, "but as for you, gather the sons of Israel one by one."

*p MT הָאֹבְדִים (*hāʾōbĕdîm*), "those lost"; 1QIsaᵃ האובדים. Syr. switches the order of Assyria and Egypt in its translation.

Commentary

On that day (v. 1) is again the day of salvation, when Yahweh with his harsh, great, and strong sword will punish Leviathan the fleeing serpent (לִוְיָתָן נָחָשׁ בָּרִחַ, *liwĕyātān nāḥāš bāriaḥ*), Leviathan the twisting serpent (לִוְיָתָן נָחָשׁ עֲקַלָּתוֹן, *liwĕyātān nāḥāš ʿăqallātôn*), and kill the sea monster (הַתַּנִּין, *hattannîn*) that is in the sea. The sea monster motif is a loose quotation ultimately derived from the Canaanite myth about Baal's battle with the sea monster. Note the repeated lines: *k tmḫṣ . ltn . bṯn . brḥ | tkly . bṯn . ʿqltn . | šlyṭ . d . šbʿy . rašm*, "When you smote Lotan, the fleeing serpent, (when) you vanquished the twisting serpent, Shalliyaṭ of the seven heads" (*KTU* 1.5 i 1-3, 27-30). Lotan is the Ugaritic form of Leviathan with contraction of the diphthongs. The word *bṯn* (*baṯnu*, "serpent, sea serpent") is cognate with Akkadian *bašmu*, later Hebrew via Aramaic פֶּתֶן (*peten*, "serpent"), and older Hebrew בָּשָׁן* (*bašan*, "serpent"). The older Hebrew בָּשָׁן* (*bašan*) was easily confused with the place name בָּשָׁן (*Bāšān*, the northern Transjordan plateau), and נָחָשׁ (*nāḥāš*, another word for "serpent") soon displaced it almost entirely. It is preserved in two old pieces of poetry where a wordplay with the geographical name protected it (Deut 33:22; Ps 68:23). In the tribal blessings in Gen 49:16-17, Dan is compared to a snake (נָחָשׁ, *nāḥāš*) on the path, while in Deut 33:22, Dan is a lion's cub that jumps back from the serpent (הַבָּשָׁן, *habbāšān*). In Ps 68:22-23, in a passage with

clear mythological overtones, God smites (יִמְחַץ, *yimḥaṣ*) the head of his enemies, and the Lord says, "I will turn back from the serpent/Bashan [מִבָּשָׁן, *mibbāšān*], I will turn back from the depth of the sea [יָם, *yām*]." In Ugaritic myth, Lotan, the serpent (*baṯnu*), the sea serpent (*tnn*; see *KTU* 1.3 iii 40-42), and Shalliyaṭ of the seven heads all referred to the same seven-headed sea monster, and the same should be said for the parallel terms in Hebrew. For the multiheaded nature of this sea monster in the Hebrew tradition, see Ps 74:13-14. In the Hebrew tradition, the sea monster was also known as רַהַב (*rahab*, "the tumultuous one," Rahab; Isa 30:7; 51:9; Ps 89:11; Job 9:13; 26:12).

The motif of the sea monster was used in Israel, as elsewhere in the Near East in general, to symbolize cosmic evil, chaos, and disorder, but it was also used from time to time to demonize particular historical enemies, much as one still hears particular nations characterized as "the evil empire" or "the great Satan." First Isaiah identified the sea monster רַהַב (*rahab*) with Egypt (Isa 30:7), and this demonization of Egypt as the sea monster is also found twice in Ezekiel (תַּנִּים, Ezek 29:3; 32:2; cf. also the faded allusion to this identification in the bland reference to Egypt as Rahab in Ps 87:4). This identification of the sea monster with a particular historical enemy of Israel raises the question of its referent in Isa 27:1. I am inclined to think that our author, in line with the earlier Isaianic tradition and with Ezekiel, his younger contemporary, is using this motif with particular reference

337

to Egypt. From Judah's point of view, Egypt was the power that thwarted the great expectations associated with Josiah's religious reform and national revival and returned the nation to chaos and subjugation. True deliverance would require that the Egyptian monster be destroyed just as Assyria had been, and admirers of Josiah, like Jeremiah, were delighted when the Egyptians were thoroughly defeated at Carchemish and Hamath (Jer 46:1-12). Our writer appears to come from the same period and reflects similar views.

The second "on that day" (v. 2) suggests again the day of salvation when Yahweh intervenes to punish his enemies. The syntax of the rest of the verse, however, seems abrupt and a bit awkward. The expression כֶּרֶם חֶמֶד (kerem ḥemed), "a vineyard of beauty," "a pleasant vineyard," could be taken as an elliptical nominal clause, "there will be a vineyard of beauty," or it could be taken as the title of the song one is commanded to sing, but then there would be no expressed antecedent for the one to whom the song was to be sung. The first possibility, therefore, seems more probable, and the following command to sing לָהּ (lāh), "to it, with reference to it," should be rendered as "sing of it" or "sing about it," not "sing to it." As syntactically abrupt as the verse is, it clearly alludes back to Isaiah of Jerusalem's eighth-century "Song of the Vineyard" (Isa 5:1-7) and suggests that the judgment on Israel and Judah announced there is about to be revised and reversed. In effect, the Song of the Vineyard is about to be rewritten in a major key on a positive note. What follows is the revised song.

Yahweh is the speaker, and he affirms that he is the vineyard's guard, will water it regularly, and lest anyone or anything should harm it, will guard it night and day (v. 3). This is in contrast to the original Song of the Vineyard, where Yahweh in anger over the failure of the vineyard to produce a vintage, removed its hedge and broke down its wall, thus allowing the vineyard to be grazed and trampled until, then uncultivated, it grew up in thorns and thistles (Isa 5:4-6). Now, however, Yahweh has no wrath toward his vineyard (v. 4). If it yields thorns and thistles (שָׁמִיר שָׁיִת—a slight variant of the שָׁמִיר וָשָׁיִת in 5:6) instead of good grapes, that is, bloodshed and violence instead of justice and righteousness (Isa 5:7), Yahweh will advance against it and burn it up together with its evil fruit. On the other hand, if it holds fast to Yahweh's refuge, it will make peace with Yahweh (v. 5).

My interpretation assumes that the subjects of the third person masculine singular verbs and the originally third person masculine singular suffixes, later misread as third person feminine singular, all refer back to the vineyard. The repetition of the phrase "it will make peace with me" implies that this is the result the singer now expects in contrast to the past judgment.

In light of this expectation the prophet promises that in days to come Jacob will take root, Israel will sprout and blossom, and the face or surface of the world will be filled with fruit (v. 6). The harvest God expected but failed to receive in the original Song of the Vineyard (Isa 5:1-7) will now fill the whole world. There is, however, a significant shift in emphasis. In 5:7 the harvest for which God was looking consisted in the moral qualities and behavior of justice and righteousness, but the fruit promised in 27:6 seems far more focused on the numeric increase in the surviving population of Jacob/Israel. For this agricultural metaphor for the increase in the human population, compare Isa 37:31. The terminology "Jacob/Israel" is a bit ambiguous. In the earlier Isaianic tradition, this terminology often refers specifically to the northern kingdom in contrast to Judah, both of whom are mentioned at the conclusion to the earlier Song of the Vineyard (5:7). The later author of the Isaiah Apocalypse may be using Jacob/Israel as a more inclusive terms for all Israel, including Judah, but he may also be thinking specifically of the people of the former northern kingdom. Jeremiah, in some of his earliest oracles, speaks of the return of the northern exiles to their home in the mountains of Samaria and the hill country of Ephraim, and of their pilgrimage to Zion to worship (Jer 31:1-14).

Following up on this promise, the prophet raises two rhetorical questions relating to Israel's earlier punishment, both questions expecting a negative answer: "Has he beaten him as his beater was beaten? Or has he been slain as his slayers were slain?" His beater (מַכֵּהוּ, makkēhû) in the earlier Isaianic tradition may at one point have referred to Aram as the oppressor of the northern kingdom (10:20), but it soon came to be a reference to Assyria, and the assumed answer to the rhetorical questions is that, though Yahweh may have beaten Israel severely in punishment (see Isa 1:5-9), compared to the total annihilation Yahweh imposed on Assyria, his staff for punishing Israel (Isa 10:5-12, 20, 24), Israel got off very lightly. Israel may have suffered severe casualties, but Assyria was killed off completely.

Then in v. 8 the prophet seems to develop his discussion of the punishment God imposed on Israel. There is a certain ambiguity in the referents of the pronominal suffixes in the verse. They are pointed as third person feminine singular suffixes, though Israel as the antecedent in v. 7 is construed as third person masculine singular. One might think of the antecedent not as Israel but as Assyria, his smiter and his slayers, but there would still be a lack of agreement in gender and for "his slayers" in number as well as gender. The suffixes are probably to be corrected to the third person masculine singular, having been misread because of a misunderstanding of the early ambiguous use of ה (-h) as a *mater* for both a final -ô, "his," and a final -â, "her." Moreover, it is unlikely that Assyria is to be understood as the antecedent, since the "expulsion and sending him away" appears to refer to the exile of Israelites and Judeans in both Assyria and Egypt that is mentioned in vv. 12-13. The sense of v. 8 seems to be that God dealt with Israel by expulsion and exile, removing him from his homeland by his harsh wind, as on a day with a harsh east wind blowing in from the desert (the Khamsin or Sirocco). There is no need to assume a reference to the Babylonian exile. Assyria had exiled many Israelites in the aftermath of the Syro-Ephraimitic War in 732 BCE, and again after the capture of Samaria in 722 and 720 BCE, and Sennacherib claims to have exiled over two hunded thousand Judean and perhaps Israelite refugees during his third campaign in 701 BCE.[1] Others may have ended up in Egypt during the Assyrian–Egyptian wars of the early seventh century, and some at least were taken into Egyptian exile by Necho after his murder of Josiah and his return from Carchemish in 609 BCE, when he replaced Josiah's successor Jehoahaz with Eliakim, Necho's own pick (2 Kgs 23:29-35).

Given such a harsh punishment, though far lighter than that imposed on Assyria, how was Jacob to find atonement for his sin? Verse 9 gives the answer. The expression "by this [זאת] the iniquity of Jacob will be atoned" (יְכֻפַּר, yĕkuppar) is clear enough, but the expression וְזֶה כָּל־פְּרִי הָסִר חַטָּאתוֹ (wĕzeh kol-pĕrî hāsīr haṭṭāʾtô, lit., "and this will be the whole fruit of the removal of his sin") is not quite as transparent.[2] The word פְּרִי (pĕrî), "fruit," is often used metaphorically for the produce or product of various parts of the body or of human actions: פְּרִי־בָטֶן (pĕrî-bāṭen), "fruit of the womb, offspring" (Gen 30:2; Deut 7:13; 28:4; et passim); פְּרִי יָדֶיהָ or פְּרִי כַּפֶּיהָ (pĕrî kappêhā /yādêhā) "the produce of her hands" (Prov 31:16, 31); פְּרִי פִי (pĕrî pî), "the fruit of the mouth" (Prov 12:14; 13:2; 18:20); פְּרִי מַעַלְלֵיהֶם (pĕrî maʿalĕlêhem), "the fruit of their deeds" (Isa 3:10; cf. Jer 17:10; 21:14; et passim); פְּרִי מַחְשְׁבוֹתָם (pĕrî maḥšĕbôtām), "the outcome of their schemes" (Jer 6:19); and פְּרִי דַרְכָּם (pĕrî darkām), "the outcome of their way of life" (Prov 1:31). Of all these metaphorical idioms, the most interesting for our passage is פְּרִי פִי (pĕrî pî), "the fruit of the mouth," because the fruit or produce of the mouth is "words" or "expression." As a token of genuine repentance in Hos 14:2-3, Israel is commanded to take words (דְּבָרִים, dĕbārîm) and return to Yahweh and say to him, "Take away all iniquity and accept the good, and we will offer the fruit of our lips" (MT has פָרִים שְׂפָתֵינוּ, pārîm sĕpātênû, "the [sacrificial] bulls of our lips," but it is clearly an intentional play on פְּרִי שְׂפָתֵינוּ, pĕrî sĕpātênû, "the fruit, that is, the words of our lips"). In other words, "the fruit [פְּרִי] of our lips" functions as the sacrificial offering, the equivalent of פָרִים, "[sacrificial] bulls." Note also Isa 10:12, where אֶפְקֹד עַל־פְּרִי־גֹדֶל לְבַב מֶלֶךְ־אַשּׁוּר (ʾepqōd ʿal-pĕrî-gōdel lĕbab melek-ʾaššûr), "I will punish the fruit of the greatness of heart of the king of Assyria," could perhaps best be rendered, "I will punish the arrogant bragging of the king of Assyria." In light of these examples, the expression וְזֶה כָּל־פְּרִי הָסִר חַטָּאתוֹ (wĕzeh kol-pĕrî hāsīr haṭṭāʾtô) in our passage, may best be rendered, "And this will be the full expression [of repentance] for the removal of his sin." The atonement for his iniquity and the full expression of repentance for removal of his sin will only be obtained when he has turned all the stones of the altars into smashed limestone, and the sacred poles (אֲשֵׁרִים, ʾăšērîm) and incense altars

---

1   See the earlier discussion and references in the commentary on Isa 11:10-16.

2   Both the feminine זֹאת and the masculine זֶה point forward to the end of the verse; the reason for the difference in gender is that the understood referent of the feminine demonstrative is presumably a feminine noun such as עֲבֹדה, "work," or פְעֻלָה, "deed," while the referent of the masculine demonstrative is the masculine noun פְּרִי, "fruit."

(חַמָּנִים, ḥammānîm) no longer remain standing. This is the type of destruction of formerly sacred objects that Josiah carried out both in Judah and to some extent in the north during his religious reform (2 Kgs 23:1-20; cf. 2 Chr 34:4, 7), and which Ezekiel, during the period between the first Babylonian exile in 597 BCE and the second capture of Jerusalem in 586 BCE, threatened God would do again in Judah (Ezek 6:4, 6). Obviously after Josiah's death, the people in both north and south reverted to the use of these cultic objects, and that is the reason why Yahweh's positive intervention has not yet come.

Absent such a genuine repentance, the situation in Israel remains bleak after God's expulsion of his people (v. 10). The fortified city sits isolated, deserted, and abandoned like the wilderness, with a calf grazing there, sleeping there, and devouring the twigs of the abandoned city's deserted orchards and vineyards. One should compare this description to Isaiah's portrayal of the future devastation of the land by Assyria and Egypt in Isa 7:18-25. The singular city hardly refers to one particular city, but simply describes the fate of all the once-fortified cities in the area. The description of the calf feeding on its (the city's) twigs presumably refers to the twigs of the abandoned orchards and vineyards associated with the city. This image leads to a further elaboration of the ruin of these once well-cultivated, expensive, and productive trees and vines (v. 11). When its branch (קְצִירָהּ, qĕṣîrāh) dries out—the noun is singular, but a collective, and the subsequent verb, following the sense rather than the grammatical form of its subject, switches to the plural—(תִּשָּׁבַרְנָה, tiššābarnâ) they are broken. Then scavenging women who come by (gather it up) making a fire with it (מְאִירוֹת אוֹתָהּ, mĕ'îrôt 'ôtāh)—reverting to the collective singular. The remnant left in the land, struggling to survive, still do not understand what they must do to atone for their sins, for it is not a people with understanding (לֹא עַם־בִּינוֹת, lō' 'am-bînôt). That is why his maker still does not show him pity (לֹא־יְרַחֲמֶנּוּ, lō'-yĕraḥămennû) and his creator still does not show him favor (לֹא יְחֻנֶּנּוּ, lō' yĕḥunnennû). Hosea's earlier oracles against Israel as a people without knowledge and understanding (Hos 4:6, 14), whom God will no longer pity (Hos 1:6; 2:6), have clearly influenced our Isaianic author here.

Nonetheless, in v. 12 the prophet again returns to the day of salvation which will eventually come. On that day, he says, Yahweh will beat out (יַחְבֹּט, yaḥbōṭ) the kernels of grain, but then he throws in a very clever double entendre with the next word מִשִּׁבֹּלֶת (miššibbōlet), "from the šibbōlet." The word שִׁבֹּלֶת (šibbōlet) can mean an ear of grain, hence immediately following the verb "to beat out" one would automatically complete the thought, "he will beat out the kernels of grain from the ear," but a homonym of שִׁבֹּלֶת (šibbōlet) also means "stream," and when the word is immediately followed by הַנָּהָר עַד־נַחַל מִצְרָיִם (hannāhār 'ad-naḥal miṣrāyim), one is forced to shift the translation to "from the stream of the river (the Euphrates) to the Wadi of Egypt." Both meanings are intended. Using the imagery of the threshing of grain, the prophet is describing how God will collect each of his people individually wherever they are scattered, from Assyria to Egypt, "And you, O sons of Israel, will be gleaned or picked up (תְּלֻקְּטוּ, tĕluqqĕṭû) one by one."

Moreover, on that day a great trumpet will be sounded, and those lost in the land of Assyria and those scattered in the land of Egypt will come and worship Yahweh on the holy mountain in Jerusalem. This is the same emphasis on Jerusalem that one finds in Isa 24:23; 25:6-10a; and 26:1-4. One should also note that the return from exile here does not mention Babylon or Babylonia at all, only Assyria and Egypt, which suggests our author is writing before the great Babylonian exile, when the concern is still for those earlier exiles to Assyria and Egypt. This same concern for those earlier exiles is found in Isa 11:11-16, and, closer to the time of our author, in Jer 31:1-12.

Bibliography

Alonso Schökel, L., "La canción de la vina: Is 27,2-5," *EstEcl* 34 (1960) 767-74.
Anderson, Bernhard W., "The Slaying of the Fleeing, Twisting Serpent: Isaiah 27:1 in Context," in Lewis M. Hopfe, ed., *Uncovering Ancient Stones: Essays in Memory of H. Neil Richardson* (Winona Lake, IN: Eisenbrauns, 1994) 3-15.
Bascom, Robert, "The Targums: Ancient Reader's Helps," *BT* 36 (1985) 301-16.

Coggins, R. J., *Samaritans and Jews: The Origins of Samaritanism Reconsidered* (Atlanta: John Knox, 1975).

Curtis, John, "Detached Note on Hereb," *Proceedings, Eastern Great Lakes and Midwest Bible Society* 4 (1984) 87–98.

Daiches, S., "An Explanation of Isaiah 27.8," *JQR* 6 (1915–16) 399–404.

Day, John, "Asherah," *ABD* 1:483–87.

———, "The Dependence of Isaiah 26:13—27:11 on Hosea 13:4—14:10 and Its Relevance to Some Theories on the Redaction of the 'Isaiah Apocalypse,'" in C. C. Broyles and C. A. Evans, eds., *Writing and Reading the Scroll of Isaiah: Studies of an Interpretive Tradition* (2 vols.; VTSup 70; Leiden: Brill, 1997) 1:357–68.

Driver, G. R., "Mythical Monsters in the Old Testament," in *Studi orientalistici in onore di Giorgio Levi Della Vida* (2 vols.; Pubblicazioni dell'Istituto per l'Oriente 52; Rome: Istituto per l'Oriente, 1956) 1:234–49.

Francke, J., *Veelkoppige Monsters: Mythologische Figuren in Bijbelteksten* (Goes: Oosterbaan & Le Cointre, 1971).

Galling, K., "Incense Altars," *IDB* 2:699–700.

Glasson, T. Francis, "Theophany and Parousia," *NTS* 34 (1988) 259–70.

Gordon, C. H., "Leviathan, Symbol of Evil," in Alexander Altmann, ed., *Biblical Motifs: Origins and Transformations* (Cambridge, MA: Harvard University Press, 1966) 1–9.

Grol, H. van, "Isaiah 27,10-11: God and His Own People," in J. van Ruiten and M. Vervenne, eds., *Studies in the Book of Isaiah: Festschrift Willem A. M. Beuken* (BETL 132; Leuven: Leuven University Press/Peeters, 1997) 195–209.

Herrmann, J., "אסאס Jes 27 8 und שאשא Hes 39 2," *ZAW* 36 (1916) 243.

Jacob, E., "Du premier au deuxième chant de la vigne du prophète Esaïe, réflexions sur Esaïe 27,2-5," in Johann Jakob Stamm, Ernest Jenni, and Hans Joachim Stoebe, eds., *Wort, Gebot, Glaube: Beiträge zur Theologie des Alten Testaments. Walther Eichrodt zum 80. Geburtstag* (ATANT 59; Zurich: Zwingli, 1970) 325–30.

Jenner, K. D., "The Big Shofar (Isaiah 27:13): A Hapax Legomenon," in H. J. Bosman, H. van Grol, et al., eds., *Studies in Isaiah 24–27: The Isaiah Workshop–de Jesaja Werkplaats* (OtSt 43; Leiden: Brill, 2000) 157–82.

———, "The Worship of Yhwh on the Holy Mountain in Light of the Idea of Return: A Short Note on the Confrontation of Theology of the Old Testament and Comparative and Applied Science of Theology," in F. Postma, et al., eds., *The New Things: Eschatology in Old Testament Prophecy. Festschrift for Henk Leene* (Amsterdamse cahiers voor exegese van de Bijbel en zijn tradities 3; Maastricht: Shaker, 2002) 129–33.

Kessler, Werner, *Gott geht es um das Ganze: Jes 56–66 und Jes. 24–27* (BAT 19; Stuttgart: Calwer, 1960) 170–72.

Leene, H., "Isaiah 27:7-9 as a Bridge between Vineyard and City," in H. J. Bosman, H. van Grol, et al., eds., *Studies in Isaiah 24–27: The Isaiah Workshop–de Jesaja Werkplaats* (OtSt 43; Leiden: Brill, 2000) 199–225.

Maag, V., "Lewjathan, Die Vorweltschlange," *Neue Zürcher Zeitung* (1959) 1775.

Ploeger, O., *Theocracy and Eschatology* (Richmond: John Knox, 1968) 71–75.

Rabin, C., "*Bariah*," *JTS* 47 (1946) 38–41.

Roberts, J. J. M., "Double Entendre."

Robertson, E., "Isaiah XXVII 2-6," *ZAW* 47 (1929) 197–206.

Sweeney, Marvin A., "New Gleanings from an Old Vineyard: Isaiah 27 Reconsidered," in Craig A. Evans and William F. Stinespring, eds., *Early Jewish and Christian Exegesis: Studies in Memory of William Hugh Brownlee* (Scholars Press Homage Series 10; Atlanta: Scholars Press, 1987) 51–66.

Wakeman, Mary K., *God's Battle with the Monster: A Study in Biblical Imagery* (Leiden: Brill, 1973).

Wallace, H., "Leviathan and the Beast in Revelation," *BA* 11 (1948) 61–68.

28

1/ Hey! Proud[a] crown of the drunkards[b] of Ephraim,
Fading rosette, the ornament of his glory!
Who/which[c] is at/on[c] the head of those proudly bloated[d] by rich food,
Those hammered with wine![e]

2/ A strong and mighty one belonging to my Lord is coming,
Like a storm of hail, a destructive gale,
Like a storm of mighty, overflowing waters.
He will cast down[f] to the ground with his hand,[g]

3/ With (his) feet you will be trampled,[h]
O proud crown of the drunkards of Ephraim.

4/ And you will become,[i] O fading rosette,[i] the ornament of his glory,
Who/which is at/on the head of those proudly bloated by rich food,
<Those hammered with wine,>[k]
Like a first-ripe fig before summer,
Which the one who spots it swallows as soon as it is in his hand.

5/ On that day Yahweh of Hosts[l] will become
A crown of beauty and a diadem of glory for the remnant of his[m] people.

6/ A spirit of justice for the one who sits in judgment,
And might for those who turn back battle at the gate.[n]

Textual Notes

a   For MT's גֵּאוּת (gēʾût), "pride, majesty"; 1QIsaᵃ has גאון (gāʾôn), "pride, exaltation."

b   LXX reads שכרי (sĕkīrê), "hired laborers," for MT's שִׁכֹּרֵי (šikkōrê), "drunkards," but that does not fit the parallelism, and none of the other ancient translations follows LXX.

c   The translation attempts to capture the intentional double entendres in the text. The grammatical antecedent of אֲשֶׁר (ʾăšer) is the crown, suggesting the translation "which," but crown is a metaphor for the Israelite king, suggesting the translation "who." A crown is worn "on" the head, but a king stands "at" the head of his servants or royal courtiers. See the use of the idiom מֵעַל רֹאשׁ (mēʿal rōʾš)," from upon the head," in 2 Kgs 2:3, 5.

d   Reading with 1QIsaᵃ, which has גאי (gēʾê), "proud of" (both here and in v. 4). MT has גֵּיא (gêʾ), "valley," both here and in v. 4, supported by Vg., Tg., and Syr., while LXX translates whatever it was reading as "mountain." Despite the support of the versions, "valley" provides no usable parallel with הֲלוּמֵי (hălûmê), "hammered, smitten of," that is, drunk with wine. The versions were apparently influenced by the idiom בְּקֶרֶן בֶּן־שָׁמֶן (bĕqeren ben-šāmen), "on a fertile spur" (Isa 5:1), but the plural שְׁמָנִים (šĕmānîm) here suggests not "fertile" but "rich foods" in parallel with "wine" just as in 25:6. The translation "proudly bloated" may be overinterpretive, but it suggests a possible double entendre; the royal court's bloated arrogance over their rich food may also reflect the food's physical impact on them, like the hammering of the wine.

e   LXX's "without wine" has perhaps been influenced by Isa 51:21.

f   1QIsaᵃ has והניח (wĕhinnîaḥ), "and he will cast down," for MT's הִנִּיחַ (hinnîaḥ), "he will cast down." This may be a secondary

change to bring the poetic idiom into line with prose syntax for the so-called converted perfect.

g   The pronominal suffix is unexpressed in Hebrew, and Syriac supplies the second person singular, "your hand," but the second person hardly fits here. LXX has the plural, "with hands," and Vg.'s terram spatiosam "broad land" appears to presuppose something like רחבת ידים (raḥăbê yādāyim) for MT's בְּיָד (bĕyad), "with the hand"; cf. Isa 33:21.

h   MT and 1QIsaᵃ both have the feminine plural תֵּרָמַסְנָה (tērāmasnâ), but LXX, Vg., Tg., and Syr., while they preserve the passive of the MT, all read a singular verb form, and Tg. and Syr. have the masculine singular. It would appear that the feminine plural is a mistake introduced by the influence of the feminine dual בְּרַגְלַיִם (bĕraglayim), "with (the) feet," as the implied subject of the trampling. Despite the final ת, the gender of עֲטֶרֶת (ʿăṭeret), "crown," is never unequivocally indicated, either by a feminine singular verb of which it is subject, or by modification with a feminine singular adjective. Even if it were feminine, the masculine referent of the image—in my opinion, the north Israelite king—could have led the prophet to use a masculine verb form. Thus, I would either read the final -נה as the energic ending on a niphal second person masculine singular verb form (first choice), or simply emend to תרמס (tērāmēs), "you will be trampled," the same form without the energic ending. If תרמסנה was the original reading, it was misunderstood as a third person feminine plural due to the implied subject רגלים; if תרמס was the original reading, it was misunderstood as a third person feminine singular because of the final ת on עטרת, and it was eventually corrupted to תרמסנה due to the implied subject רגלים.

i   1QIsaᵃ has והייתה for MT's וְהָיְתָה (wĕhāyĕtâ), "and she will be." This suggests the possibility of reading the second person masculine singular (wĕhāyîtâ), "and you will be," and seeing this as direct address. In 1QIsaᵃ the form הייתה is used both for the third person feminine singular (Isa 1:21; 6:13; 11:16; 17:9; 29:2; 34:9, 13; 50:11; 64:9) and the second person masculine singular (25:4; 58:11). The form הַיה is also used for the third person feminine singular (17:1; 19:17) and the second person feminine singular (62:3), but not for the second person masculine singular. The form היתה is also used in 1QIsaᵃ for the third person feminine singular (9:4; 13:19), but the form היה is not used at all.

j Both MT and 1QIsaᵃ have the apparently feminine form צִיצַת (ṣîṣat), "flower, rosette," instead of the clearly masculine form צִיץ (ṣîṣ), found in the parallel expression in v. 1. The alteration appears to be an attempt to make the noun agree in gender with the third person feminine singular verb היתה, but נֹבֵל (nōbēl), "fading," the masculine singular participle modifying צִיצַת, shows that this change is secondary and artificial.

k Because the text of Isaiah tends to be haplographic, particularly when phrases are repeated, I am inclined to restore the missing parallel line from v. 1 as original here as well, though it is not attested here in the surviving textual tradition.

l The Tg. makes the diadem "the Messiah of the LORD of Hosts."

m LXX reads "my people."

n 1QIsaᵃ lacks MT's ה directive on שֶׁעָר (šaʿar), "gate."

Commentary

The oracle in Isa 28:1-6 contains a host of interpretive cruxes that confused the translators of the ancient versions and continue to baffle modern scholars, but a recent creative and insightful article by Rolf A. Jacobson has pointed the way out of this morass.[1] Jacobson demonstrates that the two dominant interpretations of the metaphor עֲטֶרֶת גֵּאוּת (ʿăṭeret gēʾût), "proud crown"—the first that sees it as a reference to the walls of Samaria that resemble a crown, and the second that understands it as a reference to garlands that drunken revelers in Samaria wore—cannot be sustained,[2] and he suggests instead that the metaphor be understood as a reference to the king of Ephraim.[3] I find Jacobson's argument compelling, so I will begin from this point.

The particle הוֹי (hôy, v. 1) is a vocative particle for getting attention, and it is often followed by second person direct address. It was used in funerary addresses to the dead, and that association may sometimes have given a negative expectation to what follows; but, as Isa 55:1 shows, this was by no means always the case. The address is a fictive address to the king of Ephraim, "the proud crown of the drunkards of Ephraim," and a number

---

1 Rolf A. Jacobson, "A Rose by Any Other Name: Iconography and the Interpretation of Isaiah 28:1-6," in Martti Nissinen and Charles E. Carter, eds., *Images and Prophecy in the Ancient Eastern Mediterranean* (FRLANT 233; Göttingen: Vandenhoeck & Ruprecht, 2009), 125–46.

2 Jacobson shows from lexicographic and iconographic data that עטרת גאות can hardly be a visual simile for the city walls on a hill. In contrast to German and English, where one can speak of a hill being "crowned" by a city, in Biblical Hebrew עטרה never carries this semantic sense; it normally refers to an actual royal crown and always remains within the semantic field of the monarch or monarchy. To quote Jacobson, "In Biblical Hebrew, עטרה is so intimately connected with the person of the sovereign that it is most likely that Isaiah's original audience would have understood 'the proud crown of the drunkards of Ephraim' as a reference not to the walls of Samaria, but to the king of Ephraim" ("Iconography," 128). Moreover, a survey of the iconographic representation of royal crowns from the ancient Near East shows that these kings "did not wear the stylized, battlemented crowns that would later become popular in medieval Europe" (ibid., 130). In short, "no known Egyptian, Palestinian, or Mesopotamian crown would support the proposal that an ancient audience would have made a connection between a crown and a visual identification of the walls of a city" (ibid., 131). The second interpretation of the expression as a reference to garlands worn by drunken revelers is based primarily on texts from Greece, and it remains dubious whether this custom was even known in eighth-century Judah or Israel. Jacobson shows that the one biblical text (Ezek 23:42) cited as proof of the same custom in Israel does not speak of drunks crowning themselves with garlands. Instead, drunken men from the wilderness, that is, foreigners, come and adorn the women Oholah and Oholibah, who are never said to be drunk, with expensive bracelets and crowns. This is a quite different phenomenon.

3 Jacobson, "Iconography," 133.

of details in the oracle, including the reference to "the remnant [שְׁאָר, šĕʾār] of his people" in v. 5, suggests that it dates to the period of the Syro-Ephraimitic War. The actual audience was clearly Judean, most probably the Judean royal court. For the actual audience, it was an oracle of salvation, like most of the oracles addressed to Ahaz and his court during this crisis (see the commentary on Isa 2:2-22; 7:1-9; 7:10-17; 8:1-10; 10:16-24a; 10:27d-34; 17:1-14).

The characterization of the Israelite king as "the proud crown" and his princes and advisors as "the drunkards of Ephraim" marks both the king and his court as living in a fool's paradise of misplaced pride and drunken oblivion to the disaster that was upon them. It is analogous to what Isaiah says in Isa 9:8-9 of the reality-denying pride of the people and ruler of Samaria, who respond to disaster "in pride and arrogance of heart saying, 'The bricks have fallen, but we will rebuild with ashlars; the sycamores have been cut down, but we will replace them with cedars." The expression צִיץ נֹבֵל, "fading rosette," which stands in parallel to עֲטֶרֶת גֵּאוּת, "proud crown," contains a double entendre. The word צִיץ, "flower," probably refers to the rosette, a well-documented symbol of kingship that also decorated some ancient Near Eastern crowns.[4] The further characterization of this flower by the appositional phrase צְבִי תִפְאַרְתּוֹ (šĕbî tipʾartô), "the ornament of his glory," suggests that the Israelite king, symbolized by the ornamental rosette, was the glory of Ephraim. But the addition of the adjective נֹבֵל (nōbēl), "fading," turns this positive expression into a negative, because צִיץ (ṣîṣ), "flower," was also used as a symbol of transitoriness (Isa 40:7-8). Just as Isaiah's image of the "two smoldering stumps of firebrands" during the same Syro-Ephraimitic crisis suggested that the fire of Aram and Israel had already gone out (Isa 7:4), the sense of this metaphor of the "fading rosette" is that the haughty northern monarchy is not long for this world (cf. Isa 7:7-9, 16; 8:4).

As a crown sits on the head, so the king is over his royal courtiers who are characterized as גֵּאֵי שְׁמָנִים (gēʾê šĕmānîm), "proudly bloated with rich food," and הֲלוּמֵי יַיִן (hălûmê yāyin), "hammered with wine." The verb הלם (hālam) is used for the action of hitting with a hammer (Isa 41:7), so its metaphorical use here is similar to that of the English expression "smashed" to describe a very

drunk person. Before one dismisses this characterization of the Israelite king and his court as mere prophetic invective or Judean propaganda, one should note that the northern prophet Hosea said much the same thing about the Israelite king and his court (Hos 7:3-7). Isaiah's characterization of the excessive feasting and drinking of the Israelite court also differs little from that given by Amos who worked in the north (Amos 6:1-6).

The invocation and characterization of the Israelite king and his court are then followed by an announcement of Yahweh's impending action against them. He has a strong and mighty one who will come as his agent against the north like a hail storm, a destructive wind storm, and a rainstorm of mighty overflowing waters (v. 2). The imagery is similar to that found in the oracle against Israel from the period of the Syro-Ephraimitic War in Isa 8:6-8a. In contrast to Isaiah 8, the agent is unnamed here, but in the historical context it could hardly be any other than the same Assyrian power.

Isaiah's poetry cleverly links the actions of the hand and feet of this mighty enemy of the Ephraimite king (vv. 2-3) while subtly shifting the attention back to the northern king by shifting from this enemy as the subject of the active verb in the third person back to direct address of the Ephraimite king as the subject of the passive verb in the second person:

He will cast down to the ground with his hand,
With his feet you will be trampled,
O proud crown of the drunkards of Ephraim.
And you will become, O fading rosette, the ornament
    of his glory. . . .

If one rejects the analysis of תרמסנה as a second person masculine singular with energic ending, the correction of the verb תרמסנה to תרמס involves a textual emendation, but some emendation is required by grammar. Jacobson's translation, "Trampled underfoot will be the proud crown . . . ," makes עטרת the subject of תרמסנה, but the noun is singular while the verb is plural. Something must be corrected to get agreement in number. If one keeps the noun as singular, then the verb must be analyzed as a singular with energic ending or be corrected to תרמס, which can be read either as third person feminine

4   Ibid., 133–36.

singular or second person masculine singular. And in the parallel line, the MT's third person feminine singular verb היתה does not agree with its subject ציצת despite the altered ending of the noun from ציץ of v. 1, because the noun is still modified by the masculine singular participle נבל. In this case, there is textual evidence for emendation, since 1QIsaᵃ's הייתה suggests the possibility of reading the second person masculine singular verb, which would bring it into agreement with its subject. Since הוי oracles often introduce direct address with second person forms, it is likely that that was originally the case here, and the failure to recognize direct address is partly responsible for the subsequent corruption.

It has been suggested that Isaiah's use of so many feminine nouns in his metaphorical characterization of the king of Ephraim involved a certain polemical feminization of the Ephraimite king in contrast to Isaiah's very masculine portrait of the strong and mighty one God was bringing to destroy the northern king. Isaiah was certainly capable of making such a critique, as he does in 3:12: "O my people—whose oppressor is a child, Over whom women rule." On the other hand, most of the nouns used here, and they are by no means all feminine—עטרה "crown," גאות "pride," ציץ "rosette," צבי "ornament," תפארת "glory"—are so closely associated with kingship and royalty that the suggested "feminization" appears to be subjective overinterpretation. This judgment is confirmed, moreover, by the use of this same terminology to refer to Yahweh's royal exaltation in v. 5. One could hardly describe the language there as a polemical "feminization" of Yahweh.

There is rare artistry in Isaiah's description of what Ephraim's fading flower will become. On the one hand, it plays on the imagery of those proudly bloated with rich foods. Israel's self-indulgent court has no monopoly on the taste for rich foods. On the other hand, it plays on the natural development of fruit. First the flower, and then when it fades, the fruit (cf. Isa 18:5 with the development of the grape). Ephraim's king, whose flower is already fading, will ripen before his time, and, as with an early fig, the first to see him will pluck and swallow him almost in one motion. The imagery suggests that the Assyrian invasion is imminent and that the time frame for the destruction of Israel, the northern kingdom, was very narrow. One should note that Isaiah uses similar agricultural imagery for the devouring of Israel in another oracle from the period of the Syro-Ephraimitic War (see Isa 17:5-6).

Verses 5-6 are introduced with the phrase ביום ההוא (bayyôm hahûʾ, "on that day"), but this is hardly justification for detaching these verses as a later, secondary addition, as Jacobson points out.[5] They form the original conclusion to the oracle. On this imminent day of judgment, when Ephraim's king will be cast down and trampled, plucked and devoured, Yahweh of Hosts will replace him, becoming (יהיה ל, yihyê lě) a crown of beauty (עטרת צבי, ʿăteret ṣěbî) and a diadem of glory (צפירת תפארה, ṣěpîrat tipʾārâ) for the remnant of his people (לשאר עמו, lišʾār ʿammô). For the expression עטרת צבי (ʿăteret ṣěbî) the prophet combines v. 1's עטרת of עטרת גאות (ʿăteret gēʾût), "proud crown," and the צבי of צבי תפארתו (ṣěbî tipʾartô), "ornament of beauty," to create the new expression "crown of beauty" or "crown of ornament," that is, "ornamental crown." For צפירת תפארה (ṣěpîrat tipʾārâ), "diadem of glory," he introduces the new word צפירה (ṣěpîrâ), "diadem," but links it with תפארה (tipʾārâ), "glory," the final word of the expression צבי תפארתו (ṣěbî tipʾartô), "ornament of beauty." The word צפירה (ṣěpîrâ), "diadem," is a rare word, attested only in this passage in Isaiah in this sense; the two occurrences in Ezekiel (7:7, 10) have a different meaning. The rearrangement of the phrases from v. 1 suggests the creativity of Isaiah, not the wooden repetition of a later redactor, and it may have been motivated by the desire to avoid the negatively charged גאות (vv. 1, 3).

The remnant of his people (שאר עמו, šěʾār ʿammô) here is not an eschatological reference or a reference to the remnant of Judah returning from Babylonian exile, but a reference to the remnant of the northern kingdom who would survive the disaster of the Syro-Ephraimitic War. It is connected to the symbolic name given to Isaiah's son שאר ישוב (šěʾār yāšûb, "Shear-yashub"), who appeared before Ahaz with Isaiah as a living symbolic message at the beginning of this crisis. It also appears in a reworked fragment of an oracle originally from that period in Isa 10:20-24a. This fragment speaks of the remnant of Israel

---

5 Jacobson, "Iconography," 138–39.

or of Jacob, both designations pointing to the northern kingdom, returning to Yahweh after an overwhelming judgment. Isaiah 10:21 plays directly on Isaiah's son's name, when it says, שְׁאָר יָשׁוּב שְׁאָר יַעֲקֹב אֶל־אֵל גִּבּוֹר (šẽʾār yāšûb šẽʾār yaʿăqōb ʾel-ʾēl gibbôr), "a remnant will return [Shear-yashub], a remnant of Jacob, to Mighty God." One should note that אֵל גִּבּוֹר, "Mighty God," is one of the throne names of the Judean king in Isa 9:5. The implication would seem to be that a return to Yahweh on the part of the surviving northerners also involved a return to and reacceptance of the Judean hegemony under a Davidic monarch. While Isa 28:5 identifies Yahweh as the real crown, that is, the real king of this remnant—a thought perfectly compatible with Isaiah's Zion theology—v. 6 goes on to describe Yahweh as becoming רוּחַ מִשְׁפָּט (rûaḥ mišpāṭ), "a spirit of judgment," for the one sitting over judgment and גְּבוּרָה (gĕbûrâ), "strength," to those who turn back war at the gate. The language is remarkably similar to that in Isa 11:1-5, where Isaiah describes Yahweh's endowment of the ideal Davidic king with רוּחַ עֵצָה וּגְבוּרָה (rûaḥ ʿēṣâ ûgĕbûrâ), "a spirit of counsel and strength," so that he may judge justly and smite the wicked. The parallels suggest that the expression לַיּוֹשֵׁב עַל־הַמִּשְׁפָּט (layyôšēb ʿal-hammišpāṭ), "for the one who sits in judgment," has as its reference the Judean king, at the time Ahaz, and the expression מְשִׁיבֵי מִלְחָמָה שָׁעְרָה

(mĕšîbê milḥāmâ šāʿĕrâ), "for those who turn back battle at the gate," while it is in the plural and thus implies the Judean king's generals and troops, nonetheless should be understood as indicating that they act under the king's orders. This language of "turning back the battle at the gate" is quite appropriate to the actual circumstances of the Syro-Ephraimitic War, because the surprise attack of the Aramean and Israelite army on Jerusalem came right up to the gates of the city before it was beaten back (cf. Isa 7:1-9; 10:27d-34).

To summarize, this oracle contains a fictive address in the second person to the Israelite king, Pekah, son of Remaliah. He is warned that his transitory crown would soon be overthrown and destroyed by God's mighty agent of destruction, a reference to the Assyrian king Tiglath-pileser III. On that day of judgment Yahweh would become the true crown for the surviving remnant of the northern kingdom and would provide the judicial wisdom and strength for his human representative, the current Davidic king, Ahaz of Judah, to rule with justice and triumph in battle against his Israelite and Aramean attackers. Thus, the oracle is an oracle of judgment against Pekah and the northern kingdom, its fictive addressees, but an oracle of salvation for its real audience, Ahaz and his Judean court.

Bibliography

Asen, B., "The Garlands of Ephraim: Isaiah 28:1-6 and the Marzeah," *JSOT* 71 (1996) 73–87.

Barth, *Die Jesaja-Worte*.

Beuken, W. A. M., "Isaiah 28: Is It Only Schismatics That Drink Heavily? Beyond the Synchronic versus Diachronic Controversy," in Johannes C. de Moor, ed., *Synchronic or Diachronic? A Debate on Method in Old Testament Exegesis* (OtSt 34; Leiden: Brill, 1995) 15–38.

Childs, *Assyrian Crisis*, 28–31.

De Vries, Simon J. *From Old Revelation to New: A Tradition-Historical and Redaction-Critical Study of Temporal Transitions in Prophetic Prediction* (Grand Rapids: Eerdmans, 1995).

Gilula, M., "*Sby* in Isaiah 28,1—a Head Ornament," *TA* 1 (1974) 128.

Görg, M., "Die Bildsprache in Jes 28:1," *BN* 3 (1977) 17–23.

Jackson, Jared J., "Style in Isaiah 28 and a Drinking

Bout of the Gods (RS 24.258)," in Jared J. Jackson and Martin Kessler, eds., *Rhetorical Criticism: Essays in Honor of James Muilenburg* (PTMS 1; Pittsburgh: Pickwick, 1974) 85–98.

Jacobson, Rolf A., "A Rose by Any Other Name: Iconography and the Interpretation of Isaiah 28:1-6," in Martti Nissinen and Charles E. Carter, eds., *Images and Prophecy in the Ancient Eastern Mediterranean* (FRLANT 233; Göttingen: Vandenhoeck & Ruprecht, 2009) 125–46.

Janzen, Waldemar, *Mourning Cry and Woe Oracle* (BZAW 125; Berlin: de Gruyter, 1972).

Krause, H. J., "*Hôj* als prophetische Leichenklage über das eigene Volk im 8. Jahrhundert," *ZAW* 85 (1973) 15–46.

Löhr, M., "Jesaja-Studien 3. Schlusswort: Zur Komposition der Kapp. 28–31," *ZAW* 37 (1917–18) 59–76.

——, "Zwei Beispiele von Kehrvers in den Prophetenschriften des Alten Testaments," *ZDMG* 61 (1907) 1–6.

Loretz, Oswald, "Das Prophetenwort über das Ende der Königstadt Samaria (Jes 28:1-4)," *UF* 9 (1977) 361–63.

Montgomery, James A., "Notes on the Old Testament," *JBL* 311 (1912) 140–46.

Prinsloo, W. S., "Eighth-Century Passages from the Book of Isaiah? Reflection on Isaiah 28:1-6," *OTE* 1 (1988) 11–19.

Qimron, E., "The Biblical Lexicon in Light of the Dead Sea Scrolls," *DSD* 2 (1995) 294–329.

Roberts, J. J. M., "Double Entendre."

Rost, Leonhard, "Zu Jesaja 28,1ff.," *ZAW* 53 (1935) 292.

Vogt, E., "Das Prophetenwort Jes 28,1-4 und das Ende der Königsstadt Samaria," in L. Alvarez Verdes and E. J. Alonso Hernández, eds., *Homenaje a Juan Prado: Miscelánea de estudios bíblicos y hebráicos* (Madrid: Consejo Superior de Investigaciones Científicas, 1975) 108–30.

7/ These also[a] stagger because of wine,
   And stray because of beer;
   Priest and prophet stagger because of beer,
   They are confused by wine;
   They stagger from beer.
   They stagger in vision,[b]
   They wobble in regard to judgment.

8/ Indeed all the tables are full of vomit,
   Excrement[c] until there is no more room.[d]

9/ "To whom would he teach knowledge,
   And to whom would he explain the report?
   Those just weaned from milk,
   Those just removed from the breasts?

10/ 'Doo-doo[e] to doo-doo, doo-doo to doo-doo,
    Yuk-yuk to yuk-yuk, yuk-yuk to yuk-yuk,[f]
    A little here, a little there.'"

11/ Surely, with stammering of lip,
    And with a foreign tongue,
    Shall he speak[g] to this people

12/   To whom he said,
    "This is rest; give rest[h] to the weary.
    This is repose;[i] give repose to the needy."[j]
    But they refused to hear.[k]

13/ So the word of Yahweh will be to them,
    "Doo-doo[l] to doo-doo, doo-doo to doo-doo,
    Yuk-yuk to yuk-yuk, yuk-yuk to yuk-yuk,
    A little here, a little there,"
    So that they go and stumble back,
    And they are broken, and snared, and caught.

14/ Therefore hear[m] the word of Yahweh,
    You men of scoffing,[n]
    You rulers of this people,
    Who are in Jerusalem.

15/ Because you said,
    "We have made a covenant with death,
    And with Sheol we have made a treaty.
    The overflowing scourge,[o] when it passes by,[p]
    Will not come upon us;
    For we have made a lie our refuge,
    And in falsehood we have taken shelter."

16/ Therefore thus says my Lord Yahweh:
    "Look, I am about to lay[q] in Zion a stone,
    A massive stone, a cornerstone valuable for a foundation,
    A foundation[r] for the one who trusts that will not shake.

17/ And I will make justice the line,
    And righteousness the weight;
    And hail will sweep away the refuge of lies,
    And waters will overflow[s] the shelter.

18/ And your covenant with death will be annulled,[t]
    And your treaty with Sheol will not stand.
    When the overflowing scourge passes by,
    You will become trampled by it.

19/ As often as it passes by, it will take you,
    For morning by morning it will pass by,
    By day and by night."
    And it will be[u] nothing but terror to understand the report.

20/ For the bed is too short to stretch out,[v]
    And the cover[w] is too narrow[x] to curl up.[y]

21/ For as[z] on Mount Perazim Yahweh will rise up,
    As*[a] in the valley in Gibeon he will bestir himself,

> To perform his work;
>> Strange is his work.
> To do his labor;
>> Alien is his labor.

22/ And now*[b] do not scoff,
>> Lest your bonds*[c] be tightened.
> For a decreed destruction I have heard
>> From my Lord*[d] Yahweh of Hosts
>>> Over the whole land.

Textual Notes

a   1QIsaᵃ omits the copula on וְגַם (wĕgam), "and also."

b   The last couplet gave the versions, apart from the Vg., real difficulties; LXX, Syr., and Tg. vary widely from the Hebrew but give no indication of a variant Hebrew *Vorlage*.

c   The accents in MT would read צֹאָה (ṣōʾâ), "excrement," with the preceding line, but the line division is better if taken with the second line.

d   LXX has only a loose interpretation of this couplet: ἀρὰ ἔδεται ταύτην τὴν βουλήν· αὕτη γὰρ ἡ βουλὴ ἕνεκεν πλεονεξίας, "A curse will devour this counsel, for this counsel is for the sake of greed."

e   For MT's consistent צַו לָצָו (ṣaw lāṣāw) 1QIsaᵃ has צי לצי (ṣy lṣy) consistently.

f   Despite many attempts to translate the phrases צַו לָצָו (ṣaw lāṣāw) and קַו לָקָו (qaw lāqāw), beginning with the versions, the phrases do not appear to represent intelligible adult words. They might suggest initial attempts at teaching a young child the alphabet, but more likely they represent baby talk. Their relative unintelligibility is clear from the comparison to the unintelligible syllables of a foreign language in the next verse. Nonetheless there is an obvious play on the same sound לְקָו (lĕqāw) in v. 17, where the expression clearly means "for a plumb line."

g   LXX has the plural λαλήσουσιν, "they shall speak," but this is secondary.

h   LXX omits הָנִיחוּ (hānîḥû), "give rest," by haplography due to the similarity of the preceding הַמְּנוּחָה (hammĕnûḥâ), "rest."

i   LXX misunderstood הַמַּרְגֵּעָה (hammargēʿâ), "repose," as a word meaning destruction (τὸ σύντριμμα).

j   I restore the parallel cognate verb and indirect object וְזֹאת הַמַּרְגֵּעָה הַרְגִּיעוּ לָאֶבְיוֹן (wĕzōʾt hammargēʿâ hargîʿû lĕʾebyôn), "and this is repose; give repose to the needy"). It was lost by haplography, perhaps in stages. The object was lost because of the similarity of הרגיע[ו לאביון] to the following וְלֹא אבה. The verb הרגיעו was lost because of the repetition of the root of the

k   preceding noun המרגעה, just as the LXX omitted הניחו following המנוחה in the preceding parallel line.

   The unusual form אבוא is due to textual error influenced by the preceding corruption (see GKC, §23f.3.3).

l   As in v. 10, 1QIsaᵃ has צי consistently for MT's צו.

m   For MT and 4QIsaᶜ's plural imperative שִׁמְעוּ (šimʿû), "hear!"; 1QIsaᵃ has the incorrect singular שמע (šĕmaʿ).

n   LXX's odd reading ἄνδρες τεθλιμμένοι, "afflicted men," may be based on a misreading of a form from the root צור (ṣûr), "to confine, bind," rather than לָצוֹן (lāṣôn), "scoffing."

o   1QIsaᵃ has שוט (šôṭ), "scourge," agreeing with MT's qĕrēʾ and the same phrase in v. 18, rather than with MT's kĕtîb שיט (šîṭ).

p   MT's qĕrēʾ is יַעֲבֹר (yaʿăbōr), "when it passes by," and it is supported by 1QIsaᵃ's יבור (ya˂ă˃bôr), though the scribe inadvertently omitted the ע (ʿ). 1QIsaᵇ supports MT's more difficult and no doubt secondary perfect tense kĕtîb עָבַר (ʿābar), "when it passed by." The initial י (y) of the imperfect verb was probably inadvertently omitted because of the final י (y) on the preceding conjunction כִּי (kî).

q   Reading the *qal* participle יֹסֵד (yôsēd), "I am about to lay a foundation," with 1QIsaᵇ; 1QIsaᵃ has the *piel* participle מיסד (mĕyassēd), with basically the same meaning, and both Syr. and Tg. translate with a participle. LXX and Vg., with their future translations, also support reading a Hebrew participle here. The participle is expected after הנה (hinnê), "behold," with a pronominal suffix, especially when the suffix is the first person common singular. MT's הִנְנִי יִסַּד (hinĕnî yissad), "behold I am the one who founded," a *piel* perfect third person masculine singular verb following the first person common singular suffix on הנה would be anomalous. MT's error was perhaps influenced by the parallel statement in 14:32, יְהוָה יִסַּד צִיּוֹן (YHWH yissad ṣiyôn), "Yahweh founded Zion," where the *piel* perfect third person masculine singular fits contextually.[1]

r   The MT pointing of מוּסָּד (mûssād) as a *hophal* participle seems artificial; the repetition of אבן (ʾeben), "stone," suggests that the repetition of מוסד (mûsād), "foundation," is analogous, that in both cases the noun is repeated for poetic effect. I would point

---

1   For a fuller discussion, see my article, "Yahweh's Foundation in Zion (Isaiah 28:16)," *JBL* 106 (1987) 27–45; republished in *The Bible and the Ancient Near East: Collected Essays* (Winona Lake, IN: Eisenbrauns, 2002) 292–310.

the second occurrence of the word as the construct form מוּסַד (*mûsad*), "foundation of."

s MT and 1QIsa[b] have the correct יִשְׁטֹפוּ (*yišṭōpû*), "will overflow"; 1QIsa[b]'s ושטפו (*wĕšāṭĕpû*), "and they will overflow," is a scribal error or just a poorly written initial י (*y*).

t MT's passive construction וְכֻפַּר בְּרִיתְכֶם (*wĕkuppar bĕrîtkem*), "and your covenant will be annulled," is apparently reflected in 1QIsa[b]'s וכפר בריתכם despite the lack of agreement between the masculine verb and the feminine noun, but 1QIsa[a]'s וכפר את בריתכמה (*wĕkippēr ʾet bĕrîtkemâ*), with the introduction of the object marker, might suggest that he was reading the verb as active rather than passive, "and it/he will annul your covenant."

u 1QIsa[a] omits the verb וְהָיָה (*wĕhāyâ*), "and it will be."

v For MT's מֵהִשְׂתָּרֵעַ (*mēhiśtārēaʿ*), "to stretch out," 1QIsa[a] has the clearly corrupt משתריים (*mśtryym*). The versions had difficulty understanding the passage, so corruption was to be expected.

w 1QIsa[a] has the garbled והמסכסכה (*whmskskh*) for MT's וְהַמַּסֵּכָה (*wĕhammassēkâ*), "the cover."

x 1QIsa[a] totally omits צָרָה (*sārâ*), "is too narrow."

y For MT's כְּהִתְכַּנֵּס (*kĕhitkannēs*), "as to curl up," 1QIsa[a] has בהתכנס (*bĕhitkannēs*), "in curling up." One could debate whether the initial preposition should be restored as כְ, בְ, or מִן, though repeating the same idiom with מִן (*min*) as in the parallel line, lit., "too short from stretching out, too narrow from curling up," seems the most likely.

z For MT's כְּהַר (*kĕhar*), "as <on> mount," 1QIsa[a] has בהר (*bĕhar*), "<as>on mount."

*a For MT's כְּעֵמֶק (*kĕʿēmeq*), "as <in> the valley," 1QIsa[a] has בעמק (*bĕʿēmeq*), "<as> in the valley." The original text was probably elliptical; MT and 1QIsa[a] simply differ on which preposition was omitted in the original ellipsis.

*b For MT's וְעַתָּה (*wĕʿattâ*), "and now," supported by Vg., Syr., and Tg., 1QIsa[a] and LXX read ואתה (*wĕʾattâ*), "and you."

*c For MT's מוֹסְרֵיכֶם (*môsĕrêkem*), "your bonds," 1QIsa[a] has the feminine plural noun מוסרותיכם (*môsĕrôtêkem*), "your bonds."

*d 1QIsa[a] and LXX omit אֲדֹנָי (*ʾădōnāy*), "my Lord."

Commentary

If vv. 1-6 were originally an oracle against the northern kingdom Israel from the time of the Syro-Ephraimitic War, as I have argued above, vv. 7-22 reedit and reapply those verses to make them applicable to the leadership of the southern kingdom Judah at a much later period, probably the time of Hezekiah's revolt against Assyria with Nubian and Egyptian support in 705–701 BCE. Years ago William Holladay referred to this reuse and reapplication of one of his earlier oracles by Isaiah himself as a "self-extended" oracle, and Holladay identified several of these.[2] The extension is accomplished by the expression וְגַם־אֵלֶּה (*wĕgam-ʾēllê*), "these also." The "these" here is no longer a reference to the king and ruling oligarchs of Samaria, but to the priests, prophets (v. 7), and other royal advisors in Judah (v. 14). Interestingly, it is the advisors in the royal court, not the person of the Judean king himself, who is the subject of Isaiah's criticism. Isaiah's avoidance of a direct criticism of the king here, presumably Hezekiah, stands in striking contrast to his explicit address to Ahaz in the earlier Syro-Ephraimitic crisis (Isa 7:3, 10-13). It suggests that the bitter polemic is an internal debate between rival parties among Hezekiah's royal advisors carried on with enough deference to the king to prevent alienating the king while unmercifully castigating his advisors who currently have the king's ear. It leaves room for the king to switch policies if Isaiah's premonitions prove to be correct.

It is difficult to know how literally to take Isaiah's polemical reference to the drunkenness of his adversaries in the royal court. The Israelites were aware that drunkenness could subvert the proper exercise of priestly and governmental functions, and there were rules and admonitions against the use of alcohol while exercising those functions (Lev 10:9; Ezek 44:21; Prov 31:4-5; Eccl 10:16-17). Thus Isaiah's description of the drunken stupor of these priests, prophets, and royal advisors amid the vomit and excrement resulting from their uncontrolled binge drinking suggests that their advice and counsel are worthless. What reasonable king would listen to the advice of disgusting, drunken fools wallowing in their own vomit and excrement? Did all of the royal advisors opposing Isaiah actually get that drunk, and if they did, when did they do it? It is hard to imagine that they became so inebriated before they gave their advice to the king. It

---

2 See William L. Holladay, *Isaiah: Scroll of a Prophetic Heritage* (Grand Rapids: Eerdmans, 1978) 59–60.

is easier to assume an element of Isaianic exaggeration perhaps based on the behavior of some of his opponents at a royal banquet after their political advice had been given, perhaps a royal banquet sealing the treaty with Egypt (v. 15).

At any rate, some of his opponents are still sober enough to respond to Isaiah's criticism with a belittling polemic of their own, if vv. 9-10 are correctly analyzed as the words of Isaiah's opponents. The point is debatable, since the change of speakers involved in the rhetorical citation of an opponent's objections is often linguistically unmarked in Hebrew poetry. Some scholars see vv. 9-10 as a simple continuation of Isaiah's critique of his opponents (so Watts, *Isaiah 1–33*, 430; Hayes and Irvine, 324), but the difficulty with this view is that Isaiah refers to his opponents as "men of scoffing" and "jesters" or "makers of clever sayings" (v. 14), and in v. 22 he warns them not to continue their scoffing lest their punishment be even more severe. Unless vv. 9-10 are seen as an example of that scoffing, it would be totally unclear what Isaiah was talking about. Assuming his opponents are speaking, v. 9 is relatively clear. In this verse they complain that Isaiah's message is simplistic and infantile, more suited to young, newly weaned children than to sophisticated royal counselors. In effect, they are saying, "To whom does he think he is talking with this infantile prattle." Their characterization of that prattle in v. 10, however, is a difficult crux. The initial כִּי (*kî*), rather than being a causal particle, perhaps functions simply to introduce the following expressions as the opponents' quotation of Isaiah's message. The precise meaning of צַו לָצַו (*saw lāṣāw*) and קַו לָקָו (*qaw lāqāw*) remains hotly debated. Given the context, the words are presumably some sort of baby talk, but what sort? It has been suggested that these are names for letters used in teaching children the alphabet,[3] but if so, why pick letters from the middle of the alphabet? J. A. Emerton's suggestion that these expressions may be baby talk for shit and vomit seems more likely.[4] The

expression צַו could be an infantile expression for צֹאָה (*ṣōʾâ*), "excrement" (v. 8), and קַו could be an infantile expression for קִיא (*qîʾ*), "vomit" (v. 8). His opponents are obviously picking up on Isaiah's earlier graphic portrayal of their drunkenness, and their response suggests that Isaiah, like a naughty child, is hung up on infantile bathroom language. The expression זְעֵיר שָׁם זְעֵיר שָׁם (*zěʿêr šām zěʿêr šām*) is also difficult. The word זְעֵיר (*zěʿêr*) appears to be a phonetic variant, more common in Aramaic dialects, of Hebrew צָעִיר (*sāʿîr*), "little, small, young." Perhaps the sense is that Isaiah doles out his message in infantile portions rather than presenting his message as a complete and coherent argument appropriate to his audience of sophisticated royal advisors. "A little here, a little there," also cleverly picks up on Isaiah's complaint that excrement and vomit were everywhere, filling every table. In short, Isaiah's opponents insist that they are too advanced and sophisticated in their thinking to put up with Isaiah's simplistic, uncultured, and dirty-minded elementary education.

Isaiah then responds (v. 11) with the threat that God will speak to this people with the stammering lip of a foreign language. Note that this threat is put in the future tense. In contrast, the prior action of God expressed in v. 12 is put in the past tense. The relative particle אֲשֶׁר (*ʾăšer*) here comes close to the meaning "because." When God spoke plainly in Hebrew to the leaders of the people saying the real way to achieve national rest and security would be to provide rest and security for the weary and needy among your own people, the leaders refused to listen. Therefore, the word of Yahweh will no longer come to them in the clear syllables of their own native Hebrew, but in the confusing foreign syllables of their enemies. In v. 13 Isaiah repeats his opponents' disparaging portrayal of his prophetic word to suggest that these intellectual leaders will indeed be forced by their changed historical circumstances back into elementary education. Like very young children they will have to learn a new

---

3 See W. W. Hallo, "Isaiah 28,9-13 and the Ugaritic Abecedaries," *JBL* 77 (1958) 324–38.

4 J. A. Emerton, "Some Difficult Words in Isaiah 28:10 and 13," in Ada Rapoport-Albert and Gillian Greenberg, eds., *Biblical Hebrew, Biblical Texts: Essays in Memory of Michael P. Weitzman* (JSOTSup 333;

Sheffield: Sheffield Academic Press, 2001) 51–54; see also Christopher B. Hays, "The Covenant with Mut: A New Interpretation of Isaiah 28:1-22," *VT* 60 (2010) 212–40, esp. 234.

language, even the baby words for shit and vomit. The identity of the language is not explicitly indicated, but in the context of a rebellion against Assyria, it is most likely that it is Assyrian, the language of the attacking enemy, to which Isaiah is referring.[5] Isa 33:18-19 also speaks of the difficulty of understanding the language of an enemy who had plundered Judah, had taken tribute, and had counted the towers of Jerusalem, and there it seems clearly to refer to Assyria. A similar motif is used in the covenant curses of Deut 28:49, which may have initially had the Assyrians and then later the Babylonians in mind, and in Jer 5:15, where the Babylonians are clearly intended. Both Assyrians and Babylonians spoke variant dialects of Akkadian.

In the process of this judgment, Isaiah's opponents will stumble and be broken, snared, and caught. This language at the end of v. 13 is very similar to that in 8:15, and the underlying thought is much the same. Just as Isaiah's audience at the time of the Syro-Ephraimitic War was so caught up by the terror of the moment that it lost sight of God and failed to fear and sanctify its true source of security, so Judah's leaders in the revolt against Sennacherib dismissed God and God's demands from their considerations and sought security in their own human diplomatic machinations. The result of this refusal to fear, sanctify, and trust God enough to abide by his counsel, Isaiah says, will be another disaster depressingly similar to the one that befell Israel in the Syro-Ephraimitic War.

In v. 14, Isaiah disparagingly addresses his opponents in the royal court with designations rich with sound play and double entendre. The expression אנשי לצון (ʾanšê lāṣôn), "men of scoffing," seems an intentional sound play on אנשי ציון (ʾanšê ṣîyôn), "men of Zion."[6] The expression משלי העם הזה (mōšĕlê hāʿām hazzeh), "rulers of this people," could also be translated "jesters of this people." There are two verbs משל (māšal), one meaning "to rule," and its homonym meaning "to construct parables, to jest" (see Job 17:6). Isaiah is obviously capitalizing on this ambiguity in creating poetic parallelism with the expression "men of scoffing." These royal advisors play a "ruling" role in Zion, but Isaiah dismisses their royal advice as the work of drunken jesters and buffoons. That an allusion to Zion is intended by the sound play between lāṣôn and ṣîyôn is indicated by the relative clause, "who are in Jerusalem," since Jerusalem often occurs in parallel with Zion. Though its placement is ambiguous because of the preceding construct chain, which the relative clause may not interrupt, the relative clause actually modifies "rulers/jesters," not "this people." The "men of scoffing/Zion" and "the rulers/jesters who are in Jerusalem" are misleading "this people." "This people" includes not only the inhabitants of Jerusalem, but the inhabitants of all of Judah. It is the ruling class who are centered in Jerusalem the capital, not the majority of the Judean populace.

Isaiah's assertion in v. 15 that his opponents boasted of making a treaty with מָוֶת (māwet), "Death," has been an insoluble crux. Did his opponents actually say any such thing, or did Isaiah attribute to them words that they would automatically and emphatically deny? Political polemic based on an opponent's words needs at least a plausible connection to what the opponent actually said to be an effective argument. Otherwise, the opponent could simply dismiss the charge as a lie and tar the critic as a liar. Thus, it is likely that Isaiah is referring to an actual statement of his opponents, though his interpre-

---

5 Hays suggests that the reference to the foreign language is a reference not to the language of their enemies but to their Nubian treaty partners, since the Nubians are characterized elsewhere as גוי קו־קו ומבוסה, "a nation qaw-qāw and mĕbûsâ" (Isa 18:2) ("Covenant with Mut," 234–35), but it is not at all clear that either of these adjectives refers to the Nubians' language. One could also suggest Aramaic as a possibility, since Aramaic was fast becoming the diplomatic language of the period and the dominant language even in Assyria, but many if not most of the elite royal advisors, in contrast to the general Judean populace, probably already spoke and understood

Aramaic (see 2 Kgs 18:26-28), so a reference to Aramaic would hardly be that threatening to this educated class. The similar reference to the difficulty of understanding the language of the enemy in Isa 33:18-19 obviously cannot refer to the Nubians, since the Nubians never attacked Jerusalem.

6 This precise expression is unattested elsewhere in the OT, but the construction with the plural construct ʾanšê, "men of," followed by a city name is well attested—Sodom (Num 13:32), Ai (Josh 7:4), Gibeon (Josh 10:6), Penuel (Judg 6:30), Sukkoth (Judg 8:8), etc. There also may be a wordplay on the earlier expression לצו, that is, "men of doo-doo."

tation of that statement is hardly the meaning that his opponents would assign to the statement. The treaty Isaiah's opponents boasted of making is a treaty intended to protect Judah from the "overflowing scourge," language that in Isaiah is a standard way of referring to the military power of Assyria (Isa 8:7-8a). As a military counterweight to Assyria, Judah's most likely treaty partner would be the unified Nubian-Egyptian state under the Nubian pharaohs of the Twenty-Fifth Dynasty. Isaiah refers elsewhere to appeals to them for help and a treaty with them that he opposed (Isa 30:1-5; 30:6-7; 31:1-3). The Babylonians under Merodach-Baladan may also have been involved in anti-Assyrian treaty negotiations with Hezekiah's Judah at some point (Isa 39:1-8), but Babylon was far away, beyond Assyria, and there was no realistic expectation that a Babylonian relief force could actually reach Judah. Nubia was the only major power in close enough proximity to Judah to provide significant military support against an Assyrian invasion.

If Isaiah is referring to a defensive, anti-Assyrian treaty with Nubia, however, his opponents' boast of a treaty with מות could be plausibly explained as a reference to the high Egyptian goddess Mut. As Hays has demonstrated, the mother goddess Mut, the wife of Amun, was a very prominent goddess in the period.[7] Moreover, she is attested as participating in covenant making; she is portrayed as fiercely protective of those loyal to her; she has associations with the netherworld; and the pronunciation of her name is similar enough to the Hebrew word for "death" that it could provide the prophet with the basis for a disparaging double entendre. While his opponents boasted that they had made a covenant with the powerful Egyptian goddess Mut, Isaiah reported that they had made a covenant with Mot, the Hebrew word for death and the Canaanite god who personified death. By this play on the similarity in sound between the two words, Isaiah turned the confident boast of his opponents into an implicit threat. The parallelism with Sheol, the netherworld, would also convey a negative tone in Hebrew, though the Egyptian Mut's association with the netherworld was far more positive in Egyptian thought. Isaiah's choice of the second word for treaty (חזה, ḥōzeh) also

seems to be motivated by the desire for double entendre. The parallelism with ברית (bĕrît), "covenant," shows that חֹזֶה (ḥōzeh) means "treaty,"[8] but the word is also either cognate with or a homonym of a verbal root meaning "to see, to see a vision," and, as such, it points back to Isaiah's claim that his opponents "stagger in vision" (שגו בראה, šāgû bārōʾeh, v. 7), since ḥōzeh and rōʾeh are normally synonyms. His opponents' claim that their treaty with Egypt would protect them from the Assyrian flood, when it came, is already rendered suspect by Isaiah's reference to this covenant as a covenant with Death and as a deceptive vision/treaty with/of the netherworld. The first half of Isaiah's quotation of his opponents' words may be a fairly accurate quote, though twisted by Isaiah's interpretation of those words, but the last half of the quotation can hardly reflect what his opponents actually said. Unless there is a wordplay between כזב (kāzāb), "a lie," and שקר (šeqer), "falsehood," and two similar sounding Egyptian divine names also invoked in the treaty making, at this point Isaiah seems to put into his opponents' mouths the reality rather than their claims of what they were doing. To make a secret treaty with Nubia was to breach the preexisting treaty with Assyria and to break the sworn oaths they had made to the Assyrian overlord. This was tantamount to making a lie their refuge and taking shelter in falsehood.

Over against this false and deadly refuge, Yahweh offers a solid and secure shelter from the storm. Yahweh asserts that he is about to lay a foundation in Zion of a stone. The repetition of אבן (ʾeben), "stone," at the end of line 1 (v. 16) of Yahweh's quotation and at the beginning of line 2 is intended to further define what kind of stone God is about to lay as a foundation. The repetition specifies the stone as an אבן בחן (ʾeben bōḥan), but there is a dispute about both the meaning and the correct vocalization of the rare word בחן (bōḥan). The traditional derivation from the verb בחן (bāḥan), "to test," gives either the active meaning "a testing stone, touchstone," or the passive meaning "a tested stone,"[9] but neither meaning seems contextually appropriate, even if the prophet may be engaged in double entendre. Others have suggested a derivation from Egyptian bḥn, "schist gneiss,"[10] but this

7   Hays, "Covenant with Mut."
8   This meaning for the word is attested only here and for the cognate form חָזוּת (ḥāzût) in v. 18. Isaiah probably chose these rare synonyms for treaty for the sake of his play on words.
9   See the discussion in Clements, 231; and Wildberger, 3:1075–77.
10   Adolf Erman and Hermann Grapow, *Wörterbuch der aegyptischen Sprache* (Leipzig: Hinrichs, 1926) 1:471; T. O. Lambdin, "Egyptian Loan Words in the Old

stone is not found in Palestine, and there is no evidence that it was imported for building purposes,[11] though it is possible that the loanword could have come to designate fine building stones distinct from the original Egyptian stone designated by the term. In my opinion, however, the word should more likely be connected with *baḥan*, another loanword from Egyptian, which means "fortress, tower, watchtower."[12] This word occurs twice in Isaiah, once in 32:14 and, with slightly variant vocalizations (*bḥn* or *bḥwn*), in 23:13. The word also occurs three times in the Qumran literature in passages dependent on Isa 28:16 (1QS 8:7b-8a; 1QH 6:25d-27a; and 1QH 7:8-9). Moreover, the Qumran community vocalized *bḥn* in Isa 28:16 as *baḥan*, not *bōḥan*, and its usage in Qumran suggests that the term refers to the kind of large stones used in building a fortress, that is, "ashlars."[13]

God's "ashlar" is then further defined by the expression פִּנַּת יִקְרַת מוּסָד (*pinnat yiqrat mûsād*), "a cornerstone valuable for a foundation." The feminine adjective יקרה (*yiqrâ*) modifies פנת (*pinnat*), but it is in the construct before מוסד (*mûsād*) to indicate for what the cornerstone has value. The construction is syntactically parallel to אֵשֶׁת יְפַת-תֹּאַר (*ʾēšet yĕpat-tōʾar*), "a woman beautiful of form" (Deut 21:11). The repetition of מוסד at the end of line 2 and at the beginning of line 3 (v. 16) parallels the earlier repetition of אבן and suggests that מוסד in both its occurrences should be treated as the same word, "foundation." As with אבן, the repetition is to further define the nature of that foundation. The second מוסד is probably to be vocalized as a construct (*mûsad*) before the *hiphil* participle הַמַּאֲמִין (*hammaʾămîn*), producing a construct chain that defines the foundation as "a foundation of or for the one who trusts." The "one who trusts" can be further defined as "the one who believes God's promises and acts on that belief" (cf. Isa 7:9; 2 Chr 20:29).

The following unmarked relative clause, לֹא יָחִישׁ (*lōʾ yāḥîš*), is normally seen as modifying המאמין, the word it immediately follows, and the verbal root חוש (*ḥûš*) is normally given a meaning related to its ordinary Hebrew

sense, "to hurry," thus NRSV's rendering, "one who trusts will not panic." Such a meaning seems forced in this context, however, particularly since the emphasis in the passage is on the solidity of the refuge founded by God in Zion, not on the constancy of the believer. Despite some uncertainty about the meaning of the verbal root חוש, the Qumran passage 1QS 8:8—ובל יחישו ממקומם (*ûbal yāḥîšû mimmĕqômām*), "they [the foundations] will not *ḥûš* from their place"—suggests a meaning "waver, shake, quake," or the like, and this meaning is suggested also by the parallelism with זוע (*zûaʿ*), "to tremble, quake," in the same Qumran context. One should note that *CAD* H also lists a rare Akkadian root ḫâšu/ḫiāšu C (p. 147), found in lexical texts with precisely this connotation. The clause with לא יחיש, thus, follows the participle המאמין (*hammaʾămîn*) rather than מוסד (*mûsad*), the noun it actually modifies, because מוסד (*mûsad*) is in construct with המאמין (*hammaʾămîn*), which prohibits the clause from intervening between the two words. Thus, the foundation is defined as a foundation for the believer that will not totter or shake. The one who trusts will find true security in God's foundation in Zion.

There is a further parallel here to Isaiah's earlier oracle in 8:14-15. Just as in 8:14-15 Yahweh would be a מקדש (*miqdāš*), "a sanctuary," to those who sanctified, feared, and trusted him, but a destructive stone to those who did not, so here Yahweh's foundation stone would stand in judgment on those who treated it with disrespect. Verse 17, with its reference to justice as the line and righteousness as the weight, implies that a plumb line is being used to check whether God's people are building precisely on his foundation stone. The imagery is rooted in ancient temple theology that laid great stress on rebuilding temples precisely on the ancient foundations revealed by the deity to the first builder.[14] Even a slight error in proper alignment could provoke the deity into causing the new building to collapse prematurely. But proper alignment with Yahweh's foundation is judged by moral categories. Justice and righteousness here are simply a rewording

Testament," *JAOS* 73 (1953) 148–49; L. Koehler, "Zwei Fachwörter der Bausprache in Jesaja 28, 16," *TZ* 3 (1947) 392; *HALAT*, 115.

11   Wildberger, 3:1066; M. Tsevat, "בחן *bḥn*," *TDOT* 2:72.

12   Erman and Grapow, *Wörterbuch*, 1:471.

13   For more details, see my "Yahweh's Foundation."

14   For detailed discussion of this point, see my "Yahweh's Foundation."

of the admonition given in v. 12. If one wants security, it comes through giving relief to the weary and repose to the poor and needy. To care for the poor and defenseless members of society with justice and righteousness is to build on Yahweh's solid foundation. In contrast, the flimsy shelter Isaiah's opponents tried to construct by their treaty with Nubia, cloaked as it was in lies, deceit, and secrecy, would be washed away by the first storm. The imagery of the overflowing gully-washer points again to the coming invasion of Assyria (cf. Isa 8:8), but the choice of this imagery may also be dictated by the topography of the actual Jerusalem. The city was built on a steep hill, and, particularly on the eastern slope, poorly anchored buildings were apt to be undercut by torrential rains, resulting in their collapse into the valley below.[15]

In any case, the treaty with Mut and her Nubian devotees would be as useless a refuge as a treaty with Death and the netherworld. The use of חזות (ḥāzût) in v. 18 for treaty suggests the same double entendre as the use of חזה (ḥōzê) in v. 15. The "vision" behind the treaty was misleading (see v. 7). The treaty and the "vision" that undergirded it would collapse under the Assyrian deluge like a poorly built building on a steep slope, and the Judean royal counselors would be trampled in the process. Verses 18-19 suggest that this process of destruction would continue day after day, night after night without relief, and that the news during this whole period would be nothing but terror-inspiring. The expression הבין שמועה (hābîn šěmû῾â), "to understand the report," picks up the יבין שמועה (yābîn šěmû῾â), "[to whom] would he explain the report," of v. 9. Before the crisis, when understanding Isaiah's report or message might have helped them, they dismissed it as infantile. When the crisis hits, and the terrible news of destruction comes in day after day, night after night, understanding the report or message will only serve to excite terror or trembling (זועה zěwā῾â). As a prophetic prediction, this word no doubt captures the actuality of what it was like to live through Sennacherib's thorough devastation of Judah in the campaign of 701 BCE. The situation, Isaiah says, will be analogous to the proverbial saying about the person who tries to sleep on too short a bed with too narrow a cover

(v. 20). One can get no relief, for the bed is too short to stretch out, and the cover is too narrow to cover oneself when one curls up to stay within the length of the bed.

Such a threat against Yahweh's own royal city may have been regarded by Isaiah's opponents as heresy in the light of the Zion Tradition's promise of Yahweh's presence in and protection of Zion, so Isaiah anticipates and blocks this objection by a daring appeal to the Davidic traditions of Yahweh's participation in the battles against the Philistines at Mount Perazim (2 Sam 5:17-21) and in the Valley of Gibeon (2 Sam 5:22-25; 1 Chr 14:13-17; the Samuel text mentions Geba, not Gibeon, but the Chronicler has Gibeon). In these early traditions, Yahweh rose up to fight with David against the Philistines and to protect David's new capital, Jerusalem, but Isaiah claims that when Yahweh rises up again in analogous fashion, it will be to do a strange work (v. 21). The implication is clearly that this time Yahweh will fight against Jerusalem, not for it, a view that Isaiah explicitly spells out in 29:1-3 and 30:4 (cf. also Isa 10:5-12).

In light of God's strange plan, then, Isaiah's opponents should stop their scoffing and take Isaiah seriously. Otherwise their fetters, when they are taken into captivity, will be even harsher, for Isaiah has heard Yahweh issue a firm decree of destruction upon the whole land (v. 22). The announcement of this coming judgment, which Isaiah has heard from Yahweh, picks up much of the same vocabulary that Isaiah used in an earlier oracle against the northern kingdom at the time of the Syro-Ephraimitic War (Isa 10:20-23). The expression כִּי־כָלָה וְנֶחֱרָצָה (kî kālâ wěneḥěrāṣâ, "for a decreed destruction") is found in both passages (10:23; 28:22). Both passages then identify the divine source of this judgment as אֲדֹנָי יְהוִה צְבָאוֹת (ʾădōnāy YHWH ṣěbāʾôt), "my Lord Yahweh of Hosts." And both passages conclude with similar statements announcing that the judgment will overtake the whole land (בקרב כל־הארץ, běqereb kol hāʾāreṣ, "in the midst of the whole land" [Isa 10:23]; עַל־כָּל־הָאָרֶץ, ῾al kol hāʾāreṣ, "over the whole land" [Isa 28:22]). Given this close parallelism between Isa 10:23 and 28:22, I see no reason to dismiss the final phrase in Isa 28:22 as "dangling and no part of the flow of the verse," as Hays does.[16] The

---

15 See my more extended discussion of this point in "Yahweh's Foundation," 41–43.

16 Hays, "Covenant with Mut," 215, n. 18.

close parallelism between these verses also suggests that both at the beginning (28:1-6) and at the end (28:22) of the present oracle Isaiah is reworking old material, thus creating an interesting kind of inclusion.

Bibliography

Aitken, K. T., "Hearing and Seeing: Metamorphoses of a Motif in Isaiah 1–39," in Philip R. Davies and David J. A. Clines, eds., *Among the Prophets: Language, Image and Structure in the Prophetic Writings* (JSOTSup 144; Sheffield: JSOT Press, 1993) 12–41.

Bailey, K. E., "'Inverted Parallelism' and 'Encased Parables' in Isaiah and Their Significance for OT and NT Translation and Interpretation," in L. J. de Regt, J. de Waard, and J. P. Fokkelman, eds., *Literary Structure and Rhetorical Strategies in the Hebrew Bible* (Assen: Van Gorcum, 1996) 14–30.

Barthel, Jörg, *Prophetenwort und Geschichte: Die Jesajaüberlieferung in Jes 6–8 und 28–31* (FAT 19; Tübingen: Mohr Seibeck, 1997) 280–303.

Betz, Otto, "Firmness in Faith: Hebrews 11:1 and Isaiah 28:16," in Barry P. Thompson, ed., *Scripture: Meaning and Method. Essays Presented to Anthony Tyrrell Hanson for His Seventieth Birthday* (Hull: Hull University Press, 1987) 92–113.

——, "Zungenreden und süsser Wein: Zur eschatologischen Exegese von Jesaja 28 in Qumran und im Neuen Testament," in Siegfried Wagner, ed., *Bibel und Qumran: Beiträge zur Erforschung der Beziehungen zwischen Bibel- und Qumranwissenschaft. Hans Bardte zum 22. 9. 1966* (Berlin: Evangelische Haupt-Bibelgesellschaft,1968) 20–36.

Beuken, W. A. M., "Isaiah 28: Is It Only Schismatics That Drink Heavily? Beyond the Synchronic Versus Diachronic Controversy," in Johannes C. de Moor, ed., *Synchronic or Diachronic? A Debate on Method in Old Testament Exegesis* (OtSt 34; Leiden: Brill, 1995) 15–38.

Blenkinsopp, Joseph, "Judah's Covenant with Death (Isaiah XXVIII 14-22)," *VT* 50 (2000) 472–83.

Boehmer, J., "Der Glaube und Jesaja: Zu Jes 7,9 und 28,16," *ZAW* 41 (1923) 84–93.

Bronznick, N. M., "The Semantics of the Biblical Stem *yqr*," *HS* 22 (1981) 9–12.

Daiches, S., "Isaiah and Spiritualism: A New Explanation of Isaiah XXVIII 5-22,"*Jewish Chronicle Supplement* (1921) 1–4.

Donner, *Israel unter den Völkern*, 146–53.

Driver, G. R., "'Another Little Drink'–Isaiah 28:1-22," in Peter R. Ackroyd and Barnabas Lindars, eds., *Words and Meanings: Essays Presented to David Winton Thomas on His Retirement from the Regius Professorship of Hebrew in the University of Cambridge* (London: Cambridge University Press, 1968) 47–67.

Driver, G. R., "Hebrew Notes," *ZAW* 52 (1934) 51–56.

Evans, Craig A., "On Isaiah's Use of Israel's Sacred Tradition," *BZ* n.s. 30 (1986) 92–99.

Exum, J. Cheryl, "'Whom Will He Teach Knowledge?' A Literary Approach to Isaiah 28," in Paul Achtemeier, ed., *SBLSP 1979* (Missoula, MT: Scholars Press, 1979) 2:123–51; reprinted in David J. A. Clines, David M. Gunn, and Alan J. Hauser, eds., *Art and Meaning: Rhetoric in Biblical Literature* (JSOTSup 19; Sheffield: JSOT Press, 1982) 109–10.

Finney, Charles Grandison, "Refuges of Lies," *Fundamentalist Journal* 3, no. 6 (1984) 44–45.

Floss, Johannes Peter, "Biblische Theologie als Sprecherin der 'gefährlichen Erinnerung' dargestellt an Jes 28:7-12," *BN* 54 (1990) 60–80.

Ford, J. M., "The Jewel of Discernment," *BZ* 11 (1967) 109–16.

Fullerton, K., "The Stone of Foundation," *AJSL* 37 (1920) 1–50.

Gese, H., "Die strömende Geissel des Hadad und Jesaja 28,15 und 18," in Arnulf Kuschke and Ernst Kutsch, eds., *Archäologie und Altes Testament: Festschrift für Kurt Galling zum 8. Jan. 1970* (Tübingen: Mohr, 1970) 127–34.

Görg, Manfred, "Jesaja als 'Kinderlehrer': Beobachtungen zur Sprache und Semantik in Jes 28:10(13)," *BN* 29 (1985) 12–16.

Graffey, A., "'The Lord However Says This': The Prophetic Disputation Speech [Is 28:14-19; 49:14-25; Ezek 37:11-13]," *ScrB* 20 (1989) 2–8.

Hallo, William W., "Isaiah 28,9-13 and the Ugaritic Abecedaries," *JBL* 77 (1958) 324–38.

Halpern, Baruch, "The Excremental Vision: The Doomed Priests of Doom in Isaiah 28," *HAR* 10 (1987) 109–21.

Hays, Christopher B., "The Covenant with Mut: A New Interpretation of Isaiah 28:1-22," *VT* 60 (2010) 212–40.

Hooke, S. H., "The Corner-Stone of Scripture," in Hooke, *The Siege Perilous: Essays in Biblical Anthropology and Kindred Subjects* (London: SCM, 1956) 235–49.

Jeppesen, Knud., "The Cornerstone (Isa 28,16) in Deutero-Isaianic Rereading of the Message of Isaiah," *ST* 38, no. 2 (1984) 93–99.

Jeremias, J., "Κεφαλὴ γωνίας - Ἀκρογωνιαῖος Kephale gonias-akrogoniaios," *ZNW* 29 (1930) 264–80.

Kaiser, O., "Geschichtliche Erfahrung und eschatologische Erwartung: Ein Beitrag zur Geschichte der alttestamentlichen Eschatologie im Jesajabuch," *Neue Zeitschrift für systematische Theologie* 15 (1973) 272–85.

Klopfenstein, Martin A., *Die Lüge nach dem Alten Testament: Ihr Begriff, ihre Bedeutung, und ihre Beurteilung* (Zurich: Gotthelf-Verlag, 1964).

Köhler, L., "Zwei Fachwörter der Bausprache in Jesaja 28,16," *TZ* 3 (1947) 390–93.

———, "Zu Jes 28,15a und 18b," *ZAW* 48 (1930) 227–28.

Laberge, Léo, *La Septante d'Isaïe 28–33: Étude de tradition textuelle* (Ottawa: Laberge, 1978).

Landy, Francis, "Tracing the Voice of the Other: Isaiah 28 and the Covenant with Death," in J. Cheryl Exum and David J. A. Clines, eds., *The New Literary Criticism and the Hebrew Bible* (Valley Forge, PA: Trinity Press International, 1993) 140–62.

Lanier, D. E., "With Stammering Lips and Another Tongue: I Cor 14:20-22 and Is 28:11-12," *CTR* 5 (1991) 259–85.

Lindblom, J., "Der Eckstein in Jes 28:16," in *Interpretationes ad Vetus Testamentum Sigmundo Mowinckel* (Oslo: Forlayet Land og Kirke, 1955) 123–32.

Lucas, A., and A. Rowe, "The Ancient Egyptian Bekhen-Stone," *ASAE* 38 (1938) 127–56.

Lutz, H. M., *Jahwe, Jerusalem und die Völker* (WMANT 27; Neukirchen-Vluyn: Neukirchener Verlag, 1968).

Martin-Achard, Robert, "Esaie et Jérémie aux prises avec les problèmes politiques: Contribution á l'étude du thème, Prophétie et politique," *Cahiers de la Revue de Théologie et de Philosophie* 11 (1984) 306–22.

Melugin, R. F., "The Conventional and the Creative in Isaiah's Judgment Oracles," *CBQ* 36 (1974) 301–11.

Möller, Hans, "Abwägen zweier Übersetzungen von Jes 28:19b," *ZAW* 96 (1984) 272–74.

Mosca, P. G., "Isaiah 28:12e: A Response to J. J. M. Roberts," *HTR* 77 (1984) 113–17.

Muszyński, Henryk, *Fundament, Bild und Metapher in den Handschriften aus Qumran: Studie zur Vorgeschichte des ntl. Begriffs "Themelios"* (AnBib 61; Rome: Biblical Institute Press, 1975).

Oudenrijn, M. A. van den, "Priesters en profeten by Isaias (Is XXVII 7-13)," *Studia Catholica* 14 (1938) 299–311.

Petersen, David L., "Isaiah 28, a Redaction Critical Study," in Paul Achtemeier, ed., *SBLSP 1979* (Missoula, NT: Scholars Press, 1979) 2:101–22.

Pfeifer, G., "Entwöhnung und Entwöhnungsfest im Alten Testament: Der Schlüssel zu Jesaja 28,7-13?" *ZAW* 84 (1972) 341–47.

Quiring, H., "Der Probierstein," *FF* 25 (1949) 238–39.

Richardson, H. N., "Some Notes on *Lys* and Its Derivatives," *VT* 5 (1955) 163–79.

Roberts, J. J. M., "Double Entendre."

———, "A Note on Isaiah 28:12," *HTR* 73 (1980) 48–51.

———, "Yahweh's Foundation."

Selms, A. van, "Isaiah 28,9-13: An Attempt to Give a New Interpretation," *ZAW* 85 (1973) 332–39.

Sethe, K., "Die Bau- und Denkmalsteine der alten Ägypter und ihre Namen. 6: Der angebliche Basalt des Wadi Hammamat," SPAW (1936) 864–912.

Stewart, A. C., "The Covenant with the Dead in Isaiah 28," *ExpTim* 100 (1988–89) 375–77.

Stolz, F., "Der Streit um die Wirklichkeit in der Südreichsprophetie des 8. Jahrhunderts," *WD* 12 (1973) 9–30.

Szlaga, J., "Symbolika Kamienia I Fundamentu W Ks. Izajasza 28,16-17," *Studia Pepliÿnaskie* 2 (1971) 149–57.

Tanghe, Vincent, "Dichtung und Ekel in Jesaja XXVIII 7-13," *VT* 43 (1993) 235–60.

Terrien, S., "The Metaphor of the Rock in Biblical Theology," in Tod Linafelt and Timothy K. Beal, eds., *God in the Fray: A Tribute to Walter Brueggemann* (Minneapolis: Fortress Press, 1998) 157–71.

Tromp, Nicholas J., *Primitive Conceptions of Death and the Nether World in the Old Testament* (BibOr 21; Rome: Pontifical Biblical Institute, 1969).

Tsevat, M., "בחן *bḥn*," *TDOT* 2:72.

Virgulin, S., "Il Significato della Pietra di Fondazione in Is. 28,16," *RivB* 7 (1959) 208–20.

Xella, Paolo, "Le grand Froid: Le dieu Baradu madu . . . Ebla," *UF* 18 (1986) 437–44.

28

23/   Listen and hear my voice,
        Pay attention and hear my speech.
24/   Does the one who plows to sow plow every day,
        When he opens[a] and harrows[b] his land?
25/   When he has smoothed its surface,
        Does he not rather scatter black cumin,
            And broadcast[c] cumin;[d]
    And place wheat in a row,
        Barley in a strip,[e]
            With spelt as its borders?[f]
26/   He[g] teaches him what is appropriate;[h]
        His[g] God instructs[i] him.
27/   For black cumin is not threshed[j] with a threshing sled,
        And the wheel of a cart is not rolled[k] over cumin;
    But black cumin is beaten out with a staff,
        And cumin with a rod.[l]
28/   Bread grain[m] is crushed,
        But one does not thresh[n] it forever;
    Even when one sets in motion the wheel of his wagon and his horses,
        One does not crush[o] it.
29/   This also has gone forth[p] from Yahweh of Hosts,
        Who has made his counsel marvelous,[q]
            His wisdom surpassing.[r]

Textual Notes

a   1QIsaᵃ has ופתח (ûpittaḥ), "and he opens," for MT יְפַתַּח (yĕpattaḥ), "he opens." MT is to be preferred.

b   1QIsaᵃ has ושדד (wĕśidded), "and he harrows," corrected to MT's וִישַׂדֵּד (wîśaddēd), "and harrows."

c   For MT יְזְרֹק (yizrōq), "he broadcasts," 1QIsaᵃ appears to have וזרק (wĕzāraq), "and he broadcasts."

d   1QIsaᵃ has וכמן (wkymn) for MT וְכַמֹּן (wĕkammōn), "cumin."

e   The meaning of נִסְמָן (nismān), "strip?," is uncertain. LXX and Syr. omit the word. Vg. takes it as millet.

f   Reading the plural גבולותו (gĕbûlôtô), "its borders," for MT's גְּבֻלָתוֹ (gĕbūlātô), "its border," following 1QIsaᵃ, LXX, Vg., Syr., and Tg., though LXX has the second person common singular suffix.

g   LXX consistently reads the second person common singular here: "and you will be instructed by the judgment of your God, and you will rejoice."

h   LXX and Syr. construe למשפט (lammišpāṭ), "for the just/appropriate action," as though it were in construct with אֱלֹהָיו (ʾĕlōhāyw), "his God," though LXX reads אלהיך (ʾĕlōhêkā), "your God"—"by the judgment of your/his God."

i   LXX and Syr. misconstrue יֹרֶנּוּ (yôrennû), "he teaches him," as though it were from the verb רנן (rānan), "to rejoice"—"and you/they will rejoice."

j   For MT's *qal* passive (or less likely *hophal*) verb form יוּדַשׁ (yûdaš), "is not threshed," 1QIsaᵃ (ידשׁ, yādūš) and 4QIsaᵏ (ידוש, yādûš) have the *qal* active, "one does not thresh black cumin."

k   For MT's *qal* passive יוּסַּב (yûssāb), "is rolled," 1QIsaᵃ has the *qal* active יסוב (yissôb), "one rolls."

l   LXX garbles the last line, construing the part it preserves with the beginning of the next verse, τὸ δὲ κύμινον μετὰ ἄρτου βρωθήσεται, "and the cumin will be eaten with bread."

m   1QIsaᵃ omits לֶחֶם (leḥem), "bread grain"; 4QIsaᵏ has לחם (leḥem) with the correction to ולחם (wĕleḥem), "and bread grain," written above the line.

n   For the expected *qal* infinitive absolute דּוֹשׁ (dôš), "to thresh," MT has the unusual אָדוֹשׁ (ʾādôš) and 1QIsaᵃ has הדשׁ (hādōš).

o   For MT's יְדֻקֶּנּוּ (yĕduqqennû), "one crushes it," 1QIsaᵃ has the *hiphil* ידיקנו (yādîqennû), "one crushes it."

p   4QIsaᵏ appears to read the masculine יצא (y[yā]sāʾ) for יצאה (yāṣāʾâ, "has gone forth") in MT and 1QIsaᵃ.

q   4QIsaᵏ also has the anomalous הפיל (hipîl), the *hiphil* perfect third person masculine singular of נפל (nāpal), "he caused (counsel) to fall/fail," for MT's הִפְלִיא (hiplîʾ), "he made marvelous," and 1QIsaᵃ's הפלה (hiplâ)—the latter two being variant spellings for the *hiphil* perfect third person masculine singular of פלא (pālāʾ), "to make marvelous."

r   1QIsaᵃ has והגדיל (wĕhigdîl), "and he made great," for MT's הִגְדִּיל (higdîl), "he made great."

Commentary

It is possible that this is an independent oracle originally unconnected to the preceding material, but, if so, it fits with the preceding material remarkably well. The oracle seems to be a response to the complaint either that God's actions were irrational or at least that Isaiah's portrayal of God's imminent actions was irrational. In the light of the received religious tradition, Isaiah's opponents appear to have claimed that it made no sense for Yahweh to act in the way that Isaiah proclaimed that God would. Such a complaint could easily have been provoked by Isaiah's reference to God's strange work in Isa 28:21. For his opponents, the idea that God would attack Zion rather than defend it made no sense. One could imagine a similar response to Isaiah's oracle about Assyria as God's rod for punishing Jerusalem in Isa 10:5-15. Even long after Isaiah, when one might have thought that such an idea would have gained purchase, Habakkuk still had difficulty with the logic of Yahweh using a wicked nation, this time the Babylonians, to punish God's own, in Habakkuk's mind, far less wicked people (Hab 1:5-17).

In response to this complaint, Isaiah first calls his audience to pay attention, and then he answers their objection with a parable about farmers. Isaiah's audience wants God to always act in a consistent manner, always rescuing his chosen Davidic king and Zion, his royal city, from threatening enemies. Isaiah suggests that such boring consistency is not the mark of wisdom in other endeavors. A farmer does not spend his whole time plowing, breaking up and harrowing his field. Once that is done, the farmer changes his activity, levels the field's surface, and sows it with various crops, each of which he plants and cultivates differently as appropriate to that particular crop. According to this passage, black cumin (קצח, qeṣaḥ) and cumin (כמן, kammōn) were broadcast sown. Wheat (חטה, ḥiṭṭâ), on the other hand, appears to have been planted in rows, if שורה (śôrâ) is correctly identified with Mishnaic Hebrew שורה (śûrâ). If not, the noun may refer to another crop, a type of sorghum known as durra or Indian millet,[1] but then it is not clear how the treatment of wheat, durra, and barley differs from that for black cumin and cumin. Barley (שערה, śĕʿōrâ) is well known, but the meaning of נסמן (nismān) is unknown. "Strip" is just a guess at the meaning. Others have suggested that it is yet another crop of some sort, or perhaps just a garbled dittography of the following word.[2] Spelt (כסמת, kussemet) was either planted as the border of the field (lit., as "its

borders"), or one might also render the expression as a locative accusative, "in its patch."

The farmer's different treatment of the different crops is something that the farmer was taught by God according to v. 26. This statement strongly suggests a type of natural revelation or natural theology, because there is no indication that the farmer learned these farming techniques through the revelatory mediation of priests and prophets. Presumably he learned them from other farmers and from his own observations in the process of farming.

According to v. 27, one does not thresh out the seed of black cumin and cumin in the same fashion that one threshes out wheat and barley. Instead of using iron threshing sleds and cart wheels, one threshes black cumin and cumin with a staff. One crushes the bread grains or cereals like wheat and barley, but only up to a point (v. 28). The cart wheels and hoofs of the threshing animals do not thoroughly crush it; they simply separate the grain from the chaff. These different techniques of threshing, like the different techniques of cultivating the different crops, also come from Yahweh of Hosts as the ultimate teacher of the farmer, and they demonstrate how majestic and marvelous—and, one might add, varied—God's wisdom is (v. 29). The point of the parable, however, is that the same God who teaches the farmer the different activities appropriate to the planting, cultivating, and harvesting of different crops at different stages in that process may also take quite different but equally appropriate actions at different stages in dealing with his people. A non-farmer may find the farmer's differing activities inexplicable and strange, but they have their own divinely taught logic. In the same way, Yahweh's treatment of his people and other nations may seem inexplicable and strange to Isaiah's untutored opponents, but Yahweh's strange work also has its own internal logic, and this work too will ultimately demonstrate God's majestic and marvelous wisdom.

1 See *HALOT*, 1314.
2 See BDB, 702; *BHS*; Wildberger, 3:1084.

Bibliography

Amsler, S., and O. Mury, "Yahweh et la sagesse du paysan: Quelques remarques sur Esaïe 28,23-29," *RHPR* 53 (1973) 1–5.

Guthe, H., "Eggen und Furchen im Alten Testament," in Karl Marti, ed., *Beiträge zur alttestamentlichen Wissenschaft: Karl Budde zum siebzigsten Geburtstag am 13. April 1920* (BZAW 34; Giessen: A. Töpelmann, 1920) 75–82.

Healey, John F., "Ancient Agriculture and the Old Testament (with Special Reference to Isaiah 28:23-29)," in J. Barton et al., *Prophets, Worship and Theodicy: Studies in Prophetism, Biblical Theology, and Structural and Rhetorical Analysis and on the Place of Music in Worship* (OtSt 23; Leiden: Brill, 1984) 108–19.

Heaton, E. W., *Everyday Life in Old Testament Times* (New York: Scribner, 1956).

Jensen, *Use of tôrâ*, 50–51.

Liebreich, L. J., "The Parable Taken from the Farmer's Labors in Isaiah 28:23-29" (in Hebrew with English resumé), *Tarbiz* 24 (1945–55) 126–28.

Schuman, N. H., "Jesaja 28:23-29: Een Boerengelijkenis als politieke profetie. Ook een manier van exegetiseren," *Segmenten* 2 (1981) 83–141.

Thexton, S. C., "A Note on Isaiah XXVIII 25 and 28," *VT* 2 (1952) 81–83.

Vriezen, T. C., "Essentials of the Theology of Isaiah," in Bernhard W. Anderson and Walter Harrelson, eds., *Israel's Prophetic Heritage: Essays in Honor of James Muilenburg* (New York: Harper, 1962) 128–46.

Whedbee, J. William, *Isaiah and Wisdom* (Nashville: Abingdon, 1971) 51–68.

Wilbers, H., "Étude sur trois textes relatifs à l'agriculture: Is. 28:27,28; Amos 2:13 et 9:9," in *Melanges de l'Université Saint-Joseph* 5 (Beyrouth: Impr. catholique, 1911–12) 269–83.

The mixture of judgment and salvation in this oracle has led many critics, as early as Bernhard Duhm, T. K. Cheyne, and Karl Marti, and continuing down to the present, to dismiss all or part of vv. 5-8 as a later redactor's addition to the text. This ignores the fact, however, that precisely the same mixture of judgment and deliverance is found numerous times in Isaiah of Jerusalem. Isaiah saw a corrupted Jerusalem requiring a purging by fire, but that fiery judgment was to produce a purified Jerusalem that would once again be called a city of righteousness (Isa 1:21-28). The prophet explained Assyria's historical role as the rod Yahweh used to punish sinful nations, and Judah and Jerusalem would feel the pain of that rod just as Israel and Samaria had (Isa 10:5-11), but

that was not the end of the story. Once Yahweh had finished his disciplining work on Mount Zion, his "strange work" (cf. 28:21), Yahweh would punish the Assyrian "tool" for exceeding the divine command given him (Isa 10:6-7), as well as for the Assyrian's arrogance and undue pleasure in his task (Isa 10:12-15). The same pattern is found in Isa 31:4-5, where God first attacks Jerusalem and then delivers it from its enemies. For Isaiah, Yahweh had founded Zion (Isa 14:32) and dwelt in it (Isa 8:18), and judgment was only Yahweh's plan for urban renewal to make God's chosen city habitable again for the divine king (Isa 28:16-17; 33:13-21), whose promises to the Davidic house and Jerusalem remained inviolable (see Isa 7:1-9).

1/   Hey, Ariel, Ariel,[a]
    City where David[b] encamped!
    Add[c] year to year,
    Let the festivals circle round.[d]

2/   Then I will afflict Ariel,[e]
    And there will be[f] moaning and lamentation,[g]
    And she will become[h] to me like an Ariel.[e]

3/   And I will encamp against you like David,[i]
    And I will besiege you with a siege wall,[j]
    And I will raise[k] fortifications[l] against you.

4/   And low from the ground you will speak,
    And your speech will be from low in the dust;
    And your voice will be like a ghost from the ground,
    And from the dust your speech will chirp.

5/   And the multitude of your enemies[m] will be like fine dust,
    And the multitude of the violent will be like passing chaff,[n]
    And it will happen very suddenly,

6/   That she will be visited[o] by Yahweh of Hosts,
    With thunder and earthquake and loud noise,
    With whirlwind and storm,
    And the flame of a devouring fire.

7/   And the multitude of all[p] the nations[q] who fight[r] against Ariel,[s]
    And all[p] who fight against her,[t] and the siege works against her,[u]
    And who oppress her,[v]
    Will become like a dream, a vision of the night.

8/   And it will be as when the hungry dreams[w] that he eats,
    But he awakes, and his throat[x] is empty;
    Or as when the thirsty dreams[w] that he drinks,[y]
    But he awakes still faint, and his throat thirsty.[z]
    Thus shall be the multitude of all the nations*[a]
    Who fight against Mount Zion.

Textual Notes

a   אֲרִיאֵל (ʾărîʾēl), a poetic name for Zion that can also mean "altar hearth"; 1QIsaᵃ has ארואל (ʾărûʾēl), but LXX, Vg., and Syr.

support MT's vocalization, though LXX omits one אֲרִיאֵל. Tg. translates the word as "altar."

b   MT דָּוִד (dāwîd), "David"; 1QIsaᵃ דויד.

c MT סְפוּ (sĕpû), "add" (masculine plural imperative yāsap) is supported by Syr.; 1QIsaᵃ ספי and 4QIsaᵏ סופי (feminine singular imperative yāsap). Since the city is being addressed, the feminine singular fits the context better than the maculine plural. LXX's συναγάγετε γενήματα ἐνιαυτὸν ἐπ' ἐνιαυτόν, "gather the produce year by year," seems to presuppose the verb אסף (ʾāsap), "to gather."

d MT חַגִּים יִנְקֹפוּ (ḥaggîm yinqōpû), "let the festivals circle around," is supported by 1QIsaᵃ, Vg., and Syr. Tg.'s rendering, "the year in which the feasts cease in you," is loose, and LXX's odd reading φάγεσθε γὰρ σὺν Μωαβ, "for you will eat with Moab," remains obscure.

e See note a above.

f MT וְהָיֵתָה (wĕhāyĕtâ), "and it/she will be"; 1QIsaᵃ והייתה is just an orthographic variant, but 4QIsaᵏ has the imperfect ו.תהיה[.

g For MT's תַּאֲנִיָּה וַאֲנִיָּה (taʾănîyâ waʾănîyâ), "moaning and lamentation," LXX's erroneous καὶ ἔσται αὐτῆς ἡ ἰσχὺς καὶ τὸ πλοῦτος ἐμοί, "and her strength and wealth will be mine," seems to read two nouns with feminine suffixes, one of which must be אונה (ʾônāh), "her strength, wealth."

h Again MT and 1QIsaᵃ have the same variant orthography as in note f. While the third person feminine singular verb form will work here, it is tempting to emend to the second person feminine singular והיית (wĕhāyît), "and you will become," to prepare for the second person feminine singular suffixes in the next verse.

i MT כַּדּוּר (kaddûr), "like a ball, circle, sphere," though it is supported by Vg. and Syr., appears to be a corruption of כדוד (kĕdāwîd), "like David." LXX ὡς Δαυιδ, "like David," presupposes this reading. 4QIsaᵏ also appears to have this reading, and even 1QIsaᵃ may have כדוד rather than the commonly read כדור; see the comment in DJD 15, p. 126. The repetition of the verb חנה (ḥānâ), "to encamp," from v. 1, suggests the repetition of "David" as well.

j MT וַהֲקִימֹתִי (wahăqîmōtî), "and I will raise up"; 1QIsaᵃ והקימותי.

k MT's מֻצָּב (muṣṣāb) or the variant מ[ן]צֹּבה in 1Q8 (1QIsaᵇ) col. 11, frags. d–e, line 5 is presumably a technical military term for something set up in the process of besieging a city, though the term is attested only here. One could think either of siege instruments of various types, a siege wall, or of military outposts that encircled the city preventing either access or egress from the besieged city.

l MT מְצֻרֹת (mĕṣūrōt), "fortifications"; 1QIsaᵃ מצודות (mĕṣûdōt), "strongholds." It is hard to decide between the two readings; either would refer in this context to siegework fortifications.

m MT זָרָיִךְ (zārāyik), "your enemies, foreigners"; Vg. and Tg. appear to be reading zōrāyik, "those scattering, winnowing you" (cf. Syr.). 1QIsaᵃ has זדיך (zēdayik), "those insolent toward you." LXX reduces the parallel lines, "the multitude of your enemies" and "the multitude of the violent," to the single phrase, "the multitude of the godless."

n MT וּכְמֹץ עֹבֵר (ûkĕmōṣ ʿōbēr), "like passing chaff"; 1QIsaᵃ וכמוץ עובר.

o MT תִּפָּקֵד (tippāqēd), "she will be visited," is to be analyzed as niphal imperfect third person feminine singular, not as

second person masculine singular, since the feminine city is the addressee. The switch to the third person is continued in the following verse.

p MT כָּל (kol), "all," without the mater; 1QIsaᵃ כול, with mater.

q MT הַגּוֹיִם (haggôyīm), "the nations"; 1QIsaᵃ הגואים.

r MT הַצֹּבְאִים (haṣṣōbĕʾîm), "who fight against"; 1QIsaᵃ הצובאים.

s See note a above. Tg. here has "the city in which the altar is."

t MT צֹבֶיהָ (ṣōbêhā), "those who fight against her"; LXX has a double translation, καὶ πάντες οἱ στρατευσάμενοι ἐπὶ Ιερουσαλημ καὶ πάντες οἱ συνηγμένοι ἐπ' αὐτήν, "and all those who make war upon Jerusalem and all who are gathered against her"; Tg. seems to take the Hebrew as a noun, not a participle, "their army."

u MT וּמְצֹדָתָהּ (ûmĕṣōdātāh), "and her stronghold"; 1QIsaᵃ has ומצרתה (ûmĕṣūrōtāh), "and her siegeworks." Vg. read a verbal form et obsederunt, "and they besieged," and LXX, Tg., and Syr. all saw the Hebrew suffixed noun as referring to a "gathering" of Jerusalem's enemies. NRSV, following MT, takes the term to refer to Ariel's fortress, and the reading וּמְצֹדָתָה here would help explain the introduction of the reading in 1QIsaᵃ of מצודות in v. 3. On the other hand, the term here is in a series preceded by וְכָל־צֹבֶיהָ (wekol-ṣōbêhā), "all who fight against her," and followed by וְהַמְּצִיקִים לָהּ (wĕhammĕṣîqîm lāh), "and who oppress her," both of which refer to Ariel's enemies who were attacking her. To make it clear that וּמְצֹדָתָה stood outside that series, the writer would have needed to repeat the על, something like וכל־ צביה ועל מצדתה, "and all those fighting against her and against her fortress." Lacking such a clarifying expression, it is more likely that ומצרתה is the original reading both here and in v. 3, and that it refers to the siegeworks mentioned in v. 3 that had been set up against Ariel; cf. JPS. The introduction of מצדת in MT here, as in 1QIsaᵃ in v. 3, was simply a result of the easy confusion of ר and ד.

v MT וְהַמְּצִיקִים (wĕhammĕṣîqîm), "and who afflict"; 1QIsaᵃ והמצוקים.

w MT יַחֲלֹם (yaḥălōm), "he dreams"; 1QIsaᵃ יחלום.

x MT נַפְשׁוֹ (napšô), "his soul, his appetite, his throat"; 1QIsaᵃ נפשיו.

y MT שֹׁתֶה (šōtê), "he drinks"; 1QIsaᵃ שותה.

z MT שׁוֹקֵקָה (šôqēqâ), "it thirsts"; 1QIsaᵃ שקיקה, "it is thirsty."

*a MT כָּל־הַגּוֹיִם (kol-haggôyīm), "all the nations"; 1QIsaᵃ כול הגואים.

Commentary

The oracle begins with the attention-getting exclamation *hôy*. Isaiah uses this particle extensively (1:4, 24; 5:8-22; 10:1, 5; 17:12; 18:1; 28:1; 29:1, 15; 30:1; 31:1; 33:1). It was used in funerary laments addressed to the dead (1 Kgs 13:30; Jer 22:18; 34:5), and some scholars assume that this usage so dominated the preexilic period that anytime a prophet in this period began an oracle with this particle, the audience would immediately assume a somber announcement about death would follow.[1] I remain dubious about this generalized conclusion, particularly since in the later period the exclamation could be used to introduce the good news of salvation (Isa 55:1; Zech 2:10-11). In my opinion, the particle itself is a relatively neutral attention-getting exclamation that acquired its negative or positive charge from the following characterization of the audience being addressed, much like the colloquial English exclamation, "Hey!" In this particular passage, however, where by v. 4 Jerusalem, the addressee, is chirping like a ghost from the underworld, the associations with the funerary lament would come into play soon enough.

Jerusalem is addressed as Ariel (*ʾărîʾēl*). The word appears to mean an altar hearth (see v. 2 and Ezek 43:15-16;[2] cf. Mesha Stele, line 12), though it clearly serves as a nickname for Jerusalem (Isa 29:1, 7). The gentilic plural may also be used of the inhabitants of Jerusalem, the Arielites, if one adopts the reading אֶרְאֵלִים (*ʾărʾēlîm*) in Isa 33:7. In 2 Sam 23:20, Beniah, one of David's heros, is said to have killed אֵת שְׁנֵי אֲרִאֵל מוֹאָב (*ʾēt šĕnê ʾărîʾēl môʾāb*), generally regarded, based on the LXX, as a corruption of אֵת שְׁנֵי בְּנֵי אֲרִאֵל מוֹאָב (*ʾēt šĕnê bĕnê ʾărîʾēl môʾāb*) "the two <sons> of Ariel of Moab," taking Ariel as a personal name). One could also consider taking Ariel in this passage as a designation for an important priest serving the altar: "the two <sons> of the Ariel of Moab." Whether the Hebrew term has any connection to the Akkadian poetic name for the netherworld *arallû*,[3] remains problematic.

That Jerusalem is the addressee is made clear when Ariel is appositionally defined as "the city where David encamped." The reference is a fairly benign allusion to David's capture of Jerusalem and the establishment of his royal and religious capital there (cf. 2 Sam 5:6-9; 6:1—7:29). The following imperative, calling for the continuation of the yearly festivals, picks up on the importance of Jerusalem as the religious capital of Judah, the site of Solomon's temple, and the place of the altar, but the function of the expression is to give at least a vague time limit for the coming judgment. Adding a year to a year, and letting the festivals circle round, suggests a time span of two to three years. This oracle probably dates sometime long enough after the death of Sargon II in 705 BCE for Isaiah to realize that his warnings to Hezekiah's court not to enter into a defensive alliance with Nubian Egypt have been rejected, and that Assyria's retaliation against Judah's rebellion could be expected within three years. Thus, the oracle dates to approximately the same period as the material in Isaiah 28, sometime around 703 BCE.

Verse 2 begins with a jolt, when Yahweh says, "Then I will afflict Ariel." Zion/Jerusalem was Yahweh's chosen city (see Ps 132:13-18), and despite Isaiah's proclamation about God's purging judgment of Jerusalem, his Judean audience apparently had difficulty harmonizing Isaiah's message of refining judgment with their more optimistic, less complicated understanding of the Zion Tradition. Recognizing their difficulty, even Isaiah characterized this disciplining of the chosen city as God's "strange work" (Isa 28:21), as we have seen. Nonetheless, the prophet goes on here to characterize God's affliction of Ariel as producing moaning and lamentation. The final image in the verse picks up on Isaiah's recurring motif of a refining judgment by fire. To say that Jerusalem will be like an altar hearth suggests to me a city scorched and blackened by fire, just like the base of an altar long used for repeated burnt offerings.

If one accepts the common correction of MT's כַּדּוּר (*kaddûr*), "like a ball, circle, sphere," to כְדָוִד (*kĕdāwîd*),

---

1   See esp. Janzen, *Mourning Cry.*

2   The first occurrence in v. 15 of MT has וְהַהֲרְאֵל, but the other occurrence in v. 15 and that in v. 16 has the form הָאַרְאֵיל, and LXX, Vg., and Syr. suggest the same reading for the first occurrence in v. 15.

3   W. F. Albright, "The Babylonian Temple-Tower and the Altar of Burnt-Offering," *JBL* 39 (1920) 137-42.

"like David," following LXX and a number of Hebrew texts (see textual notes), v. 3 picks up on v. 1's benign mention of David's encamping at Jerusalem and turns it into a threatening reference to David's encamping against Jerusalem when he fought against it to capture it from the Jebusites. The notion seems to be that, just as David once fought against Jerusalem, the city of David, so Yahweh will fight against his chosen city to make it God's own again. Cf. the parallel notion in Isa 28:21. Yahweh describes his coming siege of Jerusalem as involving the typical siege equipment and tactics common at the time,[4] and while he uses the first person to attribute this action to the divine will, it seems probable in the light of v. 7 that the actual human agents God will use for these actions are the troops of the Assyrians and their supporting vassals.

According to v. 4, the resulting situation will be so dire for Jerusalem that the city will speak low from the ground or underworld—the word *ʾereṣ* can mean either—and her speech will come from down in the dust. In other words, her voice will be like that of a ghost from the underworld, chirping from the dust as one seemed to expect when the necromancers contemporary with Isaiah called up the dead for consultation with the living (Isa 8:19). If Jerusalem was not dead yet, the best one could say for her was that she already had one foot in the grave.

At this moment of gravest peril, however, the prophet announces a sudden shift in the expected deadly outcome of this judgment. Verse 5's description of the multitude of Jerusalem's enemies as like "fine dust" and the multitude of the violent as like "passing chaff" implies that the threat posed by these multitudes is transient and will soon dissipate. Chaff (*mōṣ*) that is easily blown away is a very common symbol for transience (see also Hos 13:3; Zeph 2:2; Pss 1:4; 35:5; Job 21:18), and *ʾābāq*, "dust," though not as common, is also attested elsewhere as a symbol of transience (Isa 5:24). The closest parallel to the

imagery is actually found in Isa 17:13-14 to characterize the sudden end to the threat against Jerusalem posed by the combined Aramean and Ephraimite army during the Syro-Ephraimitic War (cf. Isa 7:1-9; 10:27-34). The imagery cannot appropriately be read as heightening the threat against Jerusalem.

The last line of v. 5 goes with v. 6, "And it will happen very suddenly that she will be visited by Yahweh of Hosts." The verb תִּפָּקֵד (*tippāqēd*), "she will be visited," is ambiguous in and of itself; the verb can be used in the sense "she will be punished." But following the description of Jerusalem's enemies as "fine dust" and "passing chaff," it is clear that this sudden visitation is about to sweep away these enemies, not Jerusalem. Since Jerusalem was already at death's door, a divine intervention to finish the city off could hardly have been described as a sudden visitation. The language used to describe this divine intervention—thunder, earthquake, a loud noise, whirlwind and storm, and a flame of devouring fire—is typical theophanic language, language at home in Israel's hymnic tradition of praise to Yahweh for his appearances as the divine warrior to save his people from their enemies (see Pss 18:8-16; 77:19; 81:8; 83:14-16; 104:4-7; Job 26:14; Isa 66:15-16; Nah 1:2-6; cf. 1 Kgs 19:11-12).

When Yahweh suddenly appears in this theophany, the multitude of all those nations who fight against Ariel, the siege works against her, and all those who afflict her, that is, the human agents and their instruments that Yahweh used to attack and discipline Jerusalem (see vv. 2-3), will become as insubstantial as a dream, a vision of the night, when the dreamer awakes (v. 7).[5] The sense of the image is further elaborated in v. 8 by reference to a vivid dream such as a hungry man may have about eating, or a thirsty man may have about drinking, yet when he awakes, he finds himself still famished or still thirsty. The host of enemies attacking Mount Zion will prove to be just as insubstantial and transient as such vividly expe-

---

4   See Yigael Yadin, *The Art of Warfare in Biblical Lands, in the Light of Archaeological Study* (New York: McGraw-Hill, 1963).

5   Dreams were an accepted source of revelation in the OT, as the numerous texts about the interpretation of dreams in Genesis, Daniel, and other texts indicate (see Jean-Marie Husser, *Dreams and Dream Narratives in the Biblical World* [Biblical Seminar 63; Sheffield: Sheffield Academic Press, 1999]). Note

also the promise of future revelation in Joel 3:1-2, which includes the old men dreaming revelatory dreams. Yet despite this, some of the canonical prophets were dubious about the reliability of the supposed dreams of their opponents as a genuine word from God (Jer 23:25-32; 27:9-10; 29:8-9; Zech 10:2; cf. Eccl. 5:2 on much worry as the source of dreams).

rienced yet soon forgotten dreams of the night. Once God's judgment of his city has accomplished his purpose, the human agents of that judgment will vanish like a bad dream, forgotten when one awakens to God's new day in his redeemed and renewed city.

Bibliography

Albright, W. F., "The Babylonian Temple-Tower and the Altar of Burnt-Offering," *JBL* 39 (1920) 137–42.

Barthel, Jörg, *Prophetenwort und Geschichte: Die Jesajaüberlieferung in Jes 6–8 und 28–31* (FAT 19; Tübingen: Mohr Seibeck, 1997).

Driver, "Isaiah 1–39: Problems," 51.

Feigin, S., "The Meaning of Ariel," *JBL* 39 (1920) 131–37.

Godbey, A. H., "Ariel, or David-Cultus," *AJSL* 41 (1924) 253–66.

Irwin, William Henry, *Isaiah 28–33: Translation with Philological Notes* (BibOr 30; Rome: Biblical Institute Press, 1977).

Jeremias, Jörg, *Theophanie: Die Geschichte einer alttestamentlichen Gattung* (WMANT 10; Neukirchen-Vluyn: Neukirchener Verlag, 1965) 123–36.

Mare, W. H., "Ariel (Place)," *ABD* 1:377.

Mattingly, G. L., "Ariel (Person)," *ABD* 1:377.

May, H. G., "Ephod and Ariel," *AJSL* 55 (1939) 44–56.

North, C. R., "Ariel," *IDB* 1:218.

Petzold, H., "Die Bedeutung von Ariel im Alten Testament und auf der Mescha-Stele," *Theol* 40 (1969) 372–415.

Routledge, Robin L., "The Siege and Deliverance of the City of David in Isaiah 29:1-8," *TynBul* 43 (1991) 181–90.

Schreiner, Josef, *Sion-Jerusalem, Jahwes Königssitz: Theologie der Heiligen Stadt im Alten Testament* (SANT 7; Munich: Kösel, 1963) 255–63.

Tromp, Nicholas J., *Primitive Conceptions of Death and the Nether World in the Old Testament* (BibOr 21; Rome: Pontifical Biblical Institute, 1969).

Werlitz, J., *Studien zur literarischen Methode: Gericht und Heil in Jesaja 7,1-17 und 29,1-8* (BZAW 204; Berlin: de Gruyter, 1992).

Wong, G. C. I., "On 'Visits' and 'Visions' in Isaiah XXIX 6-7," *VT* 45 (1995) 370–76.

Youngblood, R., "Ariel, 'City of God,'" in A. I. Katsh and L. Nemoy, eds., *Essays on the Occasion of the Seventieth Anniversary of Dropsie University* (Philadelphia: Dropsie University Press, 1979) 457–62.

29

9/   Astound yourself[a] and be astounded,
    Blind yourself and be blinded![b]
    You who are drunken,[c] but not from wine,[d]
    Who stagger,[c] but not from beer.[e]

10/   For Yahweh has poured upon you[f]
    A spirit of stupor.
    He has shut your eyes,[g] the prophets;[h]
    And your heads,[i] the seers,[j] he has covered.[k]

11/   And the vision[l] of everything[m] has become[n] to you[o] like the words of the
        sealed scroll which they give[p] to one who knows how to read[q] saying,[r]
        "Read this, please!" and he says,[s] "I cannot[t] because it is sealed."

12/   Then the scroll is given[u] to[v] one who does not know[w] how to read saying,[x]
    "Read this, please!" and he says,[y] "I do not[z] know how to read."

13/   And my Lord said,*[a]
    "Because this people has drawn near with its mouth,
    And with its lips they have honored me,
    But its heart has grown distant*[b] from me,
    And their piety toward me*[c] has become*[d]
    Merely a commandment*[e] of men learned by rote,*[f]

14/   Therefore I am*[g] about to again do a marvelous work*[h] with this people,
    Performing a marvelous work and a wonder,*[i]
    And the wisdom of its wise will perish,*[j]
    And the understanding of its prudent*[k] will keep itself hidden."*[l]

Textual Notes

a   Correcting MT and 1QIsaᵃ הַתְמַהְמְהוּ וּתְמָהוּ (hitmahměhû ûtěmāhû), "tarry and be astounded!" to הִתַּמְּהוּ וּתְמָהוּ (hittamměhû ûtěmāhû), "astound yourself and be astounded!," reading the *hithpael* masculine plural imperative of *tmh*, "to be astounded," in place of MT's *hithpalpel* masculine plural imperative of *mhh*, "to tarry." The correction is suggested by the same idiom in Hab 1:5 and by the versions, most of which treat the paired imperatives as synonymous. The Vg. and Syr. support the emendation, while Tg. treats both verbs as meaning "tarry." LXX has ἐκλύθητε καὶ ἔκστητε, "be faint and amazed!" The error was probably introduced due to the following *hithpalpel* imperative.

b   MT הִשְׁתַּעַשְׁעוּ וָשֹׁעוּ (hišta'aš'û wāšō'û), "blind yourself and be blinded," has two synonymous forms of the same verb—the *hithpalpel* masculine plural imperative and the *qal* masculine plural imperative of š'' I, "to be blind." 1QIsaᵃ התשעʔשעו ושועו (hitša'aʔš'û wāšô'û) represents the same forms and same meaning with a slightly different orthography. The first word does not show the normal transposition of sibilant and dental (*tš* > *št* when they fall together), and the misplaced correction above the line was probably intended to correct that perceived error, and the second word is simply written with a *mater*. As is common in LXX, which is not fond of synonymous parallelism, this

parallel to the first pair of imperatives is omitted as redundant. Vg., Tg., and Syr. all take the expression as meaning something like "be confused and stagger."

c   The two third person masculine plural *qal* perfects, שָׁכְרוּ (šākěrû [1QIsaᵃ appears to have the same form with the addition of the paragogic *nun* (שכרון]) and נָעוּ (nā'û [1QIsaᵃ has the form, but it is run together with the following words with a corrective erasure—נעו ו>ל<ולשכר]) are often corrected to *qal* imperatives because the shift from second person to third person is felt to be abrupt. It is preferable to retain the MT and read these clauses as asyndetic relative clauses functioning as vocatives, which is not uncommon in direct address.[1]

d   MT וְלֹא־יָיִן (wělō'-yayin), "and not from wine"; 1QIsaᵃ has a plene spelling for the negative and inserts the preposition ולוא מיין (wělô' miyyayin). LXX reverses the order of this line and the following parallel, putting σικερα, "beer," before οἶνου, "wine."

e   MT וְלֹא שֵׁכָר (wělō' šēkār), "and not from beer"; 1QIsaᵃ is garbled as noted above, but before getting confused, the scribe probably intended to write ולוא שכר.

f   MT עֲלֵיכֶם ('ălêkem), "upon you"; 1QIsaᵃ has the longer form עליכמה.

g   MT אֶת־עֵינֵיכֶם ('et-'ênêkem), "your eyes"; so 1QIsaᵃ without the *maqqep*); LXX and Syr. have "their eyes."

---

1   See Irwin, *Isaiah 28–33*, 56, and note my extended discussion of this phenomenon in the commentary on Isa 5:8-24 and 22:15-19.

h MT אֶת־הַנְּבִיאִים (ʾet-hannĕbîʾîm), "the prophets"; so 1QIsaᵃ without the maqqep); LXX has "and (the eyes) of their prophets."

i MT וְאֶת־רָאשֵׁיכֶם (ʾet-rāʾšêkem), "your heads"; so 1QIsaᵃ without the maqqep; LXX has "and (the eyes) of their rulers," and Syr. has "and upon their heads."

j MT הַחֹזִים (haḥōzîm), "the seers"; 1QIsaᵃ החזים.

k MT כִּסָּה (kissâ), "he has covered"; so 1QIsaᵃ, Vg., and Tg.; LXX and Syr read the form as a noun, "the hidden things."

l MT חָזוּת (ḥāzût), "vision"; LXX omits the word in its translation.

m MT הַכֹּל (hakkōl), "of everything"; 1QIsaᵃ הכול.

n MT וַתְּהִי (wattĕhî), "has become"; 1QIsaᵃ ותהיה.

o MT לָכֶם (lākem), "to you"; so 1QIsaᵃ and most of the versions; Syr. has "among them."

p Literally, "which they give it" (MT אֹתוֹ, ʾōtô; 1QIsaᵃ אותו).

q Literally, the one who knows (the) book: the kĕtîb of MT has הַסֵּפֶר (hassēper), "the book"; the qĕrēʾ is סֵפֶר (sēper), "a book"; 1QIsaᵃ has ספר. The qĕrēʾ and 1QIsaᵃ probably represent the superior reading, though I am not convinced the presence of the article would really alter the meaning.

r MT לֵאמֹר (lēʾmōr), "saying"; 1QIsaᵃ לאמור.

s MT וְאָמַר (wĕʾāmar), "and he says"; 1QIsaᵃ ויאמר, "and he said."

t MT לֹא (lōʾ), "not"; 1QIsaᵃ לוא.

u MT וְנִתַּן (wĕnittan), the niphal third person masculine singular, "then (the book) is given"; this third person masculine singular passive is supported by all the versions; 1QIsaᵃ has the qal third person masculine plural, ונתנו, "then they give."

v MT עַל (ʿal), "to, upon"; 1QIsaᵃ אל, "to."

w MT לֹא־יָדַע (lōʾ-yādaʿ), "who does not know"; 1QIsaᵃ repeats the participial construction of the previous verse, לוא יודע.

x See note r above.

y See note s above.

z See note t above.

*a MT וַיֹּאמֶר אֲדֹנָי (wayyōʾmer ʾădōnāy), "and my Lord said"; 1QIsaᵃ ויאומר אדוני.

*b MT has the verb רָחַק (riḥaq), "has grown distant"; 1QIsaᵃ the adjective רחוק (rāḥôq).

*c MT יִרְאָתָם אֹתִי (yirʾātām ʾōtî), "their piety toward me"; 1QIsaᵃ יראת אותי, "the piety toward me." For the construction, see GKC §115d. Syr. and Tg. support MT. Vg. has et timuerunt me,

"and they fear me," while LXX has μάτην δὲ σέβονταί με, "and in vain they worship me."

*d MT וַתְּהִי (wattĕhî), "and it has become"; 1QIsaᵃ ותהיה.

*e MT מִצְוַת (miṣwat), "a commandment of"; 1QIsaᵃ כמצות, "like a commandment of," similarly Syr. and Tg. LXX has the plural, "commandments."

*f MT מְלֻמָּדָה (mĕlummādâ), "taught, learned"; so also 1QIsaᵃ. Vg. and Syr. have "and with the doctrine(s)"; LXX has διδάσκοντες ἐντάλματα ἀνθρώπων καὶ διδασκαλίας, "teaching the commandments of men and doctrines." Tg. has "like the commandment which men teach."

*g MT הִנְנִי (hinĕnî), "behold I"; 1QIsaᵃ הנה אנוכי, "behold I."

*h MT לְהַפְלִיא (lĕhaplîʾ), "to do a marvelous work"; 1QIsaᵃ has the byform להפלה. Vg. supports MT, and Syr. has the somewhat ambiguous "because of this behold I am about to again separate this people." The other versions, however, give the verb a less-ambiguous, negative interpretation. LXX has διὰ τοῦτο ἰδοὺ ἐγὼ προσθήσω τοῦ μεταθεῖναι τὸν λαὸν τοῦτον, "because of this behold I will again remove this people," and Tg. has "because of this I am about to smite this people."

*i MT הַפְלֵא וָפֶלֶא (haplēʾ wāpeleʾ), "performing a marvelous work and a wonder"; 1QIsaᵃ הפלה ופלה. Vg. has "with a great and stunning miracle," and Syr. has "with signs and wonders." LXX has καὶ μεταθήσω αὐτούς, "and I will remove them," and Tg. has "with separating blows."

*j MT וְאָבְדָה (wĕʾābĕdâ), "and (wisdom) will perish," is supported by 1QIsaᵃ and the versions, apart from LXX, which has the first person, "and I will destroy the wisdom of the wise."

*k MT וּבִינַת נְבֹנָיו (ûbînat nĕbōnāyw), "and the understanding of its prudent"; 1QIsaᵃ ובינת נבוניו, "and the understandings of its prudent," but the plural does not agree with the singular verb that follows.

*l MT תִּסְתַּתָּר (tistattār), "will keep itself hidden, will disappear," is supported by 1QIsaᵃ and the versions, apart from LXX, which has the first person, "the understanding of the prudent I will hide."

Commentary

The ironic command to Isaiah's audience in v. 9 to astound themselves and blind themselves (cf. Isa 6:9-10) is followed by the comment that they are drunk and stagger like a drunkard. The vocabulary and imagery of wine, beer, and drunken staggering call to mind Isaiah's biting criticism of the disgusting overindulgence of the priests, prophets, and political leaders of Judah in Isa 28:7-13. It suggests that Isa 29:9-14 comes from the same general historical context as 28:7-13, when, following the death of Sargon II, Judah was attempting to negotiate a defensive alliance with Nubian Egypt. Yet here in 29:9 the prophet asserts that the drunkenness of Judah's leaders is not from wine and beer. The cause of this blindness is far deeper and more frightening.

Yahweh himself has poured a spirit of stupor over the leaders, but precisely how God has done that depends on the grammatical analysis of the following, somewhat ambiguous clauses. As the text stands,[2] one could translate either as direct address to the prophets, "He has shut your eyes, O prophets, and your heads, O seers, he has covered," or, assuming a broader audience than the prophets and seers, as the appositional phrases in which "prophets" and "seers" define the society's normal means of "seeing" or "discerning" the right course of action: "He has shut your eyes, the prophets, and your heads, the seers, he has covered." Either rendering is grammatically possible. But I have opted for the second, because I think the message is addressed to the broader Judean political leadership that attempted to control the prophetic and priestly oracular responses to this political crisis. That the political elite attempted such control is clear from a number of charges the prophet makes against them: (1) Isaiah claims that they said to the seers (ראים, rōʾîm), "You shall not see!" and to the prophetic visionaries (חזים, hōzîm), "You shall not envision for us truthful visions. Speak to us pleasant things; envision for us deceptions" (Isa 30:10).[3] (2) He also claims that these royal counselors attempted to hide their plans from Yahweh: "Hey! You who would hide the plan deep from Yahweh, and whose works are in darkness, and who say, 'Who sees us?' and, 'Who knows us?'" (Isa 29:15). (3) Moreover, that charge of hiding their plans from the deity is probably connected to Isaiah's further claim that these counselors refused to seek oracular approval for their treaty with Egypt: "Who undertake to go down to Egypt, but do not inquire [šāʾal] of me" (Isa 30:2); "And who do not look upon the Holy One of Israel, and do not inquire [dāraš] of Yahweh" (Isa 31:1).

Either way, the text represents a simple variation on a recurring and well-known motif in prophetic literature—the threat of the cessation of prophetic oracles. Amos threatens a famine, not of food and water but of hearing the word of Yahweh, and he pictures a frantic wandering about through the land in a fruitless attempt to consult Yahweh (Amos 8:11-12). Micah threatens the prophets themselves with a night without a vision, with darkness without revelation, with disgrace because there will be no answer to them from God (Mic 3:5-7). Hosea describes the people as going with their flocks and their cattle to inquire of Yahweh but not finding him because he had withdrawn from them (Hos 5:6). And according to Ezekiel, God will not allow himself to be inquired of by people who do not take the prophetic word seriously, but who go to inquire of the prophet while retaining their idols and sins in their heart (Ezek 14:1-11; 20:3, 31). Such threats are a response to the people's refusal to heed an unwelcome prophetic word (Mic 2:6, 11), to official attempts to silence the prophets (Amos 2:12; 7:12-17), or to the prophets' own attempts to gain a hearing by making the prophetic word more palatable to their audience (Mic 3:5), but while such threats presuppose opposition to the prophetic word, their value as threats is utterly dependent on the assumption that the culture takes seriously the importance of prophetic communication from the divine world. The paradox between these two clashing points of view will be explored further at Isa 29:15.[4]

---

2   Many modern commentators delete the words "prophets" and "seers" from v. 10 as secondary glosses and dismiss vv. 11-12 as a prosaic expansion from a much later period (so Wildberger, 3:1112–16; Clements, 238; and Blenkinsopp, 403, 405). The evidence for such a judgment is highly subjective, however. There is not the slightest textual evidence for deleting "prophets" and "seers," and the metrical argument is not convincing. Verses 11-12 do read like prose, but the assumption that prose passages must be late expansions on the prophet's original, purely poetic oracles remains simply that, an unproven assumption.

3   This indication of political pressure on the prophets should temper one's interpretation of Isaiah's criticism of the prophets and seers, and particularly the odd notion that Isaiah tried to distance himself from being identified as a prophet. Isaiah was critical of the prophet (נביא, nābîʾ) who failed to fulfill his function in society appropriately (Isa 3:2; 9:14; 28:7), just as he was critical of the priest (כהן, kōhēn, Isa 28:7), royal official (שר, śar, Isa 1:23), or any other important member of his society who failed to perform his task appropriately. There is no evidence, however, that Isaiah regarded the נביא as an illegitimate functionary per se, or that he attempted to distance himself from being identified as a נביא. That is the title assigned to Isaiah by the tradents of the Isaiah tradition (Isa 37:2; 38:1; 39:3), and Isaiah himself had no reservations about referring to his wife with the feminine form of this noun (נביאה, nĕbîʾâ, Isa 8:3).

4   One should note that in divination as exemplified in Mesopotamia the failure to get a divine answer to an act of divination is always understood as a negative

The frightening result of the blindness that Yahweh has imposed on Judah's prophets and seers is spelled out in vv. 11-12. There is no longer any divine guidance, for there is no one who can read the sealed scroll of Yahweh's vision for the future. It is as though one hands a sealed scroll to one who can read, but he hands it back unread, presumably because he has no authority to break the seal. Then one hands it to one who presumably has the authority to remove the seal, but he hands it back still sealed and unread because he is unable to read. There is no prophetic guidance for Judah's actions, because on the heavenly level Yahweh is withholding the prophetic word. The reality on the human level probably seemed quite different. The pressure on the prophets to give oracles supporting the plans of the Judean court (Isa 30:10) may have caused some of them to offer such oracles, and it may have led others just to keep silent, but despite this pressure and his own announcement of Yahweh's withholding of the prophetic word, Isaiah (and perhaps others of like mind) continued the prophetic critique of Judah's policy. The motif of the withholding of the divine word, whether in Amos, Hosea, Micah, Ezekiel, or Isaiah, is a polemical motif to underscore the importance of listening to that prophet, who, despite the scarcity he announces, still claims to offer the true word of Yahweh to his audience. In short, the prophet is saying, "Either hear the word of Yahweh from me (and perhaps from others who agree with me), or you will not hear the word of Yahweh at all."

Nonetheless, the leaders' rejection of Isaiah's message and their pressure on other prophets to get them to support the court's foreign policy were not overtly hostile to Judah's religious traditions. As v. 13 indicates, the political leaders and their supporters maintained the appearance of honoring Yahweh and cultivating piety toward God. The outward expressions of piety remained, though the inner commitment of their heart had grown distant from God. A contemporary may have had difficulty seeing Isaiah as more religious or more devoted to God than his opponents, just as a contemporary of Jeremiah and Hananiah may have had difficulty deciding which of these two prophets was speaking the true word of Yahweh (Jer 28:1-17). Isaiah dismisses his opponents' and their followers' public display of piety, however, as mere lip service, claiming that the heart of this people was far from God. Their piety, he says, was merely a human commandment learned by rote. Precisely what that means is less than crystal clear, since the prophet does not elaborate the point. Perhaps it suggests that they were punctilious in carrying out the prescribed religious rituals (see Isa 1:10-20), while not allowing the deeper significance of those rituals to shape or affect their personal and political decisions.

In any case, Yahweh announces that Judah's alienation from God is about to provoke another miraculous divine intervention. The idiom לָכֵן הִנְנִי יוֹסִף לְהַפְלִיא (lākēn hinĕnî yôsip lĕhaplî᾽), "therefore behold I am about to again do a marvelous work (with this people)," with its note of repetition, appears to pick up on the הַפְלִיא עֵצָה (hiplî᾽ ῾ēṣâ) at the end of the parable of the farmer in Isa 28:29: "This also has gone forth from Yahweh of Hosts, *Who has made his counsel marvelous*, His wisdom surpassing." That parable was placed after the oracle concerning God's strange work of judgment in the neighborhood of Jerusalem (28:21) to justify the apparent illogic of divine judgment on his chosen city. The allusion to it here suggests that the prophet still anticipates serious resistance from his audience to any notion that God would punish his own people, in this case by destroying the wisdom of its wise counselors, no doubt the same scoffing royal advisors against whom Isaiah was engaged in bitter polemic in chap. 28. The allusion to Isa 28:21 in 29:14 thus suggests that whatever the order in which these individual oracles may originally have been given orally, the present literary order is quite ancient.

answer from the god(s). Despite the condemnation of divination and diviners in certain OT texts like Deut 18:14-22, the OT practice of seeking an oracle from God by the priest's manipulation of the sacred lots or by consulting a prophet is actually very similar to divination, perhaps even a subcategory of it. In both Israel and Mesopotamia, the refusal of the deity to answer such a query was frightening (see the example of Saul, 1 Sam 28:3-7, 15).

Bibliography

Aitken, K. T., "Hearing and Seeing: Metamorphoses of a Motif in Isaiah 1–39," in Philip R. Davies and David J. A. Clines, eds., *Among the Prophets: Language, Image and Structure in the Prophetic Writings* (JSOTSup 144; Sheffield: JSOT Press, 1993) 12–41.

Carroll, Robert P., "Blindsight and the Vision Thing," in C. C. Broyles and C. A. Evans, eds., *Writing and Reading the Scroll of Isaiah: Studies of an Interpretive Tradition* (VTSup 70; Leiden: Brill, 1997) 1:79–93.

Esbroeck, Michael van, "Une exégèse rare d'Isaïe 29, 11-12 conservée en Arménien," in Christoph Burchard, ed., *Armenia and the Bible: Papers Presented to the International Symposium Held at Heidelberg, July 16–19, 1990* (University of Pennsylvania Armenian Texts and Studies 12; Atlanta: Scholars Press, 1993) 73–78.

New, David S., "The New Confusion of Taw with Waw-Nun in Reading 1QIsa 29:13," *RevQ* 15 (October 1992) 609–10.

Roberts, J. J. M., "Blindfolding the Prophet: Political Resistance to First Isaiah's Oracles in the Light of Ancient Near Eastern Attitudes toward Oracles," in Jean-Georges Heintz, ed., *Oracles et prophéties dans l'antiquité: Actes du Colloque de Strasbourg 15–17 juin 1995* (Travaux du Centre de recherche sur le Proche-Orient et la Grèce antiques 15; Strasbourg: De Boccard, 1997) 135–46; reprinted as chap. 19 in Roberts, *The Bible and the Ancient Near East: Collected Essays* (Winona Lake, IN: Eisenbrauns, 2002) 282–91.

——, "Contemporary Worship in the Light of Isaiah's Ancient Critique," in M. Patrick Graham, Rick R. Mars, and Steven L. McKenzie, eds., *Worship and the Hebrew Bible: Essays in Honour of John T. Willis* (JSOTSup 284; Sheffield: Sheffield Academic Press, 1999) 265–75.

Schmidt, J. M., "Gedanken zum Verstockungsauftrag Jesajas (Is. VI)," *VT* 21 (1971) 68–90.

Schmidt, K. L., "Die Verstockung des Menschen durch Gott," *TZ* 1 (1945) 1–17.

Williamson, *Book Called Isaiah*, 94–115.

29

15/ Hey! You[a] who would hide the plan
Deep from Yahweh,[b]
And whose works are[c] in darkness,
And who say,[d] "Who sees us?"[e]
And, "Who knows us?"[f]

16/ Isn't this perverse of you?[g]
Shall the potter[h] be considered[i] as the clay?[j]
Or shall what is made say[k] of its maker,[l]
"He did not[m] make me"?[n]
Or the vessel say[o] of its potter,[p]
"He does not[m] understand"?[q]

Textual Notes

a Vg. recognizes in its translation that this whole verse is in direct address: *vae qui profundi estis corde ut a Domino abscondatis consilium quorum sunt in tenebris opera et dicunt quis videt nos et quis novit nos*, "woe you who are deep in heart in order that you might hide counsel from the Lord, whose works are in darkness, and who say, 'Who sees us?' and 'Who knows us?'"

b The syntactical ambiguity caused by the elliptical character of the first two lines led to a clarifying translation in LXX: οὐαὶ οἱ βαθέως βουλὴν ποιοῦντες καὶ οὐ διὰ κυρίου· οὐαὶ οἱ ἐν κρυφῇ βουλὴν ποιοῦντες, "Woe (you) who make a plan deeply and not through the Lord; Woe (you) who make a plan in secret." The Hebrew is difficult to render literally in English—"Hey! You who would make it too deep for Yahweh in order to hide the plan!"

c Both MT וְהָיָה (wĕhāyâ), "and it is," and 1QIsa[a] ויהי ("and it was") have singular verb forms with the following plural noun.

d MT וַיֹּאמְרוּ (wayyōʾmĕrû), "and who say"; 1QIsa[a] ויואמרו.

e MT רֹאֵנוּ (rōʾēnû), "sees us"; 1QIsa[a] ראנו.

f MT יֹדְעֵנוּ (yōdĕʿēnû), "knows us"; 1QIsa[a] ידענו. LXX adds the clause ἢ ἃ ἡμεῖς ποιοῦμεν, "or what we do?"

g MT הַפְכְּכֶם (hapkĕkem), "your perversity!," in its stunning brevity is a crux, leaving the strong suspicion that something has fallen out of the text. 1QIsa[a] הפך מכם, "he has overturned from you," is no improvement, and suggests that the scribe was struggling to make sense of the text. Vg.'s explanatory translation *perversa est haec vestra cogitatio*, "perverse is this your thought," is probably on track, but it remains uncertain what, if anything, to restore. LXX, followed by Syr., appears to take the phrase with the preceding verse. LXX has καὶ τίς ἡμᾶς γνώσεται ἢ ἃ ἡμεῖς ποιοῦμεν, "and who knows us or the things which we do?" Syr. has "who knows what we are overturning?" Tg. also understands the expression as a question: הֲלִמְהַפַךְ עוֹבָדֵיכוֹן אַתּוּן בָּעַן, "Are you seeking to turn your deeds upside down?" Modern scholars have been just as puzzled by the text, and many emendations have been suggested, but none of them has proved persuasive to more than a few adherents (see the long discussion in Wildberger, 3:1125–26, 1129). A common modern translation of the phrase is "You turn things upside down!" (see NRSV, RSV, AV, NIV, Luther), but it is not entirely clear how that meaning is extracted from a suffixed infinitive. If the MT is preserved unemended, it is better to take the expression

as an exclamation with a suffixed form of the noun הֵפֶךְ (hēpek), "perversity," which would yield a rendering like, "O your perversity!" This view is found in BDB (p. 246), is defended by Wildberger (3:1125), and is represented in the JPS translation. I doubt, however, whether the MT has preserved the original text uncorrupted. My suspicion is that haplography has robbed us of part of the original text, and that in turn may have led to further corruption. The context suggests that the general meaning intuited by the NRSV and similar translations is correct, but precisely what to restore remains problematic. The use of אם to introduce the following question may suggest that the original text was introduced by the interrogative particle ה, and that Syr. and Tg. were correct in understanding the text as a question.

h MT הַיֹּצֵר (hayyōṣēr), "the potter"; 1QIsa[a] היוצר.

i For the Hebrew's third person singular verb form, LXX has the second person plural, "Shall not you be considered as the clay of the potter?" Vg. takes the verb as active and makes clay its subject, *quasi lutum contra figulum cogitet*, "as though clay plotted against the potter."

j MT כְּחֹמֶר (kĕḥōmer), "as clay"; 1QIsa[a] is defective, having only כחם, "as the heat of."

k MT יֹאמַר (yōʾmar), "he will say"; 1QIsa[a] יאמר.

l MT לְעֹשֵׂהוּ (lĕʿōśēhû), "with regard to its maker"; 1QIsa[a] לעושהו.

m MT לֹא (lōʾ), "not"; 1QIsa[a] לוא.

n LXX reverses the verbs in these two couplets, putting the play on יצר in the first couplet and עשה in the second couplet, and renders with the second person, as do Vg., Syr., and Tg., μὴ ἐρεῖ τὸ πλάσμα τῷ πλάσαντι Οὐ σύ με ἔπλασας; ἢ τὸ ποίημα τῷ ποιήσαντι Οὐ συνετῶς με ἐποίησας, "What is shaped does not say to its shaper, 'You did not shape me,' does it; or what is made to its maker, 'You did not make me wisely,' does it?"

o MT וְיֵצֶר אָמַר (wĕyēṣer ʾāmar), "or the vessel say"; 1QIsa[a] ויצר חמר, "or the clay vessel," with the verb understood, though this seems an obvious error.

p MT לְיֹצְרוֹ (lĕyōṣĕrô), "with regard to its potter"; 1QIsa[a] ליוצריו, "with regard to its potters."

q LXX and Syr. repeat the cognate verb with an object and take הבין as adverbial, "You did not make/shape me wisely," while Vg. has, "You do not understand," and Tg., "You do not understand me."

Commentary

This hôy-oracle is addressed to the same royal counselors whose wisdom Yahweh threatened to destroy in the preceding verse. It challenges them to reflect on the folly of thinking that they could keep their political plans secret from Yahweh, as though God could not see or know what they were planning. But again one must distinguish between the motives that Isaiah assigns to these royal counselors in his polemic and what they may have actually thought they were doing. After all, it is dubious that any well-educated ancient Judean counselor truly believed that humans could hide anything from the mind of Yahweh. This leads us back to the paradox of a leader's desperate human need for divine guidance over against the numerous inconveniences and dangers associated with such guidance through human intermediaries such as prophets or oracle priests. Something of this paradox can be seen in the biblical narratives of Jeremiah's interactions with Zedekiah, and then with the pitiful remnant following the murder of Gedaliah. Powerful government officials under king Zedekiah were adamantly opposed to Jeremiah and wanted him killed because his message was undermining morale in Jerusalem (Jer 38:4). Though the king could not prevent these officials from putting Jeremiah under arrest (37:15-16; 38:7), and though Zedekiah himself did not heed Jeremiah's prophetic oracles, King Zedekiah continued to call for Jeremiah to hear what word Yahweh had given to the prophet (37:17; 38:14-28). Likewise, after Gedaliah was murdered, the people and their leaders approached Jeremiah with the request that he pray for them and obtain directions from Yahweh as to what they should do. But, when he returned with the prophetic word that they should remain in the land and trust Yahweh to protect them from Babylonian retaliation (Jer 42:1-22), they rejected Jeremiah's message as a lie (Jer 43:1-4). This resistance to the oracular word requested from Jeremiah cannot be explained as rooted in the belief of a rival prophetic word—at this stage in Jeremiah's career the rival prophets appear to have been discredited (see Jer 37:19). Nor can it be seen as a principled rejection of a woe oracle. In his oracles to Zedekiah, Jeremiah did urge surrender to Babylon, but this was accompanied by the promise that such a course of action would save the city from destruction and Zedekiah and his family from death. Jeremiah's oracle to the remnant after Gedaliah's murder was likewise a conditional oracle of divine protection. Both messages were apparently rejected, or at least not acted on, because of a fear that either the prophet was lying or, in the case of Zedekiah, because he was paralyzed by his fear of both his own officers and the wrath of Nebuchadnezzar—by his inability to trust Yahweh to fulfill his promises.

One finds a similar paradox in other ancient Near Eastern texts dealing with oracular communications from the divine world. It is clear from the Mari archives, for instance, that in a culture where oracles were taken very seriously, political leaders could occasionally act contrary to the oracles even when the oracles were given with some insistence. Thus, Nur-Su'en, who served as the agent of Zimri-Lim, king of Mari, in Aleppo, claims that he had written to Zimri-Lim as many as five times with regard to the zukrum-festival and the niḫlatum-property that the god Adad of Kallasu had demanded from Zimri-Lim, and though Zimri-Lim eventually gave orders to provide the zukrum-festival, he continued to delay turning over the niḫlatum-property even in the face of serious threats from Adad.[1] Kibri-Dagan, the governor of Terqa, reports the renewed demand by the god through an ecstatic that the governor begin work on a new gate, but, though the god threatens Kibri-Dagan with a plague if he does not carry out the divine command, the governor informs Zimri-Lim that he is totally involved in bringing in the barley harvest and cannot attend to the gate at the moment without assistance from the king.[2] When Zimri-Lim began peace treaty negotiations with Eshnunna in his fourth year, there was considerable religious opposition to such a treaty, and both the goddess Dîritum and the god Dagan of Terqa gave oracles warning Zimri-Lim not to conclude the treaty.[3] They warn that beneath his

---

1   *RA* 78 (1984) 7–18.
2   Jean-Marie Durand, *Archives épistolaires de Mari* 1/1 (Archives royales de Mari 26; Paris: Editions Recherche sur les civilisations, 1988) no. 221.
3   Durand, *AEM* 1/1, 400; Dominique Charpin,

"Un traité entre Zimri-Lim de Mari et Ibâl-pî-El II d'Ešnunna," in D. Charpin and F. Joannès, eds., *Marchands, diplomates et empereurs: Etudes sur la civilisation mésopotamienne offertes à Paul Garelli* (Paris: Éditions Recherches sur les civilisations, 1991) 164–65.

peaceful words the king of Eshnunna is plotting treachery, they promise victory over Eshnunna, and they urge Zimri-Lim not to conclude the treaty without first consulting the god.[4] This last point is worth stressing. Twice in text no. 199 one finds the divine admonition: *šarrum balum ilam išallu napištašu la ilappat*, "the king without consulting the god shall not touch his throat, i.e., conclude the treaty."[5] Nevertheless, despite the prophetic opposition, it is clear that Zimri-Lim went ahead with the ratification of the treaty,[6] and there is no evidence that he waited for a positive oracle from either Dîritum or Dagan of Terqa before this action.

Moreover, such political resistance to particular divine oracles is not limited to those issued by prophetic-type figures. Oracles obtained through liver omens could also be resisted. One normally did not set out on a military campaign without favorable oracles.[7] If the situation were not critical, one simply continued making inquiry until one received a favorable oracle.[8] When the situation was critical, however, one could urge action despite the lack of favorable oracles. One letter writer claims that he kept formulating inquiries for the departure of the army and the execution of battle, but the oracle did not answer him. Nonetheless, he goes on to say that, in accordance with his deliberations, he will send out the army with the prayer, "And may the god of my lord let our campaign prosper!"[9] In another text, Meptûm urges the king to come see and encourage his troops whether the oracles for such a trip are favorable or not.[10] Perhaps the most striking example of this resistance to oracular instruction is the response of a certain Ḫammânum, who was reluctant to hand over barley to another official. When that official suggested that Zikri-Ḫanat should take oracles to decide whether the barley should be handed over, Ḫammânum is purported to have replied, "When he will have taken the oracles, even if they are favorable in every regard, I will not give a single seah of barley!"[11]

One of the difficulties that reliance on oracles presented to political leaders was the problem of preserving

state secrets. It was not possible to make meaningful oracular inquiries of the deity without revealing to the divination priests or prophetic respondents a great deal of the state's secret plans and concerns. The so-called protocol of the diviners, a kind of loyalty oath taken by diviners in which, among other things, one swore not to reveal the content of oracular consultations to unauthorized persons, was an attempt to deal with such potential security leaks,[12] but it did not solve the problem. The problem was particularly acute when such oracular inquiry took place in the presence of foreign political allies who were potential enemies. During the period of joint Mari–Babylonian activity, Ibâl-pî-El, one of Zimri-Lim's commanders, complained to his king that certain servants of Išme-Dagan of Assyria, a longtime enemy of Zimri-Lim of Mari, had won the confidence of Ḫammurabi, king of Babylon. These servants of Išme-Dagan were potential spies, yet they were constantly present during the oracular consultation of the Mari diviners Ḫâlî-Ḥadûn and Inib-Šamaš—consultations that for security reasons should have been kept secret.[13] This may explain the background behind the complaint of the diviners Ḫâlî-Ḥadûn and Ilu-šu-naṣir that Ibâl-pî-El had excluded them from his secret council and refused to supply them with lambs to perform oracular inquiry.[14] In halting the inquiries Ibâl-pî-El may merely have been trying to plug a serious security leak.

Government officials also preferred secret oracles for another, though related reason. One not only feared divulging state secrets to the enemy; one was also concerned about the morale and support of one's own subjects. Oracles given publicly and thus liable to affect public opinion and morale had to be handled more carefully than those delivered to government officials in private. Thus, Yaqqîm-Addu makes a point of informing Zimri-Lim that the ecstatic of the god Dagan who threatened the town of Saggarâtum with a plague did so in public: "And it was not in secret that he spoke to me his oracle; in the assembly of the elders he gave his oracle."[15] A public oracle against government policy could have

4 Durand, *AEM* 1/1, 400.
5 Durand, *AEM* 1/1, no. 199:38-39, 49-50.
6 Charpin, "Un traité," 165.
7 Durand, *AEM* 1/1, p. 28 n. 104.
8 Ibid., no. 182:4-12.
9 Ibid., no. 190.
10 Ibid., p. 28 n. 104.
11 Ibid., no. 154:20-29.
12 Ibid., pp. 11–22.
13 Ibid., no. 104.
14 Ibid., no. 101.
15 Ibid., no. 206:32-34.

a devastating effect on public order, both demoralizing those loyal to the government policy and encouraging dissidents who might be looking for an opportune time to revolt. In the Old Testament I have already referred to the military commanders' complaints against Jeremiah, and one should also note that Amos, accused of conspiring (קשר, qāšar) against Jeroboam II because of his oracles, which Amaziah claims were too much for the land to bear (Amos 7:10), was forbidden from any further prophesying at Bethel and encouraged to flee to Judah (Amos 7:12-13). Moreover, as the story of Ahab and Micaiah ben Imlah makes clear, if a prophet had the reputation of giving negative oracles in response to royal consultations, a king would be apt to exclude him from such consultations, particularly if a positive oracle was important to gain the support of a nervous ally (1 Kgs 22:1-28).

To return to Isaiah, all these considerations would have led the Judean court in 705–703 BCE to try to exclude him from their secret negotiations with defensive allies against Assyria. Isaiah was known as a steadfast opponent of any policy of defensive alliances. In the Syro-Ephraimitic crisis of 735–732 BCE, the prophet encouraged Ahaz to trust in the promises of Yahweh to the Davidic house and the city of Jerusalem and to eschew foreign alliances, but Ahaz and the royal court obviously found his oracles unwelcome and refused to ask for the miraculous sign of their confirmation that Isaiah offered them (Isa 7:1-14). This eventually led Isaiah to withdraw from direct involvement in the court for a period of time as a critic of royal policy (Isa 8:16-18). Later, early in the reign of Hezekiah, during the Ashdod affair of 715–711 BCE, Isaiah again was an outspoken critic of the policy of defensive alliances, and his opposition to the defensive alliance with Philistia and their Nubian-Egyptian supporters against Assyria was both vigorous and embarrassingly public. Day after day he appeared in the nude before the palace to inveigh against this proposed defensive alliance as a disaster just waiting to happen (see Isaiah 20). The impact of his public demonstration against the proposed royal policy probably swayed public opinion against it, and it would certainly have alerted any Assyrian agents in Jerusalem about what was being proposed, thus reducing the time available to negotiate the alliance and prepare adequate coalition defenses against the inevitable Assyrian response. The royal advisors who had opposed

Isaiah in 735–732 BCE, and especially those whom he undermined in 715–711, would not have forgotten. If in 705–703 they wanted to negotiate a successful defensive alliance with Nubian Egypt, and perhaps with Merodach-baladan's Babylon as well, it was important to keep these negotiations secret from Isaiah as long as possible. One would certainly not go to him to consult Yahweh on the matter. One already knew his opinion, and if he started giving oracles about it, Isaiah would again undermine the public support for their plan and expose it to any halfway intelligent Assyrian agent in town. Thus, for the sake of morale and state security, it was important to keep these plans secret from Isaiah for as long as possible. When Isaiah complains that his opponents were attempting to hide their plans too deep for Yahweh so that no one could see or know, he really means that they were attempting to hide their plans from him, the true prophet of Yahweh. Whether they consulted other prophets on the issue is less clear. Isaiah's complaint that they pressured prophets to give the message they wanted to hear may suggest they did consult more compliant prophets (Isa 30:10), but it is equally possible that they simply avoided prophetic consultation altogether in the name of state security (see 30:2; 31:1).

Either way, Isaiah treats the political policy of these supposedly wise royal counselors as sheer folly. Despite the textual difficulty at the beginning of v. 16 (see the textual notes), it is clear that Isaiah regards his opponents' actions in trying to conceal their negotiations from God as tantamount to a piece of pottery dismissing the potter as not its maker, or as claiming that the potter who shaped it does not understand. Behind this imagery, of course, is the ancient Near Eastern creation traditions in which the deity forms and shapes humankind from dampened dust or moistened clay before bringing them to life (for example, Gen 2:7; Atrahasis Epic I 190-245; cf. Enuma Elish VI 1-39). If God is the potter who shaped and made humans, it is folly for these humans to think that God does not understand their actions. The perverted hubris of these royal advisors, in Isaiah's view, is the equal of the Assyrian king who misunderstood his mere instrumental role in God's plan for Jerusalem (see Isa 10:5-15).

Bibliography

Beuken, W. A. M., "Isa 29, 15-24: Perversion Reverted," in F. García Martínez, A. Hilhorst, and C. J. Labuschagne, eds., *The Scriptures and the Scrolls: Studies in Honour of A. S. van der Woude on the Occasion of His 65th Birthday* (VTSup 49; Leiden: Brill, 1992) 43–64.

Brandon, S. G. F., *Creation Legends of the Ancient Near East* (London: Hodder & Stoughton, 1963).

Evans, Craig A., "On Isaiah's Use of Israel's Sacred Tradition," *BZ* n.s. 30 (1986) 92–99.

Maag, V., "Alttestamentliche Anthropogonie in ihrem Verhältnis zur altorientalischen Mythologie," *Asiatische Studien* 9 (1955) 15–44.

——, "Sumerische und babylonische Mythen von der Erschaffung der Menschen," *Asiatische Studien* 8 (1954) 85–106.

Martin-Achard, Robert, "Esaïe et Jérémie aux prises avec les problèmes politiques: Contribution á l'étude du thème, prophétie et politique," *Cahiers de la Revue de Théologie et de Philosophie* 11 (1984) 306–22.

Pettinato, Giovanni, *Das altorientalische Menschenbild und die sumerischen und akkadischen Schöpfungsmythen* (AHAW; Heidelberg: C. Winter, 1971).

Roberts, J. J. M., "Blindfolding the Prophet: Political Resistance to First Isaiah's Oracles in the Light of Ancient Near Eastern Attitudes toward Oracles," in Jean-Georges Heintz, ed., *Oracles et prophéties dans l'antiquité: Actes du Colloque de Strasbourg 15-17 Juin 1995* (Travaux du Centre de recherche sur le Proche-Orient et la Grèce antiques 15; Strasbourg: De Boccard, 1997) 135–46; reprinted as chap. 19 in Roberts, *The Bible and the Ancient Near East: Collected Essays* (Winona Lake, IN: Eisenbrauns, 2002) 282–91.

Robinson, T. H., "Notes on the Text of Isaiah 29:16," *ZAW* 49 (1931) 322.

Virgulin, S., "Il significato della pietra di fondazione in Isa 28:16," *RivB* 7 (1959) 208–20.

Whedbee, William J., *Isaiah and Wisdom* (Nashville: Abingdon, 1971).

Williamson, H. G. M., "Isaiah and the Wise," in John Day, Robert P. Gordon, and H. G. M. Williamson, eds., *Wisdom in Ancient Israel: Essays in Honour of J. A. Emerton* (Cambridge: Cambridge University Press, 1995) 133–41.

There is a great deal of debate about the unity, date, and authorship of the material in Isa 29:17-24. The difficulties in the text give rise to these different attempts to explain them, and, given the nature of the difficulties, it is unlikely that any interpretation of this text will win universal acceptance anytime soon. Nonetheless, in my view, the text gives indications of involving an Isaianic reworking of an earlier oracle addressed to the north from the time of the Syro-Ephraimitic War, or soon afterward, similar to Isa 28:1-6. That is, a promise originally addressed to the northern exiles of 733–732 BCE has been reworked to address the battered remnant of the southern kingdom of Judah toward the end of Sennacherib's devastating campaign there. To the earlier northern exiles deported by Tiglath-pileser III (733–732), Shalmaneser V (722), and Sargon II (721–720), Sennacherib added another two hundred thousand from Judah in 701.[1] The reedited oracle is a hopeful response to this disastrous destruction and depopulation of Hezekiah's Judean kingdom, which envisions a correction of the political and religious policies that led to this disaster and a new divine blessing that will restore the fertility of the whole land and its people.

17/ Shall not in yet a little while
The Lebanon turn into a fruitful field,[a]
And Carmel[a] be considered a forest?
18/ And on that day the deaf will hear the words of a book,
And from gloom and darkness[b] the eyes of the blind will see.
19/ And the poor[c] will again have joy in Yahweh,
And the needy of humankind will rejoice in the Holy One of Israel.
20/ For the violent one is gone, and the scoffer[d] will be finished;
And all those who watch over iniquity[e] will be cut off—
21/ Those who cause a man to lose a lawsuit,
And who lay a snare for the arbiter at the gate,
With the result that they completely ruin[f] the person in the right.
22/ Therefore, thus says Yahweh to the house of Jacob[g]
The one who redeemed Abraham,[h]
"No[i] longer shall Jacob[g] be ashamed,
And no[i] longer shall his face grow pale."[j]
23/ For when he sees[k] his children
The work of my hands in his midst,
They will sanctify[l] my name,
And they will sanctify the Holy One of Jacob,[m]
And the God[n] of Israel they will fear as awesome.[o]
24/ And those who err[p] in spirit will know understanding,
And the grumblers will accept instruction."[q]

Textual Notes

a   LXX and Vg. take the noun כַּרְמֶל (*karmel*) not as "farmland" or "fruitful field" but as the proper name for Mount Carmel. It would appear that the first occurrence of the word means "fruitful field," but because of the parallelism with Lebanon, the second occurrence probably refers to Mount Carmel.

b   MT וּמֵאֹפֶל וּמֵחֹשֶׁךְ (*ûmēʾōpel ûmēḥōšek*), "and from gloom and from darkness"; 1QIsaᵃ ומאפלה ומחושך.

c   MT עֲנָוִים (*ʿănāwîm*), "the poor"; 1QIsaᵃ עניים.

d   MT לֵץ (*lēṣ*), "the scoffer"; 1QIsaᵃ ליץ.

e   MT כָּל־שֹׁקְדֵי אָוֶן (*kol-šōqĕdê ʾāwen*), "all those who watch over/plot iniquity"); 1QIsaᵃ כול שוקדי און.

f   Literally, "so that they turned aside into ruin the person in the right."

g   MT יַעֲקֹב (*yaʿăqōb*), "Jacob"; 1QIsaᵃ יעקוב.

1   Luckenbill, *Annals*, 33, iii 24. See now the edition and translation of the accounts of the third campaign in Grayson and Novotny, RINAP 3/1.

h   For MT and 1QIsaᵃ אֲשֶׁר פָּדָה אֶת־אַבְרָהָם (ʾăšer pādâ ʾet-ʾabrāhām), "who redeemed Abraham"; LXX has the odd translation ὃν ἀφώρισεν ἐξ Ἀβρααμ, "whom he set apart from Abraham."

i   MT לֹא (lōʾ), "no"; 1QIsaᵃ לוא.

j   LXX inserts "Israel" as a parallel to Jacob in the last line.

k   MT בִּרְאֹתוֹ (birʾōtô), "when he sees"; 1QIsaᵃ בראותו.

l   MT יַקְדִּשׁוּ (yaqdîšû), "they will sanctify"; 1QIsaᵃ יקדשו. Vg. understands this verb to refer to the action of the children, *sed cum viderit filios suos opera manuum mearum in medio sui sanctificantes nomen meum*, "but when he sees his children, the work of my hands, sanctifying my name in his midst. . . ." Though grammatically wrong, in a sense Vg. is exegetically correct, since the eponymous ancestor Jacob (a collective singular) and his children (plural) refer to the same reality, the people of Jacob.

m   See note g above.

n   MT אֱלֹהֵי (ʾĕlōhê), "the God of"; 1QIsaᵃ אלוהי.

o   The best commentary on the meaning of יַעֲרִיצוּ (yaʿărîṣû) "they will fear as awesome," here is Isa 8:12-13 (see commentary). LXX gets it right with its καὶ τὸν θεὸν τοῦ Ἰσραηλ φοβηθήσονται, "and the God of Israel they will fear." Vg. has the odd rendering *praedicabunt*, "they will preach."

p   MT תֹעֵי (tōʿê), "those who err"; 1QIsaᵃ תעי.

q   LXX adds a line that it apparently imported from 32:4: καὶ αἱ γλῶσσαι αἱ ψελλίζουσαι μαθήσονται λαλεῖν εἰρήνην, "and the stammering tongues will learn to speak peace."

Commentary

Verse 17 begins with a question expecting a positive answer. The same temporal use of עוֹד מְעַט מִזְעָר (ʿôd mĕʿaṭ mizʿār), "in yet a little while," is found in Isa 10:25, where God promises that his anger at his own people will soon pass and will be redirected against their enemies, the Assyrians. Here in yet a little while the current difficult situation will likewise be totally changed. The nature of that change, however, is less clear than in 10:25, because of the figurative language involved. The figure describes a transformation of the Lebanon and Mount Carmel, where the Lebanon becomes orchard land like Carmel, and Carmel becomes a forest land like Lebanon. Exactly what that is intended to signify is less than totally clear, though it is clearly intended to be positive for God's people. Isaiah 32:15 describes a positive transformation of Judah's desert (מדבר, *midbār*) to orchard land (כרמל, *karmel*) and her orchard land to forest (יער, *yaʿar*), which suggests a renewal of fertility for the land of Judah, probably following the widespread destruction and devastation of Sennacherib's campaign against Hezekiah, but whether a simple renewal of fertility is what is implied by the figure in 29:17 is less clear. In an oracle originally from the Syro-Ephraimitic War directed against Aram and Israel כְּבוֹד יַעְרוֹ וְכַרְמִלּוֹ (kĕbôd yaʿrô wĕkarmillô), "the glory of his forest and orchard land" (Isa 10:18) is used as an image for the troops of this enemy, who will be destroyed and left a pitiful remnant, so few that even a child can number them. A similar image is used in 10:33-34 for Yahweh hacking down the thick forest of his enemy's troops as a judgment on Lebanon. There, before the oracle was later reapplied to Assyria,[2] Lebanon seems to stand in part as a metaphor for Aram. See also the use of Lebanon and Bashan in Isa 2:13. If Isa 29:17 is a reworked oracle from the period of the Syro-Ephraimitic War, the original parallelism between Lebanon and Carmel might have suggested a contrast and improvement in north Israel's situation vis-à-vis Aram: Aram (Lebanon) will become orchard land and Israel (Carmel) will become the forest. When reapplied to the situation after Assyria's conquest of Aram and the north, the imagery probably lost that sense of contrast and simply indicated a restoration of fertility and growth in population for Israel after the destructive judgment.

The reference to the דִּבְרֵי־סֵפֶר (dibrê-sēper), "words of a book," in v. 18 picks up on the כְּדִבְרֵי הַסֵּפֶר הֶחָתוּם (kĕdibrê hassēper heḥātûm), "like the words of a sealed book," in

---

2   One should also note Isa 37:24//2 Kgs 19:23, where one has the well-known Mesopotamian motif of the Mesopotamian ruler on his heroic journey to the west to cut down cedars from Lebanon. In Isaiah 37, the image is part of the Assyrian king's boast. So here in chap. 29 and also in chaps. 10 and 2 that image may be present and satirized: your Lebanon will be destroyed.

v. 11. In vv. 11-12 the words of the book could not be seen or heard, because it was sealed, or because the one with the authority to break the seal could not read. The earlier passage does not mention the deaf (החרשים, haḥērĕšîm) or the blind (עורים, ʿiwĕrîm), a word pair that occurs elsewhere in Isaiah only in the later part of the book (35:5; 42:16-19; 43:8; cf. 42:7), but it does mention Yahweh shutting the eyes of prophets and covering the heads of the seers, in effect blinding those who might be expected to read the words of God's book and thereby making deaf those dependent on the prophets for hearing these words. The same notion of God's message for the future as a sealed book that his rebellious people refused to hear, demanding that their seers and prophets neither see this message nor prophesy it, is also found in Isa 30:8-10. Isaiah's motif of Israel's blindness and deafness ultimately goes back to the prophet's inaugural vision in which Israel, though having ears and eyes, refuses to see or hear God's word (6:9-10). Isaiah 29:18, however, is a reversal of those earlier judgments. On the day of the transformation shortly to be expected, those formerly deaf will now hear the words of God's book, and those formerly blind will be delivered from their gloom and darkness and see again. One should note the similarity in this motif of the deliverance from gloom and darkness by new sight to Isaiah's similar promise to the north in his coronation oracle for Hezekiah, "The people who walked in darkness [בחשך, baḥōšek] have seen a great light [ראו אור גדול, rāʾû ʾôr gādôl]; Those who dwelt in the land of gloom [צלמות, ṣalmāwet] on them light has shown" (9:1).

When this happens (v. 19), the poor and needy will again have joy (שמחה, śimḥâ) in Yahweh and rejoice (יגיל, yāgîl) in the Holy One of Israel. Note the similar play on these two roots for rejoicing in the coronation oracle in Isa 9:2. Many scholars have seen an important distinction between עֲנָוִים (ʿănāwîm), "the poor, meek," and עֲנִיִּים (ʿăniyyîm), "the poor, afflicted," arguing that the former indicates a moral or religious category over against the latter that simply indicates an economic or class category, but the distinction seems hard to maintain.[3] On the other

hand, the parallel term וְאֶבְיוֹנֵי אָדָם (wĕʾebyônê ʾādām), "and the needy of humankind," is clearly an economic or class category. Even a person of high economic or social status might wish to identify himself or herself with the "poor" for religious or political reasons, to create a sense of solidarity with and thereby support from the masses of the poor, or to demonstrate one's humility before the deity, but that is a far cry from demonstrating a religious party of the ʿănāwîm in distinction from the poor in general. The Holy One of Israel (קְדוֹשׁ יִשְׂרָאֵל, qĕdôš yiśrāʾēl) is one of Isaiah's favorite epithets for Yahweh (1:14; 5:19, 24; 10:20; 12:6; 17:7; 30:11-12, 15; 31:1), though it also remains popular in the later Isaianic tradition (Isa 37:23; 41:14, 16, 20; 43:3, 14; 45:11; 47:4; 48:17; 49:7; 54:5; 55:5; 60:9, 14).

The reason for this rejoicing of the poor and needy is that the violent oppressor (עָרִיץ, ʿārîṣ) will no longer exist, and the scoffer (לֵץ, lēṣ) and all those who watch over or plan evil (כָּל־שֹׁקְדֵי אָוֶן, kol-šōqĕdê ʾāwen) will be finished and cut off (v. 20). Precisely who is referred to by these three designations is open to debate. In Isa 29:5 the "violent oppressors" are the multitude of those who attack Jerusalem, so it is possible that, here in v. 20, the prophet is also referring to a foreign enemy. Though the occurrences of the term in Isa 13:11; 25:3-5; 49:25 cannot be attributed to Isaiah of Jerusalem, these passages also appear to refer to a violent foreign tyrant or oppressor. In contrast, the following two expressions appear to designate fellow countrymen who afflict the poor. The noun לֵץ (lēṣ), "scoffer," is not attested elsewhere in Isaiah (it occurs in Ps 1:1 and fourteen times in Proverbs), but the cognate noun lāṣôn, "scoffing," is found in Isa 28:14 in the expression אַנְשֵׁי לָצוֹן (ʾanšê lāṣôn), "O men of scoffing"/"O scoffers," and the hithpolel imperfect of the verb is found in 28:22: וְעַתָּה אַל־תִּתְלוֹצָצוּ (wĕʿattâ ʾal-titlôṣāṣû), "and now do not continue scoffing." In Isaiah 28, these references are to Isaiah's opponents, who scoffed at his prophetic word. It is likely that לֵץ (lēṣ), "scoffer," in Isa 29:20 also refers to a well-educated member of the upper class who scoffs at God's prophetic word.[4] The expression שֹׁקְדֵי אָוֶן, "those who plan evil," is not otherwise attested in Isaiah,

---

3 Wildberger mentions this discussion and dismisses the distinction as "too simple" (3:1140), but nonetheless he identifies the אביונים and ענוים in this passage as "the pious, who in a special way hold on to the traditional faith."

4 The use here of the singular, "scoffer," by no means implies that only one of this group was involved in scoffing.

but it also seems to imply fellow countrymen of the poor and needy who plot to do them wrong. It probably refers to the same elite group to which the scoffer belongs, whose secret political plans (29:15) involved rejecting the prophetic word and trusting instead in בְּעֹשֶׁק וְנָלוֹז (bĕʿōšeq wĕnālôz), "in oppression and deceit" (30:12). The prophetic word saw peace and security as the by-product of providing rest and security to the poor and oppressed (28:12) while maintaining a quiet confidence in God (30:15), but Isaiah's opponents among the political elite saw it as requiring a deceitful, secret treaty with Egypt (28:14-15), and they apparently had every intention of continuing their oppression of their own poor.

This is suggested by the following v. 21, which uses three different expressions to describe ways in which these oppressors deprive the poor of their rights in court. The expression מַחֲטִיאֵי אָדָם בְּדָבָר (maḥăṭîʾê ʾādām bĕdābār), "who declare a man in the wrong in a matter," refers to those who give an unfair verdict against the honest man in his lawsuit, ruling that he is in the wrong. The second expression וְלַמּוֹכִיחַ בַּשַּׁעַר יְקֹשׁוּן (wĕlammôkîaḥ baššaʿar yĕqōšûn), "and who lay a snare for the arbiter at the gate," refers to those who try to obstruct the work of anyone who attempts to arbitrate or intervene on behalf of the poor in a lawsuit at the city gate. Amos 5:10 indicates that the wealthy and powerful in north Israel hated such helpers of the poor in eighth-century Israel (Amos 5:10), while Isaiah described such judicial action on behalf of the poor as part of the work of the ideal Davidide (Isa 11:3-4). The third expression, וַיַּטּוּ בַתֹּהוּ צַדִּיק (wayyaṭṭû battōhû ṣaddîq), "with the result that they completely ruin the person in the right," is a variation on a common expression for blocking the party in the right from gaining justice through legal procedures. Compare Amos 2:7 and 5:12 for a similar judicial oppression of the poor in eighth-century Israel. The basis for such miscarriages of justice was often bribery (Amos 5:12; Isa 5:23), which obviously favored those who could afford bribes. The situation became so corrupt in Isaiah's time that he spoke of the powerful passing unjust laws so that they could legally turn aside the poor from their right and plunder the property of widows and orphans (Isa 10:1-2), and the elites' confiscation of the property of the poor reached epidemic proportions during this period, if we may trust the testimony of Isaiah and Micah (Isa 3:14-15; 5:8-10; Mic 2:1-2, 9).

In v. 22, the prophet returns to his theme of the deliverance soon to come. Because the foreign tyrant and the native oppressors of the Israelite poor are soon to be removed, therefore Yahweh, who redeemed Abraham, can make the solemn promise to the house of Jacob—now with that deliverance "no longer shall Jacob be ashamed; and no longer shall his face grow pale." The relative clause that further defines Yahweh as "the one who redeemed Abraham" (אֲשֶׁר פָּדָה אֶת־אַבְרָהָם, ʾăšer pādâ ʾet-ʾabrāhām) is both awkward and unexpected. It is awkward because it follows the prepositional phrase אֶל־בֵּית יַעֲקֹב (ʾel-bêt yaʿăqōb), "to the house of Jacob," rather than following immediately after Yahweh, the word that it modifies. It is unexpected, because the figure of Abraham is otherwise unmentioned in any eighth-century prophetic work, with the possible exception of Mic 7:20, depending on when one dates that text. There is little doubt the Abraham traditions were known in the eighth century, but apart from these two passages and one reference in Jeremiah (Jer 33:26) and Ezekiel (Ezek 33:24), Abraham does not receive prominent mention in prophetic literature until Second Isaiah (41:8; 51:2; 63:16). One might dismiss the relative clause, then, as a secondary gloss from the exilic period of Second Isaiah, but the statement that Yahweh redeemed (פָּדָה, pādâ) Abraham is not further explained by such dating. At least, the statement about Jacob here has a clear echo in Jer 31:11: "For Yahweh redeemed [פדה, pādâ] Jacob, and ransomed him [וגאלו, ûgĕʾālô] from a power too strong for him." The latter occurs in a context in which Jeremiah is predicting the salvation of the northern exiles, the return to their homeland on the mountains of Samaria, and their renewed pilgrimage to the height of Zion to serve Yahweh (Jer 31:1-12), an oracle probably originally given in the reign of Josiah when the restoration of the north to Judah appears to have been a goal of the Josianic royal policy.

However one explains the odd relative clause, Yahweh's address to "the house of Jacob" suggests that the message was originally intended for the oppressed of the northern kingdom. See my extended discussion of בֵּית יַעֲקֹב (bêt yaʿăqōb), "house of Jacob," in Isa 2:5-6. Jacob, the ancestor and designation for the people of the oppressed northern territories, will no longer be ashamed or his face appalled by his situation, once the external and internal oppressors have been removed. With the reediting at the time of Sennacherib's campaign against Judah in 701 BCE, however, Jacob must now be understood more inclusively to include Judah as well.

Verse 23 originally suggested the return of northern exiles to their homeland and a regrowth of the population in the north, but in the later setting it would also include the return of the exiles Sennacherib had deported from Judah. Continuing the image of the eponymous ancestor, when Jacob sees his children, the work of my (that is, God's) hands, then the descendants of Jacob will respond appropriately. Wildberger is wrong in dismissing יְלָדָיו (yĕlādāyw), "his children," as a gloss and treating מַעֲשֵׂה יָדַי (maʿăśēh yāday), "the work of my hands," as "the works that Yahweh brings to pass within history." The particular work of God's hands that the prophet is referring to is precisely the repopulation of the land, either under the imagery of the restored forests and orchard land—the cutting down of forests is an image for a radical reduction in population (Isa 9:18-19; 10:18-19; cf. 7:23-25 for destroyed vineyards as a image of depopulation)—or under the imagery of the reappearance of Jacob's children. As a parallel, note Second Isaiah's imagery of bereft mother Zion suddenly finding herself surrounded by a horde of her long-lost children (49:14-21; 54:1-3). When Jacob sees his long-lost children, a work brought about by the hands of Yahweh in Jacob's midst (בְּקִרְבּוֹ, bĕqirbô, "in his midst"), God's redemption will produce an appropriate response from his people. In contrast to their earlier behavior at the time of the Syro-Ephraimitic War (Isa 8:13), when their terror of human enemies prevented them from sanctifying Yahweh and making him their primary object of fear (וְהוּא מוֹרַאֲכֶם, wĕhûʾ môraʾăkem, "and he will be your object of fear") and terror (וְהוּא מַעֲרִצְכֶם, wĕhûʾ maʿărîṣkem, "and he will be your object of terror"), they will now sanctify (יַקְדִּישׁוּ, yaqdîšû) God's name, they will sanctify the Holy One of Jacob, and the God of Israel they will fear as awesome (יַעֲרִיצוּ, yaʿărîṣû, "they will stand in terror of").

With this sanctification of Yahweh and the focus on the God of Israel as their primary object of terror or reverence, those who formerly strayed in spirit will learn wisdom, and the grumblers will accept instruction (v. 24). Obviously in its present form, this involves more than just the northern exiles. On some level, the acquiring of בִּינָה (bînâ, "understanding") is a correction to the loss of understanding mentioned in Isa 29:14, and the learning of instruction is a correction of the refusal to be instructed by a so-called infantile prophet in Isa 28:9-13. As such, the promise has clearly been extended and adapted to what is now predominantly a Judean audience, to whom Isaiah is promising a future beyond the current Assyrian disaster.

Bibliography

Clements, R. E., "Patterns in the Prophetic Canon," in George W. Coats and Burke O. Long, eds., *Canon and Authority: Essays in Old Testament Religion and Theology* (Philadelphia: Fortress Press, 1977) 42–55.

Conrad, E. W., "Isaiah and the Abraham Connection," *AJT* 2 (1988) 382–93.

Donner, *Israel unter den Völkern*, 155–58.

Laberge, Léo, *La Septante d'Isaïe 28–33: Étude de tradition textuelle* (Ottawa: Laberge, 1978).

Padilla, C. Ren, "The Fruit of Justice Will Be Peace," *Transformation* 2, no. 1 (1985) 2–4.

Payne, J. B., "The Effect of Sennacherib's Anticipated Destruction in Isaianic Prophecy," *WTJ* 34 (1971) 22–38.

Stolz, F., "Die Bäume des Gottesgartens auf dem Libanon," *ZAW* 84 (1972) 141–56.

Williamson, *Book Called Isaiah*, 58–63.

Ziegler, J., "Zum literarischen Aufbau im Buch des Propheten Isaias," *BZ* 21 (1933) 138–41.

30

This oracle dates from sometime in the period between 705 and 701 BCE and concerns Hezekiah's treaty with Nubian Egypt, also mentioned in Isa 28:15; 31:1-3, and alluded to in Isa 29:15. Though one may distinguish between several oracles in Isaiah 30—vv. 1-5, 6-7, 8-17, 18-26, and 27-33—all of these oracles may date to this same period, to different stages in the crisis provoked by Hezekiah's rebellion against Assyria, and Sennacherib's response to that rebellion in his famous third campaign.

1/   Hey, rebellious children, says Yahweh,[a]
         Making a plan that is not[b] from me,[c]
         And forming a covenant that is not[b] from my spirit,
         So as to add sin upon sin.
2/   Who undertake[d] to go down[e] to Egypt,
         But did not[f] inquire of me;
         To take refuge in the stronghold of Pharaoh,[g]
         And to shelter in the shade of Egypt.[g]
3/   And the stronghold of Pharaoh will become an embarrassment to you,
         And the shelter[h] in the shade of Egypt a source of shame.[i]
4/   For his princes[j] are[k] in Tanis,
         And his messengers[j] have reached[l] Hanes.[m]
5/   Everyone will be ashamed/start to stink[n] because of a people who cannot[o] help him;[p]
         He will not[o] be an aid,[q] and he will not[r] be a help,[s]
         But a shame and also a reproach.

Textual Notes

a   MT נְאֻם־יְהוָה (nĕʾum-YHWH), "oracle of Yahweh/says Yahweh"; 1QIsaᵃ נואם יהוה.

b   MT וְלֹא (wĕlōʾ), "and not"; 1QIsaᵃ ולוא.

c   MT מִנִּי (minnî), "from me"; 1QIsaᵃ has the longer form ממני.

d   MT הַהֹלְכִים (hahōlĕkîm), "who go, undertake"; 1QIsaᵃ ההולכים.

e   MT לָרֶדֶת (lāredet), "to go down"; 1QIsaᵃ לרדׄ.

f   MT לֹא (lōʾ), "not"; 1QIsaᵃ לוא.

g   MT פַּרְעֹה (parʿōh), "Pharaoh"; 1QIsaᵃ פרעוה. LXX switches the order of Pharaoh and Egypt.

h   MT וְהֶחָסוּת (wĕheḥāsût), "and the shelter," so also 1QIsaᵃ, Vg., Syr.; LXX apparently read the participle והחוסים (καὶ τοῖς πεποιθόσιν ἐπʼ Αἴγυπτον, "and to those who trust in Egypt").

i   MT לִכְלִמָּה (liklimmâ), "to a shame"; 1QIsaᵃ has לכמה, either unintentionally omitting a letter, or misreading the form as a preposition with the second person masculine plural suffix.

j   MT שָׂרָיו וּמַלְאָכָיו (śārāyw ûmalʾākāyw), "his princes and his messengers," so also 1QIsaᵃ and Tg., which, like the MT, make each noun the subject of its clause; Vg. read שָׂרֶיךָ ומלאכיך, "your princes and your messengers"; LXX took both nouns as the subject of the first clause, "because there are leaders in Tanis, evil messengers" (ὅτι εἰσὶν ἐν Τάνει ἀρχηγοὶ ἄγγελοι πονηροί); Syr. takes both nouns as the subject of the second clause, "and his evil leaders and messengers will grow weary."

k   MT has the plural הָיוּ (hāyû), "they are," followed by LXX, Vg., and Tg.; 1QIsaᵃ and Syr. have the singular היה.

l   MT יַגִּיעוּ (yaggîʿû), "they reached," so 1QIsaᵃ. Both LXX and Syr. take יגע as though it was from יגע, "to labor, grow weary."

m   LXX appears to have a double translation of חנס, treating it as both "evil," followed in this by Syr., and "vain." Hanes appears to be a site in the northeastern Delta, near but east of Tanis, even closer to Jerusalem. Heracleopolis Parva in the eastern Delta has been suggested based on Herodotus's reference (2.166.137) to Anysis in the Delta (see Kitchen, *Third Intermediate*, 374 n. 749). Tg. renders the word as Tahpanes, which also supports a northeastern location, since Tahpanes was an Egyptian fortress on Egypt's eastern frontier near Tanis in the northern Delta. Others identify Hanes with Anusi, the same as Heracleopolis Magna farther south, 80 km south of Memphis at the southern end of the Delta, about 100 km south of Cairo (see H. O. Thompson, "Hanes," ABD 3:49–50). This more important southern Hanes does not work as well geographically for an embassy coming from Nubia, though that may be what is behind Vg.'s translation with the second person suffixes, which mistakenly identifies the messengers and princes as those sent by Judah.

n   MT kĕtîb is כֹּל הִבְאִישׁ (kōl hibʾîš), "everyone stinks"; the qĕrēʾ is כֹּל הֹבִישׁ (kōl hōbîš), "everyone is ashamed." 1QIsaᵃ has כלה באש. LXX and Syr. seem to omit the whole phrase. The Stuttgart editor suggests on basis of Tg. the correction to כל הבא הביש, "everyone who goes will be ashamed," but one might also consider the *qal* imperfect כל הבא יבש, with the same meaning. The verbs באש, "to stink," and בוש, "to be ashamed," often seem confused in Biblical Hebrew, though this may be more an issue

381

of intentional punning between the two similar roots rather than actual confusion.

o See note f above.

p The form לָמוֹ is normally a plural (= לָהֶם "to them"), but can, more rarely, be used for a singular (= לוֹ "to him"), as in Gen 9:26, 27; cf., e.g., Joüon-Muraoka, vol. 2, § 103f. Since the antecedent here is masculine singular, I have taken the pronominal suffix as masculine singular.

q MT לְעֵזֶר (lĕʿēzer), "for an aid"; 1QIsaᵃ has the feminine לעזרה with the same meaning.

r See note b above.

s MT לְהוֹעִיל (lĕhôʿîl), "to help," "for a help"; 1QIsaᵃ תועיל, "and she will not help."

Commentary

This *hôy*-oracle is addressed to Yahweh's בָּנִים סוֹרְרִים (*bānîm sôrĕrîm*), "rebellious children." The imagery is similar to Isa 1:2-6, where God's people are addressed as זֶרַע מְרֵעִים בָּנִים מַשְׁחִיתִים (*zeraʿ mĕrēʿîm bānîm mašḥîtîm*, "offspring who do evil, children who act corruptly," 1:4). In Isaiah 30 the nature of that rebellion is spelled out. They make a plan that does not come from God, and they conclude a covenant without God's approval. The precise meaning of the idiom וְלִנְסֹךְ מַסֵּכָה (*wĕlinsōk massēkâ*) is debated. Some take the literal sense of the cognate verb and noun to be "to weave a pattern/covering" (see the discussion of possible renderings in Watts, *Isaiah 1–33*, 462; from the sense "weaving a covering," Blenkinsopp (p. 410) renders, "seeking security." Others understand it to as "to pour out a libation" (so Wildberger, 3:1148). The second derivation seems more likely, since the verb נסך (*nāsak*), "to pour out," is used with the noun רוח (*rûaḥ*), "spirit," elsewhere in Isaiah (29:10; cf. 41:29). Both the LXX and the Vulgate take the idiom to mean, "make a plan" or "covenant," while the Syriac has "who make an offering." The analysis and literal rendering, "to pour out a libation," would agree with the Syriac and would still fit the interpretation of the LXX and the Vulgate very well. "To pour out a libation" is probably an expression for making a covenant based on one part of the covenant ritual, in which a libation confirmed the agreement. It would be similar to the Akkadian *qatālu ḫiara*, lit., "to kill a donkey" (*CAD* Ḫ, 118–19; *CAD* Q, 162) or *lapātu napišta*, lit., "to touch the throat" (*CAD* L, 84, 1b; *CAD* N 1, 303, 9.3´), both expressions referring to a particular ritual act in covenant making, but both used idiomatically to simply mean "to make a covenant." As v. 2 will make clear, the plan that was not from God and the covenant unapproved by God's spirit are clearly

a reference to the treaty the Judean court of Hezekiah concluded with Nubian Egypt for help in the proposed revolt against Assyria after the death of Sargon II in 705 BCE (see Isa 28:14-19; 29:15-16). By making this treaty, God's rebellious children just added another sin to their already long list of sins.

With the expression "who undertake to go down to Egypt," the prophet suggests that the Judean court took the initiative in making this agreement with Egypt, while the second clause, "but did not inquire of me" (lit., "of my mouth"), asserts that they began these negotiations with Egypt without first consulting Yahweh through the prophetic oracle to see if this was the divine will. Isaiah makes a similar charge in 31:1. Normally even an impious king would consult the oracles before making such an important political decision, so the failure to consult the oracles suggests special circumstances. Whether Isaiah's complaint simply indicates that he was not consulted, or whether no prophet at all was consulted, it would appear that the court was trying to keep these negotiations with Egypt as secret as possible (see Isa 29:15-16), perhaps to avoid security leaks should Isaiah or other prophets oppose the treaty, as Isaiah had done very publicly when a similar agreement was proposed during the Ashdod crisis (715–711 BCE) some years before. The last two prepositional phrases in the verse, "to take refuge in the stronghold of Pharaoh," and "to shelter in the shade of Egypt," indicate that the Judean court was seeking military support from Egypt for their revolt against Assyria.

This reliance on Egypt, however, will not yield success, but only shame and embarrassment (v. 3). Here Isaiah basically repeats the message he directed against those who wanted to make Nubia and Egypt their hope back in 715–711 BCE during the Ashdod crisis (Isa 20:5-6). The stronghold of Pharaoh and shelter in the shade of Egypt were a false hope.

Verse 4 is ambiguous enough that it raises the question, "Whose princes are in Tanis, and whose messengers are in Hanes?" The Vulgate, with its translation "your princes" and "your messengers," understands the officials and messengers as those sent to Egypt by the Judean court. The Hebrew text, however, speaks of "his princes" and "his messengers." Egypt at the time was ruled by the Nubians, whose homeland was far to the south, and their administrative capital in Egypt tended to be at Thebes, perhaps occasionally at Memphis,[1] but not in the Delta. The princes and messengers of the Nubian overlord, then, would have a long trip to meet with the representatives from Judah and possibly other Palestinian states joining in this anti-Assyrian alliance. Isaiah 18:1-2 depicts such an arduous journey of the Nubian envoys in the earlier Ashdod crisis. If the officials of the Nubian overlord were already in Tanis in the eastern Delta and their messengers had even reached Hanes, identified by Kitchen and others, as noted above, as a site even farther east than Tanis, and thus closer to Judah, it suggests that the Nubians and their Egyptian vassals in the Delta were as eager to conclude this anti-Assyrian alliance with their Palestinian supplicants as Judah and the Philistines were. Judah and the other Palestinian parties in the arrangement were eager to gain the military support of a major power as a counterweight to the impressive military might of Assyria, but the Nubians and their Egyptian vassals were eager to create a further buffer between themselves and the Assyrians, whose expansion in the west had begun to threaten both their territorial and their economic interests already in the earlier conflicts of 720 and 715–711 BCE.

Nonetheless, in v. 5 the prophet reiterates his earlier statement (v. 3): everyone will be ashamed of this people who cannot help them; Nubian Egypt will not be an aid or a help to Judah, but simply a source of shame and reproach.

Bibliography

Barthel, *Prophetenwort*, 391–427.

Beuken, W., "Isa 30: A Prophetic Oracle Transmitted in Two Successive Paradigms," in C. Broyles and C. Evans, eds., *Writing and Reading the Scroll of Isaiah: Studies of an Interpretive Tradition* (2 vols.; VTSup 70; Leiden: Brill, 1997) 1:369–97.

Childs, *Assyrian Crisis*, 32–33.

Dahood, M., "Accusative ʿēṣāh, "Wood" in Isaiah 30,1b," *Bib* 50 (1969) 57–58.

Donner, *Israel unter den Völkern*, 132–34, 159–62.

Dorsey, D. A., "On," in P. Achtemeier, ed., *Harper's Bible Dictionary* (San Francisco: Harper & Row, 1985) 730–31.

Emerton, J. A., "A Further Note on Isaiah XXX," *JTS* 33 (1982) 16.

———, "A Textual Problem in Isaiah XXX. 5," *JTS* 32 (1981) 125–28.

Fichtner, J., "Jahwes Plan in der Botschaft des Jesaja," *ZAW* 63 (1951) 16–33; reprinted in Fichtner, *Gottes Weisheit: Gesammelte Studien zum Alten Testament* (ed. K. D. Fricke; Stuttgart: Calwer, 1964) 27–43.

García de la Fuente, O., *La búsqueda de Dios en el Antiguo Testamento* (Madrid: Guadarrama, 1971).

Gerstenberger, Erhard S., "The Woe Oracles of the Prophets," *JBL* 81 (1962) 249–63.

Høgenhaven, Jesper, "Prophecy and Propaganda: Aspects of Political and Religious Reasoning in Israel and the Ancient Near East," *SJOT* 1 (1989) 125–41.

Irwin, *Isaiah 28–33*.

Kitchen, *Third Intermediate*.

Kuschke, A., "Zu Jes 30,1-5," *ZAW* 64 (1952) 194–95.

McKane, W., *Prophets and Wise Men* (Naperville, IL: Alec R. Allenson, 1965) esp. 71–72.

Roberts, J. J. M., "Egypt, Assyria, Isaiah," 265–83.

———, "Egyptian and Nubian Oracles," 201–9.

———, "Security and Justice in Isaiah," *Stone-Campbell Journal* 13 (2010) 71–79.

---

1   Later, in some inscriptions of Ashurbanipal, there is reference to various local Egyptian princes, and so on, who are said to have been appointed as rulers over Egypt by Esarhaddon, but who then scattered in fear of Tirhakah of Nubia as he moved north to try to retake Egypt. Tirhakah reached Memphis and made it his northern base of operation, before Ashurbanipal drove him back south and reappointed the Egyptian vassals who had been loyal to their Assyrian overlord (*ANET*, 294, 296).

Schmidt, W. H., "'Suchet den Herrn, So werdet ihr leben': Exegetische Notizen zum Thema 'Gott suchen' in der Prophetie," in *Ex orbe religionum: Studia Geo Widengren, XXIV mense apr. MCMLXXII* (2 vols.; SHR 21–22; Leiden: Brill, 1972) 127–40.

Thompson, H. O., "Hanes," *ABD* 3:49–50.

Turbessi, G., "Quaerere Deum," *RivB* 10 (1962) 282–96.

Werner, Wolfgang, *Studien zur alttestamentichen Vorstellung vom Plan Jahwes* (BZAW 173; Berlin: de Gruyter, 1988) 85–94.

Westermann, Claus, "Die Begriffe für Fragen und Suchen im Alten Testament," *KD* 6 (1960) 2–30, esp. 21–22.

Wonsuk, Ma., "The Spirit (*Ruah*) of God in Isaiah 1–39," *AJT* 3 (1989) 582–96.

Ziegler, J., "Zum literarischen Aufbau verschiedener Stücke im Buche des Propheten Isaias," *BZ* 21 (1933) 131–49.

30

The heading of this short saying separates it from the preceding material, but the content of the oracle shows that it comes from the same period as the foregoing material.

Like the preceding material, this oracle highlights the folly of depending on the Egyptians as an ally against Assyria.

6/   Oracle concerning the beasts of the Negeb:
   In a harsh[a] and difficult land
   Of lioness and roaring[b] lion
   Of viper and flying serpent
   They carry[c] their wealth[d] on the shoulder of donkeys,
   Their treasures[e] on the hump of camels,
   To[f] a people that cannot[g] help.[h]
7/   And the Egyptians will be a vain and empty help,
   Therefore I have named her[i] Chaos the quieted.

Textual Notes

a   MT בְּאֶרֶץ צָרָה וְצוּקָה (bĕʾereṣ ṣārâ wĕṣûqâ), "in a harsh and difficult land"; 1QIsaᵃ inserts וציה, "in a harsh *and dry* and difficult land."

b   MT's מֵהֶם (mēhem), "from them," is difficult, though supported by LXX, Vg., and Syr. 1QIsaᵃ reads ואין מים, "and without water." One could analyze the form מֵהֶם as a *hiphil* participle of a geminate root המם (hāmam; cf. מֵפֵר from פרר), perhaps meaning "to roar," though the *hiphil* of המם is not otherwise attested. Another possibility is to emend to נהם (nōhēm), the *qal* active participle of נהם (nāham), "to roar."

c   MT יִשְׂאוּ (yiśĕʾû), "they carry," so the versions; 1QIsaᵃ has the singular ישא (yiśśāʾ), "he carries."

d   MT חֵילֵהֶם (ḥêlēhem), "their wealth"; 1QIsaᵃ has the shorter suffix חילם.

e   MT אוֹצְרֹתָם (ʾôṣĕrōtām), "their wealth"; 1QIsaᵃ אוצרותמ.

f   Both MT and 1QIsaᵃ have the preposition על here, but it is clearly used as the equivalent of אֶל ("to"). The phrase "a people who cannot help" obviously refers to the same people as the identical phrase in v. 5, the Egyptians, who are then explicitly named in the following parallel v. 7.

g   MT לֹא (lōʾ), "not"; 1QIsaᵃ לוא.

h   LXX adds ἀλλὰ εἰς αἰσχύνην καὶ ὄνειδος, "but for shame and reproach," from v. 5.

i   MT לָזֹאת (lāzōʾt), "to this one, her"; 1QIsaᵃ לזואת. The feminine demonstrative here must refer to Egypt, which is sometimes construed as feminine (Exod 10:7); see commentary. The versions had difficulty with MT רַהַב הֵם שָׁבֶת (rahab hēm šābet), which 1QIsaᵃ construes as רהבהם שבת. The word רהב is the name of a mythical, presumably masculine, sea monster (see Isa 51:9; Ps 89:11; Job 9:13; 26:12), which personifies chaos—thus the translation "Chaos." I construe the rest of the phrase as הַמָּשְׁבָּת (hammošbāt), the *hophal* masculine singular participle of שבת, "to cease"—hence "the quieted, the stilled."

Commentary

The heading of this short saying characterizes it as an oracle about the beasts of the Negeb, some of which will soon be mentioned. Before that, however, there is a description of the difficult landscape of the Sinai that one must traverse to move from Judah to the Egyptian cities of the Delta. The landscape is described as harsh and difficult, which is a fair appraisal. It is also characterized as filled with dangerous wild beasts and frightening serpents. The presence of lions and vipers in the area in this period is hardly to be doubted, but the mention of a flying serpent (וְשָׂרָף מְעוֹפֵף, wĕśārāp mĕʿôpēp), the mythological winged seraphim of Isaiah 6, points more to the fear that this region engendered in those who considered crossing it than to a sober classification of its fauna. Esarhaddon, the Assyrian successor of Sennacherib, gives a similar description of this region that he crossed a few years later to attack Egypt. He mentions deadly two-headed serpents as well as an odd winged creature (for a convenient English translation, see *ANET*, 292). The stress on the difficulty and danger in crossing this region underscores the trouble the Judean court was willing to endure in order to gain Egyptian aid, and it was not free. The next lines point to the cost. Judah had to send tribute to the Egyptians to buy their assistance. The Judean tribute was loaded on the shoulder of donkeys and the hump of camels to transport it across the dangerous Sinai to the Egyptian emissaries at Hanes or Tanis. Again the imagery underscores both the trouble and the cost to Judah, but the real stinger is that the people to whom Judah has taken such pains to send their wealth cannot help them. Their labor and expense are for naught.

Verse 7 simply underscores this judgment. The Egyptians are a vain and empty help. They are so useless that Isaiah has given Egypt the name "Chaos (Rahab) the quieted." As noted above, the feminine demonstrative pronoun shows that Egypt here is construed as feminine, though in other biblical texts it is construed as masculine. This choice may be totally inadvertent, but it might suggest the notion that Egypt was terrified like a woman (cf. Isa 19:16). In contrast, Rahab is the name of a masculine sea monster that Yahweh subdued (see Isa 51:9; Ps 89:11; Job 9:13; 26:12). One should note that this Rahab is spelled differently in Hebrew (רַהַב, *rahab*, from a root meaning "to be tumultuous, rage") from the name of Rahab the prostitute (רָחָב, *rāḥāb*, from a root meaning "to be broad"). If the redivision suggested in the textual notes is correct, the feminine Egypt is like this masculine sea monster after Yahweh has stopped or quieted him, that is, totally useless to anyone seeking help from her.

Bibliography

Beuken, W., "Isa 30: A Prophetic Oracle Transmitted in Two Successive Paradigms," in C. Broyles and C. Evans, eds., *Writing and Reading the Scroll of Isaiah: Studies of an Interpretive Tradition* (2 vols.; VTSup 70; Leiden: Brill, 1997) 1:369–97.

Day, John, *God's Conflict with the Dragon and the Sea: Echoes of a Canaanite Myth in the Old Testament* (Camridge: Cambridge University Press, 1985).

Hertlein, E., "Rahab," *ZAW* 38 (1919–20) 113–54.

Høgenhaven, Jesper, "Prophecy and Propaganda: Aspects of Political and Religious Reasoning in Israel and the Ancient near East," *SJOT* 1 (1989) 125–41.

Murison, R. G., "Rahab," *ExpTim* 16 (1904) 190.

Roberts, J. J. M., "Egyptian and Nubian Oracles," 201–9.

——, "Security and Justice in Isaiah," *Stone-Campbell Journal* 13 (2010) 71–79.

Schunck, K. D., "Jesaja 30,6-8 und die Deutung der Rahab im Alten Testament," *ZAW* 78 (1966) 48–56.

This oracle again characterizes God's people as disobedient children similarly to Isa 30:1, and it comes out of the same historical context. It also reflects the same political pressure on Judah's prophets as one finds in Isa 29:9-16, not to challenge the strategic decision being formulated by the elite in the royal court to form a defensive alliance with Nubian Egypt, and concerns the same treaty with Egypt mentioned in Isa 28:14-15 and alluded to in Isa 31:1-3. It should be dated somewhere between the death of Sargon II in 705 BCE and Sennacherib's third campaign against Judah in 701 BCE.

8/ Now come in, write it[a] on a tablet,
Come,[b] inscribe it[c] on a scroll;
That it may be for a future day,
As a witness[d] forever.
9/ For he is a disobedient people,
Lying children,
Children who were unwilling[e] to hear[f]
The instruction of Yahweh.
10/ Who said to the seers,
"You shall not[g] see!"
And to the prophetic visionaries,[h]
"You shall not[g] envision for us truthful visions;
Speak to us pleasant things,
Envision for us deceptions.[i]
11/ Turn aside[j] from[k] the way;
Depart from[k] the path,
Remove from before us
The Holy One of Israel."
12/ Therefore thus[l] says the Holy One of Israel,
"Because you rejected this word,
And you trusted instead in oppression[m] and deceit,[n]
And you relied upon it,
13/ Therefore this iniquity[o] will be to you
Like a falling,[p] bulging breach in a high wall,
Whose shattering collapse comes suddenly in a moment.
14/ And its shattering collapse will be like the shattering of the vessel of potters,
Smashed beyond repair;[q]
There will not[r] be found among its fragments,
A sherd large enough to take fire from the hearth,
Or to scoop[s] water from a cistern."
15/ For thus said my Lord, Yahweh,[t] the Holy One of Israel,
"In returning[u] and rest you will be saved;
In quietness and in trust will be your strength."
But you were unwilling,[v]
16/ And you said,[w] "No,[x] but on[y] horses we will race."
Therefore[z] you will flee.
"And on*[a] a swift mount we will ride."
Therefore[z] your pursuers*[b] will be swifter.
17/ A thousand at the shout of one—
At the shout of five*[c] you shall flee.*[d]
Until you are left like a signal post on the top*[e] of the mountain,*[f]
And like a flag on the hill.

Textual Notes

a   MT כָּתְבָהּ (kotbāh), "write it," the qal imperative second person masculine singular with third person feminine singular suffix; 1QIsaᵃ has כ'תבהא.

This is presumably a fuller writing of the same form, but 1QIsaᵃ is peculiar in providing a second object with אותם (ʾôtām), "them." LXX, Vg., Tg., and Syr. omit the object suffix on כתבה, and apparently so does 4QIsaᶜ, since only the final ב is preserved on the damaged text.

b   MT אִתָּם (ʾittām), "with them"; 1QIsaᵃ has the suffixed direct object marker אותם, which is followed by LXX, Vg., and Syr., but that reading works only if one ignores the third person feminine singular object suffix on כתבה and חקה. It is better to read אֱתֵמוֹ (ʾătēmô), "come!," the qal imperative second person masculine singular with enclitic *mem* from אתה, "to come."

c   MT חֻקָּהּ (ḥuqqāh), "inscribe it," so also 1QIsaᵃ and Vg.; but LXX and Tg. omit the suffix.

d   Correct MT לָעַד עַד־עוֹלָם (lāʿad ʿad-ʿôlām), "forever and ever," to לְעֵד עַד־עוֹלָם (lĕʿēd ʿad-ʿôlām), "as a witness forever," following Vg., Syr., and Tg.

e   MT לֹא (lōʾ), "not"; 1QIsaᵃ לוא.

f   MT שְׁמֹעַ (šĕmoaʿ), "to hear"; 1QIsaᵃ לשמוע (lišmoaʿ), "to hear."

g   See note e above.

h   MT וְלַחֹזִים (wĕlaḥōzîm), "and to the prophetic visionaries"; 1QIsaᵃ and 4QIsaᶜ ולחוזים.

i   MT מַהֲתַלּוֹת (mahătallôt), "deceptions"; 1QIsaᵃ מתלות simply reflects assimilation of the ה.

j   MT and 4QIsaᶜ סוּרוּ (sûrû), "turn aside!"; 1QIsaᵃ תסירו (tāsîrû), "you shall turn aside."

k   MT מִנִּי (minnê), "from"; 1QIsaᵃ appears to have mistakenly written מנו in the first occurrence. LXX may have misinterpreted מנו as "from us"; Vg. clearly misunderstood מני as "from me."

l   MT, 1QIsaᵃ, 1QIsaᵇ כֹּה (kōh), "thus"; 4QIsaᶜ כוה.

m   MT בְּעֹשֶׁק (bĕʿōšeq), "in oppression"; 1QIsaᵃ בעושק.

n   MT and probably 4QIsaᶜ וְנָלוֹז (wĕnālôz), "and deceit"; 1QIsaᵃ ותעלוז (wattaʿălôz), "and you exulted." LXX has καὶ ὅτι ἐγόγγυσας, "and because you murmured."

o   MT הֶעָוֹן (heʿāwōn), "the iniquity"; 1QIsaᵃ העוֹן (heʿāwôn), the supralinear correction is written over an erasure of a letter that may be a ה.

p   MT נֹפֵל (nōpēl), "falling"; 1QIsaᵃ נופל.

q   MT לֹא יַחְמֹל (lōʾ yaḥmōl), "which cannot be healed, beyond repair"; 1QIsaᵃ לוא יחמיל.

r   MT וְלֹא (wĕlōʾ), "and not"; 1QIsaᵃ ולוא.

s   MT וְלַחְשֹׂף (wĕlaḥśōp), "and to scoop"; 1QIsaᵃ ולחסוף.

t   MT אֲדֹנָי יְהוָה (ʾădōnāy YHWH), "my Lord, Yahweh"; 1QIsaᵃ אֲדוני יהוה, while 4QIsaᶜ appears to have had [אדונ]י יהוה. LXX has only κύριος, "Lord," but Vg. supports MT.

u   MT and probably 4QIsaᶜ בְּשׁוּבָה (bĕšûbâ), "in returning"; 1QIsaᵃ בשיבה (bĕšîbâ), "in returning."

v   See note r above.

w   MT and 1QIsaᵃ וַתֹּאמְרוּ (wattōʾmĕrû), "and you said"; 4QIsaᶜ ו[תואמרו.

x   See note e above.

y   MT עַל (ʿal), "upon"; 1QIsaᵃ אל, "to."

z   MT עַל־כֵּן (ʿal-kēn), "therefore"; 1QIsaᵃ עלכן, "therefore."

*a   MT וְעַל (wĕʿal), "and upon"; 1QIsaᵃ ואל, "and to."

*b   MT רֹדְפֵכֶם (rōdĕpêkem), "your pursuers"; 1QIsaᵃ רודפיכם.

*c   MT מִפְּנֵי גַּעֲרַת חֲמִשָּׁה (mippĕnê gaʿărat ḥămiššâ), "at the shout of five"; 1QIsaᵃ ומפני חמשה (ûmippĕnê ḥămiššâ), "and from before five." LXX and Vg. support MT's longer reading, but with the conjunction "and" of 1QIsaᵃ.

*d   MT תָּנֻסוּ (tānūsû), "you will flee"; 1QIsaᵃ תנוסו. LXX has φεύξονται πολλοί, "many shall flee."

*e   MT רֹאשׁ (rōʾš), "the top"; 1QIsaᵃ ראש.

*f   MT הָהָר (hāhār), "of the mountain"; 1QIsaᵃ הר, "of a mountain."

Commentary

The command (v. 8) to Isaiah to come write and inscribe his prophecy on a scroll here is analogous to his sealing of his testimony in a scroll during the time of the Syro-Ephraimitic War in 8:16-17. In both cases it serves the same function, to be a witness against the people in the future when the prophet's words come to pass. The command is repeated twice with slight variation as a function of poetic parallelism, though this has been obscured by the misreading of אֱתֵמוֹ (ʾătēmô), "come!," the qal imperative second person masculine singular with enclitic *mem* from אתה, "to come," as אִתָּם (ʾittām), "with them," the suffixed preposition את, "with," or as אֹתָם (ʾōtām), "them," the suffixed direct object marker. Either of these misreadings creates syntactical problems with the feminine singular suffix on the two imperatives for writ-

ing, and thereby indicates that they are misreadings. That these feminine singular suffixes are original is indicated by the feminine singular verb וּתְהִי (ûtĕhî), "that it might be," which depends on them to supply the antecedent for its subject. The feminine noun implied by these suffixes and the feminine verb should perhaps be understood as תּוֹרַת יְהוָה (tôrat YHWH), "the instruction/oracle of Yahweh," since it is mentioned in the next verse. So by delaying the explicit mention of the antecedent to the third person feminine singular suffixes on כתבה and חקה, a certain dramatic tension—a sense of anticipation—is created. Thus, we have here a *deliberate* rhetorical device, not a textual error or confusion. This writing down of the divine instruction given to Isaiah for the people is so that it will still be around for a future day, to serve as a witness to the people forever.

The reason this permanent witness is needed is that the people to whom this message was given are a rebellious people (v. 9). In the future they will deny that the prophet ever said any such thing, so the written record is important to keep them honest. That is probably why Isaiah characterizes them as lying children, as children who are unwilling to hear the instruction of Yahweh. There is a close parallel between this characterization of God's people as disobedient children and the similar characterization of these people in Isa 1:4.

Moreover, their refusal to listen to Yahweh's instructions is exemplified by their attitude toward their own seers and prophetic visionaries (v. 10). Instead of honestly seeking the instruction of Yahweh from these intermediaries with access to the divine will, they order the seers not to see, and the visionaries they order not to have honest, reliable visions for the people, an ironic echo, perhaps, of 6:9-10. It is difficult to translate adequately in English the parallel participles רֹאִים (rōʾîm), "seers," and חֹזִים (ḥōzîm), "prophetic visionaries," and their respective verbs ראה (rāʾâ), "to see," and חזה (ḥāzâ), "to see," since they are close synonyms that mean the same thing and refer to the same figures and the same prophetic activity. I have distinguished them in translation only to indicate that two different verbal roots are being used. Isaiah's choice of חֹזִים here rather than נביאים (něbîʾîm), "prophets," is probably because of the desire to exploit the notion of seeing. It should not be taken as an implicit critique of the נביאים, contra Wildberger (3:1171). The verb חזה, however, probably implies the act of speaking, and one could certainly translate it simply as "prophesy."

Instead of hearing what God really said to these intermediaries, the people demand that these intermediaries speak to them חֲלָקוֹת (ḥălāqôt), "the smooth, soothing falsehoods,"[1] that the people want to hear. They are only to see in their visions מַהֲתַלּוֹת (mahătallôt), "deceptions." Two comments are required here. While Isaiah speaks of the people (v. 9), it is clear that he is primarily concerned with the political elite of the people. It would be the king and members of the royal court who would be consulting the intermediaries about government policy. Private citizens would also consult the intermediaries, but normally about their private concerns. The second point is that Isaiah is probably overstating what the officials said to the intermediaries to make his point. They wanted a favorable prophetic response to the plans they were hatching, and the kind of political pressure they might put on a prophet who did not support their plan with positive oracles is indicated in the story of Micaiah ben Imlah (1 Kgs 22:5-28, esp. 5-8, 13-14, 18, 26-27), but they would certainly not have used the words Isaiah puts in their mouths. His statement that they commanded the seers, "You shall not see!" may be explained by Isaiah's comments elsewhere that the political elite chose not to consult Yahweh at all (see 29:10-12, 15-16; 30:2; 31:1). This was probably for fear that prophets opposed to their policy, like Isaiah, would protest against it, thus both negatively affecting public opinion as well as alerting Assyrian agents to the plans being formed.

Similar strictures apply to Isaiah's claim in v. 11 that his opponents said, "Turn aside from the way, depart from the path, remove from before us the Holy One of Israel!" If one reads MT's intransitive סורו (sûrû), "turn aside!," the sense of the first two verbs is that the prophets should turn aside from the straight path, so as to remove God from the concerns of the elite. If, less likely, one reads 1QIsaᵃ's transitive תסירו (tāsîrû), "you shall cause to turn aside," then the sense of the first two verbs is similar to the third—the prophets should remove the Holy One of Israel from the path and cease mentioning him before the elite. In neither case is it likely that Isaiah's opponents said precisely those words. The implication of the political leadership's reticent use of only those seers who could be depended on to back their plans, or perhaps the refusal to consult any seers at all, was tantamount, in Isaiah's view, to trying to remove Yahweh, the Holy One of Israel, from their plans altogether, but it is doubtful that they stated this as blatantly as his words here might suggest. His citation of God's comment in 29:13, that this people draw near to me with their mouth, and honor me with their lips, though their heart is far

---

1 Cf. the Qumran designation, apparently of the Pharisees, as men of חֲלָקוֹת, which various modern interpreters have rightly taken as a satirical pun on the Pharisees as men of הֲלָכוֹת.

from me, shows that outwardly the political elite maintained an appearance of public piety. This is political/religious polemic, and in neither political nor religious polemic does one expect a participant to be totally fair in reporting the actual words of his or her opponents.

Yahweh's response to the leadership's attempt to remove him from the equation begins in v. 12, "therefore thus says the Holy One of Israel." The following statement, "because you have rejected this word," leaves the astute reader with the question, "What word?" Whatever the word the prophet is referring to, the following part of the verse contrasts it with trusting in "oppression and deceit" and relying on such deceitful oppression or oppressive deceit. The preceding part of the oracle does not seem to contain the expected contrasting positive word, so the mention of it is probably anticipatory, and I am inclined to identify this positive word with Yahweh's promise given in v. 15. From v. 16 it is clear that the deceit the Judean leadership was relying on, instead of God's promises, involved making arrangements with Egypt to gain additional cavalry and chariotry for the coming war with Assyria (see also 28:14-15; 30:1-5, 6-7; 31:1-3;). Oppression probably refers to the economic hardships that this national policy will impose, particularly upon the poor, in terms of higher taxation, forced labor, and confiscation of property for defense purposes (see Isa 22:8-11).

Before Isaiah comes to the positive word of God's promises, the prophet indicates the judgment that will befall the people for this sin of relying on oppression and deceit (v. 13). This sin will become like a spreading (falling) breach that bulges out in a high wall, and then suddenly collapses with shattering destruction. Its shattering will be like that of a piece of pottery that is shattered into such small pieces that no remaining piece will be found that is large enough to take fire from a hearth or scoop water from a cistern (v. 14). In the historical context of revolt against Assyria when Judah's leadership and people will have taken refuge in Judah's fortified, high-walled cities, the imagery of the collapse of such fortifications, even used figuratively, would have had an ominous sound to Isaiah's audience. Cf. his imagery in Isa 28:17-18.

In v. 15 Isaiah recites the word from Yahweh that he referred to in v. 12 as being rejected by the people. He introduces the word with an extended epithet of Yahweh, "my Lord Yahweh the Holy One of Israel," which is probably intended to lend gravitas to God's word. What God said was, "In returning and rest you will be saved, in quietness and trust will be your strength." The meaning is, "if you will turn back to Yahweh and, trusting in his promises, wait in calm and quiet patience for his intervention, you will be saved." For this imagery of calm trust and detachment in a period of frantic and fearful political maneuvering, compare the portrait of Yahweh in Isa 18:4. Pure passivity, however, was not what the prophet meant. Turning back to Yahweh and trusting in his promises implied active obedience to the commands that Yahweh had given the people. A parallel formula to the word given here is found in Isa 28:12, and there the emphasis is laid on an active providing of rest and relief to the poor and oppressed. Or, as Isa 28:17 puts it, God's line and plummet are justice and righteousness. The problem was, just as in 28:12, that the people refused God's word of promise and sought salvation on their own terms.

They said, in effect, we will not trust in God's promises, but in horses that we can race away in battle and swift mounts that we can ride (v. 16). God's response is that they will indeed race away in headlong flight, playing on an ambiguity in the meaning of the verb נוס (nûs), which normally means "to flee" but apparently could be used more positively for fast tactical movements. Isaiah threatens that, forgetting any fast tactical movement, Judah will only flee in panic, and, unfortunately for them, the horses of their pursuers will be even swifter than the ones on which the Judeans ride.

This element of panic is highlighted in v. 17, where Isaiah says in direct address to his Judean audience that a thousand of you will flee at the shout of one enemy—that at the shout of only five you will all flee in panic until your pitiful military remnant is as isolated and few as a signal post on the top of a mountain or a flag on a hill. Instead of salvation, this reliance on horses will simply contribute to the speed with which this disaster is already overtaking Judah.

Bibliography

Allegro, J. M., "More Isaiah Commentaries from Qumran's Fourth Cave," *JBL* 77 (1958) 215–21.

Beuken, "Isa 30."

Cathcart, Kevin J., "Isaiah 30:15 בשובה ונחת and Akkadian *šubat nēḫti/šubtu nēḫtu,* 'Quiet Abode,'" in Iain Provan and Mark J. Boda, eds., *Let Us Go Up to Zion: Essays in Honour of H. G. M. Williamson on the Occasion of His Sixty-Fifth Birthday* (VTSup 153; Leiden: Brill, 2012) 45–56.

Couroyer, B., "Le Nes biblique: Signal ou enseigne," *RB* 91 (1984) 5–29.

Dahood, M., "Some Ambiguous Texts in Isaiah," *CBQ* 20 (1958) 41–49.

Darr, K. P., "Isaiah's Vision and the Rhetoric of Rebellion," in *SBLSP 1994* (Atlanta: Scholars Press, 1994) 847–82.

Driver, "Isaiah 1–39: Problems," 51.

Exum, J. Cheryl, "Of Broken Pots, Fluttering Birds, and Visions in the Night: Extended Simile and Poetic Technique in Isaiah," *CBQ* 43 (1981) 331–52.

Friedländer, I., "Das hebräische סֵפֶר in einer verkannten Bedeutung," *JQR* 15 (1903) 102–3.

Galling, K., "Tafel, Buch und Blatt," in Hans Goedicke, ed., *Near Eastern Studies in Honor of William Foxwell Albright* (Baltimore: Johns Hopkins Press, 1971) 207–33.

Gordis, Robert, "Some Hitherto Unrecognized Meanings of the Verb *Shub,*" *JBL* 52 (1933) 153–62.

Huber, F., *Jahwe, Juda und die andern Völker beim Propheten Jesaja* (BZAW 137; Berlin: de Gruyter, 1976) esp. 140–47.

Jenni, E., *Die politischen Voraussagen der Propheten* (Zurich: Zwingli, 1956) esp. 83–85.

Jensen, *Use of tôrâ,* esp. 112–21.

Melugin, R. F., "The Conventional and the Creative in Isaiah's Judgment Oracles," *CBQ* 36 (1974) 301–11, esp. 303–4.

Nötscher, F., "Entbehrliche Hapaxlegomena in Jesaia," *VT* 1 (1951) 300–302.

Reymond, P., "Un tesson pour 'ramasser' de l'eau à la mare (Esaïe XXX, 14)," *VT* 7 (1957) 203–7.

Roberts, J. J. M., "Blindfolding the Prophet: Political Resistance to First Isaiah's Oracles in the Light of Ancient Near Eastern Attitudes toward Oracles," in Jean-Georges Heintz, ed., *Oracles et prophéties dans l'antiquité: Actes du Colloque de Strasbourg 15-17 juin 1995* (Travaux du Centre de recherche sur le Proche-Orient et la Grèce antiques 15; Strasbourg: De Boccard, 1997) 135–46; reprinted as chap. 19 in *The Bible and the Ancient Near East: Collected Essays.* Winona Lake, IN: Eisenbrauns, 2002) 282–91.

——, "Contemporary Worship in the Light of Isaiah's Ancient Critique," in M. P. Graham, R. R. Marrs, and S. L. McKenzie, eds., *Worship and the Hebrew Bible: Essays in Honour of John T. Willis* (JSOTSup 284; Sheffield: JSOT Press, 1999) 265–75.

——, "Egyptian and Nubian Oracles," 201–9.

——, "Isaiah, National Security, and the Politics of Fear," in Robert Jewett, Wayne L. Alloway Jr., and John G. Lacey, eds., *The Bible and the American Future* (Eugene, OR: Cascade, 2009) 72–91.

——, "Security and Justice."

Smelik, K. A. D., "Ostracon, schrijtafel of boekrol? Jeremia 36, Jesaja 30:8 en twee ostraca uit Saqqara," *NedTT* 44 (1990) 198–207.

Stegemann, U., "Der Restgedanke bei Isaias," *BZ* n.F. 13 (1969) 161–86.

Williamson, *Book Called Isaiah,* 103–6.

Wong, G. C. I., "Faith and Works in Isaiah XXX 15," *VT* 47 (1997) 236–46.

30

The dating of this oracle is more problematic than that of the preceding oracles, though it is literally connected to the immediately preceding oracle by the conjunction וְלָכֵן (wĕlākēn), "and therefore." Most scholars date the passage far later than the time of Isaiah of Jerusalem, though the evidence for attaching it to any particular later date is hardly compelling. The passage is a bit unusual, and it may indeed date to a later writer than Isaiah of Jerusalem, but I think it is worth exploring its connections to Isaiah of Jerusalem and the possibility, as improbable as that may seem to most scholars, that it offers Isaiah's hope for Jerusalem's survivors toward the end of Sennacherib's campaign in Judah.

18/ And therefore[a] Yahweh waits to be gracious[b] to you,
And therefore he rises up[c] to show you mercy,
For[d] a God of justice is Yahweh;[e]
Blessed are all[f] who wait on him.

19/ For, O people in Zion, who dwell in Jerusalem,[g]
You will no longer weep.[h]
He will be exceedingly gracious to you[i]
At the sound of your calling;
As soon as he hears,[j] he will answer you.

20/ And my Lord[k] will give to you
Bread of affliction and water of oppression,[l]
And your teacher will no longer hide himself,[m]
But your eyes will see your teacher,[n]

21/ And your ears[h] will hear a word from behind you saying,[o]
"This is the way, Go in it!"
Whenever you turn to the right,[p]
Or whenever you turn to the left.[q]

22/ And you will defile[r] the silver overlay of your idols,
And the gold veneer of your molten image.[s]
You will throw them out like[t] (the rag) of a menstruous woman,
"Go out!" you will say to it.

23/ And he will give rain for your seed
With which you sow[u] the ground;[v]
And bread, the produce of the ground,
And it will be[w] rich and abundant;
Your livestock will graze[x] a broad[y] pasture in that day,

24/ And the oxen[z] and donkeys[*a] that work[*b] the land
Will eat seasoned[*c] fodder
Which has been winnowed[*d] with shovel and with pitchfork.[*e]

25/ And there will be on every[*f] high mountain
And upon every[*f] lofty hill
Brooks running[*g] with water
On a day[*h] of great slaughter
When the towers fall.

26/ And the light of the moon will be like the light of the sun,
And the light of the sun will become sevenfold,
Like the light of seven days,
On the day that Yahweh binds up[*i] the breach of his people,
And heals the wound caused by his blow.[*j]

Textual Notes

a   MT, 1QIsaᵃ וְלָכֵן (wĕlākēn), "and therefore"; LXX renders καὶ πάλιν, "and again."

b   MT לַחֲנַנְכֶם (laḥănankem), "to be gracious to you"; 1QIsaᵃ לחונכם (lĕḥonnĕkem), "to be gracious to you."

c   MT יָרוּם (yārûm), "he rises up"; 1QIsaᵃ ירים (yārîm), "he raises up."

d   MT כִּי (kî), "for"; 1QIsaᵃ כיא.

e   MT אֱלֹהֵי מִשְׁפָּט יְהוָה (ʾĕlōhê mišpāṭ YHWH), "a god of justice is Yahweh"; 1QIsaᵃ אלוהי משפט יהוה; LXX has κριτὴς κύριος ὁ θεὸς ἡμῶν ἐστιν, "the Lord our God is a judge."

f   MT כֹּל (*kol*), "all"; 1QIsaᵃ כול.

g   MT עַם בְּצִיּוֹן יֵשֵׁב בִּירוּשָׁלָ͏ִם (*'am bĕṣiyôn yēšēb bîrûšālāim*), "O people in Zion who live in Jerusalem"; 1QIsaᵃ עם בציון ישב ובירושלם, "O people who live in Zion and in Jerusalem." LXX has λαὸς ἅγιος ἐν Σιων οἰκήσει, "a holy people shall live in Zion"; καὶ Ιερουσαλημ, "and Jerusalem," omitting the preposition, is taken with the following clause.

h   MT בָּכוֹ לֹא־תִבְכֶּה (*bākô lō'-tibkeh*), "you [sg.] will no longer weep"; 1QIsaᵃ בכו לוא תבכו (*bākô lô' tibkû*), "you [pl.] will no longer weep." LXX omits the negative and reads the verb as third person, "and Jerusalem wept with weeping." Vg. supports MT.

i   MT חָנוֹן יָחְנְךָ (*ḥānôn yāḥnĕkā*), "he will be exceedingly gracious to you"; 1QIsaᵃ חנון יחונך יהוה (*ḥānôn yĕḥonnĕkā YHWH*), "Yahweh will be exceedingly gracious to you." LXX takes the infinite absolute as an imperative spoken by the weeping Jerusalem: Ἐλέησόν με· ἐλεήσει σε, "Have mercy on me; he will show you mercy." Vg. supports MT.

j   MT כְּשָׁמְעָתוֹ (*kĕšom'ātô*), "as soon as he hears"; 1QIsaᵃ כשמותו. LXX has ἡνίκα εἶδεν, "when he sees."

k   MT אֲדֹנָי (*'ădōnāy*), "my Lord"; 1QIsaᵃ אדוני.

l   MT וּמַיִם לָחַץ (*ûmayim lāḥaṣ*), "and water of oppression"; 1QIsaᵃ has the more normal construct form ומי לחץ (*ûmê lāḥaṣ*), "and water of oppression."

m   MT וְלֹא־יִכָּנֵף עוֹד מוֹרֶיךָ (*wĕlō'-yikkānēp 'ôd môrêkā*), "and your teacher will no longer hide himself"; 1QIsaᵃ ולוא יכנפו עוד מוראיך, "and your teachers will no longer hide themselves," though it has the variant orthography מוריך in the following line. The form looks plural, as 1QIsaᵃ takes it, but MT's understanding of it as singular is probably correct. For these "apparent plurals," see Joüon-Muraoka (2006), p. 283, §96 Ce. Vg. supports MT, but LXX and Syr. render "your teachers" as "those who deceive you."

n   MT וְאָזְנֶךָ (*wĕ'oznêkā*), "and your ears"; 1QIsaᵃ ואוזניך.

o   MT לֵאמֹר (*lē'mōr*), "saying"; 1QIsaᵃ לאמור.

p   MT תַּאֲמִינוּ (*ta'ămînû*), "you turn to the right"; 1QIsaᵃ תיאמינו. The root is ימן and one expects the form תימינו (*têmînû*).

q   The versions have some interesting interpretations. LXX makes the voice that of the deceivers who say, Αὕτη ἡ ὁδός, πορευθῶμεν ἐν αὐτῇ εἴτε δεξιὰ εἴτε ἀριστερά, "This is the way, let us go in it whether to the right or to the left." Vg. has *haec via ambulate in ea neque ad dexteram neque ad sinistram*, "this is the way, walk in it neither to the right nor to the left." Syr. clari-fies, "This is the way, walk in it, and do not turn aside to the right or to the left."

r   MT וְטִמֵּאתֶם (*wĕṭimmē'tem*), "and you will defile"; 1QIsaᵃ וטמיתם.

s   MT וְאֶת־אֲפֻדַּת מַסֵּכַת זְהָבֶךָ (*wĕ'et-'ăpuddat massēkat zĕhābekā*), "and the golden veneer of your molten image"; 1QIsaᵃ ואת אפודות מסכות זהבך, "and the golden veneers of your molten images."

t   MT and 1QIsaᵃ כְּמוֹ (*kĕmô*), "like"; LXX, Vg., and Syr. appear to be reading כמי (*kĕmê*), "as the water of *a menstruous woman*."

u   MT תִּזְרַע (*tizra'*), "you sow"; 1QIsaᵃ has the same form after the erasure of an erroneous final ך.

v   MT הָאֲדָמָה (*hā'ădāmâ*), "the ground"; 1QIsaᵃ אדמה.

w   MT וְהָיָה (*wĕhāyâ*), "and it will be"; 1QIsaᵃ יהיה (*yihyeh*), "it will be."

x   MT יִרְעֶה (*yir'eh*), "will graze"; 1QIsaᵃ miscopies as זרעה.

y   MT נִרְחָב (*nirḥāb*), "broad, wide"; 1QIsaᵃ miswrites as נרהב.

z   MT and 1QIsaᵃ וְהָאֲלָפִים (*wĕhā'ălāpîm*), "and the oxen"; LXX has "your bulls" and Vg. "and your bulls."

*a   MT, 1QIsaᵃ וְהָעֲיָרִים (*wĕhā'ăyārîm*), "and the donkeys," followed by Vg.; LXX and Syr. have "and the cattle."

b   MT עֹבְדֵי ('ōbĕdê*), "who work"; 1QIsaᵃ עובדי.

*c   MT חָמִיץ (*ḥāmîṣ*), "seasoned"; 1QIsaᵃ חמיץ.

d   MT אֲשֶׁר־זֹרֶה ('ăšer-zōreh*), "which one winnows"; 1QIsaᵃ אשר יזרה (*'ăšer yizreh*), "which one winnows." MT's *qal* participle is normally emended to the *pual* perfect *zōrâ*, "which has been winnowed" (so Wildberger, 3:1192; cf. BHK and BHS).

*e   LXX and Vg. omit the names of the winnowing instruments with a loose interpretive rendering of the end of the verse: φάγονται ἄχυρα ἀναπεποιημένα ἐν κριθῇ λελικμημένα, "will eat chaff prepared with winnowed barley"; *commixtum migma comedent sic in area ut ventilatum est*, "will eat a mixed mixture as is winnowed in the threshing-floor."

*f   MT כֹּל (*kol*), "every"; 1QIsaᵃ כול.

*g   Reading with 1QIsaᵃ פלגים יובלי מים (*pĕlāgîm yôbĕlê māyim*), "brooks bringing/running with water") over against MT's פְּלָגִים יִבְלֵי־מָיִם (*pĕlāgîm yiblê-māyim*), "brooks *and* streams of water." The versions all read a participle here.

*h   MT בְּיוֹם (*bĕyôm*), "on a day"; 1QIsaᵃ בים.

*i   MT חֲבֹשׁ (*ḥăbōš*), "to bind up"; 1QIsaᵃ חבוש.

*j   MT, 1QIsaᵃ מַכָּתוֹ (*makkātô*), "his blow," so Vg., Syr., Tg.; LXX has τῆς πληγῆς σου, "of your blow."

Commentary

The וְלָכֵן (*wĕlākēn*), "and therefore," of v. 18 links the following material to the preceding oracle of judgment, and the following material continues the direct address of v. 17. In view of your (Judah's) rejection of God's word and the resultant judgment, Yahweh is now waiting for the opportunity to be gracious to you. He will rise up to show you mercy, because Yahweh is a God of justice. The statement that Yahweh is a God of justice, and the final statement in the verse, "Blessed are all who wait for him," implies that not all Judeans were complicit in or supported the plans of the political decision makers, though they suffered the consequences nonetheless. The verbal expression חכה ל (*ḥākâ lĕ*), "to wait for *God*," is the same expression used by Isaiah to describe his behavior at the time of the Syro-Ephraimitic War, when the Judean court of Ahaz rejected his oracular advice (Isa 8:17), and it is clear from that context that Isaiah had his supporters who stood with him in powerless opposition to the royal policy. In the later Sennacherib crisis, it appears there were also those who stood on Isaiah's side. Moreover, their number probably grew along with the influence of Isaiah in Hezekiah's court as the disastrous consequences of the revolt against Assyria and the reliance on Egypt became apparent with the fall of more and more Judean fortresses and the tightening blockage around Jerusalem itself. It was only then that Hezekiah appears to have initiated a consultation of Yahweh through the prophet Isaiah (37:2-7), whose earlier warnings, though ignored, had proven true. For this relatively righteous remnant, it was only just that Yahweh would seek to be gracious to them.

So Isaiah addresses the people in Zion, who live in Jerusalem (v. 19), with the promise: "You will no longer weep. God will be gracious to you. At the sound of your cry for help, as soon as he hears, he will answer you." The promise is not a promise of luxurious abundance, however, as v. 20 makes clear. God will give you scarce rations of food and water, but at least your teacher will no longer hide himself. Scarce rations of food and water correspond to the actual situation during the siege of Jerusalem, but Isaiah promises that now instruction and revelation from Yahweh will be forthcoming. Now that Isaiah is being consulted, the earlier self-imposed blackout of the prophetic word by the government has been lifted, and the people will be able to "see" their teacher. There is a certain ambiguity about the expression מוֹרֶיךָ (môrêkā), "your teacher," as the variation in the translations of the versions indicate. In and of itself, it could be taken as a plural, and the LXX and the Syriac take it that way and interpret it as referring to the false teachers who mislead the people. The MT uses the singular verb יִכָּנֵף (yikkānēp), "hide himself," with the noun, however, which shows that the noun should be construed as singular, and the promissory nature of the oracle suggests that the teacher should be a positive figure.

That is spelled out in v. 21. Whenever the people begin to stray to the right or to the left of the correct way,

they will hear a word behind them saying, "This is the way, go in it." In short, don't turn to the right, don't turn to the left; stay in the straight way. The identity of the speaker remains somewhat mysterious. Is it God himself? A prophetic spokesman for God? There is an element of perhaps intentional ambiguity here, but the prophetic spokesman is probably implied. The function of the prophetic word is to provide instruction from God to keep people walking in God's way of righteousness and justice. With the recovery of the prophetic word that had been sealed by government opposition (Isa 29:10-12), the people will once more receive such instruction when they are tempted to turn aside.

In response to this recovery of the blessing of God's prophetic word, the people will rid themselves of their idols, those false sources of security and instruction whose advice and help had proven so useless during Sennacherib's conquest of Judah (v. 22; cf. Isa 10:10-11; 28:15).[1] They will throw out these idols, even the ones plated with silver or gold, as things as polluted and unclean as an undergarment polluted by the blood of a menstruous woman. The expression is elliptical and the grammar is somewhat awkward because of the ellipsis: "You will throw them away like *the rag* of a menstruous woman. 'Get out!' you will say to it (him)." The suffix on לוֹ (lô), "to him," is masculine singular, so it cannot refer back to דָּוָה (dāwâ), "the menstruous woman," or to the idols, which are referred to with a masculine plural suffix תִּזְרֵם (tizrēm), "you will throw *them* out"; it must refer to some disposable masculine singular object, either an object of clothing or an easily replaceable household object of little worth, polluted by contact with her blood. Any object a woman sat or lay on during her period was considered unclean (Lev 15:20, 26), but expensive household objects like beds would normally be purified after her period, rather than being thrown out. The point is that these idols are considered not only polluted but valueless as well, not worth purifying. One can hardly read this passage without reflecting on the humorous story in Gen 31:34-35, where Rachel hid the idols of

---

1   Both Israel and then Judah had shown themselves more than willing to turn to necromancy, idolatry, and other pagan practices in a desperate effort to gain security, particularly in threatening times (8:19-20; 1:29-31; 2:15, 20; 17:7-8, 10; 31:6-7).

her father Laban in a camel's saddlebag and then sat on them, declining to rise for her father because she was in her period.

Following the people's repentance, Yahweh will once more give them rain for the seed with which they sow the ground, and the ground will produce bread for them in rich abundance, and their livestock will be able to graze in broad pastures (v. 23). Moreover, their working oxen and asses will be given rich, nutritious feed, cleansed from empty chaff and other filler (v. 24), and all the mountains and hills will flow with streams of water (v. 25). Such a promise of abundant food and water, good crops, broad pastures, and well-fed livestock would certainly appeal to people shut up in Jerusalem, cut off from their fields and pasture, and on siege rations of food and water. But the end of v. 25 indicates that this redemption of God's people, their coming plenty and abundance, will coincide with the slaughter of their enemies and the destruction of their enemies' towers. The "towers" probably are the fortifications and siege towers the Assyrians had set up in Judah and around Jerusalem, which obviously had to be removed before Judah could enjoy the abundance and broad pasture that Isaiah was promising them.

That day of salvation will be brighter than any day in the experience of God's people—the moon will be as bright as the sun, and the sun seven times as bright as normal (v. 26). This is poetic hyperbole to indicate how glorious and happy that day will be, not a pseudo-scientific portrait of the end-time, nor even a full-blown apocalyptic vision of a radical transformation of the physical world in which Isaiah's contemporaries lived. One could object that making the moon as bright as the sun would destroy sleep and that a sevenfold increase in the brightness of the sun would scorch the earth, but such objections simply indicate that the objector has no sense for the meaning of poetic metaphor. That day of salvation will be the day when God heals the hurt of his people that has been caused by God's punishment. The language of this last part of the verse picks up the language of Isa 1:5-6, which speaks of Yahweh's harsh discipline of his rebellious children and alludes to his use of the Assyrians as the club with which he punished his people (Isa 10:5-15). For Isaiah's use of שֶׁבֶר (šeber), "shatter," see above, Isa 30:13-14, and cf. Isa 1:28; 8:15; 14:5, 25, 29; 28:13. For his use of רָפָא (rāpā᾽), "to heal," see Isa 6:10; 19:22.

Bibliography

Allegro, J. M., "More Isaiah Commentaries from Qumran's Fourth Cave," *JBL* 77 (1958) 215–21.

Bacher, W., "Isaïe XXX, 21," *REJ* 40 (1900) 248–49.

Beuken, W. A. M., "Isa 30."

——, "What Does the Vision Hold: Teachers or One Teacher? Punning Repetition in Isa. 30:20," *HeyJ* special issue (Festschrift R. Murray) 36 (1995) 451–56.

Gordis, Robert, "Midrash in the Prophets," *JBL* 49 (1930) 417–21.

Gray, A. H., "The Beatitude of 'Them That Wait,'" *ExpTim* 48 (1936) 264–67.

Köhler, L., "בליל חמיץ Jes 30,24," *ZAW* 40 (1922) 15–17.

Laberge, L., "Isa 30,19-26: A Deuteronomic Text?" *Eglise et théologie* 2 (1971) 35–54.

Lindblom, J., "Lot-Casting in the Old Testament," *VT* 12 (1962) 164–78.

Roberts, J. J. M., "The Teaching Voice in Isaiah 30:20-21," in E. Ferguson, ed., *Christian Teaching: Studies in Honor of Lemoine G. Lewis* (Abilene, TX: Abilene Christian University, 1981) 130–37.

Tov, E., "The Nature and Background of Harmonizations in Biblical Manuscripts," *JSOT* 31 (1985) 3–29.

30

Just as with the preceding oracle, this oracle is often dated later than the time of Isaiah of Jerusalem, but with much less justification. The main argument for its later dating is the occurrence of the expression שֵׁם־יְהוָה (*šēm-YHWH*), "Name of Yahweh," which, used as a hypostatic replacement for Yahweh himself, is generally regarded as a theological innovation developed in the Deuteronomistic movement.[1] Since that movement and the book of Deuteronomy that gave it its name are generally dated much later than the time of Isaiah, this oracle is also dated similarly.[2] It is doubtful, however, whether either the Deuteronomistic movement or this expression should be dated as late as it often is. If one may judge from the place-names in the book of Deuteronomy, all of which are northern,[3] the Deuteronomistic theology developed in the north, and its emphasis on Mosaic covenant law is clearly reflected in the work of the northern prophet Hosea, a contemporary of Isaiah, in the late eighth century. Apparently many of the adherents of this Deuteronomistic theology moved south when the northern kingdom collapsed, since Hezekiah's reform seems to promote many of the theological concerns found in the book of Deuteronomy, and there are traces of Deuteronomistic covenant theology in Isa 1:2-20 and 3:13-14. The old scroll of the law found in the temple in the time of Josiah, far from being a late forgery made to look old, was probably an early edition of Deuteronomy, perhaps composed in Jerusalem and deposited in the temple there in the time of Hezekiah and then neglected and forgotten by Hezekiah's paganizing successors Manasseh and Amon. I would thus argue for a composition of this early edition of Deuteronomy in Jerusalem, for curiously enough, the *šēm-YHWH* theology seems to be a Judean innovation introduced into the Deuteronomistic tradition after its move south. While Hosea, the northern prophet, has references to covenant law, he never uses the expression שֵׁם־יְהוָה. On the other hand, it is common in the Judean J narrative in the expression קָרָא בְּשֵׁם יהוה (*qārāʾ běšēm YHWH*), "to call upon the name of Yahweh" (Gen 4:6; 12:8; 13:4; 21:33; 26:25). The mid-eighth-century Judean prophet Amos uses it in the idiom לְהַזְכִּיר בְּשֵׁם יְהוָה (*lěhazkîr běšēm YHWH*), "to mention the name of Yahweh" (6:10), Isaiah uses the expression again in his Nubian oracle (18:7), and Micah, the contemporary of Isaiah, uses it twice in passages that I regard as early and genuine (4:5; 5:3). In other words, the Deuteronomistic reform movement had become an amalgam of northern and southern theological currents as early as Hezekiah's religious reform in the late eighth century. As the following commentary will show, nothing else in the oracle requires a date later than the time of Isaiah, and much in the oracle points to the eighth-century prophet as its author.

27/ Behold the name of Yahweh comes from afar,[a]
His anger burning[b] and with a thick column of smoke;[c]
His lips are full of indignation,
And his tongue like a devouring[d] fire.
28/ And his breath is like an overflowing wadi,
Which reaches[e] up to the neck—
To shake/move[f] the nations[g] back and forth with a sieve/yoke of vanity,
And a misleading bridle upon the jaws[h] of the peoples.

1   Defenders of the authenticity of the oracle, therefore, often delete the word שם as a secondary insertion (see Wildberger, 3:1207,1214–15). One should also note, however, the related but apparently non-Deuteronomistic use of שם in Lev 24:11, 16.
2   See Clements's discussion of this and other reasons for the later dating of this oracle (p. 52).
3   Apart from the brief survey of the whole land given to Moses in Deut 34:1-3 from the top of Mount Nebo, the only sites mentioned west of the Jordan are Gaza (Deut 2:23), Mount Gerizim (11:29; 27:12), Mount Ebal (11:29; 27:4, 13), Gilgal (11:30), and the oak of Moreh (11:30), a sacred tree near Shechem (Gen 12:6), close to Mount Gerizim and Mount Ebal. Jerusalem is conspicuous by its absence from the book of Deuteronomy.

29/ You will have[i] singing as on a night when a festival is celebrated,[j]
And gladness of heart as when one sets out to the sound of the flute
To go into the mountain of Yahweh, to the Rock of Israel.

30/ And Yahweh will cause the majesty of his voice to be heard,[k]
And the descent of his arm he will cause to be seen,
In a rage of anger and a flame of devouring fire,
With a cloudburst and rainstorm and hailstones.

31/ For at the voice of Yahweh Assyria will be shattered,
When he beats[l] with the rod.

32/ And every[m] blow of his stick of punishment,[n]
Which Yahweh will bring down upon him,
Will be to the sound of tambourines and lyres,
And with brandished maces[o] he will fight against him.[p]

33/ For his Tophet[q] has long been prepared,
Indeed it[r] is prepared[s] for the king;
Its firepit[t] one has made deep and wide,[u]
With fire and wood in abundance,
The breath of Yahweh burning in it like a stream of sulfur.

Textual Notes

a   LXX understands מִמֶּרְחָק (*mimmerḥāq*), "from afar," temporally rather than spatially: Ἰδοὺ τὸ ὄνομα κυρίου διὰ χρόνου ἔρχεται πολλοῦ, "behold the name of the Lord comes after a long time."

b   MT בֹּעֵר (*bōʿēr*), "burning"; 1QIsaᵃ בוער.

c   The meaning of וְכֹבֶד מַשָּׂאָה (*wěkōbed maśśāʾâ*) is disputed. Following in the steps of Vg., Syr., and Tg., JPS renders, "with a heavy burden." LXX takes the first word as *kābōd* and renders μετὰ δόξης τὸ λόγιον τῶν χειλέων αὐτοῦ, τὸ λόγιον ὀργῆς πλῆρες, "with glory is the oracle of his lips, the oracle is full of wrath." I understand *maśśāʾâ* as a byform of *maśʾēt*, which is used in Judg 20:38, 40 to designate a rising column of smoke, hence "with a thick column of smoke."

d   MT אֹכָלֶת (*ʾōkālet*), "devouring"; 1QIsaᵃ אוכלת.

e   MT יֶחֱצֶה (*yeḥěṣeh*), "it reaches"; 1QIsaᵃ erroneously writes וחצה, "and it will reach."

f   MT לַהֲנָפָה (*lahănāpâ*), "to move back and forth"; the form appears to be a nominal substitute for the *hiphil* infinitive of נוף (*nûp*), "to move back and forth, wave." 1QIsaᵃ לנפה.

g   MT גּוֹיִם (*gôyīm*), "nations"; 1QIsaᵃ גואים.

h   MT לְחָיֵי (*lěḥāyê*), "the jaws"; 1QIsaᵃ לוחי (*lôḥāyê*), "the jaws."

i   MT יִהְיֶה לָכֶם (*yihyeh lākem*), "there will be to you, you will have"; 1QIsaᵃ היה לכמה. LXX renders the whole verse negatively as questions implying judgment: μὴ διὰ παντὸς δεῖ ὑμᾶς εὐφραίνεσθαι καὶ εἰσπορεύεσθαι εἰς τὰ ἅγιά μου διὰ παντὸς ὡσεὶ ἑορτάζοντας καὶ ὡσεὶ εὐφραινόμενους εἰσελθεῖν μετὰ αὐλοῦ εἰς τὸ ὄρος τοῦ κυρίου πρὸς τὸν θεὸν τοῦ Ἰσραηλ; "Is it necessary for you to continually rejoice and to continually enter into my holy places as if you were keeping a feast and as if you were rejoicing to enter with a flute into the mountain of the Lord to the God of Israel?"

j   MT הִתְקַדֶּשׁ (*hitqaddeš*), "to celebrate"; 1QIsaᵃ התקדישו (*hitqaddîšû*), "when they celebrate."

k   MT וְהִשְׁמִיעַ יְהֹוָה (*wěhišmîaʿ YHWH*), "and Yahweh will cause to be heard"; 1QIsaᵃ omits the initial ו and has a dittography of the verb השמיע השמיע יהוה. LXX renders Yahweh as ὁ θεός, "God."

l   MT יַכֶּה (*yakkeh*), "when he beats"; 1QIsaᵃ יאכה.

m   MT כֹּל (*kōl*), "every"; 1QIsaᵃ כול.

n   Both MT מַטֵּה מוּסָדָה (*maṭṭēh mûsādâ*), "stick of foundation," and 1QIsaᵃ מטה מוסדו (*maṭṭēh mûsādô*), "stick of his foundation," have misread a ר for ד, a very common scribal error because of the similarity of the two letters in most periods of the Hebrew script. The original reading was מטה מוסרה (*maṭṭēh mûsārô*), "the stick of his punishment," with the final ה serving as a *mater* for the ō vowel, as was common in the preexilic script.

o   MT and 1QIsaᵃ וּבְמִלְחֲמֹות תְּנוּפָה (*ûběmilḥāmôt těnûpâ*), "and with maces of brandishment." The noun *milḥāmâ* normally means "war," but in a few passages it occurs in a list with particular weapons of war (Ps 76:4; Hos 1:7; 2:20), suggesting that it could also be the name of a weapon. In the context of Yahweh's arm beating with a rod and a stick, maces seem to be the logical choice. The emendation to וּבִמְחֹלוֹת (*ûbimḥōlôt*), "and with circular dances," is no improvement to the text.

p   MT נִלְחַם־בָּהּ (*nilḥam-bāh*), "he will fight against her," and 1QIsaᵃ נלחם בה should have been read as *nilḥam bô*, "he will fight against him," the ה being the old *mater* for the ō vowel. Because it was misread as a feminine suffix, the scribes introduced the *qěrē* בָּם (*bām*, "against them") to avoid the lack of an antecedent for the feminine suffix.

q   MT תָּפְתֶּה (*topteh*) as pointed and 1QIsa תפתח are cruxes. MT has the correct consonantal text, but it has misunderstood the final ה, which is the old *mater* for the final ō vowel. The original reading would have been *toptô*, "his Tophet." The Tophet was the name of the site and its equipment where one burned human sacrifices to Molek or Melek (2 Kgs 23:10; Jer 7:31-32; 19:6-13). It was also the name used in Phoenician/Punic for the sites of human, especially child, sacrifice.[4] The name itself may mean something like "hearth" or "fireplace."

r In MT גַּם־הוּא (gam-hûʾ), "indeed it/he," there is a certain ambiguity, since the masculine pronoun could refer back to either the masculine suffix on Tophet or to Tophet itself; the qĕrēʾ הִיא (hîʾ), "it/she," is an attempt to make the pronoun agree in gender with the noun misread as a feminine form. 1QIsaᵃ has גם היה, "indeed it was."

s MT הוּכָן (hûkān), "is prepared"; 1QIsaᵃ יוכן (yûkān), "it will be prepared."

t MT מְדֻרָתָהּ (mĕdūrātāh), "its firepit," and 1QIsaᵃ מדורתה should be read with the masculine suffix mĕdū/ûrātô, because the final ה is again the old mater for the final ō vowel.

u MT הֶעְמִיק הִרְחִב (heʿmîq hirḥîb), "one has made deep and wide"; 1QIsaᵃ adds a verb and puts all three in the hiphil feminine singular imperative הכיני והעמיקי הרחיבי, "Prepare, and make deep and make wide!" Presumably the addressee is Lady Zion.

Commentary

In v. 27, the expression שֵׁם־יְהוָה (šēm-YHWH), "Name of Yahweh," which occurs elsewhere in Isaiah of Jerusalem only in his Nubian oracle in 18:7, functions as an hypostasis of Yahweh himself; thus, the sense is that Yahweh is coming from afar in burning anger, his progress marked by a thick column of smoke, while his lips are full of indignation and his tongue devours like fire (v. 27). The notion that Yahweh was coming "from afar" evokes the motif of early Israelite poetry in which Yahweh comes from his ancient home in the distant southern mountains (Sinai, Seir, Mount Paran, and Teman) to save his people in the land of Canaan (Deut 33:2, 26-29; Judg 5:4-5; Ps 68:8-9, 18; Hab 3:3-15).[5] Other poetic texts of the monarchical period have God coming from his sanctuary or temple in Zion (Ps 20:3) or heaven, which in the early monarchy were hardly distinguishable (Ps 18:7, 9). The prophet chooses the more archaic motif here, because it is Zion itself that is threatened by the foe, and his audience must have felt that Yahweh was somehow absent for these disasters to overtake Jerusalem. In effect, Yahweh will return to Zion, accompanied by the terrifying display of fire and smoke that were a traditional feature of Yahweh's theophanies (Exod 19:16-18; Ps 18:8-16).

The comparison of Yahweh's breath to an overflowing wadi whose waters reach up to a person's neck (v. 28) recalls Isaiah's description of the Assyrian enemy as the overflowing Euphrates, whose waters will reach up to the neck of his people (Isa 8:7-8; cf. also 10:22; 28:2, 17-18 for other occurrences of שטף [šāṭap], "to overflow," with Assyria as the implied agent of judgment). The allusion to this earlier passage is intentional. It suggests that Assyria will be meted out the same punishment it had inflicted on others. The second part of v. 28 switches from the flash flood metaphor to a metaphor of the enemy as a horse or work animal directed by a yoke or a bridle. Most scholars take נָפָה (nāpâ) in the expression בְּנָפַת שָׁוְא (bĕnāpat šāwʾ) as "a sieve," and render the expression as "with a sieve of destruction,"[6] and this is the initial impression of most readers. But when one reads the parallel line, a sieve seems an odd match for a רֶסֶן (resen), "bridle," in the parallel expression וְרֶסֶן מַתְעֶה (wĕresen matʿeh), "and a misleading bridle." It makes a better parallel to analyze נָפָה (nāpâ) as נָפָה II, "yoke," and to take the whole expression as meaning "with a yoke of vanity." There is a similar metaphor in the old poem in Isa 37:29. The point of the passage is that Assyria is just God's tool, and Assyria's arrogant misunderstanding of its role has irritated Yahweh, so Yahweh turns Assyria away when it

---

4 See Paolo Xella, ed., *The Tophet in the Phoenician Mediterranean.* Studi epigrafici e linguistici sul Vicino Oriente antico, Nuova serie, Ricerche storiche e filologiche sulle culture del Vicino Oriente e del Mediterraneo antico 29–30 (Verona: Essedue Edizioni, 2013).

5 In these preserved early poetic texts, the sense of distance is indicated by the place-names indicating areas remote from the Israelite settlements in Palestine, not by the root רחק.

6 So Clements, 253, and NRSV; Wildberger translates, "whirls with a destructive whirling" (3:1207–8, 1218–19); but compare JPS.

has accomplished God's purpose but before Assyria has achieved its purpose, thus, from Assyria's perspective, misleading it in a vain enterprise (cf. Isa 10:12-15). The choice of the rare נָפָה (nāpâ), "yoke," rather than the common עֹל (ʿōl), "yoke," or even the חָח (ḥāḥ), "hook," as in Isa 37:29, however, strongly suggests that this was an intentional attempt to create a double entendre with the homonym. Like a destructive sieve, it is a yoke or a misleading bridle that guides Assyria to destruction. The reference to the גוֹיִם (gôyīm), "nations,") and עַמִּים (ʿammîm), "peoples," is an allusion to the many contingents from other nations that made up parts of the Assyrian imperial army.

In v. 29, the prophet shifts from the coming of Yahweh (v. 27) and its impact on Assyria (v. 28) to the reaction of Judah and Jerusalem to this divine intervention. They will celebrate in song as on a night when a festival is celebrated, with the kind of joy one has when processing into the mount of Yahweh to the sound of the flute. Yahweh is characterized here as the צוּר יִשְׂרָאֵל (ṣûr yiśrāʾēl), "Rock of Israel," an old epithet applied to Yahweh as the refuge or protective fortress of his people (Deut 32:15, 30-31, 37; 2 Sam 22:3, 32, 47; 23:3; Isa 17:10; Ps 19:15 and passim). The parallelism here is supplementary, not synonymous. The הַר־יהוה (har-YHWH) is Mount Zion, where Yahweh lives, but ṣûr yiśrāʾēl, "Rock of Israel," refers not to the place but to God, who lives in his sacred mountain and whose presence, like an inaccessible rock cliff, provides Zion its security.

With v. 30, the scene shifts back to Yahweh. God will cause his voice to be heard and the avenging downstroke of his arm to be seen. Yahweh's intervention will be public and transparent to his people, accompanied by the typical theophanic display of rage, devouring fire, cloudburst, rainstorm, and hailstones. For at the sound of Yahweh, Assyria will be shattered, when Yahweh beats with the rod (v. 31). The verb יֵחַת (yēḥat, niphal imperfect third person masculine singular of חתת, ḥātat) can mean either "be shattered" or "be dismayed, terrified," but beating an enemy with a club, while it might produce terror, is certainly intended to shatter (see Isa 7:8 and cf.

Ps 2:9). There is an ironic allusion here back to Isa 10:5, 15, where Assyria was the שֵׁבֶט (šēbeṭ), "rod" or "club," with which Yahweh beat his own people, but here the šēbeṭ is not Assyria but a different, unidentified rod with which Yahweh beats Assyria. Grammatically one could render, "For at the sound of Yahweh Assyria will be shattered/dismayed as he (Assyria) beats with the rod," but since the preceding v. 30 describes "the downstroke of Yahweh's arm" and the following v. 32 mentions "every blow of his staff of punishment which Yahweh brings down upon him," it is far more likely that the rod or staff in God's hand here is not Assyria, since Assyria is clearly the recipient of the beating, not the club with which it is administered.

Verse 32 suggests that Yahweh administers this beating in time with the beat of the tambourines and lyres of the sacred festival mentioned in v. 29. It is as though Yahweh were the drummer in the percussion section with both hands swinging maces as drumsticks. For the meaning "maces" for וּבְמִלְחֲמוֹת תְּנוּפָה (ûbĕmilḥămôt tĕnûpâ), "and with maces of brandishing/swinging," see the textual notes. The picture of Yahweh fighting him (Assyria; see textual note) with a mace in both hands is analogous to portrayals of Baal fighting Yamm with a mace in both hands (*KTU* 1.2. i 38-40, iv 11-27; for a convenient English translation see *ANET*, p. 130, lines 38-40, p. 131, lines 11-27).

Verse 33 concludes the oracle with a striking threat that Yahweh will burn Assyria as a human sacrifice. The תֹּפֶת (tōpet) was a pagan installation, normally set up in the valley of Hinnom at the outskirts of Jerusalem, for passing one's children through the fire לַמֹּלֶךְ (lammōlek), "to Molek" (2 Kgs 23:10). The practice obviously goes back at least to Isaiah's time in the late eighth century, since Ahaz is reported to have passed his son through the fire, though the precise location where he did this is not reported (2 Kgs 16:3). There is a long-standing debate about the nature and meaning of this practice, whether it was actually a human sacrifice of a living victim, and to whom or what the sacrifice was offered.[7] I think it was a human sacrifice, analogous to the desperate Moabite king

---

7   See, for example, the discussion in the work cited in n. 4, and in the works listed in the bibliography on this section by Day, Eissfeldt, Heider, B. P. Irwin, Smelik, and Weinfeld.

offering his firstborn son as a burnt offering on the walls of Kir-hareseth (2 Kgs 3:27). That would explain why the prophets were horrified by the practice and argued either that the command for such a practice never entered Yahweh's head (Jer 7:31), or that Yahweh had given such bad, life-denying ordinances in order to punish his people (Ezek 20:25-26). The second question is to whom such offerings were made. The vocalization Molek is probably secondary, combining the consonants מלך with the vowels for בֹּשֶׁת (bōšet), "shame," to express the disapproval of later scribes. The original vocalization was probably the divine epithet מֶלֶךְ (melek), "king," but what deity was designated by the epithet is disputed. Nonetheless, the passages cited above from Jeremiah and Ezekiel suggest that the Judeans thought they were making these offer-ings to Yahweh, their divine king. In Isa 30:33, Assyria's Tophet is now prepared לַמֶּלֶךְ (lammelek), "for the king." Given the standard formulation in the passages about the Tophet, "the king" here is probably an epithet for King Yahweh, not a reference to the Assyrian king, much less a reference to a pagan deity. The text concludes with the thought that the firebox of the Tophet is both deep and wide, capable of holding a lot of wood for a very hot fire, and, moreover, just as the oracle began in vv. 27-28, the breath of Yahweh will be the igniting agent, flowing into the firebox like a wadi full of burning sulfur. The implication is the total destruction and fiery death of Assyria. This did not happen in Isaiah's time, but that is no proof against the view that the eighth-century prophet Isaiah held such prophetic expectations and hopes.

Bibliography

Barth, *Die Jesaja-Worte,* 92–103.

Beuken, "Isa 30."

Day, John, *Molech: A God of Human Sacrifice in the Old Testament* (University of Cambridge Oriental Publications 41; Cambridge: Cambridge University Press, 1989).

Driver, "Isaiah 1–39: Problems," 51.

Eissfeldt, Otto, *Molk als Opferbegriff im Punischen und im Hebräischen und das Ende des Gottes Moloch* (Beiträge zur Religionsgeschichte des Altertums 3; Halle: M. Niemeyer, 1935).

Ginsberg, H. L., "An Obscure Hebrew Word," *JQR* 22 (1931) 143–45.

Gordis, Robert, "Midrash in the Prophets," *JBL* 49 (1930) 421–22.

Görg, M., "Marginalien zur Basis *NḤT*," *BN* 32 (1986) 20–21.

Guillaume, A., "Isaiah's Oracle against Assyria (Isaiah 30:27-33) in the Light of Archaeology," *BSOAS* 17 (1956) 413–15.

Heider, George C., *The Cult of Molek: A Reassessment* (JSOTSup 43; Sheffield: JSOT Press, 1985).

Huber, Friedrich, *Jahwe, Juda und die anderen Völker beim Propheten Jesaja* (BZAW 137; Berlin: de Gruyter, 1976) 50–54.

Irwin, B. P., "Molek Imagery and the Slaughter of Gog in Ezekiel 38 and 39," *JSOT* 65 (1995) 93–112.

Irwin, W. H., "Conflicting Parallelism in Job 5:13; Isa. 30:28; 32:7," *Bib* 76 (1995) 72–74.

Kruger, P. A., "The Obscure Combination כבד משאה in Isaiah 30:27: Another Description of Anger?" *JNSL* 26 (2000) 155–62.

Milgrom, J., "An Alleged Wave-Offering in Israel and in the Ancient Near East," *IEJ* 22 (1972) 33–38.

Peña, J., "La 'fiesta solemne y santa' en Isaías 30:27-33 como pascua," *Theologika – Revista Bíblico Teológica* 14 (1999) 104–20.

Ringgren, H., "Behold Your King Comes," *VT* 24 (1974) 207–11.

Roberts, J. J. M., "Isaiah, National Security, and the Politics of Fear," in Robert Jewett, Wayne L. Alloway Jr., and John G. Lacey, eds., *The Bible and the American Future"* (Eugene, OR: Cascade, 2009) 72–91.

Sabottka, L., "Is 30, 27-33: Ein Übersetzungs-vorschlag," *BZ* 12 (1968) 241–45.

Sasson, V., "An Unrecognized 'Smoke Signal' in Isaiah xxx 27," *VT* 33 (1983) 90–95.

Schedl, C., "Gedanken zu einem 'Übersetzungs-vorschlag' (Is 30, 27-33)," *BZ* n.s. 13 (1969) 242–43.

Smelik, K. A. D., "Moloch, Molech, or Molk Sacrifice? A Reassessment of the Evidence Concerning the Hebrew Term Molekh," *SJOT* 9 (1995) 133–42.

Weinfeld, M., "The Worship of Molech and the Queen of Heaven and Its Background," *UF* 4 (1972) 133–54.

The material in Isa 31:1-9 is normally separated into two
or more distinct oracles: (1) an oracle against relying on
Egypt (vv. 1-3); (2) possibly a distinct oracle about God's
intervention for or against Jerusalem (vv. 4-5) (Duhm,
206), though some would see this as just the beginning
of the following oracle (vv. 4-9) (so Wildberger, 3:1236;
Clements, 256); and (3) a call for repentance and a threat
against Assyria (vv. 6-9), which is sometimes further
fragmented (Kaiser, *Jesaja 13–39*, 250). There is some
justification for such fragmentation of these nine verses,
as the seams are occasionally abrupt, but the material
seems to have been edited to present a coherent literary
whole, whatever the original oral context in which the
individual parts were first spoken. Within the larger context of Isaiah 28–33, that literary context would appear
to be the crisis created by Hezekiah's rebellion against
Assyria and Sennacherib's response in the years 705–701
BCE. The material in vv. 1-3 is parallel to Isa 30:1-5, 6-7,
and it deals with the same concerns that are addressed in
Isa 28:14-22 and 29:15-16. As we shall see, the material in
vv. 4-5 is of the same character as Isa 29:1-8, and thus it
makes an appropriate extension of vv. 1-4. Isaiah 30:6-7
is of a different character. It appears to be a fragment
of an earlier oracle against the northern kingdom from
the time of the Syro-Ephraimitic War of 735–732 BCE,
which has been reused like Isa 28:1-6 to address the later
Judean audience with a demand for repentance. Isaiah
30:8-9 then concludes with a promise for the fiery divine
destruction of Assyria, analogous to 29:5-8; 30:27-33; and
33:10-14. Nothing in this material requires a date later
than the time of Isaiah of Jerusalem, and I am inclined
to attribute this literary editing to the prophet himself,
probably toward the end of Sennacherib's campaign or
shortly afterward.

1/   Hey! You who go down[a] to Egypt for help,
    Who rely on horses,
    And trust upon chariotry[b]
    Because they are many,
    And upon cavalry,[c]
    Because they are very numerous,[d]
    And who do not[e] look upon[f] the Holy One of Israel,
    And do not[e] inquire of Yahweh.

2/   Yet he also is wise,
    And he brought[g] disaster,
    And he did not[h] turn aside his words;
    But he will rise against the house of evildoers,
    And against the help of those who do iniquity.[i]

3/   And the Egyptians are human, and not[j] God,
    And their horses[k] are flesh, and not[j] spirit,[l]
    And Yahweh will stretch forth his hand,
    And the helper will stumble, and the one helped will fall,
    And together they will all perish.[m]

4/   For thus said Yahweh to me,
    Just as the lion[n] or young lion growls over its prey,[o]
    And, when a band of shepherds[p] is called out against it,[q]
    Is not[r] terrified by their voice,
    And is not[r] cowed[s] by their noise,
    Thus Yahweh of Hosts will come down
    To fight against Mount Zion,
    And against its height.

5/   Like birds[t] flying (overhead)
    Thus shall Yahweh of Hosts protect Jerusalem,
    Protecting and delivering,
    Sparing and rescuing.[u]

6/   Return to the one[v] against whom you have deeply rebelled,[w]
    O sons of Israel.

7/   For on that day you will discard,[x]
    Each one his idols of silver

And his idols of gold
Which your own hands sinfully made for you.^y

8/ And Assyria shall fall by a sword not^z of man,
And a sword not of a human*^a shall devour him,*^b
And he shall flee from before the sword,*^c
And his young men shall be put to forced labor.*^d

9/ And his rock shall pass away from terror,*^e
And his commanders shall be frightened away from the standard,*^f
Says*^g Yahweh who has a fire in Zion,
And has a furnace in Jerusalem.*^h

Textual Notes

a   MT הַיֹּרְדִים (hayyōrĕdîm), "who go down"; 1QIsaᵃ היורדים.

b   MT רֶכֶב (rekeb), "chariotry"; 1QIsaᵃ has the article הרכב.

c   Hebrew פָּרָשִׁים (pārāšîm) is ambiguous; it can mean either "horsemen, cavalry" or "horses, steeds." LXX takes it as "horses," but Vg., and Tg. take it as horsemen. Syr. renders it as "chariots."

d   MT כִּי־עָצְמוּ מְאֹד (kî-ʿāṣĕmû mĕʾōd), "because they are very numerous"; 1QIsaᵃ כי עצמו מאדה; LXX has only πλῆθος σφόδρα, "a great multitude."

e   MT לֹא (lōʾ), "not"; 1QIsaᵃ לוא.

f   MT שָׁעוּ עַל (šāʿû ʿal), "look upon"; 1QIsaᵃ שעו אל, "look to." The versions all translate the verb with the sense "to trust upon" (LXX, Syr.), "be confident upon" (Vg.), or "lean upon" (Tg.).

g   MT וַיָּבֵא (wayyābēʾ), "and he brought,"; 1QIsaᵃ ויביא.

h   See note e above.

i   MT פֹּעֲלֵי אָוֶן (pōʿălê ʾāwen), "those who do iniquity"; 1QIsaᵃ פועלי און. LXX has καὶ ἐπὶ τὴν ἐλπίδα αὐτῶν τὴν ματαίαν, "and upon their vain hope," but whether this represents a different text or is just a free translation is unclear.

j   See note e above.

k   MT וְסוּסֵיהֶם (wĕsûsêhem), "and their horses"; 1QIsaᵃ וסוסיהמה.

l   MT רוּחַ (rûaḥ), "spirit"; 1QIsaᵃ has erased an initial א and then written ריח. Perhaps a similarly garbled Hebrew manuscript is behind LXX's odd rendering of this line, ἵππων σάρκας καὶ οὐκ ἔστιν βοήθεια, "the flesh of horses and there is no help."

m   MT וְיַחְדָּו כֻּלָּם יִכְלָיוּן (wĕyaḥdāw kullām yiklāyûn), "and together they will all perish"; 1QIsaᵃ omits the conjunction יחדו כולם יכלין. LXX simplifies the last two lines καὶ κοπιάσουσιν οἱ βοηθοῦντες, καὶ ἅμα πάντες ἀπολοῦνται, "and those helping will grow weary, and together they will all perish."

n   MT הָאַרְיֵה (hāʾaryê), "the lion"; 1QIsaᵃ אריה.

o   MT טַרְפּוֹ (tarpô), "its prey"; 1QIsaᵃ טרפיו, "its objects of prey."

p   MT מְלֹא רֹעִים (mĕlōʾ rōʿîm), "a band/multitude of shepherds"; 1QIsaᵃ מלאו ר'עים, probably a simple mistake. For these two

words and the following מִקּוֹלָם, "from their voice," LXX's ἕως ἂν ἐμπλησθῇ τὰ ὄρη τῆς φωνῆς αὐτοῦ, "until the mountains are filled with his voice," appears to read מלאו הרים מקולו.

q   MT אֲשֶׁר יִקְרֵא עָלָיו (ʾăšer yiqqārēʾ ʿālāyw), "which is called out against it"; 1QIsaᵃ אשר יקרא אליו. LXX reads the active qal rather than the niphal, "and he [the lion] will cry against it [the prey]."

r   See note e above.

s   MT יַעֲנֶה (yaʿănê), "he is cowed"; the scribe of 1QIsaᵃ originally repeated the preceding יחת, "is terrified," then saw his mistake, erased it, and wrote the correct יענה. LXX construes both of these verbs as plural with their subject, the people who hear the lion's roaring, καὶ ἡττήθησαν καὶ τὸ πλῆθος τοῦ θυμοῦ ἐπτοήθησαν, "and they were overcome and terrified by the fulness of his wrath."

t   MT כְּצִפֳּרִים (kĕṣippŏrîm), "like birds"; 1QIsaᵃ כצפורים.

u   MT has גָּנוֹן וְהִצִּיל פָּסֹחַ וְהִמְלִיט (gānôn wĕhiṣṣîl pāsōaḥ wĕhimlîṭ), "protecting he will deliver, sparing he will rescue," but instead of reading the infinitive absolute followed by a converted perfect, one should probably read all four forms as infinitive absolutes, as Vg. apparently does: thus gānôn wĕhaṣṣîl pāsōaḥ wĕhamlîṭ, "protecting and delivering, sparing and rescuing."

v   MT שׁוּבוּ לַאֲשֶׁר (šûbû laʾăšer), "return to the one against whom"; 1QIsaᵃ is badly garbled שובי לאש לאשר.

w   MT הֶעְמִיקוּ סָרָה (heʿmîqû sārâ), lit., "they have made deep the rebellion"; but the third person masculine plural is syntactically conditioned,[1] and the opening plural imperative makes clear that the verse involves direct address, as all the versions recognized, hence "against whom you have made deep the rebellion." Because of the use of the hiphil of עמק, as in Isa 29:15, the LXX saw this verse as referring to the same action mentioned there, ἐπιστράφητε, οἱ τὴν βαθεῖαν βουλὴν βουλευόμενοι καὶ ἄνομον, "Turn back, you who plan a deep and lawless plan."

x   MT יִמְאָסוּן (yimʾāsûn), lit., "they will discard," but direct address

---

1   See the discussion of the syntax of direct address at 1:4-9; 2:5-6; 5:8-10; 22:15-16; and the literature referred in the following n. 2.

402

is still implied, as the second person forms at the end of the verse indicate.

y   MT אֲשֶׁר עָשׂוּ לָכֶם יְדֵיכֶם חֵטְא (ʾăšer ʿāśû lākem yĕdêkem ḥēṭ), "which your hands sinfully made for you"; 1QIsaᵃ has the same text except for the erasure of a ה on the ה of חטא. LXX omits the last word and, influenced by the initial verb, drops the second person forms at the end of the verse, ἃ ἐποίησαν αἱ χεῖρες αὐτῶν, "which their hands made."

z   See note e above.

*a MT אָדָם‎-לֹא (lōʾ-ʾādām), "not of a human"; 1QIsaᵃ לוא*דם.

*b MT תֹּאכְלֶנּוּ (tōʾkălennû), "shall devour him"; 1QIsaᵃ תאכולנו.

*c MT וְנָס לוֹ מִפְּנֵי-חֶרֶב (wĕnās lô mippĕnê-ḥereb), "and he will flee for himself from before the sword"; MT's dative of interest, "for himself," was misunderstood by 1QIsaᵃ as a negative—ונס ולוא מפני חרב, "and he fled, but not from before the sword," and this reading was taken up by LXX and Vg.; Syr. and Tg. stick with MT.

*d MT and 1QIsaᵃ's לָמַס (lāmas), "to forced labor," is supported by Vg.'s "will be tributaries [vectigales]," and is probably correct. LXX's εἰς ἥττημα, "unto defeat," may be connected to mās, "discouraged," derived from מסס, "to melt, be discouraged." JPS with its "pine away" seems to opt for this understanding. Syr.'s "sign, standard" appears to be reading נס, "standard, flag," as in v. 9, not מס.

*e The first line is ambiguous because of uncertainty as to the precise reference of וְסַלְעוֹ (wĕsalʿô), "and his rock." Does it refer to the Assyrian king's elite body guard, thus being parallel to שָׂרָיו (śārāyw), "his commanders," as the most reliable part

of the Assyrian army, or does "his rock" refer to "his fortified stronghold." Vg. (et fortitudo eius a terrore transibit, "and his strength shall pass away from terror") and Tg. (wšltwnwhy mn qdm dḥlʾ yʿdwn, "and his commanders will pass away from fear") appear to lean toward the former, while LXX seems to opt for the latter with its translation, πέτρα γὰρ περιλημφθήσονται ὡς χάρακι καὶ ἡττηθήσονται, "for they shall be surrounded with a rock as a palisade, and they shall be defeated."

*f MT וְחַתּוּ מִנֵּס שָׂרָיו (wĕḥattû minnēs śārāyw), "and his commanders will be frightened away from the standard," is also ambiguous: Does this mean to desert the Assyrian flag in terror, or does it mean to be terrified by the enemy's banner? 1QIsaᵃ וחתו מנוס שריו could be rendered, "his commanders will be too frightened to flee." LXX has ὁ δὲ φεύγων ἁλώσεται, "and the one who flees shall be captured"; and Vg. has et pavebunt fugientes principes eius, "and his princes will be afraid, fleeing."

*g MT נְאֻם (nĕʾūm), lit., "oracle," traditionally rendered "says"; 1QIsaᵃ נואם.

*h The last two lines of the verse are relatively straightforward, but LXX has a unique interpretation, Τάδε λέγει κύριος Μακάριος ὃς ἔχει ἐν Σιων σπέρμα καὶ οἰκείους ἐν Ιερουσαλημ, "thus says the Lord, Blessed is he who has seed in Zion and kinfolk in Jerusalem." The translator apparently saw the image of "a fire" and "a furnace" in Jerusalem as related to the old idea that one kept a lamp burning in Jerusalem by the continuation of one's family (see 1 Kgs 11:36; 15:4; 2 Kgs 8:19).

Commentary

Isaiah 31:1 begins as a hôy-oracle, just as Isa 30:1, but while direct address is explicitly marked in 30:3 by the second person masculine plural suffix on the preposition, there is no explicit marker of direct address in Isaiah 31 until the plural imperative in v. 6 and the second person masculine plural suffixes in v. 7. Nonetheless, one should read the oracle as direct address with syntactically conditioned third person forms after the opening participle.[2] The prophet accuses his audience of going down to Egypt for military help and of relying on horses, of trusting in the sheer number of chariots and cavalry they are able to amass through their treaty with Egypt. Obviously Isaiah's primary audience is the Judean royal court, the

king and his political advisors, since ordinary Judeans did not determine Judah's foreign policy. Then the prophet continues his denunciation of the royal policy by pointing out that the king and his court did not look to the Holy One of Israel or even make oracular inquiry (dārāšû) of Yahweh. The charge that the royal court did not seek an oracle from Yahweh before making their decision is also found in 30:2, and it is reflected in Isaiah's complaint that the royal advisors were trying to hide their plans from Yahweh (29:15). The many interconnections between this material in Isaiah 28–31, with the specific mention of "the rulers of this people who are in Jerusalem" (28:24) and the siege of Jerusalem/Ariel (29:1-8), suggests that all these oracles, whatever the prehistory of certain fragments, were reedited for use in the Assyrian crisis of 705–

---

2   Delbert R. Hillers, "Hôy and Hôy-Oracles: A Neglected Syntactic Aspect," in Carol L. Meyers and M. O'Conner, eds., The Word of the Lord Shall Go Forth: Essays in Honor of David Noel Freedman in Celebration of His Sixtieth Birthday (Winona Lake, IN: Eisenbrauns, 1983) 185–88; J. J. M. Roberts, "Form, Syntax," esp. n. 43.

701 BCE and addressed specifically to Hezekiah's Judean court of that period. Israel of the Syro-Ephraimitic period is excluded as the primary, even fictive, audience of the reedited material by these references to Jerusalem. In that period, Isaiah had urged the Judean king Ahaz to trust in Yahweh's promises to Jerusalem and the Davidic dynasty, and had even offered him a miraculous confirming sign (Isa 7:1-17), but the material in chaps. 28–31 does not fit that period, since Ahaz turned to Assyria, not Egypt. Isaiah's message to Hezekiah's Judean court during the Ashdod crisis of 715–711 BCE (Isa 14:28-32; 18:1-7; 20:1-6) to rely on the promises of Yahweh and not to buy into the Philistine's false hope of Nubian/Egyptian aid is consistent with the prophet's theology in the later crisis of 705–701 BCE, but in the earlier Ashdod crisis Isaiah was apparently successful in dissuading Hezekiah from joining the Philistine revolt against Assyria. The material in Isaiah 28–31 reflects a far more desperate situation in which the prophet has been effectively excluded from Hezekiah's inner circle, and the decision to summon Nubian/Egyptian support has already been made despite the prophet's objections.

The statement in v. 2, "yet he also is wise," refers to Yahweh, from whom the royal counselors cannot hide their plans (29:15). God as the creator of these arrogant human creatures is far more "understanding" (hēbîn) than these dumb clay pots can imagine (29:16). They think they can make their plans without regard to Yahweh, but God has the last laugh. God brought the disaster his prophet predicted and did not turn aside his words. The two verbs here, wayyābēʾ, "and he brought," and hēsîr, "he turned aside," are both past tense, while the following verbs are future. It is possible that these verbs should be treated as "prophetic perfects" and translated as future threats, but it is also possible that, by the time the prophet spoke this oracle, the negative results of the court's policy was already becoming evident and the past tense should be preserved. In any case, God threatens to rise up both against the house of the evildoers and against the help summoned by these doers of iniquity.

The help of Egypt will be useless, for the Egyptians are human, not divine, and their horses are flesh, not spirit (v. 3). Against the divine power, mere humans and mortal flesh are powerless. Yahweh will stretch forth his hand, and both the helper and the helped, both Nubia/Egypt and Judah, will stumble and fall, and all of them will perish. At what was probably the outset of Sennacherib's campaign against Judah, Isaiah's message to the Judean court is both negative and bleak, and the bleakness of the message continues in v. 4.

Verse 4 compares Yahweh to a lion growling to warn intruders away from the prey he has taken. Just as a lion will not be intimidated and scared away from his kill by a whole group of shouting shepherds, so Yahweh of Hosts will come down to fight against Mount Zion and against its hill. The imagery here is hardly positive. Jerusalem is compared to the prey טַרְפּוֹ (ṭarpô), "his prey," of a lion, and Yahweh is compared to a lion. Elsewhere Isaiah refers to Assyria as a lion that seizes prey, removes it, and allows no one to deliver it (5:29). Given Isaiah's prior oracles, on first reading one might think that here, as elsewhere, Assyria was the agent for Yahweh's actions against Jerusalem (Isa 10:1-12; cf. 29:1-5). In any case, nothing in Isaiah suggests that either lion or prey imagery could have a positive twist. Taken by itself, the preposition עַל (ʿal), "upon, against" (and a variety of other related meanings), is rather ambiguous, but the verbal idiom used here (צָבָא עַל), if one may judge from the three other of its four occurrences in the Hebrew Bible, has no such ambiguity: (1) הָמוֹן כָּל־הַגּוֹיִם הַצֹּבְאִים עַל־אֲרִיאֵל וְכָל־צֹבֶיהָ, "the multitude of all the nations who fight against Ariel, and all who fight against her" (Isa 29:7); (2) כֵּן יִהְיֶה הֲמוֹן כָּל־הַגּוֹיִם הַצֹּבְאִים עַל־הַר צִיּוֹן, "thus shall be the multitude of all the nations who fight against Mount Zion" (Isa 29:8—note the same object of the preposition here and in 31:4); and (3) וְזֹאת תִּהְיֶה הַמַּגֵּפָה אֲשֶׁר יִגֹּף יְהוָה אֶת־כָּל־הָעַמִּים אֲשֶׁר צָבְאוּ עַל־יְרוּשָׁלָ͏ִם, "and this will be the plague with which Yahweh will smite all the peoples who fight against Jerusalem" (Zech 14:12). In view of these parallels, and given the negative connotations of lion and prey, I think the preposition here should clearly be translated as "against."

Verse 5, however, confounds these initial expectations with its conflicting metaphor of Yahweh as birds protecting their nest. Like birds flying about their nest, Yahweh of Hosts will protect Jerusalem (יָגֵן עַל, yāgēn ʿal, "offer protection over"; for the idiom, cf. Isa 37:35; 38:6). Despite the attempts of some scholars to turn these birds into scavenging buzzards threatening Jerusalem, the whole series of verbs used in v. 5—גָּנַן (gānan), "to protect"; הִצִּיל (hāṣîl), "to deliver"; פָּסַח (pāsaḥ), "to spare"; and הִמְלִיט (himlîṭ), "to save"—are positive verbs indicating deliverance or salvation. Michael L. Barré attempts to get

404

around this objection by finding negative connotations for these roots in Syriac,[3] but Isaiah spoke Hebrew, not Syriac. Nonetheless, Barré's attempt demonstrates the discomfort that Isaiah's mixed and conflicting metaphors have created among modern scholars. Probably the majority of modern scholars try to remove the conflict by making both metaphors either positive or negative or, failing that, by excising one of the offending metaphors as a secondary addition to the text. Neither approach is compelling. Isaiah repeatedly speaks of Yahweh's plan first to discipline harshly but ultimately to save his chosen city (1:21-28; 10:5-12; 29:1-8). Isaiah 31:4-5, with its initially conflicting metaphors, fits this paradigm to a tee. Neither the Judean court's disobedience nor the power of Yahweh's Assyrian agents of punishment will ultimately frustrate Yahweh's positive plan for Zion's future.

The masculine plural imperative in v. 6, שׁוּבוּ (šûbû), "return!," is addressed to בְּנֵי יִשְׂרָאֵל (běnê yiśrāʾēl), "O sons of Israel," which is an unusual expression for Isaiah to use of the Judean court. The expression occurs only three times in First Isaiah (17:3, 9; 31:9) and once in Third Isaiah (66:20). In 17:3 the reference is clearly to the northern kingdom as an ally of Damascus during the Syro-Ephraimitic War, as the parallel with Ephraim indicates, while 17:9 is a more general reference to the people of Israel during the premonarchic settlement period. Moreover, many other occurrences of "Israel" in First Isaiah refer to the northern kingdom in contrast to the southern kingdom Judah (5:7; 7:1; 8:14, 18(?); 9:7, 11, 13; 10:20, 22; 11:12, 16). Given this usage and the prominent place the verb שׁוּב (šûb), "return, repent," played in Isaiah's message, both spoken and embodied in the symbolic name of his son שְׁאָר יָשׁוּב (šěʾār yāšûb), Shear-jashub, "A-Remnant-Will-Return," during the Syro-Ephraimitic War (7:3; 10:20-23), it is possible that this is a reedited fragment of an oracle from that earlier period similar to the reedited fragment in 28:1-6. An earlier fictive admonition to the northerners to return to Yahweh, against whom they had deeply rebelled by abandoning their own people and joining the foreign enemies of Judah (see Isa 2:6), is now turned into a real admonition to the Judean leadership to repent and return to Yahweh, against whom they had deeply rebelled by their treaty with Egypt. As the LXX translator noted long ago (see textual notes above), there is probably an intentional allusion in the choice of the expression לַאֲשֶׁר הֶעְמִיקוּ סָרָה (laʾăšer heʿmîqû sārâ), "against whom you have deeply rebelled," to the charge made against the Judean royal advisors in Isa 29:15: הוֹי הַמַּעֲמִיקִים מֵיהוָה לַסְתִּר עֵצָה (hôy hammaʿămîqîm mēYHWH lastīr ʿēṣâ), "Hey! You who make deep to hide the plan from Yahweh . . . ."

Verse 7 may also be a part of the reworked oracle, since Isaiah accused the northerners of idolatry in his oracles from the period of the Syro-Ephraimitic War (see 2:8, 18, 20; 17:7-11). It is not clear that Judah, particularly after Hezekiah's reform, was characterized by the widespread making of silver and golden idols apparently implied by this text. Nonetheless, the Judean court was guilty of the same sin of idolatry in seeking refuge in a treaty with Egypt made in the name of the Egyptian goddess Mut (see Isa 28:15). Ultimately one will discard such humanly constructed false gods, Isaiah says, since these idols will prove useless to save one from the crises for which they were created and invoked.

In v. 8 the prophet turns back to the fate of Assyria, God's tool for disciplining his people. Assyria will fall, but it will not be through Judah's defensive alliance with Nubia/Egypt or by the mass of chariotry and cavalry that Judah and their stronger ally can muster against Assyria. Assyria's defeat will not be from human power at all, but it will be Yahweh's invisible divine sword that devours him and causes Assyria to flee and his young men to be subjected to forced labor. Whether the prophet specifically envisioned the divine imposition of a killing plague, as the tradition in Isa 37:36 (2 Kgs 19:35) suggests, or whether he simply left this coming judgment intentionally vague and mysterious, is unclear.

Despite some ambiguity in the appropriate translation of v. 9, what does seem clear is that even Assyria's strongest contingents and most loyal commanders will flee in terror from their posts before this mysterious divine sword. This is the promise of Yahweh, who has a fire in

---

3   Michael L. Barré, "Of Lions and Birds: A Note on Isaiah 31:4-5," in Philip R. Davies and David J. A. Clines, eds., *Among the Prophets: Language, Image, and* *Structure in the Prophetic Writings* (JSOTSup 144; Sheffield: JSOT Press, 1993) 55–59.

Zion and a furnace in Jerusalem. The implication seems to be that this fire and furnace may be used to refine a corrupt Jerusalem (see Isa 1:25-26), but once Yahweh has disciplined his people and purified his dwelling place, Yahweh's fire is also in Jerusalem to burn away foreign threats to Yahweh's chosen abode (see esp. Isa 30:27-33; 33:10-14).

Bibliography

Amsler, S., "Les prophètes et la politique," *RTP* 23 (1973) 14–31.

Barré, Michael L., "Of Lions and Birds: A Note on Isaiah 31:4-5," in Philip R. Davies and David J. A. Clines, eds., *Among the Prophets: Language, Image, and Structure in the Prophetic Writings* (JSOTSup 144; Sheffield: JSOT Press, 1993) 55–59.

Birch, B. C., "Old Testament Foundations for Peace-making in the Nuclear Era," *ChrCent* 102 (1985) 1115–19.

Childs, *Assyrian Crisis*.

Couroyer, B., "L'origine Égyptienne du mot 'Pâque,'" *RB* 62 (1955) 481–96.

Davis, M. T., and B. A. Strawn, "Isaiah 31:4-5 in the Light of Lion Iconography in the Ancient Near East," in *AAR/SBL Abstracts 1996* (Atlanta: Scholars Press, 1996) 293.

Dietrich, *Jesaja und die Politik*, 144–52.

Donner, *Israel unter den Völkern*, 135–39.

Driver, "Prophets and Proverbs," 162–75.

Eidevall, G., "Lions and Birds as Literature. Some Notes on Isaiah 31 and Hosea 11," *SJOT* 7 (1993) 78–87.

Exum, J. Cheryl, "Of Broken Pots, Fluttering Birds, and Visions in the Night: Extended Simile and Poetic Technique in Isaiah," *CBQ* 43 (1981) 331–52.

Geers, H., "Critical Notes," *AJSL* 34 (1917) 133–34.

Glasson, T. G., "The 'Passover,' a Misnomer: The Meaning of the Verb Pasach," *JTS* 10 (1959) 79–84.

Haag, H., *Vom alten zum neuen Pascha: Geschichte und Theologie des Osterfestes* (SBS 49; Stuttgart: Katholisches Bibelwerk, 1971).

Hehn, J., "Zum Problem des Geistes im Alten Orient und im Alten Testament," *ZAW* 43 (1925) 210–25.

Hempel, Johannes, "Jahwegleichnisse der israelitischen Propheten," in Hempel, *Apoxysmata: Vorarbeiten zu einer Religionsgeschichte und Theologie des Alten Testaments: Festgabe zum 30. Juli 1961* (BZAW 81; Berlin: A. Töpelmann, 1961).

Höffken, P., "Bemerkungen zu Jesaja 31:1-3," *ZAW* 112 (2000) 230–38.

Høgenhaven, J., "Prophecy and Propaganda: Aspects of Political and Religious Reasoning in Israel and the Ancient Near East," *SJOT* 1 (1989) 125–41, esp. 126–37.

Irwin, *Isaiah 28–33*.

Jüngling, H.-W., "Der Heilige Israels: Der erste Jesaja zum Thema 'Gott,'" in Ernst Haag, ed., *Gott, der Einzige: Zur Entstehung des Monotheismus in Israel* (QD 104; Freiburg: Herder, 1985) 91–114.

Keel, Othmar, "Erwägungen zum Sitz im Leben des vormosaischen Pascha und zur Etymologie von פֶּסַח," *ZAW* 84 (1972) 414–34.

Klassen, W., "Jesus and the Messianic War," in Craig A. Evans and William F. Stinespring, eds., *Early Jewish and Christian Exegesis: Studies in Memory of William Hugh Brownlee* (Scholars Press Homage Series 10; Atlanta: Scholars Press, 1987) 155–75.

Klijn, A. F. J., "Jerome's Quotations from a Nazoraean Interpretation of Isaiah (Isa 8:14, 19—9:1; 29:20-21; 31:6-9)," in B. Gerhardsson et al., eds., *Judéo-Christianisme: Recherches historiques et théologiques offertes en hommage au cardinal Jean Daniélou* (Paris: Recherches de science religieuse, 1972) 241–55.

Laaf, P., *Die Pascha-Feier Israels: Eine literarkritische und überlieferungsgeschichtliche Studie* (BBB 36; Bonn: P. Hanstein, 1970).

Lys, Daniel, *La chair dans L'Ancien Testament "Bâsâr"* (Paris: Éditions universitaires, 1967).

———, *Rûach: Le souffle dans l'Ancien Testament: enquête anthropologique à travers l'histoire théologique d'Israël* (Études d'histoire et de philosophie religieuses 56; Paris: Presses Universitaires de France, 1962).

McKane, William, *Prophets and Wise Men* (SBT 44; Naperville, IL: Alec R. Allenson, 1965) esp. 72–73.

Schilling, Othmar, *Geist und Materie in biblischer Sicht: Ein exegetischer Beitrag zur Diskussion um Teilhard de Chardin* (SBS 25; Stuttgart: Katholisches Bibelwerk, 1967).

Stansell, G., "Isaiah 32: Creative Redaction in the Isaiah Tradition," in *SBLSP 1983* (Chico, CA: Scholars Press, 1983) 1–12.

Strawn, Brent A., *What Is Stronger Than a Lion? Leonine Image and Metaphor in the Hebrew Bible and the Ancient Near East* (OBO 212; Fribourg: Academic Press; Göttingen: Vandenhoeck & Ruprecht, 2005).

Sweeney, Marvin A. *Isaiah 1–39,* 401–8.
——, "Parenetic Intent in Isaiah 31," in D. 'Assaf, ed., *Proceedings of the Eleventh World Congress of Jewish Studies: Division A. The Bible and Its World* (Jerusalem: World Union of Jewish Studies, 1994) 99–106.

Vermeylen, *Du prophète Isaïe,* esp. 1:420–24.
Wong, G. C. I., "Isaiah's Opposition to Egypt in Isaiah XXXI 1-3," *VT* 46 (1996) 392–401.
Wonsuk, Ma., "The Spirit (*Ruah*) of God in Isaiah 1–39," *AJT* 3 (1989) 582–96.

32

Whatever the original historical setting in which the oracle in Isa 32:1-8 was spoken, it fits well in its present literary context following the judgment on Jerusalem, the divine destruction of Assyria, and deliverance of Jerusalem in Isa 31:1-9. Isaiah urged Judah's Davidic rulers to avoid such judgment, not by frantic, fear-inspired, deceitful and oppressive political and military policies, but by trusting in God's promises to David and Jerusalem (7:9; 8:12-14). Such faith would allow Judah's kings to concentrate instead on their task of providing internal justice and easing the suffering of the poor (28:12; 30:15). When the kings failed to respond in this fashion and the threatened refining judgment came upon Judah (1:24-26), Isaiah tended to attribute the last-minute deliverance of Jerusalem to the intervention of Yahweh alone (29:5-8; 31:8-9). But the prophet assigned a more active role to the king and his officials in the following age of salvation (1:26; 11:3-4; 32:1-2).

Many critics regard this passage as secondary, though the arguments against Isaianic authorship are not very impressive. Wildberger, while admitting the weakness of these arguments, nonetheless rejects the passage on the basis that "for Isaiah the שרים would hardly have had a place next to the Davidide in such a vision of the future" (3:1253). Yet this judgment flies in the face of the clearly Isaianic 1:26, where Yahweh, following his refining judgment on Zion, promises to restore her judges and counselors as at the beginning. Isaiah's vision of the future included a place for royal officials, and it is not surprising to find them mentioned here.[1] Clements argues that 32:1 does not foretell the advent of the king who rules justly but simply describes him as a present figure (p. 259),

but against him one must insist that vv. 1-5 are all clearly construed in the future. Moreover, the oracle is placed in a context where it follows Yahweh's deliverance of Zion, just as 11:1 follows Yahweh's destruction of Zion's enemies.[2] The oracle may originally have been independent of its present context, but it had a context, and I see no reason to fault the ancient editor, who apparently understood the oracle to refer to the era of salvation after Yahweh will have destroyed Assyria.

Hans-Jürgen Hermisson, who accepts 32:1-2 as genuine, rejects vv. 3-5, since these verses deal with the altered nature of humans or particular human types in the age of salvation. He cannot see any connection between a change in human nature and the coming kingdom.[3] Wildberger similarly claims that Isaiah envisioned a particular political-social action of Yahweh, not the creation of a new humanity (3:1252). Both of them miss the point. In his critique of his contemporaries, Isaiah had blamed the leaders for misleading the people (3:12). The political and religious leadership were largely responsible for Judah's blindness, deafness, and folly.[4] The promise is that when the leaders rule justly, these defects will fall aside. It is precisely the political-social establishment of just government that will lead to a transformation of society. This is not an individualistic vision of a transformed humanity but a vision of transformed society!

---

1 See Hans-Jürgen Hermisson, "Zukunftserwartung und Gegenwartskritik in der Verkündigung Jesajas," *EvT* 33 (1973) 67; J. Skinner, *Isaiah* (Cambridge Bible for Schools and Colleges; Cambridge: Cambridge University Press, 1925) 255; Bernhard Duhm, *Das Buch Jesaia* (HKAT 3.1; Göttingen: Vandenhoeck & Ruprecht, 1892) 210–11.

2 Isaiah 31:9 contains the fire imagery so dear to Isaiah for describing Yahweh's deliverance through judgment that leads to a renewed community (cf. 1:25-26; 10:17; 30:33; 33:10-14).

3 Hermisson, "Verkündigung Jesajas," 57 n. 12.

4 Their refusal to look to the Holy One of Israel (5:12; 22:11), their desire not even to hear of him

(30:9-11), ultimately led to the loss of their wisdom (29:9-14). Precisely what the "tongue of the stammerers" refers to is not clear. The word "stammerers" (עִלְּגִים, *ʿillĕgîm*, 32:4) occurs nowhere else in the OT. The closest parallels are in the expressions בְּלַעֲגֵי שָׂפָה (*bĕlaʿăgê śāpâ*, "by those of strange lips," Isa 28:11), and נִלְעַג לָשׁוֹן אֵין בִּינָה (*nilʿag lāšôn ʾên bînâ*, "who stammer in a tongue you cannot understand," Isa 33:19). The two roots עלג and לעג may in fact be the same root with a simple metathesis, which would be quite appropriate in a root meaning "to stammer." In 32:4, however, the stammerer is not a foreigner but a Judean.

1/   See,[a] a king will reign[b] in righteousness,
    And even royal officials[c] will govern in justice.
2/   Everyone of them will be like a refuge[d] from the wind,
    And a shelter[e] from the rainstorm,
    Like streams of water in a dry land,[f]
    Like the shade[g] of a massive rock in a weary land.
3/   Then the eyes of those who see will not be closed,[h]
    And the ears of those who hear[i] will listen attentively,
4/   The heart of the thoughtless will attain understanding,
    And the tongue of the stammerers will speak clearly.[j]
5/   No[k] longer will the fool be called[l] noble,
    Nor[k] will "gentleman" be said[m] of a knave.[n]
6/   For the fool speaks folly,
    And his mind plots treachery:[o]
    To act impiously,
    And to advocate disloyalty against Yahweh.
    To leave the craving of the hungry unsatisfied
    And deprive the thirsty of drink.
7/   As for the knave,[p] his weapons are evil.
    He[q] devises wicked schemes
    To destroy the poor[r] with lies
    Even when the needy[s] speaks what is just.
8/   But the noble plans noble actions,
    And he is constant in noble deeds.

Textual Notes

a   MT הֵן (hēn), "behold, see!"; 1QIsaᵃ has the longer form הנה.

b   MT יִמְלֹךְ (yimlok), "will reign"; 1QIsaᵃ ימלוך.

c   MT supported by 1QIsaᵃ וּלְשָׂרִים (ûlĕśārîm), "and even royal officials." The versions ignore the lamed, but see the commentary ahead.

d   MT כְּמַחֲבֵא (kĕmaḥăbēʾ), "like a refuge, hiding place"; 1QIsaᵃ has the same word with a different spelling כמחבה. Apart from Syr., all the versions misunderstood this form as a participle and garbled the rest of the verse as a consequence. LXX, for example, has καὶ ἔσται ὁ ἄνθρωπος κρύπτων τοὺς λόγους αὐτοῦ καὶ κρυβήσεται ὡς ἀφʼ ὕδατος φερομένου· καὶ φανήσεται ἐν Σιων ὡς ποταμὸς φερόμενος ἔνδοξος ἐν γῇ διψώσῃ, "and the man shall be hiding his words and he shall be hidden as though from rushing water. And he shall appear in Zion as a rushing river glorious in a thirsty land."

e   MT וְסֵתֶר זָרֶם (wĕsēter zārem), "and a shelter from the rainstorm"; 1QIsaᵃ has וסתרם זרם, though the final ם on וסתר is marked as erased. It probably originated as a preposition on the following word מזרם וסתר, "and a shelter from the rainstorm," to make explicit the meaning of the adverbial accusative in MT.

f   MT בְּצָיוֹן (bĕṣāyôn), "in a dry land"; 1QIsaᵃ בציין. LXX supports MT's spelling by its misunderstanding of the form as "in Zion."

g   MT כְּצֵל (kĕṣēl), "like the shade"; 1QIsaᵃ's בצל (bĕṣēl), "in the shade," is an easy but obvious error.

h   MT וְלֹא תִשְׁעֶינָה (wĕlōʾ tišʿênâ). If the form is analyzed as the qal imperfect from שעה (šʿh), it would mean, "the eyes that look will not behold," which makes no sense with the following parallel clauses that speak of the healing of defective hearing, understanding, and stammering speech (vv. 3-4). Most critics analyze the form as either a qal or a hophal of שעע (šʿʿ), properly תְּשֹׁעֵינָה (tĕšōʿênâ) or תֻּשֹׁעֵינָה (tušoʿênâ), with the meaning, "the eyes that look will not be blinded"; 1QIsaᵃ ולוא תשעינה. LXX garbles this line: καὶ οὐκέτι ἔσονται πεποιθότες ἐπʼ ἀνθρώποις, "and they will no longer trust upon men."

i   MT שֹׁמְעִים (šōmĕʿîm), "who hear"; 1QIsaᵃ שומעים.

j   MT צָחוֹת (ṣāḥôt), "clearly"; 1QIsaᵃ צוחות.

k   MT לֹא (lōʾ), "no"; 1QIsaᵃ לוא.

l   MT יִקָּרֵא (yiqqārēʾ), "will be called," niphal imperfect third person masculine singular; 1QIsaᵃ יקראו, which in this context must be: "will they call," qal imperfect third person masculine plural.

m   MT יֵאָמֵר (yēʾāmēr), "will be said," niphal imperfect third person masculine singular; 1QIsaᵃ יומר, "one will say," qal imperfect third person masculine singular.

n   For this last line LXX has the odd reading καὶ οὐκέτι μὴ εἴπωσιν οἱ ὑπηρέται σου Σίγα, "and no longer will your servants say, 'Silence!'"

o   Reading with 1QIsaᵃ אוון חושב (hôšēb ʾāwen), "his heart plots treachery"; MT has יַעֲשֶׂה־אָוֶן (yaʿăśê-ʾāwen), "his heart does treachery," but that is an ineloquent repetition of the same verb with the following חֹנֶף לַעֲשׂוֹת (laʿăśôt ḥōnep), "to do impiety, act impiously."

p   MT וְכֵלַי (wĕkēlay), "knave"; 1QIsaᵃ וכילי.

q   MT הוּא (hûʾ), "he"; 1QIsaᵃ והוא, "and he."

r   MT kĕtîb עֲנָוִים (ʿănāwîm), "the poor"; qĕrēʾ עֲנִיִּים (ʿănîyîm), "the poor"; 1QIsaᵃ עניים.

s   MT אֶבְיוֹן (ʾebyôn), "the needy one"; 1QIsaᵃ אביונים, "the needy ones."

Commentary

The oracle begins with the shortened form of the interjection or demonstrative adverb to call attention to the new situation that God's deliverance will bring about. In contrast to the foolish, misleading rule of the past (Isa 3:12), in the age of salvation the king will rule righteously and the royal officials will officiate justly. For the meaning of the idiom לְצֶדֶק (lĕṣedeq), "in righteousness, righteously," and לְמִשְׁפָּט (lĕmišpāṭ), "in justice, justly," see Isa 11:3; 28:26; 42:3; Jer 9:2; 15:15; 30:11 (= 46:28; לַמִּשְׁפָּט, lammišpāṭ here is synonymous with בְּמִשְׁפָּט, bĕmišpāṭ, "in justice," in Jer 10:24); Hos 10:12; Joel 2:23. BDB and many commentators, following the lead of the ancient versions, omit the preposition לְ on וּלְשָׂרִים (ûlsārîm) assuming it is an error introduced by the preposition לְ on the following לְמִשְׁפָּט (lĕmišpāṭ), "justly," but I take it as the emphatic *lamed* well known in Ugaritic,[5] "even the royal officials will officiate justly." In monarchical systems of government, it is fairly common to assume that if one could just get past the corrupt royal bureaucrats to the person of the king himself, one would see justice done. That is why the Judean king swore to remove such arrogant and corrupt officials from his administration (Ps 101:4-7), and that is one reason why Isaiah's critique of the royal administration focuses more on royal officials than on the figure of the king (Isa 1:23; 3:2-4, 12-14; 7:13; 10:1-2; 28:7, 14; 29:15; 30:1-2; 31:1). Another possible reason, particularly in the case of Hezekiah, was that the prophet did not want to so alienate the king by the sharpness of his criticism that the king would be reluctant to accept the prophet's advice, even later when the policy promoted by the king's royal advisors was exposed by the unfolding course of events as the folly Isaiah had declared it to be.

Verse 2 then illustrates what righteous and just rule means. Each of these royal officials, from the king on down, will be for the needy and oppressed like a refuge from the wind and a shelter from the rainstorm, like streams of water in a dry land and like the shade of a great rock in a weary land. The imagery here is borrowed from the imagery used of God as a protector and shelter in trouble, as a source of life-giving water or of the shade that renews the hot and weary traveler in a sun-parched landscape. Much of the same imagery and identical or synonymous vocabulary are used of God in Isa 25:5 (see also Isa 4:5-6). Yahweh provides shelter (סֵתֶר, sēter) for his worshipers (Pss 27:5; 31:21; 32:7; 61:5; 81:8; 91:1; 119:114). He supplies his faithful with life-giving waters (Pss 1:3; 46:5; 65:10) or is their life-giving water (Jer 2:13). People find shelter in God's shade (Pss 17:8; 36:8; 57:2; 63:8; 91:1; 121:5). Yahweh is a rock (סֶלַע, selaʿ) for his servants (Pss 18:3; 31:4; 42:10; 71:3; 78:16). In other words, the king and his officials participate in the work of God. It is God's justice and righteousness that the king and his officials carry out (see Ps 72:1-2), thereby participating by God's gift in God's work of keeping the powers of chaos at bay (see Ps 89:26).

As a result of this righteous rule (v. 3), the eyes that once looked without seeing (Isa 6:9), that were blinded and intentionally kept from seeing by government policy (29:9-10; 30:10), would now be uncovered and see clearly. The ears that once heard without understanding (6:9), who did not want to hear (28:12; 30:9), would now listen attentively and learn from the experience. The heart of those who reacted impetuously without thought would now gain understanding (v. 4); and the tongue of the incoherent stammerers would now be able to articulate their thoughts clearly. Once the leadership embodied, enforced, and articulated a just and clear moral vision, the rest of society would own and embrace it.

When that happens, the hypocrisy of calling a fool noble, or of addressing a scoundrel or knave as a gentleman, one of the elite of the society,[6] will cease (v. 5). The thought is similar to Isaiah's earlier complaint (5:20) that his audience called evil good and good evil, pretended that dark is light and light is dark, and labeled bitter as sweet and sweet as bitter. The point is that the reformed society will judge and evaluate its members on a moral basis, not by their sheer wealth, power, or influence,

---

5   Another attractive possibility suggested to me by my editor, Peter Machinist, is to take the *lamed* here simply as a kind of ethical dative: "And as for the royal officials, they will govern in justice."

6   The word שׁוֹעַ (šôaʿ) is very rare, but the parallelism here and in Job 34:18-19 makes clear that it is an honorific term given to a rich, prominent person.

but by how well they embody the divine righteousness undergirding the society. Crooked judges and corrupt royal officials will be named for what they really are, not flattered and pandered to by fearful and obsequious seekers of favors.

Verse 6 explains that the fool speaks folly, and his heart or mind plots treachery (see the textual notes). Folly (נְבָלָה, *nĕbālâ*) in the biblical tradition is not just intellectually foolish behavior but morally wrong behavior (Gen 34:7; Deut 22:21; Josh 7:15; Judg 19:23-24; 2 Sam 13:12; Isa 9:16). The fool acts impiously and advocates disloyalty to Yahweh, and such plotting, talk, and actions find concrete expression in depriving the hungry of food and the thirsty of drink. In the context of the prophet's oracle, these fools are clearly among the nobility, who by their position and wealth were able to alleviate the suffering of the poor (see Isa 28:12; 30:15).

Then v. 7 gives a similar exposition of the behavior of the knave. There is an obvious wordplay and probably a double entendre between the word for knave (כִּילַי, *kîlay* [v. 5] or כֵּלַי, *kēlay* [v. 7]—the etymology of the word

is unknown) and כֵּלָיו (*kēlāyw*, which could be analyzed either as "his weapons" from כְּלִי, *kĕlî*, "weapon, utensil," or as the suffixed abstract plural of *kîlay* or *kēlay*, "his knaveries, his acts of knavery"). The knave's knaveries/weapons are evil. Like the fool, he devises wicked schemes to hurt the poor and needy, and he does it by perverting justice with lies in a judicial setting even when the needy is speaking the truth, and an impartial judge would acknowledge that the needy is in the right (cf. Isa 1:16-17; 3:14-15; 5:23; 10:1-2).

In contrast, the true noble plans noble actions (v. 8). The prophet does not here further define what noble actions are, but vv. 1-2 have already indicated their general character, and they are obviously the opposite of the actions of the fool and knave spelled out in vv. 6-7. Another double entendre occurs at the end of the verse. The expression וְהוּא עַל־נְדִיבוֹת יָקוּם (*wĕhûʾ ʿal-nĕdîbôt yāqûm*) could be rendered either, "and he is constant in noble deeds," or "and he will stand/remain because of noble deeds." Isaiah probably meant both.

Bibliography

Barth, *Die Jesaja-Worte*, 211–15.

Becker, Joachim, *Messiaserwartung im Alten Testament* (SBS 83; Stuttgart: Katholisches Bibelwerk, 1977; Eng. trans. *Messianic Expectation in the Old Testament* (trans. D. E. Green; Philadelphia: Fortress Press, 1980).

Fichtner, J., "Jesaja unter den Weisen," *TLZ* 74 (1949) 75–80.

Gerleman, G., "Der Nicht-Mensch: Erwägungen zur hebräischen Wurzel *nbl*," *VT* 24 (1974) 147–58.

Gosse, B., "Isaïe 28–32 et la rédaction d'ensemble du livre d'Isaïe," *JSOT* 9 (1995) 75–82.

Har-El, M., "נופי מדבר בנבואת ישעיהו," *BetM* 29 (1966) 79–82.

Hermission, Hans-Jürgen, "Zukunftserwartung und Gegenwartskritik," *EvT* 33 (1973) 54–77, esp. 67.

Hertzberg, Hans Wilhelm, "Die Nachgeschichte alttestamentlicher Texte innerhalb des Alten Testaments," in Hertzberg, *Beiträge zur Traditionsgeschichte und Theologie des Alten Testaments* (Göttingen: Vandenhoeck & Ruprecht, 1962) 69–80.

Irwin, W. H., *Isaiah 28–33*.

——, "Conflicting Parallelism in Job 5:13; Isa 30:28; Isa 2:7," *Bib* 76 (1995) 72–74.

Labuschagne, C. J., "The Particles הֵן and הִנֵּה," in Labuschagne et al., *Syntax and Meaning: Studies in Hebrew Syntax and Biblical Exegesis* (OtSt 18; Leiden: Brill, 1973) 1–14.

Olley, J. W., "Notes on Isaiah xxxii 1, xlv 19,23, and lxiii 1," *VT* 33 (1983) 446–53.

Roberts, J. J. M., "Bearers of the Polity: Isaiah of Jerusalem's View of the Eighth-Century Judean Society," in J. T. Strong and S. T. Tuell, eds., *Constituting the Community: Studies on the Polity of Ancient Israel in Honor of S. Dean McBride* (Winona Lake, IN: Eisenbrauns, 2005) 145–52.

——, "The Divine King and the Human Community in Isaiah's Vision of the Future," in F. A. Spina, H. B. Huffmon, and A. R. W. Green, eds., *The Quest for the Kingdom of God: Studies in Honor of George E. Mendenhall* (Winona Lake, IN: Eisenbrauns, 1983) 127–36.

——, "Isaiah, National Security."

Sklba, R. J., "Until the Spirit from on High Is Poured Out on Us (Is 32:15): Reflections on the Role of the Spirit in the Exile," *CBQ* 46 (1984) 1–17.

Stade, B., "Jes. 32.33," *ZAW* 4 (1884) 256–71.

Stansell, Gary, "Isaiah 32."

——, *Micah and Isaiah: A Form and Tradition Historical Comparison* (*SBLDS* 85; Atlanta: Scholars Press, 1988) 62–63.

Thompson, M. E. W., "Israel's Ideal King," *JSOT* 24 (1982) 79–88.

Waschke, E.-J., "Die Stellung der Königstexte im Jesajabuch im Vergleich zu den Königspsalmen 2, 72 und 89," *ZAW* 110 (1998) 358–60.

Wegner, Paul D., *An Examination of Kingship and Messianic Expectation in Isaiah 1–35* (Lewiston, NY: Mellen Biblical Press, 1992) 275–300.

Whedbee, *Isaiah and Wisdom*.

Williamson, H. G. M., "Isaiah and the Wise."

——, "The Messianic Texts in Isaiah 1–39," in John Day, ed., *King and Messiah in Israel and the Ancient Near East: Proceedings of the Oxford Old Testament Seminar* (JSOTSup 270; Sheffield: Sheffield Academic Press, 1998) 264–70.

The oracle addressed to the carefree women (vv. 9-12) continues with a judgment on the land (vv. 13-14) and then a reversal of that judgment by God's deliverance (vv. 15-20). The address to the carefree women is similar to the prophet's condemnation of the prominent women of Zion in 3:16—4:1, so the present verses are normally regarded as genuine and are attributed to Isaiah of Jerusalem.[1] In vv. 10 and 12 the judgment on these women affects the vintage and the pleasant fields, a thought that is expanded and continued in vv. 13-14, so there is little justification for separating these verses from the oracle against the women or for attributing them to a later editor. The date and authorship of vv. 15-18 are more problematic, but, whatever the actual date of these verses—and any specific later date is just as problematic as an eighth-century date—they appear to have been composed as a reversing word of hope in response to the word of judgment of the preceding verses. For that reason, despite the uncertainty of date and authorship, I interpret these verses as the conclusion of the preceding oracle. Verses 19-20, however, appear to be a later addendum to the text, inserting another word of judgment following the promises of vv. 15-18.

9/   You carefree[a] women,
              Rise up![b] Hear my voice!
              You confident[c] daughters,
              Listen[d] to my word!

10/   In little more than a year
              You confident (daughters)[e] will become agitated,
              Because the vintage will fail,
              The ingathering will not[f] come.

11/   Tremble, you carefree (women);[g]
              Be agitated, you confident (daughters);[h]
              Strip and make yourself naked;[i]
              And gird (sackcloth) upon the loins.[j]

12/   And beat[k] upon the breasts,
              Lamenting[l] over the pleasant fields,[m]
              Over the fruitful vine,

13/   Over the land of my people,
              which is growing up in thorns and briars,[n]
              Yes,[o] over all[p] the joyous houses
              In the exultant city.

14/   For the palace will be abandoned,
              The noisy city forsaken,
              The acropolis and tower[q] will become
              Cleared fields[r] forever:
              The joy of wild asses,
              Pasture for the flocks.[s]

15/   Until there is poured out upon us a spirit from on high,
              And the wilderness will become a fertile field,
              And Mount Carmel/the fertile field[t] will be considered a forest.

16/   And justice will dwell in the wilderness,
              and righteousness will live in the fertile field.

17/   And the product of righteousness[u] will be peace,
              And the produce[w] of righteousness will be undisturbed quiet and confidence for ever,

18/   And my people[x] will live in a pasture of peace,
              And in secure dwellings,
              And in carefree resting places.[y]

---

1   So Duhm, 210–11; Wildberger admits that the majority of present scholars assume it is Isaianic, though he dates it later (3:1265–67); and Clements (261–62), though he follows Wildberger, lists Georg Fohrer and Antoon Schoors as prominent scholars arguing for its Isaianic authorship.

19/ But the forest will come down completely,[z]
And the city*[a] will be completely laid low.
20/ Blessed are you*[b] who sow*[c] beside all*[d] waters,
Who send out*[e] the foot of the ox and the donkey.

Textual Notes

a   MT שַׁאֲנַנּוֹת (šaʾănannôt), "carefree"; 1QIsaᵃ שי*נות. LXX, Vg.,
and Syr. render as "rich/wealthy women."

b   MT קֹמְנָה (qōmnâ), "rise!"; 1QIsaᵃ קומנה.

c   MT בֹּטְחוֹת (bōṭĕḥôt), "confident"; 1QIsaᵃ בוטחות.

d   MT הַאֲזֵנָּה (haʾăzēnnâ), "listen!; 1QIsaᵃ האזינה.

e   MT בֹּטְחוֹת (bōṭĕḥôt), "confident"; 1QIsaᵃ adds the article
הבוטחות. LXX has an odd translation of the first two lines,
ἡμέρας ἐνιαυτοῦ μνείαν ποιήσασθε ἐν ὀδύνῃ μετ' ἐλπίδος, "make
mention of the days of the year in pain with hope."

f   MT בְּלִי (bĕlî), "not"; 1QIsaᵃ בל.

g   MT חִרְדוּ שַׁאֲנַנּוֹת (ḥirdû šaʾănannôt), "tremble, you carefree
women," supported by 1QIsaᵃ has a masculine plural imperative followed by a feminine adjective, but the rest of the imperatives in the verse are all feminine plural. Classical Hebrew has
a tendency to prefer masculine forms because of the male-
dominated culture, but the masculine plural form here is probably a mistake introduced in the transmission of the text, since
otherwise the text, apart from one mistake in 1QIsaᵃ (see note i
below), is consistent in using feminine plural imperatives. In its
translation, LXX omits שַׁאֲנַנּוֹת, which it translated as πλούσιαι,
"rich," in v. 9.

h   See note c above.

i   MT וְעֹרָה (wĕʿōrâ), "and make yourself naked"; 1QIsaᵃ's יערו, a
qal imperfect third person masculine plural, is clearly an error.

j   MT וַחֲגוֹרָה עַל־חֲלָצִים (waḥăgôrâ ʿal-ḥălāṣāyim), "and gird upon
the loins"; 1QIsaᵃ חגרנה וספדנה על החלצים, "gird and beat (the
breasts in mourning) upon the loins." 1QIsaᵃ's additional
imperative וספדנה obviously interrupts the natural connection
between חגרנה, "gird," and על החלצים, "upon the loins," and
thus must be misplaced. The object of the verb "gird" is not
expressed, but in the context of mourning it must be "sackcloth," and LXX adds that word in its translation: περιζώσασθε
σάκκους τὰς ὀσφύας, "gird the loins with sackcloth."

k   I restore the first two lines of this verse as:

וספדנה על שדים
ספדים על שדי חמד

The repetition of imperatives followed by the preposition ʿal, "upon," combined with the play on words between
שדים (šādayim), "breasts," and שדי (śĕdê), "fields," created an
ideal situation for haplography. In most Hebrew manuscripts
וספדנה was simply lost, but in 1QIsaᵃ or its *Vorlage* it was preserved by its vertical displacement to the preceding verse. Once
the imperative was lost, then the following masculine plural

participle of the same verb had to be read as the subject of the
first line, though the shift to the masculine, particularly with
the object of the preposition being breasts following a series of
feminine imperatives, is quite awkward. The shift to the masculine is not so awkward, if the masculine participle governs the
following "over the pleasant fields," since the men would also
be mourning over the loss of the crops.

l   MT סֹפְדִים (sōpĕdîm), "lamenting," and 1QIsaᵃ סופדים, both have
the masculine plural participle, which is either a mistake similar to the masculine plural imperative חִרְדוּ (ḥirdû), "tremble,"
in v. 11, or it is an intentional transition to include the whole
community, "As men/all lament over the pleasant fields."
From this point on neither the feminine plural nouns nor the
feminine plural verb forms recur.

m   MT עַל־שְׂדֵי־חֶמֶד (ʿal-śĕdê-ḥemed), "over the pleasant fields";
1QIsaᵃ על שדי חמדה.

n   MT קוֹץ שָׁמִיר (qôṣ šāmîr), "thorns [and] briars"; 1QIsaᵃ קוץ ושמיר.

o   The כִּי is the emphatic kî (see *HALOT*, 470).

p   MT כָּל (kol), "all"; 1QIsaᵃ כול.

q   MT עֹפֶל וָבַחַן (ʿopel wābaḥan), "acropolis and tower"; 1QIsaᵃ עופל
ובחן. The versions had difficulty with this phrase. LXX split the
phrase in two, taking the first word with the preceding verb
as οἶκους ἐπιθυμητούς, "desirable houses," and the second
with the following verb as αἱ κῶμαι, "the villages." Vg. took
the phrase as *tenebrae et palpatio*, "darkness and terror." The
Hebrew apparently understood the pair ʿopel wābaḥan as a kind
of hendiadys, considered as a single subject, since it construes
it with the singular verb הָיָה.

r   MT בְּעַד מְעָרוֹת (bĕʿad mĕʿārôt) supported by 1QIsaᵃ is a crux.
The function of the preposition bĕʿad, which normally means
"behind," "through," "out of," "round about," or "for the
benefit of," is unclear here, and many scholars suggest deleting
it.[2] LXX, Vg., and Syr. take the noun mĕʿārôt in the well-known
sense of "caves, dens," but "caves" would hardly be the choice
site for wild asses. Thus, G. R. Driver ("Hebrew Notes," 52)
suggested a מערה II (mĕʿārâ), "cleared field, bare space," a feminine counterpart of maʿărê or maʿar, "bare, naked place," from
the root ערה, "to be naked, bare."

s   MT מִרְעֵה עֲדָרִים (mirʿēh ʿădārîm), "pasture of the flock"; 1QIsaᵃ
מרעה לעדרים, "pasture for the flock." Some scholars (Driver,
"Hebrew Notes," 52; *BHS*) have suggested the emendation
of ʿădārîm to ʿărôdîm or ʿărādîm, a synonym for wild asses, the
singular of which is used in parallel with פרא (pereʾ), "wild ass,"
in Job 39:5.

---

2   So Wildberger (3:1264), who thinks it was added as a
misplaced parallel to עַד־עוֹלָם, "forever."

t   MT *kětîb* and 1QIsaᵃ וְכַרְמֶל (*wěkarmel*), "and a fertile field"; MT *qěrēʾ* והכרמל (*wěhakkarmel*), "and Carmel," or "and *the* fertile field." The versions take all the occurrences of *karmel* in vv. 15-16 as the proper name for Mount Carmel. The wordplay on the two meanings in Isa 29:17 might suggest a similar wordplay here.

u   The repetition of הַצְּדָקָה (*haṣṣědāqâ*), "righteousness," in the two parallel lines is not elegant and might suggest the emendation of the first occurrence to מַעֲשֵׂה הַמִּשְׁפָּט (*maʿăśēh hammišpāṭ*), "the product of justice," but all the versions support MT, so if a corruption occurred, it was very early.

v   MT שָׁלוֹם (*šālôm*), "peace," supported by the versions; 1QIsaᵃ לשלום, "for peace."

w   MT וַעֲבֹדַת (*waʿăbōdat*), "and the work of, the produce of"; 1QIsaᵃ ועבודת.

x   LXX is alone in having "his people."

y   MT וּבִמְנוּחֹת (*ûbimnûḥōt*), "and in resting places,"; 1QIsaᵃ ובמנוחות.

z   Reading וירד ברדת היער (*wěyārad běredet hayyāʿar*), "and the forest will come down in coming down," that is, "will come down completely" // ובשפלה תשפל העיר (*ûbaššiplâ tišpal hāʿîr*), "and in the lowness the city will be laid low," that is, "will be completely laid low." Syr. and Tg. may give some support to this emendation, but the strongest argument in its favor is the parallelism. MT, with the support of 1QIsaᵃ, actually reads וּבָרַד בְּרֶדֶת הַיַּעַר (*ûbārad běredet hayyāʿar*), "and it will hail when the forest comes down," but that creates an odd parallelism, and it would be the only occurrence of the verb *bārad*, "to hail," in the OT. LXX and Vg. support MT's reading, but LXX's translation is otherwise so remote from MT as to be useless: ἡ δὲ χάλαζα ἐὰν καταβῇ, οὐκ ἐφ᾽ ὑμᾶς ἥξει. καὶ ἔσονται οἱ ἐνοικοῦντες ἐν τοῖς δρυμοῖς πεποιθότες ὡς οἱ ἐν τῇ πεδιανῇ, "and the hail, if it falls, will not come upon you; and those who dwell in the woods will be confident just as those in the plain."

*a For MT's הָעִיר (*hāʿîr*), "the city," 1QIsaᵃ repeats the earlier היער, "forest," but this is clearly a mistake.

*b MT אַשְׁרֵכֶם (*ʾašrêkem*), "blessed are you"; 1QIsaᵃ אשריכמה.

*c MT זֹרְעֵי (*zōrěʿê*), "those who sow"; 1QIsaᵃ זורעי.

*d MT כָּל (*kol*), "all"; 1QIsaᵃ כול.

*e MT מְשַׁלְּחֵי (*měšallěḥê*), "who send out"; 1QIsaᵃ ומשלחי, "and who send out."

Commentary

In v. 9 the prophet addresses the carefree women and the confident daughters with feminine plural imperatives, commanding them to stand still and hear his voice and listen to his word. The carefree women (נָשִׁים שַׁאֲנַנּוֹת, *nāšîm šaʾănannôt*) and the confident daughters (בָּנוֹת בֹּטְחוֹת, *bānôt bōṭěḥôt*) refer to those Judean women, probably primarily resident in Jerusalem, who were so at ease and comfortable in their wealth and position that they had no worries about the health of the nation as a whole. The same parallelism of שאן and בטח is found in Amos 6:1 to address the wealthy, indolent, and self-indulgent ruling class of Samaria[3] who were not concerned about the destruction of Joseph (Amos 6:6). Isaiah may have known the Amos prophecy. In any case, he is attacking the same selfish unconcern of the ruling class for the welfare of the rest of the nation, and, curiously enough, for their own long-term well-being.

In little more than a year (יָמִים עַל־שָׁנָה, *yāmîm ʿal-šānâ*, "a few days more than a year"—for the idiom, see BDB 755, 4b), these confident women will be agitated, because the vintage will fail and no ingathering will take place (v. 10). From the verses that follow, it seems clear that this failure will be caused not by drought or crop disease but by the presence of an invading army that will cut off access to the fields. This suggests that this oracle was spoken shortly before Sennacherib's campaign against Judah, when the nobility was still optimistic of their chances of turning back any serious Assyrian threat. Thus, it would fit within the same general time frame as most of Isaiah 28–33, which dates between the death of Sargon II in 705 and shortly after the end of Sennacherib's campaign in 701 BCE. Isaiah did not share his leaders' confidence, and he warns the confident women to prepare to experience quite different emotions and a quite different style of life.

Tremble (see the textual note) and be agitated, he commands them (v. 11). "Strip off your clothes, make

---

3   The phrase בְּצִיּוֹן (*běṣîyôn*), "in Zion," in Amos 6:1 may be a later, secondary correction from בַּבִּצָּרוֹן (*babbiṣṣārôn*), "in the fortress"; see W. Rudolph, *Joel–Amos–Obadja–Jona* (KAT 13.2; Gütersloh: Gerd Mohn, 1971) 215. For a full treatment of the passage—though at that time a less positive evaluation of the emendation—see my "Amos 6.1-7," in J. T. Butler, E. W. Conrad, and B. C. Ollenburger, eds., *Understanding the Word: Essays in Honor of Bernhard W. Anderson* (JSOTSup 37; Sheffield: JSOT Press, 1985) 155–66.

yourselves naked, and then gird sackcloth on your naked loins!" he orders. These, of course, are precisely the actions the women would be expected to have taken as a sign of mourning and repentance, when such a disaster overtook the nation and clearly threatened even the wealthy's own security.

Following the textual correction, the prophet commands the women to beat upon their breasts (וּסְפֹדְנָה עַל־שָׁדַיִם, ûsĕpōdnâ ʿal-šādayim), while men and women alike mourn over the pleasant fields (סֹפְדִים עַל־שְׂדֵי־חֶמֶד, sōpĕdîm ʿal-śĕdê-ḥemed), over the fruitful vine. Beating upon one's breasts was apparently a gesture of mourning for wailing women (see Pritchard, *ANEP*, 459), and both LXX καὶ ἐπὶ τῶν μαστῶν κόπτεσθε, "and beat upon (your) breasts," and Vg. *super ubera plangite*, "beat upon (your) breasts," render with verbs that can mean both "beat" and "mourn." Because this is the only occurrence of the idiom sāpad ʿal-šādayim, "beat/mourn upon the breasts," in the OT, many critics deny this meaning to the verb and emend the noun to a form of śāde, "field" (so Wildberger, 3:1263; cf. BDB, 704), but all the ancient versions read šādayim, "breasts." Whether "beat" was a primary meaning of the verb sāpad or a secondary meaning derived from a characteristic gesture of mourning or wailing women is irrelevant; it seems to be the meaning of the verb here and allows the prophet to make an elaborate artistic play on words between the primary and secondary meaning of the verb sāpad, and between the similar sounding al-šādayim, "upon the breasts," and al-śĕdê, "upon the fields." The mourning over the fields and vines is because the besieged Judeans will only be able to look from the walls of their besieged cities at their abandoned and unharvested fields and vineyards as they go to waste or are devoured by their enemies.

The lamentation will be over the land of God's people because, left untended, it will grow up in thorns and thistles (v. 13). But the lamentation will also be over the joyous houses in the exultant city. The deprivation caused by the Assyrian campaign in Judah would not be limited to the devastation of the countryside and the resulting shortages of food and loss of income. The cities and their great houses would also be affected.

Isaiah threatens that the palace will be abandoned, the noisy city forsaken; the acropolis and tower, he says, will become bare fields forever: the joy of wild asses and pasture for the flocks (v. 14). It is unclear whether the prophet is speaking specifically of Jerusalem or of Judean cities in general. Such a fate did not befall Jerusalem in 701 BCE, but it did befall many of the great walled cities of Judah. Sennacherib claims to have captured and destroyed forty-six Judean walled cities, among them the great government center at Lachish. Though Jerusalem survived, the devastation of Judah was so great it seems dubious that many of Isaiah's contemporaries in the immediate aftermath of the disaster would have dismissed the prophet's word as false prophecy.

Verse 15 suggests that this situation of desolation will last until God intervenes—until a spirit is poured upon us from above. The choice of the verb ערה (ʿārâ, "to expose oneself," in the *niphal*, "to be poured out") is probably due to the resulting assonance with מְעָרוֹת (mĕʿārôt), "cleared fields," and מִרְעֶה (mirʿēh), "pasturage," in v. 14. One should also note the similarity in sound between עֲדָרִים (ʿădārîm), "flocks," and עַד־יֵעָרֶה (ʿad-yēʿāreh), "until there be poured out." In Isaiah, a spirit (רוּחַ, rûaḥ) from God may be poured upon someone for either ill (19:3, 14; 29:10) or positive effect (11:2; 28:6), but here it appears to be positive. When this pouring out of the spirit happens, the wilderness will become fertile farmland, and the fertile farmland (or perhaps Mount Carmel) will become a forest. It is unclear whether the second occurrence of the word refers to fertile farmland or to the specific geographical site of Mount Carmel, or both at the same time corresponding to the variation in Isa 29:17. In Isa 32:15, the transformation of Judah's desert or wilderness (מדבר, midbār) into orchard land (כרמל, karmel) would obviously be positive, but the transformation of its orchard land into forest is not so obviously positive, though the transformation of Mount Carmel into forest land, thus providing an ample supply of wood, might be so regarded. In Isaiah, however, such agricultural and arboreal imagery is often used to refer to the decrease or increase of human population rather than to the agricultural produce that supports them (6:13; 9:17-18; 10:18-19, 33-34; 17:5-6; 37:31). Nonetheless, the figure, despite its difficulties, seems to suggest a renewal of fertility and abundance for the population of the land of Judah following the widespread destruction and devastation of Sennacherib's campaign against Hezekiah.

Justice will dwell in the former wilderness, and righteousness will live in the former orchard land or Mount Carmel (v. 16). These areas devastated by the slaughter, destruction, and horrors of war imposed by the Assyrian war machine, and before that by the unjust rule of Judean fools and knaves too loosely supervised by the Judean king, will now experience the kind of rule idealized in the royal theology of the Davidic court. As a result of this just rule, initiated after the disaster by the pouring out of God's spirit (cf. Isa 11:1-2), Judeans will see that the product of righteousness is peace, and the produce of righteousness is undisturbed quiet and confidence forever (v. 17). Note how the author takes up and reasserts the claims made in Isa 28:12 and 30:15 that the true way to security, peace, and well-being is by maintaining justice and righteousness for others. Verse 18 would make a nice conclusion to the oracle, since against the false carefreeness and confidence of the leisured women castigated in 32:9-11, it promises that God's people will live in a pasture or abode of peace, and in secure dwellings (וּבְמִשְׁכְּנוֹת מִבְטַחִים, *ûbĕmiškĕnôt mibṭaḥîm*) and in carefree resting places (וּבִמְנוּחֹת שַׁאֲנַנּוֹת, *ûbimnûḥōt ša'ănannôt*)—a genuine confidence and carefreeness rooted in divine justice and the product of righteousness.

Verse 19 is less clear. It threatens that the forest will come down completely and that the city will be completely laid low, but it is not clear to what either the forest or the city refers. The announcement of judgment following the promise of secure dwellings for God's people is awkward, perhaps suggesting that the forest and city refer to a foreign power, but that would seem to go against the apparent meaning of city in v. 14 and forest in v. 15. Perhaps this is a later addition of judgment when the destruction of Judah and Jerusalem in the Babylonian era seemed imminent.

Verse 20 is even less clear. The author blesses those who sow beside all waters, and those who send out the feet of ox and ass, but to whom is the writer referring? Some take these words to indicate that Israel is no longer hindered or threatened, that one can sow wherever one pleases, and that one can let ox and ass out to pasture without worrying about raiding parties (so Wildberger, 3:1280). Perhaps one might find some support for such a reading by a comparison with Isa 7:23-25, but this interpretation is far less than obvious. If v. 19 is not a threat of judgment against an enemy power but a renewed word of judgment against Judah, v. 20 is unlikely to be a word celebrating Judah's freedom from threat. I am more inclined to take this as another addition, perhaps later than and building on v. 19. It is a message of encouragement for exiles, a blessing for those who engage in any kind of productive work that keeps God's people alive wherever they live, even if it is by the waters of Babylon. In other words, I would see it as a poetic analogy to Jeremiah's letter to the exiles in which he urged them to get on with their lives wherever they were living so that the people would not decrease in number, for the exile was going to last a long time (Jer 29:4-23, esp. vv. 5-7).

Bibliography

Ballard, Paul H., "The Kingdom of God Is Justice and Peace," *King's Theological Review* 8 (1985) 51–54.

Barth, J., "Eine verkannte hebräische Imperativform," *ZDMG* 56 (1902) 247–48.

Beuken, W. A. M., "De os en de ezel in Jesaja literair (Jes 1:3 en 32:20)," in R. Michiels, ed., *Herinnering en hoop: Herman Servotte aangeboden door de universitaire parochie van de K.U.* (Averbode: Altiora, 1995) 161–83.

Eichrodt, Walther, *Die Hoffnung des ewigen Friedens im alten Israel: Ein Beitrag zur Frage nach der israelitischen Eschatologie* (BFCT 25.3; Gütersloh: Bertelsmann, 1920).

Fensham, F. C., "The Wild Ass in the Aramean Treaty between Bar-Ga'ayah and Mati'El," *JNES* 22 (1963) 185–86.

Fohrer, G., "Entstehung, Komposition und Überlieferung von Jesaja 1–39," in Fohrer, *Studien zur alttestamentlichen Prophetie (1949–1965)* (BZAW 99; Berlin: de Gruyter, 1967) 2:122–28.

García Recio, J., "'La fauna de las ruinas,' un 'topos' literario de Isaías," *EstBíb* 53 (1995) 55–96.

Gross, H., *Die Idee des ewigen und allgemeinen Weltfriedens im Alten Orient und im Alten Testament* (TThSt 7; Trier: Paulinus-Verlag, 1956).

Har-El, M., "נופי מדבר בנבואת ישעיהו," *BetM* 29 (1966) 79–82.

Hertzberg, Hans Wilhelm, "Die Nachgeschichte alttestamentlicher Texte innerhalb des Alten Testaments," in Hertzberg, *Beiträge zur Traditionsgeschichte und Theologie des Alten Testaments* (Göttingen: Vandenhoeck & Ruprecht, 1962) 69–80.

Humbert, P., "פֶּרֶא: zèbre ou onagre?" *ZAW* 62 (1949) 202–6.

Irwin, *Isaiah 28–33*.

Köhler, L., "פֶּרֶא = Equus Grevyi Oustalet," *ZAW* 44 (1926) 59–62.

Labuschagne, C. J., "The Particles הֵן and הִנֵּה," in Labuschagne et al., *Syntax and Meaning: Studies in Hebrew Syntax and Biblical Exegesis* (OtSt 18; Leiden: Brill, 1973) 1–14.

Lofthouse, W. F., "The Beatitude of Security," *ExpTim* 48 (1936) 505–9.

Ma, W., *Until the Spirit Comes: The Spirit of God in the Book of Isaiah* (JSOTSup 271; Sheffield: Sheffield Academic Press, 1999).

Nielsen, E., "Ass and Ox in the Old Testament," in F. Hvidberg, ed., *Studia orientalia Ioanni Pedersen septuagenario dicata* (Hauniae: Munksgaard, 1953) 261–74.

Padilla, C. Ren, "The Fruit of Justice Will Be Peace," *Transformation* 2, no. 1 (1985) 2–4.

Rayan, Samuel, "Christian Participation in the Struggle for Social Justice," *Point* 7, no. 1 (1978) 37–54.

Reider, J., "Contributions to the Scriptural Text," *HUCA* 24 (1952–53) 88.

Roberts, J. J. M., "Isaiah, National Security."

———, "Security and Justice."

Schmid, H. H., *Šalôm: 'Frieden' im Alten Orient und im Alten Testament* (SBS 51; Stuttgart: Katholisches Bibelwerk, 1971).

Sklba, R. J., "Until the Spirit from on High Is Poured Out on Us (Is 32:15): Reflections on the Role of the Spirit in the Exile," *CBQ* 46 (1984) 1–17.

Stade, B., "Jes. 32.33," *ZAW* 4 (1884) 256–71.

Stansell, "Isaiah 32," 2–4, 7–11.

Vattioni, F., "I precedenti letterari di Isaia 32,17. Et erit opus iustitiae pax," *RivB* 6 (1958) 23–32.

Vollers, K., "Zu Jesajas 32,11," *ZDMG* 57 (1903) 375.

Westermann, Claus, "Der Frieden (Shalom) im Alten Testament," in Georg Picht and Heinz E. Tödt, eds., *Studien zur Friedensforschung*, vol. 1 (Stuttgart: E. Klett, 1969) 144–77.

Wonsuk, Ma, "The Spirit (*Ruah*) of God in Isaiah 1–39," *AJT* 3 (1989) 582–96.

Since Hermann Gunkel's famous article of 1924, Isaiah 33 has generally been treated as a unit, as a "prophetic liturgy"—a judgment that confirms Sigmund Mowinckel's earlier treatment of 1921 of the chapter as a "coherent eschatological piece," the "portrayal of a single author," in the "form of a liturgical lament with a prophetic response."[1] Hans Wildberger reverts to breaking the passage up into individual units, but even he admits that it is probable that the three parts of Isaiah 33 grow out of the same situation and stem from the same author (3:1286). Given that admission, it is difficult to justify his splintering the piece.

Though the chapter uses different genres, these are woven together in a way that provides a logical and coherent development of thought. Verse 1 opens with a *hôy*-oracle formally addressed to the enemy. As in Isa 10:5-22, however, the real audience is Judah; the *hôy*-oracle functions to comfort the oppressed people. In v. 2 the author moves from this word of comfort to direct petition of Yahweh. His request is bolstered by a reference to God's acts of deliverance in the past (vv. 3-6). That past security of Zion serves as a foil against which the present need brought on by the treacherous enemy stands out more clearly (vv. 7-9). This lament, in turn, is answered by an oracle in which Yahweh promises to rise up again, as he did in the past, and destroy the enemy (vv. 10-12). The oracle continues in vv. 13-16 with a renewed call to attention. Yahweh wants everyone to grasp what he is doing, because his deliverance of Jerusalem will be such as to provoke a religious reform among the city's survivors—a reform he characterizes by quoting from the entrance liturgy genre. That leads, quite logically, into a description of life in the purified Jerusalem of this age of salvation (vv. 17-24). The coherence provided by this logical development is further strengthened by recurring themes and vocabulary items that tie the different sections together.

If there has been considerable scholarly agreement to treat Isaiah 33 as a unit, there has been far less agreement concerning its date and authorship. Up until the late nineteenth century it was generally taken as Isaianic and connected to Sennacherib's assault on Jerusalem. The tide began to shift against that view with Bernhard Stade's arguments against Isaianic authorship in 1884,[2] and though such later scholars as Franz Feldmann, Joseph Ziegler, Angelo Penna, and H. L. Ginsberg still argue for its authenticity, the modern tendency is to date it much later.[3] Mowinckel placed it in the time of Josiah;[4] Clements thinks of the Babylonian exile (p. 265); Wildberger, of the Persian period (3:1288); and others, of the Hellenistic if not the Seleucid era (Kaiser, *Jesaja 13–39*, 271).

Yet, as Paul Auvray points out, the arguments against the chapter's authenticity are hardly decisive.[5] The repeated claim that the allusions to the enemy are too vague to be Isaianic is simply false. In some oracles Isaiah names the Assyrians, but in others the enemy is not named at all (1:5-9, 18-20; 3:1-15; 3:24—4:1; 5:26-30; 28:11; 29:1-8). There is no clear pattern of specificity in Isaiah's references to the enemy; it varies from oracle to oracle. Moreover, if chap. 33 were composed during the siege of Jerusalem, the original audience would have found it quite specific enough. The composite, liturgical character of Isaiah 33 is an argument against Isaianic authorship only if one persists in fragmenting Isaiah's speeches into their smallest divisible units. If one recognizes larger liturgical settings, or even speeches composed of several genres,[6] Isaiah 33 no longer appears so isolated. Stade's argument from vocabulary hinges on the antiquated notion that the Psalms are basically late postexilic compositions.[7] Once that notion is rejected, there is hardly anything left to discuss. Finally, as I will show in the following exegesis, the theology of Isaiah 33 is completely consistent with Isaiah's views. Once one has

1 Sigmund Mowinckel, *Psalmenstudien*, vol. 2, *Das Thronbesteigungsfest Yahwäs und der Ursprung der Eschatologie* (Kristiania: Jacob Dybwad, 1921) 235.

2 Bernhard Stade, "Miscellen," *ZAW* 4 (1884) 256–71.

3 Franz Feldmann, *Das Buch Isaias* (2 vols.; EHAT 14; Münster: Aschendorff, 1925) 1:396–98; Joseph Ziegler, *Isaias* (Echter-Bibel; Würzburg: Echter, 1948) 98–102; Angelo Penna, *Isaia* (La Sacra Bibbia; Rome: Marietti, 1958) 299–300; H. L. Ginsberg,

"First Isaiah," *Encyclopaedia Judaica* 9 (Jerusalem: Keter, 1971) 59.

4 Mowinckel, *Psalmenstudien*, 2:235 n. 1.

5 Paul Auvray, *Isaïe 1–39* (SB; Paris: Librairie Lecoffre, 1972) 293.

6 See Kaiser, *Jesaja 1–12*, 10, on Isa 1:1-20, and my treatment of this passage in the present commentary.

7 Stade, "Miscellen," 264–65.

recognized the temporal priority of the Zion Tradition and Isaiah's dependency on that tradition,[8] there remains no compelling reason to deny the Isaianic authorship of Isaiah 33.

1/ Hey, destroyer—you who have not[a] been destroyed,
Betrayer—you whom they have not[a] betrayed!
When you have finished[b] destroying, you will be destroyed.
When you have ceased[c] betraying, they will betray[d] you.

2/ O Yahweh, be gracious to us;[e] we wait for you,[f]
Be[g] our support[h] in the morning,
Even our salvation[i] in the time of stress.

3/ At the sound of your thunder[j] the peoples fled;
At your rising up[j] the nations were scattered;

4/ And spoil was gathered as the gathering of the grasshopper,
As the rushing of locusts, one was rushing upon it.[k]

5/ Yahweh was exalted.[l] Yes, he dwelt on the height.[l]
He filled Zion with justice and righteousness.

6/ Yahweh, faithfulness to your covenant was her wealth.
Her salvation was wisdom and devotion,
The fear of Yahweh was her treasure.[m]

7/ But now[n] the Arielites[o] cry[p] without,
The messengers of Shalem[q] weep[r] bitterly,

8/ The highways are desolate,
The wayfarer[s] has ceased.
He has broken the covenant,
He has rejected the treaty,[t]
He has not[u] considered the tribute.[v]

9/ The land[w] is dried and withered,[x]
Lebanon is disgraced[y] and moldering,[z]
Sharon has become*[a] like a desert,
And Bashan and Carmel shake off (their leaves).*[b]

10/ "Now I will arise," says*[c] Yahweh,
"Now I will exalt myself,*[d]
Now I will raise myself up.*[e]

11/ You conceive stubble,*[f]
You give birth to chaff,
My breath like a fire*[g] will devour you.

12/ And the peoples will be*[h] burnings of lime,
Cut-down thorns which are set on fire.

13/ Hear, you distant ones, what I have done;
And acknowledge,*[i] you near ones, my might."*[j]

14/ Sinners in Zion are afraid,
Trembling has seized the impious:
"Who among us can live with this devouring fire?
Who among us can live with this never-dying blaze?"

15/ The one who walks*[k] in righteousness,
And who speaks*[l] uprightly,
Who refuses the profit from oppression,

8 Gerhard von Rad, *Old Testament Theology*, vol. 2, *The Theology of Israel's Prophetic Traditions* (New York: Harper & Row, 1965) 156–60; J. J. M. Roberts, "Zion in the Theology of the Davidic-Solomonic Empire," in W. H. Ishida, ed., *Studies in the Period of David and Solomon and Other Essays: Papers Read at the International Symposium for Biblical Studies, Tokyo, 5–7 December 1979* (Winona Lake, IN: Eisenbrauns, 1982) 93–108.

Who shakes out his hands[*m] from taking a bribe,[*n]
Who closes his ears[*o] from listening to plots to shed blood,[*p]
Who shuts[*q] his eyes from contemplating evil.
16/ Such a one will dwell[*r] in the heights;
His fortress will be the citadels of the cliffs.
His bread will be given him,
And his water assured.
17/ Your eyes will gaze[*s] upon the king in his beauty;[*t]
They will see a land that stretches afar.
18/ Your hear[*u] shall muse on the terror—
Where is the one who counted?
Where is the one who weighed?
Where is the one who counted the towers?[*v]
19/ The barbarian people you[*w] will no[*x] longer see,[*y]
The people whose speech was too difficult to comprehend,
Who stammered in a tongue you could not understand.
20/ Gaze upon Zion, the city of our festivals![*z]
Your eyes shall see Jerusalem
As a secure habitation,
A tent which one does not move,
Whose tent pegs[†a] will never be pulled up,
And none[†b] of its ropes shall be broken.
21/ But there Yahweh is majestic for us,[†c]
A reservoir of rivers,[†d]
Of streams broad and wide,
Where no rowing ship[†e] can go,
Nor[†f] stately craft can pass.
22/ For Yahweh is our judge,[†g]
Yahweh is our commander,[†h]
Yahweh[†i] is our king,
He[†j] will save us.
23/ Their tackle ropes[†k] hang loose,
They cannot hold firm the socket[†l] of their mast,
They cannot spread[†m] the sail.
Then prey will be divided,
Booty in abundance;[†n]
The lame will divide the spoil.
24/ And no inhabitant will say,[†o] "I am sick."
The people who live[†p] therein will be forgiven of sin.[†q]

Textual Notes

a MT לֹא (*lō*ʾ), "not"; 1QIsa[a] consistently writes the negative with a *mater* לוא.

b MT כַּהֲתִמְךָ (*kahătīmĕkā*), "when you have finished" (*hiphil* infinitive construct with second person masculine singular suffix from תום a byform of תמם, "to make complete"); 1QIsa[a] כהתמכך appears to be a simple mistake, since neither a relevant form from מכך, "sink down, become low," nor תמך, "to take hold of," appears likely in this context.

c Reading ככלותך (*kĕkallôtĕkā*), "when you have ceased, completed," with 1QIsa[a]; MT's כַּנְּלֹתְךָ (*kannĕlōtĕkā*) is a simple scribal error, though Vg. and Tg. try to make sense of it by reading it as a *niphal* infinitive from לאה, "to grow weary." For the pairing of *tmm/klh,* see also Isa 16:4; Lam 3:22.

d MT לִבְגֹּד יִבְגְּדוּ (*libgōd yibgĕdû*), "(*when you have ceased*) betraying, they will betray"; 1QIsa[a] לבגוד יבגודו. LXX makes a hash of most of the verse: Οὐαὶ τοῖς ταλαιπωροῦσιν ὑμᾶς, ὑμᾶς δὲ οὐδεὶς ποιεῖ ταλαιπώρους, καὶ ὁ ἀθετῶν ὑμᾶς οὐκ ἀθετεῖ· ἁλώσονται οἱ ἀθετοῦντες καὶ παραδοθήσονται καὶ ὡς σὴς ἐπὶ ἱματίου οὕτως ἡττηθήσονται, "Woe to those who distress you! But no one makes you distressed, and the betrayer does not betray you; the betrayers will be caught and delivered up, and like a moth on a garment, so will they be defeated."

e MT חָנֵּנוּ (*ḥonnēnû*), "be gracious to us"; 1QIsa[a] חוננו.

f MT לְךָ (*lĕkā*), "for you"; 1QIsa[a] לכה.

g MT הֱיֵה (*hĕyê*), "be"; 1QIsa[a] והיה, "and be."

h MT זְרֹעָם (*zĕrō*ʿ*ām*), 1QIsa[a] זרעם; the MT pointing would normally be rendered "their arm," but that does not fit here. Either read *zĕrō*ʿ*-m*, a substantive with enclitic *mem*, the suffix being understood from the suffix of the parallel term *yšwᶜtnw*, "our salvation,"[9] or correct to *zrᶜnw*, "our arm, support." The Syr., Tg., and some manuscripts of the Vg. support the correction to *zrᶜnw*.

i   MT אַף־יְשׁוּעָתֵנוּ (*ʾap-yĕšûᶜātēnû*), "even our salvation"; 1QIsaᵃ אף הושעתנו with an erased ה between the two words is a garbled form. It looks as though the scribe started to write the *hiphil* imperative, *ʾp hwšᶜnw*, "yes, save us," and then switched back to the nominal form *ʾp yšwᶜtnw*, "even our salvation." The mixed form makes one think of MT's *kĕtîb/qĕrēʾ*.

j   The precise meaning of הָמוֹן (*hāmôn*), "sound, murmur, roar, abundance," depends on one's understanding of the parallel term מֵרוֹמְמֻתֶךָ (*mērômĕmûtekā*). BDB's traditional treatment of it—the preposition *mn*, followed by an abstract noun used as an infinitive formed from the *polel* stem of *rwm*, "to rise up," plus the pronominal suffix—seems preferable to the numerous emendations suggested.[10] Syr., the later Greek translations, and Vg. all understood the word as a derivative from *rwm*. Moreover, there seems to be a play on this word in v. 10, where the author uses the *polel* imperfect of *rwm* to announce just such a rising up of the deity as indicated in v. 3. Yahweh's rising up implies judgment and is traditionally clothed in the imagery of the thunderstorm (Isa 2:19, 21; 29:6; 30:27-33; Pss 46:7; 76:7, 10). In that setting the translation of *hmwn* as "thunder" seems appropriate, and the suffix is understood from its occurrence with the parallel term. 1QIsaᵃ has מדממתך, "from your silence, calm," for MT's מֵרוֹמְמֻתֶךָ, but this seems an obvious error due to the similarity of *dalet* and *resh*.

k   The text of v. 4 is very difficult. The antecedent of the second person masculine plural suffix in MT's וְאֻסַּף שְׁלַלְכֶם אֹסֶף הֶחָסִיל כְּמַשַּׁק גֵּבִים שׁוֹקֵק בּוֹ (*wĕ-ʾussap šĕlalkem ʾosep heḥāsîl kĕmaššaq gēbîm šôqēq bô*), "and your spoil was gathered *as* the gathering of the grasshopper, as the rushing of locusts one was rushing/jumping upon it," is unclear, and 1QIsaᵃ shows the loss of a ל in its rendering of the last line of the verse: משק גבים שקק בו. These two observations suggest the emendation to ואסף שלל כמו אסף החסיל כמשק גבים שוקק בו (*wĕ-ʾussap šālāl kĕmô ʾosep heḥāsîl kĕmaššaq gēbîm šôqēq bô*), "and spoil was gathered as the gathering of the grasshopper, as the rushing of locusts, one was rushing upon it [the spoil]").

l   Gunkel corrected the participles *niśgāb*, "was exalted," and *šōkēn*, "he dwelled," to perfects,[11] but since the tense of a participle must be derived from the context,[12] and since most of the preceding verbs (*nādĕdû*, "they fled"; *nāpĕṣû*, "they were scattered"; *wĕ-ʾussap*, "and was gathered") and the succeeding verb (*millēʾ*, "he filled") are perfects, one may translate *niśgāb* and *šōkēn* as referring to past time even if the vocalization as participles is preserved.

m   This verse presents a textual crux that is impossible to resolve with any degree of certainty. The present text is hardly correct, but no correction is likely to receive common assent. As it stands, MT has וְהָיָה אֱמוּנַת עִתֶּיךָ חֹסֶן יְשׁוּעֹת חָכְמַת וָדַעַת יִרְאַת יְהוָה הִיא אוֹצָרוֹ (*wĕhāyâ ʾĕmûnat ᶜittêkā ḥōsen yĕšûᶜōt ḥokmat wādāᶜat yirʾat YHWH hîʾ ʾôṣārô*), "and he will be the faithfulness of your (masc. sg.) times, the wealth of salvation (and) wisdom and knowledge, the fear of Yahweh is his treasure." 1QIsaᵃ differs slightly יהיה אמונת עתיך חסן וישעות חכמת ודעת יראת יהוה היא אוצרו, "he will be the faithfulness of your times, wealth and salvation, wisdom and knowledge, the fear of Yahweh is his treasure." The versions offer little help. Vg. and Syr. stick relatively close to the Hebrew; Tg. is too interpretive to help, and LXX is strange: ἐν νόμῳ παραδοθήσονται, ἐν θησαυροῖς ἡ σωτηρία ἡμῶν, ἐκεῖ σοφία καὶ ἐπιστήμη καὶ εὐσέβεια πρὸς τὸν κύριον· οὗτοί εἰσιν θησαυροὶ δικαιοσύνης, "In the law they will be handed over. Our salvation is in treasures; wisdom and knowledge and piety toward the Lord are there. They are the treasures of righteousness."

The verse appears to form a tricolon, and any analysis should begin with the last unit, since it is clearest: "The fear of Yahweh was her treasure" (correcting אוצרו, "his treasure," to אוצרה, "her treasure"). The third person masculine singular suffix on אוצרו (*ʾôṣārô*), "his treasure," would presumably refer to Yahweh, but it is difficult to take Yahweh as the antecedent given the second person masculine singular reference to God earlier in the verse. The antecedent should be Zion and therefore feminine. It is possible that the original suffix was the feminine -*â*, written *h*, which an early scribe misread as a *mater* for the masculine suffix -*ô*. The letter *h* was used as a *mater lectionis* for -*â*, -*ê*, and -*ô* from the time of Isaiah to the exile,[13] and there is other evidence in Isaiah for textual corruption due to uncertainty over which vowel the *mater h* represented (e.g., Isa 30:33; תפתה, *toptô*, "his tophet," instead of MT's *toptê*; מדרתה, *mĕdūrātô*, "his/its pile," instead of MT's *mĕdūrātâ*; and בה, *bô*, instead of MT's *bâ*).

If this widely accepted emendation is correct, the second line should probably be divided and corrected to read ישועתה חכמה ודעת (*yĕšûᶜâtâ ḥokmâ/at wādāᶜat*), "her salvation was wisdom and devotion." The suffix -*h* on ישעת probably dropped out by haplography after the adoption of the square script due to the similarity to the following *ḥ*. The anomalous form חכמת (*ḥokmat*) is perhaps an error due to the following ודעת (*wādāᶜat*), but one should not rule out the possibility that it is a rare but nonetheless correct form for the more common חכמה (*ḥokmâ*). Note the nominal (Phoenicianizing form, חָכְמוֹת (*ḥokmôt*, "wisdom," Prov 24:7; Ps 49:4). The present form could

---

9   Irwin, *Isaiah 28–33*, 138.

10 See Wildberger's discussion of a number of these (3:1283).

11 H. Gunkel, "Jesia 33, eine prophetische Liturgie: Ein Vortrag," *ZAW* 42 (1924) 178.

12 GKC, 356, §116d 2.

13 Frank Moore Cross and David Noel Freedman, *Early Hebrew Orthography* (AOS 36; New Haven: American Oriental Society, 1952) 49, 53.

be a defectively written variant to be vocalized חָכְמֹת (ḥokmōt, "wisdom").

Unfortunately, the first line remains problematic. Neither MT's opening third person masculine singular converted perfect or 1QIsaᵃ's third person masculine singular imperfect fits, since either clashes with the second person masculine singular suffix on עתיך (ʿittêkā), "your times." Nor does the word "your times" seem very fitting. Radical emendation seems necessary. The 1QIsaᵃ reading עדים (ʿādîm), "covenant, treaty," in v. 8 suggests the possible correction of עתיך to עדיך, "your covenant." The verb form remains a problem, but 1QIsaᵃ's reading יהיה suggests a correction to יהוה that would have the merit of preparing for the second person masculine singular suffix: יהוה אמונת עדיך חסנה (YHWH ʾĕmûnat ʿādêkā ḥosnâ), "O Yahweh, faithfulness to your covenant was her wealth").

n MT הֵן (hēn), "behold"; so also 1QIsaᵃ, LXX, Vg., and Tg.; Syr. translates as ʾen, "if."

o Reading אראלים with a few manuscripts but pointing it as אֲרִאֵלִים (ʾărîʾēlîm), "the Arielites," that is, the inhabitants of Jerusalem, which Isaiah refers to as אֲרִיאֵל (ʾărîʾēl) in 29:1. MT has אֶרְאֶלָּם (ʾerellām), perhaps for "their warriors," though the vocalization is suspect (cf. 2 Sam 23:20), but 1QIsaᵃ has ארא למ, which apparently led Vg., Tg., and Syr, to understand the first element as a form of the verb ראה, "to see," while Tg. and Syr. took the second element as the preposition with third person masculine plural suffix, "to them." LXX apparently took the first element as a form of the verb ירא, "to fear," producing the odd translation, "Behold with your fear they will be afraid; those whom you feared shall be afraid of you."

p MT צָעֲקוּ (ṣāʿăqû), "they cry out"; 1QIsaᵃ זעקו (zāʿăqû), "they cry out."

q MT and 1QIsaᵃ שָׁלֹום (šālōm), "peace." As a parallel with "the Arielites," the inhabitants of Jerusalem, I am inclined to repoint to šālēm, "Salem," attested as a poetic name for Jerusalem (Ps 76:3). Even if the reading šālōm, "peace," is correct, it probably represents a play on the proper name and should be regarded as an intentional double entendre, a device found elsewhere in Isaiah.[14] The messengers of peace/Salem were the messengers sent from Jerusalem to sue for peace. LXX and Tg. understand these messengers as sent by the nations to Israel to sue for peace.

r MT יִבְכָּיֻון (yibkāyûn), "they weep"; 1QIsaᵃ יבכוון.

s MT עֹבֵר אֹרַח (ʿōbēr ʾōraḥ), "the wayfarer"; 1QIsaᵃ עובר ארח.

t Reading עדים with 1QIsaᵃ and interpreting it in light of the Aramaic cognate (cf. the attestation in Akkadian, adê) and the parallelism with בְּרִית (bĕrît), "covenant," as ʿādîm, "treaty" (from the "oaths" that seal the treaty). MT עָרִים (ʿārîm), "cities," followed by Vg., Tg., and Syr. LXX appears to omit this clause.

u MT לֹא (lōʾ), "not"; 1QIsaᵃ לוא.

v MT and 1QIsaᵃ have the same consonantal text, which MT points as אֱנֹושׁ (ʾĕnôš), usually rendered as "man." That pro-

duces a translation such as, "He has no regard for anyone," and the versions all seem to have some variant of that general reading. In the context of a suzerain (Assyria) rejecting a treaty with his vassal (Judah), however, that reading is a little weak. I follow Delbert Hillers in seeing the form as cognate with Ugaritic ʾunt/unuššu,[15] and I would assign it the meaning "tribute." The messengers of peace from Jerusalem would naturally be upset if the Assyrian monarch broke the covenant, rejected the treaty, and disregarded the tribute that those same messengers had brought to the Assyrian king.

w MT אֶרֶץ (ʾāreṣ), "(the) land"; 1QIsaᵃ adds the article in a correction above the line ארץה.

x LXX omits אֻמְלְלָה (ʾumlĕlâ), "is withered," in its penchant for shortening or simplifying the text.

y MT הֶחְפִּיר (heḥpîr), "Lebanon feels ashamed, is abashed"; 1QIsaᵃ has the qal passive חפור, "is disgraced." The different forms vary little at all in meaning.

z LXX appears to take קָמַל (qāmal), "is moldering," used of the rotting of reeds in Isa 19:6, with the next line, ἔλη ἐγένετο ὁ Σαρων, "Sharon became marshes."

*a MT הָיָה (hāyâ), "has become"; 1QIsaᵃ had והיה, but the ו is erased.

*b MT וְנֹעֵר (wĕnōʿēr), "and he shakes off"; 1QIsaᵃ נוער. LXX omits כַּעֲרָבָה (kaʿărābâ), "like the desert," changes Bashan to Galilee, and gives an interpretive translation, φανερὰ ἔσται ἡ Γαλιλαία καὶ ὁ Κάρμηλος, "Galilee and Carmel will be visible," that is, without the foliage to obscure the view.

*c MT יֹאמַר (yōʾmar), "says (Yahweh)"; 1QIsaᵃ אמר (the perfect with no discernible difference in meaning).

*d MT אֵרֹומָם (ʾērômām), "I will exalt myself," hithpolel with assimilated -t- and compensatory lengthening of preceding vowel; 1QIsaᵃ אתרומם (regular form).

*e MT אֶנָּשֵׂא (ʾennāśēʾ), "I will raise myself up"; 1QIsaᵃ הנשא.

*f MT חֲשַׁשׁ (ḥăšaš), "stubble"; 1QIsaᵃ has the feminine חששה.

*g Reading רוחי כמו אש (rûḥî kĕmô ʾēš), "my breath like a fire (will devour you)," for MT and 1QIsaᵃ רוּחֲכֶם אֵשׁ (rûḥăkem ʾēš), "your breath is a fire (that will devour you)." The scribe was apparently influenced by the second person masculine plural suffix on the verb to misread the first kmw as the same suffix. For the presence of the comparative particle cf. Vg. and Tg.

*h MT וְהָיֻו (wĕhāyû), "and (the peoples) will be"; 1QIsaᵃ ויהיו, "and (the peoples) were."

*i MT וּדְעוּ (ûdĕʿû), "and acknowledge"; 1QIsaᵃ ידעו could be analyzed either as a jussive, "let them acknowledge," or it and the preceding שמע could both be analyzed as perfects, "(the far off) heard . . . the nearby acknowledged. . . ."

*j MT גְּבֻרָתִי (gĕbūrātî), "my might"; 1QIsaᵃ גבורתי.

*k MT הֹלֵךְ (hōlēk), "who walks"; 1QIsaᵃ הולוד with the second ו erased.

*l MT וְדֹבֵר (wĕdōbēr), "and the one who speaks"; 1QIsaᵃ וידבר.

*m MT כַּפָּיו (kappāyw), "his hands"; 1QIsaᵃ כפו, "his hand."

---

14 See my "Double Entendre," 39–48.
15 Delbert R. Hillers, "A Hebrew Cognate of unuššu/ʾunṭ in Is 33:8," *HTR* 64 (1971) 257–59.

*n MT בְּשֹׁחַד (baššōḥad), "from taking hold of the bribe"; 1QIsaᵃ בשחוד.

*o MT אֹטֵם אָזְנוֹ (ʾōṭēm ʾozĕnô), "who closes his ear"; 1QIsaᵃ אוטם אוזניו, "who closes his ears."

*p MT מִשְּׁמֹעַ דָּמִים (miššĕmōaʿ dāmîm), "from listening to plots to shed blood"; 1QIsaᵃ משמוע דמים.

*q MT וְעֹצֵם (wĕʿōṣēm), "and who shuts (his eyes)"; 1QIsaᵃ יעצם, "he will shut."

*r MT יִשְׁכֹּן (yiškōn), "he will dwell"; 1QIsaᵃ ישכן.

*s MT תֶּחֱזֶינָה (teḥĕzênâ), "(your eyes) will gaze upon/see"; 1QIsaᵃ תחזיון.

*t MT בְּיָפְיוֹ (bĕyopyô), "in his beauty"; 1QIsaᵃ ביופי.

*u MT לִבְּךָ (libbĕkā), "your heart"; 1QIsaᵃ לבכה.

*v MT אֶת-הַמִּגְדָּלִים (ʾet-hammigdālîm), "the towers"; 1QIsaᵃ את מגדלים.

*w For MT אֶת-עַם נוֹעָז (ʾet-ʿam nôʿāz), "the fierce people," 1QIsaᵃ has את עם נועז, which suggests that the first word might be better vocalized as the pronoun אַתָּה, "you." For נוֹעָז (nôʿāz), "fierce," it would be better to read לוֹעֵז (lôʿēz), "(a people) who speak an incomprehensible language/a barbarian people"). The expression עַם לֹעֵז (ʿam lōʿēz), "a barbarian people," occurs in Ps 114:1, and לֹעֵז would make a better parallel to the two following lines that concern the difficulty of understanding the speech of this people (for a similar thought, though using different language, cf. Isa 28:11; Deut 28:49).

*x See note u above.

*y MT תִּרְאֶה (tirʾê), "you [masc. sg.] will see"; 1QIsaᵃ ת'ראו, "you [masc. pl.] will see" (the correction above the line appears to be erased). The singular is preferable, since it continues the second person masculine singular suffixes of the preceding verses.

*z MT מוֹעֲדֵנוּ (môʿădēnû), "our assembly," or collective for "our festivals"; 1QIsaᵃ מועדינו, "our festivals."

†a MT יְתֵדֹתָיו (yĕtēdōtāyw), "its tent pegs"; 1QIsaᵃ יתדותו.

†b MT וְכָל (wĕkol), "and all" with negative "none"; 1QIsaᵃ וכול.

†c The correct line division and placement of לָנוּ (lānû), "for us," is problematic. MT's accentuation and most translations read it as the end the first line, but logically it goes just as well at the beginning of the second line, and its placement at the link between the two lines facilitates this ambiguity.

†d MT מְקוֹם-נְהָרִים (mĕqôm-nĕhārîm), "a place of rivers"; 1QIsaᵃ מקום נהרות with the same meaning. I follow Irwin in reading the first word as miqwē-m, מקוה plus enclitic mem, "a reservoir of."[16] But there is probably an intentional double entendre with mĕqôm (see the commentary).

†e MT אֳנִי-שַׁיִט (ʾŏnî-šayiṭ), "rowing ship, ship of oar"; 1QIsaᵃ אני שט.

†f See note u above.

†g MT שֹׁפְטֵנוּ (šōpĕṭēnû), "our judge, ruler"; 1QIsaᵃ שופטנו.

†h MT יְהוָה מְחֹקְקֵנוּ (YHWH mĕḥōqĕqēnû), "Yahweh is our commander"; 1QIsaᵃ ויהוה מחוקקנו, "and Yahweh is our commander."

†i MT יְהוָה (YHWH), "Yahweh"; 1QIsaᵃ ויהוה, "and Yahweh."

†j MT הוּא (hûʾ), "he"; 1QIsaᵃ והוא, "and he."

†k Both MT and 1QIsaᵃ have חֲבָלָיִךְ (ḥăbālāyik), "your tackle ropes," but the second person feminine singular suffix, which would refer back to Zion/Jerusalem (v. 20), cannot be correct. It should be corrected to חבליהם, "their rigging," to agree with the following תָּרְנָם (tornām), "their mast."

†l MT כֵּן-תָּרְנָם (kēn-tornām), "the socket of their mast"; 1QIsaᵃ כי תרנם, "because their mast," is a copying error.

†m MT בַּל-פָּרְשׂוּ (bal-pārĕśû), " they cannot spread"; 1QIsaᵃ בל פרש, "one cannot spread."

†n MT מַרְבֶּה (marbê), "in abundance"; 1QIsaᵃ מרובה, "abundant (spoil)."

†o MT וּבַל-יֹאמַר שָׁכֵן (ûbal-yōʾmar šākēn), "and no inhabitant will say"; 1QIsaᵃ ובל יואמר שוכן.

†p MT הַיֹּשֵׁב (hayyōšēb), "who live"; 1QIsaᵃ היושב.

†q MT עָוֹן (ʿāwōn), "sin"; 1QIsaᵃ עוון.

Commentary

The identity of the destroyer in v. 1 remains subject to debate. Duhm's equation of the enemy with Antiochus Eupator places the text too late to be credible in view of the date of the Qumran scrolls (1892 ed., 216). Wildberger thinks of the early Persian period (3:1288), but against such an identification is the fact that the Persians did not plunder Jerusalem; thus Wildberger is forced to turn this passage into a generalized judgment on a world oppressor in whose fall all, including Israel, will suffer (3:1291–92). With more reason, Clements assigns the whole of chap. 33 to the age of the Babylonian exile (p. 265). Habakkuk 2:5-8, which appears to speak of

Babylon, contains a similar thought, and Isa 21:2, which is usually dated to the Babylonian exile, also mentions in the same language הַבּוֹגֵד בּוֹגֵד וְהַשּׁוֹדֵד שׁוֹדֵד (habbôgēd bôgēd wĕhaššôdēd šôdēd), "the betrayer who betrays and the destroyer who destroys." I would date Isaiah 21 earlier, in the Assyrian period, however, and Habakkuk could be reusing a motif taken from Isaiah. The general thought of Isa 33:1 is the same as that found in Isa 10:5-22, where Assyria is expressly identified as the enemy. There the emphasis is on God's use of unwitting Assyria as his tool to punish Israel, while in chap. 33 the prophet emphasizes the destroyer's actions without specifically referring to God's motive for permitting them; but in both cases,

16 Irwin, *Isaiah 28–33*, 158–59.

when the destroyer has finished his task, he in turn will be destroyed (Isa 10:12).

The term בּוֹגֵד (bôgēd), "betrayer," includes the notion of treachery or betrayal;[17] it should not be reduced to a mere synonym of שׁוֹדֵד (šôdēd), "plunderer." That raises the issue of its referent. If one thinks of the Assyrian period and interprets v. 8 as referring to the same incident, one may find its background in the events recorded in 2 Kgs 18:17-37. The literary character of this account and its relationship to the preceding account in 2 Kgs 18:13-16 are debated.[18] A superficial reading of 2 Kgs 18:17—19:37 suggests that after Hezekiah submitted to Sennacherib's demands, Sennacherib raised them. According to 2 Kgs 18:14, Hezekiah agreed to Sennacherib's terms while Sennacherib was at Lachish, but when the Rabshakeh ends his unsuccessful negotiations with Hezekiah, he finds that Sennacherib has left Lachish for Libnah (2 Kgs 19:8). Why was the Rabshakeh still negotiating with Hezekiah if Hezekiah had already agreed to terms while Sennacherib was at Lachish? Did Sennacherib make additional demands? Of course, the relationship between the events recorded in the two accounts may be far more complex. 2 Kings 18:13-16 may simply be a brief summary account of the agreement, and 2 Kgs 18:17—19:37 may be a more detailed account of events that eventually led up to the agreement summarized in 2 Kgs 18:13-16. Sennacherib may have temporarily left the Lachish siege for Libnah to deal with the threat of the Nubian-Egyptian relief force, during which time the Rabshakeh returned to Lachish from his failed negotiations, but then later, after the Egyptian relief force had been turned back, Sennacherib may have returned to finish the siege at Lachish, and only then did Hezekiah signal his agreement to terms for tribute. Nonetheless, it is hard to dismiss 2 Kgs 18:17—19:37 as mere fiction or historicized legend. Despite Clements's claims,[19] our historical knowledge of the events of 701 BCE is not sufficient to rule out a serious check to Assyrian hopes, compatible with the highly theologized account in 2 Kgs 18:17—19:37. Sennacherib did not capture Jerusalem, as even his own bombastic account makes clear, and it should be noted that Hezekiah's tribute did not reach him until after he had returned to Nineveh.[20] Though the details are obscure, there may well have been an initial agreement between Sennacherib and Hezekiah about terms to end the conflict in 701 BCE, to which Sennacherib then, from a Judean point of view, treacherously added additional demands. Whether 2 Kgs 18:13-16 and 18:17—19:37 are read sequentially or understood in a more complex fashion, either reading is open to the historical reconstruction of a change in demands made by Sennacherib and, despite the ultimate payment of tribute by Hezekiah, a less than totally successful outcome for Sennacherib.

The difficulties in reconciling the details in Kings and various sayings of Isaiah led John Bright and others to argue for the hypothesis of a second Sennacherib campaign against Jerusalem undertaken over ten years later in connection with Sennacherib's final campaign against Babylon and attack on the Arab caravan site of Duma (691–689 BCE).[21] The lack of Assyrian historical sources for events during the last eight years of Sennacherib's reign (689–681 BCE), particularly immediately after the attack on Duma, makes it impossible to rule out this hypothesis completely, even if it seems unlikely. Nonetheless, the threat of such a campaign may have seemed real in Judah, and such a threat would provide a striking context for the group of oracles in Isaiah 21, even if it is not relevant for the interpretation of chap. 33.

---

17 Irwin, *Isaiah 28–33*, 137.
18 For the discussion and literature, see Clements, *Isaiah and the Deliverance*.
19 Ibid., 18–19.
20 Luckenbill, *Annals*, 33–34, lines 37–49. See now the edition and translation of accounts of the third campaign in Grayson and Novotny, RINAP 3/1-2.
21 John Bright, *A History of Israel* (2nd ed.; Philadelphia: Westminster, 1972) 296–308; W. H. Shea, "Sennacherib's Second Palestinian Campaign," *JBL* 104 (1985) 401–18; Shea, "The New Tirhakah Text and Sennacherib's Second Palestinian Campaign," *AUSS* 35 (1997) 181–87. For the numerous scholarly attempts to refute this theory, see, for example, Mordechai Cogan and Hayim Tadmor, *II Kings: A New Translation with Introduction and Commentary* (AB 11; Garden City, NY: Doubleday, 1988) 248–50; William R. Gallagher, *Sennacherib's Campaign to Judah: New Studies* (SHCANE 18; Leiden: Brill, 1999) 8–9. See also the articles in L. L. Grabbe, ed., *'Like a Bird in a Cage': The Invasion of Sennacherib in 701 B.C.E.* (JSOTSup 363; London: Sheffield Academic Press, 2003); and Isaac Kalimi and Seth Richardson, eds., *Sennacherib at the Gates of Jerusalem: Story, History and Historiography* (CHANE 71; Leiden: Brill, 2014).

In v. 2, the prophet switches from his fictive direct address of the enemy to invoke Yahweh on behalf of his community. In the voice of the community, he calls upon God with imperatives of supplication, "be gracious to us," "be our support in the morning, even our salvation in the time of trouble." As motivation for God to respond positively to these requests, the communal voice asserts, "we wait for you."

At v. 3, however, while maintaining the direct address of God in prayer, the communal voice switches to the narrative past. The perfects in v. 3 should be taken as indicating genuine past-tense narration, not as precative perfects continuing the imperatives of the prayer,[22] nor as a present or future description of the plight of the nations (Wildberger, 3:1289). The prophet is reciting the claims of the Zion tradition as they are found, for example, in the quite ancient Psalm 76. It is the same ancient tradition that the author of Psalm 48 refers to when he says, "As we have heard, thus we have seen" (Ps 48:9). For that psalmist, an ancient tradition was confirmed in a contemporary experience, and in similar manner our prophet is quoting the ancient tradition as a background for his following prediction of the outcome of the present conflict. His use of the *polel* of רום (*rûm*), "to be high, exalted, rise," in the oracle of salvation (v. 10) resumes מְרוֹמְמֻתֶךָ (*mĕrômĕmūtekā*), "at your rising," in this verse and is a way of underscoring his point. In the past, Yahweh saved Zion by rising up and thundering his rebuke, at which the peoples and nations threatening Zion were scattered and fled. That is the model for the salvation prayed for (v. 2) and ultimately announced (v. 10).

The image in v. 4 appears to mean that, just as grasshoppers or locusts swarm over a field, so Israel swarmed over the booty left by the nations who fled and were scattered. Again the motif of booty, if not the locust imagery, is rooted in the Zion Tradition. Note the form אֶשְׁתּוֹלְלוּ (*ʾeštôlĕlû*), "(the stouthearted) were despoiled, stripped of booty," Ps 76:6) and the division of spoil or booty (שָׁלָל, *šālāl*) mentioned in Ps 68:13.

Then v. 5 celebrates Yahweh's former victory over his enemies with hymnic participles that describe God as exalted (נִשְׂגָּב, *niśgāb*) and dwelling on the height (שֹׁכֵן מָרוֹם, *šōkēn mārôm*). The designation מָרוֹם (*mārôm*), "height," can refer either to heaven (Ps 102:20) or to an earthly height (Isa 22:16; 26:5; Hab 2:9; Obad 3), and it often refers specifically to the Temple Mount (Isa 33:16; Jer 17:12; 31:12; Ezek 20:40; 34:14). Classical temple theology did not clearly distinguish terrestrial from celestial (Amos 1:2; Joel 4:16 compared to Jer 25:30; Ps 18:10 compared to Pss 20:3, 7; 50:2),[23] but *mārôm* here undoubtedly involves the concept of God's abode on the sacred mount (Isa 8:18), since the last half of the verse speaks of God's largess to Zion. When the verb שכן (*šākan*), "to tent, dwell," is used of God's dwelling, it normally refers to his dwelling in Jerusalem (1 Kgs 6:11-13; 8:12-13 = 2 Chr 6:1; Isa 8:18; Ezek 43:5-9; Joel 4:17, 21; Zech 2:14-15; 8:3; Pss 68:17, 30; 74:2; 135:21; 1 Chr 23:25) or at least to his earthly dwelling among humans (Exod 24:16; 25:8; 29:45; Num 5:3; 35:34; Ps 78:60). Moreover, a nominal form (מִשְׂגָּב, *miśgāb*, "haven, refuge") of the root employed here to speak of Yahweh's elevation (שגב, *śāgab*, "to be high, exalted") is used in two of the Zion Songs to describe the exalted deity's protection of his city (Pss 46:8, 12; 48:4). That nominal form also occurs later in this chapter, in v. 16, where the prophet picks up on three of the terms used here (*niśgāb–miśgabbô*, *šōkēn–yiškōn*, *mārôm–mĕrômîm*). One should note that the prophet continues to play on the root רום (*rûm*), "to be high, exalted, rise."

Verse 5a prepares for 5b and 6. It was Yahweh's presence in and love for Zion that filled the city with justice and righteousness (cf. Ps 132:13-18). Verse 6 is textually uncertain, but it appears to be developing the preceding thought further. Jerusalem's wealth, salvation, and treasure were all rooted in her special relationship to Yahweh. In this context, both wisdom (*ḥokmat*, *ḥokmōt*, or *ḥokmâ*) and knowledge (*dāʿat*) have a theological specificity; it is not just any wisdom or knowledge, but what Hosea refers to as דַּעַת אֱלֹהִים (*daʿat ʾĕlōhîm*), "the knowledge of God" (Hos 4:1). In Hosea 4, "the knowledge of God" appears to involve the Ten Commandments or, stated more broadly, a special relationship governed

22   So Irwin, *Isaiah 28–33*, 140.
23   See T. Mettinger, "YHWH SABAOTH: The Heavenly King on the Cherubim Throne," in Tomoo Ishida, ed., *Studies in the Period of David and Solomon and Other Essays: Papers Read at the International Symposium for Biblical Studies, Tokyo, 5–7 December, 1979* (Winona Lake, IN: Eisenbrauns, 1982) 109–38.

by covenantal obligations. That Isaiah was familiar with Hosea's concept seems clear from a comparison of Hos 4:6 and Isa 5:12-13.

After this petition grounded in Yahweh's past graciousness to Jerusalem, the prophet turns to the situation of need that provoked the petition and in so doing picks up part of the thought of v. 1. The הֵן (hēn), "behold!" in v. 7 appears to indicate a contrast between the former happy situation of Zion and the present situation of desperate need. The word is used elsewhere to introduce a statement set in contrast to a preceding clause (Isa 50:1, 2, 9). As indicated in the textual notes, the term אֶרְאֵלִים (ʾărʾēlîm), "the Arielites," is an Isaianic designation for the inhabitants of Jerusalem, which Isaiah called אֲרִיאֵל (ʾărîʾēl) in 29:1. The "messengers of Shalem" (מַלְאֲכֵי שָׁלֵם, malʾăkê šālēm), if one accepts my emendation, or the "messengers of peace" (מַלְאֲכֵי שָׁלוֹם, malʾăkê šālôm), if one does not, is in any case an intentional double entendre playing on the similarity between שָׁלֵם (šālēm), a poetic name for Jerusalem (Ps 76:3; Gen 14:18) and שָׁלוֹם (šālôm), "peace." As a parallel to the Arielites, the messengers of Shalem/Peace, are the messengers sent from Shalem (Jerusalem) to sue for peace. Unlike in the good old days, the present inhabitants of Jerusalem cry and their messengers weep bitterly because of the danger that has stopped travel. The term חֻצָה (ḥūṣâ), "without," does not mean "outside the city," as though these mourners were exiles, but "outside, in the streets," where public mourning customarily took place (Amos 5:16; Isa 15:3; 24:11).

It is not entirely clear why the messengers of Shalem weep. The line could refer to messengers from Jerusalem who had been turned back from their mission by besieging forces,[24] in which case the reference to the ceasing of travel is particularly appropriate. Verse 7b could also refer to such messengers returning with new and harsh demands after discussions with the Assyrian overlord. Sennacherib mentions the messengers Hezekiah sent to Nineveh to bear tribute and make submission as a vassal,[25] and this background could explain the wordplay with šālôm, "messengers of peace." In any case, v. 8a

indicates that the highways were empty and travelers had abandoned traveling, presumably because the danger was too great.

In the present context, the third masculine singular perfects of v. 8b can only refer back to the treacherous destroyer of v. 1. "He has broken the treaty, / He has rejected the treaty, / He has disregarded the tribute" would be appropriately said of Sennacherib if, as 2 Kgs 18:17 suggests, Sennacherib went back on his word after the capitulation of Hezekiah. Given that scenario, Duhm's objection that it was Hezekiah, not Sennacherib, who had broken the covenant (1892 ed., 218), falls by the way.

Verse 9 introduces the imagery of the vast landscape languishing, drying up, and losing its foliage. The landscape includes not only the generic "the land," but Lebanon, Sharon—the fertile coastal plain south of Carmel as far as Jaffa, Bashan in the northern Transjordan, and Carmel, implying how widespread the devastation was. The imagery of languishing woodlands or pasture is often associated with the covenant curses (Hos 4:3; Isa 24:1-6; Jer 23:10; 12:4), but that would not fit here if the Assyrian is the covenant breaker. The imagery also appears in theophanies (Nah 1:4; Amos 1:2), and in descriptions of a land ravaged by foreign enemies (Isa 19:1-15) or by natural disaster under the figure of a foreign enemy (Joel 1:10-12). Ravaging by a foreign enemy must be what is involved here.

It is possible, however, that the present text represents Isaiah's own reworking of an originally independent oracle, thus involving what William L. Holladay calls a "self-extended oracle."[26] Verses 7-16, with slight changes, could be read as a judgment oracle against Judah, her plight described in traditional terms as due to her breach of covenant (reading three infinitive absolutes: hāpēr, māʾōs, ḥāšōb).[27] In this case, v. 11 would originally have referred to Israel's plans as worthless (cf. 30:1-5; 31:1-4), and God's devouring fire would have originally burned his own people (reading ʿammî + enclitic mem, "my people") to lime (v. 13; cf. 5:23-24). If that were the original

---

24 See Luckenbill, *Annals*, 33, lines 29–30; Grayson and Novotny, RINAP 3/1, p. 176, no. 22, iii 29–30.

25 Luckinbill, *Annals*, 34, lines 48–49; Grayson and Novotny, RINAP 3/1, p. 177, no. 22, iii 37b–49.

26 Holladay, *Scroll of a Prophetic Heritage*, 84.

27 See Delbert R. Hillers, "A Hebrew Cognate of unuššu / ʾunṭ in Is 33:8," *HTR* 64 (1971) 257–59.

setting of vv. 7-16, they have been altered and perhaps expanded to fit into the present larger context.

Finally Yahweh responds to the prayer of the community and their desperate need (v. 10). Yahweh asserts, "Now I will arise, Now I will exalt myself, Now I will raise myself up." The language of Yahweh's rising up picks up the thought of v. 3, binding the two units together. As in the past, so in the present, Yahweh, without assistance, will rise up to defeat his enemies. Yahweh, still speaking, addresses those enemies in v. 11: "You conceive stubble, you give birth to chaff." The word pair הָרָה / יָלַד (hārâ / yālad), "to conceive / to give birth," is often used in the sense of planning and bringing to fruition evil plots (Isa 59:4; Ps 7:15; Job 15:35). The sense here is that the hostile plans these enemies hatch are no more substantial than straw that is easily burned, and Yahweh continues with the assertion, "My breath will devour you like a fire" (see textual note). Not just the plans, but the enemies who birthed them will be burned up in God's judgment. The peoples who threaten Jerusalem will be burned to lime like cut-down thorns that are set ablaze (v. 12).

In v. 13, then, Yahweh calls upon all people, both those close at hand and those far away, to pay attention to what God has done. The reference is clearly to his projected judgment mentioned in the preceding verses, *pace* Vermeylen.[28] Isaiah had constantly complained that his contemporaries did not pay attention to Yahweh's work (Isa 5:12; 22:11; 28:21-22). On occasion they even mocked Isaiah by urging Yahweh to hurry it up (Isa 5:19). But once Yahweh has acted, Isaiah says, the sinners and profane ones in Zion who have seen his intervention first-hand will no longer scoff at the prophet. They will react in terror at the majesty of this devouring fire and with trembling ask who can live in this God's presence (v. 14). The reference to fire and furnace resumes the thought of vv. 11-12 and demonstrates the interconnection of these verses despite the putative introductory formula in v. 13.

The question and answer in vv. 14-16 are modeled on the entrance liturgies, such as Psalms 15 and 24. Isaiah apparently adopted this form, which was at home in the pre-Isaianic Zion Tradition and tied to its festival processions,[29] to give expression to what he understood as the result of God's purging of Jerusalem (cf. Isa 1:25-28). The moral transformation of Zion's survivors is expressed here in traditional terms, though rooted in a new experiential awareness of God's character as mediated through his actions in history. The characterization of the one who may live in God's presence is in the generic third person masculine singular (v. 14c-d), but it surely intends to include the female inhabitants of Jerusalem as well, since they were specifically included in his earlier criticisms of the corrupt Jerusalem's population (Isa 3:16—4:1; 32:9-14). The first two responses give generalized statements about the acceptable person's positive actions. The acceptable person will walk, that is, behave righteously and speak uprightly or truthfully (v. 15 a-b). The final four responses spell out positive actions the righteous person will take to avoid doing evil things. Such a one will refuse to accept profit that comes from oppression, will shake out his hands to avoid taking a bribe, will shut his ears in order not to listen to plots to commit bloodshed, and will shut his eyes rather than looking at or contemplating evil (v. 15c-f).

In v. 16, as in Pss 15:5c and 24:5-6, the characterization of the behavior of the righteous person is followed by a statement of the blessings such a one will receive. Such a person, whether male or female, will be secure, for he will dwell (יִשְׁכֹּן, yiškōn) in or on the heights (מְרוֹמִים, mĕrômîm), and his high fortress (מִשְׂגַּבּוֹ, miśgabbô) will be the citadel of the cliffs. Moreover, contrary to the judgment announced against Judah and Jerusalem's bread and water in Isa 3:1 (cf. 30:20), and the shortage of both that must have been experienced in Jerusalem during Sennacherib's campaign, this righteous person's food will be provided, and his water assured (נֶאֱמָנִים, ne'ĕmānîm, "firm, reliable, constant"). Note how the vocabulary here reiterates the description of the past security of Zion in vv. 5-6, providing another link to tie the chapter together.

---

28 Vermeylen, *Du prophete Isaïe*, 1:433.
29 Psalm 24; see Cross, *Canaanite Myth*, 91–94; J. J. M. Roberts, "Zion," 93–108; J. J. M. Roberts, "The Divine King and the Human Community in Isaiah's Vision of the Future," in H. B. Huffmon, F. A. Spina, and A. R. W. Green, eds., *The Quest for the Kingdom of God: Essays in Honor of George E. Mendenhall* (Winona Lake, IN: Eisenbrauns, 1983) 127–36.

At v. 17, the prophet switches to direct address of such a prospective individual in his audience with a vision of what he will experience in Jerusalem in this coming era of salvation after the terror has passed. Your (masc. sg.) eyes, he says, will gaze upon the king in his beauty; they will see a land stretching afar. The king here refers to the divine king Yahweh (see v. 22), and in those days the righteous inhabitant of Zion will see the true king even as Isaiah saw him in the temple, and he will also see a land stretching afar, because the presence of Yahweh in the land will mean the absence of the enemy. That absence will cause the inhabitant of Jerusalem to look around in wonder and will provoke reflection (cf. Isa 29:7-8). Your (masc. sg.) heart, Isaiah says, shall muse on the terror asking, "Where is the one who counted? Where is the one who weighed? Where is the one who counted the towers?" (v. 18). The three participles refer to different enemy figures. The last presumably refers to one who numbered the towers of Jerusalem that needed to be destroyed, the next to last refers to one who weighed the tribute to be collected, and the first may be a more general reference to a chief officer or scribe in charge of the others. That barbaric people who spoke a language impossible for the inhabitant of Jerusalem to understand will no longer be present (v. 19). This is presumably the same strange language in which Yahweh threatened to speak to Judah's leaders in Isa 28:11. Though neither chap. 28 nor chap. 33 names this people of barbaric tongue, the reference in 33:19 probably depends on 28:11, and both refer to the Assyrians, whose language the average Judean could not understand. Even the Judean officials who asked to discuss terms with the Assyrian representative in a language other than Hebrew are represented as asking for the discussion to take place in Aramaic, not Assyrian (2 Kgs 18:26).

Psalm 48:13-14, which seems close to Isa 33:18, is probably dependent on Isaiah, not the other way around. Isaiah is presenting a future projection, but the psalmist is apparently referring to something that has already happened. The psalmist has just experienced what the ancient tradition affirmed (Ps 48:9), and, as a result of God's victory, he calls upon his audience to walk around and inspect the recently delivered Zion (Ps 48:13-14). Isaiah, in contrast, is speaking of a future deliverance, and he apparently refers to the enemy's hostile inspec-

tion of Zion. The close resemblance between Psalm 48 and Isaiah 33 suggests that they date from the same period, and it is possible that the psalmist, having experienced the deliverance of Jerusalem and familiar with the slightly earlier oracle of Isaiah, formulated his hymn of thanksgiving in words appropriated from that oracle.

In v. 20, Isaiah continues with a command to his individualized audience to gaze upon Zion, but the prophet then identifies with that audience when he describes Zion as "the city of our (com. pl.) festivals." Your (masc. sg.) eyes, he says, will see Jerusalem as a secure or carefree habitation (נָוֶה שַׁאֲנָן, *nāweh šaʾănān*), picking up on the language of Isa 32:18. The imagery is developed under the metaphor of a permanently fixed tent, whose tent pegs will never be pulled out, and whose securing ropes will never be broken. Then the prophet shifts to the imagery of the city as the paradisiacal abode of Yahweh (v. 21). There, the prophet says, Yahweh will be majestic (אַדִּיר, *ʾaddîr*) for us. But the imagery is given depth by what appears to be an intentional double entendre between the identically written and similar sounding *mĕqôm*, "place," and *miqwē-m*, "reservoir." Read the first way, Jerusalem, the "there" is described as a place of rivers, of streams broad and wide. Read the second way, Yahweh is for us a reservoir of rivers, of streams broad and wide. The two senses are not mutually exclusive. The same wordplay is found in the P account of creation in Gen 1:9-10, but that can hardly be taken as compelling evidence for direct literary dependence of Isaiah 33 on the P source, and thus of a very late date. In the Zion Tradition, the origin of which is far older than P, there was a river whose streams made glad the city of God (Ps 46:5), but the living waters of that river had its source in and flowed out from the very abode of God (Ezek 47:1-2; Joel 4:18; Zech 14:8; cf. 13:1). The waters were there only because Yahweh was there. In Jeremiah's words (2:13; 17:13), Yahweh is the מְקוֹר מַיִם חַיִּים (*mĕqôr mayim ḥayyîm*), "the fountain of living waters." Note the wordplay on the different meanings of מִקְוֶה (*miqwēh*), "hope" or "collection of water," already in Jer 17:13, which certainly predates the common late dating of the P account of creation.

The water motif is then expanded by reference to another motif of the Zion Tradition, the assault of the enemy kings on Zion. In the mythological antecedents of that motif these *lim . ḥp y[m]*, "men of the seashore" (*KTU* 1.3 ii 7) apparently came by ship to attack Baal's mountain.[30] Psalm 48:8 speaks of Yahweh smashing the ships of Tarshish, and Isaiah elsewhere in a highly mythological context speaks of Yahweh's day against all the ships of Tarshish and dhows of Arabia (Isa 2:16). The motif is clearly mythological in origin and secondarily applied to Jerusalem, since Jerusalem is neither on the coast nor subject to waterborne assault. Nonetheless, Isaiah uses this motif metaphorically to underscore Zion's future security. Though Yahweh's abode will be the source and site of wide streams, those rivers will never again be the avenue for arrogant human assaults on God's city. No rowing ship or majestic vessel will be able to reach it with hostile intent.

The reason for the future security of Zion is given in v. 22: Yahweh is our judge (שֹׁפְטֵנוּ, *šōpěṭēnû*), Yahweh is our commander (מְחֹקְקֵנוּ, *měḥōqěqēnû*), Yahweh is our king (מַלְכֵּנוּ, *malkēnû*); he will save us. Each of the terms used for Yahweh's office may be used in the generic sense of ruler, but the first two, judge and commander, emphasize particular aspects of a ruler's task, while king is more general. The primary function of the king, however, was "to save" the people. In the early traditions of the formation of Israel's human kingship, Israel rejected God, who had saved them from all their evils and afflictions (1 Sam 10:19), to ask for a human king to lead them and fight their battles (1 Sam 8:19-20), though some doubted that their new king, Saul, could save them (1 Sam 10:27). Hosea, referring to these traditions, sarcastically asked the Israelites, "Where now is your king that he may save you? (Hos 13:10).

In Isaiah's prophecy, Yahweh, the true king, will once again, as in the distant past, save his people (v. 23). Any ships in potentially hostile fleets approaching Jerusalem on these broad streams will suddenly find their tackle ropes coming loose, their unsupported masts collapsing, and thus be incapable of spreading their sails and continued directed movement. Such disabled and eventually wrecked and abandoned enemy ships will then be subject to salvage and looting by Jerusalem's inhabitants. Even Zion's lame will find a share in the abundant wealth left abandoned by Zion's divinely thwarted foes. Note how the motif of plunder (שָׁלָל, *šālāl*) resumes the thought of Jerusalem's good old days in v. 4.

Finally, in v. 24, as if to correct the notion suggested by the mention of the lame in the preceding verse, Isaiah promises that the inhabitants of this purified Jerusalem will not suffer illness, for they will be a forgiven people, unlike the battered and sick Zion of the period before God's purging judgment (Isa 1:5-6).

If these words were spoken by Isaiah in the context of the Assyrian crisis, as argued in this commentary, many of Isaiah's expectations were not fulfilled. Whatever the nature of Yahweh's deliverance of Jerusalem, it did not have the permanently transforming effect upon Judah's inhabitants that Isaiah predicted. All Zion's sinners did not give up their sins, and Jerusalem did not ever after remain secure. Yahweh did not become transparently present for his people, and Jerusalem fell to her enemies again and again. The vision's failure to be realized in contemporary reality, however, is no reason to deny the vision to Isaiah. Most Old Testament prophetic visions of salvation were not realized in the time and to the extent expected by their biblical authors. Isaiah simply joins Ezekiel, Second Isaiah, and others among the prophets whose glorious visions for the future failed to materialize or, perhaps more adequately stated, are yet to be realized in a transformed and more glorious manner.[31]

Bibliography

Beuken, W. A. M., "Jesaja 33 als Spiegeltext im Jesajabuch," *ETL* 67 (1991) 5–35.
Bodenheimer, F. S., *Animal Life in Palestine* (Jerusalem: L. Mayer, 1935).

Borowski, Oded, "The Sharon—Symbol of God's Abundance," *BRev* 4 (1988) 40–43.
Childs, *Assyrian Crisis*.
Dahood, M., "Ugaritic and Phoenician or Qumran and the Versions," in Harry Hoffner Jr., ed., *Orient and Occident: Essays Presented to Cyrus H. Gordon on*

30   J. J. M. Roberts, "Zion," 93–108. See *KTU* 1.4 vii 30–37; 1.3 ii 3–39; 1.3 iii 43–iv 47.
31   See J. J. M. Roberts, "A Christian Perspective on Prophetic Prediction," *Int* 33 (1979) 240–53.

the Occasion of His Sixty-fifth Birthday (AOAT 22; Kevelaer: Butzon & Bercker; Neukirchen-Vluyn: Neukirchener Verlag, 1973) 54–55.

Delekat, Lienhard, Asylie und Schutzorakel am Zionheiligtum: Eine Untersuchung zu den privaten Feindpsalmen (Leiden: Brill, 1967).

Galling, K., "Der Beichtspiegel: Eine gattungsgeschichtliche Studie," ZAW 47 (1929) 125–30.

Gerlach, M., "Die prophetischen Liturgien des Alten Testaments" (Diss., Bonn, 1967).

Ginsburg, H. L., "Emendations in Isaiah," JBL 69 (1950) 57.

Grieshammer, R., "Zum 'Sitz im Leben' des negativen Sündenbekenntnisses," in Wolfgang Voigt, ed., XVIII Deutscher Orientalistentag vom 1. bis 5. Oktober 1972 in Lübeck (ZDMGSup 2; Wiesbaden: Steiner, 1974).

Gunkel, H., "Jesaja 33, eine prophetische Liturgie: Ein Vortrag," ZAW 42 (1924) 177–208.

Hillers, Delbert R., "A Hebrew Cognate Of unuššu / ʾunṭ in Is 33:8," HTR 64 (1971) 257–59.

Holmgren, H. R., III, "Does Isaiah 33:23 Address Israel or Israel's Enemy?" BSac 152 (1995) 273–78.

Irwin, Isaiah 28–33.

Johnson, Aubrey R., The Cultic Prophet in Israel's Psalmody. Cardiff: University of Wales Press, 1979.

Kapelrud, Arvid S., "The Prophets and the Covenant," in W. Boyd Barrick and John R. Spencer, eds., In the Shelter of Elyon: Essays on Ancient Palestinian Life and Literature in Honor of G. W. Ahlström (JSOTSup 31; Sheffield: JSOT Press, 1984) 175–83.

Koch, K., "Tempeleinlassliturgien und Dekaloge: Studien zur Theologie der alttestamentlichen Überlieferungen," in Rolf Rendtorff and Klaus Koch, eds., Studien zur Theologie der alttestamentlichen Überlieferungen (Neukirchen: Neukirchener Verlag, 1961) 45–60.

Köhler, L., "Gēbîm (Heuschrecken-)Schwärme," TZ 4 (1948) 317.

Korostovtsev, M., "Stèle de Ramsès IV," BIFAO 45 (1947) 155–73.

Laberge, L., Isaïe 28–33: Étude de tradition textuelle, d'après la Pešiṭto, le texte de Qumrân, la Septante et le texte Massorétique (Vanier, ON: Mary Nash Information Series, 1977).

——, La Septante d'Isaïe 28–33.

Mowinckel, Sigmund, Psalmenstudien, vol. 2, Das Thronbesteigungsfest Yahwäs und der Ursprung der Eschatologie (Kristiania: Jacob Dybwad, 1921; repr., Amsterdam: P. Schippers, 1966).

Murray, R., "Prophecy and the Cult." In Richard Coggins, Anthony Phillips, and Michael Knibb, eds., Israel's Prophetic Tradition: Essays in Honour of Peter R. Ackroyd (Cambridge: Cambridge University Press, 1982) 200–216.

Poynder, A., "'Be Thou Their Arm Every Morning': Isaiah 33,2," ExpTim 13 (1901) 94.

Roberts, J. J. M., "Isaiah 33: An Isaianic Elaboration of the Zion Tradition," in Carol L. Meyers and M. O'Connor, eds., The Word of the Lord Shall Go Forth: Essays in Honor of David Noel Freedman in Celebration of His Sixtieth Birthday (Winona Lake, IN: Eisenbrauns for ASOR, 1983) 15–25.

Schoeps, H. J., "Ein neuer Engelname in der Bibel? (Zur Übersetzung des Symmachus von Jes 33,3)," ZRGG 1 (1948) 86–87.

Schwantes, S., "A Historical Approach to the ʾrʾlm of Isa. 33," AUSS 3 (1965) 158–66.

Spiegel, Joachim, Die Idee vom Totengericht in der ägyptischen Religion (Leipziger ägyptologische Studien 2; Glückstadt: J. J. Augustin, 1935).

Stade, B., "Jes. 32.33," ZAW 4 (1884) 256–71.

Stansell, "Isaiah 32."

Steingrimsson, Sigurdur Örn, Tor der Gerechtigkeit: Eine literaturwissenschaftliche Untersuchung der sogenannte Einzugliturgien im AT: Ps 15; 24,3-5 und Jes 33, 14-16 (ATSAT 22; St. Ottilien: EOS-Verlag, 1984).

Thompson, M. E. W., "Vision, Reality, and Worship: Isaiah 33," ExpTim 113 (2002) 327–33.

Weis, Richard D., "Angels, Altars and Angles of Vision: The Case of ʾerʾellam in Isaiah 33:7," in Gerard J. Norton and Stephen Pisano, eds., Tradition of the Text: Studies Offered to Dominique Barthélemy in Celebration of His 70th Birthday (OBO 109; Freiburg, Switzerland: Universitätsverlag; Göttingen: Vandenhoeck & Ruprecht, 1991) 285–92.

Weiss, R., "On Ligatures in the Hebrew Bible," JBL 82 (1963) 188–94.

Williamson, Book Called Isaiah, 238–39.

Ziegler, J., "Das Heuschreckengleichnis Is. 33,4," Bib 14 (1933) 460–64.

Chapters 34–35 of Isaiah have some striking similarities to both Isaiah 24–27 and Isaiah 40–55. They do not stem from the eighth-century Isaiah of Jerusalem but appear to come from a later period, during and after the Babylonian conquest of Jerusalem. The fierce animosity toward the Edomites reflected in chap. 34 compares to the feeling toward the Edomites found in other prophetic books from that later period (Isa 63:1-6; Jer 49:7-22; Ezek 35:1-15; Joel 4:19; Obadiah 10-16; Mal 1:3-4; cf. also Ps 137:7-9). From the point of view of the Judeans, the Edomites had treacherously taken the side of the Babylonians in Judah's darkest hour, taking advantage of the calamity overtaking Judah and Jerusalem, in order to expand into former Judean territory. From the point of view of the Edomites, Edom's behavior may have been seen rather as finally enjoying a long-delayed opportunity for revenge for the many centuries of Judean hegemony and oppression over Edom. In any case, this bitter animosity fits the situation during and after the Babylonian conquest of Jerusalem in the very late seventh century and continuing on for most of the sixth century BCE far better than it would fit in the late eighth century. Amos expresses some complaints against the Edomites (1:11-12), and he envisions a restoration of Davidic hegemony over all of Edom (9:11-12), but that is in the context of a liturgy of complaints against all of Israel's neighbors and in the expectation of a restoration of Davidic hegemony over all of greater Israel's former vassals.[1] Edom is not singled out for particular hostility in the way it is in Isaiah 34, in which the virulent hatred for Edom makes it the paradigm for all enemy nations.

Isaiah 35 contains a promise for the restoration of Judah's fertility that appears to be the intentional inversion or counterpoint to the threatened destruction of Edom in chap. 34 that will leave the Edomite territory a scorched and barren wasteland forever. The linkage between the punishment of Zion's enemies in chap. 34 followed by the restoration of the fertility of Zion's territory in chap. 35 suggests that the two chapters are from the same period, and probably from the same author. There are motifs in Isa 35:8-9 that echo earlier motifs from Isaiah of Jerusalem of a pilgrimage to Zion (Isa 2:2-5), or a highway back to Zion (Isa 11:16), or a path from which one does not stray, because the divine teacher constantly alerts his people any time they threaten to stray to the right or left from the way (Isa 30:21), so the author of Isaiah 34–35 is using the earlier tradition, but his use of it is tending toward the imagery of the highway in the wilderness found in Second Isaiah (see, for example, Isa 40:3-5). There are also close links to Isaiah 24–27, where a similar impending universal judgment on all the nations and a subsequent deliverance of God's people is proclaimed in the light of an already accomplished or imminently expected destruction of particular foreign enemies—there presumably Assyria and soon to follow, Egypt. Whether the author of Isaiah 34–35 was the same as the author of Isaiah 24–27 or the same as the somewhat later author of Isaiah 40–55 is impossible to say for certain, but each of these authors, whether two or three, stood in the same Isaianic tradition, and they were not all that far removed from one another chronologically.

---

1   I take these Amos passages as genuine eighth-century oracles of the prophet.

34

1/ Draw near,[a] you nations,[b] to hear,[c]
And, you peoples,[d] pay attention;
Let the earth and what fills it[e] listen,
The world and all[f] that comes from it.

2/ For[g] Yahweh has wrath against all[h] the nations,[i]
And anger against all[h] their host;
He has dedicated them to destruction, he has given them[j] over to slaughter.[k]

3/ Their slain will be cast out,[l]
And the stench[m] of their corpses[n] will go up,
And the mountains[o] will dissolve from their blood.

4/ And all the host[p] of heaven will rot away,[q]
And the heavens will be rolled up like the scroll,
And all their host will wither[r] as a leaf withers from the vine,[s]
Or withered fruit from a fig tree.[t]

5/ For my sword has become drunk[u] in the heavens,
Behold, on Edom it will come down,
And upon the people I have doomed[v] to judgment.

6/ Yahweh has a sword;
It is full of blood,
It is greasy with fat,
From the blood of lambs and goats,
From the fat of the kidneys[w] of rams,
For[x] there is a sacrifice for Yahweh in Bozrah,[y]
And a great slaughter in the land of Edom.

7/ And the wild oxen will go down with them,
And young bulls with mighty bulls,
And their land[z] will be saturated[*a] with blood,
And their dust will be greasy with fat.

8/ For[*b] there is a day of vengeance for Yahweh,
A year of recompense for the cause of Zion.

9/ And its wadis will be turned to pitch,
And its dust to brimstone,
And its land will turn into[*c] burning pitch.[*d]

10/ Night and day it will never go out,[*e]
Forever its smoke will rise,[*f]
From generation to generation it will lie in ruins,[*g]
For ever and ever no one will pass through it.[*h]

11/ But the jackdaw and the hedgehog will possess it,[*i]
The owl and the raven[*j] will dwell in it;[*k]
And he will stretch[*l] the line of chaos[*m] over it,[*n]
And the stones of emptiness.

12/ "There is no kingdom there," they will name (it);
Its nobles[*o] and all its princes will be nothing.[*p]

13/ And thorn bushes will grow up[*q] in its citadels,[*r]
Nettles and briers in its fortifications,[*s]
And it will be[*t] a dwelling for jackals,
An abode[*u] of ostriches.

14/ And wildcats will meet hyenas,[*v]
And a goat-demon will call to its companion,
There too[*w] Lilith[*x] will repose,[*y]
And find[*z] a resting place for herself.[†a]

15/ There the arrow-snake[†b] will nest,
And lay eggs and hatch,
And brood in its shade;
Also there[†c] the vultures[†d] will gather,
Each with its companion.

16/ Search[†e] from upon the scroll of Yahweh,
And read,
Not one of them will be lacking,[†f]
They will not miss[†g] each its companion.

For it is his mouth that has commanded,[th]
And it is his spirit that has gathered them.[ti]

17/ And it is he who apportioned[tj] (it) to them[tk] by lot,
And his hand[tl] divided it[tm] to them[tn] by cord;
Forever they will possess it,[to]
For generation and generation they will dwell in it.[tp]

Textual Notes

a MT קִרְבוּ (qirbû), "draw near"; 1QIsaᵃ קרובו.

b MT גּוֹיִם (gôyīm), "nations"; 1QIsaᵃ גואים.

c MT לִשְׁמֹעַ (lišmōaʿ), "to hear"; 1QIsaᵃ לשמוע.

d MT וּלְאֻמִּים (ûlĕʾummîm), "and peoples"; 1QIsaᵃ ולאומים.

e MT וּמְלֹאָהּ (ûmĕlōʾāh), "and what fills it"; 1QIsaᵃ ומלואה.

f MT וְכָל (wĕkol), "and all"; 1QIsaᵃ וכול.

g MT כִּי (kî), "for"; 1QIsaᵃ כיא.

h See note f above.

i See note b above.

j MT נְתָנָם (nĕtānām), "he has given them"; 1QIsaᵃ ונתנם, "and he has given them."

k MT לַטֶּבַח (laṭṭābaḥ), "to slaughter"; 1QIsaᵃ לטבוח, corrected to the qal infinitive construct.

l MT יֻשְׁלָכוּ (yušlākû), "will be cast out"; 1QIsaᵃ יושלכו.

m MT בָּאְשָׁם (boʾšām), "their stench"; 1QIsaᵃ באושמה.

n MT וּפִגְרֵיהֶם (ûpigrêhem), "and their corpses"; 1QIsaᵃ ופגריהמה.

o MT הָרִים (hārîm), "(the) mountains"; 1QIsaᵃ with the article ההרים, "the mountains."

p MT כָּל־צְבָא (kol-ṣĕbāʾ), "all the host"; 1QIsaᵃ וכול צבא, "and all the host."

q MT וְנָמַקּוּ (wĕnāmaqqû), "and they will rot"; 1QIsaᵃ והעמקים יתבקעו וכול צבא השמים יפולו, "and the valleys will be split and all the host of heaven will fall." The versions do not support 1QIsaᵃ's reading, though LXX seems to lack the first line of the verse.

r MT וְכָל־צְבָאָם יִבּוֹל (wĕkol-ṣĕbāʾām yibbôl), "and all their host will wither"; 1QIsaᵃ וכול צבאם יבול. It is probably a corruption of this line that gave the earlier וכול צבא השמים יפולו, "and all the host of heaven will fall." Note that LXX has here καὶ πάντα τὰ ἄστρα πεσεῖται, "and all the stars will fall."

s MT כִּנְבֹל עָלֶה מִגֶּפֶן (kinbōl ʿāleh miggepen), "as a leaf withers from the vine"; 1QIsaᵃ כנובל עלה מגופן, reading the participle rather than the infinitive.

t MT וּכְנֹבֶלֶת מִתְּאֵנָה (ûkĕnōbelet mittĕʾēnâ), "and withered fruit from a fig tree"; 1QIsaᵃ וכנובלת מן תאנה.

u The verb in MT כִּי־רִוְּתָה בַשָּׁמַיִם חַרְבִּי (kî-riwwĕtâ baššāmayim ḥarbî), "for my sword will give drink abundantly in the heavens," should probably be corrected from the piel (riwwĕtâ) to the qal (rāwĕtâ) with LXX, Vg., Syr. ("for my sword will become drunk in the heavens"); cf. v. 7; 1QIsaᵃ כיא תראה בשמים חרביא, "for my sword will be seen in the heavens," so Tg. אֲרֵי תִתְגְּלֵי בִשְׁמַיָּא חַרְבִּי (ʾĕrê titgĕlê bišmayāʾ ḥarbî), "for my sword will be revealed in the heavens."

v Literally, wĕ-al-ʿam ḥermî lĕmišpāṭ, "and upon the people of my ban to judgment."

w MT כְּלָיוֹת (kilyôt), "kidneys"; 1QIsaᵃ כלאיות.

x MT כִּי (kî), "for"; 1QIsaᵃ כיא.

y MT בְּבָצְרָה (bĕboṣrâ), "in Bozrah"; 1QIsaᵃ בבוצרה.

z MT אַרְצָם (ʾarṣām), "their land"; 1QIsaᵃ ארצמה.

*a As in v. 5, MT's piel וְרִוְּתָה (wĕriwwĕtâ), "and she saturated," should be corrected to the qal וְרָוְתָה (wĕrāwĕtâ), "and she was saturated," with LXX, Vg., Syr. (so also BHS).

*b See note x above.

*c MT וְהָיְתָה (wĕhāyĕtâ), "and (its land) will become/turn into"; 1QIsaᵃ והיתה.

*d MT לְזֶפֶת בֹּעֵרָה (lĕzepet bōʿērâ), "to burning pitch," Vg., Syr., Tg.; 1QIsaᵃ takes the participle with the beginning of the following verse: לזפת ובערה לילה ויום, "to pitch, and it will burn night and day." LXX splits the difference καὶ ἔσται αὐτῆς ἡ γῆ καιομένη ὡς πίσσα νυκτὸς καὶ ἡμέρας, "and its land will become burning like pitch night and day."

*e MT לֹא תִכְבֶּה (lōʾ tikbê), "it will not go out," Vg., Tg., Syr.; 1QIsaᵃ ולוא תכובה לעולם (wĕlōʾ tĕkubbê lĕʿôlām), "and it will not be quenched forever," so also LXX.

*f MT לְעוֹלָם יַעֲלֶה עֲשָׁנָהּ (lĕʿôlām yaʿăleh ʿăšānāh), "forever its smoke will rise," Vg., Tg., Syr.; 1QIsaᵃ ועלה עשנה מדור לדור, "and its smoke will rise from generation to generation." LXX καὶ ἀναβήσεται ὁ καπνὸς αὐτῆς ἄνω, "and its smoke will go up."

*g MT מִדּוֹר לָדוֹר תֶּחֱרָב (middôr lādôr teḥĕrāb), "from generation to generation it will lie in ruins," Vg., Syr., Tg.; 1QIsaᵃ ותחרב לנצח נצחים, "and it will lie in ruins for ever and ever." LXX εἰς γενεὰς ἐρημωθήσεται καὶ εἰς χρόνον πολύν, "for generations it will be left desolate and for a long time."

*h MT לְנֵצַח נְצָחִים אֵין עֹבֵר בָּהּ (lĕnēṣaḥ nĕṣāḥîm ʾên ʿōbēr bāh), "for ever and ever no one will pass through it," Vg., Syr., Tg.; 1QIsaᵃ ואין עובר בה, "and no one will pass through it." LXX lacks the negated participial construction.

*i MT וִירֵשׁוּהָ (wîrēšûhā), "and they will possess it"; 1QIsaᵃ וירשוהה.

*j MT וְעֹרֵב (wĕʿōrēb), "and raven"; 1QIsaᵃ ועורב.

*k MT יִשְׁכְּנוּ־בָהּ (yiškĕnû-bāh), "will dwell in it"; 1QIsaᵃ ישכונו בהא.

*l MT וְנָטָה (wĕnāṭâ), "and he will stretch"; 1QIsaᵃ ונטא.

*m MT קַו־תֹהוּ (qaw-tōhû), "line of chaos"; 1QIsaᵃ קו ותהו, "a line and chaos."

*n MT עָלֶיהָ (ʿālêhā), "over it"; 1QIsaᵃ עליהא.

*o MT חֹרֶיהָ וְאֵין־שָׁם מְלוּכָה יִקְרָאוּ (ḥōrêhā wĕʾên-šām mĕlûkâ yiqrāʾû), "its nobles, and there is no kingdom there, they will call/name it"; 1QIsaᵃ וחריה ואין שמה מלוכה יקראו. The text is quite awkward and dubious. The initial noun ḥōrêhā, "its nobles," or wĕḥōrêhā, "and its nobles," should probably follow the verb yiqrāʾû, "they will call/name it," right before the parallel expression "and all its princes." Why the displacement took place is not as clear.

*p MT וְכָל־שָׂרֶיהָ יִהְיוּ אָפֶס (wĕkol-śārêhā yihyû ʾāpes), "and all its

434

princes will be nothing"; 1QIsaᵃ וכול שריה יהיו כאפס (wĕkôl śārêha yihyû kĕ²apes), "and all its princes will be <as> nothing," though the preposition kĕ, "as," is marked as an error to be erased.

*q There is a strange lack of agreement between the plural noun סירים (sîrîm), "thorn bushes," and the feminine singular verb וְעָלְתָה (wĕ²ālĕtâ), "and it will grow up."

*r MT אַרְמְנֹתֶיהָ (²armĕnōtêha), "its citadels"; 1QIsaᵃ ארמנותיה. The form is apparently to be taken as an adverbial accusative.

*s MT בְּמִבְצָרֶיהָ (bĕmibṣārêha), "in its fortifications"; 1QIsaᵃ במבצריהא.

*t MT וְהָיְתָה (wĕhāyĕtâ), "and it will be"; 1QIsaᵃ והייתה.

*u MT חָצִיר (ḥāṣîr), "grass," but here for ḥāṣēr, "courtyard, dwelling"; 1QIsaᵃ חצר (ḥāṣēr), "courtyard, dwelling."

*v MT אֶת־אִיִּים (²et-²îyîm), "wildcats"; 1QIsaᵃ את אייאמים.

*w MT אַף־שָׁם (²ak-šām), "there too"; 1QIsaᵃ אכ שמה.

*x MT לִילִית (lîlît), "Lilith"; 1QIsaᵃ ליליות, "the Lilith demons."

*y MT הִרְגִּיעָה (hirgî²â), "reposes," hiphil perfect third person feminine singular; 1QIsaᵃ ירגיעו (yargî²û), "they will rest," hiphil imperfect third person masculine plural.

*z MT וּמָצְאָה (²ûmāṣĕ²â), "and find," qal perfect third person feminine singular; 1QIsaᵃ ומצאו (²ûmāṣĕ²û), "and they will find," qal perfect third person masculine plural.

†a MT לָהּ (lāh), "for herself"; 1QIsaᵃ להמה (lāhēmmâ), "for themselves."

†b MT קִפּוֹז (qippôz), "arrow-snake"; 1QIsaᵃ קופד for קִפּוֹד (qippôd), "hedgehog," so also LXX, Vg., Syr., and Tg.

†c See note *w above.

†d MT דַּיּוֹת (dayyôt), "the vultures"; 1QIsaᵃ דוות. LXX has "deer," but the other versions support MT.

†e MT דִּרְשׁוּ (diršû), "seek"; 1QIsaᵃ דרושו.

†f MT אַחַת מֵהֵנָּה לֹא נֶעְדָּרָה (²aḥat mēhēnnâ lō² ne²dārâ), "one of them will not be lacking"; 1QIsaᵃ ואחת לוא נעדרה, "and one will not be lacking."

†g MT אִשָּׁה רְעוּתָהּ לֹא פָקָדוּ (²iššâ rĕ²ûtāh lō² pāqādû), "they will not miss each its companion"; 1QIsaᵃ omits lō² pāqādû, "they will not miss."

†h Reading כִּי־פִיהוּ הוּא צִוָּה (kî-pîhû hû² ṣiwwâ), "for it is his mouth that commanded it"; MT lacks the suffix on פי, but 1QIsaᵃ has כיא פיהו הוא צוה, and the parallelism with the next line requires the third person masculine singular suffix. MT has suffered a simple haplography because of the repetition of הו in פיהו הוא.

†i MT וְרוּחוֹ הוּא קִבְּצָן (wĕrûḥô hû² qibbĕṣān), "and it is his spirit that has gathered them [fem. pl.]"; 1QIsaᵃ ורוחתהו היאה קבצם, "and it is his spirit that has gathered them [masc. pl.]."

†j MT וְהוּא־הִפִּיל (wĕhû²-hippîl), "and it was he who cast (the lot for them)"; 1QIsaᵃ והואה הפיל.

†k MT לָהֶן (lāhen), "to them"; 1QIsaᵃ להנה.

†l MT וְיָדוֹ (wĕyādô), "and his hand"; 1QIsaᵃ וידיו, "and his hands."

†m MT חִלְּקַתָּה (ḥillĕqattâ), "divided it"; 1QIsaᵃ חלקת (ḥillĕqat), "divided."

†n MT לָהֶם (lāhem), "to them"; 1QIsaᵃ להמה, "to them [masc pl.]," corrected to להן, "to them [fem. pl.]."

†o MT יִירָשׁוּהָ (yîrāšûha), "they will possess it"; 1QIsaᵃ ירשוה is inserted above the line.

†p MT לְדוֹר וָדוֹר יִשְׁכְּנוּ־בָהּ (lĕdôr wādôr yiškĕnû-bāh), "for generation and generation they will dwell in it"; 1QIsaᵃ inserts this line in very small script along with 35:1-2 before continuing with 35:3 in normal script.

Commentary

Isaiah 34 opens with an appeal to all nations and peoples, the whole world and all its inhabitants, to draw near, pay close attention, and listen (v. 1), for Yahweh is angry with all nations (v. 2). His wrath is against all their host. He has dedicated them to the ban (הֶחֱרִימָם, heḥĕrîmām, "devoted them to destruction") and handed them over to slaughter. Their slain will be cast out, the stench of their corpses (פִּגְרֵיהֶם, pigrêhem) will rise up, and the mountains will flow or melt (וְנָמַסּוּ, wĕnāmassû) with their blood. The picture is of a gruesome slaughter of such a large multitude that the horrible stench of the rotting dead nauseates, and the liquid gore transforms the landscape. But not just the landscape. All the host of heaven will also rot away (וְנָמַקּוּ, wĕnāmaqqû); the heavens will be rolled up like a scroll, and all their host—the sun, moon, and stars—will wither as a leaf withers from the vine, or as withered fruit from a fig tree (v. 4). The imagery here of worldwide judg-

ment that affects the heavenly hosts as well as the human armies on earth is similar to that in Isa 24:21-23. As God says in v. 5, "My sword has saturated itself in the heavens; now it is about to descend upon Edom, upon the people I have doomed to judgment" (וְעַל־עַם חֶרְמִי לְמִשְׁפָּט, wĕ²al-²am ḥermî lĕmišpāṭ, lit., "and upon the people of my ban to judgment").

This gory imagery is continued in v. 6 with the statement that Yahweh has a sword that is covered in blood (מָלְאָה דָם, mālĕ²â dām, "full of blood") and smeared with fat (הֻדַּשְׁנָה מֵחֵלֶב, huddašnâ mēḥēleb, "greasy with fat") from sacrificial animals, blood from young rams (כָּרִים, kārîm) and billy goats (וְעַתּוּדִים, wĕ²attûdîm), fat from the kidneys (מֵחֵלֶב כְּלָיוֹת, mēḥēleb kilyôt) of rams (אֵילִים, ²êlîm). The sheep and goats mentioned are all male, because normally only male animals were sacrificed; the females were preserved to increase the flock or herd, while it was only necessary to preserve a few of the males for this purpose. That these are sacrificial animals is clear from

435

the final statement in the verse about Yahweh's sacrifice in Bozrah, his great slaughter in the land of Edom. But it is also clear that the animals mentioned are only metaphors for the human population of Edom and its important city Bozrah. There is a long convention in West Semitic of using animal names as designations for human nobility,[1] so the prophet's audience would immediately have thought of Edom's human leaders as the sacrificial animals God was slaughtering. Moreover, this motif of Yahweh's sacrifice of his human enemies is found already in Zeph 1:7-8, from the time of Josiah; in Jer 46:10, from c. 605 BCE; and in Ezek 39:17-19, from the first half of the Babylonian exile. Here this slaughter of Edom's nobility is not restricted to the mid-level nobility, the rams and billy goats. As v. 7 indicates, the most powerful of Edom's leaders, the wild oxen (רְאֵמִים, rĕʾēmîm) will go down with them, and the young bulls (וּפָרִים, ûpārîm) with the mighty bulls (עִם־אַבִּירִים, ʿim-ʾabbîrîm). The slaughter will be so great that their land will be saturated (וְרִוְּתָה, wĕriwwĕtâ) with blood, and their dust will be greasy (יְדֻשָּׁן, yĕduššān) with fat. This is coming, because Yahweh will have his day of vengeance and year of recompense for the cause of Zion (v. 8). Because Edom took advantage of Jerusalem's weakness, both helping the Babylonians and helping themselves to Zion's former territory, Yahweh will repay them in full for their treachery (cf. Isa 63:1-6; Jer 49:7-22; Ezek 35:1-15; Joel 4:19; Obad 10-16; Mal 1:3-4).

Edom's dry water-courses or wadis will be turned to pitch, its dust to brimstone, and its land to burning pitch (v. 9). The burning land will never be quenched, day or night; its smoke will rise forever; it will remain a ruin throughout the generations with no one ever crossing through it (v. 10). The imagery here of an utterly desolate, inhospitable, and abandoned landscape, burning with an unquenchable fire, comes close to the traditional descriptions of the overthrow of Sodom and Gomorrah and the cities of the plain (Gen 19:24-28; Deut 29:23; Isa 13:19-20; Jer 49:18; 50:40; Amos 4:11; Zeph 2:9), then, via the pagan *tophet*, of the sacrificial burning of children in the valley of the son of Hinnom (בְּגֵיא בֶן־הִנֹּם, bĕgêʾ ben-hinnōm, 2 Kgs 23:10; Jer 7:31-32; 19:2-6; 32:35; cf.

Isa 66:24), and of the later descriptions of hell (γέενναν, geennan, Matt 5:22, 29-30; 10:28; 18:9; 23:15, 33; Mark 9:43, 45, 47; Luke 12:5; Jas 3:6; cf. Rev 20:14-15; 21:8).

At v. 11 the prophet drops the fire imagery to elaborate on the imagery of an abandoned landscape inhabited only by wild creatures of the deserted steppe. The identification of many of these desert creatures is highly uncertain. The jackdaw (קָאַת, qāʾat, or "owl") and the hedgehog (וְקִפֹּד, wĕqippōd, or "short-eared owl"), the great owl (יַנְשׁוֹף, yanšôp, or "ibis" or "bee-eater"), and the raven (עֹרֵב, ʿōrēb) will dwell there. There will be no human builder there to stretch out a measuring line (קָו, qaw) or drop a stone plumb line to check the depth of a well or to see that the wall he is building is vertical (cf. Isa 28:17; Amos 7:7-8; Zech 4:10). The only line there will be the line of chaos that Yahweh stretches over it;[2] the only stones, those of empty badlands. They will name it, "There is no kingdom there," and its former nobles (חֹרֶיהָ, ḥōrêhā) and all its royal officials (וְכָל־שָׂרֶיהָ, wĕkol-śārêhā) will no longer exist (v. 12). Thornbushes (סִירִים, sîrîm) will grow up in its citadels, nettles (קִמּוֹשׂ, qimmôš) and briers (וָחוֹחַ, wāḥôaḥ) in its fortifications (v. 13). It will be a camping place (נָוֶה, nĕwê) for jackals and an open settlement (חָצֵר, ḥāṣēr) for ostriches. Wildcats (צִיִּים, ṣiyîm) will meet hyennas (אִיִּים, ʾiyîm, or "jackals") and a goat-demon (שָׂעִיר, sāʿîr) will call to its companion; there too the Lilith-demon (לִילִית, lîlît) will repose and find a resting place for herself (v. 14). Here the prophet leaves the actual fauna of deserted places for the common superstitious fear of them that populates them with frightful demons as well as wild and sometimes dangerous animals. The goat-demons were similar to the satyrs of the Greek world, while Lilith was a female demon feared for killing babies and otherwise creating havoc with human sexuality.

There the arrowsnake (קִפּוֹז, qippôz, a tree-dwelling snake or a type of bird) makes its nest (קִנְּנָה, qinnĕnâ), lays its eggs (וַתְּמַלֵּט, wattĕmallēṭ, "and brings forth"), and will hatch (וּבָקְעָה, ûbāqĕʿâ, "and will split open") and brood (וְדָגְרָה, wĕdāgĕrâ, "and will brood") in its shade (v. 15). Some scholars think of "brooding" only as the snake's or bird's care for the eggs until they are hatched and hence

---

1   P. D. Miller, "Animal Names as Designations in Ugaritic and Hebrew," *UF* 2 (1970) 177–86.

2   There may be an echo here of the use of תהו ובהו elsewhere (cf. Gen 1:2; Jer 4:23; and, closer to the usage here, Deut 32:10; Job 6:18; 12:24; Ps 107:40).

assume that the order of וּבָקְעָה וְדָגְרָה (*ûbāqĕ‛â wĕdāgĕrâ*) has been inadvertently transposed,[3] but if "brooding" can also refer to the care that a bird, in particular, gives to its young offspring after they hatch, there is no need to correct the text. There also the vultures (דַיּוֹת, *dayyôt*, or "birds of prey") gather, each with its companion.

The following command in v. 16 is surprising. The prophet's audience is urged to seek or search on the scroll of Yahweh and read the scroll, apparently an earlier written document with an oracle of judgment against Edom, though precisely what that document might have been remains unclear. According to our prophet, however, each of these creatures is to be found mentioned in the scroll. Not one of them will be lacking, and no one of them will miss her companion, for it is his mouth (Yahweh's) that commanded, and it is his spirit that will gather them. Using traditional Israelite terminology for the communal distribution of property, the prophet claims that Yahweh has legally given to these wild creatures and demons the Edomite territory forever. Yahweh has cast the lot (גּוֹרָל, *gôrāl*) for them, and his hand has apportioned it (וְיָדוֹ חִלְּקַתָּה, *wĕyādô ḥillĕqattāh*) to them by line (בַּקָּו, *baqqāw*), so they will possess it forever and dwell in it from generation to generation (v. 17). See the similar language for distributing property in Num 26:55-56; 33:54; 34:13; 36:2-3; Josh 14:2; 18:8-10 and passim; Mic 2:5; Pss 16:6; 60:8; 78:55; 105:11.

Bibliography

Beuken, W. A. M., "Isaiah 34: Lament in Isaianic Context," *OTE* 5 (1992) 78–102.

Bril, Jacqies, *Lilith, ou, La mère obscure* (Bibliothèque scientifique; Paris: Payot, 1984).

Caspari, W., "Jesaja 34 und 35," *ZAW* 49 (1931) 67–86.

Contenau, G., *La magie chez les Assyriens et les Babyloniens* (Bibliothèque historique; Paris: Payot, 1957).

Dicon, Bert, "Literary Function and Literary History of Isaiah 34," *BN* 58 (1991) 30–45.

Donner, H., "'Forscht in der Schrift JHWH's und lest': Ein Beitrag zum Verständnis des israelitischen Prophetie," *ZTK* 87 (1990) 285–98.

Elliger, Karl, *Deuterojesaja in seinem Verhältnis zu Tritojesaja* (BWANT 63; Stuttgart: Kohlhammer, 1933).

Emerton, J. A., "A Note on the Alleged Septuagintal Evidence for the Restoration of the Hebrew Text of Isaiah 34:11-12," *ErIsr* 16 (1982) 34–36.

Fauth, W., "Lilits und Astarten in aramäischen, mandäischen und syrischen Zaubertexten," *WO* 17 (1986) 66–94.

Gaster, T. H., *Myth, Legend, and Custom in the Old Testament: A Comparative Study with Chapters from Sir James G. Frazer's Folklore in the Old Testament* (New York: Harper & Row, 1969).

Gosse, B., "Isaïe 34–35: Le châtiment d'Edom et des Nations, salut pour Sion. Contribution à l'étude de la rédaction du livre d'Isaïe," *ZAW* 102 (1990) 396–404.

Grätz, H., "Isaiah XXXIV and XXXV," *JQR* 4 (1891) 1–8.

Gray, B., "Critical Discussions: Isaiah 26; 25 1-5; 34 12-14," *ZAW* 31 (1911) 111–27.

Grill, S., "Der Schlachttag Jahwes," *BZ* 1 (1957) 278–83.

Haag, H., "Der Tag Jahwes im Alten Testament," *BibLeb* 13, no. 14 (1972) 238–48.

Hillers, Delbert R., *Treaty-Curses and the Old Testament Prophets* (BibOr 16; Rome: Pontifical Biblical Institute, 1964).

Hommel, F., "Isaiah XXXIV 15," *ExpTim* 12 (1900) 336.

Hurwitz, S., *Lilith, die erste Eva: Eine Studie über dunkle Aspekte der Weiblichkeit* (Zurich: Daimon, 1980).

Hutter, M., "Lilith," *DDD*, 2nd ed., 520–21.

Kellermann, U., *Israel und Edom: Studien zum Edomhass Israels im 6.–4. Jahrhundert v.Chr.* Habilitationsschrift, Münster, 1975.

Killen, A. M., "La légende de Lilith et quelques interprétations modernes de cette figure légendaire," *RLC* 12 (1932) 277–311.

Koeverden, W. van, "Isaïe, XXXIV, 15," *RB* 9 (1912) 542–43.

Krebs, W., "Lilith—Adams erste Frau," *ZRGG* 27 (1975) 141–52.

Langdon, Stephen Herbert, *Semitic Mythology* (Mythology of All Races 5; Boston: Marshal Jones, 1965) 361–64.

---

3   So Duhm, Cheyne, and others according to Wildberger, 3:1329.

Levonian, L., "Isaiah XXXIV 5," *ExpTim* 24 (1913) 45–46.

Lim, Bo H., *The "Way of the Lord" in the Book of Isaiah* (LHBOTS 522; London: T&T Clark, 2010).

Lust, Johan, "Isaiah 34 and the *herem*," in J. Vermeylen, ed., *Le livre d'Isaïe: Les oracles et leurs relectures unité et complexité de l'ouvrage* (BETL 81; Leuven: Leuven University Press, 1989) 275–86.

Mailland, A., "La 'Petite apocalypse' d'Isaïe: Étude sur les chapitres XXXIV et XXXV du livre d'Isaïe" (Diss., Lyon, 1955–56).

Mathews, Claire R., *Defending Zion: Edom's Desolation and Jacob's Restoration (Isaiah 34–35) in Context* (BZAW 236; Berlin: de Gruyter, 1995).

Miscall, Peter D., *Isaiah 34–35: A Nightmare/A Dream* (JSOTSup 281; Sheffield: Sheffield Academic Press, 1999).

Morgenstern, J., "Further Light from the Book of Isaiah upon the Catastrophe of 485 B.C.," *HUCA* 37 (1966) 1–28, esp. 4–13.

———, "The Loss of Words at the Ends of Lines in Manuscripts of Hebrew Poetry," *HUCA* 25 (1954) 41–83.

Muilenburg, J., "The Literary Character of Isaiah 34," *JBL* 59 (1940) 339–65.

Orlinski, H. M., "Studies in the St. Mark's Isaiah Scroll, VI," *HUCA* 25 (1954) 85–92, esp. 88–90.

Patai, Raphael, *The Hebrew Goddess* (New York: Ktav, 1967) 207–45, 318–22.

Pope, M., "Isaiah 34 in Relation to Isaiah 35, 40–66," *JBL* 71 (1952) 235–43.

Ribichini, A., "Lilith nell' albera ḤULUPPU," in *Atti del 1. Convegno italiano sul Vicino Oriente antico (Rome, 22–24 aprile, 1976)* (Orientis antiqui collectio 13; Rome: Centro per le antichità e la storia dell'arte del Vicino Oriente, 1978) 25–33.

Rose, M., "Yahweh in Israel: Qaus in Edom?" *JSOT* 4 (1977) 28–34.

Sawyer, J. F. A., "The Role of Jewish Studies in Biblical Semantics," in H. L. J. Vanstiphout et al., eds., *Scripta signa vocis: Studies about Scripts, Scriptures, Scribes, and Languages in the Near East, Presented to J. H. Hospers by His Pupils, Colleagues and Friends* (Groningen: E. Forsten, 1986) 201–8.

Scholem, G., "Lilith," *EncJud*, 11:245–49.

Seitz, Christopher R., "On the Question of Divisions Internal to the Book of Isaiah," in *SBLSP 1993* (Atlanta: Scholars Press, 1993) 260–73.

Smart, J. D., *History and Theology in Second Isaiah* (Philadelphia: Westminster, 1965).

Stern, P. D., "Isaiah 34, Chaos, the Ban," in Robert Chazan, William W. Hallo, and Lawrence H. Schiffman, eds., *Ki Baruch Hu: Ancient Near Eastern, Biblical, and Judaic Studies in Honor of Baruch A. Levine* (Winona Lake, IN: Eisenbrauns, 1999) 387–400.

Tanghe, Vincent, "Der Schriftgelehrte in Jes 34:16–17," *ETL* 67 (1991) 338–45.

Torrey, C. C., *The Second Isaiah: A New Interpretation* (New York: Scribner, 1928).

———, "Some Important Editorial Operations in the Book of Isaiah," *JBL* 57 (1938) 109–39.

Vermeylen, *Du prophète Isaïe*, 1:439–46.

Vértesalji, P. P., "'La déesse nue élamite' und der Kreis der babylonischen '*Lilû*'-Dämonen," *Iranica Antiqua* 26 (1991) 101–48.

Weippert, M., "Studien und Materialien zur Geschichte der Edomiter auf Grund schriftlicher und archäologischer Quellen" (Diss., Tübingen, 1971).

Williamson, *Book Called Isaiah*, 116, 211–21.

Young, E. J., "Isaiah 34 and Its Position in the Prophecy," *WTJ* 27 (1964–65) 93–114.

35

1/ The wilderness and dry land will rejoice,[a]
And the steppe will be glad and blossom like a lily.

2/ It will surely blossom,
And rejoice with joy and singing;
The glory of the Lebanon[b] will be given to it,
The splendor of Carmel and Sharon;
They will see[c] the glory of Yahweh,
The splendor of our God.

3/ Strengthen[d] the weak hands,
Make firm the stumbling[e] knees.

4/ Say to the fearful of heart,
Be strong, do not be afraid;
Here is your God,[f]
Vengeance is coming,[g]
The requital of God[h]—
He[i] will come[j] and save you.[k]

5/ Then the eyes of the blind will be opened,
And the ears[l] of the deaf will be unstopped.

6/ Then the lame will leap like the deer,[m]
And the tongue of the dumb will sing for joy,[n]
For[o] waters will break forth in the wilderness,
And flowing wadis in the steppe.[p]

7/ And the scorched ground will become a pool,
And the thirsty ground, springs of water,
In the abode of jackals there will be a pasture,[q]
The home [of ostriches][q] will become reeds and rushes.

8/ And there will be[r] a highway[s] there,[t]
And the way of holiness[u] it will be named,[v]
And an unclean person[w] will not pass along it,[x]
But it will be for them,[y]
The one who walks the way,[z] even fools, will not*[a] stray.

9/ There will not*[b] be a lion there,*[c]
And no predator among the beasts will go up upon it,*[d]
It will not be found there,*[e]
But the redeemed will walk (it).

10/ And the ransomed of Yahweh will return,*[f]
And enter Zion with a shout of rejoicing,*[g]
With eternal joy upon their head;*[h]
They will attain*[i] gladness and joy,
And sorrow and sighing will flee.*[j]

Textual Notes

a   MT, 1QIsa[a] יְשֻׂשׂוּם (yĕśūśûm), "let them rejoice"; the final *mem* is either a *nun paragogicum* that has been assimilated to the initial *mem* of the following word ישׂושׂום מ < ישׂושׂון מ, or, less likely, it is an enclitic *mem*. It is not a suffix. LXX translates the verb as an imperative singular: Εὐφράνθητι, "rejoice, (O thirsty wilderness)." Verses 1-2 of 1QIsa[a] are inserted in small script along with the last four words of 34:17; there is a small space before the regular script resumes at 35:3.

b   MT הַלְּבָנוֹן (hallĕbānôn), "the Lebanon"; 1QIsa[a] לבנון, "Lebanon."

c   LXX adds "my people" as the subject of the verb: καὶ ὁ λαός μου ὄψεται τὴν δόξαν κυρίου, "and my people will see the glory of the Lord."

d   LXX treats the first *piel* imperative as if it were a *qal* and takes "hands" and "knees" as the subject: ἰσχύσατε, χεῖρες ἀνειμέναι καὶ γόνατα παραλελυμένα, "Be strong, you weak hands and

feeble knees!," though the Hebrew verb is masculine plural, while both body parts are feminine duals.

e   MT כֹּשְׁלוֹת (kōšĕlôt), "stumbling"; 1QIsa[a] כושלות.

f   MT אֱלֹהֵיכֶם (ʾĕlōhêkem), "your God"; 1QIsa[a] אלוהכמה.

g   MT נָקָם יָבוֹא (nāqām yābôʾ), "vengeance is coming"; 1QIsa[a] נקם יביא (nāqām yābîʾ), "vengeance he will bring."

h   MT אֱלֹהִים (ʾĕlōhîm), "of God"; 1QIsa[a] אלוהים.

i   MT הוּא (hûʾ), "he"; 1QIsa[a] הואה.

j   MT יָבוֹא (yābôʾ), "will come"; 1QIsa[a] יביא (yābîʾ), "will bring."

k   MT וְיֹשַׁעֲכֶם (wĕyōšaʿăkem), "and will save you"; 1QIsa[a] ויושעכמה.

l   MT וְאָזְנֵי (wĕʾoznê), "and the ears of"; 1QIsa[a] ואוני.

m   MT כָּאַיָּל (kāʾayyāl), "like the deer"; 1QIsa[a] כאיאל.

n   MT וְתָרֹן (wĕtārōn), "and will sing for joy"; 1QIsa[a] ותרון; LXX has καὶ τρανὴ ἔσται γλῶσσα μογιλάλων, "and the tongue of stammerers will be clear"; Vg.: aperta erit lingua mutorum, "the tongue of the dumb will be open"; Syr.: ntpšt lšnh dpʾsʾ, "the tongue of the dumb will be straightened."

o MT כִּי (kî), "for"; 1QIsaᵃ כיא.

p MT וּנְחָלִים בָּעֲרָבָה (ûněḥālîm bāʿărābâ), "and wadis in the steppe"; 1QIsaᵃ adds a verb ונחלים בערבה ילכו (ûněḥālîm bāʿărābâ yělěkû), "and wadis in the steppe will flow," but this addition is not supported by the versions.

q MT רִבְצָה (ribṣāh), "its resting place, pasture"; 1QIsaᵃ רבצ is ambiguous; it could be analyzed as the noun rēbeṣ ("in the home of jackals there will be a pasture, resting place [for domesticated animals]") or as the verb rābaṣ ("in the pasture where jackals rested"), assuming an unmarked relative clause and a third person masculine singular verb with a masculine plural subject. For this last meaning with tannîm, "jackals," as the subject of the verb, two slight emendations have been suggested: rāběṣâ, "where jackals rested" (3rd fem. sg. verb with masc. pl. subject)[1] and rāběṣû, "where jackals rested," have been suggested (see Wildberger, 3:1354). LXX has ἐκεῖ εὐφροσύνη ὀρνέων, "the joy of birds will be there." My rendering follows the lead of JPS in assuming that this passage is an intentional reversal of the judgment announced on Edom in Isa 34:13. The formerly productive Edomite territory will be turned into an arid wasteland and become a dwelling for jackals (נְוֵה תַנִּים, něwēh tannîm) and an abode of ostriches (חָצִיר לִבְנוֹת יַעֲנָה, ḥāṣîr libnôt yaʿānâ), but Judah, which is such a wasteland now, will be turned into a well-watered landscape. In the former dwelling place for jackals (בִּנְוֵה תַנִּים, binwēh tannîm) there will be a pasture or resting place (רֵבֶץ, rēbeṣ) (for domesticated animals), and the abode (of ostriches) ([לִבְנוֹת יַעֲנָה] חָצִיר, ḥāṣîr [libnôt yaʿānâ]) will become a swampy area of reeds and rushes.

r MT וְהָיָה (wěhāyâ), "and there will be"; 1QIsaᵃ יהיה (yihyê), "there will be."

s MT מַסְלוּל (maslûl), "a highway"; 1QIsaᵃ מסלול. LXX has ἐκεῖ ἔσται ὁδὸς καθαρά, "a pure way will be there," which has led to the emendation of the first וְדֶרֶךְ (wāderek), "and the way," in MT to ברור (maslûl bārûr), "(there will be) a pure highway (there)," but the emendation is quite uncertain.

t MT שָׁם (šām), "there"; 1QIsaᵃ שמה שמה (šammâ šammâ), "there, there," clearly involves a dittography.

u MT וְדֶרֶךְ וְדֶרֶךְ הַקֹּדֶשׁ (wāderek wěderek haqqōdeš), "and the way, and the way of holiness," clearly involves a dittography of ודרך, though Vg. follows MT; cf. 1QIsaᵃ ודרך הקודש, "and the way of holiness."

v MT יִקָּרֵא לָהּ (yiqqārēʾ lāh), "it will be named to it"; 1QIsaᵃ יקראו לה (yiqrěʾû lāh), "they will name it." The noun דֶּרֶךְ (derek) may be either feminine or masculine; but the mixture of feminine and masculine suffixes referring to it—the feminine suffix here לָהּ (lāh), "to it/her," and the masculine suffix in the following clause (יַעַבְרֶנּוּ, yaʿaběrennû, "pass along it/him")—is troubling. Since the masculine subject pronoun וְהוּא (wěhûʾ), "and it/ he," is also used with דֶּרֶךְ (derek) as the understood subject, one should probably read all the forms as masculine, thus לֹה (lô, not lāh).

w MT טָמֵא (ṭāmēʾ), "an unclean person"; 1QIsaᵃ טמה written vertically in the margin.

x MT לֹא־יַעַבְרֶנּוּ (lōʾ-yaʿaběrennû), "will not pass along it"; 1QIsaᵃ לוא יעבורנה (lôʾ yaʿbôrennâ), "will not pass along it."

y MT וְהוּא־לָמוֹ (wěhûʾ-lāmô), "and it will be for him/them"; 1QIsaᵃ הואה ולמי, "it and for whomever (?)"; Vg. et haec erit nobis, "and this will be for us"; LXX οὐδὲ ἔσται ἐκεῖ ὁδὸς ἀκάθαρτος, "there will not be there an unclean way"; cf. Syr. wlʾ thwʾ bh ʾwrḥʾ, "and there will not be in it the way." Emendations suggested have included והוא לעמו (wěhûʾ lěʿammô), "and it will be for his people," or והוא לעם (wěhûʾ lāʿām), "and it will be for the people" (see Wildberger, 3:1355).

z MT הֹלֵךְ דֶּרֶךְ (hōlēk derek), "the one walking the way/the traveler"; 1QIsaᵃ הולך דרך.

*a MT לֹא (lōʾ), "not"; 1QIsaᵃ לוא.

*b See note *a above.

*c MT שָׁם (šām), "there"; 1QIsaᵃ שמה.

*d MT בַּל־יַעֲלֶנָּה (bal-yaʿălennâ), "will not go up on it"; 1QIsaᵃ has a redundant negative בל לוא יעלנה.

*e MT לֹא תִמָּצֵא שָׁם (lōʾ timmāṣēʾ šām), "and it [fem.] will not be found there"; 1QIsaᵃ ולוא ימצא שם, "and it [masc.] will not be found there."

*f MT יְשֻׁבוּן (yěšûbûn), "they will return"; 1QIsaᵃ ישובו.

*g MT בְּרִנָּה (běrinnâ), "with a shout of rejoicing"; 1QIsaᵃ ברונה.

*h MT עַל־רֹאשָׁם (ʿal-rōʾšām), "upon their head"; 1QIsaᵃ על ראושם.

*i MT יַשִּׂיגוּ (yaśśîgû), "they will attain"; 1QIsaᵃ ישיגו בה with the בה marked for erasure.

*j MT וְנָסוּ (wěnāsû), "and they will flee"; 1QIsaᵃ ונס, "and it will flee."

Commentary

The wilderness, dry land, and steppe of Isa 35:1, which will rejoice, be glad, and blossom like a beautiful wild flower, refers to the now barren and abandoned territory of Judah and Israel. Its coming fertility stands in sharp contrast to the now inhabited territory of Edom, which will become a barren, burning wasteland, fit only for wild creatures and demons (Isaiah 34). The identification of the חֲבַצָּלֶת (ḥăbaṣṣālet) is uncertain. It is variously translated as "rose," "crocus," "asphodel" (a kind of lily), or "meadow saffron" (see *HALOT*, 287). The metaphor suggests that it is a particularly abundant wildflower. The coming fertility and abundant blooming of plants in Judah will make this territory as gloriously verdant as the Lebanon, with the splendor of the greenery of Carmel

---

1 With many manuscripts; see *BHS*.

and the plain of Sharon just south of Mount Carmel (v. 2). With this transformation of nature, the prophet asserts, the inhabitants of Judah will see the glory of Yahweh and, including himself in the community, the splendor of "our" God. It is fairly common in the psalms and the prophets for nature to break into song rejoicing over God's deliverance of his people (Isa 44:23; 49:13; 51:3; 52:9; Ps 96:12; 98:8), but the trope of nature "rejoicing" as a synonym for abundant growth is not that common. For the construct form גִּילַת (gîlat), "with joy," in place of the expected absolute form גִּילָה (gîlâ), see GKC §130b.

In vv. 3-4, the prophet admonishes his audience with the only imperatives found in the chapter. He commands them to strengthen (חַזְּקוּ, ḥazzĕqû, "strengthen," masc. pl.) the weak or drooping hands and make firm (אַמְּצוּ, ʾammēṣû, masc. pl.) the stumbling knees. They are to do this by saying (אִמְרוּ, ʾimĕrû, "say," masc. pl.) to the fearful of heart (לְנִמְהֲרֵי־לֵב, lĕnimhărê-lēb, "the panicked of heart"), "Be strong! Do not fear! Here is your God! Vengeance [נָקָם, nāqām] is coming, the requital of God [גְּמוּל אֱלֹהִים, gĕmûl ʾĕlōhîm]! He will come and save you!" In effect, the prophet is urging his audience to encourage one another precisely as the prophet by his message is encouraging his community. The time of suffering will soon be over. The oppressive enemy, of whom Edom (chap. 34) is a prime example (see the verbal echoes of 34:8 in 35:4), will soon receive God's just judgment for their treatment of Judah, while Judah will rejoice in God's salvation.

With God's intervention to save Judah a remarkable transformation in the physical and moral character and abilities of God's people will take place. If disobedient Israel had earlier been characterized as having eyes, but not able to see, as having ears, but not able to hear (Isa 6:9-10; cf. Isa 29:10-12, 18), when God comes to save his people, then the eyes of the blind will be opened, and the ears of the deaf will be opened (cf. Isa 42:18-19; 43:8). Then, instead of stumbling knees (v. 3), the lame person (פִּסֵּחַ, pissēaḥ) will leap like the deer, and the tongue of the dumb (אִלֵּם, ʾillēm, "one unable to speak") will sing for joy (וְתָרֹן, wĕtārōn). This is in response to the physical transformation of Judah back into a fertile land, "for waters will break forth in the wilderness, and flowing wadis in the steppe" (v. 6). The scorched ground will become a pool, and the thirsty ground will become springs of water (v. 7). This transformation of the Judean landscape is a direct reversal of the transformation of the landscape of its

enemy Edom (Isa 34:9-15). Edom will become a scorched wasteland, but Judah will once again become a well-watered Eden. In the place where jackals once dwelled, there will be pastureland, and in the dry places where ostriches once stayed, there will be reeds and rushes (see the direct verbal echoes of Isa 34:13 in Isa 35:7).

In contrast to Edom, through which no one will pass forever and ever (Isa 34:10), there will be a highway (מַסְלוּל, maslûl) in Judah (35:8). The word מַסְלוּל (maslûl) is a synonym of מְסִלָּה (mĕsillâ; Isa 40:3; 49:11; 62:10), and both words refer to a road that has been elevated above the level of the surrounding ground, leveled, and cleared of large stones and other obstructions. This road will be named the way or path of holiness (וְדֶרֶךְ הַקֹּדֶשׁ, wĕderek haqqōdeš), and no unclean person (טָמֵא, tāmēʾ) will pass along it. The expression וְהוּא־לָמוֹ (wĕhûʾ-lāmô), "and it will be for them," is quite ambiguous, but even if one does not emend to והוא לעמו (wĕhûʾ lĕʿammô), "and it will be for his people," or the like, the context, which prohibits the unclean from using this road, demands a sense in which the road is for the remnant of God's purified, chastened, morally transformed, and redeemed people (see also v. 10). No one who travels the road from that group, even if they are mentally challenged (lit., וֶאֱוִילִים, weʾĕwîlîm, "fools"), will stray from the path. The designation of this way as the road of holiness, the prohibition of the unclean from traveling it, and the inability of even fools to stray from it, suggest that the motif here is not limited to the idea of the road from Assyria and Egypt that the returning exiles will take (Isa 11:16; 19:23), much less to Second Isaiah's road from Mesopotamia that both God and the Babylonian exiles would take to Jerusalem (Isa 40:3; 49:11-12). The motif here also has a lot in common with the motif in Isa 30:19-21, where God's redeemed people will clearly hear their divine teacher correcting them anytime they start to turn either right or left from the appropriate path.

This road will also be safe from lions and other ravenous wild beasts (v. 9). They will not be there, they will not go up on it, and they will not be found there. Only the redeemed (גְּאוּלִים, gĕʾûlîm) will travel on it. And those ransomed by Yahweh (וּפְדוּיֵי יְהוָה, ûpĕdûyê YHWH) will use it to return and come back to Zion with singing and eternal joy on their heads (v. 10). They will obtain joy and rejoicing, and sorrow and sighing will flee away (cf. Isa 25:8; 26:1-2; 27:12-13).

441

Bibliography

Alonso Schökel, L., and C. Carnetti, "'In Testa' Is 35,10," *RivB* 34 (1986) 397–99.

Caspari, W., "Jesaja 34 und 35," *ZAW* 49 (1931) 67–86.

Clements, Ronald E., "Patterns in the Prophetic Canon: Healing the Blind and the Lame," in Gene M. Tucker, David L. Petersen, and Robert R. Wilson, *Canon, Theology, and Old Testament Interpretation: Essays in Honor of Brevard S. Childs* (Philadelphia: Fortress Press, 1988) 189–200.

Elliger, Karl, *Deuterojesaja in seinem Verhältnis zu Tritojesaja* (BWANT 63; Stuttgart: Kohlhammer, 1933).

Emerton, J. A., "A Note on Isaiah XXXV 9-10," *VT* 27 (1977) 488–89.

Frankfurter, David T. M., "The Origin of the Miracle-List Tradition and Its Medium of Circulation," in *SBLSP 1990* (Atlanta: Scholars Press, 1990) 344–74.

Gosse, B., "Isaïe 34–35: Le châtiment d'Edom et des Nations, salut pour Sion. Contribution à l'étude de la rédaction du livre d'Isaïe," *ZAW* 102 (1990) 396–404.

Grätz, H., "Isaiah XXXIV and XXXV," *JQR* 4 (1891) 1–8.

Harrelson, W., "Isaiah 35 in Recent Research and Translation," in Samuel E. Balentine and John Barton, eds., *Language, Theology, and the Bible: Essays in Honour of James Barr* (Oxford: Oxford University Press, 1994) 248–60.

Howell, Maribeth, "A Closer Look: Isaiah 35:1-10," in Lawrence Boadt and Mark S. Smith, eds., *Imagery and Imagination in Biblical Literature: Essays in Honor of Aloysius Fitzgerald, F.S.C.* (CBQMS 32; Washington, DC: Catholic Biblical Association of America, 2001) 72–80.

Hubmann, F. D., "Der 'Weg' zum Zion: Literar- und stilkritische Beobachtungen zu Jes 35:8-10," in Johannes B. Bauer and Johannes Marböck, eds., *Memoria Jerusalem: Freundesgabe Franz Sauer zum 70. Geburtstag* (Graz: Akademische Druck- u. Verlagsanstalt, 1977) 29–41.

Kraus, H.-J., "Jes 35:3-10," *Hören und Fragen* 5 (1976) 495–500.

Kuan, J. K., "The Authorship and Historical Background of Isaiah 35," *Jian Dao* 6 (1996) 1–12.

Levonian, L., "Isaiah XXXIV 5," *ExpTim* 24 (1913) 45–46.

Mailland, A., "La 'Petite apocalypse' d'Isaïe: Étude sur les chapitres XXXIV et XXXV du livre d'Isaïe" (Diss., Lyon, 1955–56).

Marx, A., "Brève note textuelle sur Esäie 35,8," *ZAW* 107 (1995) 123–28.

Mathews, Claire R., *Defending Zion : Edom's Desolation and Jacob's Restoration (Isaiah 34–35) in Context* (BZAW 236; Berlin: de Gruyter, 1995).

Miscall, Peter D., *Isaiah 34–35: A Nightmare/A Dream* (JSOTSup 281; Sheffield: Sheffield Academic Press, 1999).

Olmstead, A. T., "II Isaiah and Isaiah, Chapter 35," *AJSL* 53 (1936–37) 251–53.

Oswalt, John N., "God's Determination to Redeem His People (Isaiah 9:1-7; 11:1-11; 26:1-9; 35:1-10)," *RevExp* 88 (1991) 153–65.

Pope, M., "Isaiah 34 in Relation to Isaiah 35, 40–66," *JBL* 71 (1952) 235–43.

Scott, M., "Isaiah XXXV.7," *ExpTim* 37 (1925) 122.

Scott, R. B. Y., "The Relation of Isaiah, Chapter 35, to Deutero-Isaiah," *AJSL* 52 (1936) 178–91.

Smart, J. D., *History and Theology in Second Isaiah* (Philadelphia: Westminster, 1965).

Steck, Odil Hannes, *Bereitete Heimkehr: Jesaja 35 als redaktionelle Brücke zwischen dem Ersten und dem Zweiten Jesaja* (SBS 121; Stuttgart: Katholisches Bibelwerk, 1985).

Torrey, C. C., *The Second Isaiah. A New Interpretation* (New York: Scribner, 1928).

Wernberg-Møller, P., "Two Difficult Passages in the Old Testament," *ZAW* 69 (1957) 69–73, esp. 71–73 on Isa 35:4.

Williamson, *Book Called Isaiah.*

Apart from 2 Kgs 18:14-17, which contains the report of Hezekiah's submission to Sennacherib and the tribute imposed upon him, which is missing in Isaiah, and Isaiah 38:9-20, which contains the prayer of Hezekiah, which is missing in Kings, 2 Kgs 18:13–20:19 and Isaiah 36–39 contain slightly variant readings for what is basically the same underlying text. This has raised the question of the direction of dependency.[1] Did the editors of the book of Isaiah borrow from 2 Kings, or did the editors of 2 Kings borrow from the book of Isaiah? Or, as I am more inclined to believe, did both collections independently borrow from a third, independent source? The version in Isaiah, with the mention of only one Assyrian official at the meeting before the walls of Jerusalem over against the three officials mentioned in Kings (2 Kgs 18:17; Isa 36:2), and the ad hoc, almost supplementary mention of the cake of figs and the prophetic sign in Isa 38:21, over against the coherent inclusion of these elements in 2 Kgs 20:7-11, suggest that the account in 2 Kings is primary over against the account in Isaiah, but the reality is probably more complex than that. The account of Hezekiah's submission and the tribute he was required to pay in 2 Kgs 18:14-17 reads like an account taken from royal records, but the rest of the material common to both Kings and Isaiah has the character of prophetic stories, and it is very unlikely that the Deuteronomistic historian is the creator of these prophetic stories. It is far more likely that they originated among the disciples of the prophet and were secondarily borrowed and inserted into the Deuteronomistic history. That does not mean that the version in Isaiah is the earliest version, however. The editors of the book of Isaiah probably borrowed and adapted this material from the same source as the editors of the Deuteronomistic history.

Mordechai Cogan and Hayim Tadmor, following Bernhard Stade, Leo L. Honor, Brevard S. Childs,[2] and many others, divide the material in Kings concerning Sennacherib's campaign against Hezekiah into two discrete sources: (A) 18:13b-16 (= only Isa 36:1), a chronistic record; and (B) 18:17—19:37 (= Isa 36:2—37:38), prophetic narratives. They further divide B into B_1 (18:17—19:9a, 36) and B_2 (19:9b-35), though curiously omitting v. 37 from either strand.[3] This literary analysis may be correct, apart from the unnecessary omission of v. 37 from B_2 (see below), but the literary analysis does not solve the problem of dating the material.

The question of the date of this material is hotly debated and unlikely to be resolved to everyone's satisfaction until the eschaton. In my opinion, there is a widespread tendency to date these chapters far too late. The last detail mentioned in the traditions about Hezekiah and Isaiah in this material is the death of Sennacherib in 681 BCE, which means that the formulation of these traditions *in the shape we have them* must postdate that event. But there is no compelling reason to date these traditions long after that event. By the time of Jeremiah's conflict with King Jehoiakim of Judah, sometime after the death of Josiah in 609 BCE, the tradition of the earlier deliverance of Jerusalem under Hezekiah seems to have been a fixed part of the religious tradition in Judah (Jer 26:16-19). It appears to have been the basis for the Judeans' false confidence in the presence of Yahweh's temple among them (Jer 7:4-10) and Zedekiah's vain hope that Yahweh would perform another miracle to deliver Jerusalem in his day (Jer 21:1-2). Cogan and Tadmor claim that the information about the assassination of Sennacherib could only have been derived from a Babylonian chronicle,[4] which, given the date of these chronicles and Israelite access to them, would presumably put the creation of this account after the beginning of the Babylonian exile at the earliest, but their claim is dubious in the extreme, as I explain in the discussion on chap. 37. The death of a

---

1   Though they do not explicitly discuss the literary relationship between the text of 2 Kings and the Isaiah text, Mordechai Cogan and Hayim Tadmor have an extensive discussion of the text of Kings, Sennacherib's campaign, and the historical issues involved, along with references to earlier literature (*II Kings: A New Translation with Introduction and Commentary* [AB 11; Garden City, NY: Doubleday, 1988] 240-51).

2   Cogan and Tadmor, *II Kings,* 240; Bernhard Stade, "Anmerkungen zu 2 Kö. 15–21," *ZAW* 6 (1886)

122–92, esp. 172–83; Leo L. Honor, *Sennacherib's Invasion of Palestine: A Critical Source Study* (Contributions to Oriental History and Philology 12; New York: Columbia University Press, 1926) 45–48; Childs, *Assyrian Crisis,* 73–101.

3   Cogan and Tadmor, *II Kings,* 242–43.

4   Ibid., 244.

hated emperor is big news among the oppressed people of an imperial state, and the details of that death would spread like wildfire among the people soon after the event itself. News and basic details of Sargon II's death in 705 BCE reached Judah very quickly, as Isaiah's taunt song in chap. 14 indicates.[5] One must also assume that the exiled Judean and Israelite community in Assyrian exile in the mid-seventh century BCE corresponded with their countrymen in the old country just as the later Babylonian exiles did in the sixth century BCE, and it would be passing strange if they did not include any tidbits they had heard about the details of Sennacherib's death. In my opinion, then, nothing in these traditions requires a date later that the mid-seventh century for their formation. Even miracle stories do not require generations to be formed and become believable. Paul in 1 Cor 15:3-11, only twenty or so years after the death of Jesus, speaks of those who had seen the risen Christ, and the belief in a crucified Messiah who has been raised from the dead is a much harder miracle to sell than the belief in the miraculous deliverance of a city threatened with siege. Unexpected deliverances of threatened cities are not actually that rare in history.

---

5   Note also Eckart Frahm's important effort to tie the introduction of Gilgamesh tablet 12 to Sargon's death: "*Nabû-zaqup-bēnu*, das Gilgameš-Epos und der Tod Sargons II.," *JCS* 51 (1999) 73–90.

36

1/ In the fourteenth year[a] of King Hezekiah,[b] Sennacherib the king of Assyria went up against all[c] the fortified[d] cities of Judah and captured[e] them. **2/** And[f] the king of Assyria[g] sent (the) Rabshakeh[h] from Lachish to Jerusalem[i] to King Hezekiah[j] with a large[k] army, and he stood[l] at the channel of the upper pool on the road[m] by the laundryman's field.[n] **3/** And[o] Eliakim son of Hilkiah,[p] who was over the palace, and Shebna the secretary,[q] and Joah the son of Asaph, the recorder, went out to him.[r] **4/** And (the) Rabshakeh said to them,[s] "Say[t] to Hezekiah:[u] Thus[v] says the great king, the king of Assyria: What is this source of confidence in which you trust?[w] **5/** Do you think[x] that a mere word of the lips is counsel and strength for war? Now on whom[y] do you trust[z] that[*a] you have rebelled against me?[*b] **6/** See,[*c] you have trusted[*d] upon the staff of this broken reed, upon Egypt, which, if a man leans on it, will go into his palm and pierce it; thus is Pharaoh[*e] the king of Egypt to all[*f] those who trust[*g] upon him. **7/** And if you say[*h] to me, 'In[*i] Yahweh our God[*j] we trust,' is not he[*k] the one whose high places and altars[*l] Hezekiah[*m] removed when he said[*n] to Judah and to Jerusalem,[*o] 'Before this altar you will worship'[*p]? **8/** And now make a wager[*q] with my lord,[*r] the king[*s] of Assyria: I will give you[*t] two thousand horses if you are able on your part[*t] to put riders upon them.[*u] **9/** Then how[*v] can you repulse a single governor of the least of the servants of my lord[*w] when you put your own trust[*x] upon Egypt for chariots and for horsemen? **10/** And now[*y] is it without Yahweh that I have come up[*z] against this land[†a] to destroy it?[†b] Yahweh said to me, 'Go up to this land[†c] and destroy it!'[†d]" **11/** And Eliakim[†e] and Shebna[†f] and Joah said to (the) Rabshakeh,[†g] "Speak to your servants[†h] Aramaic, for we understand,[†i] but do not speak to us Judean[†j] in the hearing of the people[†k] who are on the wall."[†l] **12/** And (the) Rabshakeh said,[†m] "Is it only to your lord and to you[†n] that my lord[†o] sent me to speak these words? Is it not[†p] for the men who are sitting on the wall[†q] who are doomed to eat their own shit[†r] and to drink their own piss[†s] with you?[†t]" **13/** And (the) Rabshakeh[†u] stood[†v] and cried in a loud voice in Judean, and he said,[†w] "Hear the words[†x] of the great king, the king of Assyria: **14/** Thus[†y] says the king,[†z] 'Do not let Hezekiah[‡a] deceive you,[‡b] for he is not able[‡c] to deliver you.[‡d] **15/** And don't let Hezekiah[‡e] make you[‡f] trust in Yahweh saying,[‡g] "Yahweh will surely save us; this[‡h] city will not[‡i] be given into the hand of the king of Assyria."' **16/** Do not listen to Hezekiah,[‡j] for thus[‡k] says the king of Assyria,[‡l] 'Make an offering of peace with me and come out to me so that you may eat,[‡m] each from his own vine[‡n] and each from his own fig tree,[‡o] and so that you may drink, each the water from his own cistern **17/** until I come[‡p] and take you[‡q] to a land like your land,[‡r] a land[‡s] of grain and wine, a land of bread and vineyards,[‡t] **18/** lest Hezekiah mislead you[‡u] saying,[‡v] "Yahweh will save us." Did any of the gods of the nations[‡w] save his land[‡x] from the hand of the king of Assyria? **19/** Where are the gods[‡y] of Hamath and Arpad? Where are the gods[‡y] of Sepharvaim?[‡z] And did they deliver[§a] Samaria[§b] from my hand? **20/** Who[§c] among all the gods[§d] of these lands were there who delivered their land from my hand that[§e] Yahweh should deliver Jerusalem[§f] from my hand?'" **21/** But they kept silent,[§g] and did not[§h] answer him[§i] a word, for[§j] it was[§k] the command of the king, saying, "You shall not answer him."[§l] **22/** And Eliakim the son of Hilkiah[§m] who was over the palace and Shebna[§n] the secretary[§o] and Joah the son of Asaph, the recorder, went in[§p] to Hezekiah[§q] with torn garments and they reported to him[§r] the words of (the) Rabshakeh. **37:1/** And when King Hezekiah[§s] heard,[st] he tore his clothes, covered himself in sackcloth, and entered the house of Yahweh. 2/ And he sent Eliakim who was over the palace and Shebna the secretary[su] and the elders of the priests,[sv] covered with sackcloth, to the prophet Isaiah son of Amoz.[sw] 3/ And they said[sx] to him, thus[sy] says Hezekiah,[sz] "This day is a day of affliction, rebuke, and humiliation, for[¶a] children have come to the breach and there is no strength[¶b] to give birth.[¶c] 4/ Perhaps Yahweh your God[¶d] will hear the words[¶e] of (the) Rabshakeh, whom the king of Assyria his lord[¶f] sent to taunt the living God,[¶g] and will rebuke the words[¶h] that Yahweh your God[¶d] heard; therefore lift up[¶i] a prayer on behalf of the remnant that is left."[¶j] 5/ When the servants of King Hezekiah[¶k] came in[¶l] to Isaiah,[¶m] 6/ Isaiah said to them,[¶n] "Thus[¶o] you shall say to your lord:[¶p] thus[¶o] says Yahweh, 'Do not be afraid of the words[¶q] that you heard[¶r] with which the servants of the king of Assyria have reviled me. 7/ I am about to put a spirit in him,[¶s] and he will hear a report and return to his own land, and I will cause him to fall by the sword in his own land.[¶t]'" 8/ And (the) Rabshakeh returned[¶u] and found the king of Assyria fighting against Libnah, for[¶v] he had heard that[¶v] he had departed from Lachish.[¶w]

Textual Notes

a   The temporal phrase in Isaiah וַיְהִי בְּאַרְבַּע עֶשְׂרֵה שָׁנָה (wayhî bĕʾarbaʿ ʿeśrê šānâ), "and it came to pass in the fourteenth year," differs from its purported source in 2 Kings וּבְאַרְבַּע עֶשְׂרֵה שָׁנָה (ûbĕʾarbaʿ ʿeśrê šānâ), "and in the fourteenth year" (2 Kgs 18:13). Other textual issues in the verse are simply orthographic variants.

b   MT חִזְקִיָּהוּ (ḥizqîyāhû), "Hezekiah"; MT of 2 Kgs 18:13 and 1QIsaᵃ חזקיה.

c   MT כָּל (kol), "all"; 1QIsaᵃ כול.

d   MT הַבְּצֻרוֹת (habbĕṣūrôt), "the fortified"; 1QIsaᵃ הבצורות.

e   MT וַיִּתְפְּשֵׂם (wayyitpĕśēm), "and he captured them"; 1QIsaᵃ ויתפושם.

f   Isaiah omits 2 Kgs 18:14-16 from his account, whether deliberately or as the result of haplography; note that 2 Kgs 18:14 and 17 (= Isa 36:2) both begin with וישלח (wayyišlaḥ), "and he sent."

g   1QIsaᵃ אשו has accidentally omitted the last letter of אַשּׁוּר (ʾaššûr), "Assyria."

h   2 Kgs 18:17 contains a longer list of Assyrian officials, אֶת־תַּרְתָּן וְאֶת־רַב־סָרִיס וְאֶת־רַב־שָׁקֵה (ʾet-tartān wĕʾet-rab-sārîs wĕʾet-rab-šāqê), "(the) Tartan, (the) Rabsaris, and (the) Rabshakeh." These are all titles of the Assyrian officials, though the Hebrew omits the article and appears to treat the titles as personal names.

i   MT מִלָּכִישׁ יְרוּשָׁלְָמָה (millākîš yĕrûšālamāh), "from Lachish to Jerusalem"; 1QIsaᵃ omits the locative he on Jerusalem (ירושלם). The passage in 2 Kgs 18:17 has a different word order, inserting the expression "to king Hezekiah with a large army" between מִן־לָכִישׁ (min-lākîš), "from Lachish," and יְרוּשָׁלָם (yĕrûšālaim), "(to) Jerusalem."

j   See note b above, though here 2 Kgs 18:17 has the same form of the name as MT of Isa 36:2.

k   1QIsaᵃ adds מאודה (mĕʾôdâ), "a very large army."

l   MT וַיַּעֲמֹד (wayyaʿămōd), "and he stood"; 1QIsaᵃ ויעמוד. The narrative in 2 Kgs 18:17 has a plural verb because of a longer list of officials, and it is preceded by additional clauses, "and they went up and came to Jerusalem, and they went up and came and stood."

m   2 Kgs 18:17 inserts אֲשֶׁר (ʾăšer), "which (is on the road)."

n   MT שְׂדֵה (śĕdê), "field"; 1QIsaᵃ שדי.

o   2 Kgs 18:18 opens with a clause not found in Isaiah, וַיִּקְרְאוּ אֶל־הַמֶּלֶךְ (wayyiqrĕʾû ʾel-hammelek), "and they called to the king."

p   MT חִלְקִיָּהוּ (ḥilqîyāhû), "Hilkiah," as in 2 Kgs 18:18; 1QIsaᵃ חלקיה.

q   MT וְשֶׁבְנָא הַסֹּפֵר (wĕšebnāʾ hassōpēr), "and Shebna the secretary"; 1QIsaᵃ ושובנא הסופר.

r   MT and 1QIsaᵃ וַיֵּצֵא אֵלָיו (wayyēṣēʾ ʾēlāyw), "and he went out to him"—the singular verb form is not uncommon with plural subjects that follow the verb; 2 Kgs 18:18 has וַיֵּצֵא אֲלֵהֶם (wayyēṣēʾ ʾălēhem), "and he went out to them."

s   MT וַיֹּאמֶר אֲלֵיהֶם (wayyōʾmer ʾălêhem), "and he said to them"; 1QIsaᵃ ויואמר אליהמה.

t   MT אִמְרוּ (ʾimrû), "say"; 1QIsaᵃ אמרו.

u   See note b above, though 2 Kgs 18:19 has the same as Isa 36:4; following the name Hezekiah, 1QIsaᵃ inserted מלך יהודה, "king of Judah," but then he put dots about the phrase to indicate it was an expansion.

v   MT כֹּה (kōh), "thus"; 1QIsaᵃ כוה.

w   MT אֲשֶׁר בָּטָחְתָּ (ʾăšer bāṭāḥtā), "in which you trust," is expanded by 1QIsaᵃ for clarity אשר אתה בטחתה בו, "which you trust in it."

x   MT has the first person אָמַרְתִּי (ʾāmartî), "I said, thought," but both 2 Kgs 18:20 אָמַרְתָּ (ʾāmartā), "you said, thought," and 1QIsaᵃ (אמרתה) have second person singular.

y   MT and 2 Kgs 18:20 עַל־מִי (ʿal-mî), "upon whom"; 1QIsaᵃ על מיא.

z   MT and 2 Kgs 18:20 בָּטָחְתָּ (bāṭaḥtā), "do you trust"; 1QIsaᵃ בטחתה.

446

*a MT and 2 Kgs 18:20 כִּי (kî), "that"; 1QIsaᵃ כיא.

*b MT and 2 Kgs 18:20 מָרַדְתָּ בִּי (māradtā bî), "you rebelled against me"; 1QIsaᵃ מרדתה ביא.

*c MT and 1QIsaᵃ הִנֵּה (hinnê), "see"; 2 Kgs 18: 21 has an extra word עַתָּה הִנֵּה (ʿattâ hinnê), "now see."

*d MT בָּטַחְתָּ (bāṭaḥtā), "you trust"; 1QIsaᵃ בטחתה; while 2 Kgs 18:21 has בָּטַחְתָּ לְּךָ (bāṭaḥtā lĕkā), "you trust for yourself."

*e MT and 2 Kgs 18:21 פַּרְעֹה (parʿōh), "Pharaoh"; 1QIsaᵃ פרעוה.

*f MT and 2 Kgs 18:21 לְכָל (lĕkol), "to all"; 1QIsaᵃ לכול.

*g MT and 2 Kgs 18:21 הַבֹּטְחִים (habbōṭĕḥîm), "who trust"; 1QIsaᵃ הבוטחים.

*h MT וְכִי־תֹאמַר (wĕkî-tōʾmar), "and if you say"; 2 Kgs 18:22 וְכִי־תֹאמְרוּן (wĕkî-tōʾmĕrûn), "and if you say," has the plural as does 1QIsaᵃ וכיא תואמרו.

*i MT and 2 Kgs 18:22 have the preposition אֶל (ʾel), "to, in"; 1QIsaᵃ has עַל (ʿal), "upon," used with the verb in the preceding verses.

*j MT and 2 Kgs 18:22 אֱלֹהֵינוּ (ʾĕlōhênû), "our God"; 1QIsaᵃ אלוהינו.

*k MT and 2 Kgs 18:22 הֲלוֹא־הוּא (hălô-hûʾ), "is not he"; 1QIsaᵃ הלוא הואה.

*l MT and 2 Kgs 18:22 אֶת־בָּמֹתָיו וְאֶת־מִזְבְּחֹתָיו (ʾet-bāmōtāyw wĕʾet-mizbĕḥōtāyw), "his high places and his altars"; 1QIsaᵃ את במותיו ואת מזבחותיו.

*m See note b above, though 2 Kgs 18:19 has the same form as MT of Isa 36:7.

*n MT and 2 Kgs 18:22 וַיֹּאמֶר (wayyōʾmer), "and he said"; 1QIsaᵃ ויואמר.

*o MT and 2 Kgs 18:22 וְלִירוּשָׁלִַם (wĕlîrûšālaim), "and to Jerusalem"; 1QIsaᵃ ולירושלים.

*p 2 Kgs 18:22 adds בִּירוּשָׁלָם (bîrûšālāim), "(you shall worship) in Jerusalem," at the end of the verse, and 1QIsaᵃ has בירושלים, though it marks the word as an expansion by putting dots above it.

*q MT and 2 Kgs 18:23 הִתְעָרֶב נָא (hitʿāreb nāʾ), "make a wager"; 1QIsaᵃ התערבונא (the plural imperative).

*r MT and 2 Kgs 18:23 אֶת־אֲדֹנִי (ʾet-ʾădōnî), "with my lord"; 1QIsaᵃ את אדוני.

*s MT and 2 Kgs 18:23 הַמֶּלֶךְ (hammelek), "the king"; 2 Kgs 18:23 אֶת־מֶלֶךְ (ʾet-melek), "with the king." The definite article on a noun in construct: הַמֶּלֶךְ אַשּׁוּר (hammelek ʾaššûr), "the king of Assyria," is unusual, but this should probably not be explained away as textual corruption (see Joüon-Muraoka, 2:520, §140c and the literature cited there).

*t MT and 2 Kgs 18:23 לְךָ (lĕkā), "to you"; 1QIsaᵃ לכה.

*u MT and 2 Kgs 18:23 רֹכְבִים עֲלֵיהֶם (rōkĕbîm ʿālehem), "riders upon them"; 1QIsaᵃ רוכבים עליהמה.

*v MT and 2 Kgs 18:24 וְאֵיךְ (wĕ'êk), "then how"; 1QIsaᵃ ואיכה.

*w MT and 2 Kgs 18:24 עַבְדֵי אֲדֹנִי (ʿabdê ʾădōnî), "of the servants of my lord"; 1QIsaᵃ מעבדי אדוני, "from the servants of my lord."

*x MT and 2 Kgs 18:24 לְךָ (lĕkā), "for yourself"; 1QIsaᵃ לכם, "for yourselves."

*y MT and 1QIsaᵃ וְעַתָּה (wĕʿattâ), "and now"; 2 Kgs 18:25 עַתָּה (ʿattâ), "now."

*z MT, 2 Kgs 18:25, and 1QIsaᵃ עָלִיתִי (ʿālîtî), "I have come up"; LXX has ἀνέβημεν, "we have come up."

†a MT עַל־הָאָרֶץ הַזֹּאת (ʿal-hāʾāreṣ hazzōʾt), "against this land"; 1QIsaᵃ על הארץ הזואת; but 2 Kgs 18:25 has עַל־הַמָּקוֹם הַזֶּה (ʿal-hammāqôm hazzeh), "against this place." The versions support MT.

†b MT and 1QIsaᵃ לְהַשְׁחִיתָהּ (lĕhašḥîtāh), "to destroy it/her"; 2 Kgs 18:25 לְהַשְׁחִתוֹ (lĕhašḥîtô), "to destroy it/him." LXX omits the rest of the verse.

†c MT אֲלֵה אֶל־הָאָרֶץ הַזֹּאת (ʾălê ʾel-hāʾāreṣ hazzōʾt), go up to this land"; 2 Kgs 18:25 has עֲלֵה עַל־הָאָרֶץ הַזֹּאת (ʾălê ʿal-hāʾāreṣ hazzōʾt), "go up against this land"; 1QIsaᵃ עלה אל הארץ הזות. The versions appear to read עַל.

†d MT and 2 Kgs 18:25 וְהַשְׁחִיתָהּ (wĕhašḥîtāh), "and destroy it/her"; 1QIsaᵃ להשחיתה, "to destroy it/her." The versions support MT.

†e After Eliakim, 2 Kgs 18:26 adds בֶּן־חִלְקִיָּהוּ (ben-ḥilqîyāhû), "son of Hilkiah."

†f MT וְשֶׁבְנָא (wĕšebnāʾ), "and Shebna"; 2 Kgs 18:26 וְשֶׁבְנָה (wĕšebnâ); 1QIsaᵃ ושבנא (wĕšobnāʾ). LXX and Vg. read the name with the o vowel, thus Somnas (LXX) and Sobna (Vg.).

†g MT and 2 Kgs 18:26 וַיֹּאמֶר ... אֶל־רַב־שָׁקֵה (wayyōʾmer . . . ʾel-rab-šāqê), "and he said . . . to (the) Rabshakeh"; 1QIsaᵃ ויואמרו אליו, "and they said to him." LXX combines the two readings, καὶ εἶπεν πρὸς αὐτόν, "and he said to him." Vg. follows MT.

†h MT and 2 Kgs 18:26 אֶל־עֲבָדֶיךָ (ʾel-ʿăbādêkā), "to your servants"; 1QIsaᵃ עם עבדיך, "with your servants," but then in the margin has been added עמנו, "with us."

†i MT and 2 Kgs 18:26 כִּי שֹׁמְעִים אֲנָחְנוּ (kî šōmĕʿîm ʾănāḥnû), "for we hear/understand"; 1QIsaᵃ כי שומעים אנחנו.

†j MT אֵלֵינוּ יְהוּדִית (ʾēlênû yĕhûdît), "to us Judean"; 2 Kgs 18:26 עִמָּנוּ יְהוּדִית (ʿimmānû yĕhûdît), "with us Judean"; 1QIsaᵃ את הדברים האלה, "(do not speak) these words." The versions support MT.

†k MT and 2 Kgs 18:26 בְּאָזְנֵי הָעָם (bĕ'oznê hāʿām), "in the ears/hearing of the people"; 1QIsaᵃ באוני האנשים, "in the ears/hearing of the men," perhaps to be consistent with the האנשים in the next line, v. 12. LXX follows 1QIsaᵃ, while Vg. goes with MT.

†l MT אֲשֶׁר עַל־הַחֹמָה (ʾăšer ʿal-haḥômâ), "who are on the wall"; 2 Kgs 18:26 אֲשֶׁר עַל־הַחֹמָה; but 1QIsaᵃ has היושבים על החומה, "who are sitting on the wall." Again, 1QIsaᵃ seeks to be consistent with the same expression as in the succeeding v. 12.

†m MT וַיֹּאמֶר רַב־שָׁקֵה (wayyōʾmer rab-šāqê), "and (the) Rabshakeh said"; 1QIsaᵃ ויואמר רב שקה; but 2 Kgs 18:27 וַיֹּאמֶר אֲלֵיהֶם רַב־שָׁקֵה (wayyōʾmer ʾălêhem rab-šāqê), "and (the) Rabshakeh said to them"; LXX and Vg. follow the reading of 2 Kgs 18:27.

†n MT הַאֵל אֲדֹנֶיךָ וְאֵלֶיךָ (haʾel ʾădōnêkā wĕʾēlêkā), "Is it only to your lord and to you"; 2 Kgs 18:27 הַעַל אֲדֹנֶיךָ וְאֵלֶיךָ (haʿal ʾădōnêkā wĕʾēlêkā), "Is it only against your lord and to you"; 1QIsaᵃ האליכמה ועל אדוניכמה, "Is it only to you and against your lord."

†o MT and 2 Kgs 18:27 אֲדֹנִי (ʾădōnî), "my lord"; 1QIsaᵃ אדוני.

†p MT and 2 Kgs 18:27 הֲלֹא (hălōʾ), "is it not"; 1QIsaᵃ הלוא.

†q MT הַיֹּשְׁבִים עַל־הַחוֹמָה (hayyōšĕbîm ʿal-haḥômâ), "who are sitting on the wall"; 2 Kgs 18:27 but 1QIsaᵃ היושבים על החומה.

†r MT לֶאֱכֹל אֶת־חַרְאֵיהֶם (leʾĕkōl ʾet-ḥarʾêhem), "to eat their own shit"; 2 Kgs 18:27 לֶאֱכֹל אֶת חֲרֵיהֶם (leʾĕkōl ʾet-ḥărêhem), "to eat their own shit"; 1QIsaᵃ לאכול את חריהמה. The word for "shit" was considered crude or offensive, so the qĕrē', the word read in public, in

447

MT for both Isa 36:12 and 2 Kgs 18:27 is צוֹאָתָם (*ṣôʾātām*), "their dung."

†s MT and 2 Kgs 18:27 וְלִשְׁתּוֹת אֶת־שֵׁינֵיהֶם (*wĕlištôt ʾet-šênêhem*), "and to drink their piss"; 1QIsaᵃ ולשתות את שיניהמה. Again the word for "piss" was considered crude, so the *qĕrē* was מֵימֵי רַגְלֵיהֶם (*mêmê raglêhem*), "urine," lit., "the water of their feet."

†t MT and 2 Kgs 18:27 עִמָּכֶם (*ʿimmākem*), "with you"; 1QIsaᵃ עמכמה.

†u MT and 2 Kgs 18:28 רַב־שָׁקֵה (*rab-šāqê*), "(the) Rabshakeh"; 1QIsaᵃ has the article רב שקה, "the Rabshakeh."

†v MT and 2 Kgs 18:28 וַיַּעֲמֹד (*wayyaʿămōd*), "and he stood"; 1QIsaᵃ ויעמוד.

†w MT וַיֹּאמֶר (*wayyōʾmer*), "and he said"; 1QIsaᵃ ויואמר; the parallel in 2Kgs 18:28 adds another verb וַיְדַבֵּר וַיֹּאמֶר (*waydabbēr wayyōʾmer*), "and he spoke and said," but the extra verb has no versional support in Isaiah.

†x MT and 1QIsaᵃ דִּבְרֵי (*dibrê*), "the words of"; 2 Kgs 18:28 דְּבַר (*dĕbar*), "the word of."

†y MT and 2 Kgs 18:29 כֹּה (*kōh*), "thus"; 1QIsaᵃ כוה.

†z MT and 2 Kgs 18:29 הַמֶּלֶךְ (*hammelek*), "the king," so versions; 1QIsaᵃ מלך אשור, "the king of Assyria."

‡a MT and 2 Kgs 18:29 חִזְקִיָּהוּ (*ḥizqîyāhû*), "Hezekiah"; 1QIsaᵃ חזקיה.

‡b MT אַל־יַשִּׁא לָכֶם (*ʾal-yaššîʾ lākem*), "let him not deceive you"; 2 Kgs 18:29 אַל־יַשִּׁיא לָכֶם (*ʾal-yaššîʾ lākem*); 1QIsaᵃ אל ישא לכמה.

‡c MT and 2 Kgs 18:29 כִּי לֹא־יוּכַל (*kî lōʾ-yûkal*), "for he is not able"); 1QIsaᵃ כיא לוא יוכל.

‡d MT and 2 Kgs 18:29 לְהַצִּיל אֶתְכֶם (*lĕhaṣṣîl ʾetkem*), "to deliver you"); 1QIsaᵃ להציל אתכמה; but 2 Kgs 18:29 adds מִיָּדוֹ (*miyyādô*), "from his hand." LXX has the interesting, though otherwise unsupported reading, Μὴ ἀπατάτω ὑμᾶς Ἐζεκιας λόγοις, οἳ οὐ δυνήσονται ῥύσασθαι ὑμᾶς, "Let not Hezekiah deceive you with words that will not be able to save you."

‡e For חִזְקִיָּהוּ (*ḥizqîyāhû*) in MT and 2 Kgs 18:30, 1QIsaᵃ has חזקיה.

‡f MT and 2 Kgs 18:30 אֶתְכֶם (*ʾetkem*), "you"; 1QIsaᵃ אתכמה.

‡g MT and 2 Kgs 18:30 לֵאמֹר (*lēʾmōr*), "saying"; 1QIsaᵃ לאמור.

‡h MT and 2 Kgs 18:30 הַזֹּאת (*hazzōʾt*), "this"; 1QIsaᵃ הזואת.

‡i 2 Kgs 18:30 וְלֹא (*wĕlōʾ*), "and not," and 1QIsa ולוא begin the last clause with the conjunction: "*and* this city will not"; MT לֹא (*lōʾ*), "not," omits it. Vg. follows MT; LXX supports 1QIsaᵃ and 2 Kgs 18:30.

‡j See note ‡e above.

‡k MT and 2 Kgs 18:31 כִּי כֹה (*kî kōh*), "for thus"; 1QIsaᵃ כיא כוה.

‡l MT has the unexpected article on a noun in construct הַמֶּלֶךְ אַשּׁוּר (*hammelek ʾaššûr*), "the king of Assyria," as in v. 8; both 2 Kgs 18:31 מֶלֶךְ אַשּׁוּר (*melek ʾaššûr*), "the king of Assyria," and 1QIsaᵃ omit it.

‡m MT and 2 Kgs 18:31 וְאִכְלוּ (*wĕ-ʾiklû*), "and eat!"; 1QIsaᵃ ואכולו.

‡n MT and 2 Kgs 18:31 אִישׁ־גַּפְנוֹ (*ʾîš-gapnô*), "each from his vine"; 1QIsaᵃ inserts the object marker איש את גפנו.

‡o MT and 2 Kgs 18:31 וְאִישׁ תְּאֵנָתוֹ (*wĕʾîš tĕʾēnātô*), "and each from his own fig tree"; 1QIsaᵃ ואיש את תנתו.

‡p MT and 2 Kgs 18:32 עַד־בֹּאִי (*ʿad-bōʾî*), "until my coming/I come"; 1QIsaᵃ עד בואי.

‡q MT and 2 Kgs 18:32 אֶתְכֶם (*ʾetkem*), "you"; 1QIsaᵃ אתכמה.

‡r MT and 2 Kgs 18:32 כְּאַרְצְכֶם (*kĕʾarṣĕkem*), "like your land"; 1QIsaᵃ כארצכמה.

‡s MT and 2 Kgs 18:32 אֶרֶץ (*ʾereṣ*), "a land"; 1QIsaᵃ אל ארץ, "to a land."

‡t 2 Kgs 18:32 has a longer text, continuing with אֶרֶץ זֵית יִצְהָר וּדְבַשׁ וִחְיוּ וְלֹא תָמֻתוּ (*ʾereṣ zêt yiṣhār ûdĕbaš wiḥyû wĕlōʾ tāmūtû*), "a land of olive trees, oil, and honey, so that you may live and not die," but that seems never to have been a part of the Isaiah text.

‡u Over against MT פֶּן־יַסִּית אֶתְכֶם חִזְקִיָּהוּ (*pen-yassît ʾetkem ḥizqîyāhû*) and 1QIsaᵃ פן יסית אתכמה חזקיה, "lest Hezekiah mislead you," 2 Kgs 18:32 introduces the thought here differently: וְאַל־תִּשְׁמְעוּ אֶל־חִזְקִיָּהוּ כִּי־יַסִּית אֶתְכֶם (*wĕʾal-tišmĕʿû ʾel-ḥizqîyāhû kî-yassît ʾetkem*), "and do not listen to Hezekiah because he will mislead you."

‡v MT and 2 Kgs 18:32 לֵאמֹר (*lēʾmōr*), "saying"; 1QIsaᵃ לאמור.

‡w MT and 2 Kgs 18:33 אֱלֹהֵי הַגּוֹיִם (*ʾĕlōhê haggôyîm*), "gods of the nations"; 1QIsaᵃ אלוהי הגואים.

‡x MT and 2 Kgs 18:33 אֶת־אַרְצוֹ (*ʾet-ʾarṣô*), "his land"; 1QIsaᵃ ארצו omits the object marker.

‡y MT and 2 Kgs 18:34 אֱלֹהֵי (*ʾĕlōhê*), "the gods of"; 1QIsaᵃ אלוהי.

‡z MT סְפַרְוַיִם (*sĕparwāim*), "Sepharvaim"; 1QIsaᵃ ספריים; but 2 Kgs 18:34 expands as סְפַרְוַיִם הֵנַע וְעִוָּה (*sĕparwaim hēnaʿ wĕʿiwwâ*), "Sepharvaim, Hena, and Ivvah."

§a MT and 2 Kgs 18:34 וְכִי־הִצִּילוּ (*wĕkî-hiṣṣîlû*), "and did they deliver"; 1QIsaᵃ has a redundant *he* on the verb וכיא ההצילו, and 2 Kgs 18:34 omits the conjunction כִּי הִצִּילוּ (*kî-hiṣṣîlû*), "did they deliver."

§b MT and 2 Kgs 18:34 שֹׁמְרוֹן (*šōmĕrôn*), "Samaria"; 1QIsaᵃ שומרון.

§c MT and 2 Kgs 18:35 מִי (*mî*), "who"; 1QIsaᵃ מיא.

§d MT and 2 Kgs 18:35 בְּכָל־אֱלֹהֵי (*bĕkol-ʾĕlōhê*), "among all the gods"; 1QIsaᵃ בכול אלוהי.

§e MT and 2 Kgs 18:35 כִּי (*kî*), "that"; 1QIsaᵃ כיא.

§f MT and 2 Kgs 18:35 יְרוּשָׁלָ͏ִם (*yĕrûšālaim*), "Jerusalem"; 1QIsaᵃ ירושלים.

§g MT וַיַּחֲרִישׁוּ (*wayyaḥărîšû*), "but they kept silent"; 1QIsaᵃ והחרישו and 2 Kgs 18:36 וְהֶחֱרִישׁוּ הָעָם (*wĕheḥĕrîšû hāʿām*), "but the people kept silent," have the perfect, but the latter specifies the subject.

§h MT and 2 Kgs 18:36 וְלֹא (*wĕlōʾ*), "and not"; 1QIsaᵃ ולוא.

§i MT and 2 Kgs 18:36 אֹתוֹ (*ʾōtô*), "him"; 1QIsaᵃ אותה.

§j MT and 2 Kgs 18:36 כִּי (*kî*), "for"; 1QIsaᵃ כיא.

§k MT and 2 Kgs 18:36 הִיא (*hîʾ*), "it was," the third person feminine singular independent pronoun in agreement with the feminine noun מִצְוַת הַמֶּלֶךְ (*miṣwat hammelek*), "the command of the king," used as the predicate of the nominal clause; 1QIsaᵃ has an ungrammatical third person masculine singular verbal form היה.

§l MT and 2 Kgs 18:36 לֵאמֹר לֹא תַעֲנֻהוּ (*lēʾmōr lōʾ taʿănūhû*), "saying, you shall not answer him"); 1QIsaᵃ לאמור לוא תענוהו.

§m MT חִלְקִיָּהוּ (*ḥilqîyāhû*), "Hilkiah"; 2Kgs 18:37 and 1QIsaᵃ have the shorter form חלקיה (*ḥilqîyāh*).

§n MT and 2 Kgs 18:37 וְשֶׁבְנָא (*wĕšebnâ*), "Shebna"; 1QIsaᵃ ושובנא.

§o MT and 1QIsaᵃ הַסֹּפֵר (*hassōpēr*), "the scribe"; 2 Kgs 18:37 הַסֹּפֵר; LXX has ὁ γραμματεὺς τῆς δυνάμεως, "the secretary of the army."

§p MT and 2 Kgs 18:37 וַיָּבֹא (*wayyābōʾ*), "and he went in"; 1QIsaᵃ ויבוא.

§q MT and 2 Kgs 18:37 חִזְקִיָּהוּ (ḥizqîyāhû), "Hezekiah"; 1QIsaᵃ חזקיה.

§r MT וַיַּגִּדוּ לוֹ (wayyaggîdû lô), "and they reported to him"; 1QIsaᵃ ויגידו לוא; and 2 Kgs 18:23 וַיַּגְדוּ לוֹ.

§s MT and 2 Kgs 19:1 הַמֶּלֶךְ חִזְקִיָּהוּ (hammelek ḥizqîyāhû), "the king Hezekiah"; 1QIsaᵃ חזקיה המלך, "Hozekiah the king."

§t MT and 2 Kgs 19:1 כִּשְׁמֹעַ (kišmōaʿ), "when he heard"; 1QIsaᵃ כשמוע.

§u MT וְאֵת שֶׁבְנָא הַסֹּפֵר (wĕʾēt šebnāʾ hassōpēr), "and Shebna the secretary"; 2 Kgs 19:2 וְשֶׁבְנָא הַסֹּפֵר; and 1QIsaᵃ ואת שובנא הסופר.

§v MT and 2 Kgs 19:2 הַכֹּהֲנִים (hakkōhănîm), "the priests"; 1 QIsaᵃ הכוהנים.

§w MT יְשַׁעְיָהוּ בֶן־אָמוֹץ הַנָּבִיא (yĕšaʿyāhû ben-ʾāmôṣ hannābîʾ), "Isaiah son of Amoz the prophet"; similar order in 1QIsaᵃ ישעיה בן אמוץ הנביא; but 2 Kgs 19:2 has יְשַׁעְיָהוּ הַנָּבִיא בֶן־אָמוֹץ, "Isaiah the prophet son of Amoz."

§x MT and 2 Kgs 19:3 וַיֹּאמְרוּ (wayyōʾmĕrû), "and they said"; 1QIsaᵃ ויואמרו.

§y MT and 2 Kgs 19:3 כֹּה (kōh), "thus"; 1QIsaᵃ כוה.

§z MT and 2 Kgs 19:3 חִזְקִיָּהוּ (ḥizqîyāhû), "Hezekiah"; 1QIsaᵃ יחזקיה (yĕḥizqîyāh), "Jehizkiah," a variant form of the king's name; cf. Hos 1:1; Mic 1:1; Ezra 2:16).

¶a MT and 2 Kgs 19:3 כִּי (kî), "for"; 1QIsaᵃ כיא.

¶b MT and 2 Kgs 19:3 וְכֹחַ (wĕkōaḥ), "and strength"; 1QIsaᵃ וכוח.

¶c All three Hebrew texts have לְלֵדָה (lĕlēdâ), "to give birth," but after the word and above the line 1QIsaᵃ has the erased correction to ללדת.

¶d MT and 2 Kgs 19:4 אֱלֹהֶיךָ (ʾĕlōhêkā), "your God"; 1QIsaᵃ אלוהיכה.

¶e MT and 1QIsaᵃ אֵת דִּבְרֵי (ʾēt dibrê), "the words of," supported by the versions; 2 Kgs 19:4 אֵת כָּל־דִּבְרֵי (ʾēt kol-dibrê), "all the words of."

¶f MT and 2 Kgs 19:4 אֲדֹנָיו (ʾădōnāyw), "his lord"; 1QIsaᵃ אדוניו.

¶g MT and 2 Kgs 19:4 אֱלֹהִים (ʾĕlōhîm), "God"; 1QIsaᵃ אלוהים.

¶h So Tg. and many modern translations, taking God as the subject of וְהוֹכִיחַ (wĕhôkîaḥ), "and he will rebuke," and thus continuing the narrative sequence begun by the preceding יִשְׁמַע (yišmaʿ), "he will hear." LXX and Vg. appear to read the infinitive and treat it as a continuation of the previous infinitive with the Rabshakeh being the subject of both: "to reproach/blaspheme the living God and to reproach with words which the Lord your God heard."

¶i MT and 2 Kgs 19:4 וְנָשָׂאתָ (wĕnāśāʾtā), "and you will lift up"; 1QIsaᵃ ונשאת.

¶j MT and 2 Kgs 19:4 הַנִּמְצָאָה (hannimṣāʾâ), "which are found/left"; 1QIsaᵃ הנמצאים בעיר הזואת, "who are left in this city." The extra phrase is an expansion not found in the versions.

¶k As in v. 7a above, MT and 2 Kgs 19:5 הַמֶּלֶךְ חִזְקִיָּהוּ (hammelek ḥizqîyāhû), "the king Hezekiah"; 1QIsaᵃ המלך יחזקיה.

¶l MT and 2 Kgs 19:5 וַיָּבֹאוּ (wayyābōʾû), "and they went in"; 1QIsaᵃ ויבואו.

¶m MT יְשַׁעְיָהוּ (yĕšaʿyāhû), "Isaiah"; 2 Kgs 19:5 יְשַׁעַיָהוּ (yĕšaʿayāhû), "Isaiah"; 1QIsaᵃ ישעיה.

¶n MT וַיֹּאמֶר אֲלֵיהֶם יְשַׁעְיָהוּ (wayyōʾmer ʾălêhem yĕšaʿyāhû), "and Isaiah said to them"; 2 Kgs 19:6 וַיֹּאמֶר לָהֶם יְשַׁעְיָהוּ (wayyōʾmer lāhem yĕšaʿyāhû), "and Isaiah said to them"); 1QIsaᵃ ויואמר להמה ישעיה.

¶o MT and 2 Kgs 19:6 כֹּה (kōh), "thus"; 1QIsaᵃ כוה.

¶p MT and 2 Kgs 19:6 תֹּאמְרוּן אֶל־אֲדֹנֵיכֶם (tōʾmĕrûn ʾel-ʾădōnêkem), "you will say to your lord"; 1QIsaᵃ תואמרו אל אדוניכמה.

¶q MT and 2 Kgs 19:6 אַל־תִּירָא מִפְּנֵי הַדְּבָרִים (ʾal-tîrāʾ mippĕnê haddĕbārîm), "do not be afraid of the words"; 1QIsaᵃ אל תירא מפני הדברי.

¶r MT and 2 Kgs 19:6 שָׁמַעְתָּ (šāmaʿtā), "you heard"; 1QIsaᵃ שמעתה.

¶s MT הִנְנִי נֹתֵן בּוֹ רוּחַ (hinĕnî nōtēn bô rûaḥ), "I am about to put in him a spirit"; 2 Kgs 19:7 הִנְנִי נֹתֵן בּוֹ רוּחַ (hinĕnî nōtēn bô rûaḥ); 1QIsaᵃ הנני נותן רוח בוא, "I am about to put a spirit in him."

¶t In 1QIsaᵃ the last part of the verse is written vertically in the margin of the following sheet: והפלתיו בחרב בארצו, "and I will cause him to fall by the sword in his own land." In this manuscript everything in vv. 6-7 after מפני הדברי, "of the words," appears to have been crammed into a small space in a smaller script before v. 8, as though the scribe had originally accidentally omitted this verse and a half.

¶u MT and 2 Kgs 19:8 וַיָּשָׁב (wayyāšob), "and he returned"; 1QIsaᵃ וישוב.

¶v MT and 2 Kgs 19:8 כִּי (kî), "for, that"; 1QIsaᵃ כיא.

¶w LXX omits the final two clauses, but Vg. has them.

Commentary

The synchronism in v. 1 (and 2 Kgs 18:13), between Sennacherib's third campaign in 701 BCE and the fourteenth year of Hezekiah's reign, dates the beginning of Hezekiah's reign to 715 BCE, which is at odds with date formula in 2 Kgs 18:1 and the related synchronism in 2 Kgs 18:9. 2 Kings 18:1 dates the beginning of Hezekiah's reign to the third year of the Israelite king Hoshea, who, according to Assyrian sources,[1] seized the throne by murdering Pekah the son of Remaliah in 733/732 BCE (cf. 2 Kgs 15:25). This would make the beginning of Hezekiah's reign 729 BCE, or, given the different beginning and ending of our Gregorian calendar and the Assyrian, Judean, and Israelite calendars, 728 BCE, at the latest. 2 Kings 18:9-10 connects Shalmaneser V's siege of Hoshea's Samaria to the seventh through the ninth year of Hoshea (725–723/722) and to the fourth through the sixth year

---

1   Tadmor, *Inscriptions of Tiglath-pileser III*, 277.

of Hezekiah (725–723/722). E. R. Thiele accepts the later date of 715 based on the synchronism in Isa 36:1 and 2 Kgs 18:13 as the accession year of Hezekiah.[2]

On the other hand, Joachim Begrich and many scholars who follow him prefer the earlier date for Hezekiah's accession, though Begrich and many others cut the date down against the biblical text to 727 BCE in order to make the year of Ahaz's death coincide with the death of the Assyrian king Tiglath-pileser III, based on a controversial interpretation of the oracle in Isa 14:28-32.[3] This preference for the numbers in the biblical regnal formulae over against a synchronism outside the regnal formulae seems odd given the extreme difficulties in the numbers given in the regnal formulae for this period. Perhaps the preference is rooted in the assumption that the regnal formulae represent an archaic chronological framework derived from early Israelite and Judean official annals or daybooks that was used to structure the narrative. On this assumption, the regnal formulae are considered more reliable than dates in the later narrative independent of the regnal formulae. All of this, however, is just an unproven assumption, and there are some serious objections to it.

Jeffrey S. Rogers's close study of the regnal formulae in 1–2 Kings has shown that there is far more textual fluidity in the regnal formulae in Kings than there is in the synchronistic statements outside these formulae, which led him to the opposite conclusion that the regnal formulae, far from being an ancient, preexisting archival framework on which the narrative was constructed, were actually formed, shaped, and reshaped by the narrative in which they stood.[4] Rogers may overstate his conclusion, but even if the chronological framework of the regnal formulae were ancient, the freedom with which the ancient scribes, intentionally or unintentionally, corrected or altered the numbers suggests that they did not regard

them as untouchable.[5] Moreover, a close look at some of the regnal formulae for the period under discussion will show that many of these numbers are simply not reliable.

Thus, according to 2 Kgs 15:25-27, Pekah the son of Remaliah murdered his master Pekahiah son of Menahem in Samaria and ruled in his stead in Samaria for twenty years. This can hardly be correct, however. We know from Assyrian sources that Menahem of Israel was still king of Israel in 738 BCE, when he paid tribute to Tiglath-pileser,[6] and that Hoshea murdered and replaced Pekah the son of Remaliah in 733/732 BCE.[7] Since Pekahiah succeeded Menahem and ruled two years in Samaria (2 Kgs 15:23), which would be from 737 to 735, there are only three years left for Pekah the son of Remaliah to have ruled in Samaria (735–732); a twenty-year reign in Samaria is impossible. According to the regnal formula in 2 Kgs 15:32, Jotham the son of Uzziah began to reign over Judah in the second year of Pekah son of Remaliah and reigned for twenty-six years, which would mean that Jotham's reign extended, based on the regnal years for Pekah son of Remaliah (2 Kgs 15:25-27), eight years beyond the reign of Pekah, or down to 726 BCE. That can hardly be correct, because of the following regnal formula in 2 Kgs 16:1-2. Here it is said that Ahaz the son of Jotham began to rule over Judah in the seventeenth year of Pekah son of Remaliah and ruled for sixteen years. That would make Ahaz's reign, which overlaps with the last three years of Pekah's reign, extend from 735 to 719, which does not fit with an accession of Hezekiah in 729, 727, or even 715. If one assumes, however, that the scribe has confused the numbers for Ahaz's age at succession with his length of reign, one would get agreement with the Assyrian synchronism for Hezekiah. If Ahaz were sixteen when he became king and ruled for twenty years, then his death and Hezekiah's accession would both fall in 715 BCE. That would make it easier to explain why

2   Edwin Richard Thiele, *The Mysterious Numbers of the Hebrew Kings: A Reconstruction of the Chronology of the Kingdoms of Israel and Judah* (rev. ed.; Grand Rapids: Eerdmans, 1965) 118–40, 205.

3   Joachim Begrich, *Die Chronologie der Könige von Israel und Juda und die Quellen des Rahmens der Königsbücher* (BHT 3; Tübingen: Mohr, 1929); Begrich, "Jesaja 14, 28-32: Ein Beitrag zur Chronologie der israelitisch-judäischen Königszeit," *ZDMG* 83 (1929) 213–37.

4   Jeffrey S. Rogers, "Synchronism and Structure in 1–2

Kings and Mesopotamian Chronographic Literature" (Diss., Princeton Theological Seminary, 1992).

5   Cf. Thiele's characterization of the numbers in 2 Kgs 17:1; 18:1, 9-10 as "the product of a late hand and not of a contemporary recorder . . . the result of late calculation . . . not found in the original annalistic journals contemporary with the years of the kings" (*Mysterious Numbers*, 135).

6   Tadmor, *Inscriptions of Tiglath-pileser III*, 276.

7   Ibid., 277; cf. 2 Kgs 15:30.

Isaiah complained about Judah being ruled by babes and women (Isa 3:4, 12), and it would also fit with the oracle against Philistia dated to the year of Ahaz's death (Isa 14:28-32), which appears to reflect the background near the beginning of the Ashdod affair in 715 BCE (see below).

Despite the difficulty with the figure for the length of Ahaz's reign in 2 Kgs 16:1-2, the date for the beginning of Ahaz's reign in 735 BCE is probably correct, since Jotham appears to have been king at the beginning of the Syro-Ephraimitic crisis (2 Kgs 15:37) only to be replaced by Ahaz in the same year (2 Kgs 16:1-5; Isa 7:1). The regnal formula in 2 Kgs 17:1, which dates the accession of Hoshea to the twelfth year of Ahaz (723 BCE), is an obvious error for the second year of Ahaz (733/732). Finally, the regnal formula in 2 Kgs 18:1 and the related regnal synchronisms in 2 Kgs 18:9-10, which would assign the accession year of Hezekiah to 729, are obviously in error, since they would lop off most of the reign of Ahaz.

The effort to preserve the accuracy of the regnal formula in 2 Kgs 18:1 by pushing the date down to 727 BCE and making the death of Ahaz fall in the same year as Tiglath-pileser III's death does not solve this problem, and the attempt to connect the oracle in Isa 14:28-32 to the year of Tiglath-pileser's death is a blunder. That oracle against the Philistines is dated to the year of Ahaz's death, but it makes absolutely no reference to Tiglath-pileser at all.

If one dates the oracle to 715 BCE, the year of Hezekiah's accession and hence of Ahaz's death according to the synchronism in Isa 36:1 and 2 Kgs 18:13, Isaiah's hostility to the Philistines in the oracle is quite understandable.[8] In 715, the Philistines of Ashdod had begun to try to foment a rebellion against Assyria to which Ahaz had been opposed, and with the death of Ahaz the Philistines obviously felt that Hezekiah would be more receptive to their plans. Isaiah was opposed to Judean involvement in this Ashdod affair, as the material in 20:1-6 and 18:1-7 makes quite clear, and the oracle in 14:28-32 belongs in this same context. The rod that smote Philistia is not a reference to Tiglath-pileser III, but to Ahaz, their Judean enemy, who as a loyal Assyrian ally undoubtedly supported Assyria and took his own revenge during the Philistines' drubbing by both Tiglath-pileser III in the Syro-Ephraimitic War of 735–732 BCE, and by Sargon II in the Hamath-Gaza revolt of 720. The rod's being broken is simply an allusion to Ahaz's death (v. 28). The flying seraph that will emerge from the root of this serpent (Ahaz) is not a reference to another Assyrian king, but to Hezekiah, Ahaz's son, who the Philistines mistakenly thought would support their rebellion. Only the "smoke from the north" is a clear reference to the Assyrians, an allusion to Sargon II's ultimate crushing of the Ashdod rebellion in 711 BCE. If, on the contrary, one tries to put this oracle in 727, why was Isaiah upset by the Philistine attitude? There is absolutely no evidence that the Philistines were agitating for a revolt against Assyria or trying to get the new king Hezekiah to join them in this revolt in 727. Why would Isaiah care if the Philistines rejoiced over the death of Tiglath-pileser III? He himself probably rejoiced over the Assyrian king's death as well, just as he rejoiced over the death of Sargon II in 705 (see Isa 14:4-23). Isaiah was no great admirer of Assyrian kings, and any hostility he expresses toward Philistia normally comes from a political point he wants to make with a royal Judean audience.

In any case, the synchronism in Isa 36:1 and 2 Kgs 18:13, which dates Hezekiah's accession to 715 BCE, seems far more reliable on a number of grounds than the date formulae's accession in 729 (2 Kgs 18:1, 9-10). Cogan and Tadmor's dismissal of this synchronism by taking "the fourteenth year" as "the date which originally introduced the prophetic story of Hezekiah's illness and his miraculous recovery" and was thus totally unconnected to Sennacherib's invasion is pure fantasy and far more manipulative than doubting the chronological data found in the regnal formulae,[9] which in many cases are clearly unreliable as noted above—which Cogan and Tadmor admit even for 2 Kgs 18:1, 9-10.[10]

The statement that Sennacherib went up against all the fortified cities of Judah and captured them is a summary statement, anticipating some of the material in the narrative that follows, but in general it agrees with Sennacherib's own account in which he claims to have

---

8   For a full discussion of Isa 14:28-32, see my commentary on that passage above, and my earlier study, "Rod that Smote," 381–95.

9   Cogan and Tadmor, *II Kings*, 228.

10   Ibid., 216.

besieged and captured forty-six of Hezekiah's strong walled cities as well as the small cities in their neighborhood.[11] As the unfolding narrative will show, however, the phrase "all the fortified cities of Judah" does not include Jerusalem, Hezekiah's capital.

As v. 2 suggests, Sennacherib may not yet have captured Lachish, the most prominent of the forty-six cities that Sennacherib captured, the siege of which was the centerpiece of the stone reliefs that Sennacherib set up in his palace after this campaign.[12] Sennacherib may still be engaged in the siege of Lachish when he sends the Rabshakeh with a large force from Lachish to Jerusalem to parley with Hezekiah. The parallel in 2 Kgs 18:17 mentions three high government officials that were sent, אֶת־תַּרְתָּן וְאֶת־רַב־סָרִיס וְאֶת־רַב־שָׁקֵה (ʾet-tartān wĕʾet-rab-sārîs wĕʾet-rab-šāqê), "the Tartan, the Rabsaris, and the Rabshakeh." It is unclear why the narrative in Isaiah omits the Tartan, or field marshal, the highest official after the king, and the Rabsaris, the chief eunuch, the second highest official after the king, or, alternatively, why the narrative in Kings adds them, though in both narratives it is the Rabshakeh who does all the speaking for the Assyrian delegation. The term Rabshakeh (רַב־שָׁקֵה, rab-šāqê; Akkadian rab šāqî/ê) means "chief cupbearer," but the person so designated was not a household servant but a very high administrative official in the Assyrian government.[13] When he arrives at Jerusalem, he takes up a position by one of the water channels along the highway of the laundryman's field in the Kidron Valley underneath the eastern walls of Jerusalem, close to the same location where Isaiah confronted Ahaz years earlier in 735 BCE (Isa 7:3). Why he chose this, from an attacker's point of view, difficult ground rather than the easier approach from the north is not clear, but since his purpose was to parley, not to attack, the tactical difficulties of this ground did not matter. It may have been intended as an implicit threat to the security of Jerusalem's water supply, which depended on the Gihon Spring, or it may just have been that this area was closer to the temple and the palace and thus to the royal officials with whom he wished to parley. Or it may have been that this ground seemed a safe enough area for Judean officials to go out and parley with the Assyrian official.

In any case, three high Judean officials go out to him to parley (v. 3)—Eliakim the son of Hilkiah, who was over the palace (עַל־הַבָּיִת, ʿal-habbāyit), Shebna the secretary (הַסֹּפֵר, hassōpēr), and Joah the son of Asaph the recorder (הַמַּזְכִּיר, hammazkîr). The first named official, Eliakim the ʿal-habbāyit, appears to be the highest official, and it appears that he had replaced the demoted Shebna in that position only a short time before (see Isa 22:15-25). Shebna is now just the royal secretary or scribe. The precise distinction between hassōpēr and hammazkîr is not clear; both terms seem to suggest scribal activity, but, as with the Assyrian titles for high state officials, the designations may not describe their actual governmental functions.

The Rabshakeh begins the parley by commanding the Judean officials in formulaic language strikingly similar to the introductory formula in letters to tell Hezekiah what the great king, the king of Assyria, says (v. 4). He then quotes his king's words verbatim: "What is this source of confidence [הַבִּטָּחוֹן הַזֶּה, habbiṭṭāḥôn hazzeh] in which you trust [בָּטָחְתָּ, bāṭāḥtā]?" Note that he addresses Hezekiah in the second person masculine singular, making clear that the address is intended for the Judean king personally. He then continues with the sarcastic remark, "Do you [see the textual notes] think that a mere word of the lips is counsel and strength for war?" If not, then "on whom do you trust that you have rebelled against me" (v. 5)? In the continuation of the speech, the Assyrian king will try to undercut Hezekiah's trust in any source of confidence he might have for maintaining the rebellion against Sennacherib. As Peter Machinist has convincingly shown, the arguments the Assyrian king makes in this narrative are precisely the same sorts of arguments one finds in the Assyrian propaganda from the period.[14]

---

11   Luckenbill, *Annals*, 32–33, iii 19–23. See now Grayson and Novotny, RINAP 3/1-2.

12   See David Ussishkin, *The Conquest of Lachish by Sennacherib* (Publications of the Institute of Archaeology 6; Tel Aviv: Tel Aviv University, Institute of Archaeology, 1982).

13   See *CAD* 17, Š Part II, 30–32. Note also Raija Mattila, *The King's Magnates: A Study of the Highest Officials of the Assyrian Empire* (SAAS 11; Helsinki: Neo-Assyrian Text Corpus Project, 2000).

14   Peter Machinist, "Assyria and Its Image in the First Isaiah," *JAOS* 103 (1982) 719–37.

The first of these possible sources of confidence that the Assyrian king mentions is Egypt, but he dismisses Egypt as no more than a staff of a bruised or splintered reed that pierces the hand of anyone who leans on it (v. 6). Such, he says, is Pharaoh the king of Egypt to all those who put their trust in him. In commenting on Yamani and the Philistines' reliance on Egypt during the Ashdod crisis of 715–711 BCE, the Assyrian king Sargon II makes a similar disparaging comment about the king of Egypt: "To Pharaoh king of Egypt [*ᵖPi-ir-ʾu-u šàr māt*(kur) *Mu-uṣ-ri*], a ruler who could not save them [*mal-ku la mu-še-zi-bi-šú-nu*], they carried their present, and they kept asking him for military help."[15] Based on the history of the previous twenty-five years, this opinion of Egypt seemed reasonable. Egypt provided no significant help for Hoshea's rebellion against Shalmaneser V, despite Hoshea's appeal (2 Kgs 17:4). The Nubian/Egyptian relief army led by Reu sent to relieve the siege of Gaza in 720 was soundly defeated by Sargon II, and supporting Nubian troops on the walls of Raphia and Gabbatuna did not prevent those cities from falling to the Assyrians.[16] And when Sargon II attacked rebellious Ashdod and its allies in 711, the promised Nubian/Egyptian relief army did not even show up. What historical basis could a reasonable person muster for trusting in Egyptian help?

Having dismissed the Egyptians as a reliable source of help, the Assyrian envoy then raises the possibility that Hezekiah and his people may be relying on Yahweh (v. 7). There is a subtle shift here from a personal address to Hezekiah to an address to his people as well, marked by the mixture of singular and plural forms and a reference to Hezekiah in the third person that implies that the Assyrians were trying to drive a wedge between the Judean king and his people. "And if you say [masc. sg.] to me, we trust [com. pl.] in Yahweh our God, is not he the one whose high places and altars Hezekiah removed when he said to Judah and Jerusalem, 'Before this altar

you shall worship!' (v. 7)?" The Assyrian envoy is suggesting that Hezekiah has alienated Yahweh by his religious reform, and thus the deity can no longer be trusted to support Hezekiah. This negative reference to Hezekiah's restriction of sacrificial worship to Jerusalem shows that the Assyrians were very well informed by their spies on what was going on in Judah, and it also suggests that there remained inner-Judean opposition to and resentment over Hezekiah's reform that the Assyrians were attempting to exploit.[17]

At v. 8 the Assyrian envoy drops any pretense of simply quoting Sennacherib's words to Hezekiah and speaks in his own voice, "And now make a wager with my Lord, the king of Assyria." The Rabshakeh offers to give Hezekiah two thousand horses, if Hezekiah can furnish riders for them, with the clear implication that even if Hezekiah had the horses, he would be unable to muster enough horsemen to make use of them. In the Rabshakeh's opinion, Hezekiah's remaining mobile troops are too few to make any difference in the outcome of the war. With so few troops, he asks Hezekiah, how can you hope to turn back a single governor of the least of the servants of the Assyrian king when you are forced to rely on the Egyptians for chariotry and cavalry (v. 9)?

The Rabshakeh has already dismissed the Egyptians as unreliable, so now he turns back to the question of Yahweh (v. 10). He now claims that it was actually Yahweh who had commanded him to go up against this land—the land of Judah—and destroy it. Presumably his logic is that Hezekiah's radical reform had angered Yahweh, and in response Yahweh had summoned the Assyrians to punish Judah for this sin.

The discussion had apparently been taking place in Judean Hebrew in close enough proximity to the city walls that it could be overheard by the defenders on the wall, and the Judean envoys now interrupt the Rabshakeh with the request that the negotiations be continued in Aramaic

---

15 Fuchs, *Die Annalen*, 81–96; K.1668b+D.T.6 VII.b, lines 30–33.

16 See my "Egyptian and Nubian Oracles," 201–9, esp. 203.

17 See Peter Dubovský, *Hezekiah and the Assyrian Spies: Reconstruction of the Neo-Assyrian Intelligence Services and Its Significance for 2 Kings 18–19* (BibOr 49; Rome: Pontificio Istituto Biblico, 2006); Dubovský, "Sennacherib's Invasion of the Levant through the Eyes of Assyrian Intelligence Services," in Isaac Kalimi and Seth Richardson, eds., *Sennacherib at the Gates of Jerusalem: Story, History and Historiography* (CHANE 71; Leiden: Brill, 2014) 249–91; and Peter Machinist, "The *Rab šāqēh* at the Wall of Jerusalem: Israelite Identity in the Face of the Assyrian 'Other,'" *HS* 41 (2000) 151–68, esp. 163–64 and n. 30.

(אֲרָמִית, ʾărāmît),[18] which they understand (כִּי שֹׁמְעִים אֲנָחְנוּ, kî šōmĕʿîm ʾănāḥnû, lit., "for we hear it"), rather than in Judean (יְהוּדִית, yĕhûdît), because they are troubled by the possible impact of this discussion on the morale of the defenders (v. 11). This is the only attested use of yĕhûdît to refer to the Judean dialect of Hebrew, but the clear dialectal distinction between Judean Hebrew and north Israelite Hebrew has been demonstrated by F. M. Cross and D. N. Freedman.[19] Of course, the whole point of the Rabshakeh's speaking in Judean was to undermine the morale of defenders of Jerusalem, so he quickly rebuffs their request (v. 12). "Was it only to your [masc. sg.] Lord and to you [masc. sg.] that my Lord sent me to speak these words?" he says. "Was it not also for the men sitting on the wall, who are doomed to eat their own shit and to drink their own piss with you [masc. pl.]?" Then, sensing a psychological advantage, the Rabshakeh stood up and shouted in a loud voice in Judean to the men on the wall, "Hear [masc. pl.] the words of the great king, the king of Assyria (v. 13)! Thus says the king, 'Let not Hezekiah deceive you [masc. pl.], because he is not able to save you [masc. pl.].'" The Rabshakeh then warns the men on the wall not to let Hezekiah deceive them into trusting in Yahweh by saying, "Yahweh will surely save us, and this city will not be given into the hand of the king of Aššur" (v. 15). The Assyrian envoy continues by warning the men on the wall not to listen to Hezekiah, but instead to listen to the words of the king of Assyria (v. 16). If they will only make a peace offering to the king of Assyria and come out of the city to him in surrender, then instead of starvation siege rations of shit and piss, each of them will be able to eat from his own vine and fig tree and drink from his own cistern, until the king of Assyria comes and takes them to a land like their own land, a land of grain and new wine, a land of bread and vineyards (v. 17). The precise connotation of the idiom עֲשׂוּ־אִתִּי בְרָכָה (ʿăśû-ʾittî bĕrākâ)

is disputed. The general sense seems to be to surrender and make peace with the Assyrian king. Some think the word bĕrākâ here is derived from the verb ברך I, "to bow (in submission)";[20] others derive it from the normal word "blessing" but in the sense of "making an agreement with someone."[21] Cogan and Tadmor suggest that the uncommon use of עשה (ʿāśâ), "to make," as an auxiliary verb indicates an Aramaic or Akkadian calque, and they point to the use of the Akkadian expression šulmānu epēšu in the sense of "to exchange or send gifts." Thus, they argue that this is the same use of the word bĕrākâ in the sense of "gift" as a synonym of מִנְחָה (minḥâ), "offering, gift," attested in Gen 33:10-11, though they cite only Josh 15:19; 1 Sam 30:26; and 2 Kgs 5:15, and omit the Genesis passage.[22] Then the following expression וּצְאוּ אֵלַי (ûṣĕʾû ʾēlay), "and come out to me," is the equivalent of "surrender to me," since opening the gates and exiting the fortified city obviously mean submission and surrender. That seems the best explanation of the idiom, since it operates with a meaning of bĕrākâ that is actually attested in Hebrew. The Assyrian king is offering the Judean soldiers a temporary comfortable life back at home over against the threat of privation and death in the siege of Jerusalem, and then a comfortable life in a new land of exile very similar to their homeland.

The Rabshakeh is still worried, however, that Hezekiah has convinced his soldiers that Yahweh will deliver them, so he again tries to undercut this confidence. "Don't let Hezekiah deceive you saying, 'Yahweh will deliver us'" (v. 18). Now, however, instead of arguing that Yahweh himself had sent Assyria against Judah, he argues that no God had ever been able to save his land from the king of Assyria. "Where," he asks, "are the gods of Hamath, Arpad, and Sepharaim? And did they save Samaria from my hand?" (v. 19). Note the fluidity with which the Rabshakeh moves from referring to the king of Assyria

---

18 Aramaic rather than Akkadian was the language of the Assyrian empire west of the Euphrates; see Cogan and Tadmor, *II Kings*, 232; R. A. Bowman, "Arameans, Aramaic, and the Bible," *JNES* 7 (1948) 65–90; H. Tadmor, "The Aramaization of Assyria," in Hans-Jörg Nissen and Johannes Renger, *Mesopotamien und seine Nachbarn: Politische und kulturelle Wechselbeziehungen im alten Vorderasien vom 4. bis 1. Jahrtausend v. Chr.* (Berliner Beiträge zum Vorderen Orient 1; Berlin: Reimer, 1983) 449–70.

19 Frank Moore Cross and David Noel Freedman, *Early Hebrew Orthography: A Study of the Epigraphic Evidence* (AOS 36; New Haven: American Oriental Society, 1952).

20 See *HALOT*, 161.

21 A. Murtonen, "The Usage and Meaning of the Words lĕbārek and bĕrākâ in the Old Testament," *VT* 9 (1959) 158–77, esp. 73–74.

22 Cogan and Tadmor, *II Kings*, 232.

in the third person to a direct quotation of his words in the first person. Arpad fell to Tiglath-pileser III in 740 BCE and much of Hamath's former territory was taken by Tiglath-pileser at the fall of Kullani in 738, but Hamath led a rebellion against Sargon II in 720, and Sargon II reconquered it in that year. These were great cities, but their gods were not able to save them from the Assyrians. The identification of Sepharaim is more problematic. In the past it was often identified with Babylonian Sippar, on the assumption that Sippar consisted of two conjoined cities—Sippar of Shamash and Sippar of Annunitum on opposite sides of the canal—thus the dual ending -aim,[23] but others think it should refer to a city in Syria because of its listing with Arpad, Hamath, and Samaria.[24] The parallel in 2 Kgs 18:34 adds the cities Hena (הֵנַע, hēnaʿ, perhaps Anat on the middle Euphrates; so HALOT, 252) and Ivvah (עִוָּה, ʿiwwâ, location uncertain) after Sepharaim, though these seem to be a later addition to the text from 2 Kgs 19:13.[25] With the identification of Sepharaim less than certain, the date of the conquest of the city is also uncertain. The Rabshakeh ends the list of conquered cities with Samaria, whose gods could not save Samaria from the hand of the Assyrian king, because the chief god of Samaria was Yahweh. If the Yahweh of Samaria could not save Samaria, why should the Judeans trust the Yahweh of Jerusalem to save Jerusalem? "Who among all the gods of these lands," the Assyrian king asks, "saved their land from my hand that Yahweh should save Jerusalem from my hand?" (v. 20). The Assyrian argument from previous history is intended to underscore the inevitability of Jerusalem's fall and thus to encourage its defenders to opt for a quick surrender.

Nonetheless, the discipline of the Judean defenders on the wall is remarkable. They kept silent and refused to respond to the Rabshakeh's speech with so much as a word (v. 21). There is no expressed subject for the two verbs וַיַּחֲרִישׁוּ וְלֹא־עָנוּ אֹתוֹ (wayyaḥărîšû wĕlōʾ-ʿānû ʾōtô), "and they kept silent and did not answer him," but inasmuch as the Rabshakeh has been specifically addressing the defenders on the wall since v. 13 (see v. 12), they are the natural subject. The parallel in 2 Kgs 18:36 makes this understanding explicit by adding a subject וְהֶחֱרִישׁוּ הָעָם (wĕheḥĕrîšû hāʿām), "and the people kept silent." Nonetheless, Cogan and Tadmor reject this subject as secondary and understand the subject of the verbs as the Judean royal officials, since they argue that the king could hardly "have given an order to the people to remain silent before the confrontation with the Rabshakeh, when only during the negotiations did it become known to Jerusalem's defenders that they were the object of the Assyrian's speech."[26] This is hardly a serious objection, however. The Judean royal court was not made up of idiots, and they had had years to observe Assyrian siege tactics, from Tiglath-pileser III's campaigns against their close neighbors the Philistines, Israel, and Damascus, Shalmaneser V's campaign against Samaria, and Sargon II's campaign against Samaria and against Ashdod down to Sennacherib's initial conquest of Phoenician and Philistine cities and the first of the Judean fortresses. It was the standard tactic of the Assyrians, as of any intelligent besieging army including the Israelites (see 2 Sam 20:14-22; 2 Kgs 10:1-11), to try to avoid the time and expense of a drawn-out siege by turning the population of a besieged city against its own ruling class whose policies had provoked the siege and so securing a quick surrender. The "people" on the wall above the critical site where the parley was to take place were probably a contingent of Hezekiah's best troops, and it is not at all surprising that the king would have issued them a firm command not to respond at all to the Assyrian negotiators.[27]

---

23   See BDB, 709.

24   See the discussion in Cogan and Tadmor (II Kings, 212), who are dubious about any of the proposed identifications.

25   Cogan and Tadmor, however, seem to regard these two names in 2 Kgs 18:34 as a textual corruption (II Kings, 233) rather than actual city names.

26   Ibid.

27   Cogan and Tadmor (II Kings, 242) have pointed to the Nimrud letter ND 2632, published by H. W. F. Saggs ("The Nimrud Letters, 1952, Part I," Iraq 17 [1955] 23–24), in which two Assyrian officials take their stand before one of the gates of Babylon and try unsuccessfully to persuade the citizens of Babylon to abandon their support of the Chaldean king of Babylon (c. 730 BCE) as a parallel to the negotiations portrayed in this biblical passage. There is also a relief showing an Assyrian official at the wall of a city under Assyrian siege reading out something—probably surrender terms. See H. W. F. Saggs, Assyriology and the Study of the Old Testament (Cardiff: University of Wales Press, 1969) 17–18.

When the parley was over, the Judean envoys—Eliakim, Shebna, and Joah—went back into the city to Hezekiah and reported to him the words of the Rabshakeh (v. 22). They do so, however, with their garments torn as a sign of the desperate straits in which they perceive the city to be. The parley with the Rabshakeh has not reassured them but, rather, cast them into a deeper despair. When King Hezekiah hears their report, he shares their despair, rends his garments, covers himself with sackcloth as a sign of mourning, and enters the temple, presumably to pray to Yahweh (Isa 37:1). In the meantime, he sends Eliakim and Shebna, two of his three top officials who had participated in the parley, along with the elders of the priests, all covered in sackcloth to the prophet Isaiah, the son of Amoz (v. 2). Why Joah does not accompany this delegation is not said. The delegation quotes to the prophet the words of Hezekiah, requesting that Isaiah offer a prayer to Yahweh on behalf of the remnant that is left (vv. 3-4).

This appeal of the king to the prophet through his royal advisors and senior priests marks a radical shift in the royal court's attitude toward Isaiah in the brief period between the death of Sargon II in 705 and the now-frightening experience of Sennacherib's onslaught in Judah. The royal court had tried to exclude Isaiah from their deliberations and sensitive negotiations with Nubian Egypt and Merodach-Baladan's Babylon when they were setting up their defensive alliances in preparation for the revolt against Assyria, because they considered him a security threat, since they knew he would oppose these alliances. And they were right. Despite their best efforts, they could not keep their deliberations secret from Isaiah, and he viciously attacked the priests and royal officials whose policy of foreign military alliances he opposed (28:7-22; 29:9-16; 30:1-17; 31:1-3). Now, however, the

superiority of the prophet's views over the disastrously failed plans of his court opponents, and the perception that the prophet indeed had the ear of Yahweh, the ultimate cause of the failure of their defensive alliance just as the prophet had warned, made the prophet's word and his possible intercession with Yahweh important to the king.

The king appeals to Isaiah with a proverbial saying from the experience of difficult childbirth that graphically described the plight of Jerusalem, "This day is a day of affliction, rebuke, and humiliation, for children have come to the breach and there is no strength to give birth" (v. 3; see Hos 13:13; cf. Isa 26:17-18). The form מַשְׁבֵּר (mašbēr), "the breaking forth," appears to be a gerund describing the breaking forth of the fetus into the world (cf. the use of the verb פָּרַץ in Gen 38:29),[28] while the noun מִשְׁבָּר (Hos 13:13) designates the opening of the cervix. Following this proverbial saying, Hezekiah then suggests the possibility that Yahweh, whom he describes as the prophet's God, acknowledging the very close relationship between the prophet and Yahweh, may have heard the words of the Rabshakeh and been offended by the Assyrian king's blasphemous taunting of the living God. Perhaps Yahweh, the prophet's God, will rebuke these offensive words which he has heard, and, given that hope, the king asks Isaiah to lift up an intercessory prayer for the surviving remnant of Judah (v. 4). The idea that a deity could be angered by a foreign enemy's arrogance, particularly by the disparaging of the power of the deity (1 Kgs 20:28), even if the deity had himself sent the foreign enemy to punish his own people, was a common motif in the ancient Near East (Isa 10:12-15).[29]

The narrator has gotten ahead of himself, however, and at v. 5 he jumps back to the moment when the servants of Hezekiah entered into the presence of Isaiah

28   So Cogan and Tadmor, *II Kings*, 233.

29   For a full discussion of the comparable Mesopotamian material, see Patrick D. Miller Jr. and J. J. M. Roberts, *The Hand of the Lord: A Reassessment of the "Ark Narrative" of 1 Samuel* (1977; repr., Atlanta: Society of Biblical Literature, 2008) 12–26 and the literature cited there. Note particularly the explanations of Esarhaddon (Borger, *Die Inschriften Asarhaddons*, 12–18, episodes 2-15; and see now Leichty, RINAP 4) and Nabonidus (S. Langdon, *Die* neubabylonischen Königsinschriften [VAB 4; Leipzig: Hinrichs 1912] 270-80, Nabonid no. 8), translated in *ANET*, 308–11) for the Assyrian destruction of Marduk's cult places, and for Marduk's revenge. For the latest and most complete edition of Nabonidus's inscriptions, see Hanspeter Schaudig, *Die Inschriften Nabonids von Babylon und Kyros' des Grossen samt den in ihrem Umfeld entstandenen Tendenzschriften: Textausgabe und Grammatik* (AOAT 256; Münster: Ugarit, 2001).

as though he had forgotten that he had already narrated their delivery of Hezekiah's message to the prophet. This breaking of the narrative sequence seems odd, though it is attested elsewhere.[30] Perhaps the device is to focus sole attention on Isaiah's words to Hezekiah as independent of any psychological manipulation by the rhetorical cleverness of Hezekiah's message. Without any direct reference to Hezekiah's message, Isaiah commands the king's envoys to tell their lord what Yahweh says: "Do not be afraid of the words which you [masc. sg.] have heard, with which the servants of the king of Assyria have blasphemed me" (v. 6). Yahweh's response does cleverly allude to Hezekiah's message, however. Hezekiah had suggested the possibility that Yahweh might "hear" (יִשְׁמַע, yišmaʿ) the words of the Rabshakeh, whom the king of Assyria sent to "taunt" (לְחָרֵף, lĕḥārēp) God, and might rebuke (him) for the words which Yahweh "heard" (שָׁמַע, šāmaʿ). Yahweh's response shifts the hearing to Hezekiah, "Do not be afraid of the words which you have heard [שָׁמַעְתָּ, šāmaʿtā]," though God does acknowledge that those words of the servants of the king of Assyria "reviled . . . me" (גִּדְּפוּ . . . אוֹתִי, giddĕpû . . . ʾôtî). God's designation of the servants of the king of Assyria as נַעֲרֵי (naʿărê), "boys of, servants of," rather than as עַבְדֵי (ʿabdê), "servants of," may have been intended as a disparaging comment on the Assyrian officials (cf. Isa 3:4, where Judah's royal officials [śārîm] are disparaged as mere boys [nĕʿārîm]).

God continues with the statement that he is about to put a spirit (רוּחַ, rûaḥ) in the Assyrian king, and the king will hear a report that will cause him to return to his own land, where God will cause him to fall by the sword (v. 7). The divine insertion of a spirit into the Assyrian king means that God will incite him to act irrationally, against his own best interests (see Isa 19:14; 1 Kgs 22:23). The report that he will hear apparently refers to the report about Tirhaqa, the Nubian king, mentioned in v. 9b, while the account of the Assyrian king's return to his own land and his death by the sword there does not come until vv. 37-38. The editing of the larger narrative has postponed the fulfillment of God's promise, splitting it into two parts spread across the rest of the chapter.

In the meantime, however, this episode in the narrative comes to a close. The Rabshakeh, getting no response from either Hezekiah's delegation or the defenders on the wall, returns from his mission to report to Sennacherib, and, having heard that Sennacherib had departed from Lachish, the Rabshakeh finds that the king of Assyria is now fighting against Libnah. Lachish is identified with Tell ed-Duwer in the Shephelah, while Libnah is usually identified either with Tell Bornat, eight km northeast of Lachish, or Tell es-Safi, nine km northwest of Tell Bornat. Either location is closer to Jerusalem than Lachish, so it suggests that Sennacherib has captured Lachish and has moved his siege operations to another fortress city guarding the approaches to Jerusalem.

Bibliography

Abel, F. M., *Géographie de la Palestine* (2 vols.; EBib; Paris: J. Gabalda, 1933–38; repr., 1967).

Ackroyd, Peter R., "The Bibical Interpretation of the Reigns of Ahaz and Hezekiah," in W. Boyd Barrick and John R. Spencer, eds., *In the Shelter of Elyon: Essays on Ancient Palestinian Life and Literature in Honor of G. W. Ahlström* (JSOTSup 31; Sheffield: JSOT Press, 1984) 247–50.

———, "Historians and Prophets," in Ackroyd, *Studies in the Religious Tradition of the Old Testament* (London: SCM, 1987) 121–51, 278–82.

———, "Isaiah 36–39: Structure and Function," in W. C. Delsman et al., eds., *Von Kanaan bis Kerala: Festschrift für Prof. Mag. Dr. Dr. J. P. M. van der Ploeg* (AOAT 211; Kevelaer: Butzon & Bercker; Neukirchen-Vluyn: Neukirchener Verlag, 1981) 3–21.

Alt, Albrecht, "Die territorialgeschichtliche Bedeutung von Sanheribs Eingriff in Palästina," *PJ* 25 (1930) 80–88.

Begrich, Joachim, "*Sōfēr* und *Mazkîr*," *ZAW* 58 (1940) 1–29.

Ben Zvi, Ehud, "Who Wrote the Speech of Rabshakeh and When?" *JBL* 109 (1990) 84–85, 91.

30 S. R. Driver, *A Treatise on the Use of Tenses in Hebrew and Some Other Syntactical Questions* (Oxford: Clarendon, 1892) 75–76.

Berges, U., "Die Zionstheologie des Buches Jesaja," *EstBib* 58 (2000) 167–98.

Boecker, Hans Jochen, "Erwägungen zum Amt des Mazkir," *TZ* 17 (1961) 212–16.

——, *Redeformen des Rechtslebens im Alten Testament* (2nd ed.; WMANT 14; Neukirchenen-Vluyn: Neukirchener Verlag, 1970) 106–11.

Bright, John, "Le problème des campagnes de Sennachérib en Palestine," in *Hommage à Wilhelm Vischer* (Montpellier: Causse, Graille, Castlenau, 1960) 20–31.

Burney, C. F., "'The Jew's Language': 2 Kings XVIII 26 = Isa XXXVI 11," *JTS* 13 (1912) 417–20.

Camp, Ludger, *Hiskija und Hiskijabild: Analyse und Interpretation von 2 Kön 18–20* (Münsteraner theologische Abhandlungen 9; Altenberge: Telos, 1990).

Catastini, Alessandro, *Isaia ed Ezechia: Studio di storia della tradizione di II Re 18–20//Is. 36–39* (Studi semitici n.s. 6; Rome: Pontifical Biblical Institute, 1989).

——, "Le varianti greche di Isaia 36–39," *EVO* 6 (1983) 209–34.

Childs, *Assyrian Crisis.*

Clements, R. E., *Isaiah and the Deliverance.*

——, "The Prophecies of Isaiah and the Fall of Jerusalem in 587 B.C.," *VT* 30 (1980) 421–36.

——, "The Prophecies of Isaiah to Hezekiah concerning Sennacherib: 2 Kings 19:12-34/Isa 37:22-35," in Clements, *Old Testament Prophecy: From Oracles to Canon* (Louisville: Westminster John Knox, 1996) 35–48.

Cohen, C., "Neo-Assyrian Elements in the First Speech of the Biblical Rabshaqe," *IOS* 9 (1979) 32–48.

Conrad, D., "Einige (archäologische) Miszellen zur Kultgeschichte Judas in der Königszeit," in A. H. J. Gunneweg and Otto Kaiser, eds., *Textgemäss: Aufsätze und Beiträge zur Hermeneutik des Alten Testament. Festschrift für Ernst Würthwein zum 70. Geburtstag* (Göttingen: Vandenhoeck & Ruprecht, 1979) 28–32.

Conrad, E. W., "The Royal Narratives and the Structure of the Book of Isaiah," *JSOT* 41 (1988) 67–81.

Croatto, J. S., "La critica profetica a la ideologia militar imperialista: exegesis de Isaias 36–37," *RevistB* 49 (1987) 169–85.

Crown, A. D., "Messengers and Scribes: The ספר and מלאך in the Old Testament," *VT* 24 (1974) 366–70.

Darr, K. P., "No Strength to Deliver: A Contextual Analysis of Hezekiah's Proverb in Isaiah 37:3*b*," in Roy F. Melugin and Marvin A. Sweeney, eds., *New Visions of Isaiah* (JSOTSup 214; Sheffield: Sheffield Academic Press, 1996) 218–56.

Deutsch, Richard, *Die Hiskiaerzählungen: Eine formgeschichtliche Untersuchung der Texte Js 36–39 und 2 R 18–20* (Diss., Basel; Basel: Basileia, 1969).

Dietrich, Walter, *Prophetie und Geschichte: Eine redaktionsgeschichtliche Untersuchung zum deuteronomistischen Geschichtswerk* (FRLANT 108; Göttingen: Vandenhoeck & Ruprecht, 1972).

Dion, P. E., "Sennacherib's Expedition to Palestine," *Eglise et théologie* 20 (1989) 5–25.

Diringer, D., "Sennacherib's Attack on Lachish: New Epigraphical Evidence," *VT* 1 (1951) 134–36.

Ellul, Jacques, *The Politics of God and the Politics of Man* (Grand Rapids: Eerdmans, 1977) 143–89.

Fewell, D. N., "Sennacherib's Defeat: Words at War in 2 Kings 18:3–19:37," *JSOT* 34 (1986) 79–90.

Fichtner, J., "Jahwes Plan in der Botschaft des Jesajas," in Fichtner, *Gottes Weisheit: Gesammelte Studien zum Alten Testament* (AzTh 2.3; Stuttgart: Calwer, 1965) 27–43.

Fullerton, K., "Isaiah's Attitude in the Sennacherib Campaign," *AJSL* 42 (1925) 1–25.

Gallagher, William R., *Sennacherib's Campaign to Judah: New Studies* (SHCANE 18; Leiden: Brill, 1999).

Galling, Kurt, *Die israelitische Staatsverfassung in ihrer vorderorientalischen Umwelt* (AO 28; Leipzig: Hinrichs, 1929).

Gantt, C. A., "Do Not Let Your God Deceive You: The Idea of Divine Deception in the Hebrew Bible" (Diss., Harvard University, 1998).

Geyer, J. B., "2 Kings XVIII 14-16 and the Annals of Sennacherib," *VT* 21 (1971) 604–6.

Gonçalves, Francolino J., *L'expédition de Sennachérib en Palestine dans la littérature hébraïque ancienne* (Publications de l'Institut orientaliste de Louvain 34; Paris: Gabalda, 1986).

Grabbe, Lester L., ed., *"Like a Bird in a Cage": The Invasion of Sennacherib in 701 BCE* (JSOTSup 363; London: Sheffield Academic Press, 2003).

Haag, H., "La campagne de Sennachérib contre Jérusalem en 701," *RB* 58 (1951) 348–59.

Hallo, W. W., "From Qarqar to Carchemish," *BA* 23 (1960) 34–61.

Hardmeier, C., "Die Propheten Micha und Jesaja im Spiegel von Jeremia XXVI and 2 Regum XVIII–XX: Zur Prophetie-Rezeption in der nachjosianischen Zeit," in J. A. Emerton, ed., *Congress Volume: Leuven 1989* (VTSup 43; Leiden: Brill, 1991) 172–89.

——, *Prophetie im Streit vor dem Untergang Judas: Erzählkommunikative Studien zur Entstehungssituation der Jesaja- und Jeremiaerzählungen in II Reg 18–20 und Jer 37–40* (BZAW 187; Berlin: de Gruyter, 1990).

Heinz, J. G., "Lettres royales à la divinité en Mésopotomie et en Israël antiques: D'un genre littéraire," *RHR* 181 (1972) 111–13.

Helck, W., "Herold (*whmw*)," in W. Helck and E. Otto, eds., *Lexikon der Ägyptologie* (Wiesbaden: Harrassowitz, 1975–92) 2:1153–54.

458

Honor, Leo L., *Sennacherib's Invasion of Palestine: A Critical Source Study* (Contributions to Oriental History and Philology 12; New York: Columbia University Press, 1926).

Horn, S. H., "The Chronology of King Hezekiah's Reign," *AUSS* 2 (1964) 40–52.

——, "Did Sennacherib Campaign Once or Twice against Hezekiah," *AUSS* 4 (1966) 1–28.

Hurwitz, M. S., "The Septuagint of Isaiah 36–39 in Relation to That of 1–35, 40–66," *HUCA* 28 (1957) 75–83.

Hutter, Manfred, *Hiskija, König von Juda: Ein Beitrag zur judäischen Geschichte in assyrischer Zeit* (Grazer Theologische Studien 6; Graz: Im Eigenverlag des Instituts für Ökumenische Theologie und Patrologie an der Universität Graz, 1982).

Irwin, W. A., "The Attitude of Isaiah in the Crisis of 701," *JR* 16 (1936) 406–18.

Izu, Y., "The Theological Significance of the Hezekiah Narrative in Isaiah," *BV* 35 (2001) 77–86.

Jack, A. M., *Texts Reading Texts, Sacred and Secular* (JSNTSup 179; Sheffield: Sheffield Academic Press, 1999).

Janssen, J. M. A., "Que sait-on actuellement du pharaon Tarhaqa?" *Bib* 34 (1954) 23–43.

Jenkins, A. K., "Hezekiah's Fourteenth Year: A New Interpretation of 2 Kings XVIII 13—XIX 37," *VT* 26 (1976) 284–98.

Jepsen, Alfred, *Die Quellen des Königsbuches* (Halle/Saale: Max Niemeyer, 1953).

Kaiser, O., "Die Verkündigung des Propheten Jesaja im Jahre 701," *ZAW* 81 (1969) 304–15.

Kalimi, Isaac, and Seth Richardson, eds., *Sennacherib at the Gates of Jerusalem: Story, History and Historiography* (CHANE 71; Leiden: Brill, 2014).

Kooij, A. van der, "Das assyrische Heer vor den Mauern Jerusalems im Jahr 701 v. Chr.," *ZDPV* 102 (1986) 93–109.

Kruger, H. A. J., "Gods, for Argument's Sake: A Few Remarks on the Literature and Theological Intentions of Isaiah 36–37: Part I," *OTE* 9.1 (1996) 52–67.

Laato, A., "Hezekiah and the Assyrian Crisis in 701 B.C.," *SJOT* 2 (1987) 49–68.

Lambert, W. G., "Destiny and Divine Intervention in Babylon and Israel," *OtSt* 17 (1972) 65–72.

LeMoyne, J., "Les deux ambassades de Sennachérib à Jérusalem," in *Mélanges bibliques en l'honneur de André Robert* (Travaux de l'Institut Catholique de Paris 4; Paris: Bloud & Gay, 1956) 149–64.

Levine, L. D., "The Second Campaign of Sennacherib," *JNES* 32 (1973) 312–17.

——, "Sennacherib's Southern Front: 704–689 B.C.," *JCS* 34 (1982) 29–34.

Lewy, J., "Sanherib und Hiskia (Jes 38,5; 36,2ff.)," *OLZ* 31 (1928) 150–63.

Liwak, R., "Die Rettung Jerusalems im Jahr 701 v. Chr.: Zum Verhältnis und Verständnis historischer und theologischer Aussagen," *ZTK* 83 (1986) 137–66.

Lohfink, N., "Die Gattung der 'historischen Kurzgeschichte' in den letzten Jahren von Juda und in der Zeit des babylonischen Exils," *ZAW* 90 (1986) 319–47.

Machinist, "Assyria and Its Image," 719–37.

Mbuwayesango, D. R., "The Defense of Zion and the House of David in Isaiah 1–39" (Diss., Emory University, 1998).

McKenzie, Steven L., *The Trouble with Kings: The Composition of the Book of Kings in the Deuteronomistic History* (VTSup 42; Leiden: Brill, 1991) 101–9.

Meinhold, J., *Die Jesajaerzählungen Jesaja 36–39: Eine historisch-kritische Untersuchung* (Göttingen: Vandenhoeck & Ruprecht, 1898).

Millard, A. R., "Adad-Nirari III, Aram and Arpad," *PEQ* 105 (1973) 161–64.

——, "Sennacherib's Attack on Hezekiah," *TynBul* 36 (1985) 61–77.

Na'aman, N., "Sennacherib's Campaign to Judah and the Date of the *lmlk* Stamps," *VT* 29 (1979) 61–68.

Norin, S., "An Important Kennicott Reading in 2 Kings xviii 13," *VT* 32 (1982) 337–38.

Olmstead, A. T., "The Earliest Book of Kings," *AJSL* 31 (1915) 169–214.

Orlinsky, H. M., "The Kings-Isaiah Recensions of the Hezekiah Story," *JQR* n.s. 30 (1939) 33–49.

Parpola, Simo, *Neo-Assyrian Toponyms* (programming and computer printing by Kimmo Koskenniemi; AOAT 6; Kevelaer: Butzon & Bercker, 1970).

Person, R. F., Jr., *The Kings–Isaiah and Kings–Jeremiah Recensions* (BZAW 252; Berlin: de Gruyter, 1997).

Pope, M., "Isaiah 34 in Relation to Isaiah 36, 40–66," *JBL* 71 (1952) 235–43.

Provan, I. W., *Hezekiah and the Books of Kings: A Contribution to the Debate about the Composition of the Deuteronomistic History* (BZAW 172; Berlin: de Gruyter, 1988).

Reventlow, H. Graf, "Das Amt des Mazkir," *TZ* 15 (1959) 161–75.

Rofé, Alexander, *The Prophetical Stories: The Narratives about the Prophets in the Hebrew Bible, Their Literary Types and History* (Publications of the Perry Foundation for Biblical Research in the Hebrew University of Jerusalem; Jerusalem: Magnes Press, Hebrew University, 1988) 88–95.

Rogers, R. W., "Sennacherib and Judah," in Karl Marti, ed., *Studien zur semitischen Philologie und Religionsgeschichte: Julius Wellhausen zum siebzigsten Geburtstag am 17. Mai 1914* (BZAW 27; Giessen: A. Töpelmann, 1914) 317–28.

Rowley, H. H., "Hezekiah's Reform and Rebellion," *BJRL* 44 (1961) 395–461; reprinted in Rowley, *Men of God: Studies in Old Testament History and Prophecy* (London: Nelson, 1963) 98–132.

Rudman, D., "A Rhetorical Study of 2 Kings XVIII 17-35," *VT* 50 (2000) 101–10.

Ruprecht, E., "Die ursprüngliche Komposition der Hiskia-Jesaja-Erzählungen und ihre Umstrukturierung durch den Verfasser des deuteronomistischen Geschichtswerkes," *ZTK* 87 (1990) 33–66.

Saggs, H. W. F., "The Nimrud Letters, 1952: Part I," *Iraq* 17 (1955) 21–50.

Sarna, N., "The Abortive Insurrection in Zedekiah's Day (Jer. 27–29)," *ErIsr* 14 (1978) 89–96.

Seitz, Christopher R., "Account A and the Annals of Sennacherib: A Reassessment," *JSOT* 58 (1993) 47–57.

——, *Zion's Final Destiny: The Development of the Book of Isaiah. A Reassessment of Isaiah 36–39.* Minneapolis: Fortress Press, 1991.

Shea, W. H., "Sennacherib's Second Campaign," *JBL* 104 (1985) 401–18.

Smelik, K. A. D., "Distortion of Old Testament Prophecy: The Purpose of Isaiah xxxvi and xxxvii," in Johannes C. de Moor et al., *Crises and Perspectives: Studies in Ancient Near Eastern Polytheism, Biblical Theology, Palestinian Archaeology, and Intertestamental Literature. Papers Read at the Joint British–Dutch Old Testament Conference, Held at Cambridge, U.K., 1985* (OtSt 24; Leiden: Brill, 1986) 70–93.

——, "King Hezekiah Advocates True Prophecy: Remarks on Isaiah xxxvi and xxxvii/II Kings xviii and xix," *OtSt* 28 (1992) 93–128.

Smith, H. S., and A. Smith, "A Reconsideration of the Kamose Texts," *ZÄS* 103 (1976) 48–76.

Soden, Wolfram von, "Sanherib vor Jerusalem 701 v. Chr.," in von Soden, *Bibel und alter Orient: Altorientalische Beiträge zum Alten Testament* (ed. Hans-Peter Müller; BZAW 162; Berlin: de Gruyter, 1985) 149–57.

Spieckermann, Hermann, *Juda unter Assur in der Sargonidenzeit* (FRLANT 129; Göttingen: Vandenhoeck & Ruprecht, 1982).

Stade, B., "Anmerkungen zu 2 Kö. 15–21," *ZAW* 6 (1886) 122–92.

Stohlmann, S., "The Judaean Exile after 701 B.C.E.," in W. W. Hallo et al., eds., *Scripture in Context*, vol. 2, *More Essays on the Comparative Method* (Winona Lake, IN: Eisenbrauns, 1983) 147–75.

Strus, Andrzej, "Interprétation des noms propres dans

les oracles contre les nations," in J. A. Emerton, ed., *Congress Volume: Salamanca 1983* (VTSup 36; Leiden: Brill, 1985) 272–85.

Tadmor, H., "Philistia under Assyrian Rule," *BA* 29 (1966) 86–102.

——, "Sennacherib's Campaign at Judah: Historical and Historiographical Considerations" (in Hebrew), *Zion* 50 (1985) 65–80; now in English in Tadmor, "With My Many Chariots I Have Gone Up the Heights of the Mountains" in *Historical and Literary Studies in Ancient Mesopotamia and Israel* (ed. Mordechai Cogan; Jerusalem: Israel Exploration Society, 2011) 653–75.

Talmon, S., "Aspects of the Textual Transmission of the Bible in the Light of Qumran Manuscripts," *Textus* 4 (1964) 95–132.

Van Leeuwen, C., "Sanchérib devant Jérusalem," *OtSt* 14 (1966) 245–72.

Vantulli, P., *Libri Synoptici Veteris Testamenti seu Librorum Regnum et Chronicorum Loci quos hebraice graece et latine critice edidit* (Rome: Paralleli, 1931).

Vaux, Roland de, "Jérusalem et les Prophètes," *RB* 73 (1966) 481–509.

Vermeylen, J., "Hypothèses sur l'origine d'Isaïe 36–39," in J. van Ruiten and M. Vervenne, eds., *Studies in the Book of Isaiah: Festschrift Willem A. M. Beuken* (BETL 132; Leuven: Leuven University Press, 1997) 95–118.

Vogt, E., *Der Aufstand Hiskias und die Belagerung Jerusalems 701 v. Chr.* (AnBib 106; Rome: Biblical Institute Press, 1986).

——, "Jesaja und die drohende Eroberung Palästinas durch Tiglatpilesar," in Josef Schreiner, ed., *Wort, Lied und Gottesspruch: Festschrift für Joseph Ziegler* (2 vols.; FB 1–2; Würzburg: Echter, 1972) 2:249–55.

——, "Sennacherib und die letzte Tätigkeit Jesajas," *Bib* 47 (1966) 427–37.

Vuk, T., "Wiederverkaufte Freiheit: Der Feldzug Sanheribs gegen Juda nach dem Invasionsbericht 2 Kö 18.13-16" (Thesis, Pontificium Athaenaeum Antonianum Facultas Hierosolymitana Theologiae Biblicae, 1979).

Wiener, H. M., "Isaiah and the Siege of Jerusalem," *JSR* 11 (1927) 195–209.

Wieringen, A. L. H. M. van, "Notes on Isaiah 36–37 (36:5,8; 39:9,18)," *BN* 96 (1999) 32–35.

Wildberger, H., "Die Rede des Rabsake vor Jerusalem," *TZ* 35 (1979) 35–47.

Zimmerli, W., "Jesaja und Hiskia," in Hartmut Gese and Hans Peter Rüger, eds., *Wort und Geschichte, Festschrift für Karl Elliger zum 70.Geburtstag* (AOAT 18; Kevelaer: Butzon & Bercker, 1973) 199–208.

Zimmern, H., "Über Bäcker und Mundschenk im Altsemitischen," *ZDMG* 53 (1899) 115–19.

9/ And he heard concerning[a] Tirhaqa, the king of Nubia, saying,[b] "He has
come out[c] to fight with you."[d] And he again sent[e] messengers to Hezekiah
saying,[b] 10/ "Thus you shall say to Hezekiah[f] the king of Judah, saying,[g]
'Let not your God,[h] in whom[i] you are trusting, deceive you,[j] saying:[g] Jerusalem[k] shall not[l] be given into the hand of the king of Assyria. 11/ Behold
you have heard[m] what[n] the kings of Assyria did to all the lands, destroying
them utterly. And will you be delivered?[o] 12/ Did the gods of the nations[p]
deliver them whom my forefathers destroyed,[q] Gozan and Haran and
Rezeph and the Edenites who were in Telassar?[r] 13/ Where[s] is the king
of Hamath and the king of Arpad and the king of Lair, of Sepharvaim, of
Hena, and of Ivvah?'"[t] 14/ And Hezekiah[u] took the letters[v] from the hand
of the messengers and read it,[w] and he went up[x] to the house of Yahweh and Hezekiah[u] spread it[y] before Yahweh. 15/ And Hezekiah[z] prayed
to Yahweh,[*a] saying,[*b] 16/ "O Yahweh of Hosts, God of Israel[*c] who sits
enthroned upon the cherubim,[*d] you alone are God[*e] to all[*f] the kingdoms
of the earth. You made[*g] the heavens and the earth. 17/ Incline[*h] your
ear,[*i] O Yahweh, and hear;[*j] Open your eye,[*k] O Yahweh, and see. And hear
all the words[*l] of Sennacherib that he has sent[*m] to reproach the living
God.[*n] 18/ Truly, O Yahweh, the kings of Assyria have devastated all the
countries[*o] and their land.[*p] 19/ And they have put[*q] their gods[*r] into the
fire, because[*s] they were not gods,[*t] but[*s] the work[*u] of human hands,
wood and stone, and they destroyed them. 20/ And now, O Yahweh our
God,[*v] save us[*w] from his[*x] hand, that all[*y] the kingdoms of the earth may
know that[*z] you, Yahweh, are (God) alone."[†a] 21/ And Isaiah[†b] the son of
Amoz sent to Hezekiah,[†c] saying,[†d] "Thus[†e] says Yahweh the God[†f] of Israel,
What you have prayed to me[†g] concerning Sennacherib king of Assyria I
have heard.[†h] 22/ This is the word that Yahweh has spoken concerning him:

Virgin daughter Zion shows contempt for you,[†i] she derides you;[†i]
   Daughter Jerusalem[†j] shakes the head[†k] behind you.[†l]
23/ Whom[†m] have you reproached[†n] and reviled?[†o]
   And against whom[†m] have you raised the voice
   And lifted your eyes[†p] on high?
   Against the Holy One of Israel!
24/ By the hand of your servants[†q] you have reproached my Lord,[†r]
   And you said:[†s] By the multitude of my chariotry[†t]
   I have ascended the height of the mountains, the peaks of Lebanon,
   That I might cut down[†u] his tallest cedars, his choicest cypresses,[†v]
   That I might enter[†w] his most distant height,[†x] the forest of his plantation.[†y]
25/ I dug[†z] and I drank[‡a] water,[‡b]
   That I might dry up[‡c] with the sole of my feet[‡d] all[‡e] the rivers of Egypt.[‡f]
26/ Have you not heard?[‡g]
   From long ago I did it;[‡h]
   From days[‡i] of old I fashioned it.[‡j]
   Now I have brought it,[‡k] that it might come to pass,[‡l]
   To lay waste[‡m] fortified cities[‡n] in desolate heaps.[‡o]
27/ And their inhabitants,[‡p] powerless,[‡q]
   Are terrified and ashamed;[‡r]
   They have become like plants of the field,
   And green grass,[‡s]
   Grass of the rooftops, blighted[‡t] before the east wind.[‡u]
28/ Your rising up[‡v] and your sitting down,
   and your going out and your coming in[‡w] I know,[‡x]
   And your raging against me.[‡y]
29/ Because your raging against me,[‡z]
   And your arrogance[§a] has come up into my ears,[§b]
   I will place my hook in your nose[§c] and my bridle in your lips,[§d]
   And I will turn you back[§e] in the way by which you came.[§f]

461

30/ And this is the sign for you:[§g]
This year eat[§h] what grows of itself,
And in the second year what grows from it,[§i]
And in the third year sow and harvest,[§j]
And plant[§k] orchards and eat[§l] their fruit.[§m]

31/ And the surviving part of the house of Judah[§n] which remains[§o]
will again make[§p] root[§q] downward,
and make fruit upward,[§r]

32/ For[§s] from Jerusalem[§t] will go forth a remnant,
and a surviving part[§u] from Mount Zion;[§v]
The zeal of Yahweh of Hosts[§w] will do this.[§x]

33/ Therefore thus[§y] says Yahweh concerning the king of Assyria,
He will not[§z] enter[¶a] this[¶b] city,
And he will not shoot an arrow there,[¶c]
And he will not[¶d] advance upon it with a shield,
And he will not pile up siege ramps against it.[¶e]

34/ By the way which he came, by it[¶f] he will return,
And into this[¶g] city he will not enter,[¶h] says[¶i] Yahweh.

35/ And I will give protection over[¶j] this[¶k] city to save it,
for my sake and for the sake of David[¶l] my servant."

36/ And[¶m] the angel of Yahweh went out and smote[¶n] in the camp of Assyria a hundred and eighty-five thousand men,[¶o] and when they arose early in the morning,[¶p] all of these[¶q] were dead[¶r] corpses. 37/ So Sennacherib the king of Assyria departed, went, and returned,[¶s] and dwelt in Nineveh. 38/ And as he[¶t] was worshiping in the house[¶u] of Nisrok his god,[¶v] Adrammelek and Sarezer,[¶w] his sons,[¶x] smote him with the sword, and they fled to the land of Ararat,[¶y] and Esarhaddon[¶z] his son[**a] became king[**b] in his place.

Textual Notes

a MT עַל (ʿal), "concerning"; 1 Kgs 19:9 and 1QIsaᵃ אֶל (ʾel), "with respect to."

b MT and 2 Kgs 19:8 לֵאמֹר (lēʾmōr), "saying"; 1QIsaᵃ לאמור.

c MT and 1QIsaᵃ יָצָא (yāṣāʾ), "he has come out"; 2 Kgs 19:9 הִנֵּה יָצָא (hinnê yāṣāʾ), "behold he has come out."

d MT and 2 Kgs 19:9 אִתָּךְ (ʾittāk), "with you"), a pausal form for masculine singular אִתְּךָ (ʾittĕkā); 1QIsaᵃ אתכה. LXX has αὐτόν, "him."

e MT וַיִּשְׁמַע וַיִּשְׁלַח (wayyišmaʿ wayyišlaḥ), "and he heard and sent"; 2 Kgs 19:9 וַיָּשָׁב וַיִּשְׁלַח (wayyāšob wayyišlaḥ), "and he turned and sent/and he again sent"; 1QIsaᵃ וישמע וישוב וישלח, "and he heard and turned and sent/and he heard and again sent." LXX supports the longer reading of 1QIsaᵃ; Vg. follows MT. The verb וַיִּשְׁמַע (wayyišmaʿ), "and he heard," appears to be an erroneous repetition of the first verb of the verse. Read with 2 Kgs; 1QIsaᵃ and LXX are trying to correct the obvious error without deleting the erroneous repetition.

f MT and 2 Kgs 19:10 כֹּה תֹאמְרוּן אֶל־חִזְקִיָּהוּ (kōh tōʾmĕrûn ʾel-ḥizqîyāhû), "thus you shall say to Hezekiah"; 1QIsaᵃ כוה תומרו אל חזקיה.

g MT and 2 Kgs 19:10 לֵאמֹר (lēʾmōr), "saying"; 1QIsaᵃ לאמור.

h MT and 2 Kgs 19:10 אֱלֹהֶיךָ (ʾĕlōhêkā), "your God"; 1QIsaᵃ אלוהיכה.

i MT and 2 Kgs 19:10 בּוֹ (bô), "in whom"; 1QIsaᵃ בוא.

j MT and 2 Kgs 19:10 יַשִּׁאֲךָ (yaššîʾăkā), "deceive you"; 1QIsaᵃ ישיכה.

k MT and 2 Kgs 19:10 יְרוּשָׁלָ͏ִם (yĕrûšālaim), "Jerusalem"; 1QIsaᵃ ירושלים.

l MT and 2 Kgs 19:10 לֹא (lōʾ), "not"; 1QIsaᵃ לוא.

m MT and 2 Kgs 19:11 שָׁמַעְתָּ (šāmaʿtā), "you have heard"; 1QIsaᵃ שמעתה.

n MT אֲשֶׁר (ʾăšer), "what"; 2 Kgs 19:11 and 1 QIsaᵃ add the direct object marker את אשר.

o MT, 2 Kgs 19:11, 1QIsaᵃ, Vg., Syr., and Tg. all seem to have וְאַתָּה תִּנָּצֵל (wĕʾattâ tinnāṣēl), "and will you be delivered"; LXX omits the clause.

p MT and 2 Kgs 19:12 אֱלֹהֵי הַגּוֹיִם (ʾĕlōhê haggôyīm), "the gods of the nations"; 1QIsaᵃ אלוהי הגואים.

q MT and 1QIsaᵃ have the *hiphil* הִשְׁחִיתוּ (hišḥîtû), "they destroyed"; 2 Kgs 19:12 has the *piel* שִׁחֲתוּ (šiḥătû), "they destroyed."

r MT and 1QIsaᵃ בִּתְלַשָּׂר (bitlaśśār), "in Telassar"; 2 Kgs 19:12 בְּתלאשׂר (bitlaʾśśār), "in Til-assar"; LXX misread *resh* as a *dalet* to produce the place name θελσαδ, "Thelsad," but there are many other variants of this name in the Greek textual tradition.

s MT and 1QIsaᵃ אַיֵּה (ʾayyēh), "where"; 2 Kgs 19:13 אַיּוֹ (ʾayyô), "where."

t MT and 2 Kgs 19:13 סְפַרְוַיִם הֵנַע וְעִוָּה (sĕparwayim hēnaʿ wĕʿiwwâ), "Sepharvaim, Hena, and Ivvah"; 1QIsaᵃ וספריים נע ועוה ושומרון, "Sepharayim, and Na, and Ivvah, and Samaria." Sepharayim looks like a simple corruption of ספרוים by misreading the waw as a yodh, and נע looks like a simple corruption of הנע. The versions give no support to the Qumran reading.

u MT and 2 Kgs 19:14 חִזְקִיָהוּ (ḥizqîyāhû), "Hezekiah"; 1QIsaᵃ חזקיה; for the second occurrence of the name in the verse, 1QIsaᵃ originally omitted it, and then inserted it above the line.

v All the Hebrew texts have the plural הַסְּפָרִים (hassĕpārîm), "the letters, scrolls," but the LXX of Isa 37:14 renders the word as a singular, "the book, scroll, letter."

w MT וַיִּקְרָאֵהוּ (wayyiqrāʾēhû), "and read it"; 2 Kgs 19:14 and 1QIsaᵃ have וַיִּקְרָאֵם (wayyiqrāʾēm), "and read them," to make the suffix agree with the plural antecedent. LXX has the singular but radically abbreviates the end of the verse: καὶ ἤνοιξεν αὐτὸ ἐναντίον κυρίου, "and he opened it before the Lord." Tg. tries to solve the lack of agreement in number between the singular suffix and its plural antecedent by the rendering, "and he read one of them." Perhaps the confusing final mem on hassĕpārîm, "the letters, scrolls," was originally the enclitic mem, not the plural marker, and its misreading and, then, misspelling as the plural marker—hsprm > hsprym—is responsible for the textual uncertainty.

x MT and 2 Kgs 19:14 וַיַּעַל (wayyaʿal), "and he went up"; 1QIsaᵃ ויעלה.

y MT and 2 Kgs 19:14 וַיִּפְרְשֵׂהוּ (wayyipreśēhû), "and spread it"; 1QIsaᵃ ויפרושה. Vg. and Syr. have "he spread them."

z See note u above.

*a MT אֶל־יְהוָה (ʾel-YHWH), "to Yahweh," 1QIsaᵃ, LXX and Vg. similar; 2 Kgs 19:15 לִפְנֵי יְהוָה (lipnê YHWH), "before Yahweh."

*b MT לֵאמֹר (lēʾmōr), "saying"; 1QIsaᵃ לאמור; but 2 Kgs 19:15 וַיֹּאמֶר (wayyōʾmar), "and he said." Apart from Syr., the versions follow MT.

*c MT יְהוָה צְבָאוֹת אֱלֹהֵי יִשְׂרָאֵל (YHWH sĕbāʾôt ʾĕlōhê yiśrāʾēl), "Yahweh of Hosts, God of Israel"; 1QIsaᵃ יהוה צבאות אלוהי ישראל; but 2 Kgs 19:15 omits צְבָאוֹת (sĕbāʾôt), "of Hosts."

*d MT and 2 Kgs 19:15 יֹשֵׁב הַכְּרֻבִים (yōšēb hakkĕrūbîm), "who sits enthroned upon the cherubim"; 1QIsaᵃ יושב הכרובים.

*e MT and 2 Kgs 19:15 אַתָּה־הוּא הָאֱלֹהִים לְבַדְּךָ (ʾattâ-hûʾ hāʾĕlōhîm lĕbaddĕkā), "you alone are God"; 1QIsaᵃ אתה הואה האלוהים לבדכה.

*f MT and 2 Kgs 19:15 לְכֹל (lĕkōl), "to all"; 1QIsaᵃ לכול.

*g MT and 2 Kgs 19:15 עָשִׂיתָ (ʿāśîtā), "you made"; 1QIsaᵃ עשיתה.

*h MT and 2 Kgs 19:16 הַטֵּה (haṭṭēh), "incline"; 1QIsaᵃ הטא.

*i MT and 2 Kgs 19:16 אָזְנְךָ (ʾoznĕkā), "your ear"; 1QIsaᵃ אוזנכה.

*j MT וּשְׁמָע (ûšĕmāʿ), "and hear," a pausal form; 2 Kgs 19:16 וּשֲׁמָע (ûšāmāʿ), "and hear," also a pausal form; 1QIsaᵃ ושמעה.

*k MT עֵינֶךָ (ʿênekā), "your eye," 2 Kgs 19:16 עֵינֶיךָ (ʿênekā), "your eyes"; 1QIsaᵃ עיניכה.

*l MT אֵת כָּל־דִּבְרֵי (ʾēt kol-dibrê), "all the words of"; 1QIsaᵃ את כול דברי; but 2 Kgs 19:16 has only אֵת דִּבְרֵי (ʾēt dibrê), "the words of." Vg. and Tg. support MT, while Syr. has the shorter reading. LXX abbreviates the whole verse: εἰσάκουσον, κύριε, εἴσβλεψον, κύριε, καὶ ἰδὲ τοὺς λόγους, οὓς ἀπέστειλεν Σενναχηριμ

ὀνειδίζειν θεὸν ζῶντα, "Hear, O Lord, Look, O Lord, and see the words which Sennacherib sent to reproach the living God."

*m MT and 1QIsaᵃ שָׁלַח (šālaḥ), "he sent"; 2 Kgs 19:16 שְׁלָחוֹ (šĕlāḥô), "he sent it"—this reading appears to be secondary, since the suffix does not agree with its plural antecedent.

*n MT and 2 Kgs 19:16 חָי אֱלֹהִים (ʾĕlōhîm ḥāy), "the living God"; 1QIsaᵃ אלוהים חי.

*o MT אֶת־כָּל־הָאֲרָצוֹת (ʾet-kol-hāʾărāṣôt), "all the countries"; 1QIsaᵃ את כול הארצות; but 2 Kgs 19:17 אֶת־הַגּוֹיִם (ʾet-haggôyīm), "the nations."

*p MT and 2 Kgs 19:17 וְאֶת־אַרְצָם (wĕ-ʾet-ʾarṣām), "and their land"; 1QIsaᵃ omits this phrase, but the versions support it.

*q MT has the infinite absolute וְנָתֹן (wĕnātōn), "and they put"; 1QIsaᵃ ויתנו, "and they put" (converted imperfect); 2 Kgs 19:18 וְנָתְנוּ (wĕnātĕnû), "and they put" (simple perfect). MT is more original.

*r MT and 2 Kgs 19:18 אֶת־אֱלֹהֵיהֶם (ʾet-ʾĕlōhêhem), "their gods"; 1QIsaᵃ את אלוהיהמה.

*s MT and 2 Kgs 19:18 כִּי (kî), "because, but"; 1QIsaᵃ כיא.

*t MT and 2 Kgs 19:18 לֹא אֱלֹהִים (lōʾ ʾĕlōhîm), "they were not gods"; 1QIsaᵃ לוא אלוהים.

*u MT and 2 Kgs 19:18 מַעֲשֵׂה (maʿăśēh), "the work of"; 1QIsaᵃ מעשי.

*v MT and 2 Kgs 19:19 אֱלֹהֵינוּ (ʾĕlōhênû), "our God"; 1QIsaᵃ אלוהינו.

*w MT הוֹשִׁיעֵנוּ (hôšîʿēnû), "save us"; 2 Kgs 19:19 adds the particle נָא (nāʾ), "please"; 1QIsaᵃ אושיענו, the aphel imperative.

*x LXX has "their" hand.

*y MT and 2 Kgs 19:19 כָּל (kol), "all"; 1QIsaᵃ כול.

*z See note *s above.

†a MT לְבַדֶּךָ (lĕbaddĕkā), "you alone," is elliptical; the ellipsis is supplied in 2 Kgs 19:19 אֱלֹהִים לְבַדֶּךָ (ʾĕlōhîm lĕbaddĕkā), "you alone are God," and 1QIsaᵃ אלוהים לבדכה.

†b MT and 2 Kgs 19:20 יְשַׁעְיָהוּ (yĕšaʿyāhû), "Isaiah"; 1QIsaᵃ ישעיה.

†c MT and 2 Kgs 19:20 אֶל־חִזְקִיָּהוּ (ʾel-ḥizqîyāhû), "to Hezekiah"; 1QIsaᵃ על יהוקיה.

†d MT and 2 Kgs 19:20 לֵאמֹר (lēʾmōr), "saying"; 1QIsaᵃ לאמור.

†e MT and 2 Kgs 19:20 כֹּה (kōh), "thus"; 1QIsaᵃ כוה.

†f MT and 2 Kgs 19:20 אֱלֹהֵי (ʾĕlōhê), "God of"; 1QIsaᵃ אלוהי.

†g MT and 2 Kgs 19:20 אֲשֶׁר הִתְפַּלַּלְתָּ אֵלַי (ʾăšer hitpallaltā ʾēlay), "what you have prayed to me"; 1QIsaᵃ אשר התפללתה אליו, "which you prayed to him." The change to the third person was necessitated by the loss of the final verb.

†h Reading with 2 Kgs 19:20, LXX, and Syr. שָׁמָעְתִּי (šāmāʿtî), "I have heard." MT and 1QIsaᵃ are lacking this word, but this loss has produced an awkward reading in MT that led to a correction (see note †g) in 1QIsaᵃ: "Thus says Yahweh the God of Israel, 'What you prayed to me concerning Sennacherib the king of Assyria [I have heard]'" (MT) > "Thus says Yahweh the God of Israel to whom you prayed concerning Sennacherib the king of Assyria" (1QIsaᵃ).

†i MT and 2 Kgs 19:21 לְךָ (lĕkā), "to you, for you"; 1QIsaᵃ לכה.

†j MT and 2 Kgs 19:21 יְרוּשָׁלִָם (yĕrûšālāim), "Jerusalem"; 1QIsaᵃ ירושלים.

†k MT and 2 Kgs 19:21 רֹאשׁ (rōʾš), "head"; 1QIsaᵃ ראושה, "her head."

†l MT and 2 Kgs 19:21 אַחֲרֶיךָ (ʾaḥărêkā), "behind you"; 1QIsaᵃ אחריכה.

†m MT and 2 Kgs 19:22 מִי (mî), "whom"; 1QIsaᵃ מיא.

†n MT and 2 Kgs 19:22 חֵרַפְתָּ (ḥēraptā), "you reproached"; 1QIsaᵃ חרפתה.

†o MT and 2 Kgs 19:22 וְגִדַּפְתָּ (wĕgiddaptā), "and you reviled"; 1QIsaᵃ וגדפתה.

†p MT and 2 Kgs 19:22 עֵינֶיךָ (ʿênêkā), "your eyes"; 1QIsaᵃ עיניכה.

†q MT בְּיַד עֲבָדֶיךָ (bĕyad ʿăbādêkā), "by the hand of your servants"; 1QIsaᵃ ביד עבדיכה; but 2 Kgs 19:23 בְּיַד מַלְאָכֶיךָ (bĕyad malʾākêkā), "by the hand of your messengers"; Vg. and Tg. follow MT, while Syr. follows the reading of 2 Kgs 19:23, and LXX simplifies it to δι᾽ ἀγγέλων, "through messengers."

†r MT and 2 Kgs 19:23 חֵרַפְתָּ אֲדֹנָי (ḥēraptā ʾădōnāy), "you have reproached my Lord"; 1QIsaᵃ חרפתה אדונ.

†s MT and 2 Kgs 19:23 וַתֹּאמֶר (wattōʾmer), "and you said"; 1QIsaᵃ ותומר.

†t MT and 2 Kgs 19:23 בְּרֹב רִכְבִּי (bĕrōb rikbî), "by the multitude of my chariotry"; 1QIsaᵃ ברוב רכבי; the kĕtîb in 2 Kgs 19:23 בְּרֶכֶב רִכְבִּי (bĕrekeb rikbî), "by the chariotry of my chariotry," is clearly corrupt; the qĕrēʾ agrees with the text of Isaiah.

†u MT and 2 Kgs 19:23 וְאֶכְרֹת (wĕʾekrōt), "that I might cut down"; 1QIsaᵃ ואכרותה. Cogan and Tadmor (II Kings, 237) want to repoint this and the following imperfects with waw-consecutives to make all the action in the simple past tense, but the present pointing suggests a modal sense.

†v MT מִבְחַר בְּרֹשָׁיו (mibḥar bĕrōšāyw), "the choicest of his cypresses"; 2 Kgs 19:23 מִבְחוֹר בְּרֹשָׁיו (mibḥôr bĕrōšāyw); 1QIsaᵃ מבחר ברושיו.

†w MT and 1QIsaᵃ וְאָבוֹא (wĕʾābôʾ), "that I might enter"; 2 Kgs 19:23 וְאָבוֹאָה (wĕʾābôʾāh), "that I might enter."

†x MT and 1QIsaᵃ מְרוֹם קִצּוֹ (mĕrôm qiṣṣô), "his most distant height"; 2 Kgs 19:23 מְלוֹן קִצֹּה (mĕlôn qiṣṣōh), "his most distant lodging."

†y MT and 2 Kgs 19:23 יַעַר כַּרְמִלּוֹ (yaʿar karmillô), "the forest of his plantation"; 1QIsaᵃ יער כרמליו, "the forest of his plantations."

†z MT and 2 Kgs 19:24 קַרְתִּי (qartî), "I dug"; 1QIsaᵃ קראתי. All the versions in Isaiah 37 take the verb in the sense of "digging" a well. The LXX of 2 Kgs 19:24 has ἔψυξα, "I cooled myself," apparently deriving the Hebrew verb from קרר, "to cool," rather than קור, "to dig," but even there the LXX lacks the support of the other versions.

‡a LXX appears to omit וְשָׁתִיתִי (wĕšātîtî), "and I drank," and construes "waters" with the following verb: καὶ ἠρήμωσα ὕδατα, "and I made the waters desolate."

‡b MT מָיִם (māyim), "water"; 2 Kgs 19:24 and 1QIsaᵃ מַיִם זָרִים (mayim zārîm), "foreign waters."

‡c MT and 2 Kgs 19:24 וְאַחְרִב (wĕʾaḥrib), "that I might dry up"; 1QIsaᵃ ואחריבה.

‡d MT, 2 Kgs 19:24, 1QIsaᵃ בְּכַף־פְּעָמַי (bĕkap-pĕʿāmay), "with the sole of my feet"; LXX omits.

‡e MT and 2 Kgs 19:24 כֹּל (kōl), "all"; 1QIsaᵃ כול.

‡f MT, 2 Kgs 19:24, 1QIsaᵃ יְאֹרֵי מָצוֹר (yĕʾōrê māṣôr), "the rivers of Egypt." The versions did not understand māṣôr as Egypt. LXX has συναγωγὴν ὕδατος, "a gathering of water" in Isaiah and

ποταμοὺς περιοχῆς, "streams of enclosure" in 2 Kgs 19:24. Vg. has "rivers of the rampart"; Syr. has "strong rivers"; and Tg. has "deep rivers."

‡g MT הֲלוֹא־שָׁמַעְתָּ (hălôʾ-šāmaʿtā), "have you not heard"; 2 Kgs 19:25 הֲלֹא־שָׁמַעְתָּ; and 1QIsaᵃ הלוא שמעתה.

‡h MT and 1QIsaᵃ אֹתָהּ (ʾōtāh), "it"; 2 Kgs 19:25 אֹתָהּ. The third person feminine singular verbal object is presumably because the understood object is God's plan, עֵצָה (ʿēṣâ), a feminine singular noun.

‡i MT and 2 Kgs 19:25 מִימֵי (mîmê), "from days of"; 2 Kgs 19:25 לְמִימֵי (lĕmîmê), "from days of."

‡j MT and 2 Kgs 19:25 וִיצַרְתִּיהָ (wîṣartîhā), "and I fashioned it"; 1QIsaᵃ omits the conjunction יצרתיה. LXX and Vg. also appear to omit it, and this appears to be the better reading, though, if the waw is original, it may be emphatic: "indeed I fashioned it." The LXX of 2 Kgs 19:25 omits everything in the verse before this verb.

‡k MT הֲבֵאתִיהָ (hăbēʾtîhā), "I brought it"; 2 Kgs 19:25 הֲבֵאתִיהָ (hăbēʾtîhā); 1QIsaᵃ הביאותיה.

‡l MT and 2 Kgs 19:25 וּתְהִי (ûtĕhî), suggests a modal translation; one could repoint to וַתְּהִי (wattĕhî), "and it happened," to get a simple past tense, so Vg.

‡m MT לְהַשְׁאוֹת (lĕhašʾôt), "to lay waste"; 1QIsaᵃ לשאות; and 2 Kgs 19:25 לַהְשׁוֹת (lahšôt), "to lay waste," with elision of the aleph. The LXX of 2 Kgs 19:25 with its rendering εἰς ἐπάρσεις, "to a rising of," apparently understood the form as the hiphil infinitive of נשא, "to raise."

‡n MT and 2 Kgs 19:25 עָרִים בְּצֻרוֹת (ʿārîm bĕṣūrôt), "fortified cities"; 1QIsaᵃ ערים בצורות. LXX's καὶ ἐνοικοῦντας ἐν πόλεσιν ὀχυραῖς, "and who dwell in fortified cities," appears to take the initial participle of v. 27 with this verse.

‡o MT and 2 Kgs 19:25 גַּלִּים נִצִּים (gallîm niṣṣîm), "desolate heaps"; 1QIsaᵃ גלים נצורים, "guarded heaps." LXX's ἔθνη ἐν ὀχυροῖς, "nations in fortifications," appears to be reading גוים נצורים. The LXX of 2 Kgs 19:25 ἀποικεσιῶν μαχίμων, "of warlike colonies," is deriving niṣṣîm from נצה I, "to fight," and apparently taking גלים as gōlîm, "immigrants, exiles." Neither LXX reading is compelling.

‡p MT and 2 Kgs 19:26 וְיֹשְׁבֵיהֶן (wĕyōšĕbêhen), "and their inhabitants"; 1QIsaᵃ ויושביהנה.

‡q MT, 2 Kgs 19:26, 1QIsaᵃ קִצְרֵי־יָד (qiṣrê-yād), "short of hand, powerless"; LXX has ἀνῆκα τὰς χεῖρας, "I weakened the hands," but this reading is not supported in the other versions.

‡r MT וָבֹשׁוּ (wābōšû), "and they are ashamed"; 2 Kgs 19:26 וַיֵּבֹשׁוּ (wayyēbōšû), "and they became ashamed"; 1QIsaᵃ וישבשו (The initial ש is marked with dots above and below it to indicate it is an error, so with the correction, the Qumran text agrees with 2 Kings against the MT of Isa 37:27.)

‡s MT and 2 Kgs 19:26 וִירַק דֶּשֶׁא (wîraq dešeʾ), "and green grass"; 1QIsaᵃ ירק דשה.

‡t Neither MT וּשְׁדֵמָה (ûšĕdēmâ), "and a field, terrace," nor 2 Kgs 19:26 וּשְׁדֵפָה (ûšĕdēpâ), "and a scorching," can be correct. One expects an adjectival form modifying the preceding masculine noun חָצִיר (ḥāṣîr), "grass." 1QIsaᵃ provides that with חציר גגות הנשדף, "the grass of the rooftops which is blighted," though

the article on the *niphal* participle may be secondary. Read נִשְׁדָּף (*nišdāp*), "blighted." LXX, as it often does, paraphrases and shortens the text: καὶ ἐξηράνθησαν καὶ ἐγένοντο ὡς χόρτος ξηρὸς ἐπὶ δωμάτων καὶ ὡς ἄγρωστις, "and they have withered, and they have become like dry grass upon the housetops and like wild grass." Vg. supports the emendation.

‡u Reading with 1QIsaᵃ קָדִ֜ם (*qādîm*), "the east wind." MT and 2 Kgs 19:26 קָמָה (*qāmâ*), "standing grain," would give a strained though possible metaphor, "grass of the rooftops, blighted before the standing grain." NRSV's rendering of the form as a verb, "blighted before it is grown," though anticipated by Vg., is dubious, because the form is feminine, and the antecedent *ḥāṣîr*, "grass," is masculine.

‡v 1QIsaᵃ has קומכה (*qûmekâ*), "your rising up"; MT, 2 Kgs 19:27, and the versions lack this word, but it should be restored, probably written קמך. The resemblance between this form and the preceding קדים led to the haplography of קדים and the corruption of קמך to קמה that lies behind the present MT.

‡w MT וְשִׁבְתְּךָ וְצֵאתְךָ וּבֹאֲךָ (*wešibtēkā wešēʾtēkā ûbôʾākā*), "and your sitting down, and your going out and your going in"; 2 Kgs 19:27 וְשִׁבְתְּךָ וְצֵאתְךָ וּבֹאֲךָ (*wešibtēkā wešēʾtēkā ûbôʾākā*); 1QIsaᵃ ושבתכה וצאתכה ובואכה.

‡x MT and 2 Kgs 19:27 יָדָעְתִּי (*yādaʿtî*), "I know"; 1QIsaᵃ ידעתיא.

‡y MT and 2 Kgs 19:27 וְאֵת הִתְרַגֶּזְךָ אֵלָי (*weʾēt hitraggezkā ʾēlāy*), "and your raging against me"; 1QIsaᵃ has the *hiphil* infinitive ואת הרגזכה אלי. The repetition of this phrase in the following verse has led some to regard it as a dittography here (so Wildberger, 3:1419).

‡z MT and 2 Kgs 19:28 יַעַן הִתְרַגֶּזְךָ אֵלָי (*yaʿan hitraggezkā ʾēlāy*), "because your raging against me"; 1QIsaᵃ omits the phrase, but the versions appear to have it: ὁ δὲ θυμός σου, ὃν ἐθυμώθης, "And your wrath with which you have raged" (LXX); *cum furores adversum me* (Vg.), "because you have raged against me"; *ʿl dʾmrḥt qdmy*, "because you have been rash against me" (Syr.).

§a MT and 2 Kgs 19:28 וְשַׁאֲנַנְךָ (*wešaʾănankā*), "and your self-confidence, arrogance"; 1QIsaᵃ ושאננכה. LXX and Vg. could be understood as supporting this reading, but the parallelism has led many scholars to correct the text to וּשְׁאוֹנֶךָ (*ûšeʾônēkā*), "and your tumult").[1]

§b MT and 2 Kgs 19:28 בְּאָזְנָי (*beʾoznāy*), "into my ears"; 1QIsaᵃ באזני.

§c MT and 2 Kgs 19:28 בְּאַפֶּךָ (*beʾappekā*), "in your nose"; 1QIsaᵃ באפכה.

§d MT and 2 Kgs 19:28 בִּשְׂפָתֶיךָ (*bišpātêkā*), "in your lips"; 1QIsaᵃ בשפאותיכה.

§e MT וַהֲשִׁבֹתִיךָ (*wahăšibōtîkā*), "and I will turn you back"; 2 Kgs 19:28 וַהֲשִׁבֹתִיךָ (*wahăšibōtîkā*); 1QIsaᵃ והשיבותיכה.

§f MT and 2 Kgs 19:28 אֲשֶׁר־בָּאתָ בָּהּ (*ʾăšer-bāʾtā bāh*), "by which you came"; 1QIsaᵃ אשר בתה בה.

§g MT and 2 Kgs 19:29 לְךָ (*llēkā*), "for you"; 1QIsaᵃ לכה.

§h MT, 2 Kgs 19:29, and 4QIsaᵇ (אכל) have the infinitive absolute אָכוֹל (*ʾākôl*), "eat"; 1QIsaᵃ has the plural imperative אכולו.

§i MT שָׁחִיס (*šāḥîs*), "self-seeded growth"; 2 Kgs 19:29 סָחִיש (*sāḥîš*); 1QIsaᵃ שעיס. These are all phonetic variants of the same word, whose meaning is clear from context, but the correct etymology remains uncertain.

§j MT and 2 Kgs 19:29 וְקִצְרוּ (*weqiṣrû*), "and harvest"; 1QIsaᵃ וקצורו.

§k MT and 2 Kgs 19:29 וְנִטְעוּ (*weniṭʿû*), "and plant"; 1QIsaᵃ ונטוע.

§l The *kětîb* of MT and apparently 4QIsaᵇ וְאָכוֹל (*weʾākôl*), "and eat"; the *qěrē* of MT and 2 Kgs 19:29 וְאִכְלוּ (*weʾiklû*), "and eat"; 1QIsaᵃ ואכולו.

§m 4QIsaᵇ lacks פִּרְיָם (*piryām*), "their fruit," but MT, 2 Kgs 19:29, 1QIsaᵃ, and the versions all have it.

§n MT and 2 Kgs 19:30 פְּלֵיטַת בֵּית־יְהוּדָה (*pēlêṭat bêt-yěhûdâ*), "the surviving part of the house of Judah"; 1QIsaᵃ originally omitted this expression and then inserted it above the line.

§o MT and 2 Kgs 19:30 הַנִּשְׁאָרָה (*hanniš²ārâ*), "which remains"; 1QIsaᵃ's masculine singular participle והנמצא, "and which is found," is a mistake introduced by the omission of the preceding phrase.

§p MT, 2 Kgs 19:30, and probably the fragmentary 4QIsaᵇ וְיָסְפָה (*weyāsěpâ*), "and it will again make"; 1QIsaᵃ ואספה, "and it gathered." The versions support MT.

§q MT and 2 Kgs 19:30 שֹׁרֶשׁ (*šōreš*), "root"; 1QIsaᵃ שורש.

§r MT, 2 Kgs 19:30, 4QIsaᵇ לְמָעְלָה (*lěmā²ělâ*), "upward"; 1QIsaᵃ מעלה.

§s MT, 2 Kgs 19:31, 4QIsaᵇ כִּי (*kî*), "for"; 1QIsaᵃ כיא.

§t MT, 2 Kgs 19:31, 4QIsaᵇ מִירוּשָׁלַם (*mîrûšālaim*), "from Jerusalem," supported by versions; 1QIsaᵃ מציון, "from Zion."

§u MT and 2 Kgs 19:31 וּפְלֵיטָה (*ûpělêṭâ*), "and a surviving part"; 1QIsaᵃ ופליטא.

§v MT and 2 Kgs 19:31 מֵהַר צִיּוֹן (*mēhar ṣîyôn*), "from Mount Zion," supported by versions; 1QIsaᵃ מירושלים, "from Jerusalem."

§w Some manuscripts of 2 Kgs 19:31 are lacking צְבָאוֹת (*sěbā²ôt*), "of Hosts."

§x MT, 2 Kgs 19:31, 4QIsaᵇ זֹאת (*zō²t*), "this"; 1QIsaᵃ זואת.

§y MT and 2 Kgs 19:32 כֹּה (*kōh*), "thus"; 1QIsaᵃ כוה.

§z MT and 2 Kgs 19:32 לֹא (*lō²*), "not"; 1QIsaᵃ לוא.

¶a MT and 1QIsaᵃ יָבוֹא (*yābô²*), "he will enter"; 2 Kgs 19:32 יָבֹא (*yābō²*).

¶b MT and 2 Kgs 19:32 הַזֹּאת (*hazzō²t*), "this"; 1QIsaᵃ הזאות.

¶c MT and 2 Kgs 19:32 וְלֹא־יוֹרֶה שָׁם חֵץ (*wělō²-yôrê šām ḥēṣ*), "and he will not shoot an arrow there," followed by the versions; 1QIsaᵃ inserts the last line of the verse here, given as ולוא ישפוך עליהא סוללה, and then has this line as ולוא ירא שם חץ.

¶d MT and 2 Kgs 19:32 וְלֹא (*wělō²*), "and not"; 1QIsaᵃ ולוא.

¶e MT and 2 Kgs 19:32 וְלֹא־יִשְׁפֹּךְ עָלֶיהָ סֹלְלָה (*wělō²-yišpōk ʿālehā sōlělâ*), "and he will not pile up siege ramps against it"; for 1QIsaᵃ, see note ¶c above.

---

1 So Wildberger, 3:1419, *BHK*, and *BHS*, among others. Moreover, note the same root, שאה, in v. 26.

¶f   MT and 2 Kgs 19:33 בָּהּ (*bāh*), "by it, in it"; 1QIsaᵃ באה.

¶g   MT and 2 Kgs 19:33 הַזֹּאת (*hazzōʾt*), "this"; 1QIsaᵃ הזואת.

¶h   MT לֹא יָבוֹא (*lōʾ yābôʾ*), "he will not enter"; 2 Kgs 19:33 לֹא יָבֹא (*lōʾ yābōʾ*); 1QIsaᵃ לוא יבוא.

¶i   MT and 2 Kgs 19:33 נְאֻם (*nĕʾūm*), "says"; 1QIsaᵃ נואם.

¶j   MT and 1QIsaᵃ עַל (*ʿal*), "over"; 2 Kgs 19:34 אֶל (*ʾel*), "to."

¶k   MT and 2 Kgs 19:34 הַזֹּאת (*hazzōʾt*), "this"; 1QIsaᵃ הזואת.

¶l   MT and 2 Kgs 19:34 דָּוִד (*dāwīd*), "David"; 1QIsaᵃ דויד.

¶m   At the beginning of the verse, 2 Kgs 19:35 has the additional clause וַיְהִי בַּלַּיְלָה הַהוּא (*wayhî ballaylâ hahûʾ*), "and it came to pass in that night."

¶n   MT וַיַּכֶּה (*wayyakkê*), "and smote"; 2 Kgs 19:35 and 1QIsaᵃ וַיַּךְ (*wayyak*), "and smote."

¶o   MT מֵאָה וּשְׁמֹנִים וַחֲמִשָּׁא אָלֶף (*mēʾâ ûšĕmōnîm waḥămiššâ ʾālep*), "a hundred and eighty and five thousand"; 2 Kgs 19:35 מֵאָה שְׁמוֹנִים וַחֲמִשָּׁה אָלֶף (*mēʾâ šĕmônîm waḥămiššâ ʾālep*), "a hundred eighty and five thousand"; 1QIsaᵃ מאה ושמונים וחמשא אלף.

¶p   MT and 2 Kgs 19:35 בַּבֹּקֶר (*babbōqer*), "in the morning"; 1QIsaᵃ בבוקר.

¶q   MT and 2 Kgs 19:35 כֻּלָּם (*kullām*), "all of them"; 1QIsaᵃ כולם.

¶r   MT and 2 Kgs 19:35 מֵתִים (*mētîm*), "dead"; 1QIsaᵃ מיתים.

¶s   MT and 2 Kgs 19:36 וַיָּשָׁב (*wayyāšob*), "and he returned"; 1QIsaᵃ וישׁוב (the correction above the line appears to be erased). LXX translates the opening clause with only two verbs: καὶ ἀποστραφεὶς ἀπῆλθεν βασιλεὺς Ἀσσυρίων, "and the king of Assyria having turned, went away"; but, apart from the absence of the proper name, this is stylistic and does not indicate a different text.

¶t   MT and 2 Kgs 19:37 הוּא (*hûʾ*), "he"; 1QIsaᵃ הואה.

¶u   MT and 2 Kgs 19:37 בֵּית (*bêt*), "in the house of," locative accusative; 1QIsaᵃ בבית.

¶v   MT and 2 Kgs 19:37 אֱלֹהָיו (*ʾĕlōhāyw*), "his god"); 1QIsaᵃ אלוהיו.

¶w   MT and 2 Kgs 19:37 וְשַׂרְאֶצֶר (*wĕśarʾeṣer*), "and Sarezer"; 1QIsaᵃ ושראוצר.

¶x   Some manuscripts of 2 Kgs 19:37 are lacking בָּנָיו (*bānāyw*), "his sons."

¶y   MT and 2 Kgs 19:37 אֲרָרָט (*ʾărārāṭ*), "Ararat"; 1QIsaᵃ הורדט.

¶z   MT and 2 Kgs 19:37 אֵסַר־חַדֹּן (*ʾēsar-ḥaddōn*), "Esarhaddon"; 1QIsaᵃ אסרחודן.

**a   MT and 2 Kgs 19:37 בְּנוֹ (*bĕnô*), "his son"; 1QIsaᵃ בניו, "his sons."

**b   MT and 2 Kgs 19:37 וַיִּמְלֹךְ (*wayyimlōk*), "and he became king"; 1QIsaᵃ וימלוך.

Commentary

In the present literary composition, v. 9 continues the preceding narrative, but the repetition of the verb שמע, "to hear," in vv. 8-9, without an explicit subject creates a confusing ambiguity. In v. 8 he (the Rabshakeh) heard that he (the king of Assyria) had departed from Lachish. In v. 9 he (the king of Assyria) heard concerning Tirhaqa, the king of Nubia, "He has come out to fight with you. And he [the king of Assyria] again sent messengers to Hezekiah, saying . . . ." The reference to Tirhaqa as the king of Nubia appears to be an anachronism, since the standard Egyptian chronologies, including the revised chronology of D. Kahn,[2] date Tirhaqa's accession to 690 BCE. He may have been old enough, however, to have been sent by Shebitku, the Nubian king in 701 BCE, as the commander of the Nubian/Egyptian relief force. Many modern English translations render כּוּשׁ (*kûš*) as Ethiopia (so RSV and NRSV), but modern Ethiopia is too far east to correspond to biblical *kûš*. The term refers to the area of the Nile valley between Aswan and Khartoum, the area of southern Egypt and northern Sudan that used to go by the name Nubia. In its present context, it appears that Sennacherib is again sending messengers to Hezekiah because of the fear that the appearance of Tirhaqa with his relief force may embolden Hezekiah to continue his revolt.

Yet, curiously enough, the Assyrian king's message makes no mention of the Nubian/Egyptian relief force. Instead he warns Hezekiah, "Do not let your god in whom you trust deceive you," and then the Assyrian king quotes a possible oracle of Hezekiah's god, "Jerusalem will not be given into the hand of the king of Assyria" (v. 10). He then reminds Hezekiah that Hezekiah had heard what the kings of Assyria had done to all the lands, destroying them utterly, so, "Why," he asks, "do you think you will be saved?" (v. 11). As an example of all these nations, which his ancestors had destroyed and whose gods were not able to save them, he first mentions Gozan, Harran, Rezeph, and the Edenites who were in Telassar (v. 12). Gozan (Akk. *Guzāna*, modern *Tell Halaf*), on the upper Habor, was conquered by Aššurnasirpal II (883–859 BCE), but Adad-nirari III had to campaign against it again in 808 BCE, and it again revolted and

2   D. Kahn, "The Inscription of Sargon II at Tang-I Var and the Chronology of Dynasty 25," *Or* n.s. 70 (2001) 1–18; cf. A. F. Rainey and R. S. Notley, *The Sacred Bridge: Carta's Atlas of the Biblical World* (Jerusalem: Carta, 2006) 233.

was attacked by Aššur-dan III in 759–758. Haran (Akk. *Ḥarrānu*), located on the Balikh 100 km north of its confluence with the Euphrates, 80 km west of Gozan and 80 km east of Carchemish, was also conquered during the ninth century, but its fortunes also reflected the fluctuations in Assyrian power in the late ninth and early eighth centuries. Rezeph (Akk. *Raṣappa*) is probably to be identified with modern *Ruṣafa* or *Reṣafa*, north of Palmyra, 20 km or so south of the Euphrates. Tukulti-Ninurta II (890–884 BCE) took tribute from it, but it revolted in the reign of Aššurnasirpal II, and he had to campaign against it twice to subdue successive rebellions, but then it appears to have remained in Assyrian hands. The governor of Rezeph, Nergal-erish, was the Assyrian eponym official in 803 (under Adad-nirari III) and 775 (under Shalmaneser IV [782–773 BCE]), and Sin-shallimanni, appointed sometime after 775, was its Assyrian governor in 747. The בְּנֵי־עֶדֶן (*bĕnê-ʿeden*), "the sons of Eden, Edenites," refers to the kingdom referred to in the Assyrian sources as *Bīt-Adini* (see בֵּית עֶדֶן, *bêt ʿeden*, Amos 1:5), which controlled the area on both sides of the Euphrates as far east as the valley of the Balikh. Both Aššurnasirpal II and Shalmaneser III campaigned against it repeatedly before Shalmaneser III finally destroyed it (856 BCE). The capital of Bīt-Adini was Til-Barsip, modern Tell Aḥmar, on the Euphrates about 20 km south of Carchemish, which Shalmaneser III renamed Kar-Shalmaneser, "Harbor of Shalmaneser." Telassar is probably a garbled form of Til-Aššur, "the tell of (the god) Aššur," a play on Til-Barsip, which was now an Assyrian city with a new Assyrian name.

In v. 13 the Assyrian king then asks Hezekiah where the former kings of Hamath, Arpad, Lair, Sepharvaim, Hena, and Ivvah are now. Tiglath-pileser III took much of the former territory of Hamath when he captured Kullani (biblical Calneh [Amos 6:2] or Calno [Isa 10:9]) in 738 BCE, and Sargon II reconquered Hamath when it rebelled in 720. Arpad fell to Tiglath-pileser III in 740 BCE after a three-year siege. Lair (לָעִיר, *lāʿîr*, often erroneously read as "to the city of") is to be identified with the Assyrian place-name *Laḫīru*, but there are two of these, one in

northwest Babylonia north of *Zabban* on the headwaters of the Turna River, and one on the Tubliash River near the border with Elam.[3] Different scholars have identified biblical Lair with one site or the other, but there is little basis for a clear decision. The identifications of Sepharvaim and Ivvah are still disputed, but Hena is probably Anat on the middle Euphrates. The independent kings of all these areas had been replaced by Assyrian officials after their conquest by Sennacherib's predecessors, so the disappearance of these kings is a warning to Hezekiah that his continued rebellion against Sennacherib can only end badly. Just as the gods of these kings could not save them, so Hezekiah's god cannot save him.

Apparently the messengers sent this time did not attempt to negotiate with Hezekiah but simply delivered the letter from Sennacherib to him (v. 14). The pronominal suffixes on the following verbs suggest there was only one letter, so the plural ending on הַסְּפָרִים (*hassĕpārîm*), "the letters," is either a scribal error or a misunderstood enclitic *mem* (see the textual notes). Hezekiah read the letter, went up to the temple, and spread the letter before Yahweh. The imagery suggests Hezekiah spread the letter under or in front of the cherubim throne so that Yahweh could read it for himself. For an ancient parallel, compare the act of the Assyrian scribe Urad-Gula, who, having received a letter from Assurbanipal, placed it in the temple of Nabu, on the god's throne.[4] The understanding, by the author of the letter to the Hebrews, that only the high priest had access to the holy of holies, and he only once a year (Heb 9:7), is a misunderstanding of the yearly ritual of atonement that involved a cleansing of the sanctuary (Exod 30:10), perhaps influenced by the Chronicler's story of Uzziah attempting to usurp priestly privilege and being hurried out of the temple after God struck him with leprosy (2 Chr 26:16-21). From Isaiah it is clear that both the prophet (Isaiah 6) and the king (Isaiah 37) had ready access to the holy of holies as late as the end of the eighth century BCE.

Having placed the letter before Yahweh for him to read, Hezekiah then prayed to him (v. 15). The prayer

---

3   See Simo Parpola and Michael Porter, *The Helsinki Atlas of the Near East in the Neo-Assyrian Period* (Helsinki: Neo-Assyrian Text Corpus Project, 2001) 12.

4   V. A. Hurowitz, "ABL 1285 and the Hebrew Bible: Literary Topoi in Urad-Gula's Letter of Petition to Assurbanipal," *SAAB* 7, no. 2 (1993) 9–17, esp. 14–15.

follows the standard form of petitionary prayer, but that is not unusual even for extemporaneous prayer in a traditional religious culture. There are certain expectations for what acceptable prayer sounds like even in religious tradition where extemporaneous prayer is the norm; a liturgy fixed in writing is not necessary to create and maintain standard forms of prayer, as any one who grew up in a "nonliturgical" religious tradition can attest. The prayer begins with an invocation of the deity that mentions aspects of the deity relevant to the request that Hezekiah wishes to make (v. 16). The epithet "Yahweh of Hosts" underscores Yahweh's great power as the creator of the heavenly armies. His designation as "the God of Israel" underscores his particular relationship to his special people, and "who sits enthroned on the cherubim" emphasizes that Yahweh's divine throne is located in his temple in Jerusalem, the city he chose as his dwelling place. The assertions "You alone are God to all the kingdoms of the earth" and "You made the heavens and the earth" undercut Sennacherib's argument that none of the gods of the kingdoms whom the Assyrians conquered were able to save their people. Those gods, Hezekiah confesses to Yahweh, were not real gods; the only real God for all the nations is Yahweh, who is the creator of the whole universe.

The as-yet-unspoken implication is that Yahweh, this all-powerful universal God, who has a special relationship to Israel and to his temple in Jerusalem, should for the sake of his divine reputation and self-interest intervene to save Israel and Jerusalem, so proving the arrogant and boastful Assyrian king wrong. The petition in v. 17 makes this explicit. Hezekiah calls upon Yahweh to incline his ear(s) and open his eye(s) to both hear and see all the words of Sennacherib. The letter was set before Yahweh so he could see and read it, but reading in antiquity was normally done aloud, so the emphasis, even in reading, was on hearing the message.[5] This emphasis is reflected in the repetition of the imperative, "hear." What Hezekiah wants Yahweh to hear are the words that Sennacherib sent "to reproach the living God." Sennacherib has insulted and belittled Yahweh, so if Yahweh wants to preserve his respect and honor, he needs to respond vigorously to this insult.

Hezekiah admits that the kings of Assyria have indeed devastated all the countries and their lands (v. 18) and burned their gods in the fire, but that was because they were not really gods, just the work of human hands made of wood and stone, so the Assyrians were able to destroy them (v. 19). But now Hezekiah calls on Yahweh, "our God," to save us from his hand, so that all the kingdoms of the earth may know that "you alone are God" (v. 20; see the textual note). In other words, like Moses in Exod 32:12, Hezekiah appeals to Yahweh's interest in preserving his divine reputation in the world as the incentive to get God to act against the blaspheming Assyrian king.

Cogan and Tadmor claim that "the Deuteronomic echoes in Hezekiah's prayer are manifest, a clear sign of its compositional origin," but their evidence is not as impressive as the bare claim suggests.[6] One occurrence of the phrase יְהוָה הוּא הָאֱלֹהִים אֵין עוֹד מִלְבַדּוֹ (*YHWH hûʾ hāʾĕlōhîm ʾên ʿôd milbaddô*), "Yahweh is God, there is none other besides him," in Deut 4:35 does not make Deuteronomy the source for the expressions אַתָּה־הוּא הָאֱלֹהִים לְבַדְּךָ (*ʾattâ-hûʾ hāʾĕlōhîm lĕbaddĕkā*), "you alone are God" (Isa 37:16) or אַתָּה יְהוָה אֱלֹהִים לְבַדְּךָ (*ʾattâ YHWH ʾĕlōhîm lĕbaddĕkā*), "you, Yahweh, are <God> alone" (Isa 37:20; see textual note), particularly since Isaiah uses the expression יְהוָה לְבַדּוֹ (*YHWH lĕbaddô*), "Yahweh alone," to speak of the sole exaltation of Yahweh (2:11, 17). Nor does one occurrence of כֹּל מַמְלְכוֹת הָאָרֶץ (*kōl mamlĕkôt hāʾāreṣ*), "all the kingdoms of the earth," in Deut 28:25 make Deuteronomy the source for the same expression in Isa 37:16, 20, particularly since Isaiah uses the same expression in the oracle against Tyre in 23:17. Even the expression מַעֲשֵׂה יְדֵי־אָדָם (*maʿăśēh yĕdê-ʾādām*), "the work of human hands" (Isa 37:19), though attested once in Deut 4:28, need not derive from Deuteronomy, since Isaiah repeatedly used the expression מַעֲשֵׂה יָד (*maʿăśēh yād . . .*), "the work of his/my hands," to refer to both God's actions (5:12; 19:25; cf. 5:19; 10:12; 28:21; 29:23) and human actions (29:15), twice referring specifically to idols or other cultic objects made by human hands (2:8; 17:8).

---

5   See the discussion in Shigetake Yaginuma, "Did Thucydides Write for Readers or Hearers?" in Lewis Ayres, ed., *The Passionate Intellect: Essays on the Transformation of Classical Traditions* (Rutgers University

6   Studies in Classical Humanities 7; New Brunswick, NJ: Transaction, 1995) 131–42, esp. 131–32.
Cogan and Tadmor, *II Kings*, 236.

The characterization of foreign gods as עֵץ וָאֶבֶן (ʿēṣ wāʾeben), "as mere wood and stone," does sound Deuteronomic, since it is a common expression in Deuteronomy (4:28; 28:36, 64; 29:16) and is found elsewhere outside the Sennacherib narrative only in Ezek 20:32 (but cf. Jer 2:27; Hab 2:19). But even if there are traces of Deuteronomic influence on the narrative, that does not mean that the narrative must be dated later than the early seventh century. Hosea, the late-eighth-century northern prophet, reflects much of the Deuteronomic theology, and Hezekiah's religious reform (2 Kgs 18:3-6; 2 Chr 29:3-21), probably instituted relatively early in his reign, c. 715 BCE, appears to have followed Deuteronomic concerns, perhaps brought south by northern refugees. Moreover, an early version of Deuteronomy may have been deposited in the temple during his reign, only to be rediscovered in the temple in the time of Josiah, where it fueled his similar religious reform (2 Kgs 22:3–23:27).

Then Isaiah the prophet sends a message to Hezekiah giving Yahweh's response to his prayer (v. 21). In his response, Yahweh identifies himself, choosing a phrase from Hezekiah's prayer, as "Yahweh the God of Israel." God then acknowledges that he has heard (see textual note) what Hezekiah prayed to him concerning Sennacherib the king of Assyria, the implication being that God will grant Hezekiah's petition. This is made explicit by the following "word" which Yahweh has spoken against the Assyrian king (v. 22a). That word is the long, mainly poetic, oracle that follows in vv. 22b-35.

The oracle begins with Zion personified as a virgin daughter mocking and deriding the Assyrian king, with Jerusalem as a daughter shaking her head in derision behind the Assyrian king's back.[7] The expressions בְּתוּלַת בַּת־צִיּוֹן (bĕtûlat bat-ṣîyôn), "virgin daughter Zion," and בַּת יְרוּשָׁלִָם (bat yĕrûšālāim), "daughter Jerusalem," do not mean "the virgin daughter of Zion" and "the daughter

of Jerusalem" but personify Zion as "a virgin daughter"/Jerusalem as "a daughter." Zion/Jerusalem is the subject of the verbs, not the mother of the subject.[8] The actions of Zion/Jerusalem express the lack of fear or respect the city has for the Assyrian king; he is the object of her contempt and derision, and a female's derision for a warrior was very demeaning in all the cultures of the ancient Near East.

This derisive contempt is not rooted in the city's own power, however. Verse 23 makes clear that it is rooted in the city's confidence in Yahweh, Zion's God, the Holy One of Israel, whom the Assyrian king had provoked by raising his voice against him in reproach and blasphemy, and by his arrogant and haughty look on high. Zion's direct questions to the Assyrian king contain an element of astonishment that anyone could be so reckless and foolish as to challenge the power of Yahweh: "Whom have you reproached and reviled? Against whom have you raised your voice and lifted your eyes on high? Against the Holy One of Israel!" God's punishment of the exalted eyes of human arrogance is a recurrent theme in the prophet Isaiah (2:11; 10:12).

According to v. 24, Zion accuses the Assyrian king of using his servants to reproach the Lord by conveying the Assyrian king's boasts of former triumphs. The nature of those triumphs is formulated differently here, however, from in vv. 11-13 or even in the earlier speech of the Rabshakeh in 36:18-20. Here the Assyrian king is reported to have boasted, "By the multitude of my chariotry I have ascended the height of the mountains, the peaks of Lebanon, that I might cut down his tallest cedars, his choicest cypresses, and that I might enter his most distant height, the forest of his plantation." The Assyrian kings often boasted of cutting good timber in the Lebanon or Amanus for their building projects in Assyria,[9] but the nature of the boast here seems more mythological and less prac-

---

7   For a general discussion of nonverbal communication, see Mayer Gruber, *Aspects of Non-Verbal Communication in the Ancient Near East* (2 vols.; Studia Pohl 12; Rome: Biblical Institute Press, 1980).

8   See W. F. Stinespring, "No Daughter of Zion: A Study of the Appositional Genitive in Hebrew Grammar," *Encounter* 26 (1965) 133–41. A critique of his study can be found in Michael E. Floyd, "Welcome Back Daughter of Zion," *CBQ* 70 (2008) 484–504. See also David Bosworth, "Daughter Zion and Weeping in Lamentations 1–2," *JSOT* 38 (2013) 217–23,

which gives a nice summary of the scholarship on the issue.

9   See the discussion of this motif in Peter Machinist, "Assyria and Its Image in the First Isaiah," *JAOS* 103 (1983) 723; and his reference to articles by Abraham Malamat ("Campaigns to the Mediterranean by Iahdunlim and Other Early Mesopotamian Rulers," in Hans G. Güterbock and Thorkild Jacobsen, *Studies in Honor of Benno Landsberger on His Seventy-fifth Birthday, April 21, 1963* [AS 16; Chicago: University of Chicago Press, 1965] 367–69), Shalom M. Paul,

tical. It has the same mythological quality as the material in the taunt song over the death of Sargon in 14:8-14. Of course, as Peter Machinist pointed out to me, the actual journeys to the cedar forest and the Gilgamesh version of them are thoroughly intermixed: the actual journeys, in their reportage, took on a mythological character, just as the mythological version echoed the actual journeys.

In any case, the text makes one think of Gilgamesh and Enkidu's invasion of the cedar forest and the killing of Humbaba, its guardian installed by the god Enlil, in the Gilgamesh epic (tablets II–V). As Gilgamesh and Enkidu approach Mount Lebanon, they dig a well before Gilgamesh ascends the mountain (IV 37-40, 82-85, 124-27, 166-68). The cedar mountain (*šadū erēnu*) is characterized as the abode of the gods (*mušab ilī*) and the throne-dais of the goddesses (*parak irnini*, V 6). Though Enkidu fears the angry response of Enlil and the great gods (V 242-43), they slay Humbaba and cut the best timber in the forest (V 262-65, 289-97). Eventually, however, Enlil has his revenge with the premature death of Enkidu (VII 85-89). The Gilgamesh epic was known in the west; a Middle Babylonian fragment of it was actually found at Megiddo in Palestine.[10] Our Isaiah text seems to portray Sennacherib's assault on the forests of the Lebanon in the light of that epic, except that the forest is Yahweh's, not Enlil's. The third person masculine singular pronominal suffixes in v. 24 are normally taken as referring back to the noun Lebanon, "its tallest cedars, its choicest cypresses, . . . its remotest height, the forest of its plantation," but they could just as easily refer back to the more remote antecedent אֲדֹנָי (*ʾădōnāy*), "my Lord," thus designating Yahweh as the owner of the cedar forest that Sennacherib had desecrated. The expression in v. 25, "I dug (a well) and drank water," also seems to be modeled on the behavior of Gilgamesh and Enkidu in the Gilgamesh epic.[11] The rest of v. 25 seems to shift the location from the Lebanon to a different site, however. The expression יְאֹרֵי מָצוֹר (*yěʾōrê māṣor*) is normally taken as "the streams

of Egypt," referring to the numerous branches and canals into which the Nile divides in the Delta (cf. Isa 19:6), since יְאֹר (*yěʾōr*) is the normal Hebrew word for the Nile.[12] Unless one emends the pointing of וְאַחְרִב (*wěʾaḥrīb*), "that I might dry up," to וָאַחְרִב (*wāʾaḥrīb*), "and I dried up," the verb should be rendered with a modal sense, not as a simple past tense. It suggests that Sennacherib dug a well and drank water in preparation for drying up all the rivers of Egypt with the sole of his feet. The imagery would seem to be a metaphor for destroying the power of Egypt to intervene in support of Hezekiah. Similar imagery is used in Isa 19:6 for Yahweh destroying the power of Egypt to act. Since Sennacherib only engaged Egyptian forces in Palestine and never actually invaded Egypt, however, this must be regarded as either a purely metaphorical or purely prospective boast.

In v. 26, Yahweh, now speaking in his own voice in the first person, addresses Sennacherib with an incredulous question, "Haven't you heard? From long ago I did (planned) it. From days of old I fashioned it. Now I have brought it to pass that it might come to be, laying waste fortified cities in desolate heaps." The point of Yahweh's question to Sennacherib is to make clear that the real power behind Assyria's former conquests was not Sennacherib or his ancestors, but Yahweh himself. As in Isa 10:5-15, Yahweh had only used Assyria as his agent of destruction. The inhabitants of these doomed cities had no power, were terrified and ashamed, and withered like dried-up plants and grass before the scorching east wind (v. 27), not because Assyria was so invincible but because Yahweh had planned it and brought it to pass. But, as in Isa 10:5-15, Yahweh had noted Sennacherib's arrogant misunderstanding of the historical situation (v. 28). Nothing that Sennacherib did or thought escaped Yahweh's observation: "I know your rising up and your sitting down; your going out and your coming in, and your raging against me" (see textual notes). And as in Isa 10:5-15, Assyria's arrogant misunderstanding of the situation

("Deutero-Isaiah and Cuneiform Royal Inscriptions," *JAOS* 88 [1968] 182–83), and Yutaka Ikeda ("Hermon, Sirion and Senir," *Annual of the Japanese Biblical Institute* 4 [1978] 33–36).

10 A. Goetze and S. Levy, "Fragment of the Gilgamesh Epic from Megiddo," *Atiqot* 2 (1959) 121–28.

11 See SB version, tablet IV, lines 163-67, in A. R. George, *The Babylonian Gilgamesh Epic: Introduction,*

Critical Edition and Cuneiform Texts (2 vols.; Oxford: Oxford University Press, 2003) 1:596–97.

12 For a recent study of this passage, see Diana Edelman, "The Nile in Biblical Memory," in Ehud Ben Zvi and Christoph Levin, eds., *Thinking of Water in the Early Second Temple Period* (BZAW 461; Berlin: de Gruyter, 2014) 77–102, esp. 91–95.

irritated Yahweh. Because Sennacherib's raging against Yahweh and the Assyrian king's arrogant self-confidence have come up into Yahweh's ear, Yahweh threatens to intervene against Sennacherib (v. 29). Yahweh asserts, "I will put my hook in your nose, and my bridle in your lips, and I will turn you back by the way in which you came." The imagery of the hook in the nose or bridle in the lips suggests a domesticated bovine or riding horse, easily led about subject to the whim of its owner. The implication is that Sennacherib is no more than Yahweh's draft animal or riding horse, who must go where Yahweh directs, imagery little more flattering to the Assyrian king than the mere stick of Isa 10:5-15.

At v. 30, the prophet again addresses Hezekiah, this time with the sign (הָאוֹת, hāʾôt) confirming that the oracle is true. This year Hezekiah (and his people) are to eat what grows of itself; the second year, what grows from that; but in the third year they are commanded to sow and harvest and plant vineyards and eat their fruit. The sign, then, consists in a time limit as in Isa 7:14-16; 8:4 (cf. Exod 3:12).[13] Within three years, the threat from Assyria will have ended, and the survivors of Jerusalem and Judah will be able to go about life normally, with no interference to their agricultural activity, and they will be able to enjoy the fruit of their labor. Moreover, the human population of the surviving part of the house of Judah that remains will also increase again (v. 31), which is what the agricultural metaphor of taking root downward and making fruit upward means (cf. Isa 27:6; Hos 9:16; 14:6). Within that time limit a remnant will surely go forth from Jerusalem, and a surviving part from Mount Zion (v. 32), not because of Zion's inherent strength but because the zeal of Yahweh of Hosts will do this (cf. the same idiom in Isa 9:6).

In further confirmation of this promise to Hezekiah and his capital city, Yahweh adds the promises in vv. 33-35. The king of Assyria will not enter this city, he will not shoot an arrow there, he will not advance upon it with a shield, and he will not pile up siege ramps of dirt against its walls (v. 33). Instead, the king of Assyria will return by the way in which he came, and he will not enter this city (v. 34). God further promises, "I will protect [וְגַנּוֹתִי, wĕgannôtî; cf. the similar use of the verb גָּנַן in Isa 31:5] this city to deliver it for my sake and for the sake of David my servant" (v. 35). This promise is clearly rooted in the Zion Tradition's affirmations that Yahweh was the supreme God, and that he had chosen David and his dynasty as his human king and Jerusalem as his imperial city, and this is the same theological tradition that most profoundly shapes the message of the eighth-century Isaiah of Jerusalem. Such theology is no indication of a late date. Early on, Isaiah of Jerusalem had expected Jerusalem to come under a full-fledged siege (29:1-4), but that apparently never developed. According to Sennacherib's own annals, he had shut up Hezekiah in his city like a bird in a cage,[14] and the biblical account of the negotiation with the Rabshakeh under the eastern wall of the city, with the walls fully defended, suggests that Jerusalem was expecting a full-fledged siege at any minute. There is no clear indication, however, that such a full-fledged siege ever began. Sennacherib's account suggests there were Assyrian outposts around the city to prevent ingress into or egress from the city, thus preventing further provisioning of the city and blocking easy communications with any other remaining fortified city in Judah or with the Egyptian relief force, but such outposts are not the same as the onset of a full-fledged siege.

Following Isaiah's oracle of salvation, there is a brief historical notation indicating the outcome of the situation. According to v. 36, an angel of Yahweh went forth and smote 185,000 in the Assyrian camp, and when the Assyrians arose early the next morning, all of these were dead corpses. This brief note has created an enormous amount of discussion.[15] Some scholars simply dismiss it as a late, unhistorical legend (so Clements, 287–88). Others connect it to a tradition in Herodotus (2.141) in which a plague of mice devours the leather harnesses of the Assyrian chariots and cavalry, which forces the Assyrian army to turn back.[16] Based on this tradition, some suggest

---

13 For a general discussion of such signs, see my "Of Signs, Prophets, and Time Limits: A Note on Psalm 74:9," *CBQ* 39 (1977) 474–81.

14 There are multiple copies of Sennacherib's account of his third campaign giving this detail in Grayson and Novotny, RINAP 3/1-2, but see, for example, I, p. 65, text 4, lines 52–54.

15 For a relatively recent treatment of this issue with extensive references to the relevant bibliography up to that time, see Gallagher, *Sennacherib's Campaign*.

16 James A. Montgomery and H. S. Gehman, while treating the biblical account as legendary, nonetheless mention the parallel Egyptian legend and go on to say, "the two stories are a capital instance of the

that the vermin infected the Assyrian army with bubonic plague, which caused a massive die-off and resulted in the Assyrians cutting short their campaign season.[17]

Quite apart from the Herodotus tradition, which has been questioned for a number of reasons,[18] the problem of an infectious disease, whatever its precise identification, decimating a besieging army is not that unusual. Bubonic plague was known in the region; it seems to be the disease indicated in the pre-Davidic narrative about the loss of the ark of the covenant and the subsequent decimation of the Philistine population by a plague (1 Sam 4:1–7:1). The mention of mice and rats and עֳפָלִים (ʿŏpālîm), "buboes," the inflamed swelling in the lymph glands of the armpits and groins associated with bubonic plague, clearly point in that direction.[19] Such plagues had been endemic in the general region for centuries. The plague prayers of the Hittite king Mursilis II indicate that the Hittites had contracted the plague from Egyptian prisoners taken in the Lebanon region during the era of Shuppiluliuma I, and the plague had continued to decimate the population of Hatti down to the time of Mursilis II (*ANET*, 394–96). The Amarna letters mention a plague ("the hand of Nergal/Rashap/?") that was decimating the population of Cyprus (EA 35).[20] Moreover, the Assyrian eponym lists mention a plague after a campaign to the seacoast in 802 BCE, another in 765, and another in 759.[21] That Sennacherib's army, after its prolonged siege activity in the field in Philistia and Judah—involving by Sennacherib's own boast the conquest of forty-six of Hezekiah's walled cities, some of which, like Lachish, did not fall until after a long and bitterly contested siege

involving many dead—would have been susceptible to rapidly spreading infectious disease is not improbable in the slightest. The number of dead Assyrians given in the biblical narrative, 185,000, is clearly an exaggeration, as is true of most of the numbers in the biblical accounts and as is also probably true of many, if not most, of the numbers in the Assyrian accounts.[22] For that matter, the estimate of enemy dead in contemporary military accounts down to the present is usually wildly inflated. Nonetheless, the outbreak of infectious disease among his troops would help to explain why Sennacherib would be willing to return home early without conquering Jerusalem.

Hezekiah's submission to Sennacherib did not involve a surrender of Jerusalem, the Judean capital, which Sennacherib never entered, nor a personal appearance by Hezekiah before the Assyrian king, and Hezekiah's promised tribute was not sent to Sennacherib until after he had returned to Assyria. In Sennacherib's pictorial display of his campaign, the high point was the Assyrian conquest of Lachish, an important but outlying fortress, not the capital of the country. Contrast that with Tiglath-pileser's conquest of Arpad after a three-year siege (743–740 BCE), or his conquest of Kullani, the capital of Unqi/Pattina (738), or Sargon II's conquest of Ashdod (711), or Sennacherib's own conquest and destruction of Babylon in 691–689, to get some feel for how incomplete Sennacherib's defeat of Hezekiah was. Leaving Hezekiah on the throne in his uncaptured capital Jerusalem must have been almost as disappointing to Sennacherib as leaving Merodach-baladan as a tribute-paying vassal in Babylon would have been.

various development of popular legend based on historic fact," though precisely what that historic fact was, they do not say (*A Critical and Exegetical Commentary on the Books of Kings* [ICC; Edinburgh: T&T Clark, 1951] 497–98).

17 See Gallagher, *Sennacherib's Campaign*, 242; H. H. Rowley, "Hezekiah's Reform and Rebellion," in Rowley, *Men of God: Studies in Old Testament History and Prophecy* (Longon: Nelson, 1963) 125–26; Wolfram von Soden, "Sanherib vor Jerusalem 701 B.C.," in von Soden, *Bibel und alter Orient: Altorientalische Beiträge zum Alten Testament* (BZAW 162; Berlin: de Gruyter, 1985) 155–56; K. A. Kitchen, "Egypt, the Levant and Assyria in 701 B.C.," in Manfred Görg, ed., *Fontes atque pontes: Eine Festgabe für Hellmut Brunner* (AAT 5; Wiesbaden: Harrassowitz, 1983) 245, 251.

18 See Cogan and Tadmor, *II Kings*, 250–51.

19 See the discussion in Patrick D. Miller and J. J. M. Roberts, *The Hand of the Lord: A Reassessment of the "Ark Narrative" of 1 Samuel* (1977; repr., Atlanta: Society of Biblical Literature, 2008) 64–67.

20 William L. Moran, *The Amarna Letters* (Baltimore: Johns Hopkins University Press, 1992) 107–8.

21 For a convenient English translation of the lists, see E. R. Thiele, *The Mysterious Numbers of the Hebrew Kings: A Reconstruction of the Chronology of the Kings of Israel and Judah* (rev. ed.; Grand Rapids: Eerdmans, 1965) 209–15.

22 See the most recent comprehensive study, Marco De Odorico, *The Use of Numbers and Quantifications in the Assyrian Royal Inscriptions* (SAAS 3; Helsinki: Neo-Assyrian Text Corpus Project, 1995).

At any rate, following the unexpected death of many of his troops at the hand of Yahweh, Sennacherib set out and returned to Assyria, where he dwelled in Nineveh (v. 37). While living there and worshiping in the temple of his god, Nisrok, two of his sons, Adrammelek and Sarezer, murdered Sennacherib with the sword and fled to the country of Ararat, and Esarhaddon, Sennacherib's son, succeeded him on the throne of Assyria (v. 38). Sennacherib was indeed murdered by a son or sons, but not until 681 BCE, some twenty years after his campaign against Judah. The foreign names in this account are garbled. The divine name נִסְרֹךְ (nisrōk), Nisrok or, more traditionally Nisroch, is not attested in Assyrian sources and is obviously corrupted, perhaps intentionally, but from what is not self-evident. One might think of Marduk or Nusku, though Sennacherib was no great fan of Marduk,[23] the Babylonian god whom Nabonidus credits with arranging the murder of Sennacherib by his own son (ANET, 309a). The Babylonian Chronicle also mentions the murder of Sennacherib by his son,[24] as does the later tradition of Berossos.[25] Simo Parpola has argued that Sennacherib's murderer was Arad-Ninlil (pronounced Arda-milissu, virtually identical to the form Adramelos found in an excerpt from Berossus by Abydenos), an older son bypassed in the line of succession for Esarhaddon.[26] The biblical form Adrammelek would be a relatively easy corruption of Adramelos. No other source mentions the second son Sarezer as participating in the murder of Sennacherib, though Esarhaddon does mention his brothers, in the plural, as participating in the revolt in Assyria (ANET, 289b), and there is no reason to doubt that Adramilissu had an accomplice. The name is abbreviated, lacking the theophoric element, and the fuller name has been plausibly reconstructed as [Nabu]-shar-uṣur, the governor of Markasi and eponym in 682 BCE.[27] The land of Ararat, where they fled, would be the ancient country of Urartu,

or modern Armenia. The name Esarhaddon (Akk. Aššur-aḫ-iddina, "the (god) Aššur has given a brother") shows the same š > s change from Akkadian to Hebrew that one finds with the royal name Sargon (Akk. Šarru-kīn, "legitimate king"), though the place-name Aššur, "Assyria," is normally rendered in Hebrew as אַשּׁוּר (Aššûr), without this change of sibilant.[28]

Obviously these historical details at the end of the account could not have been recorded until after the events in 681 BCE, so at least some twenty years after Sennacherib's campaign against Hezekiah. It is not at all clear, however, that this account of Yahweh's deliverance of Jerusalem must date much later. Cogan and Tadmor's assertion that the information about the death of Sennacherib in the account "could only have been derived from a Babylonian chronicle" is problematic in the extreme.[29] As an Assyrian vassal after Hezekiah's submission in 701 BCE, Judah would have been eager for any news of Assyria, and news of the death of the hated Sennacherib would have captivated the Judean audience, as it probably captivated audiences throughout the vassal states of western Asia. The death of an emperor was major news, even in antiquity, and people would have wanted as much information about it from messengers from Assyria as they could obtain. The details of the death of Sargon II in 705 BCE reached Judah quickly, as both Isaiah's taunt song against him in Isaiah 14 and Hezekiah's rebellion against Assyria indicate. Why would the similar news of Sennacherib's violent death be any different? There were Judean exiles in Assyria, and, if one may judge by the later correspondence between the first Babylonian exiles and their kin remaining in Jerusalem (see Jer 29:1-32), the correspondence between Assyria and Judah was probably not insignificant. Moreover, the tradition of Yahweh's miraculous deliverance of Jerusalem in the days of Hezekiah had become a fixed part

23 He seems to have taken the Marduk statue from Esagila to the city of Aššur, or else destroyed it. See especially the article of Hayim Tadmor, with Benno Landsberger and Simo Parpola, "The Sin of Sargon, and Sennacherib's Last Will," SAAB 3, no. 1 (1989) 3–51.

24 A. K. Grayson, Assyrian and Babylonian Chronicles (TCS 5; Locust Valley, NY: J. J. Augustin, 1975) 81:34–35.

25 Stanley Mayer Burstein, The "Babyloniaca" of Berossus

(Sources from the Ancient Near East 1.5; Malibu: Undena, 1978) 24:3.

26 Simo Parpola, "The Murderer of Sennacherib," Mesopotamia 8 (1980) 171–82.

27 See Cogan and Tadmor, II Kings, 240, and the literature cited there.

28 This change of sibilants has been studied, for example, by Alan Millard, "Royal Names in Biblical Hebrew," JSS 21 (1976) 1–14.

29 Cogan and Tadmor, II Kings, 244.

of the tradition by the time of Jeremiah and is reflected both in the popular tradition about the prophet Micah (Jer 26:16-19) and in the false confidence the people placed in the presence of the temple of Yahweh in their city (Jer 7:4, 8-15). It is unlikely that even this version of the deliverance of Hezekiah's Jerusalem postdated the rise of the Neo-Babylonian kingdom of Nabopolasar in the 620s BCE, much less the fall of Assyria between 615 and 609 BCE.

Bibliography

Abel, F. M., *Géographie de la Palestine* (1933; 2 vols.; EBib; repr., Paris: J. Gabalda, 1967).

Ackroyd, P. R., "Isaiah 36–39: Structure and Function," in W. C. Delsman et al., eds., *Von Kanaan bis Kerala: Festschrift für Prof. Mag. Dr. Dr. J. P. M. van der Ploeg* (AOAT 211; Kevelaer: Butzon & Bercker; Neukirchen-Vluyn: Neukirchener Verlag, 1981) 3–21.

Alt, Albrecht, "Die territorialgeschichtliche Bedeutung von Sancheribs Eingriff in Palästina," *PJ* 25 (1930) 80–88.

Avaux, M., "La mention de Tarhaqa en 2R 19,9; Js 37,9," *Aiphos* 20 (1973) 31–43.

Barnett, R. D., "The Siege of Lachish," *IEJ* 8 (1958) 161–64.

Becker, J. P., "Wurzel und Wurzelspross," *BZ* 20 (1976) 22–44.

Begrich, Joachim, "*Sōfēr* und *Mazkîr*," *ZAW* 58 (1940) 1–29.

Boecker, H. J., "Erwägungen zum Amt des Mazkir," *TZ* 17 (1961) 212–16.

——, *Redeformen des Rechtslebens im Alten Testament* (2nd ed.; WMANT 14; Neukirchen-Vluyn: Neukirchener Verlag, 1964).

Brueggemann, Walter, "Isaiah 37:21-29: The Transformative Potential of a Public Metaphor," *HBT* 10 (1988) 1–32.

Budde, K., "The Poem in 2 Kings xix 21-28 (Isaiah xxxvii 22-29)," *JTS* 35 (1934) 307–13.

Burney, C. F., "'The Jew's Language': 2 Kings XVIII 26 = Isa XXXVI 11," *JTS* 13 (1912) 417–20.

Burstein, Stanley Mayer, *The "Babyloniaca" of Berossus* (Sources from the Ancient Near East 1.5; Malibu: Undena, 1978) 24:3.

Clements, *Isaiah and the Deliverance*.

——, "The Prophecies of Isaiah to Hezekiah concerning Sennacherib: 2 Kings 19:21-34/Isa 37:22-35," in Rüdiger Liwak and Siegfried Wagner, eds., *Prophetie und geschichtliche Wirklichkeit im alten Israel: Festschrift für Siegfried Herrmann zum 65. Geburtstag* (Stuttgart: Kohlhammer, 1991) 65–78.

Cornaly, W. A., "2 Kings XIX (Ja XXXVII 36) and Herodotus II 141," *ExpTim* 25 (1913) 379–80.

Crown, A. D., "Messengers and Scribes: The ספר and מלאך in the Old Testament," *VT* 24 (1974) 366–70.

Fewell, D. N., "Sennacherib's Defeat: Words at War in 2 Kings 18:3–19:37," *JSOT* 34 (1986) 79–90.

Fullerton, K., "Isaiah's Attitude in the Sennacherib Campaign," *AJSL* 42 (1925) 1–25.

Galling, Kurt, *Die israelitische Staatsverfassung in ihrer vorderorientalischen Umwelt* (AO 28; Leipzig: Hinrichs, 1929).

Grayson, A. K., *Assyrian and Babylonian Chronicles* (TCS 5; Locust Valley, NY: J. J. Augustin, 1975) 81:34–35.

Iwry, S., "והנמצא—a Striking Variant Reading in 1QIsa," *Textus* 5 (1966) 34–43.

Kitchen, K. A., "Egypt, the Levant and Assyria in 701 BC.," in Manfred Görg, ed., *Fontes atque pontes: Eine Festgabe für Hellmut Brunner* (AAT 5; Wiesbaden: Harrassowitz, 1983) 243–53.

——, "Late Egyptian Chronology and the Hebrew Monarchy: Critical Studies in Old Testament Mythology, I," *JANES* 5 (1973) 225–33.

——, *Third Intermediate*.

Parpola, Simo, "The Murderer of Sennacherib," *Mesopotamia* 8 (1980) 171–82; also in B. Alster, ed., *Death in Mesopotamia: Papers Read at the XXVIe Rencontre Assyriologique Internationale* (Copenhagen: Akademisk, 1980).

——. *Neo-Assyrian Toponyms* (programming and computer printing by Kimmo Koskenniemi; AOAT 6; Kevelaer: Butzon & Bercker, 1970).

Roberts, J. J. M., "Of Signs, Prophets, and Time Limits: A Note on Psalm 74:9," *CBQ* 39 (1977) 474–81.

Rofé, Alexander, *The Prophetical Stories: The Narratives about the Prophets in the Hebrew Bible, Their Literary Types and History* (Publications of the Perry Foundation for Biblical Research in the Hebrew University of Jerusalem; Jerusalem: Magnes Press, Hebrew University, 1988) 88–95.

Rowley, H. H., "Hezekiah's Reform and Rebellion," in Rowley, *Men of God: Studies in Old Testament History and Prophecy* (London: Nelson, 1963) 98–132; originally published in *BJRL* 44 (1961–62) 395–461.

Soden, Wolfram von, "Sanherib vor Jerusalem 701 v. Chr.," in von Soden, *Bibel und Alter Orient: Altorientalische Beiträge zum Alten Testament* (ed. Hans-Peter Müller; BZAW 162; Berlin: de Gruyter, 1985) 149–57.

Talmon, S., "A Case of Faulty Harmonization," *VT* 5 (1955) 206–8.

Tawil, H., "2 Kings 19:24: יארי מצור‎," *JNES* 41 (1982) 195–206.

Thiele, E. R., *The Mysterious Numbers of the Hebrew Kings: A Reconstruction of the Chronology of the Kings of Israel and Judah* (rev. ed.; Grand Rapids: Eerdmans, 1965) 209–15.

Vervenne, M., "The Phraseology of 'Knowing Yhwh' in the Hebrew Bible: A Preliminary Study of Its Syntax and Function," in van Ruiten and Vervenne, *Studies in the Book of Isaiah*, 467–92.

Zimmerli, W., *Erkenntnis Gottes nach dem Buche Ezekiel: Eine theologische Studie* (ATANT 27; Zurich: Zwingli, 1954).

38

1/ In those[a] days Hezekiah[b] became mortally sick, and
Isaiah,[c] the son of Amoz, the prophet, came[d] to
him and said[e] to him, "Thus[f] says Yahweh, 'Order[g]
your house,[h] for[i] you are going to die;[j] you will not[k]
live.'" 2/ And Hezekiah[l] turned[m] his face[n] to the wall
and prayed to Yahweh, 3/ and he said,[o] "Please,
O Yahweh, remember[p] how I walked[q] before you[r]
in faithfulness and with a whole heart[s] and how I
did what was good in your eyes."[t] And Hezekiah[u]
wept[v] profusely. 4/ And the word of Yahweh came[w]
to Isaiah[x] saying,[y] 5/ Go[z] and say*[a] to Hezekiah,*[b]
"Thus*[c] says Yahweh, the God of David,*[d] your
father,*[e] 'I have heard your prayer.*[f] I have seen*[g]
your tears.*[h] Now I will add fifteen years to your
days.*[i] 6/ And from the hand of the king of Assyria
I will deliver you*[j] and this*[k] city, and I will protect
this*[k] city.'*[l] 7/ And this is the sign to you*[m] from
Yahweh that Yahweh will do this word which he has
spoken.*[n] 8/ 'I am about to make the shadow on the
steps, which had gone down on the steps of Ahaz*[o]
because of the sun,*[p] return back*[q] ten steps,'" and
the sun returned*[r] ten steps, on the same steps
which it had gone down.*[s]

[Verses 9-20 contain the inserted Psalm of Hezekiah;
see ahead.]

21/ And Isaiah said,*[t] "Let them take*[u] a cake of figs
and let them rub*[v] (it) on*[w] the sore, that he may
recover."*[x] 22/ And Hezekiah*[y] said, "What sign is
there that I will go up to the house of Yahweh?"*[z]

Textual Notes

a MT and 2 Kgs 20:1 הָהֵם (hāhēm), "those"; 1QIsa[a] ההמה.

b MT and 2 Kgs 20:1 חִזְקִיָּהוּ (ḥizqîyāhû), "Hezekiah"; 1QIsa[a] יחזקיה.

c MT and 2 Kgs 20:1 יְשַׁעְיָהוּ (yĕšaʿyāhû), "Isaiah"; 1QIsa[a] ישעיה.

d MT and 1QIsa[a] וַיָּבֹא (wayyābôʾ), "and he came"; 2 Kgs 20:1 וַיָּבֹא.

e MT and 2 Kgs 20:1 וַיֹּאמֶר (wayyōʾmer), "and he said"; 1QIsa[a] ויואמר.

f MT and 2 Kgs 20:1 כֹּה (kōh), "thus"; 1QIsa[a] כוה.

g MT and 2 Kgs 20:1 צַו (saw), "order, command!"; 1QIsa[a] צוי.

h MT and 2 Kgs 20:1 לְבֵתֶךָ (lĕbêtekā), "to your house"; 1QIsa[a] לביתכה.

i MT and 2 Kgs 20:1 כִּי (kî), "for, because"; 1QIsa[a] כיא.

j MT and 2 Kgs 20:1 מֵת (mēt), "will die"; 1QIsa[a] מית.

k MT and 2 Kgs 20:1 וְלֹא (wĕlōʾ), "and not"; 1QIsa[a] ולוא.

l 2 Kgs 20:2 omits the proper name; for MT and 1QIsa[a] see note b above.

m MT and 2 Kgs 20:2 וַיַּסֵּב (wayyasseb), "and he turned"; 1QIsa[a] ויסוב.

n MT and 1QIsa[a] פָּנָיו (pānāyw), "his face"; 2 Kgs 20:2 אֶת־פָּנָיו (ʾet-pānāyw), "his face."

o MT וַיֹּאמַר (wayyōʾmar), "and he said"; 1QIsa[a] ויואמר; this word is omitted by 2 Kgs 20:3, which instead has לֵאמֹר (lēʾmōr), "saying," at the end of v. 2. LXX appears to reflect this last reading with its opening λέγων, "saying."

p MT and 2 Kgs 20:3 זְכָר־נָא (zĕkor-nāʾ), "remember please"; 1QIsa[a] זכורנא.

q MT and 2 Kgs 20:3 הִתְהַלַּכְתִּי (hithallaktî), "I walked about, conducted myself"; 1QIsa[a] originally had the qal הלכתי, "I walked," then inserted ת ה above the line to correct to the hithpael form of MT.

r MT and 2 Kgs 20:3 לְפָנֶיךָ (lĕpānêkā), "before you"; 1QIsa[a] לפניכה.

s MT וּבְלֵב (ûbĕlēb), "and with a heart"; 2 Kgs 20:3 and 1QIsa[a] וּבְלֵבָב (ûbĕlēbāb), "and with a heart."

t MT and 2 Kgs 20:3 בְּעֵינֶיךָ (bĕʿênêkā), "in your eyes"; 1QIsa[a] בעיניכה.

u See note b above.

v MT and 2 Kgs 20:3 וַיֵּבְךְּ (wayyēbk), "and he wept"; 1QIsa[a] ויבכא.

w MT and 1QIsa[a] וַיְהִי דְּבַר־יְהוָה (wayhî dĕbar YHWH), "and the word of Yahweh came"; 2 Kgs 20:4 has an additional introductory clause וַיְהִי יְשַׁעְיָהוּ לֹא יָצָא הָעִיר [חָצֵר] הַתִּיכֹנָה (wayhî yĕšaʿyāhû lōʾ yāṣāʾ hāʿîr [kĕtîb]/ḥāṣēr [qĕrē] hattîkōnâ, "Before Isaiah had gone out of the middle court [following the qĕrē]," and follows it with וּדְבַר־יְהוָה הָיָה אֵלָיו לֵאמֹר (ûdĕbar-YHWH hāyâ ʾēlāyw lēʾmōr), "the word of Yahweh came to him, saying."

x For the spelling of Isaiah, see note c above.

y MT and 2 Kgs 20:4 לֵאמֹר (lēʾmōr), "saying"; 1QIsa[a] לאמור.

z MT and 1QIsa[a] הָלוֹךְ (hālôk), "go!"; 2 Kgs 20:5 שׁוּב (šûb), "go back/return!"

*a MT and 2 Kgs 20:5 וְאָמַרְתָּ (wĕʾāmartā), "and you will say"; 1QIsaᵃ ואמרתה.

*b See note b above. After the royal name, 2 Kgs 20:5 adds נְגִיד־עַמִּי (nĕgîd-ʿammî), "the leader of my people."

*c See note f above.

*d MT and 2 Kgs 20:5 אֱלֹהֵי דָוִד (ʾĕlōhê dāwîd), "the God of David"; 1QIsaᵃ אלוהי דויד.

*e MT and 2 Kgs 20:5 אָבִיךָ (ʾābîkā), "your father"; 1QIsaᵃ אביכה.

*f MT and 2 Kgs 20:5 תְּפִלָּתֶךָ (tĕpillātekā), "your prayer"; 1QIsaᵃ תפלתכה.

*g MT and 2 Kgs 20:5 רָאִיתִי (rāʾîtî), "I have seen"; 1QIsaᵃ וראיתי, "and I have seen."

*h MT and 2 Kgs 20:5 אֶת־דִּמְעָתֶךָ (ʾet-dimʿātekā), "your tears"; 1QIsaᵃ את דמעתכה.

*i MT and 1QIsaᵃ הִנְנִי יוֹסִף עַל־יָמֶיךָ חֲמֵשׁ עֶשְׂרֵה שָׁנָה (hinĕnî yôsīp ʿal-yāmêkā ḥāmēš ʿeśrê šānâ), "now I am about to add upon your days fifteen years," though 1QIsaᵃ has the longer spelling for the suffix עַל ימידה, "upon your days." 2 Kgs 20:5 has a significantly different text הִנְנִי רֹפֶא לָךְ בַּיּוֹם הַשְּׁלִישִׁי תַּעֲלֶה בֵּית יְהוָה (hinĕnî rōpeʾ lāk bayyôm haššĕlîšî taʿăleh bêt YHWH), "Now I am about to heal you. On the third day you will go up to the house of Yahweh." The counterpart to MT does not occur until the beginning of v. 6: וְהֹסַפְתִּי עַל־יָמֶיךָ חֲמֵשׁ עֶשְׂרֵה שָׁנָה (wĕhōsaptî ʿal-yāmêkā ḥāmēš ʿeśrê šānâ), "and I will add upon your days fifteen years."

*j MT and 2 Kgs 20:6 אַצִּילְךָ (ʾaṣṣîlĕkā), "I will deliver you"; 1QIsaᵃ אצילכה.

*k MT and 2 Kgs 20:6 הַזֹּאת (hazzōʾt), "this"; 1QIsaᵃ הזואת.

*l 1QIsaᵃ follows 2 Kgs 20:6 in adding at the end of the verse לְמַעֲנִי וּלְמַעַן דָּוִד [dāwîd in 1QIsaᵃ] ʿabdî), "for my sake and for the sake of David my servant." None of the versions supports this contamination from Kings.

*m MT לְךָ (lĕkā), "to you"; 1QIsaᵃ לכה.

*n 2 Kgs 20:7-8 has additional material that roughly corresponds to Isa 38:21-22 and will be noted there. 2 Kgs 20:9a has וַיֹּאמֶר יְשַׁעְיָהוּ זֶה־לְךָ הָאוֹת מֵאֵת יְהוָה כִּי יַעֲשֶׂה יְהוָה אֶת־הַדָּבָר אֲשֶׁר דִּבֵּר (wayyōʾmer yĕšaʿyāhû zê-lĕkā hāʾôt mēʾet YHWH kî yaʿăśê YHWH ʾet-haddābār ʾăšer dibbēr), "and Isaiah said, 'This will be the sign to you from Yahweh that Yahweh will do the word which he spoke.'"

*o MT בְּמַעֲלוֹת אָחָז (bĕmaʿălôt ʾāḥāz), "on the steps/sundial of Ahaz"; 1QIsaᵃ במעלות עלית אחז, "on the steps of the upper room of Ahaz."

*p MT בַּשֶּׁמֶשׁ (baššemeš), "because of the sun"; 1QIsaᵃ את השמש, "the sun," seems to indicate a second object of the participle, "I am about to make the shadow on the steps, which had gone down on the steps of Ahaz, that is, the sun, return back ten steps."

*q MT אֲחֹרַנִּית (ʾăḥōrannît), "back, backwards"; 1QIsaᵃ אחרנית.

*r MT וַתָּשָׁב (wattāšob), "and (the sun) returned"; 1QIsaᵃ יתשוב.

*s 2 Kgs 20:9b-11, continuing Isaiah's word in v.9a, has a far more elaborate text which allows Hezekiah to chose the sign: "Shall the shadow advance ten steps or shall it return ten steps?" And Hezekiah said, "It is easy for the shadow to extend ten steps, but not for the shadow to return back ten steps." And Isaiah the prophet cried to Yahweh, and he made the shadow on the steps, which had gone down on the steps of Ahaz, turn back ten steps.

*t MT and 2 Kgs 20:7 וַיֹּאמֶר (wayyōʾmer), "and he said"; 1QIsaᵃ ויאמר.

*u MT and 1QIsaᵇ יִשְׂאוּ (yiśĕʾû), "let them take"; 1QIsaᵃ accidentally omits this word, leaving the syntactical anomaly of an object without any verb; 2 Kgs 20:7 has the masculine plural imperative of a different verb קְחוּ (qĕḥû), "take."

*v MT, 1QIsaᵃ, and 1QIsaᵇ וְיִמְרְחוּ (wĕyimrĕḥû), "and let them rub, apply"; 2 Kgs 20:7 differs considerably, with וַיִּקְחוּ וַיָּשִׂימוּ (wayyiqĕḥû wayyāśîmû), "and they took and placed."

*w MT, 1QIsaᵃ, 2 Kgs 20:7 עַל (ʿal), "upon"; 1QIsaᵇ אל, "to."

*x MT (and presumably 1QIsaᵃ and 1QIsaᵇ, though these texts are unpointed) וְיֶחִי (wĕyeḥî), "that he may recover"; 2 Kgs 20:7 maintains the narrative past tense וַיֶּחִי (wayyeḥî), "and he recovered."

*y MT and 2 Kgs 20:8 חִזְקִיָּהוּ (ḥizqîyāhû), "Hezekiah"; 1QIsaᵃ has the shorter form חזקיה.

*z MT, 1QIsaᵃ, 1QIsaᵇ כִּי אֶעֱלֶה בֵּית יְהוָה (kî ʾeʿĕlê bêt YHWH), "that I will go up to the house of Yahweh"; 2 Kgs 20:7 כִּי־יִרְפָּא יְהוָה לִי וְעָלִיתִי בַּיּוֹם הַשְּׁלִישִׁי בֵּית יְהוָה (kî-yirpāʾ YHWH lî wĕ-ʿālîtî bayyôm haššĕlîšî bêt YHWH), "that Yahweh will heal me and I will go up on the third day to the house of Yahweh." The verse is obviously out of place in Isa 38:22, since the sign was already given back in vv. 7-8.

Commentary

"In those days" is a very imprecise date formula, and the question of when Hezekiah suffered his illness is disputed.[1] The narrative in Isaiah 39 tells of a Babylonian embassy from Merodach-baladan to Hezekiah to congratulate him on his recovery from his illness. Since Merodach-baladan was king of Babylonia twice, once from 721 to 710 BCE and again for nine months in 703, that still leaves room for debate. Nonetheless, if Hezekiah

---

1 Wildberger (3:1447) and Hayes and Irvine (p. 383) date it to the time of the Ashdod affair (c. 713–711 BCE). Clements (p. 289) regard's Hezekiah's illness as "the kernel of fact in the story"; the rest is unrelated, unhistorical legendary accretion, which

would appear to leave the date of Hezekiah's illness irrelevant. Jensen (p. 299) and Thiele (*Mysterious Numbers*, 157–59) associate the illness with Sennacherib's campaign against Jerusalem.

became king in 715, as I have argued above, his sickness should probably be dated to sometime in 704, and thus the embassy of Merodach-baladan would be dated in 703. The Babylonians were probably even more concerned to discover whether Hezekiah remained committed to the anti-Assyrian defensive league than to congratulate him on the recovery from his illness. A date in 704 BCE for Hezekiah's illness and recovery would also fall within the general time period of the revolt against Assyria and its aftermath, so the generic "in those days" fits within the general time frame of these events. In response to Hezekiah's illness, Isaiah the prophet came to him with an unwelcome prophetic oracle from Yahweh. Hezekiah was "to command" his house, that is, make the necessary arrangements within the palace, because he was going to die and not live. It was common practice for the sick to seek an oracle from the deity whether they were going to recover or die, and if they were going to recover, how long it would take, but the negative response, "You are going to die," was no more welcome then than when it is now spoken to a patient by a medical professional.

On hearing this news, Hezekiah turned his face to the wall and prayed to Yahweh (v. 2). He implored God to remember how he had walked before God in faithfulness and with a fully committed heart, and how he had done what was good in God's eyes, and Hezekiah wept profusely as he prayed (v. 3). In response to his prayer, Yahweh again spoke to Isaiah (v. 4) and sent him back to Hezekiah to announce to the king, "Thus says Yahweh, the God of David your ancestor, 'I have heard your prayer. I have seen your tears. I am going to add fifteen years to your days'" (v. 5). God then adds, "I will deliver you and this city from the hand of the king of Assyria, and I will protect this city" (v. 6). This additional prom-ise suggests that Hezekiah's revolt against Assyria had already begun, but it is problematic, because Isaiah does not appear to have been that supportive of the revolt early on (see Isa 28:1-22; 29:1-16; 30:1-17; 31:1-5). The additional promise may have been added later in the light of Isaiah's promises to Hezekiah and Jerusalem in the later stages of the revolt. Then in order to confirm the reliability of his oracle, Isaiah offers a sign from Yahweh that Yahweh will carry out this word that he has spoken (v. 7). The sign was that God was about to cause the shadow on the steps, which had gone down on the steps of Ahaz because of the sun, to go back ten steps, and the sign occurred as God promised, the shadow going back the ten steps it had gone down (v. 8). In the parallel account in 2 Kgs 20:9b-10, Hezekiah is given a choice of signs, either having the shade going down ten more steps in response to the natural movement of the sun, or having the shade quite abnormally go back ten steps, and Hezekiah chooses the more miraculous sign. That feature is missing in Isaiah, though a fragment of a longer, more complex version is preserved in v. 22, where Hezekiah asks for a sign, rather than having Isaiah offer him one unbidden. The prayer of Hezekiah in vv. 9-20 has been inserted in the middle of the narrative, interrupting its conclusion in v. 21, but v. 21 probably originally followed immediately after v. 8. In it Isaiah commands those ministering to the sick king to take a cake of figs and apply it to Hezekiah's sore, that Hezekiah might recover. The term הַשְּׁחִין (haššĕḥîn), "the boil, sore," refers to an inflamed irruption in the skin, but such sores could have different causes, and it is not obvious precisely what medical condition Hezekiah was suffering.

Bibliography

Ackroyd, P. R., "The Death of Hezekiah—a Pointer to the Future," in Maurice Carrez, Joseph Doré, and Pierre Grelot, eds., *De la Tôrah au Messie: Études d'exégèse et d'herméneutique biblique offertes à Henri Cazelles pour ses 25 années d'enseignement à l'Institut Catholique de Paris (Octobre 1979)* (Paris: Desclée, 1981).
——, "An Interpretation of the Babylonian Exile: A Study of 2 Kings 20, Isaiah 38-39," *SJT* 27 (1974) 329-52.

Barton, John, *Oracles of God: Perceptions of Ancient Prophecy in Israel after the Exile* (London: Darton, Longman & Todd, 1986).
Borchardt, L., *Die altägyptische Zeitmessung*, in Ernst von Bassermann-Jordan, ed., *Die Geschichte der Zeitmessung und der Uhren*, Vol. 1, B (Berlin: Vereinigung wissenschaftlicher Verleger, 1920), 1-70.
Catastini, A., "Osservazioni filologische sulla cosidetta 'Meridiana de Achaz' (Isaia 38:8/II Re 20:11)," *Henoch* 5 (1983) 161-78.

Clements, *Isaiah and the Deliverance.*

Fullerton, K., "The Original Text of 2K.20,7-11 = I.38,7.8.21f.," *JBL* 44 (1925) 44–62.

Gosse, Bernard, "Un texte pré-apocalyptique du règne de Darius: Isaïe 13:1—14:23," *RB* 92 (1985) 200–222.

Hoffer, V., "An Exegesis of Isaiah 38:21," *JSOT* 56 (1992) 69–84.

Illman, Karl-Johan, *Old Testament Formulas about Death* (Publications of the Research Institute of the Åbo Academic Foundation 48; Åbo: Åbo Akademi, 1979) 24–25.

Iwry, S., "The Qumran Isaiah and the End of the Dial of Ahaz," *BASOR* 147 (1957) 27–33.

Jeremias, C., "Zu Jes XXXVIII 31f.," *VT* 21 (1971) 104–11.

Johl, Carl Hermann, *Altägyptische Webestühle und Brettchenweberei in Altägypten* (Leipzig: Hinrichs, 1924).

Konkel, A. H., "The Sources of the Story of Hezekiah in the Book of Isaiah," *VT* 43 (1993) 462–82.

Landy, D., ed., *Culture, Disease and Healing: Studies in Medical Anthropology* (New York: Macmillan, 1978) 278–85.

Lewy, J., "Sanherib und Hiskia (Jes 38,5; 36,2ff.)," *OLZ* 31 (1928) 150–63.

Ognibeni, B., "Achaz o no Achaz: A proposito del testo di Is 38:8," *RivistB* 40 (1992) 76–86.

——, "Ombra e sole in Is 38,8: Una Riposta A. Catastini," *RivistB* 41 (1993) 205–9.

Pilch, J. J., "Biblical Leprosy and Body Symbolism," *BTB* 11 (1981) 108–13.

Rofé, A., "Classes in Prophetic Stories," in *Studies on Prophecy: A Collection of Twelve Papers* (VTSup 26; Leiden: Brill, 1974) 143–64.

Sachsse, E., "Untersuchungen zur hebräischen Metrik," *ZAW* 43 (1925) 173–92.

Seitz, Christopher R., "Zion King: Death Sentence Diverted (Isaiah 38)," in Seitz, *Zion's Final Destiny: The Development of the Book of Isaiah. A Reassessment of Isaiah 36–39* (Minneapolis: Fortress Press, 1991) 149–66, 172–82.

Sloley, R. W. S., "Primitive Methods of Measuring Time," *JEA* 17 (1931) 166–78.

Smitten, W. T. in der, "Patient und Arzt: Die Welt des Kranken im Alten Testament," *Janus* 60 (1973) 103–29.

Vermeylen, J., "Hypothèses sur l'origine d'Isaïe 36–39," in van Ruiten and Vervenne, *Studies in the Book of Isaiah*, 95–118.

Weiss, R., "Textual Notes," *Textus* 6 (1968) 127–29.

Welten, P., "Sonnenuhr," in Herbert Haag, ed., *Bibel-Lexikon* (2nd ed.; Einsiedeln: Benzinger, 1968) 1616–17.

Wieringen, A. L. H. M. van, "Notes on Isaiah 38–39," *BN* 102 (2000) 28–32.

Williamson, *Book Called Isaiah*, 202–8.

Yadin, Y., "The Dial of Ahaz," *ErIsr* 5 (1959) 91–96.

Zakowitcz, Y., "2 Kings 20:7—Isaiah 38:21-22," *BetM* 50 (1972) 302–5.

38

9/ A writing[a] of Hezekiah[b], king of Judah, when he became sick[c] and
    recovered from his sickness:[d]

10/ I said,
    In the middle of my days[e] I must go;[f]
    Into the gates of Sheol
    I am consigned[g] for the rest of my years.[h]

11/ I said,
    I will not[i] see Yah,
    Yah[j] in the land of the living,[k]
    I will not[i] view humans again
    With those who inhabit the world.[l]

12/ My dwelling[m] is pulled up and rolled up[n] by me[o]
    Like a tent[p] of a shepherd;[q]
    I have folded up[r] my life like the weaver,[s]
    Who cuts me off from the loom.
    Day and night you make an end of me.

13/ I lay quietly[t] until morning,[u]
    Like a lion thus he crushes[v] all my bones,
    Day and night you make an end of me.

14/ Like a swift or a thrush[w] thus I chirp,
    I moan like the dove;[x]
    My eyes grow weak[y] (looking) to the height,
    My Lord,[z] there is oppression[*a] to me,
    Be my security.[*b]

15/ What can I say?
    I was thinking to myself;[*c]
    He is the one[*d] who did (it) to me.[*e]
    All my sleeping fled away,[*f]
    because of the bitterness of my soul.[*g]

16/ O my Lord,[*h] in spite of these things[*i]
    And from all among them[*j] the life of my spirit[*k] revives;[*l]
    You restored me to health,[*m] and revived me.[*n]

17/ Truly[*o] it was for my own good that the bitterness to me was so bitter,[*p]
    And you yourself kept[*q] my life from the pit of oblivion,[*r]
    For you threw[*s] all[*t] my sins behind your back.[*u]

18/ For[*v] Sheol cannot[*w] thank you,[*x]
    Death cannot[*w] praise you;[*y]
    Those who go down to the pit cannot[*z] wait for your faithfulness.[†a]

19/ It is[†b] the living, only the living who can thank you[†c] as I do today.[†d]
    A father makes known[†e] to the children, O God, your faithfulness.[†f]

20/ O Yahweh, save me indeed,[†g] and my stringed music we will play all[†h] the
    days of our life at the house of Yahweh.

Textual Notes

a   MT and 1QIsaᵃ מִכְתָּב (miktāb), "a writing, document, inscription," so also Vg., Syr., and Tg.; LXX has προσευχή, "the prayer (of Hezekiah)." The similarity of the idiom between miktāb lĕ + PN and the idiom in the heading of six psalms מכתם לדוד (miktām lĕdāwīd), "a miktām of David" (Pss 16:1; 60:1) or לדוד מכתם (lĕdāwīd miktām), "a miktām of David" (Pss 56:1; 57:1; 58:1; 59:1) has led many scholars, including Wildberger (3:1442, 1458), to emend מכתב (miktāb) here to מכתם (miktām), but, since the meaning of miktām is quite obscure, the argument rests on a very thin reed. LXX consistently renders miktām in the psalms references as στηλογραφία or εἰς στηλογραφίαν, "a stele inscription" or "for a stele inscription," never προσευχή, "prayer," as here. Mowinckel in Psalmenstudien IV, while accepting this emendation, argued that miktām was to be derived from the cognate root attested in Akkadian, katāmu, "to cover," and that it was a designation for the individual lament psalm, since the purpose of such psalms was to "cover" or "atone" for sin, seen as the root cause of the individual's suffering. Since all the examples were individual lament psalms, it amounted to a genre designation.[1] By the time he published his later *The*

---

1   Sigmund Mowinckel, *Psalmenstudien*, vol. 4, *Die technischen Termini in den Psalmenüberschriften* (Kristiania: Dybwad, 1922; repr., Amsterdam: P. Schippers, 1966) 4–5.

Psalms in Israel's Worship, Mowinckel had changed his mind about accepting the emendation, though he still maintained his interpretation of the term *miktām*.[2] The problem with Isa 38:9-20 is that it is a psalm of thanksgiving after illness, not an individual lament psalm, and, according to Mowinckel, "this makes the correction improbable."[3] Mowinckel's explanation of the term *miktām* remains problematic, however, because the verbal root is attested in Hebrew only in the sense of "to stain" or "be stained" by sin, blood, or the like (see the *niphal* in Jer 2:22; and cf. the Tg. there and in Isa 1:18). Moreover, the possibility that *miktām* is not a genre designation but some technical musical notation must be considered, since the Akkadian cognate *kitmu* is used for "a tuning and interval on a musical instrument" (*CAD* K, 466). There is no counterpart in 2 Kings 20 to Isa 38:9-20.

b For the variation between the spelling of Hezekiah in MT and 1QIsaᵃ see textual note b on Isa 38:1 above.

c MT בַּחֲלֹתוֹ (*baḥǎlōtô*), "when he became sick"; 1QIsaᵃ בחוליותי, "in his illnesses."

d MT מֵחָלְיוֹ (*mēḥolyô*), "from his sickness"; 1QIsaᵃ מחליו.

e MT בִּדְמִי יָמַי (*bidmî yāmay*), "in the middle of my days," so Vg. and Syr.; 1QIsaᵃ may have ברמי ימי, "in the height of my days," though ד and ר are hard to distinguish in its script. LXX's Ἐν τῷ ὕψει τῶν ἡμερῶν μου, "in the height of my days," seems to presuppose that reading. The insertion of a *waw* above the line in 1QIsaᵃ makes little sense. Tg.'s "in the sorrow of my days" is interpretive.

f MT and 1QIsaᵃ אֵלֵכָה (*ʾēlēkâ*), "I must go"; LXX simplifies and shortens by omitting this verb: "in the height of my days in the gates of Hades I will leave behind (my) remaining years."

g MT פֻּקַּדְתִּי (*puqqadtî*), "I am summoned, consigned"; 1QIsaᵃ פקודתי (*pěqûdātî*), "(is) my punishment." LXX, Vg., and Syr. understand the verb as "I will leave behind" or "I will seek," which may suggest they were reading an active form rather than MT's *pual* passive.

h MT יֶתֶר שְׁנוֹתָי (*yeter šěnôtāy*), "the rest of my years," so LXX, Vg., Syr.; 1QIsaᵃ ומר שנותי, "and bitter are my years."

i MT לֹא (*lōʾ*), "not"; 1QIsaᵃ לוא, in the second occurrence ולוא, "and (I will) not."

j MT repeats the shortened divine name יָהּ יָהּ (*yāh yāh*), "Yah, Yah," which Vg. renders with the repetition of *Dominum*, "Lord." 1QIsaᵃ has only one יה, and the other versions do not repeat the divine name. This is the only place in the OT where the shortened divine name is repeated in this fashion, but יָהּ יְהוָה (*yāh YHWH*), "Yah, Yahweh," occurs in Isa 12:2; בְּיָהּ יְהוָה (*běyāh YHWH*), "in Yah, Yahweh," in Isa 26:4; יָהּ אֱלֹהִים (*yāh ʾělōhîm*), "Yah, God," in Ps 68:19; and יָהּ אֲדֹנָי (*yāh ʾǎdōnāy*), "Yah, My Lord," in Ps 130:3 at a line division ("If you keep track of sins, O Yah//My Lord who can stand"). It is tempting to see יה as a simple scribal error due to the confusion between *yod* and *waw* for an original יהוה.

k MT בְּאֶרֶץ הַחַיִּים (*běʾereṣ haḥayyîm*), "in the land of the living"; 1QIsaᵃ omits the article חיים בארץ, which may be more original.

l MT and 1QIsaᵃ עִם־יוֹשְׁבֵי חָדֶל (*ʿim-yôšěbê ḥādel*) in parallel with "in the land of the living" is probably to be corrected to עִם־יֹשְׁבֵי חָלֶד (*ʿim-yôšěbê ḥāled*), "with those who inhabit the world" (cf. Ps 49:2), or *ḥādel* and *ḥāled* are to be seen as byforms of the same positive word meaning "world." *Ḥādel* is traditionally taken as from *ḥādal* I, "to cease," and is assigned the meaning "the land of cessation, the underworld," but despite support from Syr.'s "with the inhabitants of the pit," that does not fit the parallelism here.

m MT and 1QIsaᵃ דּוֹרִי (*dôrî*), "my dwelling," is from *dôr* I, "dwelling," as the analogy with tent indicates, though the versions derived it from *dôr* II, "generation."

n MT וְנִגְלָה (*wěniglâ*), "and was taken away (from me)," is problematic. The *niphal* of גלה normally means "to appear, show, reveal, reveal oneself, be exposed." This would be the only occurrence of the *niphal* with the meaning "to be taken away." 1QIsaᵃ has יכלה, "vanishes (from me)," which is better, but still does not fit the comparison with the shepherd's tent very well. Vg.'s *et convoluta est*, "and is rolled up," fits the comparison, since when a shepherd pulls up his tent to move, the tent must be rolled or folded up for the move. This gives support to the slight emendation suggested by Joachim Begrich: ונגל (*wěnāgal*), "and is rolled up," from the root גלל, "to roll up."[4]

o If one accepts the preceding emendation, however, the suffixed preposition מִנִּי (*minnî*), "from me," becomes a tad awkward. Wildberger feels compelled to delete it (3:1443), but one might take it as supplying the implied subject of the passive form, particularly if one retains the first person form קפדתי; see note r below.

p MT כְּאֹהֶל (*kěʾōhel*), "like a tent"; 1QIsaᵃ כאוהל.

q MT and 1QIsaᵃ רֹעִי (*rōʿî*), "of a shepherd"; the final î on the word for "shepherd" is not a suffix but the *hireq compaginis*.

r MT קִפַּדְתִּי (*qippadtî*), "I rolled up"; 1QIsaᵃ ספרתי, "I counted out," appears to be the result of a couple of scribal errors. Many critics, including Wildberger (3:1443), have been bothered by the first person form, which appears to clash with the second person form at the end of the verse. Suggested emendations include both *qippadtā*, "you rolled up," and *qippad*, "he rolled up," but I do not think any emendation is necessary.

s MT כָּאֹרֵג (*kāʾōrēg*), "like the weaver"; 1QIsaᵃ כאורג. Another possibility, perhaps to be preferred, is to read *kāʾārîg*, "like the woven cloth" (so Wildberger, 3:1443, following Begrich, *Psalm*, 31, and *HALOT*, 84).

t MT שִׁוִּיתִי (*šiwwîtî*), "I lay quietly"; 1QIsaᵃ שפותי, meaning unclear. The translation of MT is suggested by the parallel with Ps 131:1-3: "Yahweh, my heart is not proud nor my eyes haughty. I do not aspire to great things or to things that are beyond me. But I lay down and calmed my soul like a weaned child upon his mother; my soul is like a weaned child

2 Sigmund Mowinckel, *The Psalms in Israel's Worship* (2 vols.; New York: Abingdon, 1962) 1:209.

3 Ibid.

4 Joachim Begrich, *Der Psalm des Hiskia: Ein Beitrag zum Verständnis von Jesaja 38, 10-20* (FRLANT n.s. 25; Göttingen: Vandenhoeck & Ruprecht, 1926) 27–28.

upon me. Let Israel wait for Yahweh from this time forth forever" אִם־לֹא שִׁוִּיתִי וְדוֹמַמְתִּי נַפְשִׁי כְּגָמֻל עֲלֵי אִמּוֹ כַּגָּמֻל עָלַי נַפְשִׁי: יַחֵל יִשְׂרָאֵל אֶל־יְהוָה מֵעַתָּה וְעַד־עוֹלָם: *im-lō*ʾ *šiwwîtî wĕdômamtî napšî kĕgāmul ʿălê ʾimmô kaggāmul ʿălay napšî. yaḥēl yiśrāʾēl ʾel-YHWH mēʿattâ wĕ-ʿad-ʿôlām*, vv. 2-3). There is a dispute, however, whether the Hebrew verb is from שוה I, "to level, smooth," hence "still, calm," or from שוה II, "to set, place," hence "lay oneself down, lie down." Vg. has *sperabam usque ad mane*, "I hoped/waited patiently till morning," which supports the general sense of MT, but it does not resolve the issue of the root. 1QIsaᵃ's vocalization suggests a geminate root שפף, but the ease of confusing *waw* and *yod* might suggest a correction to שפיתי, which would point to the later synonymous root שפה in Middle Hebrew meaning "to be quiet, at ease." Nonetheless, many critics suggest the emendation to שועתי (*šiwwaʿtî*), "I cried for help (*until morning*)." It would fit well enough in the context, but it does not seem to be a necessary emendation.

u   MT בֹּקֶר (*bōqer*), "morning"; 1QIsaᵃ בוקר.

v   MT יְשַׁבֵּר (*yĕšabbēr*), "he crushes, crushed"; 1QIsaᵃ ישבור (*yišbôr*), "he breaks, broke."

w   MT כְּסוּס עָגוּר (*kĕsûs ʿāgûr*), "like a swift, a thrush"; 1QIsaᵃ כסוס עוגר. LXX and Syr. see only one bird here, but Jer 8:7 indicates that these are two different birds and, following the *qĕrēʾ*, suggests the reading *kĕsîs wĕʾāgûr*, "like a swift or a thrush."

x   MT כַּיּוֹנָה (*kayyônâ*), "like the dove"; 1QIsaᵃ כיונא.

y   MT and 1QIsaᵃ דַּלּוּ (*dallû*), "were poor, little"; one should perhaps emend to כלו, since כלה is often used with "eyes" for the failure of sight (for example, Deut 28:65; Pss 69:4; 119:82, 123).

z   MT אֲדֹנָי (*ʾădōnāy*), "my Lord"; אדוני.

*a   MT עָשְׁקָה (*ʿošqâ*), "oppression"; 1QIsaᵃ עושקה.

*b   MT עָרְבֵנִי (*ʿorbēnî*), "be my security"; 1QIsaᵃ וערבני, "and be my security." LXX, Tg., and Syr. apparently read this form as a perfect rather than as an imperative.

*c   MT וְאָמַר־לִי (*wĕʾāmar-lî*), "and what can he say to me," so also Vg. After the preceding imperfect, the MT verbal form should be read as a converted perfect. 1QIsaᵃ ואומר לוא, "and I said, 'No' . . . ." With the correction of לוא to ליא (see note *e below), one would get, "'What can I say?' I was saying (thinking) to myself." Tg. supports the reading of both verbs as first person, so I adopt the reading ואמר לי (*wĕʾōmar lî*) with *BHS*.

*d   MT וְהוּא עָשָׂה (*wĕhûʾ ʿāśâ*), "and he is the one who did it." The independent nominative pronoun is used here for emphasis. 1QIsaᵃ והיאה, "and she," involves the simple error of the confusion of *yod* for *waw*.

*e   1QIsaᵃ ליא, "to me," supplies the missing indirect object after the verb.

*f   This line is a difficult crux. MT has אֶדַּדֶּה כָל־שְׁנוֹתַי (*ʾeddaddê kol-šĕnôtay*), "I will walk about all my years," if one analyzes the verb as a *hithpael* of the verb דדה, "to walk," but that is hardly a common lament motif. Begrich (*Psalm*, 42–43) emended the verb אדדה to אדכה (*ʾōdekâ*), "I will praise (*you all my years*)," but this assumes that the transition in the psalm from description of past suffering to present deliverance has already been reached, which is less than self-evident. The verb form in 1QIsaᵃ's אדודה כול שנותי is difficult, but it does not seem to

support a derivation from דדה. Perhaps one should read the form as the cohortative of נדד, "I must flee/wander about all my years," though "all my years" remains problematic, since the psalmist is facing imminent death. Syr. also saw the root נדד here, though it rendered, "He caused all my sleep to flee," apparently reading שְׁנָתִי (*šēnātî*), "my sleep," rather than MT's שְׁנוֹתַי (*šĕnôtay*), "my years." A number of modern translations including RSV, NRSV, and JPS, adopt the emendation נדדה כל־שנתי (*nādĕdâ kol-šĕnātî*), "all my sleep has fled (*because of the bitterness of my soul*)"; cf. Gen 31:40; and Esth 6:1, and this is probably the original reading. MT's unusual verb form אֶדַּדֶּה (*ʾeddaddê*) is a late Aramaic-influenced third person feminine singular *ʾithpael* from נדד, not a first person singular from דדה. The same variation between the third person feminine singular of the *peal* of נדד (*Targum Onkelos*) and the third person feminine singular of the *ithpeel* of נדד (*Targum Neofiti*) is reflected in the Aramaic translations of Gen 31:40. The word for sleep does occur in the plural or as a singular abstract noun ending in *-ôt*, שְׁנוֹת, *šēnôt*, Prov 6:10; 24:33), which would be easily confused as a plural form. Thus, the first person singular suffixed form of this real or assumed plural would be identical in form with the first person singular suffixed form of "years" (שְׁנוֹתַי, *šĕnôtay*, either "my years" or "my sleeping"), which might explain the confusion and be the source for some of the corruption. Since the form is the subject of a third person feminine singular verb, however, one must either correct the pronominal suffix on the abstract שְׁנוֹתִי (*šĕnôtî*), "my sleep," or restore the singular שְׁנָתִי (*šĕnātî*), "my sleep."

*g   MT עַל־מַר נַפְשִׁי (*ʿal-mar napšî*), "because of the bitterness of my soul"; 1QIsaᵃ differs only in orthography על מור נפשיא.

*h   MT and 1QIsaᵇ אֲדֹנָי (*ʾădōnāy*), "O my Lord"; 1QIsaᵃ אדוני.

*i   MT עֲלֵיהֶם (*ʿălêhem*), "upon/by/in spite of them"; 1QIsaᵃ עליהמה.

*j   MT and 1QIsaᵇ וּלְכָל־בָּהֵן (*ûlĕkol-bāhēn*), "and with regard to/from all among them [fem. pl.]"; 1QIsaᵃ maintains the masculine plural ולכל בהמה.

*k   MT חַיֵּי רוּחִי (*ḥayyê rûḥî*), "life of my spirit"; the form *ḥayyê* is a masculine plural construct and is the subject of the plural verb יִחְיוּ (*yiḥyû*), "will revive." 1QIsaᵃ חיו רוחו is a simple orthographic error for חיי רוחי.

*l   MT supported by 1QIsaᵇ יִחְיוּ (*yiḥyû*), "(the life of my spirit) will revive"; 1QIsaᵃ appears to have וחיו, but this is probably just a mistake for יחיו.

*m   MT has וְתַחֲלִימֵנִי (*wĕtaḥălîmēnî*), "and you will restore me to health," but it is better to revocalize to the converted imperfect (*wattaḥălîmēnî*), "and you restored me to health."

*n   MT וְהַחֲיֵנִי (*wĕhaḥăyēnî*), "and revive me!" Though MT is supported by 1QIsaᵃ, the suffixed *hiphil* imperative does not fit here. Emend with Begrich (*Psalm*, 44–45) to וַתְּחַיֵּנִי (*wattaḥăyēnî*), "and you revived me."

*o   MT הִנֵּה (*hinnê*), "behold, truly"; 1QIsaᵃ has the short form הן.

*p   MT supported by the fragments of 1QIsaᵇ מַר־לִי מָר (*mar-lî mār*), "the bitterness to me was bitter"; 1QIsaᵃ מר ליא מאודה, "it was exceedingly bitter to me."

*q   MT חָשַׁקְתָּ (*ḥāšaqtā*), "you loved," seems to be reflected by the varying translations in LXX, Syr., and Tg., and is supported by 1QIsaᵃ, but one should read חשכת (ḥāśaktā), "you kept back, held back, saved," because of the following prepositional phrase.

*r MT מִשַּׁחַת בְּלִי (miššaḥat bĕlî), "from the pit of oblivion/nothing-ness"; 1QIsaᵃ משחת כלי is a simple scribal error.

*s MT כִּי הִשְׁלַכְתָּ (kî hišlaktā), "for you threw"; 1QIsaᵃ כיא השלכתה.

*t MT כָּל (kol), "all"; 1QIsaᵃ כול.

*u MT גֵּוֶךָ (gēwĕkā), "your back"; 1QIsaᵃ גוכה. LXX has ὀπίσω μου, "behind me."

*v MT כִּי (kî), "for"; 1QIsaᵃ כיא.

*w MT לֹא (lōʾ), "not"; 1QIsaᵃ לואָ.

*x MT תּוֹדֶךָּ (tôdekkā), "thank you"; 1QIsaᵃ תודכה.

*y MT יְהַלֶלֶךָּ (yĕhalĕlekkā), "praise you"; 1QIsaᵃ יהללכה.

*z 1QIsaᵃ ולוא adds the conjunction as well as fuller spelling.

†a MT אֲמִתֶּךָ (ʾămitteka), "your faithfulness"; 1QIsaᵃ אמתכה.

†b For the Hebrew text of v. 19, we have the MT, 1QIsaᵇ, and two versions in 1QIsaᵃ, one in v. 19, and another in v. 20, where, after the first two words of v. 20, there is a dittography of all of v. 19, but done by a prior scribe, since the text of the dittography differs from the text of v. 19 in orthography and other more important regards:

MT: חַי חַי הוּא יוֹדֶךָ כָּמוֹנִי הַיּוֹם אָב לְבָנִים יוֹדִיעַ אֶל־אֲמִתֶּךָ

1QIsaᵇ: חי חי הוא יודך היום כמוני אב לבנים יודע אלה אמתך

1QIsaᵃ v. 19: חי חי הוא יודכה כמונו היום אב לבנים יודיע אל אמתכה

1QIsaᵃ v. 20: חי חי יודך כמוני היום אב לבנים יהודה אלוה אמתך

The dittography in 1QIsaᵃ omits the pronoun הוא, "The living, the living <he> can thank you."

†c MT יוֹדֶךָ (yôdekā), "who can thank you"; 1QIsaᵃ יודכה, but in the dittography in v. 20 this form is written as in MT יודך.

†d MT's word order כמוני היום, "as I do today," is reversed by 1QIsaᵇ היום כמוני, "today as I do."

†e MT and v. 19 of 1QIsaᵃ have the form יודיע (yôdiaʿ), "he makes known," while 1QIsaᵇ omits the second *mater*, and v. 20 of 1QIsaᵃ preserves the ה of the *hiphil* יהודיע.

†f The most interesting variant, however, is in the last two words. MT's אֶל־אֲמִתֶּךָ (ʾel-ʾămitteka) paralleled by v. 19 of 1QIsaᵃ אל אמתכה has normally been understood in the sense of a second prepositional phrase governed by the verb: "the father makes known *to* the children *concerning* your faithfulness," but such a construction with the *hiphil* of ידע is otherwise unknown. 1QIsaᵇ's reading אלה אמתך rules out the preposition, and might suggest the demonstrative ʾēllê, "he makes known these your *acts* of faithfulness," but v. 20 of 1QIsaᵃ's אלוה אמתך clearly has the word "God," which, given the second person forms, should be read as a vocative, "the father makes known to the children your faithfulness, O God." A variant with אל, "O God," was misunderstood as the preposition, and that created the difficulty in the text.

†g MT יְהוָה לְהוֹשִׁיעֵנִי (YHWH lĕhôšîʿēnî), "Yahweh save me indeed"; 1QIsaᵇ יהוה להושיעני; and 1QIsaᵃ has יהוה להושיעני both before and after the dittography. The ל is to be understood as the emphatic *lamed*, and the verb form is to be analyzed as an imperative continuing the direct address of the preceding verse.

†h MT כָּל (kol), "all"; 1QIsaᵃ כול.

Commentary

Verse 9 characterizes the following poetic text (vv. 10-20) as a text written by or for Hezekiah when he became sick and recovered from his illness. The text belongs to the genre of the תּוֹדָה (tôdâ), or thanksgiving psalm, which was typically performed along with an accompanying thanksgiving sacrifice (also known as a תּוֹדָה, tôdâ). The genre typically includes some narrative about the preceding trouble from which the psalmist prayed for relief, before thanking God for the deliverance from that trouble. The text is clearly a preexisting unit that the editor of Isaiah has inserted into the narrative, but the source of the text is problematic. Verse 9 claims that the text was written by or for Hezekiah, and that cannot be ruled out. West Semitic rulers were known to set up stelas or other inscribed *ex voto* objects to honor the deity or deities who heard and delivered them when they cried out in need (see *ANET*, 655–58, for the Ben-Hadad, Zakir, Yehaw-milk, and Punic *ex voto* inscriptions). Normally, however, these inscriptions give the author's self-identification, since the worshiper wanted to get credit for the fulfillment of his vow. Unless that part of the text was omitted, perhaps because the Isaiah editor had already indicated, in v. 9, that Hezekiah was the author, this psalm is actually anonymous. That leaves open the alternative possibility that the editor, knowing the convention, simply selected an appropriate, though anonymous, thanksgiving psalm and attributed it to Hezekiah in order to dress up his narrative. This practice is well known in the biblical text. The prayer of Hannah in 1 Sam 2:1-10 was hardly composed by Hannah in the premonarchical period, since it mentions Yahweh's human king and anointed one (1 Sam 2:10), and the prayer of Jonah from the belly of the fish (Jonah 2) was neither composed by Jonah nor prayed in the belly of the fish, since the prayer is a prayer of thanksgiving for deliverance from trouble, not a prayer of lament or petition asking for such deliverance. With regard to the prayer of Hezekiah, we simply lack the evidence to be sure of its origin. The editor,

483

however, clearly felt that these words were appropriate in the mouth of Hezekiah.

The psalm begins with the speaker being resigned to death (v. 10). The idiom אֲנִי אָמַרְתִּי (ʾănî ʾāmartî), "I said," may refer to the psalmist's internal thought processes rather than a spoken word and could be appropriately translated with JPS as "I had thought." His thoughts or expectations were that he would enter the gates of the underworld in the prime of life, in the midpoint of his days, and be consigned there for the rest of his years. The prepositional phrase בְּשַׁעֲרֵי שְׁאוֹל (běšaʿărê šěʾôl), "into/in the gates of Sheol," stands between, and is governed by, both the preceding and the following verb. This resignation also involved the recognition that he would never see Yahweh (see textual note) again in the land of the living, nor view humans again with those who inhabit the upper world (see textual notes k–l above). The idiom רָאָה יהוה/אלהים (rāʾâ YHWH/ʾělôhîm), "to see Yahweh/God," is an ancient idiom that refers to participation in worship at the sanctuary (Exod 23:15; 34:20, 23-24; Deut 16:16; 31:11; 1 Sam 1:22; Isa 1:12; Ps 42:3), since in a pagan context one would look upon the statue of the deity there, but the idiom was initially continued in Hebrew despite the lack of divine images, though eventually the active *qal* conjugation in this idiom was often secondarily altered (see esp. Exod 34:24; Deut 31:11; Isa 1:12, where the original *niphal* infinitive should have been written לְהֵרָאוֹת not לִרְאוֹת), to the passive *niphal* (נִרְאָה, nirʾâ), giving the more appropriate meaning, at least in the mind of the correctors, "to appear before Yahweh."

At v. 12 the psalmist switches to highly metaphorical language. He asserts that his dwelling has been pulled out (נִסַּע, nissaʿ, refers to the action of pulling out the tent pegs—Isa 33:20), and rolled up (see textual note n above) like a shepherd's tent, a striking metaphor for the transiency of human life. If the suffixed preposition מִנִּי (minnî), "from me" or "by me," is preserved (see textual note o above), it suggests, depending on the translation adopted, that the psalmist saw his tent pulled down and rolled up from him by others before he was ready to move (= "from me"), or that he himself pulled it down and rolled it up in preparation for his death (= "by me"). The psalmist further asserts, if the first person form קִפַּדְתִּי (qippadtî), "I folded up," is correct (see textual note r above), that he has folded up his life like a weaver, or perhaps like woven cloth (see textual note s above),

suggesting that he was making the necessary arrangements for his imminent death. With the correction to קִפַּדְתָּ (qippadtā), "you folded up," or קִפַּד (qippad), "he folded up," the sense would be that God folded up the psalmist's life like the weaver. That would fit a bit more smoothly with the continuation, which identifies the just-mentioned weaver as the one "who cuts me off from the loom," implying that the weaver is not a figure of speech for the psalmist but refers to God, who cuts the psalmist's life from the thrum or warp prematurely. The meaning of the final clause in the verse is disputed because of uncertainty about the meaning of the *hiphil* of שלם (šālam), "to be whole, be at peace." I understand the sense to be, "from day to night you bring me to an end." That is, the psalmist has no relief from his illness day or night; during both alike, God is bringing his life to an end. This is supported by v. 13, which suggests that the psalmist waited patiently for morning to come, or, if one accepts the popular emendation to שִׁוַּעְתִּי (šiwwaʿtî), "I cried for help," that he cried for help until morning. There was an Israelite tradition that help would come with the morning (Pss 30:6; 46:6; 143:8; Isa 17:14; 33:2), and it is a common experience of the sick, even in the modern world, that the coming of morning often brings relief and new hope. Unfortunately, that was not the experience of our psalmist. When morning came, God continued, like a lion, to break all the psalmist's bones. There was no relief from his suffering, day or night, and his steady decline toward the end continued day and night.

In this pitiful condition, the psalmist chirped like a swift and a thrush and moaned like a dove, while his eyes grew weak (see textual note y above) from looking above for help from God (v. 14). The chirping and moaning imagery suggests that the psalmist was near death, since this same imagery is used for the sounds the dead make when they are called up by the necromancer (see Isa 8:19; 29:4). The psalmist appealed to God, "My Lord, I am oppressed, be my security [עָרְבֵנִי, ʿorbēnî]." This last verb calls upon God to guarantee the psalmist's debt, to pay for it out of God's own funds, that is, by divine grace to cover or atone for any wrongdoing of the psalmist that might be responsible for his sickness.

Verse 15 is riddled with text-critical problems, so any translation and interpretation are problematic (see the textual notes), but I understand the first part of the verse as the psalmist saying, "What can I say? I was thinking to myself; he is the one who did it (to me)." In other words, the psalmist was pondering what else he could say to God in his prayer to motivate God to relieve his suffering, since God was the one who afflicted the psalmist with the illness in the first place. The last part of the verse is equally difficult textually, but I accept the common emendation that results in the translation, "all my sleep has fled because of the bitterness of my soul" (see the textual notes *f, *g above). The psalmist can find no rest at night from his suffering, because the constant pain inflicted by God has embittered his soul.

Despite a difficult text that has produced a spate of widely varying translations, the transition from the narration about the psalmist's former suffering to the announcement of his salvation occurs in v. 16 (see the textual notes). Despite all his former suffering and from all these things he had endured and worried about—and spoken about in the preceding verses—the life of his spirit revived. He confesses, "You restored me to health and revived me." For this translation and understanding of the text compare the similar translation of JPS, "My Lord, for all that and despite it My life-breath is revived; You have restored me to health and revived me."

In the light of that revival and recovery, the psalmist can now see that his former bitter suffering was for his own good and well-being (v. 17), presumably to turn him from his sins. Even in that former suffering, God graciously held his life back from the pit of oblivion, that is, death as end of human existence. God graciously threw all the psalmist's sins behind God's back, refusing to punish him to the full extent those sins deserved. Nonetheless, while thanking God for his graciousness, the psalmist also reminds God that the deity also benefits from this graciousness (v. 18).

After all, Sheol, the underworld and realm of the dead, does not give thanks to God, nor does Death praise God. Those who die and go down to the pit can no longer wait for God's faithfulness. It is the living person who gives thanks and praise to God, as the psalmist is doing this very day in reciting this prayer of thanksgiving after his recovery (v. 19). Since his children would be invited to the thanksgiving sacrifice and the prayer of thanksgiving that accompanied it, it is in this fashion that a father teaches his children about God's faithfulness and passes on the faith. The implication is, in short: if God desires a community of worshipers who thank, praise, and wait upon God's faithfulness, God would be wise not to send them into death and oblivion too quickly, lest the membership in his choir drop precipitously or die out entirely. Such an appeal to God's self-interest is found as early as Moses' intercession for Israel in the wilderness (Exod 32:11-14) and is common in the Psalms (Pss 6:6; 30:9; 88:10-12).

Verse 20 ends the prayer with a renewed prayer for deliverance and a vow that the psalmist would have his stringed music played all the days of the community's life in the temple of Yahweh. The renewed request, "O Yahweh, save me indeed," is not strange coming from someone recovering from a mortal illness. There would always be the concern, even if unspoken, that one might suffer a relapse. It is worth noting the transition between the singular and plural forms in the vow. "Keep me well, O Yahweh," the psalmist says, "and my praises *we* will continually perform before you all the days of *our* lives." Such a public performance of an individual's praises would be particularly appropriate if that individual were the king or an important public official with influence over worship in the temple.

Bibliography

Ackroyd, P. R., "The Death of Hezekiah—a Pointer to the Future," in Maurice Carrez, Joseph Doré, and Pierre Grelot, eds., *De la Tôrah au Messie: Études d'exégèse et d'herméneutique biblique offertes à Henri Cazelles pour ses 25 années d'enseignement à l'Institut Catholique de Paris (Octobre 1979)* (Paris: Desclée, 1981) 219–26.

——, "An Interpretation of the Babylonian Exile: A Study of 2 Kings 20, Isaiah 38–39," *SJT* 27 (1974) 329–52.

Airoldi, N., "Nota a Is. 38,16," *BeO* 15 (1973) 255–59.

Barré, M. L., "Restoring the 'Lost' Prayer in the Psalm of Hezekiah," *JBL* 114 (1995) 385–99.

Barton, John, *Oracles of God: Perceptions of Ancient Prophecy in Israel after the Exile* (London: Darton, Longman & Todd, 1986).

Begrich, Joachim, *Der Psalm des Hiskia: Ein Beitrag zum Verständnis von Jesaja 38, 10-20* (FRLANT n.s. 25; Göttingen: Vandenhoeck & Ruprecht, 1926).

Bellinger, W. H., *Psalmody and Prophecy* (JSOTSup 27; Sheffield: JSOT Press, 1984) 79–81.

Boer, P. A. H. de, "Notes on Text and Meaning of Isaiah XXXVIII 9-20," *OtSt* 9 (1951) 170–86.

Borchardt, L., in Ernst von Bassermann-Jordan, ed., *Die Geschichte der Zeitmessung und der Uhren* (Berlin: Vereinigung wissenschaftlicher Verleger, 1920).

Calderone, J., "ḤDL - II in Poetic Texts," *CBQ* 23 (1961) 451–60.

———, "Supplementary Note on ḤDL - II," *CBQ* 24 (1962) 412–19.

Castellino, G. R., "Lamentazioni individuali Accadiche ed Ebraiche," *Salm* 10 (1948) 145–61.

Clements, *Isaiah and the Deliverance.*

Coetzee, J. E., "The 'Song of Hezekiah' (Is 38, 9-20): A Doxology of Judgement from the Exilic Period," *OTE* 2 (1989) 13–26.

Dahood, M., "ḤDL 'Cessation' in Isaiah 38,11," *Bib* 52 (1971) 215–16.

Fullerton, K., "The Original Text of 2K. 20,7-11 = I.38,7.8.21f.," *JBL* 44 (1925) 44–62.

Gillingham, S. E., *The Poems and Psalms of the Hebrew Bible* (Oxford: Oxford University Press, 1994).

Gosse, Bernard, "Un texte pré-apocalyptique du règne de Darius: Isaïe 13:1–14:23," *RB* 92 (1985) 200–222.

Hallo, W. W., "The Royal Correspondence of Larsa: I. A Sumerian Prototype for the Prayer of Hezekiah," in Barry L. Eicher, ed., *Kramer Anniversary Volume: Cuneiform Studies in Honor of Samuel Noah Kramer* (AOAT 25; Kevelaer: Butzon & Bercker, 1976) 209–24.

Hauge, M. R., *Between Sheol and Temple: Motif Structure and Function in the I-Psalms* (JSOTSup 178; Sheffield: Sheffield Academic Press, 1995).

Iwry, S., "The Qumran Isaiah and the End of the Dial of Ahaz," *BASOR* 147 (1957) 27–33.

Jensen, Peter, "Faith and Healing in Christian Theology," *Point* 11, no. 2 (1982) 153–59.

Jeremias, C., "Zu Jes XXXVIII 31f.," *VT* 21 (1971) 104–11.

Johl, Carl Hermann, *Altägyptische Webestühle und Brettchenweberei in Altägypten* (Leipzig: Hinrichs, 1924).

Kuhn, Johannes, "Krankenandacht über Jesaja 38,10-17," in Hansgeorg Kraft and Hans Mayr, eds., *Botschafter von der Versöhnung: Festschrift für Walter Arnold zum 50. Geburtstag am 11.7.1979* (N.p., 1979) 147–55.

Lewy, J., "Sanherib und Hiskia (Jes 38,5; 36,2ff.)," *OLZ* 31 (1928) 150–63.

Lindström, F., *Suffering and Sin: Interpretation of Illness in the Individual Complaint Psalms* (ConBOT 37; Stockholm: Almqvist & Wiksell, 1994).

Mathys, Hans-Peter, *Dichter und Beter: Theologen aus spätalttestamentlichen Zeit* (OBO 132; Freiburg, Schweiz: Universitätsverlag; Göttingen: Vandenhoeck & Ruprecht, 1994).

Moor, Johannes C. de, and Wilfred G. E. Watson, eds., *Verse in Ancient Near Eastern Prose* (AOAT 42; Kevelaer: Butzon & Bercker; Neukirchen-Vluyn: Neukirchener Verlag, 1993).

Newman, Judith H., *Praying by the Book: The Scripturalization of Prayer in Second Temple Judaism* (SBLEJL 14; Atlanta: Scholars Press, 1999).

Nyberg, H. S., "Hiskias Danklied Jes 38,9-21," in *Festschrift Hans Kosmala* (ASTI 9; Leiden: Brill, 1974) 85–97.

Plöger, O., "Reden und Gebete im deuteronomistischen und chronistischen Geschichtwerk," in Wilhelm Schneemelcher, ed., *Festschrift für Günther Dehn zum 75. Geburtstag am 18. April 1957* (Neukirchen-Vluyn: Kreis Moors, 1957) 39–41, 46.

Sachsse, E., "Untersuchungen zur hebräischen Metrik," *ZAW* 43 (1925) 173–92.

Seitz, Christopher R., "The Prayer of Hezekiah," in Seitz, *Zion's Final Destiny: The Development of the Book of Isaiah. A Reassessment of Isaiah 36–39* (Minneapolis: Fortress Press, 1991) 81–88.

Seybold, Klaus, *Das Gebet des Kranken im Alten Testament: Untersuchungen zur Bestimmung und Zuordnung der Krankheits- und Heilungspsalmen* (BWANT 5; Stuttgart: Kohlhammer, 1973).

Soggin, J. Alberto, "Il 'Salmo di Ezechia' in Isaia 38,9-20," *BeO* 16 (1974) 177–81.

Starbuck, S. R. A., *Court Oracles in the Psalms: The So-Called Royal Psalms in Their Ancient Near Eastern Context* (SBLDS 172; Atlanta: Society of Biblical Literature, 1999).

Tournay, R., "Relectures bibliques concernant la vie future et l'angélologie," *RB* 69 (1962) 481–505, esp. 482–89.

Venter, J., "Isaiah and Jerusalem," *OTE* 2 (1988) 27–35.

Vermeylen, J., "Hypothèses sur l'origine d'Isaïe 36–39," in van Ruiten and Vervenne, *Studies in the Book of Isaiah*, 95–118.

Watts, J. W., "Biblical Psalms outside the Psalter," in Peter W. Flint and Patrick D. Miller, eds., *The Book of Psalms: Composition and Reception* (VTSup 99; Leiden: Brill, 2004) 288–309.

———, *Psalm and Story: Inset Hymns in Hebrew Narrative* (JSOTSup 139; Sheffield: JSOT Press, 1992).

Weiss, R., "Textual Notes," *Textus* 6 (1968) 127–29.

Weitzman, Steven, *Song and Story in Biblical Narrative: The History of a Literary Convention in Ancient Israel* (Indiana Studies in Biblical Literature; Bloomington: Indiana University Press, 1997).

Wollenweber, Klaus, "Danken und Klagen als Lebensäusserung des Glaubens: Predigt: Jesaja 38,9-20," in Manfred Oeming and Axel Graupner, eds., *Altes Testament und christliche Verkündigung: Festschrift für Antonius H. J. Gunneweg zum 65. Geburtstag* (Stuttgart: Kohlhammer, 1987) 416–19.

1/ At that[a] time Merodach-baladan[b] son of Baladan, king of Babylon, sent letters and a gift to Hezekiah,[c] when he heard[d] that he
had been sick[e] and had recovered.[f]

2/ And Hezekiah[g] rejoiced[h] over them,[i] and he showed them the
treasure-house,[j] the silver, and the gold, and the incense, and
the fine oil,[k] and his whole armory,[l] and everything[m] that was
found in his treasuries;[n] there was not[o] anything that Hezekiah[p]
did not[o] show them in his house and in all[m] his kingdom.[q]

3/ And Isaiah[r] the prophet went in[s] to the king[t] Hezekiah[u] and said[v]
to him, "What did these men say, and from where were they
coming[w] to you?"[x] And Hezekiah[u] said,[y] "From a far country
they came to me, from Babylon."

4/ And he said,[y] "What did they see in your house?[z]" And
Hezekiah[*a] said,[y] "They saw everything[*b] that is in my house.
There was not[*c] anything that I did not[*c] show them[*d] in my
treasuries."[*e]

5/ And Isaiah[*f] said[*g] to Hezekiah,[*h] "Hear the word of Yahweh of
Hosts![*i]

6/ 'Days are coming when all[*j] that is in your house[*k] and that your
ancestors[*l] stored up until this day will be taken to Babylon.[*m]
Nothing[*n] will be left,' says Yahweh.

7/ 'And some of your sons[*o] who have come forth from you,[*p]
which you engendered, they will take,[*q] and they will become[*r]
eunuchs in the palace of the king of Babylon.'"

8/ And Hezekiah[*s] said[*t] to Isaiah,[*u] "The word of Yahweh which
you have spoken[*v] is good." And he said,[*w] "Because there will
be peace and stability in my days."[*x]

Textual Notes

a MT הַהוּא (written *hahû*, vocalized *hahî*); 1QIsaᵃ, 1QIsaᵇ,
4QIsaᵇ, 2 Kgs 20:12 ההיא.

b MT מְרֹדַךְ בַּלְאֲדָן (*mĕrōdak balʾădān*), "Merodach-baladan"; 1QIsaᵃ
מרודך בלאדן; but 2 Kgs 20:12 has the erroneous בְּרֹאדַךְ בַּלְאֲדָן
(*bĕrōʾdak balʾădān*), "Berodach-baladan."

c MT, 2 Kgs 20:12, 1QIsaᵇ חִזְקִיָּהוּ (*ḥizqîyāhû*), "Hezekiah"; 1QIsaᵇ
יחזקיה.

d MT, 1QIsaᵃ, 1QIsaᵇ וַיִּשְׁמַע (*wayyišmaʿ*), "when he heard"; 2 Kgs
20:12, 4QIsaᵇ כִּי שָׁמַע (*kî šāmaʿ*), "because he heard."

e MT, 1QIsaᵇ, כִּי חָלָה (*kî ḥālâ*), "that he had been sick"; 1QIsaᵃ
כיא חלה; but 2 Kgs 20:12 כִּי חָלָה חִזְקִיָּהוּ (*kî ḥālâ ḥizqîyāhû*), "that
Hezekiah had been sick."

f MT and 1QIsaᵃ וַיֶּחֱזָק (*wayeḥĕzāq*), "and had recovered"; 1QIsaᵇ
ויחיה, "and had gotten well"; 2 Kgs 20:12 omits entirely.

g See note c above.

h MT, 1QIsaᵃ, 1QIsaᵇ וַיִּשְׂמַח (*wayyiśmaḥ*), "and (Hezekiah)
rejoiced"; 2 Kgs 20:13 וַיִּשְׁמַע (*wayyišmaʿ*), "and (Hezekiah)
heard."

i MT and 2 Kgs 20:13 עֲלֵיהֶם (*ʿălêhem*), "over, concerning them";
1QIsaᵃ עליהמה.

j MT אֶת־בֵּית נְכֹתֹה (*ʾet-bêt nĕkōtōh* [qĕrēʾ: נכתו, *nĕkōtô*]), "the
treasure-house"; 2 Kgs 20:13 אֶת־כָּל־בֵּית נְכֹתֹה (*ʾet-kol-bêt nĕkōtōh*),
"the whole treasure-house"; 1QIsaᵃ את כול בית נכתיו, "his whole
treasure-house."

k 2 Kgs 20:13 is alone in erroneously omitting the article on ואת
<ה>שמן הטוב (*wĕʾet <haš>šemen haṭṭôb*), "and <the> fine oil."

l MT וְאֵת כָּל־בֵּית כֵּלָיו (*wĕʾet kol-bêt kēlāyw*), "and his whole armory";
so 1QIsaᵃ except for the orthography of בית כול; but 2 Kgs 20:13
omits כל (*kol*) altogether: "and his armory."

m 1QIsaᵃ consistently uses the fuller orthography כול (*kol*), "all,
everything."

n MT and 4 QIsaᵇ בְּאֹצְרֹתָיו (*bĕʾōṣĕrōtāyw*), "in his treasuries"; 2 Kgs
20:13 בְּאוֹצְרֹתָיו; and 1QIsaᵃ באוצרותיו.

o 1QIsaᵃ consistently writes the negative as לוא.

p 1QIsaᵃ writes Hezekiah as יחזקיה.

q MT and 2 Kgs 20:13 מֶמְשַׁלְתּוֹ (*memšaltô*), "his kingdom"; 1QIsaᵃ
ממלכתו (*mamlaktô*), "his kingdom."

r MT, 2 Kgs 20:14, 1QIsaᵇ, 4QIsaᵇ יְשַׁעְיָהוּ (*yĕšaʿyāhû*), "Isaiah";
1QIsaᵃ ישעיה.

s MT, 2 Kgs 20:14, 4QIsaᵇ וַיָּבֹא (*wayyābōʾ*), "and he went in";
1QIsaᵃ and 1QIsaᵇ ויבוא.

t MT and 2 Kgs 20:14 הַמֶּלֶךְ (*hammelek*), "the king"; 1QIsaᵃ המלך.

u For the spelling of Hezekiah, see note c above.

v MT, 2 Kgs 20:14 וַיֹּאמֶר (*wayyōʾmer*), "and he said"; 1QIsaᵃ ויואמר.

w MT, 1QIsaᵇ, 4QIsaᵇ, and 2 Kgs 20:14 יָבֹאוּ (*yābōʾû*), "(from where)
did they come"; 1QIsaᵃ יבואו.

x MT, 1QIsaᵇ, 4QIsaᵇ and 2 Kgs 20:14 אֵלֶיךָ (*ʾēlêkā*), "to you";
1QIsaᵃ אליכה.

y MT and 2 Kgs 20:15 וַיֹּאמֶר (*wayyōʾmer*), "and he said"; 1QIsaᵃ
ויואמר.

z MT and 2 Kgs 20:15 בְּבֵיתֶךָ (*bĕbêtekā*), "in your house"; 1QIsaᵃ
בביתכה.

*a For the spelling of Hezekiah, see note c above.

*b See note m above.

*c See note o above.

*d MT and 1QIsaᵃ הֶרְאִיתִם (hirʾîtîm), "I showed them"; 2 Kgs 20:15 and 1QIsaᵇ הִרְאִיתָם (hirʾîtîm).

*e MT בְּאֹצְרֹתָי (bĕʾôṣĕrōtāy), "in my treasuries"; 2 Kgs 20:15 (bĕʾōṣĕrōtāy); 1QIsaᵃ באוצרותי.

*f For the spelling of Isaiah, see note r above.

*g See note y above.

*h See note *a above.

*i MT and 1QIsaᵃ יְהוָה צְבָאוֹת (YHWH ṣĕbāʾôt), "Yahweh of Hosts"; 2 Kgs 20:16 has only "Yahweh," omitting "of Hosts."

*j See note m above.

*k See note z above.

*l MT and 2 Kgs 20:17 אֲבֹתֶיךָ (ʾăbōtêkā), "your ancestors, fore-fathers"; 1QIsaᵃ אבותיכה.

*m MT and 1QIsaᵃ have the adverbial accusative בָּבֶל (bābel), "to Babylon"; 2 Kgs 20:17 and 4QIsaᵇ (from the traces) have the ה directive בָּבֶלָה (bābelāh), "to Babylon."

*n See note o above.

*o MT and 2 Kgs 20:18 וּמִבָּנֶיךָ (ûmibbānêkā), "and some of your sons"; 1QIsaᵃ ומבניכה.

*p MT, 2 Kgs 20:18, and 4QIsaᵇ מִמְּךָ (mimmĕkā), "from you"; 1QIsaᵃ ממעיכה (mimmēʿêkâ), "from your loins."

*q MT, 1QIsaᵃ, qĕrēʾ of 2 Kgs 20:18 יִקָּחוּ (yiqqāḥû), "they will take"; the kĕtîb of 2 Kgs 20:18 has יִקָּח (yiqqāḥ), "he will take"; 4QIsaᵇ's יקחי is just an error for יקחו.

*r MT, 2 Kgs 20:18, and 4QIsaᵇ וְהָיוּ (wĕhāyû), "and they will become"; 1QIsaᵃ ויהיו (wĕyihyû), "and they will become" or "that they may become."

*s See note c above.

*t See note y above.

*u See note r above.

*v MT and 2 Kgs 20:19 דִּבַּרְתָּ (dibbartā), "which you have spoken"; 1QIsaᵃ דברתה.

*w See note y above, though here 1QIsaᵃ must insert a correction above the line ויואמ.

*x MT כִּי יִהְיֶה שָׁלוֹם וֶאֱמֶת בְּיָמָי (kî yihyê šālôm weʾĕmet bĕyāmāy), "because there will be peace and stability in my days"; 1QIsaᵃ הלוא אם־שלום ואמת בימי; but 2 Kgs 20:19 has הֲלוֹא אִם־שָׁלוֹם וֶאֱמֶת יִהְיֶה בְּיָמָי (hălôʾ ʾim-šālôm weʾĕmet yihyê bĕyāmāy), "Why not, if there will be peace and stability in my days?"

Commentary

Merodach-baladan (Akk. Marduk-apla-iddina II, "Marduk-gave-an-heir"), a descendant of an earlier king of Babylonia, Eriba-Marduk, was the leader of the Chaldean tribe of Bit-Yakin and ruled Babylon twice. As "king of the Sealand," he paid tribute to Tiglath-pileser III around 729 BCE, but with the trouble in Assyria that led to the overthrow of Shalmaneser V, Merodach-baladan seized control of Babylon and ruled as the king of Babylon from 721 to 710 BCE, successfully repulsing Sargon II's attempt to recapture the south in 720. In 710, Sargon II finally succeeded in driving Merodach-baladan from Babylon, eventually capturing Merodach-baladan's tribal capital of Dur-Yakin in 707, when Merodach-baladan was forced to flee to Elam. After Sargon II's death in battle in 705 and the installation of Sennacherib as his successor on the throne of Assyria, however, Babylon again revolted, and Marduk-zakir-šumi II seized the throne. His reign was very brief, only one month, before Merodach-baladan returned with Elamite support, replaced Marduk-zakir-šumi II, and began his second reign over Babylon, which lasted nine months in 703 BCE. Sennacherib, in his first and second campaigns, drove Merodach-baladan from Babylon, sent forces to the marshes of the Sealand where Merodach-baladan had fled and taken refuge, and eventu-

ally chased him into Elamite territory, after which Mero-dach-baladan disappears from the historical record. In his own inscriptions, Merodach-baladan never mentions his actual father, just the earlier ancestor who had been king of Babylonia, Eriba-Marduk (whose rule of at least nine years ended before 760 BCE). The name the biblical text gives for Merodach-baladan's father is a shortened name, omitting the theophoric element [DN]-apla-iddina ("The god . . . gave an heir"), and in the absence of more evidence, one may doubt the reliability of this information.

According to our text, Merodach-baladan sent letters and a gift to Hezekiah when he heard that Hezekiah had been sick and had recovered (v. 1). Given Merodach-baladan's two distinct periods as king of Babylon and the dispute on the actual dates for the reign of Hezekiah, one cannot date this event with any real certainty. Nonetheless, having dated the beginning of Hezekiah's reign to 715 BCE, I am inclined to date this Babylonian embassy to Hezekiah to the year 703, during Merodach-baladan's second period of rule over Babylon. The embassy's ostensible purpose was to congratulate Hezekiah on the recovery from his illness, but its more fundamental, underlying goal was probably to confirm his continued participation in the anti-Assyrian league that included Babylonia, the Aramean and Chaldean tribes, the Arabs, and the Elamites to the east and south of Assyria, and the

488

Syrian-Palestinian states and Nubian Egypt in the west. Hezekiah's sickness, which must then have taken place sometime in the previous year or very early in 703, may have raised questions about Judah's continued participation in this endeavor, and Merodach-baladan was understandably concerned to maintain the strength of his western allies.

Hezekiah was happy over the arrival of the Babylonian envoys, and he showed them his treasury, the silver, gold, incense, and the fine oil in his storehouses, as well as his whole armory (v. 2). There was nothing, the text says, that he did not show them in his house and his whole kingdom. Such a tour of Judah's financial resources and of its cache of weaponry would be calculated to reassure the Babylonians of Judah's readiness to engage Assyria, their common enemy, militarily. Abundant financial resources and well-stocked armories have always been a major component for successful revolt against a strong military opponent.

Apparently after this Babylonian embassy left, Isaiah the prophet came to king Hezekiah and asked about them (v. 3). Isaiah wanted to know what these men said and from where they had come. It must have been apparent that they were foreigners, but the fact that Isaiah did not know who they were, what they wanted, or from where they had come suggests that Isaiah was being intentionally kept out of the diplomatic loop. Behind his questions to Hezekiah, then, lies Isaiah's complaint that Hezekiah's royal advisors were trying to hide their plans from God and refusing to consult the prophetic oracle, which, on one level, meant that Isaiah was no longer privy to to the deliberations of the inner circle of Hezekiah's advisors.[1] From the point of view of those advisors, Isaiah was too great a security risk. During the ticklish negotiations with the Philistine and Nubian delegates in 715–711 BCE, Isaiah had made an embarrassing public spectacle of his opposition to any plans for a mutual defense pact with Nubia and Philistia, a public spectacle that would have drawn the attention of any Assyrian agent in reasonable shouting distance of Jerusalem. Better that Isaiah not know these plans at all than risk alerting Assyrian

agents before the plans were finalized even if that meant forgoing the usual consultation of the prophetic oracle.

In response to Isaiah's question, Hezekiah, who after his recovery may have been more favorably inclined toward the prophet than some of his advisors, informs Isaiah that the men came from a distant land, from Babylonia. The prophet then asks what they saw in the palace, and Hezekiah goes on to say that he had showed them everything in his storehouses (v. 4). Isaiah, who was no dummy, immediately realized the military implications of this state visit and was clearly irritated by what he had learned, though he probably suspected as much before confronting Hezekiah. In response, he announces the word of Yahweh of Hosts to Hezekiah (v. 5). In days to come, he says, one will take away everything in your palace, including what your forefathers down to the present have stored there, and carry it off to Babylon. Not a thing will be left in your palace (v. 6), and, moreover, some of your own male descendants whom you engendered will be taken away and will become eunuchs in the palace of the king of Babylon (v. 7).

Strangely enough, Hezekiah seems to take this clearly negative oracle as a positive word. He tells the prophet that the word of Yahweh which the prophet spoke is good (v. 8). The last statement in v. 8 explains the logic by which the king reached this false conclusion. He thought—the verb אָמַר, "to speak," often has the sense, "to say to oneself, to think"—there will be peace and security in my days. Apparently Hezekiah reasoned that if Babylon and its king were still going to be on the throne in days to come, that must mean that the revolt against Assyria was going to succeed, and hence there would be peace and security for the rest of Hezekiah's reign. Obviously a later reader who knows about the Babylonian conquest of Jerusalem under Nebuchadnezzar II and the Babylonian exile of most of the Judean royal family can hardly read this account without thinking of the events of 597 and 586 BCE, but that does not mean this account was originally written after these events or originally referred to them. Hezekiah's assumption was that Merodach-baladan, his ally, would remain on the

---

1 See Isa 29:15; 30:1; 31:1; and my "Blindfolding the Prophet: Political Resistance to First Isaiah's Oracles in the Light of Ancient Near Eastern Attitudes toward Oracles," in Jean-Georges Heintz, ed., *Oracles et prophéties dans l'antiquité: Actes du Colloque de Strasbourg 15–17 juin 1995* (Travaux du Centre de recherche sur le Proche-Orient et la Grèce antiques 15; Paris: De Boccard, 1997) 135–46.

throne of Babylon. But what if the king of Babylon were no longer Merodach-baladan but the victorious Assyrian king, Sennacherib? The three preceding Assyrian kings, Tiglath-pileser III, Shalmaneser V, and Sargon II, had all claimed the title "king of Babylon" during parts of their reigns, when they controlled Babylon, and Isaiah may have assumed that Sennacherib would do the same when he reconquered the region. As it turned out, Sennacherib appointed first Bel-ibni (702–700 BCE), a native Babylonian, as king of Babylon, then his own son, Aššur-nadin-šumi (699–694 BCE), and finally Sennacherib took direct control of Babylon himself (688–681 BCE), though even then he never pretended to be a true king of Babylon. Nonetheless, Esarhaddon, Sennacherib's successor, did revert to the earlier practice of the Assyrian kings in claiming the title "king of Babylon" (680–669 BCE).

Bibliography

Ackroyd, P. R., "An Interpretation of the Babylonian Exile: 2 Kings 20, Isaiah 38–39," *SJT* 27 (1974) 329–52.

Allen, L. C., "Cuckoos in the Textual Nest at 2 Kings xx 13, Isa xlii 10, xlix 24, Ps xxii 17, and 2 Chron v 9," *JTS* 22 (1971) 143–50.

Begg, Christopher T., "2 Kings 20:12-19 as an Element of the Deuteronomistic History," *CBQ* 48 (1986) 27–38.

——, "Hezekiah's Display: Another Parallel," *BN* 41 (1988) 7–8.

——, "The Reading at 2 Kings xx 13," *VT* 36 (1986) 339–41.

Borger, R., "Merodach-Baladan," in *Biblisches-Historisches Handwörterbuch* (4 vols.; Göttingen: Vandenhoeck & Ruprecht, 1962–79) 2:1195.

Brinkmann, J. A., "Elamite Military Aid to Merodach-Baladan II," *JNES* 24 (1965) 161–66.

——, "Merodach-Baladan II," in R. D. Briggs and J. A. Brinkman, eds., *Studies Presented to A. Leo Oppenheim* (Chicago: Oriental Institute, 1964) 6–53.

——, "Notes on the Aramaeans and Chaldeans in Southern Babylonia in the Early Seventh Century B.C.," *Or* 46 (1977) 304–25.

Clements, R. E., "The Isaiah Narrative at 2 Kings 20:12-19 and the Date of the Deuteronomic History," in Alexander Rofé and Yair Zakovitch, eds., *Isac Leo Seeligmann Volume* (Jerusalem: Rubinstein, 1983) 209–20.

Crown, A. D., "Messengers and Scribes: The ספר and מלאך in the Old Testament," *VT* 24 (1974) 366–70.

Dietrich, Manfried, *Die Aramäer Südbabyloniens in der Sargonidenzeit (700–684)* (AOAT 7; Kevelaer: Butzon & Bercker, 1970).

Follet, R., "Une nouvelle inscription de Merodach-Baladan II," *Bib* 35 (1954) 413–28.

Gosse, Bernard, "Un texte pré-apocalyptique du règne de Darius: Isaïe 13:1–14:23," *RB* 92 (1985) 200–222.

Höffken, P. von, "Zur Eigenart von Jes 39 par 2 Reg 20:12-19," *ZAW* 110 (1998) 244–49.

Leemans, W. F., "Marduk-Apal-Iddina II, zijn Tijd en zijn Geslacht," *JEOL* 3 (1944) 432–55.

Levine, L. D., "Sennacherib's Southern Front: 704–689 B.C.," *JCS* 34 (1982) 28–58.

Mitchell, H. G., "Isaiah on the Fate of His People and the Capital," *JBL* 37 (1918) 149–62.

Moriarty, F. L., "Hezekiah, Isaiah, and Imperial Politics," *TBT* 19 (1965) 1270–76.

Ockinga, Boyo, "Hiskias 'Prahlerei,'" in Manfred Görg, ed., *Fontes atque pontes: Eine Festgabe für Hellmut Brunner* (AAT 5; Wiesbaden: Harrassowitz, 1983) 342–46.

Seitz, Christopher R., "Final Remarks: 2 Kings 20:12 and Isaiah 39:1-8," in Seitz, *Zion's Final Destiny: The Development of the Book of Isaiah. A Reassessment of Isaiah 36–39* (Minneapolis: Fortress Press, 1991) 182–91.

Vermeylen, J., "Hypothèses sur l'origine d'Isaïe 36–39," in van Ruiten and Vervenne, *Studies in the Book of Isaiah,* 95–118.

Ackroyd, Peter, "Isaiah I–XII: Presentation of a Prophet," in *Congress Volume: Göttingen 1977* (VTSup 29; Leiden: Brill, 1978) 16–48.

Alt, Albrecht, *Kleine Schriften zur Geschichte des Volkes Israel* (3 vols.; Munich: C. H. Beck, 1953–59; 3rd ed., 1964).

Anderson, Bernhard W., and Walter Harrelson, eds., *Israel's Prophetic Heritage: Essays in Honor of James Muilenburg* (New York: Harper, 1962).

Asurmendi, Jesús María, *La guerra siro-efraimita: Historia y profetas* (Institución San Jerónimo 13; Valencia: Institución San Jerónimo para la Investigación Biblica, 1982).

Auvray, Paul, *Isaïe 1–39* (SB; Paris: Gabalda, 1972).

Baer, D. A., "It's All about Us! Nationalistic Exegesis in the Greek Isaiah 1–12," in *SBLSP 2001* (Atlanta: Society of Biblical Literature, 2001) 197–219.

——, "With Due Respect: Speaking about God in LXX Isaiah," *AAR/SBL Abstracts 1998* (Atlanta: Scholars Press, 1998) 326.

Baillet, M., J. T. Milik, and R. de Vaux, eds., *Les "petites grottes" de Qumrân* (DJD 3; Oxford: Clarendon, 1962).

Balentine, S. E., and J. Barton, eds., *Language, Theologie, and the Bible* (Oxford: Clarendon, 1994).

Barnett, R. D., *The Sculptures of Aššur-nasir-apli II, 883–859 B.C., Tiglath-pileser III, 745–727 B.C., [and] Esarhaddon, 681–669 B.C., From the Central and South-West Palaces at Nimrud* (London: Trustees of the British Museum, 1962).

Barrick, W. Boyd, and John R. Spencer, eds., *In the Shelter of Elyon: Essays on Ancient Palestinian Life and Literature in Honor of G. W. Ahlström* (JSOTSup 31; Sheffield: JSOT Press, 1984).

Bartelt, Andrew H., *The Book around Immanuel: Style and Structure in Isaiah 2–12* (Biblical and Judaic Studies from the University of California, San Diego 4; Winona Lake, IN: Eisenbrauns, 1995).

Barth, Hermann, *Die Jesaja-Worte in der Josiazeit: Israel und Asshur als Thema einer Produktiven Neuinterpretation des Jesajaüberlieferung* (WMANT 48; Neukirchen-Vluyn: Neukirchener Verlag, 1977).

Barthel, Jörg, *Prophetenwort und Geschichte: Die Jesajaüberlieferung in Jes 6–8 und 28–31* (FAT 19; Tübingen: Mohr Siebeck, 1997).

Barthélemy, D., and J. T. Milik, *Qumran Cave 1* (DJD 1; Oxford: Clarendon, 1955).

Batto, Bernard F., and Kathryn L. Roberts, eds., *David and Zion: Biblical Studies in Honor of J. J. M. Roberts* (Winona Lake, IN: Eisenbrauns, 2004).

Beck, Astrid B., et al., eds., *Fortunate the Eyes That See: Essays in Honor of David Noel Freedman in Celebration of His Seventieth Birthday* (Grand Rapids: Eerdmans, 1995).

Becker, Joachim, *Isaias: Der Prophet und sein Buch* (SBS 30; Stuttgart: Katholisches Bibelwerk, 1968).

Becker, U., *Jesaja–Von der Botschaft zum Deuterojesaja* (BWANT 4.25; Stuttgart: Kohlhammer, 1938).

Beckman, Gary, *Hittite Diplomatic Texts* (WAW; Atlanta: Scholars Press, 1996).

Benoit, P., J. T. Milik, and R. de Vaux, eds., *Les grottes de Murabba'at* (DJD 2; Oxford: Clarendon, 1961).

Berges, U., *Das Buch Jesaja: Komposition und Endgestalt* (HBS 16; Freiburg: Herder, 1998).

Beuken, W. A. M., "Isa 30: A Prophetic Oracle Transmitted in Two Successive Paradigms," in C. Broyles and C. Evans, eds., *Writing and Reading the Scroll of Isaiah: Studies of an Interpretive Tradition* (2 vols.; VTSup 70; Leiden: Brill, 1997) 1:369–97.

——, *Jesaja 1–12* (HThKAT; Freiburg: Herder, 2003).

——, *Jesaja 13–27* (HThKAT; Freiburg: Herder, 2007).

——, *Jesaja 28–39* (HThKAT; Freiburg: Herder, 2010).

Bewer, J. A., *The Book of Isaiah*, vols. 3–4 of *Harper's Annotated Bible* (New York: Harper & Bros., 1950).

Blenkinsopp, Joseph, *Isaiah 1–39: A New Translation with Introduction and Commentary* (AB 19; New York: Doubleday, 2000).

Blum, E., et al., eds., *Die hebräische Bibel und ihre zweifache Nachgeschichte: Festschrift für Rolf Rendtorff zum 65. Geburtstag* (Neukirchen-Vluyn: Neukirchener Verlag, 1990).

Böhnke, M., and H. Heinz, eds., *Im Gespräch mit dem dreineinen Gott: Elemente einer trinitarischen Theologie. Festschrift für 65. Geburtstag von Wilhelm Breuning* (Düsseldorf: Patmos, 1985).

Borger, Riekele, *Die Inschriften Asarhaddons, Königs von Assyrien* (AfOB 9; Graz: E. Weidner, 1956).

Brock, S. P., ed., *Isaiah* (Old Testament in Syriac according to the Peshiṭta Version 3.1; Leiden: Brill, 1987).

———, "Text History and Text Division in Peshiṭta Isaiah," in *The Peshiṭta: Its Early Text and History. Papers Read at the "Peshiṭta Symposium" Held at Leiden 30-31 August, 1985* (ed. P. B. Dirksen and M. J. Mulder; Monographs of the Peshiṭta Institute, Leiden 4; Leiden: Brill, 1988) 49–80.

Brownlee, W. H., *The Meaning of the Qumran Scrolls for the Bible: With Special Attention to the Book of Isaiah* (New York: Oxford University Press, 1964).

Broyles, C. C., and C. A. Evans, eds., *Writing and Reading the Scroll of Isaiah: Studies of an Interpretive Tradition* (2 vols.; VTSup 70; Leiden: Brill, 1997).

Brunet, G., *Essai sur l'Isaïe de l'histoire: Études de quelques textes, notamment dans Is 7,8 et 22 (I. l'Emmanuel: II. le Siloé)* (Paris: A. & J. Picard, 1975).

Bruno, Arvid, *Jesaja: Eine rhythmische und textkritische Untersuchung* (Stockholm: Almqvist & Wiksell, 1953).

Budde, K., *Jesaja's Erleben: Eine gemeinverständliche Auslegung der Denkschrift des Propheten (Kap. 6:1–9:6)* (Gotha: Klotz, 1928).

Buhl, Frants, *Jesaja* (2nd ed.; Copenhagen: Gyldendal, 1912).

Burrows, Millar, "Variant Readings in the Isaiah Manuscript," *BASOR* 111 (1948–49) 16–24; 113 (1949) 24–32.

Burrows, Millar, et al., eds., *The Dead Sea Scrolls of St. Mark's Monastery*, vol. 1, *The Isaiah Manuscript and the Habakkuk Commentary* (New Haven: ASOR, 1950).

Carr, David M., "Reading Isaiah from Beginning (Isaiah 1) to End (Isaiah 65–66): Multiple Modern Possibilities," in Roy F. Melugin and Marvin A. Sweeney, eds., *New Visions of Isaiah* (JSOTSup 214; Sheffield: Sheffield Academic Press, 1996) 189–96.

Carrez, M., et al., eds., *De la torah au messie* (Paris: Desclée, 1981).

Chan, Michael, "Rhetorical Reversal and Usurpation: Isaiah 10:5-34 and the Use of Neo-Assyrian Royal Idiom in the Construction of an Anti-Assyrian Theology," *JBL* 128 (2009) 717–33.

Charlesworth, James H., ed., *The Bible and the Dead Sea Scrolls*, vol. 1, *Scripture and the Scrolls. The Second Princeton Symposium on Judaism and Christian Origins* (Waco, TX: Baylor University Press, 2006).

———, ed., *The Messiah: Developments in Earliest Judaism and Christianity. The First Princeton Symposium on Judaism and Christian Origins* (Minneapolis: Fortress Press, 1992).

Cheyne, T. K., *The Book of the Prophet Isaiah* (5th ed.; New York: Dodd, Mead, 1904).

Childs, Brevard S., *Isaiah* (OTL; Louisville: Westminster John Knox, 2001).

———, *Isaiah and the Assyrian Crisis* (SBT 2/3; Naperville, IL: Allenson, 1967).

———, *The Struggle to Understand Isaiah as Christian Scripture* (Grand Rapids: Eerdmans, 2004).

Chilton, Bruce D., *The Glory of Israel: The Theology and Provenience of the Isaiah Targum* (JSOTSup 23; Sheffield: JSOT Press, 1982).

———, *The Isaiah Targum: Introduction, Translation, Apparatus, and Notes* (ArBib 11; Wilmington, DE: Glazier, 1987).

Clements, Ronald E., *Isaiah 1–39* (NCB; Grand Rapids: Eerdmans, 1980).

———, *Isaiah and the Deliverance of Jerusalem: A Study of the Interpretation of Prophecy in the Old Testament* (JSOTSup 13; Sheffield: JSOT Press, 1980).

Cogan, Mordechai, and Hayim Tadmor, *II Kings: A New Translation with Introduction and Commentary* (AB 11; Garden City, NY: Doubleday, 1988).

Coggins, Richard, et al., eds., *Israel's Prophetic Tradition: Essays in Honour of Peter R. Ackroyd* (Cambridge: Cambridge University Press, 1982).

Cohen, C., "A Philological Reevaluation of Some Significant DSS Variants of the MT in Isa 1–5," in T. Muraoka and J. F. Elwolde, eds., *Diggers at the Well: Proceedings of a Third International Symposium on the Hebrew of the Dead Sea Scrolls and Ben Sira* (STDJ 36; Leiden: Brill, 2000) 40–55.

Cohen, Raymond, and Raymond Westbrook, eds., *Isaiah's Vision of Peace in Biblical and Modern International Relations: Swords into Plowshares* (Culture and Religion in International Relations; New York: Palgrave Macmillan, 2008).

Conrad, Edgar W., "Prophet, Redactor and Audience: Reforming the Notion of Isaiah's Formation," in Roy F. Melugin and Marvin A. Sweeney, eds., *New Visions of Isaiah* (JSOTSup 214; Sheffield: Sheffield Academic Press, 1996) 305–26.

——, *Reading Isaiah* (Overtures to Biblical Theology; Minneapolis: Fortress Press, 1991).

Conrad, Edgar W., and Edward G. Newing, eds., *Perspectives on Language and Text: Essays and Poems in Honor of Francis I. Andersen's Sixtieth Birthday, July 28, 1985* (Winona Lake, IN: Eisenbrauns, 1987).

Coppens, Joseph, "Le messianisme royal," *NRT* 90 (1968) 30–49, 82–85, 225–51, 479–512, 622–50, 834–63, 936–75 = *Le messianisme royal* (LD 54; Paris: Cerf, 1968).

Cross, Frank Moore, *Canaanite Myth and Hebrew Epic: Essays in the History of the Religion of Israel* (Cambridge, MA: Harvard University Press, 1973).

Cross, Frank Moore, et al., eds., *Scrolls from Qumran Cave I: The Great Isaiah Scroll, The Order of the Community, The Pesher to Habakkuk, from Photographs by John C. Trever* (Jerusalem: Albright Institute of Archaeological Research and the Shrine of the Book, 1972).

Dalman, Gustaf, *Arbeit und Sitte in Palästina* (7 vols.; Gütersloh: C. Bertelsmann, 1928–39).

Darr, Katheryn Pfisterer, *Isaiah's Vision and the Family of God* (Literary Currents in Biblical Interpretation; Louisville: Westminster John Knox, 1994).

De Roche, Michael, "Yahweh's *rîb* against Israel: A Reassessment of the So-Called 'Prophetic Lawsuit' in the Preexilic Prophets," *JBL* 102 (1983) 563–74.

Dearman, J. Andrew, *Property Rights in the Eighth-Century Prophets: The Conflict and Its Background* (SBLDS 106; Atlanta: Scholars Press, 1981).

Delitzsch, Franz, *Biblical Commentary on the Prophecies of Isaiah* (trans. James Martin; Grand Rapids: Eerdmans, 1949).

——, *Biblischer Commentar über den Propheten Jesaia* (Leipzig: Dörffling & Frank, 1869).

Diedrich, F., and B. Willmes, eds., *Ich bewirke das Heil und erschaffe das Unheil (Jesaja 45,7): Studien zur Botschaft der Propheten* (FB 88; Würzburg: Echter, 1998).

Dietrich, Walter, *Jesaja und die Politik* (BEvT 74; Munich: C. Kaiser, 1976).

Dillmann, August, *Der Prophet Jesaja* (5th ed.; Kurzgefasstes exegetisches Handbuch zum Alten Testament 5; Leipzig: S. Hirzel, 1890; 6th ed., rev. and ed. Rudolf Kittel, 1898).

Dobbs-Allsopp, F. W., J. J. M. Roberts, C. L. Seow, and R. E. Whitaker, eds., *Hebrew Inscriptions: Texts from the Biblical Period of the Monarchy with Concordance* (New Haven: Yale University Press, 2005).

Döderlein, J. C., *Esaias, ex recensione textus Hebraei* (Altorfi, 1789).

Donner, Herbert, *Israel unter den Völkern: Die Stellung der klassischen Propheten des 8. Jahrhunderts v. Chr. zur Aussenpolitik der Könige von Israel und Juda* (VTSup 11; Leiden: Brill, 1964).

Driver, G. R., "Hebrew Notes," *VT* 1 (1951) 241–50.

——, "Hebrew Notes on Prophets and Proverbs," *JTS* 41 (1940) 162–75.

——, "Isaiah 1–39: Textual and Linguistic Problems," *JSS* 13 (1968) 36–57.

——, "Isaianic Problems," in G. Wiesner, ed., *Festschrift für Wilhelm Eilers* (Wiesbaden: Harrassowitz, 1967) 43–57.

——, "Linguistic and Textual Problems: Isaiah I–XXXIX," *JTS* 38 (1937) 36–50.

Driver, S. R., *Isaiah: His Life and Times and the Writings Which Bear His Name* (New York: Randolph, 1883).

493

Duhm, Bernhard, *Das Buch Jesaia* (3rd ed.; HKAT 3.1; Göttingen: Vandenhoeck & Ruprecht, 1914).

Durand, Jean-Marie, *Archives épistolaires de Mari 1/1* (Archives royales de Mari 26; Paris: Editions Recherche sur les civilisations, 1988).

Eaton, J. H., "The Origin of the Book of Isaiah," *VT* 9 (1959) 138–57.

Ehrlich, Arnold B., *Randglossen zur hebräischen Bibel, textkritisches, sprachliches und sachliches,* vol. 4, *Jesaia, Jeremia* (Leipzig: Hinrichs, 1912).

Eichrodt, Walther, *Der Heilige in Israel: Jesaja 1–12* (BAT 17.1; Stuttgart: Calwer, 1960).

———, *Der Herr der Geschichte: Jesaja 13–23 und 28–39* (BAT 17.2; Stuttgart: Calwer, 1967).

Erlandsson, S., *The Burden of Babylon: A Study of Isaiah 13:2–14:23* (ConBOT 4; Lund: Gleerup, 1970).

Eusebius Pamphili of Caesaria, *Der Jesajakommentar,* vol. 9 of *Eusebius Werke* (ed. J. Ziegler; Berlin: Akademie, 1975).

Exum, J. Cheryl, and H. G. M. Williamson, eds., *Reading from Right to Left: Essays on the Hebrew Bible in Honour of David J. A. Clines* (JSOTSup 373; London: Sheffield Academic Press, 2003).

Fales, F. M., and J. N. Postgate, *Imperial Administrative Records, Part II* (SAA 11; Helsinki: Helsinki University Press, 1995).

Feldmann, Franz, *Das Buch Isaias* (2 vols.; EHAT 14; Münster: Aschendorff, 1925–26).

Fey, R., *Amos und Jesaja: Abhängigkeit und Eigenständigkeit des Jesaja* (WMANT 12; Neukirchen-Vluyn: Neukirchener Verlag, 1963).

Field, F., *Origenis Hexaplorum quae supersunt,* vol. 2 (1875; repr., Oxford: Oxford University Press, 1964).

Fischer, Johann, *In welcher Schrift lag das Buch Isaias den LXX vor?* (BZAW 56; Giessen: A. Töpelmann, 1930).

Flint, Peter W., "The Book of Isaiah in the Dead Sea Scrolls," in Edward D. Herbert and Emanuel Tov, eds., *The Bible as Book: The Hebrew Bible and the Judaean Desert Discoveries* (London: British Library, 2002) 229–51.

———, "The Isaiah Scrolls from the Judean Desert," in C. C. Broyles and C. A. Evans, eds., *Writing and Reading the Scroll of Isaiah: Studies of an Interpretive Tradition* (2 vols.; VTSup 70; Leiden: Brill, 1997) 2:481–89.

Flint, P. W., E. Ulrich, and M. G. Abegg, *Qumran Cave 1.II: The Isaiah Scrolls* (2 vols.; DJD 32; Oxford: Clarendon, 2010).

Fohrer, Georg, *Das Buch Jesaja* (3 vols.; ZBK; Zurich: Zwingli, 1960–64; 2nd ed., 1962–67).

———, "Neue Literatur zur alttestamentlichen Prophetie," *TRu* 45 (1980) 1–39, 108–15.

———, *Studien zur alttestamentlichen Prophetie (1949–1965)* (BZAW 99; Berlin: A. Töpelmann, 1967).

———, *Die symbolischen Handlungen der Propheten* (ATANT 25; Zurich: Zwingli, 1953; 2nd ed., 1968).

Frame, Grant, "The Inscription of Sargon II at Tang-i Var," *Or* 68 (1999) 31–37.

———, *Rulers of Babylonia: From the Second Dynasty of Isin to the End of Assyrian Domination (1157–612 BC)* (RIMB 2; Toronto: University of Toronto Press, 1995).

Franklin, N., "The Room V Reliefs at Dur-Sharruken and Sargon II's Western Campaigns," *TA* 21 (1994) 255–75.

Fuchs, Andreas, *Die Annalen des Jahres 711 v. Chr. nach Prismenfragmenten aus Ninive und Assur* (SAAS 8; Helsinki: Neo-Assyrian Text Corpus Project, 1998).

———, *Die Inschriften Sargons II. aus Khorsabad* (Göttingen: Cuvillier, 1994).

Gallagher, William R., *Sennacherib's Campaign to Judah: New Studies* (SHCANE 18; Leiden: Brill, 1999).

García Martínez, F., "Le livre d'Isaïe à Qomrân: Les textes, l'influence," *MdB* 49 (1987) 43–45.

Gelston, A., "Was the Peshitta of Isaiah of Christian Origin?" in C. C. Broyles and C. A. Evans, eds., *Writing and Reading the Scroll of Isaiah: Studies of an Interpretive Tradition* (2 vols.; VTSup 70; Leiden: Brill, 1997) 2:563–82.

Gesenius, Wilhelm, *Hebräisches und aramäisches Handwörterbuch über das Alte Testament* (18th ed.; Berlin: Springer, 1987).

——, *Der Prophet Jesaia* (Leipzig: Vogel, 1829).

Gitay, Yehoshua, *Isaiah and His Audience: The Structure and Meaning of Isaiah 1–12* (SSN 30; Assen: Van Gorcum, 1991).

Goedicke, H., ed., *Near Eastern Studies in Honor of William Foxwell Albright* (Baltimore: Johns Hopkins Press, 1971).

Gonçalves, F. J., "Isaiah Scroll," *ABD* 3:470–72.

Gordon, Robert P., *Hebrew Bible and Ancient Versions: Selected Essays of Robert P. Gordon* (SOTSMS; Aldershot: Ashgate, 2006).

——, *"The Place Is Too Small for Us": The Israelite Prophets in Recent Scholarship* (Sources for Biblical and Theological Study 5; Winona Lake, IN: Eisenbrauns, 1995).

Goshen-Gottstein, Moshe H., ed., *The Book of Isaiah* (Hebrew University Bible; Jerusalem: Magnes Press, Hebrew University, 1995).

——, "Die Jesaja Rolle und das Problem der hebräischen Bibelhandschriften," *Bib* 35 (1954) 429–42.

Gottwald, N. K., *All the Kingdoms of the Earth: Israelite Prophecy and International Relations in the Ancient Near East* (New York: Harper & Row, 1964).

Gray, George Buchanan, *A Critical and Exegetical Commentary on the Book of Isaiah I–XXXIX* (ICC; Edinburgh: T&T Clark, 1912).

Gray, John, *The Canaanites* (New York: Praeger, 1964).

Grayson, A. Kirk, *Assyrian and Babylonian Chronicles* (TCS 5; Locust Valley, NY: J. J. Augustin, 1975).

Grayson, A. Kirk, and Jamie Novotny, *The Royal Inscriptions of Sennacherib, King of Assyria (704–681), Part 1* (RINAP 3.1; Winona Lake, IN: Eisenbrauns, 2012).

——, *The Royal Inscriptions of Sennacherib, King of Assyria (704–681 BC), Part 2* (RINAP 3.2; Winona Lake, IN: Eisenbrauns, 2014).

Gressmann, Hugo, *Der Messias* (FRLANT 43; Göttingen: Vandenhoeck & Ruprecht, 1929).

Gryson, R., "Esaias," in *Vetus Latina Beuron 12* (Freiburg im Br.: Herder, 1987).

Guthe, Hermann, *Jesaja* (Tübingen: Mohr, 1907).

Hardmeier, Christof, "Verkündigung und Schrift bei Jesaja: Zur Entstehung der Schriftprophetie als Oppositionsliteratur im alten Israel," *TGI* 73 (1983) 119–34.

Harvey, Julien, *Le plaidoyer prophétique contre Israël après la rupture de l'alliance* (Bruges: Desclee de Brouwer, 1967).

——, "Le 'Rib-Pattern': Réquisitoire prophétique sur la rupture de l'alliance," *Bib* 43 (1962) 172–96.

Hausmann, Jutta, and Hans-Jürgen Zogel, eds., *Alttestamentlicher Glaube und biblische Theologie: Festschrift für Horst Dietrich Preuss zum 65. Geburtstag* (Stuttgart: Kohlhammer, 1992).

Hayes, John H., and Stuart A. Irvine, *Isaiah, the Eighth-Century Prophet: His Times and His Preaching* (Nashville: Abingdon, 1987).

Herbert, A. S., *The Book of the Prophet Isaiah, Chapters 1–39* (CBC; Cambridge: Cambridge University Press, 1973).

Herntrich, Volkmar, *Der Prophet Jesaja: Kapitel 1–12* (ATD 17; Göttingen: Vandenhoeck & Ruprecht, 1950).

Hertzberg, Hans Wilhelm, *Der Erste Jesaja* (3rd ed.; Leipzig: Schloessmann, 1955).

Hillers, Delbert R., *Covenant: The History of a Biblical Idea* (Seminars in the History of Ideas; Baltimore: Johns Hopkins Press, 1969).

Hitzig, Ferdinand, *Der Prophet Jesaja* (Heidelberg: Winter, 1833).

Hoffmann, H. W., *Die Intention der Verkündigung Jesajas* (BZAW 136; Berlin: de Gruyter, 1974).

Høgenhaven, Jesper, *Gott und Volk bei Jesaja: Eine Untersuchung zur biblischen Theologie* (ATDan 24; Leiden: Brill, 1988).

Holladay, W. L., *Isaiah: Scroll of a Prophetic Heritage* (Grand Rapids: Eerdmans, 1978).

Huffmon, H. B., "The Covenant Lawsuit in the Prophets," *JBL* 78 (1959) 285–95.

——, et al., eds., *The Quest for the Kingdom of God: Studies in Honor of George E. Mendenhall* (Winona Lake, IN: Eisenbrauns, 1983).

Ibn Ezra (Abraham ben Meir), *Commentary of Ibn Ezra on Isaiah* (in Hebrew; trans. M. Friedlander; 2nd ed.; New York: Feldheim, 1966).

Irvine, Stuart A., *Isaiah, Ahaz, and the Syro-Ephraimitic Crisis* (SBLDS 123; Atlanta: Scholars Press, 1990).

Irwin, William Henry, *Isaiah 28–33: Translation with Philological Notes* (BibOr 30; Rome: Biblical Institute Press, 1977).

Jacobson, Rolf A., "A Rose by Any Other Name: Iconography and the Interpretation of Isaiah 28:1-6," in Martti Nissinen and Charles E. Carter, eds., *Images and Prophecy in the Ancient Eastern Mediterranean* (FRLANT 233; Göttingen: Vandenhoeck & Ruprecht, 2009) 125–46.

James, F. D., "A Critical Examination of the Text of Isaiah" (PhD diss., Boston University, 1959).

Janzen, Waldemar, *Mourning Cry and Woe Oracle* (BZAW 125; Berlin: de Gruyter, 1972).

Jensen, Joseph, *Isaiah 1–39* (OTM 8; Wilmington, DE: Michael Glazier, 1984).

——, *The Use of tôrâ by Isaiah: His Debate with the Wisdom Tradition* (CBQMS 3; Washington, DC: Catholic Biblical Association of America, 1973).

Jerome, *Commentaires de Jerome sur le prophete Isaie* (ed. R. Gryson and P.-A. Deproost; Aus der Geschichte der lateinischen Bibel 23, 27, 30, 35, 36; Freiburg: Herder, 1993–).

Joüon, P., and T. Muraoka, *A Grammar of Biblical Hebrew* (2 vols.; SubBib 14; Rome: Pontifical Biblical Institute, 1993).

Kaiser, Otto, *Isaiah 1–12* (trans. R. A. Wilson; 2nd ed.; OTL; Philadelphia: Westminster, 1983).

——, *Isaiah 13–39* (trans. R. A. Wilson; 2nd ed.; OTL; Philadelphia: Westminster, 1983).

——, *Der Prophet Jesaja: Kapitel 1–12* (2nd ed.; ATD 17; Göttingen: Vandenhoeck & Ruprecht, 1963).

——, *Der Prophet Jesaja: Kapitel 13–39* (ATD 18; Göttingen: Vandenhoeck & Ruprecht, 1973).

Katzenstein, H. J., *The History of Tyre, from the Beginning of the Second Millennium B.C.E. until the Fall of the Neo-Babylonian Empire in 539 B.C.E.* (2nd rev. ed.; Beer Sheva: Ben-Gurion University of the Negev Press, 1997).

Kautzsch, E., and A. E. Cowley, eds., *Gesenius' Hebrew Grammar* (2nd ed.; Oxford: Clarendon, 1910; repr., 1988).

Keel, Othmar, *Jahwe-Visionen und Siegelkunst: Eine neue Deutung der Majestätsschilderungen in Jes 6, Ez 1 und Sach 5* (SBS 84/85; Stuttgart: Katholisches Bibelwerk, 1977).

Kelle, Brad E., and Megan Bishop Moore, eds., *Israel's Prophets and Israel's Past: Essays on the Relationship of Prophetic Texts and Israelite History in Honor of John H. Hayes* (LHBOTS 446; New York: T&T Clark, 2006).

Kelley, P. H., "Isaiah," in *The Broadman Bible Commentary* (ed. Clifton J. Allen et al.; 12 vols.; Nashville: Broadman, 1969–72) 5:149–374.

Kilian, Rudolf, *Jesaja 1–12* (NEchtB 17; Würzburg: Echter, 1986).

——, *Jesaja 1–39* (EdF 200; Darmstadt: Wissenschaftliche Buchgesellschaft, 1983).

——, *Jesaja II: 13–39* (NEchtB 32; Würzburg: Echter, 1994).

Kimchi, David, *The Commentary of David Kimchi on Isaiah* (in Hebrew with introduction in English; ed. L. Finkelstein; Columbia University Oriental Studies 19; New York: Columbia University Press, 1926; repr., New York: AMS Press, 1966).

King, Philip J., and Lawrence E. Stager, *Life in Biblical Israel* (Library of Ancient Israel; Louisville: Westminster John Knox, 2001).

Kissane, Edward J., *The Book of Isaiah* (rev. ed.; 2 vols.; Dublin: Browne & Nolan, 1960).

Kitchen, K. A., *The Third Intermediate Period in Egypt, 1100–650 B.C.* (2nd ed. with suppl.; Warminster: Aris & Phillips, 1986; 3rd ed., 1995).

Koch, Christoph, *Vertrag, Treueid, und Bund: Studien zur Rezeption des altorientalischen Vertragsrechts im Deuteronomium und zur Ausbildung der Bundestheologie im Alten Testament* (BZAW 383; Berlin: de Gruyter, 2008).

König, Eduard, *Das Buch Jesaja* (Gütersloh: Bertelsmann, 1926).

Kooij, Arie van der, *Die alten Textzeugen des Jesajabuches* (OBO 35; Freiburg: Universitätsverlag; Göttingen: Vandenhoeck & Ruprecht, 1981).

———, "Interpretation of the Book of Isaiah in the Septuagint and Other Ancient Versions," in *SBLSP 2001* (Atlanta: Society of Biblical Literature, 2001) 220–39.

———, "Isaiah in the Septuagint," in C. C. Broyles and C. A. Evans, eds., *Writing and Reading the Scroll of Isaiah: Studies of an Interpretive Tradition* (2 vols.; VTSup 70; Leiden: Brill, 1997) 2:513–29.

———, "The Old Greek of Isaiah in Relation to the Qumran Texts of Isaiah: Some General Comments," in G. J. Brooke and B. Lindars, eds., *Septuagint, Scrolls and Cognate Writings: Papers Presented to the International Symposium on the Septuagint and Its Relations to the Dead Sea Scrolls and Other Writings, Manchester, 1990* (SCS 33; Atlanta: Scholars Press, 1992) 195–213.

———, "The Septuagint of Isaiah: Translation and Interpretation," in J. Vermeylen et al., eds., *Le livre d'Isaïe: Les oracles et leurs relectures unité et complexité de l'ouvrage* (BETL 81; Leuven: Leuven University Press, 1989) 127–33.

Kooij, Arie van der, and M. van der Meer, eds., *The Old Greek of Isaiah: Issues and Perspectives. Papers Read at the Conference on the Septuagint of Isaiah, Held in Leiden 10-11 April 2008* (CBET 55; Leuven: Peeters, 2010).

Kutsche, Ernst, *Verheissung und Gesetz: Untersuchung zum sogenannten "Bund" im Alten Testament* (BZAW 131; Berlin: de Gruyter, 1973).

Kutscher, E. Y., *The Language and Linguistic Background of the Isaiah Scroll (1QIsaᵃ)* (STDJ 6; Leiden: Brill, 1974).

Laato, Antti, *A Star Is Rising: The Historical Development of the Old Testament Royal Ideology and the Rise of the Jewish Messianic Expectations* (University of South Florida International Studies in Formative Christianity and Judaism 5; Atlanta: Scholars Press, 1997).

———, *Who Is Immanuel? The Rise and the Foundering of Isaiah's Messianic Expectations* (Åbo: Åbo Academy Press, 1988).

Laberge, Léo, *La Septante d'Isaïe 28–33: Étude de tradition textuelle* (Ottawa: L. Laberge, 1978).

Lack, Rémi, *La symbolique de livre d'Isaïe: Essai sur l'image littéraire comme élément de structuration* (AnBib 59; Rome: Biblical Institute Press, 1973).

Leichty, Erle, *The Royal Inscriptions of Esarhaddon, King of Assyria (680–669 BC)* (RINAP 4; Winona Lake, IN: Eisenbrauns, 2011).

Leslie, Elmer Archibald, *Isaiah, Chronologically Arranged, Translated and Interpreted* (New York: Abingdon, 1963).

Limburg, James, "The Root *rîb* and the Prophetic Lawsuit Speeches," *JBL* 88 (1969) 291–304.

Lindblom, Johannes, *A Study on the Immanuel Section in Isaiah: Isa. vii, 1–ix, 6* (Scripta Minora Regiae Societatis Humaniorum Litterarum Lundensis 4; Lund: Gleerup, 1957).

Loretz, Oswald, *Der Prolog des Jesaja Buches (1, 1–2, 5): Ugaritologische und kolometrische Studien zum Jesaja-Buch* (UBL 1; Altenberg: CIS-Verlag, 1984).

Luckenbill, Daniel David, *The Annals of Sennacherib* (OIP 2; Chicago: University of Chicago Press, 1924).

Luther, Martin, *Lectures on Isaiah Chs. 1–39*, vol. 16 of *Luther's Works* (ed. and trans. J. Pelikan and H. C. Oswald; St. Louis: Concordia, 1969).

———, *Der Prophet Jesaia*, vols. 25, 31.2 of *D. Martin Luthers Werke* (Kritische Gesamtausgabe 25; Weimar: H. Böhlau, 1883) 87–401.

Luzzatto, S. D., *Commentary on the Book of Isaiah* (in Hebrew; 1855; repr., Tel Aviv: Davir, 1970).

———, *Il profeta Isaia volgarizzato e commentato ad uso degli'Israelit* (Padua: A. Bianchi, 1867).

Machinist, Peter, "Assyria and Its Image in the First Isaiah," *JAOS* 103 (1982) 719–37.

Macpherson, Ann, *Prophets* (Scripture Discussion Commentary 2, 4; London: Sheed & Ward, 1971–72).

Marti, D. Karl, *Das Buch Jesaja* (KHC 10; Tübingen: Mohr Siebeck, 1900).

Mauchline, John, *Isaiah 1–39: Introduction and Commentary* (TBC; London: SCM, 1962).

McCarthy, Dennis J., *Treaty and Covenant: A Study in Form in the Ancient Oriental Documents and in the Old Testament* (AnBib 21; Rome: Pontifical Biblical Institute, 1963; rev. ed., 1978).

Meer, M. N. van der, et al., eds., *Isaiah in Context: Studies in Honour of Arie van der Kooij on the Occasion of His Sixty-fifth Birthday* (VTSup 138; Leiden: Brill, 2010).

Melugin, Roy F., and Marvin A. Sweeney, eds., *New Visions of Isaiah* (JSOTSup 214; Sheffield: Sheffield Academic Press, 1996).

Mendenhall, George E., "Ancient Oriental and Biblical Law," *BA* 17 (1954) 26–46.

——, "Covenant Forms in Israelite Tradition," *BA* 17 (1954) 50–76.

Metzger, Martin, *Königsthron und Gottesthron: Thronformen und Throndarstellungen im Ägypten und im Vorderen Orient im dritten und zweiten Jahrtausend vor Christus und deren Bedeutung für das Verständnis von Aussagen über den Thron im Alten Testament* (2 vols.; AOAT 15.1–2; Kevelaer: Butzon & Bercker; Neukirchen-Vluyn: Neukirchener Verlag, 1985).

Millard, Alan, *The Eponyms of the Assyrian Empire 910–612 B.C.* (SAAS 2; Helsinki: Neo-Assyrian Text Corpus Project, 1994).

Motyer, J. Alec, *The Prophecy of Isaiah: An Introduction and Commentary* (Downers Grove, IL: InterVarsity, 1993).

Mowinckel, Sigmund, *He That Cometh: The Messiah Concept in the Old Testament and Later Judaism* (Nashville: Abingdon, 1956).

——, "Die Komposition des Jesajabuches Kap. 1–39," *AcOr* 11 (1933) 267–92.

Nägelsbach, C. W. E., *Der Prophet Jesaja* (Leipzig: Klasing, 1877).

Neves, Joaquim Carreira Marcelino das, *A teologia da tradução grega dos setenta no livro de Isaías: (cap. 24 de Isaías)* (Lisbon: Universidade Católica Portuguesa, 1973).

Nielsen, Kirsten, *Yahweh as Prosecutor and Judge: An Investigation of the Prophetic Lawsuit (Rîb-Pattern)* (JSOTSup 9; Sheffield: Department of Biblical Studies, University of Sheffield, 1978).

O'Connell, Robert H., *Concentricity and Continuity: The Literary Structure of Isaiah* (JSOTSup 188; Sheffield: Sheffield Academic Press, 1994).

Ollenburger, Ben C., *Zion, the City of the Great King: A Theological Symbol of the Jerusalemite Cult* (JSOTSup 41; Sheffield: JSOT Press, 1987).

Olley, J. W., "Hear the Word of JHWH: The Structure of the Book of Isaiah in 1QIsaᵃ," *VT* 43 (1993) 19–49.

Olyan, Saul M., and Robert C. Culley, eds., *"A Wise and Discerning Mind": Essays in Honor of Burke O. Long* (BJS 325; Providence, RI: Brown Judaic Studies, 2000).

Oswalt, John N., *The Book of Isaiah, Chapters 1–39* (NICOT; Grand Rapids: Eerdmans, 1986).

Otte, Marianne, *Der Begriff berît in der jüngeren alttestamentlichen Forschung: Aspekte der Forschungsgeschichte unter besonderer Berücksichtigung der semantischen Fragestellung bei Ernst Kutsch* (Frankfurt am Main: P. Lang, 2005).

Parry, D. W., and E. Qimron, eds., *The Great Isaiah Scroll (1QIsaᵃ): A New Edition* (STDJ 32; Leiden: Brill, 1999).

Perlitt, Lothar, *Bundestheologie im Alten Testament* (WMANT 36; Neukirchen-Vluyn: Neukirchener Verlag, 1969).

Porter, S. L., and B. W. R. Pearson, "Isaiah through Greek Eyes: The Septuagint of Isaiah," in C. C. Broyles and C. A. Evans, eds., *Writing and Reading the Scroll of Isaiah: Studies of an Interpretive Tradition* (2 vols.; VTSup 70; Leiden: Brill, 1997) 2:531–46.

Postma, F., et al., eds., *The New Things: Eschatology in Old Testament Prophecy. Festschrift for Henk Leene* (ACBETSup 3; Maastricht: Shaker, 2002).

Procksch, Otto, *Jesaia I übersetzt und erklärt* (KAT 9.1; Leipzig: A. Deichert, 1930).

Rahlfs, A., ed., *Septuaginta* (9th ed.; Stuttgart: Württembergische Bibelanstalt, 1935).

Rainey, Anson F., and R. Steven Notley, *The Sacred Bridge: Carta's Atlas of the Biblical World* (Jerusalem: Carta, 2006) 233.

Reid, Stephen B., ed., *Prophets and Paradigms: Essays in Honor of Gene M. Tucker* (JSOTSup 229; Sheffield: Sheffield Academic Press, 1996).

Rignell, L. G., "Isaiah Chapter I: Some Exegetical Remarks with Special Reference to the Relationship between the Text and the Book of Deuteronomy," *ST* 11 (1957) 140–58.

Roberts, B. J., "The Second Isaiah Scroll from Qumran (1QIsaᵃ)," *BJRL* 42 (1959) 132–44.

Roberts, J. J. M., *The Bible and the Ancient Near East: Collected Essays* (Winona Lake, IN: Eisenbrauns, 2002).

——, "The Davidic Origin of the Zion Tradition," *JBL* 92 (1973) 329–44.

——, "Double Entendre in First Isaiah," *CBQ* 54 (1992) 39–48.

——, "Egypt, Assyria, Isaiah, and the Ashdod Affair: An Alternative Proposal," in Andrew G. Vaughn and Ann E. Killebrew, *Jerusalem in Bible and Archaeology: The First Temple Period* (SBLSymS 18; Atlanta: Society of Biblical Literature, 2003) 265–83.

——, "Egyptian and Nubian Oracles," in Brad E. Kelle and Megan Bishop Moore, eds., *Israel's Prophets and Israel's Past: Essays on the Relationship of Prophetic Texts and Israelite History in Honor of John H. Hayes* (LHBOTS 446; New York: T&T Clark, 2006) 201–9.

——, "Form, Syntax and Redaction in Isaiah 1:2-20," *PSB* 3 (1982) 293–306.

——, "The Importance of Isaiah at Qumran," in James H. Charlesworth, ed., *The Bible and the Dead Sea Scrolls: The Princeton Symposium on the Dead Sea Scrolls* (Scripture and the Scrolls 1; Waco, TX: Baylor University Press, 2006), 273–86.

——, "Isaiah, National Security, and the Politics of Fear," in Robert Jewett, ed., *The Bible and the American Future* (Eugene, OR: Cascade, 1009) 72–91.

——, "Prophets and Kings: A New Look at the Royal Persecution of Prophets against Its Near Eastern Background," in B. A. Strawn and N. R. Bowen, eds., *A God So Near: Essays on Old Testament Theology in Honor of Patrick D. Miller* (Winona Lake, IN: Eisenbrauns, 2003) 341–54.

——, "Public Opinion, Royal Apologetics, and Imperial Ideology: A Political Analysis of the Portrait of David, A Man after God's Own Heart," *Theology Today* 69 (2012) 1–17.

——, "The Rod That Smote Philistia: Isaiah 14:28-32," in David S. Vanderhooft and Abraham Winitzer, eds., *Literature as Politics, Politics as Literature: Essays on the Ancient Near East in Honor of Peter Machinist* (Winona Lake, IN: Eisenbrauns, 2013) 381–95.

——, "Security and Justice in Isaiah," *Stone-Campbell Journal* 13 (2010) 71–79.

——, "Solomon's Jerusalem and the Zion Tradition," in A. G. Vaughn and A. F. Killebrew, eds., *Jerusalem in Bible and Archaeology: The First Temple Period* (SBLSymS 18; Atlanta: Society of Biblical Literature, 2003) 163–70.

——, "Whose Child Is This? Reflections on the Speaking Voice in Isaiah 9:5," *HTR* 90 (1997) 115–29.

——, "Yahweh's Foundation in Zion (Isaiah 28:16)," *JBL* 106 (1987) 27–45; reprinted in *The Bible and the Ancient Near East: Collected Essays* (Winona Lake, IN: Eisenbrauns, 2002) 292–310.

——, "Zion in the Theology of the Davidic Solomonic Empire," in W. H. Ishida, ed., *Studies in the Period of David and Solomon and Other Essays: Papers Read at the International Symposium for Biblical Studies, Tokyo, 5–7 December 1979* (Tokyo: Yamakawa-Shuppansha; Winona Lake, IN: Eisenbrauns, 1982) 93–108.

Rohland, Edzard, "Die Bedeutung der Erwählungstraditionen Israels für die Eschatologie der alttestamentlichen Propheten" (PhD diss., Heidelberg, 1956).

Rubinstein, A., "The Theological Aspect of Some Variant Readings in the Isaiah Scroll," *JJS* 6 (1955) 187–200.

Ruiten, J. van, and M. Vervenne, eds., *Studies in the Book of Isaiah: Festschrift Willem A. M. Beuken* (BETL 132; Leuven: Leuven University Press/ Peeters, 1997).

Schoors, Antoon, *Jesaja* (De boeken van het Oude Testament; Roermond: J. J. Romen & Zonen, 1972).

Schunck, K.-D., and M. Augustin, eds., *Goldene Äpfel in silbernen Schalen: Collected Communications to the XIIIth Congress of the International Organization for the Study of the Old Testament, Leuven 1989* (BEATAJ 20; Frankfurt am Main: P. Lang, 1992).

Schweitzer, S. J., "Mythology in the Old Greek of Isaiah: The Technique of Translation," *CBQ* 66 (2004) 214–30.

Scott, R. B. Y., "The Book of Isaiah," in George A. Buttrick et al., eds., *The Interpreter's Bible* (12 vols.; Nashville: Abingdon, 1956) 5:149–381.

Seeligmann, Isac Leo, *The Septuagint Version of Isaiah: A Discussion of Its Problems* (Leiden: Brill, 1948).

———, *The Septuagint Version of Isaiah and Cognate Studies* (ed. R. Hanhart and H. Spieckermann; FAT 40; Tübingen: Mohr Siebeck, 2004).

Seitz, Christopher R., *Isaiah 1–39* (IBC; Louisville: John Knox, 1993).

Simons, J., *The Geographical and Topographical Texts of the Old Testament* (Studia Francisci Scholten memoriae dicata 2; Leiden: Brill, 1959).

Skehan, Patrick W., "Some Textual Problems in Isaiah," *CBQ* 22 (1960) 47–55.

———, "The Text of Isaias at Qumrân," *CBQ* 17 (1955) 158–63.

Skehan, P. W., and E. Ulrich, "Isaiah," in E. Ulrich et al., eds., *Qumran Cave 4.X: The Prophets* (DJD 15; Oxford: Clarendon, 1997).

Skilton, John H., ed., *The Law and the Prophets: Old Testament Studies Prepared in Honor of Oswald Thompson Allis* (Nutley, NJ: Presbyterian and Reformed, 1974).

Snijders, L. A., *Jesaja*, vol. 1 (2nd ed.; De Prediking van het Oude Testament; Nijkerk: Callenbach, 1979).

Sperber, A., ed., *The Bible in Aramaic*, vol. 3, *The Latter Prophets according to Targum Jonathan* (Leiden: Brill, 1962).

Stager, Lawrence E., "Jerusalem and the Garden of Eden," *ErIsr* 26 (1999) 183*–94.*

———, "Jerusalem as Eden," *BAR* 26, no. 3 (2000) 36–47.

Stager, Lawrence E., et al., eds., *Ashkelon 1: Introduction and Overview (1985–2006)* (Leon Levy Expedition to Ashkelon; Winona Lake, IN: Eisenbrauns, 2008).

Stansell, Gary, "Isaiah 32: Creative Redaction in the Isaian Traditions," in *SBLSP 1983* (Chico, CA: Scholars Press, 1983) 1–12.

Steinmann, Jean, *Le prophète Isaïe: Sa vie, son oeuvre et son temps* (LD 5; Paris: Cerf, 1955).

Stenning, J. F., ed. and trans., *The Targum of Isaiah* (Oxford: Clarendon, 1949).

Strong, John T., and Steven S. Tuell, eds., *Constituting the Community: Studies on the Polity of Ancient Israel in Honor of S. Dean McBride, Jr.* (Winona Lake, IN: Eisenbrauns, 2005).

Sukenik, E. L., ed., *The Dead Sea Scrolls of the Hebrew University* (Jerusalem: Magnes Press, Hebrew University, 1955).

Sweeney, Marvin A., *Isaiah 1–4 and the Post-Exilic Understanding of the Isaianic Tradition* (BZAW 171; Berlin: de Gruyter, 1988).

———, *Isaiah 1–39, with an Introduction to Prophetic Literature* (FOTL 16; Grand Rapids: Eerdmans, 1996).

Tadmor, Hayim, "The Campaigns of Sargon II of Assur: A Chronological-Historical Study," *JCS* 12 (1958) 22–40, 77–100.

———, *The Inscriptions of Tiglath-pileser III King of Assyria: Critical Edition, with Introductions, Translations, and Commentary* (Jerusalem: Israel Academy of Sciences and Humanities, 1994).

Tadmor, Hayim, Benno Landsberger, and Simo Parpola, "The Sin of Sargon and Sennacherib's Last Will," *SAAB* 3 (1989) 3–51.

Tadmor, Hayim, and Shigeo Yamada, *The Royal Inscriptions of Tiglath-pileser III (744–727 BC) and Shalmaneser V (726–722 BC), Kings of Assyria* (RINAP 1; Winona Lake, IN: Eisenbrauns, 2011).

Talmon, S., "Observations on Variant Readings in the Isaiah Scroll (1QIsaᵃ)," in Talmon, *The World of Qumrân from Within: Collected Studies* (Jerusalem: Magnes; Leiden: Brill, 1989) 117–30.

Thiele, Edwin R., *The Mysterious Numbers of the Hebrew Kings: A Reconstruction of the Chronology of the Kings of Israel and Judah* (Chicago: University of Chicago Press, 1951; 2nd ed., Grand Rapids: Eerdmans, 1965;

3rd ed., Grand Rapids: Zondervan, 1983).

Török, László, *The Kingdom of Kush: Handbook of the Nabatan-Meriotic Civilization* (HO 1: Der Nahe und Mittlere Osten 31; Leiden: Brill, 1977).

Tov, Emanuel, "The Text of Isaiah at Qumran," in C. C. Broyles and C. A. Evans, eds., *Writing and Reading the Scroll of Isaiah: Studies of an Interpretive Tradition* (2 vols.; VTSup 70; Leiden: Brill, 1997). 2:491–511.

Troxel, Ronald L., *LXX-Isaiah as Translation and Interpretation: The Strategies of the Translator of the Septuagint of Isaiah* (JSJSup 124; Leiden: Brill, 2008).

Tucker, Gene M., "Prophecy and the Prophetic Literature," in Douglas A. Knight and Gene M. Tucker, eds., *The Hebrew Bible and Its Modern Interpreters* (Philadelphia: Fortress Press; Chico, CA: Scholars Press, 1985) 325–68.

Tur-Sinai, N. H., "A Contribution to the Understanding of Isaiah I–XII," in C. Rabin, ed., *Studies in the Bible* (ScrHier 8; Jerusalem: Magnes Press, 1961) 154–88.

Ulrich, Eugene, "An Index to the Contents of the Isaiah Manuscripts from the Judean Desert," in C. C. Broyles and C. A. Evans, eds., *Writing and Reading the Scroll of Isaiah: Studies of an Interpretive Tradition* (2 vols.; VTSup 70; Leiden: Brill, 1997) 2:477.

Ulrich, Eugene, et al., eds., *Qumran Cave 4.X: The Prophets* (DJD 15; Oxford: Clarendon, 1997).

Vanel, A., "Tâbeʾél en Is VII 6 et le roi Tubail de Tyr," in *Studies on Prophecy* (VTSup 26; Leiden: Brill, 1974) 17–24.

Vermeylen, J., *Book of Isaiah = Le livre d'Isaïe: les oracles et leur relectures. Unité et complexité de l'ouvrage* (BETL 81; Leuven: Leuven University Press/Peeters, 1989).

——, *Du prophète Isaïe à l'apocalyptique* (2 vols.; EBib; Paris: Gabalda, 1977–78).

Vollmer, J., *Geschichtliche Rückblicke und Motive in der Prophetie des Amos, Hosea und Jesaja* (BZAW 119; Berlin: de Gruyter, 1971).

Waard, J. de, *A Handbook on Isaiah* (Textual Criticism and the Translator 1; Winona Lake, IN: Eisenbrauns, 1997).

Wanke, Günther, *Die Zionstheologie der Korachiten in ihrem traditionsgeschichtlichen Zusammenhang* (BZAW 97; Berlin: A. Töpelmann, 1966).

Watts, James W., and Paul R. House, eds., *Forming Prophetic Literature: Essays on Isaiah and the Twelve in Honor of John D. W. Watts* (JSOTSup 235; Sheffield: Sheffield Academic Press, 1996).

Watts, John D. W., *Isaiah 1–33* (WBC 24; Waco, TX: Word Books, 1985; rev. ed., 2005).

——, *Isaiah 34–66* (WBC 25; Waco, TX: Word Books, 1987).

Weber, O., ed., *Biblia Sacra iuxta vulgatem versionem*, vol. 2 (Stuttgart: Württembergische Bibelanstalt, 1969).

Westermann, Claus, *Basic Forms of Prophetic Speech* (trans. H. C. White; Philadelphia: Westminster, 1967; repr., Louisville: Westminster John Knox, 1991).

Whedbee, J. W., *Isaiah and Wisdom* (Nashville: Abingdon, 1971).

Wiklander, Bertil, *Prophecy as Literature: A Text-Linguistic and Rhetorical Approach to Isaiah 2–4* (ConBOT 22; Malmö: Gleerup, 1984).

Wildberger, Hans, *Isaiah 1–12; 13–27; 28–39* (trans. T. H. Trapp; 3 vols.; Continental Commentary; Minneapolis: Fortress Press, 1991–2002).

——, *Jesaja* (3 vols.; BKAT 10.1–3; Neukirchen-Vluyn: Neukirchener Verlag, 1972–82).

Williamson, H. G. M., *The Book Called Isaiah: Deutero-Isaiah's Role in Composition and Redaction* (Oxford: Clarendon, 1994).

——, *A Critical and Exegetical Commentary on Isaiah 1–27* (3 vols.; ICC 23; London: T&T Clark, 2006).

——, "Isaiah and the Wise," in John Day, Robert P. Gordon, and H. G. M. Williamson, eds., *Wisdom in Ancient Israel: Essays in Honour of J. A. Emerton* (Cambridge: Cambridge University Press, 1995) 133–41.

Willis, John T., "The First Pericope in the Book of Isaiah," *VT* 34 (1984) 63–77.

———, *Instruction Shall Go Forth: Studies in Micah and Isaiah* (ed. M. Hamilton and T. M. Willis; Eugene, OR: Pickwick, 2014.

Wong, Gordon C. I., *The Road to Peace: Pastoral Reflections on Isaiah 1–12* (Singapore: Gordon C. I. Wong, 2009).

Wood, Joyce R., et al., eds., *From Babel to Babylon: Essays on Biblical History and Literature in Honour of Brian Peckham* (LHBOTS 455; New York: T&T Clark, 2006).

Wright, George Ernest, *The Book of Isaiah* (Layman's Bible Commentary 11; Richmond: John Knox, 1964).

———, "The Lawsuit of God: A Form Critical Study of Deuteronomy 32," in Bernhard W. Anderson and Walter Harrelson, eds., *Israel's Prophetic Heritage: Essays in Honor of James Muilenburg* (New York: Harper, 1962) 26–67.

Young, E. J., *The Book of Isaiah* (3 vols.; NICOT; Grand Rapids: Eerdmans, 1965–72).

Ziegler, Joseph, ed., *Isaias* (Septuaginta 14; Göttingen: Vandenhoeck & Ruprecht, 1939).

———, ed., *Isaias* (3rd ed.; Septuaginta: Vetus Testamentum Graecum Auctoritate Academiae Scientiarium Gottingensis 14; Göttingen: Vandenhoeck & Ruprecht, 1983).

———, *Isaias* (Echter-Bibel; Würzburg: Echter, 1948).

———, *Die jüngeren griechischen Übersetzungen als Vorlagen der Vulgata in den prophetischen Schriften,* Beilage zum Personal- und Vorlesungs-Verzeichnis der Staatl. Akademie zu Braunsberg (Ostpr.) W.-S., 1943/44.

———, *Sylloge: Gesammelte Aufsätze zur Septuaginta* (Mitteilungen des Septuaginta-Unternehmens der Akademie der Wissenschaften in Göttingen 10; Göttingen: Vandenhoeck & Ruprecht, 1971).

———, *Textkritische Notizen zu den jüngeren griechischen Übersetzungen des Buches Isaias* (Septuaginta-Arbeiten 1; Göttingen: Vandenhoeck & Ruprecht, 1930).

———, *Untersuchungen zur Septuaginta des Buches Isaias* (ATA 12.3; Münster: Aschendorff, 1934).

———, "Die Vorlage der Isaias-Septuaginta (LXX) und die erste Isaias-Rolle von Qumran (1QIsaᵃ)," *JBL* 78 (1959) 34–59.

1. Passages

a / Old Testament and Apocrypha

28:10	65	12:18	145	11:33	241
28:15-68	314	12:23	147	12:21	16
28:25	468	13:7-13	147	13:3	118
28:36, 64	469	13:9, 17	234	13:5, 7	117
28:49	250, 352, 424	13:15-23	235	13:22	99
28:65	482	13:19	237	14:12-13	64
29:7	235	13:24-32	147	16:9	178
29:16	469	13:25	237, 241	19:23-24	411
29:22	15	14:2	437	20:1	145
29:23	436	15:19	454	20:38, 40	397
30:15-20	24	17:1, 5	147		
30:19	18, 19	17:5, 6	145	**Ruth**	
31:11	16, 484	17:11	147	2:15-17	241
31:24-30	18	18:8-10	437	3:16	64
31:28	19	21:36	235		
31:29	117	21:38-39	235	**1 Samuel**	
32	18	22:9, 13, 15	145	1:3	22
32:1	14, 19	22:10-34	263	1:11	22
32:2	137	22:32	145	1:22-28	119
32:4	330	24:2-3	187	1:22	484
32:5-18	20	24:11	243	2:1-10	483
32:5	14	24:14-15	187	2:2	330
32:6	21			2:11	119
32:8-9	4	**Judges**		3:14	290
32:10	436	1:27	147	3:17	290
32:11	134	2:10-23	263	3:21	16
32:14	120	3:24	90	4:1—7:1	472
32:15	137, 399	5:1-31	192	4:4	92, 255
32:18	14, 137, 330	5:4-5	255, 398	4:19	117
32:30, 31	137, 399	5:17	145	8:19-20	430
32:32	14, 20	5:20	316	10:1-7	117
32:37	137, 330, 399	5:22	29	10:19	430
32:39	14, 20	5:25	120	10:27	430
33:2, 26-29	398	5:26	314	14:37	280
33:12	71	6:3	187	15:13	179
33:22	337	6:15-18	117	17:53	80
34:1-3	396	6:22	99	17:56	118
		6:26-40	117	20:22	118
Joshua		6:30	352	21:6	197
3:10	243	6:33—8:28	149	22:11	93
7:4	352	6:33	187	24:4	90
7:15	411	7:12	187	25:22	290
7:22—8:29	175	7:25	172	25:28	114
9:1	243	8:8	352	26:19	177
9:10	147	8:10	187	28:3-25	142
10:6	352	8:21, 26	63	28:3-7, 15	369
11:2	147	9:13	314	28:6	280
12:2	235	10:4	145	28:13	142
12:4-6	147	10:8	147	30:26	454
12:8	243	11:19—26	235	30:28	241

514

516

In the design of the visual aspects of *Hermeneia*, consideration has been given to relating the form to the content by symbolic means.

The letters of the logotype *Hermeneia* are a fusion of forms alluding simultaneously to Hebrew (dotted vowel markings) and Greek (geometric round shapes) letter forms. In their modern treatment they remind us of the electronic age as well, the vantage point from which this investigation of the past begins. The Lion of Judah used as visual identification for the series is based on the Seal of Shema. The version for *Hermeneia* is again a fusion of Hebrew calligraphic forms, especially the legs of the lion, and Greek elements characterized by the geometric. In the sequence of arcs, which can be understood as scroll-like images, the first is the lion's mouth. It is reasserted and accelerated in the whorl and returns in the aggressively arched tail: tradition is passed from one age to the next, rediscovered and re-formed.

"Who is worthy to open the scroll and break its seals. . . ."
Then one of the elders said to me
"weep not; lo, the Lion of the tribe of David,
the Root of David, has conquered,
so that he can open the scroll and its seven seals."
Rev. 5:2, 5

To celebrate the signal achievement in biblical scholarship which *Hermeneia* represents, the entire series will by its color constitute a signal on the theologian's bookshelf: the Old Testament will be bound in yellow and the New Testament in red, traceable to a commonly used color coding for synagogue and church in medieval painting; in pure color terms, varying degrees of intensity of the warm segment of the color spectrum. The colors interpenetrate when the binding color for the Old Testament is used to imprint volumes from the New and vice versa.

Wherever possible, a photograph of the oldest extant manuscript, or a historically significant document pertaining to the biblical sources, will be displayed on the end papers of each volume to give a feel for the tangible reality and beauty of the source material.

The title-page motifs are expressive derivations from the *Hermeneia* logotype, repeated seven times to form a matrix and debossed on the cover of each volume. These sifted-out elements will be seen to be in their exact positions within the parent matrix.

Horizontal markings at gradated levels on the spine will assist in grouping the volumes according to these conventional categories.

The type has been set with unjustified right margins so as to preserve the internal consistency of word spacing. This is a major factor in both legibility and aesthetic quality; the resultant uneven line endings are only slight impairments to legibility by comparison. In this respect the type resembles the handwritten manuscripts where the quality of the calligraphic writing is dependent on establishing and holding to integral spacing patterns.

All of the typefaces in common use today have been designed between AD 1500 and the present. For the biblical text a face was chosen which does not arbitrarily date the text, but rather one which is uncompromisingly modern and unembellished so that its feel is of the universal. The type style is Univers 65 by Adrian Frutiger.

The expository texts and footnotes are set in Baskerville, chosen for its compatibility with the many brief Greek and Hebrew insertions. The double-column format and the shorter line length facilitate speed reading and the wide margins to the left of footnotes provide for the scholar's own notations.

Kenneth Hiebert

Category of biblical writing,
key symbolic characteristic,
and volumes so identified.

1
Law
(boundaries described)
   Genesis
   Exodus
   Leviticus
   Numbers
   Deuteronomy

2
History
(trek through time and space)
   Joshua
   Judges
   Ruth
   1 Samuel
   2 Samuel
   1 Kings
   2 Kings
   1 Chronicles
   2 Chronicles
   Ezra
   Nehemiah
   Esther

3
Poetry
(lyric emotional expression)
   Job
   Psalms
   Proverbs
   Ecclesiastes
   Song of Songs

4
Prophets
(inspired seers)
   Isaiah
   Jeremiah
   Lamentations
   Ezekiel
   Daniel
   Hosea
   Joel
   Amos
   Obadiah
   Jonah
   Micah
   Nahum
   Habakkuk
   Zephaniah
   Haggai
   Zechariah
   Malachi

5
New Testament Narrative
(focus on One)
   Matthew
   Mark
   Luke
   John
   Acts

6
Epistles
(directed instruction)
   Romans
   1 Corinthians
   2 Corinthians
   Galatians
   Ephesians
   Philippians
   Colossians
   1 Thessalonians
   2 Thessalonians
   1 Timothy
   2 Timothy
   Titus
   Philemon
   Hebrews
   James
   1 Peter
   2 Peter
   1 John
   2 John
   3 John
   Jude

7
Apocalypse
(vision of the future)
   Revelation

8
Extracanonical Writings
(peripheral records)